About Pearson

Pearson is the world's learning company, with presence across 70 countries worldwide. Our unique insights and world-class expertise come from a long history of working closely with renowned teachers, authors and thought leaders, as a result of which, we have emerged as the preferred choice for millions of teachers and learners across the world.

We believe learning opens up opportunities, creates fulfilling careers and hence better lives. We hence collaborate with the best of minds to deliver you class-leading products, spread across the Higher Education and K12 spectrum.

Superior learning experience and improved outcomes are at the heart of everything we do. This product is the result of one such effort.

Your feedback plays a critical role in the evolution of our products and you can contact us at reachus@pearson.com. *We look forward to it.*

Words of endorsement from scholars and leaders...

Businesses are undergoing massive digital transformations and disruptions. In their book, Dr. Sheth and Dr. Shainesh provide a comprehensive and contemporary guide to cope with such challenges. With a focus on South Asia, the book is a wonderful collection of insights and perspectives from the world-renowned marketing guru, Prof. Philip Kotler. It is a must-read for marketing professionals who want to cultivate impactful leadership for a better world.

Dr. Dipak C. Jain
President (European) & Professor of Marketing – CEIBS
Dean - Kellogg School of Management (2001-09) and Dean – INSEAD (2011–13)

The authors provide in-depth marketing perspectives from a growth market lens to cover the role of technology and digital media as well as traditional channels in the dynamic marketplace. The text is rich in frameworks and case studies that enable both design and implementation of proactive marketing strategies.

Dr. Rajendra Srivastava
Novartis Professor of Marketing and Innovation and Dean (2016–21) – Indian School of Business

This Indian adaptation of Philip Kotler's classic textbook will help students and managers learn the principles and applications of marketing management. Its analytical approach and managerial orientation will augment learning. The concepts, frameworks and contemporary examples of several Indian brands will provide the foundation to succeed in the emerging hyper-competitive market environment.

Harsh Mariwala
Chairman – Marico Ltd.

The South Asian adaptation of Kotler's classic text is a timely, much-needed contribution to marketing educators, students, and practitioners. It preserves the bedrock marketing principles from previous editions. At the same time, it re-examines and augments those principles from a fresh, forward-looking perspective, particularly vis-à-vis the growing impact of globalization, digitization and corporate social responsibility on marketing decisions.

Dr. A. Parasuraman
Emeritus Professor of Marketing & James W. McLamore Chair Emeritus – University of Miami and
Mentor – AIM-Parasuraman Centre for Service Excellence, Jagdish Sheth School of Management (JAGSoM)

'Marketing Management' continues to be the seminal book on the subject and, in its 16th edition, is the best example of what it quintessentially embodies - how to remain relevant and differentiated in an increasingly noisy and competitive world. With illustrations and case studies covering various products and service domains, it refreshes and reinforces why marketing continues to be the driver of value creation for businesses.

Vinita Bali
Strategy Adviser & Independent Director
Former MD & CEO, Britannia

This book incorporates the realities of the post-pandemic era and the impact of the 4th Industrial Revolution in the marketing domain. Readers will develop a better understanding of the emerging business realities in South Asia. A must-read for all marketers.

Dr Harivansh Chaturvedi
Director. Birla Institute of Management Technology

MBA students will enjoy learning from this South Asian adaptation of the classic book 'Marketing Management'. Examples of successful Indian brands and themes like business model design and socially responsible marketing make this edition very contemporary.

Sameer Suneja
Global CEO, Perfetti Van Melle Group B.V., Amsterdam

The two distinguished scholars, Prof. Jagdish Sheth and Prof. G. Shainesh, have leveraged their rich experience in marketing to adapt a "bible": Philip Kotler's 'Marketing Management' to the South Asian market.
I strongly feel it will offer significant learning on global marketing practices. Contemporary Indian cases will make it extremely useful to management students and faculty.

Dr. Rajan Saxena
Former Vice-Chancellor, NMIMS (Deemed University) and Distinguished Professor of Marketing, NMIMS (2009–2020)

The 16th edition of the marketing bible "Marketing Management" is now even more impactful, especially for Indian students. With rich case studies from India covering the fast-changing marketplace and a focus on areas like digital, e-commerce, and social media, it truly continues to be the holy grail of marketing.

Manish Tiwary
VP & Country Manager, Amazon.in

This best-selling marketing textbook builds on the authors' deep scholarship and practical insights. New concepts and frameworks, along with several examples, will enhance the understanding of the entire value delivery process for business growth.

Dr. Amit Mookerjee
Professor and Head, University School of Management and Entrepreneurship, Director, East Campus, Delhi Technological University

Wonderful effort from the authors! Timely revision to an all-time classic. Local examples and case studies will be of particular relevance to students; a must-read for any MBA graduate in India.

Dr. S. Bharadhwaj
Dr. Bala V and Vasantha Balachandran Chair Professor of Marketing, Great Lakes Institute of Management

Marketing Management's enduring appeal as one of the best business books lies in its comprehensive coverage and evolution. The 16th edition will be an important guide for students and managers as it incorporates the latest developments in concepts and practices while showcasing several leading and new-age Indian brands.

Neelesh Garg
MD & CEO, Tata AIG General Insurance Co Ltd.

This book offers a plethora of case studies and examples of brands & organizations that operate in India. These insights coupled with the conceptual foundations of marketing management, make it an essential reading for MBA students as well as experienced practitioners.

Dr. Moutusy Maity
Professor of Marketing and Dr. Ishwar Dayal Chair for Futuristic Issues in the Behavioral Sciences, Indian Institute of Management Lucknow

This edition encapsulates the interdisciplinary role of marketing in the realm of globalization & digitization through new-age technologies, data analytics, social media, and sustainability. The authors unpack these key themes in a systematic manner with real-life case studies of leading Indian brands. This is a must-read book for all learners and practitioners

Prof. Dr. Uday Salunkhe
Group Director, WeSchool

The book has been written keeping the Indian students in mind and it captures the cases, illustrations and anecdotes from across Indian corporate. The book helps the students of management in forming a clear perspective on various marketing concepts with reference to India as well as globally. This book is a must have for every student and teacher of marketing in India.

J. Mahendra Reddy
Vice Chancellor (Incharge), ICFAI Foundation for Higher Education

This book is dedicated to my wife and best friend, Nancy, with love.

—PK

This book is dedicated to my wife, Punam, and my two daughters, Carolyn and Allison, with much love and thanks.

—KLK

This book is dedicated to my parents, Irina and Christo, with love and gratitude.

—AC

This book is dedicated to Professor John A. Howard who was my thesis advisor, mentor and coauthor of The Theory of Buyer Behavior.

—JNS

This book is dedicated to my wife, Leena and our children, Priya and Aditya, with love.

—GS

Brief Contents

Contents

Preface

The 16th edition of *Marketing Management* builds on the classic examples, core concepts, and logical structure that made the first edition a landmark text. Much has changed since the 15th edition was published. Ongoing globalization; the increasing role of corporate social responsibility; advances in technology, e-commerce, and digital communication; the growing impact of social media, and the widespread use of data analytics, marketing automation, and artificial intelligence have disrupted many industries and have opened doors to new business models. Responding to these changes, the 16th edition was redesigned from the ground up to provide managers with the tools necessary to succeed in the new market environment.

Marketing Management owes its success to its maximization of three dimensions of marketing coverage: depth, breadth, and relevance. The *depth* includes its solid academic grounding; its examination of important theoretical concepts, models, and frameworks; and its ability to provide conceptual guidance to solve practical problems. The *breadth* reflects the wide range of topics addressed in the book and its emphasis on those topics that are most crucial to marketing management. The *relevance* is embodied by the ability of this book to identify the issues commonly faced by managers and present the material in a way that enables them to develop successful strategies to address these issues.

The 16th edition builds on the fundamental strengths of past editions that distinguish *Marketing Management* from all other marketing management texts:

- **Managerial orientation.** The book focuses on the major decisions that marketing managers and top management face in their efforts to harmonize the organization's objectives, capabilities, and resources with marketplace needs and opportunities.
- **Analytical approach.** The text presents conceptual tools and frameworks for analyzing recurring problems in marketing management. Cases and examples illustrate effective marketing principles, strategies, and practices.
- **Multidisciplinary perspective.** *Marketing Management* draws on the rich findings of various scientific disciplines—such as economics, behavioral science, and management theory—for fundamental concepts and tools that are directly applicable to marketing challenges.
- **Universal applications.** The book applies strategic thinking to the complete spectrum of marketing: products, services, persons, places, information, ideas, and causes; consumer and business markets; profit and nonprofit organizations; domestic and foreign companies; small and large firms; manufacturing and intermediary businesses; and low- and high-tech industries.
- **Comprehensive and balanced coverage.** *Marketing Management* covers the topics a manager must understand in order to design and execute a successful marketing campaign.

Preface to the Indian Edition

This adaptation has been enriched by incorporating scores of relevant examples and caselets of Indian brands and organizations from a variety of sectors to illustrate marketing strategies, practices, concepts and principles. Exemplifying key concepts with familiar brands from the Indian market will improve student engagement and enhance the relevance of theoretical analysis in a familiar context.

What's New in the 16th Edition

The overriding goal of the revision for the 16th edition of *Marketing Management* was to create a comprehensive, current, and engaging marketing text. We streamlined the organization of the content, added new material, cut or updated older material, and deleted material that was no longer relevant or necessary. The 16th edition allows those instructors who have used previous editions to build on past experience, while at the same time offering a text that is unsurpassed in breadth, depth, and relevance for students experiencing *Marketing Management* for the first time.

To improve the presentation of the material, individual chapters are organized into seven rather than eight major parts, as described next. We retained many of the favorably received within-chapter features that have been introduced through the years, such as topical chapter openers, examples highlighting noteworthy companies or issues, and the Marketing Insight and Marketing Spotlight features that provide in-depth conceptual and company-specific information. Most of the chapter-opening vignettes, in-text examples, and end-of-chapter features are new, reflecting current market developments.

UPDATED CHAPTER CONTENT

The content of the 16th edition has been reorganized to accommodate the introduction of new material and streamline the presentation of material retained from the previous edition. The chapters and the material in the redesigned book better reflect the ways in which marketing management is currently being taught in most business schools. The organization of the 16th edition and the ways its individual parts and chapters correspond to those from the previous edition are outlined next.

- Part I, "Fundamentals of Marketing Management," is a retitled version of Part I in the previous edition.
  - Chapter 1, "Defining Marketing for the New Realities," has been substantively rewritten to serve as an introductory chapter that defines the scope of marketing management as a business discipline.
  - Chapter 2, "Marketing Planning and Management," has also been extensively rewritten to provide an actionable framework for marketing management and marketing planning. It includes material from Chapters 2 and 23 of the previous edition, but most of the content—text and figures—is new. For example, the new section entitled "Planning and Managing Marketing Offerings," covers the G-STIC approach to action planning. New supporting Figure 2.6 illustrates the G-STIC framework and Figure 2.7 illustrates an action-planning flowchart.

will create value for collaborators. Finally, the *company value map* outlines the ways in which the offering will create value for the company's stakeholders. Note that these three value maps are intricately related as they reflect different aspects of the process of creating market value. Only by creating value for target customers, collaborators, and the company can a manager ensure the market success of an offering.

Planning and Managing Market Offerings

A company's future depends on its ability to develop successful market offerings that create superior value for target customers, the company, and its collaborators.[21] Market success typically results from diligent market analysis, planning, and management; rarely is it a lucky accident. Succeeding in the market requires a company to develop a viable business model and an action plan that allows the business model to become a reality. The process of developing such an action plan is encapsulated in the G-STIC framework described in the following sections.

THE G-STIC APPROACH TO ACTION PLANNING

The action plan, which articulates the company's goal and delineates a course of action to reach this goal, is the backbone of marketing planning. Five key activities guide the development of an action plan: These activities include setting a *goal*, developing a *strategy*, designing the *tactics*, defining an *implementation* plan, and identifying a set of *control* metrics to measure the success of the proposed action. The G-STIC (Goal-Strategy-Tactics-Implementation-Control) framework comprises these five activities and acts as the lynchpin of marketing planning and analysis. At the core of the action plan is the business model based on the offering's strategy and tactics.

The individual components of the G-STIC approach to marketing planning and management are as follows:

- The **goal** describes the company's ultimate criterion for success; it specifies the end result that the company plans to achieve. The two components of the goal are its *focus*, which defines the metric (such as net income) used to quantify the intended result of the company's actions, and the performance *benchmarks* that signal movement toward the goal and define the time frame for achieving the goal.
- The **strategy** provides the basis for the company's business model by delineating the company's *target market* and describing the offering's *value proposition* in this market.
- **Tactics** carry out the strategy by defining the key attributes of the company's offering. These seven tactics—*product, service, brand, price, incentives, communication*, and *distribution*—are the tools used to create value in the company's chosen market.
- **Implementation** consists of the processes involved in readying the company's offering for sale. Implementation includes *developing* the offering and *deploying* the offering in the target market.
- **Control** measures the success of the company's activities over time by monitoring the company's *performance* and the changes in the market *environment* in which the company operates.

The key components of the marketing plan and the key factors describing each component are outlined in Figure 2.7 and are examined in more detail in the following sections.

SETTING A GOAL

Defining the goal that the company aims to achieve sets the marketing plan in motion. The goal can be regarded as the beacon that guides all company activities. Two key decisions are involved in setting a goal: identifying the *focus* of the company's actions and specifying the performance *benchmarks* to be achieved. These decisions are discussed in more detail next.

Defining the Goal Focus. The goal's focus defines the desired outcome of the company's activities, an important criterion of a firm's success. Based on their focus, goals can be monetary or strategic.

- **Monetary goals** are based on such outcomes as net income, profit margins, earnings per share, and return on investment. For-profit firms use monetary goals as their primary performance metric.

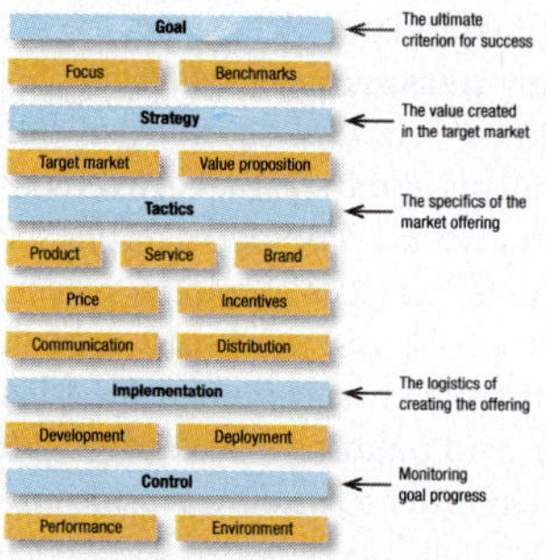

FIGURE **2.7**
The G-STIC Action-Planning Flowchart
Source: Alexander Chernev, *Strategic Marketing Management: Theory and Practice* (Chicago, IL: Cerebellum Press, 2019).

- **Strategic goals** are centered on nonmonetary outcomes that are of strategic importance to the company. Among the most common strategic goals are increasing sales volume, brand awareness, and social welfare, as well as enhancing the corporate culture and facilitating employee recruitment and retention. Nonprofit companies and for-profit companies looking to support items that are bigger revenue producers than the focal offering have strategic goals as their main performance metric. As an example, Amazon might only break even or actually take a loss on some of its Kindle devices and yet view them as a strategically important platform for its retail business.

Companies are increasingly looking beyond sales revenue and profit to consider the legal, ethical, social, and environmental effects of their marketing activities and programs. The concept of a "triple bottom line"—people, planet, and profits—has gained traction among many companies taking stock of the societal impact of their activities.[22] For example, one of Unilever's key initiatives—its Sustainable Living Plan—has three major goals: to improve people's health and well-being, to reduce our environmental impact, and to enhance livelihoods. These goals are underpinned by metrics spanning social, environmental, and economic performance in the company's value chain.[23]

Defining Performance Benchmarks. Quantitative and temporal performance benchmarks work in tandem to provide the measurements that track the progress of the company toward reaching its established goal.

- **Quantitative benchmarks** set out the specific milestones to be achieved as the company moves toward its ultimate goal. These benchmarks quantify the company's focal goal, which might, for example, include increasing market share by 5 percent, or improving retention rates by 15 percent, or growing revenues by 10 percent. Quantitative benchmarks can be stated in relative terms, such as aiming to increase market share by 20 percent, or in absolute terms, such as aspiring to achieve sales of one million units per year.
- **Temporal benchmarks** identify the time frame for achieving a specific quantitative or qualitative benchmark—e.g., revamp the company's Web site by the end of the first quarter. The timeline set for achieving a goal is a key decision that can affect the type of strategy used to implement the goal, the number of people involved, and even costs. For example, the goal of maximizing next quarter's profits is likely to require a different strategy and tactics than the goal of ensuring long-term profitability.

Implementing the company goal requires that three main objectives be specified: *what* the company aims to achieve (goal focus), *how much* the company wants to achieve (quantitative benchmark), and *when* the company wants to achieve it (temporal benchmark). Thus, a company might have the goal

- Part II, "Understanding the Market," includes most of the material from Parts II and III in the previous edition.
  - Chapters 3 and 4, "Analyzing Consumer Markets" and "Analyzing Business Markets," are updated versions of namesake Chapters 6 and 7 in the previous edition. Both chapters have been significantly revised to present a systematic view of market analysis.
  - Chapter 5, "Conducting Marketing Research" combines the content outlined in Chapters 3 and 4 in the previous edition to present a streamlined approach for gathering market insights. Chapter 5 includes a new section on "Data Mining" that covers how marketers can gather useful information about consumers, businesses, and markets.
- Part III, "Developing a Winning Marketing Strategy" is a modified version of Part IV of the previous edition.
  - Chapter 6, "Identifying Market Segments and Targets," is a substantially revised version of Chapter 9 from the previous edition. This chapter offers new content that defines the strategic and tactical aspects of segmenting the market and identifying target customers.
  - Chapter 7, "Crafting a Customer Value Proposition and Positioning," is a largely revised and updated version of Chapter 10 from the previous edition. This chapter builds on the content presented in Chapter 6 to outline a systematic approach to developing a value proposition of the chosen target market. New content examines how to develop a meaningful value proposition by creating benefits across three domains—functional, psychological, and monetary—and delineates strategies for creating a sustainable competitive advantage.
- Part IV, "Designing Value," is a modified version of Part V from the previous edition.
  - Chapter 8, "Designing and Managing Products," Chapter 9, "Designing and Managing Services," and Chapter 10, "Building Strong Brands," correspond to Chapters 13, 14, and 11 in the previous edition. All three chapters have been significantly revised to reflect new market realities.

The New Services Realities

Service firms once lagged behind manufacturers in their understanding and use of marketing because they were small or faced large demand or little competition. This has certainly changed. Some of the most skilled marketers now are service firms.

Savvy services marketers are recognizing the new services realities, such as the increasing role of technology, the importance of the increasingly empowered customer, customer coproduction, and the need to engage employees as well as customers.

INCREASING ROLE OF TECHNOLOGY

Technology is changing the rules of the game for services in a very fundamental way. Banking, for instance, is being transformed by the ability to bank online and via mobile apps; some customers rarely see a bank lobby or interact with an employee anymore. The Covid-19 pandemic accelerated the digital transformation of services by forcing many companies to change course and transform their businesses by integrating digital technology to fundamentally change how they deliver value to their customers.

Technology also has great power to make service workers more productive. However, companies must avoid pushing technological efficiency so hard that they reduce perceived quality.[21] Amazon has some of the most innovative technology in online retailing, but it also keeps customers extremely satisfied when a problem arises, even if they don't actually talk to an Amazon employee. More companies have introduced "live chat" features to blend technology with a human voice. One company that enables enterprises to connect with customers across different touch points—from text messages to emails, phone calls to video, intelligent chatbots and back—is Twilio.

Twilio Twilio, the leading cloud communications platform, is used by millions of developers around the world to "virtualize" the telecommunications infrastructure and improve the human interaction experience. Twilio has over 60,000 business customers, including high-profile clients such as Airbnb, Intuit, Salesforce, Uber, Twitter, eBay, Sony, Yelp, Hulu, and Lyft. Twilio offers its clients a comprehensive, customizable, and easy-to-use platform to automate and streamline communications to customers, collaborators, employees, and coworkers. Coca-Cola uses Twilio to rapidly dispatch service technicians, real estate site Trulia uses Twilio for its click-to-call app that enables potential buyers to connect with an agent, EMC uses Twilio to send texts to

Source: Gabby Jones/Bloomberg/Getty Images

<< To keep both its high-profile business customers and their customers happy, leading cloud communication platform Twilio offers a variety of easy-to-use, customizable services that automate, streamline, and enhance interactions between companies and their customers, collaborators, and employees.

- Chapter 11, "Managing Pricing and Sales Promotions," includes material from Chapters 16 and 20 in the previous edition. The discussion of sales promotions is now a part of the pricing chapter rather than being discussed in the chapter on managing mass communications.

- Part V, "Communicating Value," corresponds to Part VII of the previous edition. Note that the order of Parts VI and VII from the previous edition has been switched so that the topic of communications is introduced before the topic of distribution. This change is made to better align the content with the view of marketing as a process of designing, communicating, and delivering value.
  - Chapter 12, "Managing Marketing Communications," corresponds to Chapter 19 in the previous edition and introduces a streamlined approach to developing a communication campaign that spans different media.
  - Chapter 13, "Designing an Integrated Marketing Campaign in the Digital Age," includes content from Chapters 20 and 21 of the previous edition. This chapter outlines the key decisions involved in managing the media across different communication channels.
  - Chapter 14, "Personal Selling and Direct Marketing," includes substantively revised content from Chapter 22 in the previous edition. The content on personal selling is now organized into three sections: managing the sales process, designing the sales force, and managing the sales force.
- Part VI, "Delivering Value," corresponds to Part VI in the previous edition
  - Chapter 15, "Designing and Managing Distribution Channels," corresponds to Chapter 17 in the previous edition and features new chapter organization and content.
  - Chapter 16, "Managing Retailing," corresponds to Chapter 18 in the previous edition and also includes new coverage on franchising.
- Part VII, "Managing Growth," is a new capstone section that groups growth-related topics covered across different parts of the previous edition.
  - Chapter 17, "Driving Growth in Competitive Markets," offers an updated and streamlined version of the content discussed in Chapter 12 of the previous edition.

Business-Model Design

Up to this point, the product has existed only in the form of a description, a drawing, or a prototype. The next step represents a jump in investment that dwarfs the costs incurred so far, requiring the company to determine whether the product idea can be translated into a commercially feasible offering. **Business-model design** also takes the offering's *viability*—its value-creating capacity—into consideration, in addition to concept development's focus on the technological *feasibility* and the *desirability* of the offering. If the business model is validated, the concept can move to the development stage. If the business-model analysis suggests that the offering is unlikely to create market value for the company and its customers, the offering concept (and sometimes the underlying idea) must be revised and reevaluated.

DESIGNING THE BUSINESS MODEL

Designing the business model involves three key components (discussed in detail in Chapter 2): identifying the target market, articulating the offering's value proposition in that market, and delineating the key attributes of the market offering (Figure 18.3):

- The **target market** is the market in which the company has chosen to create value with its offering. Included in the target market are the target customers that the company has identified as potential purchasers of the offering, competitors that are also vying for the target customers, collaborators that will help the company distribute the offering and serve the target customers, the company itself, and the context of the market in which the company operates.
- The **value proposition** details the type of value that the company plans to create for its target customers and collaborators in the market, as well as the way in which the company plans to capture some of this value for itself.
- The **market offering** describes how the company will create, communicate, and deliver value to its target customers, collaborators, and the company stakeholders. This involves specifying the product, service, brand, price, incentives, communication, and distribution aspects of the company's offering.

The creation of market value is the ultimate goal of the business model. Accordingly, the success of an offering is determined by the degree to which it can create value for its target customers, collaborators, and the company. Thus, the design of a business model for a new offering is guided by three key questions: *Does the offering create value for target customers? Does the offering create value for the company collaborators?* and *Does the offering create value for the company?*

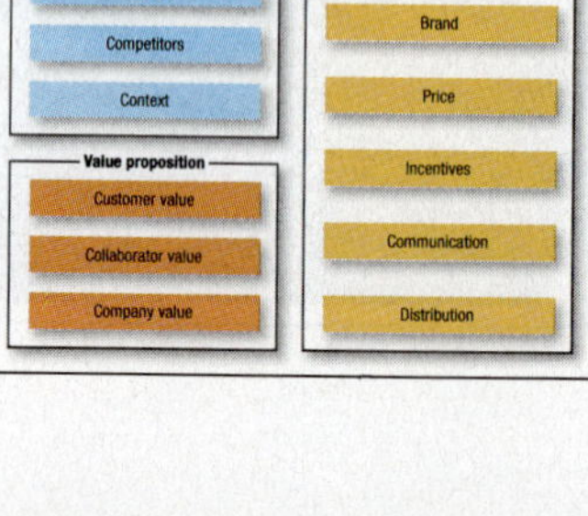

FIGURE **18.3**
The Key Components of a Business Model of a New Offering
Source: Alexander Chernev, *Strategic Marketing Management: Theory and Practice* (Chicago, IL: Cerebellum Press, 2019)

- Chapter 18, "Developing New Market Offerings," which was Chapter 15 in the previous edition, is now organized in a way that reflects the key steps of the new-product development process. Specifically, this chapter includes new coverage of idea generation, business model design, implementation of the offering, and market deployment.
- Chapter 19, "Building Customer Loyalty," covers content discussed in Chapter 5 of the previous edition and focuses on customer relationship management.
- Chapter 20, "Tapping into Global Markets," covers content discussed in Chapter 8 of the previous edition.
- Chapter 21, "Socially Responsible Marketing," is a new chapter that reflects the growing importance of corporate social responsibility in marketing management. As more companies are defining their purpose beyond profits, conducting business in a socially responsible manner becomes a key aspect of creating market value.

CHAPTER 21

Socially Responsible Marketing

TATA TRUSTS

Tata Trusts programs in healthcare, education, community & rural development and skilling have benefitted millions over more than 100 years. They are a testimony to the founder, Jamsetji Tata's vision of keeping the community at the centre of the enterprise.
Source: Tata Trusts

Healthy long-term growth for a brand requires marketers to engage in a host of marketing activities and satisfy a broad set of constituents and objectives. In doing so, marketers must also consider the societal impact of their actions. Corporate social responsibility has become a priority for many organizations and is ingrained in their business models. Some organizations, such as Tata Trusts, fully embrace this vision of social responsibility.

>>> Tata Trusts, established by eminent industrialist and pioneering philanthropist Jamsetji Tata, has been an integral part of nation-building for more than 125 years[1]. Driven by the legacy of the founder's philosophy of constructive philanthropy and selfless giving, Tata Trusts that hold two-thirds of the equity of Tata Sons, has been ploughing the dividends to support an assortment of causes for nation building such as cancer care, health, nutrition, education, water and sanitation, livelihoods, environment, digital literacy, sports, arts and culture and, institutions to name a few. The many trusts and not-for-profits operating under the umbrella of Tata Trusts have been empowering and

UPDATED CHAPTER FEATURES

In addition to the new core content, all chapters include a number of features—chapter openers, in-text examples, Marketing Insights, and Marketing Spotlights—that aim to illustrate the key concepts and enhance the relevance of the theoretical discussion. Many of these features in the 16th edition are new, and all of those that appeared in the previous edition have been updated to better reflect the current marketing environment. Some of the companies and topics highlighted in features new to the current edition are listed next.

- New chapter openers: bigbasket (Chapter 1), inMobi (Chapter 2), Flipkart (Chapter 3), Qualtrics (Chapter 5), Taj Hotels (Chapter 6), Reliance Jio (Chapter 7), Tesla (Chapter 8), Infosys (Chapter 9), Amul (Chapter 10), Netflix (Chapter 11), Fevicol (Chapter 12), Credit Access Grameen (Chapter 14),

Asian Paints (Chapter 15), Net-a-Porter (Chapter 16), Maruti Suzuki (Chapter 17), Tata Ace (Chapter 18), cult.fit (Chapter 19), Bajaj Auto (Chapter 20) and Tata Trusts (Chapter 21).

CHAPTER 8

PART 4 | DESIGNING VALUE

Designing and Managing Products

Tesla's Model 3 set out to prove that mass-produced, environmentally sound electric cars can successfully and profitably pilfer market share from producers of traditional gasoline-powered vehicles.
Source: imageBROKER/ Alamy Stock Photo

At the heart of a great brand is a great product. To achieve market leadership, firms must offer products and services of superior quality that provide unsurpassed customer value. Tesla has conquered the electric car market in the United States, thanks in part to a relentless focus on product innovation and performance.

>>> In March 2016, Tesla revealed the long-awaited Model 3, the vehicle that the company hopes will ultimately take the electric car to the mass consumer. Priced starting at $35,000 (after $8,000 credits and fuel savings were factored in), Model 3 aimed to disrupt the auto industry by proving that mass producing an environmentally friendly vehicle is both feasible and profitable. Tesla's new mass market car created a lot of excitement, generating over half a million pre-orders, 100,000 of which were placed before the Model 3 was revealed. The customer appeal of Model 3 stemmed from several factors. Perhaps the most important was the lack of direct competition. The combination of Tesla's image as a luxury brand and the (relatively) low price point made it the only option for customers who were looking for an all-electric sedan priced around $40,000. To achieve its goal of building 5,000 vehicles a week, Tesla invested close to $1 billion to build its first Gigafactory—a lithium-ion battery and vehicle assembly factory near Reno, Nevada. Tesla's efforts to scale up production of Model 3 paid off: In 2018, it became the best-selling luxury vehicle in the United States, despite the fact that electric cars made up only 1.12% of total vehicle sales. Despite its success, Tesla faces growing competition from other car manufacturers that are revamping their product lines to include an increasing number of all-electric vehicles. Yet Tesla's focus is on gaining share from the traditional car market. "Our true competition is not the small trickle of non-Tesla electric cars being produced," argued Tesla's CEO Elon Musk, "but rather the enormous flood of gasoline cars pouring out of the world's factories every day." In the fall of 2020, Elon Musk laid out a plan for Tesla to build a $25,000 electric car using drastically lower-cost batteries to potentially turn the company into the world's largest car manufacturer.[1]

Marketing planning begins with formulating an offering to meet target customers' needs or wants. The customer will judge the offering's benefits on three basic elements: product, service, and brand. In this chapter we examine product; in Chapter 9, services; and in Chapter 10, brand. All three elements—product, service, and brand—must be fused into a competitively attractive market offering.

Product Differentiation

To successfully compete in the market, products must be differentiated. At one extreme are products that allow little variation: chicken, aspirin, and steel. Yet even here some differentiation is possible: Perdue chickens, Bayer aspirin, and India's Tata Steel have carved out distinct identities in their categories. Procter & Gamble makes Tide, Cheer, and Gain laundry detergents, each with a separate brand identity. At the other extreme are products that lend themselves to high differentiation, such as automobiles, commercial buildings, and furniture. Here the seller faces an abundance of differentiation possibilities.

Well-differentiated products can create significant competitive advantages. Crafting a distinctive aura for a product that helps distance it from competitors can involve moves that range from impressive technological advances like Intuitive Surgical's da Vinci robotic system for minimally invasive surgery to simple tweaks like putting a Chiquita sticker on a banana. Some brands, such as DeBeers, differentiate their products by tying them to special occasions. Others, including Tropicana and Tiffany, use packaging to ensure that they stand out from their respective competitors.

Attributes on the basis of which to differentiate include core functionality, features, performance quality, conformance quality, durability, reliability, form, style, and customization.[2] Design has become an increasingly important differentiator, and we discuss it separately later in the chapter.

- **Core functionality.** To create customer value, products must deliver on their core benefit. Products that fail to deliver on their core value proposition will inevitably fail in the market. Consider the plight of one-time highflier Nokia.

Learning Objectives After studying this chapter you should be able to:

8.1 Explain how companies use product differentiation to create market value.
8.2 Explain the role of product design in differentiating market offerings.
8.3 Discuss the key aspects of designing product portfolios and product lines.
8.4 Describe the key decisions involved in managing product packaging.
8.5 Explain how companies design and manage product guarantees and warranties.

- New in-text examples integrated into various chapters: Wipro (Chapter 1), HDFC Bank and Biocon (Chapter 2), Allen Solly (Chapter 3), Tata Steel (Chapter 4), Titan, Aries Agro, Geico, Bandhan Bank (Chapter 7), Infosys Finacle, Maruti Suzuki (Chapter 8), Narayana Health, Kaya Skin Clinic, Clirnet, SBI Yono (Chapter 9), Treebo, Mahindra Rise (Chapter 10), Buhler, Twilio (Chapter 11), ID Vada (Chapter 13), Eureka Forbes, Tupperware (Chapter 14), Ambit Energy (Chapter 14), Mercedes Benz (Chapter 15), Fab India, Max (Chapter 16), Cadbury, SBI MF SIP (Chapter 17) Godrej Interio (Chapter 19), Starbucks, TCS (Chapter 20), and Gokaldas Exports, Naandi Foundation, Plaeto, Faguo (Chapter 21).
- New Marketing Insights: Behavioral Decision Theory (Chapter 3), Chasing the Long Tail (Chapter 6), Ethical Issues in Prescription Drug Pricing (Chapter 11), Managing the Price Image of a Retailer (Chapter 16), and Understanding the Adoption of Innovations (Chapter 18).
- New Marketing Spotlights: Aravind Eye Care and PayTM (Chapter 3), udaan (Chapter 4), LEGO (Chapter 5), mjunction (Chapter 6), Lenskart (Chapter 7), Priceline (Chapter 11), Uber (Chapter 11), Avon (Chapter 14), Titan (Chapter 15), Croma (Chapter 16), Treebo (Chapter 17), Paper Boat (Chapter 18), WeChat (Chapter 18), Infosys & Tanishq (Chapter 19), Taj Hotels (Chapter 20), Ben & Jerry's (Chapter 21), and Tiffany & Co. (Chapter 21).

Solving Learning and Teaching Challenges

Many students who take a marketing management course are creative and have strong communication skills. However, students often have difficulty developing marketing plans that blend time-tested marketing approaches with modern marketing tools to both generate new customers and maintain existing customers. The 16th edition of *Marketing Management* addresses these challenges by reflecting changes in marketing theory and practice and providing relevant examples from a variety of industries.

This edition prepares students to work in today's environment as companies increasingly (1) shift gears from managing product and service portfolios to managing *customer* portfolios; (2) move from stand-alone mass products to integrated and customized service solutions; (3) use data analytics and artificial intelligence to better create and capture customer value; (4) rely on social media rather than traditional advertising to promote their offerings; (5) improve their methods of measuring customer profitability and customer lifetime value; (6) focus on measuring the return on their marketing investment and its impact on shareholder value; and (7) concern themselves with the ethical and social implications of their marketing decisions.

To address all these different shifts, the 16th edition is organized to specifically describe and interpret the following eight functions that constitute modern marketing management in the 21st century.

1. Developing a strategic marketing plan
2. Understanding the market and capturing market insights
3. Crafting winning marketing strategies
4. Designing market value
5. Communicating market value
6. Delivering market value
7. Managing growth in a socially responsible way

As companies change, so does their marketing organization. Marketing is no longer a company department charged with a limited number of tasks; it is a company-wide undertaking. It drives the company's vision, mission, and strategic planning. Marketing includes decisions like deciding whom the company wants as its customers, which customer needs to satisfy, what products and services to offer, what prices to set, what communications to send and receive, what channels of distribution to use, and what partnerships to develop.

PEDAGOGY THAT EMPHASIZES REAL-WORLD, RELEVANT MARKETING EXAMPLES

Effective learning occurs when sound theory is complemented by relevant practical examples. To this end, the 16th edition includes a variety of features—chapter-opening vignettes, in-text examples, Marketing Insights, and Marketing Spotlights—designed to engage students by highlighting the practical application of the concepts covered in each chapter.

- Each chapter opens with a relevant real-world marketing example that engages students and sets the context of the chapter.
- Each chapter includes several in-text features with additional real-world and engaging marketing examples to illustrate key concepts within sections.
- Each chapter includes at least one Marketing Insight feature that addresses a specific marketing topic in greater detail to provide in-depth coverage and foster better understanding of this topic.

marketing INSIGHT **Managing the Price Image of a Retailer**

Price image reflects the general perception that consumers have about the level of prices at a given retailer. For example, Walmart is often regarded as being rather inexpensive, whereas Target is usually considered to be moderately priced. Price image differs from price, which is quantitatively expressed; price image is qualitative in nature. This means that consumers regard a retailer's pricing in categorical terms such as "expensive" or "inexpensive." Price image resides in the minds of the buyers; thus, it is based on consumers' perception of prices at a particular retailer compared to other retailers and may not be an accurate reflection of the actual level of a retailer's prices.

Many managers mistakenly believe that price image is based solely on the prices within a specific store and that managing price image is as simple as adjusting the prices of items the store carries. This results in the theory that a retailer can lower its price image by lowering the prices of items in its assortment.

However, this method of resetting price image has not proved effective. Low or high prices are an important factor in the formation of a retailer's price image, but prices are not the only things that consumers consider when forming a judgment about price image. Figure 16.1 depicts the key drivers of price image and their related impact on consumer behavior.

- *Average price level.* Price image does indeed hinge on the actual prices of the items carried by a particular retailer, although not entirely. A store in which prices are substantially above those of its competitors will find it difficult to convince customers that it is not high priced, regardless of other measures it may take to change its price image.
- *Known-value items.* Consumers typically do not examine all prices at a store; instead, they tend to focus on items whose prices they are familiar with, which are referred to as known-value or signpost items. Because shoppers are aware of the prices for these items at other stores, they use them to determine whether or not a particular price is competitive. Known-value items usually fall into the category of frequently purchased items like milk, soda, and snacks, allowing consumers to readily compare prices across different stores.
- *Price range.* Consumers form an assessment of price image not just from the average level of prices at a retailer, but also from the range of prices within

- Each chapter includes two Marketing Spotlight (formerly Marketing Excellence) features that use a relevant real-world company to illustrate the marketing concepts covered in the chapter. Questions give students an opportunity to confirm their understanding and apply critical thinking. Professors can assign the questions as homework or use them for class discussion.

marketing SPOTLIGHT

IKEA

IKEA—a Swedish retailing company known for furniture, home furnishings, and appliances—has been the world's largest furniture retailer since 2008. IKEA has made a name for itself worldwide because of its affordable prices and innovative design. In 75 years of business, IKEA has expanded to over 300 stores in 25 countries across the globe, adjusting its stores and products on the basis of different consumer preferences in each location.

IKEA was founded by entrepreneur Ingvar Kamprad in 1943. The name IKEA is an acronym for Ingvar Kamprad's name; Elmtaryd, the farm where he grew up; and Agunnaryd, his hometown in Sweden. Kamprad started the business by

Source: Alexander Bilnov/Alamy Stock Photo

furniture. The popularity of IKEA's first showroom inspired the company to open its first retail location 5 years later in the same city. The profitability of IKEA's Almhult showroom spurred the spread of IKEA across Europe, starting with Norway in 1963. Enjoying success in European

The preceding features capture many of the significant changes and trends in the marketplace and can greatly enhance comprehension of the material by illustrating the key marketing concepts. In addition, these real-world examples can help to stimulate student interest and engagement with the material.

INSTRUCTOR TEACHING RESOURCES

Detailed information and resources are available at www.pearsoned.co.in/PhilipKotler

Acknowledgments

The 16th edition of *Marketing Management* bears the imprint of many people.

From Philip Kotler and Kevin Lane Keller: We are thrilled to introduce Professor Alexander Chernev as coauthor of the 16th edition of *Marketing Management*. Alex has contributed to the field of marketing in many ways—as an accomplished researcher, a widely acclaimed teacher, a prolific writer, and a trusted source of expert insight to many firms and organizations. He is that rare marketing scholar who skillfully blends rigor and relevance in all he does. Alex has made a name for himself through his unique ability to develop and disseminate relevant marketing knowledge, and we couldn't be more pleased to have had the opportunity to work with him on this new edition. At the top of this game, he has brought new ideas, new thinking, and new energy that have significantly transformed and improved the book. We thank Alex for his contribution and look forward to working with him on many more editions to come.

From Philip Kotler: My colleagues and associates at the Kellogg School of Management at Northwestern University continue to have an important impact on my thinking: Eric Anderson, Jim Anderson, Robert Blattberg, Ulf Böckenholt, Bobby Calder, Gregory Carpenter, Moran Cerf, Alexander Chernev, Anne Coughlan, David Gal, Kelly Goldsmith, Kent Grayson, Karsten Hansen, Lakshman Krishnamurthi, Angela Lee, Sidney Levy, Vincent Nijs, Neil Roese, Mohan Sawhney, John Sherry Jr., Louis Stern, Brian Sternthal, Alice Tybout, Florian Zettelmeyer, and Andris Zoltners. I also want to thank the S. C. Johnson Family for its generous support of my chair at the Kellogg School. Completing the Northwestern team are my former deans, Donald P. Jacobs, Dipak Jain, and Sally Blount, who have provided generous support for my research and writing.

Several former faculty members of the marketing department had a great influence on my thinking: Steuart Henderson Britt, Richard M. Clewett, Ralph Westfall, Harper W. Boyd, Sidney J. Levy,

John Sherry, and John Hauser. I also want to acknowledge Gary Armstrong for our work on *Principles of Marketing*.

I am indebted to the following coauthors of international editions of *Marketing Management* and *Principles of Marketing*, who have taught me a great deal in adapting marketing management thinking to the problems of different nations: Swee-Hoon Ang and Siew-Meng Leong (National University of Singapore), Chin-Tiong Tan (Singapore Management University), Marc Oliver Opresnik (University of Luebeck, Germany), Linden Brown and Stewart Adam (Deakin University, Australia), Suzan Burton (Macquarie Graduate School of Management, Australia), Sara Denize (University of Western Sydney, Australia), Delphine Manceau (ESCP-EAP European School of Management, France), John Saunders (Loughborough University, United Kingdom), Veronica Wong (Warwick University, United Kingdom), Jacob Hornick (Tel Aviv University, Israel), Walter Giorgio Scott (Universita Cattolica del Sacro Cuore, Italy), Peggy Cunningham (Queen's University, Canada), and Taihong Lu (Sun Yat-sen University, China).

I also want to acknowledge how much I have learned from working with coauthors on more specialized marketing subjects: Alan Andreasen, Christer Asplund, Paul N. Bloom, John Bowen, Roberta C. Clarke, Karen Fox, David Gertner, Evert Gummesson, Michael Hamlin, Thomas Hayes, Donald Haider, David Houle, Hooi Den Hua, Dipak Jain, Somkid Jatusripitak, Hermawan Kartajaya, Milton Kotler, Neil Kotler, Nancy Lee, Sandra Liu, Suvit Maesincee, James Maken, Waldemar Pfoertsch, Gustave Rath, Irving Rein, Eduardo Roberto, Christian Sarkar, Joanne Scheff, Joel Shalowitz, Ben Shields, Francois Simon, Robert Stevens, Fernando Trias de Bes, Walter Vieira, Bruce Wrenn, and David Young.

My overriding debt continues to be to my lovely wife, Nancy, who provided me with the time, support, and inspiration needed to prepare this edition. It is truly our book.

From Kevin Lane Keller: I continually benefit from the wisdom of my marketing colleagues at Tuck. I also gratefully acknowledge the invaluable research and teaching contributions from my faculty colleagues and collaborators through the years. I owe a considerable debt of gratitude to Duke University's Jim Bettman and Rick Staelin for helping to get my academic career started and serving as positive role models to this day. I am also appreciative of all that I have learned from working with many industry executives who have generously shared their insights and experiences. Finally, I give special thanks to Punam, my wife, and Carolyn and Allison, my daughters, who make it all happen and make it all worthwhile.

From Alexander Chernev: This book has benefited from the wisdom of many of my current and former colleagues at the Kellogg School of Management at Northwestern University. I owe a considerable debt of gratitude to Philip Kotler, who sparked my interest in marketing management. I am also indebted to Jim Bettman, Julie Edell Britton, Joel Huber, John Lynch, John Payne, and Rick Staelin at the Fuqua School of Business at Duke University for their advice and support at the outset of my academic career. I also would like to thank my current and former MBA and PhD students, who helped shape many of the conceptual insights and practical examples presented in this text. Special thanks are due to Alexander Moore (University of Chicago) for his valuable input and insightful comments, and to Joanne Freeman for her creative editing of the content of this text.

We are all indebted to the following colleagues at other universities who reviewed this new edition of *Marketing Management*:

Susan Baxter, LIM College
Courtney Cothren, University of Missouri
Jacqueline Eastman, Georgia Southern University
Cristina Farmus, Purdue University
Dr. Kelli Lynn Fellows, Pfeiffer University
David Fleming, Indiana State University
William Foxx, Troy University
Paul Galvani, University of Houston
John Gironda, Nova Southeastern University
Anne Hamby, Hofstra University
Hal Kingsley, Erie County Community College
Jennifer Landis, Wilmington University
Dian O'Leary, Wilmington University
Danielle C. Pienkowski, Bryant & Stratton College
Elizabeth Purinton-Johnson, Marist College
Raj Sachdev, Columbia College
Christina Simmers, Missouri State University
Sunil Jumar Singh, University of Nebraska-Lincoln
Raphael Thomadsen, Washington University in St. Louis
George Young, Liberty University

We would also like to thank colleagues who have reviewed previous editions of *Marketing Management*:

Homero Aguirre, TAMIU
Alan Au, University of Hong Kong
Hiram Barksdale, University of Georgia
Jennifer Barr, Richard Stockton College
Boris Becker, Oregon State University
Sandy Becker, Rutgers University
Parimal Bhagat, Indiana University of Pennsylvania
Sunil Bhatla, Case Western Reserve University
Michael Bruce, Anderson University
Frederic Brunel, Boston University
John Burnett, University of Denver
Lisa Cain, University of California at Berkeley and Mills College
Surjit Chhabra, DePaul University
Yun Chu, Frostburg State University
Dennis Clayson, University of Northern Iowa
Bob Cline, University of Iowa
Brent Cunningham, Jacksonville State University
Hugh Daubek, Purdue University
John Deighton, University of Chicago
Kathleen Dominick, Rider University
Tad Duffy, Golden Gate University
Lawrence Kenneth Duke, Drexel University
Mohan Dutta, Purdue University
Barbara Dyer, University of North Carolina at Greensboro
Jackie Eastman, Georgia Southern University
Steve Edison, University of Arkansas–Little Rock
Alton Erdem, University of Houston at Clear Lake
Elizabeth Evans, Concordia University
Barbara S. Faries, Mission College
William E. Fillner, Hiram College
Barb Finer, Suffolk University
Chic Fojtik, Pepperdine University
Renee Foster, Delta State University
Frank J. Franzak, Virginia Commonwealth University
Ralph Gaedeke, California State University, Sacramento
Robert Galka, DePaul University
Betsy Gelb, University of Houston at Clear Lake
Dennis Gensch, University of Wisconsin, Milwaukee
David Georgoff, Florida Atlantic University
Rashi Glazer, University of California, Berkeley
Bill Gray, Keller Graduate School of Management
Albert N. Greco, Fordham University
Barbara Gross, California State University at Northridge
Lewis Hershey, Fayetteville State University
Thomas Hewett, Kaplan University
Mary Higby, University of Detroit–Mercy
John A. Hobbs, University of Oklahoma
Arun Jain, State University of New York, Buffalo
Michelle Kunz, Morehead State University
Eric Langer, Johns Hopkins University
Even Lanseng, Norwegian School of Management
Brian Larson, Widener University
Ron Lennon, Barry University
Michael Lodato, California Lutheran University
Henry Loehr, Pfeiffer University–Charlotte
Bart Macchiette, Plymouth University
Susan Mann, Bluefield State College
Charles Martin, Wichita State University
H. Lee Matthews, Ohio State University
Paul McDevitt, University of Illinois at Springfield
Mary Ann McGrath, Loyola University, Chicago
John McKeever, University of Houston
Kenneth P. Mead, Central Connecticut State University
Henry Metzner, University of Missouri, Rolla
Robert Mika, Monmouth University
Mark Mitchell, Coastal Carolina University
Francis Mulhern, Northwestern University
Pat Murphy, University of Notre Dame
Jim Murrow, Drury College
Zhou Nan, University of Hong Kong
Nicholas Nugent, Boston College
Nnamdi Osakwe, Bryant & Stratton College
Donald Outland, University of Texas, Austin
Albert Page, University of Illinois, Chicago
Young-Hoon Park, Cornell University
Koen Pauwels, Dartmouth College
Lisa Klein Pearo, Cornell University
Keith Penney, Webster University
Patricia Perry, University of Alabama
Mike Powell, North Georgia College and State University
Hank Pruden, Golden Gate University
Christopher Puto, Arizona State University
Abe Qstin, Lakeland University
Anthony Racka, Oakland Community College
Lopo Rego, University of Iowa
Jamie Ressler, Palm Beach Atlantic University

Richard Rexeisen, University of St. Thomas
William Rice, California State University–Fresno
Scott D. Roberts, Northern Arizona University
Bill Robinson, Purdue University
Robert Roe, University of Wyoming
Jan Napoleon Saykiewicz, Duquesne University
Larry Schramm, Oakland University
James E. Shapiro, University of New Haven
Alex Sharland, Hofstra University
George David Shows, Louisiana Tech University
Dean Siewers, Rochester Institute of Technology
Anusorn Singhapakdi, Old Dominion University
Jim Skertich, Upper Iowa University
Allen Smith, Florida Atlantic University
Joe Spencer, Anderson University
Mark Spriggs, University of St. Thomas
Nancy Stephens, Arizona State University
Michael Swenso, Brigham Young University, Marriott School
Thomas Tellefsen, The College of Staten Island–CUNY
Daniel Turner, University of Washington
Sean Valentine, University of Wyoming
Ann Veeck, West Michigan University
R. Venkatesh, University of Pittsburgh
Edward Volchok, Stevens Institute of Management
D. J. Wasmer, St. Mary-of-the-Woods College
Zac Williams, Mississippi State University
Greg Wood, Canisius College
Kevin Zeng Zhou, University of Hong Kong

The talented staff at Pearson deserves praise for their role in shaping the 16th edition. We want to thank our editor, Lynn Huddon, for her contribution to this revision, as well as our product manager, Krista Mastroianni. We also want to thank our content producer, Claudia Fernandes, and our project manager, Kelly Murphy, for making sure everything moved along and fell into place in such a personable way, both with the book and with the supplements. We benefited greatly from the superb editorial help of Lena Buonanno, whose insights considerably enhanced this edition. We also thank our marketing team, Nayke Heine and Mellissa Yokell.

Philip Kotler
Professor Emeritus of Marketing
Kellogg School of Management
Northwestern University
Evanston, Illinois

Kevin Lane Keller
E. B. Osborn Professor of Marketing
Tuck School of Business
Dartmouth College
Hanover, New Hampshire

Alexander Chernev
Professor of Marketing
Kellogg School of Management
Northwestern University
Evanston, Illinois

Acknowledgments for Indian Edition

We would like to acknowledge the meticulous efforts of Sonal Khatri, Research Associate, IIM Bangalore. For each brand story, Sonal helped identify multiple published sources for triangulation and comprehensive understanding for incorporation as chapter openers, caselets, in-text examples and spotlights.

We are grateful to all business leaders, CEOs, CMOs, Marketing Heads and Communication Heads who responded promptly and positively to our requests for images and creatives. Many took the effort to create exclusive composites and creatives to align the images with write-up on their brands and organizations.

Pearson India's professional and skilful team deserve our special thanks for their efforts in shaping this adaptation. It has been a real pleasure working with Varun Goenka, Anindita Malhotra and Swati Chauhan.

Jagdish N. Sheth

Charles H. Kellstadt Professor of Business
Goizueta Business School, Emory University
Atlanta, Georgia, US

G Shainesh

Professor of Marketing
Indian Institute of Management Bangalore (IIMB)
Bengaluru, India

About the Authors

Philip Kotler is one of the world's leading authorities on marketing. He is the S. C. Johnson & Son Distinguished Professor of International Marketing at the Kellogg School of Management, Northwestern University (emeritus). He received his master's degree at the University of Chicago and his PhD at MIT, both in economics. He did postdoctoral work in mathematics at Harvard University and in behavioral science at the University of Chicago.

Dr. Kotler is the author or coauthor of *Principles of Marketing; Marketing: An Introduction; Strategic Marketing for Nonprofit Organizations; Marketing Models; The New Competition; Marketing Professional Services; Strategic Marketing for Educational Institutions; Marketing for Health Care Organizations; High Visibility; Social Marketing; Marketing Places; The Marketing of Nations; Marketing for Hospitality and Tourism; Standing Room Only; Museum Strategy and Marketing; Marketing Moves; Kotler on Marketing; Lateral Marketing; Winning at Innovation; Ten Deadly Marketing Sins; Chaotics; Winning Global Markets; Corporate Social Responsibility; Confronting Capitalism; Democracy in Decline; Advancing the Common Good; Social Media Marketing; Brand Activism; Marketing 3.0; Marketing 4.0;* and *My Adventures in Marketing.*

In addition, he has published over 150 articles in leading journals, including *Harvard Business Review, Sloan Management Review, Business Horizons, California Management Review, Journal of Marketing, Journal of Marketing Research, Management Science, Journal of Business Strategy,* and *Futurist*. He is the only three-time winner of the Alpha Kappa Psi award for the best annual article published in the *Journal of Marketing*.

Professor Kotler was the first recipient of the American Marketing Association's (AMA) Distinguished Marketing Educator Award (1985); he was chosen as the Leader in Marketing Thought by academic members of the AMA (1975) and received the Paul Converse Award (1978). Other honors include the Prize for Marketing Excellence from the European Association of Marketing Consultants and Sales Trainers; Sales and Marketing Executives International's (SMEI) Marketer of the Year (1995); the Distinguished Educator Award from the Academy of Marketing Science (2002); the William L. Wilkie "Marketing for a Better World" Award (2013); the Sheth Foundation Medal for Exceptional Contribution to Marketing Scholarship and Practice (2013); and induction into the Marketing Hall of Fame (2014).

He has received 22 honorary doctoral degrees, among them from Stockholm University, the University of Zurich, Athens University of Economics and Business, DePaul University, the Cracow School of Business and Economics, Groupe H.E.C. in Paris, the Budapest School of Economic Science and Public Administration, the University of Economics and Business Administration in Vienna, and Plekhanov Russian Academy of Economics.

Professor Kotler has been a consultant to many major U.S. and foreign companies, including IBM, General Electric, AT&T, Honeywell, Bank of America, Merck, SAS Airlines, and Michelin. In addition, he has served as chairman of the College of Marketing of the Institute of Management Sciences, a director of the American Marketing Association, a trustee of the Marketing Science Institute, a director of the MAC Group, a member of the Yankelovich Advisory Board, and a member of the Copernicus Advisory Board. He was a member of the Board of Governors of the School of the Art Institute of Chicago and a member of the Advisory Board of the Drucker Foundation. He has traveled extensively throughout Europe, Asia, and South America, advising many companies about global marketing opportunities.

Kevin Lane Keller is the E. B. Osborn Professor of Marketing and Senior Associate Dean for Marketing and Communications at the Tuck School of Business at Dartmouth College. Professor Keller has an AB degree in math and economics from Cornell University, an MBA from Carnegie-Mellon, and a PhD in marketing from Duke University. At Dartmouth, he teaches MBA courses on strategic brand management and lectures in executive programs on those topics.

Previously, Professor Keller was on the faculty at Stanford University, where he also served as head of the marketing group. Additionally, he has been on the faculty at the University of California at Berkeley and the University of North Carolina at Chapel Hill, was a visiting professor at Duke University and the Australian Graduate School of Management, and has two years of industry experience as marketing consultant for Bank of America.

Professor Keller's general area of expertise is in understanding how theories and concepts related to consumer psychology can improve branding and marketing strategies. His research has been published numerous times in each of the four of the major marketing journals: the *Journal of Marketing*, *Journal of Marketing Research*, *Journal of Consumer Research,* and *Marketing Science*. With over 120 published papers, he is also one of the most heavily cited of all marketing academics, and he has received numerous awards for his research accomplishments.

Actively involved with industry, Professor Keller has worked on a host of different types of marketing projects. He has served as a consultant and advisor to marketers for some of the world's most successful brands, including Accenture, American Express, Disney, Ford, Intel, Levi Strauss, L.L. Bean, Nike, Procter & Gamble, and Samsung. He is a popular and highly sought-after speaker and has given keynote speeches and conducted workshops with top executives in a wide variety of forums. He has lectured all over the world, from Seoul to Johannesburg, from Sydney to Stockholm, and from Sao Paulo to Mumbai.

Professor Keller is currently conducting a variety of research studies that address strategies to build, measure, and manage brand equity. His text on those subjects, *Strategic Brand Management*, added coauthor Vanitha Swaminathan for its 5th edition. It has been adopted at top business schools and leading firms around the world and has been heralded as the "bible of branding." He has also served as an academic trustee, executive director, and executive committee member for the Marketing Science Institute.

An avid sports, music, and film enthusiast in his so-called spare time, Professor Keller has helped to manage, market, and serve as executive producer for one of Australia's great rock and roll treasures, The Church, as well as American power-pop legends Tommy Keene and Dwight Twilley. He currently serves on the Board of Directors for the Lebanon Opera House and the Doug Flutie, Jr. Foundation for Autism. He lives in Etna, New Hampshire, with his wife Punam (also a Tuck marketing professor) and two daughters, Carolyn and Allison.

Alexander Chernev is a professor of marketing at the Kellogg School of Management, Northwestern University. He holds an MA and a PhD in psychology from Sofia University and a PhD in business administration from Duke University. He is an academic thought leader, speaker, and advisor in the area of marketing strategy, brand management, consumer decision making, and behavioral economics.

Professor Chernev has written numerous articles focused on business strategy, brand management, consumer behavior, and market planning. His research has been published in the leading marketing journals and has been frequently quoted in the business and popular press, including the *Wall Street Journal*, the *Financial Times*, the *New York Times*, the *Washington Post*, *Harvard Business Review*, *Scientific American*, the *Associated Press*, *Forbes*, and *Bloomberg Businessweek*. He was ranked among the top ten most prolific scholars in the leading marketing journals by the *Journal of Marketing* and among the top five marketing faculty in the area of consumer behavior by a global survey of marketing faculty published by the *Journal of Marketing Education*.

In addition to academic and managerial articles, Professor Chernev has published a number of impactful books—*Strategic Marketing Management: Theory and Practice*, *Strategic Marketing Management: The Framework, Strategic Brand Management*, *The Marketing Plan Handbook*, and *The Business Model: How to Develop New Products, Create Market Value, and Make the Competition Irrelevant*—that have been translated into multiple languages and are used in top business schools around the world.

Professor Chernev has served as an area editor for the *Journal of Marketing* and the *Journal of Consumer Psychology* and on the editorial boards of leading research journals, including the *Journal of Marketing Research*, *Journal of Consumer Research*, *International Journal of Research in Marketing*, *Journal of the Academy of Marketing Science*, and *Journal of Marketing Behavior*.

At the Kellogg School of Management, Professor Chernev teaches marketing strategy, brand management, and behavioral decision theory in MBA, PhD, and executive education programs. He has also taught in executive programs at INSEAD in France and Singapore, at the Institute for Management Development (IMD) in Switzerland, and at Hong Kong University of Science and Technology. He has received numerous teaching awards, including the Core Course Teaching Award, the Kellogg Faculty Impact Award, and the Kellogg Executive MBA Program's Top Professor Award, which he has received 13 times.

In addition to research and teaching, Professor Chernev has served as an academic trustee, and is currently a fellow, of the *Marketing Science Institute.* He has served as an expert on numerous legal cases dealing with issues pertaining to intellectual property, consumer behavior, and marketing strategy. A consummate educator and presenter, Professor Chernev has keynoted presentations at conferences and corporate events around the globe. He advises companies worldwide—from Fortune 500 firms to start-ups—on issues of marketing strategy, brand management, strategic planning, and new-product development, as well as on ways to craft their business models, build strong brands, uncover market opportunities, develop new products and services, and gain competitive advantage.

Jagdish N. Sheth is Charles H. Kellstadt Professor of Business in the Goizueta Business School at Emory University. He is globally known for his scholarly contributions in consumer behavior, relationship marketing, competitive strategy, and geopolitical analysis. Professor Sheth has over 50 years of combined experience in teaching and research at the University of Southern California, the University of Illinois at Urbana-Champaign, Columbia University, MIT, and Emory University.

Dr. Sheth is a recipient of the 2020 Padma Bhushan Award for literature and education, one of the highest civilian awards given by the Government of India. He is also a Fellow of the Academy of International Business (AIB); Fellow of the Association of Consumer Research (ACR); Fellow of the American Psychological Association (APA); Fellow of the American Marketing Association (AMA); Distinguished Fellow of the Academy of Marketing Science (AMS); and a Distinguished Fellow of International Engineering Consortium. Dr. Sheth is the recipient of an Honorary Doctorate in Science, awarded by the University of Illinois at Urbana-Champaign (2016), and Honorary Doctor of Philosophy, awarded by Shiv Nadar University (2017). He is the recipient of all four top awards given by the American Marketing Association (AMA).

Dr. Sheth has been on the board of several companies including Norstan, Pacwest-Telecom, Cryocell International, Shasun Drugs and Chemicals, and WIPRO Limited. Over the 50 years, he has been advisor to numerous companies including Whirlpool, Motorola, Texas Instruments, Cox Communications, Rockwell International, AT&T, Bellsouth, WIPRO Consumer Care, Aditya Birla Group, L.M. Mittal (Avanta), E&Y, Square D, Ingram Micro, Hughes Corporation, and others. This has included mergers and acquisitions as well as strategic positioning or repositioning of the company.

His *Rule of Three* book has been the foundation for investment bankers and policy makers with respect to industry consolidation including horizontal mergers and acquisitions. Professor Sheth has authored or coauthored more than three hundred papers and several books including *The Global Rule of Three: Competing with Conscious Strategy* (2020), *The Howard-Sheth Theory of Buyer Behavior* (2020), *Genes, Climate and Consumption Culture: Connecting the Dots* (2017), *Breakout Strategies for Emerging Markets* (2016), *The Sustainability Edge* (2016), *The 4 As of Marketing* (2012), *Chindia Rising* (2011), *Self-Destructive Habits of Good Companies* (2007), *Firms of Endearment* (2007), *Tectonic Shift* (2006), *The Rule of Three* (2002), and *Clients for Life* (2000). His autobiography, *The Accidental Scholar* (2014), has inspired others in the areas of education and academic entrepreneurship.

Professor Sheth has been advisor to the Government of Singapore in repositioning the nation for the future. He has also been the policy advisor to the U.S. Government about the future of the telecommunications industry.

Dr. Sheth is the Founder of Center for Telecommunications Management (CTM) at University of Southern California (USC) which has now become an Institute. He is also Founder and Chairman of India, China, and America (ICA) Institute which analyzes the trilateral relationship and its impact on geopolitics, security, trade, and investment. He and his wife, Madhu Sheth, have established the Sheth Family Foundation to support several charities in India and in the United States. They have also established the Madhuri and Jagdish Sheth Foundation to support scholars and scholarship in the field of marketing. The Sheth Foundation supports the AMA-Sheth Foundation Doctoral Consortium, hosted annually by different universities. It also supports research in emerging fields through AMA, ACR, AMS, and AIB. Finally, Professor Sheth is the Founder and Chairman of the Academy of Indian Marketing (AIM) which supports research and scholarship among Indian scholars in marketing and management.

G Shainesh is a Professor of Marketing at the Indian Institute of Management Bangalore (IIMB). He is the current Chair for Executive Education at IIMB. Shainesh has over two and half decades of research and teaching experience in India and abroad. He has conducted research and teaching assignments at the University of Gothenburg (Sweden), University of St. Gallen (Switzerland), Audencia Nantes and IESEG (France), Vienna University and MCI Innsbruck (Austria), Bocconi University (Milan), and Curtin University of Technology (Perth), among others. His research and teaching focus on Digital Marketing Strategies, Relationship Marketing, Services Marketing and Service Innovations. At IIMB, Shainesh has served as Dean – Administration (2014-17), Chair – EPGP (2013-14) and Chair – Student Exchange Program (2006–09).

He leads the cross functional research initiative on consumer insights (ICI@IIMB). His case study 'Narayana Nethralaya: Expanding Affordable Eye Care' won the second prize in the GlobaLens 2014 NextBillion Case Writing Competition. He was named 'Best Professor in Marketing' by the CMO Asia Council during the 'Best B-Schools in Asia Awards', July 2011, Singapore. He is also a past winner of the Citibank Special Research Award (1994) and P D Agarwal TCI Award for Doctoral Research in Management (1995).

He has worked for several organizations in the public, the non-profit and the corporate sectors, including telecom, software, engineering, and service firms, both as an advisor and as a seminar leader. His clients include ABB, Adobe, Allstate Insurance, Aventis Pharma, Department of Pharmaceuticals, Caterpillar, Ericsson, Indian Oil, Lumen Technologies, Manipal Universal, NCSM, Philips, SKF, Indian Railways, IFFCO, ICPB, Ministry of Tourism, Power Ministry, Tata AIG, TRIFED, Sanskriti, Pradan, etc.

His books include *Social Media Marketing: Emerging Concepts and Applications* (2018), *Customer Relationship Management – A Strategic Perspective* (2006) and *Customer Relationship Management – Emerging Concepts, Tools and Applications* (21st Reprint 2017). Professor Shainesh's MOOC courses on CRM and Services Marketing are offered on edX https://www.edx.org/bio/shainesh-g

He is Editor-in-Chief of the *Journal of Indian Business Research (JIBR)*, an Emerald (UK) publication. His papers on services and relationship marketing have been published in the MIS Quarterly, *Journal of Service Research, Journal of International Marketing*, *Journal of Services Marketing, Service Industries Journal, International Journal of Bank Marketing, International Journal of Retail and Distribution Management, International Journal of Technology Management, Journal of Relationship Marketing, International Marketing Review*, among others.

Marketing Management

CHAPTER 1

Defining Marketing for the New Realities

Source: bigbasket ©Innovative Retail Concepts Pvt Ltd., used with permission

Formally and informally, people and organizations engage in a vast number of activities that we call marketing. In the face of the digital revolution and other major changes in the business environment, effective marketing today is both increasingly vital and radically new. Consider the rapid market success of the start-up bigbasket.

>>> Founded in 2011, bigbasket has rapidly emerged as India's largest online grocer, serving around 10 million customers. In 2018, the company fulfilled almost 100,000 orders every day from its wide array of over 18,000 grocery items in 25 cities.[1]

The market for grocery is highly competitive, especially in urban India where customers in cities are spoilt for choice—starting from the neighborhood *'kirana'* stores to supermarket chains like Reliance Mart, Big Bazaar, DMart, Spar and More. The options have further widened with the entry of start-ups, like Blinkit and Dunzo and e-commerce giants like Amazon and Flipkart, into home delivery of grocery and essentials. bigbasket is the brainchild of a team of dotcom bust veterans. In 1999, they had set up FabMart, a pioneering e-commerce company to sell grocery, toys and books, and later its physical extension—FabMall, a chain of food and grocery stores that scaled up to over 200 stores before being acquired by a large conglomerate. Enriched with invaluable experience and understanding of the grocery market, online as well as offline, the same team set up bigbasket in Bengaluru. Soon bigbasket gained the homemaker's trust by understanding and responding to the household needs through a user-friendly website and mobile app for easy search and order, good quality products and on-time delivery backed by a responsive service support. The company relied on 'word of mouth' to attract customers in the initial years while judiciously expanding its operations to other big cities. In 2016, the company signed up one of the leading Bollywood actors as a brand ambassador to create awareness and influence while expanding into new markets. The company's emphasis on quality fresh produce, broad assortment, competitive prices and a robust supply chain tailored for time sensitive grocery deliveries have been key differentiators.[2] A dedicated network of farmers, suppliers and employees enables bigbasket to provide a consistent customer experience in the challenging category of groceries involving perishables. The company's farm-to-fork supply chain engages with over 30,000 farmers and provides them with a direct and secure route to market.[3] bigbasket's agronomists support these farmers to adopt better practices for improving yield and producing organic and high-quality vegetables, fruits and staples. The company's end-to-end logistics system orchestrates the collection of produce from farms, processing them at collection centers and quick transportation to ensure that over 60% orders for locally grown vegetables and fruits are delivered to homes within 8-hours after harvesting. The delivery system is AI driven with a geocoding engine that provides optimized and dynamic route planning to reduce logistics costs while improving customer experience by ensuring over 99.5% of its orders are delivered on time.[4] Its contact centers support customers over calls in local languages, live chats, emails and chatbots. bigbasket has also expanded physical reach through 'BB Instant' vending machines, stocked with fast moving grocery items, at offices, technology parks and residential premises to improve availability and convenience. BB Daily, a subscription service, helps customers place last minute orders for milk, staples, and fresh groceries till 10.00 PM for delivery early next morning. The convenience and safety offered by home delivery boosted bigbasket's customer base by 84 per cent along with an increase in daily orders by 40% and larger order sizes during the pandemic in 2020.[5]

Presently, the company serves over 15 million customers in 30 cities through an assortment of around 30,000 stock keeping units (SKUs). It handles over 3 million customer orders every month. The competition in the online grocery market is intensifying with quicker delivery options from Swiggy InstaMart, Dunzo Daily and OTPxpress. bigbasket continues to innovate to stay ahead of the pack. The infusion of over $200 million by the Tata group will help the team explore more opportunities as it charts an ambitious plan to accelerate its leadership position.[6]

Good marketing is no accident. It is both an art and a science, and it results from careful planning and execution using state-of-the-art tools and techniques. Skillful marketers are continually updating classic practices and inventing new ones to find creative, practical ways to adapt to new marketing realities. In this chapter, we lay the foundation for sound marketing practices by reviewing important marketing concepts, tools, frameworks, and issues.

Learning Objectives After studying this chapter you should be able to:

1.1 Define the scope of marketing.

1.2 Describe the new marketing realities.

1.3 Explain the role of marketing in the organization.

1.4 Illustrate how to organize and manage a modern marketing department.

1.5 Explain how to build a customer-centric organization.

The Scope of Marketing

To be a successful marketer, one must have a clear understanding of the essence of marketing, what can be marketed, and how marketing works. We discuss these three aspects of marketing next.

WHAT IS MARKETING?

Marketing is about identifying and meeting human and social needs in a way that harmonizes with the goals of the organization. When Google recognized that people needed to more effectively and efficiently access information on the internet, it created a powerful search engine that organized and prioritized queries. When IKEA noticed that people wanted good furnishings at substantially lower prices, it created knockdown furniture. These two firms demonstrated marketing savvy and turned a private or social need into a profitable business opportunity.[7]

The American Marketing Association offers the following formal definition: *Marketing is the activity, set of institutions, and processes for creating, communicating, delivering, and exchanging offerings that have value for customers, clients, partners, and society at large.*[8] Coping with these exchange processes calls for a considerable amount of work and skill. Marketing management takes place when at least one party to a potential exchange thinks about the means of achieving desired responses from other parties. Thus **marketing management** *is the art and science of choosing target markets and getting, keeping, and growing customers through creating, delivering, and communicating superior customer value.*

We can also distinguish between social and managerial definition of marketing. A social definition of marketing shows the role marketing plays in society; for example, one marketer has said that marketing's role is to "deliver a higher standard of living." Our social definition of marketing: *Marketing is a societal process by which individuals and groups obtain what they need and want through creating, offering, and freely exchanging products and services of value with others.* Co-creation of value among consumers and with businesses, and the importance of value creation and sharing, have become important themes in the development of modern marketing thought.[9]

Managers sometimes think of marketing as "the art of selling products," and many people are surprised when they hear that selling is *not* the most important part of marketing. Selling is only the tip of the marketing iceberg. Peter Drucker, famed management theorist, put it this way:

> There will always, one can assume, be need for some selling. But the aim of marketing is to make selling superfluous. The aim of marketing is to know and understand the customer so well that the product or service fits him and sells itself. Ideally, marketing should result in a customer who is ready to buy. All that should be needed then is to make the product or service available.[10]

When Nintendo released its Wii game system, when Apple launched its iPad tablet computer, and when Toyota introduced its Prius hybrid automobile, these manufacturers were swamped with orders. Their success cannot be attributed merely to the great selling skills of retailers. Rather, their runaway success stemmed from the fact that they had designed the right product, based on careful marketing homework about consumers, competition, and all the external factors that affect cost and demand.

WHAT IS MARKETED?

Marketing is ubiquitous—it permeates all aspects of the society. Specifically, marketing typically involves 10 different domains: goods, services, events, experiences, persons, places, properties, organizations, information, and ideas. Let's take a quick look at these categories.

- **Goods.** Physical goods constitute the bulk of most countries' production and marketing efforts. Each year U.S. companies market billions of fresh, canned, bagged, and frozen food products and millions of cars, refrigerators, televisions, machines, and other mainstays of a modern economy.
- **Services.** As economies advance, a growing proportion of their activities focus on the production of services. The U.S. economy today produces a services-to-goods mix of roughly two-thirds to one-third. Services include the offerings of airlines, hotels, car rental firms, barbers and beauticians, maintenance and repair people, accountants, bankers, lawyers, engineers, doctors, software programmers, and management consultants. Many market offerings mix goods and services, such as a fast-food meal.
- **Events.** Marketers promote time-based events, including major trade shows, artistic performances, and company anniversaries. Global sporting events such as the Olympics and the World

Cup are promoted aggressively to companies and fans. Local events include craft fairs, bookstore readings, and farmers' markets.

- **Experiences.** By orchestrating several services and goods, a firm can create, stage, and market experiences. Walt Disney World's Magic Kingdom lets customers visit a fairy kingdom, a pirate ship, or a haunted house. Customized experiences include a week at a baseball camp with retired baseball greats, a four-day rock-and-roll fantasy camp, and a climb up Mount Everest.
- **Persons.** Artists, musicians, CEOs, physicians, high-profile lawyers and financiers, and other professionals often get help from marketers.[11] Many athletes and entertainers have done a masterful job of marketing themselves—cricket star Virat Kohli, Bollywood superstar Amitabh Bachchan, celebrity chef Sanjeev Kapoor and Olympic medal winner P V Sindhu. Management consultant Tom Peters, himself a master at self-branding, has advised each person to become a "brand."
- **Places.** Cities, states, regions, and whole nations compete to attract tourists, residents, factories, and company headquarters.[12] Place marketers include economic development specialists, real estate agents, commercial banks, local business associations, and advertising and public relations agencies. The Las Vegas Convention & Visitors Authority has met with much success with its provocative ad campaign "What Happens Here, Stays Here," portraying Las Vegas as "an adult playground."
- **Properties.** Properties involve intangible rights of ownership to either real property (real estate) or financial property (stocks and bonds). They are bought and sold, and these exchanges require marketing. Real estate agents work for property owners and sellers, or they buy and sell residential and commercial real estate. Investment companies and banks market securities to both institutional and individual investors.
- **Organizations.** Museums, performing-arts organizations, corporations, and nonprofits all use marketing to boost their public image and compete for audiences and funds. Some universities have created chief marketing officer (CMO) positions to better manage their school identity and image, encompassing everything from admission brochures and Twitter feeds to brand strategy.
- **Information.** Information is disseminated knowledge. It is produced, marketed, and distributed by TV and radio news, newspapers, the internet, think tanks, government and business entities, and schools and universities. Firms make business decisions using information supplied by organizations such as Nielsen, R.R. Donnelley & Sons, comscore, Gartner, J.D. Power and Associates, GfK, and Ipsos.
- **Ideas.** Social marketers promote such ideas as "Friends Don't Let Friends Drive Drunk" and "A Mind Is a Terrible Thing to Waste." Political parties promote social causes such as gun control, tax reform, and affordable health care. As part of their corporate social responsibility activities, many organizations promote causes focused on issues such as poverty, climate change, civil rights, social justice, racial discrimination, gender inequality, health care availability, and childhood obesity.

THE MARKETING EXCHANGE

A marketer is someone who seeks a response—attention, a purchase, a vote, a donation—from another party. Marketers are skilled at stimulating demand for their products; however, that's a limited view of what they do. They also seek to influence the level, timing, and composition of demand to meet the organization's objectives.

Traditionally, a "market" was a physical place where buyers and sellers gathered to buy and sell goods. Economists describe a market as a collection of buyers and sellers who negotiate transactions that involve a particular product or product class (such as the housing market or the grain market).

There are five basic markets: resource markets, manufacturer markets, consumer markets, intermediary markets, and government markets. The five basic markets and their connecting flows of goods, services, and money are shown in Figure 1.1. Manufacturers go to resource markets (raw material markets, labor markets, money markets), buy resources and turn them into goods and services, and sell finished products to intermediaries, who sell them to consumers. Consumers sell their labor and receive money with which they pay for the goods and services they purchase. The government collects tax revenues to buy goods from resource, manufacturer, and intermediary markets and uses these goods and services to provide public services. Every nation's economy, and the global economy itself, all consist of interacting sets of markets linked through exchange processes.

Marketers view *industry* as a group of sellers and use the term *market* to describe customer groups. There are need markets (the diet-seeking market), product markets (the shoe market), demographic markets (the "Millennium" youth market), and geographic markets (the Chinese market), as well as voter markets, labor markets, and donor markets.

Figure 1.2 shows how sellers and buyers are connected by four flows. Sellers send goods and services and communications such as ads and direct mail to the market; in return, they receive money

FIGURE **1.1**
Structure of Goods, Services, and Money Flows in a Modern Exchange Economy

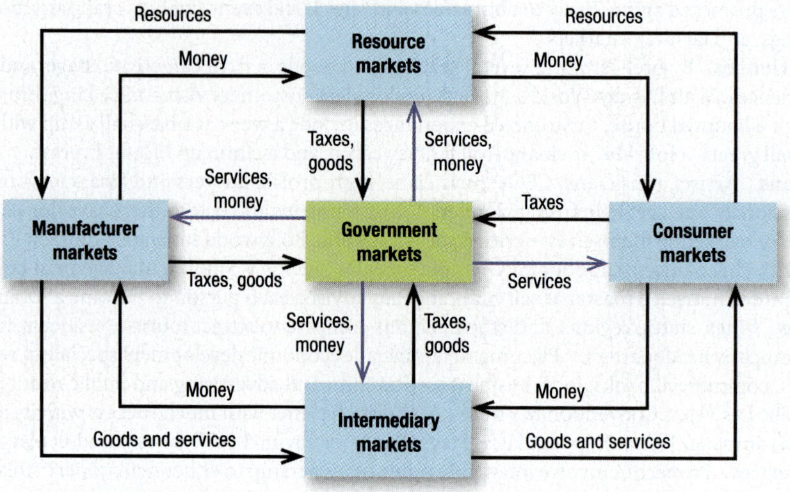

FIGURE **1.2**
A Simple Marketing System

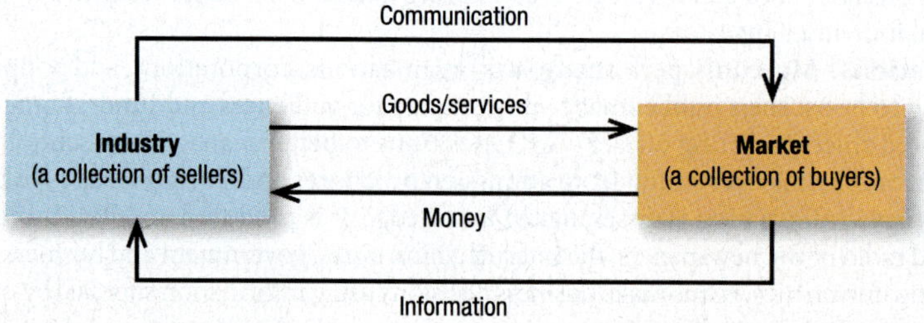

and information such as data on customer attitudes and sales. The inner loop shows an exchange of money for goods and services; the outer loop shows an exchange of information.

Finance, operations, accounting, and other business functions won't really matter without sufficient demand for products and services that enable a firm to make a profit. In other words, there must be an effective top line for there to be a healthy bottom line. Thus, financial success often depends on marketing ability. Marketing's value extends to society as a whole. It has helped introduce new or enhanced products that ease or enrich people's lives. Successful marketing builds demand for products and services, which, in turn, creates jobs. By contributing to the bottom line, successful marketing also allows firms to more fully engage in socially responsible activities.[13]

In an online- and mobile-fueled environment where consumers, competition, technology, and economic forces change rapidly and consequences quickly multiply, marketers must choose features, prices, and markets and decide how much to spend on advertising, sales, and online and mobile marketing.

There is little margin for error in marketing. Just a short time ago, MySpace, Yahoo!, Blockbuster, and Barnes & Noble were admired leaders in their industries. What a difference a few years can make! All of these brands have been completely overtaken by upstart challengers—Facebook, Google, Netflix, and Amazon, respectively—and they now struggle, sometimes unsuccessfully, for mere survival. Firms must constantly move forward. At greatest risk are those companies that fail to carefully monitor their customers and competitors and thus fail to continually improve their value offerings and marketing strategies, in the process satisfying their employees, stockholders, suppliers, and channel partners.

Innovation in marketing is critical. Imaginative ideas on strategy exist in many places within a company. Senior management should identify and encourage fresh ideas from three generally underrepresented groups: employees with youthful or diverse perspectives, employees far removed from company headquarters, and employees new to the industry. Each group can challenge company orthodoxy and stimulate new ideas.

British-based RB (formerly Reckitt Benckiser) has been an innovator in the staid household cleaning products industry by generating 35 percent of sales from products under three years old. Its multinational staff is encouraged to dig deeply into consumer habits and is well rewarded for excellent performance.

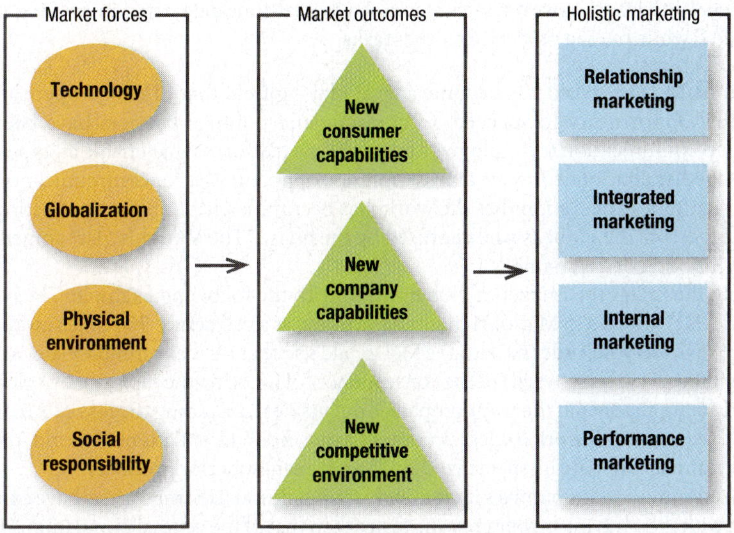

FIGURE **1.3**
The New Marketing Realities

The New Marketing Realities

The marketplace is dramatically different from even 10 years ago, with new marketing behaviors, opportunities, and challenges emerging.[14] The new market realities can be divided into three main categories: the market forces that shape the relationships among the different market entities, the market outcomes that stem from the interplay of these forces, and the emergence of holistic marketing as an essential approach to succeeding in the rapidly evolving market.

Figure 1.3 summarizes the four major market forces, three key market outcomes, and four fundamental pillars of holistic marketing that help to capture the new marketing realities. With these concepts in place, we can identify a specific set of tasks that make up successful marketing management and marketing leadership.

THE FOUR MAJOR MARKET FORCES

The business environment today has been profoundly influenced by four main forces: technology, globalization, the physical environment, and social responsibility. We discuss these four transformative forces in more detail next.

Technology. The pace of change and the scale of technological achievement can be staggering. The rapid rise of e-commerce, online and mobile communication, and artificial intelligence has offered marketers increasing capabilities. Massive amounts of information and data about almost everything are now available to both consumers and marketers.

Technological developments have given birth to new business models that take advantage of the new capabilities stemming from these technologies. Companies like Netflix, Amazon, Airbnb, and Uber that have embraced the new technologies have disrupted markets and become major players in the industries in which they compete.

Advances in data analytics, machine learning, and artificial intelligence have enabled companies not only to better understand their customers but also to tailor their offerings to consumers' needs Exponentially increasing computing power—coupled with complex data analysis algorithms that include natural language processing, object recognition, and affective computing—have provided marketers with unprecedented knowledge about their customers and enabled them to interact with these customers on a one-to-one basis. The growth of data analytics and artificial intelligence platforms have democratized these technologies by making them available to smaller companies that typically would not have had the resources to implement these technologies on their own.

Even traditional marketing activities have been profoundly affected by technology. To improve sales force effectiveness, drug maker Roche issued iPads to its entire sales team. Though the company had previously used a sophisticated customer relationship management software system, it still depended on sales reps to input data accurately and in a timely fashion, which, unfortunately, did not always happen. With iPads, however, sales teams can do real-time data entry, improving the quality of the data entered while freeing up time for other tasks.

Globalization. The world has become a level playing field that offers competitors across the globe an equal opportunity to succeed. Geographic and political barriers have been eroded as advanced telecommunication technologies and workflow platforms that enable all types of computers to work together continue to create almost limitless opportunities for communication, collaboration, and data mining. The notion that the world has become a smaller place connecting businesses and customers across the globe is well captured by the phase "The World Is Flat" coined by Thomas Friedman in his book of that name.[15]

Friedman illustrates the impact of globalization with the following example: The person taking your order at a McDonald's in Missouri might be working at a call center 900 miles away in Colorado Springs. She then zaps your order back to the McDonald's so that it's ready minutes later as you drive to the pickup window. Friedman warns of the consequences of ignoring the rapid pace of global advances that will necessitate changes in the way companies do business, including the loss of American jobs to skilled employees who will work for less. In order to succeed in this "flattened" world, the U.S. workforce must continually update its specialized skills and create superior products.

Globalization has made countries increasingly multicultural. U.S. minorities have expanding economic clout, with their buying power growing faster than that of the general population. Demographic trends favor developing markets with populations whose median age is below 25. In terms of growth of the middle class, the vast majority of the next billion people who join the middle class are likely to be Asian.[16]

Globalization changes innovation and product development as companies take ideas and lessons from one country and apply them to another. After years of little success with its premium ultrasound scanners in the Chinese market, GE successfully developed a portable, ultra-low-cost version that addressed the country's unique market needs. Later, it began to successfully sell the product throughout the developed world for use in ambulances and operating rooms where existing models were too big.[17]

Physical Environment. The physical environment in which companies operate has changed dramatically during the past decade. Two particularly far-ranging changes in the physical environment deserve special attention: climate change and changes in global health conditions.

Climate change—a term referring to lasting changes in Earth's global climate as well as changes in regional climates—can have a significant impact on a company's business activities. Climate change is not limited to global warming; it can also involve lower rather than rising temperatures (global cooling). In addition, the effects of climate change go beyond lasting changes in the temperature to trigger more frequent and more extreme weather events, fluctuations in humidity and rainfall, and rising sea levels resulting from thermal expansion of ocean waters and unprecedented melting of glaciers and the polar ice caps.

Climate change can have a profound effect on the business models of virtually all companies regardless of their size or the industry in which they operate. For example, an increase in the average annual temperature can lead to lower yields of fruits and vegetables that are accustomed to cooler temperatures and to higher yields of warm-climate vegetation. As the warm season lengthens, warm-weather activities tend to grow, whereas winter sports tend to suffer. Rising sea levels are creating major disruptions in global commerce as well as in people's daily lives. As a result of rising seas and extreme weather caused by climate change, Indonesia's government announced plans to move its endangered national capital from Jakarta to a new location on the island of Borneo. The impact of rising sea levels not only entails frequent flooding; it also means higher rates of erosion, greater damage from storms, and saltwater contamination of drinking water.

Health conditions range from short-term illnesses that are confined to a particular geographic area to pandemics that spread across the globe. Changes in health conditions can influence not only the operations of pharmaceutical, biotechnology, and health management companies but also companies that are not directly related to health care. Pandemics, such as avian influenza and swine flu, can have a profound effect on all areas of business, including food, tourism, hospitality, and transportation. A truly global pandemic such as COVID-19 could effectively paralyze most, if not all, business transactions, leading to a virtual standstill of global commerce. Because the process of globalization and the related increase in global travel have magnified the probability of localized diseases becoming pandemics, managers must be prepared to adapt their business models to account for changing health conditions that threaten their customers, employees, and the company's bottom line.

Source: ZUMA Press, Inc./Alamy Stock Photo

<< A powerful electric motor combined with a quick changeover to gas lets the Prius get over 50 mpg both in the city and on highways. It also allows owners to display their concern for the environment.

Social Responsibility. Poverty, pollution, water shortages, climate change, social injustice, and wealth concentration demand our attention. The private sector is taking some responsibility for improving living conditions, and firms all over the world have elevated the role of corporate social responsibility.

Because marketing's effects extend to society as a whole, marketers must consider the ethical, environmental, legal, and social context of their activities.[18] The organization's task is thus to determine the needs, wants, and interests of target markets and satisfy them more effectively and efficiently than competitors, while preserving or enhancing consumers' and society's long-term well-being.

As goods have become more commoditized and consumers have grown more socially conscious, some companies—including The Body Shop, Timberland, and Patagonia—have incorporated social responsibility as a way to differentiate themselves from competitors, build consumer preference, and achieve notable sales and profits.[19]

In making these shifts in marketing and business practices, firms also face ethical dilemmas and perplexing trade-offs. Consumers may value convenience but find it difficult to justify disposable products or elaborate packaging in a world trying to minimize waste. Increasing material aspirations can defy the need for sustainability. Smart companies are creatively designing with energy efficiency, carbon footprints, toxicity, and disposability in mind.

Toyota Prius Some auto experts scoffed when Toyota predicted sales of 300,000 cars within five years of launching its gas-and-electric Prius hybrid sedan in 2001. But by 2004, the Prius had a six-month waiting list. Toyota's winning formula consists of a powerful electric motor and the ability to quickly switch power sources—resulting in 55 miles per gallon for city and highway driving. It also offers the roominess and power of a family sedan and an eco-friendly design and look at a starting price of a little more than $20,000. Some consumers also appreciate that the Prius's distinctive design allows them to make a visible statement about their commitment to the environment. The lesson? Functionally successful products that consumers see as also being good for the environment can offer enticing options.[20]

Now more than ever, marketers must think holistically and craft creative win–win solutions to balance conflicting demands. They must develop fully integrated marketing programs and meaningful relationships with a range of constituents.[21] Besides doing all the right things inside their company, they need to consider the broader consequences in the marketplace, topics we turn to next.

THE THREE KEY MARKETING OUTCOMES

The four major forces shaping today's markets—technology, globalization, the physical environment, and social responsibility—are fundamentally changing the ways consumers and companies interact with each other. These forces provide both consumers and companies with new capabilities, while at the same time promoting a competitive market environment. We discuss these three market outcomes in more detail next.

New Consumer Capabilities. Consumers today have more power at their fingertips than they have ever had in the past. Expanded information, communication, and mobility enable customers to make better choices and share their preferences and opinions with others around the world. The new consumer capabilities involve several key aspects:

- **Consumers can use online resources as a powerful information and purchasing aid.** From home, office, or mobile phone, they can compare product prices and features, consult user reviews, and order goods online from anywhere in the world 24 hours a day, seven days a week, bypassing limited local offerings and realizing significant price savings. They can also engage in "showrooming": comparing products in stores but buying online. Because consumers and other constituents can fact track down virtually any kind of company information, firms now realize that transparency in corporate words and actions is of paramount importance.
- **Consumers can use mobile connectivity to search, communicate, and purchase on the go.** Consumers increasingly integrate smart phones and tablets into their daily lives. Smart device owners use their mobile phones and tablets to research products, shop for everything from groceries to gifts, contribute to social causes and disaster relief, explore insurance options, send and receive money via online banking platforms, and conduct virtual consultations between doctors and patients and among health care teams in far-flung locations. There is one cell phone for every two people on the planet—and each day10 times more cell phones are produced globally than babies are born. Telecommunications is one of the world's trillion-dollar industries, along with tourism, military, food, and automobiles.
- **Consumers can tap into social media to share opinions and express loyalty.** Social media is an explosive worldwide phenomenon that has changed the way people conduct their everyday lives. Consumers use social media such as Facebook, Twitter, Snapchat, and LinkedIn to keep in touch with family, friends, and business colleagues; tout products and services; and even engage in politics. Personal connections and user-generated content thrive on social media such as Facebook, Instagram, Wikipedia, and YouTube. Sites like Dogster for dog lovers, TripAdvisor for travelers, and Moterus for bikers bring together consumers with a common interest. At Bimmerfest, Bimmerpost, and BMW Links, auto enthusiasts talk about chrome rims, the latest BMW model, and where to find a great local mechanic.
- **Consumers can actively interact with companies.** Consumers see their favorite companies as workshops from which to draw out the offerings they want. By opting to be put on lists, they can receive marketing and sales-related communications, discounts, coupons, and other special deals. With smart phones, they can scan barcodes and QR codes to access a brand's website and other information. Many companies have developed apps that allow them to interact with customers more effectively.
- **Consumers can reject marketing they find inappropriate or annoying.** Some customers today may see fewer product differences and feel less brand loyalty. Others may become more price- and quality-sensitive in their search for value. Almost two-thirds of consumers in one survey reported that they disliked advertising. For these and other reasons, consumers can be less tolerant of undesired marketing. They can choose to screen out online messages, skip commercials, and avoid marketing appeals through the mail or over the phone.
- **Consumers can extract more value from what they already own.** Consumers share bikes, cars, clothes, couches, apartments, tools, and skills. As one sharing-related entrepreneur noted, "We're moving from a world where we're organized around ownership to one organized around access to assets." In a sharing economy, someone can be both a consumer and a producer, reaping the benefits of both roles.[22]

New Company Capabilities. In addition to enabling consumers, globalization, social responsibility, and technology have also generated a new set of capabilities to help companies create value for their customers, collaborators, and stakeholders. The key company capabilities are as follows:

- **Companies can use the internet as a powerful information and sales channel, including for individually differentiated goods.** A website can list products and services, history, business philosophy, job opportunities, and other information of interest to consumers worldwide. Solo Cup marketers note that linking the company's storefronts to its website and Facebook page makes it easier for consumers to buy Solo paper cups and plates while engaging with the brand online.[23] Thanks to advances in factory customization, computer technology, and database marketing software, companies can allow customers to buy M&M candies bearing their names, Wheaties boxes or Jones soda cans with their pictures on the front, and Heinz ketchup bottles with customized messages.
- **Companies can collect fuller and richer information about markets, customers, prospects, and competitors.** Marketers can conduct fresh marketing research by using the internet to arrange focus groups, send out questionnaires, and gather primary data in several other ways. They can assemble information about individual customer purchases, preferences, demographics, and profitability. Many retailers such as CVS, Target, and Albertsons use loyalty-card data to better understand what consumers purchase, the frequency of store visits, and other buying preferences. Recommendation engines help marketers develop purchase suggestions tailored to a user's past online behavior. Companies like Netflix, Amazon, Alibaba, and Google have created effective algorithms based on purchase and viewing data, search terms, product feedback, and location to fuel their recommendation engines for individual customers. A large share of Amazon purchases is derived from product recommendations.
- **Companies can reach consumers quickly and efficiently via social media and mobile marketing, sending targeted ads, coupons, and information.** GPS technology can pinpoint consumers' exact location, letting marketers send them messages at the mall with wish-list reminders and coupons or offers good only that day. Location-based advertising is attractive because it reaches consumers closer to the point of sale. Social media and buzz are also powerful. For example, a word-of-mouth marketing agency recruits consumers who voluntarily join promotional programs for products and services they deem worth talking about.
- **Companies can improve purchasing, recruiting, training, and internal and external communications.** Firms can recruit new employees online, and many have internet training products for their employees, dealers, and agents. Blogging has waned as companies embrace social media. "We want to be where our customers are," said Bank of America after dropping its blog in favor of Facebook and Twitter.[24] Farmers Insurance uses specialized software to help its agents nationwide maintain their own Facebook pages. Via intranets and databases, employees can query one another, seek advice, and exchange information. Popular hybrid Twitter- and Facebook-type products designed especially for business employees have been introduced by Salesforce.com, IBM, and numerous start-ups. The Houston Zoo uses the "I want to" button on its intranet to quickly accomplish mundane tasks such as ordering business cards and uniforms or communicating with the IT department, leaving employees more time for animal care. The Team Sites tab on Maxxam Analytics' intranet allows team members in different locations to exchange ideas for improving efficiency and customer service, which serves to advance both team and company goals.
- **Companies can improve their cost efficiency.** Corporate buyers can achieve substantial savings by using the internet to compare sellers' prices and purchase materials at auction or by posting their own terms in reverse auctions. Companies can improve logistics and operations to reap substantial cost savings while improving accuracy and service quality. Small businesses can especially unleash the power of the internet. Physicians maintaining a small practice can use Facebook-like services such as Doximity to connect with referring physicians and specialists.

New Competitive Environment. The new market forces have not only changed consumer and company capabilities; they have also dramatically changed the dynamics of the competition and the nature of the competitive landscape. Some of the key changes in the competitive environment are as follows:

- **Deregulation.** Many countries have deregulated industries to create greater competition and growth opportunities. In the United States, laws restricting financial services, telecommunications, and electric utilities have all been loosened in the spirit of greater competition.
- **Privatization.** Many countries have converted public companies to private ownership and management to increase their efficiency. The telecommunications industry has seen much privatization in countries such as Australia, France, Germany, Italy, Turkey, and Japan.

- **Retail transformation.** Store-based retailers face competition from catalog houses; direct-mail firms; newspaper, magazine, and TV direct-to-customer ads; home-shopping TV networks; and e-commerce. In response, customer-centric companies such as Amazon, Best Buy, and Target are building entertainment into their stores with coffee bars, demonstrations, and performances—marketing an "experience" rather than a product assortment.
- **Disintermediation.** Early dot-coms such as Amazon.com and E*TRADE successfully created *disintermediation* in the delivery of products and services by intervening in the traditional flow of goods. In response, traditional companies engaged in *reintermediation* and became "brick-and-click" retailers, adding online services to their offerings. Some with plentiful resources and established brand names became stronger contenders than pure-click firms.
- **Private labels.** Brand manufacturers are further buffeted by powerful retailers that market their own store brands, increasingly indistinguishable from any other type of brand.
- **Mega-brands.** Many strong brands have become mega-brands and extended into related product categories, including new opportunities at the intersection of two or more industries. Computing, telecommunications, and consumer electronics are converging, with Apple and Samsung releasing a stream of state-of-the-art mobile phones, tablets, and wearable devices.

THE CONCEPT OF HOLISTIC MARKETING

Holistic marketing recognizes and reconciles the scope and complexities of marketing activities and offers an integrated approach to managing strategy and tactics. Figure 1.4 provides a schematic overview of four broad components characterizing holistic marketing: relationship marketing, integrated marketing, internal marketing, and performance marketing. We'll examine these major themes throughout this text.

To succeed, marketing must be more holistic and less departmental. Marketers must achieve wider influence in the company, continuously create new ideas, and strive to gather and use customer insight. They must build their brands more through performance than promotion. They must go electronic and build superior information and communication systems.

The market value concept calls for a holistic approach to marketing that is focused on building relationships, rather than on generating transactions; on integrated marketing that is both automated and creative, rather than on manually managed piecemeal marketing actions; on internal marketing that reflects a strong corporate culture rather than disengaged employees; and on performance-focused marketing that is driven by science rather than intuition.

Relationship Marketing. Increasingly, a key goal of marketing is to develop deep, enduring relationships with people and organizations that directly or indirectly affect the success of the firm's marketing activities. **Relationship marketing** aims to build mutually satisfying long-term relationships with key constituents in order to earn and retain their business.

Four key constituents in relationship marketing are customers, employees, marketing partners (channels, suppliers, distributors, dealers, agencies), and members of the financial community (shareholders, investors, analysts). Marketers must create prosperity among all these constituents and

FIGURE **1.4**
The Concept of Holistic Marketing

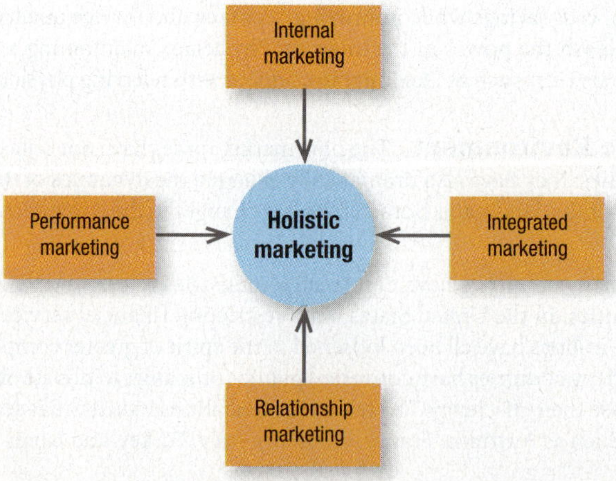

balance the returns for all key stakeholders. Forging strong relationships with constituents requires understanding their capabilities and their resources, needs, goals, and desires.

The ultimate outcome of relationship marketing is a unique company asset called a **marketing network**, which consists of the company and its supporting stakeholders—customers, employees, suppliers, distributors, retailers, and others—with whom it has built mutually profitable business relationships. The operating principle is simple: Build an effective network of relationships with key stakeholders, and profits will follow. Thus, more companies are choosing to own brands rather than physical assets and are subcontracting activities to firms that can do them better and more cheaply, while retaining core activities. Nike is a prime example: The sportswear giant's "Just Do It" marketing activities emanate from its Oregon headquarters, but it outsources all production to overseas locations. China is the largest manufacturer of its footwear and clothing, but other plants are located in Thailand, India, South Korea, and Vietnam.

Companies are also shaping separate offers, services, and messages to *individual customers* based on information about their past transactions, demographics, psychographics, and media and distribution preferences. By focusing on their most profitable customers, products, and channels, these firms hope to achieve profitable growth and capture a larger share of each customer's expenditures by building strong customer loyalty. They estimate individual customers' lifetime value and design their market offerings and prices to make a profit over this lifetime.

Wipro Established in 1945 as a manufacturer and distributor of cooking oil, Wipro has transformed into one of India's most global and diversified enterprises with its businesses spanning across consumer goods, healthcare, information technology, consulting, and software services. Being passionate about clients' success is one of its core values as articulated in the 'Spirit of Wipro'.[25] The leadership team's belief in being successful only when clients succeed is deep-rooted. This encompasses closer engagement with clients and greater focus on innovation to create a deeper impact on client's business. While the company invests in relationship with clients, they continue to focus on strengthening partnerships with global technology leaders including Microsoft, Google, Amazon, Salesforce, and SAP that is aligned with their success mantra of 'Wipro Winning Together'.[26] The company practices a shared value system that gives equal importance to all stakeholders. Collaboration, commitment and striving for excellence enhance Wipro's competitive advantge as it strengthens its leading role in technology driven customer solutions.[27] Wipro's ongoing, successful joint venture set up in 1990 with General Electric (GE) to develop high-quality, affordable healthcare solutions exemplifies the company's belief in partnerships.[28]

<< Wipro has managed to rise to the challenges in the technology field by pivoting its strategic focus to address the needs of the changing environment and by carefully listening to and working closely with its customers.

Source: ©Wipro, used with permission

The Marriott chain provides an excellent example of cultivating customer loyalty. Frequent guests at its hotels and resorts can climb a tiered rewards ladder from the basic Marriott Rewards member rung to accrue an increasing number of perks and bonus points with Lifetime Silver, Lifetime Gold, and three Lifetime Platinum levels. After Lifetime status is achieved, it can never be revoked or expire, ensuring that committed customers receive the benefits of Silver, Gold, or Platinum status with each visit.

Marketing must skillfully manage not only customer relationships but partner relationships as well. Companies are deepening their partnering arrangements with key suppliers and distributors, regarding them as allies in delivering value to end customers so that everybody benefits. Wipro has learned the value of strong customer bonds.

Integrated Marketing. **Integrated marketing** coordinates all marketing activities and marketing programs and directs them toward creating, communicating, and delivering consistent value and a consistent message for consumers, such that "the whole is greater than the sum of its parts." This requires that marketers design and implement each marketing activity with all other activities in mind. When a hospital buys an MRI machine from General Electric's Medical Systems division, for instance, it expects good installation, maintenance, and training services to go with the purchase.

An integrated channel strategy should assess each channel option for its direct effect on product sales and brand equity, as well as its indirect effect on interactions with other channel options. All company communications also must be integrated to reinforce and complement one another. A marketer might selectively employ television, radio, and print advertising, public relations events, and PR

Iceland Already reeling from some of the biggest losses in the global financial crisis of 2008, Iceland faced more misfortune when dormant volcano Eyjafjallajökull unexpectedly erupted in April 2010. Its enormous plumes of ash created the largest air-travel disruption since World War II, resulting in a wave of negative press and bad feelings throughout Europe and elsewhere. With tourism generating around 20 percent of the country's foreign exchange, and with bookings plummeting, government and tourism officials decided to launch "Inspired by Iceland." This campaign was based on the insight that 80 percent of visitors to Iceland recommend the destination to friends and family. The country's own citizens were recruited to tell their stories and encourage others to join in via a website or Twitter, Facebook, and Vimeo. Celebrities such as Yoko Ono and Eric Clapton shared their experiences, and live concerts generated positive PR. Real-time Webcams across the country showed that it was not ash-covered but green. The campaign was wildly successful—over 22 million stories were created by people all over the world—and ensuing bookings were dramatically above forecasts.[29]

Source: travellinglight/Alamy Stock Photo

>> The "Inspired by Iceland" campaign harnessed the social media power of citizens, visitors, and celebrities to overcome the negative publicity caused by a volcanic eruption that decimated both air travel and Iceland's image.

and website communications so that each contributes on its own and improves the effectiveness of the others. Each must also deliver a consistent brand message at every contact. Consider this award-winning campaign for Iceland.

Increasingly, marketing is *not* relegated only to the marketing department; every employee has an impact on the customer. Marketers now must properly manage all possible touch points: store layouts, package designs, product functions, employee training, and shipping and logistics. Creating a strong marketing organization means that marketers must think like executives in other departments, and executives in other departments must think more like marketers. Interdepartmental teamwork that includes marketers is necessary to manage key processes like production innovation, new-business development, customer acquisition and retention, and order fulfillment.

Internal Marketing. **Internal marketing**, an element of holistic marketing, is the task of hiring, training, and motivating able employees who want to serve customers well. Smart marketers recognize that marketing activities within the company can be as important as—or even more important than—those directed outside the company. It makes no sense to promise excellent service unless the company's staff is ready to provide it.

Marketing succeeds only when all departments work together to achieve customer goals: when engineering designs the right products, finance furnishes the right amount of funding, purchasing buys the right materials, production makes the right products in the right time horizon, and accounting measures profitability in the right ways. Such interdepartmental harmony can truly coalesce, however, only when senior management clearly communicates a vision of how the company's marketing orientation and philosophy serve customers. The following hypothetical example highlights some of the potential challenges in integrating marketing.

The marketing vice president of a major European airline wants to increase the airline's traffic share. Her strategy is to build customer satisfaction by providing better food, cleaner cabins, better-trained cabin crews, and lower fares, yet she has no authority in these matters. The catering department chooses food that keeps food costs down; the maintenance department uses inexpensive cleaning services; the human resources department hires people without regard to whether they are naturally friendly and service oriented; the finance department sets the fares. Because these departments generally take a cost or production point of view, the vice president of marketing is stymied in his efforts to create an integrated marketing program.

Internal marketing requires vertical alignment with senior management and horizontal alignment with other departments so everyone understands, appreciates, and supports the marketing effort. For example, the frustrated airline marketing VP might first enlist the help of senior management and department heads by illustrating how mounting a coordinated company effort to enhance the company's image will make a difference in its bottom line. This might be accomplished by making data on competitors available, as well as by compiling customer reviews of their experiences with the airline.

Management's engagement will be central in this integrated marketing effort, which must involve and motivate all employees—from reservations clerks and maintenance workers to catering department employees and cabin crews—by engaging them in a team effort to reinvigorate the airline's mission to provide excellent service. In addition to ongoing employee training that emphasizes customer service, regular internal communications to keep everyone abreast of the company's actions and single out employees who provide outstanding ideas or service can be part of the effort to get the entire company involved.

Performance Marketing. **Performance marketing** requires understanding the financial and nonfinancial returns to business and society from marketing activities and programs. As noted previously, top marketers increasingly go beyond sales revenue to examine the marketing scorecard and interpret what is happening with market share, customer loss rate, customer satisfaction, product quality, and other measures. They are also considering the legal, ethical, social, and environmental effects of marketing activities and programs.

When they founded Ben & Jerry's, Ben Cohen and Jerry Greenfield embraced the performance marketing concept by dividing the traditional financial bottom line into a "double bottom line" that also measured the environmental impact of their products and processes. That later expanded into a "triple bottom line" to represent the social impact, negative and positive, of the firm's entire range of business activities.

Many firms have failed to live up to their legal and ethical responsibilities, and consumers are demanding more responsible behavior.[31] One research study reported that at least one-third of consumers around

>> From its inception, Patagonia has striven to successfully balance an acute societal commitment to preserve the environment with its goal of ensuring ongoing benefits for company shareholders.

Source: Sundry Photography/Alamy Stock Photo

Patagonia As one of a small number of benefit (B) corporations in the United States that must each year explain how their mission is benefiting both stakeholders and society, Patagonia aims to combine environmental consciousness with maximizing shareholder returns. True to its mission and corporate culture, Patagonia not only helped develop a natural rubber material for its wetsuits (to replace petroleum-based neoprene) but also encouraged other companies to use this bio-rubber product for wetsuits and other products such as yoga mats and sneakers.[30] The company seems to have found a winning combination. According to climber, surfer, self-taught blacksmith, and Patagonia founder Yvon Chouinard, every decision he's made that was right for the environment has in the long run made the company money.

the world believe that banks, insurance providers, and packaged-food companies should be subject to stricter regulation.[32] Given the new marketing realities, organizations are challenging their marketers to find the best balance of old and new and to provide demonstrable evidence of success.

Marketers are increasingly asked to justify their investments in financial and profitability terms, as well as in terms of building the brand and growing the customer base.[33] Organizations recognize that much of their market value comes from intangible assets, especially brands, the customer base, employees, distributor and supplier relations, and intellectual capital. They are thus applying more metrics—brand equity, customer lifetime value, return on marketing investment—to understand and measure their marketing and business performance and are employing a broader variety of financial measures to assess the direct and indirect value their marketing efforts create.[34]

The Role of Marketing in the Organization

A key task for any business is defining the role that marketing will play in the organization. A company must decide what overarching philosophy will guide a company's marketing efforts, determine how to organize and manage the marketing department, and, ultimately, find the best means to build a customer-centric organization that can deliver value to company stakeholders.[35]

What philosophy should guide a company's marketing efforts? Let's first review the evolution of marketing philosophies.

- The **production concept** is one of the oldest concepts in business. It holds that consumers prefer products that are widely available and inexpensive. Managers of production-oriented businesses concentrate on achieving high production efficiency, low costs, and mass distribution. This orientation has made sense in developing countries such as China, where the largest PC manufacturer,

TABLE 1.1 Product-Oriented versus Market-Value-Oriented Definitions of a Business

Company	Product Definition	Market-Value Definition
Union Pacific Railroad	We run a railroad.	We move people and goods.
Xerox	We make copying equipment.	We help improve office productivity.
Hess Corporation	We sell gasoline.	We supply energy.
Paramount Pictures	We make movies.	We market entertainment.
Encyclopedia Britannica	We sell encyclopedias online.	We distribute information.
Carrier	We make air conditioners and furnaces.	We provide climate control in the home.

Legend (principal owner of Lenovo Group), and domestic appliances giant Haier have taken advantage of the country's huge and inexpensive labor pool to dominate the market. Marketers also use the production concept when they want to expand the market.

- The **product concept** proposes that consumers favor products offering the highest quality, the best performance, or innovative features. However, managers are sometimes caught in a love affair with their products. They might succumb to the "better-mousetrap" fallacy, believing a better product will by itself lead people to beat a path to their door. As many start-ups have learned the hard way, a new or improved product will not necessarily be successful unless it is priced, distributed, advertised, and sold properly.
- The **selling concept** holds that consumers and businesses, if left alone, won't buy enough of the organization's products. It is practiced most aggressively with unsought goods—goods buyers don't normally think of buying, such as insurance and cemetery plots—and when firms with overcapacity aim to sell what they make rather than make what the market wants. Marketing based on hard selling is risky. It assumes that customers who are coaxed into buying a product not only won't return or bad-mouth it or complain to consumer organizations, but might even buy it again.
- The **marketing concept** emerged in the mid-1950s as a customer-centered, sense-and-respond philosophy. The job of marketing is not to find the right customers for your products but to develop the right products for your customers. Dell doesn't prepare a PC or laptop for its target market. Rather, it provides product platforms on which each person customizes the features she desires in the machine. The marketing concept holds that the key to achieving organizational goals is being more effective than competitors in creating, delivering, and communicating superior customer value to your target markets. Harvard's Theodore Levitt drew a perceptive contrast between the selling and marketing concepts:[36] *Selling focuses on the needs of the seller; marketing on the needs of the buyer. Selling is preoccupied with the seller's need to convert his product into cash; marketing with the idea of satisfying the needs of the customer by means of the product and the whole cluster of things associated with creating, delivering, and finally consuming it.*
- The **market-value concept** is based on the development, design, and implementation of marketing programs, processes, and activities that recognize their breadth and interdependencies. The value-based view of marketing acknowledges that everything matters in marketing—and that a broad, integrated perspective is often necessary. Traditionally, marketers played the role of intermediary, charged with understanding customers' needs and transmitting their voice to various functional areas.[37] In contrast, the market-value concept implies that *every* functional area should be actively focused on creating value for customers, the company, and its collaborators.

The market-value concept implies that companies should define their business as a customer-satisfying process rather than in terms of their products or industries. Products are transient; basic needs and customer groups endure forever. Transportation is a need; the horse and carriage, automobile, railroad, airline, ship, and truck are products that meet that need. Viewing businesses in terms of customer needs can suggest additional growth opportunities. Table 1.1 lists companies that have moved from a product definition to a market-value definition of their business.

The market-value view of a company's activities can redefine the market in which a company competes. For example, if Pepsi adopted a product-focused view of its business, it would define its target market as everyone who drinks carbonated soft drinks, and its competitors would therefore be other carbonated soft drink companies. However, if Pepsi adopted a market-value view, it would define its market in much broader terms, targeting everyone who might drink something to quench his or her thirst. Thus, its competition would also include companies that market noncarbonated soft drinks, bottled water, fruit juices, tea, and coffee.

Organizing and Managing the Marketing Department

The structure of the marketing department plays a major role in a company's ability to create market value. Company success is determined not only by the skills of the individual marketers but also, and to a large degree, by the way the marketers are organized to create a high-performing marketing team. In this context, organizing and managing the marketing department are of utmost importance in creating a modern marketing organization.

ORGANIZING THE MARKETING DEPARTMENT

Modern marketing departments can be organized in a number of different, sometimes overlapping ways: functionally, geographically, by product or brand, by market, or in a matrix.

Functional Organization. In the most common form of marketing organization, functional specialists report to a chief marketing officer who coordinates their activities. Figure 1.5 shows seven specialists. Other specialists might include a marketing planning manager, a market logistics manager, a direct marketing manager, a social media manager, and a digital marketing manager.

The main advantage of a functional marketing organization is its administrative simplicity. However, it can be quite a challenge for the departments to develop smooth working relationships, which can result in inadequate planning as the number of products and markets increases and the functional groups vie for budget and status. The marketing vice president constantly weighs competing claims and faces a difficult coordination problem.

Geographic Organization. A company selling in a national market often organizes its sales force (and sometimes its marketing) along geographic lines. The national sales manager may supervise four regional sales managers, who each supervise six zone managers, each of whom supervises eight district sales managers, who supervise 10 salespeople apiece.

Some companies are adding *area market specialists* (regional or local marketing managers) to support sales efforts in high-volume markets. To illustrate, consider how one such market might work in Miami–Dade County, Florida, where almost two-thirds of households are Hispanic and Latinos. The Miami specialist would know Miami's customer and trade makeup, help marketing managers at headquarters adjust their marketing mix for Miami, and prepare local annual and long-range plans for selling all the company's products there. Some companies must develop different marketing programs in different parts of the country, because geography substantially alters their brand development activities.

Product or Brand Organization. Companies producing a variety of products and brands often establish a product- or brand-management organization. This does not replace the functional

FIGURE **1.5**
Functional Organization

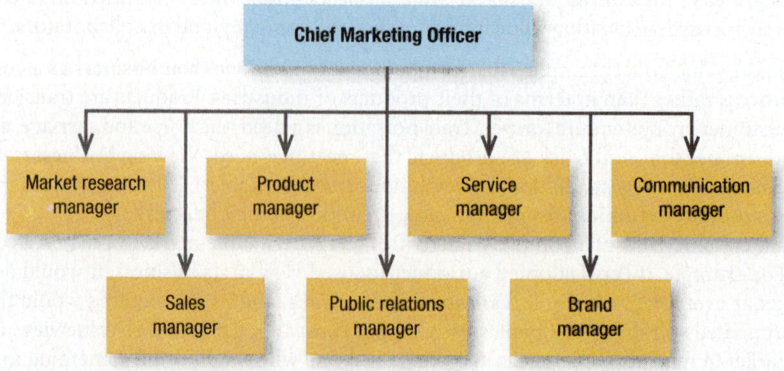

organization but serves as another layer of management. A group product manager supervises product category managers, who in turn supervise specific product and brand managers.

A product-management organization makes sense if the company's products are quite different or if there are more products than a functional organization can handle. This form is sometimes characterized as a hub-and-spoke system. The brand or product manager is figuratively at the center, with spokes leading to various departments representing working relationships (see Figure 1.6).

A manager's functions involve developing a long-range and competitive strategy for the offering; preparing an annual marketing plan and sales forecast; working with advertising, digital, and merchandising agencies to develop copy, programs, and campaigns; managing support of the product among the sales force and distributors; gathering continuous intelligence about the product's performance, customer and dealer attitudes, and new problems and opportunities; and initiating product improvements to meet changing market needs.

The product-management organization lets the product manager concentrate on developing a cost-effective marketing program and react more quickly to new products in the marketplace; it also gives the company's smaller brands a product advocate. But it has disadvantages, too. Product and brand managers may lack authority to carry out their responsibilities. They often become experts in their product area but rarely achieve functional expertise. Another challenge is that brand managers normally manage a brand for only a short time. Short-term involvement leads to short-term planning and fails to build long-term strengths. The fragmentation of markets makes it harder to develop a national strategy. Brand managers must please regional and local sales groups, transferring power from marketing to sales. Another important consideration is that product and brand managers focus the company on building market share rather than customer relationships.

The product-management organization can be structured around the company's products or, alternatively, a company can focus on product categories to manage its brands. Procter & Gamble, a pioneer of the brand-management system, and other top packaged-goods firms have made a major shift to category management, as have firms outside the grocery channel. Diageo's shift to category management was seen as a means to better manage the development of premium brands. It also helped the firm address the plight of under-performing brands.

Procter & Gamble cited a number of advantages of its shift to category management. The traditional brand-management system had created strong incentives to excel but also internal competition for resources and a lack of coordination. The new scheme was designed to ensure adequate resources for all categories. Another rationale for category management is the increasing power of the retail trade, which has thought of profitability in terms of product categories. P&G felt it only made sense to deal along similar lines. Mass market retailers and regional grocery chains such as Walmart and Wegmans embrace category management as a means to define a particular product category's strategic role within

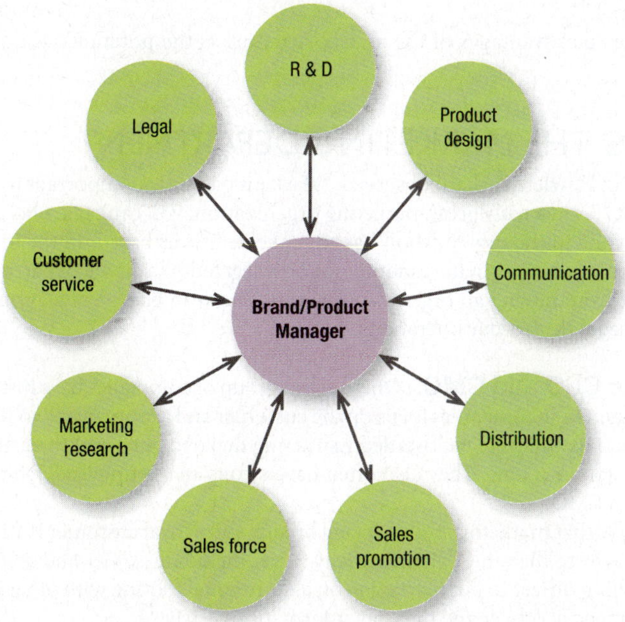

FIGURE **1.6**

The Product Manager's Interactions

the store and to address logistics, the role of private-label products, and the trade-offs between product variety and inefficient duplication.[38] In fact, in some packaged-goods firms, category management has evolved into aisle management and encompasses multiple related categories typically found in the same sections of supermarkets and grocery stores. General Mills' Yoplait Yogurt has served as category advisor to the dairy aisle for 24 major retailers, boosting the yogurt base footprint four to eight feet at a time and increasing yogurt sales by 9 percent and dairy category sales by 13 percent nationwide.[39]

Market Organization. Companies often develop diverse products and services to target distinct target markets. For example, Canon sells printers to consumer, business, and government markets. Nippon Steel sells to the railroad, construction, and public utility industries. When customers fall into different user groups with distinct buying preferences and practices, a market-management organization is desirable. Market managers supervise several market-development managers, market specialists, or industry specialists and draw on functional services as needed. Market managers of important markets might even have functional specialists reporting to them.

Market managers are staff (not line) people, with duties like those of product managers. They develop long-range and annual plans for their markets and are judged by their market's growth and profitability. Because this system organizes marketing activity to meet the needs of distinct customer groups, it shares many of the advantages and disadvantages of product-management systems. Many companies are reorganizing along market lines and becoming market-centered organizations. Xerox converted from geographic selling to selling by industry, as did IBM and Hewlett-Packard.

When a close relationship is advantageous, such as when customers have diverse and complex requirements and buy an integrated bundle of products and services, a customer-management organization that deals with individual customers, rather than with the mass market or even market segments, should prevail.[40] One study showed that companies organized by customer groups reported much higher accountability for the overall quality of relationships and greater employee freedom to take actions to satisfy individual customers.[41]

Matrix Organization. Companies that produce many products for many markets may adopt a matrix structure employing both product and market managers. The rub is that this choice is costly and often creates conflicts. There's the cost of supporting all the managers and the issue of resolving questions about where authority and responsibility for marketing activities should reside—at headquarters or in the division.[42] Some corporate marketing groups assist top management with overall opportunity evaluation, provide divisions with consulting assistance on request, help divisions that have little or no marketing, and promote the marketing concept throughout the company.

Many companies have reengineered their work flows and have built cross-functional teams that are responsible for each process.[43] AT&T, LexisNexis, and Pratt & Whitney have reorganized their employees into cross-functional teams. Cross-functional teams operate in nonprofit and government organizations as well.[44]

One of the key disadvantages of the matrix structure is the potential lack of clear focus and accountability.

MANAGING THE MARKETING DEPARTMENT

As David Packard of Hewlett-Packard observed, "Marketing is far too important to leave to the marketing department . . . . In a truly great marketing organization, you can't tell who's in the marketing department. Everyone in the organization has to make decisions based on the impact on the customer." Although marketing activities should not be relegated to a single department, many enterprises can benefit from having an organizational unit that is in charge of all company marketing activities and manages day-to-day operations.

The Role of the CEO and CMO. Only a select group of companies have historically stood out as master marketers. These companies focus on the customer and are organized to respond effectively to changing needs. They all have well-staffed marketing departments, and their other departments accept that the customer is king. They also often have strong marketing leadership in the form of a successful CEO and CMO.

CEOs recognize that marketing builds strong brands and a loyal customer base, intangible assets that contribute heavily to the value of a firm. Many firms, including service and nonprofit firms, now have a chief marketing officer to put marketing on a more equal footing with other C-level executives such as the chief financial officer and the chief information officer.[45]

What steps can a CEO take to create a market- and customer-focused company? To create a true marketing organization, the CEO must convince senior management of the importance of being customer focused. It is also important that the CEO be able to hire strong marketing talent. Most companies need a skilled chief marketing officer who not only manages the marketing department but also has the respect of, and influence with, the other C-level executives.

Given the rapidly evolving nature of today's markets, the CEO must facilitate the creation of strong in-house marketing training programs to sharpen the company's marketing skills. Many companies, such as McDonald's, Unilever, and Accenture, have centralized training facilities to run such programs. The CEO should also ensure that the company's reward system is aligned with its strategic goal of creating market value by developing a satisfied, loyal customer base. The CEO should personally exemplify strong customer commitment and reward those in the organization who do likewise.[46]

A major responsibility of the CEO is to appoint a chief marketing officer who is ultimately responsible for marketing activities in the organization. The CMO is a member of the C-suite and typically reports to the CEO. The senior marketing managers responsible for various parts of the marketing strategy typically report to the CMO. The CMO leads all marketing functions in the organization, including product development, brand management, communication, market research and data analytics, sales, promotion, distribution management, pricing, and customer service.

In the 21st century, the advancement of digital, online, and mobile marketing has changed the role of the CMO. To effectively manage the marketing functions of the organization, the CMO must also be able to handle digital technologies. The challenge CMOs face is that success factors are many and varied. CMOs must have strong quantitative *and* qualitative skills; they must have an independent, entrepreneurial attitude but work closely with other departments; and they must capture the "voice" of consumers yet have a keen bottom-line understanding of how marketing creates value. Two-thirds of top CMOs think return on marketing investment will be the primary measure of their effectiveness in the next decade.

Marketing experts George Day and Robert Malcolm believe that three driving forces will change the role of the CMO in the coming years: (1) predictable marketplace trends, (2) the changing role of the C-suite, and (3) uncertainty about the economy and organizational design. They identify five priorities for any successful CMO: act as the visionary for the future of the company, build adaptive marketing capabilities, win the war for marketing talent, tighten the alignment with sales, and take accountability for returns on marketing spending.[47]

Perhaps the most important role for any CMO is to infuse a customer perspective in business decisions affecting any customer *touch point* (where a customer directly or indirectly interacts with the company). Increasingly, these customer insights must have a global focus. As the leader of one top executive search firm has said, "Tomorrow's CMO will have to have global and international experience. You can do it without living abroad, . . . but you have to get exposure to those markets. It opens your eyes to new ways of doing business, increases cultural sensitivity and increases flexibility."[48]

Relationships with Other Departments. The firm's success depends not only on how well each department performs its work, but also on how well the company coordinates departmental activities to conduct core business processes. Under the marketing concept, all departments need to "think customer" and work together to satisfy customer needs and expectations. Yet departments define company problems and goals from their own viewpoints, so conflicts of interest and communication problems are unavoidable. The marketing vice president or the CMO must usually work through persuasion, rather than through authority, to coordinate the company's internal marketing activities and coordinate marketing with finance, operations, and other company functions to serve the customer.[49]

Many companies now focus on key processes rather than on departments because departmental organization can be a barrier to smooth performance. They appoint process leaders who manage cross-disciplinary teams that include marketing and salespeople. Marketers thus may have a solid-line responsibility to their teams and a dotted-line responsibility to the marketing department.[50]

Given the goal of providing positive customer experiences from start to finish, all areas of the organization need to work effectively together. In particular, because of the growing importance of understanding the needs of individual customers, marketers must work closely with the customer insights and data analytics teams. Furthermore, to be able to reach consumers in an effective and cost-efficient manner, marketers must work closely with different communication agencies—from traditional advertising agencies to social media, publicity, and event-management companies. Finally, to be able to deliver the company's offerings to the right place at the right time, marketers must work closely with a company's channel partners, both in the brick-and-mortar space and in the e-commerce space.

One advantage—perhaps a somewhat subtle one—of a customer-driven focus is that it aids a certain type of proactivity. When we're at our best, we don't wait for external pressures. We are internally driven to improve our services, adding benefits and features, before we have to. We lower prices and increase value for customers before we have to. We invent before we have to. These investments are motivated by customer focus rather than by reaction to competition. We think this approach earns more trust with customers and drives rapid improvements in customer experience—importantly—even in those areas where we are already the leader.

Building a Customer-Oriented Organization

Creating a superior customer experience has become a priority for companies in nearly every industry.[51] The proliferation of products, services, and brands; increased consumer knowledge about market offerings; and consumers' ability to influence public opinion about companies and their offerings—all have underscored the importance of building a customer-oriented organization. Most companies now realize that the path to creating stakeholder value begins with re-envisioning the organization as focused on creating long-term customer value.[52] In his letter to shareholders, Jeff Bezos defines Amazon's customer-centricity as follows.

Managers who believe the customer is the company's only true "profit center" consider the traditional organization chart in Figure 1.7(a)—a pyramid with the president at the top, management in the middle, and frontline people and customers at the bottom—to be obsolete.[53]

Successful marketing companies transform the traditional organization-hierarchy chart to look like the chart in Figure 1.7(b). A company's top priority are customers; next in importance are the frontline people who meet, serve, and satisfy these customers; then come service managers, whose job is to support the frontline people so they can serve customers well; and finally, there is the top management, whose job is to hire and support good service managers. The key to developing a customer-oriented company is that managers at every level must be personally engaged in understanding, meeting, and serving customers. Table 1.2 lists the main characteristics of a customer-centric organization.

Some companies have been founded on a customer-focused business model, and customer advocacy has been their strategy—and competitive advantage—all along. With the rise of digital technologies, increasingly informed consumers expect companies to do more than connect with, satisfy, and even delight them. They expect companies to *listen* and *respond* to them.

Traditionally, marketers played the role of intermediary, charged with understanding customers' needs and transmitting their voice to various functional areas of the company.[54] But in a networked enterprise, *every* functional area can interact directly with customers. Marketing no longer has sole ownership of customer interactions; it now must integrate all customer-involving processes so that customers see a single face and hear a single voice when they interact with the firm.[55]

FIGURE **1.7**

Traditional Organization versus Modern Customer-Oriented Company Organization

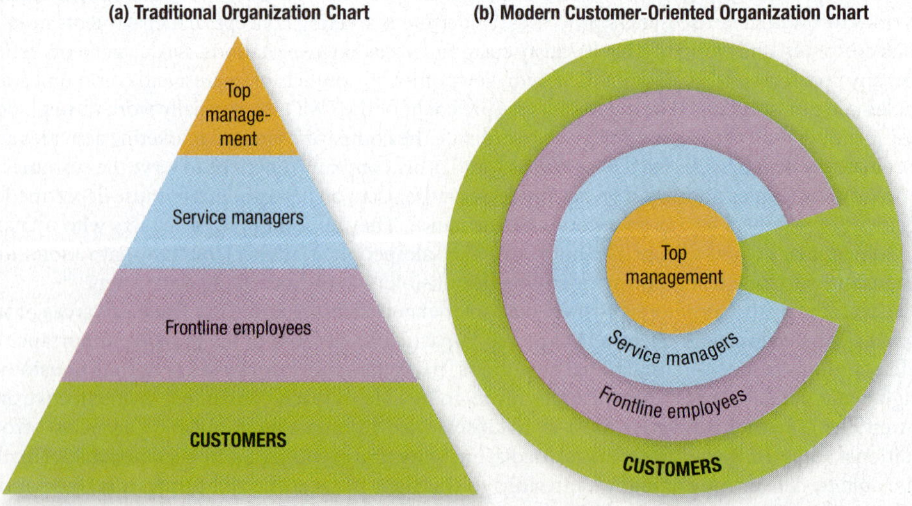

TABLE 1.2 Characteristics of a Customer-Centric Organization

Low Customer-Centricity	High Customer-Centricity
Product driven	Market driven
Mass market focused	Customer focused
Process oriented	Outcome oriented
Reacting to competitors	Making competitors irrelevant
Price driven	Value driven
Hierarchical organization	Teamwork

Many companies realize they're not yet really market and customer driven; rather, they are product and sales driven. Transforming into a true market-driven company requires (among other actions) developing a company-wide passion for customers, organizing around customer segments instead of products, and understanding customers through qualitative and quantitative research.[56]

Although it's *necessary* to be customer oriented, it's not *enough*. The organization must also be creative.[57] Companies today copy one another's advantages and strategies with increasing speed, making differentiation harder to achieve and lowering margins as firms become more alike. The best answer to this dilemma is to build capability in strategic innovation and imagination. This capability comes from assembling tools, processes, skills, and measures that let the firm generate more and better new ideas than its competitors.[58] To encourage such capability, companies should strive to put together inspiring work spaces that help stimulate new ideas and foster imagination.

Companies must be alert to trends and stand ready to capitalize on them. Nestlé was late seeing the trend toward coffeehouses, which paved the way for chains such as Starbucks. Coca-Cola was slow to pick up on beverage trends toward fruit-flavored drinks such as Snapple, energy drinks such as Gatorade, and designer water brands. Market leaders can miss trends when they are risk averse, obsessed about protecting their existing markets and physical resources, and more interested in efficiency and profit than innovation.[59]

marketing INSIGHT — The 10 Deadly Marketing Sins

Focused on their day-to-day activities, many marketers ignore the big picture: designing, communicating, and delivering offerings that create superior market value for their customers, collaborators, and stakeholders. Exhibiting a number of "deadly sins" signals that the marketing program is in trouble. Here are 10 deadly sins, the telltale signs, and some solutions.

Deadly Sin #1: The company is not sufficiently market focused and customer driven.

Signs: There is evidence of poor identification and poor prioritization of market segments. There are no market segment managers, no employees who think it is the job of marketing and sales to serve customers, no training program to create a customer culture, and no incentives to treat the customer especially well.

Solutions: Use more advanced segmentation techniques, prioritize segments, specialize the sales force to serve each market segment, develop a clear statement of company values, foster more "customer consciousness" in employees and company agents, make it easy for customers to reach the company, and respond quickly to any customer communication.

Deadly Sin #2: The company does not fully understand its target customers.

Signs: The latest study of customers is three years old, customers are not buying your product like they once did, competitors' products are selling better, and there is a high level of customer returns and complaints.

Solutions: Conduct more sophisticated consumer research, use more analytical techniques, establish customer and dealer panels, use customer relationship software, and engage in data mining.

(continued)

marketing insight *(continued)*

Deadly Sin #3: The company needs to better define and monitor its competitors.

Signs: The company focuses on near competitors, misses distant competitors and disruptive technologies, and has no system for gathering and distributing competitive intelligence.

Solutions: Establish an office to collect competitive intelligence, hire competitors' employees, watch for technology that might affect the company, and prepare offerings like those of competitors.

Deadly Sin #4: The company does not properly manage relationships with stakeholders.

Signs: Employees, dealers, and investors are not happy, and good suppliers are reluctant to partner with the company.

Solutions: Move from zero-sum thinking to positive-sum thinking, and do a better job of managing employees, supplier relations, distributors, dealers, and investors.

Deadly Sin #5: The company is not good at finding new opportunities.

Signs: The company has not identified any exciting new opportunities for years, and the new ideas the company has launched have largely failed.

Solutions: Set up a system for stimulating the flow of new ideas.

Deadly Sin #6: The company's marketing planning process is deficient.

Signs: The marketing plan format does not have the right components, there is no way to estimate the financial implications of different strategies, and there is no contingency planning.

Solutions: Establish a standard format including situational analysis, SWOT, major issues, objectives, strategy, tactics, budgets, and controls; ask marketers what changes they would make if they were given 20 percent more or less budget; and run an annual marketing awards program with prizes for best plans and performance.

Deadly Sin #7: Product and service policies need tightening.

Signs: There are too many products, and many are losing money, the company is giving away too many services, and the company is poor at cross-selling products and services.

Solutions: Establish a system to track weak products and fix or drop them, offer and price services at different levels, and improve processes for cross-selling and up-selling.

Deadly Sin #8: The company's brand-building and communication skills are weak.

Signs: The target market does not know much about the company, the brand is not seen as distinctive, the company allocates its budget to the same marketing tools in much the same proportion each year, and there is little evaluation of the ROI impact of marketing communications and activities.

Solutions: Improve brand-building strategies and measurement of results, shift money into effective marketing instruments, and require marketers to estimate the ROI impact in advance of funding requests.

Deadly Sin #9: The company is not organized for effective and efficient marketing.

Signs: Staff lacks 21st-century marketing skills, and there are bad vibes between marketing/sales and other departments.

Solutions: Appoint a strong leader to build new skills in the marketing department, and improve relationships between marketing and other departments.

Deadly Sin #10: The company has not made maximum use of technology.

Signs: There is evidence of minimal use of the internet, the sales automation system is outdated, and there are no market automation, no decision-support models, and no marketing dashboards.

Solutions: Use the internet more, improve the sales automation system, apply market automation to routine decisions, and develop formal marketing decision models and marketing dashboards.[60]

summary

1. Marketing is an organizational function and a set of processes for creating, communicating, and delivering value to customers and for managing customer relationships in ways that benefit the company, its customers, and its collaborators. Marketing management is the art and science of choosing target markets and getting, keeping, and growing customers through creating, delivering, and communicating superior customer value.
2. Companies aim to create value by marketing goods, services, events, experiences, persons, places, properties, organizations, information, and ideas. They also operate in five basic markets: resource markets, manufacturer markets, consumer markets, intermediary markets, and government markets.
3. Today's marketplace is fundamentally different as a result of major market forces. In particular, technology,

globalization, and social responsibility have created new opportunities and challenges and have significantly changed marketing management. Companies seek the right balance of tried-and-true methods and breakthrough new approaches to achieve marketing excellence.

4. Four major market forces—technology, globalization, the physical environment, and social responsibility—have forged new consumer and company capabilities and have dramatically altered the competitive landscape. These changes require companies to re-evaluate their current business models and adapt the way they create market value to the new environment.
5. The holistic marketing concept is based on the development, design, and implementation of marketing programs, processes, and activities that are based on breadth and interdependencies. Holistic marketing recognizes that everything matters in marketing and that a broad, integrated perspective is often necessary. Four components of holistic marketing are relationship marketing, integrated marketing, internal marketing, and performance marketing.
6. There are five competing concepts under which organizations can choose to conduct their business: the production concept, the product concept, the selling concept, the marketing concept, and the market-value concept. The more sophisticated a company's understanding of the market, the more likely that it will adopt the market-value concept as an overarching philosophy of doing business.
7. Companies use different approaches to organize the marketing department: functional, geographic, product/brand, market, and a matrix structure. The choice of a particular approach depends on the market in which a company operates, its organizational structure, and its strategic goals.
8. Marketing is not conducted by the marketing department alone. To create a strong marketing organization, marketers must think like executives in other departments, and executives in other departments must think more like marketers.
9. A customer-centric company must be market driven rather than product driven, it must aim to cater to individual customer needs rather than mass market needs, and it must strive to make the competition irrelevant rather than merely reacting to competitors' actions. To succeed, a company should focus on delivering superior value to target customers in a way that benefits the company and its collaborators.

marketing SPOTLIGHT

Nike

Source: Wisanu Boonrawd/ Alamy Stock Photo

When Phil Knight, a former college track athlete, and his former coach, Bill Bowerman, started a shoe company in 1962, they couldn't have known that they would ultimately create one of the world's most valuable brands. Originally known as Blue Ribbon Sports, the company started out as a distributor for the Japanese shoe maker that today is known as Asics. It wasn't until 1971 that Blue Ribbon changed its name to Nike, after the Greek goddess of victory, and started designing its own shoes.

Nike focused on providing affordable, high-quality running shoes designed for athletes by athletes. To keep the cost of the shoes competitive, the company outsourced its production to lower-cost manufacturers in Asia. Through this combination of innovative design, a commitment to serious athletes, and competitive prices, Nike built a cult following among U.S. consumers.

Although Nike had a great product on its hands, the company knew that deft management was vital to the growth of the brand. Central to the company's branding was its belief in a "pyramid of influence," with the preferences of a small group of top athletes influencing the product and brand choices of consumers. Following through with the theme of victory embedded in its name, Nike in 1972 signed Olympic track star Steve Prefontaine as its first spokesperson—the beginning of a long line of accomplished athletes who have touted the company's products.

One of Nike's greatest successes with this approach came in 1985 with the signing of rookie basketball player Michael Jordan as a spokesperson. Jordan was still an up-and-comer, but he personified superior performance. Thanks to Jordan's meteoric rise over the next few years, Nike's bet paid off as consumers clamored for the Air Jordan line of basketball shoes with the distinctive Nike swoosh. As one reporter stated, "Few marketers have so reliably been able to identify and sign athletes who transcend their sports to such great effect."

In addition to associating itself with the best athletes, Nike also showed a talent for creating iconic advertising campaigns. In 1988, Nike aired the first ads in its influential "Just Do It" ad campaign, which subtly challenged a generation of athletic enthusiasts to chase their goals. The slogan

(continued)

was a natural offshoot of Nike's attitude of self-empowerment through sports.

While expanding overseas, Nike adapted its marketing to face new challenges. The company quickly learned that its U.S.-style ads were too aggressive for consumers in Europe, Asia, and South America and adjusted its tone. Furthermore, it needed to tailor its marketing for different countries so consumers would feel that the brand was authentic. To this end, Nike focused on promoting soccer (called football outside the United States), becoming an active supporter of youth leagues, local clubs, and national teams around the world. It also searched for opportunities to sponsor soccer teams and leagues in an attempt to replicate the company's earlier success with U.S. sponsorships.

In the late 1990s, Nike moved into soccer in a big way. It secured marketing rights for several major soccer federations, including those in powerhouse countries like Brazil and Italy. It also started pouring money into marketing campaigns focused on the World Cup. Nike's heavy investment in soccer helped propel the brand's growth internationally as its image morphed from that of a sneaker company into a brand that represented emotion, allegiance, and identification. In 2003, overseas revenues surpassed U.S. revenues for the first time, and in 2007 Nike acquired Umbro, a British maker of soccer-related footwear, apparel, and equipment. The acquisition made Nike the sole supplier to more than 100 professional soccer teams around the world and boosted Nike's international presence and authenticity in soccer.

As Nike's global brand continued to grow, its managers realized that, across countries, players and fans of a given sport have a lot in common. Thus, the company began to focus its marketing efforts more on categories than on geographic location. With this principle in mind, Nike has successfully expanded its brand into many sports and athletic categories and increased its presence across the globe.

Nike continues to partner with high-profile and influential athletes, coaches, teams, and leagues to build credibility with consumers as it expands into more categories. It has sponsored tennis stars like Maria Sharapova, Roger Federer, and Rafael Nadal to push its line of tennis clothing and gear. In golf, Nike's swoosh gained prominence when Tiger Woods won tournament after tournament while wearing the company's products. In the years since Nike first partnered with Woods, Nike Golf has grown into a multi-million-dollar business and changed the way golfers dress. Of course, Nike hasn't forgotten its roots. To promote its line of basketball shoes and apparel, Nike has partnered with generations of basketball superstars like Kobe Bryant and LeBron James. Today, Nike is the biggest sponsor of athletes in the world, spending hundreds of millions of dollars a year on athletic endorsements.

While Nike's athletic endorsements help attract and inspire consumers, its recent innovations in technology have resulted in more loyal and emotionally connected customers. Delving into wearable technology, Nike has developed a running application and community called NIKE+ that allows runners to engage in the ultimate running experience. By linking a Nike+ kit to a smartphone app, runners can view their real-time pace, distance, route, and coaching tips, which they can then share online. Nike has expanded NIKE+ to areas like basketball and general exercise tracking. It has also co-branded with Apple to create the Apple Watch Nike+ edition, which gives users access to special watch faces and bands unavailable to other Apple Watch purchasers.

In addition to its foray into technology, Nike, like many companies, is trying to make its company and products more eco-friendly. Unlike many companies, though, it does not promote these efforts. As one brand consultant explained, "Nike has always been about winning. How is sustainability relevant to its brand?" Nike executives agree that promoting an eco-friendly message would distract from its slick high-tech image, so efforts such as recycling old shoes are kept quiet.

Thanks to its successful expansion across product categories and geographic markets, Nike is the top athletic apparel and footwear manufacturer in the world. Swooshes abound on everything from wristwatches to skateboards to swimming caps. Looking to the future, Nike sees some challenges ahead. Nike has traditionally thrived in brick-and-mortar retail channels, but increasing numbers of consumers are shopping online. Nike is searching for a winning strategy for promoting its brand in a digital age dominated by websites like Amazon. Despite its focus on new forms of promotion and distribution, the firm's long-term strategy remains the same: to produce innovative, high-quality products that help athletes win.[61]

Questions

1. What are the key components of Nike's marketing strategy?
2. What are Nike's strengths and weaknesses?
3. If you were Adidas, how would you compete with Nike?

marketing SPOTLIGHT

Disney

Source: D. Hurst/Alamy Stock Photo

Few companies have been able to connect with their audience as well as Disney has. Since its founding in 1923, the Disney brand has been synonymous with quality entertainment for the entire family. The company, originally founded by brothers Walt and Roy Disney, stretched the boundaries of entertainment during the 20th century to bring classic and memorable family entertainment around the world. Walt Disney once stated, "I am interested in entertaining people, in bringing pleasure, particularly laughter, to others, rather than being concerned with 'expressing' myself with obscure creative impressions." Beginning with simple black-and-white animated cartoons, the company grew into the worldwide phenomenon that today includes theme parks, feature films, television networks, theatre productions, consumer products, and a growing online presence.

In its first two decades, Walt Disney Productions was a struggling cartoon studio that introduced its most famous character, Mickey Mouse, to the world. Few believed in Disney's vision at the time, but the smashing success of cartoons with sound and the first-ever full-length animated film, *Snow White and the Seven Dwarfs*, in 1937, led to other animated classics throughout the 1940s, 1950s, and 1960s, including *Pinocchio*, *Bambi, Cinderella,* and *Peter Pan*, live action films such as *Mary Poppins* and *The Love Bug,* and television series like *Davy Crockett*.

When Walt Disney died in 1966, he was considered the best-known person in the world. Walt had expanded the Disney brand into film, television, consumer products, and Disneyland in southern California—its first theme park, where families could experience the magic of Disney in real life. After Walt's death, Roy Disney took over as CEO and realized his brother's dream of opening the 24,000-acre Walt Disney World theme park in Florida. Roy died in 1971, but the two brothers left behind a brand that stood for trust, fun, and entertainment and resonated with children, families, and adults, and some of the most moving and iconic characters, stories, and memories of all time.

The Walt Disney Company stumbled for several years without the leadership of its two founding brothers. It wasn't until the late 1980s that the company reconnected with its audience and restored trust and interest in the Disney brand. It all started with the release of *The Little Mermaid*, which turned an old fairy tale into a magical animated Broadway-style movie that won two Oscars. Between the late 1980s and 2000, Disney entered an era known as the Disney Renaissance, as it released ground-breaking animated films such as *Beauty and the Beast* (1991), *Aladdin* (1992), *The Lion King* (1994), *Toy Story* (with Pixar, 1995), and *Mulan* (1998). In addition, the company thought of creative new ways to target its core family-oriented consumers and expand into areas that would reach an older audience. Disney launched the Disney Channel, Touchstone Pictures, and Touchstone Television. The company made its classic films available on *The Disney Sunday Night Movie* and sold them on video at extremely low prices, reaching a whole new generation of children. Disney tapped into publishing, international theme parks, and theatrical productions that helped reach a variety of audiences around the world.

Today, Disney comprises four business units: (1) *Media Networks* encompasses a vast array of broadcast, cable, radio, publishing, and digital businesses across two divisions—the Disney/ABC Television Group and ESPN Inc. (2) *Parks, Experiences and Consumer Products* brings Disney's stories, characters, and franchises to life through parks and resorts, toys, apps, apparel, books, and stores. (3) *Studio Entertainment* brings movies, music, and stage plays to consumers around the world through the company's core business unit, The Walt Disney Studios, along with Marvel Studios, Pixar Animation Studios, and LucasFilm. (4) The *Direct-To-Consumer & International* division includes digital subscription streaming services and international holdings.

Disney's greatest challenge today is keeping its 90-year-old brand relevant and current, while retaining its core audience and staying true to its heritage and fundamental brand values. Disney's CEO Bob Iger explained, "As a brand that people seek out and trust, it opens doors to new platforms and markets, and hence to new consumers. When you deal with a company that has a great legacy, you deal with decisions and conflicts that arise from the clash of heritage versus innovation versus relevance. I'm a big believer in respect for heritage, but I'm also a big believer in the need to innovate and the need to balance that respect for heritage with a need to be relevant."

Internally, Disney has focused on the value-creation dynamic that sets it apart from its competitors. The *Disney Difference,* based on high standards of quality and recognition, stems from one of Walt Disney's most recognizable quotations: "Whatever you do, do it well. Do it so well that when people see you do it they will want to come back and see you do it again and they will want to bring others and show them how well you do what you do."

(*continued*)

Disney works hard to connect with its customers on a multitude of levels and through every single detail. For example, when visiting Disney World, employee "cast members" are trained to be "assertively friendly" and greet visitors by waving big Mickey Mouse hands, giving maps to adults and stickers to kids, and cleaning up the park so diligently that it's difficult to find a piece of garbage anywhere. Every little magical detail matters to Disney, right down to the custodial workers who are trained by Disney's animators to take their broom and bucket of water and quietly "paint" a Goofy or Mickey Mouse in water on the pavement. It's a moment of magic for the guests that lasts just a minute before it evaporates in the hot sun.

With so many brands, characters, and businesses, Disney uses technology to ensure that a customer's experience is consistent across every platform. Disney connects with its consumers in innovative ways through e-mail, blogs, and its website to provide insight into movie trailers, television clips, Broadway shows, and virtual theme park experiences. Disney was one of the first companies to begin regular podcasts of its television shows and to release ongoing news about its products and interviews with Disney's employees, staff, and park officials. The My Disney Experience app enables users to order food remotely from fast-food restaurants and pay in advance, allowing consumers to avoid lines when visiting Disney Parks and Resorts.

A key aspect of Disney's business model and culture is adherence to high standards of corporate social responsibility. Disney is committed to always act ethically, create content and products responsibly, maintain respectful workplaces, invest in communities, and be good stewards of the environment. The company's commitment to doing well by doing good has made it one of the world's most admired companies.[62]

Questions

1. How does Disney create value for its customers?
2. What are the core strengths of the Disney brand?
3. What are the risks and benefits of expanding the Disney brand to new products and services?

CHAPTER 2

Marketing Planning and Management

Enabling brands seamlessly integrate their products into mobile content, InMobi cloud platform provides mobile marketing solutions for global brands.

Source: ©InMobi, used with permission

Developing the right marketing strategies over time requires a blend of discipline and flexibility. Firms must stick to a strategy but also constantly improve it. In today's fast-changing marketing world, identifying the best long-term strategies is crucial. At the core of any successful marketing strategy is the development of an enduring value proposition that addresses a real customer need. One company that has developed distinct offerings designed to address unmet customer needs is InMobi.

>>> InMobi, founded in 2007, is a leading mobile marketing cloud platform that delivers advertising solutions, mobile app analytics and consumer insights to global brands. It has partnered with thousands of publishers of mobile websites and apps, enabling brands and app developers seamlessly integrate their products into mobile content. Launched initially as an advertising provider offering text-based local search service that updated subscribers on information about neighborhood vendors, deals and promotions, the company pivoted to a mobile ad platform in 2009 for brands to advertise on mobile versions of websites.[1,2] Its cloud-based marketing solutions help businesses develop market insight and identify target audience while its proprietary technology to deploy mobile ads, with the click of a button, allows clients to remotely publish their ads on sites and apps of their

choice.[3] The platform offers end-to-end solutions to brands to understand, identify, engage and acquire customers. Listed among the top innovative and disruptive companies owing to its distinctive offerings to global clients, InMobi attracted eminent investors—including Softbank, Sherpaloo and Google—thereby emerging as India's first B2B unicorn.[4] The unprecedented growth of users and time spent by over 3 billion gamers on mobile games attracted the company to launch in-game advertising on InMobi Exchange. The company's partnerships with all industry-leading platforms in the native in-game advertising space permits brands to interact with consumers in an intuitive way through high impact creatives and non-disruptive ad formats to a very engaged audience. Gaming-based mobile ads is expected to further consolidate InMobi's leadership position in the rapidly growing global mobile advertisement market.[5]

InMobi's flagship app 'Glance', a consumer facing mobile-first content platform, serves news, videos and games on the lock screens of Android phones. Created as a skunkworks project by a few engineers in 2016, Glance amassed over 115 million daily active users in less than 18 months post its launch. These users spend approximately 25 minutes every day on the platform.[6] Partnerships with Samsung, Xiomi, Vivo and Gionee to preinstall the service on mobile devices ensured that Glance is available on over 65% smartphones sold in India.[7] The combined valuation of InMobi and Glance is expected to be $15 billion at the end of 2021.[8] It is noteworthy that in 2020, Glance raised $145 million in funding led by Google.

This chapter begins by examining some of the strategic marketing implications involved in creating customer value. We'll look at several perspectives on planning and describe how to draw up a formal marketing plan.

Corporate and Business Unit Planning and Management

To ensure that they execute the right activities, marketers must prioritize strategic planning in three key areas: managing the company's businesses as an investment portfolio, assessing the market's growth rate and the company's position in that market, and developing a viable business model. The company must develop a game plan for achieving the long-run objectives of each business unit.

Generally speaking, marketing planning and management can occur on three different levels: corporate, business unit, and specific market offering. Corporate headquarters is responsible for designing a corporate strategic plan to guide the whole enterprise. It makes decisions on the amount of resources to allocate to each business unit, as well as on which businesses to start or eliminate. Each business unit develops a plan to carry that business unit into a profitable future. Finally, each market offering involves a marketing plan for achieving its objectives (Figure 2.1).

Learning Objectives After studying this chapter you should be able to:

2.1 Identify the key tasks required for company and business unit planning.

2.2 Describe the process of developing a market offering.

2.3 Explain the process of marketing planning.

2.4 Describe the key components of an actionable marketing plan.

2.5 Explain how and when to modify the marketing plan.

FIGURE **2.1**
The Strategic Planning Processes

This section addresses the key issues involved in analyzing, planning, and managing a company or distinct business units. The remainder of the chapter examines the process of analyzing, planning, and managing a company's offerings.

Companies undertake four planning activities: defining the corporate mission, building the corporate culture, establishing strategic business units, and assigning resources to each strategic business unit. We'll briefly look at each process.

DEFINING THE CORPORATE MISSION

An organization exists to accomplish something: make cars, lend money, provide a night's lodging. Over time, the mission may change to respond to new opportunities or market conditions. Amazon.com changed its mission from being the world's largest online bookstore to aspiring to be the world's largest online store; eBay changed from running online auctions for collectors to running online auctions that offer all kinds of goods; and Dunkin' Donuts switched its emphasis from doughnuts to coffee.

A **mission** is a clear, concise, and enduring statement of the reasons for an organization's existence. Often referred to as its *core purpose*, a company's mission is a long-term goal that provides company employees and management with a shared sense of purpose, direction, and opportunity.[9]

To define its mission, a company should address Peter Drucker's classic questions:[10] What is our business? Who is the customer? What is of value to the customer? What will our business be? What should our business be? These simple-sounding questions are among the most difficult a company will ever face. Successful companies continuously ask and answer them.

A clear, thoughtful mission statement, developed collaboratively with managers, employees, and often customers, provides a shared sense of purpose, direction, and opportunity. At its best, it reflects a vision, an almost "impossible dream," that provides direction for the next 10 to 20 years. Sony's former president, Akio Morita, wanted everyone to have access to "personal portable sound," so his company created the Walkman and the portable CD player. Fred Smith wanted to deliver mail anywhere in the United States before 10:30 AM the next day, so he created FedEx.

Consider the following mission statements:

> Google's mission is to organize the world's information and make it universally accessible and useful.[11]
>
> At IKEA our vision is to create a better everyday life for the many people. Our business idea supports this vision by offering a wide range of well-designed, functional home furnishing products at prices so low that as many people as possible will be able to afford them.[12]
>
> Facebook's mission is to give people the power to build community and bring the world closer together.[13]
>
> Tesla's mission is to accelerate the world's transition to sustainable energy.[14]
>
> To inspire and nurture the human spirit – one person, one cup and one neighborhood at a time (Starbucks).[15]
>
> Our mission is to empower every person and every organization on the planet to achieve more (Microsoft).[16]

Good mission statements have five major characteristics.

- **They focus on a limited number of specific goals.** Mission statements containing a laundry list of unrelated activities tend to be less effective than focused mission statements that clearly articulate their ultimate goals.
- **They stress the company's major policies and values.** Narrowing the range of individual discretion lets employees act consistently on important issues.
- **They define the major markets that the company aims to serve.** Because the choice of target market defines a company's strategy and tactics, it should be defined by and follow from the company's mission statement.
- **They take a long-term view.** The corporate mission defines the ultimate strategic goal of the company; it should be changed only when it ceases to be relevant.

- **They are as short, memorable, and meaningful as possible.** Three- to four-word corporate mantras are typically more effective than long-winded mission statements.

BUILDING THE CORPORATE CULTURE

Strategic planning happens within the context of the organization. A company's organization consists of its structures, policies, and corporate culture, all of which can become dysfunctional in a rapidly changing business environment. Whereas managers can change structures and policies (though with difficulty), the company's culture is very hard to change. Yet creating a viable corporate culture is often the key to market success, as the experience of HDFC Bank shows.

>> HDFC Bank's customer-centric approach is backed by the commitment to foster a culture of camaraderie, fairness, respect, pride, and credibility among its employees

Source: Casimiro / Alamy Stock Photo

HDFC Bank HDFC Bank, incorporated in 1994 with a mission to be a world-class Indian bank, adopted customer centric innovation and disciplined risk management to deliver shareholder returns of more than 16,000 per cent in the next two and half decades.[17] The bank has stayed true to its founding principles of customer focus, risk management and technology-led innovation, and in 2020, it's founder-CEO has been rated by the Economist as the world's best banker.[18] Aditya Puri, the founder-CEO of HDFC Bank, explained the consistency in its customer-centric approach as, "*The ultimate person we are here for is the consumer. In everything we do, the only way we'll succeed is if you bring your expertise together to provide a differentiated product to the customer.*" The leader's unwavering commitment motivates the bank's employees to deliver the brand promise during every interaction with customers. The conservative approach to risk meant that the bank finances its assets through deposits from its retail customers rather than debts. The bank serves retail and commercial clients in cities and semi-urban centers through one of the largest networks of branches and ATMs among private banks. Shunning investments in infrastructure projects as well as foreign ventures resulted in a steady and profitable growth with low defaults and the lowest non-performing assets among India's banks. Interestingly, the bank's core values not just include customer focus but also operational excellence, product leadership, people and sustainability.[19] Several awards and accolades recognizes the bank's employee-engagement experience, including the 'Great Place to Work' certification for mega employers with more than 50,000 employees.[20] The award acknowledges the bank's commitment to foster a culture of camaraderie, fairness, respect, pride, and credibility among its employees.[21] By creating and sustaining a culture that empowers employees and balances the freedom to work with responsibility, HDFC bank is able to attract the best talent and retain the most competent.[22]

What exactly is a **corporate culture**? Some define it as "the shared experiences, stories, beliefs, and norms that characterize an organization." Walk into any company and the first thing that strikes you is the corporate culture—the way people dress, talk to one another, and greet customers.

A customer-centric culture can affect all aspects of an organization. Enterprise Rent-A-Car features its own employees in its latest "The Enterprise Way" ad campaign. Through its "Making It Right" training program, Enterprise empowers all employees to make their own decisions. One ad in the campaign, themed "Fix Any Problem," reinforces how any local Enterprise outlet has the authority to take actions that maximize customer satisfaction.[23]

DEFINING STRATEGIC BUSINESS UNITS

Many large companies manage a portfolio of different businesses often referred to as strategic business units, each requiring its own strategy. A **strategic business unit (SBU)** has three characteristics: (1) It is a single business, or a collection of related businesses, that can exist separately from the rest of the company; (2) It has its own set of competitors; and (3) It has a manager responsible for strategic planning and profit performance, who controls most of the factors affecting profit.

Strategic business units make up a company's portfolio. Based on the diversity of the individual strategic business units within the portfolio, these units can be defined as specialized or diversified.

A **specialized portfolio** involves SBUs with fairly narrow assortments consisting of one or a few product lines. To illustrate, Ferrari (high-performance sports cars), Glacéau (bottled water), GoPro (action camcorders), and Roku (digital media streaming) have strategically limited their product mix to a fairly narrow product line.

In contrast, a **diversified portfolio** involves SBUs with fairly broad assortments containing multiple product lines. For example, companies like Amazon, General Electric, Johnson & Johnson, and Unilever offer a wide variety of product lines. The primary rationale for a diversified business mix is to take advantage of growth opportunities in areas in which the company has no presence.

Each business unit needs to define its specific mission within the broader company mission. Thus, a company that manufactures and markets lighting equipment for television studios might define its mission as "To target major television studios and become their vendor of choice for lighting technologies that represent the most advanced and reliable studio lighting arrangements." Note that this mission statement does not mention winning business from smaller television studios, offering the lowest price, or venturing into non-lighting products.

The purpose of identifying the company's strategic business units is to develop separate strategies and assign appropriate funding. Senior management knows its portfolio of businesses usually includes a number of "yesterday's has-beens" as well as "tomorrow's winners." Liz Claiborne has put more emphasis on some of its younger businesses, such as Juicy Couture, Lucky Brand Jeans, Mexx, and Kate Spade, while selling businesses without the same buzz (Ellen Tracy, Sigrid Olsen, and Laundry).

ALLOCATING RESOURCES ACROSS BUSINESS UNITS

Once it has defined its SBUs, management must decide how to allocate corporate resources to each unit.[24] This is often done by assessing each SBU's competitive advantage and the attractiveness of the market in which it operates. When assessing individual business units, a company might also consider

>> Biocon's entrepreneurial approach to strategic management constantly seeks opportunities to make its offerings affordable and accessible to over a billion

Source: ©Biocon, used with permission

existing synergies among them. Such synergies can be related to company processes (e.g., research and development, manufacturing, and distribution) or to personnel (e.g., experienced management, qualified engineers, and knowledgeable sales force). Based on the assessment of its portfolio of business units, the company could decide whether to grow, "harvest" (or draw cash from), or hold on to a particular business.

Portfolio management focuses on two types of factors: (1) opportunities presented by a particular industry or market and (2) the company's resources, which determine its ability to take advantage of the identified opportunities. Here, market opportunities are typically defined in terms of overall market/industry attractiveness factors such as its size, growth, and profitability. A company's resources, on the other hand, reflect its competitive position in the marketplace and are often measured in terms of factors such as strategic assets, core competencies, and market share.

Because the principles for making resource-allocation decisions across different business units are very similar across industries, many companies have developed generalized strategies for making such decisions. These generalized strategies are often integrated into formal portfolio models that offer guidance on how to allocate resources across multiple SBUs.

Biocon Biocon, India's most successful biopharmaceutical company straddles the entire drug value chain, from pre-clinical discovery to clinical development and finally commercialization,[25] The company has adopted a hybrid model to manage its four businesses comprising of generics, biosimilars, research services and novel biologics. Low-hanging revenue-earning, low-risk and predictable businesses like research services and generics serve as cash cows that generate surplus to run the higher-risk and longer-stream business of novel therapeutic programs for oral insulin, cancer vaccines, and autoimmune diseases, among others.[26] Biocon keeps refining its business model to manage its global business spanning emerging markets in Asia and Africa to the highly regulated markets in North America, Europe, Japan and Australia. Even in the generics segment, the company has adopted a differentiated approach of branded formulations anchored by biologics, unlike its Indian peers who are largely focused on off-patent small molecule generics. The company has harnessed the collaborative route to partner with global pharma giants including Pfizer, Mylan, Novartis and Bristol-Myers Squibb. Such collaborations allow sharing of risk and reward of drug development while extending its global footprint through local marketing alliances. The company's entrepreneurial approach to strategic management constantly seeks opportunities to make its offerings affordable and accessible to billions. In July 2020, as part of its global strategy, the company diversified into the rapidly growing digital therapeutic segment by partnering with Voluntis, a French healthcare solutions company. The partnership develops and distribute Insulia, a digital product, for at-home management of diabetes patients.[27] The digital app allows physicians to remotely monitor patients who receive automated and customized insulin dose recommendations. The treatment plan based on each patient's specific needs will lower treatment costs and improve health outcomes. Biocon plans to create a comprehensive digital therapeutics portfolio by extending the Insulia platform to its range of insulin products in its key global markets. The company believes that tapping into the growing digital therapeutics solutions will transform patient experiences through personalization.

As part of the global strategy for its biosimilars business, the company has diversified into vaccines by partnering with Serum Institute of India, the world's largest manufacturer of vaccines. While Biocon Biologics, which houses Biocon's biosimilars business, continues to have a broad and robust pipeline of biosimilars that target non-communicable diseases, it has also made a strategic move into the communicable disease segment through the partnership with Serum Institute for vaccines and infectious disease antibodies. This strategic alliance provides Biocon Biologics an asset-light and accelerated entry into the vaccines segment. It also complements the strengths and resources of the two leading players in vaccines and biologics, to address inequitable access in emerging and developed markets for life saving vaccines and biologics. The companies aim to make a significant positive impact on global healthcare through their alliance.

A key aspect in developing portfolio models involves identifying the metrics underlying the performance of a given business unit. Depending on the assumptions of the model, these metrics can include factors such as return on investment, market share, and industry growth rate. One widely used—albeit somewhat oversimplified and subjective—approach to portfolio analysis is the BCG matrix developed by the Boston Consulting Group. Newer portfolio-management methods use a more comprehensive approach to assess the potential of a business based on growth opportunities from global expansion, repositioning or retargeting, and strategic outsourcing.

Developing Market Offerings

In order to create value for target customers, collaborators, and company stakeholders, it is necessary for a company to clearly identify the target market in which it will compete and to design an offering that will deliver a meaningful set of benefits to target customers.[28] These activities encompass the two key components of a company's business model: strategy and tactics.

Strategy involves choosing a well-defined market in which the company will compete and determining the value it intends to create in this market. **Tactics**, also called the marketing mix, make the company's strategy come alive: They define the key aspects of the offering developed to create value in a given market. The tactics logically follow from the company's strategy and reflect the way the company will make this strategy a market reality. Tactics shape everything from the offering's benefits and costs to the means by which target customers learn about and buy the offering.

Strategy and tactics are fundamentally intertwined. A company's strategy specifies the target market and the value the company aims to create in this market, while the tactics detail the actual attributes of the offering that will create value in the chosen market. Deciding on the specific tactical aspects of an offering—its features, brand image, and pricing, and the means of promoting, communicating, and distributing the offering—is not possible without understanding the needs of the target marketing and the competing options that exist to fulfill these needs.

The key aspects of an offering's strategy and tactics are discussed in more detail in the following sections.

DEVELOPING THE MARKETING STRATEGY

Marketing strategy incorporates two key components: the *target market* in which the company will compete and the *value proposition* for the relevant market entities—the company, its target customers, and its collaborators. A carefully chosen target market and a well-crafted value proposition provide the foundation of the company's business model and serve as the guiding principles for determining the tactical decisions that define the company's offering.

Identifying the Target Market. The **target market** in which a company aims to create and capture value comprises five factors: the *customers* whose needs the company intends to fulfill, the *competitors* that aim to fulfill the same needs of the same target customers, the *collaborators* that help the company fulfill the needs of customers, the *company* that develops and manages the offering, and the *context* that will affect how the company develops and manages the offering.

These five market factors—the *Five Cs*—are visually represented in the *5-C framework* as a set of concentric ellipses: Target customers are in the center, with collaborators, competitors, and the company in the middle and the context on the outside (Figure 2.2). The central placement of target customers in the 5-C framework reflects their defining role in the market. The other three market entities—the company, its collaborators, and its competitors—work to create value for the target customers. Forming the outer layer of the 5C framework is the market context, which defines the environment in which customers, the company, collaborators, and competitors operate.

The Five Cs and the relationships among them are discussed in more detail in the following sections.

- **Target customers** are the individuals or organizations whose needs the company plans to fulfill. Target customers in business-to-consumer markets are typically the end users of the company's offerings, whereas in business-to-business markets, target customers are other businesses that use the company's offerings. Two key principles determine the choice of target customers: The company and its collaborators must be able to create superior value for target customers relative to the competition, and the target customers chosen should be able to create value for the company and its collaborators.
- **Collaborators** work with the company to create value for target customers. A company should base the choice of collaborators on the complementary resources they can offer to help the company fulfill customer needs. Collaboration involves outsourcing (rather than developing) the resources that the company lacks but that it requires to create an offering that fulfills the needs of target customers. Instead of building or acquiring resources that are lacking, a company can gain access to necessary resources by partnering with entities that have them and can benefit from sharing them. Collaborators can include suppliers, manufacturers, distributors (i.e., dealers, wholesalers, and retailers), research-and-development entities, service providers, external sales forces, advertising agencies, and marketing research companies.
- **Competitors** aim to fulfill the same needs of the same customers that the company is targeting.[29] Companies should avoid falling prey to the myopic view of competition that defines their rivals using traditional category and industry terms.[30] A company should examine the main competitors and their strategies by asking the following questions: What is each competitor seeking in the marketplace? What drives each competitor's behavior? This helps clarify the company's position since many factors are involved a competitor's objectives, including its size, history, current management, and financial situation. For example, it's important to know whether a competitor that is a division of a larger company is being run for growth or for profits, or is just being milked.[31]

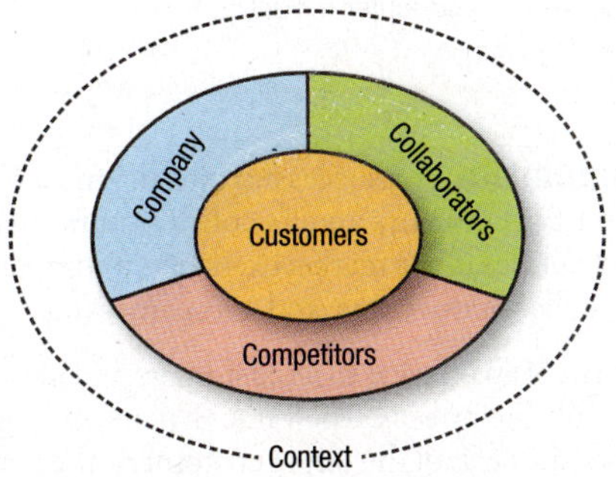

FIGURE **2.2**

Identifying the Target Market: The 5-C Framework

Source: Alexander Chernev, *Strategic Marketing Management: Theory and Practice* (Chicago, IL: Cerebellum Press, 2019).

- The **company** develops and manages a given market offering. For organizations with diverse strategic competencies and market offerings, the term *company* typically refers to the particular business unit that manages a specific offering. Each strategic business unit can be viewed as a separate company that requires its own business model. For example, GE, Alphabet (Google's parent company), and Facebook have multiple strategic business units.
- The **context** is the environment in which the company and its collaborators operate. It encompasses five factors. The *sociocultural context* is characterized by social and demographic trends, value systems, religion, language, lifestyles, attitudes, and beliefs. The *technological context* consists of new techniques, skills, methods, and processes for developing, communicating, and delivering market offerings. The *regulatory context* includes taxes, import tariffs, and embargoes, as well as product specification and pricing, communication regulations, and intellectual property laws. The *economic context* is made up of economic growth, money supply, inflation, and interest rates. The *physical context* comprises natural resources, geographic location, topography, climate trends, and health conditions. Context can have a dramatic impact on a company's ability to create market value. Many recent developments—including the advancements in artificial intelligence, the initiation of trade wars, global warming, and the coronavirus pandemic—have forced many companies to completely rethink the way they operate and pivot their business models.

The key component of the target market is the selection of target customers, which determines all other aspects of the market: This includes specifying the competition, choosing collaborators, defining the company resources needed to develop a superior offering for customers, and outlining the context in which the company will create market value. It follows that a change in target customers typically leads to a change in competitors and collaborators, different resource requirements, and a change in context factors. Because of its strategic importance, the choice of the right target customers is the foundation for building a successful business model.

The Five Cs and the Five Forces of Competition

The Five-C framework is similar to the Five Forces framework originated by Michael Porter.[32] The Five Forces framework identifies industry competitiveness according to five factors: the bargaining power of suppliers, the bargaining power of buyers, the threat of new entrants, the threat of substitutes, and rivalry among existing competitors. These five factors jointly define the competitive environment in which a firm operates. The Five Forces framework suggests that competition within an industry increases along with greater bargaining power of suppliers and buyers, a higher threat of new competitors and substitute products, and intensified rivalry among existing competitors.

The Five Forces framework is similar to the 5-C framework in that both are meant to facilitate analysis of the market in which a company operates. The difference between these frameworks is the way in which each defines the market. The Five Forces framework analyzes the competition in the market from an industry perspective. The 5-C framework, on the other hand, defines the market based on customer needs rather than on the industry in which the company competes. Accordingly, it defines competitors in terms of their ability to fulfill customer needs and create market value. The 5-C framework is not concerned with whether the company and its competitors operate within the same industry, which makes the concept of substitutes superfluous because from a customer's point of view, substitutes are merely cross-category competitors that aim to fulfill a particular need.

The Five Forces framework's focus on industry makes it particularly relevant for marketers analyzing the competitive structure within a given industry. However, the Five Forces approach has much less relevance when it comes to analyzing an offering's ability to create market value. In this case, the 5-C framework is typically more useful because of its customer focus and its market perspective based on customer needs rather than on a particular industry.[33]

Developing a Value Proposition. A successful offering must create superior value not only for target customers but also for the company and its collaborators. Accordingly, when developing market offerings for the relevant entities in the market exchange, a company needs to consider all three types of value: customer value, collaborator value, and company value.

- **Customer value** is the worth of an offering to its customers and hinges on customers' assessment of how well an offering fulfills their needs. The value that an offering creates for its customers is based on three main factors: the *needs* of the target customers, the benefits customers receive and

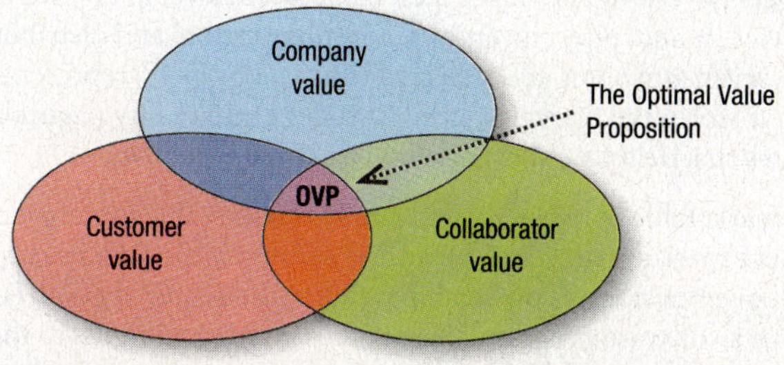

FIGURE 2.3
The 3-V Market Value Principle
Source: Alexander Chernev, *Strategic Marketing Management: Theory and Practice* (Chicago, IL: Cerebellum Press, 2019).

the costs they incur when they purchase the company's offering, and the benefits and costs of the alternative means—competitive offerings—that target customers can use to fulfill their needs. Thus, the customer value proposition should be able to explain why target customers would choose the company's offering instead of the available alternatives.

- **Collaborator value** is the worth of an offering to the company's collaborators. It sums up all benefits and costs that an offering creates for collaborators and reflects how attractive an offering is to collaborators. The collaborator value proposition should explain why collaborators would choose the company's offering instead of competitive alternatives to achieve their goals.
- **Company value** is the worth of the offering to the company. The value of an offering is defined relative to all benefits and costs associated with it, its affinity with the company's goal(s), and the value of other opportunities that could be pursued by the company—for example, other offerings that the company could launch. Therefore, the company value proposition determines why the company would choose this offering instead of selecting alternative options.

The market value principle is also referred to as the 3-V principle because it underscores the importance of creating value for the three key market entities—target customers, collaborators, and the company itself. The market value principle defines the viability of a business model by posing three sets of questions that must be addressed:

What value does the offering create for target customers? Why would target customers choose this offering? What makes this offering superior to the alternative options?

What value does the offering create for the company's collaborators (suppliers, distributors, and co-developers)? Why would collaborators partner with the company instead of with other entities?

What value does the offering create for the company? Why should the company invest resources in this offering rather than pursuing other options?

The need to manage value for all three of these market entities begs the question of which value to prioritize. This requires the creation of an **optimal value proposition** that balances the value for customers, collaborators, and the company. The term *optimal value* as used here means that the value of the offering is connected across the three entities, such that it creates value for target customers and collaborators in a way that enables the company to achieve its strategic goals. The market value principle optimizes customer, collaborator, and company value and is the basis of market success (Figure 2.3). Failure to create superior value for any of the three market entities inevitably leads to an unsustainable business model and dooms the business venture.

Consider the means that Starbucks uses to create market value. Customers receive the functional benefit of a variety of coffee beverages and the psychological benefit of expressing their personality by choosing a customized beverage, for which they deliver monetary compensation to Starbucks. Collaborators (coffee growers) receive monetary payments from Starbucks for the coffee beans they provide and derive the strategic benefit of having a consistent demand for their product; in return, they invest resources in growing coffee beans that conform to Starbucks' standards. Starbucks receives revenues and profits from investing company resources in developing and offering its products and services to consumers, in addition to deriving the strategic benefits of building a brand and enhancing its market footprint.

DESIGNING THE MARKETING TACTICS

The **market offering** is the actual good that the company deploys in order to fulfill a particular customer need. Unlike the target market and the value proposition, which reflect the company's strategy, the market offering reflects the company's tactics—the specific way the company will create value in the market in which it competes.

Marketing managers have seven tactics at their disposal to develop an offering that creates market value: product, service, brand, price, incentives, communication, and distribution. Also called the **marketing mix**, these seven attributes (also referred to as tactics or Ts) represent the combination of activities required to transform the market offering's strategy into reality (Figure 2.4).

The seven attributes that delineate the market offering are as follows:

- The **product** is a marketable commodity that aims to create value for target customers. Products can be tangible (like food, apparel, and furniture) or intangible (like music and software). Purchase of a product gives customers ownership rights to the acquired good. For example, with the purchase of a car or a software program, the owner is granted all rights to the acquired product.
- The **service** also aims to create value for its customers, but it does so without entitling them to ownership. Examples of services include appliance repairs, movie rental, medical procedures, and tax preparation. At times, the same offering can be positioned as a product or a service. This occurs, for example, when a software program can be offered as a product that gives purchasers the rights to a copy of the program, or as a service that allows customers to lease the program and temporarily receive its benefits.
- The aim of the **brand** is to identify the products and services produced by the company and differentiate them from those of the competition, in the process creating unique value over and above the product and service aspects of the offering. The Rolls-Royce brand identifies the cars manufactured by BMW subsidiary Rolls-Royce to differentiate these cars from those made by Bentley, Maserati, and Bugatti, as well as to evoke a distinct emotional reaction from its customers, who use the Rolls-Royce brand to call attention to their wealth and socioeconomic status.
- The **price** is the monetary charge that customers and collaborators incur to receive the benefits provided by the company's offering.
- **Incentives** are targeted tools designed to enhance the value of the offering by reducing its costs or increasing its benefits. Incentives are typically offered in the form of volume discounts, price reductions, coupons, rebates, premiums, bonus offerings, contests, and monetary and recognition rewards. Incentives can be directed to consumers or to the company's collaborators—for example, its channel partners.
- **Communication** apprises target customers, collaborators, and the company stakeholders of the specifics of the offering and where to acquire it.
- **Distribution** encompasses the channel(s) used to deliver the offering to target customers and company collaborators.

Again, a Starbucks example can illustrate these attributes. Starbucks' *product* includes the variety of beverage and food items available. The *service* consists of the assistance that Starbucks offers to customers before, during, and after purchase. The *brand* consists of the Starbucks name and logo, as well as the associations it evokes in customers' minds. The *price* is the amount of money that Starbucks charges customers for its offerings. *Incentives* include promotional tools such as loyalty programs, coupons, and temporary price reductions that provide additional benefits for customers. *Communication* consists of

FIGURE **2.4**

Marketing Tactics: The Seven Tactics (7 Ts) Defining the Market Offering

Source: Alexander Chernev, *Strategic Marketing Management: Theory and Practice* (Chicago, IL: Cerebellum Press, 2019).

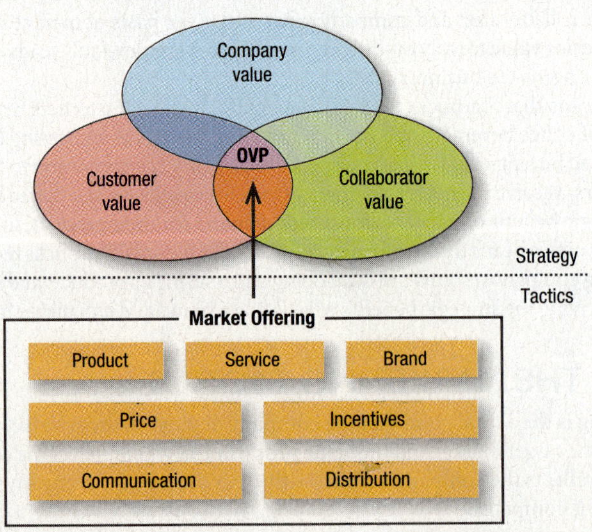

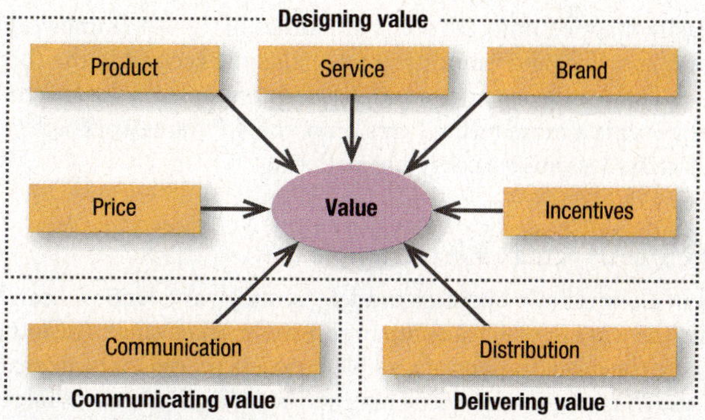

FIGURE 2.5
Marketing Tactics as a Process of Designing, Communicating, and Delivering Customer Value

Source: Alexander Chernev, *Strategic Marketing Management: Theory and Practice* (Chicago, IL: Cerebellum Press, 2019).

the information Starbucks disseminates via advertising, social media, and public relations to inform the public about its offerings. *Distribution* includes company-owned stores and company-licensed retail outlets that deliver Starbucks' offerings to its customers.

The seven marketing tactics—product, service, brand, price, incentives, communication, and distribution—can be regarded as a *process of designing, communicating, and delivering* customer value. The value-design aspect of the offering comprises the product, service, brand, price, and incentives, while communication and distribution form the information-value and delivery-value aspects of the process (Figure 2.5). Thus, even though the different tactical attributes play distinct roles in the value-creation process, they optimize customer value across all three dimensions.

The value-creation process can be considered from the perspectives of both the company and the customer. The company regards value creation as a process of *designing, communicating*, and *delivering* value; however, the customer looks at the value-creation process from a different perspective, viewing it in terms of the *attractiveness, awareness*, and *availability* of the offering.[34] Attractiveness reflects the benefits and costs that target customers associate with the product, service, brand, price, and incentives aspects of the offering. Awareness highlights the methods through which target customers are informed about the specifics of the offering. Availability consists of the ways in which target customers can acquire the offering.

THE SEVEN Ts AND THE FOUR Ps

The view of marketing tactics as a process of defining the seven key attributes of an offering can be related to the widely popular 4-P framework. Introduced in the 1960s, the 4-P framework identifies four key decisions that managers must make when designing an offering: the features to include in the *product*, the *price* of the product, the best way to *promote* the product, and the retail outlets in which to *place* the product. These four decision areas are represented by the Four Ps: product, price, promotion, and place.

Because it is simple, intuitive, and easy to remember, the 4-P framework enjoys wide popularity. However, because of that very simplicity, the 4-P framework has significantly limited relevance in the contemporary business environment. One of its limitations is that it fails to distinguish between the product and service aspects of the offering, which is a key drawback in today's service-oriented business environment, where a growing number of companies are switching from a product-based to a service-based business model. Another important limitation of the 4-P framework is that it does not regard the *brand* as a separate factor, instead viewing the brand as part of the product. The product and brand are two distinct aspects of the offering, and each can exist independently of the other. In fact, a growing number of companies outsource their product manufacturing so they can focus their efforts on building and managing their brands.

Another area in which the 4-P framework comes up short is in its treatment of the term *promotion*. Promotion is a broad concept that comprises two distinct promotional activities: *incentives*, which include price promotions, coupons, and trade promotions, and *communication*, which encompasses advertising, public relations, social media, and personal selling. Incentives and communication make disparate contributions to the value-creation process: Incentives enhance an offering's value, whereas communication serves to inform customers about the offering but does not necessarily enhance the offering's value. The 4-P framework's use of the term *promotion* to refer to both of these discrete activities can obscure the unique role that each plays in creating market value.

The limitations of the 4-P framework can be avoided by regarding the offering in terms of seven factors—product, service, brand, price, incentives, communication, and distribution—instead of four.

The four Ps can be easily mapped onto the seven attributes of the 7-T framework: The first P (product) comprises product, service, and brand; price remains the second P; the third P (promotion) is expanded to incentives and communication; and distribution replaces the fourth P (place). Thus, the 7-T marketing mix represents a more refined version of the 4-P framework, offering a more accurate and actionable approach to designing a company's offering.

CREATING A MARKET VALUE MAP

The two key aspects of a company's business model—strategy and tactics—can be represented as a value map that defines the ways in which a company creates market value. The ultimate purpose of the value map is to facilitate the development of a viable business model that can enable the company to achieve market success. Thus, the market value map can be thought of as a visual representation of the key components of a company's business model and the ways in which they are related to one another.

The market value map mirrors the structure of the business model and contains three key components that define the company's strategy and tactics—*the target market, the value proposition,* and *the market offering*. The target market is, in turn, defined by the Five Cs—customers, collaborators, company, competitors, and context—with customers playing the key role in defining the market. The value proposition then represents the three types of value that the company must create in the market: customer value, collaborator value, and company value. Finally, the offering component of the market value map delineates the seven key attributes—product, service, brand, price, incentives, communication, and distribution—that represent the tactical aspect of a company's business model. The components of the market value map and the key questions defining each component are shown in Figure 2.6.

The value proposition component of the market value map is central to ensuring the viability of the company's business model. The market success of the company's offering is determined by its ability to create value for the three key entities: target customers, the company's collaborators, and the

FIGURE **2.6**

The Market Value Map

Source: Alexander Chernev, *Strategic Marketing Management: Theory and Practice* (Chicago, IL: Cerebellum Press, 2019).

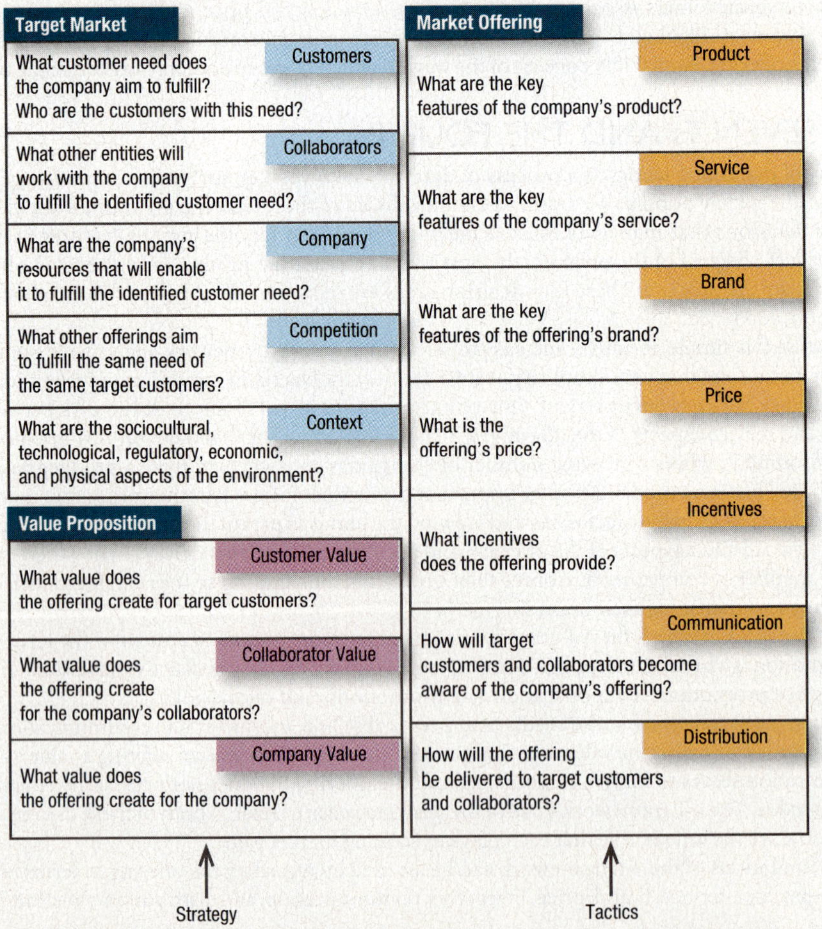

company itself. Because these entities have distinct needs and require different value propositions, the marketing planning process can be better served by developing a separate value map for each entity. Thus, in addition to having a single value map, managers might benefit from developing three value maps: a customer value map, a collaborator value map, and a company value map.

These three value maps depict the distinct aspects of the company's business model that concern the key entities involved in the value-creation process. The *customer value map* captures the ways in which the company's offering will create value for its target customers and outlines the strategic and tactical aspects of the customer-focused aspect of the company's business model. The *collaborator value map* delineates the strategic and tactical aspects of the ways in which the company's offering will create value for collaborators. Finally, the *company value map* outlines the ways in which the offering will create value for the company's stakeholders. Note that these three value maps are intricately related as they reflect different aspects of the process of creating market value. Only by creating value for target customers, collaborators, and the company can a manager ensure the market success of an offering.

Planning and Managing Market Offerings

A company's future depends on its ability to develop successful market offerings that create superior value for target customers, the company, and its collaborators.[35] Market success typically results from diligent market analysis, planning, and management; rarely is it a lucky accident. Succeeding in the market requires a company to develop a viable business model and an action plan that allows the business model to become a reality. The process of developing such an action plan is encapsulated in the G-STIC framework described in the following sections.

THE G-STIC APPROACH TO ACTION PLANNING

The action plan, which articulates the company's goal and delineates a course of action to reach this goal, is the backbone of marketing planning. Five key activities guide the development of an action plan: These activities include setting a *goal*, developing a *strategy*, designing the *tactics*, defining an *implementation* plan, and identifying a set of *control* metrics to measure the success of the proposed action. The G-STIC (Goal-Strategy-Tactics-Implementation-Control) framework comprises these five activities and acts as the lynchpin of marketing planning and analysis. At the core of the action plan is the business model based on the offering's strategy and tactics.

The individual components of the G-STIC approach to marketing planning and management are as follows:

- The **goal** describes the company's ultimate criterion for success; it specifies the end result that the company plans to achieve. The two components of the goal are its *focus*, which defines the metric (such as net income) used to quantify the intended result of the company's actions, and the performance *benchmarks* that signal movement toward the goal and define the time frame for achieving the goal.
- The **strategy** provides the basis for the company's business model by delineating the company's *target market* and describing the offering's *value proposition* in this market.
- **Tactics** carry out the strategy by defining the key attributes of the company's offering. These seven tactics—*product, service, brand, price, incentives, communication*, and *distribution*—are the tools used to create value in the company's chosen market.
- **Implementation** consists of the processes involved in readying the company's offering for sale. Implementation includes *developing* the offering and *deploying* the offering in the target market.
- **Control** measures the success of the company's activities over time by monitoring the company's *performance* and the changes in the market *environment* in which the company operates.

The key components of the marketing plan and the key factors describing each component are outlined in Figure 2.7 and are examined in more detail in the following sections.

SETTING A GOAL

Defining the goal that the company aims to achieve sets the marketing plan in motion. The goal can be regarded as the beacon that guides all company activities. Two key decisions are involved in setting a goal: identifying the *focus* of the company's actions and specifying the performance *benchmarks* to be achieved. These decisions are discussed in more detail next.

FIGURE 2.7

The G-STIC Action-Planning Flowchart

Source: Alexander Chernev, *Strategic Marketing Management: Theory and Practice* (Chicago, IL: Cerebellum Press, 2019).

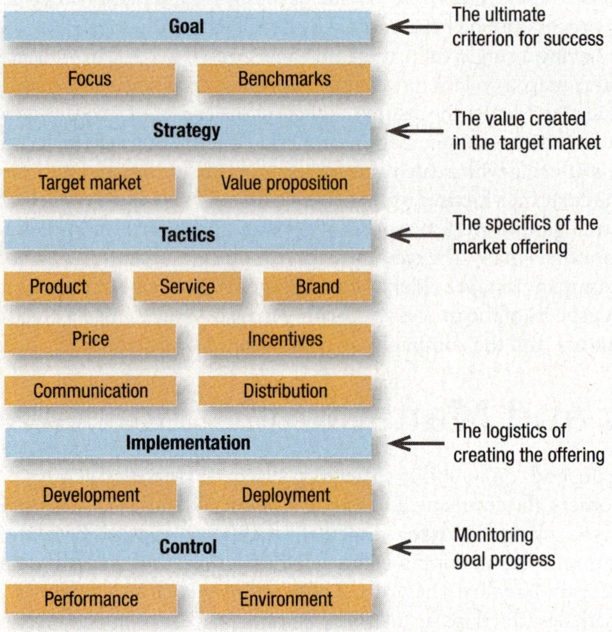

Defining the Goal Focus. The goal's focus defines the desired outcome of the company's activities, an important criterion of a firm's success. Based on their focus, goals can be monetary or strategic.

- **Monetary goals** are based on such outcomes as net income, profit margins, earnings per share, and return on investment. For-profit firms use monetary goals as their primary performance metric.
- **Strategic goals** are centered on nonmonetary outcomes that are of strategic importance to the company. Among the most common strategic goals are increasing sales volume, brand awareness, and social welfare, as well as enhancing the corporate culture and facilitating employee recruitment and retention. Nonprofit companies and for-profit companies looking to support items that are bigger revenue producers than the focal offering have strategic goals as their main performance metric. As an example, Amazon might only break even or actually take a loss on some of its Kindle devices and yet view them as a strategically important platform for its retail business.

Companies are increasingly looking beyond sales revenue and profit to consider the legal, ethical, social, and environmental effects of their marketing activities and programs. The concept of a "triple bottom line"—people, planet, and profits—has gained traction among many companies taking stock of the societal impact of their activities.[36] For example, one of Unilever's key initiatives—its Sustainable Living Plan—has three major goals: to improve people's health and well-being, to reduce our environmental impact, and to enhance livelihoods. These goals are underpinned by metrics spanning social, environmental, and economic performance in the company's value chain.[37]

Defining Performance Benchmarks. Quantitative and temporal performance benchmarks work in tandem to provide the measurements that track the progress of the company toward reaching its established goal.

- **Quantitative benchmarks** set out the specific milestones to be achieved as the company moves toward its ultimate goal. These benchmarks quantify the company's focal goal, which might, for example, include increasing market share by 5 percent, or improving retention rates by 15 percent, or growing revenues by 10 percent. Quantitative benchmarks can be stated in relative terms, such as aiming to increase market share by 20 percent, or in absolute terms, such as aspiring to achieve sales of one million units per year.
- **Temporal benchmarks** identify the time frame for achieving a specific quantitative or qualitative benchmark—e.g., revamp the company's website by the end of the first quarter. The timeline set for achieving a goal is a key decision that can affect the type of strategy used to implement the goal, the number of people involved, and even costs. For example, the goal of maximizing next quarter's profits is likely to require a different strategy and tactics than the goal of ensuring long-term profitability.

Implementing the company goal requires that three main objectives be specified: *what* the company aims to achieve (goal focus), *how much* the company wants to achieve (quantitative benchmark), and *when* the company wants to achieve it (temporal benchmark). Thus, a company might have the goal of generating net income (goal focus) of $40 million (quantitative benchmark) in one year (temporal benchmark). Clearly delineating the goal that is to be achieved and establishing realistic quantitative and temporal benchmarks help fine-tune the company's strategy and tactics.

DEVELOPING THE STRATEGY

Because the processes involved in developing a sound marketing strategy were covered in detail previously in this chapter, this section contains only a brief mention of strategy in relation to the G-STIC framework. The strategy denotes the value that the company intends to create in a particular market and includes the company's *target market* and its *value proposition* for this market.

- The **target market** in which the company aims to create value is defined by five factors: *customers* whose needs will be fulfilled by the offering, *competitors* whose offerings aim to fulfill the same needs of the same target customers, *collaborators* that help the company meet the needs of target customers, the *company* managing the offering, and the *context* in which the company operates.
- The **value proposition** defines the benefits and costs of the market offering with which the company plans to meet target customers' needs. The three components of the value proposition are *customer value, collaborator value,* and *company value*. The value proposition is often complemented by a *positioning statement* that highlights the key benefit(s) of the company's offering in a competitive context.

DESIGNING THE TACTICS

The development of marketing tactics was also discussed in greater detail earlier in this chapter, so here we briefly mention tactics as they relate to the G-STIC framework. Tactics, or the *marketing mix*, are a logical sequence of components of the company's strategy that make this strategy a market reality. They define the actual offering that the company introduces in the target market through seven attributes—*product, service, brand, price, incentives, communication,* and *distribution*—that work together to create the market value embodied by the company's offering.

Implementation is a direct outcropping of the company's strategy and tactics. After the strategy is translated into a set of tactics, it is converted into an implementation plan that spells out the activities that will give life to the business model. Implementation consists of three key components: *development of the company resources, development of the offering,* and *commercial deployment of the offering*.

- **Resource development** entails securing the competencies and assets needed to implement the company's offering. Resource development may involve developing manufacturing, service, and technology infrastructure; securing reliable *suppliers*; recruiting, training, and retaining skilled employees; creating *products, services,* and *brands* that serve as a platform for the new offering; acquiring the skills necessary for development, production, and management of the offering; developing the communication and distribution channels that inform target customers about the company's offering and make it available to them; and securing the necessary capital to make resource development possible.
- **Development of the offering** transforms the company's strategy and tactics into an actual good that will be offered to target customers. This involves overseeing the flow of information, materials, labor, and money that will create the offering the company brings to the market. Offering development includes designing the *product* (procurement, inbound logistics, and production) and specifying the service (installation, support, and repair activities); building the brand; setting retail and wholesale prices and incentives (coupons, rebates, and price discounts); designing the manner of communication (message, media, and creative execution); and procuring distribution channels (warehousing, order fulfillment, and transportation).
- **Commercial deployment** is the logical outcome of offering development and establishes the company's offering in the market. Deployment includes setting the timing of the offering's market launch, as well as determining the resources involved and the scale of the market launch. Initial deployment can be selective, focusing on specific segments of the target market to allow the company to assess market reaction to the offering. Alternatively, deployment can involve a large-scale rollout across all target markets. Selective commercial deployment calls for the marketing plan to define the primary market in which the offering will first be introduced and to outline the key activities associated with the offering's initial launch. The marketing plan then spells out the

timing and the processes involved in expanding the offering beyond the primary market, allowing it to reach all target customers and achieve its full market potential.

IDENTIFYING CONTROLS

Because the business environment undergoes constant change, companies must be agile in order to consistently realign their actions with current market realities. Controls steer a company in the direction of its ultimate goal by ensuring that company actions are in line with its strategy and tactics. Furthermore, controls make marketing operations more effective and cost efficient, and they make it possible to better assess the return on marketing investment by helping companies determine whether they are on the right track to achieve their goals.

Controls have one primary function: to inform the company whether it should stay with its current course of action, modify the underlying strategy and tactics, or completely abandon its current course of action and develop an offering that better reflects the realities of the market. Controls have two key components: *evaluating the company's performance* and *monitoring the market environment.*

Evaluating Performance. Evaluating a company's performance means using benchmarks to track the company's progress toward its goal. For example, evaluating a company's monetary performance might consist of comparing the desired and actual sales revenue outcomes or assessing desired and actual net income to identify operational inefficiencies. Here are some common performance measures:[38]

- Sales metrics such as sales volume, sales growth, and market share
- Customer readiness-to-buy metrics such as awareness, preference, purchase intent, trial rate, and repurchase rate
- Customer value metrics such as customer satisfaction, customer acquisition costs, customer churn, customer lifetime value, customer profitability, and return per customer
- Distribution metrics such as number of outlets, average stock volume, out-of-stock frequency, share of shelf space, and average sales per channel
- Communication metrics such as brand awareness, gross rating points (GRP), and response rate

Evaluating the company's performance can reveal either adequate progress toward its goal or a performance gap between the desired and the actual performance. If the progress is deemed adequate, the company can stay the course with its current action plan. However, when performance evaluation reveals a discrepancy and shows a gap between company performance and the benchmarks set, the company's action plan must be reevaluated and modified to put the company back on a path that will enable it to achieve its goal.

Monitoring the Environment. Monitoring the environment allows early identification of changes in the market context that have implications for the company. It enables the company to take advantage of opportunities such as favorable government regulations, a decrease in competition, or an increase in consumer demand. In addition, it alerts a company of impending threats such as unfavorable government regulations, an increase in competition, or a decline in customer demand.

When a company is vigilant about identifying opportunities and threats, it can take corrective measures to modify the current action plan in a timely manner, taking advantage of available opportunities and counteracting impending threats. Because keeping a close eye on the market environment helps coordinate company actions with market conditions, it enhances business agility, which is a prerequisite for sustainability of the company's value-creation model.

The importance of controls in marketing management and, specifically, the significance of monitoring the environment in which the company operates are perhaps best exemplified by the profound market changes stemming from advancements in technology. Companies like Amazon, Google, Netflix, Salesforce, Uber, and Express Scripts were among the first to recognize the benefits of the various technology-driven innovations and realign their business models to take advantage of the impending market changes. Thus, they were able to gain ground on companies that were oblivious to the changes in the environment around them.

Developing a Marketing Plan

The marketing plan directs and coordinates all company marketing efforts.[39] It is a tangible outcome of a company's strategic planning process, outlining the company's ultimate goal and the means by which it aims to achieve this goal. In order to serve its ultimate purpose of guiding a company's actions, the marketing plan must effectively communicate the company's goal and its proposed course of action to relevant stakeholders—company employees, collaborators, shareholders, and investors.

The scope of the marketing plan is narrower than that of the business plan because marketing covers only one aspect of a company's business activities. A company's business plan addresses not only the marketing aspect of the company's activities but also the financial, operations, human resources, and technological aspects of the company. The marketing plan may briefly touch on other aspects of the business plan, but only if they are relevant to the marketing strategy and tactics.

The marketing plan serves three main functions: It describes the company's goal and proposed course of action, informs the relevant stakeholders about the goal and action plan, and persuades the relevant decision makers of the viability of the goal and the proposed course of action.

Marketing plans typically start with an executive summary followed by a situation overview. The plan then describes the company's goal, the value-creation strategy it has devised, the tactical aspects of the offering, and its plan to implement the offering's tactics. This is followed by delineation of a set of control measures that will monitor the company's progress toward its goals, and the plan concludes with a roster of relevant exhibits. Figure 2.8 illustrates the key components of the marketing plan and the main decisions underlying its individual components.

- The **executive summary** can be regarded as the "elevator pitch" for the marketing plan. It presents a streamlined and succinct overview of the company's goal and the proposed course of action. Typically, the executive summary consists of one or two pages that outline the pertinent issues faced by the company—an opportunity, a threat, or a performance gap—and the proposed action plan.

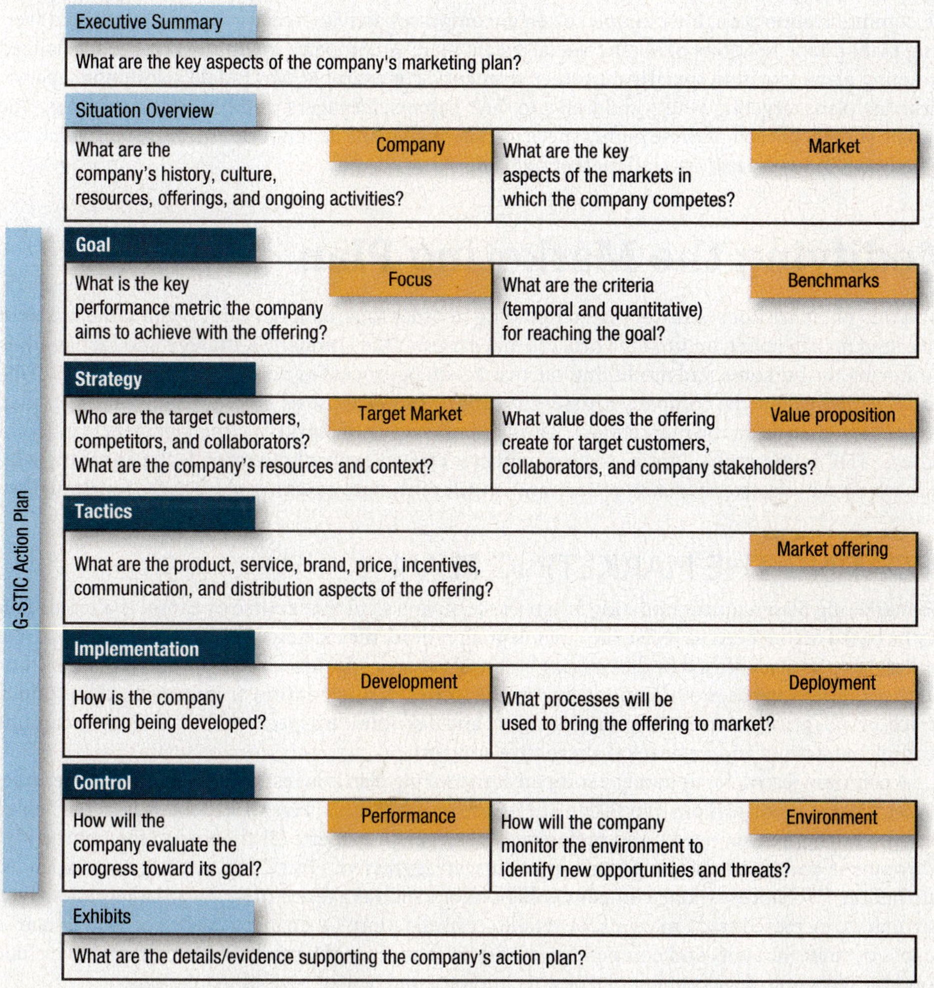

FIGURE **2.8**
The Organization of the Marketing Plan
Source: Alexander Chernev, *The Marketing Plan Handbook*, 6th ed. (Chicago, IL: Cerebellum Press, 2020).

- The **situation overview** provides an overall evaluation of the environment in which the company operates, as well as of the markets in which the company competes and/or will compete. Thus, the situation overview is composed of two sections: the *company overview* that outlines the company's history, culture, resources (competencies, assets, and offerings, and the *market overview* that outlines the markets in which the company currently manages offerings and those that the company could potentially target for future offerings.
- The **G-STIC** section forms the core of the marketing plan. It includes (1) the *goal* the company aims to achieve; (2) the *strategy*, which defines the offering's target market and value proposition; (3) the *tactics* defining the product, service, brand, price, incentives, communication, and distribution aspects of the offering; (4) the *implementation*, which lays out the aspects of executing an offering's strategy and tactics; and (5) *control* procedures that evaluate the performance of the company's offering and analyze the environment in which the company operates.
- **Exhibits** streamline the marketing plan by keeping tables, charts, and appendices in a distinct section to separate the less important and/or more technical aspects of the plan from the essential information.

The ultimate goal of the marketing plan is to guide a company's actions. Therefore, the core of the marketing plan is contained in the key elements of the G-STIC framework that delineate the company's goal and the course of action it proposes. The other elements of the marketing plan—the executive summary, situation overview, and exhibits—elucidate the logic underlying the plan and provide specifics of the proposed course of action.

In addition to the overall marketing plan, companies often develop more specialized plans. These can include a product development plan, service management plan, brand management plan, sales plan, promotion plan, and communication plan—which, in turn, can breed even more specific plans. The communication plan, for example, often encompasses activity-specific plans such as an advertising plan, public relations plan, and social media plan. A company might also create specialized marketing plans targeting specific customer segments. For example, McDonald's develops separate marketing plans targeting young children and their parents, teenagers, and business customers. The ultimate success of each of these highly specific individual plans depends on the degree to which it is aligned with the company's overall marketing plan.

Modifying the Marketing Plan

Marketing plans are not static; they need updating in order to remain relevant.[40] The same is true of marketing management, an iterative process that executes the company's strategy and tactics while monitoring the outcome and modifying the management process as needed. Continual monitoring and adjustment allow the company to assess its progress toward the set goals while tweaking its plan to reflect the changes in the marketplace. The dynamic nature of marketing management is inherent in the G-STIC framework's control section, which is crafted explicitly to provide the company with feedback on the effectiveness of its actions and on relevant changes taking place in the target market.

UPDATING THE MARKETING PLAN

The marketing plan requires updating when the company's current course of action is altered. This may be based on the need to revise the current goal; rethink the existing strategy because new target markets have been identified or the offering's overall value proposition for customers, collaborators, and the company needs modification; change the tactics by augmenting or improving the product, service, brand, price, incentives, communication, and distribution aspects of the offering; streamline the implementation; and/or develop alternative controls.

A common reason for updating a company's marketing plan is in response to changes in the target market. Market modifications can take place in one or more of the Five Cs: (1) changes in the demographics, buying power, needs, and preferences of target customers; (2) changes in the competitive environment, such as a new competitor, price cuts, an aggressive advertising campaign, or expanded distribution; (3) changes among company collaborators, such as a threat of backward integration from distributors, increased trade margins, or retailer consolidation; (4) changes in the company, such as the loss of strategic assets and competencies; and (5) changes in the market context that can include economic recession, development of a new technology, and new or revised regulations.

Some examples of updated marketing plans: In response to the shifting needs and preferences of their *customers*, McDonald's and other fast-food restaurants have redefined their offerings to include healthier options. In response to increasing *competition* from online retailers, many traditional brick-and-mortar retailers—including Walmart, Macy's, Barnes & Noble, and Best Buy—have redefined their business models and become multichannel retailers. Similarly, many manufacturers have redefined their product lines to include lower-cost offerings in response to the widespread adoption of private labels by *collaborators'* (retailers). Developing or acquiring *company* assets, such as patents and proprietary technologies, can signal the need to redefine the underlying business models in virtually any industry. And changes in the market context, such as the ubiquitous spread of mobile communication, e-commerce, and social media, have disrupted existing value-creation processes, making it necessary for companies to redefine their business models.

The ways in which a company creates market value must keep up with the changes in the market in which it operates if a company is to succeed at achieving its goal. Inattention to changing environments has rendered a number of formerly successful business models obsolete. Companies that do not adapt their business models and market plans to the new market conditions tend to be supplanted by companies with superior business models that are better equipped to create market value. Ultimately, the key to market success is not only to conceive a viable market plan but also to modify this plan as often as needed to adapt to market changes.

CONDUCTING A MARKETING AUDIT

A marketing audit is a comprehensive examination of the marketing aspect of an offering or a company's marketing department. It is intended to identify overlooked opportunities and problems areas and to recommend a plan of action to improve the company's performance. An effective marketing audit should be *comprehensive, systematic, unbiased,* and *periodic.*

- **Comprehensive.** A marketing audit should cover all major marketing activities of a business, not just a few trouble spots (these are covered by functional audits, which focus on a particular aspect of marketing activity, such as pricing, communication, or distribution). Although functional audits can be useful, they may be unable to accurately discern the cause-and-effect relationships that drive the company's performance. For example, excessive turnover in the sales force could result from inferior company products, inappropriate pricing, and limited distribution, rather than from poor training or inadequate compensation. A comprehensive marketing audit can locate the real root of problems and can suggest solutions to effectively address these problems.
- **Systematic.** The marketing audit should examine the operating environment of the organization in an orderly manner—from the company's marketing objectives and strategies to its specific activities. To achieve this systematic approach, the marketing audit should follow the G-STIC guidelines to analyze the soundness of the company's goals, strategy, tactics, implementation, and controls. This enables the marketing audit to identify problems and opportunities at each step of the design and implementation of the marketing plan and to integrate them into a meaningful action plan.
- **Unbiased.** It may be more beneficial to have marketing audits conducted by an external entity. Intra-company audits conducted by managers who rate their own operations tend to be overly subjective, making it easier to miss problems that would be readily apparent to a more impartial observer. Even when managers try their best to be impartial, internal assessments may still be biased because they reflect the views, theories, and motives of the managers. Third-party auditors can offer the needed objectivity, cross-category and cross-industry experience, and undivided time and attention to ensure a thorough look into marketing activities.
- **Periodic.** Many firms consider marketing audits only when they encounter a problem, which often presents itself in terms of the company's inability to reach its goals. Waiting until an audit is necessary has two main drawbacks. First, focusing solely on existing problems precludes early identification of potential issues. This means problems are detected only when they have already had a negative impact large enough to be noticed. Second, and more important, concentrating only on problems can cause the company to overlook promising opportunities that could represent fruitful areas for growth. The bottom line: A periodic marketing audit can benefit companies in good health as well as those in trouble.

Because the marketing audit resembles the organization of the marketing plan, it follows the G-STIC framework and comprises five key components: *goal audit, strategy audit, tactics audit, implementation audit*, and *controls audit*. The key difference between the marketing audit and the marketing plan is that the marketing plan faces forward toward the future and plots a course of action that the company should undertake; the marketing audit consolidates the company's past, present, and future by examining the company's current and past performance to determine the right course to ensure its future.

marketing INSIGHT A Template for Writing a Marketing Plan

The development of a marketing plan can be greatly facilitated by following a logical structure that enables the reader to understand the company's goals, the specific activities that the company intends to undertake, and the rationale for the proposed course of action. Such an approach to organizing the marketing plan is outlined in Figure 2.7, and a template for writing a marketing plan following this organization is outlined below.[41]

Executive Summary

Provide a brief overview of the situation, the company's goal, and the proposed course of action.

Situation Overview

Provide an overview of the situation—current/potential customers, collaborators, competitors, and context—in which the company operates, and identify relevant opportunities and threats.

Goal

Identify the company's primary goal and its market-specific objectives.

- *Primary Goal.* Identify the company's ultimate goal by defining its focus and key performance benchmarks.
- *Market Objectives.* Identify the relevant customer, collaborator, company, competitive, and context objectives that will facilitate achieving the primary goal. Define the focus and key benchmarks for each objective.

Strategy: Target Market

Identify the target market in which the company will launch its new offering.

- *Customers.* Define the need(s) to be fulfilled by the offering, and identify the profile of customers with such needs.
- *Collaborators.* Identify the key collaborators (suppliers, channel members, and communication partners) and their strategic goals.
- *Company.* Define the business unit responsible for the offering, the relevant personnel, and key stakeholders. Outline the company's core competencies and strategic assets, its current product line, and its market position.
- *Competitors.* Identify the competitive offerings that provide similar benefits to the same target customers and collaborators.
- *Context.* Evaluate the relevant economic, technological, sociocultural, regulatory, and physical contexts.

Strategy: Value Proposition

Define the offering's value proposition for target customers, collaborators, and the company.

- *Customer value proposition.* Define the offering's value proposition, positioning strategy, and positioning statement for target customers.
- *Collaborator value proposition.* Define the offering's value proposition, positioning strategy, and positioning statement for collaborators.
- *Company value proposition.* Outline the offering's value proposition, positioning strategy, and positioning statement for company stakeholders and personnel.

Tactics

Outline the key attributes of the market offering.

- *Product.* Define relevant product attributes.
- *Service.* Identify relevant service attributes.
- *Brand.* Determine the key brand attributes.
- *Price.* Identify the price(s) at which the offering is provided to customers and collaborators.
- *Incentives.* Define the incentives offered to customers, collaborators, and company employees.
- *Communication.* Identify the manner in which the key aspects of the offering are communicated to target customers, collaborators, and company employees and stakeholders.
- *Distribution.* Describe the manner in which the offering is delivered to target customers and collaborators.

Implementation

Define the specifics of implementing the company's offering.

- *Resource development.* Identify the key resources needed to implement the marketing plan, and

(*continued*)

marketing insight *(continued)*

outline a process for developing/acquiring deficient resources.

- *Offering development.* Outline the processes for developing the market offering.
- *Commercial deployment.* Delineate the process for bringing the offering to target customers.

Control

Identify the metrics used to assess the offering's performance and to monitor the environment in which the company operates.

- *Performance evaluation.* Define the criteria for evaluating the offering's performance and progress toward the set goals.
- *Analysis of the environment.* Identify metrics for evaluating the environment in which the company operates, and outline the processes for modifying the plan to accommodate changes in the environment.

Exhibits

Provide additional information—market research data, financial analyses, offering specifics, and implementation details—to support specific aspects of the marketing plan.

summary

1. Market-oriented strategic planning is the managerial process of developing and maintaining a viable fit between the organization's objectives, skills, and resources and its changing market opportunities. The aim of strategic planning is to shape the company's businesses and products so that they yield target profits and growth. Strategic planning takes place on three levels: corporate, business unit, and market offering.
2. The corporate strategy establishes the framework within which the divisions and business units prepare their strategic plans. Setting a corporate strategy means defining the corporate mission, establishing strategic business units (SBUs), assigning resources to each, and assessing growth opportunities.
3. Strategic planning for individual business units includes defining their mission, analyzing external opportunities and threats, analyzing internal strengths and weaknesses, and crafting market offerings that will enable the company to achieve its mission.
4. Marketing planning and management can occur on two levels. They can focus on analyzing, planning, and managing the company (or a specific business unit within the company), or they can focus on analyzing, planning, and managing one or more of the company's offerings.
5. From the point of view of designing a particular offering, marketing planning is a process defined by five main steps: setting a *goal*, developing the *strategy*, designing the *tactics*, defining the *implementation* plan, and identifying the *control* metrics to measure progress toward the set goal. These five steps constitute the G-STIC framework, which is the backbone of market planning.
6. The *goal* identifies the ultimate criterion for success that guides all company marketing activities. Setting a goal involves identifying the *focus* of the company's actions and defining the specific quantitative and temporal performance *benchmarks* to be achieved. A company's ultimate goal is translated into a series of specific market objectives that stipulate the market changes that must occur in order for the company to achieve its ultimate goal.
7. The *strategy* delineates the value created by the company in a particular market; it is defined by the company's target market and its value proposition for this market. The *target market* defines the offering's target customers, collaborators, company, competitors, and context (the Five Cs). The *value proposition* specifies the value that an offering aims to create for the relevant market entities—target customers, the company, and its collaborators.
8. The *tactics* outline a set of specific activities employed to execute a given strategy. The tactics define the key attributes of the company's offering: product, service, brand, price, incentives, communication, and distribution. These seven tactics are the means that managers have at their disposal to carry out a company's strategy.
9. The *implementation* plan lays out the logistics of executing the company's strategy and tactics. This involves developing the resources necessary to implement the company's offering, developing the actual offering that will be introduced in the market, and deploying the offering in the target market.
10. The *control* delineates the criteria for evaluating the company's goal progress and articulates a process for analyzing the changes in the environment in which the company operates, in order to align the action plan with market realities.
11. The *marketing plan* can be formalized as a written document that communicates the proposed course of action to

relevant entities: company employees, stakeholders, and collaborators. The core of a company's marketing plan is the G-STIC framework, which is complemented by an executive summary, a situation overview, and a set of relevant exhibits. To be effective, the marketing plan must be actionable, relevant, clear, and succinct. Once developed, marketing plans must be updated to remain relevant.

12. To ensure that its marketing plan is adequately implemented, a company must periodically conduct a *marketing audit* to identify overlooked opportunities and problem areas and to recommend a plan of action to improve the company's marketing performance.

marketing SPOTLIGHT

Google

Source: Valeriya Zankovych/Alamy Stock Photo

From smart phones to maps to e-mail to search, today Google is everywhere. This ubiquity makes it easy to forget that the company was founded in 1998 by two Stanford University PhD students, Larry Page and Sergey Brin. They named the company Google as a play on "googol," the term for the number 1 followed by a hundred zeroes. The name expressed the duo's ambition to help users sift through the nearly limitless amounts of information on the internet. Page and Brin further elucidated their goals in Google's corporate mission statement: "To organize the world's information and make it universally accessible and useful." To this end, they started by focusing their energy on the nascent field of internet search. The result of their effort was the PageRank algorithm, which counted the number and quality of links to a given website to rate its relevance and importance. This algorithm proved to be far superior to those used at the time by competing search engines such as Yahoo, and Google quickly became the dominant company in Web search.

Google's revenues revolved around advertising early on. It realized that the information from searches on its website could be used to deliver highly targeted advertisements to consumers and took advantage of this opportunity in 2000 by launching AdWords. This service allowed companies to pay Google to have their text advertisements show up alongside search results to queries containing specific words. Hundreds of thousands of companies grew to rely on AdWords by buying these "search ads." Google also moved into displaying advertisements beside Web content. In 2003 the company launched AdSense, which scanned the text on a website and automatically displayed targeted advertisements relevant to its contents. Website publishers could earn money every time their visitors clicked on these ads. Prior to this innovation, most websites were unable to automatically display highly specific ads to match their content.

Google also provided free tools to better serve advertisers and content providers. In 2005, the company launched a suite of tools called Google Analytics that allowed content providers to see custom reports on the way people behaved on their websites. Among other details, these reports showed how many people visited the website, how they found it, how long they spent there, and what ads they responded to while browsing content. Google also integrated tools into its AdWords platform to help advertisers better understand the effectiveness of their marketing campaigns. With these tools, advertisers on Google's platform could constantly monitor and optimize their advertisements. Google called this approach "marketing asset management," implying that advertisements should be managed like assets in a portfolio depending on market conditions. Companies could use the real-time data that Google collected to adjust their campaigns to market conditions, instead of following marketing plans developed months in advance.

Google came to dominate search and online advertising thanks to its ability to collect and process enormous amounts of data from the internet and make them useful. It used this capability to provide consumers and businesses alike with the information they needed. Despite its early successes, Google never stopped innovating. It continued to expend significant energy to develop and refine algorithms that could be used to squeeze more information out of the internet and keep Google ahead of the competition. In addition to refining existing products, Google developed a series of free online services for consumers. By applying its computer science and design skills to new problems, Google helped users get things done more efficiently and effectively. In many cases, rather than coming up with novel products, Google applied

(*continued*)

its expertise to existing categories to create a superior product offering. By entering a slew of new categories, Google gave advertisers access to consumers in an increasing number of contexts. Furthermore, the company gained access to increasing amounts of information on consumers that it could further monetize in the future.

Through continuous internal development and a series of acquisitions, Google rapidly expanded its product offerings. In 2004, Google launched Gmail, an advertising-supported e-mail service that by 2016 numbered over a billion active users every month. In 2005, the company launched Google Maps to compete with existing online mapping services. The company repeatedly impressed consumers as it upgraded its map service with features such as Street View, which gave users 360-degree views of map locations. In 2006, Google branched into streaming video when it acquired YouTube and grew it into a service that generated billions of dollars in advertising revenues. That same year the company also launched Google Docs, Sheets, and Slides—free online alternatives to elements of the Microsoft Office suite. Google continues to expand its online product offerings with everything from translation tools to calendars to specialized searches.

As Google developed into an internet giant, it realized that to continue growing, it would need to expand beyond products used only on computers. Google identified mobile technology as one of the ways forward and developed the open source Android mobile operating system. Whereas companies like Apple created proprietary operating systems for their hardware, Google gave its operating system away free to handset makers. As part of its strategy, Google partnered with companies like Samsung to improve and expand Android. These partners were free to modify Android and use its branding if they stuck to guidelines laid out by Google. In 2008, one year after Apple introduced the iPhone, Google launched Android on handsets from a variety of companies. Today Android is used on over 80 percent of smart phones globally. All Android users have access to Google Play, the official app store for the operating system. Google gets a cut of all sales. In addition to developing Android, Google became the leader in the rapidly expanding mobile advertising space, garnering nearly a third of 2017 U.S. mobile ad revenues in a market worth over $50 billion.

Google has also broadened its reach into other growing markets like hardware and cloud computing. With cloud computing, Google is competing with the likes of Amazon and Microsoft to provide remote storage capacity, data processing, and programming tools for enterprises and start-ups alike. Companies like HSBC have signed on with Google as it has rushed to embed itself in this rapidly growing sector. Google has also introduced a variety of hardware products, including the 2016 release of its high-end Pixel phones, designed to compete directly with the iPhone. In the same year it debuted Google Home, a smart speaker that not only connects to smart devices but also responds to voice commands and interacts with home automation systems.

Google has moved into many categories over its short lifetime, but all of its products are drawn together by the company's desire to harness the power of data to create better customer experiences. In an effort to continue innovating, Google has invested heavily in machine learning and artificial intelligence. These rapidly developing technologies offer the company a way to automatically sift through ever-increasing amounts of data to extract useful information. Google sees the further development of AI capabilities as pivotal to its future growth. From translation software to Web search to smart-phone cameras, artificial intelligence has come to underpin an increasing number of the company's product offerings and innovation.

Today Google has grown into a multinational company with almost $100 billion in revenue, almost 90 percent of which is from advertising. So far, though, Google's dependence on advertising revenue hasn't hurt growth. Google continues to dominate the online advertising market, capturing large share of the increased spending on online ads during the previous year. In addition, its annual revenue continued to soar by double digits. In the future, Google aims to create a more varied range of income streams from its investments in sectors like cloud computing, hardware, and artificial intelligence.[42]

Questions

1. What is Google's core business? What are the pros and cons of managing a diverse portfolio of businesses?
2. With a portfolio as diverse as Google's, what are the company's core brand values?
3. What's next for Google? Where should the company focus its resources?

marketing
SPOTLIGHT

Source: opturadesign/Alamy Stock Photo

Zappos

The 1999 creation of popular online retailer Zappos was inspired by founder Nick Swimmurn's inability to find a specific pair of shoes at his local mall. What started as an online retailing venture that primarily sold footwear has diversified to become a leading online vendor of shoes, handbags, clothing, sunglasses, and accessories.

Zappos has made customer service one of its core competencies. CEO Tony Hsieh believed that a strong customer-service experience leads to lasting customer loyalty. In addition, instead of viewing the lifetime value of a customer as a fixed amount, Zappos's management believes that the value of a customer can grow because of excellent customer service.

Zappos places high priority on its customer call team compared to other retailing companies. Specifically, Zappos takes a uniquely human approach to customer calls and e-mails to create a memorable and high-quality customer-service experience. Many online retailers (such as Amazon) use telephone contact as a last resort, with many clicks required for a customer to find a service number. However, Zappos invites customers to call by placing a button with its telephone number right at the top of the homepage. Whereas some companies are straying from call-based customer service, Zappos believes that the telephone is a valuable service tool with a powerful ability to create more intimate human contact.

Zappos management believes that the best candidates for its call and e-mail team are permanent employees trained in house, rather than lower-cost temporary or outsourced workers. Permanent employees are more likely to adopt the corporate culture and company values. Zappos combined its headquarters in Las Vegas, Nevada, with its call center team to fully integrate customer service-employees with other departments, creating a more unified atmosphere.

Zappos identified its biggest problem in creating a strong customer-service experience as finding the best potential employees to staff the call center. Zappos's hiring process is very selective. Unlike other companies, Zappos bases its successful process largely on its perception of candidates' "cultural fit," which accounts for 50 percent of the hiring decision. Current employees are encouraged to voice their opinions on whether or not potential hires can fit within the Zappos family culture and exhibit strong customer-service skills.

The company has created its own style and methodology for training its call center employees. Once hired, Zappos employees spend their first weeks in the call center learning how to serve the customer's needs. During this period, a training team also instills in each employee Zappos's 10 core values, which are expected to be seen in the workplace every day. Many of these values—which range from "Deliver WOW Through Service" to "Be Adventurous, Creative, and Open-Minded"—are what makes the service experience different at Zappos. New and old employees take part in a variety of team-building and bonding activities throughout the year. These include activities like scavenger hunts, picnics, and trips to the bowling alley to make all employees feel comfortable with one another. After the call center training and scavenger hunt, new employees are celebrated at a graduation ceremony, accompanied by the strains of Pomp and Circumstance. If new employees feel they cannot commit fully to the company culture and values, Zappos offers them $3,000 to leave—no questions asked. Zappos is fully committed to hiring only dedicated members as part of its service team.

Zappos's scrupulous hiring process and its approach of teaching the ten core values to new call and email center employees have resulted in a highly rated customer service experience. Zappos' employees do not work from a script and use their own judgment to determine what is needed to make the customer satisfied. Employees are not forced to ask supervisors for permission about delivering the "WOW" factor and are known to go above and beyond for customers at their own discretion. In the past, Zappos employees have upgraded shipping speeds for free, sent postcards to travelers, and even gifted flowers and cookies to customers to provide the "WOW" factor. The reward for Zappos's customer-centric mentality is customer retention: 75 percent of sales are from repeat buyers.

In addition to a uniquely trained call center team, Zappos offers many other features to ensure that the service experience is satisfying for potential customers. Shipping is fast and free on all products, and the company offers a 365-day return policy to guarantee that customers are pleased with their purchases.

(continued)

Since 2009, Zappos has operated as a subsidiary of Amazon and brings in over $1 billion in revenue every year. Amazon acquired Zappos because of its one-of-a-kind company culture and its dedication to customer service, which are both valuable assets. Recognizing this, Amazon has allowed Zappos to operate as an independent entity and to maintain its customer-centric culture. Zappos employees are still trained on the same 10 core values and encouraged to keep putting a human face on the company. With over 1,500 employees, a majority of them working in the call and e-mail centers, Zappos is considered one of the top companies in the customer-service domain.[43]

Questions

1. How does Zappos create value for its customers?
2. What are the key aspects of Zappos's corporate culture?
3. Can a company stay profitable by being customer-centric? Is Zappos's business model sustainable?

CHAPTER 3

Analyzing Consumer Markets

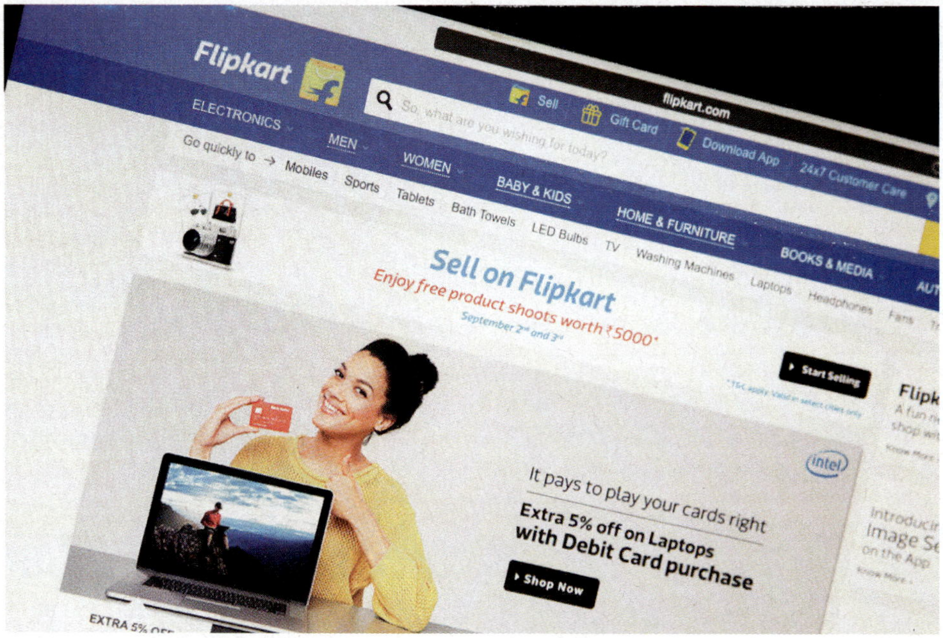

Flipkart's 'human approach to technology' revolves around customer satisfaction and loyalty. The company's research focuses on understanding factors that affect consumers decision and pain points.

Source: Pawan Kumar / Alamy Stock Photo

Marketers must have a thorough understanding of how consumers think, feel, and act and must offer clear value to each and every target consumer. Understanding consumer needs is the key to designing a value proposition that creates value for each and every customer. One of India's fastest growing brands, Flipkart, has achieved phenomenal market success by developing offerings tailored to the needs of its customers.

>>> Flipkart, founded by the IIT Delhi alumni duo—Binny Bansal and Sachin Bansal, started as an online bookstore in 2007.[1] Its technology driven customer-centric approach soon gained popularity, and the company moved into new categories including music, movies, games, electronics and mobiles. The company introduced the 'cash-on-delivery' (COD) option[2] to gain customers' confidence. COD attracted buyers who were reluctant to use credit cards for prepaid transactions because of widespread online financial frauds. No-questions-asked returns policy, no-cost instalment schemes, easy product exchange and 24×7 contact centres for round the clock service were some of the other customer-friendly initiatives introduced by the company. In 2018, Flipkart reached the milestone of being the first Indian e-commerce company with 100 million registered users and 50 million mobile app users.[3] Flipkart's 'human approach to technology' revolves around customer satisfaction

and loyalty. All key decisions related to research & development, innovation and technology are driven by a keen desire to understand the changing needs of customers. Its Flipkart Lite, a progressive web app, is primarily designed to support the app browsing for low-speed Internet users. Exclusive online-only product launches and easy product exchange for the value seeking customers exemplify its commitment to meet the evolving customer needs.[4] In 2018, Walmart acquired a majority stake for $16 billion in Flipkart, and the latter's growth accelerated by investing in logistics, distribution and fulfilment centres to help sellers on its marketplace.[5] It launched Brand Pulse, an insights tool to make the online shopping experience more seamless for consumers and valuable for brands on Flipkart's platform.[6] The sellers on Flipkart can use insights, gleaned from millions of consumers' digital journey including search, response to banners, page views and purchase, to develop timely and focused marketing plans. Going forward as competition rises from the likes of Amazon and JioMart, Flipkart needs to have even greater focus on customer needs and choices.

This chapter explores the buying dynamics of individual consumers. Adopting a holistic marketing orientation requires fully understanding customers and gaining a 360-degree view of both their daily lives and the changes that occur during their lifetimes to ensure that the right products are marketed to the right customers in the right way at the right time.

The Model of Consumer Behavior

Research on consumer behavior explores how individuals, groups, and organizations select, buy, use, and dispose of goods, services, ideas, or experiences to satisfy their needs and wants.[7] To create customer value, marketers must fully understand both the theory and the reality of consumer behavior.

The starting point for understanding consumer behavior is the model shown in Figure 3.1. The tactics shaping the offering and the context of the market in which the offering will be sold are filtered through the cultural, social, and personal lenses of target customers, as well as being influenced by consumer motivation, perception, emotions, and memory. This, in turn, influences the consumer buying process—a journey that entails recognition of a need, a search for the best means to fulfill that need, and evaluation of the available options to finally arrive at the ultimate decision of what, when, where, and how much to buy, and how to pay for these purchases.[8]

We discuss the key consumer characteristics and the psychological processes underlying consumer behavior in the following sections.

Consumer Characteristics

A consumer's buying behavior is influenced by cultural, social, and personal factors. Of these, cultural factors exert the broadest and deepest influence on people's perceptions and desires and on how they go about fulfilling their needs and wants.

Learning Objectives After studying this chapter you should be able to:

3.1 Identify the key factors that influence consumer behavior.

3.2 Explain the role cultural, social, and personal factors play in consumer behavior.

3.3 Explain how consumers' needs, emotions, and memory influence their behavior.

3.4 Illustrate the key stages of the buying decision process.

FIGURE **3.1**
Model of Consumer Behavior

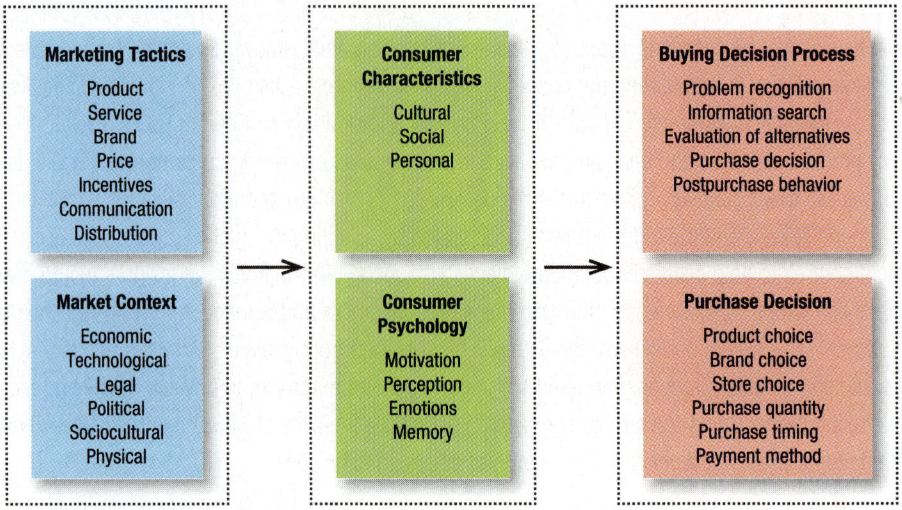

CULTURAL FACTORS

A culture is a way of life among a group of people—the behaviors, beliefs, values, and symbols that they accept, generally without thinking about them, and that are passed along by communication and imitation from one generation to the next.[9]

Culture, subculture, and social class are particularly important influences on consumer buying behavior. Culture is a fundamental determinant of a person's wants and behavior. Through family and other key institutions, a child growing up in the United States is exposed to values such as achievement and success, activity, efficiency and practicality, progress, material comfort, individualism, freedom, humanitarianism, and youthfulness.[10] A child growing up in another country might have a different view of self, relationship to others, and rituals.

Cultures can differ on a variety of dimensions, such as the extent to which people prioritize close (vs. distant) others and whether they behave as if they are part of a collective (i.e., collectivistic cultures) or see themselves as independent agents who value their autonomy (i.e., individualistic cultures). Marketers must closely attend to cultural values in every country to understand how best to market their existing products and find opportunities to develop new products. Each culture also consists of subcultures that provide members with more specific identification and socialization. Subcultures include nationalities, religions, racial groups, and geographic regions. When subcultures grow sufficiently large and affluent, companies often design specialized marketing programs to serve them.

To determine the effect of culture on purchases, a recent longitudinal study examined data from 30,000 customers of a global fashion retailer in 30 countries. The study analyzed demographic background, shopping behavior, participation in loyalty programs, types of products bought, product returns, and advertising costs—including e-mail and catalogs—using a framework that enabled national culture to be examined according to the importance of individualism and collectivism, level of indulgence or restraint, type of offerings bought, loyalty to companies/brands, tendency to embrace new technologies, and use of media. Among the findings: Consumers in individualistic societies like Australia and the United States are more likely to buy for themselves, follow trends, use multiple purchase channels (including online and catalog) to find the best deal, and return items that fall below expectations, whereas consumers in collectivist countries (e.g., Portugal, Mexico, and Turkey) tend to follow the crowd, value long-term reputation, shop for their families, buy from trusted retailers, and prefer traditional brick-and mortar stores.[11]

Virtually all human societies exhibit *social stratification,* most often in the form of social classes—relatively homogeneous, enduring, and hierarchically ordered divisions in a society whose members share similar values, interests, and behavior. For example, the United States has lower, middle, and upper classes. Social class members show distinct product and brand preferences in many areas.

They may at times want to communicate that they belong to a specific social class by purchasing products that can be viewed as status symbols.[12] The rigidity of social hierarchies and how difficult it is to move up the social ladder also differ across cultures. For example, places like India and Brazil have relatively rigid social hierarchies, with people's positions on the various rungs being determined at birth.

Pervasive inequality still exists among the upper, middle, and lower classes in Brazil, which are often divided into A-B-C-D-E socioeconomic segments by statisticians and marketers. Although it is relaxing slightly, this strict social stratification still divides wealthier and better-educated property owners, and those with special technical skills and expertise (A and B classes), from the large and disproportionately poor E-class segment of the population that has limited access to employment, education, and even basic government services like health and sanitation. C-class individuals typically have at least a high school degree and provide services to those in the A & B classes as teachers, managers, nurses, and the like. Individuals in the D class serve the C class as maids, drivers, bartenders, mechanics, etc. Those in the lowest economic stratum typically have not completed elementary school, are often illiterate, and, when employed, are usually found in jobs such as cleaner and street sweeper that pay meager wages.[13]

SOCIAL FACTORS

In addition to cultural factors, social factors such as reference groups, including family, affect our buying behavior. We address these factors in more detail next.

Reference Groups. **Reference groups** include all the groups that have a direct or indirect effect on a person's beliefs, decisions, and behavior. Family members typically constitute the most influential primary reference group. Parents and siblings have a major influence in forming an individual's beliefs, value system, and behavior. An individual's spouse and children, on the other hand, have a more direct impact on everyday buying decisions, especially in the case of high-ticket items and items that are used by different members of the household.

Reference groups include not only those that individuals belong to, such as friends, neighbors, coworkers, and religious and interest-based groups. Individuals may also be influenced by groups to which they do *not* belong, such as aspirational groups that they hope to join and dissociative groups whose values or behavior they reject.

Where reference group influence is strong, marketers must determine how to reach and influence the group's opinion leaders. An **opinion leader**, or an **influencer**, is a person who offers informal advice or information about a specific product or product category, such as which of several brands is best or how a particular product may be used.[14] Opinion leaders are often highly confident, socially active, and frequent users of the product category. Marketers try to reach these leaders by identifying their demographic and psychographic characteristics and the media they read, as well as by directing messages to them.[15]

All of us participate in many groups—family, clubs, organizations—that often influence our norms of behavior. We can define a person's position in each group in terms of role and status. A *role* consists of the activities a person is expected to perform. Each role in turn connotes a *status.* A senior vice president of marketing may have more status than a sales manager, and a sales manager may have more status than an office clerk. People choose products that reflect and communicate their role and their actual or desired status in society. Thus, marketers must be aware of the status-symbol and self-defining potential of products and brands.

Family. The family, as the most influential primary reference group,[16] is the most important consumer buying organization in society. There are two families in the buyer's life. The *family of orientation* consists of parents and siblings. From parents a person acquires an orientation toward religion, politics, and economics, along with a sense of personal ambition, self-worth, and love.[17] Even if the buyer no longer interacts very much with his or her parents, parental influence on behavior can be a significant determinant of purchases.

A more direct influence on everyday buying behavior is the *family of procreation*—namely, the person's spouse and children. In the United States, purchases have in the past varied widely by product category, with the wife usually acting as the family's main purchasing agent, especially for food, sundries, and clothing items. Traditional purchasing roles are now changing, and marketers now see both men and women as viable targets.

For expensive products and services such as cars, vacations, or housing, the vast majority of spouses engage in joint decision making.[18] Men and women may respond differently to marketing messages, however. Research has shown that women tend to place greater value connections and relationships with family and friends and place a higher priority on people than on companies.[19] Accordingly, marketers have customized the positioning of many products such as Quaker's Nutrition for Women cereals and Crest rejuvenating and whitening toothpaste.

Another shift in buying patterns is an increase in the amount of dollars spent by children and teens and the direct and indirect purchasing influence they wield. Direct influence takes the form of children's hints, requests, and demands: "I want to go to McDonald's." Indirect influence means that parents know the brands, product choices, and preferences of their children without hints or outright requests: "I think Jake and Emma would prefer to go to Panera."

A recent survey of the social media habits of 13- to 33-year-olds reveals that only 2 percent say they do not use any social platform, and Millennials report that they use their smartphones more than 11 hours each day, mostly for messaging and social networking. The majority of participants say they have friended or followed a brand on social media; 38 percent have posted about a brand, with 54 percent of these posts being positive and only 22 percent negative.[20]

PERSONAL FACTORS

Personal characteristics that influence buyers' decisions include their age and stage in the life cycle, occupation and economic circumstances, personality and self-concept, and lifestyle and values. Because many of these factors have a direct impact on consumer behavior, it is important for marketers to follow them closely.

Our taste in food, clothes, furniture, and recreation is often related to our age. Consumption is also shaped by the *family life cycle* and the number, age, and gender of people in the household at any given time. U.S. households are evolving: The traditional family of four with a husband, wife, and two kids makes up a much smaller percentage of total households than it once did.

In addition, *psychological* life-cycle stages may matter. Adults experience certain passages, or transformations, as they go through life,[21] causing their behavior during these intervals to adapt to changing circumstances. Marketers should consider *critical life events or transitions*—marriage, childbirth, illness, relocation, divorce, first job, career change, retirement, death of a spouse—as giving rise to new needs. Companies should be alert to these needs and provide products and services that can best meet them.

It's not surprising that the baby industry attracts many marketers, given the enormous amount parents spend and the life-changing nature of parenthood.

The Baby Market Although they may not yet have reached their full earning potential, expectant and new parents seldom hold back when spending on their loved ones, making the baby industry more recession-proof than most. Spending tends to peak between the second trimester of pregnancy and the twelfth week after birth. First-time mothers-to-be are especially attractive target customers since they will be unable to use many hand-me-downs and will need to acquire a full range of new furniture, strollers, toys, and baby supplies. Recognizing the importance of reaching expectant parents early to win their trust—industry pundits call it a "first in, first win" opportunity—marketers use a variety of media, including direct mail, inserts, space ads, e-mail marketing, and websites. Product samples are especially popular, and kits are often distributed at childbirth education classes and other places. Many hospitals have banned the traditional bedside gift bag, however, because of concerns with privacy and potentially adverse effects on a vulnerable audience (e.g., distributing baby formula may discourage new mothers from breastfeeding). Other avenues of access exist: For example, Disney Baby partners with a company that sells baby bedside photos, hands out playful Disney Cuddly Bodysuits, and solicits sign-ups for e-mail alerts from DisneyBaby.com. Not all expenditures go directly to baby-related purchases. Such a fundamental life change gives expectant or new parents a whole new set of needs that has them thinking differently about life insurance, financial services, real estate, home improvement, and automobiles.[22]

Occupation also influences consumption patterns. Marketers try to identify the occupational groups that have above-average interest in their products and services, and they even tailor products for certain occupational groups. Computer software companies, for example, design different products for brand managers, engineers, lawyers, and physicians. Michigan-based Carhartt Inc., founded in 1889, has become a global work-clothing dynasty with 800 products, a network of some 100 metro-Detroit retail stores, and corporate stores in seven states, as well as Carhartt Europe and Australia. Carhartt's line of durable industrial, farm, and outdoor clothing is known for quality fabrics and workmanship and through the years has gained traction as streetwear.[23]

Both product choice and brand choice are greatly affected by economic circumstances like the level, stability, and pattern of spendable income; savings and assets, including the percentage that is liquid; debts and borrowing power; and attitudes toward spending and saving. If economic indicators point to a recession, marketers can take steps to redesign, reposition, and reprice their products or emphasize discount brands so they can continue to offer value to target customers.

Source: Carolyn Jenkins/Alamy Stock Photo

>> Brands like Disney Baby know that reaching expectant and new parents early is essential to success in the baby market.

Personality and Self-Concept. By **personality** we mean a set of distinguishing human psychological traits that lead to relatively consistent and enduring responses to environmental stimuli, including buying behavior. We often describe personality in terms of such traits as self-confidence, dominance, autonomy, deference, sociability, defensiveness, and adaptability.[24]

Consumers typically choose and use brands with a brand personality consistent with their *actual self-concept* (how we view ourselves), although the match may instead be based on the consumer's *ideal self-concept* (how we would like to view ourselves) or even on *others' self-concept* of us (how we think others see us).[25] These effects may be more pronounced for publicly consumed products than for privately consumed goods.[26] On the other hand, consumers who are high "self-monitors"—that is, are sensitive to the way others see them—are more likely to choose brands whose personalities fit the consumption situation.[27]

Finally, multiple aspects of self (serious, professional, caring family member, active fun-lover) may often be evoked differently in different situations or around different types of people. Some marketers, like Joie de Vivre Hotels, carefully orchestrate their brand experiences to appeal to a variety of different personalities.

Joie de Vivre Named one of best boutique hotel chains by the editors of *Smarter Travel* magazine, San Francisco-based Joie de Vivre boasts the largest collection of lifestyle boutique hotels in California, with additional locations in Chicago, Baltimore, and New York City. The chain views itself as "a collection of heartfelt stories brought to life" and aims to inspire "the spirt of playful travel through neighborhood connections." Guests at Joie de Vivre's sleek and intimate, pet- and family-friendly, community-focused hotels have the option to donate $1 a night, which goes directly to each hotel's philanthropic partners. The chain donates almost $1.5 million each year to neighborhood organizations in the form of gift certificates, cash and in-kind donations, and events. All hotels participate in recycling, composting, and textile and food donation programs, and all work to conserve water and energy, use environmentally safe products, and purchase organic, fair trade food.[28]

Values and Lifestyle. Consumer behavior is guided by a *value system*—a set of principles and notions of "right and wrong"—that determines what is meaningful and important to consumers and how they choose to live and interact with others. Consumer decisions are also influenced by these *core values*, which go much deeper than behavior or attitude and, at a basic level, guide people's choices and

Late 1990's →

ESTABLISHED 1744 Allen Solly NOTTINGHAM • ENGLAND

Friday Dressing

Allen Solly rode the semi-formal workwear adoption wave, courtesy 'Casual Fridays'

2008 →

ALLEN SOLLY

My World. My Way.

The brand matched the fashion sensibilities of a young & dynamic workforce that viewed success differently

2018 →

Allen Solly

OPEN WORK CULTURE

Allen Solly was reintroduced as the brand for young, fashion forward leaders of the future.

>> Market research and consumer understanding spurred Allen Solly to keep introducing new range and collections that reflected changing consumer lifestyle and ramped-up sales.

Source: Allen Solly©Aditya Birla Fashion & Retail Limited, used with permission

Allen Solly Allen Solly is a prominent example of a brand that aligns with the evolving values and lifestyle of its target audience. Established in 1744, the brand was introduced in India in the early 1990s. Strategically positioning itself as 'work casuals', Allen Solly stood out in the premium, formal office wear market. The brand attracted the young professionals, aged between 21 to 30 years, employed in the booming services and software businesses in India. The brand image reinforced through the 'Friday Dressing' concept transformed the office wear range from formal plain and striped shirts and trousers to relaxed casuals.[31] The success of Allen Solly's office apparel in colourful shirts and khaki trousers paved way for it to become one of India's leading fashion brand. In response to the changing lifestyle needs of its target audience—the millennials, Allen Solly later extended its positioning to 'casual brand for all occasions' in 2008. The brand's redesigned logo and a new tag line— 'My World, My Way'—reflected the young, independent spirited and dynamic millennials.[32] In 2018, the brand launched its 'New Age Work Wear Collection' to celebrate the emergence of open work culture in organisations emphasizing work-life balance and employee friendly policies. Driven by a deep understanding of the ever-evolving young professionals, Allen Solly continues to lead in defining fashion at work through its distinct offerings.[33]

desires over the long term. Marketers who target consumers on the basis of their values believe that appealing to people's inner selves makes it possible to influence their outer selves—their purchase behavior.

People from the same subculture, social class, and occupation may adopt quite different lifestyles. A *lifestyle* is a person's pattern of living in the world, as expressed in activities, interests, and opinions. It portrays the "whole person" interacting with his or her environment.[29]

Lifestyles are shaped partly by whether consumers are *money-constrained* or *time-constrained*. Companies that aim to serve the money-constrained will create lower-cost products and services. By appealing to thrifty consumers, Walmart has become the largest company in the world. Its "everyday low prices" have wrung tens of billions of dollars out of the retail supply chain, passing the larger part of savings along to shoppers in the form of rock-bottom bargain prices.

Consumers are prone to multitasking. Some will also pay others to perform tasks because time is more important to them than money. Companies aiming to serve them will create products and services that offer multiple time-saving benefits. For example, multitasking beauty balm (BB) skin creams offer an all-in-one approach to skin care, incorporating a moisturizer, anti-aging ingredients, sunscreen, and sometimes even a whitening agent.[30]

Consumer Psychology

When marketing and environmental stimuli enter the consumer's consciousness, a set of psychological processes combine with certain consumer characteristics to result in decision processes and purchase decisions. The marketer's task is to understand what happens in the consumer's consciousness between the arrival of the outside marketing stimuli and the ultimate purchase decisions. Four key psychological processes—motivation, perception, learning, and memory—fundamentally influence consumer responses.

CONSUMER MOTIVATION

Understanding consumer motivation begins with understanding the needs consumers aim to fulfill with their actions. Thus, we first discuss the essence of consumer needs and then address the way these needs motivate consumer behavior.

Consumer Needs. *Needs* are the basic human requirements, such as air, food, water, clothing, and shelter. Some needs are *biological* and arise from physiological states of tension such as hunger, thirst, or discomfort. Other needs are *psychological* and arise from psychological states of tension such as the need for recognition, esteem, or belonging.

One of the best-known theories of human motivation, that of Abraham Maslow, carries important implications for consumer analysis and marketing strategy. Maslow sought to explain why people are driven by particular needs at particular times.[34] His answer is that human needs are arranged in a hierarchy from most to least pressing—from physiological needs to safety needs, social needs, esteem needs, and self-actualization needs (see Figure 3.2). People try to satisfy their most important needs first and then move to the next important. For example, a starving man will not take an interest in the latest happenings in the art world (need 5), or in the way he is viewed by others (need 3 or 4), or even in whether he is breathing clean air (need 2) until he has enough food and water (need 1), after which the next most important needs will become salient.

Needs become *wants* when directed to specific objects that might satisfy the need. Our wants are shaped by our society. A U.S. consumer needs food but may want a Chicago-style "deep-dish" pizza and a craft beer. A consumer in India needs food but may want chole, tandoori chicken, and naan.

Demands are wants for specific products backed by an ability to pay. Many people want a Mercedes but only relatively few can buy one. Companies must measure not only how many people want their product but also how many are willing and able to buy it. These distinctions shed light on the criticism that "marketers get people to buy things they don't want." Marketers do not create needs: Needs preexist marketers. Marketers might promote the idea that a Mercedes satisfies a person's need for social status. They do not, however, create the need for social status.

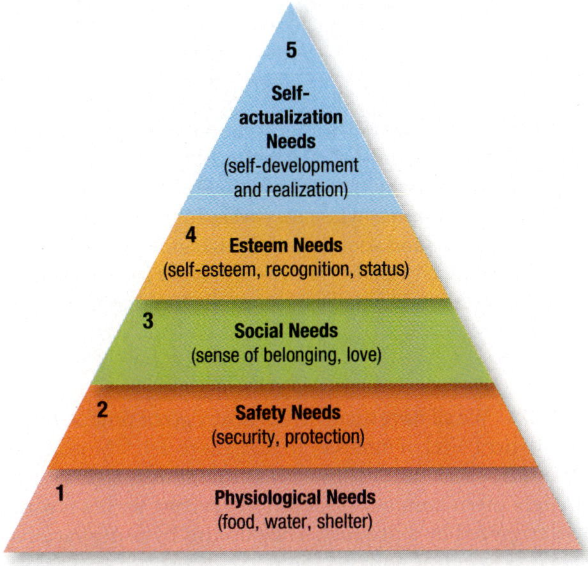

FIGURE **3.2**

Maslow's Hierarchy of Needs

Source: A. H. Maslow, *Motivation and Personality*, 3rd ed. (Upper Saddle River, NJ: Prentice Hall, 1987). Printed and electronically reproduced by permission of Pearson Education, Inc., Upper Saddle River, NJ.

>> Since she sprang into being a century ago, Betty Crocker has lent her name to more than 200 General Mills products and has even hosted her own radio and TV cooking shows.

Source: Chronicle/Alamy Stock Photo

Some customers have needs that they are not fully conscious of or cannot articulate. What does the customer mean when asking for a "powerful" lawn mower or a "peaceful" hotel? The marketer must probe further. Responding only to the stated need may shortchange the customer.[35] Consumers did not know much about tablet computers when they were first introduced, but Apple worked diligently to shape consumer perceptions and adoption of this technological innovation. To gain an edge, companies must help customers learn what they want—and make it convenient for them to obtain it. Dollar Shave Club's subscription service helped customers realize they could pay less for razors and Blue Apron helped people overcome a lack of confidence in their culinary skills that made cooking at home appear difficult.

Consumer Motivation. We all have many needs at any given time. A need becomes a motivation when aroused to a sufficient level of intensity to drive us to act.[36] Motivation has both direction (we select one goal over another) and intensity (we pursue the chosen goal with more or less vigor).

Motivation researchers often conduct in-depth interviews with a few dozen consumers to uncover deeper motives triggered by a product. They do this by using various psychology-based *projective techniques* such as word association, sentence completion, picture interpretation, and role play to probe consumers' mindset indirectly, which can yield information not elicited by explicit questioning.

Betty Crocker The name Betty Crocker, synonymous with cooking and baking, came into being in 1921 to personalize responses to consumer inquiries resulting from a promo for Gold Medal Flour. Betty catapulted to fame via a popular radio show and, according to *Fortune* magazine, in 1945 was second only to First Lady Eleanor Roosevelt in popularity. Betty's image has morphed from the first rather motherly figure in 1936 to that of a modern working woman, and she has managed to stay relevant throughout the years through painstaking research. For example, when sales of its instant Betty Crocker cake mix began to plateau in the 1950s, General Mills looked to Viennese-American psychologist and behavioral marketer Ernest Dichter. The dry cake mix required only the addition of water. Using Freudian methods to query focus groups of women, Dichter concluded that the ritual of baking a cake was rife with relationship and fertility symbolism and suggested removing the powdered egg from the mix, instead making housewives add their own fresh eggs. Sales soared after General Mills followed this advice.[37]

Another motivation researcher and cultural anthropologist, Clotaire Rapaille, worked on breaking the "code" behind product behavior—the unconscious meaning people give to a particular market offering. Rapaille worked with Boeing on its 787 "Dreamliner" to identify features in the airliner's interior that would have universal appeal. Based in part on his research, the Dreamliner has a spacious foyer; larger, curved luggage bins closer to the ceiling; larger, electronically dimmed windows; and a ceiling discreetly lit by hidden LEDs.[38] The opposite occurred with Chrysler's PT Cruiser, which reached the end of the road in less than a decade.

PT Cruiser When introduced at the beginning of the 21st century, the PT (Personal Transportation) Cruiser's retro looks and accessible price proved to be a hit with consumers in all age groups, although the polarizing design ("a cross between an old-time milk truck and luxurious sedans of the 1930s") had its critics as well as its imitators, like the Chevrolet HHR. The PT Cruiser was the first DaimlerChrysler vehicle designed using archetype research, a qualitative method developed by French medical anthropologist Clotaire Rapaille. Rapaille's approach focused on uncovering the deep-seated psychological drivers of consumers' behavior that go beyond such specific product attributes as color, size, and convenience to capture the feelings and emotions that define the "cultural unconscious" (or, in the words of Rapaille, consumers' "reptilian hot button") that defines product choice. The result was a five-door, tall-roofed hatchback that was

Source: imageBROKER/Alamy Stock Photo

<< The PT Cruiser was DaimlerChrysler's first foray into vehicle design using archetype research intended to trigger an emotional appeal and lead to purchase.

intended to evoke a nostalgic emotional reaction. Upon its launch, the PT Cruiser was considered a massive success, selling 145,000 vehicles in 2001. But by 2009, sales had plummeted to 18,000. The reason for the PT's decline came down to Chrysler's failure to invest in improving and updating the car, as well as its failure to release new models in response to consumer demand. In addition, the design appealed to a distinctly American audience during a time when globalization was becoming increasingly important to recouping research and development costs.[39]

PERCEPTION

Perception is the process by which we select, organize, and interpret information inputs to create a meaningful picture of the world.[40] A motivated person is ready to act. *How* this person will act is influenced by his or her perception of the situation. In marketing, perceptions are more important than reality because they affect consumers' actual behavior.

Perception depends not only on physical stimuli but also on the stimuli's relationship to the surrounding environment and on conditions that exist within each of us. One person might perceive a fast-talking salesperson as aggressive and insincere, whereas another might regard the salesperson as intelligent and helpful. Each will respond to the salesperson differently. People emerge with different perceptions of the same object because of three perceptual processes: selective attention, selective distortion, and selective retention.

Selective Attention. Attention is the allocation of processing capacity to some stimulus. Voluntary attention is something we do purposefully; involuntary attention occurs when our attention is grabbed by someone or something. It's estimated that the average person may be exposed to thousands of ads or brand communications every day. Because we cannot possibly attend to all these, we screen out most stimuli, a process called selective attention. **Selective attention** means that marketers must work hard to attract the notice of consumers. The real challenge is to determine which stimuli people will notice. Here are some findings:

- *People are more likely to notice stimuli that relate to a current need.* A person who is motivated to buy a smartphone will notice smartphone ads and be less likely to notice non-phone-related ads.
- *People are more likely to notice stimuli they anticipate.* You are more likely to notice laptops than portable radios in a computer store because you don't expect the store to carry portable radios.
- *People are more likely to notice stimuli whose deviations are large in relationship to the normal size of the stimuli.* You are more likely to notice an ad offering $100 off the list price of a computer than one offering $5 off.

Although we screen out much information, we are influenced by unexpected stimuli, such as unanticipated offers in the mail, over the internet, or from a salesperson. Marketers may attempt to promote their offers intrusively in order to bypass selective attention filters.

Selective attention mechanisms require active engagement and thought on the part of the consumer. **Subliminal perception** has long fascinated armchair marketers, who argue that marketers embed covert, subliminal messages in ads or packaging that consumers are not consciously aware of but that affect their behavior. Although it's clear that mental processes include many subtle subconscious effects,[41] no evidence supports the notion that marketers can systematically control consumers at that level, especially enough to change strongly held or even moderately important beliefs.[42]

Selective Distortion. Ever noticed that stimuli don't always come across in the way the senders intended? **Selective distortion** is the tendency to interpret information to fit our preconceptions. Consumers will often distort information to make it consistent with prior brand and product beliefs and expectations. For a stark demonstration of the power of consumer brand beliefs, consider taste tests in which one group of consumers samples a product without knowing the brand, while another group is aware of the brand during sampling. Invariably, the groups will have different opinions despite consuming *exactly the same product.*

When consumers report different opinions of branded and unbranded versions of identical products, it must be that their brand and product beliefs, created by whatever means (e.g., past experiences, brand promotions, familial preferences), have somehow changed their product perceptions. We can find examples of this for virtually every type of product. When Coors changed its label from "Banquet Beer" to "Original Draft," consumers claimed the taste had changed even though the formulation remained the same.

In another study, Frédéric Brochet, at the University of Bordeaux, gave glasses of red and white wine to wine science students and asked for descriptions. At a follow-up tasting, the students received glasses of the same white wine, with the catch that half the wine was dyed red. They described the white wine as they had previously but described the same red-tinted white wine in terms of red wine, showing that visual cues can override smell, taste—and expertise.[43]

Selective distortion can work to the advantage of marketers with strong brands when consumers distort neutral or ambiguous brand information to make it more positive. In other words, coffee may seem to taste better, a car may seem to drive more smoothly, and the wait in a bank line may seem shorter, depending on the brand.

EMOTIONS

Emotions are mental states that arise spontaneously rather than from conscious effort and reflect people's positive or negative reactions to internal and external stimuli. We typically have little control of feelings such as joy, sorrow, anger, fear, and ambivalence, which vary in intensity and complexity depending on our personal reactions and can be accompanied by physiological and behavioral changes.

Consumer response is not all cognitive and rational. Many responses may be emotional and evoke different kinds of feelings. A brand or product may make a consumer feel proud, excited, or confident. An ad may create feelings of amusement, disgust, or wonder. Brands like Hallmark, McDonald's, and Coca-Cola have made an emotional connection with loyal customers for years. Marketers increasingly recognize the power of emotional appeals, especially if they are rooted in some functional or rational aspects of the brand.

To help teen girls and young women feel more comfortable talking about feminine-hygiene and feminine-care products, Kimberly-Clark used four different social media networks in its "Break the Cycle" campaign for its U by Kotex brand. With overwhelmingly positive feedback, the campaign helped Kotex move into the top spot in terms of word-of-mouth share for that feminine-care target market.[44]

An emotion-filled brand story has been shown to trigger's people desire to pass along things they hear about brands through either word of mouth or online sharing. Firms are giving their communications a stronger human appeal to engage consumers in their brand stories.[45] Ray-Ban's 75th anniversary campaign, "Never Hide," showed a variety of stand-out and stylish hipsters to suggest that wearers of the brand's aviator glasses and sunglasses feel attractive and cool. Some brands have tapped into the hip-hop culture and music to market a brand in a modern multicultural way, as Apple did with its iPod.[46]

Many marketers like Ray-Ban have leveraged the emotional appeal of the past to connect with current customers, particularly younger ones. Although e-mail, Webinars, and social media platforms have seriously displaced direct mail, seminars, and trade shows, the latter can still play an effective role in marketing efforts. Retro marketing tactics and products have shown that nostalgia can pay, as costumed mascots, spinning signs, community gatherings, and billboards continue to capture the attention of customers. Products like the revived Beetle, the Fiat 500, and Cadbury's resurrected Wispa chocolate bar show that products steeped in the aura of days gone by enjoy a visceral connection with customers. Fashion houses base new designs on those of past eras. MillerCoors announced a retro marketing campaign for Miller Lite beer, along with a version of the original Miller Lite label from the 1970s. Cartier, Motel 6, and Life Savers are among other major brands that have gone retro with ad campaigns. Even football players cash in on nostalgia marketing: The NFL Pittsburgh Steelers have worn jerseys that are a throwback to the team's 1932 uniforms.[47]

Just as products and brands can elicit certain emotions, different emotional states can influence people's judgments and decisions. For example, emotions such as fear can increase or decrease the effectiveness of different marketing strategies that include social proof (e.g., communicating a product's popularity) and scarcity (e.g., "limited edition").[48] Similarly, seeing the emotions of others can also be used as a marketing tool. For example, displaying sad (vs. neutral or happy) faces of victims could increase the likelihood that people will donate to a charity.[49]

MEMORY

Memory—the brain's ability to record, store, and retrieve information and events—also plays a role in consumers' purchasing decisions. The different types of memory and the way memory processes work are described in the following sections.

Memory Models. Cognitive psychologists distinguish between **short-term memory**—a temporary and limited repository of information—and **long-term memory**—a more permanent, potentially unlimited repository. All the information and experiences we encode as we go through life can end up in our long-term memory.

Researchers distinguish three types of long-term memory: episodic, semantic, and procedural.

- *Episodic memory* is responsible for storing information about events (i.e., episodes) that we have experienced in our lives. It is an individual's memory of autobiographical events that capture the context—such as times, places, and associated emotions—in which a particular event has occurred.
- *Semantic memory* is responsible for storing information about the world, such as facts, meanings, and concepts. Unlike episodic memory, which is directly linked to an individual's personal experience, semantic memory captures general knowledge that is independent of personal experience.
- *Procedural memory* is responsible for knowing how to perform certain procedures such as walking, talking, and riding a bike. It is a memory of motor skills typically acquired through repetition and involves automatic sensorimotor activities that are so deeply embedded in our minds that they do not involve conscious thought.

Most widely accepted views of the structure of long-term memory assume we form some kind of associative model. For example, the *associative network memory model* views long-term memory as a set of nodes and links. *Nodes* are stored information connected by *links* that vary in strength. Any type of information can be stored in the memory network, including verbal, visual, abstract, and contextual information.

An activation process that spreads from node to node determines how much information we retrieve and can recall in any given situation. When a node becomes activated because we're encoding external information (when we read or hear a word or phrase) or retrieving internal information from long-term memory (when we think about some concept), other nodes are also activated if they're associated strongly enough with the initially activated node.

Based on the associative network memory model, we can think of consumer brand knowledge as a node in memory with a variety of linked associations. The strength and organization of these associations are important determinants of the information we can recall about the brand. **Brand associations** consist of all brand-related thoughts, feelings, perceptions, images, experiences, beliefs, and attitudes that become linked to the brand node. For example, the Adidas brand can conjure thoughts of soccer, shoes, running, tennis, sports apparel, health, fitness, active lifestyle, and outdoor adventures. It also might evoke associations with competitive brands such as Nike, Puma, and Reebok; brand ambassadors such as Lionel Messi and Kylie Jenner; and country of origin—Germany.

In this context, we can think of marketing as a way of making sure consumers have product and service experiences that create the right brand knowledge structures and maintain them in memory. Companies such as Procter & Gamble like to create maps that depict the key associations likely to be triggered in consumers' minds by a particular brand in a marketing setting and their relative strength, favorability, and uniqueness.

Memory Processes. Memory is very much a process of construction, because people don't remember information completely and accurately. Often, we remember just bits and pieces and fill in the rest based on whatever else we know. In general, memory can be described as a process of encoding and retrieval.

Memory encoding describes how and where information gets into memory. The strength of the resulting association depends on the degree to which we process the information we're encoding (e.g., how much we think about it) and in what way.[50] In general, the more attention we pay to the meaning of information during encoding, the stronger the resulting memory associations. And the more we are able to associate new information with other information already encoded in our memory, the better we will be able to remember it.

Memory retrieval is the way we reclaim information from memory. Three facts are important about memory retrieval.

- Cognitive psychologists believe that once information is encoded and stored in long-term memory it is extremely durable and its strength of association decays very slowly.
- Information may be *available* in memory but not be *accessible* for recall without the proper retrieval cues or reminders. The effectiveness of retrieval cues is one reason why marketing *inside* a supermarket or retail store is so critical: The product packaging and use of in-store mini-billboard

displays remind us of information already conveyed outside the store and become prime determinants of consumer decision making. Accessibility of a brand in memory is important for another reason: People talk about a brand when it is top of mind.[51]

- Information about other offerings can produce interference effects and cause us to either overlook or confuse new data. One marketing challenge in a category crowded with many competitors—e.g., airlines, financial services, and insurance companies—is that consumers may mix up brands.

Because of *selective retention*, we're likely to remember only the positive aspects of a product we like, forgetting its negative aspects and the good points about competing products.

The Buying Decision Process

The basic psychological processes we've reviewed play an important role in consumers' actual buying decisions. Here are some key consumer-behavior questions that marketers should ask in terms of who, what, when, where, how, and why:

Who buys our product or service? Who makes the decision to buy the product or service?

Who influences the decision to buy the product or service? How is the purchase decision made? Who assumes what role in the decision process?

What does the customer buy? What needs must be satisfied? What wants are fulfilled?

Why do customers buy a particular brand? What benefits do they seek?

Where do customers go or look to buy the product or service? Online and/or offline? When do they buy? Any seasonality factors? Any time of day/week/month?

How is our product or service perceived by customers? What are customers' attitudes toward our product or service?

What social factors might influence the purchase decision? Do customers' lifestyles influence their decisions? How do personal, demographic, or economic factors influence the purchase decision?[45]

Smart companies try to fully understand a customer's buying decision process, which involves all the experiences in learning, choosing, using, and even disposing of a product. Marketing scholars have developed a "stage model" of this decision process (see Figure 3.3), in which the consumer typically passes through five stages: problem recognition, information search, evaluation of alternatives, purchase decision, and postpurchase behavior.[52]

The process by which consumers make purchase decisions and their postpurchase behavior are often referred to as the *consumer decision journey*.[53] The reference to a journey stems from the fact that the manner in which consumers make purchase decisions is not always linear, as depicted in Figure 3.3. Instead, it is often an iterative process in which consumers are influenced by the new information they encounter at the different stages of their decision, which can involve the need to go back and revisit their earlier judgments. Recognizing this, marketers must develop activities and programs that reach consumers through different touchpoints at all stages of the decision process.

Consumers don't always pass through all five stages; they may skip or reverse some. When you buy your regular brand of toothpaste, you go directly from the problem-recognition stage to the purchase decision, skipping information search and evaluation. The model in Figure 3.3 provides a good frame of reference, however, because it captures the full range of considerations that arise when a consumer contemplates a new purchase or a high-involvement product that entails functional, psychological, or monetary risk. Later in the chapter, we will consider other ways in which consumers make decisions that are less calculated.

PROBLEM RECOGNITION

The buying process starts when the buyer recognizes a problem or need triggered by internal or external stimuli. With an internal stimulus, one of the person's basic needs—hunger, thirst, sex—rises to a threshold level and becomes a drive. A need can also be aroused by an external stimulus. A person

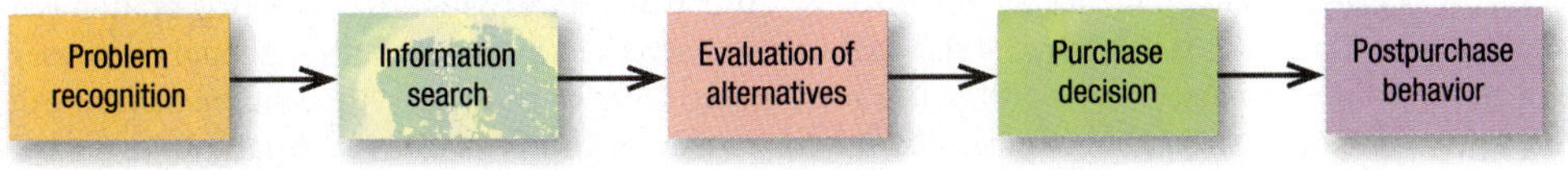

FIGURE **3.3**
Five-Stage Model of the Consumer Buying Process

may admire a friend's new car or see a television ad for a Hawaiian vacation, which inspires thoughts about the possibility of making a similar purchase.

Marketers should identify the circumstances that trigger a particular need by gathering information from a number of consumers. They can then develop marketing strategies and effective advertising campaigns that spark consumer interest. Increasing consumer motivation can be particularly important to encourage serious consideration of discretionary purchases such as luxury goods, vacation packages, and entertainment options. The drivers behind consumers' recognition of a need that they want fulfilled include factors such as *natural depletion*—e.g., the need to replace a regularly used item like toothpaste; *dissatisfaction with the current offering*, which causes consumers to seek other means of fulfilling their need; *lifestyle and goal changes*—e.g., the birth of a child or a job promotion, which can have a significant impact on purchasing habits; and *social influences*—e.g., the opinions of family, friends, and colleagues or competition from peers.

INFORMATION SEARCH

Surprisingly, consumers often search for only limited information. Surveys have shown that half of all consumers look for durable goods at just one store, and a mere 30 percent look at more than one brand of appliances. We can distinguish between two levels of engagement in the search. The milder search state is called *heightened attention*. At this level a person simply becomes more receptive to information about a product. At the next level, the person may enter an *active information search:* looking for reading material, phoning friends, going online, and visiting stores to learn about the product.

Marketers must understand what type of information consumers seek—or are at least receptive to—at different times and places. Unilever, in collaboration with Kroger, the largest U.S. retail grocery chain, has learned that meal planning goes through a three-step process: discussion of meals and what might go into them (heightened attention), choice of exactly what will go into a particular meal (information search), and, finally, purchase. Monday, it turns out, is the critical meal-planning day for the week ahead. Conversations at breakfast time tend to focus on health, but later in the day, at lunchtime, discussion centers more on how meals can be repurposed for leftovers.[54]

Information Sources. Major information sources to which consumers turn fall into four groups: *personal*, such as family, friends, neighbors, acquaintances; *commercial*, such as advertising, websites, e-mails, salespersons, dealers, packaging, displays; *public*, such as mass media, social media, consumer-rating organizations; and *experiential*, such as handling, examining, or using the product.

The relative amount of information obtained from these sources and their influence vary with the product category and the buyer's characteristics. Generally speaking, although consumers receive the greatest amount of information about a product from commercial—that is, marketer-dominated—sources, the most effective information often comes from personal or experiential sources or public sources that are independent authorities.[55] The ubiquity of social media has forever blurred the boundaries and widened the range of information sources. People sharing information about their purchases on Facebook or writing product reviews on Amazon can be viewed by others as independent authorities whose opinions carry great weight and far-ranging influence.

Each source performs a different function in influencing the buying decision. Commercial sources normally perform an information function, whereas personal sources perform a legitimizing or evaluation function. For example, physicians often learn of new drugs from commercial sources but turn to other doctors for evaluations. Many consumers alternate between going online and offline (in stores) to learn about products and brands.

Consumers rely on both internal and external information to help them arrive at a decision. Internal information is based on one's own individual experiences. For example, an individual who wants to go out for dinner might recall having a great meal at a local Italian restaurant or seeing an ad for a recently opened French bistro. External information sources are typically sought for high-involvement decisions such as purchasing a car or buying a high-end appliance. External sources can include the suggestions and opinions of family, friends, and work colleagues; making trips to dealers and searching online to compare models and prices; and consulting sources like *Consumer Reports*.

Search Dynamics. By gathering information, the consumer learns about competing brands and their features. The first box in Figure 3.4 shows the *total set* of brands available. The individual consumer will come to know a subset of this group, the *awareness set*. Only some brands, the *consideration set*, will meet the consumer's initial buying criteria. As the consumer gathers more information, just a few options, the *choice set*, will remain strong contenders. The consumer makes a final choice from these.[56]

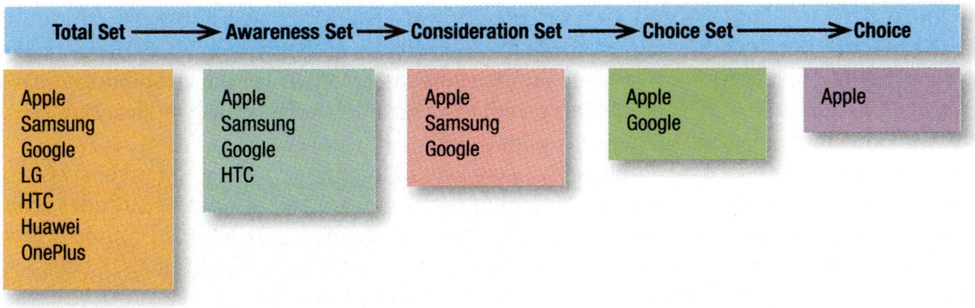

FIGURE **3.4**
Successive Sets Involved in Consumer Decision Making

Marketers need to identify the hierarchy of attributes that guide consumer decision making in order to understand different competitive forces and how various decision sets are formed. The process of identifying this attribute hierarchy is called *market partitioning*. Years ago, most car buyers first decided on the manufacturer and then on one of its car divisions (*brand-dominant hierarchy*). A buyer might favor General Motors cars and within this set choose a Chevrolet model. Today, many buyers decide first on the nation or nations from which they want to buy a car (*nation-dominant hierarchy*). Buyers may first decide they want to buy a German car and then opt for an Audi before zeroing in on the Audi A6.

The hierarchy of attributes also can reveal customer segments. Buyers who first decide on price are price dominant; those who first decide on the type of car (sedan, coupe, SUV, hybrid) are type dominant; those who choose the brand first are brand dominant. Type/price/brand-dominant consumers make up one segment; quality and service buyers make up another. Each segment may have distinct demographics, psychographics, and behaviors, as well as different awareness, consideration, and choice sets.

Figure 3.4 implies that a company must strategize to get its brand into the prospect's awareness, consideration, and choice sets. If a food store owner arranges yogurt first by brand (such as Dannon and Yoplait) and then by flavor within each brand, consumers will tend to select their flavors from the same brand. However, if all the strawberry yogurts are put together, then all the vanilla, and so forth, consumers will probably choose the flavors they want first and then choose the brand they want for that particular flavor.

Search behavior can vary online, in part because of the manner in which product information is presented. For example, product alternatives may be presented in order of their predicted attractiveness for consumers, who then may choose not to search as extensively as they otherwise would have.[57] Increasingly sophisticated recommendation engines use algorithms and data to uncover patterns in consumer choices and recommend the most relevant offerings for a particular consumer's needs and interests.

Amazon's item-to-item collaborative filtering algorithm presents recommendations to customers based on product lines and subject areas that match a customer's purchases to similar products. This involves the analysis of billions of data points derived from viewing online customer behavior, from purchase history to abandoned carts. Recommendations appear in several places: in personalized recommendations and previously viewed products links, as well as in a "Frequently Bought Together" section that helps Amazon cut delivery costs. Studies suggest that more than a third of consumer purchases on Amazon come from product recommendations.

The company must also identify the other brands in the consumer's choice set so that it can plan the appropriate competitive appeals. In addition, marketers should identify the consumer's information sources and evaluate their relative importance. Asking consumers how they first heard about the brand, what information they learned later, and the relative importance of these different information sources will help the company prepare effective communications for the target market. Digital marketing allows for easier detection and analysis of the other sites that are sending potential customers to the company's website. For instance, Amazon's affiliate network shows which websites and blogs are driving traffic not only to Amazon's site but also to specific products.

EVALUATION OF ALTERNATIVES

The way consumers decipher the pros and cons of available options is affected by the beliefs and attitudes they hold, whether these are valid or erroneous. These perceptions and the differing ways in which consumers process information weigh heavily in the purchase decision, as the following sections show.

Beliefs and Attitudes. Through experience and learning, people acquire beliefs and attitudes. These in turn influence buying behavior. A **belief** is a conviction that something is true or real, regardless of whether or not it is. Just as important are **attitudes**, a person's enduring favorable or unfavorable evaluations, emotional feelings, and behavioral tendencies toward an object or idea. People have attitudes about almost everything: religion, politics, clothes, music, food.

Attitudes put us into a frame of mind: liking or disliking an object, moving toward or away from it. They lead us to behave in a fairly consistent way toward similar objects. Because attitudes economize on energy and thought, they can be very difficult to change. As a general rule, a company is well advised to adapt its product to existing attitudes, rather than trying to change attitudes. If beliefs and attitudes become too negative, however, it may be necessary for the company to take more active steps.

Understanding consumers' attitudes is beneficial for marketers, because attitudes may at times predict behavior during the consideration and choice set stages of the customer decision process. For example, attitudes that are developed from interacting with a product during a trial can more accurately predict the likelihood of consumers purchasing the product than attitudes formed from exposure to a product ad.[58]

Information Processing. How does the consumer process the information about the available options and make a final value judgment? No single process is used by all consumers or by one consumer in all buying situations. The most current models see the consumer forming judgments largely on a conscious and rational basis.

Some basic concepts will help us understand the consumer evaluation process. First, the consumer is trying to satisfy a need. Second, the consumer is looking for certain benefits from the product offering a solution for that need. Third, the consumer sees each product as a bundle of attributes with varying abilities to deliver the benefits desired. The attributes of interest to buyers vary by product: for example, *hotels*—location, cleanliness, atmosphere, price; *mouthwash*—color, effectiveness, germ-killing capability, taste/flavor, price; *tires*—safety, tread life, ride quality, price. Consumers will pay the most attention to attributes that deliver the sought-after benefits. We can often segment the market for a product according to attributes and benefits important to different consumer groups.

More choice seems like a good thing, but this isn't always so—particularly when a consumer has no marked preferences or when no superior option exists in the awareness/consideration sets. Negligible differences among the options and time constraints further complicate the decision. Also, consumers will expend brainpower, time, and effort only in proportion to the importance of the decision task. The astute marketer must know when to reduce choice overload (and the cognitive effort imposed) by adding a superior option to the assortment (total set), reducing the amount of information customers must sift through, asking pertinent questions that aid in decision making, and alleviating time constraints involving sales or special offers.

Expectancy-Value Model. The consumer arrives at attitudes toward various brands through an attribute-evaluation procedure, developing a set of beliefs about where each brand stands on each attribute.[59] The **expectancy-value model** of attitude formation posits that consumers evaluate products and services by combining their brand beliefs—both positive and negative—according to importance.

Suppose a consumer has narrowed her choice set to four laptops (A, B, C, and D). Assume she's interested in four attributes: memory capacity, graphics capability, size and weight, and price. Table 3.1

TABLE 3.1 Laptop Computer Choice Set

Laptop Computer	Attribute			
	Memory Capacity	Graphics Capability	Size and Weight	Price
A	8	9	6	9
B	7	7	7	7
C	10	4	3	2
D	5	3	8	5

Note: Each attribute is rated from 0 to 10, with 10 representing the highest level on that attribute. Price, however, is indexed in a reverse manner, with 10 representing the lowest price, which consumers prefer.

shows her beliefs about how each brand rates on the four attributes. If one computer dominated the others on all the criteria, we could predict that this consumer would choose it. But, as is often the case, her choice set consists of brands that vary in their appeal. If she wants the best memory capacity, she should buy C; if she wants the best graphics capability, she should buy A; and so on.

If we knew the weight this consumer attaches to each of the four attributes, we could more reliably predict her choice. Suppose she assigned 40 percent of the importance to the laptop's memory capacity, 30 percent to graphics capability, 20 percent to size and weight, and 10 percent to price. To find this consumer's perceived value for each laptop according to the expectancy-value model, we would multiply these weights by her beliefs about each computer's attributes. This computation leads to the following perceived values:

$$\text{Laptop A} = 0.4(8) + 0.3(9) + 0.2(6) + 0.1(9) = 8.0$$
$$\text{Laptop B} = 0.4(7) + 0.3(7) + 0.2(7) + 0.1(7) = 7.0$$
$$\text{Laptop C} = 0.4(10) + 0.3(4) + 0.2(3) + 0.1(2) = 6.0$$
$$\text{Laptop D} = 0.4(5) + 0.3(3) + 0.2(8) + 0.1(5) = 5.0$$

An expectancy-model formulation predicts that this consumer will favor Laptop A, which (at 8.0) has the highest perceived value.[60] The expectancy-value model implies several strategies that a company can use to increase the probability that consumers will choose its offering. Suppose most laptop buyers form their preferences the same way. Knowing this, the marketer of Laptop B, for example, could apply the following strategies to stimulate greater interest in Brand B. First, the company might choose to redesign the laptop—for example, by changing its functional attributes, modifying its form, and improving service. Alternatively, the company can alter consumers' beliefs about the laptop, without necessarily modifying the laptop itself, by better communicating its benefits. The company might also alter consumers' beliefs about competitors' offerings by communicating the drawbacks of the competitive products. Finally, the company might alter consumers' beliefs about the importance of the different product attributes by persuading buyers to attach more weight to the attributes in which the brand excels.[61]

PURCHASE DECISION

In the evaluation stage, the consumer forms preferences among the brands in the choice set and may also form an intention to buy the most preferred brand. In executing a purchase intention, the consumer may make as many as five purchase decisions: brand (Brand A), distribution channel (Retailer X), quantity (one computer), timing (weekend), and payment method (credit card). This decision complexity often leads consumers to use mental shortcuts, or heuristics.

Decision Heuristics. The expectancy-value model is a compensatory model, in that perceived good things about a product can help to overcome perceived bad things. Thus, even though Brand A in the previous example lacked the graphics capability of Brand C, had the second lowest size/weight evaluation, and was more expensive than any other brand, its overall memory and graphics capacity won out relative to the other computers in the choice set. With non-compensatory models of consumer choice, positive and negative attribute considerations don't necessarily net out. Evaluating attributes in isolation facilitates decision making for consumers, but it also increases the likelihood that they would have made a different choice if they had deliberated in greater detail.

Rather than calculating the perceived importance of every attribute across products in a consideration set, consumers often take "mental shortcuts," called **heuristics** or rules of thumb, in the decision process. This is especially true when people are short on time or cognitive resources.[62] Our brand or product knowledge, the number and similarity of brand choices, time pressures, and the social context (such as the need for justification to a peer or boss) may affect whether and how we use choice heuristics. Consumers don't necessarily use only one type of choice rule. For example, they might use a non-compensatory decision rule.

A number of factors will determine the manner in which consumers form evaluations and make choices. University of Chicago professors Richard Thaler and Cass Sunstein show how marketers can influence consumer decision making through what they call *choice architecture*—designing the environment in which consumer decisions are structured and buying choices are made. According to these researchers, presenting choices in the right environment can give consumers a "nudge" via some small feature that attracts attention and leads to a specific desired behavior. They maintain that Nabisco is employing smart choice architecture by offering 100-calorie snack packs, which have solid profit margins, while nudging consumers to make healthier choices.[63]

The Level of Consumer Involvement. The expectancy-value model assumes a high level of consumer involvement and active processing by the consumer in response to a marketing stimulus. Richard Petty and John Cacioppo's **elaboration likelihood model**, an influential model of attitude formation and change, describes how consumers make evaluations in both low- and high-involvement circumstances.[64]

There are two means of persuasion in their model: the *central route*, in which attitude formation or change stimulates much thought and is based on the consumer's diligent, rational consideration of the most important product information; and the *peripheral route*, in which attitude formation or change provokes much less thought and results from the consumer's association of a brand with either positive or negative peripheral cues. *Peripheral cues* for consumers might include a celebrity endorsement, a credible source, or any object that generates strong emotional response.

Consumers follow the central route only if they possess sufficient motivation, ability, and opportunity. In other words, they must want to evaluate a brand in detail, have the necessary brand and product or service knowledge in memory, and have sufficient time and the proper setting. If any of those factors is lacking, consumers tend to follow the peripheral route and consider less central, more extrinsic factors in their decisions. We buy many products under conditions of low involvement and without significant brand differences. Consider salt. If consumers keep reaching for the same brand in this category, it may be out of habit, not strong brand loyalty.

Evidence suggests there is low involvement with most low-cost, frequently purchased products. Low-involvement products carry little cost or risk and are not well differentiated, which also means that it's easy for consumers to switch to other products in this category or indulge in impulse buying to satisfy their need for variety. Marketers can boost habituation to the purchase of these products by stressing quality and brand affiliation and by ensuring effective distribution so that consumers aren't forced to look elsewhere if, for example, their usual bath gel or soap is not available.

Marketers use four techniques to try to convert a low-involvement product into one that encourages higher involvement. First, they can link the product to an engaging issue, as when Crest linked its toothpaste to cavity prevention. Second, they can link the product to a personal situation—for example, fruit juice makers began to include vitamins and calcium to fortify their drinks. Third, marketers might design advertising to trigger strong emotions related to personal values or ego defense, as when cereal makers began to advertise to adults the heart-healthy nature of cereals and the importance of living a long time to enjoy family life. Fourth, they might add an important feature—for example, GE's introduction of "Soft White" lightbulbs. These strategies at best raise consumer involvement from a low to a moderate level: They do not necessarily propel the consumer into highly involved buying behavior.

If consumers have low involvement with a purchase decision regardless of what the marketer does, they are likely to follow the peripheral route. Marketers must give consumers one or more positive cues to justify their brand choice, such as frequent ad repetition, visible sponsorships, and vigorous PR to enhance brand familiarity. Other peripheral cues that can tip the balance in favor of the brand include a beloved celebrity endorser, attractive packaging, and an appealing promotion.

Intervening Factors. Even if consumers form an evaluation, two general factors can intervene between the purchase intention and the purchase decision (see Figure 3.5). The first factor is the *attitudes of others*. The degree to which we're influenced by another person's attitude depends on two factors: (1) the intensity of the other person's attitude toward our preferred alternative and (2) our motivation to comply with the other person's wishes.[65] The more intense the other person's attitude and the closer he or she is to us, the more we will adjust our purchase intention. The converse is also true.

FIGURE **3.5**

Steps between Evaluation of Alternatives and a Purchase Decision

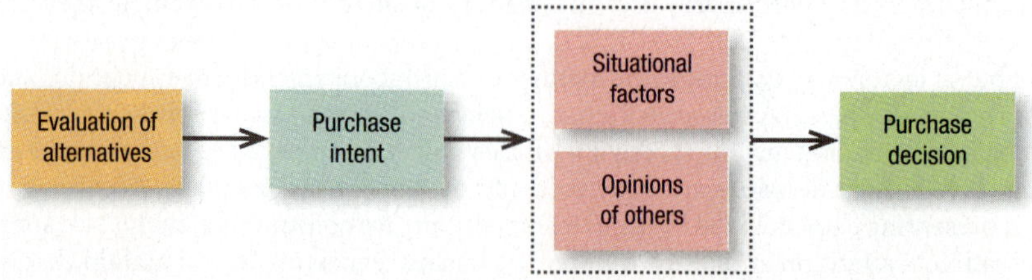

Related to the attitudes of others is the role played by infomediaries' evaluations: The *New York Times* Wirecutter website, which offers recommendations for tech and electronic products; *Consumer Reports*, which provides unbiased expert reviews of all types of products and services; J. D. Power, which provides consumer-based ratings of cars, financial services, and travel products and services; professional movie, book, and music reviewers; customer reviews of products, books, and music on such sites as Amazon.com; and the increasing number of chat rooms, bulletin boards, blogs, and other online sites like Angie's List where people discuss products, services, and companies.[66]

The second intervening factor involves the *situational considerations* that may erupt to change the purchase intention. The consumer might lose her job before she purchases a laptop, some other purchase might become more urgent, or a store salesperson might turn her off. Preferences and even purchase intentions are not completely reliable predictors of purchase behavior.

A consumer's decision to modify, postpone, or avoid a purchase decision is heavily influenced by one or more types of *perceived risk*.[67] These involve the *functional risk* that the product does not perform to expectations, the *physical risk* that the product poses a threat to the physical well-being or health of the user or others, the *financial risk* that the product is not worth the price paid, the *social risk* that the product results in embarrassment in front of others, the *psychological risk* that the product affects the mental well-being of the user, and the *opportunity risk* that the failure of the product results in spending more time and money to find another, more satisfactory product.

The degree of perceived risk varies with the amount of money at stake, the amount of attribute uncertainty, and the level of consumer self-confidence. Consumers develop routines for reducing the uncertainty and negative consequences of risk, such as avoiding decisions, gathering information from friends, and developing preferences for national brand names and warranties.[68] Marketers must understand the factors that provoke a feeling of risk in consumers and provide information and support to reduce it.

POSTPURCHASE BEHAVIOR

After the purchase, the consumer might experience dissonance from noticing certain disquieting features or hearing favorable things about other brands and will be alert to information that supports his or her decision. Marketing communications should supply beliefs and evaluations that reinforce the consumer's choice and help her or him feel good about the brand. The marketer's job doesn't end with the purchase. Marketers must monitor postpurchase satisfaction, postpurchase actions, and postpurchase product uses and disposal.

Satisfaction is a function of the closeness between consumer expectations and the product's perceived performance.[69] If performance falls short of expectations, the consumer is disappointed; if it meets expectations, the consumer is satisfied; if it exceeds expectations, the consumer is delighted. These feelings make a difference in whether the customer buys the product again and talks favorably or unfavorably about it to others. The larger the gap between expectations and performance, the greater the dissatisfaction. This is where the consumer's coping style comes into play. Some consumers magnify the gap when the product isn't perfect and are highly dissatisfied; others minimize it and are less dissatisfied.

Satisfaction influences customers' *postpurchase actions*. A satisfied consumer is more likely to purchase the product again and will also tend to say good things about the brand to others. In fact, one can argue that the highest level of success is achieved when a customer becomes an advocate and recommends the company's offering to others. Dissatisfied consumers may abandon or return the product. They may take public action by complaining to the company, going to a lawyer, complaining directly to other groups (such as business, private, or government organizations), or expressing their dissatisfaction to others online. Private actions include deciding to stop buying the product (exit option) or warning friends (voice option).[70]

Postpurchase communications to buyers have been shown to result in fewer product returns and order cancellations. Computer companies, for example, can send a letter to new owners congratulating them on having selected a fine new tablet computer. They can place ads featuring satisfied brand owners. They can solicit customer suggestions for improvements and list the location of available services. They can write intelligible instruction booklets. They can send owners e-mail updates describing new tablet applications. In addition, they can provide effective channels for speedy redress of customer grievances.

An important aspect of postpurchase behavior that marketers should monitor involves the *use* and *disposal* of the product. A key driver of sales frequency is the product consumption rate: The more

>> Quip created a sleek and simple toothbrush that relies on a subscription service that mails replacement batteries and brush heads to users every three months.

Source: ZikG/Shutterstock

quickly buyers consume a product, the sooner they may be back in the market to repurchase it. Consumers may fail to replace some products soon enough because they overestimate product life.[71]

One strategy to speed replacement is to tie the act of replacing the product to a certain holiday, event, or time of year (such as promoting changing the batteries in smoke detectors when Daylight Savings ends). Another is to offer the product on a subscription basis like Dollar Shave Club, whose razors are shipped monthly, and Quip, which delivers its electric toothbrush head refills every three months. Companies send monthly boxes to subscribers containing a variety of related products in areas that range from cosmetics (Birchbox) to clothing (Le Tote), food (Blue Apron), and dog care (BarkBox).

Another strategy is to provide consumers with better information about when they need to replace the product to sustain its current level of performance. Batteries have built-in gauges that show how much power they have left; razors have colored lubricating strips to indicate when blades may be worn; toothbrushes have colored bristles to indicate wear; and so on. Perhaps the simplest way to increase usage is to learn where actual usage is lower than recommended and persuade customers about the benefits of regular usage or of increasing the amount of product used on each occasion, which is behind the "shampoo, rinse, and repeat" instructions on everyone's favorite shampoo bottle.

marketing INSIGHT

Behavioral Decision Theory

Consumers don't always process information or make decisions in a deliberate, rational manner. One of the most active academic research areas in marketing over the past three decades has been behavioral decision theory, which studies how consumers make decisions in these situations. Behavioral decision theorists have identified many scenarios in which consumers make seemingly irrational choices. Here we review some of the decision issues in two broad areas: (1) heuristics and biases and (2) framing effects.

Heuristics are simple decision rules (or mental shortcuts) that people use to save time and minimize cognitive effort when forming judgments and making decisions. Thus, heuristics tend to focus only on the most relevant aspects of the problem, while paying little or no attention to other factors. This simplified approach to decision making often leads to choices characterized by lower accuracy and systematic errors that could result in suboptimal outcomes. These systematic errors, also referred to as *decision biases*, are particularly common in complex

(*continued*)

marketing insight *(continued)*

decisions when consumers have limited information while facing time constraints. Some of the most common decision heuristics are outlined below.

- The *availability heuristic* reflects people's tendency to judge that an event is more likely to occur if they can recall more instances of that event. For example, if asked whether more people in the United States die from homicide or emphysema, most people would attribute a greater number of deaths to homicide because it more easily comes to mind (news media give more coverage to homicide than to emphysema), even though in reality emphysema causes more deaths than homicide.
- The *representativeness heuristic* reflects people's tendency to judge the likelihood of an event occurring based on the degree to which this event is similar to the category it represents. A pale, meek, quiet person wearing glasses is more likely to be considered a computer geek than an active, outgoing, and outspoken one. This heuristic leads to a number of decision biases, including base-rate neglect, which ignores the actual probability of an event occurring.
- The *conjunction fallacy* results from people's erroneous belief that the probability of two events occurring jointly is greater than the probability of either event occurring independently. A classic example of the conjunction fallacy provided respondents with a description of Linda as bright, outspoken, and concerned with discrimination and social justice as a student. When asked to evaluate whether Linda is (A) a bank teller or (B) a bank teller and active in the feminist movement, most respondents chose the latter, even though a conjunction (B) cannot be more probable than one of its constituents (A).

Decision framing is the manner in which choices are presented to and seen by a decision maker. A $200 cell phone may not seem that expensive when compared to a $400 phone, but it may seem very expensive when compared to a phone costing $50. Framing effects are pervasive and can be powerful.

We find *framing effects* in comparative advertising, where a brand compares itself favorably to another brand with inferior features ("twice the cleaning power"); in pricing, where unit prices can make the product seem less expensive ("only pennies a day"); in product information, where larger units can seem more desirable (a 24-month warranty versus a two-year warranty); and in pitting a new product against existing products so consumers can better understand its superior functions and features.

When making financial decisions, consumers use a specific form of framing called *mental accounting*. Research has found that consumers tend to place different transactions into different mental accounts, even though there is no logic to doing so because money from any of these accounts can be used toward achieving any of the goals. Mental accounting is based on a set of core principles:

- Consumers tend to *segregate gains.* When a seller has a product with more than one positive dimension, it's desirable to have the consumer evaluate each dimension separately. Listing the multiple benefits of a large industrial product, for example, can make the sum of the parts seem greater than the whole.
- Consumers tend to *integrate losses.* Marketers have a distinct advantage in selling something if its cost can be added to another large purchase. For example, house buyers are more inclined to view additional expenditures favorably given the already high price of buying a house.
- Consumers tend to *integrate smaller losses with larger gains.* The "cancellation" principle might explain why withholding taxes from monthly paychecks is less painful than making large, lump-sum tax payments: The smaller withholdings are more likely to be overshadowed by the larger pay amount.
- Consumers tend to *segregate small gains from large losses.* The "silver lining" principle might explain the popularity of rebates on big-ticket purchases such as cars.

Consider a choice between two scenarios. In Scenario A, you spend $50 to buy a ticket for a concert. As you arrive at the show, you realize you've lost your ticket. You decide to buy a replacement. And in Scenario B, you decide to buy a ticket to a concert at the door. As you arrive at the show, you realize somehow you lost $50 along the way. You decide to buy the ticket anyway.

Which loss would you feel less keenly? Most people choose Scenario B. Although the loss is the same, in the first case you may have mentally allocated $50 for the concert, and buying another ticket would exceed your mental concert budget. In the second case, the money you lost did not belong to any account, so you have not exceeded any mental budget.[72]

marketing INSIGHT Circular Customer Decision Journey

Proliferation of products and digital channels coupled with rise of more informed and discerning customers has changed the way customers search for information, evaluate options and make buying decisions.[73] In many buying situations, the traditional funnel-based, mostly linear buying process has evolved into a circular decision-making process. The alternatives being considered expand as well as reduce at different stages of the decision-making process, unlike the funnel approach where the options being evaluated shrink with each succeeding stage. This new circular and iterative journey is more complex as 'word of mouth' and reviews from digital and social channels play a major role in the decision process.[74]

The different stages of the decision process, namely initial consideration, active evaluation, purchase and post purchase decision are connected with each other in a circular manner with an additional loyalty loop.

Initial consideration is driven by brand perception, recent exposures, touch points, and prior experience. Empowered with information from digital and social media, consumers add or subtract options as they assess and refine their needs during the active evaluation stage.

The customers take the final decision by selecting the product for purchase in the third phase. Word-of-mouth and reviews play a major role in influencing the purchase decision at every stage. The technology driven, digital consumer is increasingly influenced by non-commercial sources like reference groups and review sites.

Post-purchase experience updates the brand perception driven by consumer's usage experience. A satisfactory experience can potentially turn the customer into a loyal user who will re-purchase without going through the entire cycle again.

The circular decision-making process is complex as consumer behaviour differs across product categories. It reinforces the need for an integrated marketing approach with a systematic and scientific blend of marketing activities across multiple touch points to reach the prospects and customers. Firms that align their marketing approach with consumer's purchase journey, have better chance to reach them at the right time, at the right place with the right message, influencing each stage of the decision-making process.[75]

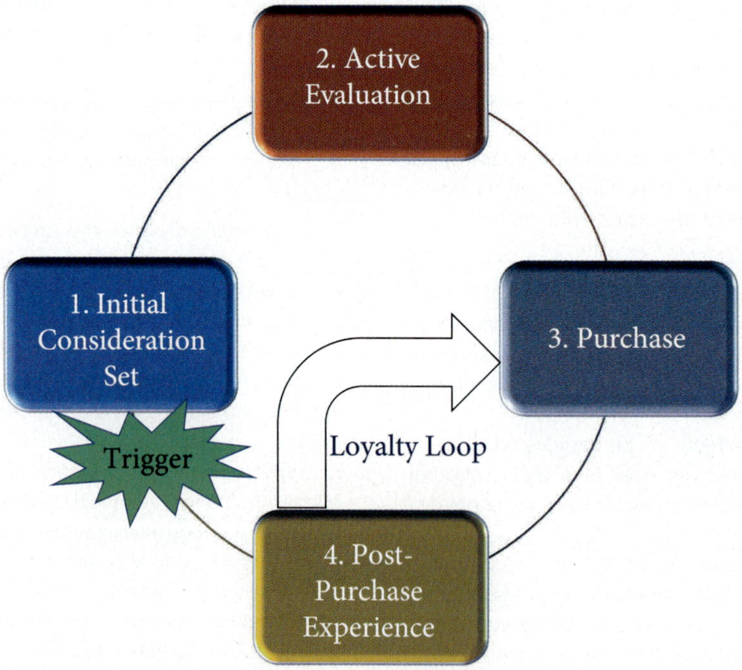

Exhibit 1: Consumer Decision Journey (Adapted)*

summary

1. To successfully compete in the market and create customer value, managers must fully understand both the theory and the reality of consumer behavior.
2. Consumer behavior is influenced by three factors: cultural, social, and personal. Research into these factors can provide clues to help companies reach and serve consumers more effectively. Of these, cultural factors exert the broadest and deepest influence on people's perceptions and desires and on how they go about fulfilling their needs and wants.
3. Four main psychological processes affect consumer behavior: motivation, perception, learning, and memory.
4. Understanding consumer motivation begins with understanding the needs that consumers aim to fulfill with their actions. Some needs are biological and arise from physiological states of tension such as hunger, thirst, or discomfort. Other needs are psychological and arise from psychological states of tension such as the need for recognition, esteem, or belonging. A need becomes a motivation when it is aroused to a sufficient level of intensity to drive us to act. Motivation has both direction and intensity.
5. Perception is the process by which we select, organize, and interpret information inputs to create a meaningful picture of the world. In marketing, perceptions are more important than reality because they affect consumers' actual behavior. People emerge with different perceptions of the same object because of three perceptual processes: selective attention, selective distortion, and selective retention.
6. Consumer response is not all cognitive and rational; much may be emotional and evoke different kinds of feelings. Emotions are mental states that arise spontaneously rather than from conscious effort and reflect people's positive or negative reactions to internal and external stimuli.
7. Memory—the brain's ability to record, store, and retrieve information and events—plays an important role in consumers' purchasing decisions. There are two types of memory: *short-term memory*—a temporary and limited repository of information—and *long-term memory*—a more permanent, potentially unlimited repository. The *associative network model* views long-term memory as a set of nodes and links. *Nodes* are stored information connected by *links* that vary in strength.
8. The typical *buying process* consists of the following sequence of events: problem recognition, information search, evaluation of alternatives, purchase decision, and postpurchase behavior. Consumers will not necessarily go through the buying process in an orderly fashion: They may skip and reverse stages and alternate between shopping online and offline. The marketers' job is to understand the buyer's behavior at each stage.
9. Consumers are constructive decision makers and are subject to many contextual influences. They often exhibit low involvement in their decisions, using many heuristics as a result. The attitudes of others and unanticipated situational factors may influence the decision to buy. A consumer's decision to modify, postpone, or avoid a purchase decision is heavily influenced by one or more types of *perceived risk*.
10. Marketers must monitor customer satisfaction and the ways in which customers use the company's offerings. Satisfaction is a function of the match between consumer expectations and the product's perceived performance. Monitoring satisfaction is important because it reflects the value customers receive from the company's offering. Examining customers' postpurchase behavior aims to capture the *use* and *disposal* of the offering both to detect potential problems and to identify new market opportunities.

marketing SPOTLIGHT

Aravind Eye Care System

Aravind Eye Care System, globally renowned for restoring eyesight to millions—especially for the poor and needy, is the world's largest eyecare provider that conducts over half a million surgeries every year. Set up by Dr. Govindappa Venkataswamy (Dr.V) in 1976, Aravind has pioneered a high quality, large volume and low-cost service delivery model led by Dr. V's enduring vision to provide compassionate and quality eyecare affordable to everyone. Aravind removes the roadblocks for the poor in receiving the required treatment, and simultaneously, generates enough surplus to make the solution sustainable and scalable. The pioneering eyecare system has handled more than 68 million out patients visits and conducted over 8.2 million surgeries till date. While more than fifty per cent of the patients at Aravind receive free or subsidised treatment at its eyecare camps, vision centres and hospitals, the paid services are also offered at affordable prices. Surplus generated from paying customers finance the hospitals' operations of offering free and subsidized services

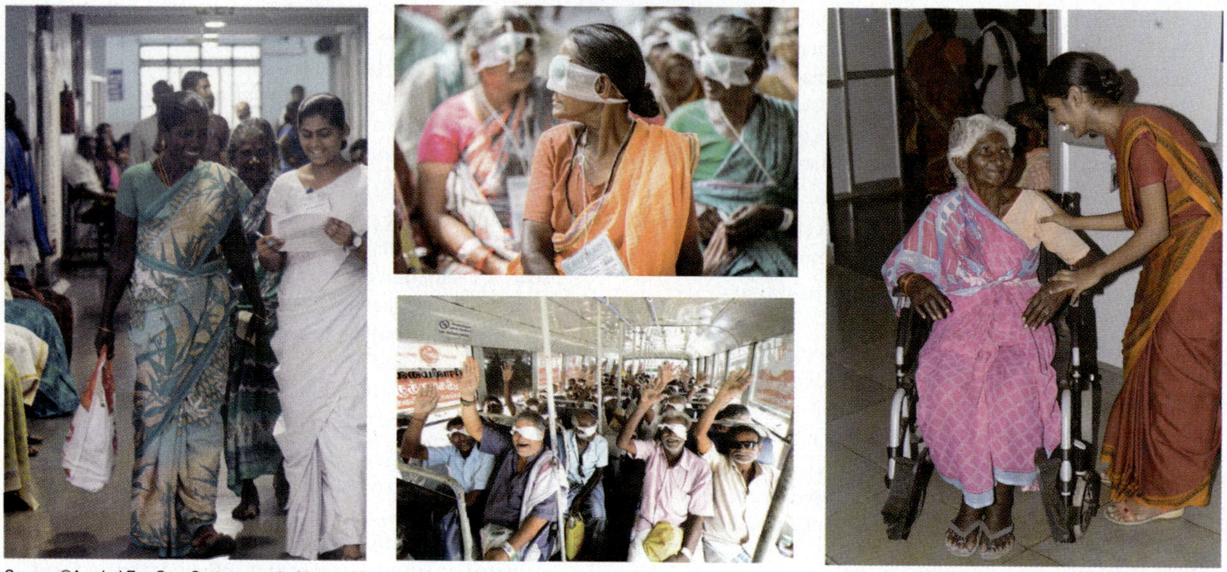

Source: ©Aravind Eye Care System, used with permission

to the poor. High quality services are provided with dignity to all users irrespective of their economic and social strata.[76]

It all started when after retiring from the local public medical college at the age of 58, Dr. V converted a home into a eyecare clinic with 11 beds in Madurai, Tamil Nadu. The visionary's inspiring leadership has successfully shaped Aravind into the world's largest and most efficient eyecare system with 14 hospitals, 6 community eye clinics and 95 primary eyecare facilities in Tamil Nadu, Puducherry (Pondicherry) and Hyderabad (Telangana). In addition to consultation, treatments and surgeries, Aravind is also engaged in research, education, training, consultancy and capacity building.

The hospital chain has also invested in facilities to manufacture ophthalmic supplies and equipment to reduce cost by substituting imported goods. High quality but affordable ophthalmic products are produced by Aurolab, a non-profit trust and manufacturing division of Aravind, set up in 1992.[77] A wide range of ophthalmic consumables like intraocular lenses, eye drops, sutures, blades, ophthalmic instruments and specialty products are manufactured at their modern production facilities. These products are exported to 160 countries around the world. During 1990s, Intraocular Lens (IOL) used for cataract procedures used to be imported. Priced at $100, most patients in India could not afford them. Support from the California-based Seva Foundation helped Aurolab start manufacturing high quality IOLs at $5—literally, at a small fraction of the cost of the imported ones. Aurolab now produces around 9% of the global volume of intraocular lenses.

Aravind's unique operational model was conceptualized by Dr. V to fulfil his mission to eliminate avoidable blindness. The assembly line approach of Ford to reduce costs and standardization achieved by McDonald's across its outlets around the world were his inspirations. Enabling large volume, high quality and affordable service, with a a patient-centric approach is unique. Designed to maintain equity, Aravind ensures that all patients are treated and served with high quality services regardless of their financial or social status.

One of the most critical aspects of Aravind's operational model is its ability to manage a large number of patients. The free eye screening camps conducted in rural areas, usually during the weekends, in partnership with the local community and voluntary organizations attract large numbers.[78] Consultations and basic treatments are provided at these eye camps. Patients requiring surgeries or more complex treatments are transported to the nearest Aravind hospital at the end of the eye camp. This structured process allows Aravind to schedule treatments and achieve maximum utilization of its resources including doctors, surgeons, operation theatres and hospital beds. Costs are optimised due to the high volume through economies of scale. The functional model is well-equipped to provide efficient quality services with value and financial sustainability for a large number of people.[79] In 2019-20 alone, surgeons across Aravind's 14 hospitals conducted over 5.19 lakh surgeries and 4.6 million patients received consultations and treatment.[80]

The secret of the highly successful operation model of Aravind Eyecare System lies in its assembly line operations which increases the overall productivity of the system, making it extremely frugal and efficient[81]. On an average, a surgeon at Aravind Eyecare System performs 2000 surgeries per year—five times the global average of 400 surgeries per year. With its unique operations and management system, Aravind is an inspiration—its system being studied and explored for its quality, productivity and financial self-reliance even as it allows patients to decide for themselves how much they would pay[82]. Even with such a generous arrangement, Aravind manages a surplus that is ploughed back to expand patient services and set up new projects. Its successful model demonstrates the power of integrating innovation with empathy, business principles with service, and outer transformation with inner change.

Nurses form the backbone of Arvind's efficient system. Mostly female, these nurses are recruited from rural areas, trained extensively and equipped for multi-tasking in opthalmic nursing, counselling and other support functions. Ingrained with compassion for patients, the nurses are proficient in what they do and serve with empathy.

Aravind regularly conducts free eye screening camps to reach the underserved. Teams of doctors, nurses and volunteers set up eye camps in rural areas for free check-up and treatment services. On an average, they conduct 2,500 camps every year[83]. These eye camps continue to be popular and attract thousands of eyecare seekers, but there always remains the need for permanent facilities to offer regular services. Aravind adopted tele-medicine to overcome the shortage of doctors in rural areas and set up vision centres (VC). The VCs are located in a rural town, with easy access to 15-20 villages within a distance of 5-7 kms, covering a population of 50,000 to 75,000. Managed by a coordinator, a technician, and a field worker, every VC is connected to a base hospital. Awareness and education programs conducted by field workers at schools, community centres and door-to-door home visits encourage patient footfall at the VCs. The trained technician performs basic tests for patients visiting the VC and then connects them to a doctor at the base hospital for a video consultation. All these services are provided for a nominal fee of ₹20. In addition, Aravind's large scale centralised procurement system allows patients to buy low-cost medicines and prescription spectacles at these centres. Aravind steadily scaled up its VCs after the success of its pilot centre set up in 2004. By 2020, the eyecare giant recorded consultation and treatment to around 6.88 lakh patients in its 79 vision centres then. Easy and affordable access to eyecare has significantly improved healthcare outcomes in these rural areas. It has also changed the healthcare-seeking behaviour.[84]

Aravind has been constantly scaling up its mass outreach through inclusiveness and affordability. Following a business model driven by productivity, quality, scalability and transferability, the eyecare chain is built on a strong foundation of compassion and committed leadership. The focus on standardisation and volume leads to effective cost-control. Aravind sets the example of a competent human–process collaboration, wherein a team of dedicated and motivated individuals equipped with high quality, efficient procedures and technology, ensures that Dr V's vision is realized and benefits thousands of patients every day.[85]

Questions

1. Explain why Aravind is exceptional at serving patients. What value does Aravind create for patients?
2. What are the key points differentiating Aravind from other hospitals and medical facilities?
3. Can other service providers adopt Aravind's operational and financial model to scale up? Why or why not?

marketing SPOTLIGHT

Paytm

Paytm, arguably the leading fintech firm in India, was founded in 2010 by Vijay Shekhar Sharma. Set up as a bill payment service provider app, Paytm steered the mobile wallet revolution in India. Paytm is now transforming into a digital financial supermarket serving a network of over 20 million merchants and 300 million customers.

Driven by its mission to bring half a billion Indians into the mainstream economy through payments, banking,

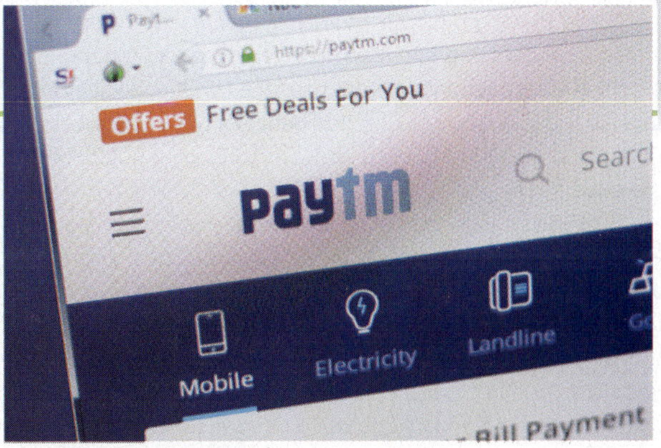

Source: Sharaf Maksumov@shutterstock.com

investments and financial services, Paytm is playing a leading role in building trust on the digital payments and financial system. Its user-friendly and interactive features have made Paytm one of the most popular mobile apps in India. Services ranging from mobile recharges, utility bill payments, travel bookings, buy tickets for movies and events, to making hassle free instant in-store payments continue to attract users. Paytm's success mantra is simple—identify users' pain points and then solve them efficiently.[86]

Prior to the e-wallet revolution, India's mobile phone consumer, of whom 85% being pre-paid users, needed to visit a physical store to buy recharge coupons that provided a long password to top-up talk time and validity period of their mobile service. Paytm's wallet eased the customers' efforts by allowing them to instantly pay into their mobile accounts for phone recharge and top-ups. This instant top-up service helped Paytm build brand awareness and a loyal customer base.

The company's broad portfolio of services cover digital banking solutions, investment products, mobile games, and insurance. These services address the evolving needs of its young and tech savvy customers.

With effective services, in a short span of time Paytm could win over the trust of Indian customers. In March 2021, the company recorded 1.2 billion monthly transactions led by offline payments and financial services. It has also achieved a benchmark of serving 150 million active customers with highest market share in offline payments. Offline payment options for its 17 million merchants include Paytm All-In-One QR (quick response), Paytm All-In-One Android PoS (point of sale), Soundbox and Paytm for Business application. The offline payment market share continues to grow at the rate of 15% per month.

Product innovation and refinement focused on changing needs of its customers are at the core of Paytm's business model. With an emphasis on meeting the needs of all of its users (merchants and consumers), Paytm regularly keeps adding new solutions to its portfolio. The journey of becoming a financial services conglomerate included several milestones like launch of Paytm wallet, Paytm UPI, Paytm Insurance, Paytm Digital payment, and the latest ones being multiple offline payment options for its merchant partners.

Each Paytm product is the result of extensive research, aimed to understand the altering preferences and requirements of the customers. Paytm uses the latest analytical tools to capture the consumption behavior of its customers, to develop an understanding about the changing needs of the customers.

The leadership counts 'speed' as its greatest asset. Paytm's quick reaction to the Indian Government's surprise announcement to demonetize currency notes of denomination ₹500 and ₹1,000, contributed significantly to its rapid growth[87]. The sudden announcement sucked out about 86% of India's cash in circulation in the latter part of 2016. People shifted to digital transactions using QR codes on mobile wallet apps. While merchants looked for alternatives to cash transactions, Paytm released newspaper ads that merchants could post on their storefronts "Paytm Accepted" as a notification of cashless transactions for customers. There was a remarkable surge in the app download and Paytm's wallet customer base grew from 125 million before demonetization to 185 million three months later.[87] By June 2017, over five million offline merchants signed up to accept payments through Paytm's QR. The multilingual feature of the app attracts merchants from small towns and tier II & tier III cities. Over a quarter of its users prefer using regional language apps that were strategically rolled out by Paytm. The government's push for digital payments has further helped accelerate adoption among the masses and small merchants.

In addition to expanding the digital payments ecosystem by enabling small merchants accept payments digitally, Paytm started exploring opportunities in the broader financial services landscape. Paytm's entry into the payments bank business in May 2017 created an opportunity for the company to build a primary deposit relationship with its customers. In addition, the app is turning into a distribution channel for financial services for its users to access a wide range of financial products, from home and life insurance policies to investment assets and products on its merchant store.

Paytm Money has become one the fastest growing investment platforms for stock broking, dematerialization and pension services. It is the largest contributor of new systematic investment plans (SIPs) in the mutual funds industry. The recognitions helped Paytm gain customer's faith in the brand.

Paytm launched its subscription-based loyalty program 'Paytm First', to cater to entertainment needs of the customers. The gaming and entertainment platforms attracted millions of users. Paytm has now emerged as a leading player in the competitive market for digital games.

Its e-commerce venture, Paytm Mall, after an initial growth fuelled by cashback deals, offers and promotional campaigns, however, could not sustain in the hyper-competitive market with well-established players, Amazon and Flipkart.[88]

Paytm's growth and expansion strategies are analysed in leading business schools as case studies. The company is a leader in the fintech industry with its wide portfolio of offerings that meet the evolving needs of a large customer base through multiple solutions ranging from wealth management, insurance, digital market space, digital payment platform and online entertainment & gaming platform.

Prone to adaptability, one of its recent strategic moves to address the need of online food delivery during COVID-19 pandemic, included the partnership with 'Tata Starbucks', offering an online food delivery service platform.[89]

Questions

1. Why is consumer research critical to Paytm's success?
2. What value does Paytm's offerings in financial services create for customers?
3. What challenges Paytm will face in the near future?

CHAPTER 4

Analyzing Business Markets

A strong focus on innovation and product expansion has propelled Caterpillar from a firm selling tractors to the world's largest manufacturer of earth-moving equipment and engines.
Source: Daniel Acker/Bloomberg/Getty Images

Business markets, although often less visible than consumer markets, are substantially larger than consumer markets. Business markets include all businesses, organizations, and governments who buy and sell vast quantities of raw materials, manufactured components, plants and equipment, supplies, and services in order to help them develop offerings for other businesses and consumers. At its core, business marketing—much like consumer marketing—aims to create market value by developing offerings that meet the needs of business customers. A company that has been able to consistently meet needs and often exceed customer expectations is Caterpillar.

>>> Caterpillar was founded in 1925 when two California-based tractor companies merged. The Caterpillar name, however, dates back to the early 1900s when Benjamin Holt, one of the company's founders, designed a tractor crawler with wide, thick tracks instead of wheels. These tracks prevented the machine from sinking into California's deep, rich soil, which was impassable when wet. The new farm tractor crept along the farmland in such a way that one observer said it "crawled like a caterpillar." Holt sold the tractor under the Caterpillar brand, and after the merger, the newly formed company became Caterpillar Tractor Company. The company grew steadily at first, hitting a

few critical milestones that included the use of Caterpillar's trademark farm treads on Army tanks in World War I and World War II. Huge postwar construction and strong overseas demand kept sales strong through the mid-20th century, as did innovations like the diesel tractor and rubber-tired tractors. Since then, Caterpillar Inc., or CAT, has grown into the largest manufacturer of earth-moving equipment and engines in the world. Today, Caterpillar ranks number one or number two in every industry it serves. Its products have a reputation for high quality and reliability, and the company has maintained a strong focus on innovation while expanding its product portfolio. Its distinctive yellow machines are found all over the globe and have helped make the brand a U.S. icon.[1]

Some of the world's most valuable brands belong to business marketers: ABB, Caterpillar, DuPont, FedEx, HP, IBM, Intel, and Siemens, to name a few. Many principles of basic marketing also apply to business marketers. They need to embrace holistic marketing principles, such as building strong loyalty relationships with their customers, just like consumer marketers. But they also face some unique challenges in selling to other businesses. In this chapter, we will highlight some of the crucial similarities and differences for marketing in business markets.[2]

The Organizational Buying Process

Organizational buying is the decision-making process by which formal organizations establish the need for purchased products and services and by which they identify, evaluate, and choose among alternative brands and suppliers.[3]

UNDERSTANDING BUSINESS MARKETS

Business markets consist of all the organizations that acquire goods and services used in the production of products or services that are sold, rented, or supplied to others. Any firm that supplies components for products is in the business-to-business (B2B) marketplace. Some of the major industries making up the business market are aerospace; agriculture, forestry, and fisheries; chemical; computer; construction; defense; energy; mining; manufacturing; construction; transportation; communication; public utilities; banking, finance, and insurance; distribution; and services.

More dollars and items change hands in sales to business buyers than to consumers. Consider the process of producing and selling a simple pair of shoes.[4] A broad spectrum of materials and material combinations are used today in shoe manufacturing. Leathers, synthetics, rubber, and textile materials are counted among the basic upper materials. Each material has its own specific character, which differs not only in appearance but also in physical properties, service life, and treatment needs. The choice of shoe material significantly influences the life of the footwear and in many cases dictates its use. For leather shoes, hide dealers must sell hides to tanners, who sell leather to shoe manufacturers, who sell

Learning Objectives After studying this chapter you should be able to:

- **4.1** Explain the key aspects of the organizational buying process.
- **4.2** Define the role of the buying center in an organization.
- **4.3** Describe the stages of the decision process in business markets.
- **4.4** Explain how organizations develop marketing programs to attract and retain business customers.
- **4.5** Describe how business-to-business marketers build and maintain relationships with customers.

shoes to wholesalers, who sell shoes to retailers, who finally sell them to consumers. Each party in the supply chain also buys many other goods and services to support its operations.

Given the highly competitive nature of business-to-business markets, the biggest enemy to marketers here is commoditization, whereby customers perceive products from different companies as offering identical benefits.[5] Commoditization eats away margins and weakens customer loyalty. It can be overcome only if target customers are convinced that meaningful differences exist among the products in the marketplace and that the unique benefits of the firm's offerings are worth the additional cost. Thus, a critical step in business-to-business marketing is to create and communicate relevant differentiation from competitors.

Business marketers face many of the same challenges as consumer marketers, especially when it comes to understanding their customers and what they value. The well-respected Institute for the Study of Business Markets (ISBM) notes that the three biggest hurdles for B2B marketing involve integrating sales and marketing departments, managing innovation, and gathering and utilizing customer and market insights. Four additional imperatives cited by ISBM are demonstrating marketing's contribution to business performance, engaging more deeply with customers and customers' customers, identifying the right mix of centralized versus decentralized marketing activities, and finding and grooming marketing talent and competencies.[6]

Business markets contrast sharply with consumer markets in some ways, however. They have

- ***Fewer but larger buyers.*** The business marketer normally deals with far fewer and buyers of much larger quantities than the consumer marketer does, particularly in such industries as aircraft engines and defense weapons. The fortunes of Goodyear tires, Cummins engines, Delphi control systems, and other automotive part suppliers depend in large part on getting big contracts from just a handful of major automakers.
- ***Close supplier–customer relationships.*** Because of the smaller customer base and the size, importance, and power of the customers, suppliers are frequently expected to customize their offerings for individual business customer needs. On an annual basis, Pittsburgh-based PPG Industries purchases more than $7 billion in materials and services from thousands of suppliers. PPG rewards its suppliers for superior performance on attributes such as product quality, delivery, documentation, innovation, responsiveness, and continuous improvement. With the Supplier Added Value Effort ($AVE) program, PPG challenges its suppliers of maintenance, repair, and operating goods and services to deliver on annual value-added and cost-savings proposals equaling at least 5 percent of their total annual sales to PPG.[7] Business buyers also often select suppliers that also buy from them. A paper manufacturer might buy chemicals for its pulp and paper making from a chemical company that in turn buys a considerable amount of paper from the manufacturer.
- ***Professional purchasing.*** Business goods are often purchased by trained purchasing agents, who must follow their organizations' purchasing policies, constraints, and requirements. Much of the documentation used in business buying—for example, requests for quotations, proposals, and purchase contracts—are not typically found in consumer buying. Many professional buyers belong to the Institute for Supply Management (ISM), which seeks to improve the profession's effectiveness and status. This means business marketers must provide more technical data about their product and its competitive advantages.
- ***Multiple buying influences.*** More people typically influence business-buying decisions. Buying committees that include technical experts and even senior management are common in the purchase of major goods. Business marketers need to send well-trained sales representatives and teams to deal with these equally well-trained buyers.
- ***Derived demand.*** The demand for business goods is ultimately derived from the demand for consumer goods. For this reason, the business marketer must closely monitor the buying patterns of end users. Pittsburgh-based Consol Energy's coal and natural gas business largely depends on orders from utilities and steel companies, which, in turn, depend on consumer demand for electricity and for steel-based products such as automobiles, machines, and appliances. Business buyers must also pay close attention to economic factors like the level of production, investment, and consumer spending, as well as to the interest rate. Business marketers can do little to stimulate total demand. They can only fight harder to increase or maintain their share.
- ***Inelastic demand.*** The total demand for many business goods and services is inelastic—that is, it is not much affected by price changes. Shoe manufacturers are not going to buy much more leather if the price of leather falls or much less if the price rises (unless they find satisfactory substitutes). Demand is especially inelastic in the short run because producers cannot make quick

changes in production methods. Demand is also inelastic for business goods that represent a small percentage of the item's total cost, such as shoelaces.

- ***Fluctuating demand.*** The demand for business goods and services tends to be more volatile than the demand for consumer goods and services. A given percentage increase in consumer demand can lead to a much larger percentage increase in the demand for plant and equipment. Demand for plant and equipment is more volatile because it reflects the normal year-to-year replacement demand as well as the need to satisfy increased or decreased consumer demand.
- ***Geographically concentrated buyers.*** For years, more than half of U.S. business buyers have been concentrated in seven states: New York, California, Pennsylvania, Illinois, Ohio, New Jersey, and Michigan. The geographic concentration of producers often helps to reduce costs. At the same time, business marketers need to monitor regional shifts of certain industries, such as the automobile industry, which is no longer concentrated around Detroit.
- ***Direct purchasing.*** Business buyers often buy directly from manufacturers rather than through intermediaries, especially items that are technically complex or expensive, such as agricultural equipment, industrial machinery, and aircraft.

TYPES OF BUYING DECISIONS

The business buyer faces many decisions in making a purchase. How many depends on the complexity of the problem being solved, the newness of the buying requirement, the number of people involved, and the time required to complete the purchase. There are three types of business-buying situations: the straight rebuy, the modified rebuy, and the new buy.[8]

- ***Straight rebuy.*** In a straight rebuy, the purchasing department reorders items like office supplies and bulk chemicals on a routine basis and chooses from suppliers on an approved list. The suppliers make an effort to maintain product and service quality and often propose automatic reordering systems to save time. Suppliers attempt to offer prospective customers something new or exploit dissatisfaction with a current supplier. Their goal is to get a small order and then enlarge their purchase share over time.
- ***Modified rebuy.*** The buyer in a modified rebuy wants to change product specifications, prices, delivery requirements, or other terms. This usually requires additional negotiation and can lead to a new purchase agreement or, in some cases, to a disruption of the business relationship and a change in suppliers.
- ***New buy.*** A new-buy purchaser faces some risk when acquiring a product or service for the first time (e.g., an office building, a new security system). The greater the risk or cost, the larger the number of buying-decision participants, the greater their information gathering—and the longer the time it takes to make a decision.[9]

The business buyer makes the fewest decisions in the straight-rebuy situation and the most in the new-buy situation. Over time, new-buy situations become straight rebuys and routine purchase behavior.

New-buy purchasing is the marketer's greatest opportunity and challenge. The buying process passes through several stages: awareness, interest, evaluation, trial, and adoption. Mass media can be most important during the initial awareness stage, salespeople often have their greatest impact at the interest stage, and technical sources can be most important during evaluation. Online selling efforts may be useful at all stages.

In the new-buy situation, the buyer must determine product specifications, price limits, delivery terms and times, service terms, payment terms, order quantities, acceptable suppliers, and the selected supplier. Different participants influence each decision, and the order in which these decisions are made varies.

Because of the complicated selling required, many companies use sales force consisting of their most effective salespeople. The brand promise and the manufacturer's name recognition will be important in establishing trust and persuading the customer to consider change. The marketer also tries to reach as many key participants as possible with information and assistance.

Once a customer has been acquired, a company's sales force continually seeks ways to add value to its market offer to facilitate rebuys. EMC (now Dell EMC) has successfully acquired a series of computer software leaders to reposition the company to manage and protect—not just store—information, thus helping companies "accelerate their journey to cloud computing." One hardware product once made up 80 percent of its sales, but Dell now gets the majority of its revenue from software and services.

The Buying Center

Who buys the trillions of dollars' worth of goods and services needed by business organizations? Purchasing agents are influential in straight-rebuy and modified-rebuy situations, whereas other employees are more influential in new-buy situations. Engineers are usually influential in selecting product components, and purchasing agents dominate in selecting suppliers.[10]

THE COMPOSITION OF THE BUYING CENTER

The decision-making unit of a buying organization is often referred to as *the buying center*. It consists of "all those individuals and groups who participate in the purchasing decision-making process, who share some common goals and the risks arising from the decisions."[11] The buying center includes all members of the organization who play one or more of seven roles in the purchase decision process.

- *Initiators*—Users or others in the organization who request that something be purchased.
- *Users*—Those who will use the product or service. In many cases, the users initiate the buying proposal and help define the product requirements.
- *Influencers*—People who influence the buying decision, often by helping to define specifications and providing information for evaluating alternatives. Technical people are particularly important influencers.
- *Deciders*—People who decide on product requirements or on suppliers.
- *Approvers*—People who authorize the proposed actions of deciders or buyers.
- *Buyers*—People who have formal authority to select the supplier and arrange the purchase terms. Buyers may help shape product specifications, but their major role is to select vendors and negotiate terms and price. In more complex purchases, buyers might include high-level managers.
- *Gatekeepers*—People who have the power to prevent sellers or information from reaching members of the buying center. For example, purchasing agents, receptionists, and telephone operators may prevent salespersons from contacting users or deciders.

Several people can occupy a given role such as user or influencer, and one person may play multiple roles.[12] A purchasing manager, for example, is often buyer, influencer, and gatekeeper simultaneously. She can decide which sales reps can call on other people in the organization, what budget and other constraints to place on the purchase, and which firm will actually get the business, even though others (deciders) might select two or more potential vendors that can meet the company's requirements.

A buying center typically has five or six members and sometimes dozens. Some may be outside the organization, such as government officials, consultants, technical advisors, and members of the marketing channel.

THE ROLE OF THE BUYING CENTER IN THE ORGANIZATION

In the past, purchasing departments occupied a humble position in the management hierarchy, in spite of often managing more than half of the company's costs. Recent competitive pressures have led many companies to upgrade their purchasing departments and elevate administrators to vice-presidential rank. These new, more strategically oriented purchasing departments have a mission to seek the best value from fewer and better suppliers.

Some multinationals have even elevated purchasing departments to "strategic supply departments" with responsibility for global sourcing and partnering. At Caterpillar, purchasing, inventory control, production scheduling, and traffic have been combined into one department. Here are two other companies that have benefited from improving their business-buying practices:

Rio Tinto Rio Tinto is a world leader in finding, mining, and processing the earth's mineral resources, with a significant presence in North America and Australia. Coordinating with its suppliers was time consuming, so Rio Tinto embarked on an electronic commerce strategy with one key supplier. Both parties have reaped significant benefits. In many cases, orders are filled in the supplier's warehouse within minutes of being transmitted, and the supplier can now use a pay-on-receipt program that has shortened Rio Tinto's payment cycle to about 10 days.[13]

Medline Industries Medline Industries, the largest privately owned manufacturer and distributor of health care products in the United States, used software to integrate its view of customer activity across online and direct sales channels. The results? The firm enhanced its product margin, improved customer retention, reduced revenue lost to pricing errors, and increased the productivity of its sales representatives.[14]

The upgrading of purchasing departments means business marketers must upgrade their sales staff to match the higher caliber of today's business buyers.

BUYING CENTER DYNAMICS

Buying centers usually include participants with differing interests, authority, status, and susceptibility to persuasion, and sometimes with very different decision criteria. Engineers may want to maximize the performance of the product, production people may stress ease of use and reliability of supply, financial staff will focus on the economics of the purchase, purchasing may be concerned with operating and replacement costs, and union officials may emphasize safety issues.

Business buyers also have personal motivations, perceptions, and preferences influenced by their age, income, education, job position, personality, attitude toward risk, and culture. Some are "keep-it-simple" buyers, or "own-expert," "want-the-best," or "want-everything-done" buyers. Some younger, highly educated buyers are technically proficient and conduct rigorous analyses of competitive proposals before choosing a supplier. Other buyers are "toughies" from the old school who pit competing sellers against one another. And in some companies, the purchasing powers-that-be are legendary.

Purchasing decisions are ultimately made by individuals, not organizations.[15] Individuals are motivated by their own needs and perceptions in attempting to maximize the organizational rewards they earn (pay, advancement, recognition, and feelings of achievement). However, organizational needs legitimize the buying process and its outcomes.

Businesspeople are not buying just "products." They are buying solutions to two problems: the organization's economic and strategic problem and their own personal need for achievement and reward. In this sense, industrial buying decisions are both "rational" and "emotional," serving the needs of the organization as well as those of the individual.[16]

Research by one manufacturer of industrial components found that even though top executives at its small- and medium-size customers were comfortable buying from other companies, they appeared to harbor subconscious insecurities about buying the manufacturer's product. Constant changes in technology had left them concerned about issues such as product performance, reliability, and compatibility. Recognizing this unease, the manufacturer retooled its selling approach to emphasize a more emotional appeal and the way its product line enabled the customer's employees to improve their performance, relieving management of the perceived complications and stress of using its components.[17]

SELLING TO BUYING CENTERS

Successful business-to-business marketing requires that marketers determine not only the types of companies on which to focus their selling efforts but also whom to concentrate on within the buying centers in those organizations.

Once marketers identify the type of businesses on which to focus marketing efforts, they must then decide how best to sell to these businesses. Who are the major decision participants? What decisions do they influence, and how deeply? What evaluation criteria do they use? Consider the following example:

> A company sells nonwoven disposable surgical gowns to hospitals. The hospital staff who participate in the buying decision include the vice president of purchasing, the operating-room administrator, and the surgeons. The vice president of purchasing analyzes whether the hospital should buy disposable or reusable gowns. If disposable, the operating-room administrator compares various competitors' products on absorbency, antiseptic quality, design, and cost and normally buys the brand that meets functional requirements at the lowest cost. Surgeons influence the decision retroactively by reporting their satisfaction with the chosen brand.

The business marketer is not likely to know exactly what kind of group dynamics take place during the decision process, though whatever information he or she can obtain about personalities and interpersonal factors is useful.

Small sellers concentrate on reaching the key buying influencers. Larger sellers often go for in-depth selling to reach as many participants as possible. Their salespeople virtually "live with" high-volume customers. Companies must rely more heavily on their communications programs to reach hidden buying influencers and keep current customers informed.[18]

Business marketers must periodically review their assumptions about buying center participants. Traditionally, SAP sold its software products to CIOs at large companies. A shift in selling focus from CIOs to individual corporate units lower on the organizational chart significantly raised the volume of software license sales to new SAP customers.

Insights into customers and buying centers are critical. GE's ethnographic research into the plastic-fiber industry revealed that the firm wasn't in a commodity business driven by price, as it had assumed. Instead, it was in an artisanal industry whose customers wanted collaboration at the earliest stages of development. This resulted in GE completely reorienting the way it interacted with companies in the industry. Ethnographic research also can be very useful in developing markets, especially in far-flung rural areas where marketers often do not know the consumers well.

In developing selling efforts, business marketers can also consider their customers' customers, or end users, if appropriate. Many B2B sales are to firms that use the products they purchase as components in products they sell to the ultimate consumers. Business marketers can seek out opportunities to interact with their customers' customers and improve their offerings or even their business model. When Xsens, a Dutch supplier of three-dimensional motion-sensor technology, helped solve the problems of one of its customers' customers, it also developed a new operating procedure that improved the accuracy of its products by an order of magnitude.[19]

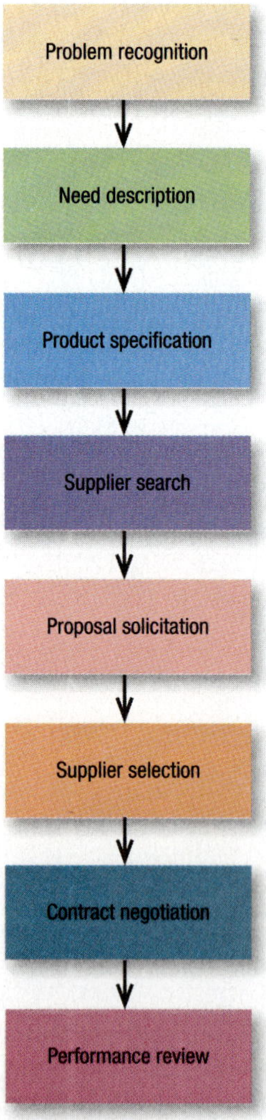

FIGURE **4.1**
Stages in the Business-Buying Process

Understanding the Buying Process

The business-buying process encompasses a number of explicit stages. One popular model delineates eight distinct stages of the decision process in business markets.[20] These stages are shown in Figure 4.1, and the important considerations in each of the eight stages are discussed in more detail in the following sections. Note that in modified-rebuy or straight-rebuy situations, some stages are compressed or bypassed. For example, the buyer normally has a favorite supplier or a ranked list of suppliers and can skip the search and the proposal solicitation.

PROBLEM RECOGNITION

The buying process begins when someone in the company recognizes a problem or need that can be met by acquiring a good or service. The recognition can be triggered by internal or external stimuli. The internal stimulus might be a decision to develop a new product that requires new equipment and materials, or it might be a machine that breaks down and requires new parts. Or purchased material may turn out to be unsatisfactory and cause the company to search for another supplier, lower prices, or better quality. Externally, the buyer may get new ideas at a trade show, see an ad, receive an e-mail, read a blog, or take a call from a sales representative who offers a better product or a lower price. Business marketers can stimulate problem recognition by direct marketing in many different ways.

NEED DESCRIPTION

Next, the buyer determines the needed item's general characteristics and the required quantity. The goal here is to identify the specific need(s) that the company aims to fulfill and the benefits it seeks to receive from the offering. For standard items, this is simple. For complex items, the buyer will work with others—engineers, users—to define characteristics such as reliability, durability, or price. Business marketers can help by describing how their products meet or even exceed the buyer's needs.

PRODUCT SPECIFICATION

The buying organization now develops the item's technical specifications. Often, the company will assign a product-value-analysis engineering team to the project. **Product value analysis** is an approach to cost reduction that studies whether components can be redesigned, standardized, or made by cheaper methods of production without adversely affecting product performance. The value analysis team will identify overdesigned components, for instance, that last longer than the product itself. Tightly written specifications allow the buyer to refuse components that are too expensive or that fail to meet specified standards.

Suppliers can use product value analysis as a tool for positioning themselves to win an account. Whatever the method, it is important to eliminate excessive costs. Mexican cement giant Cemex is famed for "The Cemex Way," which uses high-tech methods to squeeze out inefficiencies.[21]

SUPPLIER SEARCH

The buyer next tries to identify the most appropriate suppliers through trade directories, contacts with other companies, trade advertisements, trade shows, and the internet. The move to online purchasing has far-reaching implications for suppliers and will change the shape of purchasing for years to come.

To facilitate supplier search and gain power in negotiations with suppliers, companies often form buying alliances. Such alliances involve several companies that are buying the same goods joining together to form purchasing consortia in order to streamline the search for suppliers and gain deeper discounts on volume purchases. Topco is the largest American retail food GPO (group purchasing organization); this GPO represents a consortium of firms in the retail and wholesale food-related businesses.

Companies that purchase online utilize electronic marketplaces in several forms.

- *Catalog sites.* Companies can order thousands of items through electronic catalogs, such as W.W. Grainger's, distributed by e-procurement software.
- *Vertical markets.* Companies buying industrial products such as plastics, steel, or chemicals, or services such as logistics or media, can go to specialized websites called e-hubs. Plastics.com allows plastics buyers to search the best prices among thousands of plastics sellers.
- *"Pure Play" auction company.* Ritchie Bros. Auctioneers is the world's largest industrial auctioneer, with 40-plus permanent auction sites in North America, Europe, the Middle East, Asia, and Australia. At 400-plus unreserved auctions with online bidding in 2017, it sold $4.5 billion of used and unused equipment, including a wide range of heavy equipment, trucks, and other assets for the construction, transportation, agricultural, material handling, oil and gas, mining, forestry, and marine industry sectors. Although some people prefer to bid in person at Ritchie Bros. auctions, they can also do so online in real time at rbauction.com—the company's multilingual website.[22]
- *Spot (or exchange) markets.* In spot electronic markets, prices change by the minute. Intercontinental Exchange (ICE) owns exchanges for financial and commodity markets with trillions of dollars in sales.
- *Private exchanges.* HP, IBM, and Walmart operate private online exchanges to link with specially invited groups of suppliers and partners.

A growing number of companies are moving to online buying. Online business buying can be organized around e-hubs, including *vertical hubs* centered on industries (plastics, steel, chemicals, paper) and *functional hubs* (logistics, media buying, advertising, energy management). Online business buying offers several advantages: It shaves transaction costs for both buyers and suppliers, reduces

Source: Courtesy of Ritchie Bros. Auctioneers

<< Ritchie Bros., the world's largest industrial auctioneers, conducts numerous online as well as in-person auctions for its customers.

time between order and delivery, consolidates purchasing systems, and forges more direct relationships between partners and buyers. On the downside, online business buying may tend to erode supplier–buyer loyalty and create potential security problems.

PROPOSAL SOLICITATION

The buyer next invites qualified suppliers to submit written proposals. After evaluating these proposals, the buyer will invite a few suppliers to make formal presentations.

Business marketers must be skilled in researching, writing, and presenting marketing proposals that describe value and benefits in customer terms. In addition, oral presentations must inspire confidence and must position the company's capabilities and resources so they stand out from the competition.

Proposals and selling efforts are often team efforts that leverage the knowledge and expertise of coworkers. Pittsburgh-based Cutler-Hammer, part of Eaton Corp., developed "pods" of salespeople focused on a particular geographic region, industry, or market concentration.

SUPPLIER SELECTION

Business buyers seek the highest benefit package (economic, technical, service, and social) in relationship to a market offering's costs. The strength of their incentive to purchase is a function of the difference between perceived benefits and perceived costs.[23] The attributes that buyers commonly use to evaluate vendors include price, reputation, reliability, and agility. Before selecting a supplier, the buying center will specify and rank desired supplier attributes, often using a supplier-evaluation model to rate suppliers based on their performance on the attributes valued by the buyer.

Business marketers must therefore ensure that customers fully appreciate how the firm's offerings are different and better. To this end, sellers often present or "frame" their offerings in a way that enables them to underscore the benefits they provide. It can be as simple as making sure customers recognize all the benefits or cost savings afforded by the firm's offerings or becoming more influential in the customers' thinking about the economics of purchasing, owning, using, and disposing of product offerings.

To develop compelling value propositions, business marketers need to better understand how business buyers arrive at their valuations.[24] The choice of attributes and their relative importance vary with the buying situation. Delivery reliability, price, and supplier reputation might be important for some companies. For others, the most important attributes might be technical service, supplier flexibility, and product reliability. Clearly identifying a company's priorities when choosing a supplier and identifying suppliers that meet these criteria are key to market success.

Companies are increasingly reducing the number of their suppliers. There is even a trend toward single sourcing, though companies that use multiple sources often cite the threat of a labor strike, natural disaster, or any other unforeseen event as the biggest deterrent to single sourcing. Companies may also fear that single-source suppliers will become too comfortable in the relationship and lose their competitive edge.

CONTRACT NEGOTIATION

After selecting suppliers, the buyer negotiates the final order, which includes listing the technical specifications, the quantity needed, the expected time of delivery, return policies, and warranties. Many industrial buyers lease rather than buy heavy equipment such as machinery and trucks. The lessee gains a number of advantages: the latest products, better service, conservation of capital, and some tax advantages. The lessor often ends up with a larger net income and the chance to serve customers that could not afford outright purchase.

For maintenance, repair, and operating items, buyers are moving toward blanket contracts rather than periodic purchase orders. A blanket contract establishes a long-term relationship in which the supplier promises to resupply the buyer as needed, at agreed-upon prices, over a specified period of time. Because the seller holds the stock, blanket contracts are sometimes called *stockless purchase plans.* They lock suppliers in tighter with the buyer and make it difficult for out-suppliers to break in unless the buyer becomes dissatisfied.

Companies that fear a shortage of key materials are willing to buy and hold large inventories. They will sign long-term contracts with suppliers to ensure a steady flow of materials. DuPont, Ford, and several other major companies regard long-term supply planning as a major responsibility of their purchasing managers. For example, General Motors wants to buy from fewer suppliers, which must be willing to locate close to its plants and produce high-quality components. Business marketers are also setting up extranets with important customers to facilitate and lower the cost of transactions. Customers enter orders that are automatically transmitted to the supplier.

Some companies go further and shift the ordering responsibility to their suppliers, using systems called vendor-managed inventory. These suppliers are privy to the customer's inventory levels and take responsibility for continuous replenishment programs. Performance Pipe, a division of Chevron Phillips Chemical Company, supplies audio, lighting, and vision systems to the world's leading automakers. Its vendor-managed inventory program, with its 40 suppliers, resulted in significant time and cost savings and allowed the company to use former warehouse space for productive manufacturing activities.[25]

PERFORMANCE REVIEW

The buyer periodically reviews the performance of the chosen supplier(s) using one of three methods. The buyer may contact end users and ask for their evaluations, rate the supplier on several criteria using a weighted-score method, or aggregate the cost of poor performance to come up with adjusted costs of purchase, including price. The performance review may lead the buyer to continue, modify, or end a supplier relationship.

Many companies have set up incentive systems to reward purchasing managers for good buying performance, leading them to increase pressure on sellers for the best terms.

Developing Effective Business Marketing Programs

Business-to-business marketers are using every marketing tool at their disposal to attract and retain customers. They are embracing systems selling, adding valuable services to their product offerings, employing customer reference programs, and utilizing a wide variety of online and offline communication and branding activities.

TRANSITIONING FROM PRODUCTS TO SOLUTIONS

Many business buyers prefer to buy a total problem solution from one seller. This practice of **systems buying** originated with government purchases of major weapons and communications systems. The government solicited bids from prime contractors that, if awarded the contract, became responsible for bidding out and assembling the system's subcomponents from second-tier contractors. The prime contractor thus provided a turnkey solution, so called because the buyer simply had to turn one key to get the job done.[26]

Sellers increasingly recognize that buyers like to purchase in this way, and many have adopted **systems selling** as a marketing tool. Technology giants such as HP, IBM, Oracle, and Dell are all transitioning from specialists to competing one-stop shops that can provide the core technology necessary as businesses shift to the cloud.

One variant of systems selling is systems contracting, in which a single supplier provides the buyer with *all* its maintenance, repair, and operating MRO requirements. During the contract period, the supplier also manages the customer's inventory. Shell Oil manages the oil inventories of many of its business customers and knows when they require replenishment. The customer benefits from reduced procurement and management costs, as well as from price protection over the term of the contract. The seller achieves lower operating costs thanks to steady demand and reduced paperwork.

Systems selling is a key industrial marketing strategy in bidding for large-scale industrial projects such as the construction of dams, steel factories, irrigation systems, sanitation systems, pipelines, utilities, and even new towns. Project engineering firms must compete on price, quality, reliability, and other attributes to win contracts. Suppliers, however, are not just at the mercy of customer demands. Ideally, they're active early in the process to influence the actual development of the specifications. Or they can go beyond the specifications to offer additional value in various ways, as the following example shows.

Selling to the Indonesian Government The Indonesian government requested bids to build a cement factory near Jakarta. A U.S. firm made a proposal that included choosing the site, designing the factory, hiring the construction crews, assembling the materials and equipment, and turning over the finished factory to the Indonesian government. A Japanese firm, in its proposal, included all these services, plus hiring and training the workers to run the factory, exporting the cement through its trading companies, and using the cement to build roads and new office buildings in Jakarta. Although the Japanese plan involved more money, it won the contract. Clearly, the Japanese viewed the problem not just as building a cement factory (the narrow view of systems selling) but as contributing to Indonesia's economic development. They took the broadest possible view of the customer's needs, which is true systems selling.

ENHANCING SERVICES

Services play an increasing strategic and financial role for many business-to-business firms that sell primarily products. Adding high-quality services to their product offerings allows companies to provide greater value and establish closer ties with customers.

A classic example is Rolls-Royce, which has invested heavily in developing giant jet engine models for the new jumbo planes being introduced by Boeing and Airbus. An important source of profits for Rolls-Royce, beyond selling engines and replacement parts, is the add-on "power by the hour" long-term repair and maintenance contracts it sells. Margins are higher because customers are willing to pay a premium for the peace of mind and predictability the contracts offer.[27]

Technology firms are also bundling services to improve customer satisfaction and increase profits. Like many software firms, Adobe Systems is making the transition to a digital-marketing business with cloud-based monthly subscriptions. For example, Adobe products such as Photoshop, Illustrator, and InDesign have moved online to become subscription-based services. A particular benefit for companies offering such services is that the subscription model eliminates the need to constantly try to convince users who have purchased the product in the past to upgrade to the new version; in the subscription model it happens automatically. Revenue is also increasing because the company is able to sell support services to its cloud customers.

BUILDING BUSINESS-TO-BUSINESS BRANDS

Business marketers are increasingly recognizing the importance of their brands. Brands give managers peace of mind by ensuring product quality and thus make it easier to justify the purchase of established brands to the company stakeholders. As the old saying goes: "Nobody gets fired for buying IBM."

Swiss-based ABB is a global leader in power and automation technologies, with 110,000 employees in more than 100 countries. The company spends $1 billion in R&D annually to fuel a long tradition of groundbreaking and nation-building projects. ABB undertook an extensive rebranding project that evaluated five alternative positioning platforms, concluding that ABB should stand for "Power and Productivity for a Better World." In a "one company, one brand" approach, magazines, posters, brochures, digital communication, and even exhibits were all revamped to give the brand a unified look and strengthen its global market position. Most of ABB business advertising contains images of actual projects, with business-specific messages that explain technologies.[28]

In business-to-business marketing, the corporate brand is often critical because it is associated with so many of the company's products. At one time Emerson Electric—a global provider of power tools, compressors, electrical equipment, and engineering solutions—was a conglomerate of 60 autonomous, and sometimes anonymous, companies. To achieve a broader presence so it could sell locally while leveraging its global brand name, Emerson aligned the brands under a new global brand architecture and identity. Global consolidation cut the number of company websites in half, online content and marketing campaigns were translated into local languages around the globe, and social media platforms were built out.[29] SAS is another firm that recognized the importance of its corporate brand.

SAS With a huge "fan club" of IT customers in 147 countries, business analytics software and services firm SAS seemed to be in an enviable position at the turn of the century. Yet its image was what one industry observer called "a geek brand." To extend the company's reach beyond IT managers with PhDs in math or statistical analysis, the company needed to connect with C-level

Source: Kristoffer Tripplaar/Alamy Stock Photo

<< To shed its image as a brand solely for IT managers and achieve solid growth, business analytics software firm SAS geared a TV and print ad campaign to executives who were unaware of the benefits of SAS software or the merits of business analytics in general.

executives in the largest companies—people who either didn't have a clue what SAS software was or didn't think business analytics was a strategic issue. Working with its first outside ad agency ever, SAS emerged with a new logo; a new slogan, "The Power to Know"; and a series of TV spots and print ads in business publications such as *BusinessWeek, Forbes,* and the *Wall Street Journal*. Highly profitable and now one of the world's largest privately owned software companies, SAS has more than doubled its revenue stream since the brand change and has met with just as much success inside the company. For more than 15 years, *Fortune* magazine has ranked it as one of the best U.S. companies to work for.[30]

OVERCOMING PRICE PRESSURES

Despite moves toward strategic sourcing, partnering, and participation in cross-functional teams, buyers still spend a large chunk of their time haggling with suppliers on price. The number of price-oriented buyers can vary by country, depending on customer preferences for different service configurations and the characteristics of the customer's organization.[31]

Marketers can counter requests for a lower price in a number of ways, including the use of framing, as noted previously. They may also be able to show that the total cost of ownership—that is, the life-cycle cost of using their product—is lower than that for competitors' products. They can cite the value of the services the buyer now receives, especially if it is superior to that offered by competitors.[32] Research shows that service support and personal interactions, as well as a supplier's know-how and ability to improve customers' time to market, can be useful differentiators in achieving key-supplier status.[33]

Improving productivity helps alleviate price pressures. Some companies handle price-oriented buyers by setting a lower price but establishing restrictive conditions such as limited quantities, no refunds, no adjustments, and no services.[34] Others seek solutions that increase benefits and reduce costs enough to overcome any price concerns. Consider the following example.

TATA Steel Tata Steel, India's oldest and largest steel manufacturer, was founded in 1907. The company operated in a controlled and protected industry with limited competition and price controls imposed by the government until the economic liberalization of the early 1990s. Entry of new players and consequent increase in competition led to the transition from a seller's to a buyer's market and pricing switched from cost-based to market-based. Realizing the potential of a customer-centric approach to understand customer needs, Tata Steel re-engineered its entire marketing and sales strategies to remain competitive. A product mix changeover during 1992 to 2000, ensured that high-volume, low-margin products like semi-finished steel in its product mix reduced from 54 percent to 3 percent while high value flat products used in automobiles and consumer durables increased

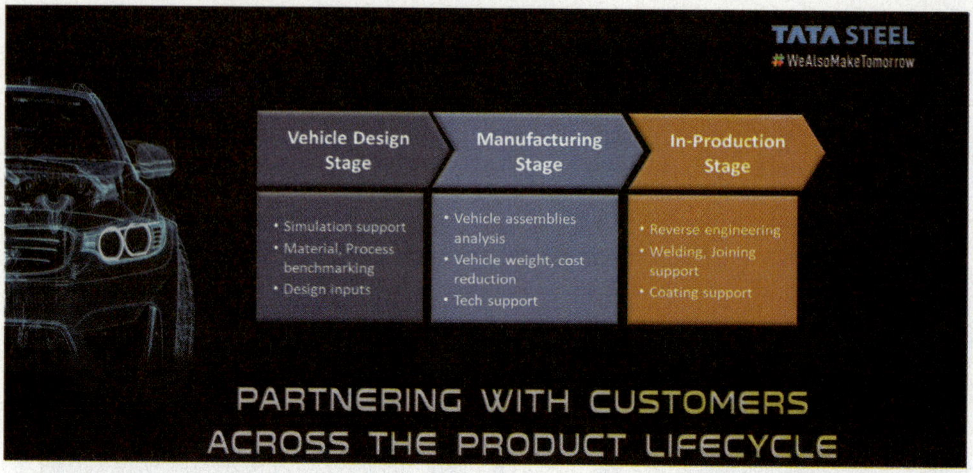

>> Rather than lowering prices to meet those of its competitors, Tata Steel worked closely with its strategic customers to identify opportunities for cost reductions that meet or exceed price differences.

Source: ©Tata Steel Limited, used with permission

from 40 to 65 percent. In parallel, the company initiated a branding program for the retail market to develop application specific products for roofing, reinforcing and general engineering requirements. These newly launched brands—Shaktee, Tiscon and Steelium— emerged as leaders with the highest brand equity in their respective categories.[35] Retail branding improved product identification and boosted brand recall while ensuring a price premium of 5% over competitive offerings.

In its business segment, characterized by growing competition and price wars, the leadership adopted an innovative partnership approach to retain and grow the share of business from existing, profitable customers to escape the downward spiral of price pressures.[36] Tata Steel initiated a multi-year, multi-phase customer value management (CVM) program with the top 25 out of its over 1500 business customers to find a long-term solution to combat product commoditization. Migrating select customers from transaction selling to strategic partnerships helped Tata Steel jointly improve their competitiveness and performance by streamlining multiple interfaces across the entire value chain, eliminating value drains and harness value creation and sharing opportunities collaboratively. CVM aided Tata Steel's growth into one of the most reliable, responsive and trustworthy partners for these industry-leading customers in automobile, durables, office furniture, and construction.

Collaboration can further help alleviate price pressure. Suppose that 3M Healthcare, a hospital supplier, signs an agreement with *India's largest private healthcare chain, Apollo Hospitals* promising ₹2 crores in savings over the first 18 months in exchange for getting a twofold increase in the hospital's share of supplies. If 3M achieves less than this promised savings, it will make up the difference. If it achieves substantially more, it will participate in the extra savings. To make such arrangements work, the supplier must be willing to help the customer build a historical database, reach an agreement for measuring benefits and costs, and devise a mechanism for resolving disputes.

Lowering the price and increasing benefits are not the only ways to overcome price pressures. In some cases, the issue is not improving the offering but better communicating the benefits that the offering already delivers to customers. A popular approach to making the value of the offering more transparent to customers is the *economic value analysis*. Economic value analysis (EVA) is a tool that helps monetize the functional benefits of a company's offering, such as performance, reliability, and warranty.

Suppose the buyer for a large construction company wants to buy a tractor for residential construction from either Caterpillar or Komatsu. He wants the tractor to deliver certain levels of reliability, durability, performance, and resale value. The competing salespeople carefully describe their respective offers. The buyer decides Caterpillar has greater product benefits based on his perceptions of those attributes. He also perceives differences in the accompanying services—delivery, training, and maintenance—and decides Caterpillar provides better service as well as a more knowledgeable and responsive staff. Finally, he places higher value on Caterpillar's corporate image and reputation. He adds up all the economic, functional, and psychological benefits from these four sources—product, services, people, and image—and decides he believes that Caterpillar delivers greater customer benefits.

Does he buy the Caterpillar tractor? Not necessarily. He also examines the total cost of transacting with Caterpillar versus Komatsu, a cost that involves more than money. As Adam Smith observed more than two centuries ago in *The Wealth of Nations*, "The real price of anything is the toil and trouble of acquiring it." Thus total customer cost also includes the buyer's time, energy, and psychological costs expended in product acquisition, usage, maintenance, ownership, and disposal. The buyer evaluates these elements, together with the monetary cost, to form a total customer cost. Then he considers whether Caterpillar's total customer cost is too high compared to total customer benefits. If it is, he might choose Komatsu. The buyer will choose whichever source delivers the highest perceived value.

Now let's use this decision-making theory to help Caterpillar succeed in selling to this buyer. Caterpillar can improve its offer in three ways. First, it can increase total customer benefit by improving the economic, functional, and psychological benefits of its product, services, people, and/or image. Second, it can reduce the buyer's nonmonetary costs by reducing the time, energy, and psychological investment needed to acquire the product. Third, it can reduce its product's monetary cost to the buyer.

Suppose Caterpillar concludes that the buyer sees its offer as worth $20,000. Further, suppose Caterpillar's cost of producing the tractor is $14,000. This means Caterpillar's offer generates $6,000 over its cost, so the firm needs to charge between $14,000 and $20,000. If it charges less than $14,000, it won't cover its costs; if it charges more, it will price itself out of the market.

Caterpillar's price will determine how much value it delivers to the buyer and how much flows to Caterpillar. If the company charges $19,000, it is creating $1,000 of customer-perceived value and keeping $5,000 for itself. The lower Caterpillar sets its price, the higher the customer's perceived value and, therefore, the higher the customer's incentive to purchase. To win the sale, the firm must offer more customer-perceived value than Komatsu does.[37]

MANAGING COMMUNICATION

Although marketing communication is usually associated with consumer markets, it also plays an important role in business markets. Companies need to inform business customers about the benefits of their offerings as well as coordinating their activities with collaborators.[38] As is the case in consumer markets, business communications are increasingly moving into the online space, using search engine optimization (SEO) and search engine marketing (SEM) to connect with buyers.

Here are some examples of the way top firms are redesigning their online presence, employing search engine optimization, engaging in social media, and launching Webinars and podcasts to improve their business performance through B2B marketing.

Chapman Kelly A subsidiary of HMS Business Services, Chapman Kelly provides medical, dental, and pharmacy claims and dependent auditing services to help firms reduce their health care and insurance costs. The company originally tried to acquire new customers through traditional cold calling and outbound selling techniques. After it redesigned its website and optimized the site so that the company's name moved close to the top of relevant online searches, revenue nearly doubled.[39]

Makino Machinery manufacturer Makino builds relationships with end-user customers by hosting an ongoing series of industry-specific Webinars, averaging three a month. The company uses highly specialized content, such as how to get the most out of machine tools and how metal-cutting processes work, to appeal to different industries and different styles of manufacturing. Its database of Webinar participants has allowed the firm to cut marketing costs and improve its effectiveness and efficiency.[40]

Kinaxis Canadian supply chain management company Kinaxis uses a fully integrated approach to communications—including blogs, white papers, and a video channel that hinges on specific keywords to drive traffic to its website and generate qualified leads. With research suggesting that 93 percent of all B2B purchases start with search, Kinaxis puts much emphasis on search engine optimization (SEO), reusing and repurposing content as much as possible to make it relevant and user-friendly.[41]

Some business-to-business marketers are adopting marketing practices from business-to-consumer markets to build their brand.[42] Xerox ran a fully integrated communication campaign to cleverly reinforce the fact that 50 percent of its revenue comes from business services, not copiers. Here is how its Marriott ad unfolded:[43]

Two Marriott bellmen are sitting in an office. "Did you finish last month's invoices?" one asks the other. "No, but I did pick up your dry cleaning and have your shoes shined," the second replies. "Well, I made you a reservation at the sushi place around the corner!" the first bellman says. This voiceover follows: "Marriott knows it's better for Xerox to automate their global invoice processes so they can focus on serving their customers."

Sometimes a more personal touch can make all the difference. Customers that are considering dropping six or seven figures on one transaction for big-ticket goods and services want all the information they can get, especially from a trusted, independent source.

Managing Business-to-Business Relationships

Business suppliers and customers are exploring different ways to manage their relationships.[44] Loyalty is driven in part by supply chain management, supplier involvement, and purchasing alliances.[45] Business-to-business marketers are using more focused approaches to attract and retain customers, homing in on their targets, and developing one-to-one marketing approaches.[46]

UNDERSTANDING THE BUYER–SUPPLIER RELATIONSHIP

Much research has advocated greater vertical coordination between buying partners and sellers so that they can transcend merely transacting and instead create more value for both parties.[47]

A number of forces influence the development of a relationship between business partners. Four relevant forces are availability of alternatives, importance of supply, complexity of supply, and supply market dynamism. Based on these forces, buyer–supplier relationships can range from basic buying and selling that involves simple, routine exchanges with moderate levels of cooperation and information exchange, to a collaborative relationship in which trust and commitment lead to true partnership.[48]

Over time, however, relationship roles may shift.[49] Some needs can be satisfied with fairly basic supplier performance if buyers neither want nor require a close relationship with a supplier. Similarly, some suppliers may not find it worth their while to invest in customers with limited growth potential.

One study found that the closest relationships between customers and suppliers arose when supply was important to the customer and there were procurement obstacles such as complex purchase requirements and few alternative suppliers.[50] Another study suggested that greater vertical coordination between buyer and seller through information exchange and planning is usually necessary only when high environmental uncertainty exists and specific investments are modest.[51]

MANAGING CORPORATE TRUST, CREDIBILITY, AND REPUTATION

Building trust is one prerequisite to enjoying healthy long-term relationships.[52] *Trust* is a firm's willingness to rely on a business partner. It depends on a number of interpersonal and interorganizational factors, such as the firm's perceived competence, integrity, honesty, and benevolence. Personal interactions with employees of the firm, opinions about the company as a whole, and perceptions of trust will evolve with experience.

A firm is more likely to be seen as trustworthy when it provides full, honest information, when employee incentives are aligned with customer needs, when it partners with customers to create market value, and when it offers valid comparisons with competitive products.[53]

Building trust can be especially tricky in online settings, and firms often impose more stringent requirements on their online business partners than on others. Business buyers worry that they won't get products of the right quality delivered to the right place at the right time. Sellers worry about getting paid on time—or at all—and debate how much credit they should extend. To this end, many firms use automated credit-checking applications and online trust services to assess the creditworthiness of trading partners.

Corporate credibility is the extent to which customers believe a firm can design and deliver products and services that satisfy their needs and wants. It reflects the supplier's reputation in the marketplace and is the foundation of a strong relationship. Corporate credibility depends on three factors. *Corporate expertise* reflects the extent to which a company is seen as able to make and sell products or conduct services. *Corporate trustworthiness* reflects the extent to which a company is seen as motivated to be honest, dependable, and sensitive to customer needs. *Corporate likability* reflects the extent to which a company is seen as likable, attractive, prestigious, and dynamic.

In other words, a credible firm is good at what it does; it keeps its customers' best interests in mind and is enjoyable to work with.

RISKS AND OPPORTUNISM IN BUSINESS RELATIONSHIPS

Researchers have noted that establishing a customer–supplier relationship creates tension between safeguarding (ensuring predictable solutions) and adapting (allowing for flexibility for unanticipated events). Vertical coordination can facilitate stronger customer–seller ties but may also increase the risk to the customer's and supplier's specific investments.[54]

Specific investments are those expenditures tailored to a particular company and value-chain partner (investments in company-specific training, equipment, and operating procedures or systems).[55] For example, a manufacturer might invest in developing an order-placing and inventory-tracking system tailored to the needs of a particular retailer. Such specific investments help improve the effectiveness and cost efficiency of the collaboration between business entities.[56]

Specific investments, however, also entail considerable risk to both customer and supplier. Transaction theory from economics maintains that because initial investments in specific investments can be high, firms can be locked into a particular relationship. Furthermore, sensitive information on cost and processes may need to be exchanged. A buyer may be vulnerable to holdup because of switching costs; a supplier may be more vulnerable because it has dedicated assets and/or technology/knowledge at stake. In terms of the latter risk, consider the following example.

An automobile component manufacturer wins a contract to supply an under-hood component to an original equipment manufacturer (OEM). A one-year, sole-source contract safeguards the supplier's OEM-specific investments in a dedicated production line. However, the supplier may also be obliged to work (noncontractually) as a partner with the OEM's internal engineering staff, using linked computing facilities to exchange detailed engineering information and coordinate frequent design and manufacturing changes over the term of the contract. These interactions could reduce costs and/or increase quality by improving the firm's responsiveness to marketplace changes. But they could also magnify the threat to the supplier's intellectual property.

When buyers cannot easily monitor supplier performance, the supplier might shirk or cheat and not deliver the expected value. *Opportunism* is a "form of cheating or undersupply relative to an implicit or explicit contract."[57]

A more passive form of opportunism might be a refusal or unwillingness to adapt to changing circumstances or negligence in satisfying contractual obligations. When Peanut Corporation of America, a peanut-processing company with only $25 million in sales, was found to have a contaminated product, a $1 billion recall resulted because the ingredient was found in 2,000 other products. The company subsequently ceased all manufacturing and business operations, and its CEO was imprisoned for knowingly shipping tainted food.[58]

Opportunism is a concern because firms must devote resources to control and monitoring that they could otherwise allocate to more productive purposes. Contracts may be inadequate to govern supplier transactions when supplier opportunism becomes difficult to detect, when firms make specific investments in assets they cannot use elsewhere, and when contingencies are harder to anticipate. Customers and suppliers are more likely to form a joint venture (which implies a greater level of commitment to the collaborative relationship than signing a simple contract) when the supplier's degree of asset specificity is high and monitoring the supplier's behavior is difficult.[59]

The presence of a significant future time horizon and/or strong solidarity norms typically causes customers and suppliers to strive for joint benefits. Their specific investments shift from expropriation (increased opportunism on the receiver's part) to bonding (reduced opportunism).[60]

MANAGING INSTITUTIONAL MARKETS

Our discussion has concentrated largely on the buying behavior of profit-seeking companies. Much of what we have said also applies to the buying practices of institutional and government organizations. However, we want to highlight certain special features of these markets.

The **institutional market** consists of schools, hospitals, nursing homes, prisons, and other institutions that must provide goods and services to people in their care. Many of these organizations are characterized by low budgets and captive clienteles. For example, hospitals must decide what quality of food to buy for patients. The buying objective here is not profit because the food is provided as part of the total service package; nor is cost minimization the sole objective because poor food will cause patients to complain and hurt the hospital's reputation. The hospital purchasing agent must search for institutional food vendors whose quality meets or exceeds a certain minimum standard and whose prices are low. In fact, many food vendors set up a separate sales division to cater to institutional buyers' special needs and characteristics. Heinz produces, packages, and prices its ketchup differently to meet the requirements of hospitals, colleges, and prisons. Aramark—which provides food services for stadiums, arenas, campuses, businesses, and schools—also has a competitive advantage in providing food for the nation's prisons, a direct result of refining its purchasing practices and supply chain management.

Aramark Where Aramark once merely selected products from lists provided by potential suppliers, it now collaborates with suppliers to develop products customized to meet the needs of individual segments. In the corrections segment, quality has historically been sacrificed to meet limits on food costs that operators outside the market would find impossible to work with. "When you go after business in the corrections field, you are making bids that are measured in hundredths of a cent," says John Zillmer, the president of Aramark Food & Support Services, "so any edge we can gain on the purchasing side is extremely valuable." Aramark sourced a series of protein products with unique partners at price points it never could have imagined before. These partners were unique because they understood the chemistry of proteins and knew how to lower the price while still creating a product acceptable to Aramark's customers, allowing the company to drive down costs. Aramark replicated this process with 163 different items formulated exclusively for corrections. Rather than reducing food costs by the usual 1 cent or so per meal, Aramark took 5 to 9 cents off—while maintaining or even improving quality.[61]

In most countries, government organizations are a major buyer of goods and services. They typically require suppliers to submit bids and often award the contract to the lowest bidder, sometimes making allowance for suppliers known for superior quality or for completing contracts on time. Governments may also buy on a negotiated-contract basis, primarily for complex projects with major R&D costs and risks and projects for which there is little competition.

Because their spending decisions are subject to public review, government organizations require considerable paperwork from suppliers, who often complain about bureaucracy, regulations, decision-making delays, and frequent shifts in procurement staff. Different types of agencies—defense, civilian, intelligence—have different needs, priorities, purchasing styles, and time frames. In addition, vendors often do not pay enough attention to cost justification, a major activity for government procurement professionals. Companies hoping to become government contractors need to help government agencies see the bottom-line impact of products. Demonstrating useful experience and successful past performance through case studies, especially with other government organizations, can be influential.

Just as companies provide government agencies with guidelines about how best to purchase and use their products, governments provide would-be suppliers with detailed guidelines describing how to sell to the government. Failure to follow the guidelines or to fill out forms and contracts correctly can create a legal nightmare.

Fortunately for businesses of all sizes, the federal government has been trying to simplify the contracting procedure and make bidding more attractive. Reforms place more emphasis on buying off-the-shelf rather than customized items, communicating with vendors online to eliminate paperwork, and debriefing losing vendors to improve their chances of winning the next time around.

Several federal agencies that act as purchasing agents for the rest of the government have launched web-based catalogs that allow authorized defense and civilian agencies to buy everything from medical and office supplies to clothing online. The General Services Administration (GSA), for example, not only sells stocked merchandise through its website but also creates direct links between buyers and contract suppliers. A good starting point for any work with the U.S. government is to make sure the company is in the System for Award Management (SAM) database, which collects, validates, stores, and disseminates data in support of agency acquisitions.

summary

1. Organizational buying is the process by which formal organizations establish the need for purchased products and services, and then identify, evaluate, and choose among alternative brands and suppliers. The business market consists of all the organizations that acquire goods and services used in the production of other products or services that are sold, rented, or supplied to others.
2. Compared with consumer markets, business markets generally have fewer and larger buyers, a closer customer–supplier relationship, and more geographically concentrated buyers. Demand in the business market is derived from demand in the consumer market and fluctuates with the business cycle. Nonetheless, the total demand for many business goods and services is quite price inelastic.
3. The buying center is the decision-making unit of a buying organization. It consists of initiators, users, influencers, deciders, approvers, buyers, and gatekeepers. To influence these parties, marketers must consider environmental, organizational, interpersonal, and individual factors.
4. Successful business-to-business marketing requires that marketers determine not only the types of companies on which to focus their selling efforts but also whom to concentrate on within the buying centers in those organizations. In developing selling efforts, business marketers can also consider their customers' customers, or end users.
5. The buying process consists of eight stages: problem recognition, need description, product specification, supplier search, proposal solicitation, supplier selection, contract negotiation, and performance review. Business marketers must ensure that the value of their offerings comes through at each stage of the buying process.
6. Business-to-business marketers are using a variety of marketing tools to attract and retain customers. They are strengthening their brands and using technology and other communication tools to develop effective marketing programs. They are also using systems selling and are adding services to provide customers added value.
7. Business marketers must form strong bonds and relationships with their customers. Building trust is one prerequisite to enjoying healthy long-term relationships. *Trust* depends on factors such as the firm's perceived competence, integrity, honesty, and benevolence. Business marketers need to be aware of the role of professional purchasers and their influencers, the need for multiple sales calls, and the importance of direct purchasing, reciprocity, and leasing.
8. The institutional market consists of schools, hospitals, retirement communities, nursing homes, prisons, and other institutions that provide goods and services to people in their care. Buyers for government organizations tend to require a great deal of paperwork from their vendors and to favor open bidding and domestic companies. Suppliers must be prepared to adapt their offers to the special needs and procedures found in institutional and government markets.

marketing SPOTLIGHT

udaan

udaan, India's fastest growing B2B e-commerce start up, was founded in 2016 by former Flipkart executives—Amod Malaviya, Vaibhav Gupta and Sujeet Kumar. The logistics and supply chain related challenges faced by Flipkart to deliver products to customers in small towns and rural markets prompted the founders to set up udaan.[62] Launched as an online platform, it helps businesses by solving India's core trading problems involving access to good quality mass products and trade credit availability. udaan enables the small and medium enterprises (SMEs) to grow by connecting retailers, traders, and wholesalers from India's small towns with manufacturers and brand owners.[63] The company is accelerating domestic trade through its full-stack online marketplace with digital tools for brands, retailers and manufacturers to discover, trade and grow their business. udaan has a network of over 3 million retailers and 25,0000–30,000 sellers across 1000 + cities in the country covering over 12,000 pin codes undertaking over 5 million transactions per month, making udaan a leader in the B2B eCommerce business.

Entrepreneurs and producers use the platform to market and sell products while leveraging udaan's credit and financing plans to boost capacity. Retailers can easily access credit up to ₹5 lakhs to meet working capital needs and improve cash flows.[64]

The founders invested almost half a year in 2016 studying the market challenges faced by retailers in managing the supply chain, cash flows and accessing information on product availability and price. Launched after extensive research, the beta site was fine-tuned for a year by inviting manufacturers and retailers to trade on the platform. Incorporating the users' experiences, learnings and insights into their platform,

(continued)

Source: ©udaan, used with permission

logistics and delivery system led to rapid adoption when the online platform finally rolled out its services in 2017.[65]

Offering logistics at low rates helped udaan build strong relationships with the buying and selling communities and assess demand for mass produced products like staples, garments, and electronics in different markets. Quality products at low prices fueled growth and soon the company was able to establish its presence across the country. Daily doorstep deliveries, safe and secure payment interface, easy returns, and credit facilities made udaan a perfect partner for retailers from small towns. The firm's ability to source directly from mass producers eliminates multiple intermediaries, the savings from this can be passed on to retailers as low procurement costs boosts margins.

Recognizing the need for quick and easy access to low-cost funds, udaan obtained a license to operate as a non-banking finance company (NBFC)—udaan Capital—for offering loans to its users. Retailers, who earlier depended on money lenders, could now be offered credit to meet their working capital needs at significantly lower rates. In addition, the platform usage and transaction history allows udaan to assess the financial health and risk of sellers as well as retailers, based on which the app offers them working capital finance and loans for capacity enhancement and expansion. udaan Capital has lent around $1 billion through its lending platform to over 200,000 merchants.[66] These fast-rotating loans, with tenures of 1-8 weeks, carry very limited credit risk as retailers use them for buying goods from udaan itself. Merchants can also use the online tools in the app for accounting, order management and payment management too.

udaan follows a commission-based model that charges the sellers a percentage of their revenue generated on its platform. Sellers promote their catalogue on the udaan platform to attract retailers and grow their business. The firm continues to charge subsidized costs for logistics.

Acceptance of a digital platform by small and medium enterprises was one of the key challenges faced by the company initially. Its field force created awareness and educated business owners about the benefits of digital tools before convincing them to register and conduct transactions on udaan's app. Gaining customer's trust for digital payments was another key challenge. udaan made the know your customer (KYC) norms mandatory to enable safe and secure payment on its network. Public campaigns, under the government's Digital India initiatives, as well as onset of the pandemic resulted in faster adoption adoption of digital payments.

(*continued*)

Establishing a viable supply chain and logistics network to reach small towns and rural areas was a major challenge. So the company set up udaan Express to expand its reach to small towns. Now its extensive supply chain and logistics system enables daily deliveries in over 1000 towns. The network includes 200 warehouses providing over 10 million square feet of storage space, equivalent to 175 football fields in size.

udaan's user-friendly mobile app is designed to work with low speed and unreliable Internet connectivity in rural areas. Its lite applications can be operated by users with low-speed data connections. Growing use of mobile apps along with affordable data packages complemented the rapid adoption of online and app services offered by udaan.

While retailers can choose to buy from traditional wholesalers and distributors, or from e-commerce giants like Amazon, Flipkart and retail specialists like ZoomTail, BigTrade, TradeKosh with similar offerings; udaan's scale, extensive network, lending capabilities and relationship management helps increase retailers' loyalty udaan creates value by growing the business of its users who are treated as business partners.[67] Its business model, based on volume of business handled, committed to growing SMEs and retailers at its core with excellent customer service, economies of scale and support offerings gives udaan an edge over competition. Almost 90% of udaan's retailers place 10–12 repeat orders per month. from a catalogue of over 2500 brands and half a million products.[68]

Product categories have eventually expanded and spans across segments such as lifestyle, electronics, home & kitchen, staples, packaged goods, medicines, and general merchandise. The company has transformed into a full stack trading platform offering marketplace, logistics, and lending services to its users, and has raised over $1 billion from global investors–DST Global, GGV Capital, Lightspeed Venture Partners, Altimeter Capital and Tencent.

The company currently handles gross merchandise value (GMV) worth $4.5 billion.[69] Expertise, backed by a strong and shared vision, has created a professionally run institution that encourages speed, rapid experimentation, and potential learning. As the organization rapidly scales up to tap a $100 billion GMV opportunity, it continues to invest in boosting agility, efficiency, innovation and customer centricity. The strong foundation—of sheer talent, superb technological know-how and visionary leadership —is expected to enable udaan achieve its aim of transforming India's over $1 trillion trade market into a digitized super hub.

Questions

1. What factors have contributed to udaan's market success?
2. How does udaan create value in business markets?
3. Which of the three offerings—marketplace, logistics and financing—should udaan prioritize in the future? Why?

marketing SPOTLIGHT

Salesforce.com

Salesforce.com, Inc. is a customer relationship management company that provides cloud-based applications as a service. CRM applications help companies manage customer data, track customer interactions, forecast sales, and facilitate many other business functions. Former Oracle executive Marc Benioff founded Salesforce.com in 1999 with the motto "The End of Software," which positioned the web-based CRM platform as a simpler and more efficient alternative to traditional packaged software licenses. Four years after the company launch, Salesforce.com had become the world's largest CRM software provider.

Prior to the launch of Salesforce.com, CRM software offered by companies such as Oracle, SAP, and Siebel Systems were sold as licenses. This software included functions such as sales management, call centers, and customer support. CRM software was installed and configured on the purchaser's premises by IT companies such as PwC, IBM, and Arthur Andersen. This system posed many difficulties for customers.

Source: Courtesy of Salesforce.com.

The first issue was that CRM software was expensive. For example, a CRM software license for a company of 200 users cost approximately $350,000. In addition to the licensing fees, companies had to spend money on hardware,

(*continued*)

$45,625 ($125 × 365) annually. Given an investment of $90,000 per plane, it would take two years for the service on each plane to break even.

- Offering ultra-high-speed Wi-Fi service would strengthen American Airlines' image as an innovative and progressive carrier and earn it some new passengers and customer goodwill.

The American Airlines managers who commissioned the research need to weigh the evidence. If their confidence in the findings is low, they may decide against introducing ultra-high-speed Wi-Fi service. If they are predisposed to launching it, the findings support their inclination. They may even decide to study the issue further and do more research. The decision is theirs, but rigorously done research provides them with insight into the matter.

When analyzing the available information and making a decision, it is important to draw a line between market data and market insights. Information is not knowledge, noted Albert Einstein. Likewise, market data alone are typically is not very useful unless they offer insights that improve managers' understanding of the problem and enhance the cost-effectiveness of their actions. Thus, interpreting the data and relating them to the problem at hand play a crucial role in managerial decision making.

Measuring Market Demand

Understanding the marketing environment and conducting marketing research can help to identify marketing opportunities. The company must then measure and forecast the size, growth, and profit potential of each new opportunity. Sales forecasts prepared by marketing are used by finance to raise cash for investment and operations; by manufacturing to establish capacity and output; by purchasing to acquire the right amount of supplies; and by human resources to hire the needed workers. If the forecast is off the mark, the company will face excess or inadequate inventory. Because it is based on estimates of demand, managers need to define exactly what they mean by "market demand."

DuPont's Performance Materials group knew that even when DuPont Tyvek had the dominant share of the $100-million market for air-barrier membranes in construction, there was greater opportunity to tap into the entire multi-billion-dollar U.S. home construction market with additional products and services.

KEY CONCEPTS IN DEMAND MEASUREMENT

The major concepts in demand measurement are market/company demand, market forecast, company sales forecast, market potential, and company sales potential. We discuss these concepts in more detail next.

Market demand for an offering is the total volume that could be bought by a defined customer group in a defined geographic area in a defined time period in a defined marketing environment under a defined marketing program.

Company demand is the company's estimated share of market demand at alternative levels of company marketing effort in a given time period. It depends on how the company's products, services, prices, and communications are perceived relative to those of competitors. Other things equal, the company's market share depends on the relative scale and effectiveness of its market expenditures. As noted previously, marketing model builders have developed sales response functions to measure how a company's sales are affected by its marketing expenditure level, marketing mix, and marketing effectiveness.[25]

The market demand corresponding to the actual level of industry marketing expenditure is called the **market forecast**.

The **company sales forecast** is the expected level of company sales based on a chosen marketing plan and an assumed marketing environment. Two other concepts are important here. A *sales quota* is the sales goal set for a product line, company division, or sales representative. It is primarily a managerial device for defining and stimulating sales effort, and it is often set slightly higher than estimated sales to stretch the sales force's effort. A *sales budget* is a conservative estimate of the expected volume of sales, primarily for making current purchasing, production, and cash flow decisions. It's based on the need to avoid excessive risk and is generally set slightly lower than the sales forecast.

Total **market potential** consists of the *maximum* sales available to all firms in an industry during a given period, under a given level of industry marketing effort, and under extant environmental conditions. The market forecast shows *expected* market demand, not maximum market demand. For the latter, we need to visualize the level of market demand resulting from a very high level of industry marketing expenditure, where further increases in marketing effort would have little effect. Market potential is the limit approached by market demand as industry marketing expenditures approach infinity for a given marketing environment. The phrase "for a given market environment" is crucial.

Consider the market potential for automobiles. It's higher during prosperity than during a recession. A common way to estimate total market potential is to multiply the potential number of buyers by the average quantity each buyer purchases and then by the price.

Company sales potential is the sales limit approached by company demand as company marketing effort increases relative to that of competitors. The absolute limit of company demand is, of course, the market potential. The two would be equal if the company captured 100 percent of the market. In most cases, company sales potential is less than the market potential, even when company marketing expenditures increase considerably. Each competitor has a hard core of loyal buyers unresponsive to other companies' efforts to woo them, which makes it challenging to capture all competitors' customers in the market.

FORECASTING MARKET DEMAND

Forecasting is the art of anticipating what buyers are likely to do under a given set of conditions. For major consumer durables such as appliances, research organizations conduct periodic surveys of consumer buying intentions, asking questions like *Do you intend to buy an automobile within the next six months?* Surveys also inquire into consumers' present and future personal finances and expectations about the economy. They combine bits of information into a consumer confidence measure (Conference Board) or a consumer sentiment measure (Survey Research Center of the University of Michigan). In most markets, good forecasting is a key factor in success.

Companies commonly prepare a macroeconomic forecast first, followed by an industry forecast, followed by a company sales forecast. The macroeconomic forecast projects inflation, unemployment, interest rates, consumer spending, business investment, government expenditures, net exports, and other variables. The end result is a forecast of gross domestic product (GDP) that the firm uses, along with other environmental indicators, to forecast industry sales. The company derives its sales forecast by assuming it will win a certain market share.

How do firms develop forecasts? They may create their own or buy forecasts from outside sources, such as marketing research firms that interview customers, distributors, and other knowledgeable parties. Specialized forecasting firms produce long-range forecasts of particular macroenvironmental components such as population, natural resources, and technology. Examples are IHS Global Insight (a merger of Data Resources and Wharton Econometric Forecasting Associates), Forrester Research, and the Gartner Group. Futurist research firms such as the Institute for the Future, Hudson Institute, and the Futures Group produce speculative scenarios.

All forecasts are built on one of three information bases: what people say, what people do, or what people have done. Using what people say requires surveying buyers' intentions, composites of sales force opinions, and expert opinion. Building a forecast on what people do means putting the product into a test market to measure buyer response. To use the final basis—what people have done—firms analyze records of past buying behavior or use time-series analysis or statistical demand analysis.

- **Industry Sales and Market Shares.** The industry trade association will often collect and publish total industry sales, although it usually does not list individual company sales separately. With this information, however, each company can evaluate its own performance against that of the industry as a whole. If a company's sales are increasing by 5 percent a year and industry sales are increasing by 10 percent, the company is losing its relative standing in the industry.

  Another way to estimate sales is to buy reports from a marketing research firm that audits total sales and brand sales. Nielsen Media Research audits retail sales in various supermarket and drugstore product categories. A company can purchase this information and compare its performance to that of the total industry or of any competitor to see whether it is gaining or losing share, overall or by brand. Because distributors typically will not supply information about how many competitors' products they are selling, business-to-business marketers operate with less knowledge of their market share results.
- **Survey of Buyers' Intentions.** For business buying, research firms can carry out buyer-intention surveys for plant, equipment, and materials, usually falling within a 10 percent margin of error. These surveys are useful in estimating demand for industrial products, consumer durables, product purchases that require advance planning, and new products. Their value increases to the extent that buyers are few, the cost of reaching them is low, and they have clear intentions that they willingly disclose and implement. One popular survey-based statistical technique used in market research is conjoint analysis, which helps determine how consumers value different attributes (product features, service benefits, and price) that make up a particular offering.[26]
- **Composite of Sales Force Opinions.** When interviewing buyers is impractical, the company may ask its sales representatives to estimate their future sales. Sales force forecasts do yield a

number of benefits. Sales reps might have better insight into developing trends than any other group, and forecasting might give them greater confidence in their sales quotas and more incentive to achieve them. A "grassroots" forecasting procedure provides detailed estimates broken down by product, territory, customer, and sales rep.

Few companies use these estimates without making some adjustments, however. Sales representatives might be pessimistic or optimistic, they might not know how the company's marketing plans will influence future sales in their territory, and they might deliberately underestimate demand so the company will set a low sales quota. To encourage better estimating, the company could offer incentives or assistance, such as information about marketing plans or how past forecasts compared with actual sales.

- **Expert Opinion.** Companies can also obtain forecasts from experts, including dealers, distributors, suppliers, marketing consultants, and trade associations. Dealer estimates are subject to the same strengths and weaknesses as sales force estimates. Many companies buy economic and industry forecasts from well-known economic-forecasting firms that have more data available and offer more forecasting expertise.

  Occasionally, companies will invite a group of experts to prepare a forecast. The experts exchange views and produce an estimate as a group (*group-discussion method*) or individually, in which case another analyst might combine the results into a single estimate (*pooling of individual estimates*). Further rounds of estimating and refining follow (the Delphi method).[27]
- **Past-Sales Analysis.** Firms can develop sales forecasts on the basis of past sales. *Time-series analysis* breaks past sales into four components (trend, cycle, seasonal, and erratic) and projects them into the future. *Exponential smoothing* projects the next period's sales by combining and the most recent sales, giving more weight to the latter. *Statistical demand analysis* measures the impact of a set of causal factors (such as income, marketing expenditures, and price) on the sales level. *Econometric analysis* builds sets of equations that describe a system and statistically derives the different parameters that make up the equations. Advanced machine learning techniques are revolutionizing marketing by automating and speeding up tasks that range from analyzing sales and revenue to spotting industry trends.
- **Market-Test Method.** When buyers don't plan their purchases carefully or experts are unavailable or unreliable, a direct market test can help forecast new-product sales or the sales of established products in a new distribution channel or territory.

Measuring Marketing Productivity

Although we can easily quantify marketing expenses and investments as inputs in the short run, the resulting outputs (such as broader brand awareness, enhanced brand image, greater customer loyalty, and improved new-product prospects) may take months or years to manifest themselves. Meanwhile, internal changes within the organization and external changes in the marketing environment may coincide with the marketing expenditures, making it hard to isolate their effects.[28]

Nevertheless, marketing research must assess the efficiency and effectiveness of marketing activities. Two complementary approaches to measuring marketing productivity are (1) *marketing metrics* to assess marketing effects and (2) *marketing-mix modeling* to estimate causal relationships and measure how marketing activity affects outcomes. **Marketing dashboards** are a structured way to disseminate the insights gleaned from these two approaches.

MARKETING METRICS

Marketers employ a wide variety of measures to assess marketing effects.[29] Marketing metrics is the set of measures that help marketers quantify, compare, and interpret their performance.[30]

> The CMO of Mary Kay cosmetics would focus on four long-term brand strength metrics—market awareness, consideration, trial, and 12-month beauty consultant productivity—as well as a number of short-term, program-specific metrics such as ad impressions, website traffic, and purchase conversion.
>
> The VP of marketing at Virgin America would look at a broad set of online metrics—cost per acquisition, cost per click, and cost per thousand page impressions (CPM). She would also look at total dollars driven by natural and paid search and online display advertising, as well as at tracking results and other metrics from the offline world.

Marketers choose one or more measures based on the particular issues or problems they face. Mindbody, a Web-based business management software provider for wellness and beauty industries worldwide, tracks numerous online analytics, including landing-page conversions, click-through rates for online ads, and rankings on Google search. In addition, Mindbody monitors the following online metrics on a weekly basis: (1) *Website analytics* detail site navigation and online interaction. (2) *Social media presence* shows demographic and geographic responses to social media channels across different markets. (3) *Permission marketing statistics* measure interactions and engagement with consumers from automated emails.

London Business School's Tim Ambler believes that firms can split evaluation of marketing performance into two parts: short-term results and changes in brand equity.[31] Short-term results often reflect profit-and-loss concerns as shown by sales turnover, shareholder value, or some combination of the two. Brand-equity measures could include customer awareness, attitudes, and behaviors; market share; relative price premium; number of complaints; distribution and availability; total number of customers; perceived quality, and loyalty and retention.[32]

Companies can also monitor an extensive set of internal metrics, such as innovation. For example, 3M tracks the proportion of sales resulting from its recent innovations. Ambler also recommends developing employee measures and metrics, arguing that "end users are the ultimate customers, but your own staff are your first; you need to measure the health of the internal market."

MARKETING-MIX MODELING

Marketing accountability also means that marketers must more precisely estimate the effects of different marketing investments. **Marketing-mix models** analyze data from a variety of sources such as retailer scanner data, company shipment data, as well as pricing, media, and promotion expenditure data, to understand more precisely the effects of specific marketing activities.[33] To deepen understanding, marketers can conduct multivariate analyses, such as regression analysis, to investigate how each marketing element influences marketing outcomes such as brand sales or market share.

Especially popular with packaged-goods marketers such as Procter & Gamble, Clorox, and Colgate, the findings from marketing-mix modeling help allocate or reallocate expenditures. Analyses explore which part of ad budgets are wasted, what optimal spending levels are, and what minimum investment levels should be.

Although marketing-mix modeling helps to isolate effects, it is less effective at assessing how different marketing elements work in combination. Wharton's Dave Reibstein also notes that it has three other shortcomings:[34] (1) Marketing-mix modeling focuses on incremental growth instead of on baseline sales or long-term effects. (2) The integration of important metrics such as customer satisfaction, awareness, and brand equity into marketing-mix modeling is limited. (3) Marketing-mix modeling generally fails to incorporate metrics related to competitors, the trade, or the sales force (the average business spends far more on the sales force and trade promotion than on advertising or consumer promotion).

MARKETING DASHBOARDS

Firms also employ organizational processes and systems to make sure they maximize the value of all these different metrics. Management can assemble a summary set of relevant internal and external measures in a marketing dashboard for synthesis and interpretation. Marketing dashboards are like the instrument panel in a car or plane, visually displaying real-time indicators to ensure proper functioning. Formally, marketing dashboards are "a concise set of interconnected performance drivers to be viewed in common throughout the organization."[35] Company input to the marketing dashboard should include two key market-based scorecards: one that reflects performance and one that provides possible early warning signals.

Dashboards are only as good as the information on which they're based, but sophisticated visualization tools are helping bring data alive. Color-coding, symbols, and different types of charts, tables, and gauges are easy to use and effective. Some companies are also appointing marketing controllers to review budget items and expenses. Increasingly, these controllers use business intelligence software to create digital versions of marketing dashboards that aggregate data from internal and external sources.

Marketing dashboards provide all the up-to-the-minute information necessary to run the business operations for a company—such as sales versus forecast, distribution channel effectiveness, brand-equity evolution, and human capital development. An effective dashboard will focus thinking, improve internal communications, and reveal where marketing investments are paying off and where they aren't. There are four common measurement "pathways" marketers pursue today.[36]

- The *customer metrics pathway* looks at how prospects become customers, from awareness to preference to trial to repeat purchase, or some less linear model. This area also examines how the customer experience contributes to the perception of value and competitive advantage.

- The *unit metrics pathway* reflects what marketers know about sales of product/service units—how much is sold by product line and/or by geography, the marketing cost per unit sold as an efficiency yardstick, and where and how margin is optimized in terms of characteristics of the product line or distribution channel.
- The *cash-flow metrics pathway* focuses on how well marketing expenditures are achieving short-term returns. Program and campaign ROI models measure the immediate impact or net present value of profits expected from a given investment.
- The *brand metrics pathway* tracks the longer-term impact of marketing through brand-equity measures that assess both the perceptual health of the brand from customer and prospective customer perspectives and the overall financial health of the brand.

Ideally, over time the number of metrics on the dashboard will be reduced to a few key drivers. Meanwhile, the process of developing and refining the marketing dashboard will undoubtedly raise and resolve many key questions about the business.

Some executives worry that they'll miss the big picture if they focus too much on a set of numbers on a dashboard. Critics are concerned about privacy and the pressure the technique places on employees. But most experts feel the rewards offset the risks.

marketing INSIGHT

Six Ways to Draw New Ideas from Your Customers

Customers—consumers and businesses—can be an effective source for generating new ideas that could lead to successful market offerings. Several popular strategies for gathering insights from current and potential customers are outlined below.

- Observe how customers are using your product. Medtronic, a medical device company, has salespeople and market researchers regularly observe spine surgeons who use their products and competitive products to learn how the company's products can be improved. After living with lower-middle-class families in Mexico City, Procter & Gamble researchers devised Downy Single Rinse, a fabric softener that removed an arduous step from the partly manual laundry process there.
- Ask customers about their problems with your products. Komatsu Heavy Equipment sent a group of engineers and designers to the United States for six months to ride with equipment drivers and learn how to make Komatsu products better. Procter & Gamble, recognizing the frustration of consumers with potato chips that break and are difficult to save after opening the bag, designed Pringles to be firmer and uniform in size so as to be encased in a protective, tennis-ball-type can.
- Ask customers about their dream products. Ask your customers what they want your product to do, even if the ideal sounds impossible. One 70-year-old camera user told Minolta he would like the camera to make his subjects look better and not show their wrinkles and aging. In response, Minolta produced a camera with two lenses, one for rendering softer images of the subjects.
- Actively solicit feedback from customers. Levi Strauss uses youth panels to discuss lifestyles, habits, values, and brand engagements, Cisco runs Customer Forums to improve its offerings, and Harley-Davidson solicits product ideas from its one million H.O.G. (Harley Owners Group) members. P&G's corporate global website includes a Share Your Thoughts section to solicit advice and feedback from customers.
- Form a brand community of enthusiasts who discuss your product. Harley-Davidson and Apple have strong brand enthusiasts and advocates. Sony engages in collaborative dialogs with consumers to co-develop its PlayStation products. LEGO draws on kids and influential adult enthusiasts for feedback on new product concepts in early stages of development.
- Encourage or challenge your customers to change or improve your product. Salesforce.com wants its users to develop and share new software applications using simple programming tools. International Flavors & Fragrances gives a toolkit to its customers to modify specific flavors, which IFF then manufactures. LSI Logic Corporation also provides customers with do-it-yourself toolkits so customers can design their own specialized chips. And BMW posted a toolkit on its website to let customers develop ideas using telematics and in-car online services.[37]

summary

1. Marketing research is all about generating insights. Marketing insights provide diagnostic information about how and why we observe certain effects in the marketplace and what that means to marketers. Good marketing research is characterized by the scientific method, creativity, multiple research methods, accurate model building, cost–benefit analysis, healthy skepticism, and an ethical focus.
2. The marketing research process consists of defining the problem, developing the research plan, collecting information, analyzing the information, and making the decision. In conducting research, firms must decide whether to collect their own (primary) data or use data that already exist (secondary data). They must also choose a research approach (observational, focus group, survey, or behavioral) and research instruments (questionnaires, qualitative measures, or technological devices). In addition, they must decide on a sampling plan, contact methods (online, in person, mail or e-mail, or telephone), and data-mining strategies.
3. To estimate current demand, companies need to determine the size, growth, and profit potential of each market opportunity. To estimate future demand, companies survey buyers' intentions, solicit the input of their sales forces, gather expert opinions, analyze past sales, or engage in market testing. Mathematical models, advanced statistical techniques, and computerized data collection procedures are essential to all types of demand and sales forecasting.
4. Marketing research must assess the efficiency and effectiveness of marketing activities. Two complementary approaches to measuring marketing productivity are (1) marketing metrics to assess marketing effects and (2) marketing-mix modeling to estimate causal relationships and measure how marketing activity affects outcomes. The insights gleaned from these two approaches must be disseminated within the organization. Marketing dashboards provide all the up-to-the-minute information necessary to run the business operations for a company—such as actual sales versus forecast, distribution channel effectiveness, brand-equity evolution, and the development of human capital. Company input to the marketing dashboard should include two key market-based scorecards that reflect performance and provide possible early warning signals.

marketing SPOTLIGHT

IDEO

IDEO is an international design company with studios in North America, Asia, and Europe. It works with a diverse roster of clients across business, governmental, and social sectors to create positive impact through design. IDEO uses a human-centered approach to problem-solving known as design thinking, which prioritizes the needs of people as central drivers in creating products, services, and experiences. IDEO has designed products and services including Apple's first computer mouse; a network of world-class, affordable schools in Peru; and an inclusive and accessible voting system for Los Angeles County.

IDEO has roots dating back to 1978, but took its name in 1991 as a design firm that focused on product design and engineering. Like many other firms, it initially employed engineers from the industrial, electrical, manufacturing, and chemical fields to create and improve client products. However, IDEO set itself apart from other design firms through its multidisciplinary approach and by popularizing design thinking. As IDEO grew, the company took on a greater array of projects and employed people with a much wider breadth of skills. It sought the perspectives of

Source: Courtesy of IDEO

marketers, anthropologists, doctors, teachers, architects, and experts in other fields.

Every aspect of the company—from the organizational structure and physical spaces to the hiring, training, and managing of employees—reflects a set of seven core values that IDEO articulated with the goal of fostering a creative and collaborative community within the company. The values are Talk Less, Do More; Make Others Successful; Learn from Failure; Embrace Ambiguity; Be Optimistic; Collaborate; and Take Ownership. In IDEO offices, the desks of partners and senior leaders are interwoven with the desks of junior designers to create the conditions for

(continued)

collaboration across all levels. Open, flexible spaces allow employees to showcase their prototypes and host brainstorming sessions.

IDEO has applied its design thinking approach to a variety of innovative products, services, and experiences spanning industries and sectors. When Oral-B asked IDEO to design a new toothbrush for young children in 1996, IDEO began by observing kids brushing their teeth. During their observations, IDEO noticed that children hold their toothbrushes differently than adults do. Whereas adults have the fine motor skills to move their toothbrushes with just their fingers, children grip the toothbrush with their fist to move it around. Adult toothbrushes posed problems for children because they were thin and hard to hold. IDEO used this realization to create a toothbrush with a thick, squishy grip. This simple innovation was widely adopted and has become the dominant form-factor for children's toothbrushes.

Another example comes from Los Angeles, where county leaders wanted to revamp their antiquated voting system, which dated back to the 1960s. Los Angeles County hired IDEO to design the concept, look, and feel of its updated system, a modular solution that could adapt over time. With nearly 5 million registered voters, LA County represents the largest voting jurisdiction in the United States. IDEO researchers organized prototyping events at community centers around the county, hearing from voters of all ages and backgrounds. IDEO created a voting system that would be useful and accessible to all types of voters: those who are vision and hearing impaired, are in wheelchairs, have learning disabilities, are unfamiliar with technology, and speak languages other than English. The new system debuted during the 2020 Presidential Primary.

IDEO has also partnered with The North Face to help build the outdoor-product company's brand story in China. The North Face wanted to expand its presence in China but found that the extreme-sport and adventuring narratives used in the company's U.S. brand story did not resonate with Chinese consumers. IDEO researchers found that Chinese consumers responded better to a brand story that encouraged them to escape big-city life and enjoy the relaxing freedom of spending time with others in nature. IDEO researchers and designers helped build the company's Chinese marketing campaign, and they collaborated on digital platforms and in-store displays to attract new customers.

Working with the J.M. Smucker Company, IDEO helped Folgers, America's leading at-home coffee brand, to better connect with a millennial audience. The collaboration resulted in 1850, a brand inspired by the heritage and history of Folgers. IDEO helped design the go-to-market product experience, including packaging, retail, and merchandise. Introduced in 2018, 1850 was considered the top launch in the Coffee Category for 2019.

The one constant behind IDEO's many solutions is its application of human-centered design. IDEO continues to uphold its philosophy that the best design solutions are found by orienting the process around the user's desires and needs. IDEO has applied human-centered design to a multitude of fields, including financial services, nonprofit organizations, brand building, health care, learning and education, and consumer goods.[38]

Questions

1. Why has IDEO been so successful?
2. What is the most difficult challenge that IDEO faces in conducting its research and designing its products?
3. In the end, IDEO creates great solutions for companies that then receive all the credit. Should IDEO try to create more brand awareness for itself? Why or why not?

marketing SPOTLIGHT

LEGO

LEGO is one of the world's most recognizable toys. The small, colorful building blocks have spawned countless sets, figurines, video games, and even movies and theme parks. LEGO is built on a very simple concept: Each block fits together with every other block, which creates an endless combination of buildings, robots, cars, and anything else the user can think of. LEGO employs a design-thinking approach to its product innovation, keeping things fresh with new releases that utilize the colorful bricks in creative ways. In 2017, LEGO became the world's largest toy manufacturer and is one of the strongest brands across all industries.

Source: Hemis/Alamy Stock Photo

The LEGO company began in 1932, in a small shop located in Billund, Denmark. Carpenter Ole Kirk Christiansen sold wooden toys, stepladders, and ironing boards with his

(*continued*)

son Godtfred. Two years later, the pair named their business LEGO, short for the Danish words *leg godt*, which translate to "play well." During the next several years, LEGO expanded its product line to include wooden ducks, clothes hangers, and simple wooden bricks. It wasn't until 1947, when LEGO purchased a plastic injection-molding machine, that it began to mass produce plastic toys that served as the predecessor of the modern LEGO brick. In 1957, LEGO created the interlocking plastic brick, and the following year it introduced the stud-and-tube coupling mechanism that became the model for all future LEGO toys. LEGO bricks became wildly popular among customers, and the company began expanding worldwide in the early 1960s. In 1964 the company started selling sets, which included the parts and instructions to construct a particular model. Soon thereafter, theme sets from movies and books such as the *Harry Potter, Star Wars*, and *Jurassic Park* series became some of the most sought-after children's toys in the world.

LEGO's growth and expansion slowed at the end of the 20th century. Birth rates had declined, and children were less interested in toys that didn't offer instant gratification. The many theme parks that LEGO opened around the world failed to turn a profit because of the company's unfamiliarity with the hospitality industry. LEGO began churning out increasingly complex and unique sets to draw in more customers, but sales failed to grow. The increased complexity of LEGO bricks also made production more complicated and inventory harder to manage. Major retailers ended up with large portions of inventory unsold, even during holiday seasons. In 1998, the company suffered its first financial loss, and by 2003, LEGO was on the verge of bankruptcy.

In 2004, Jorgen Knudstorp was promoted to CEO, only three years after arriving at the company. Knudstorp, who had previously worked at McKinsey & Company, began turning the company around and improving businesses processes, cutting costs, and better managing cash flow, which stabilized the company. To revive the popularity of LEGO toys, Knudstorp focused heavily on innovation and emphasized market and consumer research. Knudstorp believed that in order to rekindle the emotional connection between customers and LEGO toys, LEGO had to deeply understand each customer's desires and behavior.

LEGO's shift toward basing decisions on extensive research reduced complexity in production and ensured the success of its product releases. In 2011, the company launched the LEGO Friends line, an effort to attract more girls to the brand. The company's market research led to the insight that girls preferred to use their LEGO sets for roleplay, whereas boys enjoyed strong narratives and backstories, such as those offered by the Ninjago and Legends of Chima sets. Both girls and boys enjoyed the building aspect of LEGOs. The LEGO Friends line offered more sets and locations like shopping malls, juice bars, and creative labs, so girls could use their figurines to roleplay. The line caught on strongly in markets worldwide, including China, Germany, and the United States.

LEGO also established the Future Lab, a secretive research and development team that is responsible for creating some of its most innovative and successful toy lines ever. Future Lab teams are made up of industrial designers, programmers, marketers, and even master builders, who brainstorm to generate modern products. During an annual one-week field trip to Barcelona, Future Lab teams extensively brainstorm and produce prototypes from the bins of bricks, animation software, and professional-quality digital cameras available. The most successful prototypes generated are pursued back in Denmark, where viable ideas are launched into production. LEGO toy lines created by the Future Lab include LEGO Mindstorms, a robotics platform created in partnership with MIT; LEGO Fusion, an augmented-reality application; and LEGO Architecture, collections that model the world's most famous buildings.

In 2017, LEGO surpassed rival Mattel to become the biggest toy manufacturer in the world. Though LEGO has enjoyed great financial success since its all-time low in 2003, company studies have indicated that kids spend less and less time playing with physical toys every year. In an increasingly digital age, LEGO must continue researching its customers and experimenting with innovative product lines to stay at the top of the toy industry.[39]

Questions

1. How does LEGO manage to constantly reinvent its business?
2. What role did marketing research play in LEGO's market success?
3. What differentiates LEGO from its competitors? Is LEGO's competitive advantage sustainable?

CHAPTER 6

Identifying Market Segments and Target Customers

Taj Hotels adopted a new branding strategy to realign its brandscape with distinct brands, each with its own value proposition to suit the different needs of its customer segments

Source: ©THE INDIAN HOTELS COMPANY LIMITED, used with permission

Companies cannot connect with all customers in large, broad, or diverse markets. They need to identify the market segments they can serve effectively. Identifying these market segments requires a keen understanding of consumer behavior and careful strategic thinking about what makes each segment unique and different. Identifying and uniquely satisfying the right market segments are key to marketing success. Taj Hotels is one of many companies trying to come to grips with the younger Millennial consumer.

>>> The Tata group's hospitality arm, Indian Hotels operates one of the most recognizable and decorated chains of luxury hotels and resorts under the brand—Taj Hotels. This iconic company, with a legacy of over hundred years, suffered a double whammy. First, it lost its leadership crown to Marriott group in terms of greater number of rooms.[1] Second, it is facing the brunt of the rapidly growing popularity of digital-first apps like Airbnb and OYO among the profitable millennials.[2] The company has taken conscious steps to better understand this customer base ranging between the age group of 25–35 years—a segment that typically takes at least two annual holidays in 5-star hotels or luxury stays, including at least one international. In the process, the company discovered their growing need for experientials and a seamless integrated digital experience.

The company started offering curated packages that consists of tailored services and unique experiences to match guests' expectations. Personalizing the experiences, through a deep understanding, created opportunities for guests to immerse in the local art, craft and culture, interact with the locals and enjoy unique experiences from dining to wellness. Aligning with the growing trend of guests using digital and social media platforms during all stages of their journey from planning, booking, and communicating with hotels, the company invested heavily in digital infrastructure. Integrating all its digital touch points, including the upgraded website, a new mobile app and creating active social media handles on Facebook and Instagram, helped improve the guest experience while planning, booking, pre-arrival, stay, review sharing and loyalty program. Its new social media command centre—Taj.Live—enabled social media listening, omni-channel trend tracking and analysis to improve engagements with its target segments.

In 2017 the group adopted a new branding strategy to realign its brandscape with distinct brands, each with its own value proposition to suit the different needs of its customer segments.[3] The new portfolio includes 'Taj Hotels, Resorts and Palaces'—positioned as the hallmark of luxury hospitality, 'SeleQtions'—a named collection of landmark hotels with legacy and charm for the experiential traveler to celebrate individuality by offering unique experiences, 'Vivanta'— a smart collective of sophisticated upscale hotels for smart travelers, and 'Ginger'—a chain of lean luxe hotels for millennials and centennials to seamlessly switch between work and play. Its branded homestay service—'amã Stays & Trails'—offers a group of heritage bungalows, guesthouses and home-stays at unique locations across the country.

All these initiatives helped the company win the coveted rank as the strongest global hotel brand in 2021 by Brand Finance, the UK-based brand valuation consultancy.[4]

To compete more effectively, many companies are now embracing target marketing. Instead of scattering their marketing efforts, they're focusing on those consumers they have the greatest chance of satisfying. Effective targeting requires that marketers:

1. Identify distinct groups of buyers who differ in their needs and wants (segmentation).
2. Select one or more market segments to enter (targeting).
3. For each target segment, establish, communicate, and deliver the right benefit(s) for the company's market offering (developing a value proposition and positioning).

This chapter will focus on the first two steps: how to segment the market and identify target customers. Chapter 10 discusses the third step: how to develop a value proposition and positioning to build viable market offerings that grow over time and withstand competitive attacks.

Identifying Target Customers

There are many techniques for identifying target customers.[5] Once the firm has identified its market opportunities, it must decide how many and which ones to target. Marketers are increasingly combining several variables in an effort to identify smaller, better-defined target groups in order to develop an offering that can fulfill these customers' needs better than the competition. Thus, a bank may not

Learning Objectives After studying this chapter you should be able to:

6.1 Explain the essence of targeting.

6.2 Define the key principles of strategic targeting.

6.3 Describe how to effectively communicate and deliver offerings to target customers.

6.4 Explain how to develop strategies to target multiple market segments.

6.5 Describe how to segment consumer markets.

6.6 Describe how to segment business markets.

only identify a group of wealthy retired adults but also, within that group, distinguish several segments depending on current income, assets, savings, and risk preferences. This has led some market researchers to advocate a *needs-based targeting approach.*

Targeting is the process of identifying customers for whom the company will optimize its offering. Simply put, targeting reflects the company's choice of which customers it will prioritize and which customers it will ignore when designing, communicating, and delivering its offering. The logic of identifying target customers and the strategic and tactical aspects of this process are discussed in more detail in the following sections.

THE LOGIC OF TARGETING

In **mass marketing**, the firm ignores segment differences and goes after the whole market with one offer. It designs a marketing program for a product with a superior image that can be sold to the broadest number of buyers via mass distribution and mass communications. Undifferentiated marketing is appropriate when all consumers have roughly the same preferences and the market shows no natural segments. Henry Ford epitomized this strategy when he offered the Model-T Ford in one color, black.

The argument for mass marketing is that it creates the largest potential market, which leads to the lowest costs, which in turn can lead to lower prices or higher margins. The narrow product line keeps down the costs of research and development, production, inventory, transportation, marketing research, advertising, and product management. The undifferentiated communication program also reduces costs. However, many critics point to the increased splintering of the market and the proliferation of marketing channels and communication, which make it difficult and increasingly expensive to reach a mass audience.

When different groups of consumers have different needs and wants, marketers can define multiple segments. The company can often better design, price, disclose, and deliver the product or service and also fine-tune the marketing program and activities to better counter competitors' marketing. In targeted marketing, the firm sells different products to all the different segments of the market. Cosmetics firm Estée Lauder markets brands that appeal to women (and men) of different tastes: The flagship brand, the original Estée Lauder, appeals to older consumers; Clinique and M·A·C cater to young women; Aveda to aromatherapy enthusiasts; and Origins to eco-conscious consumers who want cosmetics made from natural ingredients.[6]

The ultimate level of targeting is the *one-to-one approach* in which each market segment comprises a single customer.[7] As companies have grown proficient at gathering information about individual customers and business partners (suppliers, distributors, retailers), and as their factories have been designed more flexibly, they have increased their ability to individualize market offerings, messages, and media.

Consumers can buy customized jeans, cowboy boots, and bicycles that cost thousands of dollars. Peter Wagner started Wagner Custom Skis in Telluride, Colorado, in 2006. His company now makes about 1,000 snowboards and pairs of skis a year, with prices that start at $1,750. Each ski or snowboard is unique and precisely fitted to the preferences and riding style of its owner. Strategies such as using NASA-like materials and making adjustments of thousands of an inch send a strong performance message, matched by the attractive aesthetic of the skis.[8]

One-to-one marketing is not for every company. It works best for firms that normally collect a great deal of individual customer information and carry a lot of products that can be cross-sold, need periodic replacement or upgrading, and offer high value. For others, the required investment in information collection, hardware, and software may exceed the payout. The cost of goods is raised beyond what the customer is willing to pay.

Mass customization is the ability of a company to meet each customer's requirements—to prepare on a mass basis individually designed products, services, programs, and communications.[9] MINI Cooper's online "configurator" enables prospective buyers to virtually select and try out many options for a new MINI. Coke's Freestyle vending machine allows users to choose from more than 100 Coke brands or custom flavors, and even to create their own.

Services are also a natural setting for customized marketing. Airlines, hotels, and rental car agencies are attempting to offer more individualized experiences. Even political candidates are embracing customized marketing. On Facebook, politicians can find an individual's preferences by observing the groups or causes he or she joins. Then, using Facebook's ad platform, the campaign team can test hundreds of ad messages designed to reflect the theme of these other interests. Hikers may get an

Source: Scott Keeler/ZUMAPRESS/Newscom

<< As part of a broad trend toward personalization, Coca-Cola has introduced Freestyle dispensing machines that allow users to customize their soft drink choices.

environmentally themed message; members of particular religious groups may get a Christian-themed message.

STRATEGIC AND TACTICAL TARGETING

Targeting can be strategic or tactical based on the criteria a company uses to zero in on target customers. **Strategic targeting** focuses on customers whose needs the company can fulfill by ensuring that its offerings are customized to their needs. *Tactical targeting* identifies the ways in which the company can reach these strategically important customers. Strategic and tactical targeting are not mutually exclusive; they are two integrally related components of the process of identifying target customers.

The goals of strategic and tactical targeting, however, do differ. Strategic targeting calls for a trading market size that yields a better fit between the offering's benefits and the customers' needs. Thus, rather than trying to reach the target audience with one offering that endeavors to lure a wide range of customers with diverse needs, strategic targeting is based on the deliberate choice to ignore some customers to better serve other customers with an offering that matches their specific needs. Tactical targeting takes the opposite approach. Rather than excluding any potential customers, tactical targeting strives to reach *all* strategically important customers in an effective and cost-efficient manner.

Because of their divergent goals, strategic and tactical targeting have different priorities. Whereas the focus of strategic targeting is on the *value* that the company can create for and capture from target customers, tactical targeting concentrates on the *means* the company can use to reach these customers. Together, strategic and tactical targeting seek to answer two questions, the first focusing on strategy and the second on tactics: *Who* are the customers that the company can establish a mutually beneficial relationship with? and *How* can the company reach these customers most effectively and efficiently?

The two aspects of targeting, strategic and tactical, are discussed in more detail in the following sections.

Strategic Targeting

Identification of target customers is directed by the company's capability to develop an offering that can meet the needs of these customers more effectively than the competition, while also creating value for the company.[10] This requires that strategic targeting start with pinpointing the customer need(s) that the company's offering will be designed to fulfill.

Effective strategic targeting requires the company to make an important but difficult tradeoff: the calculated decision to deliberately forgo some potential customers to more effectively meet the needs of other customers. Companies have failed because of their unwillingness to sacrifice market breadth and focus only on customers for whom their offering could create superior value. Targeting is not based solely on identifying customers that the company intends to serve: It must also be based on a meaningful assessment of customers it deliberately chooses *not* to serve, and without such an assessment, a viable market strategy is impossible.

A manager must address two key questions when evaluating the viability of a particular customer segment: *Can the company create superior value for these customers? Can these customers create superior value for the company?*

The answer to the first question hinges on the degree to which company resources are compatible with target customers' needs. The company must have the assets and competencies necessary to design an offer that creates customer value. The answer to the second question is determined by the attractiveness of the target customers. That is, do they have the ability to create value for the company? These two principles of strategic targeting—target compatibility and target attractiveness—are discussed in greater detail in the following sections.

TARGET COMPATIBILITY

Target compatibility is a reflection of the company's ability to outdo the competition in fulfilling the needs of target customers—in other words, to create superior customer value. Target compatibility is a function of the company's resources and its capacity to use these resources in a way that creates value for target customers. The right resources are important because they allow the company to create an offering that can deliver superior value to customers in a manner that is both effective and cost efficient.

Essential resources for the success of a company's targeting strategy include factors such as:

- **Business infrastructure**, which includes assets such as manufacturing infrastructure that houses the company's production facilities and equipment; service infrastructure like call centers and customer relationship management solutions; supply-chain infrastructure that includes procurement infrastructure and processes; and management infrastructure that encompasses the company's business management culture.
- **Access to scarce resources** gives the company a distinct competitive edge because it restricts the strategic options of competitors. For example, securing unique natural resources, prime manufacturing and retail locations, and a memorable web domain can be highly beneficial for the company.
- **Skilled employees** with technological, operational, and business expertise—especially those involved in research and development, education, and consulting—are prime strategic assets.
- **Technological expertise**, the expertise required to develop an offering that addresses a particular customer need, includes a company's proprietary processes, its technological processes, and its intellectual property such as patents and trade secrets.
- **Strong brands** enhance value by conferring unique identification on the offering and generating meaningful associations that create value over and above the value created by the offering's attributes. Brands are of particular importance in commoditized industries where only minor differences exist among the competitive products and services.
- **Collaborator networks** include vertical networks of collaborators in the company's supply chain (suppliers and distributors) and horizontal networks of research and development, manufacturing, and promotion collaborators that help the company create its offering and inform customers about it.

An important aspect of assessing a company's resources is identifying its core competencies.[11] A **core competency** has three characteristics: (1) it is a source of competitive advantage and makes a significant contribution to perceived customer benefits, (2) it has applications in a wide variety of markets, and (3) it is difficult for competitors to imitate.[12] Companies today outsource less critical resources if they can obtain better quality or lower cost. Many textile, chemical, and computer/electronic product firms use offshore manufacturers and focus on product design and development and marketing, their core competencies. The key to success is to own and nurture the resources and competencies that make up the *essence* of the business.[13]

Although the ability of a company to create value for target customers is an essential component, successful targeting necessitates another important criterion: Target customers also must be able to create value for the company, meaning the target must be attractive to the company. The following section discusses the main factors involved in evaluating target attractiveness.

TARGET ATTRACTIVENESS

Target attractiveness reflects the ability of a market segment to create superior value for the company. Thus, the company must carefully select customers for whom to tailor its offering based on the degree to which they can contribute value to the company and assist the company in reaching its goal. Target customers can create two kinds of value for a company: *monetary* and *strategic.*

Monetary Value. Monetary value consists of the capability of customers to engender profits for the company. Monetary value includes both the *revenues* a particular customer segment generates and the *costs* of serving these customers.

- **Customer revenues** involve money received by the company from customers for the right to own or use its offering. A number of market and customer factors influence revenue volume. These include market size and rate of growth, as well as the buying power of customers, their brand loyalty, and their price sensitivity; the pricing power of the company; the intensity of competition in the market; and context factors such as the economy, government regulations, and the physical environment.
- **Costs of serving target customers** include the expense of tailoring the offering's benefits to the needs of target customers, along with communicating and delivering the offering to them. In addition, the cost of serving target customers can include the expense of acquiring and retaining these customers, providing them with post-purchase support, and offering incentives and loyalty programs.

Many companies tend to focus almost exclusively on the monetary aspect of value created by target customers because customer revenues and costs are more easily quantified. By espousing this narrow view, they overlook the fact that the strategic value that target customers create can be a significant factor in the value they contribute to the company.

Strategic Value. Strategic value refers to nonmonetary benefits that customers bring to the company. The three main types of strategic value are *social value, scale value,* and *information value.*

- **Social value** reflects the influence of target customers on other potential buyers. Customers might be as attractive to the company for their social networks and ability to impact the opinions of other buyers as for the revenues they offer to the company. Companies routinely target opinion leaders, trendsetters, and mavens because of their capacity to promote and endorse the company's offering via social networking.
- **Scale value** denotes the benefits derived from the scale of the company's operations. The economics of its business model might lead a company to target low-margin or sometimes even unprofitable customers, as is the case with airlines, hotels, and cruise lines that have large fixed costs and smaller variable costs. A company in its early growth stages might decide to target low-margin customers to build a product and user base that will serve as a platform for future growth. The rapid growth of Uber, Airbnb, Microsoft, eBay, and Facebook illustrates the benefits of building large-scale user networks.
- **Information value** is the worth of the information that customers provide. One reason why a company might target customers is for the wealth of data they can furnish the company about their needs and profile. This information can help the company design, communicate, and deliver value to other customers with similar needs. A company might also target customers who are likely to be early adopters of the company's offering, preceding mass market adoption. These "lead users" allow the company to glean feedback on how it can modify and enhance the offering to attract more buyers.

Assessing the strategic value of different customer segments is more challenging than assessing their monetary value. Strategic value is not as readily observable and can be difficult to quantify. A customer's ability to influence others often cannot be discerned directly, and even if it can be quantified by assessing the number of followers on social media, the customer's impact on the preferences of others is difficult to gauge. In spite of the difficulty of determining strategic value, when choosing target customers it cannot be overlooked, either as a complement to their monetary value or as the main component of their value to the company. Some highly influential customers who might never generate a dollar for the company directly may exert significant influence on broader and more profitable segments of the market that decide to purchase the company's offering.

Tactical Targeting

Although **tactical targeting** involves identifying target customers, as does strategic targeting, it has a different objective: to determine which customers to target and which to ignore, and to determine how the company's offering can be effectively and cost-efficiently communicated and delivered to the target customers that have already been selected. The following sections discuss the key aspects of tactical targeting in more detail.

DEFINING THE CUSTOMER PROFILE

After the company decides on a strategically viable target market, it must garner information on the profile of these customers to communicate the offering's attributes and deliver it to them. Tactical targeting identifies the most cost-effective ways to accomplish this by linking the customer need that the offering wants to fulfill with observable customer characteristics. These observable factors—the **customer profile**—involve demographic, geographic, behavioral, and psychographic descriptors.

- **Demographic factors** include age, gender, income, occupation, level of education, religion, ethnicity, nationality, employment status, population density (urban or rural), social class, household size, and stage in the life cycle. If the company's target customers are not individuals but other companies, they are identified by factors referred to as firmographics, which include size, organizational structure, industry, growth, revenues, and profitability.
- **Geographic (geolocation) factors** reflect the physical location of target customers. Geographic data describe *where* the customers are located, in contrast to demographic data, which describe *who* the target customers are. Some geographic indicators can be relatively enduring (e.g., a customer's permanent address), whereas other geolocation factors are dynamic and change frequently (e.g., the current location of a customer at a particular time). The ubiquity of mobile devices that identify individual customers and can pinpoint their exact location in real time has dramatically increased the importance of geographic factors in targeting.
- **Behavioral factors** describe customers' actions. These factors can include customers' prior experience with the company's offering, which can be as current customers, competitors' customers, or new-to-the-category customers. Behavior factors also categorize customers by the frequency with which they purchase the offering, the quantity they purchase, their price sensitivity and sensitivity to the company's promotional activities, their loyalty, their online versus offline purchases, and the retail outlets they patronize most often. Other behavioral factors of interest are customers' role in the decision process (e.g., as initiator, influencer, decider, buyer, or user), and what stage of the customer decision journey they are in. Behavioral factors can also include the manner in which customers learn about new products, how they socialize, and what they do in their spare time.
- **Psychographic factors** involve aspects of an individual's personality—such as attitudes, value system, interests, and lifestyle. Psychographics link observable and unobservable characteristics of target customers, which is where they differ from demographic, geographic, and behavioral factors. Whereas values, attitudes, interests, and lifestyles can be established by directly questioning customers, psychographic factors often are not readily discernable and must be inferred from the observable characteristics and behavior of customers. A customer's interest in sports, which is a psychographic factor, can be confirmed by behaviors such as subscribing to sports magazines, viewing sports programming, membership in a tennis club, and the purchase of sports equipment and tickets to sports events.

The importance of psychographics, like that of geolocation factors, has been sharpened by the proliferating use of online communication and e-commerce, which have made the moral values, attitudes, interests, and lifestyles of customers more transparent to companies. Social media companies such as Facebook, Google, YouTube, and Twitter can construct actionable psychographic customer profiles from the demographic, geographic, and behavioral data of their customers. The same can be said for traditional media companies, credit card providers, and online retailers that accrue data linking individuals' demographics, geographics, and behavioral profiles with their value system, attitudes, interests, and lifestyle.

ALIGNING CUSTOMER VALUE AND CUSTOMER PROFILE

An essential element of tactical targeting is ascertaining the profile characteristics of strategically important customer segments. Although strategic targeting's focus on creating market value is crucial to the success of the company's offering, it has an important disadvantage: Value is not observable, which means it cannot readily be acted on to reach target customers. Tactical targeting addresses this shortcoming by identifying the demographic, geographic, psychographic, and behavioral characteristics of strategically selected target customers so that the company can reach out to them. Thus, strategic and tactical targeting are complementary and inseparable facets of the process of identifying target customers.

An example of this process is a company that decides to launch a new credit card with a loyalty program that rewards customers with travel benefits such as airline tickets and hotel stays. The company's strategically important customers are those who want a credit card and would appreciate the card's travel benefits (customer value), would use the card frequently, and would not default on payments (company value). Because customer needs are unobservable, it is difficult to pinpoint those consumers who might enjoy the travel benefits offered by the card. Also unobservable are customers' future use of the credit card and the likelihood that they will not default on paying for their purchases. In addition to complicating the process of targeting attractive and compatible customer segments, these unobservable characteristics make it harder for the company to effectively communicate with and deliver the card to target customers.

Solving this dilemma entails linking the value-based customer segment with the observable characteristics of customers in this segment. To identify customers who would probably use the card often without defaulting on payments, the company might consider customers' credit scores, demographics, and geolocation, as well as their purchase behavior, including buying patterns, type and quantity of items purchased, and frequent payment by credit card. To identify those customers seeking travel rewards for whom it can create value, the company might look for customers who read travel magazines, watch travel shows, purchase luggage, frequent online travel sites, and seek the help of travel agents. Thus, the company might use travel-related communication channels to promote its new card and its offerings. By focusing on customers with profiles that are aligned with the value-based target segment, a company can optimize its targeting activities.

To achieve optimal outcomes when evaluating the company's tactical targeting options, marketing managers should follow the two main principles of tactical targeting: *effectiveness* and *cost efficiency*. The effectiveness principle reflects the degree to which the company is able to reach *all* strategically viable customers whose needs can be fulfilled in a way that benefits the company and its collaborators, make them aware of the company's offering, and give them access to the offering. The cost-efficiency principle mandates that the company's communication and distribution reach *only* the customers it has targeted. The goal of the cost-efficiency principle is to curtail the waste of resources on customers whose needs the company's offering cannot effectively address and who are unable to create value for the company.[14]

BRINGING TARGET SEGMENTS TO LIFE WITH PERSONAS

To bring all their acquired information and insights to life, some researchers develop personas. **Personas** are detailed profiles of one, or perhaps a few, hypothetical target consumers, imagined in terms of demographic, psychographic, geographic, or other descriptive attitudinal or behavioral information. Photos, images, names, or short bios help convey how the target customer looks, acts, and feels so that marketers can incorporate a well-defined target-customer point of view in all their marketing decision making. Many software companies have used "personas" to help improve user interfaces and experiences, and marketers have broadened the application. For example:

> Unilever's biggest and most successful hair care launch, for Sunsilk, was aided by insights into the target consumer the company dubbed "Katie." The Katie persona personified the 20-something female's hair care needs along with her perceptions and attitudes and the way she dealt with her everyday "dramas."

Specialty tool and equipment maker Campbell Hausfeld relied on the many retailers it supplied, including Home Depot and Lowe's, to help it keep in touch with consumers. After developing eight consumer profiles, including a female do-it-yourselfer and an elderly consumer, the firm was able to successfully launch new products such as drills that weighed less or that included a level for picture hanging.

Although personas provide vivid information to aid marketing decision making, it's important not to overgeneralize. Any target market may have a range of consumers who vary along a number of key dimensions, so marketers often account for these differences by developing multiple personas, each reflecting the characteristics of a particular consumer segment. Using quantitative, qualitative, and observational research, Best Buy developed five customer personas to guide the redesign and relaunch of GeekSquad.com, its national computer-support service: "Jill"—a suburban mom who uses her computer daily and depends on the Geek Squad as on a landscaper or plumber; "Charlie"—a 50-plus male who is curious about technology but needs an unintimidating guide; "Daryl"—a technologically savvy, hands-on experimenter who occasionally needs a helping hand; "Luis"—a time-pressed small business owner whose primary goal is to complete tasks as expediently as possible; "Nick"—a prospective Geek Squad agent who views the site critically and needs to be challenged.

Clearly, the customer persona does not represent all target customers. Characterizing the target segment with a representative individual, however, makes it easier to visualize the company's target customers and better understand how likely they are to respond to the company's offering.[15]

Single-Segment and Multi-Segment Targeting

The discussion so far has focused on a scenario in which a firm identifies and targets a single customer segment. Single-segment marketing, however, is the exception rather than the rule. Most offerings exist as part of a product line, with different offerings targeting different customer segments. Single-segment and multi-segment targeting, as well as the key principles underlying the decision to target multiple segments, are discussed in the following sections.

SINGLE-SEGMENT TARGETING

With single-segment concentration, the firm markets to only one particular segment. Porsche concentrates on the sports car enthusiast and Volkswagen on the small-car market; its foray into the large-car market with the Phaeton was a failure in the United States. Through concentrated marketing, a firm gains deep knowledge of the segment's needs and achieves a strong market presence. It also enjoys operating economies by specializing its production, distribution, and promotion.

Companies targeting single segments often focus on smaller, well-defined groups of customers that seek a distinctive mix of benefits. For example, whereas Hertz, Avis, Alamo, and others specialize

Allegiant Air When the prolonged recession that began in 2008 wreaked havoc on the financial performance of all the major U.S. domestic airlines, up-and-comer Allegiant Air managed to turn a profit quarter after quarter. Founded in Eugene, OR, in 2007, Allegiant has developed a highly successful niche strategy by providing leisure travelers with affordable nonstop flights from smaller markets such as Great Falls, MT; Grand Forks, ND; Knoxville, TN; and Plattsburgh, NY, to popular vacation spots in Florida, California, and Hawaii and to Las Vegas, Phoenix, and Myrtle Beach. By staying off the beaten track, it avoids competition on all but a handful of its 100-plus routes. Much of its passenger traffic is additive and incremental, attracting tourist travel that might not otherwise have happened. If a market doesn't seem to be taking hold, Allegiant quickly drops it. The carrier carefully balances revenues and costs. It charges for services—such as in-flight beverages and overhead storage space—that are free on other airlines. It also generates additional revenue by cross-selling vacation products and packages. Allegiant owns its 64 used MD-80 planes and also cuts costs by flying to specific destinations only a few times a week, instead of a few times a day like most airlines. It even fixes its seats at a pitch halfway between fully upright and fully reclined, because adjustable seats add weight, burn fuel, and are a "maintenance nightmare."[16]

Source: Michael Matthews/Alamy Stock Photo

<< While major U.S. airlines suffered during the recession that began in 2008, Oregon-based Allegiant Air stayed profitable with a niche strategy that offered affordable nonstop flights from smaller markets to popular vacation spots, skirting the competition and attracting customers who otherwise might not have traveled at all.

in airport rental cars for business and leisure travelers, Enterprise has focused on the low-budget, insurance-replacement market by primarily renting to customers whose cars have been wrecked or stolen. By offering low cost and convenience in an overlooked niche market, Enterprise has been highly profitable. Another up-and-coming niche marketer is Allegiant Air.

What does an attractive niche segment look like? Niche customers have a distinct set of needs; they will pay a premium to the firm that best satisfies them. The niche market is fairly small but has size, profit, and growth potential. It also is unlikely to attract many competitors, and it gains certain economies through specialization. As marketing efficiency increases, niches that seemed too small may become more profitable.

TARGETING MULTIPLE SEGMENTS

As markets become more fragmented, an increasing number of companies develop offerings targeting a greater number of smaller customer segments. Even companies that start with a single offering aimed at a specific target market achieve wider customer adoption over time. As their customer base becomes more diverse, these companies transition from a single offering to a product line containing offerings that fit the needs of the diverse customers it serves.

The process of identifying multiple customer segments is similar to that of identifying a single customer segment, the main difference being that the targeting analysis yields several viable segments. Thus, a direct consequence of the decision to target multiple customer segments is the need to develop unique offerings that satisfy the disparate requirements of each segment. Indeed, because different customer segments vary in their needs and in the value they can create for the company, the company must develop a portfolio of offerings that address these distinct needs in a way that benefits the company.

With selective specialization, a firm selects a subset of all the possible segments, each objectively attractive and appropriate. There may be little or no synergy among the segments, but each segment promises to be a moneymaker. When Procter & Gamble launched Crest Whitestrips, for example, initial target segments included newly engaged women and brides-to-be, as well as gay males. The multi-segment strategy also has the advantage of minimizing the firm's risk by diversifying its offerings across different customer segments.

A firm can increase the appeal of its offerings to target customers by focusing on different products and/or markets. With *product specialization*, the firm sells a certain product to several different market segments. A microscope manufacturer, for instance, sells to university, government, and commercial laboratories, making different instruments for each and building a strong reputation in the specific product area. The downside risk is that the product may be supplanted by an entirely new technology. With *market specialization*, on the other hand, the firm concentrates on serving many needs of a particular customer group, such as by selling an assortment of products only to university

Hallmark Hallmark's personal expression products are sold in more than 40,000 retail outlets nationwide and in 100 countries worldwide. Each year the company produces 10,000 new and redesigned greeting cards, as well as related products including party goods, gift wrap, and ornaments. Its success is due in part to its vigorous segmentation of the greeting

>> In little more than three decades, Titan has expanded its offerings from watches to jewelry, eye wear, perfumes and sarees with a growing online and social media presence complementing the extensive reach of its modern retail stores.

Source: ©Titan Company Ltd, used with permission

A well-positioned brand should be distinctive in its meaning and execution. If a sport or music sponsorship, for example, would work as well if it were for a leading competitor, then either the positioning is not sharply enough defined or the sponsorship as executed does not tie closely enough to the brand positioning.

A good positioning has one foot in the present and one in the future. It needs to be somewhat aspirational so that the brand has room to grow and improve. Positioning on the basis of the current state of the market is not sufficiently forward-looking, but at the same time the positioning cannot be so removed from reality that it is essentially unobtainable. The real trick is to strike just the right balance between what the brand is and what it could be.

Positioning requires that marketers define and communicate similarities and differences between their brand and its competitors. Specifically, deciding on a positioning involves

1. Choosing a frame of reference by identifying the target market and relevant competition
2. Identifying the optimal points of parity and points of difference given that frame of reference

These two aspects of positioning are discussed in more detail in the following sections.

Choosing a Frame of Reference

Consumers determine the value of an offering relative to a reference point used to assess its benefits and costs. An offering can be viewed as attractive in comparison to an inferior offering, but the same offering can be perceived as unattractive when compared to a superior offering. Therefore, a **frame of reference** can serve as a benchmark against which customers can evaluate the benefits of a company's offering.

Given the fact that consumers naturally construct frames of reference to evaluate the available options, a skilled marketer can design these frames of reference in a way that highlights the value of the offering. Decisions about the frame of reference are closely linked to target market decisions. Deciding to target a certain type of consumer can define the nature of competition, either because certain firms have decided to target that segment in the past (or plan to do so in the future) or because consumers in that segment may already look to certain products or brands in their purchase decisions.

A good starting point in defining a competitive frame of reference for brand positioning is *category membership*—the products or sets of products with which a brand competes and that function as close substitutes. It would seem a simple task for a company to identify its competitors. PepsiCo knows Coca-Cola's Dasani is a major bottled-water competitor for its Aquafina brand; Wells Fargo knows Bank of America is a major banking competitor; and Petsmart.com knows a major online retail competitor for pet food and supplies is Petco.com.

The range of a company's actual and potential competitors, however, can be more extensive than the obvious ones. To enter new markets, a brand with growth intentions may need a broader—or maybe even a more aspirational—competitive frame. Furthermore, the brand may be more likely to be hurt by emerging competitors or new technologies than by current competitors.

The energy-bar market created by PowerBar ultimately fragmented into a variety of subcategories, including some directed at specific segments (such as Luna bars for women) and some possessing specific attributes (such as the protein-laden Balance and the calorie-control bar Pria). Each represented a subcategory for which the original PowerBar may not be as relevant.[16]

Firms should choose their competitive frame to evoke more advantageous comparisons. Consider these examples:

In the United Kingdom, the Automobile Association positioned itself as the fourth "emergency service"—along with police, fire, and ambulance—to convey greater credibility and urgency.

The International Federation of Match Poker is attempting to downplay some of the gambling image of poker to emphasize the similarity of the card game to other "mind sports" such as chess and bridge.

The U.S. Armed Forces changed the focus of its recruitment advertising from the military as patriotic duty to the military as a place to learn leadership skills—a much more rational than emotional pitch that better competes with private industry.[17]

In stable markets where little short-term change is likely, it may be fairly easy to define one, two, or perhaps three key competitors. In dynamic categories where competition may exist or arise in a variety of different forms, multiple frames of reference may be present.

Identifying Potential Points of Difference and Points of Parity

Once marketers have fixed the frame of reference for positioning by defining the customer market and the nature of the competition, they can define the appropriate points of difference (attributes or benefits that are unique to the company's offering) and points of parity (attributes or benefits that the company's offering has in common with the competition).[18] We discuss points-of-parity and points-of-difference associations in the following sections.

IDENTIFYING POINTS OF DIFFERENCE

Points of difference (PODs) are attributes or benefits that differentiate the company's offering from the competition. These are attributes or benefits that consumers strongly associate with a brand, that they positively evaluate, and that they believe could not be found to the same extent with a competitive brand.

Associations that make up points of difference can be based on virtually any type of attribute or benefit.[19] Louis Vuitton may seek a point of difference as having the most stylish handbags, Energizer as having the longest-lasting battery, and Fidelity Investments as offering the best financial advice and planning.

Successfully establishing meaningful points of difference can provide financial payoffs. As part of its IPO, the UK mobile phone operator O2 was rebranded from British Telecom's struggling BT Cellnet, based on a powerful emotional campaign about freedom and enablement. When customer acquisition, loyalty, and average revenue soared, the business was quickly acquired by Spanish multinational Telefonica for more than three times its IPO price.[20]

An increasingly important aspect of differentiation is brand authenticity—the extent to which consumers perceive a brand to be faithful to its essence and its reason for being.[21] Brands such as Hershey's, Kraft, Crayola, Kellogg's, and Johnson & Johnson that are seen as authentic and genuine can evoke trust, affection, and strong loyalty. Welch's—owned by the National Grape Cooperative, which is made up of 1,150 Concord and Niagara grape farmers—is seen by consumers as "wholesome, authentic and real." The brand reinforces those credentials by focusing on its local sourcing of ingredients, an attribute that is increasingly important for consumers who want to know where their foods come from and how they were made.[22]

Strong brands often have multiple points of difference. Some examples are Apple (*design, ease of use,* and *irreverent attitude*), Nike (*performance, innovative technology,* and *winning*), and Southwest Airlines (*value, reliability,* and *fun personality*).

Creating strong, favorable, and unique associations is a real challenge, but it is essential for competitive brand positioning. Although successfully positioning a new product in a well-established market may seem particularly difficult, Aries Agro shows that it is not impossible.

Aries Agro Founded in 1969, Aries Agro was initially set up to produce mineral feed additives for animals and birds. In 1975, the company expanded into nutrition for plants to tap into the growing demand for plant nutrients and supplements. With its expertise in mineral nutrients and strong R&D base, the firm offers customized micro-nutrient nutrient solutions for the specific needs of 107 different crops by providing all 16 nutrients required in agriculture.[23] For example, Aries Chelamin provides inert, non-reactive, water-soluble zinc—an essential micronutrient for balanced nutrition in crops—at a slow and sustained release dose, 20 times lower than traditional zinc applications in its chelated form, avoids reactions, fixation, leaching, etc. As the price does not increase proportionately, the farmer's cost of application per acre of land is significantly lower while being environmentally sensitive. Aries Zinc high density tablet is the most recent upgrade of Chelamin with 10 effervescent tablets sufficient to cover 1 acre of land as compared to 20 kilos of traditional zinc fertilizer. The company's offerings of 65 brands reach farmers through a network of over 90,000 retail outlets across India and 11 countries. Its unique packaging, designed for ease of use, creates a distinct sensory experience for its customers when dissolved in water. These water soluble, eco-friendly, single dose packs ensure accurate dosage while helping the farmers save on labor. Each pack is designed to take care of micro aspects related to the nutritional health of the cultivation field, such as the precise quantity of product used, efficient processing as well as accuracy of timing.[24] The company's training programs and nutritional solutions, tailored to the soil composition and crop requirements, benefit millions of farmers.[25] Agronomists at Aries work with farmers through extension services and soil testing to improve yield and grow healthy crops. Crop management consultation, micro-nutrient recommendations, loyalty programs and regular communication are being increasingly offered through digital channels. With environment-friendly products and customer-oriented agri-extension service solutions, Aries Agro has become one of the most trusted agriculture companies, clocking an impressive annual growth rate of 25 per cent.[26]

<< R to L – The original packaging of Aries brand (Chelamin), converted to the water soluble sachet (held above beaker) and the pouch dissolving in the centre beaker, seamlessly releasing the material into the solution (centre beaker). The upgraded high density effervescent tablet packed in recyclable tubes (Zinc HD on extreme left) with the dissolving tablet in the beaker alongside. Use of nano technology reduces the requirement to 1 tablet in a spray tank (instead of 1 dissolvable pouch). 10 tablets are sufficient for one acre of land.

Source: ©Aries Agro Ltd., used with permission

Three criteria determine whether a brand association can truly function as a point of difference: desirability, deliverability, and differentiability. Some key considerations follow.

- **Desirable to consumer.** Consumers must see the brand association as personally relevant to them. Select Comfort made a splash in the mattress industry with its Sleep Number beds, which allow consumers to adjust the support and fit of the mattress for optimal comfort with a simple numbering index. Consumers must also be given a compelling reason to believe and an understandable rationale for why the brand can deliver the desired benefit. Mountain Dew may argue that it is more energizing than other soft drinks and support this claim by noting that it has a higher level of caffeine. Chanel No. 5 perfume may claim to be the quintessentially elegant French perfume and support this claim by noting the long association between Chanel and haute couture. Substantiators can also come in the form of patented, branded ingredients, such as NIVEA Wrinkle Control Crème with coenzyme Q10.
- **Deliverable by the company.** The company must have the internal resources and commitment to feasibly and profitably create and maintain the brand association in the minds of consumers. The product design and the way the product is marketed must support the desired association. Does communicating the desired association require actual changes to the product itself or just perceptual shifts in the way the consumer thinks of the product or brand? Creating the latter is typically easier. General Motors has had to work to overcome public perceptions that Cadillac is not a youthful, modern brand and has done so through bold designs, solid craftsmanship, and active, contemporary images. The ideal brand association is preemptive, defensible, and difficult to attack. It is generally easier for market leaders such as ADM, Visa, and SAP to sustain their positioning, based as it is on demonstrable product or service performance, than it is for market leaders such as Fendi, Prada, and Hermès, whose positioning is based on fashion and thus subject to the whims of a more fickle market.
- **Differentiating from competitors.** Finally, consumers must see the brand association as distinctive and superior to relevant competitors. Splenda sugar substitute overtook Equal and Sweet'N Low to become the leader in its category by differentiating itself as a product derived from sugar without the associated drawbacks of an artificial low-calorie sweetener. In the crowded energy-drink category, Monster has become a nearly $2 billion brand, and a threat to category pioneer Red Bull, by differentiating itself on its innovative 16-ounce can and an extensive line of products targeting nearly every need state related to energy consumption.[27]

IDENTIFYING POINTS OF PARITY

Points of parity (POPs), on the other hand, are attribute or benefit associations that are not necessarily unique to the brand but may in fact be shared with other brands.[28] These types of associations come in three basic forms: category, correlational, and competitive.

- **Category points of parity** are attributes or benefits that consumers view as essential to a legitimate and credible offering within a certain product or service category. In other words, they represent necessary—but not sufficient—conditions for brand choice. Consumers may not consider a travel agency truly a travel agency unless it is able to make air and hotel reservations, provide advice about leisure packages, and offer various ticket payment and delivery options. Category points of parity may change over time because of technological advances, legal developments, or consumer trends, but to use a golfing analogy, they are the "greens fees" necessary to play the marketing game.
- **Correlational points of parity** are potentially negative associations that arise from the existence of positive associations for the brand. One challenge for marketers is that many attributes or benefits that make up their POPs or PODs are inversely related. In other words, if your brand is good at one thing, such as being inexpensive, consumers can't see it as also good at something else, like being "of the highest quality." Consumer research into the trade-offs consumers make in their purchasing decisions can be informative here.
- **Competitive points of parity** are associations designed to overcome perceived weaknesses of the brand in light of competitors' points of difference. One way to uncover key competitive points of parity is to role-play competitors' positioning and infer their intended points of difference. Competitor's PODs will, in turn, suggest the brand's POPs.

Regardless of the source of perceived weaknesses, if, in the eyes of consumers, a brand can "break even" in those areas where it appears to be at a disadvantage *and* achieve advantages in other areas, it should be in a strong—and perhaps unbeatable—competitive position. Consider the introduction of Miller Lite beer, the first major light beer in North America.

Miller Lite The initial advertising strategy for Miller Lite beer had two goals: ensuring parity with key competitors in the regular, full-strength beer category by stating that Miller Lite "tastes great," while at the same time creating a point of difference around the fact that it contained one-third fewer calories and was thus "less filling." As often happens, the point of parity and point of difference were somewhat conflicting because consumers tend to equate taste with calories. To overcome potential resistance, Miller employed credible spokespeople, primarily popular former professional athletes, who would presumably not drink a beer unless it tasted good. These ex-jocks humorously debated which of the two product benefits—"tastes great" or "less filling"—was more descriptive of the beer. The ads ended with the clever tagline "Everything You've Always Wanted in a Beer . . . and Less." As time went on, the brand positioning evolved to encompass "Miller Time" in its advertising, an emotional appeal about the brand's "sociability" and capacity to serve as a catalyst for good times with friends.[29]

For an offering to achieve parity on a particular attribute or benefit, a sufficient number of consumers must believe the brand is "good enough" on that dimension. There is a zone or range of tolerance or acceptance with points of parity. The brand does not literally need to be seen as equal to competitors, but consumers must feel it does well enough on that particular attribute or benefit. If they do, they may be willing to base their evaluations and decisions on other factors more favorable to the brand. A light beer presumably would never taste as good as a full-strength beer, but it would need to taste close enough to be able to effectively compete.

Often, the key to positioning is not so much achieving a point of difference as achieving points of parity! Consider the competition between Visa and American Express in the card industry:

Visa and American Express Visa's point of difference in the credit card category is that it is the most widely available card, which underscores the category's main benefit—convenience. American Express, on the other hand, has built the equity of its brand by highlighting the prestige associated with the use of its card. Visa and American Express now compete to create points of parity by attempting to blunt each other's advantage. Visa offers gold and platinum cards to enhance the prestige of its brand, and for years it advertised, "It's Everywhere You Want to Be," showing desirable travel and leisure locations that accept only the Visa card to reinforce both its own exclusivity and its acceptability. American Express has substantially increased the number of merchants that accept its cards and created other value enhancements, while also reinforcing its cachet through advertising that showcases celebrities such as Robert De Niro, Tina Fey, Ellen DeGeneres, and Beyoncé, as well as promotions for exclusive access to special events.[30]

>> While Visa strives to match the prestige of competitor American Express by offering gold and platinum cards, American Express is aiming to extend the reach of its card to erase Visa's advantage as the most widely available credit card.

Source: Oliver Hoffmann/Alamy Stock Photo

ALIGNING THE FRAME OF REFERENCE, POINTS OF PARITY, AND POINTS OF DIFFERENCE

It is not uncommon for a brand to identify more than one actual or potential competitive frame of reference if competition widens or the firm plans to expand into new categories. For example, Starbucks could define very distinct sets of competitors, suggesting different possible POPs and PODs as a result:[31]

Quick-serve restaurants and convenience shops (McDonald's and Dunkin' Donuts)—Intended PODs might be quality, image, experience, and variety; intended POPs might be convenience and value.

Home and office consumption (Folgers, NESCAFÉ instant, and Green Mountain Coffee K-Cups)—Intended PODs might be quality, image, experience, variety, and freshness; intended POPs might be convenience and value.

Local cafés—Intended PODs might be convenience and service quality; intended POPs might be product quality, variety, price, and community.

Note that some potential POPs and PODs for Starbucks are shared across competitors; others are unique to a particular competitor.

Under such circumstances, marketers have to decide what to do. There are two main options with multiple frames of reference. One is to first develop the best possible positioning for each type or class of competitors and then see whether there is a way to create one combined positioning robust enough to effectively address them all. If competition is too diverse, however, it may be necessary to prioritize competitors and then choose the most important set of competitors to serve as the competitive frame. One crucial consideration is not to try to be all things to all people; this leads to "lowest common denominator" positioning, which is typically ineffective.[32]

Finally, if there are many competitors in different categories or subcategories, it may be useful to develop the positioning either at the category level for all relevant categories ("quick-serve restaurants" or "supermarket take-home coffee" for Starbucks) or with an exemplar from each category (McDonald's or NESCAFÉ for Starbucks).

Occasionally, a company will be able to *straddle* two frames of reference with one set of points of difference and points of parity. In these cases, the points of difference for one category become points of parity for the other, and vice versa. Subway restaurants are positioned as offering healthy, good-tasting sandwiches. This positioning allows the brand to create a POP on taste and a POD on health with respect to quick-serve restaurants such as McDonald's and Burger King and, at the same time, to create a POP on health and a POD on taste with respect to health food restaurants and cafés!

Straddle positions allow brands to expand their market coverage and potential customer base. One example of such straddle positioning is BMW.

Source: BMW of North America

<< By combining the seemingly incompatible benefits of luxury and performance, BMW has found great success in the American automotive market.

BMW When BMW first made a strong competitive push into the U.S. market in the late 1970s, it positioned the brand as the only automobile that offered both luxury *and* performance. At that time, consumers saw U.S. luxury cars as lacking performance and U.S. performance cars as lacking luxury. By relying on the design of its cars, its German heritage, and other aspects of a well-conceived marketing program, BMW was able to simultaneously achieve: (1) a point of difference on luxury and a point of parity on performance with respect to U.S. performance cars like the Chevy Corvette and (2) a point of difference on performance and a point of parity on luxury with respect to U.S. luxury cars like Cadillac. The clever brand motto "The Ultimate Driving Machine" effectively captured the newly created umbrella category: luxury performance cars.[33]

Although a straddle positioning is often attractive as a means of reconciling potentially conflicting consumer goals and creating a "best of both worlds" solution, it also carries an extra burden. If the points of parity and points of difference are not credible, the brand may not be viewed as a legitimate player in either category. Many early personal digital assistants (palm-sized computers) such as the Palm Pilot and Apple's Newton, which unsuccessfully tried to straddle categories ranging from pagers to laptop computers, provide a vivid illustration of this risk.

Often a good positioning will have several PODs and POPs. Of those, two or three often really define the competitive battlefield and should be analyzed and developed carefully. A good positioning should also follow the "80–20" rule and be highly applicable to 80 percent of the products carrying the brand. Attempting to position based on 100 percent of a brand's products often yields an unsatisfactory, "lowest common denominator" result. The remaining 20 percent of products should be reviewed to ensure that they have the proper branding strategy and to see how they could be changed to better reflect the brand positioning.

Perceptual maps, also called positioning maps, may be useful for choosing specific benefits as POPs and PODs to position a brand. **Perceptual maps** are visual representations of consumer perceptions and preferences. They provide quantitative pictures of market situations and the way consumers view different products, services, and brands along various dimensions. By overlaying consumer preferences on brand perceptions, marketers can reveal "holes" or "openings" that suggest unmet consumer needs and marketing opportunities.[34]

Creating a Sustainable Competitive Advantage

An offering's competitive advantage reflects its ability to satisfy a customer need to a greater degree than alternative means of satisfying the same need. Thus, creating a competitive advantage gives customers a reason to choose a given offering rather than an available alternative.

SUSTAINABLE COMPETITIVE ADVANTAGE AS A MARKETING CONCEPT

To build a strong brand and avoid the commodity trap, marketers must start with the belief that it is possible to differentiate an offering by creating a sustainable competitive advantage.[35] **Competitive advantage** is a company's ability to perform in one or more ways that competitors cannot or will not match.

Some companies are finding success. Pharmaceutical companies are developing biologics—medicines produced by using the body's own cells rather than through chemical reactions in a lab—because it is difficult for copycat pharmaceutical companies to make generic versions of biologics when they go off patent. Roche Holding will enjoy an advantage of at least three years with its $7-billion-a-year-in-sales biologic rheumatoid arthritis treatment Rituxan before a biosimilar copycat version is introduced.[36]

Few competitive advantages are inherently sustainable; in the long run, they are often replicated by the competition. Instead, a competitive advantage may be leverageable. A *leverageable advantage* is one that a company can use as a springboard to new advantages, much as Microsoft has leveraged its operating system with Microsoft Office and networking applications. In general, a company that hopes to endure must be in the business of continuously inventing new advantages that can serve as the basis of points of difference.

Any product or service benefit that is sufficiently desirable, deliverable, and differentiating can serve as a point of difference for a brand. The obvious, and often the most compelling, means of differentiation for consumers are benefits related to performance. Swatch offers colorful, fashionable watches; GEICO offers reliable insurance at discount prices.

GEICO GEICO has spent hundreds of millions of dollars on TV advertising. Has it been worth it? Warren Buffet, chairman and CEO of GEICO's parent company Berkshire Hathaway, thinks so. GEICO became the fastest-growing auto insurance company in the United States by selling directly to consumers with a basic message: "15 Minutes Could Save You 15% or More on Your Car Insurance." Partnering with The Martin Agency, GEICO has run a series of highly creative and award-winning ad campaigns to emphasize different aspects of the brand. TV ads featuring the Cockney-speaking Gecko lizard spokes-character reinforce GEICO's brand image as credible and accomplished. The "Happier Than" campaign comes up with exaggerated situations to describe how happy GEICO customers are, such as a camel on Wednesday (hump day) and Dracula volunteering at a blood drive. A third campaign featuring Maxwell, a talking pig, focuses on specific products and service features. The fourth campaign, "Did You Know," starts with a person commenting on the company's famous 15-minute slogan to a companion, who replies, "Everyone knows that." The first speaker then tries to save face with a twist on some other conventional wisdom, such as Pinocchio was a poor motivational speaker or Old McDonald was a really bad speller. The multiple campaigns complement each other and build on one another's success. The company dominates the TV airwaves with so many varied car insurance messages that competitors' ads are lost.[37]

Sometimes changes in the marketing environment can open up new opportunities to create a means of differentiation. Eight years after it launched Sierra Mist, when sales began stagnating, PepsiCo tapped into rising consumer interest in natural and organic products to reposition the lemon-lime soft drink as all-natural with only five ingredients: carbonated water, sugar, citric acid, natural flavor, and potassium citrate.

Often a brand's positioning transcends its performance considerations. Companies can fashion compelling images that appeal to consumers' social and psychological needs. The primary explanation for Marlboro's extraordinary worldwide market share (about 30 percent) is that its "macho cowboy" image struck a responsive chord with much of the cigarette-smoking public. Wine and liquor companies also work hard to develop distinctive images for their brands. Even a seller's physical space can be a powerful image generator. Hyatt Regency Hotels aims to develop a distinctive image with its atrium lobbies.

To identify possible means of differentiation, marketers have to match consumers' desire for a benefit with their company's ability to deliver it. For example, they can design their distribution channels to make buying the product easier and more rewarding. Back in 1946, pet food was cheap, not very nutritious, and available exclusively in supermarkets and the occasional feed store. Dayton, Ohio–based Iams found success selling premium pet food through regional veterinarians, breeders, and pet stores.

STRATEGIES FOR CREATING A SUSTAINABLE COMPETITIVE ADVANTAGE

Three core strategies are integral to designing a value proposition that makes an offering stand out from the competition. These are to *differentiate on an existing attribute, introduce a new attribute,* and *build a strong brand.*[38]

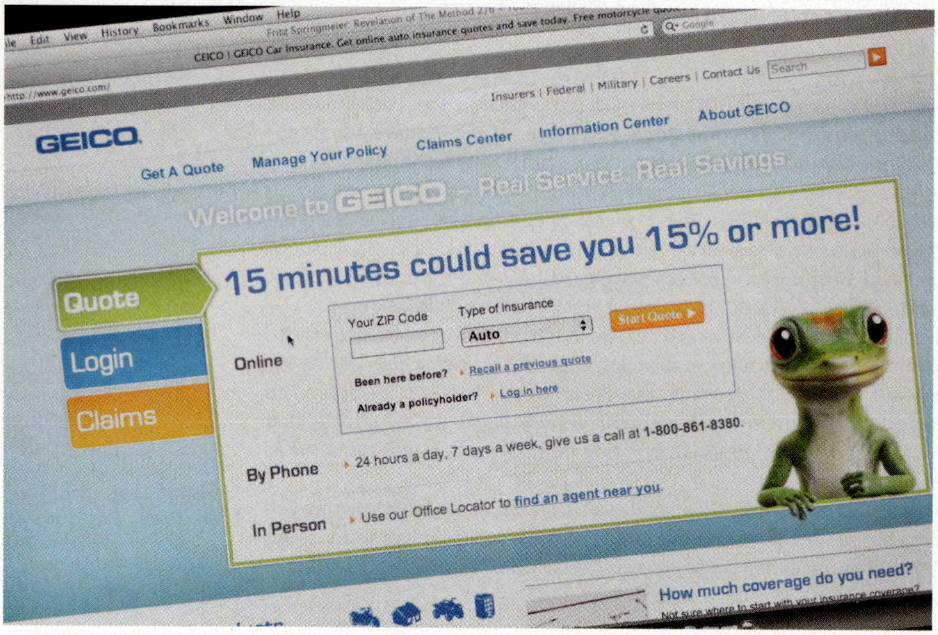

Source: NetPhotos/Alamy Stock Photo

<< Geico has successfully drowned out the voices of its competitors and become the fastest-growing U.S. auto insurance company with ongoing multimillion-dollar TV ad campaigns that feature a gecko with a cockney accent spouting money-saving advice.

Differentiate on an Existing Attribute. This is the quintessential strategy for creating an advantage over competitors. Gillette has differentiated itself from competitors by stressing the quality of its shave. Online shaving supplies retailer Dollar Shave Club stresses price as its competitive advantage over premium brands such as Gillette. Zappos differentiates itself from other online shoe retailers by the level of customer service it provides. BMW uses the driving experience delivered by its vehicles as a point of differentiation from the competition. Volvo differentiates itself by focusing on safety, while Rolls-Royce sets itself apart by emphasizing luxury.

Differentiating on an attribute that is meaningful to customers is the most intuitive way to create a competitive advantage. However, it is often difficult to achieve, because offerings in a product category start to become more similar as their overall performance improves. Television sets are a good example: As technical advancements have improved the overall quality of television sets, differences among the available options have become less apparent to consumers, who perceive TVs as similar to one another.

Introduce a New Attribute. In lieu of enhancing an offering's performance on an existing attribute, a company can distinguish its offering by introducing a new attribute—one that competitors don't have. examples abound: TOMS chose to differentiate itself from traditional shoe manufacturers by its "buy one, give one" social responsibility program. PepsiCo used only all-natural ingredients to differentiate its lemon-lime soft drink Sierra Mist from other soft drinks. Dollar Shave Club chose to set itself apart through subscription-based, direct-to-consumer shipping of shaving supplies. Uber streamlined the monetary transaction between riders and drivers by introducing cash-free payment. And Nest incorporated machine learning into its thermostats as an alternative approach to controlling the temperature in a home.

It is noteworthy that introducing a new attribute does not necessarily involve the invention of a completely innovative attribute. It can also involve tweaking an existing attribute that has been more or less neglected by competitors to transform it into a point of difference. Method Products, manufacturer of household cleaning products, did just that when it designed aesthetically pleasing packaging as a distinguishing attribute in a category in which packaging was viewed as a purely functional attribute. In the same vein, Apple introduced design as a key point of difference in the personal computer category when it came out with the egg-shaped, multi-colored iMac encased in translucent plastic.

Although the introduction of a new attribute can offer a powerful advantage to a company, such a move is rarely sustainable. Competitors will lose no time copying a new attribute that is valued by customers, thus greatly diminishing the competitive advantage of the company that pioneered the attribute. Creating a sustainable competitive advantage requires that a company constantly find fresh and unique ways of creating customer value.

Build a Strong Brand. A valuable source of sustainable competitive advantage is a powerful brand that gives customers a reason to choose the company's offering. An example of brand power is Harley-Davidson, which probably owes its success as much to the strength of its brand as to the design of its motorcycles. Taste is not what sets Coca-Cola apart from other cola drinks; rather, it is Coke's brand image, which has transcended national borders and cultural barriers to become known by almost everyone on the planet.

Differentiation through brand power is of particular value in commoditized product categories such as cereal, soft drinks, and alcoholic beverages. Grey Goose, for example, has successfully positioned its product as the World's Best Tasting Vodka, which allows the company to command a significant price premium compared to many competitive brands. The success Grey Goose has had in achieving this distinction is especially notable because vodka is effectively a commodity, designed as a "neutral spirit" that has no "distinctive character, aroma, taste, or color."[39] Because most customers cannot tell taste the difference among different premium vodkas, the Grey Goose brand is obviously the factor driving its purchase.

In addition to being viewed as an attribute of the company's offering, brand also has a singular role in creating a competitive advantage: It influences perceptions of the offering on such dimensions as quality, reliability, and durability—dimensions that are not readily visible to customers. Thus, brands can infuse the company's offering with a unique and meaningful message that resonates beyond the actual characteristics of the company's product and service and creates added value for customers. In other words, customers are buying not just Harley-Davidson, Coca-Cola, and Warby Parker products; they are buying the meaning implied by these brands.

Brands also have another facet. Besides influencing customer beliefs about the offering, a strong brand can actually drive customer behavior when it is the first option that pops into a customer's mind as a way to fulfill a given need. For instance, Budweiser consistently promotes its product so that when its customers think of beer, "Bud" is the first brand that comes to mind. GEICO is another company that spends tens of millions of dollars each year to ensure that drivers think of GEICO first when they consider car insurance. McDonald's aims to be the first fast-food restaurant that comes to customers' minds, edging out competitors Burger King, Wendy's, and Taco Bell. Tylenol, Advil, and Aleve have gained top-of-mind awareness in the category of non-prescription pain-relief, which allows these brands to sustain their market leadership in a product category filled with functionally identical low-priced generics.

Top-of-mind brand awareness also creates a competitive advantage in that the brand considered first often becomes a reference point for consumers, the default option against which the other brands are evaluated. This is an important benefit, because unless they are given a strong reason to choose an alternative option, buyers are likely to select the default option.

Communicating the Offering's Positioning

Once they have fashioned the brand positioning strategy, marketers should communicate it to everyone in the organization so that it will guide their words and actions. This is usually achieved by developing a **positioning statement**. The key aspects of crafting an effective positioning statement—communicating an offering's category membership along with points of parity and points of difference, and developing a narrative to convey the offering's positioning—are discussed in the following sections.

CRAFTING A POSITIONING STATEMENT

A positioning statement clearly articulates the offering's target customers and the key benefit that will provide customers with a reason to choose the company's offering. Consider the following positioning statements for Hertz, Volvo, and Domino's, respectively, which have guided their communication campaigns through the years with their target customers.

> For busy professionals (target customers), Hertz offers a fast, convenient way to rent the right type of car at an airport (value proposition).
>
> For safety-conscious upscale families (target customers), Volvo offers the safest, most durable automobile in which your family can ride (value proposition).
>
> For convenience-minded pizza lovers (target customers), Domino's offers a delicious hot pizza, delivered promptly to your door (value proposition).

An important question in developing a positioning statement is deciding whether to promote the specific attributes describing a company's offering or to focus on the ultimate benefits delivered by these attributes. Many marketers tend to focus on the *benefits* as the pillars of the offering's positioning. This is because consumers are usually more interested in benefits and in what exactly they will get from a product.

Offering *attributes*, on the other hand, generally play more of a supporting role. Multiple attributes may support a certain benefit, and they may change over time. Attributes provide "reasons to believe" or "proof points" for why a brand can credibly claim it offers certain benefits. Marketers of Dove soap, for example, will talk about how its attribute of one-quarter cleansing cream uniquely creates the benefit of softer skin. Singapore Airlines can boast about its superior customer service because of its highly trained flight attendants and strong service culture.

COMMUNICATING CATEGORY MEMBERSHIP

Category membership may be obvious. Target customers are aware that Lakme is a leading brand of cosmetics, Kellogg's is a leading brand of cereal, McKinsey is a leading consulting firm, and so on. But when a product is new, marketers must inform consumers of the brand's category membership.

Sometimes consumers may know the category membership but not be convinced that the brand is a valid member of the category. They may be aware that HP produces digital cameras, but they may not be certain whether HP cameras are in the same class as those made by Canon, Nikon, and Sony. In this instance, HP might find it useful to reinforce category membership.

Brands are sometimes affiliated with categories in which they do *not* hold membership. This approach is one way to highlight a brand's point of difference, providing that consumers know its actual membership. Instead of putting Amul's ice creams in the competitive frozen dessert category, marketers have positioned it in the milk based ice cream category with ads that proclaim, "Real Milk, Real Ice Cream" Similarly, pay channel HBO has developed original, edgy programming to justify its premium fee, adopting the slogan "It's Not TV, It's HBO."

The typical approach to positioning is to inform consumers of a brand's membership before stating its point of difference. Presumably, consumers need to know what a product is and what function it serves before deciding whether it is superior to the brands against which it competes. For new products, initial advertising often concentrates on creating brand awareness, and subsequent advertising attempts to create the brand image. While the new banks in India were targeting specific socio-economic

>> After Bandhan microfinance transformed into a universal bank, its ad campaigns touted doorstep banking to attract customers. Bandhan Bank serves over 25 million customers from its 5628 banking outlets and digital channels.

Source: ©Bandhan Bank, used with permission

Bandhan Bank In rebranding Bandhan, India's largest microfinance institution, as Bandhan Bank, a universal bank, the firm ran campaigns to tell real stories of its customers with narratives that resonate with viewers as they could relate to the characters and their experiences while seeking loans.[40] To convey the idea that the bank invests in the customer's dream and helps it come to life, an ad showed a boutique owner offering to gift a saree to a woman who couldn't afford to buy it within her budget. Insisting that it was not a favour, the boutique owner reminds the woman, who was a Bandhan Bank employee, had earlier shown confidence in the owner and approved a loan to set up the boutique. The ads positioned Bandhan as a universal bank, accessible to everyone, especially the lower income households and small businesses. To convey the idea of earning more through higher interest rates, the bank's well-crafted ads showcased the savings account as a new earning member of a middle-class family of professionals. Another advertisement captured the over-the-top benefits of fixed deposit, exclusively for senior citizens without active income. Promotions focusing on easy accessibility, prompted growth in its home loan and business loan portfolio. An advertisement creatively narrated the heart-warming story of a lower middle-class family, that lives in a rented house, buying a home with hassle-free process and low-cost loan from Bandhan Bank. The messaging effectively convey the category membership in banking with the help of stories that its target audience can relate with.[41] The ads reflect Bandhan Bank's philosophy of 'Aapka Bhala. Sabki Bhalai.' (Your benefit. Everyone's welfare.) underlining its core purpose of making banking inclusive.

segments, Bandhan Bank aimed to be a bank for all – from affluent large deposit customers to granular small deposit customers; from mid-sized enterprise borrowers to micro business owners.

There are three main ways to convey a brand's category membership:

- *Announcing category benefits.* To reassure consumers that a brand will deliver on the fundamental reason for using a category, marketers frequently use benefits to announce category membership. Thus, industrial tools might claim to have durability, and antacids might announce their efficacy. A brownie mix might attain membership in the baked desserts category by claiming to offer the benefit of great taste and might support this claim by including high-quality ingredients (performance) or by showing users delighting in its consumption (imagery).
- *Comparing to exemplars.* Well-known, noteworthy brands in a category can also help a brand specify its category membership. When Tommy Hilfiger was an unknown, advertising announced his status as a great U.S. designer by associating him with Geoffrey Beene, Calvin Klein, and Perry Ellis, recognized members of that category.
- *Relying on the product descriptor.* The product descriptor that follows the brand name is often a concise means of conveying category origin. Ford Motor Co. invested more than $1 billion in a radical new 2004 model called the X-Trainer, which combined the attributes of an SUV, a minivan, and a station wagon. To communicate its unique position—and to avoid association with its Explorer and Country Squire models—the vehicle, eventually called Freestyle, was designated a "sports wagon."

COMMUNICATING CONFLICTING BENEFITS

As we saw earlier, one common challenge in positioning is that many of the benefits that make up points of parity and points of difference are negatively correlated. ConAgra must convince consumers that Healthy Choice frozen foods both taste good *and* are good for you. Consider these examples of negatively correlated attributes and benefits: low price versus high quality, powerful versus safe, taste versus low calories, strong versus refined, nutritious versus good tasting, ubiquitous versus exclusive, efficacious versus mild, and varied versus simple.

Moreover, individual attributes and benefits often have positive *and* negative aspects. For example, consider a long-lived brand such as La-Z-Boy recliners, Burberry outerwear, or the *New York Times*. The brand's heritage could suggest experience, wisdom, and expertise as well as authenticity. On the other hand, it could also imply being old-fashioned and not contemporary or up to date.

The challenge is that consumers typically want to maximize *both* of the negatively correlated attributes or benefits. Much of the art and science of marketing consists of dealing with trade-offs, and positioning is no different. The best approach clearly is to develop a product or service that performs well on both dimensions. GORE-TEX was able to overcome the conflicting product images of "breathable" and "waterproof" through technological advances. When in-depth and quantitative interviews and focus groups suggested that consumers wanted the benefits of technology without the hassles, Royal Philips launched its "Sense and Simplicity" campaign for its Philips brand of electronics, which touted its products as easy to use.

Other approaches include launching two different marketing campaigns, each devoted to a different brand attribute or benefit: one linking the brand to a person, place, or thing that possesses the right kind of equity to establish an attribute or benefit as a POP or POD; and the other convincing consumers that the negative relationship between attributes and benefits, if they consider it differently, is in fact positive.[42]

POSITIONING AS STORYTELLING

Rather than outlining specific attributes or benefits, some marketing experts describe positioning a brand as telling a narrative or story. Consumers like the richness and imagination they can derive from thinking of the story behind a product or service.

To help sharpen its marketing and positioning, Jim Beam, with its namesake Jim Beam and Maker's Mark brands, hired The Moth, a group of professional storytellers best known for a weekly public radio

Source: Alko/Alamy Stock Photo

>> Jim Beam has used professional storytellers to sharpen its marketing and positioning.

broadcast, to kick off a three-day biannual gathering of its marketing teams. The Moth team broke down the structure of a story, identified the parts that were particularly meaningful, and had Beam employees tell tales to one another. This approach enabled the company to come up with a compelling story articulating its customer value proposition.[43]

Some researchers see *narrative branding* as based on deep metaphors that connect to people's memories, associations, and stories.[44] They identify five elements of narrative branding: the brand story in terms of words and metaphors; the consumer journey or the way consumers engage with the brand over time, and touch points where they come into contact with the brand; the visual language or expression for the brand; the manner in which the narrative is expressed experientially or the brand engages the senses; and the role the brand plays in the lives of consumers. Based on literary convention and brand experience, they also identify four key aspects of a brand story: (1) setting (the time, place, and context), (2) cast (the brand as a character, including its role in the life of the audience, its relationships and responsibilities, and its history or creation myth), (3) narrative arc (the way the narrative logic unfolds over time, including actions, desired experiences, defining events, and the moment of epiphany), and (4) language (the authenticating voice, metaphors, symbols, themes, and leitmotifs).

A related concept referred to as "primal branding" views brands as complex belief systems. Proponents of primal branding argue that diverse brands such as Google, MINI Cooper, the U.S. Marine Corps, Starbucks, Apple, UPS, and Aveda all have a "primal code" or DNA that resonates with their customers and generates their passion and fervor. There are seven assets that make up this belief system or primal code: a creation story, creed, icon, rituals, sacred words, a way of dealing with nonbelievers, and a good leader.[45]

marketing INSIGHT

Positioning a Start-Up

Building brands is a challenge for a small business with limited resources and budgets. Nevertheless, numerous success stories exist of entrepreneurs who have built their brands up essentially from scratch to become powerhouse brands. When resources are limited, focus and consistency in marketing programs become critically important. Creativity is also paramount—finding new ways to market new ideas about products to consumers. Here are some specific branding guidelines for small businesses:

- *Find a compelling product or service performance advantage.* As for any brand, demonstrable, meaningful differences in product or service performance can be the key to success. Dropbox has carved out a strong position in the face of a slew of competitors that also offer consumers a means to conveniently store massive amounts of documents, photos, videos, and other files, in part by virtue of its convenient single-folder approach to accommodate multiple devices for a user.[46]
- *Focus on building one or two strong brands based on one or two key associations.* Small businesses often must rely on only one or two brands and key associations as points of difference for them. These associations must be consistently reinforced across the marketing program and over time. Rooted in the snowboarding and surfing cultures, Volcom has adopted a "Youth Against Establishment" credo that has resulted in steady sales of its music, athletic apparel, and jewelry.
- *Encourage product or service trial in any way possible.* A successful small business has to distinguish itself in ways consumers can learn about and experience. One way is to encourage trial through sampling, demonstrations, or any means to engage consumers with the brand. See's Candies allows walk-in customers to sample any piece of candy in the shop they choose. As one senior executive noted, "That's the best marketing we have, if people try it, they love it." See's uses all fresh ingredients and no added preservatives to create its enticing flavors.[47]
- *Develop a cohesive digital strategy to make the brand "bigger and better."* Social media, online advertising, and e-commerce allow small firms to have a larger profile than they might otherwise. Urbane Apartments, a property investment and management company in Royal Oak, Michigan, has a virtual prominence that far exceeds its real-world scope. The company boasts a resident-penned blog touting favorite Royal Oak destinations, its own Urbane Lobby social networking site for tenants, and active YouTube, Facebook, and Twitter profiles.[48] Mobile marketing can be especially important given the local nature of many small businesses.
- *Create buzz and a loyal brand community.* Small businesses often must rely on word of mouth to establish their positioning, but they can find public relations,

(continued)

marketing insight *(continued)*

social networking, and low-cost promotions and sponsorship to be inexpensive alternatives. Creating a vibrant brand community among current and prospective customers can also be a cost-effective way to reinforce loyalty and help spread the word to new prospects. Evernote has several dozen "power users" who serve as passionate ambassadors to spread the word about the personal-organization application brand touted by the online company as the everything-in-one-place "external brain" for its customers.[49]

- *Employ a well-integrated set of brand elements.* Tactically, it is important for small businesses to maximize the contribution of all types of brand-equity drivers. In particular, they should develop a distinctive, well-integrated set of brand elements—brand names, logos, packaging—that enhances both brand awareness and brand image. Brand elements should be memorable and meaningful, with as much creative potential as possible. Innovative packaging can substitute for ad campaigns by capturing attention at the point of purchase. SMARTFOOD introduced its first product without any advertising by means of both a unique package that served as a strong visual symbol on the shelf and an extensive sampling program that encouraged trial. Proper names or family names, which often characterize small businesses, may provide some distinctiveness but can suffer in terms of pronounceability, meaningfulness, memorability, or other branding considerations.
- *Leverage as many secondary associations as possible.* Secondary associations—any persons, places, or things with potentially relevant associations—are often a cost-effective shortcut to building brand equity, especially those that help to signal quality or credibility. In 1996, J. Darius Bickoff launched an electrolyte-enhanced line of bottled water called Smartwater, followed in two years by the introduction of Vitaminwater, a vitamin-enhanced and flavored alternative to plain bottled water, and by Fruitwater two years after that. Clever marketing (including endorsement deals with rapper 50 Cent, singer Kelly Clarkson, actress Jennifer Aniston, and football star Tom Brady) helped drive success. Less than 10 years after its launch, Bickoff's Energy Brands company, also known as Glacéau, was sold to the Coca-Cola company for $4.2 billion.[50]

summary

1. A key aspect of marketing strategy is the development of a value proposition and positioning a company's offering to target customers. By clearly articulating its value proposition and positioning, companies can deliver high customer value and satisfaction, which lead to high repeat purchases and ultimately to greater company profitability.
2. Depending on the needs of consumers, an offering can create value across three domains: *functional value,* which consists of the benefits and costs that are directly related to an offering's performance; *psychological value,* which encompasses the psychological benefits and costs associated with the offering; and *monetary value,* which includes the financial benefits and costs associated with the offering. Across all three dimensions, consumer value is the difference between the consumers' evaluation of all the benefits and costs of an offering and their evaluation of the benefits and costs of the perceived alternatives.
3. The *value proposition* consists of the whole cluster of benefits the company promises to deliver. It is based on the difference between benefits customers get and costs they assume with respect to the company's offering. The value proposition is customer specific; customer segments with different needs require distinct value propositions.
4. *Positioning* is the act of designing a company's offering and image to occupy a distinctive place in the minds of the target customers. Unlike the value proposition, which articulates all benefits and costs of the offering, the positioning zeroes in on the key benefits that will provide consumers with a reason to choose the company's offering.
5. Consumers determine the value of an offering relative to a *frame of reference* used to assess its benefits and costs. An offering can be viewed as attractive in comparison to an inferior offering, and the same offering can be perceived as unattractive when compared to a superior offering. Marketers must carefully select a frame of reference that highlights the value of their offering.
6. A key component of developing a positioning strategy is identifying the *points of difference*—attributes or benefits that are unique to the company's offering—and the *points of parity*—attributes or benefits that the company's offering has in common with the competition. Three criteria determine whether a brand association can truly function as a point of difference: desirability, deliverability, and differentiability.
7. *Competitive advantage* is a company's ability to perform in one or more ways that competitors cannot or will not match. An offering's competitive advantage gives customers a reason to choose this offering rather than the available alternatives. The competitive advantage reflects the offering's points of difference that are valued by customers. Any product or service benefit that is sufficiently desirable, deliverable, and differentiating can serve as a point of difference and hence create a competitive advantage.
8. Three core strategies are integral to designing a value proposition that makes an offering stand out from the

competition and creates a competitive advantage. These strategies are differentiating on an existing attribute, introducing a new attribute, and building a strong brand.

9. Once marketers have designed an offering's positioning strategy, they develop a *positioning statement* to communicate this positioning to everyone in the organization and ensure that it guides their market actions. The key aspects of crafting an effective positioning statement include communicating an offering's category membership and points of parity and points of difference, and developing a narrative to convey the offering's positioning.

marketing SPOTLIGHT

Unilever: Axe and Dove

Unilever—manufacturer of home care, food, and personal-care brands—effectively uses marketing communication strategies to target specific age groups, demographics, and lifestyles. The company has developed some of the most successful brands in the world, including Axe, a male grooming brand, and Dove, a personal-care brand aimed at women.

The Axe brand (known as Lynx in the UK, Ireland, Australia, and China) launched in 1983, was introduced in the United States in 2002, and is now sold in over 70 different countries. Axe offers young male consumers a wide range of personal-care products such as body sprays, body gel, deodorant, and shampoo, which come in a variety of different scents. Today, Axe is the most popular male grooming brand in the world. Axe effectively broke through the clutter by finding the right target group and luring these customers with personal marketing messages that hit home.

Unilever categorized the male population into several different profile groups and decided that the biggest opportunity existed in the segment—dubbed "The Insecure Novice"—composed of geeks and nerds who needed help attracting the opposite sex and could easily be persuaded to buy products to help their appearance. Most Axe ads targeting this segment use humor and sex, often featuring skinny, average guys attracting beautiful girls by the dozens, hundreds, or even thousands after dousing themselves with Axe. The result: the brand is aspirational and approachable, and the light-hearted tone hits home with young men.

Axe has won numerous advertising awards not only for its creativity but also for its effective use of unconventional media channels. From edgy online videos to video games, mating game tool kits, chat rooms, and mobile apps, the Axe brand engages young adult males at relevant times, locations, and environments. In Colombia, for example, a female Axe Patrol scopes out the bar and club scene and sprays men with Axe body sprays. Unilever marketing director Kevin George explained, "This is all about going beyond the 30-second TV commercial to create a deeper bond with our guy."

Axe knows where to reach its consumers. It advertises only on male-dominated networks such as MTV, ESPN, Spike, and Comedy Central. It partners with the NBA and NCAA, which draw in young male audiences, and also runs ads during big sporting events. Print ads appear in

Source: Retro AdArchives/Alamy Stock Photo

Playboy, *Rolling Stone*, *GQ*, and *Maxim*. Axe's online efforts via Facebook and Twitter help drive consumers back to its website, TheAxeEffect.com.

Unilever understands that it must keep the brand fresh, relevant, and cool in order to stay current with its fickle young audience. As a result, the company launches a new fragrance annually and refreshes its online and advertising communications constantly, realizing that new males enter and exit its target market each year. Perhaps even more important than updating its product line is keeping the brand relevant and in tune with the social trends. As a result, in a matter of just a few years, Axe has made a U-turn, moving away from celebrating male stereotypes to forcefully opposing them.

The "Is It OK for Guys?" commercial that is part of Axe's "Find Your Magic" campaign is urging men to scrap traditional male stereotypes and instead embrace a more contemporary version of masculinity. The ad depicts guys who privately struggle with masculinity asking questions such as *Is it OK to be a virgin? Is it OK to experiment with other guys? Is it OK to be the little spoon in bed?* The questions, which are based on actual Google searches, underscore the degree to which young men feel anxious about adhering to, as well as straying from, societal stereotypes of masculinity. The campaign aims to let customers know they're not alone

(*continued*)

in questioning the boundaries of the traditional image of manhood and thus establishes an emotional connection with the brand.

On the other side of the personal marketing spectrum, Unilever's Dove brand speaks to women with a different tone and message. In 2003, Dove shifted away from its historical advertising, which touted the brand's benefit of one-quarter moisturizing cream, and launched the "Dove Campaign for Real Beauty." "Real Beauty" celebrated "real" women and spoke personally to women about the notion that beauty comes in all shapes, sizes, ages, and colors. The campaign arose from research revealing that only 4 percent of women worldwide think they are beautiful.

The first phase of the "Real Beauty" campaign featured nontraditional female models and asked viewers to judge their looks online and decide whether they were 'Wrinkled or Wonderful?' or 'Oversized or Outstanding?' The personal questions shocked many but created such a large PR buzz that Dove continued the campaign. The second phase of the campaign featured candid and confident images of curvy, full-bodied women. Again, the Dove brand smashed stereotypes of what usually appeared in advertising and, as a result, touched a chord with the majority of women worldwide. The third phase of the campaign, called "Pro-Age," featured older, nude women and asked questions like "Does beauty have an age limit?" Immediately, the company heard positive feedback from its older consumers. Dove also started a Self-Esteem Fund, aimed at helping women feel better about their looks.

As part of the "Real Beauty" campaign, Dove released a series of short Dove Films, one of which, *Evolution*, won both a Cyber and a film Grand Prix at the International Advertising Festival in Cannes in 2007. The film shows a rapid-motion view of an ordinary-looking woman transformed by makeup artists, hairdressers, lighting, and digital retouching to end up looking like a billboard supermodel. The end tagline is "No wonder our perception of beauty is distorted." The film instantly became a viral hit.

Dove followed up with *Onslaught*, a short film that showed a young, innocent, fresh-faced girl being bombarded with images of sexy, half-dressed women and promises of products to make her look "smaller," "softer," "firmer," and "better." Dove's 2013 film called *Sketches* featured a police sketch artist who drew two pictures of the same woman. In one, the woman described herself to the sketch artist from behind a curtain, and in the other picture a total stranger described the woman she had just met to the sketch artist. The difference in language and descriptions revealed how women are often their own harshest beauty critics and ended with the tagline "You are more beautiful than you think." The *Sketches* film has become the most watched video advertisement of all time and attracted over 175 million views in its first year alone.

Although the Axe and Dove campaigns couldn't be more different, and both have sparked much controversy and debate, the two brands have been credited with effectively targeting their consumer base with personal marketing strategies and spot-on messages. Axe's success in personal marketing has lifted the brand to become the leader in what many had thought was the mature deodorant category. And, in the 15 years that Dove focused on changing the attitudes of women and promoting positive self-esteem, sales jumped from $2.5 billion to $6 billion.[51]

Questions

1. What are the customer value propositions for Dove and Axe? What are the similarities and differences between the brands?
2. Is there a conflict in the way Unilever markets to women and the way it markets to young men? Is making women sex symbols in Axe ads undoing all the good that might be done in the "Dove Campaign for Real Beauty"?
3. How should Unilever manage these brands in the future? Should it try to find a universal positioning that fits both brands?

marketing SPOTLIGHT

Lenskart

Peyush Bansal, Amit Chaudhary and Sumeet Kapahi founded Lenskart in 2010, to offer affordable range of designer and trendy eyewear and related accessories. Peyush's first venture, searchmycampus set up in 2008, focused on classifieds for college students looking for jobs, accommodation, car pool or any such service.[52] After completing a program on entrepreneurship at IIM Bangalore in 2009, he started an online retail store—Flyrr—to sell spectacles, sunglasses and contact lenses to customers in the US. After the initial success, he started encountering challenges in product delivery. Realizing the need to control operations and delivery, he shifted focus to the domestic market and set up Lenskart in 2010 to sell a wide range of eyewear products at discounted prices, thereby, making the export-quality products affordable to all. The eyewear market was then by and large dominated by unorganized retail—offering low quality and low-cost products—with around 95% market share. The organized retail served high-end customers with international brands such as Ray-Ban and Ralph Lauren at premium prices. Lenskart started its business with a mission 'to provide every Indian access to high-quality designer glasses without shelling out their pocket.'

(*continued*)

Source: picsjockey.shutterstock.com

Lenskart took control over the complete supply chain to maintain quality as well as manage costs. The company invested in backward integration by setting up its own manufacturing unit. In addition, it also manages the end-to-end logistics to ensure timely delivery.

The company acquired high end machinery for 'zero error tolerance', 3D try-on software and robotics technologies from reputed American and German suppliers. These automated equipment ensure perfection with robotic systems to inspect lenses, determine geometric center, and load the lenses for edging without the need of a finishing block. Shaping by laser machines delivers micro-precision glasses with 0.00 degree power error enabling Lenskart keep its promise of high quality products.

The company set up chat lines to clarify customer queries and offered a 14-day, no-questions-asked returns policy for all its products, including lenses. Lenskart products are accompanied with an authenticity card and a one-year warranty. The authenticity card stands as a proof of quality and reinforces legitimacy. These customer-centric approaches instilled confidence in first-time online buyers.

Customers are used to physical touching, feeling and trying out different eyeglasses frames before buying eyewear. Lenskart started setting up retail outlets to manage the offline experiences and switched to an omni-channel model with its physical presence complementing online retail. The trust and assurance expressed about the quality of frames and lens before purchase resulted in reduced reluctance and improved product offtake. Customers can visit the stores to try out the spectacles. They can also use Lenskart's '3D Try-on' feature in the mobile app to get a feel of how they will appear with different models of spectacles online. Furthermore, the company's 'Try frames@home' service allows customers to try different frames in the comfort of their homes. An eye specialist carries over 100 types of stylish frames for trial at customer's doorstep. A membership program—Lenskart Gold Membership program— for regular and loyal customers is an annual subscription plan of ₹600 with multiple benefits like additional discount, fast delivery, extended warranty and much more.[53] Lenskart started attracting he customers from the unorganized retailers by making designer eyewear solutions available to them directly. With its omni-channel model and clear positioning, Lenskart soon captured a large share of eyewear market by serving more than 100,000 customers per month. The prices offered by Lenskart ranges between ₹345 to ₹30,000, with a vast range of products to meet the requirements of everyone. In addition, Lenskart's exclusive offer of 'the first frame for free' to all its customers continues since inception.

The company has a wide reach with 750 outlets across India to complement its online and app-based services. The physical presence created an image of Lenskart being a friendly neighborhood eyewear store that is available, accessible, and affordable to all its customers. Lenskart also emphasizes its 'no middle-man' based supply chain model that reduces costs for its fast delivery, high quality and affordability of products.[54]

With a portfolio of more than 5000 styles of eye glasses and 45 types of contact lenses at affordable prices, Lenskart justifies its tagline 'Aur Dikhao' (show more), which fits the

(*continued*)

Indian customer's mindset, to try out as many options as possible. The brand is known for its quality and unique services to ensure all possible support a customer might require before purchase. The eye test facility is also made available at the doorsteps.

Lenskart's commitment to customer satisfaction and innovative technology has developed trust and brand loyalty in its customers. With their quality products and affordable offerings, Lenskart have grown by more than 200% in the last couple of years and is amongst the top three players in India's rapidly growing market for eyewear. The company has successfully created an image of a brand which offers 'value for money'. Its designer products at affordable prices, make customers believe that "not all good things in the world are expensive".

With their 'all under one roof' concept, Lenskart has ensured the availability of a wide product portfolio with all varieties of fashionable eyewear and accessories. The variety and types of styles offered by Lenskart is more than five times the variety offered by other retailers. With its strategic position and unique offerings, Lenskart is also working towards its vision 'to reduce the number of people with avoidable blindness by extending their service in each corner of India".[55]

After a decade's experience in the Indian market, Lenskart received the unicorn status in FY2020, after raising $275 million from SoftBank. In the same financial year, it turned profitable while generating a topline of ₹894.22 crore.[56]

Questions

1. What is LensKart's customer value proposition? Is this value proposition sustainable?
2. What are the points of parity and the points of difference for LensKart relative to its competitors?
3. What role does direct-to-consumer distribution play in LensKart's business model? What are the pros and cons of LensKart making its products available in traditional eyewear stores?

CHAPTER 8

Designing and Managing Products

Tesla's Model 3 set out to prove that mass-produced, environmentally sound electric cars can successfully and profitably pilfer market share from producers of traditional gasoline-powered vehicles.

Source: imageBROKER/ Alamy Stock Photo

At the heart of a great brand is a great product. To achieve market leadership, firms must offer products and services of superior quality that provide unsurpassed customer value. Tesla has conquered the electric car market in the United States, thanks in part to a relentless focus on product innovation and performance.

>>> In March 2016, Tesla revealed the long-awaited Model 3, the vehicle that the company hopes will ultimately take the electric car to the mass consumer. Priced starting at $35,000 (after $8,000 credits and fuel savings were factored in), Model 3 aimed to disrupt the auto industry by proving that mass producing an environmentally friendly vehicle is both feasible and profitable. Tesla's new mass market car created a lot of excitement, generating over half a million pre-orders, 100,000 of which were placed before the Model 3 was revealed. The customer appeal of Model 3 stemmed from several factors. Perhaps the most important was the lack of direct competition. The combination of Tesla's image as a luxury brand and the (relatively) low price point made it the only option for customers who were looking for an all-electric sedan priced around $40,000. To achieve its goal of building 5,000 vehicles a week, Tesla invested close to $1 billion to build its first Gigafactory—a lithium-ion battery and vehicle assembly factory near Reno, Nevada. Tesla's efforts to scale up

production of Model 3 paid off: In 2018, it became the best-selling luxury vehicle in the United States, despite the fact that electric cars made up only 1.12% of total vehicle sales. Despite its success, Tesla faces growing competition from other car manufacturers that are revamping their product lines to include an increasing number of all-electric vehicles. Yet Tesla's focus is on gaining share from the traditional car market. "Our true competition is not the small trickle of non-Tesla electric cars being produced," argued Tesla's CEO Elon Musk, "but rather the enormous flood of gasoline cars pouring out of the world's factories every day." In the fall of 2020, Elon Musk laid out a plan for Tesla to build a $25,000 electric car using drastically lower-cost batteries to potentially turn the company into the world's largest car manufacturer.[1]

Marketing planning begins with formulating an offering to meet target customers' needs or wants. The customer will judge the offering's benefits on three basic elements: product, service, and brand. In this chapter we examine product; in Chapter 9, services; and in Chapter 10, brand. All three elements—product, service, and brand—must be fused into a competitively attractive market offering.

Product Differentiation

To successfully compete in the market, products must be differentiated. At one extreme are products that allow little variation: chicken, aspirin, and steel. Yet even here some differentiation is possible: Perdue chickens, Bayer aspirin, and India's Tata Steel have carved out distinct identities in their categories. Procter & Gamble makes Tide, Cheer, and Gain laundry detergents, each with a separate brand identity. At the other extreme are products that lend themselves to high differentiation, such as automobiles, commercial buildings, and furniture. Here the seller faces an abundance of differentiation possibilities.

Well-differentiated products can create significant competitive advantages. Crafting a distinctive aura for a product that helps distance it from competitors can involve moves that range from impressive technological advances like Intuitive Surgical's da Vinci robotic system for minimally invasive surgery to simple tweaks like putting a Chiquita sticker on a banana. Some brands, such as De Beers, differentiate their products by tying them to special occasions. Others, including Tropicana and Tiffany, use packaging to ensure that they stand out from their respective competitors.

Attributes on the basis of which to differentiate include core functionality, features, performance quality, conformance quality, durability, reliability, form, style, and customization.[2] Design has become an increasingly important differentiator, and we discuss it separately later in the chapter.

- **Core functionality.** To create customer value, products must deliver on their core benefit. Products that fail to deliver on their core value proposition will inevitably fail in the market. Consider the plight of one-time highflier Nokia.

Learning Objectives After studying this chapter you should be able to:

8.1 Explain how companies use product differentiation to create market value.

8.2 Explain the role of product design in differentiating market offerings.

8.3 Discuss the key aspects of designing product portfolios and product lines.

8.4 Describe the key decisions involved in managing product packaging.

8.5 Explain how companies design and manage product guarantees and warranties.

Source: Lenscap/Alamy Stock Photo

>> Failure to keep innovating and stay relevant allowed competitors to oust pioneer Nokia from its perch as the former leader in the technology-intense mobile phone industry.

Nokia For 14 years, Nokia dominated cell phone sales as the world's industry leader, before being surpassed by Samsung. Once the pride of Finland, the company has found itself outsold by Samsung even on its home soil. How could such a high-flying brand come crashing to earth? In a nutshell, it failed to innovate and stay relevant. Nokia did not respond to the wildly successful iPhone and the shifting consumer demand that accompanied it. The company thought the iPhone was too expensive to manufacture and was not up to its own product standards. The iPhone reportedly failed Nokia's "drop test," in which a phone is dropped on concrete from a height of five feet at different angles. Nokia had actually spent $40 billion on R&D over the preceding decade and was a smart-phone pioneer, but it chose not to invest in devices that anticipated what the iPhone eventually became. Without the right new products, Nokia began to be associated by consumers with an earlier era of technology, a fatal blow in the fast-moving, technologically intensive smart-phone market.[3]

- **Features.** Most products can be offered with varying features that supplement their basic function. A company can identify and select appropriate new features by surveying recent buyers and then calculating *customer value* versus *company cost* for each potential feature. Marketers should consider how many people want each feature, how long it would take to introduce it, and whether competitors could easily copy it.[4] To avoid "feature fatigue," the company must prioritize features and tell consumers how to use and benefit from them.[5] For example, although Apple's sleek looks attracted attention, it was the simplified and more intuitive user interface that lured even technophobic customers to the computer market and gained it a cult following. Marketers must also think in terms of feature bundles or packages. Auto companies often manufacture cars at several "trim levels." This lowers manufacturing and inventory costs. Each company must decide whether to offer feature customization at a higher cost or a few standard packages at a lower cost.
- **Performance quality** is the level at which the product's primary characteristics operate. Quality is growing increasingly important for differentiation as companies adopt a value model and provide higher quality for less money. Firms should design a performance level appropriate to the target market and competition—however, not necessarily the highest level possible. They must also manage performance quality through time. Continuously improving the product can produce high returns and market share; failing to do so can have negative consequences. The latter proved to be the case for Kodak and Commodore.
- **Conformance quality.** Buyers expect high **conformance quality**, the degree to which all produced units are identical and meet promised specifications. Suppose a Porsche 911 is designed to accelerate to 60 miles per hour within 10 seconds. If every Porsche 911 coming off the assembly line does this, the model is said to have high conformance quality. A product with low conformance quality will disappoint some buyers. Firms thoroughly test finished products to ensure conformance. Although men account for almost three-quarters of the world's beer sales, SABMiller found that women were actually more sensitive to levels of flavor in beer and thus were better product testers.[6]
- **Durability,** a measure of the product's expected operating life under natural or stressful conditions, is a valued attribute for vehicles, kitchen appliances, and other durable goods. The extra price for durability must not be excessive, however, and the product must not be subject to overly rapid technological obsolescence, as personal computers, televisions, and cell phones have sometimes been.
- **Reliability** is a measure of the probability that a product will not malfunction within a specified time period. Maytag has an outstanding reputation for creating reliable home appliances. Its long-running "Lonely Repairman" ad campaign was designed to highlight that attribute. Buyers normally will pay a premium for more reliable products.

Mercedes-Benz In the midst of the first decade of this century, Mercedes-Benz endured one of the most painful stretches in its history. The company saw its reputation for stellar quality take a beating in J. D. Power and other surveys, and BMW surpassed it in global sales. To recover, a new management team was organized around functional elements—motors, chassis, and electronic systems—instead of model lines. Engineers now begin testing electronic systems a year earlier and put each new model through 10,000 diagnostics that run 24 hours a day for three weeks. Mercedes-Benz also tripled its number of prototypes for new designs, allowing engineers to drive them 3 million miles before production. With these and other changes, the number of flaws in the company's cars dropped 72 percent from the 2002 peak, and warranty costs decreased 25 percent. As an interesting side effect, Mercedes-Benz dealers have had to contend with a sizable drop in their repair and service businesses.[7]

- **Form** Many products can be differentiated by form—the size, shape, or physical structure of a product. Consider the many possible forms of aspirin. Although essentially a commodity, aspirin can be differentiated by dosage, size, shape, color, coating, or action time.
- **Style** describes the product's look and feel to the buyer and creates distinctiveness that is hard to copy. Car buyers pay a premium for Jaguars because of their extraordinary looks. Aesthetics plays a key role for such brands as Apple computers, Godiva chocolate, and Harley-Davidson motorcycles.[8] Strong style does not always mean high performance, however. A car may look sensational but spend a lot of time in the repair shop.
- **Customization** Customized products and marketing enable firms to differentiate strategically by finding out exactly what a person wants—and doesn't want—and delivering on that.[9] Online retailers such as Zazzle and CafePress allow users to upload images and create their own clothing and posters or to buy merchandise created by other users. NikeiD, which allows customers to personalize and design their own shoes and clothing either online or in store at NikeiD Studios, generates hundreds of millions of dollars in revenue. The demand for customization is certainly there. One Forrester study found that more than a third of U.S. online consumers were interested in customizing product features or in purchasing build-to-order products that use their specifications. And companies have responded: M&M's allows you to print specialized messages on your candies; Pottery Barn Kids allows you to personalize a children's book; and for $2,000 or so, Burberry allows you to select the fabric, color, style, and five other features for your own personalized trench coat.[10]

Product Design

As competition intensifies, design offers a potent way to differentiate and position a company's products and services. **Design** is the totality of features that affect the way consumers perceive a product's look, feel, and function. Design offers functional and aesthetic benefits and appeals to both our rational and emotional sides.[11]

Source: Ekaterina_Minaeva/Shutterstock

<< Many different products, such as M&Ms, can now be customized by consumers.

POWER OF DESIGN

In our visually oriented culture, transmitting brand meaning and positioning through design is critical. Eye-catching form, color, and graphics can help an offering separate itself from competitive products. "In a crowded marketplace," writes Virginia Postrel in *The Substance of Style*, "aesthetics is often the only way to make a product stand out."[12] Design is especially important with long-lasting durable goods such as automobiles. Cognizant of consumers' desire for both form and functionality, Tesla excelled in developing a car that is both good for the environment and aesthetically appealing.

Design can shift consumer perceptions to make brand experiences more rewarding. Consider the lengths Boeing went to in making its 787 aircraft seem roomier and more comfortable. Raised center bins, side luggage bins, divider panels, gently arched ceilings, and raised seats make the aircraft interior seem bigger. One design engineer noted, "If we do our jobs, people don't realize what we have done. They just say they feel more comfortable."

As holistic marketers recognize the emotional power of design and the importance to consumers of look and feel as well as function, design is exerting a stronger influence in categories where it once played a small role. Herman Miller office furniture, Viking ranges and kitchen appliances, and Kohler kitchen and bathroom fixtures and faucets are among the brands that now stand out in their categories, thanks to attractive looks added to efficient and effective performance.

Some countries have developed strong reputations for their design skills and accomplishments, such as Italy in apparel and furniture and Scandinavia in products designed for functionality, aesthetics, and environmental consciousness. Finland's Marimekko fabrics, which brought the breadth of colorful and unusual Finnish textiles to the attention of the world, are still being made using environmentally safe techniques. And the Finnish firm Fiskars, which dates back to the 17th century, is known around the world not only for Fiskars products but also for such other internationally recognized brands as Wedgwood, Waterford, Arabia, and Royal Doulton. Dyson put the United Kingdom on the international product design map by elevating the form and efficiency of such "homely" products as vacuums, fans, and hair dryers to a high art.

APPROACHES TO DESIGN

Design is not just a phase in creating a product, service, or application. It's a way of thinking that penetrates all aspects of the marketing program so all design aspects work together. For the company, a well-designed product is easy to manufacture and distribute. For the customer, it is pleasant to look at and easy to open, install, use, repair, and dispose of. The designer must take all these goals into account.[13]

Given the creative nature of design, it's no surprise there isn't one widely adopted approach. Some firms employ formal, structured processes. **Design thinking** is a very data-driven approach with three phases: observation, ideation, and implementation. Design thinking requires intensive ethnographic studies of consumers, creative brainstorming sessions, and collaborative teamwork to decide how to bring the design idea to reality. Whirlpool used design thinking to develop the KitchenAid Architect kitchen appliances with a more harmonized look than had previously existed in the category. Another company known for its design prowess is Bang & Olufsen.

Bang & Olufsen The Danish firm Bang & Olufsen (B&O)—which has received many kudos for the design of its stereos, TV equipment, and telephones—trusts the instincts of a handful of designers who rarely consult with consumers. The company does not introduce many new products in any given year, so each one is expected to be sold for a long time. Its BeoLab 8000 speakers sold for $3,000 a pair when introduced in 1992 and retailed for more than $5,000 almost 20 years later. When the company was the subject of a special exhibition at the Museum of Modern Art in New York City, the museum noted, "Bang & Olufsen design their sound equipment as beautiful objects in their own right that do not inordinately call attention to themselves." Today, 15 B&O products are part of MOMA's permanent design collection.[14]

Design needn't involve extensive remodeling. "Universal design" and "incremental improvement" are the watchwords at Oxo, maker of kitchen and office supplies. Oxo appeals to users from grandparents to grandchildren with small, frustration-relieving improvements that make everyday objects a pleasure to use. Its clever redo of the salad spinner, inspired by a child's toy carousel, lets users operate it by pushing a button instead of pulling a string or manually rotating a knob while holding the spinner down with the other hand. Oxo's rectangular, easy-to-grab storage containers also open with a top button, eliminating the need to tug on a corner. Oxo added thickly padded handles to the lowly kitchen peeler to make it easier to use, and its tongs have a non-slip handle and lock to keep them closed for easier storing.[15]

Source: Grzegorz Czapski/Alamy Stock Photo

<< Well-thought-out, timeless design ensures that TV and sound products from Danish firm Bang & Olufsen have a long life span.

The International Design and Excellence Awards (IDEA) are given each year based on benefit to the user, benefit to the client/business, benefit to society, ecological responsibility, appropriate aesthetics and appeal, and usability testing. IDEO has been one of the more successful design companies through the years. Samsung's recent design accomplishments have been the result of a concerted effort.

Samsung Much of Samsung's remarkable marketing success comes from innovative new products that have captured the imagination of consumers all over the world. The company has invested heavily in R&D and in design capabilities, with big payoffs. It has a clear design philosophy it calls "Design 3.0" and an internal design slogan, "Make it Meaningful," that reflects its relentless focus on making beautiful and intuitive products that will be integrated into customers' lifestyles. Samsung applies three design criteria. Its products are (1) simple and intuitive, (2) efficient and long lasting, and (3) adaptive and engaging. Like its chief rival, Apple, the company organizes its design efforts through a cross-divisional Corporate Design Center that reports directly to the CEO. The Corporate Design Center aligns the design efforts of various divisions and analyzes cultural trends to help forecast the future of design. It also coordinates the work done at Samsung's five Global Design Centers, located in London, San Francisco, Shanghai, Tokyo, and Delhi.[16]

Source: Sundry Photography/Alamy Stock Photo

<< With a design philosophy underpinned by an internal "Make it Meaningful" slogan, Samsung is focused on making beautiful and functional products that can be integrated into consumers' lifestyles.

Product Portfolios and Product Lines

Most products exist as a part of a company's product portfolio and/or product line. Each product must be related to other products to ensure that a firm is offering the optimal set of products to fulfill the needs of its different customer segments.

PRODUCT PORTFOLIO DESIGN

A **product portfolio** encompasses all products offered by a company, including various product categories and product lines. For example, the extensive iPhone product portfolio includes headphones and headsets, cables and docks, armbands, cases, power and car accessories, and speakers. NEC's (Japan) portfolio consists of communication products and computer products. Michelin has three product lines: tires, maps, and restaurant-rating services. At Northwestern University, separate academic deans oversee the schools of medicine, law, business, engineering, music, journalism, and liberal arts, among others.

A company's product portfolio has a certain width, length, depth, and consistency. These concepts are illustrated in Figure 8.1 for selected Procter & Gamble consumer products.

- The **width** of a product portfolio is the number of different product lines the company carries. Figure 8.1 shows a product portfolio width of three lines. (In fact, P&G produces many additional lines.)
- The **length** of a product portfolio is the total number of items in the mix. In Figure 8.1, it is 12. We can also talk about the average length of a line. We obtain this by dividing the total length (here 12) by the number of lines (here 3), for an average product line length of 4.
- The **depth** of a product portfolio consists of the number of variants offered for each product in the line. If Tide came in two scents (Clean Breeze and Regular), in two formulations (liquid and powder), and with two additives (with and without bleach), it would have a depth of six because there are six distinct variants.[17] We can calculate the average depth of P&G's product mix by averaging the number of variants within the brand groups.
- The **consistency** of the product portfolio reflects how closely related the various product lines are in end use, production requirements, distribution channels, or some other way. P&G's product lines are consistent in that they are consumer goods that go through the same distribution channels. The lines are less consistent in the functions they perform for buyers.

These four product mix dimensions permit a company to expand its business in four ways. It can add new product lines, thus widening its product mix. It can lengthen each product line. It can add more product variants to each product and thereby deepen its product mix. Finally, a company can pursue more product line consistency. To make these product, service, and brand decisions, marketers can conduct product line analysis.

PRODUCT LINE ANALYSIS

A **product line** is a group of related products sold by the same company. In offering a product line, companies normally develop a basic platform and modules that can be added to meet different customer requirements and lower production costs. Car manufacturers build cars around a basic platform. Homebuilders show a model home to which buyers can add additional features. Product line managers

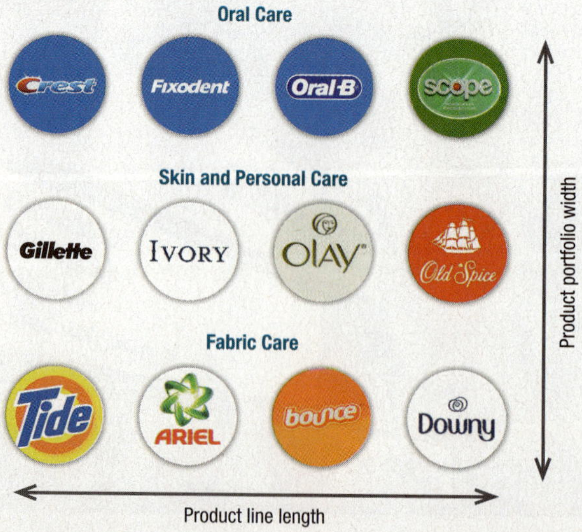

FIGURE **8.1**

Product Portfolio Width and Product Line Length for Procter & Gamble Products

Sources: REUTERS/Lucy Nicholson/Alamy Stock Photo; Keith Homan/Alamy Stock Photo; Malcolm Haines/Alamy Stock Photo; Keith Homan/Alamy Stock Photo; GK Images/Alamy Stock Photo; Courtesy of Kelly Murphy; Keith Homan/Alamy Stock Photo; GK Images/Alamy Stock Photo; rvlsoft/Alamy Stock Photo; rvlsoft/Alamy Stock Photo; Betty LaRue/Alamy Stock Photo; Helen/Alamy Stock Photo need to know the sales and profits of each item in their line to determine which items to build, maintain, harvest, or divest.[18] They also need to understand each product line's market profile and image.[19]

A company's product line typically contains products that appeal to different layers of customer needs. Supermarkets make almost no margin on bread and milk, reasonable margins on canned and frozen foods, and better margins on flowers, ethnic food lines, and freshly baked goods. Companies should recognize that different items will allow for different margins and develop strategies for maximizing the profitability of the entire product line.

The product line manager must review how the line is positioned against competitors' lines. Consider Paper Company X with a paperboard product line.[20] Two paperboard attributes are weight and finish quality. Paper is usually offered at standard levels of 90, 120, 150, and 180 weights. Finish quality is offered at low, medium, and high levels.

A product map allows a company to see its main competitors at a glance. It also helps planners to identify market segments and spot market opportunities. The map in Figure 8.2 shows the location of the various product line items of Company X and four competitors, A, B, C, and D. Competitor A sells two product items in the extra-high-weight class ranging from medium to low finish quality. Competitor B sells four items that vary in weight and finish quality. Competitor C sells three items in which the greater the weight, the greater the finish quality. Competitor D sells three items, all lightweight but varying in finish quality. Company X offers three items that vary in weight and finish quality.

The product map also shows which competitors' items are competing against Company X's items. For example, Company X's low-weight, medium-quality paper competes against competitor D's and B's papers, but its high-weight, medium-quality paper has no direct competitor. The map also reveals possible locations for new items. No manufacturer offers a high-weight, low-quality paper. If Company X estimates a strong unmet demand and can produce this paper at low cost and price it accordingly, it could consider adding this paper to its line.

Another benefit of product mapping is that it identifies market segments. Figure 8.2 shows the types of paper, by weight and quality, preferred by the general printing industry, the point-of-purchase display industry, and the office supply industry. The map shows that Company X is well positioned to serve the needs of the general printing industry but less effective in serving the other two markets.

Multibrand companies all over the world try to optimize their brand portfolios. This often means focusing on core brand growth and concentrating resources on the biggest and most established brands. Hasbro has designated a set of core toy brands to emphasize in its marketing, including GI Joe, Transformers, and My Little Pony. Procter & Gamble's "back to basics" strategy has concentrated on brands with more than $1 billion in revenue, such as Tide, Crest, Pampers, and Pringles. Every product in a product line must play a role, as must every brand in the brand portfolio.

Volkswagen Volkswagen has four different core brands of particular importance in its European portfolio. Initially, Audi and Seat had a sporty image, and VW and Škoda had a family-car image. Audi and VW were in a higher price–quality tier than Škoda and Seat, which had spartan interiors and utilitarian engine performance. To reduce costs, streamline part/systems designs, and eliminate redundancies, Volkswagen upgraded the Seat and Škoda brands, which captured market share with splashy interiors, a full array of safety systems, and reliable power trains. Clearly, the danger is that by borrowing from its upper-echelon Audi and Volkswagen products, Volkswagen could dilute its cachet. Frugal European consumers may convince themselves that a Seat or Škoda is almost identical to its VW sister, at several thousand euros less.[21]

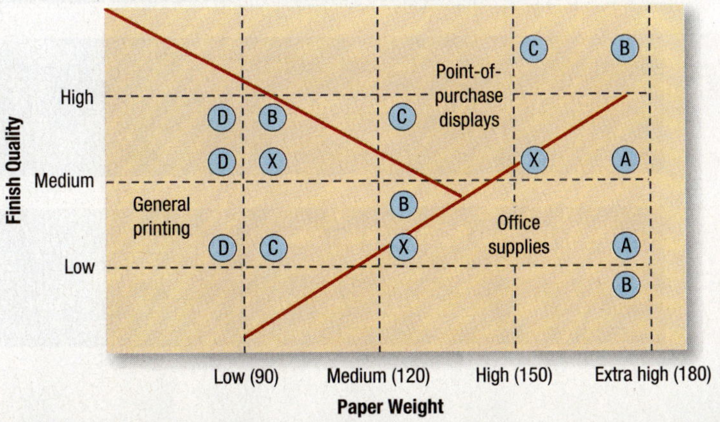

FIGURE **8.2**

Product Map for a Paper-Product Line

Source: Benson P. Shapiro, *Industrial Product Policy: Managing the Existing Product Line* (Cambridge, MA: Marketing Science Institute Report No. 77–110). Copyright © 2003. Reprinted by permission of Marketing Science Institute and Benson P. Shapiro.

>> Volkswagen's upgrade of its European Škoda and Seat family sedans may end up diluting the image of its sportier, higher-priced Audi and VW brands.

Sources: Bodnar Photodesign/Shutterstock; Dmitry Orlov/Alamy Stock Photo

Product lines regularly need to be modernized. The question is whether to overhaul the line piecemeal or all at once. A piecemeal approach allows the company to see how customers and dealers take to the new style. It is also less draining on the company's cash flow, but it lets competitors see changes and start redesigning their own lines. Consider Infosys Finacle's product line innovation.

Infosys Finacle Launched in 1999, Infosys Finacle is a leading banking solution. It pioneered the network-based core banking system to enable round the clock automated operations. By 2005, Finacle had established prominence offering complete banking solutions in 42 countries, and further expanded its services to corporate and retail banking. Its flagship product— 'Bank-in-a-Box'—provides core banking solutions enabling several small and medium size banks adopt automated banking systems. In 2008, Finacle launched its universal banking solutions with multi-entity capabilities like wealth management, mobile and analytics solutions.[22] It developed a digital wallet solution for banks, retailers, financial and telecom service providers to offer a secure, intuitive, and convenient payment experience to their customers. The launch of Finacle 11E in 2011 marked the emergence of a new era of simplified banking, and it also led to Finacle's phenomenal rise as the most scalable banking solution managing over 1.9 billion customer accounts by its banking clients. Banks processed over 50,000 transactions per second using Finacle, 6 times the volume of transactions processed by the entire US banking system.[23] In 2015, Finacle became a part of Edgeverve, a wholly-owned subsidiary of Infosys, offering industry-leading digital banking solutions. Finacle eventually transformed into a cloud-first

>> Finacle, which started as a packaged software, has been an extremely successful offering from Infosys which has been traditionally known for its custom software services and solutions. Investing in innovations and regular upgradations have transformed Finacle into one of the leading global cloud based banking platforms.

Source: The logo / brand name in the image is proprietary to Infosys Finacle

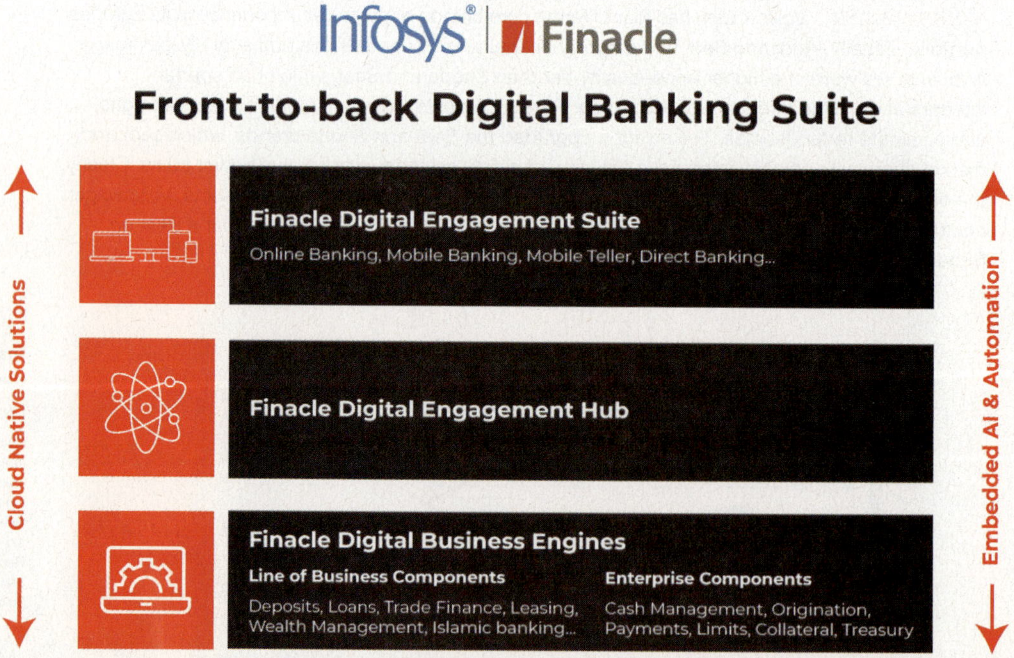

platform, expanded its offering from core banking modernization to simplified and customized digital banking solution using data analytics, machine learning and artificial intelligence. Today, Finacle handles accounts of over 16.5% of the world's banking population servicing more than a billion consumers and 1.7 billion accounts in 100 countries.[24]

In rapidly changing markets, modernization is continuous. Companies plan improvements to encourage customer migration to higher-value, higher-priced items. Microprocessor companies such as Intel and Qualcomm and software companies such as Microsoft, Oracle, and SAP continually introduce more advanced versions of their products. Marketers want to time improvements so they do not appear too early (damaging sales of the current line) or too late (giving the competition time to establish a strong reputation).[25]

PRODUCT LINE LENGTH

Company objectives influence product line length—the total number of items in the product line. One objective is to create a product line to induce up-selling. The Mercedes C-Class plays a critical role as an entry point to the brand. As one industry analyst noted, "The C-Class is critical for the luxury race because it creates the most amount of volume for Benz. It also opens the Benz brand to potential future buyers by catching them while they're young with the hopes that they upgrade as they get more affluent and older."[26]

A different objective is to create a product line that facilitates cross-selling: Hewlett-Packard sells printers as well as computers. Still another is to protect against economic ups and downs: Electrolux sells household appliances such as refrigerators, dishwashers, and vacuum cleaners under different brand names in the discount, middle-market, and premium segments, in part as a hedge against the economy moving up or down. Companies seeking high market share and market growth generally carry longer product lines. Those emphasizing high profitability carry shorter lines consisting of carefully chosen items.

Product lines tend to lengthen over time. Excess manufacturing capacity puts pressure on the product line manager to develop new items. The sales force and distributors also lobby for a fuller product line to satisfy customers. But as items are added, costs rise for design and engineering, inventory carrying, manufacturing changeover, order processing, transportation, and new-item promotions. Eventually, top management may stop development because of insufficient funds or manufacturing capacity. A pattern of product line growth followed by massive pruning may repeat itself many times. Increasingly, consumers are growing weary of dense product lines, overextended brands, and feature-laden products (see "Marketing Insight: When Less Is More").[27] Using sales and cost analysis, product line managers must periodically review the line for deadwood that depresses profits.[28]

Crocs The signature plastic clogs or "boat shoes"—colorful, comfortable, perfect for summer—succeeded soon after their introduction in Boulder, Colorado, in 2002. The company's 2006 IPO was the largest ever in U.S. footwear, raising $208 million. Its stock peaked a year later when Crocs' sales reached $847 million. But the recession and consumer fatigue with the brand were a double whammy that led to a steep drop in sales and drove the stock price down to a mere $1 in what Crocs CFO later called a "near-death experience." By 2011, however, Crocs had rebounded with more than $1 billion in revenue and growth goals of 15 percent to 20 percent. What happened? The company had diversified into more than 300 models of stylish, comfortable boots, loafers, sneakers, and other shoes that helped to reduce its reliance on clogs to less than 50 percent of sales. It also adopted a multichannel distribution approach to sell wholesale through retailers like Kohl's and Dick's Sporting Goods (60 percent of

Source: mozakim/Shutterstock

>> When the quick success achieved by Crocs' signature plastic clogs was threatened by the 2008 recession and lackluster sales, the company rebounded by diversifying with hundreds of stylishly comfortable footwear designs and adopting multichannel distribution.

business), as well as directly online (10 percent) and through more than 500 of its own retail stores (30 percent). International sales now make up more than half of its sales, including in emerging markets and the growing middle-class markets in Asia and Latin America.[29]

A company lengthens its product line in two ways: line stretching and line filling.

Line Stretching. Every company's product line covers a certain part of the total possible range. For example, Mercedes automobiles are located in the upper price range of the automobile market. **Line stretching** occurs when a company lengthens its product line beyond its current range, whether down-market, up-market, or both ways.

Down-Market Stretch. A company positioned in the middle market may want to introduce a lower-priced line for several reasons. First, a company may notice strong growth opportunities in the lower-tier market and enter this market to capture some of this growth. Alternatively, a company might be forced to move downscale because the middle market is stagnating or declining. Finally, a company might stretch its product line downscale to tie up lower-end competitors who might otherwise try to move up-market. Indeed, when a company has been attacked by a low-end competitor, it often decides to counterattack by entering the low end of the market.

When launching downscale product line extensions, companies face a number of branding choices. One option is to use the parent brand name on all its offerings. Sony has used its name on products in a variety of price tiers. An alternative approach is to introduce lower-priced offerings using a sub-brand name, such as P&G's Charmin Basic and Bounty Basic. Yet another option is to introduce the lower-priced offerings under a different name, such as the Gap's Old Navy brand. This strategy is expensive to implement and means brand equity will have to be built from scratch, but the equity of the parent brand name is protected.

Moving down-market carries risks that include dilution of the core brand's image and cannibalization of the core brand's sales. P&G introduced Tide Basic in test markets—priced lower but also lacking some of the latest detergent technology of its famous parent brand—and decided against rolling it out.[30] On the other hand, Mercedes successfully introduced its C-Class cars at $30,000 without impairing its ability to sell other Mercedes cars for $100,000. John Deere introduced a lower-priced line of lawn tractors called Sabre from John Deere, while still selling its more expensive tractors under the John Deere name. In these cases, consumers may have been better able to compartmentalize the different offerings and understand the functional differences between them.[31]

Up-Market Stretch. Companies may wish to enter the high end of the market to achieve more growth, realize higher margins, or simply position themselves as full-line manufacturers. Many markets have spawned upscale segments: Starbucks in coffee, Häagen-Dazs in ice cream, and Evian in bottled water. The leading Japanese auto companies each introduced a highly successful upscale automobile nameplate: Toyota's Lexus, Nissan's Infiniti, and Honda's Acura. They invented entirely new names because consumers might not have given the brand "permission" to stretch upward when those lines were first introduced. Moving up-market is not without risks, however. A company might lack the resources—infrastructure, know-how, and people—to develop a superior product that will fit the needs of its upscale target customers.

Some companies have used their core brands in moving up-market. Gallo sells Gallo Family Vineyards (priced at $10 to $30 a bottle) with a hip, younger image to compete in the premium wine segment. General Electric introduced the GE Profile brand for its large-appliance offerings in the upscale market. In order to signal consumers that there's been a quality improvement, some brands have used modifiers like "new" or "enhanced." Consider Ultra Dry Pampers, Extra Strength Tylenol, and Power Pro Dustbuster Plus.

Two-Way Stretch. Companies serving the middle market might stretch their line in both directions to effectively blanket the market with products and "sandwich" their competition. This carries the risks involved in both down-market and up-market stretches. However, this strategy can work, as evidenced by Robert Mondavi Winery, now owned by Constellation Brands. Mondavi sells $35 bottles of wine as the first premium "New World" wine; it also sells $125 bottles of Mondavi Reserve at high-end wineries, restaurants, and vineyards and through direct order, as well as $11 bottles of Woodbridge created during the grape oversupply of the mid-1990s. Maruti Suzuki further illustrates how simultaneous up- and down-market extension can be effective.

>> Maruti Suzuki strengthened its market position by extending its product line with differentiated offerings that provide different levels of benefits at different price points and reached a wider customer base through separate channels.

Source: ©Maruti Suzuki, used with permission

Maruti Suzuki Maruti Suzuki, largest player in India's passenger car segment capturing almost a half of the market share, offers an extensive variety of cars ranging from hatchbacks (Alto Ritz, A-Star, Swift, Ignis) to sedans (DZire, Ciaz and SX4) and utility vehicles (Ertiga and Grand Vitara). A traditional leader in small cars segment, the company by far has the largest offering in hatchbacks. The last decade, however, has witnessed increased competition in the small cars segment with the launch of new brands, like Eon & i10 from Hyundai, Kwid from Renault, and Zest from Tata, among others. To continue its position as the market leader, Maruti decided to strengthen its portfolio by introducing new and upgraded versions of its small cars. In addition, it expanded its product line upwards by introducing sedans and utility vehicles (UV) as the market trended towards more premium products. Retail outlets, Arena and NEXA, were designed to cater to two distinct categories of customer segments, respectively. Maruti Suzuki Arena provides value-for-money offerings of hatchbacks and sedans that target mostly first-time car buyers belonging to the mid and upper middle-class households. NEXA with its premium showrooms offers a superior buying experience for more expensive sedans and UV that carry the best of features for safety, comfort and convenience. Brands—Ignis, Ciaz, Baleno, S-Cross and XL6—carrying the Suzuki badge, are retailed through NEXA. These upmarket showrooms provide enhanced digital experience like car configurator, mirroring screens, and service data facility tablets for customers in a plusher and modern setting.[32] True Value, Maruti's channel for pre-owned cars, helped expand the market by attracting first time buyers as well as car owners seeking to replace their cars. Twenty years since its inception in 2001, a record number of 4 million pre-owned cars have exchanged hands through True Value.[33]

Line Filling. A firm can also lengthen its product line through **line filling**—that is, by adding more items within the existing range. Motives for line filling include reaching for incremental profits, satisfying dealers who complain about lost sales because of items missing from the line, addressing consumers' desire for variety,[34] trying to become the leading full-line company, and plugging holes to keep out competitors. Consider the way BMW has been filling the gaps in its product line.

BMW AG Over time, BMW has morphed from a one-brand, five-model carmaker into a powerhouse with three brands, 14 series, and roughly 30 distinct models. Not only has the carmaker expanded its product range downward with MINI Coopers and its compact 1-series models, but it has also built it upward with Rolls-Royce and filled in the gaps with its sports activity vehicles, roadsters, and coupes. The company has used line filling successfully to boost its appeal to the rich, the super-rich, and the hope-to-be-rich, all without departing from its pure premium positioning. BMW has also built a clear brand migration strategy within its product line, trying to move its customers from lower-end to higher-end vehicles.[35]

Line filling is overdone if it results in cannibalization, causes confusion, or merely does not address the needs of any customer segment. Indeed, if the offerings are too similar to one another, customers are likely to be confused about which to choose. And if offerings vary in price, they may overwhelmingly buy the cheaper one. In addition to avoiding confusion and cannibalization, the proposed offering should meet a genuine market need, rather than being added simply to satisfy an internal need. The infamous Edsel automobile, on which Ford lost $350 million in the late 1950s, met Ford's internal positioning need for a car between its Ford and Lincoln lines, but it clearly did not meet the market's needs at all.

Managing Packaging and Labeling

Many marketers view packaging and labeling as an important element of product strategy. Some product packages—such as the Coke bottle, Tiffany's blue box, and the Red Bull can—are world famous.

PACKAGING

Packaging includes all the activities of designing and producing the container for a product. Packages might have up to three layers, with one or more of these layers designed to capture the purchaser's attention and ensure that the product is distinct from the competition. Cool Water cologne by Davidoff For Men comes in a signature blue bottle with white lettering (*primary package*) inside a blue cardboard box with white lettering (*secondary package*), shipped in a corrugated box (*shipping package*) to protect the six dozen bottles in cardboard boxes.

Packaging is important because it is the buyer's first encounter with the product. A good package draws the consumer in and encourages product choice. In effect, it can act as a "five-second commercial" for the product. Some packages can even be attractively displayed at home. Distinctive packaging like that for Kiwi shoe polish, Altoids mints, and Absolut vodka is an important part of a brand's equity.

Several factors contribute to the growing use of packaging as a marketing tool.

- **Self-service.** In an average supermarket, which may stock 15,000 items, the typical shopper passes some 300 products per minute. Given that 50 percent to 70 percent of all purchases are made in the store, effective packaging must perform many sales tasks: attract attention, describe the product's features, create consumer confidence, and make a favorable overall impression.
- **Consumer affluence.** Affluent consumers are willing to pay a little more for the convenience, appearance, dependability, and prestige of better packaging.
- **Company and brand image.** Packaging contributes to instant recognition of the company or brand. In the store, they can create a billboard effect, as Garnier Fructis does with its bright green packaging in the hair care aisle.
- **Innovation opportunity.** Unique or innovative packaging can bring big benefits to consumers and profits to producers. Companies are always looking for a way to make their products more convenient and easier to use—often charging a premium when they do so. The SC Johnson Smart Twist Cleaning System has a handheld sprayer and carousel that rotates among concentrated versions of three different cleaning products; Kleenex hand towels use a dispenser that fits upside down on a bathroom towel rack; and Kiwi Express Shine shoe polish has a dispenser and applicator to shine shoes without the need to spread newspaper, wear a glove, or use a brush.

Packaging must achieve a number of objectives: It must identify the brand; convey descriptive and persuasive information; facilitate product transportation, protection, and storage; and aid consumption. To achieve these objectives and satisfy consumers' desires, marketers must ensure that the functional and aesthetic components of packaging are aligned with one another and, at the same time, are optimized to create value for customers and the company. Functionally, structural design is crucial. The packaging elements must harmonize with one another and with pricing, advertising, and other parts of the marketing program.[36] Aesthetic considerations involve a package's size and shape, material, color, text, and graphics.[37]

Color is a particularly important aspect of packaging and carries different meanings in different cultures and market segments. As one expert says, "Color is all-pervasive. It is language-neutral, but loaded with meaning. It's completely overt, yet each person sees color through different eyes, both literally and figuratively."[38] Color can define a brand, from Tiffany's blue box to Cadbury's purple wrapping and UPS's brown trucks. Orange, the telecom mobile operator, uses color as both its look and its very name!

One of the reasons why color is important is that different colors can have different meanings and convey different emotions. Consider the following interpretations of different colors that some marketing experts believe are common in Western culture.[39]

> *Red* symbolizes excitement, energy, passion, courage, and being bold. *Orange* connotes friendliness and fun, combining the energy of red and the warmth of yellow. *Yellow*, the color of the sun, is equated with warmth, joy, and happiness. *Green*, the color of nature, connotes health, growth, freshness, and renewal. *Blue*, the color of the sky and sea, is associated with dependability, trust, competence, and integrity. *Purple* symbolizes nobility, wealth, and wisdom, combining the stability of blue and the energy of red. *Pink* is considered to have soft, peaceful, comforting qualities. *Brown*, the color of the earth, connotes honesty and dependability. *Black* is seen as classic, strong, and balanced. *White* connotes purity, innocence, and cleanliness.

Packaging updates and redesigns can occur frequently to keep the brand contemporary, relevant, or practical. Although these changes can have an immediate impact on sales, they also can have a downside, as PepsiCo learned for its Tropicana brand.

Tropicana PepsiCo experienced great success with its Tropicana brand, acquired in 1998. Then, in 2009, the company launched a redesigned package to "refresh and modernize" the brand. The goal was to create "emotional attachment by 'heroing' the juice and trumpeting the natural fruit goodness." Arnell Group led the extreme makeover, which culminated in an entirely new look, downplaying the brand name, highlighting the phrase "100 percent orange pure & natural," and replacing the "straw in an orange" graphic on the front with a close-up of a glass of orange juice. Consumer response was swift and negative. The package was deemed "ugly" or "stupid," and some even confused the product with a store brand. Sales dropped 20 percent. After only two months, PepsiCo management announced it would revert to the old packaging.[40]

After a company designs its packaging, it must test that packaging. *Engineering tests* ensure that the package stands up under normal conditions; *visual tests* confirm that the script is legible and the colors harmonious; *dealer tests* determine that dealers find the packages attractive and easy to handle; and *consumer tests* establish that buyers will respond favorably.

When developing effective packaging, companies must consider its environmental impact. Japan's tendency to overpackage everything from groceries to cosmetics is in direct contrast to its reputation as a stellar recycler. A lone banana can come wrapped in several layers of cellophane. Squares of chocolate are individually wrapped, put together in a cardboard wrapper, and then encased in plastic. Hygiene and regulations are factors, but tradition and consumer expectations count more. Product wrapping is viewed as an added touch of luxury and often carries the store or brand name. Thus, the designing of environmentally friendly packaging will need to address customer expectations.[41]

Fortunately, addressing growing environmental concerns has become an important element in developing effective packaging in other

>> Cadbury's unique full-colour plastic wrapper is distinctly appealing

Source: Cadbury©Mondelez International, used with permission parts of the world. Although this may consume more of a company's time and resources, many firms have "gone green" and are finding creative new ways to package their wares, which can lead to unexpected benefits. Nespresso, Keurig, and others have developed recyclable coffee pods, which should attract new ecologically minded customers to its coffee-brewing machines. Dell introduced bamboo packaging as an alternative to corrugated cardboard, foam, molded paper pulp, and plastic and took other steps to reduce the overall volume of packaging used.[42] And yet, developing environmentally friendly packaging that also satisfies customers' needs can be challenging, as Frito-Lay found out.

Source: Keith Homan/Alamy Stock Photo

>> Frito-Lay decided to eliminate the entirely compostable bag it had painstakingly developed for its healthier alternative to potato chips after sales slid amid consumer complaints about the bag's high noise level.

Sun Chips Frito-Lay's Sun Chips multigrain snacks, containing 30 percent less fat than potato chips, have succeeded as a healthier, "good for you" snack option. Part of the firm's effort to support a "healthier planet" as well was to run its factory in Modesto, California, on solar power and unveil a novel 100 percent compostable bag made of plant-based materials. Much research went into the development of the bag, and it was launched with fanfare in 2010. Unfortunately, it included polymers that made it "kind of crispy and crunchy" at room temperature, and consumers began to complain about how noisy it was. One Air Force pilot said it was louder than the cockpit of his jet. To prove his point, he squeezed the new Sun Chips bag and recorded a 95-decibel level with a sound meter, considerably more than the 77-decibel level recorded when he squeezed a conventional Tostitos bag. When thousands of people chose to friend a Facebook page called "Sorry But I Can't Hear You Over This Sun Chips Bag"—and with sales sliding—Frito-Lay decided to drop the compostable bag after an 18-month run.[43]

LABELING

The label can be a simple attached tag or an elaborately designed graphic that is an inherent part of the package. It might carry a great deal of information or only the brand name. Even if the seller prefers a simple label, the law may require more.

A label performs several functions. First, it *identifies* the product or brand, as does the name Sunkist stamped on oranges. It might also *grade* the product; canned peaches are grade-labeled A, B, and C. The label might *describe* the product: who made it, where and when, what it contains, how it is to be used, and how to use it safely. Finally, the label might *promote* the product through attractive graphics. For example, advanced technology allows 360-degree shrink-wrapped labels to replace glued-on paper labels, so containers can be surrounded with bright graphics and accommodate more product information.

Labels eventually need freshening up. The label on Ivory soap has been redesigned at least 18 times since the 1890s, with gradual changes in the size and design of the letters. As Tropicana found out, companies with labels that have become icons need to tread very carefully in order to preserve key branding elements when undertaking a redesign.

A long history of legal concerns surrounds labels and packaging. In 1914, the Federal Trade Commission Act held that false, misleading, or deceptive labels or packages constitute unfair competition. The Fair Packaging and Labeling Act, passed by Congress in 1967, set mandatory labeling requirements, encouraged voluntary industry packaging standards, and allowed federal agencies to set packaging regulations in specific industries.

The Food and Drug Administration (FDA) has required processed-food producers to include nutritional labeling that clearly states the amounts of protein, fat, carbohydrates, and calories contained in products, as well as vitamin and mineral content as a percentage of the recommended daily allowance. The FDA has also taken action against potentially misleading uses of such descriptions as "light," "high-fiber," "natural," and "low-fat."

Not all countries apply such strict definitions. In the United Kingdom, "light" and "lite" do not have an official meaning in law, although "low-fat" does—the food product must be less than 3 percent fat to qualify. As a result, some foods branded "light" there have been found to contain up to seven times more fat than those described as "low-fat."[44]

Managing Guarantees and Warranties

All sellers are legally responsible for fulfilling a buyer's normal or reasonable expectations. Guarantees and warranties are explicit or implicit promises by sellers that the product will perform as specified or that the seller will fix it or refund the customer's money during a specified period. Products under warranty or guarantee can be returned to the manufacturer or a designated repair center for repair, replacement, or refund. Whether expressed or implied, guarantees and warranties are legally enforceable.

A **guarantee** ensures that if a product fails to function as promised by the company or as customers expect, the company will provide some type of compensation to the purchaser. Detailing the process of addressing potential product failures up front adds credibility to the company's claims, reduces the functional and monetary risk associated with using the product, and creates peace-of-mind value for customers. Besides creating customer value, guarantees also can be beneficial to the company: They intensify its focus on the customer experience, establish accountability, expedite the development of performance standards, and provide guidelines for recovering from failures.[45]

Many sellers offer either general or specific guarantees. A company such as Procter & Gamble promises general or complete satisfaction without being more specific: "If you are not satisfied for any reason, return for replacement, exchange, or refund." A.T. Cross guarantees its Cross pens and pencils for life. The customer mails the pen to A.T. Cross (mailers are provided at stores), and the pen is repaired or replaced at no charge.

A company can provide customers with an *overall satisfaction* guarantee that applies to any facet of the product experience, whether it involves the actual quality of the product or the customer's assessment of product quality. Or the company might provide a *specific attribute* guarantee that applies to a particular aspect of the product, such as performance, reliability, or durability. Product guarantees can be valid for a specified time period such as one year, or they might involve a variable time frame—for example, the life of the product or the customer.

Warranties provide customers and the company with much the same benefits as guarantees do. However, warranties and guarantees differ on two key dimensions. Warranties usually cover the repair or replacement of the purchased item and usually do not allow the customer to return the product for a refund, which is the case with guarantees. Furthermore, whereas guarantees are always provided free of charge and require no additional payment from customers, warranties are available to extend the free warranty that comes with the product. Such extended warranties do require added payment and can be acquired at the time the product is purchased or at a later date.[46]

Extended warranties and service contracts can be extremely lucrative for manufacturers and retailers. Analysts estimate that warranty sales have accounted for a large percentage of Best Buy's operating profits. Despite evidence that buying extended warranties does not pay off, some consumers value the peace of mind they offer.[47] These warranties still generate billions of dollars in revenue for U.S. suppliers of electronic goods, although the total has declined as consumers have become more comfortable seeking solutions to technical problems online or from friends.[48]

Guarantees and warranties reduce the buyer's perceived risk. They suggest that the product is of high quality and that the company and its service performance are dependable. They can be especially helpful when the company or product is not well known or when the product's quality is superior to that of competitors. Hyundai's and Kia's highly successful 10-year or 100,000-mile power train warranty programs were designed in part to assure potential buyers of the quality of the products and the stability of the companies.

Effective product guarantees and warranties should have three traits: They need to be *relevant*, *easily understood*, and *easy for the customer to invoke*. For a guarantee to be relevant, the guaranteed feature of the offering should be of importance to customers. Guarantees and warranties are of limited or no value to customers when they apply to features that customers do not perceive as important or that rarely malfunction. Guarantees and warranties are easy for customers to understand when the company's promise and the measures that customers need to take in the event that the product fails are stated in a simple, straightforward manner. Guarantees and warranties are easy for customers to invoke—and are more easily communicated to customers—when they contain a limited number of exclusions and limitations. This reduces the amount of time and effort needed for customers to exercise their recourse to satisfaction should the product fail to live up to the stipulations of the guarantee or warranty.[49]

marketing INSIGHT

When Less Is More

Among the decisions that managers at both manufacturers and retailers must make is how to design and manage their product lines and product assortments. Even though conventional wisdom suggests that offering an extensive variety of options will be more beneficial and, therefore, more attractive to a greater number of consumers, it is also more costly for the company. Research-backed surveys indicate that consumers prefer retailers and brands that offer the greatest variety, so managers typically try to maximize the number of options offered to consumers within the cost constraints imposed by the company.

There are several factors underlying the belief among most managers that variety facilitates choice:

- **Increased ability to match preferences and options.** Larger assortments offer an opportunity to better match consumer preferences with the options available in the choice set. The more options contained in an assortment, the greater the chance that individual consumers will find their optimal choice.
- **Increased flexibility for consumers.** Larger assortments allow consumers to keep their options open and offer them greater flexibility when making a selection. Lack of variety might make consumers feel that their choice is restricted by there being an inadequate number of options, which can create an aura of negativity.
- **Increased opportunity to explore available options.** The mere fact that a choice set contains a large variety of options may convince consumers that they have been given the chance to explore the complete roster of options available in the product category. This gives them confidence that they understand the different features and benefits among the choice alternatives before making a decision.

Thus there are impressive reasons why larger assortments are likely to be of benefit to consumers, but this is not always true. In some instances, more options can hinder rather than facilitate consumers' ability to decide among the options. There are several reasons why this can occur:

- **Information overload.** Consumers choosing from large assortments can find themselves hampered by information overload, because they have to process more information than they have to consider when they choose from less extensive assortments. Consumers often find it less taxing to deal with smaller assortments simply because they have to consider and evaluate fewer options and attributes.
- **Choice overload.** Larger assortments are more likely to lead to choice overload, which can occur when the consumer finds more than one satisfactory option in the available choice set. This compounds the difficulty of making a decision: In addition to processing a large amount of information, the consumer needs to make a trade-off, giving up performance on one attribute in order to gain performance on another.
- **High consumer expectations.** Larger assortments can complicate choice by leading consumers to expect that they are likely to find the "perfect" option. When consumers have high expectations of finding their ideal choice among the available options but it fails to materialize, there is a greater probability that they will walk away from the assortment without making a decision.

Assembling the optimal assortment size from which target customers can choose is not a simple task. Some market conditions favor large assortments that will enhance consumer choice, whereas in other scenarios, larger assortments may be detrimental to consumer choice. The question that must be answered: When will more or fewer options benefit consumer choice? Recent research suggests that consumers' reaction to assortment size is dependent on their expertise, particularly their knowledge of the attributes and attribute levels of the choice alternatives and the degree to which they already have preferences among these options. This will allow them to more easily trade off the benefits and costs of different option attributes. What this means is that "expert" consumers with product knowledge and readily articulated preferences are more likely to benefit from the variety offered by larger assortments than are "novices" who are unfamiliar with the product category and have no ready preferences.

Thus, when it comes to managing product assortments, more variety is not always the best way to go. Empirical research shows that there are many instances when fewer options can make purchase more likely, lower the rate of return, and lead to more satisfied customers. Research on assortment size emphasizes that managers should consider two key factors when designing product lines: consumer goals and consumer expertise. Managers need to take these two essential factors into account in order to develop a product line strategy that creates customer-centric offerings and achieves market success.[50]

summary

1. The product is a key element of the marketing mix. Along with services and brands, products are the core drivers of customer benefits and are the reason why consumers are willing to purchase a particular offering.
2. To successfully compete in the market, products must be differentiated. Attributes on the basis of which to differentiate include core functionality, features, performance quality, conformance quality, durability, reliability, form, style, and customization.
3. Product design—the way a product looks, feels, and functions—offers a potent way to differentiate and position a company's products and services. Design is not just a phase in creating a product, service, or application. It's a way of thinking that permeates all aspects of the marketing program so that all design aspects work together. Design offers functional and aesthetic benefits and influences both the rational and the emotional aspects of consumers' decision making.
4. Most products exist as a part of a company's product portfolio and/or product line. Each product must be related to other products to ensure that a firm is offering the optimal set of products to fulfill the needs of its different customer segments.
5. A product portfolio encompasses all products offered by a company, including various product categories and product lines. A company's product portfolio has a certain width, length, depth, and consistency. These four dimensions are the tools for developing the company's marketing strategy and deciding which product lines to grow and which to maintain, harvest, or divest.
6. A product line is a group of related products sold by the same company. A company's product line typically contains products that appeal to different layers of customer needs. In offering a product line, companies normally develop a basic platform and modules that can be added to meet different customer requirements and lower production costs. To analyze a product line and decide how many resources to invest in it, product line managers need to look at sales, profits, and market profile.
7. Company objectives influence product line length—the total number of items in the product line. Product lines tend to lengthen over time. A company lengthens its product line in two ways: line stretching and line filling. Line stretching occurs when a company lengthens its product line beyond its current range, whether down-market, up-market, or both. Line filling occurs when a firm adds more items within the existing range.
8. Packaging includes all the activities of designing and producing the container for a product. Packaging must achieve a number of objectives: identify the brand, convey descriptive and persuasive information, facilitate product transportation/protection/storage, and aid consumption. A good package draws the consumer in and encourages product choice.
9. The label can be a simple attached tag or an elaborately designed graphic that is an inherent part of the package. A label performs several functions: It *identifies* the product or brand; it might *describe* the product (who made it, where and when, what it contains, how it is to be used, and how to use it safely), and it might *promote* the product through persuasive messaging.
10. Guarantees and warranties are explicit or implicit promises by sellers that the product will perform as specified or the seller will fix it or refund the customer's money during a specified period. Guarantees reduce the buyer's perceived risk by suggesting that the product is of high quality and that the company and its service performance are dependable. Whether expressed or implied, warranties and guarantees are legally enforceable.

marketing SPOTLIGHT

Apple

Source: Sean Xu/Alamy Stock Photo

Apple Computers was founded, in 1976, by college dropouts Steve Jobs and Steve Wozniak, who wanted to make computers more user-friendly so people could use them at home and at work. The company's first major success—Apple II launched in 1977—revolutionized the computer industry with the introduction of the first-ever color graphics. On the heels of explosive growth, Apple went public in 1980. Several years later, in 1983, Jobs hired John Sculley, CEO of PepsiCo at

(*continued*)

the time, as Apple's CEO—a decision that backfired when, in 1985, Scully ended up firing Jobs.

Apple's focus on short-term profits rather than innovation led to a gradual deterioration of its market position, and by 1996, experts were raising questions about the company's viability. To make up for lack of innovation, Apple bought out NeXT Software—the company founded by Jobs after he left Apple—and brought back Jobs as an interim CEO (he officially became CEO in 2000). Once back at the helm of Apple, Jobs forged an alliance with Microsoft to develop a Mac version of its popular Office software, introduced iBook—an entry-level laptop for consumer and education markets, and launched iMac—a suite of all-in-one computers featuring distinctly colored, translucent egg-shaped cases.

Over the past two decades, Apple has continued to invest heavily in research and development to become a world leader in innovative new-product launches. The company transformed the way people listen to music, play video games, talk on the phone, and even read books. Apple's revolutionary product innovations include the iPod, iMac, iPhone, and iPad and are the reason why the company topped *Fortune* magazine's World's Most Admired Companies list for many years.

One of Apple's early and most important innovations was the iPod MP3 player. Not only did the iPod become a cultural phenomenon; it introduced many consumers to Apple and initiated a series of monumental product innovations. The iPod exemplified Apple's leading-edge design skills and looked, felt, and operated like no other device. To the delight of Apple (and the chagrin of competitor Sony), the iPod became "the Walkman of the 21st century." The dynamic duo of the iPod and the newly launched iTunes Music store helped drive iPod sales through the roof.

The iPod was also central in changing the way people listened to and used music. According to musician John Mayer, "People feel they're walking through musicology" when they use their iPods, leading them to listen to more music, and with more passion. The iPod has gone through a series of generations, and along the way Apple has added features like photo, video, and radio capabilities. Realizing the success of its foray into the music industry in general and the iPod in particular, Apple launched iTunes—a software-based digital marketplace for music. Introduced in 2003, the iTunes store became the largest music vendor in the United States by 2008 and the largest music vendor in the world by 2010.

Apple achieved its impressive market domination through a combination of shrewd product innovation and clever marketing. The marketing effort appealed both to Apple fans and to people who had not used Apple products in the past. To reach such a broad consumer base, the company had to shift its channel strategies. Apple added "mass electronic" retailers such as Best Buy and (the now obsolete) Circuit City to its existing channels, which quadrupled its number of outlets.

Besides this enhanced "push" effort, Apple also developed memorable, creative "pull" advertising that helped drive the popularity of the iPod. The Silhouettes, which featured silhouettes of people listening to and dancing with their iPods, appeared all over the world. This simple message worked across cultures, portraying the iPod as cool but not beyond the reach of anyone who enjoyed music.

As the iPod's popularity grew, a halo effect helped increase the market share of Apple's other products. As a result, in 2007 Apple officially changed its name from Apple Computer Inc. to Apple Inc. to help communicate the company's expanded focus on non-computer products. Apple's next-largest product launch after the iPod was the iPhone, its 2007 entry into the cell phone industry. The iPhone, with its touch-screen pad, virtual keyboard, and internet and e-mail capabilities, launched to huge consumer excitement: People lined up for hours to be among the first to buy one. Investment analysts initially feared that Apple's two-year contract with AT&T and high initial price would hinder the iPhone's success. Seventy-four days after the product's debut, however, Apple had sold its one-millionth iPhone. It had taken the iPod two years to reach the cumulative sales ($1.1 million) that the iPhone had reached in its first quarter. In fact, half the iPod buyers switched to AT&T from a different wireless carrier, some incurring fees to break their contracts, just to have a chance to own an iPhone.

The launch of the iPad also created a media frenzy in 2013. The multitouch device combined the look and feel of the iPhone with the power of a MacBook and gave consumers access to music, books, movies, pictures, video games, documents, and hundreds of thousands of applications at the touch of a finger, without mouse or keyboard. Apple followed up with the launch of the iPad mini, a smaller version of the original, and the iPad Air, which corresponded with a powerful marketing campaign that inspired consumers to feel they could do anything with their iPad, including creating movies, building wind turbines, studying coral reefs, and making mountain climbing safer.

On the heels of the success of the iPad, in 2015 Apple introduced its first wearable device, Apple Watch, offering fitness tracking and health-oriented capabilities. After a sluggish start, Apple Watch ultimately became one of Apple's fastest-growing product categories, selling over 30 million units in 2019. True to its mission of staying at the forefront of user-friendly consumer technologies, Apple now invests heavily in artificial intelligence and machine learning. Indeed, in the past several years, the use of artificial intelligence in consumer products has exploded through the rise of digital assistants such as Amazon's Alexa, Google's Assistant, and Apple's own Siri.

Apple's investment in research and development is one way the company remains a leader in this cutthroat industry. Apple spent over $18 billion on research and development in 2020 and continues to increase its R&D budget in order to stay ahead of the competition. Creating, producing, and

(continued)

launching new products is a top priority for Apple. Supported by creative marketing, the company's pioneering is the reason why consumers and analysts stay on their toes awaiting news of Apple's latest products.[51]

Questions

1. What are the key factors contributing to Apple's phenomenal success?
2. Apple's product launches over the past decade have been monumental. What makes the company so good at innovation?
3. How important was the iPhone to Apple's current success? Discuss the significance of the iPad and Apple Watch launches to Apple's new-product development strategy.

marketing SPOTLIGHT

Casper

Casper is an American e-commerce company that primarily sells mattresses. The idea of Casper was thought up by four members of a New York City venture accelerator in 2013. The company aimed to be an alternative to what they called "Big Mattress," the dominant manufacturers and retailers at the time.

The four brands that made up "Big Mattress" were Serta, Simmons, Tempur-Pedic, and Sealy. The Casper founders believed that mattresses sold by these companies were priced too high. The price of a queen mattress at the time from one of these companies could go as high as $2500. In addition, most mattresses were purchased in stores. Casper's founders believed that the in-store purchasing process was one of the worst buying experiences found anywhere. Customers weren't able to do much more than lie on the mattress in the store for a couple of minutes.

Casper applied the business model of Warby Parker to the mattress industry. The four founders particularly admired Warby Parker's success in offering designer sunglasses at radically low prices and its online sales model. By selling mattresses online, Casper eliminated the traditional painful consumer experience of purchasing a mattress in stores. Casper also distinguished its mattresses by offering them at one-third of "Big Mattress" prices.

Casper designed its first mattress to be the "One Perfect Mattress for Everyone." The first Casper mattress was composed of a resilient foam that could be compressed into the largest box size that could be handled by UPS. The combination of one mattress and a simple delivery method meant that consumers had an easy decision-making process and the company enjoyed logistical benefits. Casper also offered free delivery and a 100-night free trial to customers. If customers were not happy with the mattress, a customer service agent retrieved the mattress and the money was refunded with no questions asked.

Source: McClatchy-Tribune/Tribune Content Agency LLC/Alamy Stock Photo

The combination of providing a well-designed mattress and a superior shopping experience, all at a low price point, made Casper an attractive choice for customers. To create awareness for its product, Casper first focused on word of mouth and outdoor advertising. The company invested in advertisements that featured colorful ensembles of cartoon people and animals enjoying their sleep on a Casper mattress. These advertisements were located on billboards, subways, and taxis all over the country. Casper's advertising imagery was designed to be playful and lighthearted, while also emphasizing the importance of a quality mattress. Compared to competitors, Casper was careful not to overwhelm potential customers with excessive statistics and specifications.

Casper enjoyed rapid growth in sales after launch—earning over $600 million in revenue in three short years. Casper grew its product portfolio to include three different types of mattresses and began selling pillows, sheets, and bed frames to capture new customers. Casper partnered with retailers such as Nordstrom, Target, and Amazon to increase its distribution.

As Casper grew, the company shifted its advertising efforts to digital platforms. Digital advertisements were less expensive, and television advertisements were dominated by "Big Mattress" companies. Casper invested in the common practice of using internet "cookies" to track consumer visits to the online website and showing them targeted ads as

(continued)

they browsed other websites. Casper has also sponsored numerous popular podcasts and radio shows, including *This Week in Tech, My Brother, The Howard Stern Show*, and *The Dr. Laura Show*.

Casper's social media team frequently engaged with costumers on platforms such as Facebook, Instagram, and Twitter. Casper uploaded popular "unboxing" videos on these platforms that showed consumers how their tiny mattress remarkably unfurls and expands to full size when moved from the box. Casper also ran a weekly series on the Instagram Stories platform, where the company appealed to customers suffering from Monday morning blues by destroying alarm clocks in spectacular fashion. Casper launched the website Insomnobot 3000, where a chatbot sends funny text messages to those who have trouble falling sleep at night. The customer engagement and advertising efforts resulted in high net promoter scores, a common metric for consumer satisfaction.

Casper's innovative business model inspired competitors to follow in its footsteps, including the Big Mattress companies. Serta-Simmons and Tempur-Sealy began offering "beds-in-a-box" in 2016. In 2018 Walmart introduced Allswell, a digital home brand that specialized in mattresses and bedding. That same year. Amazon added its own memory foam mattress to the popular AmazonBasics line. Faced with these new competitors, Casper opened its first physical retail location to increase visibility and build customer loyalty. Casper announced that it plans to expand to over 200 stores by 2021. Although many mattress companies have followed Casper's business model, Casper aims to continue its initial success by increasing its product line, engaging with customers, and expanding its physical retail presence.[52]

Questions

1. What makes Casper's products desirable to consumers? What are the specific product attributes that are particularly valued by consumers?
2. How should Casper compete with established companies and start-ups ramping up their direct-to-consumer offerings? Should Casper shift some of its efforts from product innovation to more aggressive communication and brand building?
3. Should Casper focus on extending its product line to try to offer a mattress "for every purse and purpose"? Or should it focus on offering a single type of mattress (in different sizes) in order to streamline innovation efforts and simplify consumer choice?

marketing SPOTLIGHT

Toyota

Source: tomas devera photo/ Shutterstock

Toyota, one of the world's three largest automakers (along with Renault Nissan and Volkswagen), has come a long way over the course of its 75-year history. The company launched its first passenger car, the Model AA, in 1936. For it, Toyota copied the body design of Chrysler's landmark Airflow and modeled its engine after a 1933 Chevrolet engine. Toyota suffered several challenges in its early years, including a financial crisis in 1950. However, during the oil crisis of 1973, consumers wanted smaller, more fuel-efficient automobiles. Toyota answered with two smaller cars—the Toyota Corona and Toyota Corolla—that came with basic features and also acted as Toyota's new entry-level vehicles. The company also launched the Toyota Cressida, which combined the fuel efficiency consumers desired with additional space and luxury amenities such as air conditioning and an AM–FM radio.

During the 1980s and 1990s, Toyota gradually added more types of vehicles, ranging widely in price, size, and amenities, in order to give customers more options to fit their driving needs. In 1982 Toyota introduced the Camry, a four-door, mid-sized car that offered consumers more space than the Corona. The Camry would go on to become the best-selling passenger car in North America. The first of Toyota's popular SUVs was introduced with the 4Runner in 1984. At first the 4Runner wasn't much different from Toyota's pickup trucks in both design and performance. Eventually, however, the 4Runner morphed into looking more like a passenger vehicle and led the way for the launch of other SUVs, including the Rav4, Highlander, and LandCruiser. Around the same time, Toyota introduced a full-sized pickup truck, which later became today's Tundra, as well as several sporty and affordable cars that targeted young adults.

(continued)

In 1989, Toyota launched Lexus, its luxury division. Lexus promised to give consumers an unparalleled luxurious experience, starting with the dealerships, which offered white-glove treatment. Toyota understood, however, that each country defines perfection differently. In the United States, perfection and luxury meant comfort, size, and dependability. In Europe, luxury meant attention to detail and brand heritage. As a result, the company varied its advertising depending on the country and culture.

In 1997, Toyota innovated and launched the Prius, the first mass-produced hybrid car. The Prius was initially priced at $19,995, which fell between the Corolla and Camry. The company's keen focus on developing a clean-energy car was brilliant. By 2002, when the second-generation Prius hit showrooms, dealers received 10,000 orders before the car was even available. Over the next decade, competitors like Ford, Nissan, GM, and Honda would follow in Toyota's footsteps and enter the hybrid market with models of their own.

Toyota also started creating vehicles for specific target groups. To this end, Toyota launched the Scion brand in 2000 to target young adults aged 16 to 21 years old. After the first few years of carefully listening to feedback, Toyota learned that the Scion's target group wanted more personalization. Using this insight, Toyota designed the car "mono-spec" at the factory, with just one well-equipped trim level, and let customers choose from dozens of customization elements—ranging from stereo components to wheels and even floor mats—at dealerships. Toyota marketed the Scion at music events and in showrooms where younger consumers would feel comfortable spending time while learning more about the car.

Another important reason behind Toyota's success is its manufacturing. The firm is a master of lean manufacturing and continuous improvement. Its plants can make as many as eight different models at the same time, effecting huge increases in productivity and market responsiveness. Toyota also innovates relentlessly. A typical Toyota assembly line makes thousands of operational changes in the course of a single year. Toyota employees see their purpose as threefold: making cars, making cars better, and teaching everyone how to make cars better. The company encourages problem solving, always looking to improve the process by which it improves all other processes.

Toyota has integrated its assembly plants around the world into a single giant network. The plants customize cars for local markets and shift production quickly to satisfy any surges in demand from markets worldwide. With its manufacturing network, Toyota can build a wide variety of models much more inexpensively. That means the company is able to fill market niches as they emerge without building entirely new assembly operations. This, in turn, has enabled the company to establish a foothold across a variety of diverse market segments.

Over the years, Toyota's automobiles have consistently ranked high in quality and reliability. The company suffered some major challenges in 2009 and 2010 when it experienced a massive recall of over 8 million vehicles. A variety of problems, ranging from sticking accelerator pedals to sudden acceleration to software glitches in the braking system, affected many Toyota brands, including Lexus, Prius, Camry, Corolla, and Tundra. Despite these challenges, Toyota recouped its losses and three years later retook the lead as the largest automaker in the world. Toyota's strong focus on hybrid vehicles has proved to be profitable and helped the company rebound.

Today, Toyota offers a full line of cars for the global market, from family sedans and sport utility vehicles to trucks and minivans. Designing these different products means listening to different customers in different regions, building the cars that customers want, and then crafting marketing to reinforce the image of each make.[53]

Questions

1. Toyota has built a huge manufacturing company that can produce millions of cars each year for a wide variety of consumers. Why was it able to grow so much bigger than any other auto manufacturer?
2. Has Toyota done the right thing by manufacturing a car brand for everyone? Why or why not?
3. What should the company do over the next year, the next five years, and the next decade? How can growing companies avoid quality problems in the future?

CHAPTER 9

Designing and Managing Services

In line with its vision to be a globally respected corporation, Infosys has set very high standards in business and transactions to be an exemplar for the industry. Its tagline 'Powered by Intellect, Driven by Values' focused on competence and values. Surpassing client expectations consistently has resulted in the software giant earning an impressive customer loyalty with repeat business generating 93% of its $13.56 bn topline in 2021.

Source: Infosys

As companies find it harder to differentiate their physical products, they turn to service differentiation, whether that involves on-time delivery, better and faster response to inquiries, or quicker resolution of complaints. Top service providers are well aware of the advantages of service differentiation and its value in creating memorable customer experiences.[1] One service business that understands how to keep customers satisfied is Infosys.

>>> Narayana Murthy and the founding team of six engineers started Infosys in 1981 with an initial capital of $250 to develop software for a US-based client. Over the next four decades, the firm set a new standard for transparent value systems, ethical business practices and principles in the software service industry.[2] The company differentiated itself on a strong foundation of core value system 'C-LIFE – Client focus, Leadership by example, Integrity and transparency, Fairness, and Excellence. Following a value system based on legal, ethical, and transparent business is believed not to be a very prevalent practice in India. But the leadership at Infosys persisted and earned the trust of investors, clients and other stakeholders. Complementing its vision to be India's one of the most

respected companies delivering best-of-breed technology solutions and employing best-in-class professionals, Infosys followed a consistent strategy for brand building. As Narayana Murthy explained, *"Strategy is what we have to do to create and maintain sustainable differentiation vis-à-vis competitors. One aspect of our differentiation is our emphasis on values. Our values give our clients confidence that we will deliver on our promises, stand by them in every situation, and that we will spare no efforts to make them look good in front of their customers. Still, values cannot be just part of the strategy process; they have to be second nature for everyone in the organization."*[3] With its ethical and transparent image, Infosys gained clients' trust and many of whom continue to do business with Infosys for more than a decade.[4] Infosys has now turned onto one of the most valuable companies with market capitalization of US $100 billion as of 2021.[5]

Because it is critical to understand the special nature of services and what that means to marketers, in this chapter we systematically analyze services and how to market them most effectively.

The Nature of Services

A **service** is an act that one entity performs for another that is essentially intangible and does not result in the ownership of anything. It may or may not be tied to a physical product. Increasingly, manufacturers, distributors, and retailers are providing value-added services, or simply excellent customer service, to differentiate themselves.

Services are everywhere. The *government sector*—with its courts, employment services, hospitals, loan agencies, military services, police and fire departments, postal service, regulatory agencies, and schools—is in the service business. The *private nonprofit sector*—museums, charities, churches, colleges, foundations, and hospitals—is in the service business. A good part of the *business sector*—with its airlines, banks, hotels, insurance companies, law firms, management consulting firms, medical practices, motion picture companies, plumbing repair companies, and real estate firms—is in the service business. Many workers in the *manufacturing sector*—such as computer operators, accountants, and legal staff—are really service providers. In fact, they make up a "service factory" providing services to the "goods factory." And those in the *retail sector*—such as cashiers, clerks, salespeople, and customer-service representatives—are also providing a service.

THE SERVICE ASPECT OF AN OFFERING

Service can be a major or minor component of a company's offering. Based on the degree to which they involve a service, we distinguish five categories of offerings:

- **A pure tangible good**, such as soap, toothpaste, or salt, with virtually no accompanying services.
- **A tangible good with accompanying services**, like a car, computer, or cell phone with a warranty or specialized customer-service contract. Typically, the more technologically advanced the product, the greater the need for high-quality supporting services.

Learning Objectives After studying this chapter you should be able to:

9.1 Define the distinctive characteristics of services.

9.2 Explain the new realities that service firms face.

9.3 Identify the key strategies to achieve service excellence.

9.4 Explain how service firms can manage quality effectively.

- **A hybrid offering**, like a restaurant meal, of equal parts goods and services. People patronize restaurants for both the food and its preparation.
- **A major service with accompanying minor goods and services**, like air travel with supporting goods such as snacks and drinks. This offering requires a capital-intensive good—an airplane—for its realization, but the primary item is a service.
- **A pure service**, primarily an intangible service, such as consulting, babysitting, psychotherapy, or massage.

Restaurants are good examples of hybrid offerings combining products and services. Narayana Health is one of the most successful Indian healthcare brands

Narayana Health Narayana Health was founded in 2001 by Dr. Devi Shetty as Narayana Hrudalaya—a super-speciality cardiac hospital engaged in offering affordable services related to heart health. Eventually, Dr. Shetty's mission translated into a broader perspective of delivering high-quality affordable healthcare services through a chain of hospitals in India. Dr. Shetty banked on the transformative power of technology to develop an asset-light business model, and strategically worked with governments and private owners for land lease and renting premises, respectively. The healthcare group's purpose-driven approach helped it commission hospitals and clinics rapidly to bring the promise of quality healthcare at reasonable budget to the doorstep of the country's millions. Presently, it offers care in over 30 specialties including cardiology, oncology, neurology, orthopedics, nephrology and gastroenterology across its 21 hospitals with 6000 beds. Narayana Health optimizes productivity while minimizing costs by combining innovative technology with a highly efficient delivery system, thereby enabling its healthcare facilities increase treatment capacity and expand the number of specialty services offered[6]. The low investment and low cost, high-volume model coupled with an assembly line approach to operations helped the healthcare group leverage economies of scale while delivering high quality. Attracting large number of patients through innovative schemes such as micro-insurance and telemedicine ensured higher utilization of capital-intensive diagnostic equipment and operation theatres. Treating more patients enhance quality as skills of doctors and surgeons improve with more practice. Higher volumes enable reduction in unit cost of surgeries. Standardization of procedures, centralized purchasing, digitization, data driven business intelligence model, and motivated doctors and skilled employees drive improvements in patient outcomes and satisfaction.[7] Narayana Health has won the admiration of health system leaders through its innovative care delivery model that lowers costs, improves quality, and increases access to its services.[8]

Customers sometimes cannot judge the quality of some services even after they have received them. Based on the difficulty of evaluation, service benefits can be classified into three categories. *Search benefits* are characteristics the buyer can evaluate before purchase, *experience benefits* are characteristics the buyer can evaluate after purchase, and finally, *credence benefits* are characteristics the buyer finds hard to evaluate even after consumption.[9]

>> Narayana Health has achieved success by combining high quality with affordable price to improve healthcare access.

Source: ©Narayana Health, used with permission

Source: Debbie Ann Powell/Alamy Stock Photo

<< Carnival found out the hard way how quickly a company's image and customer loyalty can be undermined when an engine fire on its Carnival Triumph left more than 3,000 passengers with limited access to food, water, and working toilets.

Because services are generally high in experience and credence qualities, there is more risk involved in their purchase, with several consequences. First, service consumers generally rely on word of mouth rather than advertising. Second, they rely heavily on price, provider, and physical cues to judge quality. Third, they are highly loyal to service providers who satisfy them. Finally, because switching costs are high, consumer inertia can make it challenging to entice business away from a competitor.

Although customer loyalty can be strong for services, in today's modern communications environment, a service failure can be a PR nightmare and undermine that loyalty, as Carnival Cruises found.

Carnival The *Carnival Triumph* was on the third day of a four-day cruise from Galveston, Texas, to Mexico when an engine room fire disabled the boat and set it adrift, leaving 3,100 passengers with little access to food, water, and restrooms. Waste spilled into the hallways, and decks below became insufferably hot. When the boat returned to shore after a long five days, the CEO greeted passengers as they disembarked and gave each of them $500, a free flight home, a refund for the trip, and credit for another cruise. Nevertheless, given the publicity surrounding what the media called the "poop cruise," the damage had been done. Public opinion of cruises as a whole dropped. Carnival found its bookings declining by a hefty 20 percent, forcing the company to pass along steep discounts to fill boats. To avoid future problems, the cruise line invested $600 million to upgrade its fleet and hired a new VP of Technical Operations to oversee its safety initiatives. Seven years later, amid the COVID outbreak in March 2020, Carnival faced a similar challenge when it experienced several high-profile outbreaks on its ships, which spurred a congressional inquiry into the company's safety practices.[10]

DISTINCTIVE CHARACTERISTICS OF SERVICES

Researchers delineate four key characteristics that distinguish services from products: *intangibility, inseparability, variability*, and *perishability*.[11] Understanding these unique aspects of service delivery is important, because they can greatly affect the design of marketing programs. We discuss these four aspects of services in more detail next.

Intangibility. Unlike physical products, services cannot be seen, tasted, felt, heard, or smelled before they are bought. A person getting cosmetic surgery cannot see the results beforehand, and the patient in the psychiatrist's office cannot know the exact outcome of treatment. To reduce uncertainty, buyers will look for evidence of quality by drawing inferences from the place, people, equipment, communication material, symbols, and price. Therefore, the service provider's task is to "manage the evidence"—to "tangibilize the intangible."[12]

Service companies can try to demonstrate their service quality by emphasizing their tangible aspects. Because there is no physical product, the service provider's facilities—such as its primary and secondary signage, environmental design and reception area, employee apparel, and collateral material—are especially important. All aspects of the service delivery process can be branded, which is why Allied Van Lines is concerned about the appearance of its drivers and laborers, why UPS has developed such strong equity with its brown trucks, and why Doubletree by Hilton Hotels & Resorts offers fresh-baked chocolate chip cookies to symbolize care and friendliness.

Service providers often choose brand elements such as logos, symbols, characters, and slogans to make the service and its key benefits more tangible; consider the "friendly skies" of United, the "good hands" of Allstate, and the "bullish" nature of Merrill Lynch. Disney is a master at "tangibilizing the intangible" and creating magical fantasies in its theme parks. So are retailers such as Dick's Sporting Goods and Bass Pro Shops.[13] Apple tangibilized its customer service by creating its "Genius Bar"—a tech support station inside Apple's stores, aiming to provide concierge-style customer support.

Banks and financial institutions are particularly inclined to add a tangible dimension to their services—by securing a prestigious office address and an imposing building structure—in order to convey a sense of stability and instill trust. In addition, many financial institutions, including Scotiabank, MetLife, Chase, Citi, SunTrust, US Bank, Barclays, and Bank of America, have paid upwards of $100 million (and in some cases over $500 million) for the naming rights to major stadiums and sports arenas.[14]

Inseparability. Whereas physical goods are manufactured, inventoried, distributed, and later consumed, services are typically produced and consumed simultaneously.[15] A haircut can't be stored, nor can it be produced without the barber. The provider is part of the service. Because the client is also often present, provider–client interaction is a special feature of services marketing. When clients have strong provider preferences, the provider can raise its price to ration its limited time.

Several strategies exist for getting around the limitations of inseparability. The service provider can work with larger groups. Some psychotherapists have moved from one-on-one therapy to small-group therapy to groups of more than 300 people in a large hotel ballroom. The service provider can work faster; the psychotherapist can spend 30 more efficient minutes with each patient instead of 50 less structured minutes and thus see more patients. The service organization can train more service providers and build client confidence, as H&R Block has done with its national network of trained tax consultants.

A common approach to addressing the inseparability aspect of services is yield management—a pricing strategy that aims to optimize customer demand based on the available capacity of the service provider. Because services cannot be inventoried to increase availability at times of greater demand, service providers use variable pricing to influence consumer behavior by setting a price point at which consumer demand matches a company's capacity. For example, resorts are subject to seasonal fluctuations in demand, restaurants tend to be busier on weekends, and airlines experience higher than usual demand around holidays such as Thanksgiving, Christmas, and New Year's Eve. By varying their price, companies are able to influence customer demand in a way that matches their capacity.

Variability. The quality of services depends on who provides them—as well as on when, where, and to whom; thus, services are highly variable. Because service delivery is an interactive experience, the actual service received by customers varies across individual customers and service providers. Service firms know that variability in their performance puts them at risk. Hilton initiated a major program to create more uniformity in guest experiences.

Hilton Hotels Between 1964, when Hilton Hotels sold its foreign licensee Hilton International Co., and 2006, when it bought Hilton International Co. back, the two companies operated largely independently. As a result, the Hilton brand was no longer providing customers with a uniform high-quality experience. One research analyst said, "The brand standards in Europe were always very different from those in the U.S. I think they were, quite frankly, a bit slacker in Europe. To address this inconsistency, Hilton initiated H360, a project to review everything from breakfast fare to bath amenities, the décor of lobbies, Wi-Fi service, hotel architecture, and handling of customer complaints at all the company's hotels. As a result of H360—whose motto was "One brand. One vision. One culture"—independent owners of Hilton-branded hotels in the United States and abroad have been forced to upgrade to Hilton standards where necessary or be dropped from the Hilton system. Protecting the brand seems to have served the company well, helping increase its revenues and strengthening its brand equity.[16]

Source: Newscast Online Limited/Alamy Stock Photo

>> To ensure that Hilton properties in both Europe and the United States provide its guests with uniformly high-quality services or be purged from its system, Hilton launched a project to review all aspects of the guest experience—from property architecture to customer complaints.

Service buyers are aware of potential variability and often talk to others or go online to collect information before selecting a specific service provider. To reassure customers, some firms offer *service guarantees* that may reduce consumer perceptions of risk.[17] Here are three steps that service firms can take to increase quality control.

- **Invest in good hiring and training procedures.** Recruiting the right employees and giving them excellent training are crucial elements of quality control, whether employees are highly skilled professionals or low-skilled workers. Better-trained people exhibit six characteristics that improve service quality: competence, courtesy, credibility, reliability, responsiveness, and communication skill.
- **Standardize the service-performance process throughout the organization.** A **service blueprint** can map out the service process, the points of customer contact, and the evidence of service from the customer's point of view.[18] Figure 9.1 shows a service blueprint for an overnight guest at a hotel.[19] Behind the scenes, the hotel must skillfully help the guest move from one step to the next. Service blueprints can be helpful in identifying potential "pain points" for customers, developing new services, supporting a zero-defects culture, and devising service recovery strategies.
- **Monitor customer satisfaction.** Reduce service variability by employing suggestion and complaint systems, customer surveys, and third-party comparison shopping. Customer needs may vary in different areas, allowing firms to develop region-specific customer satisfaction programs.[20] Firms can also develop customer information databases and systems for more personalized service, especially online.[21]

Perishability. Services cannot be stored, so their perishability can be a problem when demand fluctuates. To accommodate rush-hour demand, public transportation companies must own more equipment than if demand were even throughout the day. Some doctors charge patients for missed appointments because the service value (the doctor's availability) exists only at the time of the appointment.

Demand or yield management is critical; the right services must be available to the right customers at the right places at the right times and at the right prices to maximize profitability. Several

FIGURE **9.1**

Blueprint for Overnight Hotel Stay

Source: Valarie Zeithaml, Mary Jo Bitner, and Dwayne D. Gremler, *Services Marketing: Integrating Customer Focus across the Firm*, 7th ed. (New York: McGraw-Hill, 2017).

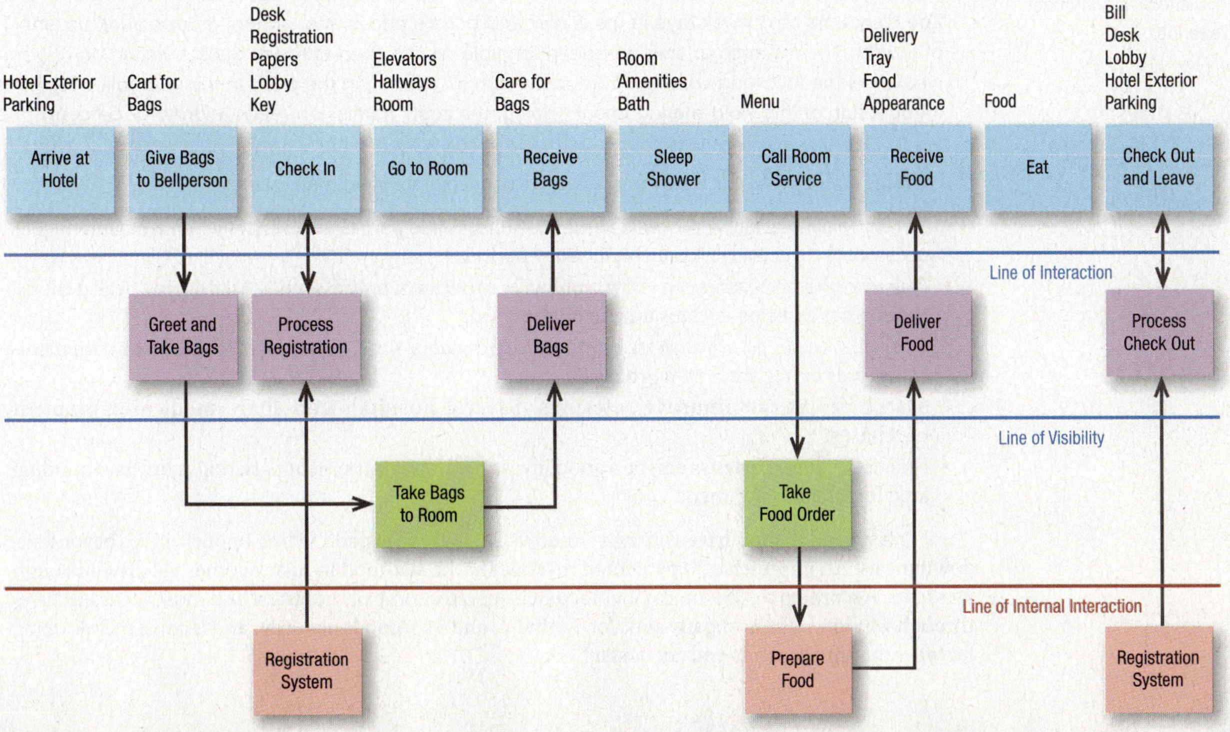

Source: Wm. Baker/GhostWorx Images/Alamy Stock Photo

>> Dynamic pricing based on advance sales and anticipated demand has helped the Indianapolis Zoo to simultaneously control the number of visitors and increase revenue.

strategies can produce a better match between service demand and supply.[22] On the demand (customer) side, we can identify the following strategies:

- *Differential pricing* will shift some demand from peak to off-peak periods. Examples include lower matinee movie prices and weekend discounts for car rentals.[23]
- *Nonpeak demand* can be cultivated. McDonald's pushes breakfast service, and hotels promote minivacation weekends.
- *Complementary services* can provide alternatives for waiting customers, such as cocktail lounges in restaurants and automated teller machines in banks.
- *Reservation systems* are a way to manage the demand level. Airlines, hotels, and physicians employ them extensively.

Perhaps one of the most popular approaches to balancing supply and demand in service delivery is **yield pricing**. For example, ride-hailing firms such as Ola and Uber use dynamic pricing when there is a demand-supply imbalance during normal peak hours, adverse weather conditions, large public events, traffic congestions or emergencies. Prices are calculated using real time algorithms depending on demand and supply at different locations in each city at any point of time. The prices charged may sometimes surge up to four times the base price during these peak demand hours. The price increase motivates drivers to take advantage of the surge thereby increasing the supply while customers, willing to pay a higher price, do not experience non-availability. Surge pricing attracts adverse reactions from many customers so governments step-in and cap the percentage increase for surge pricing[24]. In the same vein, sports teams, bands, ski resorts, and theme parks have begun adjusting prices based on demand. Dynamic pricing can produce results. Consider the Indianapolis Zoo.

Indianapolis Zoo The Indianapolis Zoo adopted dynamic pricing in part to limit crowds after opening a new orangutan center. As a result, adult passes that used to cost $16.95 were priced between $8 and $30, based on advance sales and expected demand. For example, the Zoo discounts cold weekdays in the winter and boosts prices after school groups book dozens of tickets. The dynamic pricing produced tangible results: Two-thirds of guests visited on weekdays the following summer, compared with 57 percent in the past. In the year following the introduction of this yield-management pricing, the zoo's admission revenue grew 12 percent.[25]

On the supply side, the following strategies can facilitate yield management:

- *Part-time employees* can serve peak demand. Colleges add part-time teachers when enrollment goes up; stores hire extra clerks during holiday periods.
- *Peak-time efficiency routines* can allow employees to perform only essential tasks during peak periods. Paramedics assist physicians during busy periods.
- *Increased consumer participation* frees up service providers' time. Consumers fill out their own medical records or bag their own groceries.
- *Shared services* can improve offerings. Several hospitals can share medical-equipment purchases.
- *Facilities for future expansion* can be a good investment. An amusement park might buy surrounding land for later development.

For fast-food chains, drive-through windows are a way to expand selling opportunities beyond sit-down meals. An impressive 70 percent of revenue for the fast-food industry comes via drive-through windows. According to *QSR* magazine, Taco Bell operates some of the fastest and most accurate drive-through windows. The company aims for 3 minutes and 30 seconds per order and is constantly looking for ways to shave seconds and cut costs.[26]

The New Services Realities

Service firms once lagged behind manufacturers in their understanding and use of marketing because they were small or faced large demand or little competition. This has certainly changed. Some of the most skilled marketers now are service firms.

Savvy services marketers are recognizing the new services realities, such as the increasing role of technology, the importance of the increasingly empowered customer, customer coproduction, and the need to engage employees as well as customers.

INCREASING ROLE OF TECHNOLOGY

Technology is changing the rules of the game for services in a very fundamental way. Banking, for instance, is being transformed by the ability to bank online and via mobile apps; some customers rarely see a bank lobby or interact with an employee anymore. The Covid-19 pandemic accelerated the digital transformation of services by forcing many companies to change course and transform their businesses by integrating digital technology to fundamentally change how they deliver value to their customers.

Technology also has great power to make service workers more productive. However, companies must avoid pushing technological efficiency so hard that they reduce perceived quality.[27] Amazon has some of the most innovative technology in online retailing, but it also keeps customers extremely satisfied when a problem arises, even if they don't actually talk to an Amazon employee. More companies have introduced "live chat" features to blend technology with a human voice. One company that enables enterprises to connect with customers across different touch points—from text messages to emails, phone calls to video, intelligent chatbots and back—is Twilio.

Twilio Twilio, the leading cloud communications platform, is used by millions of developers around the world to "virtualize" the telecommunications infrastructure and improve the human interaction experience. Twilio has over 60,000 business customers, including high-profile clients such as Airbnb, Intuit, Salesforce, Uber, Twitter, eBay, Sony, Yelp, Hulu, and Lyft. Twilio offers its clients a comprehensive, customizable, and easy-to-use platform to automate and streamline communications to customers, collaborators, employees, and coworkers. Coca-Cola uses Twilio to rapidly dispatch service technicians, real estate site Trulia uses Twilio for its click-to-call app that enables potential buyers to connect with an agent, EMC uses Twilio to send texts to

Source: Gabby Jones/Bloomberg/Getty Images

<< To keep both its high-profile business customers and their customers happy, leading cloud communication platform Twilio offers a variety of easy-to-use, customizable services that automate, streamline, and enhance interactions between companies and their customers, collaborators, and employees.

employees when an IT service goes down, and Airbnb uses it to automatically text information about potential renters to hosts. Building on its communications platform for text, voice, video, chats, and messaging apps, Twilio expanded its portfolio of services to include a cloud-based call-center service and a pay app that allows companies to process payments over the phone without having to read a card number to a representative. To add e-mail capabilities to its portfolio of offerings, Twilio in 2019 acquired SendGrid, the leading e-mail API platform, which bolstered the company's ability to deliver consistent messaging based on its customers' preferred form of communication.[28]

The internet and cloud computing enable firms to improve their service offerings and strengthen their relationships with customers by allowing for true interactivity, customer-specific and situational personalization, and real-time adjustments of the firm's offerings. But as companies collect, store, and use more information about customers, concerns about security and privacy arise. Companies must incorporate the proper safeguards and reassure customers about their efforts to keep customers' private information secure.

CUSTOMER EMPOWERMENT

The digital era has clearly altered customer relationships. Customers are becoming more sophisticated about buying product-support services and are pressing for "unbundled services" and the right to select the elements they want. They increasingly dislike having to deal with a multitude of service providers handling different types of products or equipment. With that in mind, some third-party service organizations now service a greater range of equipment. A plumbing business may also service air conditioners, furnaces, and other components of a household infrastructure.

Most important, social media have empowered customers by letting them send their comments around the world with a mouse click. A person who has a good customer experience is more likely to talk about it, but someone who has a bad experience will talk to more people. Ninety percent of angry customers reported sharing their story with a friend; they can now share it with strangers too. Online sites such as Angie's List, Yelp, and TripAdvisor are other popular means to spread the word about customer-service adventures. Even more challenging for firms, unhappy customers may choose to upload a damaging video to share their customer-service miseries with others.

When a customer complains, most companies now respond quickly. Many companies allow contact 24/7 by phone and e-chat, but they also reach out to customers and monitor blogs, websites, and social media. If employees see a customer report a problem on a blog, they get in touch and offer help. Clear, helpful e-mail replies to customers' queries can be very effective. Delta Airlines introduced Delta Assist to monitor customer Twitter tweets and Facebook posts around the clock with a 10-person team that provides real-time replies to any queries or problems.

More important than simply responding to a disgruntled customer, however, is preventing dissatisfaction from occurring in the future. That may mean simply taking the time to nurture customer relationships with attention from a real person. Solving a customer's problem quickly and easily goes a long way toward winning long-term loyal customers.[29]

CUSTOMER COPRODUCTION

The reality is that customers do not merely purchase and use a service; they play an active role in its delivery. Their words and actions affect the quality of their service experiences and those of others, as well as the productivity of frontline employees.[30]

Customers often believe they derive more value, and feel a stronger connection to the service provider, if they are actively engaged in the service process. This coproduction can put stress on employees, however, and reduce their satisfaction, especially if they do not share the same values, interests, or knowledge with their customers.[31] Moreover, one study estimated that one-third of all service problems are caused by the customer.[32] The growing shift to self-service technologies is likely to increase this percentage.

Preventing service failures is crucial because recovery is always challenging. One of the biggest problems is attribution. Customers often feel that the firm is at fault or that, even if it is not at fault, it is still responsible for righting any wrongs. Unfortunately, even though many firms have well-designed and well-executed procedures to deal with their own failures, they find managing *customer* failures—service problems arising from a customer's mistake or lack of understanding—much more difficult. Solutions come in all forms, as the following examples show.[33]

- *Redesign processes and redefine customer roles to simplify service encounters.* Staples transformed its business with its "Easy" program to take the hassle out of ordering office supplies.
- *Incorporate the right technology to aid employees and customers.* Comcast, the largest U.S. cable operator, introduced software to identify network glitches before they affected service and to better inform call center operators about customer problems.
- *Create high-performance customers by enhancing the clarity of their role, their motivation, and their ability to perform their role.* USAA reminds enlisted policyholders to suspend their car insurance when they are stationed overseas.
- *Encourage "customer citizenship" so customers will help one another.* At golf courses, players not only can follow the rules by playing and behaving appropriately; they can also encourage others to do so.

SATISFYING EMPLOYEES AS WELL AS CUSTOMERS

Excellent service companies know that positive employee attitudes will strengthen customer loyalty.[34] Instilling a strong customer orientation in employees can also increase their job satisfaction and commitment, especially if they have extensive customer contact. Employees thrive in customer-contact positions when they have an internal drive to (1) pamper customers, (2) accurately read their needs, (3) develop a personal relationship with them, and (4) deliver high-quality service to solve customers' problems.[35]

Given the importance of positive employee attitudes to customer satisfaction, service companies must attract the best employees they can find. They need to market a career rather than just a job, design a sound training program, provide support for employees, and reward them for good performance. Companies can use an intranet, internal newsletters, daily reminders, and employee roundtables to reinforce customer-centered attitudes. Finally, they must audit employee job satisfaction regularly.

Zappos has built a customer-focused organization admired by many.

Zappos Online retailer Zappos was founded with superior customer service at the core of its culture. With free shipping and returns, 24/7 customer service, and fast turnaround on the numerous products and thousands of brands offered on the site, the company works hard to create repeat customers. Unlike many other companies, it has not outsourced its Zappos.com call centers, and half the interview process is devoted to finding out whether job candidates are sufficiently outgoing, open-minded, and creative to be a good cultural fit. Zappos empowers

Source: dpa picture alliance/Alamy Stock Photo

<< Building customer loyalty by providing outstanding service are at the center of Zappos' corporate culture, a culture fostered by its former longtime CEO, Tony Hsieh.

its customer-service reps to solve problems. When a customer called to complain that a pair of boots was leaking after a year of use, the rep sent a new pair, even though the company's policy is that only unworn shoes are returnable. Every employee has a chance each year to contribute to the company's Culture Book about life at Zappos and how each department—from selling to warehousing, delivery, pricing, and billing—implements superior customer service. Thanks to its success, Zappos even offers two-day seminars to business executives eager to learn the secrets behind its unique corporate culture and approach to customer service.[36]

Achieving Service Excellence

The increased importance of the service industry has sharpened the focus on what it takes to excel in the marketing of services.[37] The superior marketing of services requires excellence in three broad areas: external marketing, internal marketing, and interactive marketing.[38] **External marketing** is the normal work of preparing, pricing, distributing, and promoting the service to customers. **Internal marketing** consists of training and motivating employees to serve customers well. Arguably the most important contribution the marketing department can make is to be "exceptionally clever in getting everyone else in the organization to practice marketing."[39] **Interactive marketing** reflects employees' skill in serving the client. In interactive marketing, teamwork is often key. Delegating authority to frontline employees can allow for greater service flexibility and adaptability because it promotes better problem solving, closer employee cooperation, and more efficient knowledge transfer.[40]

BEST PRACTICES OF TOP SERVICE COMPANIES

Well-managed service companies that achieve marketing excellence share a focus on customer-centricity, a commitment to service quality, an understanding of the need to cater to high-value customers, and the implementation of strategies for managing customer complaints.

Customer-Centricity. Top service companies are "customer obsessed." They have a clear sense of their target customers and their needs, and they have developed a distinctive strategy for satisfying them. At the Four Seasons luxury hotel chain, employees must pass four interviews before being hired. Each hotel also employs a "guest historian" to track guest preferences. With more than 10,000 branches in the United States (more than any other brokerage firm), Edward Jones stays close to customers by assigning a single financial advisor and one administrator to each office. Although costly, maintaining such small teams fosters personal relationships.[41]

Customer-centricity means seeing the world in general, and a company's services in particular, from the customer's point of view. Customer-centricity goes beyond providing the services that the company performs to delivering solutions that customers need. The customer-centric company is proactive in identifying and addressing customer needs (rather than being merely reactive and offering services that customers explicitly requested). Companies like The Ritz-Carlton, Four Seasons, REI, and Zappos have embraced customer-centricity as the underlying principle of their business models. One company that wins consistent praise for its brand-building success is Singapore Airlines.

Singapore Airlines Singapore Airlines (SIA) has been consistently recognized as the world's "best" airline, in large part thanks to its stellar marketing. The carrier wins so many awards that it has to update its website monthly. Famous for pampering passengers, it continuously strives to create a "wow effect" and surpass customers' expectations. SIA was the first to launch on-demand entertainment systems in all classes, Dolby sound systems, and a book-the-cook service that allows business- and first-class passengers to order meals before boarding. Thanks to a first-of-its-kind $1 million simulator the airline built to mimic the air pressure and humidity inside a plane, it found that taste buds change in the air and that, among other things, it needed to cut back on spices in its food. New SIA recruits receive four months of training (twice the industry average), and existing staff get nearly three weeks of refresher training a year (costing $70 million). With its reputation for excellence, the carrier attracts some of the best local graduates and staffs each flight with more attendants and other cabin crew members than other airlines. SIA applies a 40–30–30 rule: 40 percent of resources go to training and motivating staff, 30 percent to reviewing process and procedures, and 30 percent to creating new product and service ideas.[42]

Source: TRISTAR PHOTOS/Alamy Stock Photo

<< Singapore Airlines has achieved high-flying marketing success and earned plaudits by continuously working to delight its passengers and exceed their expectations.

Service Quality. Companies such as Marriott, Disney, and Ace Hardware have a thorough commitment to service quality. Their managers look monthly not only at financial performance but also at service performance. Ray Kroc of McDonald's insisted on continually measuring each McDonald's outlet on its conformance to QSCV: quality, service, cleanliness, and value. Some companies insert a reminder with employees' paychecks: "Brought to you by the customer." Sam Walton of Walmart required the following employee pledge: "I solemnly swear and declare that every customer that comes within 10 feet of me, I will smile, look them in the eye, and greet them, so help me Sam." Allstate, Dunkin' Brands, Oracle, and USAA have high-level senior executives with titles such as chief customer officer, chief client officer, or chief experience officer, who have the power and authority to improve customer service across every customer interaction.[43]

The best service providers set superior quality standards. In the highly regulated banking industry, Citibank still aims to answer customer phone calls within 10 seconds and letters within two days; it also has been an industry leader in using social media for customer service. The standards must be set *appropriately* high. A 98 percent accuracy standard may sound good, but it would result in 64,000 lost FedEx packages a day; six misspelled words on each page of a book; 400,000 incorrectly filled prescriptions daily; 3 million lost pieces of USPS mail each day; no phone, internet, or electricity for eight days per year, or 29 minutes per day; 1,000 mislabeled or (mispriced) products at a supermarket; and 6 million people unaccounted for in a U.S. census.

Top firms audit their own service performance, as well as that of competitors, on a regular basis. They collect *voice of the customer measurements* to probe customer satisfiers and dissatisfiers using comparison shopping, mystery or ghost shopping, customer surveys, suggestion and complaint forms, service-audit teams, and customers' letters. We can judge services on *customer importance* and *company performance*. *Importance–performance analysis* rates the various elements of the service bundle and identifies required actions.

Because U.S. consumers generally have high expectations about service delivery, they often feel their needs are not being adequately met. Service providers receive low marks for many reasons. Customers complain about inaccurate information; unresponsive, rude, or poorly trained workers; and long waits. Even worse, many find their complaints never reach a human ear because of slow or faulty phone or online reporting systems. Consumers report that companies mishandle online complaints by responding selectively or inconsistently (or not at all) and by "cutting and running," appearing insincere, or attempting to just "bribe" the consumer. It doesn't have to be that way. Consider the case of Butterball, the largest producer of turkey products in the United States.

Source: Sheila Fitzgerald/Shutterstock

>> Trained experts have been talking turkey to thousands of U.S and Canadian households every fall as they answer more than 100,000 queries on how to prepare, cook, and serve this focal element of Thanksgiving meals.

Butterball Talk Line Available every November and December, the 50+ experts at the company's talk line answer more than 100,000 questions about how to prepare, cook, and serve turkeys from thousands of households around the United States and Canada; 12,000 people call on Thanksgiving Day alone. Trained at Butterball University, the operators have all cooked turkeys dozens of different ways and can handle any queries that come up, including why turkeys shouldn't be stashed in snow banks and how to tell when the turkey is done. The Talk Line began in 1981 with six volunteers who worked the phones that holiday season to answer 11,000 turkey-cooking questions. Most recently, the company expanded the ways in which customers can connect with the Talk Line to include social media, live chat, texting—and even Amazon Alexa.[44]

Catering to High-Value Customers. Many firms have decided to coddle big spenders to retain their patronage as long as possible. Customers in high-profit tiers get special discounts, promotional offers, and lots of special service; those in lower-profit tiers, who barely pay their way, may get more fees, stripped-down service, and voice messages to process their inquiries.

When the 2008 recession hit, Zappos decided to stop offering complimentary overnight shipping to first-time buyers and to offer it to repeat buyers only. The money saved was invested in a new VIP service for the company's most loyal customers.[45] Companies that provide differentiated levels of service must be careful about claiming superior service, however; customers who receive lesser treatment will bad-mouth the company and injure its reputation. One type of company that is expert at identifying and catering to high-value customers is the bank.

Leading banks in India including HDFC, Kotak Mahindra, ICICI and SBI have set up private banking and wealth management units specifically to serve their richest clients[46]. Dedicated relationship managers advise the rich and ultra-high net worth individuals (UHNI) by analyzing the client's needs and their financial goals to develop a wealth management charter for financial planning and investments. These clients are pampered with lower rates on loans, exclusive benefits and lifestyle privileges on credit cards and concierge-like service, guaranteeing them instant access to their relationship managers to complete just about any transaction. The best wealth managers use proprietary due diligence tools and evaluation frameworks for rigorous analysis and deep understanding to offer superior products and bespoke solutions including financial planning, investment portfolio management, estate and tax planning, legal resources, business succession, risk management, among others[47]. Research-driven and expert-curated customized services often involve investment advisors and product specialists. Banks pursue wealthy clients as they generate significant profit, guarantees repeat business and brings in new business. Such high value service offerings, through a continuous investment advisory process, is an extremely profitable business in India's rapidly growing financial market.[48,49]

Delivering services that maximize both customer satisfaction and company profitability can be challenging. On the one hand, a company needs to make sure that it creates meaningful benefits for its high-value customers. On the other hand, providing too many benefits could have a negative impact on the company's profits and thus prove counterproductive. Consider the experience of Atlantic City's Tropicana casino.

Eager to attract big spenders, Atlantic City's Tropicana casino offered Don Johnson, a high roller and experienced blackjack player, a special deal that modified the rules of the game in a way that reduced the casino's advantage, in addition to offering him a 20 percent discount on losses (meaning that if he lost $500,000, he only had to pay $400,000). In their zeal to entice Johnson to play in their casino, managers did not realize that they had given up too much by offering Johnson an edge in betting against the house. With the odds on his side, Johnson won nearly $6 million in one night—an amount equal to the casino's monthly revenue. The Tropicana was not alone in offering overly generous benefits to high rollers; Atlantic City's Borgata and Caesars casinos succumbed to the same fate, losing $9 million to Johnson.[50]

Managing Customer Complaints. On average, 40 percent of customers who suffer through a bad service experience with a company stop doing business with it.[51] However, if those customers were willing to complain first, they would actually offer the company a gift—provided that the complaint is handled well. Companies that encourage disappointed customers to complain—and also empower employees to remedy the situation on the spot—have been shown to achieve higher revenues and greater profits than companies without a systematic approach for addressing service failures.[52]

Frontline employees who adopt *extra-role behaviors*, advocate the interests and enhance the image of the firm to consumers, and take the initiative to engage in conscientious behavior in dealing with customers can be a critical asset in handling complaints.[53] Customers evaluate complaint incidents in terms of the outcomes they receive, the procedures used to arrive at those outcomes, and the nature of interpersonal treatment during the process.[54] Companies are also looking to improve the way they handle complaints by increasing the quality of their *call centers* and their *customer-service representatives*. "Marketing Insight: Improving Company Call Centers" at the end of this chapter illustrates what top companies are doing.

DIFFERENTIATING SERVICES

When the physical product cannot easily be differentiated, the key to competitive success may lie in adding valued services and constantly improving their quality. Rolls-Royce PLC has ensured that its aircraft engines are in high demand by continuously monitoring the health of its airplane engines in use around the world through live satellite feeds. Under its TotalCare and CorporateCare programs, airlines pay Rolls a fee for every hour an engine is in flight, and Rolls assumes the risks and costs of downtime and repairs.

The main service differentiators are ease of ordering; speed and timing of delivery; installation, training, and consulting; maintenance and repair; and returns.

Ease of Ordering. Ordering ease reflects how simple it is for the customer to place an order with the company. As markets become increasingly competitive, many companies focus on making the ordering process as convenient as possible. This involves streamlining all aspects of a customer's interaction with the company—from the initial evaluation of the available options to the actual purchase. Voice assistants such as Alexa, Google Home, and Siri have helped make the ordering process even easier by using artificial intelligence to predict consumer preferences.

Striving to simplify the ordering process is not limited to consumer markets. It plays a major role in business markets as well. Baxter Healthcare supplies hospitals with computer terminals through which they send orders directly to the firm, thus streamlining the ordering process. Another example of simplifying the ordering process is Align Technology.

Align Technology Align Technology pioneered the invisible orthodontics market with the introduction of the Invisalign system—transparent dental braces used to adjust teeth. The company was born from the simple observation that the dental retainers commonly prescribed after orthodontic procedures could be used not only to prevent teeth from moving but also to realign teeth. This observation led to the idea that a series of custom-designed aligners could be used to straighten misaligned teeth. By 2018, the company's Invisalign system had been used to treat over 5 million patients and enjoyed wide adoption by dental professionals. To streamline the treatment process, the company introduced a digital scanner that replaced the cumbersome and time-consuming process of taking physical impressions. The use of digital scanning technology enabled the company to speed up the ordering process, increase the quality of the impressions, and improve the overall customer experience.[55]

>> By using digital scanning technology to obviate the need for taking physical impressions, Align Technology has streamlined, sped up, and improved the orthodontic process for both dental professionals and customers.

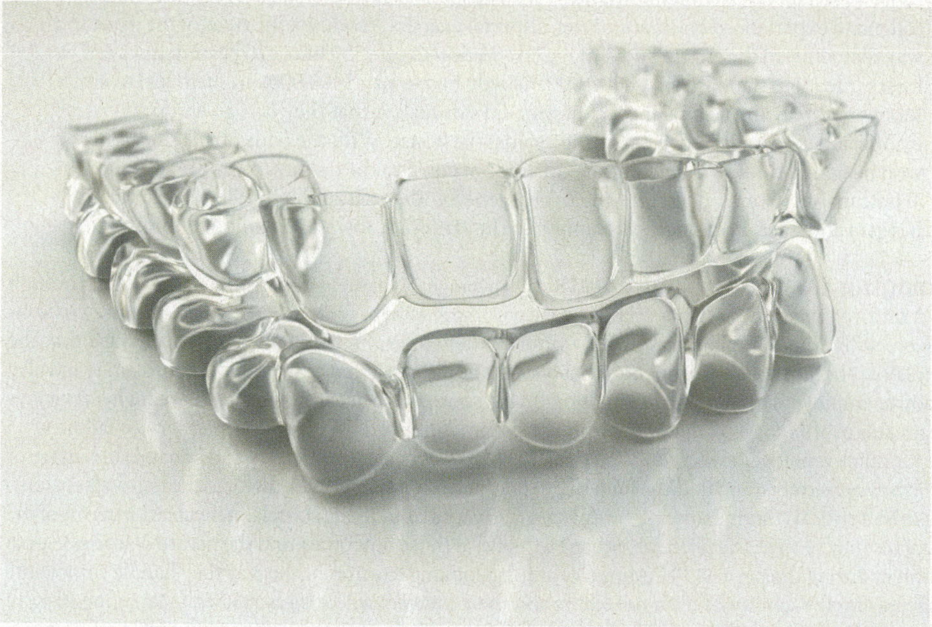

Source: Andreas Fülscher Schliemann/Alamy Stock Photo

Many companies, especially those offering subscription services, look beyond a single transaction to ensure that customers continue using the service. Harry's—a razor blade and shaving cream subscription service—simplified shoppers' decisions by offering a three-step process that helps buyers choose a razor and determine the frequency with which to receive replacements. Gillette introduced text ordering for its subscription service, enabling members to text "BLADES" when they're ready for a new shipment. In the same vein, Amazon introduced Dash—a Wi-Fi device that reorders a particular product (such as razors, laundry detergent, or dog food) with the press of a button.

Speed and Timing of Delivery. Delivery entails how well the product or service is brought to the customer, including the speed, accuracy, and care that characterize the process. Today's customers have grown to expect speed: pizza delivered in half an hour, eyeglasses made in 60 minutes, and cars lubricated in 15 minutes. Many firms have computerized *quick-response systems* that link the information systems of their suppliers, manufacturing plants, distribution centers, and retailing outlets to improve delivery.

In the consumer space, Amazon has led the charge in the speed-of-delivery game among online retailers, offering delivery options ranging from a week to only a couple of hours. Food delivery services such as Uber Eats help many restaurants and vendors offer fast and reliable delivery to their customers without having to invest in developing their own delivery infrastructure.

In business markets, Cemex, a giant cement company based in Mexico, has transformed its business by promising to deliver concrete faster than pizza and equipping every truck with a global positioning system so dispatchers know its real-time location. Its 24/7 LOAD service program guarantees delivery within a 20-minute window, providing important flexibility in an industry where delays are costly but common.[56]

Installation, Training, and Consulting. Installation consists of the work done to make a product operational in its planned location. Ease of installation is a true selling point for technology novices and for buyers of complex products like heavy equipment.

Customer training helps the customer's employees use the vendor's equipment properly and efficiently. General Electric not only sells expensive X-ray equipment to hospitals and installs it but also provides users with extensive training. McDonald's requires its new franchisees to attend Hamburger University in Oak Brook, Illinois, for two weeks to learn how to manage the franchise properly.

Customer consulting includes data, information systems, and advice services that the seller offers to buyers. Technology firms like IBM, Oracle, and SAP have learned that such consulting is an essential—and profitable—part of their business. Many industrial equipment manufacturers, such as Haas Automation, offer additional installation and training services to educate operators on how to use the machinery. Some of these additional services are part of a maintenance program that that can be purchased by customers. In the consumer space, a number of companies, including IKEA, Home Depot, and Best Buy, offer assembly and installation services to their customers for an additional fee.

Maintenance and Repair. Maintenance and repair programs help customers keep purchased products in good working order. These services are critical in business-to-business settings. Goodyear's TVTrack program helps its fleet customers monitor and manage tires more effectively. Many firms offer online technical support, or "e-support," for customers, who can search an online database for fixes or seek online help from a technician. Appliance makers such as LG, Kenmore, and Miele have introduced products that can transmit self-diagnostic data over the phone to a customer-service number that electronically describes the nature of any technical problems.

Makers of luxury products especially recognize the importance of a smooth repair process. Although Movado's watches are high-end, its repair process had been anything but, requiring time-consuming manual labor and entailing customer inconvenience. Recognizing the need to offer more digital services in general, Movado created a website where customers can buy products directly from the company as well as execute many of the initial steps in the repair process online (such as registering any problems and identifying possible repair options) before contacting customer service directly. The database created by users of the site has also allowed the company to recruit potential focus-group participants and to identify repair trends that may suggest recurring production problems.[57]

Returns. A nuisance to customers, manufacturers, retailers, and distributors alike, product returns are also an unavoidable reality of doing business, especially for online purchases. Free shipping, which is growing more popular, makes it easier for customers to try out an item—but also increases the likelihood of its being returned.

Returns can add up. One estimate is that 10 percent to 15 percent of overall holiday sales come back as returns or exchanges, and the total annual cost of dealing with them may be $100 billion.[58] For the consumer, returns can be inconvenient, embarrassing, or difficult to complete. Returns have a downside for merchants, too, especially when the returned merchandise is not in resellable condition, lacks proper proof of purchase, or is returned to the wrong store. It may even be used or stolen. Yet if the merchant is reluctant to accept returns, customers can become annoyed.

However, product returns do have an upside. Physically returning a product can get the consumer into the store, maybe for the first time. One research study found that a lenient return policy left customers more willing to make other purchases and to refer the company to others.[59]

We can think of product returns in two ways:[60] *Controllable returns* result from problems or errors made by the seller or customer; they can be largely eliminated with improved handling or storage, better packaging, and more effective transportation and logistics by the seller or its supply chain partners. *Uncontrollable returns* result from the need for customers to actually see, try, or experience products in person to determine suitability; these returns can't be eliminated by the company in the short run.

One basic strategy is to eliminate the root causes of controllable returns while developing processes for handling uncontrollable returns. The goal is to have fewer products returned and put a higher percentage back into the distribution pipeline to be sold again. San Diego–based Road Runner Sports—which sells running shoes, clothing, and equipment through multiple stores, catalogs, and a website—trains its salespeople to be as knowledgeable as possible in order to recommend the right products. As a result, its return rate on running shoes has been 12 percent, noticeably below the industry average of 15 percent to 20 percent.[61]

>> New service categories are always being created, as with Kaya, a chain of clinics to enhance the look and feel of skin and hair beautifully.

Source: Kaya Clinic (Marico)©Kaya Clinic, used with permission

INNOVATION WITH SERVICES

Innovation is as vital in services as in any industry.[62] New service categories are constantly being introduced to satisfy unmet needs and wants. Examples include Kaya, that runs clinics created around fulfilling customers' desire for beautiful skin and gorgeous hair; Reddit, a giant online digital bulletin board with tens of thousands of active forums where registered users can post content or links; and CareLinx, which functions as a matchmaking site for families with elderly members and nonmedical caregivers who can provide home care.

Online Travel Online travel agents such as Expedia and Travelocity offer customers the opportunity to conveniently book travel at discount prices. However, they make money only when visitors go to their websites and book travel. Kayak successfully entered the category later by applying the Google business model of collecting money on a per-click basis. Kayak's marketing emphasis is on building a better search engine by offering more alternatives, flexibility, and airlines. Kayak makes search simpler for travelers by ranking flights using artificial intelligence algorithm that factors in price, duration, and number of stops and offers information about, and discounts on, nearby hotels.[63]

Retail Health Clinics One of the hardest areas in which to innovate is health care. But whereas the current health care system is designed to treat a small number of complex cases, retail health clinics address a large number of simple cases. Retail health clinics such as Quick Care, RediClinic, and MinuteClinic are often found in drugstores and other retail chain stores such as Target and Walmart. They typically use nurse practitioners to handle minor injuries and illnesses such as colds, flu, and ear infections; to offer various health and wellness services such as physicals and exams for high school sports; and to administer vaccinations. The clinics seek to offer convenient, predictable service and transparent pricing, without an appointment, seven days (and evenings) a week. Most visits take no more than 15 minutes, and costs vary from $25 to $100.[64]

Consider how the following service categories emerged and how, in some cases, organizations found creative solutions in existing categories.

Innovation in existing services can also have big payoffs. When Ticketmaster introduced interactive seat maps that allowed customers to pick their own seats instead of being given one by a "best seat available" function, the conversion rate from potential to actual buyers increased to 30 percent, a 25 percent jump. Persuading a ticket buyer to add an "I'm going . . ." message to Facebook adds an extra $5 in ticket sales on average; adding reviews of a show on the site doubles the conversion rate.[65]

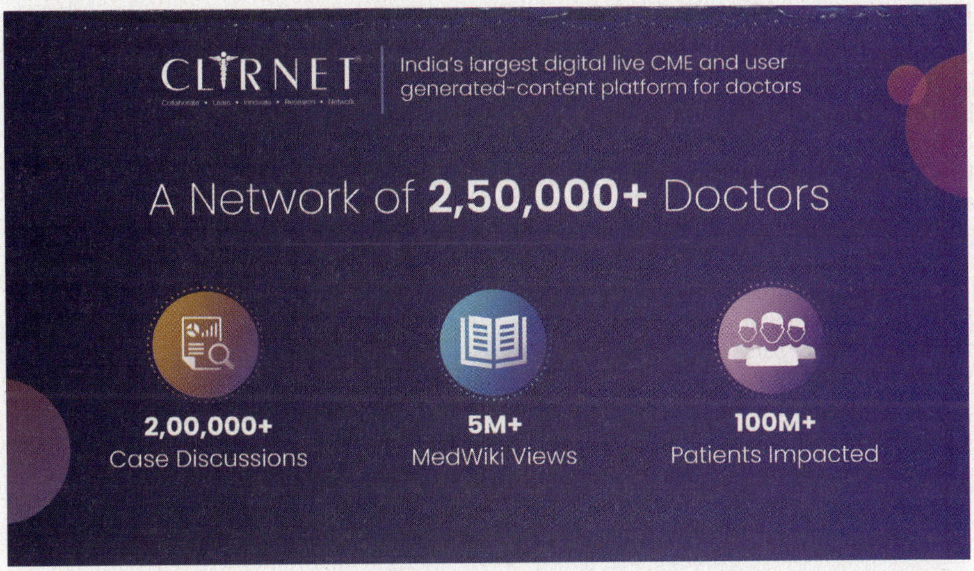

<< Clirnet is a digital platform for doctors to collaborate, share knowledge and improve healthcare solutions to enhance patient outcomes.

Source: ©Clirnet, used with permission

The service company that regularly introduces innovations can intrigue customers and stay a step ahead of its competitors.[66] Sometimes it can even reinvent a service category, as Clirnet is trying to transform the continuing medical education service for doctors.

Clirnet Clirnet offers continuing medical education (CME) services to the time-starved doctors by connecting them with specialists over phone and video. Pioneering the concept of collaborative treatment has helped the company create a large community network of more than 250,000 + doctos who connect, consult, and collaborate with each other to improve patient health outcomes. Working towards its mission to support the medical practitioners in making the healthcare services 'accessible, affordable and standardized', Clirnet has emerged as India's fastest growing doctors' network in a short span of time.[67] Doctors post queries on patient condition or treatment related issues. These queries are matched with specialists and connected over a phone call for a discussion through Clirnet's MasterConnect service.

Doctors connect to Clirnet for master sessions with experts, collaborative CME sessions, one to one discussion sessions and to access the digital encyclopaedia—MedWiki—for a wide range of audio and video driven, experiential medical content over digital media. Doctors communicate and collaborate on Clirnet platform to explore and improve healthcare solutions. Clirnet reaches out to the doctors over SMS, WhatsApp messages and emails to keep the communication mode simple, flexible and easily accessible. Clirnet's solutions like voice call facility and digital connectivity are designed to reach out to even the small towns and rural areas of the country.

As Clirnet scales up its solution by integrating the medical and healthcare industry, its services continue to be free for doctors. Leading pharmaceutical companies use Clirnet to conduct CME sessions and promote their products among doctors.[68] Clirnet is gaining popularity, especially amidst young doctors in small towns and rural areas as they can easily connect with experts for advice and improve their practice.[69]

Managing Service Quality

The service quality of a firm is tested at each service encounter. If employees are bored, cannot answer simple questions, or are visiting with each other while customers are waiting, customers will think twice about doing business there again. Flawless service delivery is the ideal output for any service organization. Two important activities are managing customer expectations and incorporating self-service technologies.

MANAGING CUSTOMER EXPECTATIONS

Customers form service expectations from many sources, including past experiences, word of mouth, and advertising. In general, they compare perceived and expected service. If the perceived service falls below the expected service, customers are disappointed. Successful companies add benefits to their offering that not only satisfy customers but surprise and delight them by exceeding expectations.[70] One company that has built its business around exceeding customer expectations is American Express.

American Express American Express has embraced a relationship-building approach in which customer-service reps are judged in part based on customer feedback. Reps—called customer care professionals—can see all kinds of relevant data on their screen when a customer calls, including name, age, address, and buying and payment habits. Whether a cardmember loses a wallet or purse while traveling or needs assistance finding a missing child in a foreign country, American Express has empowered its customer care professionals to do whatever it takes to help. This exemplary customer service brings financial benefits too. Cardmembers who positively rate their customer experience tend to increase their AmEx card spending by10 percent to 15 percent and are four to five times more likely to remain customers, increasing shareholder value. Not least, because of its strong service culture and support, American Express boasts some of the highest employee retention rates in the industry.[71]

The service-quality model in Figure 9.2 highlights the main requirements for delivering high service quality.[72] It also identifies five gaps that prevent successful delivery.

1. *Gap between consumer expectation and management perception*—Management does not always correctly perceive what customers want. Hospital administrators may think patients want better food, but patients may be more concerned with nurse responsiveness.
2. *Gap between management perception and service-quality specification*—Management might correctly perceive customers' wants but not set a uniform performance standard. Hospital administrators may tell the nurses to give "fast" service without specifying speed in minutes.
3. *Gap between service-quality specifications and service delivery*—Employees might be poorly trained; they might be incapable of meeting, or unwilling to meet, the standard; or they may be held to conflicting standards. Nurses might be confused about whether they should take time to listen to customers or give them fast service.
4. *Gap between service delivery and external communications*—Consumer expectations are affected by statements made by company representatives and ads. If a hospital brochure shows a beautiful room but the patient finds it cheap and tacky-looking, external communications have distorted the customer's expectations.

>> Customer-service reps are empowered to do whatever it takes to maintain and increase customer satisfaction among American Express cardholders, in the bargain yielding financial benefits for the company.

Source: Chris Pearsall/Alamy Stock Photo

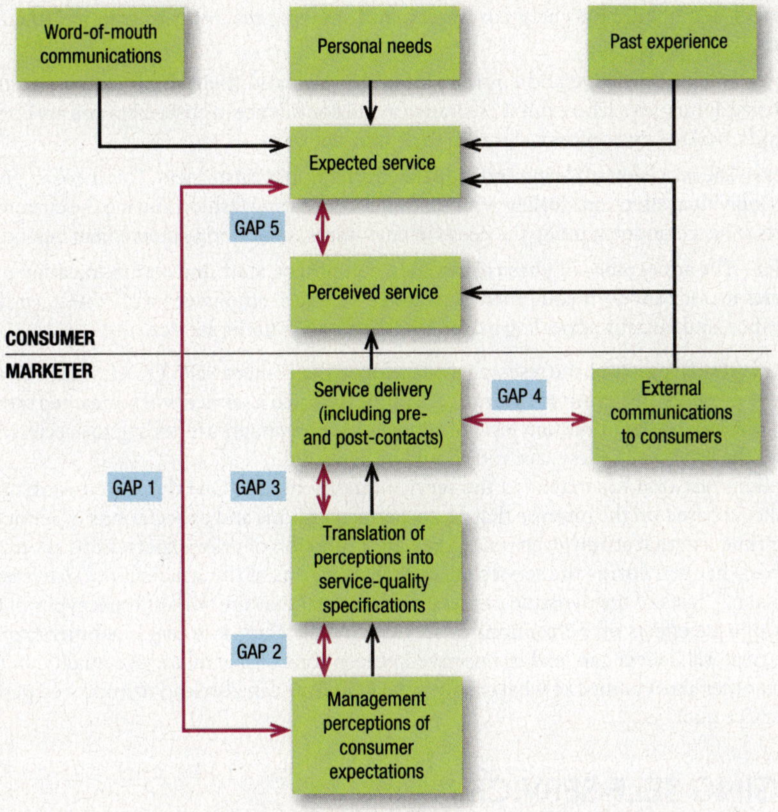

FIGURE **9.2**

Service-Quality Model

Source: A. Parasuraman, Valarie A. Zeithaml, and Leonard L. Berry, "A Conceptual Model of Service Quality and Its Implications for Future Research," *Journal of Marketing*, Fall 1985, p. 44.

5. *Gap between perceived and expected service*—The consumer may misperceive the service quality. The physician may keep visiting the patient to show care, but the patient may interpret this as an indication that something is really wrong.

Much work has validated the role of expectations in consumers' interpretations and evaluations of the service encounter and in the relationship they adopt with a firm over time.[73] Consumers are often forward-looking in terms of their likely behavior and interactions with a firm when deciding whether to keep or drop a service relationship. Any marketing activity that positively affects current or expected future usage can help to solidify a service relationship.

For continuously provided services such as public utilities, health care, financial and computing services, insurance, and other professional, membership, or subscription services, customers have been observed to mentally calculate the perceived economic benefits relative to the economic costs. In other words, customers ask themselves, "Am I using this service enough, given what I pay for it?" A negative response will lead to a change in behavior and the possible termination of an account.

Long-term service relationships can have a dark side. An ad agency client may feel that over time the agency is losing objectivity, becoming stale in its thinking, or beginning to take advantage of the relationship.[74]

MANAGING SERVICE QUALITY

Based on the service-quality model described above, researchers have identified five determinants of service quality—reliability, responsiveness, assurance, empathy, and tangibles—in descending order of importance.[75]

- *Reliability*—The ability to perform the promised service dependably and accurately. This involves providing the service as promised, offering dependability in handling customers' service problems, performing services right the first time, providing services at the promised time, maintaining error-free records, and hiring employees who have the knowledge to answer customers' questions.
- *Responsiveness*—The willingness to help customers and provide prompt service. This involves keeping customers informed about when services will be performed, giving prompt service to

customers, being willing to help customers, and showing readiness to respond to customers' requests.

- *Assurance*—The knowledge and courtesy of employees and their ability to convey trust and confidence. Employees who exhibit assurance instill confidence in customers and are consistently courteous, making customers feel safe in their transactions.
- *Empathy*—The provision of caring, individualized attention to customers. This involves giving customers individual attention, dealing with customers in a caring fashion, having the customer's best interests at heart, understanding the needs of customers, and offering convenient business hours.
- *Tangibles*—The appearance of physical facilities, equipment, staff, and communication materials. Tangibles include modern equipment, attractive facilities, employees with a neat, professional appearance, and visually appealing materials associated with the service.

Based on these five factors, the researchers developed the 21-item SERVQUAL scale.[76] In addition, they noted the presence of a **zone of tolerance**, a range in which a service will be deemed satisfactory, anchored at one end by the minimum level of service that consumers are willing to accept and, at the other end, by the level they believe can and should be delivered.

Subsequent research has extended the service-quality model. One dynamic process model of service quality is based on the premise that customer perceptions and expectations of service quality change over time, but that at any given point, they are a function of prior expectations about what *will* and what *should* happen during the service encounter, as well as of the *actual* service delivered during the last contact.[77] Tests of the dynamic process model reveal that the two different types of expectations have opposite effects on perceptions of service quality. Thus, *increasing* customer expectations of what the firm *will* deliver can lead to improved perceptions of overall service quality. In contrast, *decreasing* customer expectations of what the firm *should* deliver can also lead to improved perceptions of overall service quality.

MANAGING SELF-SERVICE

Consumers value convenience in services,[78] and many person-to-person service interactions are being replaced by self-service technologies intended to provide that convenience. To traditional vending machines, we can add automated teller machines (ATMs), self-service at gas pumps, self-checkout at hotels, and a variety of activities on the internet, such as ticket purchasing, investment trading, and customization of products.

To streamline its operations and speed up customer service, Chili's installed tabletop computer screens in its restaurants so customers can order directly and pay by credit card. The restaurant chain found that users of the service spend more per check, in part because they buy more desserts and coffee when the screen is present. As another example, SBI's YONO application lets customers conduct most banking transactions online on a smartphone.

Every company needs to think about improving its service using self-service technologies. Comcast's need for customer service has been reduced because 40 percent of its installations are done by the customer and 31 percent of customers now manage their accounts completely online.[79]

SBI YONO State Bank of India's YONO (You Only Need One) is an integrated digital banking, investments, and shopping platform. In less than five years after its launch, YONO attracted over 37 million subscribers with over 2.3 million online transactions every month.[80] It's convenient and integrated self-service solution serves the banking and shopping needs of customers from the comforts of their homes. With SBI YONO, one can access more than 100 e-commerce websites, book tickets, pay bills, make investments, and transfer funds on the move using its mobile application. Features such as 24×7 online banking services, instant account opening, quick loans, card-less cash withdrawal, spend analyzer, etc. turned YONO into one of the most convenient and popular mobile applications.[81] YONO continues to grow rapidly with 9 million logins per day after attracting 2 million new customer accounts and sourcing loans of over ₹5000 crores during FY2021.[82] Recently the bank extended YONO to seven foreign markets and onboarded 40,000 customers. Its new services include YONO Agri for farmers and YONO Business for corporates and small and medium enterprises to meet their respective banking and business needs like letter of credit, cash management supply chain finance, and foreign exchange, among others.[83]

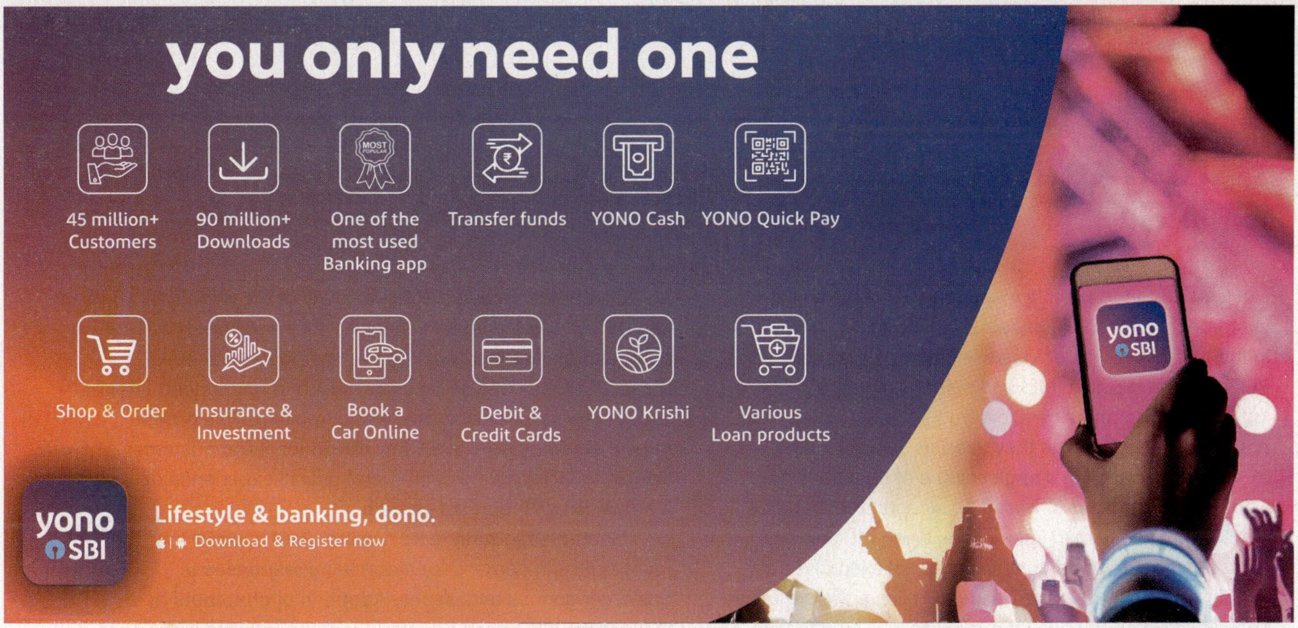

<< SBI YONO is a rapidly growing digital application that offers convenient self -service options for banking, investments and shopping.

Source: SBI YONO©State Bank of India, used with permission

Successfully integrating technology into the workforce requires a comprehensive reengineering of the front office to identify what people do best, what machines do best, and how to deploy them separately and together.[84] Some companies have found that the biggest obstacle is not the technology itself but convincing customers to use it, especially for the first time.

Customers must have a clear sense of their roles in the self-service process, must see a clear benefit, and must feel they can actually use the technology.[85] Self-service technology is not for everyone. Although some automated voices are actually popular with customers, many can provoke frustration and even rage at being unable to speak with an actual person.

MANAGING PRODUCT–SERVICE BUNDLES

No less important than service industries are product-based industries that must provide a service bundle.[86] Manufacturers of equipment—ranging from small appliances and office machines to tractors, mainframes, and airplanes—must all provide product-support services, now a battleground for competitive advantage. Many product companies also have a stronger online presence than before and must ensure that they offer adequate, if not superior, service online as well.

Products can be augmented with key service differentiators in areas such as ordering, delivery, installation, customer training, customer consulting, maintenance, and repair. Some equipment companies, such as Caterpillar and Deere, make a significant percentage of their profits from these services.[87] In the global marketplace, companies that make a good product but provide poor local service support are seriously disadvantaged.

The quality of customer-service departments varies greatly. At one extreme are those that simply transfer customer calls to the appropriate person for action with little follow-up. At the other extreme are departments that are eager to receive customer requests, suggestions, and even complaints and that handle them expeditiously. Some firms even proactively contact customers to provide service after the sale is complete.[88]

Manufacturers usually start by running their own parts-and-service departments. They want to stay close to the equipment and understand its problems. They also find it expensive and time-consuming to train others and typically discover that they can make good money from parts and service if they are the only supplier and can charge a premium price. In fact, many equipment manufacturers price their equipment low and compensate by charging high prices for parts and service.

Over time, manufacturers switch more maintenance and repair service to authorized distributors and dealers. These intermediaries are closer to customers, operate in more locations, and can offer quicker service. Still later, independent service firms emerge and offer a lower price or faster service. A significant percentage of auto-service work is now done outside franchised automobile dealerships by independent garages and chains such as Midas Muffler and Jiffy Lube. Independent service organizations handle servers, telecommunications equipment, and a variety of other equipment lines.

Customer-service choices are increasing rapidly, however, and equipment manufacturers increasingly must figure out how to make money on their equipment, independent of service contracts. Some new-car warranties now cover 100,000 miles before customers have to pay for servicing. The increase in disposable or never-fail equipment makes customers less inclined to pay 2 percent to 10 percent of the purchase price every year for service. A company with several hundred laptops, printers, and related equipment might find it cheaper to have its own service people on-site.

marketing INSIGHT

Emergence of Contact Centers with Chat Bots

Customer support plays a major role in strengthening customer relationships, especially in the service industry. In the technology-driven digital era of artificial intelligence (AI), machine learning (ML) and natural language processing (NLP), call centers have evolved into contact centers. Equipped with chat bots they support customer care executives in handling a large volume of customer queries. Chatbot's automated AI-based application tool handles tasks as well as human interactions using ML and NLP. Most chatbots support customer service executives by handling routine tasks and queries. It allows the organizations improve operational efficiency as well as effectiveness of their contact systems with chatbots connecting to its employees or customers, thus reducing the headcount for customer care executives. While chatbots resolve frequently asked queries and initiate troubleshooting guides, customer care executives, thereby, get more bandwidth and time to handle complex issues.

Upgrades in AI technology has transformed the human engagements with chatbots by enhancing the quality of interactions between business and customers. Chatbots are being designed to handle the 'Mobile-first' population with its messaging applications for instant real-time response to customer queries.

Chatbots improve the productivity of the organization and bring cost effectiveness to businesses with its automated support system. Many chatbots are used in the initial stages of a service interaction to understand the customer's requirement, query or complaint. This preliminary understanding plays a key role in resolving customer issues, thus improving customers' overall experience of interactions with contact centers.

Chatbots facilitate rapld scaling up of support to meet spikes in demand by automating responses to customer queries and issues. Adoption of chaptbots by businesses have been boosted by improvements in the underlying technologies, declining costs and improving effectiveness in handling routine queries. They are emerging as an efficient and low cost technology option to offer personalized and real time solutions to millions of customers in a cost-effective way

As chatbots get integrated with other advanced AI tools and technologies, their enhanced capabilities will help them easily handle more complex service tasks. Contact centers will depend on the AI-based conversational chatbots with the roll out of 5G networks, offering faster solutions to improve customer service and interactions.[89]

summary

1. A service is an act that one entity performs for another that is essentially intangible and does not result in the ownership of anything. It may or may not be tied to a physical product.
2. Because services are generally high in experience and credence qualities, there is more risk in their purchase, and consumers tend to rely heavily on price, provider, and physical cues to judge quality. Switching costs for many services tend to be high because customers are very loyal to service providers who satisfy them.
3. Services are intangible, inseparable, variable, and perishable. Each characteristic poses challenges and requires certain strategies. Marketers must find ways to give tangibility to the intangible, increase the productivity of service providers, enhance and standardize the quality of the service provided, and match the supply of services with market demand.
4. The marketing of services faces new realities in the 21st century because of customer empowerment, customer coproduction, and the need to satisfy employees as well as customers. The digital era has clearly altered customer relationships. Customers do not merely purchase and use a service; they play an active role in its delivery.
5. Achieving excellence in service marketing calls not only for external marketing, but also for internal marketing to motivate employees and for interactive marketing to emphasize the importance of both "high tech" and "high touch."
6. Top service companies adopt a strategic concept, have a history of top-management commitment to quality, institute high standards, establish profit tiers, and pay attention to their systems for monitoring service performance and customer complaints. They also differentiate their brands through primary and secondary service features and continual innovation.
7. Superior service delivery requires managing customer expectations and incorporating self-service technologies. Customers' expectations play a critical role in their service experiences and evaluations. Companies

must manage service quality by understanding the effects of each service encounter. Well-managed service companies that achieve marketing excellence have in common a focus on customer-centricity, a commitment to service quality, and the aim of catering to high-value customers.

8. Service differentiation is a crucial component of a company's marketing success. The main service differentiators are ease of ordering; speed and timing of delivery; installation, training, and consulting; maintenance and repair; and returns.

9. Service quality is a key driver of customer satisfaction. There are five determinants of service quality: reliability, responsiveness, assurance, empathy, and tangibles. To create customer value, a company must strive to deliver superior service on all of these dimensions, while focusing on those services that customers value most.

marketing SPOTLIGHT

The Ritz-Carlton

Source: Richard Croft/Alamy Stock Photo

The Ritz-Carlton Hotel is an American luxury hotel chain that operates 91 luxury hotels and resorts in 30 countries. The company receives high praise for its excellent service and is recognized as the gold standard in the customer-service department. By exceeding customer expectations, The Ritz-Carlton has become one of the leading companies in luxury hospitality.

The Ritz-Carlton, which began as The Ritz-Carlton Investing Company, was founded by Albert Keller in the 1900s. The company had built several hotels along the East Coast in cities such as Boston, Philadelphia, Atlantic City, and Boca Raton. However, by 1940 the company disbanded; all but one hotel had been closed down and sold off because of financial difficulties brought on by the Great Depression. The Ritz-Carlton in Boston continued operating (it was sold in 2006 to Taj Hotels) and built the foundation for future hotels. It featured private baths in each guest room, gourmet cuisine, personalized guest experiences, and many more amenities that contributed to a premier luxury experience. In 1983, The Ritz-Carlton Hotel Company was formed. Led by new management, Ritz-Carlton expanded around the globe, adding new properties across the United States, Asia, and Europe.

The cornerstone of The Ritz-Carlton's success is customer loyalty achieved through exceptional customer service. The customer-service experience is defined by The Ritz-Carlton's Gold Standards, which reflect the values and philosophy by which The Ritz-Carlton operates. The Gold Standards can best be described by its mission statement: "The Ritz-Carlton is a place where the genuine care and comfort of our guests is our highest mission."

To ensure consistency in its interactions with customers, in the 1980s The Ritz-Carlton standardized the language used by its employees. Management created a distinct style of speech with phrases like "my pleasure," "right away," and "We're fully committed tonight." Over time, these phrases began to sound insincere because employees used them in situations where they didn't fit. When employees said that it was their pleasure to unclog sinks or clean bathrooms, guests took notice. Surveys indicated that guests believed interactions with Ritz-Carlton employees had become too robotic. The Ritz-Carlton acted on this feedback and shifted its language standard to focus on more authentic, unscripted conversation. The Ritz-Carlton now features more relaxed guidelines for addressing guests; these are still thoughtful and respectful but feel genuine.

A distinct feature of The Ritz-Carlton's customer service is that employees are fully empowered to provide unique and personalized service. Employees are encouraged to make guests happy using any means, without having to consult a supervisor first. There are many stories of employees going above and beyond to provide the "Wow!" factor. For example, when one hotel's food and beverage director noticed a stain on the back of a returning guest's coat and asked what happened, the guest said it was an old stain he couldn't get out and mentioned that the coat was one of his favorites. After the conversation, the hostess collected the coats of the guest and his family to hang up while they ate lunch. Meanwhile, the restaurant team whisked the coat to housekeeping, which managed to remove the stain. The guest left delighted.

At The Ritz-Carlton, each and every employee is allowed to spend up to $2,000 per day per guest to solve customer problems or make their experience memorable. One of the most famous incidents occurred at The Ritz-Carlton,

(continued)

Shanghai. A guest came into the hotel wearing a business jacket matched with casual Hawaiian shorts. The guest told the front desk agent that his slacks had been ripped at the airport. Because the guest had an important business meeting the next morning at 10 AM, the agent offered to see whether housekeeping could repair the pants. When the pants proved irreparable, the agent headed to a shopping area in Shanghai early the next morning to resolve the problem. After searching through many stores, the agent found and purchased a pair of pants that matched the original pair almost exactly.

To constantly improve its customer-service practices, The Ritz-Carlton gathers a massive amount of data on hotel operations, services, employee behavior, and general feedback, which is used to create a customer management system referred to as the "The Ritz-Carlton Mystique." These data on specific aspects of guest behavior enable The Ritz-Carlton to craft personalized experiences prior to guests' arrival at its locations across the globe. Employees take note of guests' preferences such as temperature settings, food and drink choices, room arrangement, and amenity selection.

The unwavering dedication to perfecting the customer experience has made The Ritz-Carlton a symbol of customer-service excellence. In return, The Ritz-Carlton enjoys lasting customer loyalty, with the average Ritz customer spending more than $250,000 in the course of a lifetime. The Ritz-Carlton also has added The Ritz-Carlton Residences to its portfolio. These residential condominiums in cities and resort destinations are characterized by the same Ritz-Carlton service, management, and amenities offered by its hotel locations.[90]

Questions

1. How does The Ritz-Carlton service match up against competitive hotels? What are the key differences?
2. Discuss the importance of the "Wow!" stories in customer service for a luxury hotel like The Ritz-Carlton.
3. What are the key aspects of The Ritz-Carlton corporate culture? What role does the corporate culture play in enabling the company to deliver a superior customer experience?

marketing SPOTLIGHT

Nordstrom

In 1901, John W. Nordstrom founded a small shoe store in Seattle, which would eventually grow into a fashion specialty chain store called Nordstrom. Nordstrom has remained in the family for four generations and now sells top-quality, brand-name clothing, accessories, jewelry, cosmetics, and fragrances.

John Nordstrom set a strong foundation for the company back in the early 1900s. He built Nordstrom on the belief that the company should always provide the highest level of customer service possible, along with top-of-the-line merchandise. As a shoe retailer, Nordstrom offered a wide range of products to fit most everyone's needs and price point.

When John Nordstrom retired, his sons Everett, Elmer, and Lloyd continued to run the business with the same customer-focused attitude. As the company expanded into fashion, stores were stocked with a wide range of high-quality clothes at various prices to appeal to most shoppers. Nordstrom believed it was better to carry too many sizes in each style than not to carry enough, so that customers wouldn't get frustrated by their size not being available. The brothers also instituted a policy of "decision-by-consensus," which helped move the company along even when disagreements arose.

Nordstrom grew into the billion-dollar retailer it is today under the leadership of the family's third generation—Bruce,

Source: Chuck Pefley/Alamy Stock Photo

John, and Jim Nordstrom—and Jack McMillan. Their philosophy focused on empowering the managers and salesforce to make decisions that favored the customer, not the company. The company rewarded energetic individuals with an entrepreneurial spirit and preferred to hire "nice" people who could be trained to sell, rather than seasoned salespeople who weren't nice.

It was during this time that the company also decentralized its purchasing process. Regional managers were given the freedom to purchase styles and clothes that fit the needs and tastes of that particular area—that is, managers in Minnesota bought very differently than managers in southern California. To cater to each region, the company encouraged its sales force to regularly ask customers for feedback about what products and styles they would like to see in Nordstrom stores. Jim Nordstrom explained, "When we go into a market, our first buy is the worst."

(*continued*)

Today, Nordstrom continues to set the standard in customer service and loyalty. The company is so well known for its customer service that true tales of "heroics," or unusual acts of customer service, still circulate today. Perhaps the best-known story is how, in 1975, a customer came into a Nordstrom store wanting to return a set of tires originally bought at Northern Commercial Company, an Alaskan firm that Nordstrom had purchased. Although Nordstrom had never carried or sold tires, it happily accepted the return and instantly refunded the customer cash for his purchase. In another example, a saleswoman noticed that a customer had left her plane ticket on the store's counter. She called the airport and asked for the customer to be issued another ticket, but the airline refused. The saleswoman immediately jumped into a cab and hand-delivered the ticket to the customer at the airport.

There are many other examples of such exceptional customer service, and Nordstrom's "no questions asked" return policy remains intact today. Its sales representatives send thank-you cards to customers who shop there, warm up their customers' cars on cold days, and have hand-delivered special orders to customers' homes. Nordstrom installed a tool called Personal Book at its registers that enables salespeople to record and (later) review and recall customers' specific preferences to better personalize their shopping experiences. Nordstrom's sales associates have the freedom to sell merchandise in any department, giving them even more opportunities to develop their relationship with the customers. Nordstrom also provides customers with multiple channels for shopping, allowing them to buy something online and pick it up at a store within an hour.

The moment one enters a Nordstrom location, it is evident that the stores were developed with the customer in mind to create a pleasant, efficient experience—"a memorable experience." The company believes that it has 15 seconds to capture the excitement of a customer who walks in the door. Aisles are kept neat and uncluttered, big display windows create a bright and open atmosphere, and the layout is easily navigated. The dressing rooms are large and well lit with fixtures that imitate natural light; escalators are significantly wider than elsewhere, to allow both couples and parents with children to stand next to each other; and every component is positioned to create a more residential feeling. The layout of the stores is efficient and free of clutter, a strategy that has been copied by retailers around the world.

Nordstrom's customer loyalty program, The Nordy Club, rewards customers on four different levels based on their annual spending: members ($0–$499), insiders ($500+), influencers ($2,000+), and ambassadors ($5,000+). All members receive free basic alterations on regular-priced items, access to free styling workshops that help them curate their own look, curbside pickup of online purchases, and reward points that can be used as store credit. Higher-level members receive more points for each dollar spent, early access to sales events, and in-home stylists who come to customers' homes to offer expert styling advice and tailoring services.

Nordstrom currently operates 380 full-price and off-price stores in 40 U.S. states, Puerto Rico, and Canada. Full-price outlets include Nordstrom full-line stores, Nordstrom.com, Trunk Club (a personalized mid-level to high-end men's and women's apparel boutique acquired by Nordstrom in 2014), Jeffrey (luxury fashion boutiques in which Nordstrom bought a majority stake in 2005), and Nordstrom Local (no-inventory stores launched by Nordstrom in 2017). Off-price outlets include Nordstrom Rack stores, Nordstromrack.com, HauteLook (an online retailer that offers flash sales on designer goods, acquired by Nordstrom in 2011), and Last Chance clearance stores.

The company's long-term and often costly customer focus has reaped great benefits for the company. Not only has Nordstrom emerged over the past 100+ years as a luxury brand known for quality, trust, and service, but its customers remain loyal even in hard times. Many customers choose to shop at Nordstrom, rather than at its competitors, because of their existing relationship and the hassle-free return policy. Nordstrom remains strategically focused on customer service and constantly looks for new ways to deepen and develop its customer–salesperson relationship.[91]

Questions

1. What role does service play in Nordstrom's positioning? Does service play the same role in online and in-store experiences?
2. How else can Nordstrom continue to provide exceptional customer service and increase brand loyalty?
3. How should Nordstrom address the growing popularity of online shopping? Can it successfully compete in the online space? Who are Nordstrom's biggest competitors, and how do they stack up?

CHAPTER 10

Building Strong Brands

Market leader Amul has rapidly expanded with revenues growing by almost 5 times during 2010 to 2020 driven by new product launches and entry into new markets.

Source: Amul©GCMMF Limited, used with permission

Brands are one of the most valuable intangible assets of a firm, and it is incumbent on marketers to properly manage their value. Building a strong brand is both an art and a science. It requires careful planning, a deep long-term commitment, and creatively designed and executed marketing. A strong brand commands intense consumer loyalty—and at its heart is a great product or service. Building a strong brand is a never-ending process, as demonstrated by the marketers of Amul during the last 75 years.

>>> Amul, a brand that resonates trust among Indian consumers, was established in 1946 as a cooperative dairy to protect the rights of farmers and rural milk producers. The Amul model of dairy development helped India transition from a milk-deficient nation to the world's largest milk producer. The secret behind the success of Amul representing its tagline 'The Taste of India', lies in its strategic brand positioning as a domestic, homegrown brand for everyone right from its inception.[1] Its diversified product portfolio has a wide range of milk based offerings for everyone's need, irrespective of their economic status. With its authentic taste, quality products and competitive pricing, Amul has evolved into an exemplary brand. Amul follows a 3-layered intensive distribution system with 6000 exclusive distributors that ensures the reach of its products—such as milk, curd, buttermilk, sweets, ice-creams—to even small towns with around 10,000 population. Its innovative product-specific and topical advertisements helped the brand to win over the trust of its customers across all product categories. The universally

familiar 'Utterly Butterly Delicious' slogan and 'Blue-haired Amul Girl' connect all products under Amul's umbrella branding approach. Amul, ranked among the top five advertisers in India, spent 1% of its ₹52,000 crore turnover in 2019–20[2] on advertisements on TV, print, outdoors, radio and digital. The brand has invested in strengthening its social media presence and its live recipe content on Amul's Facebook page attracts over 10 million views daily. Content and communication in regional languages and Arabic through social media handles have built stronger bonds with customers across the country and in the Middle East. In 2020, Amul launched 60 new products and 120 stock keeping units (SKU and introduced another 33 new products in 2021 as it aims to double the turnover in the next five years.[3] A comprehensive portfolio of quality products, intensive distribution, affordable pricing and brand visibility drives Amul's special connect with millions of consumers in India and abroad.[4]

Marketers of successful 21st-century brands must excel at the strategic brand management process. **Strategic brand management** combines the design and implementation of marketing activities and programs to build, measure, and manage brands to maximize their value. It has four main steps:[5] identifying and establishing brand positioning, planning and implementing brand marketing, measuring and interpreting brand performance, and growing and sustaining brand value.

How Does Branding Work?

Perhaps the most distinctive skill of professional marketers is their ability to create, maintain, enhance, and protect brands, whether established brands such as Mercedes, Sony, and Nike or new ones like Warby Parker, Casper, and Tovala.

The American Marketing Association defines a **brand** as "a name, term, sign, symbol, or design, or a combination of them, intended to identify the goods or services of one seller or group of sellers and to differentiate them from those of competitors." The ultimate purpose of the brand is to create, for consumers, the company, and its collaborators, value that goes beyond the value created by the product and service aspects of the offering.

THE ESSENCE OF BRANDING

Branding is the process of endowing products and services with the power of a brand. It's all about creating differences between products. Marketers use brand names and other brand elements to inform consumers "who" and "what" the product is—and why consumers should care. Effective branding creates mental structures that help consumers organize their knowledge about products and services in a way that clarifies their decision making and, in the process, provides value to the firm.

Branding has been around for centuries as a means to identify the goods of one producer and distinguish them from those of another. Medieval guilds in Europe required that craftspeople put trademarks on their products to protect themselves and their customers against inferior quality. In the fine

---

Learning Objectives After studying this chapter you should be able to:

10.1 Explain the role of brands in creating market value.

10.2 Describe the key principles in designing brand elements and associations.

10.3 Discuss how a company should design the hierarchy of its brands.

10.4 Explain how a company should manage its brands over time.

10.5 Describe the key aspects of luxury branding.

arts, branding began with artists signing their works. Brands today play a number of important roles that improve consumers' lives and enhance the financial value of firms.

How do you "brand" a product or a service? Although firms provide the impetus for brand creation through marketing programs and other activities, ultimately a brand resides in the minds and hearts of consumers. It is a perceptual entity rooted in reality but reflecting the views and idiosyncrasies of consumers.

For branding strategies to be successful and create brand value, consumers must be convinced that there are meaningful differences among brands in the product or service category. Brand differences are often related to attributes or benefits of the product itself. Gillette, Merck, and 3M have led their product categories for decades, in part because of continual innovation. Other brands create competitive advantages through non–product-related means. Gucci, Chanel, and Louis Vuitton have become category leaders by understanding consumer motivations and desires and creating relevant and appealing imagery around their stylish products.

Successful brands are seen as genuine and authentic in what they sell and who they are.[6] A successful brand makes itself an indispensable part of its customers' lives. Once a faded preppy afterthought, J.Crew tripled its revenue by becoming a highly creative force in fashion. By constantly introducing new styles while retaining a cohesive look, the brand enjoys intense loyalty, numerous fan blogs, and high-profile celebrity supporters like Michelle Obama and Anna Wintour.

Marketers can apply branding virtually anywhere a consumer has a choice. It's possible to brand a physical good (Tesla automobile or Lipitor cholesterol medication), a service (Singapore Airlines or Blue Cross Blue Shield medical insurance), a store (Nordstrom or Dick's Sporting Goods), a place (the city of Sydney or the country of Ireland), an organization (U2 or the American Automobile Association), or an idea (abortion rights or free trade).

Branding has become of great importance in sports, arts, and entertainment. One of the world's top sports brands comes from Madrid, Spain.

Real Madrid Real Madrid surpassed Manchester United in 2013 to become the world's most valuable team in soccer—or football, as it is known outside the United States—with an estimated value of $3.3 billion. Also known by fans as "Los Merengues," the iconic but floundering club began to thrive when the billionaire construction tycoon Florentine Perez took over in 2000. Perez's strategy was to attract some of the very top players in the game, brand names in their own right, such as David Beckham, Zinedine Zidane, and, later, Cristiano Ronaldo. Success on the pitch (field) allowed Perez to develop three distinct and lucrative lines of business: broadcast rights, sponsorship and endorsement revenue, and match-day revenue. Real Madrid is truly a global brand and derives much of its revenue abroad. Sponsorship includes high-profile deals with Adidas, Emirates Airlines, and Spanish banking group BBVA.[7]

THE ROLE OF BRANDS

Brands identify the maker of a product and allow consumers to assign responsibility for its performance to that maker or distributor. Brands perform a number of functions for both consumers and firms.

Brands' Role for Consumers. A brand is a promise the firm makes to the consumer. It is a means to set consumers' expectations and reduce their risk. In return for customer loyalty, the firm promises that its products or services will reliably deliver a predictably positive experience and set of desirable benefits. A brand may even be "predictably unpredictable" if that is what consumers expect, but the key is that it fulfills or exceeds customer expectations in satisfying their needs and wants.

Consumers may evaluate the identical product differently depending on how it is branded. For example, consumers might be willing to pay $100 for a generic (unbranded) leather bag but ten times more for the same bag carrying the brand of Louis Vuitton, Hermès, or Gucci. They learn about brands through past experiences with the product and its marketing program, finding out which brands satisfy their needs and which do not. As consumers' lives become more rushed and complicated, a brand's ability to simplify decision making and reduce risk becomes invaluable.[8]

Brands can also take on personal meaning for consumers and become an important part of their identity.[9] They can express who consumers are or who they would like to be. For some consumers, brands can even take on human-like characteristics.[10] Brand relationships, like any relationship, are not cast in stone, and marketers must be sensitive to all the words and actions that might strengthen or weaken consumer ties with the brand.[11]

Source: Xinhua/Alamy Stock Photo

<< Signing top players who were brands in their own right rocketed football (soccer) team Real Madrid into a multibillion-dollar global brand.

Treebo Founded in 2015 by Sidharth Gupta (CEO), Rahul Chaudhary, and Kadam Jeet Jain, Treebo is an app-based aggregator of budget hotels. The hospitality sector in India offers a wide range of star-rated high quality hotels as well as thousands of stand-alone budget hotels providing cheap and low-quality accommodation. Customers wary about staying in budget hotels had but limited choice. Treebo tapped this gap as an opportunity to develop an asset light, franchisee-based business model with a mission to put dignity in to budget travel. It signed up with owners of small hotels, typically with 20–25 rooms, standardized the facilities, amenities and services, introduced technology-driven systems for property management and trained personnel to offer quality accommodation at affordable prices. Harnessing mobile applications and social media platforms, Treebo attracted customers who wanted a quality experience within limited budget. In 2018, Treebo divided its portfolio of over 400 hotels into three sub-brands—Trip, Trend, and Tryst—while retaining Treebo as a parent umbrella brand. The sub-brands offer a tiered level of amenities with differential prices ranging from ₹1000–₹1500 for Trip, ₹1500 –₹2500 for Trend, and ₹2500–₹4,000 for Tryst.[12] Sidharth believes that the new branding initiatives will help them forge a deeper relationship with customers by giving them more transparency on what they can expect when they check into a Treebo property.[13] The company also expanded into travel-related services for local events and activities and had more than 600 hotels and 12,000 rooms operational in 113 cities in 2021.[14]

<< Budget hotel chain Treebo ran a very successful quality guarantee campaign titled 'perfect stay or don't pay' to convey the confidence in its brand's promise of a premium experience.

Source: ©Treebo Hotels, used with permission

>> The hue and cry raised by passionately loyal fans forced Coca-Cola to ditch its heavily researched launch of New Coke and reinstate the company's century-old formula.

Source: Todd Gipstein/Getty Images

Coca-Cola Battered by a nationwide series of taste-test challenges from sweeter-tasting Pepsi-Cola, Coca-Cola decided in 1985 to replace its old formula with a sweeter variation dubbed New Coke. The company spent $4 million on market research, and blind taste tests showed that Coke drinkers preferred the new formula. But the launch of New Coke provoked a national uproar. Market researchers had measured the taste but failed to adequately measure the emotional attachment consumers had to Coca-Cola. There were angry letters, formal protests, and even lawsuit threats to force the retention of "The Real Thing." Ten weeks later, the company reintroduced its century-old formula as "Classic Coke." Efforts to resuscitate New Coke eventually failed, and the brand disappeared around 1992. Ironically, the failed introduction of New Coke ended up giving the old formula measurably stronger status in the marketplace, with more favorable attitudes and greater sales as a result. Interestingly, 34 years later, New Coke made a brief comeback as part of a promotional campaign with Netflix, when it was featured in several episodes of the third season of the sci-fi thriller "Stranger Things" and was made available in retail channels for a limited time.[15]

Brands' Role for Firms. Brands also perform valuable functions for firms.[16] First, they simplify product handling by helping to organize inventory and accounting records. A credible brand signals a certain level of quality so that satisfied buyers can easily choose the product again.[17] Brand loyalty provides predictability and security of demand for the firm and creates barriers to entry that make it difficult for other firms to enter the market. Loyalty also can translate into customer willingness to pay a higher price—often even 20 percent to 25 percent more than the price of competing brands.[18]

Although competitors may duplicate manufacturing processes and product designs, they cannot easily match the lasting impressions left in the minds of individuals and organizations by years of favorable product experiences and marketing activity. In this sense, branding can be a powerful means to secure a competitive advantage. Sometimes marketers don't see the real importance of brand loyalty until they change a crucial element of the brand, as the classic tale of New Coke illustrates.

For firms, brands represent enormously valuable pieces of legal property that can influence consumer behavior, can be bought and sold, and offer their owner the security of sustained future revenues.[19] Companies have paid dearly for brands in mergers or acquisitions, often justifying the price premium on the basis of the extra profits expected and the difficulty and expense of creating similar brands from scratch.[20] Wall Street believes strong brands result in better earnings and profit performance for firms, which, in turn, create greater value for shareholders.[21]

BRAND EQUITY AND BRAND POWER

The value created by a brand is captured by two key concepts: brand equity and brand power. We discuss these two concepts and the relationship between them next.

Brand Equity. The monetary value of a brand is called **brand equity** and reflects the premium that is placed on a company's valuation because of its ownership of the brand. Brand equity encompasses the net present value of the total financial returns that the brand will generate over its lifetime. Understanding the concept of brand equity, managing its antecedents and consequences, and developing methodologies to assess brand equity are of the utmost importance for ensuring a company's financial well-being.

Prior to the wave of mergers and acquisitions in the 1980s, including the $25 billion RJR Nabisco buyout, companies spent millions of dollars on brand building with no established accounting procedures in place to assess the value of the brands they created. The spate of mergers and acquisitions spiked interest in brand valuation and led to more accurate ways to measure brand equity. Putting a fair dollar amount on the brand assets that a firm has accrued through the years is vital, because the value of its brands is not reflected in the company's books and could exceed its tangible assets.

Brand equity is included in the accounting term **goodwill**, which is the monetary value of all intangible assets of a company. Goodwill not only documents the company's tangible assets, such as property, infrastructure, materials, and investments, but also incorporates the intangible assets that a company owns, including brands, patents, copyrights, know-how, licenses, distribution arrangements, company culture, and management practices. Thus, goodwill is a much broader term than brand equity and includes both the value of the company's brand and the value of the company's other intangible assets.

Measuring Brand Equity. Although the importance of brand equity is undisputed, there is no universally agreed-on method for assessing the equity of a brand accurately.[22] Several alternative methods exist, all of which emphasize different means of gauging brand equity. The *cost approach*, the *market approach*, and the *financial approach* are the three most common methods of measuring brand equity.

- The **cost approach** calculates brand equity by examining the costs of developing the brand, such as marketing research, brand design, communication, management, and legal costs. The cost method can hinge on the historical costs of creating the brand, which include an estimate of all relevant brand-building expenditures; alternatively, it can be based on the brand's replacement cost—the monetary expense of rebuilding the brand—at the time of valuation.
- The **market approach** estimates brand equity by measuring the difference between the sales revenues from a branded offering against those of an identical unbranded offering, adjusted for the expense of building the brand. Assessing the value of the Morton Salt brand, for example, would entail comparing the sales revenues generated by the Morton product with the sales revenues generated by its generic equivalent—regular salt—minus the cost of building and managing the brand.
- The **financial approach** evaluates brand equity as the net present value (NPV) of a brand's future earnings and usually encompasses three key steps: computing the company's future cash flow, estimating the brand's contribution to the company's future cash flow, and adjusting this cash flow using a risk factor that accounts for the volatility of the earnings that are attributable to the brand.

Each of the three approaches has its advantages and shortcomings. Therefore, a company can benefit from using multiple methods and alternative approaches to measuring brand value. Such approaches must take into account the strategic value of the brand and, specifically, the brand's power to influence the behavior of different market entities.

Brand Power. **Brand power**, also referred to as customer-based brand equity, is the ancillary value contributed by the brand to a product or a service.[23] Brand power reflects the degree to which the brand influences the way consumers think, feel, and act with respect to the brand.

Brand power is thus the differential effect that brand knowledge has on consumer response to the marketing of that brand.[24] A brand has positive power if consumers react more favorably to a product and the way it is marketed when the brand is identified than when it is not identified. A brand has negative power if consumers react less favorably to marketing activity for the brand under the same circumstances.

Brand power arises from differences in consumer response that a brand evokes. If no differences occur, the brand-name product is essentially a commodity, and competition will probably be based on price. Furthermore, differences in response are a result of consumers' brand knowledge, as well as of all the thoughts, feelings, images, experiences, and beliefs associated with the brand. Brands must create strong, favorable, and unique brand associations with customers, as have Toyota (reliability), Hallmark (caring), and Amazon.com (convenience and wide selection). Finally, brand equity is reflected in perceptions, preferences, and behavior related to all aspects of the marketing of a brand. Stronger brands earn greater revenue.[25]

The key benefits of brand power include improved perception of product performance, greater loyalty, less vulnerability to competitive marketing actions and marketing crises, larger margins, more inelastic consumer response to price increases and more elastic consumer response to price decreases, greater trade cooperation and support, increased effectiveness of marketing communications, expanded licensing opportunities, additional brand extension opportunities, improved employee recruiting and retention, and greater financial market returns.

The challenge for marketers, therefore, is ensuring that customers have the right kinds of experiences with products, services, and marketing programs to create the desired thoughts, feelings, and brand knowledge. In an abstract sense, we can think of brand equity as providing marketers with a vital strategic bridge from their past to their future.

Marketers should also think of the marketing dollars spent on products and services each year as investments in consumer brand knowledge. The quality, rather than the quantity, of that investment is the critical factor. It's possible to overspend on brand building if money is not spent wisely.

Customers' brand knowledge dictates appropriate future directions for the brand. Consumers will decide, based on what they think and feel about the brand, where (and how) they believe the brand should go, and they will (or will not) grant permission to any marketing action or program. New-product ventures such as Bengay aspirin, Cracker Jack cereal, Frito-Lay lemonade, Fruit of the Loom laundry detergent, and Smucker's premium ketchup all failed because consumers found them inappropriate extensions of the brand.

Measuring Brand Power. How do we measure brand power? An *indirect* approach assesses potential sources of brand power by identifying and tracking consumer brand knowledge.[26] A *direct* approach assesses the actual impact of brand knowledge on consumer response to different aspects of the marketing.

The two general approaches are complementary, and marketers can employ both. In other words, for brand power to perform a useful strategic function and guide marketing decisions, marketers need to fully understand (1) the sources of brand equity and how they affect outcomes of interest and (2) how these sources and outcomes change, if at all, over time. Brand audits are important for the former, brand tracking for the latter.

- A **brand audit** is a focused series of procedures to assess the health of the brand, uncover its sources of brand equity, and suggest ways to improve and leverage its equity. Marketers should conduct a brand audit when setting up marketing plans and when considering shifts in strategic direction. Conducting brand audits on a regular basis, such as annually, allows marketers to keep their finger on the pulse of their brands so they can manage them more proactively and responsively. A good brand audit provides keen insights into consumers, brands, and the relationship between the two.
- In **brand tracking**, the brand audit is used as input to collect quantitative data from consumers over time, providing consistent, baseline information about how brands and marketing programs are performing. Brand-tracking studies help us understand where, to what degree, and in what ways brand value is being created to facilitate day-to-day decision making.

One group that conducted a major brand audit and redefined its brand positioning is Mahindra and Mahindra.

Mahindra and Mahindra Mahindra and Mahindra, a leading conglomerate with a legacy of more than seven decades, operates in 100+ countries with over 150 companies in sectors ranging from aerospace, automobiles, farm equipment to financial services, real estate and software services. In 2011, the company initiated a new brand positioning program 'Rise' to project a singular voice for all its businesses.[27] Extensive studies across the globe helped the marketing team at Mahindra identify its customers' desire to rise, to succeed and create a better future for themselves. Mahindra Rise was chosen to reflect the customers desire as a company that empowers them to 'Rise'. Founded on the three pillars of accepting no limits, alternative thinking and driving positive change, 'Rise' also sought to unite over 100,000 employees of the group as creators of world-class offerings. The company spent ₹120 crore in the next three years to promote the new initiative across employees and customers of its global entities.[28] With its

<< Driven by its expanding global footprint, the diversified Mahindra group initiated a major brand repositioning exercise in 2011 that resulted in a new logo with a tag 'Rise'. The 3-year transformation involved incorporating 'Rise' in performance management systems to the company's websites, offices, sales and service outlets.

Source: Mahindra Rise©Mahindra, used with permission

new logo, the group created an identity of a 'technology and innovation – led global, federation of companies that provide a wide range of products, services and possibilities to people, enabling them to 'Rise'. The repositioning campaign reinforced the identity of a new, emerging global brand while preserving its heritage attributes and contemporary value system.[29]

Marketers should distinguish brand equity from brand valuation, which is the job of estimating the total financial value of the brand. In well-known companies, brand value is typically more than half the total company market capitalization. John Stuart, cofounder of Quaker Oats, said, "If this business were split up, I would give you the land and bricks and mortar, and I would take the brands and trademarks, and I would fare better than you." U.S. companies do not list brand equity on their balance sheets, in part because of differences in opinion about what constitutes a good estimate. However, companies do give it a value in countries such as the United Kingdom, Hong Kong, and Australia.

Designing the Brand

Marketers build brand equity by creating the right brand associations in consumers' minds. The success of this process depends on *all* brand-related contacts with consumers—whether marketer-initiated or not.[30]

DEFINING THE BRAND MANTRA

To focus brand positioning and guide the way their marketers help consumers think about the brand, firms can define a brand mantra. A **brand mantra** is a three- to five-word articulation of the heart and soul of the brand and is closely related to other branding concepts like "brand essence" and "core brand promise." The mantra's purpose is to guide the actions of all employees within the organization, and of all external marketing partners, by ensuring that they understand what the brand fundamentally should represent to consumers.

Brand mantras are powerful devices. By highlighting points of difference, they provide guidance about what products to introduce under the brand, what ad campaigns to run, and where and how to sell the brand. Their influence can even extend beyond these tactical concerns. Brand mantras can guide the most seemingly unrelated or mundane decisions, such as the look of a reception area and the way phones are answered. In effect, they create a mental filter to screen out brand-inappropriate marketing activities or actions of any type that may have a negative effect on customers' impressions.

Brand mantras must economically communicate what the brand is and what it is *not*. What makes a good brand mantra? McDonald's "Food, Folks, and Fun" captures its brand essence and core brand promise. Two other high-profile and successful examples, from Nike and Disney, show the power and utility of a well-designed brand mantra.

Nike The Nike brand has a rich set of associations for consumers, based on its innovative product designs, its sponsorship of top athletes, its award-winning communications, its competitive drive, and its irreverent attitude. Internally, Nike marketers adopted the three-word brand mantra "authentic athletic performance" to guide their marketing efforts. Thus, in Nike's eyes, its entire marketing program—its products and the way they are sold—must reflect that key brand value. Over the years, Nike has expanded its brand associations from "running shoes" to "athletic shoes" to "athletic shoes and apparel" to "all things associated with athletics (including equipment)." Each step of the way, however, it has been guided by its "authentic athletic performance" brand mantra. For example, as Nike rolled out its successful apparel line, one important hurdle was that the products' material, cut, and design must be innovative enough to truly benefit top athletes. At the same time, the company has been careful to avoid using the Nike name to brand products that do not fit with the brand mantra (such as casual "brown" shoes).

Disney Disney developed its brand mantra in response to its incredible growth through licensing and product development during the mid-1980s. In the late 1980s, Disney became concerned that some of its characters, such as Mickey Mouse and Donald Duck, were being used inappropriately and becoming overexposed. The characters were on so many products, and were marketed in so many ways, that in some cases it was difficult to discern what the rationale behind the deal could have been to start with. Moreover, because of the characters' broad exposure in the marketplace, many consumers had begun to feel Disney was exploiting its name. Disney moved quickly to ensure that a consistent image—reinforcing its key brand associations—was conveyed by all third-party products and services. To that end, Disney adopted the internal brand mantra "fun family entertainment" to filter proposed ventures. Opportunities that were not consistent with the brand mantra—no matter how appealing—were rejected. (As useful as that mantra was to Disney, adding the word *magical* might have made it even more so.)

Unlike brand slogans meant to engage consumers, brand mantras are designed with internal purposes in mind. Nike's internal mantra, "authentic athletic performance," was not directly communicated to consumers, who were presented, instead, with the slogan "Just Do It" that aimed to capture the brand mantra. There are three key criteria for a brand mantra. First, a good brand mantra should *communicate* what is unique about the brand. It may also need to define the brand's category (or categories) and set brand boundaries. Second, it should simplify the essence of the brand: It should be short, crisp, and vivid in meaning. Finally, it should inspire by staking out ground that is personally meaningful and relevant to as many employees as possible.

For brands anticipating rapid growth, it is helpful to define the product or benefit space in which the brand would like to compete, as Nike did with "athletic performance" and Disney with "family entertainment." Words that describe the nature of the product or service, or the type of experiences or benefits the brand provides, can be critical to identifying appropriate categories into which to extend. For brands in more stable categories where extensions are less likely to occur, the brand mantra may focus exclusively on points of difference.

Other brands may be strong on one, or perhaps even a few, of the brand associations that make up the company's brand mantra. However, for a mantra to be effective, no other brand should singularly excel on *all* its dimensions. Part of the key to the success of both Nike and Disney is that for many years, no competitor could really deliver on the combined promise suggested by their brand mantras.

CHOOSING BRAND ELEMENTS

Brand elements are devices that identify and differentiate the brand. Most strong brands employ multiple brand elements, which can be trademarked. Nike has the distinctive "swoosh" logo, the empowering "Just Do It" slogan, and the "Nike" name from the Greek winged goddess of victory. Marketers should choose brand elements that build as much brand equity as possible. The test of the appropriateness of a particular brand element is what consumers would think or feel about the product or service *if the brand element were all they knew*. Based on its name alone, for instance, a consumer might expect SnackWell's products to be healthful snack foods and Panasonic Toughbook laptop computers to be durable and reliable.

There are several factors to consider when choosing brand elements. They should be memorable, meaningful, and likable, as well as transferable, adaptable, and protectable. The first three characteristics are brand-building. The latter three are defensive; they help maintain leverage and preserve brand equity against challenges.

- *Memorable*—How easily do consumers recall and recognize the brand element, and when? At both purchase and consumption? Names such as Tide, Crest, and Puffs are memorable brand elements.[31]
- *Meaningful*—Is the brand element evocative? Consider the inherent meaning in names such as DieHard auto batteries, Mop & Glo floor wax, and Lean Cuisine low-calorie frozen entrées. The brand name of New Zealand's 42BELOW vodka refers to both a latitude that runs through New Zealand and the drink's alcohol content. The packaging and other visual cues are designed to leverage the perceived purity of the country to communicate the positioning for the brand.[32]
- *Likable*—How aesthetically appealing is the brand element? A recent trend is toward playful names that also offer a readily available URL, especially for online brands like Flickr, Instagram, Pinterest, Tumblr, and Dropbox.
- *Transferable*—Can the brand element introduce new products in the same or different categories? Does it add to brand equity across geographic boundaries and market segments? Although initially an online bookseller, Amazon.com was smart enough not to call itself "Books 'R' Us." Choosing the name of the world's biggest river allowed the company to grow into its now staggeringly diverse range of products.
- *Adaptable*—How adaptable and updatable is the brand element? Logos can easily be updated. The past 100 years have seen the Shell logo updated 10 times.
- *Protectable*—How legally protectable is the brand element? How competitively protectable? When names are in danger of becoming synonymous with product categories—as has happened to Kleenex, Kitty Litter, Jell-O, Scotch Tape, Xerox, and Fiberglass—their makers should retain their trademark rights and not allow the brand to become generic.

Brand elements can play a number of brand-building roles.[33] If consumers don't examine much information in making product decisions, brand elements should be easy to recall and inherently descriptive and persuasive. The likability of brand elements can also increase awareness and associations.[34] But choosing a name with inherent meaning may make it harder to later add a different meaning or update the positioning.[35]

Often, the more important brand elements are those that capture intangible, less concrete characteristics. Many insurance firms use symbols of strength for their brands (the Rock of Gibraltar for Prudential and the stag for Hartford) or symbols of security (the "good hands" of Allstate, the Traveler's umbrella, and the hard hat of Fireman's Fund).

Like brand names, slogans are an extremely efficient means of building brand equity.[36] They can function as useful "hooks" to help consumers grasp what the brand is and what makes it special, as in "Like a Good Neighbor, State Farm Is There," "Nothing Runs Like a Deere," and "Every Kiss Begins with Kay" for the jeweler.

Firms should be careful about replacing a good slogan. Citi walked away from its famous "Citi Never Sleeps" slogan, replacing it with "Let's Get It Done," only to return to the old slogan when the new one failed to catch on. After 50 years, Avis Car Rental dropped "We Try Harder" for "It's Your Space." The new slogan had much less staying power—to say nothing of the inherent message—of the one it replaced.

The brand name and other identifiers can be protected through registered trademarks, manufacturing processes can be protected through patents, and packaging can be protected through copyrights and proprietary designs. These intellectual property rights ensure that the firm can safely invest in the brand and reap the benefits of a valuable asset.[37]

CHOOSING SECONDARY ASSOCIATIONS

To build strong brands, marketers link brands to other meaningful information in the memories of consumers. These linked associations become secondary sources of brand knowledge (see Figure 10.1).

The Magic of Brand Characters

Brand characters have a long and important history in marketing. The Keebler elves reinforce home-style baking quality and a sense of magic and fun for the company's line of cookies. In the insurance industry, the Aflac duck competes for consumer attention with GEICO's gecko, and Progressive's chatty Flo competes with Met Life's adorable Peanuts characters. Michelin's friendly tire-shaped Bibendum—the "Michelin Man"—conveys safety for the family and is credited with helping the brand achieve 80 percent awareness around the world. Each year Michelin distributes a "Passport" for Bibendum that sets boundaries on the character's advertising use by marketers. Bibendum is never aggressive, for example, and never delivers a sales pitch.[38]

Brand characters represent a special type of brand symbol—one with human characteristics that both enhance likability and tag the brand as interesting and fun. Consumers can more easily form relationships with a brand when it is represented by a human or other character. Brand characters typically are introduced through advertising and can play a central role in ad campaigns and package designs. M&M's "spokescandies" are an integral part of all advertising, promotion, and digital communications for the brand. Some brand characters are animated, like the Pillsbury Doughboy, Peter Pan (peanut butter), and numerous cereal characters such as Tony the Tiger and Snap, Crackle, & Pop. Others are live-action figures like Juan Valdez (Colombian coffee) and Ronald McDonald.[39]

Because they are often colorful and rich in imagery, brand characters can help brands break through marketplace clutter and communicate a key product benefit in a soft-sell manner. Characters also avoid many of the problems associated with human spokespeople: They don't demand pay raises or misbehave. Offering the opportunity to shape the brand's personality and facilitate consumer interactions, brand characters play an increasingly important role in a digital world. The success of Mr. Peanut in viral videos led to the introduction of a new peanut butter line. Even old-timers are making their way onto the web. First introduced in 1957, Mr. Clean has amassed over a million Facebook fans.

FIGURE **10.1**
Secondary Sources of Brand Knowledge

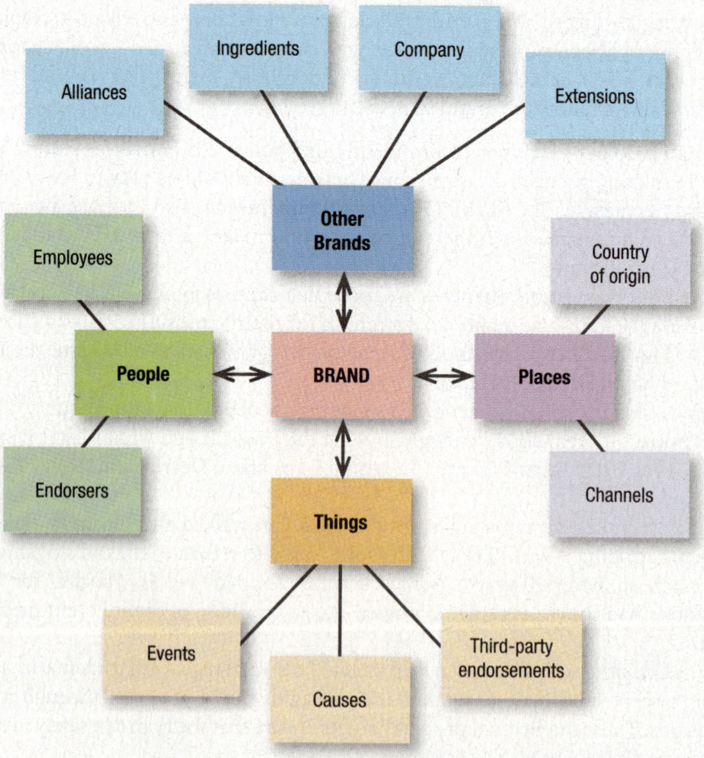

These "secondary" brand associations can link the brand to sources such as the company itself (through branding strategies), to countries or other geographic regions (through identification of product origin), and to channels of distribution (through channel strategy), as well as to other brands (through ingredient or cobranding), characters (through licensing), spokespeople (through endorsements), sporting or cultural events (through sponsorship), or some other third-party sources (through awards or reviews).

Suppose Burton—the maker of snowboards, snowboard boots, bindings, clothing, and outerwear—decided to introduce a new surfboard called the Dominator. Burton has gained more than a third of the snowboard market by closely aligning itself with top professional riders and creating a strong amateur snowboarder community around the country.[40] To support the new surfboard, Burton could leverage secondary brand knowledge in a number of ways.

First, it could "sub-brand" the surfboard, calling it "Dominator by Burton." In this case, consumers' evaluations of the new product would be influenced by how they felt about Burton and by whether they felt that such knowledge predicted the quality of a Burton surfboard. Alternatively, Burton could rely on its rural New England origins, but this geographic location would seem to have little relevance to surfing. Burton could also sell through popular surf shops in the hope that their credibility would rub off on the Dominator brand. Burton could co-brand by identifying a strong ingredient brand for its foam or fiberglass materials (as Wilson did by incorporating Goodyear tire rubber on the soles of its Pro Staff Classic tennis shoes).

Another approach for Burton would be to find one or more top professional surfers to endorse the surfboard, or it could sponsor a surfing competition or even the entire Association of Surfing Professionals (ASP) World Tour. Finally, Burton could secure and publicize favorable ratings from third-party sources such as the magazines *Surfer* and *Surfing*. Thus, independent of the associations created by the surfboard itself, its brand name, or any other aspects of the marketing program, Burton could build equity by linking the brand to these other entities.

Leveraging secondary associations can be an efficient and effective way to strengthen a brand. But linking a brand to someone or something else can be risky, because anything bad that happens to that other entity may also be linked to the brand. When popular endorsers Tiger Woods and Lance Armstrong got into trouble, many of the firms that were using them to promote their brands chose to cut ties.

A brand's secondary associations must be aligned with the brand's personality. A **brand personality** is the specific mix of human traits that we can attribute to a particular brand. Defining the personality of a brand is important because consumers tend to choose brands whose personalities match their own. Researchers have identified the following brand personality traits:[41] Sincerity (down to earth, honest, wholesome, and cheerful), Excitement (daring, spirited, imaginative, and up-to-date), Competence (reliable, intelligent, and successful), Sophistication (upper-class and charming), and Ruggedness (outdoorsy and tough). A brand personality may have several attributes: Levi's suggests a personality that is youthful, rebellious, authentic, and American.

A cross-cultural study exploring the generalizability of the brand personality scale outside the United States found that three of the five factors applied in Japan and Spain, but that a "peacefulness" dimension replaced "ruggedness" in both countries, and a "passion" dimension emerged in Spain instead of "competence."[42] Research on brand personality in Korea revealed two culture-specific factors—"passive likableness" and "ascendancy"—reflecting the importance of Confucian values in the Korean social and economic systems.[43]

Brand Hierarchy

Brand hierarchy reflects the way in which a company's brands are related to a company's products and services, as well as to one another. Developing a meaningful brand hierarchy is particularly important for companies that are managing diverse brand portfolios.

MANAGING BRAND PORTFOLIOS

A brand can be stretched only so far, and it is possible that not all segments that the firm would like to target view the brand in an equally favorable light. Marketers often need multiple brands in order to pursue multiple consumer segments. Other reasons for introducing multiple brands in a category include increasing shelf presence and retailer dependence in the store, retaining variety-seeking consumers who may otherwise switch to another brand, increasing competition within the firm, and exploiting economies of scale in advertising, sales, merchandising, and physical distribution.[44]

The **brand portfolio** is the set of all brands and brand lines that a particular firm offers for sale in a particular category or market segment. Building a good brand portfolio requires careful thinking and creative execution. The hallmark of an optimal brand portfolio is the ability of each brand it contains to maximize equity in combination with all the other brands. Marketers generally need to trade off market coverage with costs and profitability. If they can increase profits by dropping brands, a portfolio is too big; if they can increase profits by adding brands, it's not big enough.

The basic principle in designing a brand portfolio is to maximize market coverage so that no target customers are ignored but to minimize brand overlap so company brands are not competing for customer approval. Each brand should be clearly differentiated and appealing to a sufficiently sizable marketing segment to justify its marketing and production costs. Consider these examples:

Dow Corning Dow Corning has adopted a dual-brand approach to sell its silicon, which is used as an ingredient by many companies. Silicon sold under the Dow Corning name uses a "high touch" approach that gives customers much attention and support; silicon sold under the Xiameter name uses a "no frills" approach emphasizing low prices.[45]

Unilever Unilever, partnering with PepsiCo, sells four distinct brands of ready-to-drink iced tea. Brisk Iced Tea is an "on ramp" brand that serves as an entry point and a "flavor-forward" value brand; Lipton Iced Tea is a mainstream brand with an appealing blend of flavors; Lipton Pure Leaf Iced Tea is a premium and "tea-forward" brand for tea purists; and Tazo is a super-premium, niche brand.[46]

Marketers carefully monitor brand portfolios over time to identify weak brands and kill unprofitable ones.[47] Brands associated with poorly differentiated offerings are likely to be characterized by cannibalization and brand dilution. Such overextended and undifferentiated offerings might require pruning in order to ensure the health of the brand and its ability to create market value.

Three general brand portfolio strategies are popular:

- A **house-of-brands strategy** involves individual or separate family brand names. Consumer packaged-goods companies have a long tradition of branding different products by different names. General Mills largely uses individual brand names, such as Bisquick, Gold Medal flour, Nature Valley granola bars, Old El Paso Mexican foods, Progresso soup, Wheaties cereal, and Yoplait yogurt. If a company produces quite different products, one blanket name is often not desirable. Swift & Company developed separate family names for its hams (Premium) and fertilizers (Vigoro). Companies often use different brand names for different quality lines within the same product class. A major advantage of separate family brand names is that if a product fails or appears to be of low quality, the company has not tied the reputation of its other offerings to that product.[48]
- A **branded-house strategy** involves a corporate umbrella or company brand name. Many firms, such as Heinz and GE, use their corporate brand as an umbrella brand across their entire range of products.[49] Development costs are lower with umbrella names, because there's no need to research a name or spend heavily on advertising to build recognition. Campbell Soup introduces new soups under its brand name with extreme simplicity and achieves instant recognition. Sales of the new product are likely to be strong if the manufacturer's name is good. Corporate-image associations of innovativeness, expertise, and trustworthiness have been shown to directly influence consumer evaluations.[50] Finally, a corporate branding strategy can lead to greater intangible value for the firm.[51] On the downside, however, there is a greater change of a negative spillover effect if consumers' bad experience with one product contaminates their perceptions of other products associated with the same brand.
- A **sub-brand strategy** combines two or more corporate, family, or individual product brand names. Kellogg employs a sub-brand or hybrid branding strategy by combining the corporate brand with individual product brands (as with Kellogg's Rice Krispies, Kellogg's Raisin Bran, and Kellogg's Corn Flakes). Many durable-goods makers such as Honda, Sony, and Hewlett-Packard use sub-brands for their products. The corporate or company name legitimizes the new product, and the sub-brand name individualizes it.

The house-of-brands and branded-house strategies represent two ends of a continuum. A sub-brand strategy falls somewhere between, depending on which component of the sub-brand receives more emphasis. A good example of a house-of-brands strategy is used by United Technologies.

With a branded-house strategy, it is often useful to have a well-defined flagship product. A **flagship product** is one that best represents or embodies the brand as a whole to consumers. It often is the first product by which the brand gained fame, a widely accepted best-seller, or a highly admired or award-winning product.[52]

Source: David Gee/Alamy Stock Photo

<< United Technologies (now Raytheon Technologies) relies on the power of its individual brands—which include Pratt & Whitney, Goodrich, Otis, Carrier, and Kidde—to garner recognition and respect for the parent organization.

United Technologies United Technology Corporation (UTC) provides a broad range of high-technology products and services for the aerospace and commercial building industries, generating nearly $63 billion in revenues. Its aerospace businesses include Sikorsky helicopters, Pratt & Whitney aircraft engines, and UTC Aerospace Systems (which includes Goodrich Corporation and Hamilton Sundstrand aerospace systems). UTC Building & Industrial Systems, the world's largest provider of building technologies, includes Otis elevators and escalators; Carrier heating, air-conditioning, and refrigeration systems; and fire and security solutions from brands such as Kidde and Chubb. Most of its in-market brands are the names of the individuals who invented the product or created the company decades ago. These names have more power and are more recognizable in the business-buying marketplace than the name of the parent brand, and employees are loyal to the individual companies. The UTC name is advertised only to small but influential audiences—the financial community and opinion leaders in New York and Washington, DC. "My philosophy has always been to use the power of the trademarks of the subsidiaries to improve the recognition and brand acceptance, awareness, and respect for the parent company itself," said UTC's former CEO George David. In early 2020, United Technologies merged with the defense contractor Raytheon, forming the Raytheon Technologies Corporation.[53]

Flagship products play a key role in the brand portfolio in that marketing them can have short-term benefits (increased sales) as well as long-term benefits (improved brand equity for a range of products). Certain models play important flagship roles for many car manufacturers. Besides generating the most sales, family sedans Toyota Camry and Honda Accord represent brand values that all cars from those manufacturers share. In justifying the large investments incurred in launching its new 2014 Mercedes S-class automobiles, Daimler's chief executive Dieter Zetsche explained, "This car is for Mercedes-Benz what the harbor is for Hamburg, the Mona Lisa for Leonardo da Vinci and 'Satisfaction' for the Rolling Stones: the most important symbol of the reputation of the whole."[54]

Many companies are introducing **branded variants**, which are specific brand lines supplied to specific retailers or distribution channels. They result from the pressure retailers put on manufacturers to provide distinctive offerings. A camera company may supply its low-end cameras to mass merchandisers, while limiting its higher-priced items to specialty camera shops. Valentino may design and supply different lines of suits and jackets to different department stores.[55]

COBRANDING

Marketers often combine their brands with brands from other companies to create superior market value. **Cobranding**—also called dual branding—involves two or more brands marketed together.

The Essence of Cobranding. One form of cobranding is *same-company cobranding*, as when General Mills advertises Trix cereal and Yoplait yogurt. Another form is *joint-venture cobranding*, such as General Electric and Hitachi lightbulbs in Japan or the Citi Platinum Select AAdvantage Visa Signature credit card in which three different parties are involved. There is *multiple-sponsor cobranding*, such as Taligent, a one-time technological alliance of Apple, IBM, and Motorola. Finally, there is *retail cobranding* in which two retail establishments use the same location to optimize space and profits, such as jointly owned Pizza Hut, KFC, and Taco Bell restaurants.

The main advantage of cobranding is that a product can be convincingly positioned by virtue of the multiple brands. Cobranding can generate greater sales from the existing market and can open opportunities to attract new consumers and channels. It can also reduce the cost of product introduction because it combines two well-known images and speeds adoption. And cobranding may be a valuable means to learn about consumers and how other companies approach them. Companies in the automotive industry have reaped all these benefits.[56]

The potential disadvantages of cobranding are the risks and lack of control involved in becoming aligned with another brand in consumers' minds. Consumer expectations of co-brands are likely to be high, so unsatisfactory performance could have negative repercussions for both brands. And if one of the brands enters into a number of cobranding arrangements, overexposure may dilute the transfer of any meaningful association.[57]

For cobranding to succeed, the two brands must separately have brand equity—adequate brand awareness and a sufficiently positive brand image. The most important requirement is a logical fit between the two brands, to maximize the advantages of each while minimizing disadvantages. Consumers are more apt to perceive co-brands favorably if they are complementary and offer unique quality, rather than being overly similar and redundant.[58]

Managers must enter cobranding ventures carefully, looking for the right fit in values, capabilities, and goals, along with an appropriate balance of brand equity. There must be detailed plans to legalize contracts, make financial arrangements, and coordinate marketing programs. As one executive at Nabisco put it, "Giving away your brand is a lot like giving away your child—you want to make sure everything is perfect." Financial arrangements between brands vary; one common approach is for the brand more deeply invested in the production process to pay the other a licensing fee and royalty.

Brand alliances require a number of decisions. What capabilities do you *not* have? What resource constraints do you face (people, time, money)? What are your strategic goals? Does partnering help strengthen brand equity? Is there any risk of diluting brand equity? Does the opportunity offer strategic advantages such as knowledge transfer?

Ingredient Branding. Ingredient branding is a special case of cobranding. It creates brand equity for materials, components, or parts that are necessarily contained within other branded products. For host products whose brands are not that strong, ingredient brands can provide differentiation and important signals of quality.[59]

Successful ingredient brands include Dolby noise-reduction technology, the GORE-TEX water-resistant fibers, and Scotchgard fabrics. Vibram is the world leader in high-performance rubber soles for outdoor, work, military, recreation, fashion, and orthopedic shoes. Look under your shoe and you may find Vibram soles. They are used by a wide range of footwear manufacturers, including The North Face, Saucony, Timberland, Lacoste, L.L. Bean, Wolverine, Rockport, Columbia, Nike, and Frye.

An interesting take on ingredient branding is *self-branded ingredients* that companies advertise and even trademark.[60] Westin Hotels advertises its own "Heavenly Bed"—an ingredient that is critically

Source: page frederique/Shutterstock

>> The cobranding of Milka and Oreo, both Mondelēz brands, is aimed at gaining a stronger foothold for Swiss-based Milka in the U.S. market.

important to a guest's good night's sleep. The brand has been so successful that Westin now sells the mattress, pillows, sheets, and blankets via an online catalog, along with other "Heavenly" gifts, bath products, and even pet items. The success of the bed has also created a halo for the Westin brand as a whole. Heavenly Bed enthusiasts are more likely to rate other aspects of their room or stay as positive.[61] If it can be done well, using self-branded ingredients makes sense because firms have more control over them and can develop them to suit their purposes.

Ingredient brands try to create enough awareness and preference for their product so consumers will not buy a host product that doesn't contain it. DuPont has introduced a number of innovative products, such as Corian® solid-surface material, for use in markets ranging from apparel to aerospace. Many of its products, such as Tyvek® house wrap, Teflon® non-stick coating, and Kevlar® fiber, became household names as ingredient brands in consumer products manufactured by other companies.

Many manufacturers make components or materials that are used in branded products but lose their individual identity. One of the few companies that avoided this fate is Intel. Intel's consumer-directed brand campaign convinced many personal computer buyers to purchase only brands with "Intel Inside." As a result, major PC manufacturers—Dell, HP, Lenovo—typically purchase their chips from Intel at a premium price rather than buying equivalent chips from an unknown supplier.

What are the requirements for successful ingredient branding?[62] First, consumers must believe the ingredient matters to the performance and success of the end product. Ideally, this intrinsic value is easily seen or experienced. Second, consumers must be convinced that the ingredient is superior. To this end, the company must coordinate a communication campaign—often with the help of the manufacturers of the final products and the retailers carrying these products—that helps consumers understand the advantages of the branded ingredient. Finally, a distinctive symbol or logo must clearly signal that the host product contains the ingredient. Ideally, this symbol or logo functions like a "seal" and is simple and versatile, credibly communicating quality and confidence.[63]

The Brand Value Chain

The **brand value chain** is a structured approach to assessing the sources and outcomes of brand equity and the way marketing activities create brand value (Figure 10.2). It is based on several premises.[64]

First, brand value creation begins when the firm targets actual or potential customers by investing in a marketing program to develop the brand, including marketing communications, trade or intermediary support, and product research, development, and design. This marketing activity will change customers' mindsets—customers' thoughts and feelings that become linked to the brand. Next, these customer mindsets will affect buying behavior and the way consumers respond to all subsequent marketing activity—pricing, distribution channels, communication, and the product itself—which will affect the resulting market share and profitability of the brand.

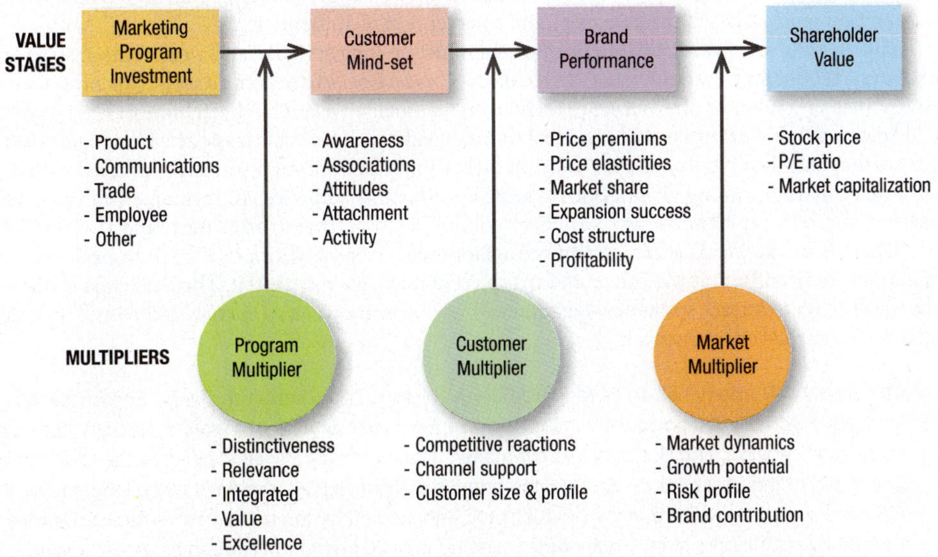

FIGURE **10.2**

Brand Value Chain

Source: Kevin Lane Keller and Vanitha Swaminathan, *Strategic Brand Management*, 5th ed. (Upper Saddle River, NJ: Pearson Education, 2020), chapter 3.

(*continued*)

Finally, the investment community will consider the market performance of the brand when assessing shareholder value in general and the value of a brand in particular.

The model also assumes that three multipliers increase or decrease the value that can flow from one stage to another:

- The *program multiplier* determines the marketing program's ability to affect the customer mindset and is a function of the quality of the program investment.
- The *customer multiplier* determines the extent to which the value created in the minds and hearts of customers affects market performance. This result depends on competitive superiority (the effectiveness of the marketing investment of other competing brands), channel and other intermediary support (the amount of brand reinforcement and selling effort that various marketing partners contribute), and customer size and profile (the number and types of customers, profitable or not, attracted to the brand).
- The *market multiplier* determines the extent to which the value shown by the market performance of a brand is manifested in shareholder value. It depends, in part, on the actions of financial analysts and investors.

Brand Dynamics

Most brands don't stay the same; they evolve over time. The two most common ways in which brands evolve are through brand repositioning and brand extensions.

BRAND REPOSITIONING

Any new development in the marketing environment can affect a brand's fortunes. Nevertheless, a number of brands have managed to make impressive comebacks in recent years.[65] After some hard times in the automotive market, Cadillac, Fiat, and Volkswagen have all turned their brand fortunes around to varying degrees. General Motors's rescue of its fading Cadillac brand was fueled by a complete overhaul of its product lineup with new designs that redefined its look and styling, such as the SRX crossover, the XTS and CTS sedans, the Escalade SUV, and the ATS sports sedan. A healthy dose of breakthrough marketing, including the first use of Led Zeppelin's music in advertising, also helped.

Often, the first thing to do in repositioning a brand is to understand what the sources of brand equity were to begin with. Are positive associations losing their strength or uniqueness? Have negative associations become linked to the brand? Then decide whether to retain the same positioning or to create a new one (and, if so, what new positioning to create).[66]

Sometimes the actual marketing program is the source of the problem because it fails to deliver on the brand promise. Then a "back to basics" strategy may make sense. We've mentioned that Harley-Davidson regained its market leadership by doing a better job of living up to customer expectations for product performance. Pabst Brewing Company did the same by returning to its roots and leveraging iconic packaging and imagery and a perception of authenticity.

In other cases, however, the old positioning is just no longer viable, and a reinvention strategy is necessary. Mountain Dew completely overhauled its brand image to become a soft-drink powerhouse. As its history reveals, it is often easier to revive a brand that is alive but has been more or less forgotten. Old Spice is another example of a brand that transcended its roots as the classic aftershave and cologne gift set that baby boomers gave their dads on Father's Day to become positively identified with contemporary male grooming products for a younger Millennial audience. To revitalize Old Spice, P&G used product innovation and tongue-in-cheek communications that stressed the brand's "experience."

There is obviously a continuum of repositioning strategies, with pure "back to basics" at one end, pure "reinvention" at the other, and many combinations in between. The challenge is often to change enough to attract some new customers, but not so much as to alienate old ones.[67] Consider how Burberry made its comeback.

Burberry Burberry has an incredible 150-year history. The company's classic English trench coats were worn by British soldiers in World War I; Sir Ernest Shackleton wore a Burberry during his Antarctic expedition; and Burberry has even been designated an official supplier to the royal family. By the turn of the 21st century, though, the brand's distinctive plaid pattern was no longer cool. It had been splashed over too many products and knocked off by too many counterfeiters. Despite the trench coat's iconic status, outerwear made up only 20 percent of Burberry's global business.

Source: iDubai/Alamy Stock Photo

<< To cement its luxury status among contemporary consumers, Burberry removed the ubiquitous signature plaid from many of its core products, created hundreds of new coat designs, and revamped its online presence to increase appeal to Millennials.

To address this issue, Burberry decided to reinforce its heritage by emphasizing, innovating, and growing its core luxury products. Targeting the luxury customer of the future, Burberry removed the overworked plaid pattern from 90 percent of its products. The brand was repositioned to gain a more unified and contemporary sensibility, resulting in the creation of more than 300 different coats, from capes and cropped jackets to classic trenches in a variety of colors and styles. New stores were opened in desirable locations, and training for sales associates was increased. Burberry's online presence was redesigned to be more appealing to Millennials, featuring emotive brand content like music, movies, heritage, and storytelling, including simulcasts of Burberry's runway shows. As a result, the company has become one of the most valuable luxury brands worldwide.[68]

BRAND EXTENSIONS

When a firm uses an established brand to introduce a new product in a different category or price tier, the resulting offering is called a **brand extension**. Honda has used its company name to cover such different products as automobiles, motorcycles, snowblowers, lawn mowers, marine engines, and snowmobiles. This suite of products allows the firm to advertise that it can fit "six Hondas in a two-car garage."

When marketers combine a new brand with an existing brand, the brand extension can also be called a *sub-brand*, such as Hershey Kisses candy, Adobe Acrobat software, Toyota Camry automobiles, and Courtyard by Marriott hotels. The existing brand that gives birth to a brand extension or sub-brand is the *parent brand*. If the parent brand is already associated with multiple products through brand extensions, it can also be called a *master brand* or *family brand*.

Brand extensions are distinct from line extensions. Unlike brand extensions, in which a company stretches its brand to a product category with which it is not currently associated, in a **line extension**, the parent brand covers a new product within a product category it currently serves, such as with new flavors, forms, colors, ingredients, and package sizes. Dannon has introduced several types of Dannon yogurt line extensions through the years—Fruit on the Bottom, All Natural flavors, Danonino, and Light & Fit. As we have noted, in a brand extension, marketers use the parent brand to enter a different product category, such as Swiss Army watches.

Many firms have decided to leverage their most valuable asset by introducing a host of new products under their strongest brand names. Most new products—typically 80 percent to 90 percent in any one year—are brand extensions. Moreover, many of the most successful new products, such as Dunkin' Donuts coffee, Progresso Light soups, and Hormel Compleats microwave meals, are brand extensions. Nevertheless, many new products are introduced each year as new brands.

>> Armani's three price tiers within its product lines help the company survive and prosper in good and bad times.

Source: Michael Kemp/Alamy Stock Photo

When to Extend a Brand? Marketers must judge each potential brand extension by how effectively it leverages existing brand equity from the parent brand, as well as by how effectively it contributes to the parent brand's equity. Crest Whitestrips leveraged the strong reputation of Crest in dental care to provide reassurance in the teeth-whitening arena, while also reinforcing its image of dental authority. Jewelry maker Bulgari has moved into hotels, restaurants, fragrances, chocolate, and skin care.

Armani Armani has extended its brand from high-end Giorgio Armani and Giorgio Armani Privé to mid-range luxury with Emporio Armani and affordable luxury with Armani Jeans and Armani Exchange. Clear differentiation exists between these brand extensions, minimizing the potential for consumer confusion and brand cannibalization. Each also lives up to the core promise of the parent brand, reducing the chances of hurting the parent's image.

Ralph Lauren Ralph Lauren has successfully marketed an aspirational luxury brand with wholesome all-American lifestyle imagery across a wide range of products. Besides clothing and fragrances, Lauren boutiques sell linens, candles, beds, couches, dishware, photo albums, and jewelry. Calvin Klein has adopted a similarly successful extension strategy, though with different lifestyle imagery.

Marketers should ask a number of questions when weighing the potential success of an extension.[69] *Does the parent brand have significant power? Is there a strong basis of fit? Will the extension have the optimal points of parity and points of difference? How can marketing programs enhance extension equity? What implications will the extension have for parent brand equity and profitability?*

Some of the key research insights on brand extensions are summarized as follows:[70]

- Successful brand extensions occur when the parent brand is seen as having favorable associations and there is a perception of fit between the parent brand and the extension product. This fit can involve product-related attributes and benefits, as well as attributes and benefits related to common usage situations or user types. For example, Ralph Lauren extended its brand from fashion apparel to perfume, furniture, and even paint.
- A brand that is seen as prototypical of a product category can be difficult to extend outside the category. For example, extending the Coca-Cola brand to fresh-squeezed juices might be challenging because of the prototypical nature of the brand in the carbonated cola category. Thus, brand associations that are positive in the original product category can become negative in the extension context. In addition, concrete attribute associations tend to be more difficult to extend than abstract benefit associations.
- Vertical extensions often require sub-branding strategies to prevent negative brand associations (in the case of upscale extensions) and brand dilution and product cannibalization (in the case of downscale extensions). For example, rather than using its core brand to launch a downscale product-line extension, Giorgio Armani introduced a sub-brand—Armani Exchange—which helped mitigate the likelihood of brand dilution and sales cannibalization.

Source: PATRICK KOVARIK/AFP/ Getty Images

<< Although Bic touted its $5 perfumes for men and women as extending Bic's heritage of convenience and affordable quality, the product extension was doomed to failure by its incongruity with consumers' image of the company.

One major mistake in evaluating extension opportunities is failing to take *all* consumers' brand knowledge into account and focusing instead on one or a few brand associations as a potential basis of fit.[71] Bic offers a classic example of that mistake.

Bic By emphasizing inexpensive, disposable products, French company Société Bic was able to create markets for nonrefillable ballpoint pens in the late 1950s, disposable cigarette lighters in the early 1970s, and disposable razors in the early 1980s. It unsuccessfully tried the same strategy to market Bic perfumes in the United States and Europe. The perfumes—"Nuit" and "Jour" for women and "Bic for Men" and "Bic Sport for Men"—were packaged in quarter-ounce glass spray bottles that looked like fat cigarette lighters and sold for $5 each. The products were displayed on racks at checkout counters throughout Bic's extensive distribution channels. At the time, a Bic spokeswoman described the new products as extensions of the Bic heritage—"high quality at affordable prices, convenient to purchase, and convenient to use." The brand extension was launched with a $20 million advertising and promotion campaign containing images of stylish people enjoying the perfume and using the tagline "Paris in Your Pocket." Nevertheless, Bic was unable to overcome its lack of cachet and negative image associations, and the extension was a failure.[72]

Advantages of Brand Extensions. Consumers form expectations about a new product based on what they know about the parent brand and the extent to which they feel this information is relevant. When Sony introduced a new personal computer tailored for multimedia applications, the VAIO, consumers may have felt comfortable with its anticipated performance because of their experience with and knowledge of other Sony products. Once the VAIO brand gained customer recognition, it was spun off from Sony, and it now operates as a stand-alone brand, with Sony maintaining a minority stake in the company as well as the trademark for the VAIO brand and logo.

By setting up positive expectations, extensions reduce risk. It also may be easier to convince retailers to stock and promote a brand extension because of anticipated increased customer demand. An introductory campaign for an extension doesn't need to create awareness of both the brand *and* the new product; it can concentrate on the new product itself.[73]

Extensions can thus reduce launch costs, which is important because establishing a major new brand name for a consumer packaged good in the U.S. marketplace can cost more than $100 million! Extensions also can avoid the difficulty—and expense—of coming up with a new name, thus allowing packaging and labeling efficiencies. Similar or identical packages and labels can lower production costs for extensions and, if coordinated properly, provide more prominence in the retail store via a "billboard" effect.[74] Stouffer's offers a variety of frozen entrées with identical orange packaging that increases their visibility when stocked together in the grocer's freezer. With a portfolio of brand variants within a product category, consumers who want a change can switch to a different product type without having to leave the brand family.

Coca-Cola To break away from its traditional image and shift to health-focused trends, Coca-Cola decided to launch a range of energy drinks, for the first time using its own brand name. The new energy drink branded "Coca-Cola Energy" and "Coca-Cola Energy No Sugar" and made with naturally derived caffeine and guarana extract. This move puts the company's energy drinks in direct competition with Monster Energy, a brand partially owned and distributed by Coca-Cola. The new energy drink also faces an uphill battle trying to change consumers' perception of the Coca-Cola brand, which has traditionally been associated with carbonated colas.[75]

Besides facilitating acceptance of new products, brand extensions can help to clarify the meaning of a brand and its core values or improve consumer loyalty to the company creating the extension. Through their brand extensions, Crayola means "colorful arts and crafts for kids" and Weight Watchers means "weight loss and maintenance."

A successful category extension may not only reinforce the parent brand and open up a new market but also facilitate even more new category extensions. The success of Apple's iPod and iTunes products opened up a new market, boosted sales of core Mac products, and paved the way for the launch of the iPhone and iPad.

Disadvantages of Brand Extensions. On the downside, line extensions may cause the brand name to be less strongly identified with any one product.[76] By linking its brand to mainstream food products such as mashed potatoes, powdered milk, soups, and beverages, Cadbury ran the risk of losing its more specific meaning as a chocolate and candy brand.[77]

Brand dilution occurs when consumers no longer associate a brand with a specific or highly similar set of products and start thinking less of the brand. Porsche found sales success with its Cayenne sport utility vehicle and Panamera four-door sedan, which accounted for three-quarters of its vehicle sales in 2012, but some critics felt the company was watering down its sports car image in the process. Porsche subsequently dialed up its on- and off-road test tracks, driving courses, and roadshow events to help customers get the adrenaline rush of driving a legendary Porsche 911.

If a firm launches extensions that consumers deem inappropriate, they may question the integrity of the brand or become confused or even frustrated: Which version of the product is "the right one" for them? Do they know the brand as well as they thought they did? Retailers reject many new products and brands because they don't have the shelf or display space for them. And the firm itself may become overwhelmed.

Even if sales of a brand extension are high and meet targets, the revenue may be coming from consumers switching to the extension from existing parent-brand offerings—in effect cannibalizing the parent brand. Within-brand shifts in sales may not necessarily be undesirable if they're a form of preemptive cannibalization. In other words, consumers who switched to a line extension might otherwise have switched to a competing brand instead. Tide laundry detergent maintains the same market share it had 50 years ago because of the sales contributions of its various line extensions—scented and unscented powder, pods, liquid, and other forms.

One easily overlooked disadvantage of brand extensions is that the firm forgoes the chance to create a new brand with its own unique image and equity. Consider the long-term financial advantages to Disney of having introduced more grown-up Touchstone films, to Levi's of creating casual Dockers pants, and to Black & Decker of introducing high-end DeWalt power tools.

MANAGING A BRAND CRISIS

Marketing managers must assume a brand crisis will someday arise. Chick-fil-A, BP, Domino's, and Toyota have all experienced damaging—and even potentially crippling—brand crises. Bank of America, JPMorgan, AIG, and other financial services firms have been rocked by scandals that significantly eroded investor trust. Repercussions include lost sales, reduced effectiveness of marketing activities, increased sensitivity to rivals' marketing activities, and reduced impact of the firm's marketing activities on competing brands. To protect the brand, key executives and sometimes even company founders might have to step down.[78]

In general, the stronger the brand and corporate image—especially for credibility and trustworthiness—the more likely the firm can weather the storm. Careful preparation and a well-managed crisis management program are also critical, however. As Johnson & Johnson's legendary and nearly flawless handling of the Tylenol product-tampering incident taught marketers everywhere, consumers must see the firm's response as both *swift* and *sincere*. They must immediately sense that the company truly cares.

The longer the firm takes to respond, the more likely consumers are to form negative impressions from unfavorable media coverage or word of mouth. Perhaps worse, they may find they don't like the brand after all and permanently switch. Getting in front of a problem with public relations, and perhaps even ads, can help avoid those problems.[79]

A classic example is Perrier—the one-time brand leader in the bottled water category. In 1994, Perrier was forced to halt production worldwide and recall all existing product when traces of benzene, a known carcinogen, were found in excessive quantities in its bottled water. Over the next weeks it offered several explanations, creating confusion and skepticism. Perhaps more damaging, the product was off shelves for more than three months. Despite an expensive relaunch featuring ads and promotions, the brand struggled to regain lost market share, and a full year later sales were less than half what they had been. With its key association with purity tarnished, Perrier had no other compelling points of difference. Consumers and retailers had found satisfactory substitutes, and the brand never recovered. Eventually it was taken over by Nestlé SA.[80]

The more sincere the firm's response—ideally a public acknowledgment of the impact on consumers and willingness to take necessary steps—the less likely it is that consumers will form negative attributions. When shards of glass were found in some jars of its baby food, Gerber tried to reassure the public that there were no problems in its manufacturing plants but adamantly refused to withdraw products from stores. After market share slumped from 66 percent to 52 percent within a couple of months, one company official admitted, "Not pulling our baby food off the shelf gave the appearance that we aren't a caring company."

If a problem exists, consumers need to know without a shadow of a doubt that the company has found the proper solution. One of the keys to Tylenol's recovery was Johnson & Johnson's introduction of triple tamper-proof packaging, successfully eliminating consumer worry that the product could ever be undetectably tampered with again.

Not all crises stem from a company's own actions. External crises such as economic recessions, natural disasters, and major geopolitical events can threaten the brand and require an appropriate brand response. For example, during the difficulties precipitated by the Covid-19 pandemic, many organizations looked to their marketers to retain customers and sustain brands. Marketing spending as a share of revenue rose to an all-time high of 11.4 percent in May 2020, up from 8.6 percent only four months earlier and topping the previous high of 9.3 percent six years previously.[81] Brand marketers were challenged like never before by this global predicament. The best marketers responded quickly and took bold action to protect brand health and customer loyalty. Consider Nike's response:

Nike Based on prevailing market conditions and factors, Nike implemented a four-phase global response to Covid-19: Containment, Recovery, Normalization, and Return to Growth. The company used its innovation and marketing teams to help in the development of Personal Protective Equipment (PPE) for frontline doctors, nurses, and medical workers. It also reassured staff and employees that there would be pay continuity despite the closing of many of its retail outlets. For consumers, Nike launched an engaging "Play Inside" digital campaign, encouraging people to stay healthy and active while they sheltered at home. The firm also offered consumers the premium component of its popular exercise app free for 90 days. Continuing a selling shift that had been building in previous years, Nike drove even more of its business online with a proprietary e-commerce app.[82]

The pandemic forced all brands to rethink what and how they were selling. Already important, digital marketing became even more so. Social media as a percentage of the marketing budget rose from 13 percent in January 2020 to 23 percent in May 2020. Successful firms, however, employed a well-rounded digital strategy that also emphasized websites, apps, and e-commerce options. As sales rose for home-related products, some brands enjoyed unprecedented demand and growth. King Arthur Flour— known for its pure, organic, and high-quality product—found that many of its infrequent customers, who previously baked only a few times a year, began to bake a few times *a month*. With exploding demand and interest in its products, the employee-owned company began to sell smaller bags to reach more customers and brought in staff reinforcement to deal with the thousands of questions on its Baker's Hotline, as well as its booming social media interactions and web traffic.[83]

No easy solutions exist for successfully navigating a brand through such marketplace turbulence, but the following four guidelines may help firms that find themselves managing a brand through an economic, health, or other crisis.

- *Empathy*: Get even closer to consumers and customers. What are they thinking and feeling now, and what are they doing differently? Are these changes temporary or permanent?
- *Value*: Put forth the most compelling value proposition. Recognize the totality of value, and communicate all possible economic, functional, and psychological benefits and all possible savings in time, money, energy, and psychological wear-and-tear.
- *Strategy*: Be authentic and true to the brand promise. Find ways to develop programs that address short-term needs in a brand-faithful manner.
- *Innovation*: Engage in "Stop, Start, and Continue (But Improve)" exercises and activities. Take advantage of the opportunity to "clean house" to prune and focus brand and product offerings. Rethink budgets, go-to-market plans, and consumer targets.

Although a crisis can put a severe strain on even the strongest brands, the best brand marketers step up in these and many other ways to thoughtfully provide clear strategic direction and creatively find new ways to implement their plans.

Luxury Branding

Luxury brands are one of the purest examples of the role of branding, because the brand and its image frequently offer key competitive advantages that create immense value for both the company and its customers. Marketers for luxury brands like Prada, Gucci, Cartier, and Louis Vuitton manage lucrative franchises that have endured for decades in what some believe is now a $300 billion industry.[84]

CHARACTERISTICS OF LUXURY BRANDS

Priced significantly higher than typical items in their categories, luxury brands for years were about social status and who a customer was—or perhaps wanted to be. Times have changed, and luxury in many developed countries has become more about style and substance, combining personal pleasure and self-expression.

A luxury shopper must feel he or she is getting something truly special. Thus, the common denominators of luxury brands are quality and uniqueness. A winning formula for many is craftsmanship, heritage, authenticity, and history (often critical to justifying a high price). Hermès, the French luxury leather-goods maker, sells its classic designs for hundreds or even thousands of dollars, "not because they are in fashion," as one writer put it, "but [because] they never go out of fashion."[85] Here is how several luxury brands have become enduring market successes:

Sub-Zero Sub-Zero sells refrigerators that range from $2,000 for small, under-counter models to $15,000 and up for high-end models. The target is customers with high standards of performance and design who cherish their home and what they buy to furnish it. Sub-Zero extensively surveys this group, as well as the kitchen designers, architects, and retailers who recommend and sell its products.[86]

>> In keeping with its name, which denotes "the boss," Patrón, sold in numbered hand-blown decanters, has ascended to the top of the high-end tequila market that it essentially created.

Source: Serebral360/Stockimo/Alamy Stock Photo

Patrón Cofounded by Paul Mitchell hair care founder John Paul DeJoria, Patrón came about after a 1989 trip to a distillery in the small Mexican state of Jalisco. Named Patrón to convey "the boss, the cool guy," the smooth agave tequila comes in an elegant hand-blown decanter and is sold in individually numbered bottles for $45 or more. Patrón, which essentially created the high-end tequila market, has generated more than $600 million in retail sales, surpassing Jose Cuervo to become the world's largest tequila brand. In 2018, Patrón was acquired by Bacardi for $5.1 billion.[87]

Montblanc The goal of Montblanc, whose products now range from pens to fragrances, is to be a strong luxury brand to as many classes of luxury customers as possible, while still retaining a prominent public image. The brand promise is that "Montblanc unites fine European craftsmanship with time-honoured designs, bringing pieces to life that emanate classic heritage and refined creation. Just as a soul remains long after its body is gone, our pieces are crafted to perform superbly and symbolize elegance for many lifetimes." The company branched out from its origins in writing instruments into categories such as leather goods and timepieces, where it could leverage its brand power and its philosophy of manufacturing competence, highest quality, sustainable value, and creativity.[88]

Much of the growth in luxury brands in recent years has been geographic. China has overtaken the United States as the world's largest luxury market. Although initially very "logo-driven" and interested in conspicuous brand signals, Chinese luxury consumers have become more conscious of quality and design, like luxury consumers in other parts of the world.

MANAGING LUXURY BRANDS

Luxury marketers have learned that luxury is not viewed the same way everywhere around the world. But in the end, luxury brand marketers have to remember they are often selling a dream, anchored in product quality, status, and prestige.[89]

Just like marketers in less expensive categories, those guiding the fortunes of luxury brands operate in a constantly evolving marketing environment. Globalization, new technologies, shifting consumer cultures, and other forces require them to be skillful and adept at their brand stewardship. To ensure success in such a dynamic environment, marketers must adhere to the general principles that

Source: Marek Slusarczyk/Alamy Stock Photo

<< Offerings in Montblanc's expanding product line combine exceptional craftsmanship with refined, classic designs that promise its customers superb and elegant performance for generations.

apply in managing luxury brands. Some of the key principles of luxury brand management are as follows:[90]

- All marketing decisions associated with luxury brands—product, service, pricing, sales incentives, communication, and distribution—must be aligned to ensure that purchase and consumption experiences are consistent with the image of the brand.
- Luxury branding typically includes the creation of a premium, aspirational image.
- Luxury brands frequently span categories, and as a result, their competitors are often defined broadly.
- Luxury brands must protect their identity and aggressively combat trademark infringement and counterfeits.
- All attributes of luxury brands must be aligned with the image of the brand. This includes brand identifiers such as names, logos, symbols, and packaging, as well as brand associations such as personalities, events, countries, and other entities.

One trend for luxury brands is to wrap personal experiences around the products. Top-end fashion retailers are offering such experiences alongside their wares, expecting that customers who have visited a workshop or met the designer will feel closer to the brand. Gucci invites its biggest spenders to fashion shows, equestrian events, and the Cannes Film Festival.

Porsche Sport Driving Schools and Experience Centers in Germany, the United States, and other parts of the world allow Porsche drivers to "train their driving skills and enjoy the all-out pleasure of driving, on-road, off-road, or on snow and ice." To this end, Porsche opened a state-of-the-art facility in southern California that features 45-degree off-road inclines and a simulated ice hill.

In an increasingly connected world, some luxury marketers have struggled to find the appropriate online selling and communication strategies for their brand. Some fashion brands have gone beyond glossy magazine spreads to listening to and communicating with consumers through Facebook, Twitter, Instagram, WeChat, and other digital and social media channels. E-commerce has also taken hold for some luxury brands. Sites such as Net-a-Porter (now Yoox Net-a-Porter), Gilt Groupe, and Farfetch now offer new ways for fashion brands to move high-end goods.

Ultimately, luxury marketers are learning that success for them, and indeed for all marketers, depends on getting the right balance of classic and contemporary imagery, and of continuity and change, in marketing programs and activities.

Given the lengths to which they go to pamper customers in their stores—with doormen, glasses of champagne, and extravagant surroundings—luxury brands have had to work hard to provide a high-quality digital experience. They are increasingly blending the two. Gucci partnered with Samsung Electronics to create an immersive in-store experience for its timepieces and jewelry that combines physical and mobile commerce. Stores feature transparent displays that show images on the screen without obscuring the products behind them and a digital shop-in-shop section where customers

Source: Agencja Fotograficzna Caro/Alamy Stock Photo

>> Porsche Sport Driving Schools and Experience Centers in Germany, the United States, and elsewhere encourage Porsche drivers to rev up their road skills and capture the fun of putting vehicles through their paces in various conditions.

can use tablet computers to browse. To reach affluent customers who work long hours and have little time to shop, many high-end fashion brands such as Dior, Louis Vuitton, and Fendi have unveiled e-commerce sites that allow customers to research items before visiting a store—and offer a means to combat fakes sold online.

marketing INSIGHT

Constructing a Brand Positioning Bull's-Eye

The key to developing a meaningful brand positioning is using a systematic approach to design the different aspects of the brand in a way that is relevant and meaningful to the customers the firm is targeting. Such a systematic approach is offered by the Bull's-Eye Framework. We discuss this framework in the context of a hypothetical Starbucks example illustrated in Figure 10.3.

The inner circle of the bull's-eye is the brand mantra defining the essence of the brand and the core brand promise. It guides the actions of company employees and collaborators by ensuring that they have a clear understanding of what the brand should represent to consumers. The brand mantra is at the heart of the bull's-eye and is the guiding principle for all other aspects of brand positioning. One could define the Starbucks brand mantra as "a rich, rewarding coffee experience." Although Starbucks has extended its offerings to include non-coffee drinks, snacks, and even wine, coffee and the experience of its consumption are at the core of the brand. "Rich" and "rewarding" capture both the physical and the psychological aspects of the ideal Starbucks experience.

The circle surrounding the one that contains the brand mantra encompasses the brand's points of difference and points of parity that make up its positioning. Points of parity and points of difference should be made as specific as possible without being too narrow, and they should be constructed in terms of the benefits a customer can actually derive from the product or service.

Different competitors will suggest different points of difference and points of parity. With competitors such as mom-and-pop coffee shops, fast-food restaurants like McDonald's, and at-home coffee brands in mind, benefits such as offering fresh, high-quality coffee, providing a variety of coffee drinks, and delivering fast, personalized service can be viewed as potential points of difference for Starbucks, whereas fair prices, the availability of convenient locations, and social responsibility can be viewed as important points of parity for the brand.

In the next concentric circle are the substantiators, or reasons to believe—attributes or benefits that provide factual or demonstrable support for the points of parity and points of difference. Substantiators are also referred to as reasons

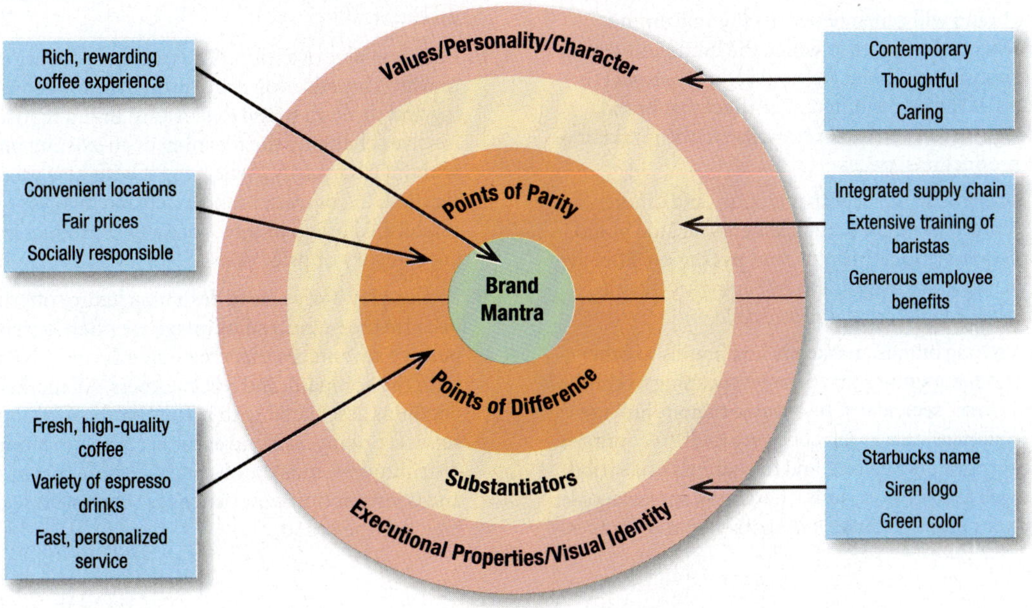

FIGURE 10.3
A Hypothetical Example of a Starbucks Brand Positioning Bull's-Eye

(continued)

marketing insight *(continued)*

to believe because they are sometimes used in a company's communication campaign to provide customers with facts that validate the company's brand messaging. Starbucks's integrated supply chain, extensive training of baristas, and generous employee benefits program are among the factors that enable it to substantiate its positioning.

Finally, the outer circle contains two additional relevant aspect of brand positioning. The first involves the brand values, personality, or character—intangible associations evoked by words and actions that help to establish the tone of the brand. In the case of Starbucks, one might think of the brand as contemporary, thoughtful, and caring. The second aspect involves executional properties and visual identity—more tangible components of the brand that affect the way customers perceive it. For Starbucks this includes its brand name, the siren logo, and the dark green and white color scheme characterizing the brand's visual appearance.

summary

1. A brand is a name, term, sign, symbol, design, or some combination of these elements that is intended to identify the goods and services of one seller or group of sellers and to differentiate them from those of competitors. The ultimate purpose of the brand is to create, for consumers, the company, and its collaborators, value that goes beyond the value created by the product and service aspects of the offering.
2. Brands are valuable intangible assets that offer a number of benefits to customers and firms and that need to be managed carefully.
3. The value created by a brand is captured by two key concepts: brand equity and brand power. Brand equity reflects the premium that is placed on a company's valuation because of its ownership of the brand. It encompasses the net present value of the total financial returns that the brand will generate over its lifetime. Brand power reflects the degree to which the brand influences the way consumers think, feel, and act with respect to the brand. It is thus the differential effect that brand knowledge has on consumer response to the marketing of that product or service.
4. Brand elements are devices that identify and differentiate the brand. Common brand elements include brand names, logos, symbols, mottos, and packaging. Effective brand elements are memorable, meaningful, likable, transferable, adaptable, and protectable.
5. To build strong brands, marketers link brands to other information in memory that conveys meaning to consumers. These "secondary" brand associations link the brand to sources such as the company itself, to countries or other geographic regions, and to channels of distribution, as well as to other brands, characters, spokespeople, sporting or cultural events, or other third-party sources.
6. Brand hierarchy reflects the way a company's brands are related to a company's products and services, as well as to one another. Developing a meaningful brand hierarchy is particularly important for companies that are managing diverse brand portfolios. The hallmark of an optimal brand portfolio is the ability of each brand to maximize equity in combination with all the other brands in the portfolio. Three general brand-portfolio strategies are house-of-brands, branded-house, and sub-branding strategies.
7. Marketers often combine their brands with brands from other companies to create superior market value. Cobranding involves two or more brands marketed together. Ingredient branding is a special case of cobranding involving materials, components, or parts that are necessarily contained within other branded products.
8. Brands evolve over time. The two most common ways in which brands evolve are through brand repositioning and through brand extensions. Brand repositioning involves changing the meaning of an existing brand without necessarily associating it with new products or services. In contrast, brand extension involves using an established brand to introduce a new product in a different category or price tier.
9. Brands play a key role in designing luxury offerings, because the brand and its image are often key competitive advantages that create significant value for both the company and its customers. All marketing decisions associated with luxury brands—product, service, pricing, sales incentives, communication, and distribution—must be aligned to ensure that purchase and consumption experiences are consistent with the image of the brand.

marketing SPOTLIGHT

Louis Vuitton

Source: Images & Stories/Alamy Stock Photo

Louis Vuitton's roots go back to when he set out from his small village, Anchay, to Paris in 1837 to begin his trunk-making business. Training as an apprentice, under master trunk maker Monsieur Marechal at the age of 16, Louis Vuitton learned the skills needed to craft quality luggage on his own. After his apprenticeship, Louis Vuitton opened his first store in Paris in 1854. Word of Louis Vuitton's skill and craftsmanship spread quickly. Louis Vuitton trunks were notable for being waterproof and stackable (because of their rectangular design). By the early 1860s, his trunks had become so popular that he was able to open the world's largest luggage store in the heart of Paris.

When Napoleon III's wife, Empress Eugenie, hired Louis Vuitton to be her personal luggage maker, his trunks started becoming popular among Parisian elites. As Louis Vuitton customers traveled abroad and showed off their luggage, demand for Louis Vuitton products skyrocketed. The Louis Vuitton brand became a symbol of luxury as his clientele expanded to some of the most influential figures of the 19th century. Royalty, industry giants, and art buffs all began traveling with Vuitton, including the Duke and Duchess of Windsor, J. P. Morgan, and Henri Matisse.

Attracted by the increasing popularity of Louis Vuitton luggage, many imitators entered the market and began producing lookalike models. To make his creations distinct, Louis Vuitton designed the famous two-tone brown checkered pattern (called the Damier canvas) in 1888. Four years later, Louis Vuitton died and his son, Georges, took over the company.

Georges Vuitton took Louis Vuitton global when he purchased a spot at the 1893 Chicago World's Fair. In the same year, Georges toured across America, hitting cities such as New York City and Philadelphia. His exhibition efforts resulted in department stores beginning to carry Louis Vuitton luggage, which established Louis Vuitton internationally. In 1986, Georges Vuitton introduced LV's signature monogram, an interlocked L and V, which would eventually become the most iconic symbol of Louis Vuitton products.

In the early 20th century, Louis Vuitton continued expanding across the world and added new bag styles to accompany its best-selling trunks. When airplanes became a more conventional way to travel in the mid-20th century, the demand for Louis Vuitton bags and trunks became even greater as famous figures traveled more often. As women entered the workforce, Louis Vuitton introduced handbags and purses, which quickly became symbols of high class and taste in the workplace. This marked the start of the company's transition into a luxury fashion brand. Louis Vuitton expanded its product line to include male suitcases and wallets shortly after.

The luxury status and financial success of Louis Vuitton throughout the 20th century caught the eye of businessman Bernard Arnault who, through a series of mergers and acquisitions turned it into the world's most valuable luxury goods company. As part of this expansion strategy, in 1987, Louis Vuitton merged with Moët et Chandon and Hennessy, leading manufacturers of champagne and cognac, respectively, and created LVMH.

Louis Vuitton began selling luxury clothing in 1997 when the company hired Marc Jacobs, one of the world's best-known fashion designers at the time. Jacobs applied the signature Damier and Monogram designs to *prêt-a-porter* (ready to wear) clothing lines, along with belts and other accessories. Through frequent collaborations with celebrities and fashion icons, Louis Vuitton's clothing and accessories were embraced by Hollywood and pop culture stars all over the world. With these new changes, LVMH became the world's largest luxury conglomerate.

Over the years, Louis Vuitton has employed many different strategies to maintain its luxury brand status. Louis Vuitton does not advertise sales or offer sales promotions. Its pricing strategy reflects the concept that owning an LV product is a true luxury. When Louis Vuitton goods fail to sell, the company discontinues the item line. Excess inventory is burned to stop products from being stolen or sold at a lower price. Prices are kept high because customers are willing to pay a premium for the status associated with owning a Louis Vuitton product.

Louis Vuitton is also careful not to dilute its brand through excessive communications. This presents the company with the challenge of trying to sell as much as possible, while maintaining an aura of exclusivity and luxury. Louis Vuitton doesn't use television for mass advertising. Instead, it advertises on billboards and in fashion magazines featuring high-profile imagery displaying the prestige of owning an LV product. Over the years, Louis Vuitton has continued using supermodels and celebrities (such as Madonna, Angelina

(*continued*)

Jolie, and Jennifer Lopez) as brand ambassadors. It has also sponsored its own international regatta, the Louis Vuitton Cup, to promote its products.

Louis Vuitton has built the world's most valuable luxury brand by maintaining a fine balance of timeless design and fresh products. The legendary LV monogram appears on all its products, whether luggage, a handbag, or a belt. By modifying its product line to fit the needs of its elite customers while preserving its iconic designs, Louis Vuitton has continued offering products that are synonymous with luxury, wealth, and fashion.[91]

Questions

1. What are the key aspects of the Louis Vuitton brand? How does it create value for customers?
2. How does an exclusive brand such as Louis Vuitton grow and sell more, while remaining fresh and retaining its cachet?
3. Is the counterfeiting of Louis Vuitton products always a negative? Are there any circumstances in which counterfeiting can be seen as having some positive aspects?

marketing SPOTLIGHT

MUJI

Source: Dennis Gilbert-VIEW/Alamy Stock Photo

MUJI was founded in 1980 as a private label for Japanese supermarket The Seiyu. At the time, foreign brands were becoming increasingly popular as the economy grew. As a result, cheaper, low-quality imitation goods became attractive alternatives for budget-conscious consumers. MUJI goods were created to fill the growing market for quality goods that were affordable and long-lasting. MUJI started with 9 household and 31 food products, which were advertised with the slogan "lower priced for a reason." Products were packaged in simple materials such as clear cellophane and brown paper. Over the next couple of years, MUJI expanded its product line to include stationery, clothing, kitchen appliances, and home furnishings. It also began opening its own stores across Japan.

The company's full name, Mujirushi Ryohin, means "no-brand quality goods," a design philosophy that reflects the simplicity and functionality of its products. MUJI claims that its products are "brandless," which means that they do not have logos or distinct markings. They are designed not to stand out, but rather to look minimalist—as MUJI describes them, to be just "enough" to deliver the one function they were designed for. This can be seen in MUJI socks, which are made with a 90-degree angle rather than the normal 120. The right angle helps with heel slippage when the socks are worn inside boots and increases overall comfort. MUJI intends its products to be simple in both function and style, so they can be mixed and matched to suit any user's needs and lifestyle.

MUJI follows three core principles to create quality, minimalist products that anyone can afford. First, MUJI carefully selects the materials used to manufacture its products. The company has been known to use industrial materials that it can buy in bulk at low cost. This concept started with the food that MUJI carried in the early 1980s; MUJI sold U-shaped pasta after buying the ends of spaghetti cut off after manufacturing, as well as canned salmon made from undesirable parts of the fish. Second, MUJI streamlines its manufacturing process; products typically use natural or unfinished materials that don't have to be painted or dyed. This not only makes MUJI products uniform in color and material but also creates less waste and reduces costs. Third, MUJI uses bulk packaging for its products, placing them in plain containers. Besides being in line with MUJI's "brandless" philosophy, the minimalist packaging saves resources and keeps the company environmentally friendly.

MUJI's "no brand" philosophy can also be seen in its promotional strategy. The company keeps its advertising budget modest by relying on word of mouth to spread awareness. Instead of running huge advertising campaigns on TV and print media, MUJI prefers to reach people through press and in-store events. Resources are invested in the salespeople employed in its physical locations. Locally hired store managers are sent to MUJI offices in Tokyo for training on how to sell MUJI products. By ensuring that customers

(*continued*)

receive a good in-store experience, MUJI has fostered sustainable brand awareness. And by keeping marketing costs low, MUJI can keep its prices low and channel more resources into product development.

By promoting itself as the "no brand" brand, MUJI has created a niche that has allowed the company to successfully expand globally. Even though the company offers over 7,000 items, MUJI does not customize its products for particular countries and regions. Rather, MUJI products are designed to fit into households all over the world. Each MUJI product is built for a specific purpose, so it is simple to use. MUJI also employs the same style of store design, layout, and merchandising for all its locations around the world. The uniformity in both retail location and products cuts the costs of regional adaptation. MUJI has stuck to a policy of adding more stores in new countries only when existing ones are running profitably, which has kept profits high and growth stable. Overseas business locations account for the majority of MUJI's stores, with East Asia accounting for the largest share.

MUJI's insistence that its brand values permeate all aspects of the company has contributed to a strong, consistent brand and a sustainable business model. The "brandless" design of its products creates a unique aesthetic: Although MUJI intends its products to look indistinct, they are at the same time recognizable among heavily branded products. Adherence to its three core principles keeps the price of MUJI products low. Combining these advantages with the products' simplicity in function and form, MUJI has created a winning combination for global expansion. Since its first store opened in 1983, MUJI has added over 1,000 locations worldwide.[92]

Questions

1. What are the key drivers of MUJI's market success? What are MUJI's points of parity and points of difference relative to the competition?
2. What are the pros and cons of using the "no brand" strategy?
3. How should MUJI grow its brand?

CHAPTER 11

Managing Pricing and Sales Promotions

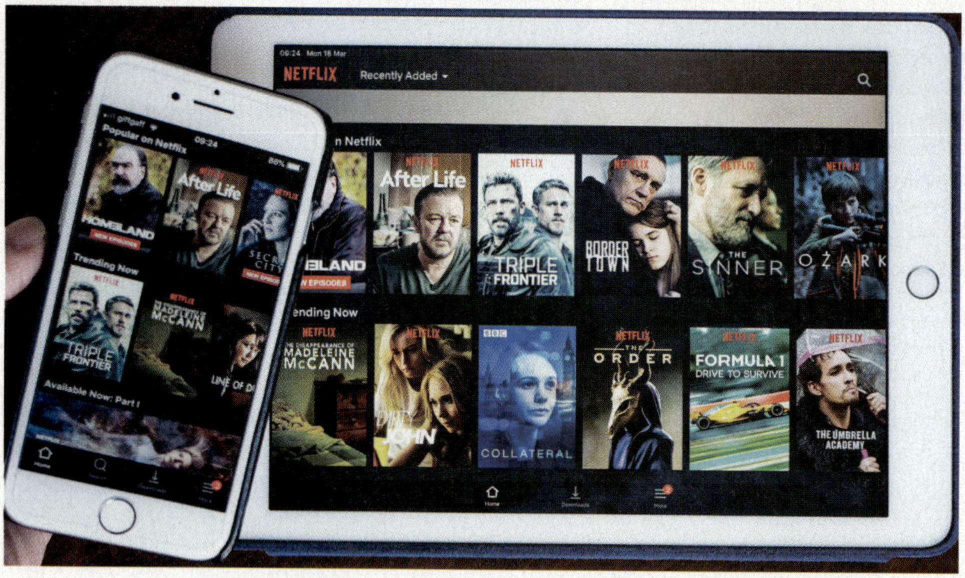

Netflix has accompanied a series of price hikes with heavy investment in developing original content to complement the extended array of streaming programming it offers.

Source: M. Unal Ozmen/Shutterstock

Price is the one element of the marketing mix that produces revenue; the other elements produce costs. Price also communicates the company's intended value positioning of its product or brand. A well-designed and marketed product can still command a price premium and reap big profits. But new economic realities have caused many consumers to reevaluate what they are willing to pay for products and services, and companies have had to carefully review their pricing strategies as a result. One company that has caught the attention of consumers and businesses is Netflix, with its unorthodox pricing strategy.

>>> Founded in 1997 by Reed Hastings and Marc Randolph, Netflix provides a subscription-based streaming service that offers online streaming of films and television programs. An over-the-top video content provider, Netflix distributes programming as a stand-alone product directly to viewers over the internet, bypassing traditional media carriers such as cable and broadcast television. Since its inception, the company's subscriber base has grown rapidly, reaching 74 million in the United States and 210 million worldwide in 2018. Starting at the very beginning, two of the key decisions that Netflix had to grapple with were selecting (and later developing) content that customers would be willing to pay for on an ongoing basis and setting a price that would appeal to customers while enabling Netflix to secure the desired content. As the competition from other streaming services (such as Amazon, Apple, and Hulu) intensified and licensing costs for original content increased, Netflix began to invest heavily in developing original content. In 2018 alone, Netflix had approximately 700 original shows, with more

in the pipeline. To pay for new content, Netflix had to augment its services and pricing structure. Since the introduction of its streaming service in November 2010, Netflix has extended the portfolio of service offerings, while at the same time raising the price. Three years after the launch of the $7.99-a-month streaming service, it introduced a premium version priced at $11.99. A year later, in May 2014, Netflix introduced a lower-tier basic service priced at $7.99, while raising the price of its standard service to $8.99. The following year, Netflix raised the price of the standard service to $9.99, followed by another price increase to $10.99 in 2017 that was combined with raising the premium service price to $13.99. Then, in 2019, Netflix announced another price hike—the largest since the inception of its streaming services—with the basic subscription priced at $8.99, the standard subscription at $10.99 (increased to $12.99 in 2020), and the premium subscription at $15.99. This pricing structure reflects the company's belief that the consumer benefits provided by its streaming service outweigh the corresponding costs. "Price is all relative to value," said CEO Hastings. "We're continuing to increase the content offering and we're seeing that reflected in viewing around the world."[1]

Netflix adopted a content localization strategy to enter and expand in international markets across the globe. The company retains its premium pricing but adapted its prices for its audience in the Indian subcontinent. In 2016, Netflix launched its services in India to tap into opportunities provided by the huge Internet userbase, driven by high smart phone penetration and affordable mobile data service packs. Alongside content localization, Netflix also changed its pricing approach for a highly price-sensitive India market by introducing a mobile-only subscription plan for ₹199 in 2019. In India, Netflix's monthly subscription plans range between ₹499 to ₹799. The company has partnered with Reliance Jio, the largest mobile service provider, for free 'mobile-only subscription' to Jio's postpaid customers. This price penetration strategy helped Netflix grow rapidly.[2] As of July 2021, Netflix recorded 5 million subscribers accounting for 14% of market share of the OTT market in India.[3]

Pricing decisions are complex and must take into account many factors—the company, the customers, the competition, and the marketing environment. Holistic marketers know their pricing decisions must also be consistent with the firm's marketing strategy and with its target markets and brand positions. In this chapter, we provide concepts and tools to facilitate setting initial prices and adjusting prices over time and markets.

Understanding Pricing

Price is not just a number on a tag. The prices you pay for goods and services perform many functions and come in many forms: rent, tuition, fares, fees, rates, tolls, retainers, wages, and commissions. Price also has many components. If you buy a new car, the sticker price may be adjusted by rebates and dealer incentives. Some firms allow customers to pay through multiple forms, such as using points, frequent flier miles, and bitcoins.

Learning Objectives After studying this chapter you should be able to:

11.1 Describe the role that pricing plays in marketing management.

11.2 Identify the key psychological factors that influence how consumers perceive prices.

11.3 Explain the factors that a manager must consider when setting prices.

11.4 Discuss how to respond to competitive prices cuts.

11.5 Explain how to design and manage incentives.

Throughout most of history, prices were set by negotiation between buyers and sellers. Bargaining is still a sport in some areas. Setting one price for all buyers is a relatively modern idea that arose with the development of large-scale retailing at the end of the 19th century. F.W. Woolworth, Tiffany & Co., John Wanamaker, and others advertised a "strictly one-price policy," an efficient approach because they carried so many items and supervised so many employees.

Traditionally, price has operated as a major determinant of buyer choice. Consumers and purchasing agents who have access to price information and price discounters put pressure on retailers to lower their prices. Retailers in turn put pressure on manufacturers to lower *their* prices. The result can be a marketplace characterized by heavy discounting and sales promotion.

For over 25 years, the internet has been changing the way buyers and sellers interact. The internet has enabled buyers to make instant price comparisons from thousands of vendors. Moreover, using smart mobile devices, customers can easily make price comparisons in stores before deciding whether to purchase, pressure the retailer to match or better the price, or buy elsewhere. Using promotional platforms such as Groupon, customers can also pool their resources to get better pricing.

Groupon Groupon was launched in 2008 to help businesses leverage the internet and e-mail to use promotions as a form of advertisement. Specifically, the company sends its large base of subscribers a humorously worded daily deal—a specific percentage or dollar amount off the regular price—for a specific client's branded product or service. With these e-mailed discounts, Groupon offers client firms three benefits: increased consumer exposure to the brand, the ability to price-discriminate, and the creation of a "buzz factor." Groupon takes 40 percent to 50 percent of the revenues in each deal in the process. Many promotions are offered on behalf of local retailers such as spas, fitness centers, and restaurants, but Groupon also manages deals on behalf of some national brands. Some businesses have complained that Groupon attracts only deal-seekers and is not effective in converting them to regular customers. One study found that 32 percent of companies lost money and that 40 percent said they would not utilize such a promotion again, with restaurants faring the worst among service businesses and with spas and salons being the most successful. Groupon has tried to innovate in several ways. Leveraging its massive sales force to sell Groupon Now, the company enlists local businesses to offer time- and location-specific deals via the Web or smartphones. The iPhone app for the new service has two buttons, "I'm Bored" and "I'm Hungry," to trigger deals in real time. For businesses, the service is a way to boost traffic at otherwise slow times. Even a popular restaurant might still consider some mid-day and mid-week discounts, knowing it is rarely full then. After a hyped IPO, Groupon's stock has not performed well, and the company is still struggling to find the right business formula.[4]

>> Via a daily deal to its large subscriber base, Groupon attempts to help businesses, many of them local, tap into the burgeoning online market in exchange for a hefty percentage of sales.

Source: seewhatmitchsee/Alamy Stock Photo

In addition to empowering buyers, the internet also enables sellers to optimize their pricing. Thus, sellers now can monitor market demand and adjust prices accordingly. For example, Uber is using "surge" pricing, charging higher fares at times of high demand. In addition, companies are now able to offer custom-tailored sales promotions based on the profile of a given market segment or an individual buyer. Online retailers such as Amazon, Wayfair, and Target offer promotional incentives to consumers based on their demographic, psychographic, and behavioral characteristics. Likewise, many brick-and-mortar retail outlets use geolocation to offer promotions to customers who are in close proximity to the store.

Companies vary in the way they set their pricing. In many small companies, the owner sets prices. In large companies, division and product line managers do. Even here, top management sets general pricing objectives and policies and often approves lower management's proposals.

Where pricing is a key competitive factor, companies often establish a pricing department to set, or assist others in setting, appropriate prices. This department reports to the marketing department, the finance department, or top management. Others who influence pricing include sales managers, production managers, finance managers, and accountants. In B2B settings, pricing performance tends to improve when pricing authority is spread horizontally across the sales, marketing, and finance units and when there is a balance in centralizing and delegating that authority between individual salespeople and teams and central management.[5]

Many companies do not handle pricing well and fall back on "strategies" such as "We calculate our costs and add our industry's traditional margins." Other common mistakes are not revising prices often enough to capitalize on market changes; setting prices independently of the rest of the marketing program, rather than as an intrinsic element of market-positioning strategy; and not varying prices enough for different product items, market segments, distribution channels, and purchase occasions.

For any organization, effectively designing and implementing pricing strategies requires a thorough understanding of buyers' pricing psychology and a systematic approach to setting, adapting, and changing prices.

Consumer Psychology and Pricing

Many economists traditionally assumed that consumers were "price takers" who accepted prices at face value or as a given. Marketers, however, recognize that consumers often actively process price information, interpreting it in the context of prior purchasing experience, formal communication (advertising, sales calls, and brochures), informal communication (friends, colleagues, or family members), point-of-purchase or online resources, and other factors.[6]

Purchase decisions are based on how consumers perceive prices and what they consider the current actual price to be—*not* on the marketer's stated price. Customers may have a lower price threshold, below which prices signal inferior or unacceptable quality, and an upper price threshold, above which prices are prohibitive and the product seems not to be worth the money. Different people interpret prices in different ways.

Consider the consumer psychology involved in buying a simple pair of jeans and a T-shirt. Why does a black T-shirt for women that looks pretty ordinary cost $275 from Armani but only $14.90 from the Gap and $7.90 from Swedish discount clothing chain H&M? Customers who purchase the Armani T-shirt are paying for a more stylishly cut T-shirt made of 70 percent nylon, 25 percent polyester, and 5 percent elastane with a "Made in Italy" label from a luxury brand known for suits, handbags, and evening gowns that sell for thousands of dollars. The Gap and H&M shirts are made mainly of cotton. Choices abound for pants to go with these T-shirts. The Gap sells its "Original Khakis" for $44.50, whereas Abercrombie & Fitch's classic button-fly chinos cost $70. But that's a comparative bargain compared to Michael Bastian's plain khakis for $480 or Giorgio Armani's for $595. High-priced designer jeans may use expensive fabrics such as cotton gabardine and require hours of meticulous hand-stitching to create a distinctive design, but equally important are the image and the sense of exclusivity they come with.[7]

Understanding how consumers arrive at their perceptions of prices is an important marketing priority. Here we consider three topics pertaining to the psychology of pricing—reference prices, image pricing, and pricing cues.

Reference Prices. Although consumers may have fairly good knowledge of price ranges, surprisingly few can accurately recall specific prices. When examining products, however, they often employ **reference prices**, comparing an observed price to an internal reference price they remember or an external frame

>> Abercrombie & Fitch's consumer image enables it to charge higher prices than many of its rivals.

of reference such as a posted "regular retail price."[8] Possible reference prices include "fair price" (what consumers feel the product should cost), typical price, last price paid, upper-bound price (reservation price, or the maximum most consumers would pay), lower-bound price (lower price threshold, or the minimum most consumers would pay), competitor price, expected future price, and usual discounted price.[9]

Sellers often attempt to manipulate reference prices. For example, a seller can situate its product among expensive competitors to imply that it belongs in the same class. Department stores will display women's apparel in separate departments differentiated by price; dresses in the more expensive department are assumed to be of better quality.[10] Marketers also encourage reference-price thinking by stating a high manufacturer's suggested price, indicating that the price was much higher originally, or by pointing to a competitor's high price.

When consumers evoke one or more of these frames of reference, their perceived price can vary from the stated price. Research has found that unpleasant surprises—when perceived price is lower than the stated price—can have a greater impact on purchase likelihood than pleasant surprises.[11] Consumer expectations can also play a key role in price response. On internet auction sites such as eBay, when consumers know similar goods will be available in future auctions, they will bid less in the current auction.[12]

Clever marketers try to frame the price to signal the best value possible. For example, a relatively expensive item can look less expensive if the price is broken into smaller units, such as a $600 annual membership for "$50 a month," even though the totals are the same.[13]

Image Pricing. Many consumers use price as an indicator of quality. **Image pricing** is especially effective with ego-sensitive products such as perfumes, expensive cars, and designer clothing. A $100 bottle of perfume might contain $10 worth of scent, but gift givers pay $100 to communicate their high regard for the recipient.

Price and quality perceptions of cars interact. Higher-priced cars are perceived to possess high quality. Higher-quality cars are likewise perceived to be higher priced than they actually are. When information about true quality is available, price becomes a less significant indicator of quality. When this information is not available, price acts as a signal of quality.

Some brands adopt exclusivity and scarcity to signify uniqueness and justify premium pricing. Luxury-goods makers of watches, jewelry, perfume, and other products often emphasize exclusivity in their communication messages and channel strategies. High prices may actually increase demand among luxury-goods customers who desire uniqueness, because they then believe fewer other customers can afford the products.[14]

To maintain its air of exclusivity, Ferrari deliberately restricts sales of its iconic, $200,000-plus Italian sports car to below 7,000 despite growing demand in China, the Middle East, and the United States. But even exclusivity and status can vary by customer. Brahma beer is a no-frills light brew in its home market of Brazil but has thrived in Europe, where it is seen as "Brazil in a bottle." Pabst Blue Ribbon is a retro favorite among U.S. college students, but its sales have exploded in China, where an

Source: Ian Shaw/Alamy Stock Photo

<< Despite booming demand, Ferrari limits production and the number of sports cars that it sells to maintain the brand's exclusivity.

upgraded bottle and claims of being "matured in a precious wooden cask like a Scotch whiskey" allow it to command a $44 price tag.[15]

Pricing Cues. **Pricing cues** are also important in the psychology of pricing. Many sellers believe prices should end in an odd number. Customers perceive an item priced at $299 to be in the $200 rather than the $300 range; they tend to process prices "left to right" rather than by rounding. Price encoding in this fashion is important if there is a mental price break at the higher, rounded price.

Another explanation for the popularity of "9" endings is that they suggest a discount or bargain, so if a company wants a high-price image, it should probably avoid the odd-ending tactic. One study showed that demand actually increased when the price of a dress *rose* from $34 to $39 but was unchanged when it rose from $34 to $44.[16]

Prices that end with 0 and 5 are also popular and are thought to be easier for consumers to process and retrieve from memory. "Sale" signs next to prices spur demand, but only if not overused. Thus total category sales are highest when some—but not all—items in a category have sale signs; past a certain point, sale signs may cause total category sales to fall.[17]

Pricing cues such as sale signs and prices that end in 9 are more influential when consumers' price knowledge is poor; when they purchase the item infrequently or are new to the category; and when product designs vary over time, prices vary seasonally, or quality or sizes vary across stores.[18] They are less effective the more they are used. Limited availability (for example, "three days only") also can spur sales among consumers actively shopping for a product.[19]

Setting the Price

A firm must set a price for the first time when it develops a new product, when it introduces its regular product into a new distribution channel or geographic area, and when it enters bids on new contract work. The firm must decide where to position its product on quality and price.[20]

Most markets have three to five price points or tiers. Marriott Hotels is good at developing different brands or variations of brands for different price points: JW Marriott (highest price), Marriott Marquis (high price), Marriott (high-medium price), Renaissance (medium-high price), Courtyard (medium price), TownePlace Suites (medium-low price), and Fairfield Inn (low price). Firms devise their branding strategies to help convey to consumers the price–quality tiers of their products or services.[21]

The firm must consider many factors in setting its pricing policy. The pricing process involves six main steps: defining the pricing objective; determining demand; estimating costs; analyzing competitors' costs, prices, and offers; selecting a pricing method; and setting the final price.

DEFINING THE PRICING OBJECTIVE

An offering's price is determined by a firm's overall pricing objective. The clearer a firm's objective, the easier it is to set price. Four common pricing objectives are current profit, market penetration, market skimming, and quality leadership.

- **Short-term profit.** Many companies try to set a price that will *maximize current profits.* They estimate the demand and costs associated with alternative prices and choose the price that produces maximum current profit, cash flow, or rate of return on investment. This strategy assumes the firm knows its demand and cost functions, but in reality, these are difficult to estimate. Furthermore, in emphasizing current performance, the company may sacrifice long-run performance by ignoring the effects of other marketing variables, competitors' reactions, and legal restraints on price.
- **Market penetration.** Companies that choose **penetration pricing** want to *maximize their market share.* They believe a higher sales volume will lead to lower unit costs and higher long-run profit, so they set a very low price, assuming the market is price sensitive. Texas Instruments famously practiced this market-penetration pricing for years. The company would build a large plant, set its price as low as possible, win a large market share, experience falling costs, and cut its price further as costs fell.

  The following conditions favor adopting a market-penetration pricing strategy: (1) the market is highly price sensitive, and a low price stimulates market growth; (2) production and distribution costs fall with accumulated production experience; and (3) a low price discourages actual and potential competition.
- **Market skimming.** Companies unveiling a new technology favor setting high prices to *maximize market skimming*. In **market skimming**, a company is setting a relatively high price in an attempt to "skim the cream" off the market by making the offering affordable only to customers with the highest willingness to pay. Sony has been a frequent practitioner of market-skimming pricing, in which prices start high and slowly drop over time.

  Market skimming is beneficial under the following conditions: (1) a sufficient number of buyers signal a high current demand; (2) the high initial price does not attract more competitors to the market; and (3) the high price communicates the image of a superior product.
- **Quality leadership.** A company might aim to be the *quality leader* in the market. To maintain quality leadership, a company must charge a relatively high price in order to be able to invest in research and development, production, and service delivery. Brands such as Starbucks, Aveda, Victoria's Secret, BMW, and Viking have positioned themselves as quality leaders in their categories, combining quality, luxury, and premium prices with an intensely loyal customer base. Grey Goose and Absolut carved out a super-premium niche in the essentially odorless, colorless, and tasteless vodka category through clever on-premise and off-premise marketing that made the brands seem hip and exclusive.

Nonprofit and public organizations may have other pricing objectives. A university aims for partial cost recovery, knowing that it must rely on private gifts and public grants to cover its remaining costs. A nonprofit hospital may aim for full cost recovery in its pricing. A nonprofit theater company may price its productions to fill the maximum number of seats. A social service agency may set a service price geared to client income.

Whatever the specific objective, businesses that use price as a strategic tool will profit more than those that simply let costs or the market determine their pricing. For art museums, which earn an average of only 5 percent of their revenues from admission charges, pricing can send a message that affects their public image and the amount of donations and sponsorships they receive.

DETERMINING DEMAND

Each price will lead to a different level of demand and have a different impact on a company's marketing objectives. The normally inverse relationship between price and demand is captured in a demand curve: The higher the price, the lower the demand. For prestige goods, the demand curve sometimes slopes upward. Some consumers take the higher price to signify a better product. However, if the price is too high, demand may fall.

To estimate the demand for a company's offering, marketers need to know how responsive, or elastic, demand is to a change in price. **Price elasticity of demand** reflects the degree to which a change in price leads to a change in quantity sold. The lower the price elasticity, the less sensitive consumers are to price increases, and the more likely it is that raising the price can increase sales revenues.[22]

Consider the two demand curves in Figure 11.1. In demand curve (a), a price increase from $10 to $15 leads to a relatively small decline in demand from 105 to 100. In demand curve (b), the same price increase leads to a substantial drop in demand from 150 to 50. If demand hardly changes with a

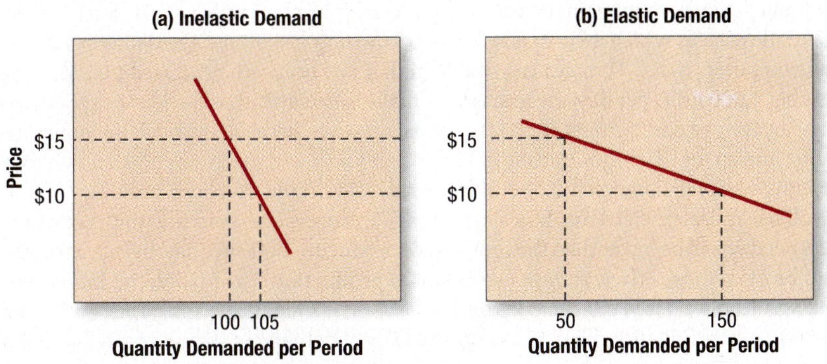

FIGURE **11.1**
Inelastic and Elastic Demand

small change in price, we say it is *inelastic*. If demand changes considerably in response to changes in price, it is *elastic*.

The higher the elasticity, the greater the volume growth resulting from a 1 percent price reduction. If demand is elastic, sellers will consider lowering the price to produce more total revenue. This makes sense as long as the costs of producing and selling more units do not increase disproportionately.

Price elasticity of demand depends on the magnitude and direction of the contemplated price change. It may be negligible with a small price change and substantial with a large price change. It may differ for a price cut than for a price increase, and there may be a **price indifference band** within which price changes have little or no effect.

Long-run price elasticity may differ from short-run elasticity. Buyers may continue to buy from a current supplier after a price increase but eventually switch suppliers; here demand is more elastic in the long run than in the short run. Or the reverse may happen: Buyers may drop a supplier after a price increase but return later. The distinction between short-run and long-run elasticity means that sellers will not know the total effect of a price change until time passes.

Generally speaking, price elasticity is low when (1) the product is distinctive and there are few or no substitutes or competitors; (2) consumers do not readily notice the higher price; (3) consumers are slow to change their buying habits; (4) consumers think the higher prices are justified by factors such as the cost of creating the product, product scarcity, and government taxation; (5) the expenditure is a smaller part of the buyer's total income or of the total cost of the end product; and (6) part or all of the cost is borne by another party.[23]

One comprehensive review of a 40-year period of academic research on price elasticity found that the average price elasticity across all products, markets, and time periods studied was –2.62.[24] In other words, a 1 percent decrease in prices led to a 2.62 percent increase in sales. Furthermore, price elasticity was higher for durable goods than for other goods and was higher for products in the introduction/growth stages of the product life cycle than for products in the mature/decline stages. Finally, promotional price elasticities were higher than actual price elasticities in the short run (although the reverse was true in the long run).

ESTIMATING COSTS

Demand sets a ceiling on the price the company can charge for its product. Costs set the floor. The company wants to charge a price that covers its cost of producing, distributing, and selling the product, including a fair return for its effort and risk.

Fixed, Variable, and Total Costs. A company's costs take two forms: fixed and variable. **Fixed costs** are costs that do not vary with production level or sales revenue. A company must pay bills each month for rent, heat, interest, salaries, and so on, regardless of output.

Variable costs vary directly with the level of production. For example, each tablet computer produced by Samsung incurs the cost of plastic and glass, microprocessor chips and other electronics, and packaging. These costs tend to be constant per unit produced, but they're called variable because their total varies with the number of units produced.

Total costs consist of the sum of the fixed and variable costs for any given level of production. **Average cost** is the cost per unit at that level of production; it equals total costs divided by production. Management wants to charge a price that will at least cover the total production costs at a given level of production.

To price intelligently, management needs to know how its costs vary with different levels of production. Take the case in which a company such as Samsung has built a fixed-size plant to produce 1,000 tablet computers a day. The cost per unit is high if few units are produced per day. As production approaches 1,000 units per day, the average cost falls because the fixed costs are spread over more units. Short-run average cost *increases* after 1,000 units, however, because the plant becomes inefficient: Workers must line up for machines, getting in each other's way, and machines break down more often.

If Samsung believes it can sell 2,000 units per day, it should consider building a larger plant. The plant will use more efficient machinery and work arrangements, and the unit cost of producing 2,000 tablets per day will be lower than the unit cost of producing 1,000 per day. In fact, a 3,000-capacity plant would be even more efficient, but a 4,000-daily production plant would be less so because of increasing diseconomies of scale: There are too many workers to manage, and paperwork slows things down. A 3,000-daily production plant is the optimal size if demand is strong enough to support this level of production.

There are more costs than those associated with manufacturing. To estimate the real profitability of selling to different types of retailers or customers, the manufacturer needs to use activity-based cost accounting instead of standard cost accounting.

Experience Curve Effects. Suppose Samsung runs a plant that produces 3,000 tablet computers per day. As the company gains experience producing tablets, its methods improve. Workers learn shortcuts, materials flow more smoothly, and procurement costs fall. The result is that average cost falls with accumulated production experience. Thus the average cost of producing the first 100,000 tablets is $100 per tablet, but when the company has produced the first 200,000 tablets, the average cost has fallen to $90. After its accumulated production experience doubles again to 400,000, the average cost is $80. This decline in the average cost with accumulated production experience is called the **experience curve**.

Now suppose three firms compete in this particular tablet market: Samsung, Firm A, and Firm B. Samsung is the lowest-cost producer at $80, having produced 400,000 units in the past. If all three firms sell the tablet for $100, Samsung makes a $20 profit per unit, A makes $10 per unit, and B breaks even. The smart move for Samsung would be to lower its price to $90. This will drive B out of the market, and even A may consider leaving. Samsung will pick up the business that would have gone to B (and possibly A). Furthermore, price-sensitive customers will enter the market at the lower price. As production increases beyond 400,000 units, Samsung's costs will drop still further and faster, more than restoring its profits, even at a price of $90.

Experience-curve pricing nevertheless carries major risks. Aggressive pricing might give the product a cheap image. It also assumes competitors are weak followers. The strategy leads the company to build more plants to meet demand, but a competitor may choose to innovate with a lower-cost technology. The market leader is now stuck with the old technology.

Most experience-curve pricing has focused on manufacturing costs, but all costs can be improved on, including marketing costs. If three firms are each investing a large sum of money in marketing, the firm that has been doing it longest might achieve the lowest costs. This firm can charge a little less for its product and still earn the same return, all other costs being equal.

ANALYZING COMPETITORS' PRICES

Within the range of possible prices identified by market demand and company costs, the firm must take competitors' costs, prices, and possible reactions into account. If the firm's offer contains features not offered by the nearest competitor, it should evaluate their worth to the customer and add that value to the competitor's price. If the competitor's offer contains some features not offered by the firm, the firm should subtract their value from its own price. Now the firm can decide whether it can charge more than, the same as, or less than the competitor.[25]

Companies offering the powerful combination of low price and high quality are capturing the hearts and wallets of consumers all over the world.[26] Value players such as Aldi, Lidl, JetBlue Airways, and Southwest Airlines are transforming the way consumers of nearly every age and income level purchase groceries, apparel, airline tickets, financial services, and other goods and services.

Traditional players are right to feel threatened. Upstart firms often rely on serving one or a few consumer segments, providing better delivery or just one additional benefit, and matching low prices with highly efficient operations to keep costs down. They have changed consumer expectations about the trade-off between quality and price.

One school of thought is that companies should set up their own low-cost operations to compete with value-priced competitors only if (1) their existing businesses will become more competitive as a result and (2) the new business will derive some advantages it would not have gained if it were independent.[27]

Low-cost operations set up by HSBC, ING, Merrill Lynch, and Royal Bank of Scotland—First Direct, ING Direct, ML Direct, and Direct Line Insurance, respectively—succeed in part thanks to synergies between the old and new lines of business. Major airlines have also introduced their own low-cost carriers. But Continental's Lite, KLM's Buzz, SAS's Snowflake, and United's Ted have all been unsuccessful, partly because of a lack of synergies. The low-cost operation must be designed and launched as a moneymaker in its own right, not just as a defensive play.

SELECTING A PRICING METHOD

Given the customers' demand schedule, the cost function, and competitors' prices, the company is now ready to select a pricing method. There are three major considerations in price setting: costs, competitors, and customers. Costs set a floor for the price. Competitors' prices and the price of substitutes provide an orienting point. Customers' assessment of unique features establishes the price ceiling.

Companies select a pricing method that includes one or more of these three considerations. We will examine five price-setting methods: markup pricing, target-rate-of-return pricing, economic-value-to-customer pricing, competitive pricing, and auction-type pricing.

Markup Pricing. The most elementary pricing method, **markup pricing**, is to add a standard markup to the product's cost. Construction companies submit job bids by estimating the total project cost and adding a standard markup for profit. Lawyers and accountants typically price by adding a standard markup on their time and costs.

Suppose a toaster manufacturer has the following costs and sales expectations:

Variable cost per unit	\$ 10
Fixed costs	\$300,000
Expected unit sales	50,000

The manufacturer's unit cost is then given by

$$\text{Unit cost} = \text{variable cost} + \frac{\text{fixed cost}}{\text{unit sales}} = \$10 + \frac{\$300{,}00}{\$50{,}000} = \$16$$

Now assume the manufacturer wants to earn a 20 percent markup on sales. The manufacturer's markup price is given by

$$\text{Markup price} = \frac{\text{unit cost}}{(1 - \text{desired return on sales})} = \frac{\$16}{1-0.2} = \$20$$

The manufacturer will charge dealers \$20 per toaster and make a profit of \$4 per unit. If dealers want to earn 50 percent on their selling price, they will mark up the toaster 100 percent to \$40. Markups are generally higher on seasonal items (to cover the risk of not selling), specialty items, slower moving items, items with high storage and handling costs, and demand-inelastic items, such as prescription drugs.

Does the use of standard markups make logical sense? Generally, no. After all, buyers often do not care about a manufacturer's costs. In fact, any pricing method that ignores current demand, perceived value, and competition is not likely to lead to the optimal price. Still, markup pricing remains popular. First, sellers can determine costs much more easily than they can estimate demand. By tying the price to cost, sellers simplify the pricing task. Second, when all firms in the industry use this pricing method, prices tend to be similar and price competition is minimized. Third, many people feel cost-plus pricing is fairer to both buyers and sellers. Sellers do not take advantage of buyers when the latter's demand becomes acute, and sellers earn a fair return on investment.

Target-Rate-of-Return Pricing. In **target-rate-of-return pricing** (or target-return pricing), the firm starts with a rate-of-return objective (e.g., 10 percent of sales revenue) and then sets a price that will yield the desired rate of return. Because it does not take into account customer demand and competitive offerings, target-rate-of-return pricing is often used in regulated industries. For example, public utilities, which need to make a fair return on investment, often use this method.

Suppose the toaster manufacturer has invested $1 million in the business and wants to set a price to earn a 20 percent ROI, specifically $200,000. The target-return price is given by the following formula:

$$\text{Target@return price} = \text{unit cost} + \frac{\text{desired return} \times \text{invested capital}}{\text{unit sales}}$$

$$= \$16 + \frac{.20 \times \$1{,}000{,}000}{50{,}000} = \$20$$

The manufacturer will realize this 20 percent ROI, provided its costs and estimated sales turn out to be accurate. But what if sales don't reach 50,000 units? The manufacturer can prepare a break-even chart to learn what would happen at other sales levels (see Figure 11.2). Fixed costs are $300,000 regardless of sales volume. Variable costs, not shown in the figure, rise with volume. Total costs equal the sum of fixed and variable costs. The total revenue curve starts at zero and rises with each unit sold.

The total revenue and total cost curves cross at 30,000 units. This is the break-even volume. We can verify it by the following formula:

$$\text{Break@even volume} = \frac{\text{fixed cost}}{(\text{price} - \text{variable cost})} = \frac{\$300{,}000}{\$20 - \$10} = 30{,}000$$

The manufacturer, of course, is hoping the market will buy 50,000 units at $20, in which case it will earn $200,000 on its $1 million investment; however, much depends on price elasticity and competitors' prices. Unfortunately, target-return pricing tends to ignore these considerations. The manufacturer needs to consider different prices and estimate their probable impacts on sales volume and profits.

Economic-Value-to-Customer Pricing. An increasing number of companies now base their price on the customer's economic value. **Economic-value-to-customer pricing** takes into account a host of inputs, such as the buyer's image of the product performance, the channel deliverables, the warranty quality, customer support, and softer attributes such as the supplier's reputation, trustworthiness, and esteem. Companies must deliver the value promised by their value proposition, and the customer must perceive this value. Firms use the other marketing program elements, such as advertising, the sales force, and the internet, to communicate and enhance perceived value in buyers' minds.

A seller can successfully charge a higher price than competitors if it can convince customers that it offers the lowest total cost of ownership. Marketers often treat the service elements in a product offering as sales incentives rather than as value-enhancing augmentations for which they can charge.

FIGURE **11.2**
Break-Even Chart for Determining Target-Return Price and Break-Even Volume

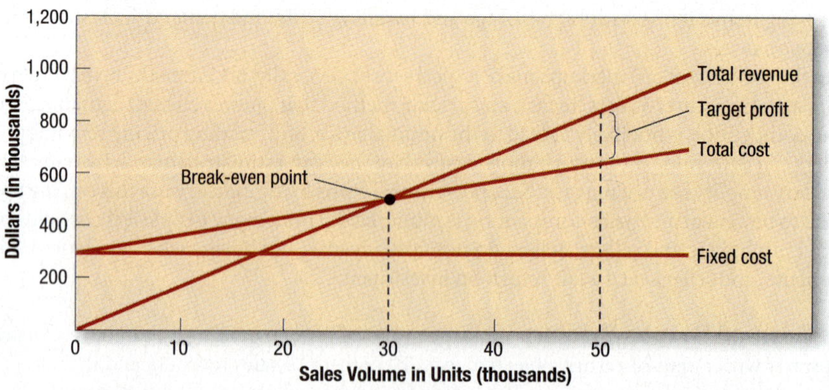

In fact, one of the most common mistakes manufacturers tend to made is to offer all sorts of services to differentiate their products without charging for them.

Caterpillar uses perceived value to set prices on its construction equipment. It might price its tractor at $100,000, even though a similar competitor's tractor might be priced at $90,000. When a prospective customer asks a Caterpillar dealer why he or she should pay $10,000 more for the Caterpillar tractor, the dealer explains as follows:

$ 90,000	is the tractor's price if it is only equivalent to the competitor's tractor
$ 7,000	is the price premium for Caterpillar's superior durability
$ 6,000	is the price premium for Caterpillar's superior reliability
$ 5,000	is the price premium for Caterpillar's superior service
$ 2,000	is the price premium for Caterpillar's longer warranty on parts
$110,000	is the normal price to cover Caterpillar's superior value
	Discount
–$ 10,000	
$100,000	final price

The Caterpillar dealer is able to show that although customers are asked to pay a $10,000 premium for this tractor, they are actually getting $20,000 extra value! The customer chooses the Caterpillar tractor because he or she is convinced that its lifetime operating costs will be lower.

Ensuring that customers appreciate the total value of a product or service offering is crucial. Consider the experience of Buhler.

Bühler A leading global food processing company, Bühler is a trusted solutions provider known for its value-added services and solutions. Bühler Insights is a connected platform that optimizes a plant's efficiency by reducing maintenance times, energy consumption, and wastage for customers. Bühler Insights generates higher returns from plants with a structured approach that increases yield and thereby improves revenues. The Insights Gateway connects machines in the plant to the Insights Platform. An integrated dashboard provides secure access to real-time plant performance with analysis of historical data and trend detection. Troubleshooting and instant support minimize interruptions to production. These and other value-added solutions from Bühler help the company justify its pricing while maintaining a competitive advantage.[28]

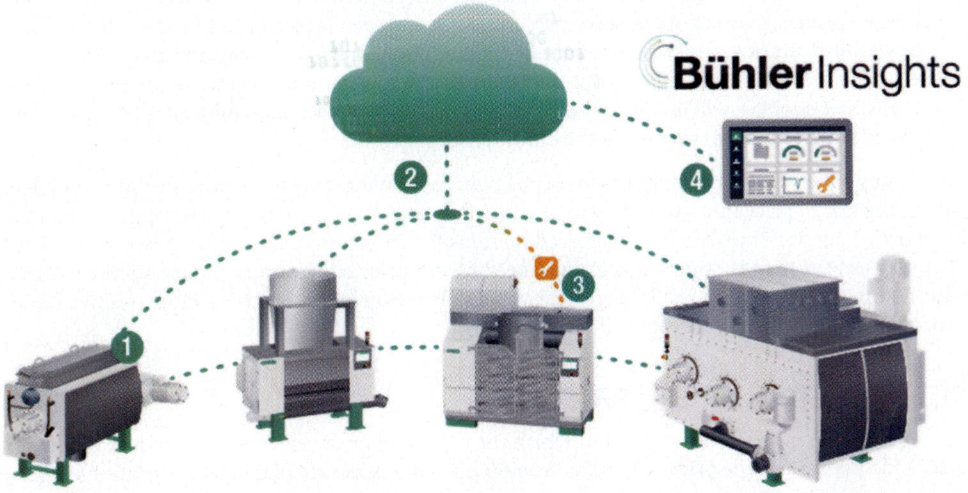

<< The additional value provided by Bühler Insights reinforces the brand's premium positioning and pricing while retaining its competitive edge.

Source: Buhler, used with permission

Even when a company claims its offering delivers more total value, not all customers will respond positively. Some care only about price. But there is also typically a segment that cares about quality. Umbrellas are essential during the three months of near-nonstop monsoon rain in Indian cities such as Mumbai, and the makers of Stag umbrellas there found themselves in a bitter price war with cheaper Chinese competitors. After realizing that they were sacrificing quality too much, Stag's managers decided to increase quality with new colors, new designs, and features such as built-in high-power flashlights and prerecorded music. Despite higher prices, sales of the improved Stag umbrellas actually increased.[29]

The key to economic-value-to-customer pricing is to deliver more unique value than competitors and to demonstrate this to prospective buyers. Thus, a company needs to fully understand the customer's decision-making process. For example, Goodyear found it hard to command a price premium for its more expensive new tires, despite innovative features to extend tread life. Because consumers had no reference price to compare tires, they tended to gravitate toward the lowest-priced offerings. Goodyear's solution was to price its models on the basis of expected miles of wear, rather than their technical product features, making product comparisons easier.[30]

Competitive Pricing. In **competitive pricing** (or going-rate pricing), the firm bases its price largely on competitors' prices. All firms in industries that sell a commodity such as steel, paper, or fertilizer normally charge the same price. Smaller firms "follow the leader," changing their prices when the market leader's prices change, rather than when their own demand or costs change. Some may charge a small premium or discount, but they preserve the difference. Thus, minor gasoline retailers usually charge a few cents less per gallon than the major oil companies, without letting the difference increase or decrease. Competitive pricing is quite popular. Where costs vary and/or are difficult to measure, when the demand fluctuates, or when competitive response is uncertain, firms feel competitive pricing is a good solution because they believe it reflects the industry's collective wisdom.

Auction Pricing. **Auction pricing** is growing more popular, especially with scores of electronic marketplaces selling everything from pigs to used cars, as firms dispose of excess inventories or used goods. Here are the three major types of auctions and their separate pricing procedures:[31]

- **English auctions (ascending bids)** have one seller and many buyers. On sites such as eBay and Amazon.com, the seller puts up an item and bidders raise their offer prices until the top price is reached. The highest bidder gets the item. English auctions are used today for selling antiques, cattle, real estate, and used equipment and vehicles. Kodak and Nortel sold hundreds of patents for wireless and digital imaging via auctions, raising hundreds of millions of dollars.[32]
- **Dutch auctions (descending bids)** feature one seller and many buyers or one buyer and many sellers. In the first kind, an auctioneer announces a high price for a product and then slowly decreases the price until a bidder accepts. In the other, the buyer announces something he or she wants to buy, and potential sellers compete to offer the lowest price. SAP Ariba runs business-to-business auctions to help companies acquire low-priced items as varied as steel, fats, oils, name badges, pickles, plastic bottles, solvents, cardboard, and even legal and janitorial work.[33]
- **Sealed-bid auctions** let would-be suppliers submit only one bid without any knowledge of the other bids. The U.S. and other governments often use this method to procure supplies or grant licenses. A supplier will not bid below its cost but cannot bid too high for fear of losing the job. The net effect of these two pulls is the bid's *expected profit*.[34]

To buy equipment for its drug researchers, Pfizer uses online reverse auctions in which suppliers submit the lowest price they are willing to be paid. If the increased savings that a buying firm obtains in an online auction translate into decreased margins for an incumbent supplier, however, the supplier may feel the firm is opportunistically squeezing out price concessions. Online auctions with a large number of bidders can result in greater overall satisfaction for both parties, more positive future expectations, and fewer perceptions of opportunism.[35]

SETTING THE FINAL PRICE

Pricing methods narrow the range from which the company must select its final price. Companies usually do not set a single price but rather develop a pricing structure that reflects variations in geographic demand and costs, market-segment requirements, purchase timing, order levels, delivery frequency, guarantees, service contracts, and other factors. As a result of discounts, allowances, and promotional support, a company rarely realizes the same profit from each unit of a product that it sells.

The phenomenon of offering different pricing schedules to different consumers and dynamically adjusting prices is exploding. Merchants are adjusting process based on inventory levels, item velocity (how fast an item sells), competitors' pricing, and advertising. Even sports teams are adjusting ticket prices to reflect the popularity of the competitor and the timing of the game. Online merchants that sell their products on Amazon.com are changing their prices on an hourly or even minute-by-minute basis, in part so they can secure the top spot on search results.

Price discrimination occurs when a company sells a product or service at two or more prices that do not reflect a proportional difference in costs. In *first-degree price discrimination*, the seller charges each customer a separate price, depending on the intensity of his or her demand. In *second-degree price discrimination*, the seller charges less to buyers of larger volumes. With certain services such as cell phone service, however, tiered pricing results in consumers actually paying *more* with higher levels of usage.

In *third-degree price discrimination*, the seller charges different amounts to different consumer segments, as in the following cases:[36]

- **Customer-segment pricing.** Different customer segments pay different prices for the same product or service. For example, museums often charge a lower admission fee to students and senior citizens. When online travel agency Orbitz found that people using Apple Mac computers spent as much as 30 percent more a night on hotels, it began to show them different—and sometimes costlier—travel options than Windows users saw. Orbitz also considers a user's location and history on the site, as a well as a hotel's overall popularity and promotions.[37]
- **Product-form pricing.** Different versions of the product are priced differently, but not in proportion to their costs. Evian prices a 2-liter bottle of its mineral water as low as $1 but sells 5 ounces of the same water in a moisturizer spray for as much as $12.
- **Channel pricing.** Coca-Cola carries a different price depending on whether the consumer purchases it from a fine restaurant, a fast-food restaurant, or a vending machine.
- **Location pricing.** The same product is priced differently at different locations, even though the cost of offering it is the same at all locations. A theater varies its seat prices according to audience preferences for different locations. Some firms store computer IP addresses and zip codes and use their proximity to a competitor's store to adjust their prices.
- **Time pricing.** Prices vary by season, day, or hour. Restaurants charge "early bird" customers less, and some hotels charge less on weekends. Retail prices for roses increase by as much as 200 percent in the lead-up to Valentine's Day.

The airline and hospitality industries use yield management systems and yield pricing, by which they offer discounted but limited early purchases, higher prices for late purchases, and the lowest rates for unsold inventory just before it expires. Airlines charge different fares to passengers on the same flight, depending on the seating class; the time of day (morning or night coach); the day of the week (workday or weekend); the season; the person's employer, past business, or status (youth, military, senior citizen); and so on. That's why, on a flight from New York City to Miami, you might pay $200 and sit across from someone who paid $1,290.

Constant price variation can be tricky, however, where consumer relationships are concerned. One way to make it work is to offer customers a unique bundle of products and services to meet their needs precisely, making it harder to make price comparisons. Another tactic that companies favor is to use variable prices as a reward rather than a penalty. Shipping company APL rewards customers who can better predict how much cargo space they'll need with cheaper rates for booking early.

Although some forms of price discrimination are illegal (such as offering different prices for the same item to different customers within the same trade group), the practice is legal if the seller can prove its costs are different when selling different volumes or different qualities of the same product to different retailers. Predatory pricing—selling below cost for the purpose of obliterating competition—is unlawful, however.

For price discrimination to work, certain conditions must exist. First, the market must be segmentable, and the segments must show different intensities of demand. Second, members in the lower-price segment must not be able to resell the product to the higher-price segment. Third, competitors must not be able to undersell the firm in the higher-price segment. Fourth, the cost of segmenting and policing the market must not exceed the extra revenue derived from price discrimination. Finally, the practice must not breed customer resentment and ill will.

PRODUCT-MIX PRICING

Marketers must modify their price-setting logic when the product is part of a product mix. In **product-mix pricing**, the firm searches for a set of prices that maximize profits on the total mix. The process is challenging, because the various products have demand and cost interrelationships and are subject to different degrees of competition. We can distinguish six main situations calling for product-mix pricing: loss-leader pricing, optional-feature pricing, captive-product pricing, two-part pricing, by-product pricing, and product-bundling pricing.

- **Loss-leader pricing.** A company can set the price of a specific product or service in a way that maximizes the profitability of its entire product line. A common product-line pricing approach is **loss-leader pricing**. Supermarkets and department stores often drop the price on well-known brands to stimulate additional store traffic. This approach pays if the revenue on the additional sales compensates for the lower margins on the loss-leader items. Manufacturers of brands that retailers use as loss leaders typically object, because this practice can dilute the brand image and bring complaints from retailers who charge the list price. Manufacturers have tried to keep intermediaries from using loss-leader pricing by lobbying for retail-price-maintenance laws, but these laws have been revoked.
- **Optional-feature pricing.** Many companies offer optional products, features, and services with their main product. The pricing of options is a sticky problem, because companies must decide which to include in the standard price and which to offer separately. Many restaurants price their beverages high and their food low. The food revenue covers costs, and the beverages—especially liquor—produce the profit. This explains why servers often press hard to get customers to order drinks. Other restaurants price their liquor low and their food high to draw in a drinking crowd.
- **Captive pricing.** Some products require the use of ancillary or captive products. Manufacturers of razors often price them low and set high markups on razor blades. Movie theaters and concert venues often make more from concessions and merchandise sales than from ticket receipts.[38] Verizon may give a free cell phone to the person who commits to buying two years of phone service. If the captive product is priced too high in the aftermarket, however, counterfeiting and substitutions can erode sales. Consumers now can buy cartridge refills for their printers from discount suppliers and save 20 percent to 30 percent off the manufacturer's price.
- **Two-part pricing.** Service firms engage in two-part pricing, consisting of a fixed fee plus a variable usage fee. Cell phone users may have to pay a minimum monthly fee plus charges for calls that exceed their allotted minutes. Amusement parks charge an admission fee plus fees for rides over a certain minimum. The service firm faces a problem similar to captive-product pricing—namely, how much to charge for the basic service and how much for the variable usage. The fixed fee should be low enough to induce purchase; profit can then come from the usage fees.
- **By-product pricing.** The production of certain goods—meats, petroleum products, and other chemicals—often yields by-products that should be priced on their value. Any income earned on the by-products will make it easier for the company to charge a lower price for its main product if competition forces it to do so. Formed in 1855, Australia's CSR was originally named Colonial Sugar Refining Company and forged its early reputation as a sugar company. The company began to sell by-products of its sugar cane; waste sugar cane fiber was used to manufacture wallboard. Today, through product development and acquisition, the renamed CSR has become one of the top 10 companies in Australia selling building and construction materials.
- **Product-bundling pricing.** Sellers often bundle products and features.[39] *Pure bundling* occurs when a firm offers its products only as a bundle. Providers of aftermarket products for automobiles increasingly are bundling their offerings in customizable three-in-one and four-in-one programs, especially second-tier products such as tire-and-wheel protection and paintless dent repair. A talent agency might insist that an in-demand actor can be signed to a film only if the film company also accepts other talent, such as directors or writers, that the agency represents. This is a form of *tied-in sales*. In *mixed bundling*, the seller offers goods both individually and in bundles, normally charging less for the bundle than if the items were purchased separately. A theater will price a season subscription lower than the cost of buying all the performances separately. Customers may not have planned to buy all the components, so savings on the price bundle must be enough to induce them to buy it.[40] Some customers want less than the whole bundle in exchange for a lower price.[41] These customers ask the seller to "unbundle" or "rebundle" its offer. If a supplier saves $100 by not supplying unwanted delivery and reduces the customer's price by $80, it has kept the customer happy while increasing its profit by $20.

Initiating and Responding to Price Changes

To gain market position, increase sales revenues, and grow profits, companies often take aggressive pricing actions, either lowering their prices, typically to lure competitors' customers, or raising prices to capture greater value from its current customers.

INITIATING PRICE CUTS

Several circumstances might lead a firm to cut prices. One is excess capacity: The firm needs additional business and cannot generate it through increased sales effort, product improvement, or other measures. Companies sometimes initiate price cuts in a drive to dominate the market through lower costs. Either the company starts with lower costs than its competitors, or it initiates price cuts in the hope of gaining market share and lower costs.

Cutting prices to keep customers or beat competitors often encourages customers to demand price concessions, however, and trains salespeople to offer them.[42] A price-cutting strategy can lead to other possible drawbacks, such as consumers assuming quality is low. Furthermore, low price buys market share but not market loyalty—the same customers will shift to any lower-priced firm that comes along. In addition, competitors might respond by lowering their prices even more, triggering a price war. There is also the possibility that higher-priced competitors will match the firm's lower prices but will have greater staying power because of lower cost structure.

Customers often question the motivation behind price changes.[43] They may assume that the item is about to be replaced by a new model, the item is faulty and is not selling well, the firm is in financial trouble, the price will come down even further, or the quality has been reduced. The firm must monitor these attributions carefully.

INITIATING PRICE INCREASES

A successful price increase can raise profits considerably. If the company's profit margin is 3 percent of sales, a 1 percent price increase will increase profits by 33 percent if sales volume is unaffected. Thus, if a company charged $10, sold 100 units, and had costs of $970, it generated a profit of $30, or 3 percent on sales. By raising its price by 10 cents (a 1 percent price increase), it could boost its profits by 33 percent, assuming the same sales volume.

A major circumstance provoking price increases is **cost inflation**, wherein rising costs unmatched by productivity gains squeeze profit margins and lead companies to regular rounds of price increases. Companies often raise their prices by more than the cost increase in anticipation of further inflation or government price controls, a practice called **anticipatory pricing**. Another factor leading to price increases is high demand that exceeds a company's production capabilities. When a company cannot supply all its customers, it can raise its prices, ration supplies, or both.

Although there is always a chance that a price increase can convey some positive meanings to customers—for example, that the item is "hot" and represents an unusually good value—consumers generally dislike higher prices. In passing price increases on to consumers, the company must avoid looking like a price gouger. Coca-Cola's proposed smart vending machines that would raise prices as temperatures rose and Amazon's dynamic pricing experiment that varied prices by purchase occasion both became front-page news. The more similar the products or offerings from a company, the more likely consumers are to interpret any pricing differences as unfair. Product customization and differentiation, as well as communications that clarify differences, are thus critical.[44]

Several techniques help avoid sticker shock and a hostile consumer reaction when prices rise. One is maintaining a sense of fairness, such as by giving consumers advance notice so they can do forward buying or shop around. Sharp price increases also need to be explained in understandable terms. Making low-visibility price moves first is also a good technique. Eliminating discounts, increasing minimum order sizes, and curtailing production of low-margin products are examples. And contracts or bids for long-term projects should contain escalator clauses based on such factors as increases in recognized national price indexes.

RESPONDING TO COMPETITORS' PRICE CHANGES

The introduction or change of any price can provoke a response from customers, competitors, distributors, suppliers, and even government. Competitors are most likely to react when the number of firms in the category is low, the product is homogeneous, and buyers are highly informed.

How can a firm anticipate a competitor's reactions? One way is to assume the competitor reacts in the standard way to a price being set or changed. Another is to assume that the competitor treats each price difference or change as a fresh challenge and reacts according to self-interest at the time. Now the company will need to research the competitor's current financial situation, recent sales, customer loyalty, and corporate objectives. If the competitor has a market share objective, it is likely to match price differences or changes.[45] If it has a profit-maximization objective, it may react by increasing its advertising budget or improving product quality.

The problem is complicated because the competitor can put different interpretations on lowered prices or a price cut: that the company is trying to steal the market, that it is doing poorly and trying to boost its sales, or that it wants the whole industry to reduce prices to stimulate total demand. When Walmart began to run ads claiming lower prices than Publix, the regional supermarket chain dropped its prices below Walmart's on roughly 500 essential items and launched its own advertising campaign in retaliation.[46]

How should a firm respond to a competitor's price cut? It depends on the situation. A firm needs to consider the following: (1) Why did the competitor change the price? To steal the market, to utilize excess capacity, to meet changing cost conditions, or to lead an industry-wide price change? (2) Does the competitor plan to make the price change temporary or permanent? (3) What will happen to the company's market share and profits if it does not respond? Are other companies going to respond? (4) What are the competitors' and other firms' likely responses to each possible reaction?

Market leaders often face aggressive price cutting by smaller firms trying to build market share. Using price, T-Mobile attacked AT&T and Verizon, AMD has attacked Intel, and Dollar Shave Club has attacked Gillette. Market leaders also face lower-priced store brands. Three possible responses to low-cost competitors are to further differentiate the product or service, to introduce a low-cost venture, or to reinvent oneself as a low-cost player.[47] The right strategy depends on the ability of the firm to generate more demand or cut costs.

An extended analysis of alternatives may not always be feasible when the attack occurs. The company may have to react decisively within hours or days, especially where prices change with some frequency and it is important to react quickly, such as in the meatpacking, lumber, or oil industries. It would make better sense to anticipate possible competitors' price changes and prepare contingent responses.

Managing Incentives

Incentives are sales promotion tools, mostly short-term, designed to stimulate quicker or greater purchase of particular products or services by consumers or the trade.[48]

INCENTIVES AS A MARKETING DEVICE

Sales promotion expenditure increased as a percentage of budget expenditure for a number of years, with the fastest-growing area being digital coupons and discounts, redeemed via smartphone or downloaded to a consumer's printer. Digital coupons eliminate printing costs, reduce paper waste, are easily updatable, and have higher redemption rates. Many retailers are now offering customized coupons based on consumer purchase histories.[49]

Sales promotions can produce a high sales response in the short run but little permanent gain over the longer term. Price promotions usually do not build permanent total-category volume. Having turned to zero percent financing, hefty cash rebates, and special lease programs during sluggish economic times, auto manufacturers have found it difficult to wean consumers from discounts ever since.[50] Sales promotions often prompt consumers to engage in stockpiling—purchasing earlier than usual (purchase acceleration) or buying extra quantities. As a result, after the initial peak, sales often hit a post-promotion dip.[51] And while their impact on sales is often temporary, incessant price reductions, coupons, deals, and premiums can have a longer-term negative impact by devaluing the company's offering in buyers' minds.

Not all sales promotions are detrimental to the company's brand image. Some sales promotion tools are *consumer franchise building*. They impart a selling message along with the deal, such as frequency awards, coupons that advertise product features, and premiums related to the product. Sales promotion tools that are typically *not* brand building include price-off packs, consumer premiums not related to a product, contests and sweepstakes, consumer refund offers, and trade allowances.

Promotional pricing has become the modus operandi of a large number of companies offering both products and services. Salespeople in particular are quick to give discounts to close a sale. But word can get around fast that the company's list price is "soft," and discounting becomes the norm, undermining the perceived value of the offerings. Some product categories self-destruct by always being on sale.

Some companies with overcapacity are tempted to give discounts or even begin to supply a retailer with a store-brand version of their product at a deep discount. Because the store brand is priced lower, however, it may start making inroads into sales of the manufacturer's brand. Manufacturers should consider the implications of supplying retailers at a discount, because they may end up losing long-run profits in an effort to meet short-run volume goals.

Managers need to monitor the proportion of customers receiving discounts, the average discount, and any tendency for salespeople to rely too heavily on discounting. To this end, managers should conduct a **net price analysis** to arrive at the "real price" of the offering. The real price is affected not only by discounts but also by other expenses that reduce the realized price. Suppose the company's list price is $3,000. The average discount is $300. The company's promotional spending averages $450 (15 percent of the list price). Retailers are given co-op advertising money of $150 to back the product. In this case the company's net price is $2,100, not $3,000.

MAJOR INCENTIVE DECISIONS

In using incentives, a company must establish its objectives, select the tools, develop the program, implement and control it, and evaluate the results.

Establishing the Objectives of Incentives. The objectives of incentives derive from basic marketing objectives for the offering. Depending on whether a manufacturer's promotional activity is focused on consumers or retailers, incentives have different objectives:

For *consumer* incentives, objectives include encouraging more frequent purchases or the purchase of larger-sized units among users, fostering trial of one's product among nonusers, and attracting switchers away from competitors' brands. If some of the brand switchers would not have otherwise tried the brand, incentives can yield long-term increases in market share.[52] Ideally, consumer incentives have short-run sales impact and long-run effects on brand equity.[53]

For *retailer* incentives, objectives include persuading the retailer or wholesaler to carry the brand; persuading the retailer or wholesaler to carry more units than the normal amount; inducing retailers to promote the brand by featuring, display, and price reductions; and motivating retailers and their sales clerks to push the product.

Defining the Size and Approach for Incentives. In deciding to use a particular incentive, marketers must first determine its *size*. The incentive must be meaningful to target customers if the promotion is to succeed. Second, the marketing manager must establish *conditions* for participation. Incentives might be offered to everyone or to select groups. Third, the marketer must decide on the *duration* of the promotion. Fourth, the marketer must choose a *distribution vehicle*. A 50-cents-off coupon can be distributed in the product package, in stores, by mail, online, or in advertising. Fifth, the marketing manager must establish the *timing* of the promotion. And finally, the *total sales promotion budget* must be set. The cost of a particular promotion consists of the administrative cost (printing, mailing, and promoting the deal) and the incentive cost (cost of premium or cents-off, including redemption costs), multiplied by the expected number of units sold. The cost of a coupon deal recognizes that only a fraction of consumers will redeem the coupons.

In addition to determining the size of incentives, a firm must decide how to allocate resources and, specifically, how much effort to devote to push activities and how much to pull activities.

A **push strategy** uses the manufacturer's sales force, trade promotion money, or other means to induce intermediaries to carry, promote, and sell the product to end users. This strategy is particularly appropriate when there is low brand loyalty in a category, brand choice is made in the store, the product is an impulse item, and product benefits are well understood.

In a **pull strategy** the manufacturer uses advertising, promotion, and other forms of communication to persuade consumers to demand the product from intermediaries, thus inducing the intermediaries to order it. This strategy is particularly appropriate when there is high brand loyalty and high involvement in the category, when consumers are able to perceive differences between brands, and when they choose the brand before they go to the store.

Top marketing companies such as Apple, Coca-Cola, and Nike skillfully employ both push *and* pull strategies. A push strategy is more effective when accompanied by a well-designed and well-executed pull strategy that activates consumer demand. On the other hand, without at least some consumer interest, it can be very difficult to gain much channel acceptance and support—and vice versa for that matter.

Selecting Consumer Incentives. The sales promotion planner should take into account the type of market, the sales promotion objectives, competitive conditions, and each tool's cost-effectiveness.[54] The main **consumer incentives** include the following:

- *Price reductions* are temporary price discounts that aim to foster sales. Price reductions can be initiated by the manufacturer seeking to increase sales or by the retailer trying to move the merchandise and clear the inventory. Price reductions can be framed in terms of specific monetary amounts or as a percentage.[55]
- *Coupons* are certificates entitling the bearer to a stated saving on the purchase of a specific product. They can be mailed, enclosed in or attached to other products, inserted in magazine and newspaper ads, e-mailed, or made available online.[56]
- *Cash refunds* provide a price reduction after purchase rather than at the retailer: The consumer sends a specified "proof of purchase" to the manufacturer, who "refunds" part of the purchase price by mail. Auto companies and other consumer-goods companies offer cash rebates to encourage purchase of the manufacturers' products within a specified time period. Rebates can help clear inventories without cutting the stated list price.[57]
- *Price packs* offer savings off the regular price of a product, flagged on the label or package. A *reduced-price pack* is a single package sold at a reduced price (such as two for the price of one). A *banded pack* is two related products banded together (such as a toothbrush and toothpaste).[58]
- *Premiums* (bonus offerings) are merchandise offered at a relatively low cost or free as an incentive to purchase a particular product. A premium can accompany the product (packed inside or affixed to the package), or it can be distributed via a different channel (such as by mail).
- *Frequency programs* provide rewards related to the consumer's frequency and intensity in purchasing the company's products or services.
- *Prizes* are offers of the chance to win cash, trips, or merchandise as a result of purchasing something. A *contest* calls for consumers to submit an entry to be examined by a panel of judges who will select the best entries. A *sweepstakes* asks consumers to submit their names in a drawing. A *game* presents consumers with something every time they buy—bingo numbers, missing letters—which might help them win a prize.[59]
- *Tie-in promotions* involve a scenario in which two or more brands or companies team up on coupons, refunds, and contests to increase pulling power.
- *Seasonal discounts* are price reductions for those who buy merchandise or services out of season. Hotels, motels, and airlines offer seasonal discounts in slow selling periods.
- *Financing* involves providing favorable financing terms in order to increase the attractiveness of an offering for consumers. Alternatively, sellers (especially mortgage banks and auto companies) offer extended payment terms by stretching loans over longer periods and thus lowering the monthly payments.

Selecting Trade Incentives. Manufacturers award money to distribution channel members in the form of trade incentives. Unlike consumer incentives that aim to create greater value for buyers, **trade incentives** aim to increase the attractiveness of the offering for the members of the distribution channel—wholesalers, retailers, and dealers. Specifically, manufacturers use a number of trade promotion tools:[60]

- *Allowances* are extra payments offered in return for the retailer's performing certain functions, such as promoting the offering at the point of sale, keeping a larger inventory to ensure product availability, and providing additional value-added services.
- *Free goods* are free merchandise to intermediaries who buy a certain quantity or who feature a certain flavor or size.
- *Price-off* is a straight discount off the list price on each case purchased during a stated time period.
- A *payment discount* is a price reduction to buyers who pay bills promptly. A typical example is "2/10, net 30," which means payment is due within 30 days but the buyer can deduct 2 percent by paying within 10 days.

The growing power of large retailers has increased their ability to demand trade promotions.[61] The manufacturer's sales force and its brand managers are often at odds here. The sales force says local retailers will not keep the company's products on the shelf unless they receive more trade promotion money, whereas brand managers want to spend their limited funds on consumer promotion and advertising.

Manufacturers, who often find it difficult to police retailers to make sure they are doing what they agreed to do, increasingly insist on proof of performance before paying any allowances. Manufacturers face several challenges in managing trade promotions. Some retailers are doing **forward buying**—that is, buying a greater quantity during the deal period than they can immediately sell. The manufacturer must then schedule more production than planned and bear the costs of extra work shifts and overtime. Other retailers are *diverting*—that is, buying more than needed in a region where the manufacturer offers a deal and shipping the surplus to their stores in non-deal regions. Manufacturers handle forward buying and diverting by limiting the amount they will sell at a discount or producing and delivering less than the full order in an effort to smooth production.

Selecting Sales Force Incentives. Companies spend billions of dollars on sales force promotion tools to gather leads, impress and reward customers, and motivate the sales force. **Sales force incentives** aim to encourage the sales force to support a new product or model, boosting prospecting and stimulating off-season sales. Sales contests are one popular type of sales force incentive. A sales contest aims at inducing the sales force or dealers to increase sales results over a stated period, with prizes (money, trips, gifts, or points) going to those who succeed.

The budgets that companies develop for incentive tools typically remain fairly constant from year to year. For many new businesses that want to make a splash with a targeted audience, especially in the B2B world, trade shows are an important tool, but the cost per contact is the highest of all communication options. The topic of managing sales force and personal selling is discussed in more detail in Chapter 15.

marketing INSIGHT

Ethical Issues in Prescription Drug Pricing

The United States spends nearly $330 billion a year on prescription drugs. In the past three decades, the share spent for pharmaceuticals nearly doubled, to reach about 10 percent of total health care spending. The U.S. government spends more on health care than it spends on any other single segment of the federal budget, including defense and Social Security. The United States spends more on drugs than any other country and twice as much as the average of the other major industrialized countries.

Pricing prescription drugs raises the ethical question of how much pharmaceutical companies should charge for their products. Some companies look at drug pricing from a purely financial perspective. To justify the decision to raise the price of nitrofurantoin (a drug listed by the World Health Organization as an "essential" medicine for lower urinary tract infections) from about $500 per bottle to more than $2,300. Nirmal Mulye, founder of Nostrum Pharmaceuticals, argued that his company had "a moral requirement to make money and sell the product for the highest price."

Examples of companies raising the prices of proprietary drugs abound. EpiPen—a medical device for injecting a measured dose of epinephrine as an emergency treatment of serious allergic reactions to insect stings/bites, foods, drugs, or other substances—went from $100 for a two-pack in 2009 to $608 in 2016. With nearly a 90 percent market share, EpiPen accounted for about 40 percent of the profits of Mylan, its parent company. EpiPen was generating a net profit margin of about 55 percent, significantly higher than the company's overall profit margin of 8.9 percent.

Perhaps the most extreme example of purely profit-driven pricing is that of Turing Pharmaceuticals. After acquiring the rights to the 60-year-old Daraprim—the only medication available for treating several rare life-threatening diseases—the company increased the price from $13.50 per tablet to $750 per tablet, a 5,000 percent jump. Turing's actions resulted in a public outcry about price-gouging, followed by resignation of its CEO and a congressional inquiry into the company's pricing practices.[62]

Unlike pricing discretionary consumer products, pricing prescription drugs can have a direct impact on social welfare. Raising prices can lead to the inability of economically disadvantaged patients to afford

(continued)

marketing insight *(continued)*

critical medicine, causing them to skip doses of their medications, take smaller doses, or abandon treatment altogether. The societal impact of drug pricing calls for developing an approach that goes beyond merely optimizing corporate profits.

A particular challenge is the rather opaque process of drug pricing. To add transparency to prescription drug pricing, the American Marketing Association launched the TruthinRx campaign in 2016. This grassroots campaign enables patients and physicians to share their experiences with prescription drug pricing to gather public support for regulations requiring drug price transparency. The TruthinRx campaign is focusing on three major market players that significantly impact drug prices: (1) pharmaceutical companies that make and market drugs, (2) pharmacy benefit managers who work on behalf of health insurance companies or employers to negotiate upfront discounts on the prices of prescription drugs with pharmaceutical companies, and (3) health insurance companies that approve prescriptions, set co-pays, and work with pharmacy benefit managers to determine how much patients pay for drugs.[63]

summary

1. Price is the only marketing element that produces revenue; the others produce costs. Pricing decisions have become more challenging in a changing economic and technological environment.
2. Purchase decisions are based on how consumers perceive prices, rather than just on the offering's stated price. Understanding how consumers arrive at their perceptions of prices—and, specifically, the role of reference prices, price–quality inferences, and price endings—can help the company set the optimal market price.
3. In setting pricing policy, a company follows a six-step procedure. It selects its pricing objective. It estimates the demand curve, the probable quantities it will sell at each possible price. It estimates how its costs vary at different levels of output, at different levels of accumulated production experience, and for differentiated marketing offers. It examines competitors' costs, prices, and offers. It selects a pricing method, and it sets the final price.
4. When setting a price, a company can pursue different objectives: current profit, market penetration, market skimming, and leadership in product quality. The clearer a firm's objectives, the easier it is to set price.
5. The demand curve shows the market's probable purchase quantity at alternative prices, summing the reactions of many individuals with different price sensitivities. Marketers need to know how responsive, or elastic, demand is to a change in price.
6. Price setting is driven by three major considerations: costs, competitors, and customers. Costs set a floor for the price. Competitors' prices and the price of substitutes provide an orienting point. Customers' assessment of unique features establishes the price ceiling. Common price-setting methods include markup pricing, target-rate-of-return pricing, economic-value-to-customer pricing, competitive pricing, and auction pricing.
7. Marketers must modify their price-setting logic when the product is part of a product mix and the company's goal is to maximize the profits on the total mix. Common scenarios for product-mix pricing include loss-leader pricing, optional-feature pricing, captive-product pricing, two-part pricing, by-product pricing, and product bundling.
8. To gain market position and grow profits, companies often take aggressive pricing actions, either lowering their prices, typically to lure competitors' customers, or raising prices to capture greater value from its current customers. Companies must anticipate competitor price changes and prepare contingent responses, which may include maintaining or changing price or quality.
9. The firm facing a competitor's price change must try to understand the competitor's intent and the probable duration of the change. A market leader attacked by lower-priced competitors can seek to better differentiate itself, to introduce its own low-cost competitor, or to transform itself completely.
10. Incentives consist of a collection of incentive tools, mostly short-term, designed to stimulate quicker or greater purchase of particular products or services by consumers or the trade. In using incentives, a company must establish its objectives, select the tools, develop the program, implement and control it, and evaluate the results.
11. In designing incentives, a firm must decide how much effort to devote to push strategies and to pull strategies. A push strategy uses the manufacturer's sales force, trade promotion money, or other means to induce intermediaries to carry, promote, and sell the product to end users. In a pull strategy, the manufacturer uses advertising and incentives to persuade consumers to demand the product from intermediaries, thus inducing the intermediaries to order it. Selecting the right mix of push and pull strategies is an important ingredient in securing trade support.

marketing
SPOTLIGHT

Priceline

Priceline launched in 1998 when Jay S. Walker first introduced its "Name Your Own Price" service for purchasing airline tickets online. Priceline flipped the conventional system of purchasing goods by having the buyer "set" prices. Typically, sellers advertise a good in the marketplace at a specific price, and buyers decide whether they want it. Priceline designed a mechanism whereby customers logged on to the company website, posted an "advertisement" that indicated where they wanted to go, the dates of travel, and the price they were willing to pay. Priceline then searched the databases of partnered airlines for compatible tickets. Customers had to be flexible about the carrier and the time of day for their flight; they received their ticket and carrier information only after the transaction was completed.

At the start of its airline ticket service, Priceline partnered only with America West and TWA. A year after inception, Priceline had sold tickets to over 1 million individuals. Shortly after, big-name air carriers such as United, American, and Delta joined as partners. Priceline's model of online bookings proved valuable to airlines, because the carrier is anonymous throughout the buying process and doesn't have to dilute its brand by selling tickets at large discounts while also maintaining its own established prices. The model was also attractive to budget-conscious travelers because, on average, customers found lower prices than they otherwise would have through their own online searches.

The company grew at a dramatic pace, and Priceline hired William Shatner to spearhead its advertising campaigns. Priceline spent millions to feature Shatner in newspaper and radio advertisements. Its advertising efforts proved successful in increasing brand awareness. Priceline became one of the top 10 best-known internet websites by 1999. Revenues in 1999 reached approximately $500 million, and Priceline's IPO was $12.9 billion, the highest first-day value at the time. Throughout that year, Priceline expanded its Name Your Own Price system to selling automobiles, hotel rooms, home financing, and even groceries. Priceline partnered with various companies and was on its way to becoming an internet megabrand.

Priceline took a nosedive when the dot-com bubble burst in the early 2000s. The stock lost over 99 percent of its value, falling from a peak of $974 to approximately $7. Jay Walker left the company as well, choosing to focus on a different company. To recover from the financial disaster, the company quit the non-travel businesses and ironically became profitable for the first time in 2001.

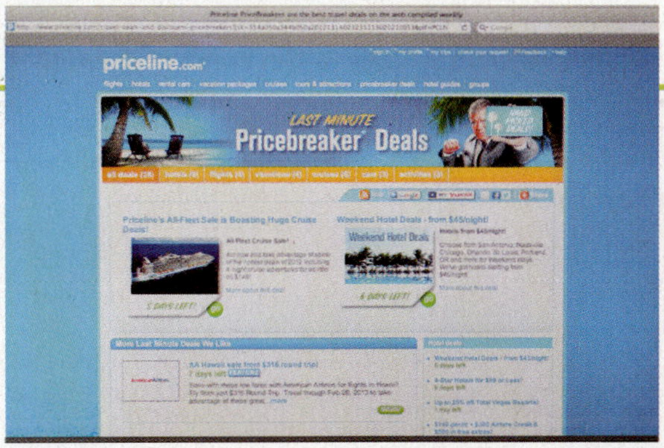

Source: NetPhotos/Alamy Stock Photo

In 2002, the company started to expand its travel operations beyond the Name Your Own Price model. Priceline acquired the European hotel-booking sites Active Hotels and Booking.com in 2004 and 2005, respectively, a move that would eventually be hailed as one of the most successful acquisitions in internet history. Priceline acquired Agoda.com, an online travel agency in Southeast Asia, in 2007; Rentalcars.com, a car rental service, in 2010; Kayak, a meta-search company, in 2013; and OpenTable, a restaurant reservation service, in 2014. Priceline's business expansion caused its stock to surpass the peak it had reached in 1999.

Much of Priceline's success can be attributed to the company's focus on businesses in the most profitable segments of online travel. Hotels account for over 85 percent of Priceline's gross bookings, compared to 48 percent for Expedia, Priceline's closest competitor. The hotel market is less concentrated than air travel, so Priceline can generate more profit by concentrating on hotel bookings, for which it can charge a 15 percent to 20 percent commission, compared to about 3 percent for air bookings. In addition, much of Priceline's gross bookings are in Europe. In contrast to the United States, European hotel markets consist mostly of independent properties, which means that they have a more difficult time attracting customers. By properly indexing European hotels, Priceline achieves greater bargaining power in its commission.

Priceline's data analytics processes also create a competitive advantage. Priceline carefully researches how and where it purchases online ads. This approach across all of its businesses has created industry-leading advertising effectiveness. The company spends an average of $7.50 per booked hotel room, compared to $16.00 for Expedia. In addition, Priceline uses data analytics to maximize its website "conversions"—when a consumer moves from browsing the website to booking a service. Priceline's research of customer demographics and behaviors allows it to leverage personalized ads on websites and in e-mails. Priceline achieved

(*continued*)

the industry's highest conversion rate in 2019; the high conversion increases profit margins on each booking.

Priceline has led the online travel industry by a wide margin. Its market capitalization is over three times that of its next closest competitor. The foundation of Priceline's success is its focus on profitable market segments and rigorous dedication to data analytics, enables the company to achieve high profit margins.[64]

Questions

1. How important was the Name Your Own Price approach to Priceline's market success?
2. What are the pros and cons of the Name Your Own Price approach to setting an offering's price?
3. Is setting prices based on one's willingness to pay fair? Does it create value for customers? Does it create value for the firm?

marketing SPOTLIGHT

Uber

The origins of Uber trace back to 2008, when Travis Kalanick and Garrett Camp, both start-up entrepreneurs, were having trouble finding a taxi on a snowy winter day. The two were inspired to create a smart-phone app that would call a taxi cab. Returning to San Francisco, Camp bought the domain name UberCab.com, and the company officially launched two years later. UberCab was initially a private luxury car service for San Francisco and Silicon Valley executives. Interested customers first had to e-mail Kalanick for access to the application. After entering their payment information, customers were able to summon a private black car. Unlike traditional black car services, the UberCab app allowed passengers to track the arriving car's location and also guided the driver to the rider's destination.

Uber began building traction almost immediately after the app launched. Executives were particularly drawn by the sheer convenience of Uber. Most executives had to book an expensive private car well in advance. Uber allowed them to quickly book a ride wherever they were. UberBlack was priced lower than private limousines but was more expensive than a typical cab ride. By the end of the year, Uber had dropped the Cab from its name and had thousands of users riding around San Francisco. As Uber attracted more and more customers and drivers, investors also became interested in the company. In February 2011, Uber raised $11 million from venture-capital firm Benchmark. Convinced that the concept it had created could scale, Uber began to expand across the nation and worldwide. In May of 2011, Uber launched in New York City. Later that year, Uber launched its service in Paris.

In 2012, Uber introduced a new service called uberX, a cheaper version that allowed drivers to use their personal vehicles instead of black cars to pick up passengers. The qualifications to be an uberX driver were much less strict than those for UberBlack, which required that drivers be licensed limousine operators and that their vehicles meet Uber's

Source: digitallife/Alamy Stock Photo

criteria for a black car service. All uberX drivers needed were a driver's license, auto insurance, and a clean driving record. UberX was priced at around 10 percent less than the cost of a traditional taxi. In 2014, Uber revealed its UberPOOL service, which paired riders who were going in the same direction so they could share a ride. Uber's version of carpooling saved customers around 50 percent of the cost of a taxi cab ride.

The key to Uber's success is its ease of use. Riders simply need to download the app, create an account, and enter their payment information. The app displays available drivers nearby. To summon one, riders simply input their destination and press a button to be matched with a driver. The customer can track the location of the matched driver, view the driver's name and car information, and look at the driver's quality rating. Customers are able to refuse drivers with low ratings. Like riders, drivers have the right to refuse customers with sufficiently low ratings. The driver app also shows locations with higher numbers of customers requesting rides. Within minutes of being matched with a driver, the customer can be on his or her way.

At the end of the ride, the cost is automatically deducted from the rider's payment method, with Uber retaining 25 percent of the fare in addition to a booking fee—a flat fee that covers regulatory, safety, and operational costs. Prices are determined by the time and distance of the ride. To balance supply and demand, Uber also charges a "Surge Pricing

(continued)

Premium" during times with high rider traffic, a practice that can multiply the normal fare by as much as seven times. Uber's surge pricing has been met with some customer dissatisfaction and concerns about price fairness. When the East Coast was experiencing heavy snow in 2013, customers submitted screen shots of their surged bills on social media; some were as high as $400 for a single ride. Despite customer concerns, Uber has retained surge pricing as a source of customer segmentation and as an incentive to attract drivers to specific locations during times of high demand.

Uber's rapid expansion across the world has been met with opposition from policy makers and the taxi industry. Many officials have questioned the legality of Uber's ride service and whether Uber should be subject to the same laws that taxi and limousine services are. Uber has been partially banned in France, Italy, and Finland, and in some other locations, such as Australia, Hong Kong, and Bulgaria, it has been banned altogether. Because uberX and UberPool's prices are often lower than the average taxi cab fare, taxi cab drivers have found themselves losing a significant portion of their customers. Many taxi drivers also find it unfair that they are required to undergo more stringent background checks and purchase a license (medallion) to legally drive customers, whereas Uber's requirements are much more relaxed.

Uber's growth in the decade after the company launched has been staggering. In 2019, Uber was available in over 700 metropolitan areas worldwide. Uber is estimated to have more than 100 million worldwide users, and it generated over $11 billion in revenue in 2018. Uber's combination of convenience and fair pricing has completely transformed transportation across the world. In addition to car ridesharing, Uber has branched off into food delivery service with the creation of UberEATS. The company has also announced plans to introduce an aerial ridesharing service called Uber Elevate.[65]

Questions

1. What were the key factors that contributed to Uber's phenomenal market success?
2. What was Uber's customer value proposition? What role did Uber's pricing play in its ability to attract riders?
3. Is surge pricing fair? What alternative strategies could Uber use to balance supply and demand?

CHAPTER **12**

Managing Marketing Communications

Fevicol's impactful campaigns, during the pandemic, urged people to wear a mask and maintain the social distance of two meters while reinforcing the brand message of adhesive's strength.

Source: Fevicol©Pidilite Industries, used with permission

Modern marketing calls for more than developing a good product, pricing it attractively, and making it accessible. Companies must also communicate with current and potential stakeholders and the general public to inform them about the attributes of their offerings. For most marketers, therefore, the question is not *whether* to communicate but rather *what* to say, *how* and *when* to say it, to *whom*, and *how often*. Consumers can turn to hundreds of cable and satellite TV channels, thousands of magazines and newspapers, and millions of internet pages and are actively deciding what communications they want to receive. To achieve their strategic goals, holistic marketers must craft communication campaigns that can break through the clutter and reach customers on a personal level. Consider Pidilite's advertisement to reinforce the positioning of its Fevicol brand as a contemporary brand by encouraging everyone to maintain social distance during the pandemic.

>>> Pidilite's Fevicol is the leading brand of adhesive used for carpentry and art & craft applications. A household name, synonymous with unbreakable bonds, Fevicol is the preferred choice of the wood-work community.[1] This popular brand is reputed for its quality product as well as its brilliant award-winning advertisements. Its recent ad-campaigns on social distancing exemplify advertisements blending the brand's value proposition of firm adhesion with a valuable

public-service message to create awareness about the importance of Covid-19 precautionary protocols such as maintaining a distance of at least two metres and wearing masks in public spaces. As the first phase pandemic lockdown eased in July 2020, Fevicol ran an advert urging caution to combat the pandemic by altering its traditional logo with the elephants in it wearing masks on their trunks.[2] Another campaign in this series involved a social experiment conducted in the food court of a shopping mall.[3] Alternate tables were kept empty with a signage stating, *"Please leave this table vacant to maintain social distancing"*. Fevicol's representatives observed that guests tend to ignore the message and would occupy all tables, thus, compromising everyone's safety. In the next stage of the experiment, alternate tables were glued to their respective sets of chairs with Fevicol. Unaware of the glued tables and chairs, people would try to move the chairs to pull them out and occupy the vacant seats. The perplexed expressions of the people on being unable to draw the chairs were recorded by the Fevicol team. Towards the end of the video, the food court's manager would step in and turn the signage to show the message "Stuck by Fevicol to ensure your safety". Hence, even during the pandemic, Fevicol continued to spread an essential message through its signature ad campaigns that are earthy, humorous and contemporary while reinforcing the brand promise of trust and reliability.[4] Pidilite has extensively used creative advertisements to successfully grow Fevicol into a market leadership position. In the last two decades, the company has strengthened its engagements with its stakeholders including carpenters, contractors, interior designers and end consumers. The Fevicol Champions' Club (FCC), with 180,000 members across 1800 clubs, is a community-based program that helps carpenters and contractors learn new techniques, build networks, and earn recognition for their work. Fevicol Design Ideas (FDI) is a platform for over thousands of interior designers to showcase their work while helping consumers to search for home décor design ideas and even hire a contractor. Fevicol continues to uphold its leadership position by directly communicating and engaging with its stakeholders through the FCC and FDI[5] as well as social media platforms including Facebook and YouTube.

Done right, marketing communications can have a huge payoff. This chapter describes how they work and what they can do for a company. It also addresses how holistic marketers combine and integrate marketing communications.

Learning Objectives After studying this chapter you should be able to:

12.1 Explain the role of marketing communications.

12.2 Define meaningful communication objectives.

12.3 Describe how a company should identify target customers and craft the communication message.

12.4 Explain how a company should decide on the communication media mix and develop a media plan.

12.5 Describe the creative strategies involved in developing an effective communication campaign.

12.6 Identify actionable metrics for measuring communication effectiveness.

The Role of Marketing Communication

Marketing communication is the means by which firms attempt to inform, persuade, and remind consumers—directly or indirectly—about the products and brands they sell. In a sense, it represents the voice of the company and its brands; it is a means by which the firm can establish a dialog and build relationships with consumers. By strengthening customer loyalty, marketing communication can contribute to customer equity.

Marketing communication also works by showing consumers how and why a product is used, by whom, where, and when. Consumers can learn who makes the product and what the company and brand stand for, and they can become motivated to try or use it. Marketing communication allows companies to link their brands to other people, places, events, brands, experiences, feelings, and things. It can contribute to brand equity by establishing the brand in memory and creating a brand image, as well as by driving sales and affecting shareholder value.

THE COMMUNICATION PROCESS

Marketers should understand the fundamental elements of effective communication. The communication process can be viewed from two perspectives: a more general macro perspective delineating the key aspects of communication as an interactive process, and a more specific micro perspective focusing on the way the message recipient responds to the communication. These two perspectives are reflected in the two models of communication: a macromodel and a micromodel.

Macromodel of the Communication Process. The **macromodel of marketing communication** articulates the interaction between the sender (company) and the recipient (consumer) of the communication message. Figure 12.1 shows a macromodel denoting nine key factors in effective communication. Two represent the major parties—*sender* and *receiver*. Two represent the major tools—*message* and *media*. Four represent major communication functions—*encoding, decoding, response*, and *feedback*. And the last element in the system is *noise*, random and competing messages that may interfere with the intended communication.

Senders must know what audiences they want to reach and what responses they want to evoke. They must encode their messages so the target audience can successfully decode them. In other words, the sender must express the message in a particular tangible form—words, images, sounds, or movements—so that the intended message can later be retrieved by the recipient. Senders must transmit the message through media that reach the target audience and develop feedback channels to monitor the responses. The more the sender's field of experience overlaps with the receiver's, the more effective the message is likely to be. Note that selective attention, distortion, and retention processes (discussed in Chapter 4) may affect how recipients receive and interpret the message.

Micromodel of Marketing Communication. A **micromodel of marketing communication** concentrates on consumers' specific responses to communications.[6] Classic response hierarchy models assume that the buyer passes through cognitive, affective, and behavioral stages, in that order.[7] This "learn–feel–do" sequence is more appropriate when the audience has high involvement with a product category perceived to have meaningful differentiation, such as an automobile or a house. An alternative sequence, "do–feel–learn," is relevant when the audience has high involvement but perceives little or no differentiation within the product category, as is the case with airline tickets or personal

FIGURE **12.1**
Elements in the Communication Process

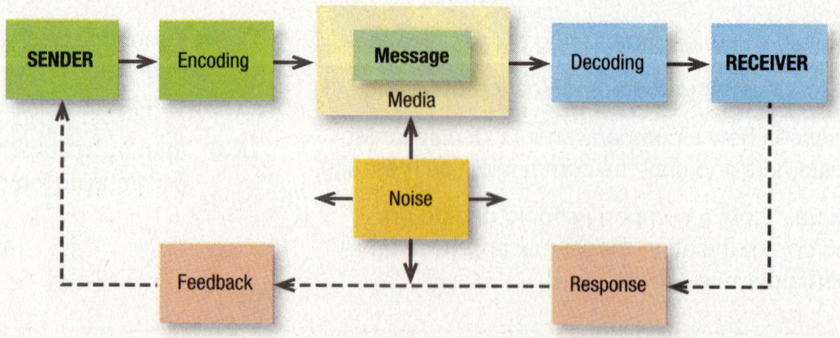

computers. A third sequence, "learn–do–feel," is relevant when the audience has low involvement and perceives little differentiation, such as with salt or batteries. By choosing the right sequence, the marketer can do a better job of planning communications.

Regardless of their specific sequence, several steps are involved in generating a consumer response.

- *Awareness.* In order to take any kind of action, customers must be aware of the existence of the company's offering. If most of the target audience is unaware of the offering, the communicator's task is to build awareness.
- *Knowledge.* The target audience might have awareness but not know much more about the offering.
- *Liking.* Members of the target audience may know the brand, but how do they feel about it?
- *Preference.* The target audience might like the product but not prefer it to other products. The communicator must then try to build consumer preference by comparing the product's quality, value, performance, and other features to those of likely competitors.
- *Conviction.* The target audience might prefer a particular product but not develop a conviction about buying it.
- *Purchase.* Finally, some members of the target audience might have conviction but not quite get around to making the purchase. The communicator must lead these consumers to take the final step, perhaps by offering the product at a low price, offering a premium, or letting them try it out.

To increase the odds of success for a communication campaign, marketers must attempt to increase the likelihood that *each* step occurs. Thus, the communication campaign must ensure (1) that the right consumer is exposed to the right message at the right place and at the right time, (2) that the offering is correctly positioned in terms of desirable and deliverable points of difference and points of parity, (3) that the consumer pays attention to the campaign and adequately comprehends the intended message, and (4) that consumers are motivated to consider purchasing and using the offering.

DEVELOPING AN EFFECTIVE COMMUNICATION PROGRAM

To develop an effective communication program, a company must follow a systematic process that starts with setting the goals to be achieved by the communication campaign and concludes with assessing the outcome of the campaign. The key steps in developing effective communications are shown in Figure 12.2. These include setting the communication objectives, identifying the target audience, crafting the communication message, selecting the communication channels, developing the creative aspect of communication, and measuring communication effectiveness.

The ultimate success of a company's communication campaign depends on the viability of the overall strategy and tactics for managing the company's offering, which serve as a basis for developing a communication plan. Thus communication objectives, the choice of target audience, and the design of the communication message typically follow from the company's overarching marketing plan that defines the offering's goals, its target customers, and its value proposition.

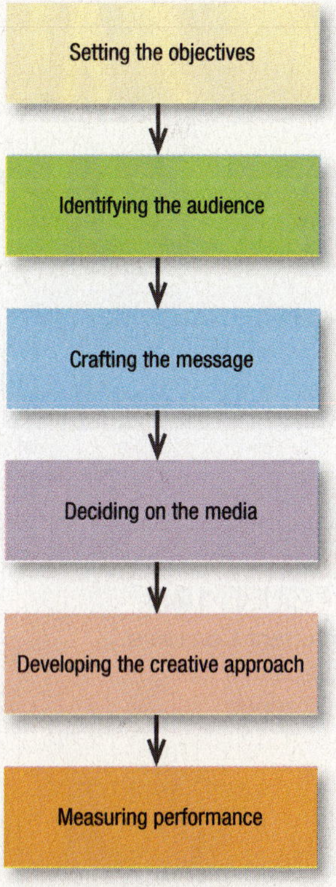

FIGURE **12.2**
Developing a Communication Program

Setting the Communication Objectives

Setting the objectives of a communication campaign involves three key decisions: defining the focus of company communications, setting communication benchmarks, and determining the communication budget. We discuss these decisions in more detail in the following sections.

DEFINING THE FOCUS OF COMPANY COMMUNICATIONS

A **communication objective** is a specific task and achievement level to be accomplished with a specific audience in a specific period of time.[8] We classify communication objectives according to whether they aim to create awareness by informing the target audience about the offering, to build preferences by persuading the audience of the benefits of the offering, or to incite action by nudging the audience to act in a way that benefits the company and its offering.

- **Creating awareness** provides a foundation for brand equity. Creating awareness involves fostering the consumer's ability to recognize or recall the brand in sufficient detail to make a purchase. Recognition is easier to achieve than recall—consumers who are asked to think of a brand of frozen entrées are more likely to recognize Stouffer's distinctive orange packages than to recall the brand without seeing it. *Brand recall* tends to be important for consumers who have received marketing communications outside the store when the company's offerings are not readily visible and available for purchase. In contrast, *brand recognition* tends to be important inside the store when consumers can readily see and purchase the company's offering. Creating awareness can involve highlighting awareness of the need (stimulating primary demand) or awareness of the specific offering (stimulating selective demand).

- **Building preferences** involves communicating an offering's ability to meet a currently relevant consumer need. Some relevant needs are negatively oriented (problem removal, problem avoidance, incomplete satisfaction, normal depletion). For example, many household cleaning products communicate their ability to solve problems. Other needs are positively oriented (sensory gratification, intellectual stimulation, or social approval). For example, food products often use sensory-oriented ads emphasizing appetite appeal. Persuasive communication aims to create liking and preference for a product or service and conviction of its benefits. Some persuasive communication is comparative in nature: It explicitly compares the attributes of two or more brands, such as the Chrysler TV ad for the Dodge Ram that asked, "What if you were to take away horsepower, torque and warranty coverage from a Ram? Well, you'd end up with a Ford F-150."[9] Comparative communication works best when it elicits cognitive and affective motivations simultaneously and when consumers process the advertising in a detailed, analytical mode.[10] In contrast, reinforcement communication aims to convince current purchasers that they made the right choice. Automobile ads often depict satisfied customers enjoying special features of their new car.
- **Inciting action** involves motivating consumers to decide to purchase the brand or take purchase-related action. Promotional offers like coupons or two-for-one deals encourage consumers to make a mental commitment to buy. But many consumers do not have an expressed category need and may not be in the market when exposed to an ad, so they are unlikely to form purchase intentions. In any given week, only about 20 percent of adults may be planning to buy detergent, only 2 percent to buy a carpet cleaner, and only 0.25 percent to buy a car. Action-focused communication aims to stimulate purchase of products and services.

The communication objective should emerge from a thorough analysis of the current marketing situation.[11] If the product class is mature, the company is the market leader, and brand usage is low, the objective might be to stimulate more frequent usage. If the product class is new, the company is not the market leader, and the brand is superior to the leader, the objective might be to convince the market of the brand's superiority.

Communication objectives for the company's offering also depend on the current consumer state of awareness. Consider the two offerings depicted in Figure 12.3. We find that 80 percent of the consumers in the total market are aware of Brand A, 60 percent have tried it, and only 20 percent who tried it are satisfied. This indicates that the communication program is effective in creating awareness, but the product fails to meet consumer expectations. Hence, in this case the company might benefit from focusing on improving the product. In contrast, 40 percent of the consumers in the total market are aware of Brand B and only 30 percent have tried it, but 80 percent of them are satisfied. In this case, the communication program might benefit from focusing on creating awareness and encouraging brand trial.

FIGURE **12.3**
Current Consumer States for Two Offerings

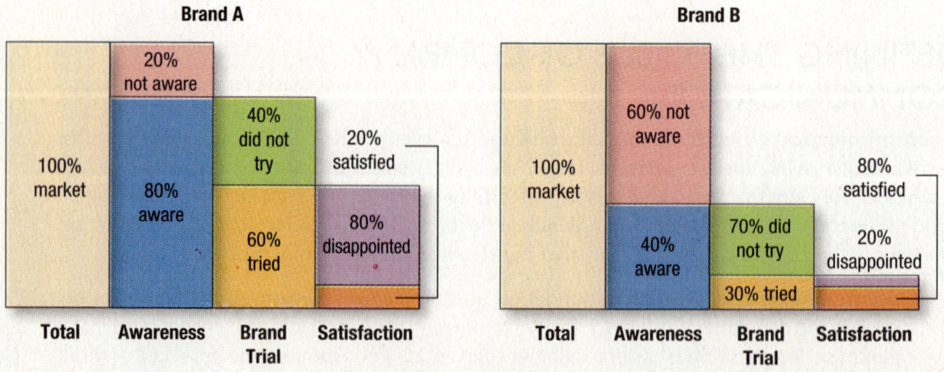

SETTING THE COMMUNICATION BENCHMARKS

In addition to defining the focus of the communication campaign, a company must set clear benchmarks that define the magnitude of the desired impact and the time frame within which a particular outcome—awareness, preference, or action—must be achieved. Without such well-articulated benchmarks, a company will find it challenging to design an effective communication campaign that is aligned with its strategic goals.

Broadly speaking, there are two types of communication benchmarks: quantitative and temporal. Quantitative benchmarks quantify a particular objective. For example, quantitative benchmarks might determine the level of awareness that the communication campaign must achieve, the desired strength of preferences among the target audience, and the specifics of the action that the communication campaign must create. Temporal benchmarks, on the other hand, define the timeframe within which a particular outcome has to be achieved. Quantitative and temporal benchmarks are closely related and interdependent: Setting a particular timeframe is contingent on the magnitude of the desired outcome, and vice versa.

To be actionable, a communication objective must have a clearly articulated focus as well as clearly defined quantitative and temporal benchmarks. To illustrate, consider the following communication objectives:

> Create awareness of the new James Bond movie (focus) among 40 percent of Millennial consumers (quantitative benchmark) prior to the movie premiere (temporal benchmark).
>
> Increase the number of consumers who believe that toothpaste Brand X has superior whitening power (focus) from 10 percent to 40 percent (quantitative benchmark) in one year (temporal benchmark).

Defining quantitative and temporal benchmarks is important, because without knowing what particular outcome needs to be achieved and the timeframe for achieving it, a company will find it difficult to design an effective communication program. In addition to guiding the development of a communication campaign, quantitative and temporal benchmarks are important for determining the effectiveness of the company's communication activities. In this context, performance benchmarks act as reference points against which the accomplishments of the communication campaign are assessed.

DETERMINING THE COMMUNICATION BUDGET

One of the most difficult marketing decisions is choosing how much to spend on marketing communications. How does a company know it's spending the right amount? John Wanamaker, the department store magnate, once said, "I know that half of my advertising is wasted, but I don't know which half." Industries and companies vary considerably in how much they spend on marketing communications. Expenditures might be 50 percent of sales in the cosmetics industry, but only 5 percent in the industrial equipment industry. Even within a given industry, there are low- and high-spending companies.

A practical approach for defining the communication budget is **objective-and-task budgeting**. This approach calls for marketers to develop a communication budget by defining specific objectives, identifying the tasks that must be performed to achieve these objectives, and estimating their costs. The sum of these costs is the proposed communication budget. The overarching principle is that the total communication budget must be set so the marginal profit from every communication dollar is greater than or equal to the marginal profit from every dollar spent on other marketing activities.

How much resources should a company allocate to marketing communications compared to alternatives such as product improvement, lower prices, or better service? There is no universal rule. How much to spend on marketing communications depends on a variety of factors. The main factors to consider when setting the communication budget follow.[12]

- *Stage in the product life cycle.* New products typically merit large communication budgets to build awareness and encourage consumer trial. Established brands usually are supported by relatively lower communication budgets, measured as percentage of sales.
- *Product differentiation.* Offerings in less differentiated categories (beer, soft drinks, banks, and airlines) often require more advertising to establish a unique image than do offerings that provide distinct benefits.
- *Market share.* High-market-share brands usually require less advertising expenditure, measured as a percentage of sales, to maintain share. Building share by increasing market size requires larger expenditures.

- *Message complexity.* The number of repetitions needed to get the company's message across to consumers has a direct impact on the communication budget. More complex messages tend to require more repetition and, hence, a larger communication budget.
- *Reach.* A company's ability to reach consumers in an effective and cost-efficient manner. Communications to customers who are more difficult to reach tend to require a larger communication budget.
- *Competitive communication.* In markets with a large number of competitors and high communication spending, a brand must advertise more heavily to be heard. Even communications not directly competitive to the brand create clutter and a need for heavier advertising.
- *Available resources.* The communication budget is limited by the company's resources. After all, a company cannot spend something it does not have.

To set a meaningful communication budget, a company must take into account all of these factors. Yet some companies fail to consider all factors and instead single out one particular metric: setting their communication budgets at parity with competitors. This approach, also referred to as **competitive-parity budgeting**, is problematic because there are no grounds for believing competitors are more knowledgeable about what the optimal communication budget should be. Company reputations, resources, opportunities, and objectives differ so greatly that communication budgets are hardly a guide for others. And there is no evidence that budgets based on competitive parity discourage communication wars.

Another group of companies set the communication budget at what they think they can afford. This approach completely ignores the role of marketing communication as an investment and its immediate impact on sales volume. It also leads to an uncertain annual budget, which makes long-range planning difficult, and it yields a budget set by the availability of funds rather than by market opportunities. Available resources certainly play an important role in determining the overall communication budget, but basing the communication budget exclusively on the available resources is likely to lead to overspending (for large companies) or underspending (for smaller firms).

Finally, some companies set communication expenditures at a specified percentage of current or anticipated sales revenues. Automobile companies often allocate to marketing communication a fixed percentage based on the planned car price. Oil companies appropriate a fraction of a cent for each gallon of gasoline sold under their own labels. Though practical in terms of implementation, when such an approach is used in isolation from the communication task to be achieved, it can lead to impractical allocation of a company's resources, ultimately yielding an ineffective communication campaign.

Although marketing communication is treated as a current expense, part of it can be considered an investment in building brand equity and customer loyalty. When a company spends $5 million on capital equipment, it can call the equipment a five-year depreciable asset and write off only one-fifth of the cost in the first year. When it spends $5 million on advertising to launch a new product, however, it must write off the entire cost in the first year, reducing its reported profit, even if the advertising benefits will persist for many years to come.

Identifying the Target Audience and Crafting the Communication Message

Identifying the target audience and developing the communication message are the two key components that define the strategy of a company's communication campaign. These two decisions, in turn, define the tactical aspects of the communication campaign, including selecting the right media and developing an effective creative solution.

IDENTIFYING THE TARGET AUDIENCE

The process must start with a clear target audience in mind: potential buyers of the company's products, current users, deciders, and influencers, as well as individuals, groups, particular sectors, or the general public. The target audience critically affects the communicator's decisions about what to say and about how, when, where, and to whom to say it.

It is possible to profile the target audience in terms of any of the identified market segments, but it's often useful to do so in terms of usage and loyalty. Is the target new to the category or a current user? Is the target loyal to the brand, loyal to a competitor, or someone who switches between brands?

If a brand user, is he or she a heavy or a light user? Communication strategy will differ depending on the answers.

The choice of target audience for the communication campaign is directly related to the choice of the target market for the company's offering. Indeed, the ultimate goal of the communication campaign is to facilitate awareness, preference, purchase, and usage of the company's offering. Yet the target market and the target audience do not always fully overlap. And on some occasions, the target audience can differ from the target market.

For example, a cereal manufacturer might develop a communication campaign to promote its products to kids even though the actual purchase is often made by adults. In the same vein, a milk producer might choose to promote its products to adults even though most of the consumption is likely to be done by kids.

The target audience for a company's communication campaign is likely to diverge from the company's target customers when purchase and usage decisions are made by a group rather than by a single individual. In this case, the communication campaign might target different members of the decision-making unit who are likely to exert influence over the end user's actions.

CRAFTING THE COMMUNICATION MESSAGE

Marketers are always seeking the "big idea" that resonates with consumers rationally and emotionally, distinguishes the brand from competitors, and is broad and flexible enough to translate into different media, markets, and time periods. Fresh insights are important for creating unique appeals and position.

A good ad normally focuses on one or two core selling propositions. As part of refining the brand positioning, the advertiser should conduct market research to determine which appeal works best with its target audience and then prepare a **creative brief**, typically one or two pages. This elaboration of the positioning strategy includes considerations such as key message, target audience, communication objectives (to do, to know, to believe), key brand benefits, support for the brand promise, and media.

How many communication messages should the advertiser create before choosing one? The more messages explored, the higher the probability of finding an excellent one. To this end, a company might rely on its own marketing team, engage an external advertising agency, or rely on crowdsourcing by recruiting consumers to come up with an effective communication message.[13]

Although entrusting consumers with a brand's marketing effort can be pure genius, it can also be a regrettable failure. When Kraft sought a hip name for a new flavor of its iconic Vegemite product in Australia, it labeled the first 3 million jars "Name Me" to enlist consumer support. But when, from among 48,000 entries, Kraft selected the name "iSnack 2.0," sales plummeted. The company had to pull iSnack jars from the shelves and start from scratch in a more conventional fashion, finally choosing the new name Cheesybite.[14]

In selecting a message strategy, management searches for appeals, themes, or ideas that will tie in to the brand positioning and help establish points of parity or points of difference. Some of these appeals or ideas may relate directly to product or service performance (the quality, economy, or value of the brand); others may relate to more extrinsic considerations (the brand as being contemporary, popular, or traditional).

Deciding on the Communication Media

Companies must allocate their marketing communication budget over the nine major modes of communication—advertising, online and social media, mobile communication, direct marketing, events and experiences, word of mouth, publicity and public relations, personal selling, and packaging. Within the same industry, companies can differ considerably in their media and channel choices. Avon concentrates its promotional funds on personal selling, whereas Revlon spends heavily on advertising. Electrolux spent heavily on a door-to-door sales force for years, whereas Hoover relied more on advertising.

Companies are always searching for ways to gain efficiency by substituting one communication tool for others. Many are replacing some field sales activity with ads, direct mail, and telemarketing. Substitutability among communication tools explains why marketing functions need to be coordinated.

DEFINING THE COMMUNICATION MEDIA MIX

Communication is not limited to advertising. Customers come to know a brand through a range of touch points, including online clubs and consumer communities, trade shows, event marketing, sponsorship, factory visits, public relations and press releases, and social cause marketing. To effectively communicate its value proposition to its target audience, a company should develop an integrated marketing communication campaign that spans different media. Consider how BMW has built the MINI Cooper brand in the United States by attracting attention through its creative use of diverse media formats.

MINI Cooper When BMW launched the modernized MINI Cooper in the United States, it employed a broad mix of media: billboards, posters, the internet, print, PR, product placement, and grassroots activities. Many media were linked to a cleverly designed website with product and dealer information. The imaginative, integrated campaign built a six-month waiting list for the MINI Cooper. Despite its relatively limited communication budget, the brand has continued to develop innovative, award-winning campaigns ever since. The MINI has especially used outdoor advertising creatively: Two curved palm trees planted next to a speeding MINI on a billboard created an illusion of speed and power; a digital billboard personally greeted passing MINI drivers by using a signal from a radio chip embedded in their key fobs; and a real MINI on the side of a building was able to move up and down like a yo-yo. A worldwide campaign, "Not Normal," spotlights MINI's strong, independent character through classic and digital media. Now sold in 100 countries around the world, the MINI has expanded into a six-model lineup, including a convertible, a coupe, the Clubman four-door, and the Countryman wagon. These product introductions reinforce the idea that the MINI is agile, versatile, and fun to drive, and the marketing campaign as a whole builds strong emotional connections with drivers.[11]

We can evaluate integrated marketing activities in terms of the effectiveness and efficiency with which they affect brand awareness and create, maintain, or strengthen brand associations and image. Although Volvo may invest in research and development, and may engage in advertising, promotion, and other communication to reinforce its "safety" brand association, it also sponsors events to make sure it is seen as active, contemporary, and up to date. Notable Volvo sponsorships include golf tournaments and the European professional golf tour, the Volvo Ocean Race, the famed Gothenburg Horse Show, and cultural events.

The communication media mix identifies the different modes of communication that a company will use to inform the target audience about its offerings. The most common media formats include advertising, online and social media communication, mobile communication, direct marketing, events

Source: culture-images GmbH/Alamy Stock Photo

>> The communication campaign for the U.S. launch of BMW's MINI Cooper used a broad mix of media in an imaginative way that maximized the budget and built a six-month waiting list for the vehicle.

and experiences, word of mouth, publicity and public relations, personal selling, and packaging. The key aspects of these communication formats are summarized as follows:[16]

- **Advertising** is any paid form of nonpersonal presentation and promotion of ideas, goods, or services by an identified sponsor via print media (newspapers, magazines, brochures, books, leaflets, directories), broadcast media (radio and television), network media, and display media (billboards, signs, posters, outer packaging, packaging inserts, ad reprints, and point-of-purchase displays). Advertising can build up a long-term image for a product (Coca-Cola ads) or trigger quick sales (a Macy's ad for a weekend sale). Certain forms of advertising, such as TV, can require a large budget, whereas other forms, such as targeted online ads, do not. The mere presence of mass-media advertising might have an effect on sales: Consumers might believe a heavily advertised brand must be of good quality.[17]
- **Online and social media communication** involves online activities and programs designed to engage customers or prospects and directly or indirectly raise awareness, improve image, or elicit sales of products and services (websites, e-mails, search ads, display ads, company blogs, third-party chat rooms, forums, Facebook and Twitter messages, and YouTube channels and videos). Online marketing and messages can take many forms to interact with consumers when they are in active search mode or when they are just browsing and surfing online for something to do.
- **Mobile communication** is a special form of online communication that places messages on consumers' cell phones, smart phones, or tablets (text messages, online communication, and social media communication). Increasingly, online marketing and social media rely on mobile forms of communication such as smart phones or tablets. Mobile communication is *timely*—messages can be very time-sensitive and reflect when and where a consumer is—and *pervasive*, meaning that messages are always at consumers' fingertips.
- **Direct marketing** involves the use of mail, phone, e-mail, online messaging, or in-person interaction to communicate directly with, or solicit response or dialog from, specific customers and prospects. The advent of data analytics has given marketers the opportunity to learn even more about consumers and develop more personal and relevant marketing communications.
- **Events and experiences** are company-sponsored activities and programs designed to create brand-related interactions with consumers. Examples include sports, arts, entertainment, festivals, factory tours, company museums, and street activities, as well as events for causes and less formal activities. Events and experiences offer many advantages as long as they are *engaging* and *implicit*, meaning that they involve indirect soft sell.
- **Word of mouth** involves the passing of information from person to person by oral communication. Social media can be viewed as a specific instance of word of mouth, where personal communication occurs online and is observable by others. Marketers can influence naturally occurring word of mouth as well as help to create word of mouth by "seeding" a message that is likely to engage consumers and lead to word-of-mouth communication related to the company and its offerings.
- **Publicity and public relations** involve a variety of programs directed internally to employees of the company or externally to consumers, other firms, the government, and media to promote or protect a company's image or its individual product communications (press kits, speeches, seminars, annual reports, charitable donations, publications, community relations, lobbying, identity media, and company magazines). Marketers tend to underuse publicity and public relations, yet a well-thought-out program coordinated with the other elements of the communication mix can be extremely effective, especially if a company needs to challenge consumers' misconceptions. The appeal of public relations and publicity is based on its high credibility: News stories and features are more authentic and credible to readers than ads.
- **Personal selling** is a process in which a seller tries to convince a buyer to purchase a particular product or service. Personal selling typically involves face-to-face communication and is highly dependent on the persuasion skills and abilities of the seller. Personal selling often takes place in one of two formats—through retail, where a salesperson interacts with potential customers who come to inquire about a product, and through direct-to-consumer marketing, where a salesperson visits potential buyers to make them aware of a company's offering.
- **Packaging** is an effective form of communication, especially in the case of decisions that are made at the point of purchase. The product's styling, the shape and color of the package, the store décor, and the company's stationery all communicate an image to buyers and deliver an impression that can strengthen or weaken a customer's view of a company.

The rise of digital media gives marketers a host of new ways to interact with customers and prospective customers. We can group communication options into three categories.[18] *Paid media* include TV, magazine and display ads, paid search, and sponsorships, all of which allow marketers to show their ad or brand for a fee. *Owned media* are communication channels that marketers actually own, such as a company or brand brochure, product packaging, website, blog, Facebook page, or Twitter account. *Earned media* are streams in which consumers, the press, or other outsiders voluntarily communicate something about the brand via word of mouth, buzz, or viral marketing methods. Social media play a key role in earned media.[19]

The different communication media formats and the ways in which they work in concert to create an *integrated marketing communication* campaign are discussed in more detail in Chapter 14. Issues pertaining to personal selling and managing a company's sales force are discussed in more detail in Chapter 15.

DEVELOPING A MEDIA PLAN

The media planner must determine the most cost-effective vehicles within each chosen media type. The advertiser who decides to buy 30 seconds of advertising on network television can pay $100,000 for a new show, $500,000 for a popular prime-time show such as *The Voice*, or over $5 million for the Super Bowl. These choices are critical: The average cost to produce a national 30-second television commercial is about $300,000,[20] so it can cost as much to run an ad once on network TV as to create and produce it! Media planners are using more sophisticated measures of effectiveness and employing them in mathematical models to arrive at the best media mix.[21]

Media planners must consider factors such as audience size, composition, and media cost and then calculate the cost per thousand persons reached. First, consider *audience quality*. For a baby lotion ad, a magazine read by 1 million young parents has an exposure value of 1 million potential buyers; if read by 1 million teenagers, it has an exposure value of almost zero. Second, consider *audience-attention probability*. Readers of some magazines may pay more attention to ads than do readers of others. Third is the medium's *editorial quality*, meaning its prestige and believability. People are more likely to believe a TV or radio ad when it appears within a program they like. Fourth, consider the value of *ad placement policies and extra services*, such as regional or occupational editions, as well as the lead-time requirements for magazines.

Communication programs involve a range of different media that should seamlessly convey the desired message to the target audience. Ocean Spray—an agricultural cooperative of cranberry growers—has used a variety of communication vehicles to turn sales around.

>> Ocean Spray turned around a decade of declining sales with its Straight from the Bog campaign that introduced product innovations and ran the gamut from TV and print ads to mini-bog tours and a pop-up restaurant.

Source: Douglas Graham/CQ Roll Call/Getty Images

Ocean Spray Facing stiff competition, adverse consumer trends, and nearly a decade of declining sales, Ocean Spray decided to reintroduce the cranberry as the "surprisingly versatile little fruit that supplies modern-day benefits," through a 360-degree campaign that used all facets of marketing communications to reach consumers in a variety of settings. The intent was to support the full range of products—cranberry sauce, fruit juices, and dried cranberries in different forms—and leverage the fact that the brand was born in the cranberry bogs and remains there still. The authentic and perhaps surprising campaign, "Straight from the Bog," was designed to also reinforce two key brand benefits—that Ocean Spray products taste good and are good for you. PR played a crucial role. Miniature bogs were brought to Manhattan and featured on an NBC *Today* morning segment. A "Bogs across America Tour" brought the experience to Los Angeles and Chicago. Television and print advertising featured two growers (played by actors) standing waist deep in a bog and talking, often humorously, about what they did. The campaign also included a website, in-store displays, and events for consumers and members of the growers' cooperative itself. Product innovation was crucial, too: New flavor blends were introduced, along with a line of 100 percent juices in diet and light versions, and Craisins—sweetened dried cranberries. Other elements included a pop-up restaurant in a bog created in New York's Rockefeller Center, where winners of a Facebook cranberry-pairings contest were treated to appetizers and drinks made from Ocean Spray products. In addition, a leap-year promotion urged consumers to "leap" to Craisins. The campaign hit the mark, lifting sales an average of 10 percent in its first five years, in spite of continued decline in the fruit juice category.[22]

Winning the Super Bowl of Advertising

The Super Bowl attracts the largest audience on television: More than 100 million viewers tune in to watch the broadcast. With an audience that large, a 30-second ad slot sold for over $5.5 million.[23] Despite their high cost, one can argue that compared to regular television spots, Super Bowl ads are in fact a bargain when their huge audience is taken into account. Indeed, recent Super Bowls have been watched by between 110 and 115 million people each year, which means that at a cost of $5 million, a 30-second Super Bowl ad works out to between 4 and 5 cents per viewer. This actually could be lower than the average cost of advertising on a national network, where the perviewer cost ranges from 8 to 10 cents or more.[24]

In addition to its relative cost efficiency, Super Bowl advertising tends to be more impactful, given that the game is often viewed on a large high-definition screen. Moreover, thanks to the iconic status of Super Bowl advertising, many of the commercials are played indefinitely over social media, thus reaching a much larger audience than the directly purchased airtime. In fact, many Super Bowl advertisers develop sophisticated publicity and social media campaigns that can attract millions of additional viewers.

Many Super Bowl ads now have a new purpose: to create curiosity and interest so consumers will go online and engage in social media and word of mouth to glean more detailed information. The most popular ads—like a Honda CR-V ad with Matthew Broderick spoofing his Ferris Bueller film role, a VW ad with a young kid playing Darth Vader, and Amazon's "Alexa loses its voice"—drew tens of millions of YouTube views. Increasingly, Super Bowl ads are released online before the game as firms attempt to maximize their social media and PR power.

Determining the Media Reach, Frequency, and Impact. Media selection aims to find the most cost-effective media to deliver the desired number and type of exposures to the target audience. What do we mean by the desired number of exposures? The advertiser seeks a specified communication objective and response from the target audience—which usually involves the degree of brand awareness generated. The number of exposures needed to reach a certain level of audience awareness is contingent on the reach, frequency, and impact of the media chosen:

- *Reach (R).* The number of different persons or households exposed to a particular media schedule at least once during a specified time period
- *Frequency (F).* The number of times within the specified time period that an average person or household is exposed to the message
- *Impact (I).* The qualitative value of an exposure through a given medium (for example, a food ad should have a higher impact in *Bon Appétit* than in *Fortune* magazine)

Audience awareness will be greater the higher the exposures' reach, frequency, and impact. There are important trade-offs here. Suppose the planner has a communication budget of $1,000,000, and the cost per thousand exposures of average quality is $5. This allows for 200,000,000 exposures $1,000,000 [$1,000,000 ÷ [$5/1,000]). If the advertiser seeks an average exposure frequency of 10, it can reach 20,000,000 people (200,000,000 ÷ 10) with the given budget. But if the advertiser wants higher-quality media costing $10 per thousand exposures, it will be able to reach only 10,000,000 people, unless it is willing to lower the desired exposure frequency.

The relationship between reach, frequency, and impact is captured in the following concepts:

- *Total number of exposures (E).* This is the reach times the average frequency—that is, $E = R \times F$, also called the *gross rating points* (GRP). If a given media schedule reaches 80 percent of homes with an average exposure frequency of 3, the media schedule has a GRP of 240 (80×3) If another media schedule has a GRP of 300, it has more weight, but we cannot tell how this weight breaks down into reach and frequency.
- *Weighted number of exposures (WE).* This is the reach times average frequency, times average impact—that is, $WE = R \times F \times I$.

Reach is most important when launching new products, extensions of well-known brands, or infrequently purchased brands, or when going after an undefined target market. Frequency is most important when there are strong competitors, a complex story to tell, high consumer resistance, or a frequent purchase cycle. A key reason for repetition is consumer forgetfulness. The higher the "forgetting rate" associated with a brand, product category, or message, the higher the warranted level of repetition.[25]

Selecting Media Timing and Allocation. When choosing media, the advertiser must make both a macroscheduling and a microscheduling decision. The **macroscheduling decision** is related to seasons and the business cycle. Suppose 70 percent of a product's sales occur between June and September. The firm can vary its communication expenditures to follow the seasonal pattern, to oppose the seasonal pattern, or to be constant throughout the year. The **microscheduling decision** calls for allocating communication expenditures within a short period to obtain maximum impact. Suppose the firm decides to buy 30 radio spots in September. Communication messages for the month can be concentrated, dispersed continuously throughout the month, or dispersed intermittently.

The chosen pattern should meet the marketer's communication objectives and consider three factors. *Buyer turnover* expresses the rate at which new buyers enter the market; the higher this rate, the more continuous the communication should be. *Purchase frequency* is the number of times the average consumer buys the product during the period; the higher the purchase frequency, the more continuous the communication should be. The *forgetting rate* is the rate at which the buyer forgets the brand; the higher the forgetting rate, the more continuous the communication should be.

When launching a new product, the advertiser must choose among four strategies: continuity, concentration, flighting, and pulsing.

- *Continuity* means exposures appear evenly throughout a given period. Generally, advertisers use continuous communication in expanding markets, with frequently purchased items, and in tightly defined buyer categories.
- *Concentration* calls for spending all the communication dollars in a single period. This makes sense for products with one selling season or one related holiday.
- *Flighting* calls for communication during a period, followed by a period with no communication, followed by a second period of communication activity. It is useful when funding is limited, the purchase cycle is relatively infrequent, or items are seasonal.
- *Pulsing* is continuous communication at low levels, reinforced periodically by waves of heavier activity. It draws on the strengths of continuous communication and flighting to create a compromise scheduling strategy. Those who favor pulsing believe it results in the audience learning the message more thoroughly and at a lower cost to the firm.[26]

A company must allocate its communication budget over space as well as over time. It makes "national buys" when it places ads on national TV and radio networks or in nationally circulated magazines. It makes "spot buys" when it buys TV time in just a few markets or in regional editions of magazines. These markets are also called **areas of dominant influence**. The company makes "local buys" when it advertises in local newspapers, radio, or outdoor sites.

Developing the Creative Approach

The impact of a company's communication campaign depends not only on what it says but also, and often more crucially, on *how* it says it. Creative execution can be decisive.[27]

DETERMINING THE MESSAGE APPEAL

The effectiveness of a communication depends on how well its message is expressed in addition to its content. If a communication is ineffective, it may mean the wrong message was used or the right one was poorly expressed. Marketers use different creative strategies to translate their messages into a specific communication. We can broadly classify them as either informational or transformational appeals.[28]

Informational Appeals. An **informational appeal** elaborates on product or service attributes or benefits. Examples in advertising include problem-solution ads (Aleve offers the longest-lasting relief for aches and pains); product demonstration ads (Thompson Water Seal can withstand intense rain, snow, and heat); product comparison ads (AT&T offers the largest 4G mobile network); and testimonials from unknown or celebrity endorsers (NBA player LeBron James pitching McDonald's, Nike, Samsung, Sprite, and others). Informational appeals assume strictly rational processing of the communication on the consumer's part. Logic and reason rule.

Academic research has shed light on informational appeals and their relationship to one-sided versus two-sided arguments. One might expect one-sided presentations that praise a product to be more effective than two-sided arguments that also mention shortcomings. Yet two-sided messages may be more appropriate, especially when negative associations must be overcome.[29] Two-sided messages are more effective with better-educated audiences and those who are initially opposed.[30]

The order in which arguments are presented is also important.[31] In a one-sided message, presenting the strongest argument first arouses attention and interest, which is important in media where the audience often does not attend to the whole message. With a captive audience, a climactic presentation might be more effective. For a two-sided message, if the audience is initially opposed, it is better to start with the other side's argument and conclude with your own strongest argument.

Transformational Appeals. A transformational appeal elaborates on a non–product-related benefit or image. It might depict the kind of person who uses a brand (VW advertised to active, youthful people with its famed "Drivers Wanted" campaign) or the kind of experience that results from use (Pringles advertised "Once You Pop, the Fun Don't Stop" for years). Transformational appeals often attempt to stir up emotions that will motivate purchase.[32]

Communicators use negative appeals such as fear, guilt, and shame to get people to do things (brush their teeth, have an annual health checkup) or stop doing things (smoking, abusing alcohol, overeating). Fear appeals work best when they are not too strong, when source credibility is high, and when the communication promises, in a believable and efficient way, that the product or service will relieve the fear it arouses. Messages are most persuasive when they moderately disagree with audience beliefs. Stating only what the audience already believes at best merely reinforces beliefs, and messages too much at variance with those beliefs will be rejected.[33]

Communicators also use positive emotional appeals such as humor, love, pride, and joy. Motivational or "borrowed interest" devices—such as cute babies, frisky puppies, popular music, and provocative sex appeals—are often employed to attract attention and raise involvement with an ad. These techniques are thought necessary in the tough new media environment of low-involvement processing and competing messages. Attention-getting tactics may also detract from comprehension, however, and they can wear out their welcome fast or overshadow the product. Thus, one challenge is figuring out how to break through the clutter *and* deliver the intended message.

The magic of advertising is to bring abstract concepts to life in the minds of the consumer target. In a print ad, the communicator must decide on headline, copy, illustration, and color.[34] For a radio message, the communicator must choose words, voice qualities, and vocalizations. The sound of an announcer promoting a used automobile should be different from the sound of one promoting a new luxury car. If the message is to be carried on television or in person, all these elements plus body language must be planned. For the message to go online, the marketer must specify layout, fonts, graphics, and other visual and verbal information.

SELECTING THE MESSAGE SOURCE

Research has shown that the credibility of the source is crucial to a message's acceptance. The three most often identified characteristics of credibility are expertise, trustworthiness, and likability.[35] *Expertise* is the specialized knowledge the communicator possesses to back the claim being made. *Trustworthiness* reflects how objective and honest the source is perceived to be. Friends are trusted more than strangers or salespeople, and people who are not paid to endorse a product are viewed as more trustworthy than people who are paid. *Likability* describes the source's attractiveness, measured in terms of candor, humor, and naturalness.

The most credible source will score high on all three dimensions—expertise, trustworthiness, and likability. Pharmaceutical companies want doctors to testify about product benefits because doctors have high credibility. Charles Schwab became the centerpiece of ads for his $4 billion-plus discount brokerage firm via the "Talk to Chuck" and "Own Your Tomorrow" corporate advertising campaigns that stressed integrity and likability.

Messages delivered by knowledgeable, trustworthy, and likable sources can achieve higher attention and recall, which is why some advertisers use celebrities as spokespeople.[36] "Marketing Insight: Celebrity Endorsements" focuses on the use of testimonials in a communication campaign. On the other hand, some marketers feature ordinary people to give their ads more realism and overcome consumer skepticism. Ford featured actual customers being thrust into a press conference to describe their vehicles. Red Lobster used chefs from its restaurants to extol the virtues of its menu.[37]

If a person has a positive attitude toward a message and its source (or a negative attitude toward both), a state of *congruity* is said to exist. But what happens when a celebrity praises a brand that a consumer dislikes? Some researchers believe an attitude change will take place that increases the amount of congruity between the two evaluations.[38] Thus, the consumer will end up respecting the celebrity somewhat less *or* the brand somewhat more. If the consumer encounters the same celebrity praising other disliked brands, she will eventually develop a negative view of the celebrity and maintain negative attitudes toward the brands. The **principle of congruity** implies that communicators can use their good image to reduce some negative feelings toward a brand but that, in the process. they might lose some esteem with the audience.

DEVELOPING THE CREATIVE EXECUTION

A practical tool to facilitate discussion about the creative output is given by the ADPLAN framework developed by Kellogg School of Management advertising expert Derek Rucker.[39] Once an agency or creative team supplies a storyboard or advertising execution, ADPLAN helps a strategist consider important factors that facilitate success and/or point out where missteps can take place. The ADPLAN acronym encompasses six dimensions: Attention, Distinction, Positioning, Linkage, Amplification, and Net Equity.

- **Attention** indicates whether an advertisement will garner interest from the target audience. This reflects both initial capture as well as sustained interest. For example, if a consumer who begins listening to an ad airing on YouTube hits the "skip ad" message after five seconds, the ad has failed to capture sufficient attention. and the company's message probably will not be heard. Recognizing this problem, Geico created a 5-second advertisement that was not skippable. Other brands have addressed this issue by using engaging creative content that people want to watch to completion.
- **Distinction** assesses whether an advertisement uses themes, content, or creative devices that distinguish it from other advertisements in the category or in general. For example, Apple's historic "1984" Super Bowl ad, despite being aired only once, achieved massive distinction because it featured high production values that represented Apple as a hero in a technological dystopia. In contrast, many local automotive commercials seem redundant.
- **Positioning** describes whether an advertisement situates the brand in the right category, provides a strong benefit, and anchors the benefit with a reason for customers to believe the message. This dimension is a check that the desired positioning is ultimately conveyed in the execution. For example, Old Spice ran a famous campaign that emphasized that it was the most masculine body wash available.
- **Linkage** communicates whether the target audience will remember the creative execution. Often, it is not enough that the target audience recalls seeing an advertisement. A strong linkage between creativity and message will ensure that target customers remember the brand that was presented. It is possible, for example, for a person to remember an ad but forget its message. For a number of years Ameriquest Mortgage ran Super Bowl commercials that people loved but could not remember what brand they promoted.
- **Amplification** captures whether individuals' thoughts about an advertisement are positive or negative. For example, Nike aired an ad featuring Collin Kaepernick following the former NFL

player's refusal to stand for the national anthem to protest racial injustice that received both positive and negative reactions from consumers. Brands typically seek to elicit primarily positive thoughts from their target audience. Amplification of positive thoughts is important because they can lead to the formation of favorable attitudes—and ultimately to purchase.

- **Net equity** pertains to how an advertisement fits with a brand's heritage and established associations. For example, the BMW brand is associated with high performance. As a consequence, one of BMW's objectives is to make sure that new advertisements do not threaten or undermine this equity.

Although the ADPLAN tool is meant to guide strategic discussions of advertisements, each element of the ADPLAN tool can be measured empirically. Thus the framework serves as a means to foster deeper conversations around advertising, as well as to direct where test and measurement might occur. Note that the ADPLAN is meant to function as just one aspect of a strategist's effort to evaluate creative output. Strategists must also develop a proper creative brief and consider the purpose of the advertisement (for example, whether awareness or persuasion is the desired outcome), the appropriateness of the media channel, and the company's advertising budget.[40]

Measuring Communication Effectiveness

Senior managers want to know the *outcomes* and *revenues* resulting from their communication investments. Too often, however, their communication managers supply only *inputs*, like press clippings or the number of ads, and *expenses*, like media costs. In fairness, communication managers try to translate inputs into intermediate outputs, such as reach and frequency (the percentage of the target market exposed to a communication and the number of exposures), recall and recognition scores, persuasion changes, and cost-per-thousand calculations.

After implementing the communication plan, marketers must measure its effectiveness. Research on the impact of communication seeks to determine the degree to which a company's communication has been effective in achieving its goals.[41] Communication effectiveness can be measured from two perspectives: supply side and demand side.

On the *supply side*, measuring communication effectiveness aims to assess the media coverage—for example, the number of seconds the brand is clearly visible on a television screen or the column inches of press clippings that mention the brand.

Although supply-side methods provide quantifiable measures, equating media coverage with advertising exposure ignores the content of the respective communications.[42] The advertiser uses media space and time to communicate a strategically designed message. Media coverage and telecasts only expose the brand and don't necessarily embellish its meaning in any direct way. Although some public relations professionals maintain that positive editorial coverage can be worth five to 10 times the equivalent advertising value, sponsorship rarely provides such favorable treatment.

On the *demand side*, measuring communication effectiveness aims to assess the effect a company's campaign has on the target audience. To this end, members of the target audience are asked whether they recognize or recall the message, how many times they saw it, what points they recall, how they felt about the message, what their previous attitudes toward the product and the company were, and what their current attitudes are.

For example, marketers can survey spectators to measure their recall of the event and their resulting attitudes and intentions toward the sponsor. Many advertisers use posttests to assess the overall impact of a completed campaign. If a company hoped to increase brand awareness from 20 percent to 50 percent and succeeded in increasing it only to 30 percent, then it is not spending enough, its ads are poor, or it has overlooked some other factor. Marketers also collect behavioral measures of audience response, such as how many people bought the product, liked it, and talked to others about it. Thus, most advertisers try to measure the communication effect of an ad—that is, its potential impact on awareness, knowledge, or preference.

Companies often examine the effectiveness of their communication campaigns to determine whether they are overspending or underspending on advertising. One way to answer this question is to work with the formulation shown in Figure 12.4. A company's *share of advertising expenditures* produces a *share of voice* (proportion of company advertising of that product to all advertising of similar competitive products) that earns a *share of consumers' minds and hearts* and, ultimately, a *share of market.*

To increase the effectiveness of its communication campaign, marketers often pretest their advertisements.[43] Based on the outcome of such pretests, the advertisement can be modified in a way that makes it more likely to achieve its ultimate goal. Pretest critics maintain that agencies can

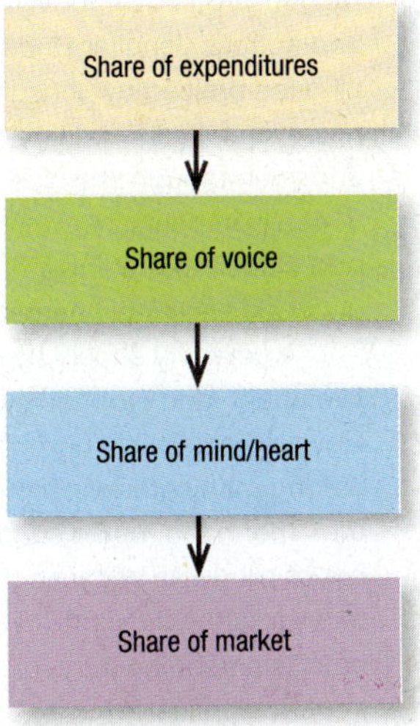

FIGURE **12.4**
Formula for Measuring Different Stages in the Sales Impact of Advertising

design ads that test well but do not necessarily perform well in the marketplace. Proponents maintain that useful diagnostic information can emerge from pretests but that they should not be used as the sole decision criterion. Nike, widely acknowledged as one of the best advertisers around, is known for doing very little ad pretesting.

In addition to pretesting their communication campaigns, marketers might measure whether and how the communication campaign influences sales. Researchers can measure sales impact with the *historical approach*, which uses advanced statistical techniques to correlate past sales to past advertising expenditures. Other researchers use *experimental data* to measure advertising's sales impact. A growing number of researchers measure the *sales effect* of advertising expenditures, instead of settling for measures of communication effect.[44] Millward Brown International has conducted tracking studies for years to help advertisers decide whether their advertising is benefiting their brand.

marketing INSIGHT Celebrity Endorsements

A well-chosen celebrity can draw attention to a product or brand—as Priceline found when it picked *Star Trek* icon William Shatner to star in campy ads reinforcing its low-price image. Other prominent celebrity endorsers include Tom Brady for Under Armour, Mark Wahlberg for AT&T, Kristen Bell for Old Navy, Reese Witherspoon for Crate and Barrel, and Drew Barrymore for Crocs.

Priceline's quirky campaigns have run for more than a decade, and Shatner's decision to receive stock options as compensation reportedly has netted him millions of dollars for his work. The right celebrity can also lend her or his image to a brand. To reinforce its high status and prestige image, American Express has used movie legends Robert De Niro and Martin Scorsese in ads.

Celebrities are likely to be effective when they are credible or personify a key product attribute. Statesman-like Dennis Haysbert for State Farm insurance, rugged Brett Favre for Wrangler jeans, and popular singer and actress Jennifer Hudson for Weight Watchers have all been praised by consumers as good fits. Celine Dion, however, failed to add glamour—or sales—to Chrysler, and even though she was locked into a three-year, $14 million deal, she was let go. Ozzy Osbourne seems an odd choice to advertise "I Can't Believe It's Not Butter," given his seemingly perpetual confusion.

A celebrity should have high recognition, high positive affect, and high "fit" with the product. Paris Hilton and Howard Stern have high recognition but negative affect among many groups. Tom Hanks and Oprah Winfrey, on the other hand, could successfully advertise a large number of products because they have extremely high ratings for familiarity and likability (known as the Q factor in the entertainment industry).

Celebrities can play a more strategic role, too, not only endorsing but also helping to design, position, and sell merchandise and services. Nike often brings its elite athletic endorsers in on product design. Tiger Woods, Paul Casey, and Stewart Cink have helped to design, prototype, and test new golf clubs and balls at Nike Golf's research and development facility. Beyoncé (Pepsi), will.i.am (Intel), Justin Timberlake (Bud Light Platinum), Alicia Keys (BlackBerry), and Taylor Swift (Diet Coke) have all been designated "ambassadors" for their brands with various creative duties and responsibilities.

Some celebrities lend their talents to brands without directly using their fame. A host of movie and TV stars do uncredited commercial voice-overs, including Jon Hamm (Mercedes-Benz), Morgan Freeman (Visa), Matt Damon (TD Ameritrade), Jeff Bridges (Duracell), and George Clooney (Budweiser). Although advertisers assume that some viewers will recognize the voices, the main rationale for using them is the actors' incomparable voice talent and skill.

Using celebrities poses certain risks. The celebrity might hold out for a larger fee at contract renewal or might even withdraw. And just like movies and album releases, celebrity campaigns can be expensive flops. The celebrity might lose popularity or, even worse, get caught in a scandal or embarrassing situation, as did Tiger Woods, Michael Phelps, and Lance Armstrong. Besides carefully checking endorsers' backgrounds, some marketers are choosing to use more than one to reduce their brand's exposure to any single person's flaws.

Another solution is for marketers to create their own brand celebrities. Dos Equis beer, imported from Mexico, boosted U.S. sales by more than 20 percent during the last recession by riding on the popularity of its "Most Interesting Man in the World" ad campaign. Suave and debonair, with a distinct voice and a silver beard, the character has hundreds of thousands of Facebook friends, despite being completely fictitious. Videos of his exploits log millions of views on YouTube. Dos Equis has made it possible for customers to "call" him and listen to a series of automated voicemail messages.[45]

summary

1. Modern marketing calls for more than developing a good product, pricing it attractively, and making it accessible to target customers. Companies must also communicate with current and potential stakeholders and with the general public.
2. The marketing communication mix consists of nine major modes of communication: advertising, online and social media, mobile communication, direct marketing, events and experiences, word of mouth, publicity and public relations, personal selling, and packaging.
3. The communication process consists of nine elements: sender, receiver, message, media, encoding, decoding, response, feedback, and noise. To get their messages through, marketers must take into account how the target audience usually decodes messages. They must also transmit the message through efficient media that reach the target audience and develop feedback channels to monitor response to the message.
4. Developing effective communication requires eight steps: (1) identify the target audience, (2) choose the communication objectives, (3) design the communication, (4) select the communication channels, (5) set the total communication budget, (6) choose the communication mix, (7) measure the communication results, and (8) manage the integrated marketing communication process.
5. In identifying the target audience, the marketer needs to close any gap that exists between current public perception and the image sought. Communication objectives can be to create a need for the category, to increase brand awareness, to improve attitude toward the brand, or to boost intension to purchase the brand.
6. Designing effective communication requires making three key decisions: what to say (message strategy), how to say it (creative strategy), and who should say it (message source). Communication channels can be personal (advocate, expert, and social channels) or nonpersonal (media, atmosphere, and events).
7. Although other methods exist, the objective-and-task method of setting the communication budget, which calls on marketers to develop their budgets by defining specific objectives, is typically the most effective.
8. In choosing the marketing communication mix, marketers must examine the distinct advantages and costs of each communication tool and the company's market rank. They must also consider the type of market in which they are selling, how ready consumers are to make a purchase, and the offering's stage in the company, brand, and product life cycle.
9. Measuring the effectiveness of the marketing communication mix requires asking members of the target audience whether they recognize or recall the communication, how many times they saw it, what points they recall, how they felt about the communication, what their previous attitudes toward the company, brand, and product were, and what those attitudes are now.

marketing SPOTLIGHT

Red Bull

Source: chara_stagram/ Shutterstock

In 1982, businessman Dietrich Mateschitz was suffering from jet lag while on a trip to Bangkok. Locals told him about a popular tonic beverage called Krating Daeng that could relieve his symptoms of drowsiness and tiredness. He tried the beverage and found that it did alleviate his fatigue. Impressed, Mateschitz launched Red Bull GmbH two years later with Thai businessman Chaleo Yoovidhya, who owned a tonic drink company. It took three years for the company to create a drink formula that adapted the tonic beverage's taste to Western palates. Red Bull was sold for the first time in Austria in 1987.

Red Bull was advertised as having three main benefits: increasing concentration for students, enhancing performance for athletes, and alleviating fatigue symptoms for business travelers. In addition to these uses, Red Bull was commonly sold as an alcohol mixer. Clubs began embracing Red Bull as a safer way for people to party longer without having to resort to drugs. Red Bull noted this unintended usage and used guerilla marketing to further entrench the product in the party scene. The company hired students and DJs to serve Red Bull at parties, which encouraged other patrons to try out the drink.

(continued)

After enjoying domestic success, Red Bull in 1992 expanded outside of Austria to Hungary and Slovenia. Red Bull continued its international expansion to Germany and Switzerland shortly after. Five years later, Red Bull began selling in the United States. Despite its popularity in Austria, Red Bull initially found limited success in these new markets, because it was one of the first beverages to be labeled as an energy drink. Many customers were unsure of when and why they should drink Red Bull.

To address costumer confusion, Red Bull focused its product positioning around an adventurous lifestyle. Red Bull employed extensive advertisements that featured the famous slogan "Red Bull gives you wings" to make the beverage and its effects better-known in newer markets. In 1995, Red Bull began sponsoring athletes and teams in various sports across the world, and in just a couple of years, its list of sponsorships had grown to hundreds of athletes as well as many teams and sporting events. The company became very active in the motorsports scene and sponsored a racing team in Formula One, which at the time attracted one of the highest annual television audiences of all sporting events. Years later, the company purchased its own Formula One team. The Red Bull F1 team eventually became one of the most successful racing teams in the world, garnering four successive championships from 2010 to 2013. Red Bull has expanded its list of sports sponsorships and ownership to include, among others, NASCAR, the NFL, football, BMX, motocross, and skateboarding. Red Bull's endeavors in sponsoring international athletes and sporting events helped make Red Bull a global brand.

In addition to sports marketing, Red Bull has invested heavily in content marketing to promote the drink and its associated lifestyle. Red Bull established the Red Bull Media House, a collection of media companies that create content in magazines, films and television, video games, social media, and music. The various platforms have released thousands of photos, videos, and articles of people and ideas that align with the image the Red Bull brand promotes. Fans are also encouraged to upload their own content showcasing the Red Bull lifestyle. Red Bull Media House released a feature film called *The Art of Flight* that quickly rose to the top of the iTunes chart. Red Bull's in-house record company has helped bring fame to artists such as AWOLNATION and Twin Atlantic. The company's own publication, *The Red Bulletin*, reported a distribution of over five million magazines in 2017. The social media team of the Red Bull Media House has released numerous viral videos showcasing the action sports lifestyle of Red Bull users on its own YouTube channel. With over five million subscribers, Red Bull's YouTube channel is home to thousands of featurettes on Red Bull athletes and sporting events. Red Bull's content marketing has pushed awareness of its brand to greater heights and has further increased the association between an active lifestyle and the company.

Red Bull's nontraditional approach to marketing has made the company one of the world's most recognized brands. What's remarkable is that the original beverage has stayed more or less the same throughout the years—with one size, one form factor, and a handful of flavors. Red Bull continues to sponsor famous athletes, teams, and events across the world, and it has generated massive awareness through stunts such as the Red Bull Stratos space dive and the annual Red Bull Rampage cliff-jumping event. Red Bull's sales reached approximately $6.8 billion in 2018. Red Bull has kept its product line narrow, but its expansive marketing portfolio continues to grow the brand.[46]

Questions

1. What are Red Bull's greatest competitive strengths as more companies (like Coca-Cola, Pepsi, and Monster) enter the energy drink category and gain market share? What are the risks of competing against such powerhouses?
2. Discuss the pros and cons of Red Bull's nontraditional marketing tactics. Should Red Bull do more traditional advertising? Why or why not?
3. Discuss the effectiveness of Red Bull's sponsorships. Where should the company draw the line?

marketing
SPOTLIGHT

The Best Job in the World

Source: Genevieve Vallee/Alamy Stock Photo

Arguably the most famous natural wonder of the world, the Great Barrier Reef is the world's largest reef and the only object that can be identified from space. The Great Barrier Reef is located next to Queensland, Australia, which is known for its sandy beaches and tranquil rainforests. One would think that the close proximity of the two hotspots would be a winning combination for tourism. However, Queensland is located far away from major cities such as Melbourne and

Sydney, which most travelers prioritized in a trip to Australia. In addition, the 2008 financial crisis caused international tourism to drop significantly.

Tourism Queensland, the Queensland government's department of tourism and events, aimed to challenge other popular tourist destinations such as the Caribbean and the Greek Islands as the top island attraction. The greatest challenge that Tourism Queensland identified was building international awareness. To do this, Tourism Queensland tasked marketing agency SapientNitro in 2009 with creating a successful global advertising campaign on a limited budget of $1.2 million.

SapientNitro came up with its now-legendary "The Best Job in the World" campaign. The campaign consisted of Tourism Queensland advertising an opening for the position of "Island Caretaker." Applicants needed no previous work experience, and their only duty was to write a single blog post about the islands once a week. The lucky applicant selected would receive free living accommodations on the island and a six-figure salary for six months. The position was billed as "The Best Job in the World," and interested candidates had to upload a 60-second application video on Tourism Queensland's website.

To create international publicity, Tourism Queensland invited influential travel journalists and bloggers from across the globe to the islands and held a media conference that featured a luxury villa and a sunny tropical paradise. The change in scenery was a stark contrast to many of the conference attendees in the Northern Hemisphere, who were experiencing a cold, dark winter.

Public interest in the advertisement campaign exploded shortly afterward. Within one day of launch, the website received over 200,000 website views. Within the six-week application period, Tourism Queensland received over 34,000 applicants from nearly 200 countries. The website had drawn over 6.8 million unique monthly visitors, who generated approximately 54 million page views and spent an extremely high average of 8.25 minutes viewing the website. More than 46,000 mainstream media articles were written about the promotion. In total, it was estimated that the campaign had reached nearly 3 billion people worldwide.

The $1.2 million campaign had exceeded Tourism Queensland's wildest expectations. Three main reasons help explain to why the low-budget promotion resulted in explosive numbers of views. For one thing, the promotion was hosted almost exclusively on their website. Whereas $1.2 million could have purchased only a small amount of TV advertisement time, the money invested resulted in a website that reached across the globe with ease. Second, the overwhelming majority of the content in the advertising campaign was provided by the numerous applicants, who submitted over 550 hours of videos to the website; none of them were created by the SapientNitro or Tourism Queensland teams. The most notable applicants received millions of views on YouTube and widespread social media attention. The popularity of these videos persisted even after the application period ended. Third, Tourism Queensland earned media coverage, instead of having to buy it. Media companies assumed the responsibility of following top candidates and telling their story. BBC Television created a one-hour documentary featuring the final 16 candidates in the competition, which received the highest viewer ratings during the week of its release in the UK.

The winner of the competition was a British man named Ben Southall. After receiving the job, Southall conducted the largest number of interviews in a 24-hour period at the time—124 in TV broadcasts all over the world. During his six-month position, Southall was interviewed by Oprah Winfrey and was featured in a six-part National Geographic series. Southall became an ambassador for Queensland tourism after his position ended. In total, the clever advertising campaign generated over $250 million in media value and brought worldwide attention to Queensland tourism. "The Best Job in the World" received 8 Cannes Lions awards for distinguished creativity in advertising and marketing and was inducted into PR News's Platinum Hall of Fame in 2014.[47]

Questions

1. What were the key reasons for the phenomenal popularity of SapientNitro's "The Best Job in the World" campaign?
2. Was the campaign successful in generating tourist traffic to Queensland? How should one measure the success of this publicity campaign?
3. What should Queensland do in the future to promote tourism?

CHAPTER 13

Designing an Integrated Marketing Campaign in the Digital Age

Product placement in music videos, celebrity endorsements from top artists, and partnering with companies like Chrysler, HP, and HTC to incorporate its sound technology in their products were key components in the success of Beats by Dre.

Source: Akio Kon/ Bloomberg/Getty Images

As the communication landscape becomes ever more complex, companies are faced with the growing challenge of coordinating communication activities to ensure that they deliver a consistent message across different channels—and do so in a way that enables them to achieve their strategic goals. As a result, companies are adopting integrated marketing communications as an approach to designing, communicating, and delivering a message through multiple strategies that work together and reinforce one another. One company that has successfully used diverse means of disseminating its message is Beats by Dr. Dre.

>>> Born Andre Young, famed rap producer Dr. Dre was a founding member of hip-hop group N.W.A. and had made an indelible mark on the music scene before becoming an entrepreneur. His Beats by Dre headphones, launched in 2006 with music mogul Jimmy Iovine, have become a must for many music lovers despite costing $300, nearly 10 times what ordinary earbuds sell for. Their appeal is in the thumping, bass-heavy sound and sleek look, even if the reviews among audiophiles are somewhat mixed. With strong adoption among celebrity musicians and athletes,

Beats became as fashionable as they were practical and an essential modern lifestyle item. Product placement, celebrity endorsements, and joint (co-op) advertising were key components of Beats's marketing strategy. Dre and Iovine, who at the time was the chairman of Interscope Records, had relationships with most of the top musicians and were able to arrange for Beats headphones to appear in music videos of some of the best-selling music artists, such as Lady Gaga, Miley Cyrus, Snoop Dogg, and Nicki Minaj. The endorsement by Dr. Dre brought Beats credibility among artists who might otherwise have been unwilling to endorse a commercial product. The exclusivity and the high cost associated with creating music videos also helped make Beats a status symbol and moved them closer to becoming a cultural phenomenon. Dre and Iovine's expertise and connections in the industry enabled them to identify hit songs and ensure placement for Beats headphones in the music video. In addition to celebrity endorsements, Beats developed celebrity special editions: purple JustBeats with Justin Bieber, jewelry-like HeartBeats with Lady Gaga, and DiddyBeats with P. Diddy. Beats also partnered with firms like Chrysler, HP, and HTC to build its sound technology into their cars, computers, and smartphones, and it has introduced its own version of earbuds and other products. "We sold half a billion worth of product before we paid for one ad," commented Iovine. Beats's success did not remain unnoticed by the large industry players. In 2011, Korean smartphone manufacturer HTC bought a majority stake in the company (financial pressures later forced HTC to sell its stake back to Dre and Iovine), and in 2014 Beats was acquired by Apple for $3.2 billion.[1]

To facilitate one-stop shopping for marketers, media companies and ad agencies have acquired promotion agencies, public relations firms, package-design consultancies, website developers, social media experts, and direct-mail houses. They are redefining themselves as *communication companies* that help clients improve their overall communication effectiveness by offering strategic and practical advice on many forms of communication. These expanded capabilities make it easier for marketers to assemble various media properties—as well as related marketing services—in an integrated communication program.

Learning Objectives After studying this chapter you should be able to:

13.1 Describe the key principles in managing an integrated marketing campaign.

13.2 Define the key aspects of managing an effective advertising campaign.

13.3 Explain how to design and manage online communications.

13.4 Describe the key aspects of managing social media.

13.5 Explain how to manage mobile communications.

13.6 Explain how to design meaningful events and experiences.

13.7 Describe the role of word of mouth in marketing communications.

13.8 Summarize how to manage publicity and public relations.

13.9 Discuss the role of product packaging as a communication tool.

Managing Integrated Marketing Communications

Integrated marketing communications (IMC) is an approach to managing a communication campaign through a coordinated use of different communication tools that work in concert and reinforce one another to enable the company to achieve its strategic goals. IMC ensures that a company's communication activities are consistent with one another and can achieve the company's communication goals in an effective and cost-efficient manner. IMC can occur on four distinct levels: horizontal, vertical, internal, and external.

- *Horizontal integration* involves coordinating all relevant marketing actions—including packaging, pricing, sales promotions, and distribution—with the communication campaign to achieve maximum customer impact.
- *Vertical integration* involves aligning the communication objectives with the higher-level goals that guide the company's overarching marketing strategy.
- *Internal integration* involves sharing the relevant information from different departments—including product development, market research, sales, and customer service—with the communication team to create an effective and cost-efficient campaign.
- *External integration* coordinates a company's communication activities with those of the external collaborators—including advertising, social media, and public relations agencies; event organizers; and campaign co-sponsors.

Having a well-integrated communication campaign is crucial to the company's market success.[2] Indeed, without an explicit focus on consistency, a company's communication can easily become a random compilation of unrelated (and sometimes even conflicting) messages, designed by different creative teams working in isolation from one another, and distributed though disparate media channels in a way that fails to emphasize their joint impact and might ultimately confuse rather than inform and persuade target customers.

The wide range of communication tools, messages, and audiences available to marketers makes it imperative that companies move toward integrated marketing communications. They must adopt a 360-degree view of consumers to fully understand all the different ways that communications can affect behavior. When done well, integrated marketing communications evaluate the strategic roles of a variety of communication disciplines and combine them seamlessly to provide clarity, consistency, and maximum impact of messages.

In developing an integrated marketing communications program, the marketer's overriding goal is to create the most effective and efficient communication program possible. The following criteria can help ensure that communications are truly integrated.[3]

- *Coverage*. Coverage is the proportion of the audience reached by each communication option employed, as well as the amount of overlap among those options. In other words, to what extent do different communication options reach the designated target market and the same or different consumers making up that market?
- *Contribution*. Contribution is the inherent ability of a marketing communication to elicit the desired response from consumers, and to exert communication effects on them, in the absence of exposure to any other communication option. How much does a communication affect consumer processing and build awareness, enhance image, elicit responses, and induce sales?
- *Commonality*. Commonality is the extent to which *common* associations are reinforced across communication options—that is, the extent to which different communication options share the same meaning. The consistency and cohesiveness of the brand image are important because they determine how easily existing associations and responses can be recalled and how easily additional associations and responses can become linked to the brand in memory.
- *Complementarity*. Communication options are often more effective when used in tandem. Complementarity involves emphasizing *different* associations and linkages across communication options. For effective positioning, brands typically need to establish multiple brand associations. Different marketing communication options may be better suited to establishing a particular brand association. For example, sponsorship of a cause may improve perceptions of a brand's trust and credibility, but TV and print advertising may be needed to communicate its performance advantages.

- *Conformability.* In any integrated communication program, the message will be new to some consumers and familiar to others. Conformability reflects the extent to which a marketing communication option works for both groups of consumers. The ability to work at two levels—effectively communicating to consumers who have seen other communications and to those who have not—is critically important.
- *Cost.* Marketers must evaluate marketing communications on all these criteria against their cost to arrive at the most effective *and* most efficient communications program.

An integrated marketing communication effort can produce greater message consistency, help build strong brands, and create more sales impact. It forces management to think about all the ways the customer comes in contact with the company, how the company communicates its positioning, the relative importance of each vehicle, and timing issues. It gives someone the responsibility—where none existed before—to unify the company's brand image and messages as they are sent through thousands of company activities. Integrated marketing communications should improve the company's ability to reach the right customers with the right messages at the right time and in the right place.[4]

The development of an integrated communication campaign requires a clear understanding of the specifics of alternative media formats in order to create a consistent experience for target customers. We briefly outline some of the key aspects of the most popular communication formats: advertising; online, social media and mobile communication; events and experiences; word of mouth; publicity and public relations; and packaging. Then, in the next chapter, we discuss personal selling and direct marketing.

Advertising

Advertising consists of any presentation and promotion of ideas, goods, services, and brands by an identified sponsor using paid media. Typically, the advertiser purchases media time (in the case of television and radio advertising) or space (in the case of print advertising) in order to convey the company's message to its target audience. The most popular forms of advertising—television, print, radio, online, and place advertising—are discussed in more detail in the following sections.

TELEVISION ADVERTISING

Television is generally acknowledged as the most powerful advertising medium and reaches a broad spectrum of consumers. TV advertising has three particularly important strengths. First, it can vividly demonstrate product attributes and persuasively explain their corresponding consumer benefits. Second, it can dramatically portray user and usage imagery, brand personality, and other intangibles. Third, television has the opportunity to tap a captive audience during live programming at important events (e.g., the Super Bowl, Oscars, and unfolding news stories).

Aflac Aflac (which stands for American Family Life Assurance Company), the largest supplier of supplemental insurance, was relatively unknown until a highly creative ad campaign made it one of the most widely recognized brands in recent history. Created by the Kaplan Thaler ad agency, the lighthearted campaign features an irascible duck incessantly squawking the company's acronymous name, "Aflac!" while consumers or celebrities discuss its products. The duck's frustrated bid for attention appealed to consumers. Sales were up 28 percent in the first year the duck aired, and name recognition went from 13 percent to 91 percent. Aflac has stuck with the duck in its advertising, even incorporating it into its corporate logo in 2005. Social media have enabled marketers to further develop the duck's personality: It has 515,000 Facebook fans and counting. The Aflac duck is not just a U.S. phenomenon. It also stars in Japanese TV ads—with a somewhat brighter disposition—where it has been credited with helping drive sales in Aflac's biggest market.[5]

Because of the fleeting nature of commercials, however, and the distracting creative elements often found in them, product-related messages and the brand itself can be overlooked.[6] Furthermore, the high volume of competitive advertisements and other nonprogramming material on television creates clutter that makes it easy for consumers to ignore or forget ads.

Source: Brendan McDermid/Reuters/Alamy Stock Photo

>> Name recognition for American Family Life Assurance Company shot up, along with sales, after a creative TV ad campaign featured a cantankerous duck interminably quacking the company's Aflac acronym.

Another consideration is the relatively high cost of television advertising. A commercial during a popular show on a national network might cost $200,000 to $500,000 per 30-second spot and deliver 2 to 7 million viewers. That equates to 8 to 10 cents or more per viewer. In contrast, online ads with video can cost around $25 per 1000 impressions, which is equal to 2.5 cents per viewer, although their impact may be diminished because they are often viewed on a much smaller computer or mobile device screen.[7]

With the advancement of online streaming, television programming has expanded beyond the actual television screen to include streaming to computers, laptops, tablets, and mobile phones. This shift has given consumers greater control over when and how to view a company's communications. In addition, the growing popularity of alternative commercial-free entertainment programming, such as Netflix, Amazon, and Hulu, is changing the communication landscape traditionally dominated by 30-second television ads. In response, marketers are seeking novel ways to engage viewers across the various types of programming and across different devices on which customers view television advertising.

Despite its drawbacks, television advertising can be a powerful way to inform customers about the company and its offerings, strengthen customer preferences and brand loyalty, and generate sales and profits. Savvy marketers take advantages of the benefits of television advertising and use it in combination with other forms of advertising and marketing communication to maximize its customer impact.

PRINT ADVERTISING

Print media offer a stark contrast to broadcast media. Because readers consume them at their own pace, magazines and newspapers can provide detailed product information and effectively communicate user and usage imagery. At the same time, the static nature of the visual images in print media makes dynamic presentations or demonstrations difficult, and print media can be fairly passive.

The two main print media—magazines and newspapers—share many advantages and disadvantages. Although newspapers are timely and pervasive, magazines are typically more effective at building user and usage imagery. Newspapers are popular for local—especially retailer—advertising. On an average day, roughly one-half to three-quarters of U.S. adults read a newspaper, although they are increasingly doing so online. Print advertising has steadily declined in recent years.[8] Advertisers have some flexibility in designing and placing newspaper ads, but relatively poor reproduction quality and short "shelf life" can diminish the impact.

Researchers report that the *picture, headline,* and *copy* in print ads matter, in that order of importance. The picture must draw attention. The headline must reinforce the picture and lead the person to read

Source: Luxottica

<< Magazine advertising can be an effective way to build or reinforce user imagery for a brand, as with Ray-Ban's "Never Hide" campaign.

the copy. The copy must be engaging and the brand's name prominent. Even then, less than 50 percent of the exposed audience will notice even a really outstanding ad. About 30 percent might recall the headline's main point, some 25 percent register the advertiser's name, and fewer than 10 percent read most of the body copy. Ordinary ads don't achieve even these modest results.

A print ad should be clear, consistent, and well branded. In an award-winning campaign, ads for the iPad Mini on the back covers of *Time* and *The New Yorker* compared the actual sizes of the device and the magazine. To celebrate its 75th anniversary, Ray-Ban's award-winning "Never Hide" print ad campaign featured seven ads showing how Ray-Ban wearers flouted convention and stood out from the crowd through seven different decades.

RADIO ADVERTISING

Radio is a pervasive medium: About 93 percent of all U.S. citizens age 12 and older listen daily and for about 20 hours a week on average—numbers that have held steady in recent years. Much radio listening occurs in the car and out of the home. To be successful, radio networks are going multiplatform with a strong digital presence to allow listeners to tune in anytime, anywhere.

Perhaps radio's main advantage is flexibility: Stations are very targeted, ads are relatively inexpensive to produce and place, and short closings for scheduling them allow for quick response. Radio can engage listeners through a combination of popular brands, local presence, and strong personalities. It is a particularly effective medium in the morning; it can also let companies achieve a balance between broad and localized market coverage. In addition, radio advertising is benefiting from the growing popularity of podcasts, which provide listeners with a wide array of options to choose from and the ability to choose when to listen to the desired content.

Radio's obvious disadvantages are its lack of visual images and the relatively passive nature of the consumer processing that results. Nevertheless, radio ads can be extremely creative. Clever use of music, sound, and other creative devices can tap into the listener's imagination to create powerfully relevant images.

ONLINE ADVERTISING

Given that internet users spend only a small portion of their time online actually searching for information, display ads still hold great promise compared to popular search ads. But ads need to be more attention-getting and influential, better targeted, and more closely tracked.[9]

Online ads offer several advantages. Marketers can easily trace their effects by noting how many unique visitors click on a page or ad, how long they spend with it, what they do on it, and where they go afterward.[10] This enables companies to test different messages and creative solutions, which in turn allows them to optimize the advertising campaign in a way that is most likely to elicit the desired consumer response. Online advertising also has the advantage of **contextual placement**, which means marketers can buy ads on sites related to their own offerings. They can also place advertising based on keywords that customers type into search engines to reach people when they've actually started the buying process.[11] Furthermore, online advertising allows for a plethora of content types—from text-only ads to print-style advertisements, video commercials, and fully interactive experiences.

Going online has disadvantages too. Consumers can effectively screen out most messages. Marketers may think their ads are more effective than they really are if bogus clicks are generated by software-powered websites. Advertisers also lose some control over their online messages, which can be hacked or vandalized. But the pros clearly can outweigh the cons, and the share of online advertising has shown continuous growth in the past decade.

An increasingly popular form of online advertising is **native advertising**, which involves materials resembling the publication's editorial content but is intended to promote the advertiser's product. In other words, native ads are paid commercial messages that match the look and feel of the publication in which they appear. Unlike traditional advertising, native advertising is designed to be non-disruptive and to look like part of the editorial flow of the publication.

Native ads come in three common formats: (1) content recommendations, such as suggested articles that appear below an article featuring editorial content, (2) "in-feed" advertisements that appear in the news feed on social networks, and (3) search listings and promoted listings that appear above the results of an organic Google search.

With its non-disruptive approach, native advertising has grown in popularity worldwide. Although it is utilized primarily in online communications, native advertising is also used in traditional media formats including print, television, and radio. For example, a magazine might feature an article that is developed jointly with the editorial staff and the advertiser in an informative, engaging, and highly readable way that promotes a particular product, service, or brand.

PLACE ADVERTISING

Place advertising is a broad category that includes many creative and unexpected forms to grab consumers' attention where they work, play, and, of course, shop. Popular options include billboards, public spaces, product placement, and point of purchase.

Billboards. Billboards use colorful, digitally produced images, graphics, backlighting, sounds, and movement. Outdoor advertising is often called the "15-second sell" because consumers have a fleeting exposure to the ad and must grasp its message almost instantly. In New York, manhole covers have been reimagined as steaming cups of Folgers coffee; in Belgium, eBay posted "Moved to eBay" stickers on empty storefronts; and in Germany, imaginary workers toiling inside vending machines, ATMs, and photo booths were justification for a German job-hunting website to proclaim, "Life Is Too Short for the Wrong Job."[12]

A strong creative message can make all the difference. Chang Soda Water in Bangkok had enough money in its budget for only one digital billboard. To maximize impact, it built a giant bubbling bottle onto the billboard to illustrate the product's carbonation. Word-of-mouth buzz quintupled bottle sales from 200,000 to 1 million.[13]

Public Spaces. Ads are appearing in such unconventional places as movie screens, airplane bodies, and fitness equipment, as well as in classrooms, sports arenas, office and hotel elevators, and other public places. Transit ads on buses, subways, and commuter trains have become a valuable way to reach working men and women. "Street furniture"—bus shelters, kiosks, and public areas—is another fast-growing option.

As the effectiveness of many traditional means of communication is declining, advertisers turn to using public spaces to create a memorable impression of the company and its offerings in customers' minds. As a result, a growing number of advertisers buy space in stadiums and arenas and on garbage cans, bicycle racks, parking meters, airport luggage carousels, elevators, gasoline pumps, the bottom of golf cups and swimming pools, airline snack packages, and supermarket produce in the form of tiny labels on apples and bananas. And more firms than ever are using their names to sponsor arenas, stadiums, and other venues that hold events, spending billions of dollars for naming rights to major North American sports facilities.

Source: PictureLux/The Hollywood Archive/Alamy Stock Photo

<< In addition to Heineken doling out a hefty sum so James Bond would choose its beer instead of a shaken-not-stirred martini, other brands opted to feature their products in the film *Skyfall*.

Product Placement. Marketers pay hundreds of thousands of dollars for their products to make cameo appearances in movies and on television.[14] Sometimes such product placements are the result of a larger network advertising deal, but small product-placement shops also maintain ties with prop masters, set designers, and production executives.

Some firms get product placement at no cost. Nike does not pay to be in movies but often supplies shoes, jackets, bags, and so on. Increasingly, products and brands are being woven directly into the story, as when a new iPad for the gadget-loving dad of *Modern Family* became the story arc of a whole episode. In some cases, however, brands pay for the rights to appear in a movie. Consider the case of *Skyfall:*

Skyfall With *Skyfall*, the 23rd film in the franchise, Heineken reportedly paid almost $40 million for James Bond to drink its beer instead of his traditional vodka martini—a sum that covered one-third of the film's estimated production budget. Marketers with the most on-screen presence after Heineken's in the film included Adidas, Aston Martin, Audi, Omega, Sony, and Tom Ford. One research firm estimated that brands recognized in the film received more than $7.6 million worth of exposure during its opening weekend. Some brands featured their product placement in the movie off screen, too. Heineken shot an extravagant 90-second ad featuring an inventive chase on a train that ended with a cameo appearance by Daniel Craig, the British actor playing Bond at that time. More than 22 million people viewed the campaign online, and Heineken's "Crack the Case" promotion invited consumers in major cities to demonstrate their Bond-like skills in a game.[15]

Point of Purchase. The appeal of point-of-purchase advertising is that consumers make many brand decisions in the store. There are many ways to communicate at the point of purchase (P-O-P), including ads on shopping carts, cart straps, aisles, and shelves and with in-store demonstrations, live sampling, and instant coupon machines.[16] Some supermarkets are selling floor space for company logos and experimenting with talking shelves. Mobile marketing reaches consumers via smartphones when in store. P-O-P radio provides programming and commercial messages to thousands of food stores and drugstores nationwide.

Online Communication

Marketers must go where the customers are, and increasingly that's online. Of the total time U.S. consumers spend with all media, more than half is spent online. Customers define the rules of engagement, however, and insulate themselves with the help of agents and intermediaries if they so choose. They define what information they need, what offerings they're interested in, and what they're willing to pay.

COMPANY WEBSITE

Companies must design websites that embody or express their purpose, history, products, and vision—and that are attractive on first viewing and interesting enough to encourage repeat visits.[17] Beauty pioneer Estée Lauder, in a reflection of times gone by, famously said she relied on three means of communication to build her multimillion-dollar cosmetics business—"telephone, telegraph, and tell a woman." She would now have to add the internet, where the company's official site describes new and old products, announces special offers and promotions, and helps customers locate stores where they can buy Estée Lauder products.

Visitors will judge a site's performance on ease of use and physical attractiveness. *Ease of use* typically means that the content is easy to understand and navigate. *Physical attractiveness* reflects the aesthetic appeal of the website, including factors such as layout, fonts, and color coordination. These features of a website can help facilitate sales. For example, J. D. Power found that consumers who were "delighted" with an automotive manufacturer's website were more likely to test drive one of its vehicles as a result.[18]

As we describe in more detail later, firms such as comscore and Nielsen track where consumers go online through measures like number of page views, number of unique visitors, length of visit, and so on. Companies must also be sensitive to online security and privacy-protection issues. One set of researchers recommends transforming various "touch points" related to website privacy into a positive customer experience by developing user-centric privacy controls that avoid multiple intrusions and prevent human intrusion by using automation whenever possible.[19]

Besides their websites, companies may employ microsites: individual pages or clusters of pages that function as supplements to a primary site. People rarely visit an insurance company's website, for example, but the company can create a microsite on used-car sites that offers advice for buyers of used cars—and a good insurance deal at the same time.

DRIVING ONLINE TRAFFIC

An important component of online marketing is driving traffic to the company's own media. There are two common approaches to drive traffic: search engine optimization and search engine marketing.

Search engine optimization (SEO) describes activities designed to improve the likelihood that a link for a brand ranks as high as possible in the order of all nonpaid links when consumers search for relevant terms. Because SEO involves optimizing the company's own website without paying a third party to generate traffic, it is significantly less costly to implement than search engine marketing.

Search engine marketing (SEM) describes activities whereby the company pays search engine companies to be featured in the results of particular keyword searches that serve as a proxy for the consumer's product or consumption interests. When consumers search for any of these words with Google, the marketer's ad may appear above or next to the results, depending on the amount the company bids and an algorithm the search engines use to determine an ad's relevance to a particular search. For example, McDonald's might pay Google for its information to appear among the results generated when consumers search for a particular word or phrase, such as "burger," "French fries," or "fast food."

Advertisers typically pay only if people click on the links, but marketers believe consumers who have already expressed interest by engaging in search are prime prospects. The cost per click depends on how high the link is ranked on the page and the popularity of the keyword. The ever-increasing popularity of paid search has increased competition among keyword bidders, significantly raising search ad prices and putting a premium on choosing the best possible keywords, bidding on them strategically, and monitoring the results for effectiveness and efficiency.

A number of guidelines have been suggested as part of SEO and SEM.[20] For example, broader search terms ("iPhone" or "burger") are useful for general brand building; more specific ones identifying a particular product model or service ("Apple iPhone XS Max") are useful for generating and converting sales leads. Search terms need to be spotlighted on the appropriate pages of the marketer's website so search engines can easily identify them. Any one product can usually be identified by means of multiple keywords, but marketers must bid on each keyword according to its probable return on revenue.

Social Media

An important component of digital marketing is social media. Social media are a means for consumers to share text, images, audio, and video information with one another and with companies, and vice versa.

Social media enable marketers to establish a public voice and presence online. They can also cost-efficiently reinforce other communication activities. In addition, because of their day-to-day immediacy, they can encourage companies to stay innovative and relevant. Marketers can build or tap into online communities, inviting participation from consumers and creating a long-term marketing asset in the process.

THE GROWTH OF SOCIAL MEDIA

Social media allow consumers to become engaged with a brand at perhaps a deeper and broader level than ever before. Marketers should do everything they can to encourage willing consumers to engage productively. But as useful as they may be, social media are rarely the sole source of marketing communications for a brand.

Research suggests that brands and products vary widely in how social they are online. Consumers are most likely to engage with media, charities, and fashion and least likely to engage with consumer goods.[21] Although consumers may use social media to get useful information, deals, and promotions or to enjoy interesting or entertaining brand-created content, a much smaller percentage use social media to engage in two-way "conversations" with brands. In short, marketers must recognize that when it comes to social media, only *some* consumers want to engage with *some* brands—and even then, only *some* of the time.

One challenge faced by social media marketers is the speed with which they are expected to react to relevant news and events. The "always-on" connectivity has conditioned consumers to expect an almost instant company response. This, in turn, forces companies to develop new communication capabilities enabling them to react to problems and opportunities in real time by shaping the social media conversation and taking actions to rectify problems and take advantage of opportunities.

Embracing social media, harnessing word of mouth, and creating buzz also require companies to take the good with the bad.[22] When Frito-Lay's "Do Us a Flavor" contest invited U.S. fans to suggest new potato chip flavors for a chance to win a huge cash prize, the Facebook app for submissions crashed the first day due to high traffic. The promotion got back on track, though, with the winner, Cheesy Garlic Bread–flavored chips, joining earlier winners from other countries, such as Caesar salad–flavored chips in Australia and shrimp chips in Egypt.[23]

The Frito-Lay example illustrates the power and speed of social media, but also the challenges they pose to companies. The reality, however, is that whether a company chooses to engage in social media or not, the internet will always permit scrutiny and criticism from consumers and organizations. By using social media and the internet in a constructive, thoughtful way, firms at least have a means to create a strong online presence and to offer credible alternative points of view if negative feedback occurs. And if the firm has built a strong online community, members of that community will often rush to defend the brand and play a policing role regarding inaccurate or unfair characterizations.

SOCIAL MEDIA PLATFORMS

There are four main platforms for social media: online communities and forums, blogs, social networks, and customer reviews.

Online Communities and Forums. Online communities and forums come in all shapes and sizes. Many are created by consumers or groups of consumers with no commercial interests or company affiliations. Others are sponsored by companies whose members communicate with the company and with one another through postings, text messaging, and chat discussions about special interests related to the company's products and brands. These online communities and forums can be a valuable resource for companies and perform multiple functions by both collecting and conveying key information.

A key for success in online communities is to create individual and group activities that help form bonds among community members. Apple hosts a large number of discussion groups organized by product line and type of user (consumer or professional). These groups are customers' primary source of product information after warranties expire.

The two-way information flow in online communities and forums can provide companies with useful, hard-to-get customer information and insights. When GlaxoSmithKline prepared to launch its first weight-loss drug, Alli, it sponsored a weight-loss community. The firm felt the feedback it gained was more valuable than what it could have received from traditional focus groups. Likewise, LEGO begun crowdsourcing product ideas from consumers by enabling fans to create and vote on designs that LEGO then took to market as formal products. LEGO's global crowdsourcing platform produced a number of successful products, including a series of sets based on the hugely popular Minecraft game.[24]

Blogs. Blogs, regularly updated online journals or diaries, have become an important outlet for word of mouth. There are millions in existence, and they vary widely; some are personal for close friends and families, and others are designed to reach and influence a vast audience. One obvious appeal of blogs is that they bring together people with common interests.

Corporations are creating their own blogs and carefully monitoring those of others.[25] Because many consumers examine product information and reviews contained in blogs, the Federal Trade Commission has also taken steps to require bloggers to disclose their relationship with marketers whose products they endorse. At the other extreme, some consumers use blogs and videos as a means of getting retribution for a company's bad service or faulty products.

Social Networks. Social networks such as Facebook, LinkedIn, Instagram, YouTube, Twitter, and WeChat have become an important force in both business-to-consumer and business-to-business marketing.[26]

Marketers are still learning how best to tap into social networks and their huge, well-defined audiences.[27] Given networks' noncommercial nature—users are generally there looking to connect with others—attracting attention and persuading are challenging. Also, given that users generate their own content, ads may appear beside inappropriate or even offensive material.

Much online content is not necessarily shared and does not go viral. Only a small fraction of content ends up "cascading" to more than one person beyond the initial recipient. In deciding whether to contribute to social media, consumers can be motivated by intrinsic factors such as whether they are having fun or learning, but more often they are swayed by extrinsic factors such as social and self-image considerations.[28]

Harvard Business School viral video expert Thales Teixeira offers the following advice for getting a viral ad shared. Utilize brand pulsing: Display the brand for short periods of time in a way that doesn't make the brand too intrusive within the story, open with joy or surprise to hook those fickle viewers who are easily bored, build an emotional roller coaster within the ad to keep viewers engaged throughout, and surprise but don't shock; if an ad makes viewers too uncomfortable, they are unlikely to share it.[29]

Viral marketing tries to create a splash in the marketplace to showcase a brand and its noteworthy features. Some believe viral marketing efforts are driven more by the rules of entertainment than by the rules of selling. Consider these examples: Quicksilver puts out surfing videos and surf-culture books for teens, Johnson & Johnson and Pampers both have popular websites with parenting advice, Walmart places videos with money-saving tips on YouTube, Grey Goose vodka has an entire entertainment division, Mountain Dew has a record label, and Hasbro is joining forces with Discovery to create a TV channel.[30] Ultimately, however, the success of any viral or word-of-mouth buzz campaign depends on the willingness of consumers to talk to other consumers.

An increasingly important component of a company's online communication is the use of social media influencers. The term **influencer marketing** refers to the use of a popular online figure to promote a product, service, or brand within his or her social media feed. Strictly speaking, influencer marketing can be viewed as a mix of publicity and paid endorsement that takes place in the context of social media. Here, the company pays the endorser to promote its offerings, but rather than using this endorsement in its own communications, the company relies on the influencer's own social media networks to disseminate the message.

Influencer marketing has grown rapidly in recent years to become a multibillion-dollar industry. This rapid growth has presented marketers with several challenges. As an increasing number of companies realize the value of using influencers to promote their offerings, the demand for influencers has gone up, and the price of securing an endorsement has increased manyfold to reach over $100,000 for some of the top influencers.[31]

The high fees collected by influencers and the lack of accurate measures of their market impact have also created a global marketplace for social media fraud. A growing number of companies specialize in selling Twitter followers and retweets, views on YouTube, and endorsements on LinkedIn to users who want to appear more popular and influential in the social media space. In one case a single company was found to be using over 3.5 million automated accounts, each sold to multiple customers, to provide influencers with more than 200 million Twitter followers.[32] Many of these influencers then used their inflated follower numbers to negotiate higher fees from advertisers for their endorsements. As advertisers become aware of the importance of authenticating the influencers' real impact, they employ companies that serve as social media detectives. These companies evaluate influencers' social media activity, looking for signs of bot activity to determine the percentage of "real" followers, views, and visitors.

Customer Reviews. Customer reviews can be especially influential in shaping customer preferences and buying decisions.[33] One Nielsen survey found that online customer reviews were the second most trusted source of brand information (after recommendations from friends and family).[34] Research has shown that social influence can lead to disproportionately positive online ratings, and subsequent raters are more likely to be influenced by previous positive ratings than by negative ones. Consumers posting reviews are susceptible to conformity pressures and to adopting the norms of others.[35] On the other hand, positive online reviews or ratings are often not as influential or valued as negative ones.[36]

Consumers are also influenced by the online opinions and recommendations of other consumers. The informal social networks that arise among consumers complement the product networks set up by the company.[37] Online "influentials" who are one of a few people—or maybe even the only person—to influence certain consumers are particularly important and valuable to companies.[38]

Mobile Communication

U.S. consumers spend a considerable amount of time on mobile—more than on radio, magazines, and newspapers combined.[39] Given the omnipresence of smartphones and tablets, and marketers' ability to personalize messages based on demographics and other consumer behavior characteristics, the appeal of mobile marketing as a communication tool is obvious.

Wharton's David Bell notes four distinctive characteristics of a mobile device: (1) It is uniquely tied to one user. (2) It is virtually always "on" since it is typically carried everywhere. (3) It allows for immediate consumption because it is in effect a channel of distribution with a payment system. (4) It is highly interactive, given that it allows for geotracking and picture and video taking.[40]

Mobile ad spending has grown dramatically worldwide. With the increased capabilities of smartphones, however, mobile ads can be more than just a display medium using static "mini-billboards." Much recent interest has been generated in mobile apps adding convenience, social value, incentives, and entertainment and making consumers' lives a little or a lot better.[41]

Smart mobile devices are also conducive to boosting loyalty programs in which customers can track their visits to and purchases from a merchant and receive rewards. By tracking the whereabouts of receptive customers who opt to receive communications, retailers can send them location-specific promotions when they are near shops or outlets. Sonic Corp. used GPS data and proximity to cell towers in Atlanta to identify when those customers who had signed up for company communications were near one of roughly 50 Sonic restaurants in the area. When that was the case, the company sent customers a text message with a discount offer or an ad to entice them to visit the restaurant.[42]

Because traditional coupon redemption rates have been declining for years, the ability of mobile to make more relevant and timely offers to consumers at or near the point of purchase has piqued the interest of many marketers. These new coupons can take many forms, and digital in-store signs can dispense them to smartphones. With user privacy safeguards in place, marketers' greater knowledge of cross-screen identities (online and mobile) can permit more relevant, targeted ads.

Understanding how consumers want to use their smart phones is critical to understanding the role of advertising. Given the small screen and fleeting attention paid, fulfilling advertising's traditional role of informing and persuading is more challenging on mobile devices. On the plus side, consumers are more engaged and attentive when using their smartphones than when they are online. Nevertheless, a number of m-commerce companies are eliminating ads to allow consumers to make purchases with as few clicks as possible.[43]

Events and Experiences

Becoming part of a personally relevant moment in consumers' lives through sponsored events and experiences can broaden and deepen a company's or brand's relationship with the target market. Daily encounters with brands may also affect consumers' brand attitudes and beliefs.

MANAGING EVENTS

Marketers report a number of reasons to sponsor events:

- *To identify with a particular target market or lifestyle.* Old Spice sponsors college sports—including its college basketball Old Spice Classic in late November—to highlight product relevance and sample among its target audience of 16- to 24-year-old males.
- *To increase the salience of a company or product name.* Events offer sustained exposure to a brand, a necessary condition for reinforcing brand salience. Top-of-mind awareness for soccer World Cup sponsors Emirates Airlines, Hyundai, Kia, and Sony benefited from the repeated brand and ad exposure over the month-long tournament.
- *To create or reinforce perceptions of key brand image associations.* Events themselves have associations that help to create or reinforce brand associations.[44] To toughen its image and appeal to the heartland, Toyota Tundra sponsors B.A.S.S. fishing tournaments and has sponsored Brooks & Dunn country music tours.
- *To enhance corporate image.* Sponsoring and organizing events can improve perceptions that the company is likable and prestigious. Although Visa views its long-standing Olympic sponsorship as a means of enhancing international brand awareness and increasing usage and volume, it also engenders patriotic goodwill and taps into the emotional Olympic spirit. McDonald's sponsors community-based programs to build goodwill, including Black & Positively Golden, which celebrates Black culture.
- *To create experiences and evoke feelings.* The feelings engendered by an exciting or rewarding event may indirectly link to the brand. Audi models featured prominently in the blockbuster film franchise *Iron Man*, including main character Tony Stark's personal R8 Spyder, the A8 and A3, as well as the Q5 and Q7 SUVs.
- *To express commitment to the community or on social issues.* Cause-related events sponsor nonprofit organizations and charities. Firms such as Timberland, Stonyfield Farms, Home Depot, Starbucks, American Express, and Tom's of Maine have made their support of causes an important cornerstone of their marketing programs.
- *To entertain key clients or reward key employees.* Many events include lavish hospitality tents and other special services or activities for sponsors and their guests only. These perks engender goodwill and establish valuable business contacts. From an employee perspective, events can also build participation and morale or serve as an incentive. BB&T Corp., a major banking and financial services player in the U.S. South and Southeast, used its NASCAR Busch Series sponsorship to entertain business customers and its minor league baseball sponsorship to generate excitement among employees.
- *To permit merchandising or promotional opportunities.* Many marketers tie contests or sweepstakes, in-store merchandising, direct response, or other marketing activities to an event. Ford and Coca-Cola have used their sponsorship of the popular TV show *American Idol* in this way.

Despite these potential advantages, the result of an event can still be unpredictable and beyond the sponsor's control. And although many consumers credit sponsors for providing the financial assistance to make an event possible, some may resent their commercialization of the event.

CREATING EXPERIENCES

Experiential marketing not only communicates features and benefits but also connects a product or service with unique and interesting experiences. Rather than focusing on selling, experiential marketing aims to let customers experience how the company's offering fits in their life. Many firms are creating their own events and experiences to stimulate consumer and media interest and involvement.

A popular form of experiential marketing involves event sponsorship. Making sponsorships successful requires choosing the appropriate events, designing the optimal sponsorship program, and measuring the effects of sponsorship. Because of the number of sponsorship opportunities and their huge cost, marketers must be selective. The event must meet the marketing objectives and communication strategy defined for the brand. It must have sufficient awareness, possess the desired image, and be able to create the desired effects. The audience must match the target market and must have a favorable attitude toward the sponsor's engagement. An ideal event also is unique but not encumbered by many sponsors, lends itself to ancillary marketing activities, and reflects or enhances the sponsor's brand or corporate image.[45]

Companies can even create a strong image by inviting prospects and customers to visit their headquarters and factories.[46] Ben & Jerry's, Boeing, Crayola, and Hershey's all sponsor excellent company tours that draw millions of visitors a year. Hallmark, Kohler, and Beiersdorf (maker of NIVEA) have built, at or near their headquarters, corporate museums that display their history and the drama of producing and marketing their products. Many firms are also creating off-site product and brand experiences. These include the World of Coca-Cola in Atlanta and Las Vegas and M&M's World in Times Square in New York City.

To promote customer loyalty, some European car manufacturers offer customers the option to fly to the factory to pick up the car they ordered from the local dealer, tour the factory, and take their new ride on a road trip around Europe. At the end of the trip, customers can drop off their car for transatlantic shipment. For example, Mercedes-Benz offers up to 7 percent off the purchase price for European delivery and waives the usual destination charge. It also offers an airfare voucher, one night's hotel accommodations, and a tour of the factory and museum.[47]

Word of Mouth

Consumers use *word of mouth* to talk about dozens of brands each day, from media and entertainment products such as movies, TV shows, and publications to food products, travel services, and retail stores. Companies are acutely aware of word-of-mouth power. Hush Puppies shoes, Krispy Kreme doughnuts, and (more recently) Crocs shoes were built through strong word of mouth, as were companies such as Red Bull, Starbucks, and Amazon.com.

Viral marketing relies on word of mouth that encourages consumers to pass along audio, video, or written information about company-developed products and services to others online.[48] With user-generated content sites such as YouTube, Facebook, and Instagram, consumers and advertisers can upload ads and videos to be shared by millions of people.[49] Online videos can be cost-effective, and marketers can take more freedom with them, as Blendtec has done.

Blendtec Utah-based Blendtec used to be known primarily for its commercial blenders and food mills. The company wasn't really familiar to the general public until it launched a series of hilarious "Will It Blend?" online videos to promote some of its commercial products for home use. The videos feature founder and CEO Tom Dickson wearing a white lab coat to pulverize objects ranging from golf balls and pens to beer bottles, all in a genial but deadpan manner. The genius of the videos (www.willitblend.com) is that they tie into current events. As soon as the iPhone was launched with huge media fanfare, Blendtec aired a video in which Dickson smiled and said, "I love my iPhone. It does everything. But will it blend?" After the blender crushed the iPhone to bits, Dickson lifted the lid on the small pile of black dust and said simply, "iSmoke." The clip drew more than 3.5 million views on YouTube. Dickson has appeared on *Today* and other network television shows and has had a cameo in a Weezer video. One of the few items *not* to blend: a crowbar![50]

Outrageousness is a two-edged sword. The Blendtec website clearly puts its comic videos in the "*Don't* try this at home" category and developed another set showing how to grind up vegetables for soup, for instance, in the "*Do* try this at home" category. Another product that has greatly benefited from word of mouth is iD's Vada.

iD Vada iD Vada was a relatively lesser-known brand until its parent company, iD Freshfoods, turned a viral video into a highly creative ad campaign, making it one of the most widely recognized food brands. iD Freshfoods is a frontrunner in the category of ready-to-cook batters of traditional south Indian snacks and breakfast items like *idli* and *dosa*. iD's readymade batters, with their authentic taste and unique packaging, make the cooking process convenient. The product team also wanted to develop batter for *vada*, a round crispy fried snack with a hole in the centre. A major challenge associated with making a *vada* is perfecting the art of its shape with the hole in it. Hence, the team realized that providing *vada* batter alone would not be as appealing unless the consumer gets to make the snack as desired in terms of taste and shape. After around three and half years of trial and errors, the iD team was able to resolve the issue with an innovative *vada* batter packaging. Each iD Vada Batter pack is designed with a spout mechanism at the nozzle that helps make crispy, golden-brown *vada* in three easy steps—squeeze, cut and fry. iD Vada Batter's ergonomic packaging retains the ingredients' freshness while shaping the batter into a

>> Recognition for iD's Vada batter shot up, along with sales, after a creative YouTube video made by the company for a talk on innovation by its CEO, PC Mustafa, went viral.

Source: iD Vada Batter©iD FRESH FOOD (INDIA) PVT. LTD., used with permission

vada with a hole in the centre. The nozzle on the pack creates a hole in the centre of the batter making it easy to use without creating any mess. Fortuitously, iD Vada became the talk of the country overnight even without the company spending a penny on promotions. The product video, leaked through a family WhatsApp group, went viral within a few hours. PC Mustafa, the CEO and co-founder, had created the video for a talk on his entrepreneurial journey. The video showcased iD Vada's innovative packaging designed to help everyone cook the perfect round shaped *vada* with a hole in the centre. The distinctive squeeze-and-fry pack that forms the perfect *vada* shape as the batter is squeezed through the spout, along with its tagline – "Everybody can Vada" – turned into a sensation overnight, forcing the company to advance the product launch and capitalize on the market demand, driven by the overwhelming response for the video.[51]

A classic example of the use of word of mouth is the way Dollar Shave Club used social media to create a viral communication campaign that helped build its brand.

Dollar Shave Club E-commerce start-up Dollar Shave Club sells a low-priced monthly supply of razors and blades online based on three different plans. The key to the company's launch was an online video. Dubbed by some the "best startup video ever," and the winner of multiple awards, the 90-second Dollar Shave Club video garnered millions of views on YouTube and gained thousands of social media followers in the process. In the quirky, irreverent video, CEO Michael Dubin rides a forklift, plays tennis, and dances with a fuzzy bear while touting the quality, convenience, and price of the company's razors and blades. Dubin has observed, "We are presenting a new business, a good idea, a funny video and tapped the pain point for a lot of consumers." While it was securing several hundred thousand customers, the company was also able to raise more than $20 million in venture capital and was ultimately sold to Unilever for $1 billion.[52]

Positive word of mouth sometimes happens organically with little advertising, but it can also be managed and facilitated.[53] Without question, more advertisers now seek greater earned media—unsolicited professional commentary, personal blog entries, social network discussion—as a result of their paid media and owned media efforts.

Products don't have to be outrageous or edgy to generate word-of-mouth buzz. More interesting brands are more likely to be talked about online, but whether a brand is seen as novel, exciting, or surprising has little effect on whether it is discussed in face-to-face, oral communications.[54] The brands discussed offline are often those that are salient and visible and come easily to mind. Research has shown that consumers tend to generate positive word of mouth themselves and to share information about their *own* positive consumption experiences. They tend to transmit negative word of mouth only by passing on information they have heard about *others'* negative consumption experiences.[55]

Publicity and Public Relations

Publicity aims to promote a company and its offerings. Unlike advertising, where the company pays for the media, *publicity* uses editorial space and does not incur media costs. Common forms of publicity include news stories, articles, and editorials. The primary goal of publicity is to attract attention to the company or its offerings. In contrast, public relations (PR) focuses on more than just public attention. The ultimate goal of public relations is to manage the overall reputation of the company and its offering, while building relationships with the community.

PUBLICITY

Many companies are turning to publicity to support corporate or product promotion and image making. **Publicity** involves securing editorial space—as opposed to paid space—in the media to promote a product, service, idea, place, person, or organization.

As the power of mass advertising weakens, marketing managers are turning to publicity to build awareness and brand knowledge for both new and established products. Publicity is also effective in blanketing local communities and reaching specific groups, and it can be more cost-effective than advertising. Increasingly, publicity takes place online, but it must be planned jointly with advertising and other marketing communications.

Publicity has important advantages over traditional advertising. First, publicity is free—even though the advertiser might have to pay an agency to secure media coverage, the advertiser does not pay for cost of the media itself (e.g., television and radio time or newspaper and magazine space). In addition, because the source of the message is a third party rather than the company, publicity is more credible and is more likely to influence the target audience. The main downside of publicity is that it cannot be directly controlled by the company and, as a result, it might end up being irrelevant or can even hurt the company and its offerings. Thus, the lack of a predictable outcome is the price associated with the low cost and credibility of publicity.

Publicity can achieve multiple objectives. It can build *awareness* by placing stories in the media to bring attention to a product, service, person, organization, or idea. It can build *credibility* by communicating the message in an editorial context. It can help boost sales force and dealer *enthusiasm* with stories about a new product before it is launched. It can hold down *promotion cost* because publicity costs less than direct mail and media advertising.

Publicity plays an important role in a variety of tasks:

- *Launching new products.* The amazing one-time commercial success of toys such as LeapFrog, Beanie Babies, and Silly Bandz owes a great deal to strong publicity.
- *Repositioning mature products.* In a classic case, New York City had extremely bad press in the 1970s until the "I Love New York" campaign.
- *Building interest in a product category.* Companies and trade associations have used publicity to rebuild interest in declining commodities such as eggs, milk, beef, and potatoes and to expand consumption of such products as tea, pork, and orange juice.
- *Defending products that have encountered public problems.* Publicity professionals must be adept at managing crises, such as those weathered by such well-established brands as Tylenol, Toyota, and BP in recent years.
- *Building the corporate image in a way that reflects favorably on its products.* The late Steve Jobs's heavily anticipated Macworld keynote speeches helped to create an innovative, iconoclastic image for Apple Corporation.

Clearly, creative publicity can influence public awareness at a fraction of the cost of advertising. The company doesn't pay for media space or time, but only for a staff to develop and circulate stories and manage certain events. An interesting story picked up by the media can be worth millions of dollars in equivalent advertising. Some experts say consumers are five times more likely to be influenced by editorial copy than by advertising. The following is an example of an award-winning publicity campaign.

Meow Mix A heritage brand, Meow Mix Cat Food decided to tap into its roots and bring back one of its most identifiable brand elements—a jingle with a repetitive meow refrain that had been off the air for over 20 years. Marketers chose singer and TV reality coach CeeLo Green and his Persian cat Purrfect to do the honors. The video with Green singing a remixed version of the jingle in a duet with Purrfect garnered attention from all kinds of outlets. The story received 1,200 media placements and 535 million media impressions, including exclusives with AP and *Access Hollywood*. Web traffic for the brand rose 150 percent, and more than 10,000 fans downloaded the song or ringtone. For each download, a pound of Meow Mix was donated to a local pet charity in Los Angeles.[56]

PUBLIC RELATIONS

Not only must the company relate constructively to customers, suppliers, and dealers; it must also relate to relevant publics. **Public relations (PR)** includes a variety of programs to promote or protect a company's image among the relevant stakeholders.

The wise company takes concrete steps to manage successful relationships with its key publics. Most have a PR department that monitors the attitudes of the organization's publics and distributes information and communications to build goodwill. The best PR departments counsel top management to adopt positive programs and eliminate questionable practices so negative publicity doesn't arise in the first place.

Many companies have PR departments that perform three main functions. They provide press coverage by presenting news and information about the organization in the most positive light. They also manage corporate communications by promoting understanding of the organization through internal and external communications. Finally, PR departments can engage in lobbying by dealing with legislators and government officials to promote or defeat legislation and regulation.

Public relations can involve different media formats. Some of the most popular PR media formats are publications, events, news, speeches, public service activities, and identity media.

- **Publications.** Companies rely extensively on published materials to reach and influence their target markets. These include annual reports, brochures, articles, company newsletters and magazines, and audiovisual materials.
- **Events.** Companies can draw attention to new products or other company activities by arranging and publicizing special events such as news conferences, seminars, outings, trade shows, exhibits, contests and competitions, and anniversaries that will reach the target publics.
- **News.** One of the major tasks of PR professionals is to find or create favorable news about the company, its products, and its people and to get the media to accept press releases and attend press conferences.
- **Speeches.** Increasingly, company executives must field questions from the media or give talks at trade associations or sales meetings, appearances that can build the company's image.
- **Public service activities.** Companies can build goodwill by contributing money and time to good causes.
- **Identity media.** Companies need a visual identity that the public immediately recognizes. The visual identity is carried by company logos, stationery, brochures, signs, business forms, business cards, buildings, uniforms, and dress codes.

Public relations helps companies shape their public image and manage their relationships with the community. Furthermore, public relations are particularly relevant in minimizing the damage to the corporate image during a marketing crisis, as well as in helping rebuild this image after the crisis has been resolved.

Packaging

Because packaging is usually perceived during a buyer's first encounter with the product, it can be a determining factor in piquing the buyer's interest. It will also shape the buyer's subsequent evaluation of the product and the final purchase decision. Because of its ability to influence consumer perceptions and choice, many companies use packaging to create distinct customer value and differentiate their products from those of the competition.[57]

The *label* is a highly visible and important element of packaging. Labels include written, electronic, or graphical communication placed directly on the packaging, as well as anything associated with and attached to the product, such as an information tag. The label's primary functions are to communicate, to consumers, channel members, and the company, information that facilitates identification of the offering; describes the offering's key attributes; highlights the offering's benefits; instructs buyers on the proper use, storage, and disposal of the product; increases the offering's aesthetic appeal; and leverages and enhances the brand associated with the offering.

Following a set of three core packaging principles can help develop effective packaging that contributes to the product's ultimate success in the market. These core principles are *visibility*, *differentiation*, and *transparency*.

- **Visibility.** Companies endeavoring to promote their offerings often overwhelm consumers with a constant barrage of information. This information overload can be counterproductive, causing customers to tune out and ignore the information they don't think will be immediately relevant to the decision at hand. This surfeit of information can also cause shoppers to overlook data that might be useful to them. Effective packaging can cut through the information clutter, arrest the attention of shoppers, and induce them to consider the offering favorably and ultimately to purchase it. Creative packaging and in-store displays helped Araku Coffee, marketed by Naandi Foundation, attract discerning coffee lovers in the retail outlets in Europe.
- **Differentiation.** Another facet of effective packaging is that it can help differentiate the company's offering from the competition. When confronted with multiple options, customers who are under time constraints frequently look to packaging as a key source of information about the offerings they are evaluating. Many companies use distinctive packaging to promote their brands, which can make it easier for loyal consumers to pinpoint at a glance the brand they're seeking.
- **Transparency.** In addition to attracting consumers' attention and differentiating the company's offerings from the competition, effective packaging clearly communicates the value of the offering to its target customers. Shoppers typically interact with the packaging at the time of purchase, which means that packaging must transparently communicate the offering's value proposition by touting the offering's virtues and giving shoppers a reason to purchase it. For example, many sustainable products feature the color green on their packaging to visually communicate their environmentally friendly nature.

>> Attractive colors, unusual shape and the creative packaging allowed Araku Coffee to effectively differentiate its high-end, premium 'specialty coffee' and make them instantly recognizable to discerning coffee lovers in France. The product, exported to the European markets, is retailed in over 50 outlets in France in addition to an Araku Café and store in the heart of Paris on rue de Bretagne in the fashionable Marais district.
Source: ©Naandi Foundation, used with permission

Many of the functions of packaging are akin to those of advertising. Both act as a means of communication that informs buyers about the salient aspects of a company's offering. However, packaging and advertising communicate different types of information and impart this information in different ways. Advertising typically aims to create a memorable impression of an offering in the minds of future purchasers. On the other hand, the impact of packaging on the purchase decision is much more immediate—in fact, nearly instantaneous—because buyers usually react to a product's packaging at the point of purchase. Thus, packaging often is designed to have a more direct visual impact on the buyer. What's more, customers typically don't spend much time or energy evaluating familiar low-cost products and tend to rely on the visual properties of packaging, and of the products themselves, when making their purchase decision.

marketing INSIGHT

Measuring Social Media ROI

Companies are spending more time, effort, and money on social media than ever. According to a survey of CMOs by MDG Advertising, social media now account for 12 percent of marketing budgets, a figure that is expected to increase to more than 20 percent in five years. When you're spending lots of time and money on social media, it's important to know just how much it's helping your brand. But that is easier said than done. Of the CMOs surveyed, 44 percent say they have been unable to measure social media's overall impact on their business. And although 36 percent feel they have a good sense of the qualitative impact of their social media activities, only 20 percent have actually quantified the impact of social media on their business.

Digital tools are available to help monitor a company's social media presence, starting with the free Google Alerts, which will e-mail you automated search results for up to 1,000 terms you choose. The catch is that Alerts monitors only Google sites. At less than $100 a month, BuzzSumo lets you set up alerts for mentions of things like your company or brand name, as well as those of competitors; it also allows unlimited content and social-influencer searches to make it easier for marketers to develop their own content and reach those who influence others. A more sophisticated option is Nuvi, whose expert data visualization enables companies to easily see how their business is perceived online and the effectiveness of their social media efforts, and gives companies the ability to capture negative comments.

The dilemma is measuring the actual sales that come from social media. MDG Advertising says that even though 58 percent of brands state that they measure social engagement, only 21 percent measure goal or revenue conversions. When Audi ran the first Super Bowl ad featuring a Twitter hashtag in 2011, it had no idea how much the high engagement of its Facebook fan base translated into sales of more cars. One report showed that 50 percent of Fortune 1000 companies did not benchmark or measure the payback of their social CRM projects. Initially, the focus of measuring social media effects was on easily observed quantities such as the number of Facebook "likes" and Twitter tweets per week. These did not always correlate with marketing or business success, so researchers began digging deeper.

Assessing the value of social media is no easy task. Some marketing pundits compare social media to a phone: How would you assess the ROI of all the different calls you make? Josh Bernoff, Forrester Research's acclaimed digital marketing guru, sees short-term and long-term benefits of social media as falling into four categories:

- *Short-term financial benefits*, such as increased revenue or decreased costs. On the revenue side, when NetShops.com added ratings and reviews to its site, sales increased 26 percent within six months. On the cost side, National Instruments, makers of sophisticated technical engineering products, found that members of its user community answered 46 percent of other users' questions, saving NI its typical $10 service cost per call. Similarly, AT&T's revamped online community saved the firm 16 percent in telephone customer support in one month.
- *Short-term overall digital benefits*. When Swanson Health Products improved the visibility of its product reviews, it became more accessible to search engines, and traffic to its product pages rose 163 percent. Online videos, communities, blogs, and Twitter can similarly boost search performance.
- *Long-term brand lift*. Social media can improve long-term brand performance measures. When P&G created a Facebook page to support ski jumper Lindsey Vonn, it solicited 40,000 signatures on a

(continued)

marketing insight *(continued)*

petition to make ski jumping an Olympic sport. Surveys of participating Facebook users found an 8 percent to 11 percent increase in brand preference and purchase intent.

- *Long-term risk avoidance*. Dealing with a crisis can cost a firm millions of dollars over time. It is better to avoid or avert a crisis before it creates brand damage. Firms such as McDonald's and AT&T have teams who monitor tweets about their products or services to nip any alleged problems in the bud.

The easiest way to create and measure social media's payoff is to include a contest, sweepstake, or promotion. Silicon Valley ad agency Wildfire created a promotion for Jamba Juice where the value of a "lucky coupon" was revealed only in the store. Tens of thousands of customers entered. The promotion was successful, but social media results can still be unpredictable.[58]

summary

1. Managing and coordinating the entire communications process calls for *integrated marketing communications*. Effective marketing communications recognizes the added value of a comprehensive plan to evaluate the strategic roles of a variety of communication disciplines and combines these disciplines to provide clarity, consistency, and maximum impact through the seamless integration of discrete messages.
2. The development of an *integrated communication campaign* requires a clear understanding of the specifics of the alternative media formats in order to create a consistent consumer experience. The most popular communication formats are advertising; online, social media, and mobile communication; events and experiences; word of mouth; publicity and public relations; and packaging.
3. *Advertising* is any paid form of nonpersonal presentation and promotion of ideas, goods, or services by an identified sponsor. Advertisers include not only business firms but also charitable, nonprofit, and government agencies. The advertiser typically purchases media time or space to convey the company's message to its target audience. The most popular forms of advertising are television, print, radio, online, and place advertising.
4. An important form of online communication is a company's *owned media*. There are two common approaches to drive traffic: (1) search engine optimization (SEO), which aims to boost the likelihood that a link to a company's content will appear at the top of the organic (nonpaid) search results and (2) search engine marketing (SEM), which involves paying search engine companies to feature one's content in the results of a particular keyword search.
5. *Social media* have become an influential form of marketing communication. They come in many forms: online communities and forums, blogs, social networks, and customer reviews. Social media reinforce other communications and offer marketers the opportunity to have a public voice and presence online for their brands. Marketers can build or tap into online communities, inviting participation from consumers and creating a long-term marketing asset in the process.
6. *Mobile communications* are an increasingly important form of interactive marketing by which marketers can use text messages, apps, and ads to connect with consumers via their smartphones, tablets, and wearable devices. A key appeal of this form of interactive marketing is that it enables marketers to personalize messages on the basis of demographics, geolocation, and behavior.
7. *Events and experiences* are a means to become part of special and more personally relevant moments in consumers' lives. Events can broaden and deepen the sponsor's relationship with its customers by connecting a company's product or service with unique and engaging experiences.
8. *Word-of-mouth marketing* aims to engage customers to share with others their views and experiences about products, services, and brands. Positive word of mouth sometimes happens organically with little advertising, but it can also be managed and facilitated. Viral marketing relies on word of mouth that encourages consumers to pass along audio, video, or written information about company-developed products and services to others online.
9. *Publicity* aims to promote a company and its offerings. Unlike advertising, where the company pays for the media, publicity uses editorial space and does not incur media costs. Common forms of publicity include news stories, articles, and editorials. The primary goal of publicity is to attract attention to the company or its offerings.
10. *Public relations* (PR) aims to manage the overall reputation of the company and its offerings, while building relationships with the community. The main tools of PR are publications, events, sponsorships, news, speeches, public service activities, and identity media. PR departments perform several functions: fostering positive press coverage about the organization, managing internal and

external corporate communications, and lobbying legislators and government officials to gain favorable legislation and regulation.

11. *Packaging* is similar to advertising in that it aims to inform buyers about the benefits of the company's offering. Unlike advertising, which typically aims to create a memorable impression of an offering in the minds of future purchasers, packaging often is designed to have a more direct visual impact on the buyer. Because of its ability to influence consumer perceptions at the point of purchase, many companies use packaging strategically to create distinct customer value and differentiate their products from those of the competition.

marketing SPOTLIGHT

Burger King

Source: Cum Okolo/Alamy Stock Photo

Burger King was founded in 1954 in Miami, Florida, when James McLamore and David Edgerton invented a flame broiler and introduced the original Whopper hamburger. Burger King and its Whopper sandwich began to spread across the United States, and by the late 1970s Burger King had become the second largest fast-food chain, behind McDonald's. However, in the next three decades, Burger King saw 13 CEOs come in and out of the company, each one taking the company in a different direction. With constant changes to management, Burger King faced different challenges, which were followed by a decline in revenues. Some of these issues included a series of ineffective advertising campaigns, an overly complicated menu, and changes in customer preferences.

Burger King's communications evolved significantly throughout its history. In the early 1960s, Burger King's slogan was "Where kids are king," a theme that introduced the famous paper crown seen in restaurants. The company's advertising changed years later to focus on the larger size and superior freshness of its burgers. The famous slogan "Have it your way" was launched in 1974. In the 1980s and 1990s, Burger King released a series of campaigns that failed to resonate with customers. The "Where's Herb?" campaign, launched in 1986, focused on a man who had never tasted a Whopper before. Burger King offered $5,000 to any guest who could find Herb as he toured across the country. The campaign was meant to rival Wendy's famous "Where's the Beef" campaign but failed to garner the same amount of national attention. *Advertising Age* declared the campaign the biggest promotional flop of the decade.

Following a change of management in the early 2000s, Burger King revamped its advertising style to be riskier and incorporate more tongue-in-cheek humor. In 2004, Burger King launched its "Subservient Chicken" website, where people could watch a human-sized chicken act out their commands, reviving the "Have it your way" tagline. The website received over 20 million hits in the week it debuted. In 2007, Burger King released the "Whopper Freakout" campaign, where angry customers were secretly filmed after being told by employees that the Whopper had been discontinued. The campaign went viral and was followed by a 4.5 percent increase in store sales.

Whereas some of Burger King's campaigns were successful and helped build the company's brand, others backfired and reflected poorly on the company's image. The advertisement for the "Texican Whopper" sandwich in 2009 outraged the Mexican government because of its stereotypical caricature of a tall white cowboy living with a small Mexican wrestler. The "SpongeBob Square Butt" advertisement was also controversial because the highly sexualized ad primarily targeted young consumers. Mental health organizations also took offense at advertisements such as "The King's Gone Crazy" because of its crude depiction of mental illness. In 2011, *Time* magazine called The King mascot one of the 10 creepiest product mascots. In short, although some advertisements succeeded in increasing sales, Burger King was becoming less and less successful at leaving a good impression on fans.

In 2010, Burger King was sold to 3G Capital, which looked to optimize operations and overhaul the company's advertising strategy in order to increase profitability. After its acquisition by 3G Capital, Burger King began streamlining its operations. The company employed a strategy of cost cutting and zero-base budgeting, which involved heavily scrutinizing its expenses and resetting its budget to zero every planning period. These new initiatives included redesigning restaurants to improve the guest experience,

(continued)

reducing the menu to focus on the burgers and fries, and selling some of the company-owned restaurants back to franchisees.

Alongside 3G Capital's acquisition came a new partnership with marketing agency McGarryBowen, which revamped Burger King's advertising strategy, taking it back to its tongue-in-cheek roots. The media team launched a series of creative campaigns that offered topical political or cultural commentary. One of the most successful campaigns revolved around the "Whopper Neutrality" video, which was released shortly after the repeal of net neutrality in the United States. The video explains the effects of a net neutrality ban, using Whopper pricing as an analog. The controversial advertisement became Burger King's most shared ad of all time, garnering over 4 billion hits and a reference during a congressional hearing. Burger King mocked artificial intelligence's capacity for creativity by releasing a bizarre set of advertisements completely generated by machine-learning algorithms.

Other communications released by Burger King offered social commentary on topics such as the "pink tax" (the fact that women's products cost more than men's), bullying, and inclusion of deaf customers. Many advertisements were also more lighthearted and humorous: Burger King offered Whoppers with holes cut out of the center to celebrate National Donut Day, hid Whoppers in popcorn bags to bypass theater rules in Romania, and even traded boarding passes for burgers in Romania. These campaigns generated global clout on social media networks.

Burger King began to grow once more after rediscovering its roots and streamlining its marketing communications. The chain has focused heavily on maintaining relevance in the minds of customers, constantly releasing topical and impressionistic advertising campaigns. Burger King's approach to managing integrated marketing communications was also recognized by industry professionals, and in 2017 Burger King was named the Cannes Lions Creative Marketer of the Year.[59]

Questions

1. What were the key factors that undermined the effectiveness of Burger King's communications over the years?
2. How should Burger King balance cost-cutting initiatives with investing in an integrated marketing campaign to create and sustain top-of-mind awareness and gain market share?
3. How should Burger King use traditional, online, and mobile communications to build a loyal customer base?

marketing SPOTLIGHT

AccorHotels

Source: Kristoffer Tripplaar/Alamy Stock Photo

AccorHotels was established in 1967 when the founders, Paul Dubrule and Gerard Pelisson, opened their first hotel, Novotel, in Lille Lesquin, France. They soon formed the Société d'investissement et d'exploitation hôteliers (SIEH) group and grew the company by opening and acquiring new hotels across the globe. In 1983, SIEH owned 400 hotels and 1,500 restaurants and renamed the company Accor Group.

Starting in 2010, Accor began shifting its operating strategy from owning to franchising and managing hotel properties. This strategy, called "asset-light," allowed the company to focus on investing and expanding its numerous brands instead of spending capital on purchasing real estate. Accor was made up of two businesses: HotelInvest, a real estate business that focused on owning and leasing hotels, and HotelServices, which focused on running Accor hotel operations. Becoming asset-light helped Accor open 2,018 new hotels in 2014, many of which were in new markets. By 2019, Accor managed 26 in-house brands targeting different segments of the hotel market. Its luxury brands include Raffles, Fairmont, and Sofitel. Its midrange brands include Swissotel and Mercure, while ibis and Formula 1 are its two main budget brands.

The digital revolution presented Accor with new challenges. Customers were now able to share their travel experiences on a much larger scale, book travel plans at a moment's notice, and interact with hotel social media accounts. In addition, there was an increase in the number of ways to book travel arrangements. Prior to the digital revolution,

(continued)

brick-and-mortar travel agents typically handled flight, hotel, and tour booking. New players entered the travel market, including online travel agencies (e.g., Booking, Expedia), review sites (e.g., TripAdvisor), travel blogs (e.g., Lonely Planet), social media websites (e.g., Facebook, Twitter), and alternative hospitality services (e.g., Airbnb). Competitors such as Airbnb, which offered affordable lodging in private residences, became serious threats to Accor. Online travel agencies, which enabled customers to easily book Accor hotels for a commission, also posed a threat to Accor's profits.

To increase direct bookings, Accor invested heavily in its website, mobile application, social media accounts, and advertisements to personally connect with customers. In 2014, Accor purchased over 12 million keywords and paid search ads. That year, Accor also sent more than 570 million targeted e-mails to prospective customers. This resulted in online sales that amounted to 5 percent of total sales in 2014, shy of Accor's ultimate goal of increasing that number to 50 percent. To drive growth, Accor set out to improve the customer experience, starting with booking the trip and ending after the hotel stay. Accor's attempts to improve its digital hospitality contained both consumer-focused and employee-focused elements.

To grow mobile bookings, Accor acquired the French mobile traveling companion application Wipolo. Accor's purchase of Wipolo in 2014 provided the company with a dynamic mobile application that could function as the primary customer-booking channel and increase the share of mobile bookings, which at the time accounted for only 12 percent of Accor's online sales. The Wipolo application allowed customers to browse different properties, easily book a room, use hotel digital services, give feedback, and utilize Accor's loyalty program. Accor also centralized its customer relationship management databases into one single platform, called "Voice of the Guests." The new database aided employees in providing personalized service for guests and featured a recommendation engine that automatically generated custom offers to customers based on their profile and traveling behavior. In addition, Accor streamlined its customer experience to include one-click booking, online check-in and check-out, targeted offers, and personalized welcomes. Accor reported that over 93 percent of customers who tried the welcome service wanted to use it again.

Accor has experienced new competitors, such as online travel agencies and new hospitality companies, but the company has stayed competitive by investing heavily in modernizing its digital experience. By streamlining its website and mobile application, customers can easily book, check into, and review a hotel room with a click of a button. Accor's upgraded CRM database also allows employees to deliver a personalized experience to every guest. In 2019, AccorHotels operated 4,200 hotels in over 100 countries worldwide and was the largest hotel group in the world outside of the United States.[60]

Questions

1. What was the key to Accor's market success?
2. What role did Accor's online strategy play in its ability to gain and retain loyal customers?
3. How should Accor balance its resources across traditional, online, and mobile communications?

CHAPTER 14

Personal Selling and Direct Marketing

Credit Access Grameen, the largest microfinance institution in India uses its field executives to form groups of rural women who use the micro-loans through its group lending model.

Source: ©CreditAccess Grameen Limited, used with permission

Companies seeking to expand profits and sales must invest time and resources searching for new customers. To generate leads, they advertise in media that will reach new prospects, send direct mail and e-mails to possible new prospects, purchase names from list brokers, and use data-mining techniques to identify prospects. Although mass and digital communications provide many benefits, there are times when personal communications are needed to be relevant and close a sale. Personal selling is at the core of many multibillion-dollar businesses such as Amway.

>>> Inspired by Nobel Laureate Professor Mohamed Yunus's success in transforming rural livelihood through micro-finance, Credit Access Grameen was originally set up in India as an NGO in 1999 to offer micro-credit to women from poor rural households and support their income-generating activities. With a customer-centric approach and an efficient delivery model, this micro-finance organization rapidly grew and expanded operations into several districts of Karnataka, Tamil Nadu and Maharashtra. Subsequently, registering itself as a non-banking financial company and a micro-finance institution (NBFC–MFI) to raise capital for its lending operations, the organization got listed on the stock exchanges as a public limited company. The company has continued to grow rapidly under the leadership of Udaya Kumar, MD and CEO in 2018.[1] A strong belief in holistic development drives the company's business model. This involves a comprehensive development of low-income

rural clients, employees, and society through social and customer welfare practices. The company's field executives, during their weekly visits for meetings with customer groups, offer need-based micro-finance solutions to clients at their doorsteps. With customization as its core, key elements of the service like tailored loan amounts, repayment tenures and service delivery help meet the customer requirements. In addition, the field executives train and mentor clients on bookkeeping, cash-flow management and growing one's business. These field executives, with profiles usually similar to that of their clients, are dedicated individuals passionately engaged with the communities' welfare.[2] The firm presently handles its business with a direct selling model in 157 districts across 9 states, with 4 million loans to serve 2.5 million customers as India's largest micro -finance institution.[3 & 4]

Personalizing communications and saying and doing the right thing for the right person at the right time are critical for marketing effectiveness. In this chapter, we consider how companies personalize their marketing communications to have more impact. We begin by evaluating personal selling and then move on to consider direct marketing.

Personal Selling

Personal selling involves direct interaction with one or more prospective buyers for the purpose of making presentations, answering questions, and procuring orders (sales presentations, sales meetings, incentive programs, samples, and fair and trade shows). Personal selling is the most effective tool at later stages of the buying process, particularly in influencing buyer preferences, conviction, and action.[5]

Well-known companies that use a personal-selling model are Avon and Electrolux. Tupperware and Mary Kay cosmetics are sold one-to-many: A salesperson goes to the home of a host who has invited friends; the salesperson demonstrates the products and takes orders. The multilevel (network) marketing sales system works by recruiting independent businesspeople who act as distributors. The distributor's compensation includes a percentage of sales made by those he or she recruits, as well as earnings on his or her own direct sales to customers.

Personal selling has three notable qualities:

- It is *customized,* meaning that the message can be designed to appeal to any individual.
- It is *relationship oriented,* meaning that personal-selling relationships can range from a matter-of-fact selling relationship to a deep personal friendship.
- It is *response oriented,* meaning that the buyer is often given personal choices and encouraged to respond directly.

Personal selling is an ancient art. Effective salespeople today have more than instinct to guide them, however. Companies now spend hundreds of millions of dollars each year to train them in methods of analysis and customer management and to transform them from passive order-takers into active order-getters.

Learning Objectives After studying this chapter you should be able to:

14.1 Define the key aspects of the selling process.

14.2 Explain how to design an effective sales force organization.

14.3 Explain how to manage a sales force.

14.4 Discuss the role of direct marketing, and identify the key direct marketing channels.

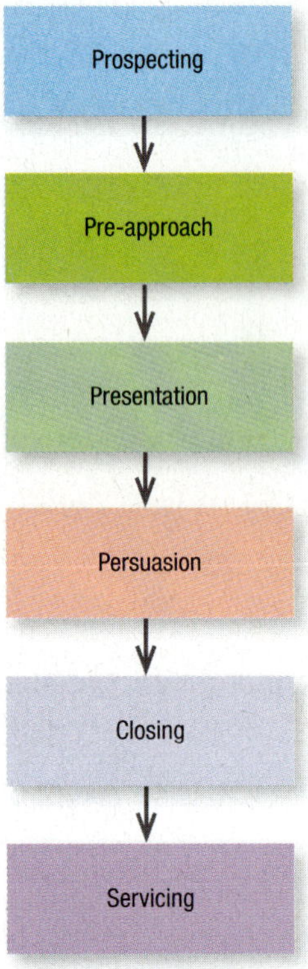

FIGURE **14.1**
Major Steps in Effective Selling

PERSONAL SELLING AS A PROCESS

Most sales training programs agree on the major steps in any effective sales process. These steps are prospecting, pre-approach, presentation, persuasion, closing, and servicing. We show these steps in Figure 14.1 and discuss their application to industrial selling next.[6]

Prospecting and Qualifying. The first step in selling is to identify and qualify prospects. More companies are taking responsibility for finding and qualifying leads so that salespeople can use their expensive time doing what they do best: selling.[7] Some companies, including IBM, qualify leads according to the acronym BANT: Does the customer have the necessary *budget*, the *authority* to buy, a compelling *need* for the product or service, and a *timeline* for delivery that aligns with what is possible?

Many marketers are going beyond the BANT approach and getting increasingly sophisticated in their pursuit of qualified leads. Using inputs as diverse as prospects' hiring practices, job boards, and sample tweets from customers and employees, companies use data analytics and artificial intelligence to classify prospects as worth a call or offer—or not.

Marketers must find the right balance between the quantity and quality of leads. Too many leads, even of high quality, and the sales force may be overwhelmed and allow the most promising opportunities to fall through the cracks; too few or low-quality leads and the sales force may become frustrated or demoralized.

To generate high-quality leads, suppliers need to know their customers. Suppliers that qualify may be visited by the buyer's agents, who will examine the suppliers' manufacturing facilities and meet their staff. After evaluating each company, the buyer will end up with a short list of qualified suppliers. Many professional buyers have forced suppliers to make adjustments to their marketing proposals to increase their likelihood of making the cut.

Pre-approach. The salesperson should learn as much as possible about the prospect company (what it needs, who takes part in the purchase decision) and its buyers (personal characteristics and buying styles). How is the purchasing process conducted at the company? How is it structured?

Companies can vary in their purchasing process and company structure. At many large companies, salespeople interact with purchasing departments tasked with procuring goods for the organization. Many purchasing departments in larger companies have been centralized and elevated to strategic supply departments with more professional practices. Centralized purchasing may put a premium on dealing with larger suppliers that are able to meet all the company's needs. At the same time, some companies are decentralizing purchasing for smaller items such as coffeemakers, office supplies, and other inexpensive necessities. The sales rep must thoroughly understand the purchasing process in terms of "who, when, where, how, and why" in order to set call objectives: to qualify the prospect, gather information, or make an immediate sale.

Another challenge is to choose the best contact approach—a personal visit, phone call, e-mail, or letter. The right approach is crucial because it has become harder for sales reps to get into the offices of purchasing agents, physicians, and other time-starved and internet-enabled potential customers. Finally, the salesperson should plan an overall sales strategy for the account.

Presentation and Demonstration. A common way of telling the product "story" to the buyer is captured by the FABV approach, which focuses on articulating the *features, advantages, benefits,* and *value* of the company's offering.

- *Features* describe the physical characteristics of a market offering. For example, a computer's features include processing speed and memory capacity.
- *Advantages* describe why the features give the customer an edge.
- *Benefits* describe the economic, technical, service, and social payback delivered.
- *Value* describes the offering's worth (often in monetary terms).

The FABV approach helps the sales force adequately allocate the effort when promoting different aspects of the product. This is important because salespeople often spend too much time on product features (a product orientation) and not enough time stressing benefits and value (a customer orientation), especially in highly competitive markets or when selling individualized or premium-priced products.[8] To be effective, the pitch to a prospective client must be highly relevant, engaging, and compelling. There is always another company waiting to take that business.

Persuasion. Selling is not a unidirectional process in which sellers simply present information to buyers. Rather, selling is an interactive process where buyers typically raise questions and pose objections. Most objections stem from two sources: psychological resistance and logical resistance.

- **Psychological resistance** includes resistance to interference, preference for established supply sources or brands, apathy, reluctance to give up something, unpleasant associations created by the sales rep, predetermined ideas, dislike of making decisions, and an anxious attitude toward money.
- Logical resistance might consist of objections to the price, delivery schedule, or product or company characteristics.

To handle psychological and logical objections, the salesperson maintains a positive approach, asks the buyer to clarify the objection, questions in such a way that the buyer answers his own objection, denies the validity of the objection, or turns it into a reason for buying.[9]

Although price is the most frequently negotiated issue—especially in tight economic times—others include contract completion time, quality of goods and services offered, purchase volume, product safety, and responsibility for financing, risk taking, promotion, and title. Salespeople sometimes give in too easily when customers demand a discount.[10]

One company recognized this problem when sales revenues went up 25 percent but profit remained flat. The company decided to retrain its salespeople to "sell the price" rather than "sell through price." Salespeople were given richer information about each customer's sales history and behavior. They received training to recognize value-adding opportunities rather than price-cutting opportunities. As a result, the company's sales revenues climbed and so did its margins.[11]

Closing. Closing is an essential component of the selling process. Without closing the deal, there is no sale. A skillful salesperson knows when and how to close the sale in a way that will not only secure the deal at hand but also help establish a long-term relationship with the buyer.[12]

To determine when to start closing, sellers pay close attention to buyers' behavior, looking for signs that the buyer is ready to finalize the purchase decision. Closing signs from the buyer include physical actions, statements or comments, and questions. Sales representatives can ask for the order, recapitulate the points of agreement, offer to help write up the order, ask whether the buyer wants A or B, get the buyer to make minor choices such as color or size, or indicate what the buyer will lose by not placing the order now.

The salesperson might offer specific inducements to close, such as an additional service, an extra quantity, or a token gift. If the client still isn't budging, perhaps the salesperson is not interacting with the right executive; a more senior person may have the necessary authority. The salesperson also may need to find other ways to reinforce the value of the offering and how it alleviates financial or other pressures the client faces.

Servicing. Follow-up and maintenance are necessary to ensure customer satisfaction and repeat business. Immediately after closing, the salesperson should cement any necessary details about delivery time, purchase terms, and other matters important to the customer. When relevant, the salesperson might schedule a follow-up call after delivery to ensure proper installation, instruction, and servicing. In addition, the salesperson might try to detect any potential problems with the offering, suggest solutions, alleviate concerns, and reaffirm the buyer's positive attitude toward the purchase.

While servicing the account, the salesperson should have a plan on how to maintain and grow the account. Providing a service that goes beyond the actual sale can demonstrate to customers that the seller stands behind its products and services and is committed to building a relationship with the buyer. Using after-sale servicing can help build a long-term relationship that benefits both parties by improving the overall purchase experience and creating a sense of trust between the buyer and seller.

MANAGING THE SALE

Many of the principles of personal selling and negotiation are largely transaction oriented because their purpose is to close a specific sale. But in many cases, the company seeks not an immediate sale but rather a long-term supplier–customer relationship. Today's customers prefer suppliers who can sell and deliver a coordinated set of products and services to many locations, who can quickly solve problems in different locations, and who can work closely with customer teams to improve products and processes.[13]

Salespeople working with key customers must do more than e-mail or call when they think customers might be ready to place orders. They should also get in touch at other times and make useful suggestions about the business to create value. They should monitor key accounts, know customers' problems, and be ready to serve them in a number of ways, adapting and responding to different customer needs or situations.[14] A popular approach for managing the sale process is SPIN, an acronym derived from the types of questions that a salesperson should ask prospects: situation questions, problem questions, implication questions, and need-payoff questions.

Designing the Sales Force

The original and oldest form of direct marketing is visiting target customers (prospects) in person. To locate prospects, develop them into customers, and grow the business, most industrial companies rely heavily on a professional sales force or hire manufacturers' representatives and agents. Many consumer companies such as Allstate, Amway, Avon, Mary Kay, Merrill Lynch, and Tupperware use a direct-selling force.

Tupperware Tupperware was founded in 1946, when inventor Earl Tupper introduced his airtight seals, patterned after the inverted rim on a can of paint, to prevent food from drying out. Despite their breakthrough nature, his products didn't sell well in retail outlets, mainly because their advantage over regular storage containers was not readily visible to buyers. Realizing that consumers needed demonstrations in order to understand how the product worked, Tupper introduced the Tupperware Home Party as a way for his products to reach consumers. Demonstrations proved an extremely effective way of communicating the benefits of the revolutionary seal, and several years later all Tupperware products were taken off store shelves to be distributed through direct selling alone. In addition to being a source of income, home parties were also a welcome diversion for women whose social circles revolved around their family. As consumers relocated to homes in the suburbs, backyard parties became a favorite way for families and neighbors to socialize. Tupperware products addressed needs created by this increasingly popular pastime by helping to keep food fresh outdoors as well as transporting it to and from parties. When microwaves became commonplace kitchen appliances, Tupperware introduced products designed specifically for microwaves, enabling consumers to warm up leftovers or cook the frozen foods that were growing in popularity. In addition to constantly innovating and extending its product line, Tupperware also introduced classes and demonstrations where customers learned about microwave cooking and food preparation, as well as ways to save money on their grocery bills, optimize cabinet space, and manage time. To fit the busy schedules of time-pressed customers, Tupperware introduced in-office demonstrations. Be it at home or office parties, personal selling has always been the defining aspect of Tupperware. With the help of its more than 3 million sales force members, Tupperware now is found in nearly 100 markets around the world, offering culturally distinct items such as the Kimchi Keeper, the Kimono Keeper, and the Japanese Bento Box.[15]

U.S. firms spend more than a trillion dollars annually on sales forces and sales force materials—more than on any other promotional method. More than 10 percent of the total workforce works in sales occupations, both nonprofit and for profit. Hospitals and museums, for example, use fundraisers to contact donors and solicit donations. In asserting that selling is the core function of every company, Boston Beer founder Jim Koch notes, "Without sales, there is no business to manage."[16]

Although no one debates the importance of the sales force in marketing programs, companies are sensitive to the high and rising costs of maintaining one, including salaries, commissions, bonuses, travel expenses, and benefits. Not surprisingly, companies are trying to increase sales force productivity through better selection, training, supervision, motivation, and compensation.[17]

Salespeople are the company's personal link to its customers. In designing the sales force, the company must develop sales force objectives, strategy, structure, size, and compensation (see Figure 14.2).

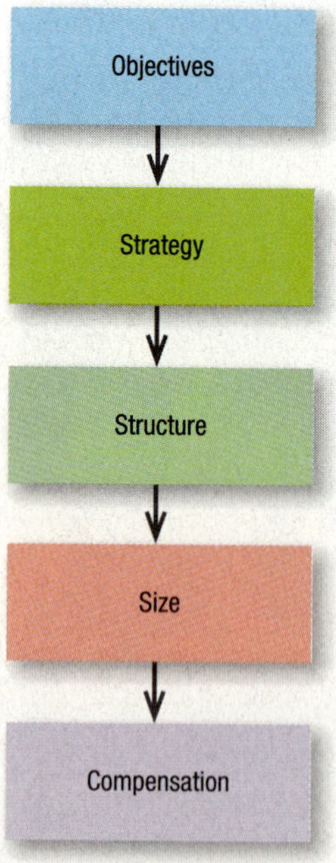

FIGURE **14.2**
Designing the Sales Force

SALES FORCE OBJECTIVES

The days when all the sales force did was "sell, sell, and sell" are long gone. Sales reps need to know how to diagnose a customer's problem and propose a solution that can help improve the customer's profitability. The best salespeople even go beyond the customer's stated problems to offer fresh

Source: Anton Starikov/Alamy Stock Photo

<< Tupperware initiated the concept of direct sales parties in homes (and later offices) to effectively demonstrate the benefits of its storage containers and encourage personal interaction with customers.

insights into the customer's business model and identify unrecognized needs and unarticulated problems.[18]

In performing their jobs, salespeople complete one or more specific tasks:

- *Information gathering* involves conducting market research and doing intelligence work.
- *Targeting* involves deciding how to allocate their time among prospects and customers.
- *Communicating* involves conveying information about the company's products and services.
- *Selling* entails approaching, presenting, answering questions, overcoming objections, and closing sales.
- *Servicing* involves providing various services to the customers—consulting on problems, rendering technical assistance, arranging financing, and expediting delivery.
- *Allocating* involves deciding which customers will get scarce products during product shortages.

Too often marketing and sales are in conflict: The sales force complains that marketing isn't generating enough leads, and marketers complain that the sales force isn't converting them. Improved collaboration and communication between these two can increase revenues and profits.[19]

Jim Farley, executive vice president at Ford, notes that "the coolest thing about my job at Ford is that I'm in charge of both marketing and sales" and maintains that it is a mistake to have separate people in charge. He sees the best salespeople at Ford as a cross between *problem solvers,* who help explain and customize all the sophisticated automobile electronics, and *concierges,* who help with all the steps in the complicated process of buying a car.[20] To improve mutual understanding, some companies move marketers into sales (and vice versa) when appropriate, as well as getting them together for joint meetings throughout the year.

SALES FORCE STRATEGY

An important aspect of developing a sales strategy is deciding whether to use a direct or a contractual sales force. A direct (company) sales force consists of full- or part-time paid employees who work exclusively for the company. Inside salespeople conduct business from the office and receive visits from prospective buyers, and field salespeople travel and visit customers. A contractual sales force consists of manufacturers' reps, sales agents, and brokers who earn a commission based on sales.

Eureka Forbes Eureka Forbes, established in 1982, is one of India's leading health and hygiene brands, in addition to being one of the largest relationship based "direct to customer" companies in Asia today. A trendsetter for direct sales in India, the company's digitally enabled sales force reaches out to over a million homes every year for product demonstrations and sell water purifiers, vacuum cleaners and air purifiers.[21]

From being a pioneer of direct sales in India, the company has now evolved into a multi-product, multi-channel organization backed by a nationwide after sales network.

Anticipating the changing needs of digital and tech-savvy customers and to changes in customer behavior, the firm developed a multi-channel approach. Eureka Forbes continues to reach out to customers through the direct sales team, complemented by other channels like retail, institutional and e-commerce. Eureka Forbes has also established a franchisee business partner network (FBP) and an exclusive network (FDO) to reach Tier I & Tier II towns and expand its direct sales operations across India.

With its innovative and customised selling skills, Eureka Forbes continues to evolve and expand, by anticipating trends, focusing on execution and keeping relationships at the heart of its business.

<< Eureka Forbes' marketing strategy for its health and hygiene products rely largely on a direct sales organization to sell directly to consumers who seek a product demonstration before purchase.

Source: ©Eureka Forbes, used with permission

Consider the following situation: A North Carolina furniture manufacturer wants to sell its line to retailers on the West Coast. One alternative is to hire 10 new sales representatives to operate out of a sales office in San Francisco and receive a base salary plus commissions. The other alternative is to use a San Francisco manufacturer's sales agency that has extensive contacts with retailers. Its 30 sales representatives would receive a commission based on their sales.

The first step is to estimate the dollar volume of sales each alternative is likely to generate. A company sales force will concentrate on the company's products, be better trained to sell them, be more aggressive, and be more successful because many customers will prefer to deal directly with the company. The sales agency has 30 representatives, however, not just 10; it may be just as aggressive, depending on the commission level; customers may appreciate its independence; and it may have extensive contacts and market knowledge. The marketer needs to evaluate all these factors in formulating a demand function for the two different channels.

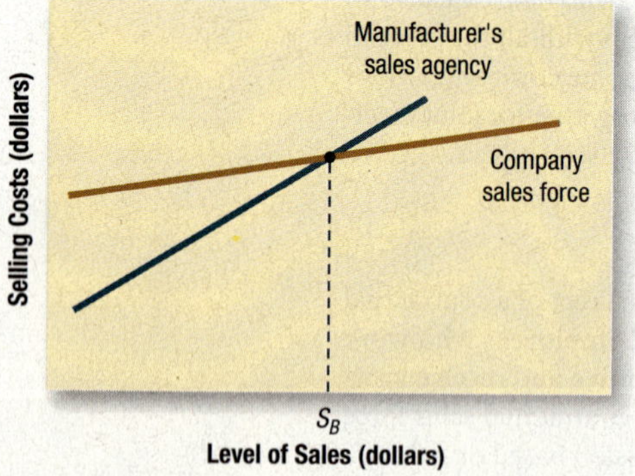

FIGURE **14.3**

Break-Even Cost Chart for the Choice between a Company Sales Force and a Manufacturer's Sales Agency

The next step is to estimate the costs of selling different volumes through each channel. The cost schedules are shown in Figure 14.3. Engaging a sales agency is initially less expensive than using the company's sales force, but costs rise faster because the sales agents get larger commissions. The final step is comparing sales and costs. As Figure 14.3 shows, there is one sales level (S_B) at which selling costs for the two channels are the same. The sales agency is thus the better channel for any sales volume below S_B, and the company sales branch is better at any volume above S_B. Given this information, it is not surprising that sales agents tend to be used by smaller firms or by large firms in smaller territories where the volume is low.

Using a sales agency can pose a control problem. Agents may concentrate on the customers who buy the most, not necessarily on those who buy the manufacturer's goods. And they might not master the technical details of the company's product or handle its promotion materials effectively.

SALES FORCE STRUCTURE

The sales force strategy also has implications for its structure. A company that sells one product line to one industry with customers in many locations would organize its sales force around geographic territories. On the other hand, a company that sells many products to customers with diverse needs might organize its sales force around specific products, services, or customer needs.

Some companies need a more complex structure and adopt some combination of four types of sales force: a strategic market sales force assigned to major accounts (see "Marketing Insight: Major Account Management"), a geographic sales force calling on customers in different territories, a distributor sales force calling on and coaching distributors, and an inside sales force marketing and taking orders online and via phone.

To manage costs, companies often choose a leveraged sales force that focuses reps on selling the company's more complex and customized products to large accounts and uses inside salespeople and online ordering for low-end selling. Salespeople handle fewer accounts and are rewarded for key account growth; lead generation, proposal writing, order fulfillment, and post-sale support are turned over to others. By motivating salespeople to sell to every possible account, this approach helps overcome some of the limitations of geographically based sales forces.[22]

Companies must deploy sales forces strategically so that they call on the right customers at the right time in the right way, acting as "account managers" who arrange fruitful contact between people in the buying and selling organizations. Selling increasingly calls for teamwork and the support of others, such as top management, especially when national accounts or major sales are at stake; technical people, who supply information and service before, during, and after product purchase; customer-service representatives, who provide installation, maintenance, and other services; and office staff, consisting of sales analysts, order expediters, and assistants.[23]

SALES FORCE SIZE

Sales representatives are one of the company's most productive and expensive assets. Increasing their number increases both sales and costs. Once the company establishes the number of customers it wants to reach, it can use a *workload approach* to establish sales force size. A streamlined version of this method has five steps:

1. Group customers into size classes according to annual sales volume.
2. Establish desirable contact frequencies (number of calls on an account per year) for each customer class.
3. Multiply the number of accounts in each size class by the corresponding call frequency to arrive at the total workload for the country, in sales calls per year.
4. Determine the average number of customer interactions a sales representative can make per year.
5. Divide the total annual calls required by the average annual customer interactions made by a sales representative to arrive at the number of sales representatives needed.

Suppose the company estimates that it has 1,000 "A" accounts and 2,000 "B" accounts. "A" accounts require 36 calls a year, and "B" accounts require 12, so the company needs a sales force that can make 60,000 sales calls a year. If the average full-time rep can make 1,000 calls a year, the company needs 60 reps.

SALES FORCE COMPENSATION

To attract top-quality reps, the company must develop an attractive compensation package. Sales reps want income regularity, extra reward for above-average performance, and fair pay for experience and longevity. Management wants control, economy, and simplicity. Some of these objectives will conflict. No wonder compensation plans vary tremendously among, and even within, industries.[24]

The company must quantify four components of sales force compensation. The *fixed amount*, a salary, satisfies the need for income stability. The *variable amount*—whether commissions, quotas, bonus, or profit sharing—serves to stimulate and reward effort.[25] *Expense allowances* enable sales reps to meet the costs of travel and entertaining on the company's behalf. *Benefits*—such as paid vacations, sickness or accident benefits, pensions, and health and life insurance—provide security and job satisfaction.[26]

Fixed compensation is common in jobs with a high ratio of non-selling to selling duties and in jobs where the selling task is technically complex and requires teamwork. Variable compensation works best where sales are cyclical or depend on individual initiative. Fixed and variable compensation give rise to three basic types of compensation plans—straight salary, straight commission, and combination salary and commission. It is not uncommon for sales reps to receive a significant part of their compensation in variable rather than fixed pay.

Straight-salary plans provide a secure income, encourage reps to complete non-selling activities, and reduce incentive to overstock customers. For the firm, these plans deliver administrative simplicity and lower turnover. When semiconductor company Microchip dropped commissions for its sales force, sales actually increased.[27] Straight-commission plans attract higher performers, provide more motivation, require less supervision, and control selling costs. On the negative side, they emphasize getting the sale over building the relationship. Combination plans feature the benefits of both plans, while limiting their disadvantages.

Plans that combine fixed and variable pay link the variable portion to a wide variety of strategic goals. One current trend deemphasizes sales volume in favor of gross profitability, customer satisfaction, and customer retention. Other companies reward reps partly on sales team performance or even company-wide performance, motivating them to work together for the common good.

Managing the Sales Force

Various policies and procedures guide the firm's activities directed at managing the sales force. Some of the key activities—recruiting, selecting, training, supervising, motivating, and evaluating sales representatives—are shown in Figure 14.4 and outlined in more detail in the next sections.

RECRUITING THE SALES FORCE

At the heart of any successful sales force are appropriately selected representatives. It's a great waste to hire the wrong people. The average annual turnover rate of sales reps for all industries is almost 20 percent. Sales force turnover leads to lost sales, the expense of finding and training replacements, and (often) pressure on existing salespeople to pick up the slack.[28]

Studies have not always shown a strong relationship between sales performance, on the one hand, and background and experience variables, current status, lifestyle, attitude, personality, and skills, on the other. More effective predictors of high performance in sales are composite tests and assessment centers that simulate the working environment and assess applicants in an environment similar to the one in which they would work.[29]

To maintain a market focus, salespeople should know how to analyze sales data, measure market potential, gather market intelligence, and develop marketing strategies and plans. Especially at the higher levels of sales management, they need analytical marketing skills. Marketers believe that sales forces are more effective in the long run if they understand and appreciate marketing as well as selling.

Although scores from formal tests are only one element in a set that includes personal characteristics, references, past employment history, and interviewer reactions, they have been weighted quite heavily by companies such as IBM, Prudential, and Procter & Gamble. Gillette claims that tests have reduced turnover and scores have correlated well with the progress of new reps.

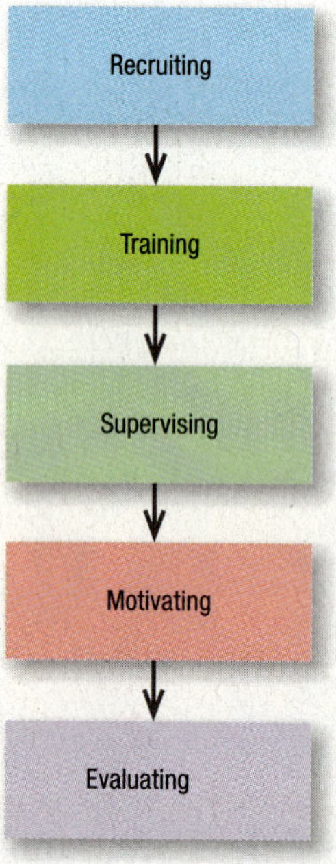

FIGURE **14.4**
Managing the Sales Force

TRAINING AND SUPERVISING THE SALES FORCE

Today's customers expect salespeople to have deep product knowledge, add ideas to improve operations, and be efficient and reliable. These demands have required companies to make a much greater investment in sales training.

New reps may spend a few weeks to several months in training. The median training period is 28 weeks in industrial-products companies, 12 in service companies, and 4 in consumer-products companies. Training time varies with the complexity of the selling task and the type of recruit. New methods of training are continually emerging, such as the use of programmed learning, distance learning, and videos. Some firms use role playing and sensitivity or empathy training to help reps identify with customers' situations and motives.[30]

Reps paid mostly on commission generally receive less supervision. Those who are salaried and must cover definite accounts are likely to receive substantial supervision. With multilevel selling, which Avon, Sara Lee, Virgin, and others use, independent distributors are also in charge of their own sales force selling company products. These independent contractors or reps are paid a commission not only on their own sales but also on the sales of people they recruit and train.

MANAGING SALES FORCE PRODUCTIVITY

How many calls should a company make on a particular account each year? Some sales reps often spend too much time selling to smaller, less profitable accounts instead of focusing on larger, more profitable ones.

Left to their own devices, many reps will spend most of their time with current customers, who are known quantities. Reps can depend on them for some business, whereas a prospect might never deliver any. Companies therefore often specify how much time reps should spend prospecting for new accounts.[31] Spector Freight wants its sales representatives to spend 25 percent of their time prospecting and to stop after three unsuccessful calls. Some companies rely on a missionary sales force to create new interest and open new accounts.

In the course of a day, reps plan, travel, wait, sell, and perform administrative tasks (writing reports and billing, attending sales meetings, and talking to others in the company about production, delivery, billing, and sales performance). The best sales reps manage their time efficiently. **Time-and-duty analysis** and hour-by-hour breakdowns of activities help them understand how they spend their time and how they might increase their productivity.

Companies constantly try to improve sales force productivity.[32] To cut costs, reduce time demands on their outside sales force, and leverage technological innovations, many have increased the size and responsibilities of their inside sales force.

Inside selling is less expensive than in-person selling, and it is growing faster. Each contact made by an inside salesperson might cost a company $25 to $30, compared with $300 to $500 for a field staff person with travel expenses. Virtual meeting software such as Webex, communication tools such as Skype, and social media sites such as LinkedIn, Facebook, and Twitter make it easier to sell with few if any face-to-face meetings. And inside sellers don't even need to be in the office—a growing percentage work at home.[33]

The inside sales force frees outside reps to spend more time selling to major accounts, identifying and converting new major prospects, and obtaining more blanket orders and systems contracts. Inside salespeople spend more time checking inventory, following up on orders, and phoning smaller accounts. They typically earn a salary or salary-plus-bonus pay.

The salesperson today has truly gone digital. Not only is sales and inventory information transferred much more quickly, but specific computer-based decision support systems have been created for sales managers and sales representatives. Going online with a tablet or laptop, salespeople can prime themselves on backgrounds of clients, call up prewritten sales letters, transmit orders, and resolve customer-service issues on the spot, as well as send samples, pamphlets, brochures, and other materials to clients.

One of the most valuable digital tools for the sales rep is the company's online presence. It can help define the firm's relationships with individual accounts and identify those whose business warrants a personal interaction. It provides an introduction to self-identified potential customers and a way to contact the seller; it might even receive the initial order.

Social media are a valuable digital selling tool. Social networking is useful in "front end" prospecting and lead qualification, as well as in "back end" relationship building and management. When one B2B sales rep for virtual-meetings company PGi was monitoring Twitter tweets for various keywords, he noticed that someone from a company tweeted about dissatisfaction with "web conferencing." The sales rep got in touch with the company's CEO and was able to quickly convince him of the merits of PGi's products, securing an agreement within a few hours.[34]

MOTIVATING THE SALES FORCE

The majority of sales representatives require encouragement and special incentives, especially those in the field who encounter daily challenges.[35] Most marketers believe that the higher the salesperson's motivation, the greater the effort and the resulting performance, rewards, and satisfaction—all of which in turn further increase motivation.[36]

Marketers reinforce *monetary and nonmonetary rewards* of all types. One research study found that the employee reward with the highest value was pay, followed by promotion, personal growth, and sense of accomplishment.[37] Least valued were liking and respect, security, and recognition. In other words, salespeople are highly motivated by pay and the chance to get ahead and satisfy their intrinsic needs, and they may be less motivated by compliments and security. Some firms use sales contests to increase sales effort.[38]

Compensation plans may even need to vary depending on salesperson type—that is, on whether the salespersons are stars, core or solid performers, or laggards.[39] *Stars* benefit from no ceiling or caps on commissions, overachievement commissions for exceeding quotas, and prize structures that allow multiple winners. Core performers benefit from multitier targets that serve as stepping stones for achievement and sales contests with prizes that vary in nature and value. Laggards respond to consistent quarterly bonuses and social pressure.[40]

Many companies set annual sales quotas, developed from the annual marketing plan, for dollar sales, unit volume, margin, selling effort or activity, or product type. Compensation is often tied to the degree of quota fulfillment. The company first prepares a sales forecast that becomes the basis for planning production, workforce size, and financial requirements. Management then establishes quotas for regions and territories, which typically add up to more than the sales forecast to encourage managers and salespeople to perform at their best level. Even if they fail to make their quotas, the company may nevertheless reach its sales forecast.[41]

Conventional wisdom says profits are maximized by sales reps focusing on the more important products and more profitable products. Reps are unlikely to achieve their quotas for established products when the company is launching several new products at the same time. The company may need to expand its sales force for new-product launches.

Setting sales quotas can create problems. If the company underestimates and the sales reps easily achieve their quotas, it has overpaid them. If it overestimates sales potential, the salespeople will find it very hard to reach their quotas and will be frustrated or quit. Another downside is that quotas can drive reps to get as much business as possible, often ignoring the service side of the business. The company gains short-term results at the cost of long-term customer satisfaction. For these reasons, some companies are dropping quotas.

EVALUATING THE SALES FORCE

We have been describing the *feed-forward* aspects of sales supervision—how management communicates what the sales reps should be doing and motivates them to do it. But good feed-forward requires good *feedback*, which means getting regular information about reps to evaluate their performance.

An important source of information about reps is sales reports. Additional information comes through personal observation, salesperson self-reports, customer letters and complaints, customer surveys, and conversations with other reps.

Sales reports are divided between *activity plans* and *write-ups of activity results*. The best example of the former is the salesperson's work plan, which reps submit a week or month in advance to describe intended calls and routing. This report forces sales reps to plan and schedule their activities and inform management of their whereabouts. It provides a basis for comparing their plans and accomplishments, or their ability to "plan their work and work their plan."

Many companies require representatives to develop an annual territory-marketing plan in which they outline their program for developing new accounts and increasing business from existing accounts. Sales managers study these plans, make suggestions, and use them to develop sales quotas. Sales reps write up completed activities as call reports. They also submit expense reports, new-business reports, lost-business reports, and reports on local business and economic conditions.

These reports provide raw data from which sales managers can extract key indicators of sales performance: average number of sales calls per salesperson per day, average sales call time per contact, average revenue per sales call, average cost per sales call, entertainment cost per sales call, percentage of orders per hundred sales calls, number of new customers per period, number of lost customers per period, and sales force cost as a percentage of total sales.

Even if she or he is effective in producing sales, the rep may not rate highly with customers. Success may come because competitors' salespeople are inferior, the rep's product is better, or new customers are always found to replace those who dislike the rep. Sales reps can analyze the success or failure of a sales call and how they would improve the odds during subsequent calls. Their performance could be related to internal factors (effort, ability, and strategy) and/or external factors (task and luck).

Direct Marketing

Today, many marketers build long-term relationships with customers. They send birthday cards and informational materials and offer free products and services. Airlines, hotels, and other businesses adopt frequency reward programs and club programs.[42] **Direct marketing** is the use of consumer-direct channels to reach and deliver goods and services to customers without using intermediaries.

Direct marketing offers companies several advantages. By eliminating the intermediary, it often proves to be more cost-effective than traditional marketing. Directly connecting with customers also can provide the company with invaluable information about customers' current and potential needs, the ways in which they use the company's offerings, as well as what aspects of the company's offerings they find particularly beneficial and what aspects need improvement. In addition, having the ability to directly interact with customers enables the company to offer a superior service experience and build a stronger brand image.

Direct marketers can use a number of channels to reach individual prospects and customers: direct mail, catalog marketing, telemarketing, kiosks, websites, and mobile devices. They often seek a measurable response, typically a customer order, through direct-order marketing.

>>> Established in 2017 by Kamesh Goyal with a mission of "making insurance simple", Digit Insurance is one of the fastest growing cloud-based insurance companies in the world. Pioneering digital insurance solutions in India, the company's business model is built around transparency and simplicity that has redefined the otherwise complex insurance products for consumers. To ensure ease of policy purchase, renewal as well as claims, Digit Insurance introduced a paperless process that uses self-service tools. For instance, its motor insurance is supported by video and photo-based self-service inspection apps that shorten the claim process time from seven days to seven minutes. More than 95% of its claims are processed directly by its customers using a mobile application and over 80% of the claims are approved within 24 hours. Its innovative and simple direct marketing approach helped the company acquire 1.5 lakh customers in less than 4 months.[43] It also offers many complementary tools like SME buddy (for small and medium enterprises), Home Loan Calculator (helps to calculate the monthly instalments), and Insurance Dictionary (helps to understand the complicated terms) to deliver trusted, effortless, and transparent insurance service experience, right from selection of a product to claims processing. Customer convenience, trust and simplicity based digital model has helped Digit attract several marquee investors at a valuation of $1.9 billion in January 2021.[44]

Direct marketing has been a fast-growing avenue, partly in response to the high and increasing costs of reaching business markets through a sales force. Sales produced through traditional direct marketing channels (direct mail, catalogs, and telemarketing) have been growing rapidly, along with direct-mail sales, which include sales to the consumer market, B2B sales, and fundraising by charitable institutions.

DIRECT MARKETING CHANNELS

We next consider some of the issues that characterize the key direct marketing channels: direct mail, catalog marketing, telemarketing, and infomercials.

Direct Mail. Direct-mail marketing involves sending an offer, announcement, reminder, or other item to an individual consumer. Using highly selective mailing lists, direct marketers send out millions of mail pieces each year—letters, fliers, foldouts, and other "salespeople with wings."

Direct mail is a popular medium because it permits target-market selectivity, can be personalized, is flexible, and allows early testing and response measurement. Although the cost per thousand is higher than for mass media, the people reached are much better prospects. The success of direct mail, however, has also become its liability: So many marketers are sending out direct-mail pieces that mailboxes are becoming stuffed, leading some consumers to disregard the blizzard of solicitations they receive. Direct mail can also produce prospect leads, strengthen customer relationships, inform and educate customers, remind customers of offers, and reinforce recent customer purchase decisions.

Most direct marketers apply the RFM (recency, frequency, monetary amount) formula to select customers according to how much time has passed since their last purchase, how many times they have purchased, and how much they have spent since becoming a customer. Suppose the company is offering a leather jacket. It might make this offer to the most attractive customers—those who made their last purchase between 30 and 60 days ago, who make three to six purchases a year, and who have spent at least $100 since becoming customers. Points are established for varying RFM levels; the more points, the more attractive the customer.[45]

The company's best prospects are customers who have bought its products in the past. The direct marketer can also buy lists of names from list brokers, but these lists often have problems, including name duplication, incomplete data, and obsolete addresses. Better lists include overlays of demographic and psychographic information. Direct marketers typically buy and test a sample before buying more names from the same list. They also can build their own lists by advertising a promotional offer and collecting responses.[46]

One of the great advantages of direct marketing is the ability to test, under real marketplace conditions, different elements of an offer strategy, such as products, product features, copy platform, mailer type, envelope, prices, or mailing lists. The Teaching Company mails 50 million catalogs and sends 25 million e-mails to sell educational lectures and courses. Every element of the offer is tested. Replacing an image of Michelangelo's hand of God with one depicting the ruins of Petra improved sales by more than 20 percent.[47]

Response rates typically understate a campaign's long-term impact. Suppose only 2 percent of the recipients who receive a direct-mail piece advertising Samsonite luggage place an order. A much larger percentage became aware of the product (direct mail has high readership), and some percentage may have formed an intention to buy at a later date (either by mail or at a retail outlet). Some may mention Samsonite luggage to others as a result of the direct-mail piece. To better estimate a promotion's impact, some companies measure the impact of direct marketing on awareness, intention to buy, and word of mouth.

Direct mail can involve regular mail or e-mail. E-mail allows marketers to inform and communicate with customers at a fraction of the cost of regular mail. E-mails can be very productive selling tools. The rate at which they prompt purchase has been estimated to be at least three times that of social media ads. To be effective, e-mails must be timely, targeted, and relevant. The Gilt Groupe sends more than 3,000 variations of its daily e-mail for its flash-sale site based on recipients' past click-throughs, browsing history, and purchase history.[48]

Privacy concerns are growing—many consumers refuse to share any personal details with brands even if doing so would bring them better targeted offers and discounts. Some firms are asking consumers to indicate whether and when they would like to receive e-mails. FTD, the flower retailer, allows customers to choose whether to receive e-mail reminders to send flowers for virtually any holiday, as well as specific birthdays and anniversaries.

Catalog Marketing. Companies using catalog marketing may send full-line merchandise catalogs, specialty consumer catalogs, and business catalogs, usually in print form but also online. Thousands of small businesses also issue specialty catalogs. Many direct marketers find combining catalogs and websites an effective way to sell. For example, W.W. Grainger every year publishes a massive, nearly 3000-page printed catalog, while at the same time posting a digital, searchable version of the catalog online along with supplemental content that goes beyond the printed version of the catalog.[49]

Catalogs are a huge business. The internet and catalog retailing industry includes 37,000 companies with combined annual revenue of $460 billion.[50] Successfully marketing a catalog business depends on managing customer lists carefully to avoid duplication or bad debts, controlling inventory, offering quality merchandise so that returns are low, and projecting a distinctive image.

Some companies add literary or information features, send swatches of materials, operate a special online or telephone hotline to answer questions, send gifts to their best customers, and donate a percentage of profits to good causes. Putting their entire catalog online also provides business marketers with better access to global consumers than ever before, saving printing and mailing costs.

Telemarketing. Telemarketing is the use of the telephone and call centers to attract prospects, sell to existing customers, and provide service by taking orders and answering questions. It helps companies increase revenue, reduce selling costs, and improve customer satisfaction. Companies use call centers for *inbound telemarketing*—receiving calls from customers—and *outbound telemarketing*—initiating calls to prospects and customers.

Over time, telemarketing has lost much of its effectiveness, although it is still heavily used in political campaigns. Business-to-business telemarketing is increasing, however. This is partly due to the use of videoconferencing, which will increasingly replace, though never eliminate, more expensive field sales calls.

Source: HORST OSSINGER/EPA/Newscom

<< TV infomercials have been used with great success to sell the George Foreman grill, backed by the former heavyweight boxing champion.

A popular form of telemarketing involves robo-calls—telephone calls that use a computer-based autodialer to deliver a prerecorded message. In the United States, calls using prerecorded messages are legal only if they deliver relevant information, such as doctor appointment reminders, flight change notifications, and credit card fraud alerts, or if they involve election campaigns. Robo-calls to sell products and services are not deemed legal.[51]

Infomercials. Some companies prepare 30- and 60-minute *infomercials* to combine the selling power of television commercials with the draw of information and entertainment. Infomercials promote products that are complicated or technologically advanced or that require a great deal of explanation. Some of the most successful are for Proactiv acne system, P90X workout program, and the George Foreman grill. At-home shopping channels are dedicated to selling goods and services through a toll-free number or via the internet for delivery within 48 hours.

THE FUTURE OF DIRECT MARKETING

The rise of direct marketing has resulted in an ever-increasing number of market niches. Consumers short of time and tired of traffic and parking headaches appreciate toll-free phone numbers, always-open websites, next-day delivery, and direct marketers' commitment to customer service. In addition, many chain stores have dropped slower-moving specialty items, creating an opportunity for direct marketers to promote these to interested buyers instead.

Sellers can benefit from direct marketing as well. Direct marketers can buy a list containing the names of almost every group imaginable: left-handed people, tall people, millionaires, or you-name-it. They can customize and personalize messages and build a continuous relationship with each customer. New parents inevitably receive periodic mailings describing new clothes, toys, and other goods as their child grows.

Direct marketing can reach prospects at the moment when they want a solicitation, so they are noticed by more highly interested prospects. It lets marketers test alternative media and messages to find the most cost-effective approach. Direct marketing also makes the company's offer and strategy less visible to competitors. Finally, direct marketers can measure responses to their campaigns to decide which have been the most profitable.

Direct marketing must be integrated with other communications and channel activities. Eddie Bauer, Lands' End, and the Franklin Mint made fortunes building their brands in the direct marketing mail-order and phone-order business before opening retail stores. They cross-promote their stores, catalogs, and websites—for example, by putting their internet addresses on their shopping bags.

Successful direct marketers view a customer interaction as an opportunity to up-sell, cross-sell, or just deepen a relationship. They make sure they know enough about each customer to customize and personalize offers and messages and develop a plan for lifetime marketing to each valuable customer, based on their knowledge of life events and transitions. They also carefully orchestrate each element of their campaigns.

marketing INSIGHT — Major Account Management

Marketers typically single out for attention major accounts (also called key accounts, national accounts, global accounts, or house accounts). These are important customers with multiple divisions in many locations that use uniform pricing and coordinated service for all divisions. A major account manager usually reports to the national sales manager and supervises field reps calling on customer plants within their territories. The average company manages about 75 key accounts. If a company has several such accounts, it's likely to organize a major account management division, in which the average major account manager handles nine accounts.

Large accounts are often handled by a strategic account management team with cross-functional members who integrate new-product development, technical support, supply chain, marketing activities, and multiple communication channels to cover all aspects of the relationship. Procter & Gamble has a strategic account management team of 300 staffers to work with Walmart in its Bentonville, Arkansas, headquarters, and more are stationed at Walmart headquarters in Europe, Asia, and Latin America. P&G has credited this relationship with saving the company billions of dollars.

Major account management is growing. As buyer concentration increases through mergers and acquisitions, fewer buyers are accounting for a larger share of sales. Many are centralizing their purchases of certain items, gaining more bargaining power. And as products become more complex, more groups in the buyer's organization participate in the purchase process. The typical salesperson alone might not have the skill, authority, or coverage to sell effectively to the large buyer.

In selecting major accounts, companies look for those that purchase a high volume (especially of more profitable products), purchase centrally, require a high level of service in several geographic locations, may be price sensitive, and want a long-term partnership. Major account managers act as the single point of contact, develop and grow customer business, understand customer decision processes, identify added-value opportunities, provide competitive intelligence, negotiate sales, and orchestrate customer service.

Many major accounts look for added value more than for a price advantage. They appreciate having a single point of dedicated contact, single billing, special warranties, electronic data interchange (EDI) links, priority shipping, early information releases, customized products, and efficient maintenance, repair, and upgraded service. And then there's the value of goodwill. Personal relationships with people who value the major account's business and have a vested interest in its success are compelling reasons for the major account to remain a loyal customer.[52]

summary

1. *Personal selling* involves a direct interaction with one or more prospective purchasers for the purpose of making presentations, answering questions, and procuring orders. Personal selling has three notable qualities: It is customized, relationship oriented, and response oriented.
2. There are several major steps in any effective *sales process*: prospecting, pre-approach, presentation, persuasion, closing, and servicing. Effective salespeople are trained in methods of analysis and customer management, as well as in the art of sales professionalism.
3. The *sales force* is a company's link to its customers. The salesperson *is* the company to many of its customers, and it is the rep who brings back to the company much-needed information about the customer. Thoughtful design and management of the sales force is of utmost importance in maximizing the effectiveness and cost efficiency of a company's sales efforts.
4. *Designing the sales force* requires choosing objectives, strategy, structure, size, and compensation. Objectives may include prospecting, targeting, communicating, selling, servicing, information gathering, and allocating. The strategy requires choosing the most effective mix of selling approaches. Structuring the sales force entails dividing territories by geography, product, or market (or some combination of these). To estimate how large the sales force needs to be, the firm estimates the total workload and how many sales hours (and hence salespeople) will be needed. Compensating sales reps requires deciding what types of salaries, commissions, bonuses, expense accounts, and benefits to give and how much weight customer satisfaction should have in determining total compensation.
5. *Managing the sales force* involves five key components: (1) recruiting and selecting sales representatives; (2) training the representatives in sales techniques and in the company's products, policies, and customer-satisfaction orientation; (3) supervising the sales force and helping reps to use their time efficiently; (4) motivating the sales force and balancing quotas, monetary rewards, and supplementary motivators; and (5) evaluating individual and group sales performance.

6. *Direct marketing* is the use of consumer-direct channels to reach and deliver goods and services to customers without using marketing intermediaries. Direct marketers can use a number of channels to reach individual prospects and customers: direct mail, catalog marketing, telemarketing, kiosks, websites, and mobile devices. They often seek a measurable response, typically a customer order, through direct-order marketing.

7. Major *direct marketing channels* include direct mail, catalog marketing, telemarketing, and infomercials. These channels offer several benefits to companies: (1) They provide companies with the option not only to inform target customers about the benefits of the offering but also to generate a sale. (2) Relative to other forms of communication, they are less visible to competitors. And (3) they enable marketers to measure responses to their campaigns to decide which have been the most profitable.

marketing SPOTLIGHT

Avon

Source: Home Bird/Alamy Stock Photo

Avon, the world's oldest direct-sales beauty company, got its start in 1886 after door-to-door book salesman David McConnell began offering free perfume to attract female customers. When the perfume proved more popular, McConnell ditched the books and started the California Perfume Company, which his son later renamed after Shakespeare's birthplace. McConnell hired 50-year-old Mrs. P. F. E Albee to peddle perfume and recruit a sales team, giving women one of the first opportunities to work outside the home and earn an income in an era when this was far from the norm. Avon's first catalog was printed in 1905 and its first print advertisement appeared the following year in *Good Housekeeping*, which 25 years later gave its seal of approval to eleven Avon products, a record for one company.

The Avon Ladies who knocked on doors, hosted parties, and enlisted friends were ensured a niche in popular culture when the company's "Ding Dong, Avon Calling" TV commercials appeared in the 1950s and 1960s. Avon's basic direct-selling model hasn't changed drastically through the years. The buy-in for an Avon rep is inexpensive. Reps can choose one of three starter kits—$25, $50, and $100—containing catalogs, product samples, order pads, delivery bags, and recruiting forms. Avon prints a new catalog for every two-week "campaign" period. Reps shop the catalogs around to customers and prospects and take orders that they fill from inventory shipped to them from Avon. Customers now can also order directly online. Commissions start at 20 percent for individual and team sales up to $150, and go up to 40 percent for sales exceeding $500; sales of more than $10,000 earn 50 percent commission. Ten "leadership" levels offer bonuses and incentives depending on campaign sales levels.

Sales reps also recruit others to join their team, who then recruit new reps of their own, on down the line, adding up to more commissions for the team leader. But there are boundaries. Avon caused a stir when it quit the Direct Selling Association, citing the need for stricter ethics for multi-level marketing, sometimes viewed as Ponzi schemes. The company has placed a limit on the amount of profit that can be reaped from recruiting others. Avon allows reps to claim commissions from only three downline generations of their personal sales organizations, rather than from an infinite number, which puts the focus on customer sales rather than on team-building.

Avon was an early entrant into international markets; Brazil became Avon's biggest sales market in 2010. But the company faced increasingly stiff competition both internationally and at home. Multinationals like P&G and Unilever made inroads in developing nations, while department and drug stores expanded their selection of affordable cosmetics, and retailers like Ulta Beauty and Sephora appeared. While Ulta's sales rose from $1.45 billion to $3.2 billion between 2010 and 2014, Avon's North American sales fell from $2.2 billion to $1 billion during that time.

One of the reasons for the decline in Avon's market share was that the company was slow to pick up on the proliferation of online marketing and social networking. Only in 2014 did Avon attempt to refurbish its website, which hadn't had a makeover in a decade, and create marketing materials specifically for its Hispanic reps, who far outsold their non-Hispanic counterparts. Social media and online selling were becoming more important as face-to-face contact became increasingly difficult in a world where women make up almost 50 percent of the workforce. In addition, Millennials, a rapidly growing market with annual spending power estimated to reach $1.4 trillion by 2020, preferred online to in-home events and were paying attention to Facebook, Instagram, and Twitter influencers—the type of social media marketing that Avon had failed to facilitate.

(*continued*)

In 2015, Avon split its operations by selling most of its North American business to private investment firm Cerberus Holdings (its U.S., Canada, and Puerto Rico businesses now operate as "New Avon LLC") and moving its headquarters to London. By 2017, Avon's stock market value had fallen to $1.3 billion—a dramatic decline from its over $21 billion market valuation a little more than a decade earlier. Many of the causes sprang from an unclear marketing strategy that dated from the early 2000s, which saw Avon straddling the line between direct sales and retailing, having difficulty implementing a workable software platform that could facilitate the transition to online sales, engaging in a number of corporate restructurings that were more about cost-cutting than strategic vision, and facing regulatory challenges in the rapidly growing Chinese market.

Realizing that Avon had lost its way and needed to step up its ability to capitalize on emerging trends and opportunities in order to grow and prosper, Jan Zijderveld, the former president of Unilever's European business unit who became Avon's CEO in February 2018, partnered with Salesforce.com and announced an investment of approximately $300 million in IT, new products, and marketing, training, and digital tools. To bring Avon into the digital age, chief beauty and brand officer James Thompson, formerly with Diageo, resolved to intensify ongoing training for reps on how to use Facebook and Instagram platforms effectively, in addition to growing Avon's own platform that connects direct online purchases with reps. Avon also appointed its first-ever chief digital officer to develop personalized beauty apps that link customers with reps via a phone camera and focus on data analytics to take the guesswork out of cosmetics purchases. By building on its direct-selling roots, while embracing new technologies and the changes in the way consumers socialize, exchange information, and shop, Avon is seeking to revamp its business model and regain its market position.

In January 2020, Avon was acquired by Natura &Co, a Brazilian multinational cosmetics and personal care company, creating the world's fourth-largest pure-play beauty company. The acquisition adds Avon to Natura &Co portfolio of brands which, in addition to the company's own brand Nature, includes The Body Shop and Aesop. The acquisition enabled Natura &Co to gain leading position in relationship selling, on and offline, with over 6.3 million consultants and representatives for the Avon and Natura brands.[53]

Questions

1. What factors contributed to Avon's initial market success? How did these factors evolve over time?
2. What is Avon's value proposition for its customers, its sales force, and its stakeholders?
3. How did the role of personal selling change during the past several decades? Can personal selling continue to be a viable business model, given the ubiquity of social media and mobile communications?

marketing SPOTLIGHT

Progressive Insurance

Progressive Corporation is one of the largest providers of auto, motorcycle, boat, and RV insurance in the United States. Founded in 1937, the company is considered one of the most innovative insurance agencies in the industry. From the beginning, Progressive's philosophy has been to approach auto insurance "like no other company had."

Progressive attracts new customers through its unique product offerings and services. For example, it was the first insurance company to offer drive-thru claim service, 24-hour claim service, and reduced rates for low-risk drivers. In 1994, Progressive introduced a comparison insurance shopping service, encouraging customers to call 800-AUTO-PRO (now 800-PROGRESSIVE) and receive a Progressive quote as well as comparison quotes from three competitors. Progressive extended this service when it launched comparison-rate shopping on the internet. Progressive was also the first insurance company to introduce the Immediate Response Vehicle (IRV), a special vehicle that brings trained claims professionals to wherever customers need them, including the scene of an accident.

Source: NetPhotos/Alamy Stock Photo

Today, the company has expanded its IRV service to thousands of IRVs across the country.

The insurance industry has changed a lot over the years as consumers have become more educated, increasingly cost-conscious, and less likely to use an agent during the buying process. Jonathan Beamer, marketing strategy and innovation business leader at Progressive, explained the company's media strategy: "As a company, we've always had the belief that customers should be able to interact with us in their channel of choice. In the past, that was by phone, online, or through an agent. Social media is another means for customers to engage with our brand." The company has a network of 35,000 independent agents but also gives customers the opportunity to interact with the company via the internet or mobile devices. Progressive offers consumers several options to manage their service claims as well. Policy holders can choose to bring their damaged vehicle to a Progressive service center or can call Progressive roadside assistance to take care of problems ranging from flat tires to locksmith needs.

Consumers have responded positively to Progressive's marketing campaigns in recent years, thanks to the company's iconic character named Flo. Flo is a quirky, witty, animated Progressive employee dressed in a white uniform and white apron that bears the company's logo. She represents the Progressive brand and its employees. The Flo commercials are often set in an imaginary insurance superstore and aimed at consumers who are considering a new insurance policy or changing insurers. The company has found that using a person to represent Progressive insurance helps consumers envision the intangible act of buying and selling insurance as a tangible one. Progressive often includes a white-and-blue "insurance package" in its commercials as well. Again, this reinforces the concept that Progressive sells something concrete rather than something abstract. In every commercial, Flo goes out of her way to help customers and their businesses. She works alongside plumbers, lugs shrubbery with landscapers, and finds stranded cars and drivers in pouring rain. Flo, her packages of insurance, and the Progressive supercenters have all helped differentiate Progressive in a competitive industry.

Flo has become one of the most recognized advertising icons in marketing today and has made "Progressive" a household name. However, Progressive's marketing team is careful to keep her modern and relevant. She appears across all types of screens—including those on TVs, computers, mobile devices, smartphone apps, video games like Sims Social, and animated YouTube videos. She even has her own Facebook page (along with millions of fans). Progressive's marketing has also won multiple awards, including *Adweek's* "Brand Genius: Marketer of the Year Award" and an Effie award for marketing efficiency.

Progressive is a leader in using technology to streamline the process of selling insurance. The company's technology-enabled features include the following:

- *Policy service and management* enables customers to update information, make payments, get vehicle recall information, and more.
- *Online claims reporting* enables customers to report auto accidents and claims in minutes using a proprietary visual reporting tool. It even lets them schedule an appointment at a nearby repair shop.
- *Rate ticker* displays actual Progressive auto insurance rates side by side with those of other top auto insurers.
- *Agent locator* enables customers who prefer to buy insurance through an agent to search for local independent insurance agents.
- *Talk to me* offers online customer service that allows online shoppers with questions about their auto insurance quote to talk to a representative over the internet or have a representative call them directly.

To make it more convenient for customers to learn about Progressive, the company also created a Flo Chatbot experience on Facebook Messenger, thus becoming the first top-10 U.S. insurance company to allow users to interact with Progressive in a familiar, natural, and conversational way. If the Flo Chatbot can't answer a particular question, a Progressive representative picks up the conversation via phone or private message.

In addition to streamlining customer experience, Progressive also invests heavily in developing solutions to empower its independent agents nationwide. Introduced in 2018, Progressive's "For Agents Only" (FAO) state-of-the-art portfolio-quoting platform contains multiple features designed to enhance the effectiveness and efficiency of sales agents. These features include

- *Integrated third-party data* to help agents identify and quickly add additional vehicles, drivers, and products registered to the customer's address.
- *Auto-filling of repeat information* across product quotes to reduce work.
- *Simplified quote and buy experience* with home, condo, renters, auto, and recreational lines products supported in a single workflow.
- *Side-by-side comparison screens* to help agents counsel their customers on the right coverage.
- *In-quote training* to highlight discount opportunities and features that can add customer and agent value.

Progressive's growth has been impressive over the past two decades because of its innovative and affordable insurance solutions and its effective direct marketing campaigns. Between 1996 and 2019, the company grew from $3.4 billion to $39 billion. Progressive now is the third largest auto insurer in the country, a leading seller of motorcycle and commercial auto insurance, and one of the top-20 homeowners' insurance carriers.[54]

Questions

1. What has Progressive done well over the years to attract new insurance customers?
2. Discuss Progressive's direct marketing campaign, which primarily revolves around the character Flo. Why does it resonate so well with consumers?
3. What else should Progressive be doing to ensure that it remains "top of mind" in the competitive insurance industry?

CHAPTER 15

Designing and Managing Distribution Channels

Asian Paints has expanded beyond its famed retail outlets with tinting machines for custom shades of paints to sell online with easy tools for product selection that match the home's decor.

Source: ©Asian Paints Ltd, used with permission

Successful value creation needs successful value delivery. Instead of limiting their focus to their immediate suppliers, distributors, and customers, holistic marketers are examining the whole supply chain as a value network, including their suppliers' suppliers upstream and their distributors' customers downstream. They are also looking at how technology is changing the way customers shop and retailers sell and finding new and different means to distribute and service their offerings. Consider how Asian Paints develops strong customer ties with a well-executed channel strategy.

>>> Asian Paints, founded in 1942, is one of the world's biggest paint companies known for its wide range of products and extensive distribution channel. In its legacy of eight decades, the company has maintained the leader's position since 1967, offering painting, home improvement and décor solutions. It follows a multi-channel distribution system, driven by strong customer focus and the spirit of innovation. Its integrated distribution system plays a significant role in effectively managing its worldwide customer base spread in 60 countries. The group operates offline as well as online distribution channels, with a very strong focus on its retail outlets. Asian Paints' multiple offerings and store formats, including Signature stores, ColourIdeas and AP Beautiful Homes serve different customer segments. The key factor responsible for its successful and effective supply

chain management is the company's ability to offer quick solutions to cope with a varied range of demand through its robust network of over 50,000 dealers. These dealers are equipped with tinting machines to enable them to quickly offer any shade of colour demanded. Mixing and matching the colours within dealer's premises, create a significant point of differentiation by reducing the lead time for any colour sought by its customers. With a share of more than 50%, the market leader generated revenues of over ₹20,000 crore for 2020–21.[1]

With the advent of e-commerce (selling online) and m-commerce (selling via mobile devices), customers are buying in ways they never have before. Companies today must build and manage a continuously evolving and increasingly complex channel system and value network. In this chapter, we consider strategic and tactical issues in integrating marketing channels and developing value networks. We will examine marketing channel issues from the perspective of retailers in Chapter 17.

The Role of Distribution Channels

Most producers do not sell their goods directly to the final users; between them stand a set of intermediaries performing a variety of functions. These intermediaries constitute a marketing channel (also called a trade channel or distribution channel). **Distribution channels** are sets of interdependent organizations participating in the process of making a product or service available for use or consumption. They are the set of pathways a product or service follows after production, culminating in purchase and consumption by the final end user.[2]

Some intermediaries—such as wholesalers and retailers—buy, take title to, and resell the merchandise; these intermediaries are called **merchants**. Others—brokers, manufacturers' representatives, sales agents—search for customers and may negotiate on the producer's behalf but do not take title to the goods; they are called **agents**. Still others—transportation companies, independent warehouses, banks, advertising agencies—assist in the distribution process but neither take title to goods nor negotiate purchases or sales; they are called **facilitators**.

Channels of all types play an important role in the success of a company and affect all other marketing decisions. Marketers should judge them in the context of the entire process by which their products are made, distributed, sold, and serviced. One of the chief roles of marketing channels is to convert potential buyers into profitable customers. Marketing channels must not just *serve* markets, they must also *make* them.

The channels chosen affect all other marketing decisions. The company's pricing depends on whether it uses online discounters or high-quality boutiques. Its sales force and advertising decisions depend on how much training and motivation dealers need. In addition, channel decisions include relatively long-term commitments with other firms, as well as a set of policies and procedures. When an automaker signs up independent dealers to sell its automobiles, it cannot buy them out the next day and replace them with company-owned outlets. But at the same time, channel choices themselves depend on the company's marketing strategy. Holistic marketers ensure that marketing decisions in all these different areas are made to maximize value overall.

Learning Objectives After studying this chapter you should be able to:

15.1 Define the roles of marketing channels.

15.2 Explain the key channel-management decisions.

15.3 Discuss how firms manage channel cooperation and conflict.

15.4 Discuss how firms manage market logistics.

Why does a producer delegate some of the selling job to intermediaries, relinquishing control over how and to whom its products are sold? Through their contacts, experience, specialization, and scale of operation, intermediaries make goods widely available and accessible to target markets, offering more effectiveness and efficiency than the producing firm could achieve on its own.

Many producers lack the financial resources and expertise to sell directly to their customers. The William Wrigley Jr. Company would not find it practical to establish small retail gum shops throughout the world or to sell gum online or by mail order. It is easier to work through the extensive network of privately owned distribution organizations. Even Ford would be hard pressed to replace all the tasks done by its 8,000+ dealer outlets worldwide.

DISTRIBUTION CHANNEL FUNCTIONS

A distribution channel performs the work of moving goods from producers to consumers. It overcomes the time and place gaps that separate goods and services from those who need or want them. Members of the marketing channel perform a number of key functions:

- Gather information about potential and current customers, competitors, and other actors and forces in the marketing environment.
- Develop and disseminate persuasive communications to stimulate purchasing and foster brand loyalty.
- Negotiate and reach agreements on price and other terms so that transfer of ownership or possession can be effected.
- Place orders with manufacturers.
- Acquire the funds to finance inventories at different levels in the marketing channel.
- Assume risks connected with carrying out channel work.
- Provide buyers with financing and facilitate payment.
- Provide for buyers' payment of their bills through banks and other financial institutions.
- Oversee actual transfer of ownership of goods from one organization or person to another.

All channel functions have three characteristics in common: They use up scarce resources, they can often be performed better through specialization, and they can be shifted among channel members. Channel functions can be illustrated in terms of flows of goods and services across distribution channels. Five of the most common flows are illustrated in Figure 15.1. If these flows

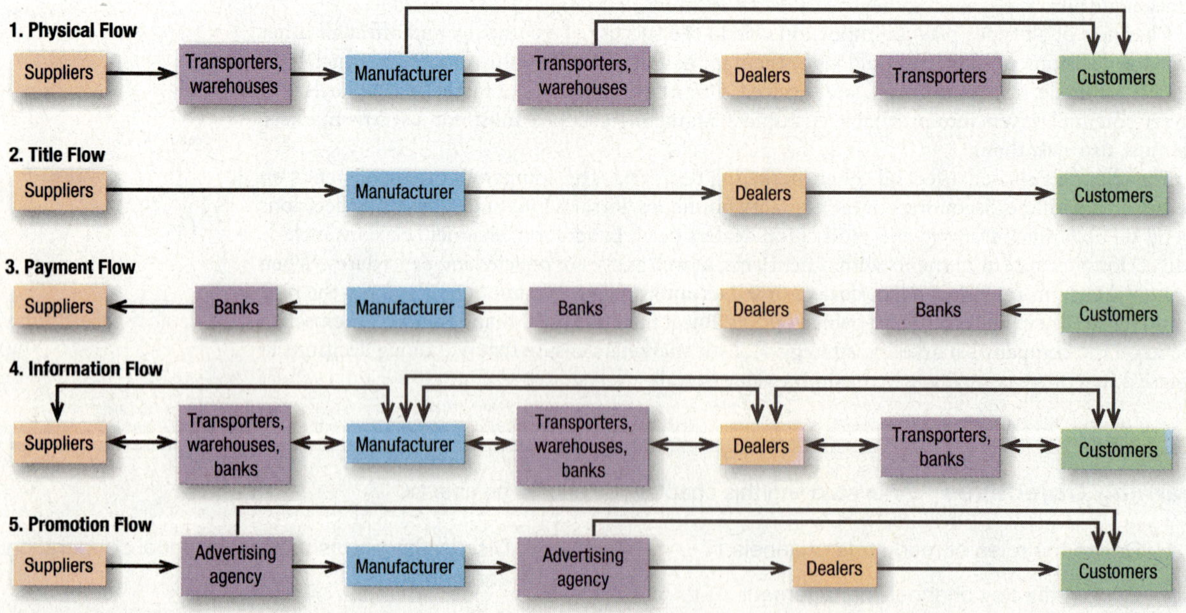

FIGURE **15.1**

Five Marketing Flows in the Marketing Channel

were superimposed in one diagram, we would see the tremendous complexity of even simple marketing channels.

Many of the channel functions involve bi-directional flows of goods and services. Some of these functions (storage and movement, title, and communications) constitute a *forward flow* of activity from the company to the customer; others (ordering and payment) constitute a *backward flow* from customers to the company. Still others (information, negotiation, finance, and risk taking) occur in both directions.

The question for marketers is not *whether* various channel functions need to be performed—they must be—but, rather, *who* is to perform them. Shifting some functions to intermediaries lowers the producer's costs and prices, but the intermediary must add a charge to cover its work. If the intermediaries are more efficient than the manufacturer, prices to consumers should be lower. If consumers perform some functions themselves, they should enjoy even lower prices. Changes in channel institutions thus largely reflect the discovery of more efficient ways to combine or separate the economic functions that provide assortments of goods to target customers.

CHANNEL LEVELS

Distribution channels can be described by the number of intermediaries that exist between the producer and the final customer. The number of intermediaries, also referred to as channel levels, define the length and breadth of the distribution channel. Figure 15.2(a) illustrates several consumer-goods marketing channels of different lengths.

A **zero-level channel**, also called a **direct marketing channel**, consists of a manufacturer selling directly to the final customer. The major examples are mail order, online selling, TV selling, telemarketing, door-to-door sales, home parties, and manufacturer-owned stores. Traditionally, Franklin Mint sold collectibles through mail order; Red Envelope sold gifts online; Time-Life sold music and video collections through TV commercials or longer infomercials; nonprofits and political organizations and candidates used the telephone to raise funds; Avon sales representatives sold cosmetics door to door; Tupperware sold its containers via in-home parties; and Apple sold computers and other consumer electronics through its own stores. Many of these firms now sell directly to customers online and via catalogs. Even traditional consumer-product firms are considering adding direct-to-consumer e-commerce sites to their channel mix. Kimberly-Clark has launched an online Kleenex Shop in the United Kingdom.

A **single-level channel** contains one selling intermediary, such as a retailer. A **dual-level channel** contains two intermediaries, typically a wholesaler and a retailer. In Japan, where density of the urban population is high and retail outlets are fragmented, food distribution may include as many as six

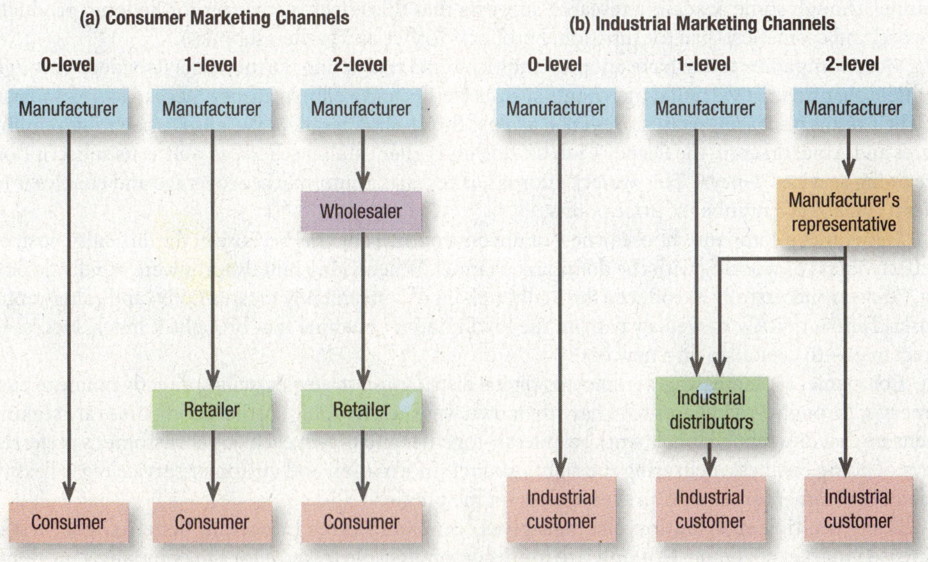

FIGURE **15.2**
Consumer and Industrial Marketing Channels

levels! Obtaining information about end users and exercising control become more difficult for the producer as the number of channel levels increases.

Figure 15.2(b) shows channels commonly used in B2B marketing. An industrial-goods manufacturer can use its sales force to sell directly to industrial customers, or it can sell to industrial distributors who sell to industrial customers, or it can sell through manufacturers' representatives or its own sales branches directly to industrial customers or indirectly to industrial customers through industrial distributors. Zero-, one-, and two-level marketing channels are quite common.

Channels normally describe a forward movement of products from source to user, but **reverse-flow channels** are also important. Reverse-flow channels perform several important functions, such as to reuse products or containers (such as refillable chemical-carrying drums), refurbish products for resale (such as circuit boards or computers), recycle products, and dispose of products and packaging. Reverse-flow intermediaries include manufacturers' redemption centers, community groups, trash-collection specialists, recycling centers, trash-recycling brokers, and central processing warehousing.

MULTICHANNEL DISTRIBUTION

Today's successful companies typically employ multichannel distribution, using two or more marketing channels to reach customer segments in one market area. HP uses its sales force to sell to large accounts, outbound telemarketing to sell to medium-sized accounts, direct mail with an inbound phone number to sell to small accounts, retailers to sell to still smaller accounts, and the internet to sell specialty items. Each channel can target a different segment of buyers, or different need states for one buyer, to deliver the right products in the right places in the right way at the least cost.[3]

When different channels target the same customers, channel conflict, excessive cost, or insufficient demand can result. Dial-a-Mattress successfully grew for three decades by selling mattresses directly over the phone and later online. A major expansion into 50 brick-and-mortar stores in major metro areas was a failure, however. Secondary locations, chosen because management considered prime locations too expensive, could not generate enough customer traffic. The company eventually declared bankruptcy.[4]

On the other hand, when a major catalog and internet retailer invested significantly in brick-and-mortar stores, different results emerged. Customers near the store purchased through the catalog less frequently, but their online purchases were unchanged. As it turned out, customers who liked to spend time browsing were happy to either use a catalog or visit the store; those channels were interchangeable. Customers who shopped online, on the other hand, were more transaction focused and interested in efficiency, so they were less affected by the introduction of stores. Returns and exchanges at the stores were found to increase because of ease and accessibility, but extra purchases made by customers returning or exchanging at the store offset any revenue deficit.[5]

Research has shown that multichannel customers can be more valuable to marketers.[6] Nordstrom found that its multichannel customers spend four times as much as those who shop only through one channel, though some academic research suggests that this effect is stronger for hedonic products (apparel and cosmetics) than for functional products (office and garden supplies).[7]

Most companies today have adopted multichannel marketing. Disney sells its videos through multiple channels: movie rental merchants such as Netflix and Redbox, Disney Stores (owned and run by The Children's Place), retail stores such as Best Buy, online retailers such as Disney's own online stores and Amazon.com, the Disney Club catalog and other catalog sellers, as well as its subscription streaming service Disney+. This variety affords Disney maximum market coverage and enables it to offer its videos at a number of price points.

Sometimes a company chooses a new or unconventional channel because of the difficulty, cost, or ineffectiveness of working with the dominant channel. When video rental stores were rapidly declining, Coinstar successfully introduced the Redbox chain of conveniently located DVD- and game-rental kiosks. Netflix quickly moved away from the revolutionary channel that brought it much success—direct mail—to capitalize on a new one.

Companies are increasingly employing digital distribution strategies, selling directly online to customers or through e-merchants who have their own websites. In doing so, these companies are seeking to ensure that different channels work seamlessly together and match each target customer's preferred ways of doing business, delivering the right product information and customer service regardless of whether customers are online, in the store, or on the phone.

Using multiple distribution channels gives companies three important benefits. The first is increased market coverage. Not only are more customers able to shop for the company's products in more places, as noted previously, but those who buy in more than one channel are often more profitable than single-channel customers.[8] The second benefit is lower channel cost. Selling online or by catalog and phone is cheaper than using personal selling to reach small customers. The third is the ability to do more customized selling—such as by adding a technical sales force to sell complex equipment.

Using a single channel is typically not very efficient. Consider a direct sales force. A salesperson would have to find leads, qualify them, presell, close the sale, provide service, and manage account growth. With an integrated multichannel approach, however, the company's marketing department could run a preselling campaign informing prospects about the company's products through advertising, direct mail, and e-mails; generate leads through telemarketing, more e-mails, and trade shows; and qualify leads as hot, warm, or cool. The salesperson enters when the prospect is ready to talk business and invests his or her costly time primarily in closing the sale. This multichannel architecture optimizes coverage, customization, and control while minimizing cost and conflict.

There is a trade-off, however. New channels typically introduce conflict and problems with control and cooperation. Two or more may end up competing for the same customers.[9] Clearly, companies need to think through their channel architecture and determine which channels should perform which functions.[10]

Managing the online and offline channels has thus become a priority for many firms.[11] There are at least three strategies for trying to gain acceptance from intermediaries. One option involves offering different brands or products online and offline. The second option entails offering offline partners higher commissions to cushion the negative impact on sales. The third option involves taking orders on the website but having retailers deliver and collect payment. Mercedes-Benz decided to tread carefully before going online.

Mercedes-Benz Mercedes-Benz launched its new distribution model, 'Retail of the future' (ROTF) in India in June 2021. Launching a direct distribution channel is a path-breaking move in the luxury car retail segment. Mercedes-Benz started using digital channels to sell its products with the help of new channel partners called 'franchise Partners'. With its new channel, Mercedes-Benz offers 'hassle-free and transparent' purchase experience to its customers. The direct sales approach is designed to create a win-win experience for both customers and franchisee partners. The franchise partners are primarily responsible for establishing and maintaining customer contacts, developing the market, and facilitating the sales, while Mercedes-Benz will hold and own the inventories, order processing and other sales-related processes. The new approach renders the franchise partners free from any liability. This new direct-to-customer distribution model offers transparency and stock visibility to customers through a central order management system. Under this sales and distribution system, standard prices are offered with added benefits managed by the company for each product category. Mercedez-Benz's Indian market is the fourth one to have ROTF after South Africa, Sweden, and Austria. The company invested around ₹60 crores in the entire process. Initial results were very positive as the company received bookings of over 1700 units through the new ROTF model.[12]

Companies should use different sales channels for different-sized business customers—a direct sales force for large customers, a digital strategy or telemarketing for midsize customers, and distributors for small customers—but should be alert for conflict over account ownership. For example, territory-based sales representatives may want credit for all sales in their territories, regardless of the marketing channel used.

Multichannel marketers also need to decide how much of their product to offer in each of the channels. Patagonia views the Web as the ideal channel for showing off its entire line of goods, given that limited space at its retail locations means they can offer only a selection, and even its catalog promotes less than 70 percent of its total merchandise.[13] Other marketers prefer to limit their online offerings, theorizing that customers look to websites and catalogs for a "best of" array of merchandise and don't want to have to click through dozens of pages. REI is a company that has carefully managed its multiple channels.

>> Apple created a dynamic atmosphere in which to experience its full line of products by opening its own stores, where the focus of the sales staff is to help customers solve problems.

Source: Olaf Schuelke/Alamy Stock Photo

accessories; and a "Genius Bar" staffed by specialists who provide technical support, often free of charge. Apple's meticulous attention to detail is reflected in the preloaded music and photos on demo devices, innovative touches such as roving credit-card swipers to minimize checkout lines, and hours invested in employee training. Employees receive no sales commissions and have no sales quotas. They are told their mission is to "help customers solve problems." Although the stores initially upset existing Apple retailers and authorized service providers, the company worked hard to smooth relationships, in part justifying its decision as a natural evolution of its online sales channel.[19]

More sophisticated companies try to forge a long-term partnership with distributors.[20] The manufacturer clearly communicates what it wants from its distributors in the way of market coverage, inventory levels, marketing development, account solicitation, technical advice and services, and marketing information and may introduce a compensation plan for adhering to the policies.

SELECTING CHANNEL MEMBERS

To customers, the channels are the company. Consider the negative impression customers would get of McDonald's, Shell Oil, or Mercedes-Benz if one or more of their outlets or dealers consistently appeared dirty, inefficient, or unpleasant.

To facilitate channel member selection, producers should determine what characteristics distinguish the better intermediaries—number of years in business, other lines carried, growth and profit record, financial strength, cooperativeness, and service reputation. If the intermediaries are sales agents, producers should evaluate the number and character of other lines carried and the size and quality of the sales force. If the intermediaries are department stores that want exclusive distribution, then their locations, future growth potential, and type of clientele will matter.

Identifying Major Channel Alternatives. Each channel—from sales force to agents, distributors, dealers, direct mail, telemarketing, and traditional retailers—has unique strengths and weaknesses. Sales forces can handle complex products and transactions, but they are expensive. Online retailing is inexpensive but may not be as effective for complex products. Distributors can create sales, but the company loses direct contact with customers. Several clients can share the cost of manufacturers' reps, but the selling effort is less intense than company reps provide.

Based on the number of intermediaries, there are three core distribution strategies: *exclusive, selective,* and *intensive* distribution. We discuss these strategies next.

Exclusive distribution severely limits the number of intermediaries. It's appropriate when the producer wants to ensure more knowledgeable and dedicated efforts by the resellers, and it often requires a closer partnership with them. Exclusive distribution is used for new automobiles, some major appliances, and luxury apparel and accessories. When the legendary Italian designer label Gucci found its image tarnished by overexposure from licensing and discount stores, it decided to end contracts with third-party suppliers, control its distribution, and open its own stores to bring back some of the luster.

Both channel partners benefit from exclusive arrangements: The producer obtains more loyal and dependable outlets, and the retailer gets a steady supply of special products and stronger seller support. Exclusive arrangements are legal as long as they do not substantially lessen competition or tend to create a monopoly and as long as both parties enter into them voluntarily.

Exclusive dealing often includes exclusive territorial agreements. The producer may agree not to sell to other dealers in a given area, or the buyer may agree to sell only in its own territory. The first practice increases dealer enthusiasm and commitment. It is also perfectly legal; a seller has no legal obligation to sell through more outlets than it wishes. The second practice, whereby the producer tries to keep a dealer from selling outside its territory, has become a major legal issue.

Selective distribution relies on some but not all of the intermediaries willing to carry a particular product. Unlike exclusive distribution, in which individual retailers do not directly compete with one another (for example, because they are assigned non-overlapping geographic areas), selective distribution might include retailers that compete for the same customers. STIHL is a good example of successful selective distribution.

STIHL STIHL manufactures handheld outdoor power equipment. All its products are branded under one name, and it does not make private labels for other companies. Best known for its chain saws, the company has expanded into string trimmers, blowers, hedge trimmers, and cut-off machines. It sells exclusively to six independent U.S. distributors and six company-owned marketing and distribution centers, which sell to a nationwide network of more than 8,000 independent retail dealers offering service. STIHL also exports to 80 countries and is one of the few outdoor power equipment companies that does not sell through mass merchants, catalogs, or the internet. It even ran an ad campaign called "Why" that touted the strength and support of its independent dealers with headlines such as "Why is the World's No. 1-selling brand of chain saw not sold at Lowe's or The Home Depot?" and "What makes this handblower too powerful to be sold at Lowe's or The Home Depot?"[21]

Source: dpa picture alliance archive/Alamy Stock Photo

<< STIHL shuns mass merchandisers and limits distribution channels to a half-dozen independent U.S. distributors and the company's own marketing and distribution centers, which supply independent U.S. retailers and export to 80 countries.

Intensive distribution places the goods or services in as many outlets as possible. This strategy works well for snack foods, soft drinks, newspapers, candies, and gum—products that consumers buy frequently or in a variety of locations. Convenience stores such as 7-Eleven and Circle K and gas station outlets like ExxonMobil's On the Run survive by providing simple location and time convenience.

Manufacturers are constantly tempted to move from exclusive or selective distribution to more intensive distribution to increase coverage and sales. This strategy may help in the short term, but if not done properly, it can hurt long-term performance by encouraging retailers to compete aggressively. Price wars can then erode profitability, dampening retailer interest and harming brand equity. Some firms do not want their products to be sold everywhere. After Sears acquired discount chain Kmart, Nike pulled all its products from Sears to make sure Kmart could not carry the brand.

To develop a channel, members must commit to each other for a specified period of time. Yet these commitments invariably reduce the producer's ability to respond to change and uncertainty. The producer needs channel structures and policies that provide high adaptability.

Producers are free to select their dealers, but their right to terminate them is somewhat restricted. In general, sellers can drop dealers "for cause," but not if, for example, a dealer refuses to cooperate in a doubtful legal arrangement such as exclusive dealing or tying agreements.

Franchising. An increasingly popular way to grow distribution channels is **franchising**. In a franchising system, individual *franchisees* are a tightly knit group of enterprises whose systematic operations are planned, directed, and controlled by the operation's owner, the *franchisor*. Franchise businesses such as McDonald's, Hampton, Jiffy-Lube, Subway, Supercuts, 7-Eleven, and many others are an integral component of the business landscape.

Franchises are distinguished by three main characteristics:

- The franchisor owns a trade or service mark and licenses it to franchisees in return for royalty payments. For example, McDonald's Corporation owns the intellectual property associated with the McDonald's brand and the logistics associated with operating its franchises.
- The franchisee pays for the right to be part of the system. Start-up costs include rental and lease equipment and fixtures and (usually) a regular license fee. McDonald's franchisees typically invest upward of $1.5 million in total start-up costs and fees. The franchisee then pays McDonald's a certain percentage of sales plus a monthly rent.
- The franchisor provides its franchisees with a system for doing business. McDonald's requires franchisees to attend "Hamburger University" in Oak Brook, Illinois, for two weeks to learn how to manage the business. Franchisees must follow certain procedures in buying materials.[22]

Franchising benefits both parties. Franchisors gain the motivation and hard work of employees who are entrepreneurs rather than "hired hands," as well as the franchisees' familiarity with local communities and conditions, and the enormous purchasing power of being a franchisor. Franchisees benefit from buying into a business with a proven business model and a well-known and accepted brand name. They find it easier to borrow money for their business from financial institutions, and they receive support in areas ranging from marketing and advertising to site selection and staffing.

Franchisees do walk a fine line between independence and loyalty to the franchisor. Some franchisors give their franchisees freedom to run their own operations, from personalizing store names to adjusting offerings and price. Great Harvest Bread believes in a "freedom franchise" approach that encourages its franchisee bakers to create new items for their store menus and to share these with other franchisees if they are successful.[23]

Although franchising is a well-established business practice, it can take different formats depending on the entity sponsoring the franchise. The *manufacturer-sponsored retailer franchise* is the traditional system. To sell its cars, Ford licenses independent businesspeople who agree to meet specified conditions of sales and services. Another system is the *manufacturer-sponsored wholesaler franchise*. Coca-Cola licenses bottlers (wholesalers) in various markets that buy its syrup concentrate and then carbonate, bottle, and sell it to retailers in local markets.

Another form of franchising system is the *service-firm-sponsored retailer franchise*, organized by a service firm to bring its service efficiently to consumers. We find examples in auto rental (Hertz and Avis), fast food (McDonald's and Burger King), and the motel business (Howard Johnson and Ramada Inn). In a dual distribution system, firms use both vertical integration (the franchisor actually owns and runs the units) and market governance (the franchisor licenses the units to other franchisees).[24]

MOTIVATING CHANNEL MEMBERS

A company needs to view its intermediaries the same way it views its end users. It should determine their needs and wants and tailor its channel offering to provide them with superior value.

Carefully implemented training, market research, and other capability-building programs can motivate and improve intermediaries' performance. The company must constantly communicate to intermediaries that they are crucial partners in a joint effort to satisfy end users of the product. Microsoft requires its third-party service engineers to complete a set of courses and take certification exams. Those who pass are formally recognized as Microsoft Certified Professionals and can use this designation to promote their own business. Other firms use customer surveys rather than exams.

Channel Power. Producers vary greatly in their skill in managing distributors. **Channel power** is the ability to alter channel members' behavior so they take actions they would not have taken otherwise.[25] Manufacturers can draw on the following types of power to elicit cooperation:[26]

- *Coercive power.* A manufacturer threatens to withdraw a resource or terminate a relationship if intermediaries fail to cooperate. This power can be effective, but its exercise produces resentment and can lead intermediaries to organize countervailing power.
- *Reward power.* The manufacturer offers intermediaries an extra benefit for performing specific acts or functions. Reward power typically produces better results than coercive power, but intermediaries may come to expect a reward every time the manufacturer wants a certain behavior to occur.
- *Legal power.* The manufacturer requests a behavior that is warranted under the contract. As long as the intermediaries view the manufacturer as a legitimate leader, legal power works.
- *Expert power.* The manufacturer has special knowledge that intermediaries value. Once the intermediaries acquire this expertise, however, expert power weakens. The manufacturer must continue to develop new expertise so that intermediaries will want to continue cooperating.
- *Referent power.* The manufacturer is so highly respected that intermediaries are proud to be associated with it. Companies such as IBM, Caterpillar, and HP have high referent power.

These forms of channel power vary depending on the degree to which they are readily observable. Coercive and reward power are objectively observable; legal, expert, and referent power are more subjective and depend on the ability and willingness of parties to recognize them.

Most producers see gaining intermediaries' cooperation as a huge challenge. They often use positive motivators, such as higher margins, special deals, premiums, cooperative advertising allowances, display allowances, and sales contests. At times, they will apply negative sanctions, such as threatening to reduce margins, slow down delivery, or terminate the relationship. The weakness of this approach is that the producer is using crude, stimulus–response thinking.

In many cases, retailers hold the power. One estimate is that manufacturers offer the nation's supermarkets between 150 and 250 new items each week, of which store buyers reject more than 70 percent. Manufacturers need to know the acceptance criteria that buyers, buying committees, and store managers use. Nielsen interviews found that store managers were most influenced by strong evidence of consumer acceptance, a well-designed advertising and sales promotion plan, and generous financial incentives.

Channel Partnerships. Based on the nature of the relationship among the members of the marketing channel, there are three basic types of channels: conventional channels, vertical marketing systems, and horizontal marketing systems.

Conventional marketing channels consist of an independent producer, wholesaler(s), and retailer(s). Each is a separate business seeking to maximize its own profits, even if this goal reduces profit for the system as a whole. No channel member has complete or substantial control over other members. Channel coordination occurs when channel members are brought together to advance the goals of the channel instead of their own potentially incompatible goals.

Vertical marketing systems, by contrast, include the producer, wholesaler(s), and retailer(s) acting as a unified system. One channel member, the **channel captain**, who is sometimes called a *channel steward*, owns or franchises the others or has so much power that they all cooperate. Stewards accomplish channel coordination without issuing commands or directives by persuading channel partners to act in the best interest of all.[27]

A channel steward might be the maker of the product or service (Procter & Gamble), the maker of a key component (Intel), the supplier or assembler (Arrow Electronics), or the distributor (W.W. Grainger) or retailer (Walmart). Within a company, stewardship might rest with the CEO, a top manager, or a team of senior managers.

Channel stewardship has two important outcomes. First, it expands value for the steward's customers, enlarging the market or increasing existing customers' purchases through the channel. Second, it creates a more tightly woven and yet adaptable channel in which valuable members are rewarded and the less valuable are weeded out.

Vertical marketing systems arose from strong channel members' attempts to control channel behavior and eliminate conflict over independent members pursuing their own objectives. These systems achieve economies through size, bargaining power, and elimination of duplicated services. Business buyers of complex products and systems value the extensive exchange of information they can offer.[28] Vertical marketing systems have become the dominant mode of distribution in the U.S. consumer marketplace, serving 70 percent to 80 percent of the market. There are three types: corporate, administered, and contractual.

- A **corporate vertical marketing system** combines successive stages of production and distribution under single ownership. For years, Sears obtained more than half the goods it sold from companies it partly or wholly owned. Sherwin-Williams makes paint but also owns and operates 3,500 retail outlets.
- An **administered vertical marketing system** coordinates successive stages of production and distribution through the size and power of one of the members. Manufacturers of dominant brands can secure strong trade cooperation and support from resellers. Thus Frito-Lay, Procter & Gamble, and Campbell Soup command high levels of cooperation from their resellers in the matter of displays, shelf space, promotions, and price policies. The most advanced producer–distributor arrangement for administered vertical marketing systems relies on distribution programming, which builds a planned, professionally managed, vertical marketing system that meets the needs of both manufacturer and distributors.
- A **contractual vertical marketing system** consists of independent firms at different levels of production and distribution integrating their programs on a contractual basis to obtain more economies or sales impact than they could achieve alone.[29] Sometimes thought of as "value-adding partnerships," contractual vertical marketing systems come in three types: (1) In *wholesaler-sponsored voluntary chains*, wholesalers organize voluntary chains of independent retailers to help standardize their selling practices and achieve buying economies. (2) In *retailer cooperatives*, retailers take the initiative and organize a new business entity to carry on wholesaling and possibly some production. (3) In *franchise organizations*, a channel member (franchisor) might link several successive stages in the production–distribution process.

Many independent retailers that have not joined a vertical marketing system have developed specialty stores serving special market segments. The result is a polarization in retailing between large vertical marketing organizations and independent specialty stores, which creates a problem for manufacturers. They are strongly tied to independent intermediaries but must eventually realign themselves with the high-growth vertical marketing systems on less attractive terms. Furthermore, vertical marketing systems constantly threaten to bypass large manufacturers and set up their own manufacturing. The new competition in retailing is no longer between independent business units but between whole systems of centrally programmed networks (corporate, administered, and contractual) competing against one another to achieve the best cost-economies and customer response.

Horizontal marketing systems involve two or more unrelated companies putting together resources or programs to exploit an emerging marketing opportunity. Each company lacks the capital, know-how, production, or marketing resources to venture alone, or it is afraid of the risk. The companies might work together on a temporary or permanent basis or create a joint venture company.

For example, many supermarket chains have arrangements with local banks to offer in-store banking. Citizens Bank has more than 500 branches in supermarkets, making up a little less than half of its branch network. Citizens' staff members in these locations are more sales oriented and more likely to have some retail sales background than staff in the traditional brick-and-mortar branches.[30]

EVALUATING CHANNEL MEMBERS

Producers must periodically evaluate intermediaries' performance against such standards as sales-quota attainment, average inventory levels, customer delivery time, treatment of damaged and lost goods, and cooperation in promotional and training programs. A producer will occasionally discover it is overpaying particular intermediaries for what they are actually doing. One manufacturer that had been compensating a distributor for holding inventories found its goods were being held in a public warehouse at its own expense. Producers should set up functional discounts in which they pay specified amounts for the trade channel's performance of each agreed-upon service. Underperformers need to be counseled, retrained, motivated, or terminated.

A new firm typically starts as a local operation selling in a fairly circumscribed market, using a few existing intermediaries. Identifying the best channels might not be a problem; the problem is often to convince the available intermediaries to handle the firm's line.

If the firm is successful, it might branch into new markets with different channels. It might sell directly to retailers in smaller markets and through distributors in larger markets. It might work with general-goods merchants in rural areas and with limited-line merchants in urban areas. It may choose to create its own online store to sell directly to customers. It might grant exclusive franchises or sell through all willing outlets. In one country, the firm might use international sales agents; in another, it might partner with a local firm.

Early buyers might be willing to pay for high-value-added channels, but later buyers will switch to lower cost channels. Small office copiers were sold first by manufacturers' direct sales forces, later through office equipment dealers, still later through mass merchandisers, and more recently by mail-order firms and internet marketers. In short, the channel system evolves as a function of local opportunities and conditions, emerging threats and opportunities, company resources and capabilities, and advancements in technology.

No channel strategy remains effective over the whole product life cycle. In competitive markets with low entry barriers, the optimal channel structure will inevitably change over time. New technologies have created digital channels undreamed of years ago. The change could mean adding or dropping individual market channels or channel members or developing a totally new way to sell goods. When new competition from Best Buy and Costco forced one-third of Leica's U.S. dealers to close, the high-end camera maker decided to open its own stylish stores to appeal to serious photographers.[31]

A producer must periodically review and modify its channel design and arrangements.[32] The distribution channel may not work as planned, consumer buying patterns change, the market expands, new competition arises, innovative distribution channels emerge, and the product moves into later stages in the product life cycle.[33]

To add or drop individual channel members, the company needs to make an incremental analysis. A basic question is "What would the firm's sales and profits look like with and without this intermediary?" Perhaps the most difficult decision is whether to revise the overall channel strategy. Avon's door-to-door system for selling cosmetics was modified as more women left the house and entered the paid workforce.

Channel Cooperation and Conflict

No matter how well channels are designed and managed, there will be some conflict, if only because the interests of independent business entities do not always coincide. **Channel conflict** occurs when one channel member's actions prevent another channel member from achieving its goal. Companies distributing their offerings through different channels are likely to face a certain level of channel conflict. In this context, a manager's goal is to reduce the channel conflict by minimizing the frictions between channel members.

A common source of channel conflict is a manufacturer's desire to sell directly to its customers, bypassing its traditional channel partners. By opening its own retail stores, Apple created a challenge for many of its authorized solution-provider and channel partners by effectively "stealing" many of their current customers. Likewise, in the business-to-business space, Apple has stepped up its direct sales force in enterprise accounts, including forming direct partnerships with companies such as Cisco and IBM that have effectively limited the scope of services provided by many of their independent solution providers.[34]

Here we examine three questions: What types of conflict arise in channels? What causes conflict? What can channel members do to resolve it?

THE NATURE OF CHANNEL CONFLICTS

To be able to effectively manage channel conflict, managers must understand the key types of channel conflict and the factors that often lead to conflicts among channel partners.

Types of Channel Conflict. Suppose a manufacturer sets up a vertical channel consisting of wholesalers and retailers, hoping for channel cooperation and greater profits for each member. Despite a desire by all parties to cooperate, horizontal, vertical, and multichannel conflict can occur.

- **Horizontal channel conflict** occurs between channel members at the same level. For example, franchisees might provide poor customer service, which harms brand value and results in poor consumer reviews that damage sales across all other channels. For example, some Pizza Inn franchisees complained about other franchisees cheating on ingredients, providing poor service, and hurting the overall brand image.
- **Vertical channel conflict** occurs between different levels of the channel. For example, a vertical conflict is likely to occur when a manufacturer sells to wholesalers and retailers directly. It is likely to be especially intense when the manufacturer sells directly to one of a wholesaler's largest customers. For example, when Estée Lauder set up an online store to sell its Clinique and Bobbi Brown brands, some department stores reduced the space it allotted to the company's products.
- **Multichannel conflict** exists when the manufacturer has established two or more channels that sell to the same market. For example, multichannel conflict is likely to occur when a restaurant chain allows two franchise locations within close proximity to each other. Multichannel conflict can be especially intense when the members of one channel get a lower price (based on larger-volume purchases) or work with a lower margin. When Goodyear began selling its popular tire brands through Sears, Walmart, and Discount Tire, it angered its independent dealers. Goodyear eventually placated them by offering exclusive tire models not sold in other retail outlets.[35]

Causes of Channel Conflict. Even though each channel conflict has unique antecedents and consequences, there are several general factors that can contribute to the creation of a channel conflict. Some of the most common reasons for channel conflict are as follows:

- *Goal incompatibility.* Channel conflict can stem from the conflicting goals of different channel members. For example, a manufacturer may want to achieve rapid market penetration through a low-price policy. Dealers, in contrast, may prefer to work with high margins and pursue short-run profitability.
- *Differences in strategies and tactics.* Channel conflict may also occur when channel members adopt different strategies and tactics to achieve their goals. The manufacturer may be optimistic about the short-term economic outlook and want dealers to carry higher inventory, while the dealers may be pessimistic. In the beverage category, it is not uncommon for disputes to arise between manufacturers and their distributors about the optimal advertising strategy.
- *Power imbalance.* Greater retailer consolidation—the 10 largest U.S. retailers account for more than 80 percent of the average manufacturer's business—has led to increased retailer influence that often spawns channel conflict. Walmart, for example, is the principal buyer for the products of many manufacturers, including Disney, Procter & Gamble, and Revlon, and is able to command reduced prices or quantity discounts from these and other suppliers.[36] Power imbalance can also be caused by distributors' reliance on the manufacturer. The fortunes of exclusive dealers, such as auto dealers, are profoundly affected by the manufacturer's product and pricing decisions.
- *Unclear roles and rights.* Territory boundaries and credit for sales often produce conflict. HP may sell laptops to large accounts through its own sales force, but its licensed dealers may also be trying to sell to large accounts.[37]

MANAGING CHANNEL CONFLICT

Some channel conflict can be constructive and lead to better adaptation to a changing environment, but too much is dysfunctional.[38] The challenge is not to eliminate all conflict, which is impossible, but to manage it better. Reprimands, fines, withheld bonuses, and other remedies can help minimize channel conflict.[39] Common mechanisms for effective conflict management include strategic justification, dual compensation, superordinate goals, employee exchange, joint memberships, and co-optation, as well as diplomacy, mediation, or arbitration and legal recourse.[40]

- *Strategic justification.* In some cases, a convincing strategic justification that channel members serve distinctive segments and do not compete as much as they might think can reduce potential for conflict. Developing special versions of products for different channel members—branded variants—is a clear way to demonstrate that distinctiveness.[41]
- *Dual compensation.* A company can mitigate channel conflict by paying existing channel members for sales made through new channels. When Allstate started selling insurance online, it agreed to pay agents a 2 percent commission for face-to-face service to customers who got their quotes online. Although lower than the agents' typical 10 percent commission for offline transactions, this commission did reduce tensions.[42]
- *Superordinate goals.* Channel members can come to an agreement on the fundamental or superordinate goal they are jointly seeking, whether it is survival, market share, high quality, or customer satisfaction. They usually do this best when the channel faces an outside threat, such as a more efficient competing channel, an adverse piece of legislation, or a shift in consumer desires.
- *Employee exchange.* Exchanging personnel between two or more channel levels can reduce channel conflict. GM's executives might agree to work for a short time in some dealerships, and some dealership owners might work in GM's dealer policy department. Thus, participants can grow to appreciate each other's point of view.
- *Joint memberships.* Marketers can encourage joint memberships in trade associations. Good cooperation between the Grocery Manufacturers of America and the Food Marketing Institute, which represents most of the food chains, led to the development of the universal product code (UPC). The associations can consider issues between food manufacturers and retailers and resolve them in an orderly way.
- *Co-optation.* An organization can win the support of its channel members by including its leaders in advisory councils, boards of directors, and the like. If the organization treats invited leaders seriously and listens to their opinions, co-optation can reduce conflict, although the initiator may need to compromise its policies and plans to win outsiders' support.
- *Diplomacy, mediation, and arbitration.* When conflict is chronic or acute, the parties may need to resort to stronger means. Diplomacy takes place when each side sends a person or group to meet with its counterpart to resolve the conflict. Mediation relies on a neutral third party skilled in conciliating the two parties' interests. In arbitration, two parties agree to present their arguments to one or more arbitrators and accept their decision.
- *Legal recourse.* Rather than pursuing other strategies, a channel partner may choose to rely on legal means to resolve the conflict.[43] When Coca-Cola decided to distribute Powerade thirst quencher directly to Walmart's regional warehouses, 60 bottlers complained that the practice would undermine their core direct-store-distribution duties and filed suit. A settlement allowed for the mutual exploration of new service and distribution systems to supplement the direct-store-distribution system.[44]

Managing Market Logistics

Market logistics includes planning the infrastructure to meet demand and then implementing and controlling the physical flows of materials and final goods from points of origin to points of use to meet customer requirements at a profit. Physical distribution starts at the factory. Managers choose a set of warehouses (stocking points) and transportation carriers that will deliver the goods to final destinations in the desired time or at the lowest total cost.

Physical distribution has now been expanded into the broader concept of supply chain management. **Supply chain management** starts before physical distribution and includes strategically procuring the right inputs (raw materials, components, and capital equipment), converting them efficiently into finished products, and dispatching them to the final destinations. An even broader perspective looks at how the company's suppliers themselves obtain their inputs.

The supply chain perspective can help a company identify superior suppliers and distributors and then help it improve productivity and reduce costs. Firms with top supply chains include Apple, McDonald's, Amazon.com, Unilever, Intel, Procter & Gamble, Toyota, Cisco Systems, and Samsung Electronics.[45] Some companies choose to partner with and outsource to third-party logistics specialists for help with transportation planning, distribution center management, and other valued-added services that go beyond shipping and storing.

Studying market logistics leads managers to find the most efficient way to deliver value. For example, a software company traditionally produced and packaged software disks and manuals, shipped them to wholesalers, which shipped them to retailers, which sold them to customers, who brought them home to install the software on their computers. Market logistics offered two superior delivery systems. The first let customers download the software directly onto their computers. The second allowed the computer manufacturer to download the software onto its products. Both solutions eliminated the need for printing, packaging, shipping, and stocking millions of disks and manuals and have quickly become the norm of the industries.

MARKET-LOGISTICS OBJECTIVES

Many companies state their market-logistics objective as "getting the right goods to the right places at the right time for the least cost." Unfortunately, this objective provides little practical guidance. No system can simultaneously maximize customer service and minimize distribution cost. Maximum customer service implies large inventories, premium transportation, and multiple warehouses, all of which raise market-logistics costs. Nor can a company achieve efficient market logistics by asking each market-logistics manager to minimize his or her own logistics costs.

Minimizing market-logistics costs can influence the overall market success of an offering and, in some cases, can even be counterproductive. Consider these examples:

The traffic manager favors rail shipment over air shipment because rail costs less. However, because the railroads are slower, rail shipment ties up working capital longer, delays customer payment, and might send customers to competitors that offer faster service.

The shipping department uses cheap containers to minimize shipping costs. Cheaper containers lead to a higher rate of damaged goods and customer ill will.

The inventory manager favors low inventories. This increases stock-outs, back orders, paperwork, special production runs, and high-cost, fast-freight shipments.

Given these trade-offs, managers must make decisions on a total-system basis. The starting point is to study what customers require and what competitors are offering. Customers are interested in on-time delivery, help meeting emergency needs, careful handling of merchandise, and quick return and replacement of defective goods.

The wholesaler must then research the relative importance of these service outputs. For example, service-repair time is very important to buyers of copying equipment. Xerox developed a service delivery standard that "can put a disabled machine anywhere in the continental United States back into operation within three hours after receiving the service request." It then designed a service division of technicians, parts, and locations to deliver on this promise.

The company must also consider competitors' service standards. It will normally want to match or exceed these, but the objective is to maximize profits, not sales. Some companies offer less service and charge a lower price; other companies offer more service and charge a premium price.

The company ultimately must establish some promise it makes to the market. Some companies define standards for each service factor. One appliance manufacturer promises to deliver at least 95 percent of the dealer's orders within seven days of order receipt, to fill them with 99 percent accuracy, to deal with inquiries about order status within three hours, and to ensure that merchandise damaged in transit does not exceed 1 percent.

MARKET-LOGISTICS DECISIONS

The firm must make four major decisions about its market logistics: How should we handle orders (order processing)? Where should we locate our stock (warehousing)? How much stock should we hold (inventory)? and How should we ship goods (transportation)?

Order Processing. Most companies are trying to shorten the **order-to-payment cycle**—that is, the time between an order's receipt, delivery, and payment. This cycle has many steps, including order transmission by the salesperson, order entry and customer credit check, inventory and production scheduling, order and invoice shipment, and receipt of payment. The longer this cycle takes, the lower the customer's satisfaction and the lower the company's profits.

Warehousing. Most companies must store finished goods until they are sold because production and consumption cycles rarely match. In order to make use of existing resources and speed transportation times, some companies have decentralized their inventory. For example, to better manage inventory, many department stores (such as Nordstrom and Macy's) now ship online orders from individual stores. More stocking locations mean that goods can be delivered to customers more quickly, but warehousing and inventory costs are higher. Alternatively, to reduce costs, a company might centralize its inventory in one place and use fast transportation to fill orders.

Some warehouses are now taking on activities formerly done in the plant, including product assembly, packaging, and construction of promotional displays. Moving these activities to the warehouse can save costs and match the offerings more closely to demand.

Inventory. Salespeople would like their companies to carry enough stock to fill all customer orders immediately. However, this is not cost effective. Inventory cost increases at an accelerating rate as the desired level of customer satisfaction approaches 100 percent. Management needs to know how much sales and profits would increase as a result of carrying larger inventories and promising faster order fulfillment times and then make a decision.

As inventory draws down, management must know at what stock level to place a new order. This stock level is called the *order* (or *reorder*) *point*. An order point of 20 means reordering when the stock falls to 20 units. The order point should balance the risks of stock-out, where the company runs out of a particular good and is unable to meet customer demand, against the costs of overstock, where the company has to bear the cost of carrying an inventory for a long period of time. The other decision is how much to order. The larger the quantity ordered, the less frequently an order needs to be placed.

The company needs to balance order-processing costs and inventory-carrying costs. *Order-processing costs* for a manufacturer consist of *setup costs* (costs of setting up the processes required to produce one item) and *running costs* (operating costs when production is running) for the item. If setup costs are low, the manufacturer can produce the item often, and the average cost per item is stable and equal to the running costs. If setup costs are high, however, the manufacturer can reduce the average cost per unit by producing a long run and carrying more inventory.

Order-processing costs must be compared with *inventory-carrying costs*, which include storage charges, cost of capital, taxes and insurance, and depreciation and obsolescence. Carrying costs might run as high as 30 percent of inventory value and are higher the larger the average stock carried. This means marketing managers who want to carry larger inventories need to show that incremental gross profits will exceed incremental carrying costs.

Companies are using different strategies to manage their inventory costs. One approach involves keeping slow-moving inventory items in a central location and carrying fast-moving items in warehouses closer to customers. Alternatively, a company can switch to carrying near-zero inventory and acquiring stock based on orders. In addition to saving on warehousing costs, this approach—referred to as **just-in-time inventory management**—helps the company improve its cash flow. Thus, by asking consumers to pay for the purchased items in advance, a company can use customers' money to pay suppliers to ship the product or the necessary components.

Despite its obvious cost advantages, the just-in-time inventory management approach has an important drawback in that it assumes uninterrupted distribution logistics. Simply put, just-in-time inventory does not have sufficient flexibility should anything go wrong, as it often does—whether it's a dock strike in California, an earthquake in Japan, or political turmoil in North Africa and the

Middle East. In an interconnected world, one weak link, if not properly managed, can bring down the entire supply chain. The limitations of just-in-time inventory management came prominently into focus during the coronavirus pandemic, as disruptions in procurement, manufacturing, and shipping resulted in demand outstripping supply in many categories, culminating in product shortages and longer delivery times than usual.

To balance the effectiveness and the cost-efficiency of their logistics, companies need to re-evaluate their logistics networks periodically to guard against extreme demand shocks. Accordingly, many companies are securing additional warehousing space and modernizing their distribution operations. Merchants are also moving their warehouses closer to large population centers to ensure not only that they have the required inventory on hand but also that they are able to deliver it to their customers faster than the competition.

Transportation. Transportation choices affect product pricing, on-time delivery performance, and the condition of the goods when they arrive, all of which affect customer satisfaction.

In shipping goods to its warehouses, dealers, and customers, a company can choose rail, air, truck, waterway, or pipeline. Shippers consider such criteria as speed, frequency, dependability, capability, availability, traceability, and cost. For speed, the prime contenders are air, rail, and truck. If the goal is low cost, then the choice is water or pipeline.

Shippers are increasingly combining two or more transportation modes, thanks to containerization. **Containerization** consists of putting the goods in boxes or trailers that are easy to transfer between two transportation modes. The term *piggyback* describes the use of rail and trucks; *fishyback,* water and trucks; *trainship,* water and rail; and *airtruck,* air and trucks. Each coordinated mode offers specific advantages. For example, piggyback is cheaper than trucking alone but provides flexibility and convenience.

Shippers can choose private, contract, or common carriers. If the shipper owns its own truck or air fleet, it becomes a *private carrier.* A *contract carrier* is an independent organization selling transportation services to others on a contract basis. A *common carrier* provides services between predetermined points on a scheduled basis and is available to all shippers at standard rates. Some contract carriers are investing and innovating to create strong value propositions.

Contract Carriers With so many transportation options available, shipping firms are constantly competing to cut costs, improve services, and offer even more value to their customers. Copenhagen-based Maersk Group is the world's largest global shipper, with around 550 container ships and 225 tankers. To improve efficiency, the firm commissioned 20 of the largest ships ever built. Costing $185 million each, these giant ships can cost effectively carry 18,000 containers, emitting 50 percent less CO_2 in the process. Schneider, one of the country's largest full-truckload freight haulers with more than $3 billion in revenue, developed a fleet-wide "tactical simulator" that has saved the company tens of millions of dollars. Besides helping in the crucial day-to-day route scheduling of drivers, the simulator has also helped with specific decisions ranging from when to raise prices for certain customers to how many drivers to hire (and where). Little changes can make big differences for shippers. Global logistics leader UPS calculated that by having its drivers use a fob instead of a key to operate its trucks, it is cutting out on average 1.7 seconds per stop, or 6.5 minutes per day, saving an estimated $70 million a year in the process.[46]

To reduce costly handing at arrival, some firms are putting items into shelf-ready packaging so they don't have to unpack them from a box and place them individually on a shelf. In Europe, Procter & Gamble has used a three-tier logistics system to schedule deliveries of fast- and slow-moving goods, bulky items, and small items in the most efficient way. To reduce damage in shipping, the size, weight, and fragility of the item must be reflected in the crating technique used and the density of foam cushioning. With logistics, every little detail must be reviewed to see how it might be changed to improve productivity and profitability.

Source: Greg Balfour Evans/Alamy Stock Photo

<< Looking to improve efficiency, global shipper Maersk Group commissioned giant ships able to carry thousands of containers while substantially cutting CO_2 emissions.

marketing INSIGHT

Understanding the Showrooming Phenomenon

Consumers have always shopped around to get the best deal or broaden their options, and now e-commerce and m-commerce (selling via mobile phone and tablet) offer them a new twist. **Showrooming** lets consumers physically examine a product and collect information in a store but make their actual purchase from the retailer later online—or, in the store's least desirable outcome, from a different retailer altogether, typically to secure a lower price.

Showrooming has been given a boost by smartphones. Thanks to their mobile devices, consumers in stores have never been better equipped to decide whether they should buy. One study showed that more than half of U.S. mobile phone users, especially younger ones, have used their phones, while shopping, to ask for purchase advice from a friend or family member or to look for reviews or lower prices.

Retailers used to worry about getting consumers into the store, but experts note that they now need to worry instead about selling to consumers who are bringing other stores in with them. Amazon's Price Check phone app, for instance, allows shoppers to instantly compare prices while in a brick-and-mortar store. Online retailers that mobile users can tap offer traditional brick-and-mortar chains serious competition because of their wider selections, lower prices (often with no taxes), and 24/7 convenience.

Addressing showrooming head-on, Best Buy and Target announced they would permanently match the prices of online retailers. Others have more closely linked their stores and websites in response to the trend. Walmart, Macy's, and Best Buy allow in-store pickup of online orders and returns of online purchases.

Many retailers are making the in-store experience more informative and rewarding. Guess, PacSun, and Aéropostale are equipping in-store sales staff with iPads or tablets for collecting more in-depth product information to share with shoppers. Shoppers enrolled in loyalty programs can also quickly download their purchase histories, product preferences, and other useful background.

The main goal of all these efforts is to hold on to the customer. One study found that 70 percent of a showrooming audience was more likely to buy from retailers with well-designed websites and apps, strong multichannel support, and price comparisons via QR (Quick Response) codes. Shifting sales from a store to online can actually be more profitable for a retailer if it prevents the customer from buying elsewhere.[47]

summary

1. Most producers do not sell their goods directly to final users. Between producers and final users stands one or more marketing channels, with a host of marketing intermediaries performing a variety of functions. Distribution channels are sets of interdependent organizations participating in the process of making a product or service available for use or consumption.
2. Companies use intermediaries when they lack the financial resources to carry out direct marketing, when direct marketing is not feasible, and when they can earn more by doing so. Effective channel management calls for selecting intermediaries and training and motivating them. The goal is to build a long-term partnership that will be profitable for all channel members.
3. Members of the marketing channel perform a number of key functions. Some of these functions (storage and movement, title, and communications) constitute a *forward flow* of activity from the company to the customer; others (ordering and payment) constitute a *backward flow* from customers to the company; and some (information, negotiation, finance, and risk taking) occur in both directions.
4. Manufacturers have many alternatives for reaching a market. They can sell direct or use one-, two-, or multilevel channels. Deciding which type(s) of channel to use calls for analyzing customer needs, establishing channel objectives, and identifying and evaluating the major alternatives, including the types and numbers of intermediaries involved in the channel.
5. A growing number of companies employ *multichannel distribution*, using two or more marketing channels to reach customer segments in one market area. In addition, companies are increasingly employing digital distribution strategies, selling directly online to customers or through e-merchants who have their own websites. Multichannel distribution calls for the development of an integrated distribution strategy where the activities involved in selling through one channel are aligned with the activities involved in selling through one or more other channels.
6. To design a marketing-channel system, marketers analyze customer needs and wants, establish channel objectives and constraints, and identify and evaluate major channel alternatives. Based on the number of intermediaries, there are three core distribution strategies: exclusive, selective, and intensive distribution. Following the choice of channel intermediaries, a company must select, train, motivate, and evaluate its channel partners.
7. An increasingly popular form of growing distribution channels is franchising. In a franchising system, individual franchisees are a tightly knit group of enterprises whose systematic operations are planned, directed, and controlled by the operation's innovator, the franchisor. Franchisees benefit from buying into a business with a well-known and accepted brand name. They find it easier to borrow money for their business from financial institutions, and they receive support in areas ranging from marketing and advertising to site selection and staffing.
8. A company needs to motivate its channel partners by identifying their needs and wants and tailor its channel offering to provide them with superior value. An important factor here is channel power, which reflects the ability to alter channel members' behavior so they take actions they would not have taken otherwise. Based on the nature of the relationship between the members of the marketing channel, there are three basic forms of channel coordination that can help motivate channel partners: conventional channels, vertical marketing systems, and horizontal marketing systems.
9. All marketing channels have the potential for conflict and competition resulting from goal incompatibility, poorly defined roles and rights, perceptual differences, and interdependent relationships. Companies can try to manage conflict through dual compensation, superordinate goals, employee exchange, co-optation, and other means.
10. Producers of physical products and services must decide on market logistics—the best way to store and move goods and services to market destinations and to coordinate the activities of suppliers, purchasing agents, manufacturers, marketers, channel members, and customers. Major gains in logistical efficiency have come from advances in information technology.
11. The supply-chain approach to managing market logistics can help a company identify superior suppliers and distributors, as well as help it improve productivity and reduce costs. The firm must make four major decisions about its market logistics: How should we handle orders (order processing)? Where should we locate our stock (warehousing)? How much stock should we hold (inventory)? and How should we ship goods (transportation)?

marketing SPOTLIGHT

Zara

Source: Mira/Alamy Stock Photo

Zara began in 1975 when Amancio Ortega and Rosalia Mera opened their first store in Galicia, Spain. The original store sold low-priced lookalikes of high-end, popular fashion products. Zara's business model of imitating the latest fashion and providing their designs at low prices appealed to Spanish consumers. In the next eight years, Zara expanded to nine more stores in popular shopping centers in Spain. During this period, Ortega had created a design, manufacturing, and distribution process he called "instant fashion," which could respond to fashion trends very quickly. Using this process, Zara spent the next decade expanding into the global market, which included the United States, France, Belgium, and Sweden. After achieving similar success with its expansions, Zara eventually became the world's largest apparel retailer.

Zara famously views clothes as a "perishable commodity," something that should be enjoyed for a couple of weeks or months. Zara's apparel appeals to consumers who are looking to keep up with all the latest fashion trends. When a new style becomes popular, Zara can imitate it and release a new collection in less than two weeks. Other fashion companies can take as long as six months to put out a new design. Unlike companies that focus on quantity over style, Zara does the opposite. Zara releases over 12,000 styles per year; this wide variety creates a greater likelihood that consumers will find an item they like.

The majority of Zara's designs stay on shelves for only three to four weeks. The constant refreshing of styles on store shelves also incentivizes customers to visit Zara stores more frequently. This can be seen in consumer behavior in Central London. Consumers visit other clothing stores and average of up to four times per year. Zara's customers visit shops an average of 17 times per year. The full racks of clothes always give shoppers something new to choose from. Zara produces lower quantities of each style to create artificial scarcity, which makes their offerings seem more desirable and luxurious. An added benefit of this scarcity is that if a style is not successful, Zara doesn't have to dispose of a high volume of inventory.

Zara's clothing starts with the design process, which includes a heavy focus on consumer input. Store employees and managers listen to customers' comments and suggestions and take note of what they're wearing in stores. Design teams visit universities, nightclubs, shopping centers, and other areas frequented by fashion trendsetters to observe new fashion choices that could potentially be successful. The trends team follows popular fashion bloggers and tracks Zara customers for new insights. The data gathered by Zara's research team span new trends that differ by gender, culture, and season. This allows Zara to create product offerings that reflect the different needs of the global market. Zara offers smaller-sized clothing in Japan, hijab headscarves and long dresses for women in Arab countries, and more breathable apparel for countries in South America. Understanding the varied needs of its customers allows Zara to release a wide variety of successful styles on a frequent basis.

What enables Zara to release new collections quickly is its fast and vertically integrated supply chain. Zara's in-house production facilities allow the company to control processes such as dyeing, fabric cutting, and processing. When new designs come into the factory, clothing items are manufactured, processed, and in stores within 15 days. Zara tends to manufacture only fashionable and trendy items that have a short selling cycle. Items that tend to stay on shelves, like basic T-shirts and pants, are outsourced to low-cost suppliers in Asia. When items are released and fail to meet sales expectations, factories quickly cancel production. Zara's fast and efficient flow of information and data can result in large fluctuations in orders. Zara can adjust orders up to 40 to 50 percent, avoiding potential overproduction. Zara's flexible production process attempts to offer consumers what they want to buy at any given time.

Zara combines an understanding of its customers with a highly efficient supply chain to create its global success. The company is aware that the consumer is an invaluable resource in the design of its trendy apparel and collections. Coupling this insight with a well-managed and highly profitable inventory strategy, Zara aims to stay on top of fashion retailing.[48]

Questions

1. Would Zara's model work for other retailers? Why or why not?
2. What can Zara do to ensure successful growth around the world that maintains the same level of speed and instant fashion?
3. Who are Zara's biggest competitors? What should Zara do to build, enhance, and sustain its competitive advantage?

marketing
SPOTLIGHT

Titan

Titan Industries Limited, established in 1984 as Titan Watches, is a joint venture between the Tata Group and the Tamil Nadu Industrial Development Corporation (TIDCO). In its 37 years of rich and classic legacy, Titan has positioned itself as a trusted, fashion brand, and currently stands as the fifth largest watch manufacturer in the world. The company's contemporary designs, outstanding advertisements and smart channel management have proven to be key contributors to Titan's success in building a strong brand.

Beginning with watches positioned as fashion accessories, Titan has emerged a leading player in multiple segments with frontrunner brands—Titan for watches, Tanishq, Mia and Carat Lane for jewelry, Titan Eye+ for eyewear. The company also expanded its product portfolio by launching 'SKINN'– a perfume brand and 'Fast track' – fancy watches and eyewear for the youth. Quality products and innovative design backed by strong branding, retailing and service support have been key factors in making Titan a lifestyle major.

Since its inception, Titan adopted an aggressive production and distribution strategy, revolving around its strong value system, and to build that classic image the company followed a tailor-made marketing approach. Its product portfolio consists of a vast variety of contemporary products, exclusively designed to fit the requirements of its target segments. To reach out to its multi-segment target audience, Titan established a very extensive distribution network, designed to complement its product and positioning strategy. Titan's channel management strategy sets itself a class apart. Aligned with the value system of the company as well as with its products, the company adopted a multi-layered distribution system designed to cater to the high volume market. Titan set up exclusive showrooms titled 'The World of Titan' designed to create a premium shopping experience for its customers. It expanded its channel with franchisee operated exclusive outlets replicating the 'The World of Titan' feel with complete control over major functions such as store design, location, recruitment, and training of the staff. Titan introduced other channel members in its network while expanding through multi-brand watch outlets and department stores for further

TANISHQ
A TATA PRODUCT

Source: Tanishq©Titan Company Ltd, used with permission

(continued)

market penetration. To reach out to other newly added markets in semi-urban areas and small towns, the company added Titan shops and Titan distributors, while opting for digital channels to capture the millennials.

Titan manages one of the largest retail networks in India through its well-crafted distribution network. It has products for all, and therefore, the channel member and distribution strategy are designed accordingly. 'The World of Titan' and 'Tanishq' are designed for its high-end customers looking for elegant fashion wear accessories and jewelry[49]. The company ensures quality services, product differentiation, standard pricing, and value proposition in both categories of outlets viz. company-owned and franchisee-owned showrooms. In the beginning, Titan preferred company-owned showrooms over franchisees to establish the retailing concept while exercising greater control over its distribution. Today the number of franchisee-owned showrooms have outnumbered the company-owned showroom. All its showrooms exclusively retail Titan brands.

For the price-sensitive and quality-conscious market, Titan introduced the 'Titan Shops'. This category is now known as 'Titan Time Zone'. It is a semi-exclusive distribution category, which focuses mainly on Titan brands. Over 70 per cent of the products are Titan brands and while the remaining nearly 30 per cent products belong to competing brands. These outlets attract customers who want to compare Titan with other brands before buying a watch. Multi-brand stores draw the price-sensitive middle class customers in the semi-urban markets.

The third category of Titan's multi-mode distribution includes 'Titan dealers'. Two categories of dealers help the company reach out to its expanded market segments. First, the traditional dealers carry Titan brands along with competing brands to capture the low-end segments. Second, the non-traditional dealers that serve the high-end customers through restaurants, gift shops and boutiques, and carry exclusive products.[50]

Titan has strangthened its online presence to cater to the millennials. The company supports its omnichannel presence amongst youth with brands like Fast track and Mia. Titan has come up with facilities like selling through video calls during the Covid-19 pandemic. The entire distribution network has been refurbished looking at the changing needs of its customers. It has also started offering the home delivery option to ensure seamless availability of its products.[51]

Today, Titan is among the country's largest retailers with 1,078 stores and 1.5 million sq ft of retail space, operating through multi-mode distribution. Its franchisee-led model has helped the business to be very asset light. The very 'face' of the company -The World of Titan showrooms – remains an integral part of the Titan family and every care is taken to ensure that similar "customer bonding" takes place with these franchisee-owners as the company's valuable primary customers. The partnership approach with franchisees has brought significant success to Titan, which has continued to enjoy rapid growth in sales and profitability. From fun-filled annual business meets to a rewards system for target achievement, this relationship although different, also helps sustain a long-term mutually profitable association. Every aspect of this relationship is reviewed and appraised in a systematic manner through processes designed for only that purpose. Like Nikhil Vora of Sixth Sense Ventures comments on Titan, *"They really are the masters of 2,000 sq ft retail,*.[52]

Questions

1. What are the key aspects of Titan's distribution model?
2. What are the key benefits of franchising for Titan's brands viz. Titan, Titan Eye+, Tanishq, Mia, etc. and their franchisees?
3. How much leeway should Titan offer to individual franchisees in deciding on the store design merchandise, staff training and advertising? Should Titan take a centralized approach, or should it let franchisees adapt their strategy to local conditions?

CHAPTER **16**

Managing Retailing

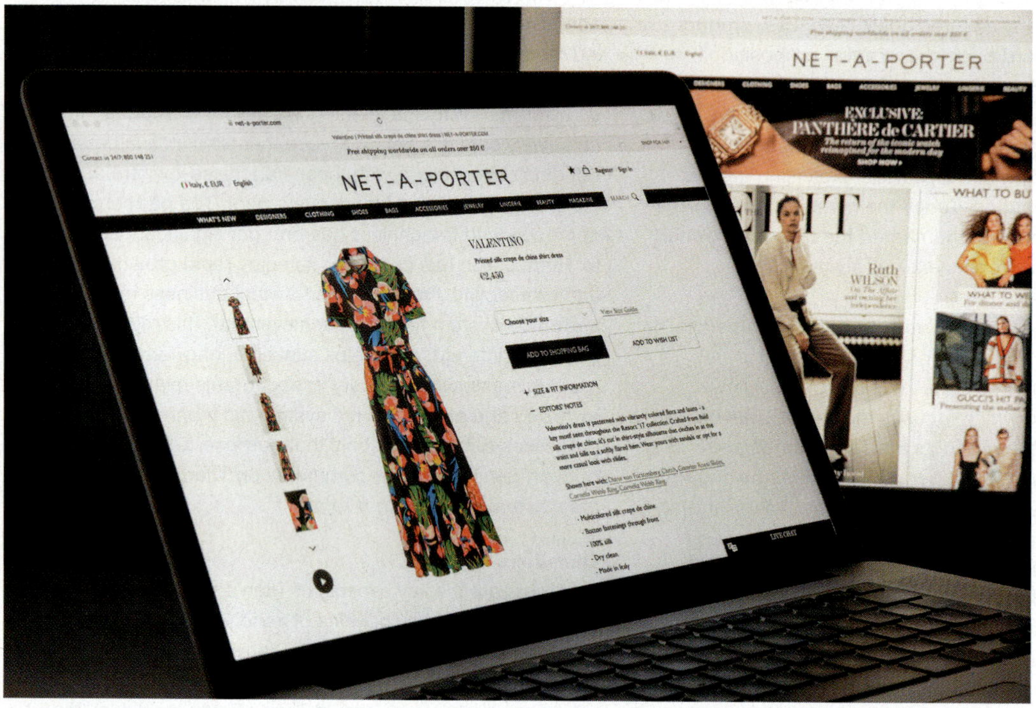

Net-a-Porter created a luxury online shopping experience by merging editorial content and magazine-quality images to showcase products in its portfolio of 800-plus designer brands.

Source: Casimiro/Alamy Stock Photo

In the preceding chapter, we examined marketing intermediaries primarily in their capacity as manufacturers that want to build and manage marketing channels. In this chapter, we view these intermediaries—retailers, wholesalers, and logistical organizations—as requiring and forging their own marketing strategies in a rapidly changing world. Intermediaries also strive for marketing excellence and can reap the benefits like any other type of company. Consider the success of Net-a-Porter.

>>> Net-a-Porter was founded in London in 2000 by fashion journalist Natalie Massenet. At a time when most luxury brands were intimidated by online retailers, Net-a-Porter set out to create a superior yet convenient shopping experience to bring luxury items to high-net-worth buyers. Since its launch, Net-a-Porter has established itself as the world's premier luxury fashion retailer, offering a portfolio of over 800 designer brands, including Gucci, Prada, Dolce & Gabbana, Chloe, Alexander McQueen, Balenciaga, Valentino, and Stella McCartney. A key to the company's success was its business model, which called for merging editorial content and retail capability to create a fashion magazine selling luxury brands. "People always say to me, 'You've really strived to redefine

retail,'" shared Massenet, "but the reality is I wanted to redefine magazines. From the beginning, we were always trying to blend the two, to buy [clothes and labels] in the same way a fashion editor would choose them." Net-a-Porter aimed to display its offerings in a manner similar to the way it would look in a magazine—but to let readers buy them online. This involved producing high-quality images and videos to showcase the brands, and developing luxury packaging to recreate the luxury shopping experience online. Net-a-Porter's approach proved to be successful, and the company turned a profit four years after its launch, despite the difficult economic climate following the internet bubble burst. Several years later, in 2010, Switzerland-based luxury goods holding company Richemont acquired a majority stake in Net-a-Porter in a deal that valued the online retailer at over $500 million. In 2015, Net-a-Porter merged with Yoox, an online retailer of off-season luxury goods, to create the world's leading online luxury fashion retailer, Yoox Net-a-Porter Group.[1]

The retail market can be unforgiving. Although innovative retailers such as Zappos, Sweden's H&M, Spain's Zara and Mango, and Britain's Topshop have thrived in recent years, others, such as former U.S. stalwarts JCPenney, Kohl's, and Kmart, have struggled. The more successful companies use strategic planning, state-of-the-art technology, advanced information systems, and sophisticated marketing tools. They segment their markets, improve their market targeting and positioning, and connect with their customers through memorable experiences, relevant and timely information, and, of course, the right products and services. In this chapter, we discuss marketing excellence in retailing.

The Modern Retail Environment

Retailing includes all the activities involved in selling goods or services directly to final consumers for personal, nonbusiness use. A retailer or retail store is any business enterprise whose sales volume comes primarily from retailing. Any organization selling to final consumers—no matter whether it is a manufacturer, a wholesaler, or a retailer—is doing retailing. It also doesn't matter *how* the goods or services are sold (in person, by mail, by telephone, by vending machine, or online) or *where* (in a store, on the street, or in a consumer's home).

The retail marketing environment is dramatically different today from what it was just a decade ago. The retail market is very dynamic, and a number of new types of competitors and competition have emerged in recent years.

- **New retail forms and combinations.** To better satisfy customers' need for convenience, a variety of new retail forms have emerged. Bookstores feature coffee shops. Gas stations include food stores. Loblaws supermarkets have fitness clubs. Grocery stores such as Whole Foods and

Learning Objectives After reading this chapter you should be able to:

16.1 Explain the key changes defining modern retailing.

16.2 Discuss the marketing decisions that retailers face.

16.3 Describe how a company manages omnichannel retailing.

16.4 Explain the key principles in building and managing private labels.

16.5 Describe the key aspects of wholesaling.

Kroger are adding bars to their locations. Shopping malls and bus and train stations have peddlers' carts in their aisles. Retailers are also experimenting with "pop-up" stores that let them promote brands to seasonal shoppers for a few weeks in busy areas. Pop-up stores are designed to create buzz, often through interactive experiences. Google uses pop-up stores as an easy way to establish a physical presence during holiday shopping seasons. In addition to gaining a retail footprint by acquiring Whole Foods, Amazon has launched its own brick-and-mortar stores.

- **Retailer consolidation.** Through their superior information systems, logistical systems, and buying power, giant retailers such as Walmart are able to deliver good service and immense volumes of product to masses of consumers at appealing prices. They are crowding out smaller manufacturers that cannot deliver enough quantity, and they often dictate to the most powerful ones what to make, how to price and promote it, when and how to ship, and even how to improve production and management. Without these accounts, manufacturers could lose a significant portion of their sales. Because consolidated retailers have power over manufacturers, they tend to charge a variety of allowance fees for listing, stocking, and promoting new brands.
- **Growth of mobile retailing.** Consumers are fundamentally changing the way they shop, increasingly using a cell phone to text a friend or relative about a product while shopping in stores. Over 50 percent of all Google searches are done on mobile phones. In some parts of the world, m-commerce is well established. Asian consumers use their mobile phones as their main computers and benefit from a well-developed mobile infrastructure. Mobile ads are accepted by consumers and relatively inexpensive for firms. In South Korea, Tesco created virtual subway stores for commuters traveling on Seoul's underground transportation system. Interactive, life-like store aisles with a wide range of product and brand images were superimposed on walls. Consumers could order products for home delivery by simply snapping photos with their phones.
- **Growth of omnichannel retailing.** Retailing has evolved from a purely brick-and-mortar format to a scenario in which retailers have augmented their physical locations with online stores designed to cater to consumers who prefer shopping online. In this physical + online format, brick-and-mortar stores and online stores perform the same functions, with online sales partially cannibalizing the sales in physical stores. Realizing the potential inefficiencies in managing two independent distribution channels, many retailers have moved to an omnichannel model in which physical locations complement one another rather than competing. For example, many retailers—including Best Buy, Target, and Nordstrom—are integrating their online and offline operations to offer a seamless customer experience in a way that is effective and cost-efficient for the company. For example, Home Depot enables customers to search online the available inventory at each of its stores and have the items that are not locally available shipped to the local store or to customers' homes. Customers may also return unwanted items by either shipping them back or bringing them to a nearby store.
- **Growth of fast retailing.** An important trend in fashion retailing in particular, but with broader implications as well, is the emergence of fast retailing. Here retailers develop completely different supply chain and distribution systems in order to offer consumers constantly changing product choices. Fast retailing requires thoughtful decisions in a number of areas, including new-product development, sourcing, manufacturing, inventory management, and selling practices. Consumers have been attracted to fast-fashion retailers such as H&M, Zara, Uniqlo, TopShop, and Forever 21 because of the novelty, value, and fashion sense of their offerings and have made these retailers successful.
- **Increasing role of technology.** Technology is profoundly affecting the way retailers conduct nearly every facet of their business. Nearly all now use technology to produce forecasts, control inventory costs, and order from suppliers, reducing the need to discount and run sales to clear out languishing products. Technology is also directly affecting the consumer shopping experience inside the store. Electronic shelf labeling allows retailers to change price levels instantaneously. In-store programming can run continual demonstrations or promotional messages. Retailers are experimenting with virtual shopping screens, audio/video presentations, and QR code integration. They are also developing fully integrated digital communication strategies with well-designed websites, e-mails, search strategies, and social media campaigns. Social media are especially important for retailers during the holiday season, when shoppers are seeking information and sharing successes. Amazon has opened cashier-less stores that use cameras and artificial intelligence to detect what items customers put in their carts, and charge them accordingly, without their having to go through a check-out process.

- **Decline of middle-market retailers.** The retail market today is hourglass shaped: Growth seems to be centered at the top (with luxury offerings from retailers like Tiffany and Neiman Marcus) and at the bottom (with discount pricing from retailers like Walmart and Dollar General). As discount retailers have improved their quality and image, consumers have been willing to trade down. Target offers Phillip Lim, Jason Wu, and Missoni designs, and Kmart sells an extensive line of Joe Boxer underwear and sleepwear. At the other end of the spectrum, Coach converted 40 of its nearly 300 stores to a more upscale format that offers higher-priced bags and concierge services. Opportunities are scarcer in the middle, where once-successful retailers such as JCPenney, Kohl's, Sears, CompUSA, RadioShack, and Montgomery Ward have struggled or even gone out of business. Supermarket chains like SuperValu and Safeway have found themselves caught in the middle between the affluent appeal of chains like Whole Foods and Wegmans and the discount appeal of Aldi and Walmart. Compounding problems is the plight of middle-class shoppers, who have seen their buying power shrink as a consequence of slumping housing prices and stagnating incomes.

Key Retailing Decisions

With this new retail environment as a backdrop, we now examine retailers' marketing decisions in some key areas: target market, product assortment, procurement, services, store atmosphere and experiences, pricing, incentives, and communication. We discuss private labels later in this chapter.

TARGET MARKET

Until it defines and profiles the target market, the retailer cannot make consistent decisions about product assortment, store décor, advertising messages and media, price, and service levels. Whole Foods has succeeded by offering a unique shopping experience to a customer base interested in organic and natural foods.

> **Whole Foods Market** In over 480 stores in North America and the United Kingdom, Whole Foods (acquired by Amazon in 2017) creates celebrations of food. Its markets are bright and well staffed, and food displays are colorful, bountiful, and seductive. Whole Foods is the largest U.S. organic and natural foods grocer. Whole Foods also provides lots of information about its food. If you want to know, for instance, whether the chicken in the display case lived a happy, free-roaming life, you can get a booklet and an invitation to visit the farm in Pennsylvania where it was raised. For other help, you have only to ask a knowledgeable and easy-to-find employee. A typical Whole Foods store has more than 200 employees, almost twice as many as Safeway. The company works hard to create an inviting store atmosphere, with prices scrawled in chalk, cardboard boxes and ice everywhere, and other creative display touches to make the shopper feel at home. Its approach is working, especially for consumers who view organic and artisanal food as an affordable luxury.[2]

Mistakes in choosing target markets can be costly. When historically mass market jeweler Zales decided to chase upscale customers, it replaced one-third of its merchandise, dropping inexpensive, low-quality diamond jewelry for high-margin, fashionable 14-karat gold and silver pieces and shifting its ad campaign in the process. The move was a disaster. Zales lost many of its traditional customers without winning over the new customers it hoped to attract.[3]

To better hit their targets, retailers are slicing the market into ever-finer segments and introducing new lines of stores to exploit niche markets with more relevant offerings. For example, in recent years, children's clothing retailing has become segmented into a large number of niche markets. Gymboree launched Janie and Jack, selling apparel and gifts for babies and toddlers; Hot Topic introduced Torrid, selling trendy fashions for women who wear sizes 10 to 30; and Limited Brand's Tween Brands began to sell lower-priced fashion to tween girls through its Justice stores and to tween boys through its Brother shops.

>> Informative, colorful displays and knowledgeable employees provide a welcoming atmosphere for patrons of Whole Foods, the largest U.S. organic and natural foods grocer.

Source: Maurice Savage/Alamy Stock Photo

PRODUCT ASSORTMENT AND PROCUREMENT

The retailer's product assortment must match the target market's shopping expectations in both *breadth* and *depth*.[4] A restaurant can offer a narrow and shallow assortment (small lunch counters), a narrow and deep assortment (delicatessens), a broad and shallow assortment (cafeterias), or a broad and deep assortment (large restaurants).

Identifying the right product assortment can be especially challenging in fast-moving industries such as technology and fashion. At one point, Urban Outfitters ran into trouble when it strayed from its "hip but not too hip" formula, embracing new styles too quickly. In the same vein, active and casual apparel retailer Aéropostale faced head winds trying to match its product assortment to its young teens' needs in a way that was profitable for the company. Forced into bankruptcy in 2016, Aéropostale had to streamline its product offerings and close more than two-thirds of its 800 stores in order to avoid extinction.

Developing a product-differentiation strategy is a key challenge in defining the store's product assortment. *Destination categories* may play a particularly important role because they have the greatest impact on where households choose to shop and how they view a particular retailer. A supermarket could be known for the freshness of its produce or for the variety and deals it offers in soft drinks and snacks.[5]

After deciding on the product-assortment strategy, the retailer must establish merchandise sources, policies, and practices. In the corporate headquarters of a supermarket chain, specialist buyers (sometimes called *merchandise managers*) are responsible for developing brand assortments and listening to presentations from their suppliers' salespeople.

Retailers are rapidly improving their skills in demand forecasting, merchandise selection, stock control, space allocation, and display. They use sophisticated software to track inventory, compute economic order quantities, order goods, and analyze dollars spent on vendors and products. Supermarket chains use scanner data to manage their merchandise mix on a store-by-store basis.

Some stores are using radio frequency identification (RFID) systems made up of "smart" tags—microchips attached to tiny radio antennas—and electronic readers to facilitate inventory control and product replenishment. The smart tags can be embedded on products or stuck on labels so that when the tag is near a reader, it transmits a unique identifying number to its computer database. Coca-Cola and Gillette have used RFID systems to monitor inventory and track goods in real time as they move from factories to supermarkets to shopping baskets.

Stores are using direct product profitability to measure a product's handling costs (receiving, moving to storage, tracking paperwork, selecting, checking, loading, and space cost) from the time it reaches the warehouse until a customer buys it in the retail store. Sometimes they find that a product's gross margin bears little relationship to the direct product profit. Some high-volume products may have such high handling costs that they are less profitable and deserve less shelf space than low-volume products—unless customers buy enough other, more profitable products to justify the loss involved in pushing the high-volume products.

Trader Joe's has differentiated itself on its innovative product assortment and procurement strategy.

Trader Joe's Los Angeles-based Trader Joe's has carved out a special niche as a "gourmet food outlet/discount warehouse hybrid," selling a constantly rotating assortment of unique upscale specialty food and wine at lower-than-average prices at its 474 stores. Roughly 80 percent of what the company stocks sells under private labels (compared with only 16 percent at most supermarkets), from Belgian waffle cookies to Thai lime-and-chili cashews. For procurement, it has adopted a "less is more" philosophy. Every store carries only 2,000 to 3,000 products, compared with 55,000 at a conventional supermarket—and then only what it can buy and sell at a good price, even if that means changing stock weekly. Trader Joe's expert buyers go directly to hundreds of suppliers, not to intermediaries, and about a quarter of these suppliers are overseas. Always thinking about what customers want and engaging them in the process, the company introduces as many as 20 products a week to replace unpopular items. With thousands of vendor relationships all around the world, Trader Joe's has built a success formula that's difficult to copy. Experts praise its ability to be a storyteller and create uniquely friendly experiences. As one expert says, "It really comes down to the small formats, well-edited assortments and value pricing of unique private brand products."[6]

SERVICES

Another differentiator is unerringly reliable customer service, whether face to face, across phone lines, or via online chat. Retailers also encounter widely different consumer preferences for service levels and specific services. Specifically, they position themselves as offering one of three levels of service:

Self-service. Self-service is the cornerstone of all discount operations. Many customers are willing to carry out their own "locate–compare–select" process to save money.

Source: Randy Duchaine/Alamy Stock Photo

<< Most of Trader Joe's offerings are private labels carefully curated to provide the level and mix of benefits sought by their customers.

Limited service. These retailers carry more shopping goods and offer services such as credit and merchandise-return privileges. Customers typically find their own goods, though they can ask for assistance.

Full service. Salespeople are ready to assist in every phase of the "locate–compare–select" process. Customers who like to be waited on prefer this type of store. The high staffing cost and many services, along with the higher proportion of specialty goods and slower-moving items, result in high-cost retailing.

Retailers must also decide on the *services mix* to offer customers. Such services might involve *pre-purchase services* such as providing product information and enabling shoppers to try and experience products, as well as *postpurchase services* such as shipping, delivery, and installation, gift wrapping, alterations and tailoring, installation, and adjustments and returns.

fabindia
CELEBRATE INDIA

>> FabIndia's classic yet contemporary nature of its products and a stress on tradition creates an emotional connection with customers. Customers enjoy shopping in its retail outlets that offer convenience, and the décor represents the rich culture of India.

Source: ©FabIndia, used with permission

FabIndia FabIndia, established in 1960 by John Bissell, is one of India's oldest organized retail company known for its iconic handmade products and classic store decor representing the rich culture of rural India. Fabindia opened its first retail outlet in 1976, showcasing hand-crafted handloom products designed to match the urban market taste and preferences. Over the last six decades, Fabindia has grown from a handloom export company to India's leading handmade garment and home furnishing company with more than 320 retail outlets across India, Dubai, Singapore, Italy, Malaysia and Mauritius. The feel of the stores, from inception, complement the classic designs of its fashion products. Fabindia operates three store formats—Premium Stores (4000+ sq ft) for entire range of products focusing on exclusive high-end products, Standard Stores (2000-4000 sq ft) mixed range of regular and high-end products and Concept Stores (800-1500 sq ft) with fewer SKU of fast selling products.[8] All these stores carry the warmth of Indian ethos and culture. Each corner of the stores enhances the shopping experience with a warm and welcoming effect. The store interiors and decor showcase Fabindia's collections in an elegant way. Be it the selection of the floral wall decor, classic lamps, unique shelf designs and elegant furniture, every corner reflects Indian ethnicity and design.[9] In 2017, Fabindia launched a new category of Experience Stores (8000-10000 sq ft) that carry the full range of its products with additional features like café (Fabcafe), kids' zone and wellness zone apart from apparel to capture the changing needs and preferences of the youth and millennials. These Experience stores offer a complete bouquet of complementary features and services to enrich the retail shopping experience. Keeping the health-conscious youth in mind, Fabcafe offers healthy and ecofriendly food. With dedicated staff at the kids' zone to look after the children, parents can enjoy their shopping undisturbed. In the era of one click shopping, Fabindia is doing a wonderful job to keep the retail shopping experience alive and young with its classic and inviting store atmospherics.[10]

Source: dbimages/Alamy Stock Photo

<< Bass Pro Shops' Outdoor World superstores, billed as attractions as well as retail spaces, offer product demonstrations and classes in surroundings that closely mirror those encountered by fans of the outdoors, converting them into loyal customers.

Bass Pro Shops Bass Pro Shops, a retailer of outdoor sports equipment, caters to hunters, campers, anglers, boaters, and outdoors fans of any type. Its Outdoor World superstores feature 200,000 square feet or more of giant aquariums, waterfalls, trout ponds, archery and rifle ranges, fly-tying demonstrations, indoor driving range and putting greens, and classes in everything from ice fishing to conservation—all free. Every department is set up to replicate the corresponding outdoor experience in support of product demonstrations and testing. During the summer, parents can bring their kids to the free in-store Family Summer Camp with a host of activities in all departments. Bass Pro Shops builds a strong connection to its loyal customers from the moment they enter the store—through a turnstile designed to highlight that "they are entering an attraction, not just a retail space"—and are greeted by the irreverent sign saying "Welcome Fishermen, Hunters, and Other Liars." Bass Pro Shops draws more than 120 million visitors annually. The average customer drives more than 50 miles and stays for more than two hours. The Bass showroom in Missouri is the number-one tourist destination in the state.[12]

STORE ATMOSPHERE

Retailers must consider all the senses in shaping the customer's experience. Varying the tempo of music affects average time and dollars spent in the supermarket; slow music can lead to higher sales. Bloomingdale's uses different essences or scents in different departments: baby powder in the baby store, suntan lotion in the bathing suit area, lilacs in lingerie, and cinnamon and pine scent during the holiday season. Other retailers such as Victoria's Secret and Juicy Couture use their own distinctive branded perfumes, which they also sell.[7]

The growth of e-commerce has forced traditional brick-and-mortar retailers to respond. In addition to their natural advantages (such as products that shoppers can actually see, touch, and test; real-life customer service; and no delivery lag time for most purchases), brick-and-mortar stores also provide a shopping experience as a strong differentiator.

The store atmosphere should match shoppers' basic motivations. If customers are likely to be in a task-oriented and functional mind-set, then a simpler, more restrained in-store environment may be better.[11] On the other hand, some retailers of experiential products are creating in-store entertainment to attract customers who want fun and excitement. REI, seller of outdoor gear and clothing products, allows consumers to test climbing equipment on 25-foot or even 65-foot walls in the store and to try GORE-TEX raincoats under a simulated rain shower. Bass Pro Shops also offers rich customer experiences.

PRICING

Prices are a key positioning factor and must be set in relationship to the target market, product-and-service assortment mix, and competition.[13] Different formats of store retailers will have different competitive and price dynamics. Discount stores, for example, historically have competed much more directly with one another than with other formats, although that is changing.[14]

All retailers would like high *turns + earns* (high volumes and high gross margins), but the two don't usually go together. Most retailers fall into the *high-markup, lower-volume* group (fine specialty stores) or the *low-markup, higher-volume* group (mass merchandisers and discount stores). Within each of these groups are further gradations.

At one end of the price spectrum is by-appointment-only Bijan on Rodeo Drive in Beverly Hills, known as one of the most expensive stores in the world. The original cost of its cologne was $1,500 for six ounces, and its suits are priced at $25,000, ties at $1,200, and socks at $100.[15] At the other end of the scale, Target has skillfully combined a hip image with discount prices to offer customers a strong value proposition. It first introduced a line of products from renowned designers such as Michael Graves, Isaac Mizrahi, and Liz Lange and has continued to enlist high-profile names, such as singer Gwen Stefani, to sell hip children's clothes. Another company following the low-margin, high-volume strategy is Lumber Liquidators.

Lumber Liquidators Lumber Liquidators is the largest hardwood flooring specialty retailer in the United States. It began in 1993 when Tom Sullivan, a building contractor, began purchasing excess wood that other companies didn't need and reselling it from the back of a trucking yard in Stoughton, Massachusetts. The first store opened in 1996 in West Roxbury, Massachusetts, and a second store opened the same year in Hartford, Connecticut. Over the past 20+ years, Lumber Liquidators has grown steadily, with hundreds of locations in the United States and Canada. The company found its niche market in hardwood flooring by buying excess wood directly from lumber mills at a discount and reselling it to customers at lower prices than those charged by larger home improvement retailers such as Lowe's and The Home Depot. It can sell at lower prices because it keeps operating costs down by cutting out intermediaries and locating stores in inexpensive locations. Lumber Liquidators also knows a lot about its customers, such as the fact that shoppers who request product samples have a 30 percent likelihood of buying within a month and that most tend to renovate one room at a time, not the entire home at once.[16]

When setting prices, retailers consider a variety of factors. Some retailers put low prices on some items to serve as traffic builders (or loss leaders) or to signal their pricing policies.[17] Others plan markdowns on slower-moving merchandise to free up inventory. Shoe retailers, for example, expect to sell 50 percent of their shoes at the normal markup, 25 percent at a 40 percent markup, and the remaining 25 percent at cost. A store's average price level and discounting policies will affect its price image with consumers, but non-price-related factors such as store atmosphere and levels of service also matter.[18]

In addition to managing their prices, retailers must manage their price image, which reflects the overall perception that consumers have about the level of prices at a given retailer. For example, Walmart is often viewed as being rather inexpensive, whereas Target is typically considered to have somewhat higher prices. Because consumers are often unaware of the actual prices of the items they seek to purchase across different retailers, they often rely on retailers' price image to determine the attractiveness of a given price. In this context, when setting its prices, retailers must take into account the impact of each individual price on their price image (see "Marketing Insight: Managing the Price Image of a Retailer").

Source: REUTERS/Alamy Stock Photo

<< Lumber Liquidators has achieved steady growth in the hardwood flooring market by buying excess wood directly from lumber mills, keeping costs down, and passing the savings on to customers.

INCENTIVES

To make their offerings more attractive to customers, retailers often use incentives such as price discounts, volume discounts (such as buy one–get one free), bonus offerings, and coupons. These incentives, also referred to as sales promotions, aim to generate store traffic and "nudge" customers toward making a purchase.

Retailers vary in the degree to which they use incentives. Two extreme strategies stand out: everyday low pricing and high–low pricing. A retailer using **everyday low pricing (EDLP)** charges a constant low price with little or no price promotion or special sales. Constant prices eliminate week-to-week price uncertainty and the high–low pricing of promotion-oriented competitors. In **high–low pricing**, the retailer charges higher prices on an everyday basis but runs frequent promotions featuring prices temporarily lower than prices at the EDLP level.[19]

In recent years, high–low pricing has given way to EDLP at such widely different venues as Toyota Scion car dealers and upscale department stores such as Nordstrom. But the king of EDLP is surely Walmart, which practically defined the term. Except for a few sale items every month, Walmart promises everyday low prices on major brands.

Retailers like Walmart have avoided "sale pricing" in favor of EDLP. This approach has led to greater pricing stability, a stronger image of fairness and reliability, and higher retail profits. Those supermarket chains that practice everyday low pricing can be more profitable than those that practice high–low sale pricing, but only in certain circumstances, such as when the market is characterized by many "large basket" shoppers who tend to buy many items on any one trip.[20]

The most important reason why retailers adopt EDLP is that constant sales and promotions are costly and have eroded consumer confidence in everyday shelf prices. Some consumers also have less time and patience for past traditions such as watching for supermarket specials and clipping coupons. Yet promotions and sales do create excitement and draw shoppers, so EDLP does not guarantee success and is not for everyone.[21] JCPenney learned that lesson the hard way.

While shopping in brick-and-mortar stores, consumers often use their smart phones to find deals or capitalize on promotions: The redemption rate for mobile coupons (10 percent) far exceeds that for

JCPenney When JCPenney hired Apple's retailing guru Ron Johnson as CEO, there was much anticipation about how he would transform the venerable department store giant. When Johnson found that the company had held 590 sales events the previous year and that almost three-quarters of its sales revenue was from merchandise marked down 50 percent or more, he decided to embark on a simplified pricing strategy. Coupons and sales were eliminated and replaced by across-the-board price decreases of 40 percent. The everyday low pricing plan turned out to be a disaster, however, and with sales and stock price plunging, Johnson was quickly shown the door. A number of reasons have been suggested for the program's failure. Competitors like Macy's and Sears continued to offer sales and discounts, giving the perception of good deals. Penney's customers missed the coupons and weekly sales events. Everyday low prices are thought to be more effective with more functional products, but they may actually harm more image-oriented products like fashion, an important category for JCPenney. One commentator might have said it best when he stated, "At the end of the day, people don't want a fair price. They want a great deal."[22]

Source: Sundry Photography/Shutterstock

>> JCPenney's attempt to switch from a plethora of coupon and sales events to everyday low pricing proved painful when customers made it clear that they missed the weekly deals and competitors continued to offer sales and discounts.

paper coupons (1 percent).[23] For retailers, research has shown that mobile promotions can get consumers to travel greater distances within a store and make more unplanned purchases.[24]

Companies are trying to give their customers more control over their shopping experiences by bringing digital technologies into the store, especially via mobile apps. Consider Nordstrom. Although Nordstrom expected its app to be used remotely, many customers launch it while shopping in a store, rather than approaching a salesperson. As one executive noted, "A lot of customers like to touch and feel and try on the merchandise, but they also want the information they get online." Nordstrom has added Wi-Fi to nearly all its stores, in part so its app will work fast.

An increasingly popular tool among brick-and-mortar retailers is **geofencing**, which involves targeting customers with a mobile promotion when they are within a defined geographic space, typically near or in a store. Consider these applications:[25]

Neiman-Marcus is using geofencing in its stores so that its salespeople will know when their more valuable customers are on the premises and can review their purchase history to provide more personalized service.

Outdoor supplier North Face uses geofences around parks and ski resorts in addition to its stores.

Cosmetics brand retailer Kiehl's uses geofencing around its free-standing stores and its kiosks within other stores. It advertises the alerts at its cash register and on social media pages and e-mail lists, and it offers customers a free lip balm for enrolling. Thousands have done so, but the company limits its texts to three a month to avoid being intrusive.

COMMUNICATIONS

Retailers use a wide range of communication tools to generate traffic and purchases. They place ads, run special sales, issue money-saving coupons, send e-mail promotions, present frequent-shopper reward programs and in-store food sampling, and put coupons on shelves or at check-out points. Retailers work with manufacturers to design point-of-sale materials that reflect both their images. They time the arrival of their e-mails and design them with attention-grabbing subject lines, animation, and personalized messages and advice.

Retailers also use interactive and social media to pass on information and create communities around their brands. They study the way consumers respond to their e-mails, not only where and how messages are opened but also which words and images led to a click.

With 15 percent of a retailer's most loyal customers accounting for as much as half of its sales, reward programs are becoming increasingly sophisticated. Consumers who choose to share personal information can receive discounts, secret or advance sales, exclusive offers, and store credits. CVS has over 9,800 retail locations and more than 90 million loyalty club members who can use in-store coupon centers and receive coupons with their sales receipts.[26]

For flagship stores in Taipei, Hong Kong, London, and Chicago, Burberry made "virtual rain" with a 360° film as part of its digital "Burberry World Live" program showcasing its rain gear. The UK's Marks & Spencer installed virtual mirrors in some of its stores so that, just as on its website, customers can see what an eye shadow or lipstick would look like for them without having to physically put it on.[27]

Buoyed by research suggesting that the majority of purchase decisions are made inside the store, firms are increasingly recognizing the importance of influencing consumers at the point of purchase. This form of influence is accomplished through *shopper marketing*, where manufacturers and retailers use stocking, displays, and promotions to affect consumers actively shopping for a product.

Where and how a product is displayed and sold can have a significant effect on sales. A strong proponent of shopper marketing, Procter & Gamble calls the store encounter the "first moment of truth" (product use and consumption are the second).[28] P&G observed the power of displays in a Walmart project designed to boost sales of premium diapers such as Pampers. As the first baby center in which infant products—previously spread across the store—were united in a single aisle, the new shelf layout encouraged parents to linger longer and spend more money, increasing Pampers sales. Another successful promotion, this one for P&G's Cover Girl cosmetics brand, tapped into a fashion trend for a "smoky eye" look by developing kits for Walmart and connecting with potential customers on Facebook with instructions, blogs, and a photo gallery.

Retailers are also using technology to influence customers as they shop. Many retailers are employing mobile phone apps or "smart" shopping carts that help customers locate items in the store, find out about sales and special offers, and pay more easily. Some companies, such as Mondelēz, use "smart shelf" technology by putting, on shelves near the check-out, sensors that can detect the age and sex of a consumer and, by virtue of advanced analytics, target them with ads and promotions for a likely snack candidate on a video screen.

Managing Omnichannel Retailing

Based on a target market analysis, retailers must decide which channels to employ to reach their customers. Increasingly, the answer is multiple channels. Staples sells through its traditional retail brick-and-mortar channel, its own website (staples.com), virtual malls, and thousands of links on affiliated sites.

This increased reliance on multiple channels means that channels should be designed to work together effectively. Although some experts predicted otherwise, catalogs have actually grown in an internet world as more firms have revamped them to serve as branding devices and to complement online activity. Victoria's Secret's integrated multichannel approach of retail stores, catalog, and internet has played a key role in its brand development.

Victoria's Secret Victoria's Secret, purchased by Limited Brands in 1982, has become one of the most identifiable brands in retailing through skillful marketing of women's clothing, lingerie, and beauty products. After witnessing women buying expensive lingerie as fashion items from small boutiques in Europe, Limited Brands founder Leslie Wexner felt that a similar store model could work on a mass scale in the United States, even though such a store format was unlike anything the average shopper would have encountered at department stores. Wexner, however, had reason to believe U.S. women would relish the opportunity to have a European-style lingerie shopping experience with soft pink wallpaper, inviting fitting rooms, and attentive staff. "Women need underwear, but women want lingerie," he observed. Wexner's assumption proved correct: A little more than a decade after he bought the business, Victoria's Secret's average customer bought eight to 10 bras per year, compared with the national average of two. The growth of digital media and e-commerce forced Victoria's Secret to boost its online presence. During the past two decades, the company has reduced the number of physical catalogs it mails out from 450 million to 300 million copies, allocating more and more resources to digital means of communication.[29]

Source: Sorbis/Shutterstock

>> While Victoria's Secret still relies on retail locations and catalogs to market its European lingerie, the growth of digital media and e-commerce has induced it to boost its online presence.

We can distinguish among *brick-and-mortar* retailers, *online* (pure-click) retailers that have ventured into e-commerce without a physical retail location, and *omnichannel* (brick-and-click) companies that have both a physical and an online presence. We discuss these three types of retailers next.

BRICK-AND-MORTAR RETAILERS

Perhaps the best-known type of brick-and-mortar retailer is the department store. Japanese department stores such as Takashimaya and Mitsukoshi attract millions of shoppers each year and feature art galleries, restaurants, cooking classes, fitness clubs, and children's playgrounds. The most common types of brick-and-mortar retailers are summarized as follows:

Department stores such as JCPenney, Macy's, and Bloomingdale's carry several product lines.

Specialty stores such as The Limited, The Body Shop, and Sephora carry a single product line (or a few related product lines).

Supermarkets such as Kroger, Albertsons, and Safeway are large, low-cost, low-margin, high-volume, self-service stores designed to meet a family's total needs for food and household products.

Convenience stores such as 7-Eleven, Circle K, and Oxxo are small stores in residential areas, often open 24/7, carrying a limited line of high-turnover convenience products.

Drugstores such as CVS Pharmacy and Walgreens carry prescription drugs, health and beauty aids, and other personal-care, small durable, and miscellaneous items.

Mass merchandisers such as Walmart and Carrefour are low-price, low-margin, high-volume stores that sell routinely purchased food and household items, plus services (laundry, shoe repair, dry cleaning, check cashing).

Category killers such as The Home Depot, Staples, and PetSmart carry a narrow but deep assortment in one category.

Extreme value or hard-discount stores such as Aldi, Lidl, Dollar General, and Family Dollar carry a very limited merchandise mix offered at heavily discounted prices.

Off-price retailers such as TJ Maxx and factory outlets offer leftover goods, overruns, and irregular merchandise sold at less than retail.

Warehouse clubs such as Costco, Sam's Club, and BJ's offer larger quantities (e.g., mega-packs) at low prices.

Automatic vending offers a variety of merchandise, including impulse goods such as soft drinks, coffee, candy, newspapers, and magazines. Vending machines are found in factories, offices, large retail stores, gasoline stations, hotels, restaurants, and many other places. With more than 5 million units, Japan has the highest per capita coverage of vending machines in the world.

The three keys to retail success are often said to be "location, location, and location." Retailers can place their stores in any of the following locations.

Central business districts. The oldest and most heavily trafficked city areas, often known as "downtown."

Regional shopping centers. Large suburban malls containing 40 to 200 stores, typically featuring one or two nationally known anchor stores such as Macy's or Bloomingdale's or a combination of big-box stores such as PETCO, Designer Shoe Warehouse, or Bed Bath & Beyond, and a number of smaller stores.

Community shopping centers. Smaller malls with one anchor store and 20 to 40 smaller stores.

Shopping strips. A cluster of stores, usually in one long building, serving a neighborhood's needs for groceries, hardware, laundry, shoe repair, and dry cleaning.

A location within a larger store. Smaller concession spaces taken by well-known retailers such as McDonald's, Starbucks, Nathan's, and Dunkin' Donuts within larger stores, airports, or schools, or "store-within-a-store" specialty retailers located within a department store, such as Gucci within Neiman Marcus.

Stand-alone stores. Some retailers, such as Kohl's and JCPenney, are avoiding malls and shopping centers in favor of free-standing storefronts so that they are not connected directly to other retail stores.

Department store chains, oil companies, and fast-food franchisers exercise great care in selecting regions of the country in which to open outlets, then in selecting particular cities, and then particular sites. In view of the relationship between high traffic and high rents, retailers must determine the most advantageous locations for their outlets, using traffic counts, surveys of consumer shopping habits, and analysis of competitive locations.

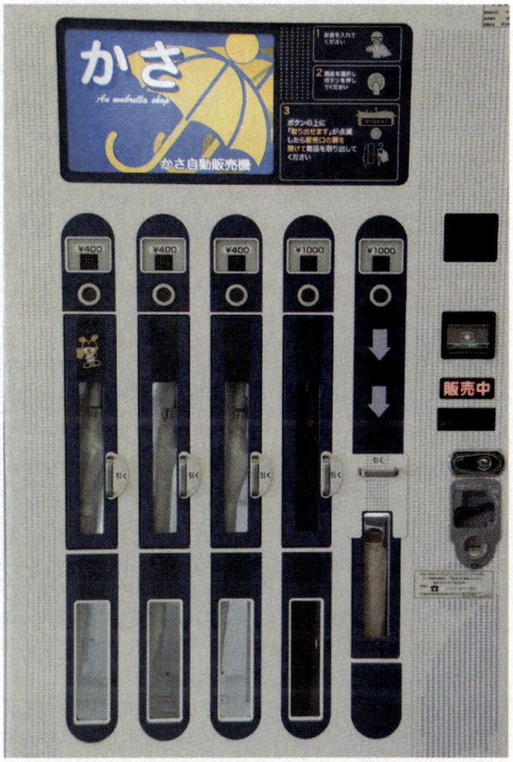

Source: VisualJapan/Alamy Stock Photo

>> Vending machines can be found almost anywhere in Japan, selling almost any kind of merchandise, including umbrellas.

ONLINE RETAILERS

Online retail sales have exploded, and it is easy to see why. Online retailers can predictably provide convenient, informative, and personalized experiences for vastly different types of consumers and businesses. By saving the cost of retail floor space, staff, and inventory, they can also profitably sell low-volume products to niche markets. Consider the success of online retailers such as Gilt.

Gilt During economic downturns, many designer brands find themselves with excess inventory that they badly needed to move. Third-party "flash-sales" sites, offering deep discounts for luxury products and other goods, for only a short period of time each day, allow them to do so in a controlled manner less likely to hurt their brands. Modeled in part after France's flash-sales pioneer Vente-Privée, Gilt was launched in November 2007 to sell fashionable women's clothing from top designer labels for up to 60 percent off, but on a limited-time basis and only to those who joined the online site. Members were alerted of deals and their deadlines via e-mails that conveyed a sense of immediacy and urgency. Adding luxury brands such as Theory and Louis Vuitton, the firm grew to more than 8 million members. As the economy improved, however, Gilt found itself challenged by dwindling inventory, growing competition from other sites, and its own aggressive expansion strategy, which included men's clothes, kids' products, home products, travel packages, and food. The company responded by focusing more on its core strength in women's fashion and developing tighter relationships with customers via personalized e-mails to announce its sales. In 2016, Gilt was acquired for $250 million by Hudson's Bay Company, owner of luxury department store chains Hudson's Bay, Lord & Taylor, and Saks Fifth Avenue.[30]

To drive traffic to a site, many firms employ affiliate marketing, paying online content providers to drive business to their brands' sites. Consumers often go online to try to find lower prices, but online retailers in fact compete on multiple dimensions: product assortment, convenience, shopping experience, speed of delivery, return policies, and ability to address problems when they occur. Consumer surveys suggest that the most significant inhibitors of online shopping are the absence of pleasurable experiences, social interaction, and personal consultation with a company representative.[31] Ensuring security and privacy online remains important.

>> Gilt, which began by selling discounted designer clothes and other products online for limited time periods, tweaked its business model when competition tightened by focusing on its strength in women's fashions and deepening its connection with customers via personalized e-mails.

Source: 360b/Alamy Stock Photo

Although business-to-consumer websites have attracted much attention in the media, even more activity is being conducted on business-to-business sites, which are changing the supplier–customer relationship in profound ways. In the past, buyers exerted a lot of effort to gather information about worldwide suppliers. Business-to-business sites make markets more efficient, giving buyers easy access to a great deal of information from a variety of sources including *supplier websites*; *infomediaries*, third parties that add value by aggregating information about alternatives; *market makers*, third parties that link buyers and sellers; and *customer communities*, where buyers can swap stories about suppliers' products and services.

Firms such as Alibaba—the largest of the business-to-business market makers—are using business-to-business auction sites, spot exchanges, online product catalogs, barter sites, and other online resources to obtain better prices. The effect of these business-to-business mechanisms is to make prices more transparent. For undifferentiated products, price pressure will increase. For highly differentiated products, buyers will gain a better picture of the items' true value. Suppliers of superior products will be able to offset price transparency with value transparency; suppliers of undifferentiated products will need to drive down their costs in order to compete.

OMNICHANNEL RETAILING

Although many brick-and-mortar companies once hesitated to open an e-commerce channel for fear of conflict with their channel partners, most have added the internet after seeing how much business is generated online. Even Procter & Gamble, which used traditional physical channels of distribution exclusively for years, is selling some big brands such as Tide, Pampers, and Olay online via its P&G e-store, in part to be able to examine consumer shopping habits more closely. As consumers are becoming more comfortable shopping online using their computers, tablets, and mobile phones, many traditional retailers, including Landmark Group, are also rapidly adopting the omnichannel format.

Landmark Group is one of the most popular and fastest growing retailers with a footprint of over 550 stores in India. Retail brands include fashion and apparel chains—Max, Lifestyle and Easybuy, grocery and supermarket chain—Spar, home retailer—Home Centre, among others. Max is a mono-brand which offers customers a one-stop shop for clothing, accessories and footwear needs for the entire family. Max has adopted an omnichannel distribution strategy to make its fashion products easily accessible across the country, including smaller cities. In addition to its 383 stores in 156 cities, Max ensures greater access with strong online presence enabling deliveries in 19,000 postal pin codes across India. Max's "Click and Collect" option allows customers to

>> The Landmark Group is prioritizing its digital strategy to give customers anytime/anywhere access to its products via mobile, online, and store sales, including warehouse-to-store shipping and digital payment. Digital applications such as Max Buddy and Spar Genie are enhancing the customers' shopping experience.

Source: Surya Nair / Alamy Stock Photo

shop online and collect from the nearest store offers convenience and faster access. Max has also partnered with Amazon and Myntra to serve a larger base of customers. Landmark introduced AI and IoT-based solutions such as Max Buddy, Self-Checkout Kiosk, and Mobile POS to create value for its customers and ensure a seamless shopping experience. Max Buddy is an in-store digital assistant which can be opened on a customer's mobile and offers personalized recommendations and fashion inputs based on customers' past purchases. It also enables customers to seamlessly look for "missing sizes" at the stores and fulfil them using its website. Features such as "self-checkout" enable customers to do contactless checkout while saving time. Max Fashion's 'voice search' for its online customers eases the shopping experience. To complement its in-store facilities, Lifestyle has introduced some unique features such as 'Fitting Room Assistance' and 'Visual Voice search' facilities for its online customers. Both the features are designed to elevate online shopping experience to the next level.[32] With its strategy to ensure Omnipresence with technology and personalized shopping experience, Landmark Group is expecting 40% of its sales from India by 2025.[33] Spar India which is the grocery and supermarket arm, has introduced Spar Genie which is an in-store digital assistant, and includes features such as a digital wallet, shopping list and offer discovery, to enable an enjoyable and easy in-store shopping experience for its customers. Each brand in the Landmark Group stable leverages its customer loyalty program – Landmark Rewards, to better understand its customers across their in-store and online behaviour and create a more personalized, omni-channel experience, in sync with the brand's product offerings.

In addition to combined brick-and-mortar and online retailers, omnichannel retailers include non-store retailers that have extended their reach to include online retailing in their portfolio. One example of such multichannel retailing includes direct-mail marketing, catalog marketing (Lands' End, L.L. Bean), telemarketing (1-800-FLOWERS), and infomercial direct-response marketing (HSN, QVC). Most of these companies have added e-commerce as another channel to connect with customers and generate sales.

The transition to omnichannel retailing was greatly facilitated by the COVID pandemic when many brick-and-mortar-only retailers found their sales revenues quickly evaporating as their customers became increasingly cautious of in-person shopping. Government regulations on business operations exacerbated the situation by further restricting consumers' access to retail stores. This dramatic change in the dynamics of shopping behavior forced many retailers to reevaluate their business models and embrace ecommerce as an integral aspect of their operations. While some companies such as Amazon, Walmart, and Target beefed up their internal delivery networks, many smaller size retailers relied on intermediaries such as Instacart and FreshDirect, GrubHub, DoorDash, Postmates, and UberEats to facilitate logistics and delivery.

Managing Private Labels

A **private label** (also called a reseller, store, or house brand) is a proprietary brand that retailers and wholesalers develop. Benetton, The Body Shop, and Marks & Spencer carry mostly own-brand merchandise. In grocery stores in Europe and Canada, store brands account for as much as 40 percent of the items sold. In Britain, roughly half of what Sainsbury's and Tesco, the largest food chains, sell is store-label goods. Germany and Spain are also European markets with a high percentage of private-label sales.

For many manufacturers, retailers are both collaborators and competitors. According to the Private Label Manufacturers' Association, store brands now account for one of every five items sold in U.S. supermarkets, drug chains, and mass merchandisers. In one study, seven of 10 shoppers believed the private-label products they bought were as good as, if not better than, their national-brand counterparts, and virtually every household purchases private-label brands from time to time.[34] The stakes in private-label marketing are high. A one-percentage-point shift from national brands to private labels in food and beverages is estimated to add $5.5 billion in revenue for supermarket chains.[35]

Private labels are rapidly gaining ground in a way that has many manufacturers of name brands running scared. Recessions increase private-label sales, and once some consumers switch to a private label, they don't always go back.[36] However, some experts believe 50 percent is the natural limit on how much private-label volume to carry because consumers prefer certain national brands, and many product categories are not feasible or attractive on a private-label basis. In supermarkets, private labels are big sellers in milk and cheese, bread and baked goods, medications and remedies, paper products, fresh produce, and packaged meats.[37]

Why do retailers sponsor their own brands? First, these brands can be more profitable. Retailers may be able to use manufacturers with excess capacity that will produce private-label goods at low cost. Other costs (such as research and development, advertising, sales promotion, and physical distribution) are also much lower, so private labels can generate a higher profit margin.[38] Retailers also develop exclusive store brands to differentiate themselves from competitors. Many price-sensitive consumers prefer store brands in certain categories. These preferences give retailers increased bargaining power with marketers of national brands.[39]

We should distinguish private-label or store brands from generics. *Generics* are unbranded, plainly packaged, less expensive versions of common products such as spaghetti, paper towels, and canned peaches. They offer standard or lower quality at a price that may be as much as 20 percent to 40 percent lower than nationally advertised brands and 10 percent to 20 percent lower than the retailer's private-label brands. The lower price is made possible by lower-cost labeling and packaging and minimal advertising, and sometimes by lower-quality ingredients.

Retailers are building better quality into their store brands and emphasizing attractive, innovative packaging. Supermarket retailers are adding premium store-brand items. When Kroger's switched to new vendors to supply higher-quality cheeses, meats, and veggies for its upscale private-label pizza, sales soared; the supermarket chain now owns 60 percent of the premium pizza market in its stores.[40] One of the most successful supermarket retailers with private labels is Canada's Loblaws.

Loblaws Since 1984, when its President's Choice line of foods made its debut, the term *private label* has brought Loblaws instantly to mind. The Toronto-based company's Decadent Chocolate Chip Cookie quickly became a Canadian leader and showed how innovative store brands could compete effectively with national brands by matching or even exceeding their quality. A finely tuned brand strategy for its premium President's Choice line and its no-frills, yellow-labeled

Source: Helen Sessions/Alamy Stock Photo

<< Loblaws' line of distinctively packaged President's Choice foods is indicative of the increasing quality and success of private-label brands.

No Name line has helped differentiate its stores and has built Loblaws into a powerhouse in Canada and the United States. The President's Choice line has become so successful that Loblaws is licensing it to noncompetitive retailers in other countries. To complete a "good, better, best" brand portfolio, Loblaws has also introduced an "affordable luxury" line of more than 200 President's Choice food products under a distinctive "Black Label" design. Each one—from eight-year-old cheddar and ginger-spiced chocolate sauce to bacon marmalade—is marketed with a story about where it's from, who produces it, and why it was chosen. To capitalize on the overall strength of its private labels, Loblaws launched a Food Network reality TV show, *Recipe to Riches*, where contestants compete to have their homemade recipes developed into an actual President's Choice product available to purchase the very next day at Loblaws stores.[41]

Although retailers get credit for the success of private labels, the growing power of store brands has also benefited from the weakening of national brands. Many consumers have become more price sensitive, a trend reinforced by the continuous barrage of coupons and price specials that has trained a generation to buy on price. Competing manufacturers and national retailers copy and duplicate the quality and features of the best brands in a category, reducing physical product differentiation. Moreover, by cutting marketing communication budgets, some firms have made it harder to create any intangible differences in brand image. A steady stream of brand extensions and line extensions has blurred brand identity at times and led to a confusing amount of product proliferation.

Bucking these trends, many manufacturers of national brands are fighting back. To stay a step ahead of store brands, leading brand marketers are investing significantly in research and development to bring out new brands, line extensions, features, and quality improvements. They are also investing in strong "pull" advertising programs to maintain high brand recognition and consumer preference and to overcome the in-store marketing advantage that private labels can enjoy.

Top-brand marketers also are seeking to partner with major mass distributors in a joint search for logistical economies and competitive strategies that produce savings for both sides. Cutting all unnecessary costs allows national brands to command a price premium, although price can't exceed consumers' perception of value.

Researchers offer four strategic recommendations for manufacturers to compete against or collaborate with private labels.[42]

- *Fight selectively* when manufacturers can win against private labels and add value for consumers, retailers, and shareholders. This typically occurs when the brand is number one or two in the category or occupies a premium niche position. Procter & Gamble rationalized its portfolio, selling off various brands such as Sunny Delight juice drink, Jif peanut butter, and Crisco shortening, in part so it could concentrate on strengthening its 20-plus brands with more than $1 billion in sales.

- *Partner effectively* by seeking win–win relationships with retailers through strategies that complement the retailer's private labels. Estée Lauder created four brands (American Beauty, Flirt, Good Skin, and Grassroots) exclusively for Kohl's to help the retailer generate volume and protect its more prestigious brands in the process. Manufacturers selling through hard discounters such as Lidl and Aldi have increased sales by finding new customers who have not previously bought the brand.
- *Innovate brilliantly* with new products to help beat private labels. Continuously launching incrementally new products keeps the manufacturer brands looking fresh, but the firm must also periodically launch radically new products and protect the intellectual property of all brands. Kraft doubled the number of its patent lawyers to make sure its innovations were legally protected as much as possible.
- *Create winning value propositions* by imbuing brands with symbolic imagery as well as functional quality that beats private labels. Too many manufacturer brands have let private labels equal them, and sometimes better them, on functional quality. In addition, to have a winning value proposition, marketers need to monitor pricing and ensure that perceived benefits equal the price premium.

Creating strong consumer demand is crucial. When Walmart decided to pull Hefty and Glad food bags from its shelves, selling just Ziploc and its own Great Value brand, Hefty and Glad stood to lose because the retail giant accounted for a third of their sales. When consumers complained about the loss of these and other brands and switched some of their shopping to other stores, Walmart relented and put Hefty and Glad back on the shelves.

Wholesaling

Wholesaling includes all the activities involved in selling goods or services to those who buy for resale or who make large purchases for business use. Wholesalers buy large quantities of goods from various producers or vendors, warehouse them, and resell them to retailers who, in turn, sell them to the general public.

THE BUSINESS OF WHOLESALING

Wholesalers differ from retailers in a number of ways. First, wholesalers pay less attention to promotion, atmosphere, and location because they are dealing with business customers rather than final consumers. Second, wholesale transactions are usually larger than retail transactions, and wholesalers usually cover a larger trade area than retailers. Third, wholesalers and retailers are subject to different legal regulations and taxes.

Based on their transactions with buyers and sellers, wholesalers can be divided into two main groups:

- **Merchant wholesalers** typically buy directly from the manufacturer, take title to the merchandise they handle, store the product, and then sell it to the customer. Merchant wholesalers vary in the level of service they offer. *Full-service wholesalers* can provide a vast array of supplementary functions, such as maintaining a sales force to promote the products, offering credit, making deliveries, and providing management assistance. In contrast, *limited-service wholesalers* offer few if any extra services and instead aim to offer lower prices on merchandise. For example, *cash and carry wholesalers* sell a limited line of fast-moving goods to small retailers in a no-frills environment, only for cash, and with limited return privileges or no-return policies.
- *Brokers and agents* differ from merchant wholesalers in that they typically do not take ownership of the goods they buy and sell. Instead, they arrange for the sale of goods between the merchant wholesaler and the retailer and receive a fee for the arrangement of the sale. Brokers bring buyers and sellers together and assist in negotiation; they are paid by the party hiring them—food brokers, real estate brokers, insurance brokers. Agents represent buyers or sellers on a more permanent basis and aim to facilitate buying and selling, on commission typically based on the selling price.

Wholesalers play a key role by serving as an intermediary between manufacturers and retailers. They are particularly important in industries with fragmented retail outlets, where they provide distribution and related services, helping to improve the effectiveness and cost efficiency of operations. Consider AmerisourceBergen—one of the largest wholesalers in the United States.

Source: Kristoffer Tripplaar/Alamy Stock Photo

<< Drug wholesaler AmerisourceBergen handles about 20 percent of all pharmaceuticals sold in the United States and also supplies Walgreens Boots Alliance, which operates 18,000 pharmacies throughout the world.

AmerisourceBergen Corporation AmerisourceBergen Corporation is an American drug wholesale company that distributes brand name and generic pharmaceuticals, as well as over-the-counter (OTC) health care products and equipment, to a wide variety of health care providers such as hospitals and health systems, retail pharmacies, mail-order facilities, physicians, clinics, and assisted-living centers. The company was formed in 2001 by the merger of Bergen Brunswig and AmeriSource Health Corporation—two of the largest U.S. wholesale drug companies. In 2013, AmerisourceBergen became the supplier for Walgreens Boots Alliance—one of the world's largest pharmacy retailers and drug distributors, which operates over 18,000 pharmacy stores around the world. The leading provider of specialty logistics for the biopharmaceutical industry, AmerisourceBergen has more than 150 offices and over 20,000 employees worldwide and ships over 3 million products each day. It is a market leader in pharmaceutical distribution, handling about 20 percent of all of the pharmaceuticals sold in the United States, with over $153 billion in annual revenue.[43]

KEY FUNCTIONS PERFORMED BY WHOLESALERS

Why do manufacturers not sell directly to retailers or final consumers? Why use wholesalers at all? In general, wholesalers can more efficiently perform one or more of the following functions.

- *Providing access to individual retailers.* Wholesalers' sales forces help manufacturers reach many small retailers and business customers at a relatively low cost. They have more contacts, and buyers often trust them more than they trust a distant manufacturer.
- *Buying and assortment building.* Wholesalers are able to select items and build the assortments their customers need, saving them considerable time, money, and effort.
- *Bulk breaking.* Wholesalers achieve savings for their customers by buying large carload lots and breaking the bulk into smaller units.
- *Warehousing.* Wholesalers hold inventories, thereby reducing inventory costs and risks to suppliers and customers.
- *Transportation.* Wholesalers can often provide quicker delivery to buyers because they are closer to the buyers.
- *Financing.* Wholesalers finance customers by granting credit, and they finance suppliers by ordering early and paying bills on time.
- *Risk bearing.* Wholesalers absorb some risk by taking title to goods and bearing the cost of theft, damage, spoilage, and obsolescence.
- *Market research.* Wholesalers provide both suppliers and customers with information about competitors' activities, such as new products and price developments.

- *Management services and consulting.* Wholesalers often help retailers improve their operations by training sales clerks, helping with store layouts and displays, and setting up accounting and inventory-control systems. They may help industrial customers by offering training and technical services.

Wholesaler–distributors have faced mounting pressure in recent years from new sources of competition, including digital platforms such as Alibaba, demanding customers, new technologies, and more direct-buying programs by large industrial, institutional, and retail buyers. Manufacturers' major complaints against wholesalers are that they do not aggressively promote the manufacturer's product line and act more like order takers; that they do not carry enough inventory and therefore do not fill customers' orders fast enough; that they do not supply the manufacturer with up-to-date market, customer, and competitive information; and that they charge too much for their services.

Savvy wholesalers have rallied to the challenge and adapted their services to meet their suppliers' and target customers' changing needs. They recognize that they must add value to the channel. Arrow Electronics has done just that.

Arrow Electronics Arrow Electronics is a global wholesaler of electronics and office products. It serves as a supply channel partner for more than 150,000 original-equipment manufacturers, value-added resellers, contract manufacturers, and commercial customers through a global network. Arrow maintains over 300 sales facilities and 45 distribution and value-added centers, serving over 80 countries. With huge contract manufacturers buying more parts directly from suppliers, however, distributors like Arrow are being squeezed out. To better compete, the company has embraced services, providing financing, on-site inventory management, parts-tracking software, and chip programming.[44]

Wholesalers have worked to increase asset productivity by better managing inventories and receivables. They are also reducing operating costs by investing in more advanced information systems, materials-handling technology, and digital technologies. Finally, they are improving their strategic decisions about target markets, product assortment and services, price, communication, and distribution.

The wholesaling industry remains vulnerable to one of the most enduring trends: fierce resistance to price increases and the winnowing out of suppliers based on cost and quality. The trend toward vertical integration, in which manufacturers try to control or own their intermediaries, is still strong.

marketing INSIGHT

Managing the Price Image of a Retailer

Price image reflects the general perception that consumers have about the level of prices at a given retailer. For example, Walmart is often regarded as being rather inexpensive, whereas Target is usually considered to be moderately priced. Price image differs from price, which is quantitatively expressed; price image is qualitative in nature. This means that consumers regard a retailer's pricing in categorical terms such as "expensive" or "inexpensive." Price image resides in the minds of the buyers; thus, it is based on consumers' perception of prices at a particular retailer compared to other retailers and may not be an accurate reflection of the actual level of a retailer's prices.

Many managers mistakenly believe that price image is based solely on the prices within a specific store and that managing price image is as simple as adjusting the prices of items the store carries. This results in the theory that a retailer can lower its price image by lowering the prices of items in its assortment.

However, this method of resetting price image has not proved effective. Low or high prices are an important factor in the formation of a retailer's price image, but prices are not the only things that consumers consider when forming a judgment about price image. Figure 16.1 depicts the key drivers of price image and their related impact on consumer behavior.

(continued)

marketing insight *(continued)*

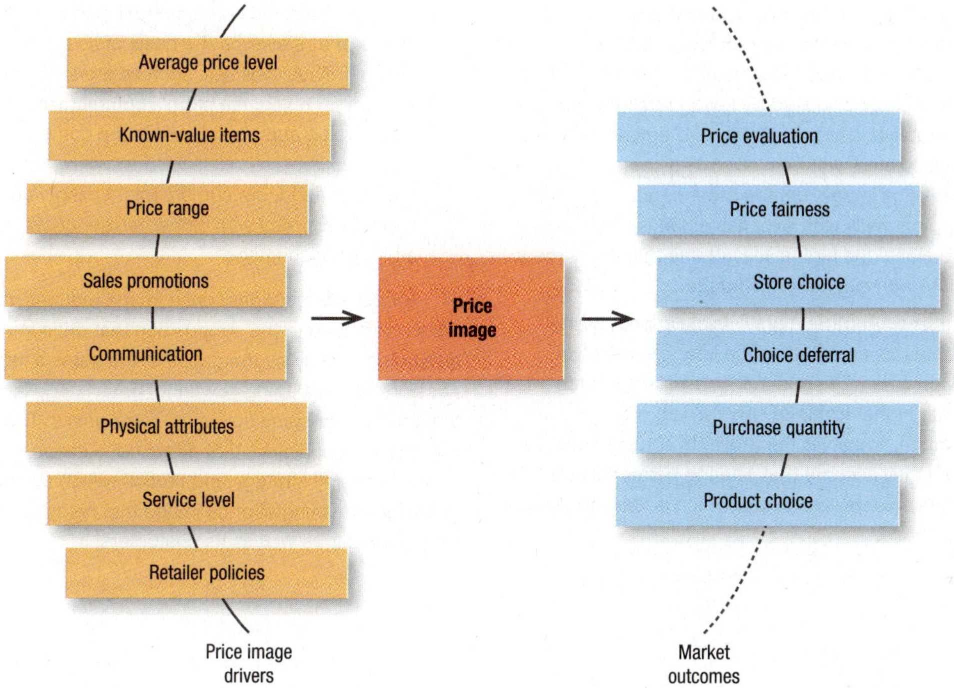

FIGURE **16.1**

Price Image Drivers and Market Outcomes

Source: Alexander Chernev, *Strategic Marketing Management: Theory and Practice* (Chicago, IL: Cerebellum Press, 2019).

- *Average price level.* Price image does indeed hinge on the actual prices of the items carried by a particular retailer, although not entirely. A store in which prices are substantially above those of its competitors will find it difficult to convince customers that it is not high priced, regardless of other measures it may take to change its price image.
- *Known-value items.* Consumers typically do not examine all prices at a store; instead, they tend to focus on items whose prices they are familiar with, which are referred to as known-value or signpost items. Because shoppers are aware of the prices for these items at other stores, they use them to determine whether or not a particular price is competitive. Known-value items usually fall into the category of frequently purchased items like milk, soda, and snacks, allowing consumers to readily compare prices across different stores.
- *Price range.* Consumers form an assessment of price image not just from the average level of prices at a retailer, but also from the range of prices within the store. If, in addition to commonly purchased known-value items, a retailer carries a few extremely high-priced items, that retailer is likely to have a higher price image than a retailer that carries a few extremely low-priced items along with the most commonly purchased items.
- *Sales promotions.* Consumers' price image might also be affected by how prices vary over time, particularly because of sales promotions. No consistent empirical evidence exists to support the conventional wisdom suggesting that everyday low pricing (EDLP) conveys a lower price image to consumers than high–low (HiLo) pricing, with its temporary deep discounts on high-priced items. Actually, HiLo pricing can often elicit a lower price image than EDLP, even when the average price level is the same.
- *Price communication.* Because shoppers can't examine all prices of all items at all retailers, it is extremely important for retailers to effectively communicate their prices to consumers, enabling them to form a more accurate price image. Consumers' price sensitivity tends to be heightened by price communication that increases their focus on price. Furthermore, communication that underscores savings (such as by providing reference prices or enumerating the money saved) encourages the formation of a low price image.

(continued)

marketing insight *(continued)*

- *Physical attributes.* The physical features of a retailer can impact price image by conveying a message about store costs and sales volume. A store located in a prime area populated by luxury retailers and featuring exquisite décor and high-end amenities is likely to be associated with high operating costs that signal a higher price image. On the other hand, large stores in shopping malls with expansive parking lots are likely to signal the high sales volume that consumers associate with a lower price image.
- *Service level.* Another highly visible aspect that contributes to a retailer's price image is the level of service offered. In general, consumers tend to associate higher levels of service with a higher price image, whatever the retailer's actual prices, because they assume that offering better service increases the retailer's costs, which is likely to elevate retailer prices.
- *Store policies.* Customers might also form their price image of a retailer on the basis of its price-related policies. Thus, policies, such as a price-match guarantee, that reveal the store's commitment to customer value and confidence in the competitiveness of its prices, are likely to lead to a lower price image. On the other hand, consumers might associate a generous return policy with higher retailer costs, leading to a higher price image.

Effectively managing price image requires managers to look beyond the supposition that price image is determined solely by the prices of the items a retailer carries and that managing (lowering) price image is merely a matter of managing (lowering) retail prices. Thoughtful alignment of *all* factors that affect price image with the retailer's overall strategy and tactics will go far toward building a meaningful price image that helps create value for the retailer as well as its customers.[45]

summary

1. *Retailing* includes all the activities involved in selling goods or services directly to final consumers for personal, nonbusiness use. Any organization selling to final consumers—whether it is a manufacturer, wholesaler, or retailer—is doing retailing, regardless of how and where the goods or services are sold.
2. The retail market is very dynamic, and a number of new types of competitors and competition have emerged in recent years. The important *developments in retailing* include the emergence of new retail forms and combinations; retailer consolidation; the growth of mobile, omnichannel, and fast retailing; the increasing role of technology in retailing; and the decline of middle-market retailers.
3. Key *retailing decisions* include identifying the target market, selecting the product assortment; developing procurement, determining the types and level of services to be offered, designing the store atmosphere and experiences, setting the prices, defining the incentives, and managing communication.
4. Based on the degree to which they have established a physical presence, we can distinguish among *brick-and-mortar* retailers, *online* retailers that engage in e-commerce without a physical retail location, and *omnichannel* companies that have both a physical and an online presence. Managing both online and offline channels has become a priority for many retailers.
5. *Private labels* are brands developed and managed by retailers and wholesalers. Private labels are typically (but not always) priced lower than national brands. Retailers sponsor their own brands because it enables them to differentiate themselves from competitors, while at the same time reaching price-sensitive consumers. Because of lower research and development, advertising, sales promotion, and physical distribution costs, private labels can also generate a higher profit margin.
6. *Wholesaling* includes all the activities involved in selling goods or services to those who buy for resale or business use. Wholesalers can perform functions better and more cost effectively than the manufacturer can. These functions include selling and promoting, buying and assortment building, bulk breaking, warehousing, transportation, financing, risk bearing, dissemination of market information, and provision of management services and consulting.
7. Like retailers, wholesalers must decide on target markets, product assortment and services, price, promotion, and place. The most successful are those that adapt their services to meet suppliers' and target customers' needs.

marketing SPOTLIGHT

Uniqlo

Source: mauritius images GmbH/Alamy Stock Photo

Uniqlo is a Japanese casual wear designer, manufacturer, and retailer. The name is a portmanteau that combines the words *unique* and *clothing*, which reflects the company's philosophy of creating simple yet stylish casual clothing. Uniqlo has quickly developed a presence around the globe, expanding to over 1,500 stores worldwide and competing with Zara and H&M to become the world's largest fashion retailer. In 2017, Uniqlo reported over $7 billion in revenue.

Founder Tadashi Yanai inherited his father's chain of tailoring stores in Ube, Yamaguchi, in 1972. Inspired by large clothing chains in Europe and the United States, Yanai saw potential in the Japanese casual wear market and changed his family's business strategy from tailoring to selling casual clothing at low cost. After becoming company president in 1984, Yanai opened the first "Unique Clothing Warehouse" in Naka-ku, Hiroshima, which later was rebranded as Uniqlo. One of Uniqlo's first business challenges was to overcome customer perception. Because Uniqlo sold casual clothing at low cost, people believed that its garments were of low quality. It wasn't until 1998, when Uniqlo opened a three-story store in Harajuku, one of Tokyo's most popular shopping destinations, that consumer perception changed. Consumers noticed that Uniqlo was selling high-quality fleece jackets at affordable prices. This precipitated a complete shift in customer perception of the brand—from cheap apparel to high-quality, affordable casual wear. By the end of 1998, Uniqlo had expanded to over 300 stores across Japan.

Compared to other popular clothing retailers, Uniqlo's brand philosophy takes a very simple and inclusive approach. Its brand message is that "Uniqlo is a modern Japanese company that inspires the world to dress casual." Unlike clothing retailers such as Zara and H&M, Uniqlo does not seek to follow fashion trends. Instead, Uniqlo designs and markets its clothing to be accessible and universal, a key ingredient in the company's success. This is embodied in Uniqlo's brand motto, "Made for All." Uniqlo has designed its clothing to appeal to all consumers, regardless of age, ethnicity, or gender. The clothing is basic but still allows wearers to express their own sense of style by pairing it with other garments and accessories.

Uniqlo creates products for three primary segments: women, men, and children, including babies. In each of these three segments, Uniqlo sells five different types of clothing: outerwear, tops, bottoms, inner-wear, and home-wear. In the outerwear category, Uniqlo is known for its Ultra-Light Down jacket, which is light and thin but still provides excellent insulation. Tops include mainly basic dresses, blouses, T-shirts, polos, and sweaters. Uniqlo's bottoms include pants, shorts, skirts, and leggings. Uniqlo offers designer collections in the tops and bottoms categories, for those seeking a more stylish flair to their wardrobes. Most Uniqlo inner-wear and home-wear is specifically designed with comfort in mind, varying in breathability and warmth.

Another aspect of Uniqlo's success is its clothing design and innovation. Yanai frequently affirms that Uniqlo is not a fashion company, but rather a technology company. Uniqlo has invested in improving the performance of its clothes through technological innovations. HeatTech fabric creates heat from moisture and locks in the heat with air pockets embedded in the fabric. AIRism fabric is light and stretchy and maintains breathability across many temperatures. Lifewear crosses sportswear and casual wear and is designed to be an everyday piece of clothing. By branding these fabric innovations and emphasizing superior performance and functionality, Uniqlo distinguishes its clothing from that of other low-cost value retailers.

Yet another factor in Uniqlo's success is that it is able to sell functional and quality clothing at low prices. After discovering that many of the popular foreign clothing chains (such as Gap and Benetton) were vertically integrated, Tadashi Yanai followed suit to take full control of product design, production, and retailing. Fast-fashion retailers design their supply chain to respond to rapidly changing fashion trends in as little as two weeks. Uniqlo instead plans its production of essentials and basics months in advance. The company aligns production with its marketing campaigns to adjust quantities based on consumer demand, and staff members visit production plants to ensure that new clothes are of Uniqlo quality.

To build its brand, Uniqlo uses many different methods beyond traditional TV commercials and flyers. One approach is a strong emphasis on the in-store experience. Bright lights, combined with neatly stacked displays and efficient organization, convey Uniqlo's message of simplicity and accessibility. Digital screens that explain the benefits of Uniqlo's innovations and styles are strategically placed in open areas. Uniqlo has also committed to creating distinct customer service. It trains its in-store staff for three months, significantly longer than the industry average. Yanai also is planning the launch of Uniqlo University, where more than

(*continued*)

1,500 managers will be trained and sent out across the globe every year. Employees are trained to go out of their way to interact with customers and help them find the right product, using six standard phrases that include "Did you find everything you were looking for?" and "Let me know if you need anything. My name is _________." Greeters at the entrances of stores wish customers a warm welcome and a friendly goodbye.

Uniqlo's strong brand positioning and "Made for All" philosophy—reflected in its marketing, design, operations, and service—have helped make the company a giant in global clothing retailing and one of the world's most valuable clothing retailers.[46]

Questions

1. What are the key aspects of Uniqlo's customer value proposition?
2. Should Uniqlo stay vertically integrated? Or should it rely more heavily on outsourcing to improve flexibility and achieve economies of scale?
3. What role does the company culture play in delivering superior customer experience?

marketing SPOTLIGHT

Croma

Croma, launched in 2006, is owned and operated by Tata's Infiniti Retail that records as India's first large format specialist retail chain for electronic appliances and gadgets. In its journey of more than a decade, Croma became one of the most sought electronic retail outlets known for its tech-savvy staff, customer relationship management, omnichannel presence, value-added pricing, strategic partnerships, and customized product offerings with over 6,000 products across 200 brands, 150+ stores spread across 40+ cities in India.[47]

Croma has undergone major shifts in its business model and strategic management. It has grown from a brick-and-mortar company to a huge network with omnipresence, to compete with major e-commerce companies like Amazon. In

Source: Paulose NK.shutterstock.com

(continued)

2008, Croma launched its own-labelled products—air-conditioners, televisions, refrigerators, home appliances, digital accessories like earphones—at affordable prices, targeting the young crowd below 30 years. The company reported 300 percent growth in its private label product portfolio in a span of three years (2015–2018).[48]

Year 2018 marked the comeback for Croma after experiencing major losses in 2016 due to fierce competition by the e-commerce players offering a huge range of products at steeply discounted prices. Croma now entered the market with a much stronger network and a differentiated omni-channel approach including strategic product partnerships and improved customer support services.

This approach helped the company match up to the changing needs and preferences of the consumers in the digital era. With its prime focus to improve the overall customer shopping experience, Croma enhanced its service-offerings through all possible means such as online service portal, mobile applications and retail outlets.

Croma has changed its targeting and promotional strategy with social media campaigns and promotions to establish better connect with the customers and improve visibility. It also helped them to understand the needs and concerns of its target customers. Croma revamped its store design, interiors, layout and display with enhanced focus on high-selling products like smart phones and sound systems, to increase the footfall and improve the conversion rate. The display areas of Croma are now transformed as 'interactive space', where customers can experience and engage with the products. As a result, Croma reported an increase in conversion rate from 13% in 2017 to 16% in 2018.

With its omnichannel model, Croma leveraged digital marketing to improve its market share through a value-added pricing strategy. Unlike the discounted pricing offered by e-commerce players, Croma decided to stick to its value-add pricing approach. It offers high quality products with added benefits like free installation and post purchase services, easy finance options, extended warranty, buyback facility and customized value-added offerings etc. With its 24×7 support system, Croma has emerged as one of the most trusted electronics brands in India.

To grab exclusive selling rights and other competitive perks from companies, Croma signed up partnerships with several leading brands—Hitachi, Samsung and Apple. Croma offers dynamic and exclusive display for their products with trained and knowledgeable staff. In turn, Croma gets exclusive sales rights for products along with customization and several value-added features. A few specific models and colors from these partner brands are sold exclusively at Croma stores. Its partnership for exclusive product offerings provides Croma an advantage as well as stability.

With its smart product display, personalized promotions, omni channel model and strategic partnership, Croma has emerged as one of the leading specialist retail stores for electronics and digital gadgets in India. The company continues to strive for leadership by providing value-added product offerings complemented with personalized post-purchase customer support services.[49]

Questions

1. What were the keys to Croma's success? What are the challenges it faces in today's retail environment?
2. How else can Croma compete against both retail competitors like Reliance Digital and online competitors like Amazon and Flipkart?
3. Should Croma focus on expanding brand partnerships? What are the pros and cons of this approach?

CHAPTER 17

Driving Growth in Competitive Markets

Maruti Suzuki, which had introduced many automotive "firsts" since its founding looked to innovation to maintain its leadership position. Its recently launched Celerio will be India's most fuel efficient car.

Source: © MARUTI SUZUKI INDIA LIMITED,used with permission

Growth is essential for the success of any firm. To be a long-term market leader is the goal of any marketer. Today's challenging marketing circumstances often dictate that companies frequently reformulate their marketing strategies and offerings. Economic conditions change, competitors launch new assaults, and buyer interest and requirements evolve. Through the years, as an interesting competitive battle has been fought between car manufacturers, Maruti Suzuki has sought to differentiate its vehicles to ensure sustained growth.

>>> Maruti Suzuki, India's leading automotive player, has played a stellar role in transforming the passenger cars market throughout its innovation-led growth journey of nearly four decades. A joint venture between the Japanese auto-giant – Suzuki Motor Corporation and the Government of India, the company kicked off in 1981 as a small-car manufacturing company. In 1983 it launched a hatchback car, Maruti 800. Designed and priced for the middle-class Indian families of the 1980's seeking ownership of a value-for-money car, Maruti 800 – people's car, became the most popular choice. With its compact design and high quality at an affordable price, great fuel-efficiency and low running costs, Maruti 800 proved to be a best seller and catapulted the company to a leadership position. The company continued to gain market share by expanding its dealership and service networks and launching new flagship brands – Alto and Wagon R. In 2003, the company's partnership

with State Bank of India, the largest Indian bank with over 25,000 branches, to offer car loans with tenure up to 7 years, effectively reduced the price barriers for first-time car buyers.[1] Another innovative outreach include launching a 24×7 call center – `Anytime Maruti', to provide convenience to customers. Its vast network of service centers across India makes after-sales service accessible to customers even in smaller cities and towns as well. Ranked numero-uno for 17 consecutive years in J D Power's Customer Service study for after-sales service, underlines the company's strong customer focus and service orientation.[2] Maruti Suzuki has successfully become one of the most trusted Indian brands known for its great products, seamless services, and 24×7 support. In recent years, the company launched its premium models – Ciaz, S-Cross, XL6 and Baleno, – that are exclusively retailed through its upmarket `NEXA' outlets. Driven by innovation, these modern outlets aspire to create exciting experiences for customers. The success of these new brands helped Maruti Suzuki create a niche in the premium car segment. Balancing its traditional product portfolio of small and mid-size cars through newly launched premium cars, Maruti Suzuki leads with over 50% market share in India, leveraging its customer-oriented and innovation-driven growth strategy.[3] The company has outlined its future plan to continue its focus on research and development in commercializing new green technology categories like CNG, mini-Hybrid systems and Electric Vehicles.[4]

This chapter examines growth, the role competition plays, and how marketers can best manage their brands given their market position and stage of the product life cycle. Competition grows more intense every year. Global competitors are eager to enter new markets, online competitors seek cost-efficient ways to expand distribution, private-label and store brands offer low-price alternatives, and brand extensions are moving mega-brands into new categories. For these reasons and more, product and brand fortunes change over time, and marketers must respond accordingly.

Assessing Growth Opportunities

Assessing growth opportunities includes planning new businesses, downsizing, and terminating older businesses. If there is a gap between future desired sales and projected sales, corporate management will need to develop or acquire new businesses to fill it.

There are two main considerations in assessing growth opportunities. The first concerns the types of products and markets a company should focus on. The second involves the ways in which a company can manage its product–market growth strategy over time. We discuss these options in the following sections.

PRODUCT–MARKET GROWTH STRATEGIES

Corporate management should constantly review opportunities for improving existing businesses. One popular framework is the **Product–Market Growth framework**, also known as the Ansoff matrix. It outlines four key sales-growth strategies that tie the company's customer segments to opportunities for product development.[5] The framework evaluates the strategic growth opportunities

Learning Objectives After reading this chapter you should be able to:

17.1 Summarize how a company assesses its growth opportunities.

17.2 Explain how a company gains market position.

17.3 Summarize the strategies a company can use to defend its market position.

17.4 Discuss the key product-cycle marketing strategies.

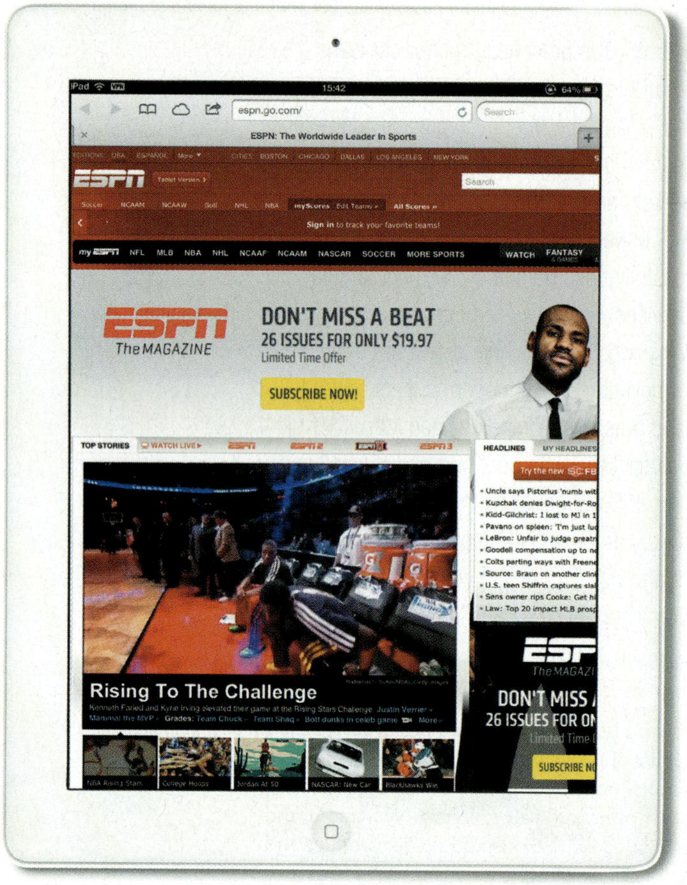

Source: IanDagnall Computing/Alamy Stock Photo

>> A vow to expand its brand by being wherever fans watched, read about, and discussed sports took ESPN from a regional broadcaster to the biggest name in sports, operating a variety of media and other businesses in nearly 200 countries and territories.

for a firm in terms of current and new products and markets.

The company first considers whether it could gain more market share with its current products in their current markets using a market-penetration strategy. Next, it considers whether it can find or develop new markets for its current products using a market-development strategy. Then it considers whether it can develop new products for its current markets with a product-development strategy. Later, the firm will also review opportunities to develop new products for new markets through a diversification strategy. The four strategies that make up the Product–Market Growth framework are illustrated in Figure 17.1.

Consider how ESPN has pursued a variety of growth opportunities.

The **market-penetration strategy**, which involves growing sales of the company's current offerings to its existing customers, is often the easiest to implement. To implement this strategy, the company could try to encourage its customers to buy more by demonstrating the benefits of its products. Alternatively, it might identify new uses for its current products and educate customers to use these products to fulfill different needs.

How can a company use a **market-development strategy**? First, it might try to identify potential user groups in the current sales areas. If it has been selling only to consumer markets, it might go after office and factory markets. Second, it might seek additional distribution channels by adding mass merchandising or online channels. Third, the company might sell in new locations in its home country or abroad.

ESPN Through its singular focus on sports programming and news, ESPN grew from a small regional broadcaster into the biggest name in sports. In the early 1990s, the company crafted a well-thought-out plan: Wherever sports fans watched, read, and discussed sports, ESPN would be there. It pursued this strategy by expanding its brand, and it now encompasses 10 cable channels, a magazine, a few restaurants (ESPN Zone), more than 600 local radio affiliates, original movies and television series, book publishing, a sports merchandise catalog and online store, music and video games, and a mobile service. ESPN International partly or wholly owns multiple television networks outside the United States and a variety of additional businesses that reach sports fans in more than 200 countries and territories across all seven continents. Now owned by The Walt Disney Company and Hearst Communications, ESPN contributes a significant portion of Disney's total cable network revenues.[6]

FIGURE **17.1**
The Product–Market Growth Framework

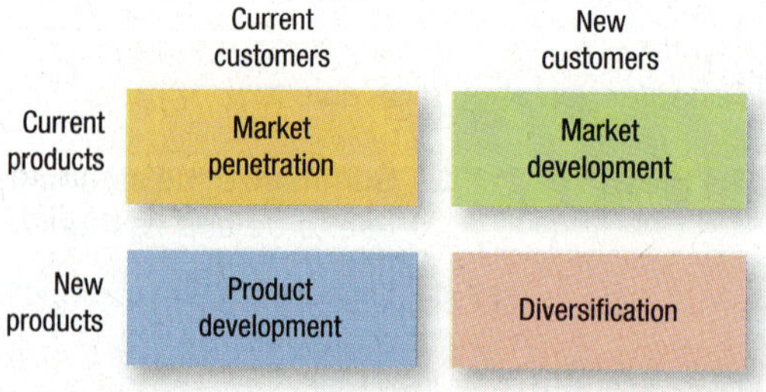

Management should also consider a **product-development strategy**. Thus, a company could develop new product features, offer different sets of benefits at different price tiers, or research an alternative technology to develop a viable substitute for its current products.

Finally, growth via a **diversification strategy** makes sense when good opportunities exist outside the present businesses—i.e., the industry is highly attractive, and the company has the right mix of business strengths to succeed. From its origins as an animated film producer, The Walt Disney Company has moved into licensing characters for merchandised goods, publishing general-interest fiction under the Hyperion imprint, entering the broadcast industry with its own Disney Channel as well as ABC and ESPN, developing theme parks and vacation and resort properties, and offering cruise and commercial theatre experiences.

Several types of diversification are possible. First, the company could choose a concentric strategy and seek new products that have technological or marketing synergies with existing product lines, even though they appeal to a different group of customers. Second, it might use a horizontal strategy and produce complementary products, even though they might require a different manufacturing process. Finally, the company might seek new businesses with no relationship to its current technology, products, or markets, adopting a conglomerate strategy.

GROWTH THROUGH MERGERS AND ACQUISITIONS

A company can grow in two ways: by increasing output and enhancing revenues and profits internally (an approach that is commonly referred to as **organic growth**) or by relying on mergers and acquisitions. Market-penetration and market-development strategies typically follow the path of organic growth, whereas product development and diversification can involve both organic growth and growth by mergers and acquisitions. Here we focus on using mergers and acquisitions to grow the company's market position.

A business can increase sales and profits through backward, forward, or horizontal integration within its industry. Merck formed joint ventures as far back as 1989 with Johnson & Johnson to sell over-the-counter pharmaceuticals and then, in 1991, with DuPont to expand basic research. In 1997, Merck and Rhône-Poulenc S.A. (now Sanofi S.A.) combined their animal health and poultry genetics businesses to form Merial Limited, a fully integrated animal health company. Merck then acquired Schering-Plough in 2009, Cubist Pharmaceuticals in 2014, Afferent Pharmaceuticals in 2016, and Antelliq in 2018.[7]

Horizontal mergers and alliances don't always work out. The merger between Sears and Kmart didn't solve either retailer's problems. Nextel Communications Inc. merged with Sprint in 2005 in what was considered one of the worst mergers of the decade, in part because of their incompatible networks.[8] In the same vein, United's merger with Continental made sense strategically and financially, but logistical problems seemed endless because the two airlines ran their businesses in very different ways, from boarding procedures to the manner in which they brought planes into the gate.

How might a company use mergers and acquisitions to grow its business? The company might acquire one or more of its suppliers to gain more control or generate more profit through backward integration. It might acquire some wholesalers or retailers, especially if they are highly profitable, in forward integration. Finally, the company might acquire one or more competitors, provided the government does not bar this horizontal integration.[9] However, these new sources may not deliver the desired sales volume. In that case, the company must consider diversification.

In addition to considering new market opportunities, a company must carefully prune, harvest, or divest itself of tired old businesses to release needed resources for other uses and reduce costs. To focus on its travel and credit card operations, American Express spun off American Express Financial Advisors, which provided insurance, mutual funds, investment advice, and brokerage and asset-management services (it was renamed Ameriprise Financial). American International Group (AIG) agreed to sell two of its subunits—American General Indemnity Co. and American General Property Insurance Co.—to White Mountains Insurance Group as part of a long-term growth strategy to discard redundant assets and focus on its core operations.

The more diversified a company's business portfolio is, the greater the likelihood that at some point it will need to downsize its business operations and/or divest itself of business units. Thus, to streamline its business and meet its current financial obligations, GE divested itself of multiple divisions, including its transportation-finance unit sold to Canada's Bank of Montréal, its appliance division sold to Chinese consumer electronics and home appliances company Haier Group, and its Industrial Solutions Business sold to the Swiss–Swedish multinational conglomerate ABB. GE also agreed to sell its distributed power unit to private equity firm Advent and merged its transportation business, which includes its locomotive-manufacturing operations, with locomotive manufacturer Wabtec.

GROWTH THROUGH INNOVATION AND IMITATION

Theodore Levitt argues that a strategy of *product imitation* might be as profitable as a strategy of *product innovation.*[10] In "innovative imitation," as he calls it, the innovator bears the expense of developing the new product, getting it into distribution, and informing and educating the market. The reward for all this work and risk is normally market leadership. However, another firm can come along and copy or improve on the new product. Although it may not overtake the leader, the follower can achieve high profits because it did not bear any of the innovation expense.

Many companies prefer to follow rather than challenge the market leader. Patterns of "conscious parallelism" are common in capital-intensive, homogeneous-product industries such as steel, fertilizers, and chemicals. The opportunities for product differentiation and image differentiation are low, service quality is comparable, and price sensitivity runs high. The mood in these industries is against short-run grabs for market share because that only provokes retaliation. Instead, most firms present similar offers to buyers, usually by copying the leader. Market shares show high stability.

That's not to say market followers lack strategies. They must know how to hold current customers and win a fair share of new ones. Each follower tries to bring distinctive advantages to its target market—location, services, financing—while defensively keeping its manufacturing costs low and its product quality and services high. It must also enter new markets as they open up.

Followers must define a growth path, but one that doesn't invite competitive retaliation. We distinguish three broad strategies:

- *Cloner.* The cloner emulates the leader's products, name, and packaging with slight variations. Technology firms are often accused of being cloners: Similar-sounding knockoffs copy mobile-messaging app maker WhatsApp's products, and Berlin-based Rocket Internet has copied competitors' business models and attempted to out-execute them.[11] Ralston Foods, now owned by ConAgra, sells imitations of name-brand cereals in look-alike boxes as part of its "Value+Brands" platform. Its Apple Cinnamon Tasteeos (versus Cheerios), Cocoa Crunchies (versus Cocoa Puffs), and Corn Biscuits (versus Corn Chex) take aim at successful General Mills brands, but with much lower price points.[12]
- *Imitator.* The imitator copies some things from the leader but differentiates on packaging, advertising, pricing, or location. The leader doesn't mind as long as the imitator doesn't attack aggressively. Fernandez Pujals grew up in Fort Lauderdale, Florida, and took Domino's pizza home delivery idea to Spain, where he borrowed $80,000 to open his first store in Madrid. His Telepizza chain operates more than 1600 locations including company stores and franchise stores in twenty-three countries.[13]
- *Adapter.* The adapter takes the leader's products and adapts or improves them. The adapter may choose to sell to different markets, but often it grows into a future challenger, as many Japanese firms have done after improving products developed elsewhere.

Note that these three follower strategies are *not* to be confused with illegal and unethical follower strategies. Counterfeiters duplicate the leader's product and packages and sell them on the black market or through disreputable dealers. High-tech firms like Apple and luxury brands like Rolex have been plagued by the counterfeiter problem for years, especially in Asia. Pharmaceutical counterfeits have become an enormous and potentially lethal $75 billion business. Unregulated, drug fakes have been found to contain traces of chalk, brick dust, paint, and even pesticides.[14]

Followership is often a rewarding path. Some follower firms have found success, but in another industry. Les Wexner, who used to run Limited Brands and its Victoria's Secret lingerie retailer, fully embraces imitation. One month a year, he travels the world looking for ideas he can borrow from other companies ranging from airlines to consumer-goods makers.[15]

Gaining Market Position

An important function of marketing is to drive the growth of company sales and revenue. Good marketing can help to attract consumers, induce them to try out the company's products, and promote word of mouth and diffusion.

A company's **market position** can be defined on three dimensions:

- *Share of market.* Market share is measured by the company's sales revenue or the number of company units sold relative to the total revenue or total units sold in a specific market.

Source: Boris Fedorenko/Alamy Stock Photo

<< Blue-chip company Xerox has avoided complacency through the years, transforming itself from a copier company to one offering a broad range of imaging and printing products, along with business-related services that help company clients reduce costs.

- *Share of mind.* This is defined by the percentage of customers who regard the company as the first company that comes to mind in a specific industry.
- *Share of heart.* The percentage of customers who name the company as the company from which they would prefer to buy a specific product.

Market share typically reflects the share of mind and heart. We could generalize as follows: *Companies that make steady gains in mind share and heart share will inevitably make gains in market share and profitability.* Firms such as Apple, Netflix, Uber, Airbnb, and Warby Parker are all reaping the benefits of providing emotional, experiential, social, and financial value to satisfy customers and all their constituents.[16]

A **market leader** has the largest market share and usually leads in price changes, new-product introductions, distribution coverage, and promotional intensity. Some historical market leaders include Microsoft (computer software), Gatorade (sports drinks), Best Buy (retail electronics), McDonald's (fast food), Blue Cross Blue Shield (health insurance), and Visa (credit cards).

Although marketers assume well-known brands are distinctive in consumers' minds, unless a dominant firm enjoys a legal monopoly, it must maintain constant vigilance. A powerful product innovation might come along, a competitor might find a fresh marketing angle or commit to a major marketing investment, or the leader's cost structure might spiral upward. One well-known brand and market leader that has worked hard to stay on top is Xerox.

Xerox Xerox has had to become much more than just a copier company. Now a blue-chip company with the name that became a verb, the company sports the broadest array of imaging products and dominates the market for high-end printing systems, while also offering a new range of printing and business-related services. It has made a product-line transition from the old light lens technology to digital systems and is finding ways to make color copying less expensive and even to print in 3-D. Xerox provides broad document and print-manager services to help companies lower costs by eliminating desktop printers, reducing paper use, and installing multifunction multi-user devices that are more efficient, break down less, and use cheaper supplies. Xerox is also becoming more of a services company, providing bill processing, business processing, and IT outsourcing. The acquisition of Affiliated Computer Services (ACS) allowed Xerox to plunge its technology into back-office operations. A call to an airline's customer service, a paper or online submission of a health insurance claim, and a query to solve a smart-phone problem all might be handled by a Xerox employee. In early 2017, Xerox spun off its business services division into a separate corporation, Conduent, enabling Xerox to focus on its document technology and document outsourcing business.[17]

To gain and defend market position, a firm might first find ways to grow sales from current customers. Second, it might expand total market demand by creating new markets. Third, it must protect its current share through effective defensive and offensive actions. Let's look at each strategy.

GROWING SALES TO CURRENT CUSTOMERS

Marketers can try to increase the amount, level, or frequency of consumption. They can sometimes boost the *amount* through packaging or product redesign. Larger package sizes increase the amount of product that consumers use at one time.[18] Consumers also use more impulse products, such as soft drinks and snacks, when the product is made more readily available.

Ironically, some food firms such as Hershey's have developed smaller packaging sizes that have actually increased sales volume through more frequent usage.[19] In general, increasing *frequency* of consumption requires either identifying additional occasions to use the company's offerings or identifying completely new and different ways to use the offerings.

>> Cadbury advertises its Dairy Milk chocolates as gifts for special occasions.

Cadbury©Mondelez International, used with permission

Identifying New Occasions for Usage. A marketing program can communicate the appropriateness and advantages of using the brand for several different occasions. Market leader Cadbury has expanded use occasions for its Dairy Milk chocolates by promoting them as gifts for special occasions. Specially created gift packs for birthdays, anniversaries and festivals like Holi and Diwali boost sales. The brand has also run several campaigns on the theme of generosity, including a heart-warming campaign where an elder brother sacrifices his bar of chocolate to make his younger brother happy.[20] Another generosity themed campaign enabled the company to sponsor insurance for around 15,000 domestic workers from the sales of over 15 million 'Thank You' bars during the pandemic in 2020.

Another opportunity to increase usage arises when consumers' perceptions of their usage differ from reality. Consumers may fail to replace a short-lived product when they should, simply because they overestimate how long it stays fresh or operates effectively.[21] One strategy is to tie the act of replacing the product to a holiday, event, or time of year. Marketers of household products such as batteries for smoke alarms and filters for vacuum cleaners, furnaces, and air conditioners use the beginning and end of Daylight Savings Time as points to remind consumers to replace old batteries with new ones.

Other approach are (1) to provide consumers with better information about when they first used the product or need to replace it and (2) to incorporate a gauge of the current level of product performance. Gillette razor cartridges feature colored stripes that slowly fade with repeated use, signaling the user to move on to the next cartridge. Marketers for Monroe shock absorbers and struts launched the clever, fully integrated "Everything Gets Old. Even Your Shocks." campaign, which drew comparisons between worn shocks and struts and familiar consumer items that eventually wear out and need to be replaced, such as shoes, socks, tires, and even bananas![22]

Identifying New Uses. The second approach to increasing frequency of consumption is to identify completely new and different applications. Food product companies have long advertised recipes that use their branded products in different ways. After discovering that some consumers used Arm & Hammer baking soda as a refrigerator deodorant, the company launched a heavy promotion campaign focusing on this use and succeeded in getting half the homes in the United States to adopt it. Next, the company expanded the brand into a variety of new-product categories such as toothpaste, antiperspirant, and laundry detergent.

CREATING NEW MARKETS

Companies that plan to introduce a new product must decide when to do so. To be first in a market can be rewarding, but it can also be risky and expensive. To come in later makes sense if the firm can bring superior technology, quality, and/or brand strength to create a market advantage.

Gaining a Pioneering Advantage. Studies show that a market pioneer can gain great advantage. Campbell's, Coca-Cola, Hallmark, and Amazon.com have enjoyed sustained market dominance. Nineteen of 25 market leaders in 1923 were still the market leaders 60 years later![23] In a sample of industrial-goods businesses, 66 percent of pioneers survived at least 10 years, compared with 48 percent of early followers.[24]

What are the sources of the pioneer's advantage? Early users will recall the pioneer's brand name if the product satisfies them. The pioneer's brand also establishes what attributes the product class should possess.[25] It normally aims at the middle of the market and so captures more users. Customer inertia also plays a role, with customers displaying a reluctance to switch from their current option. There are also producer advantages: economies of scale, technological leadership, patents, ownership of scarce assets, and the ability to erect other barriers to entry.

Researchers have identified five factors underpinning long-term market leadership: vision of a mass market, persistence, relentless innovation, financial commitment, and strategic assets.[26] Other research has further highlighted the role of disruptive innovation.[27] When a pioneer starts a market with a really new product, such as the Segway Human Transporter, surviving can be very challenging. For incremental innovators, survival rates are much higher.

Speeding up innovation is essential in an age of shortened product life cycles. Being early has been shown to pay. And yet, moving too quickly can be counterproductive. Companies should not move rapidly at the expense of careful design and execution of product-launch marketing. General Motors rushed out its newly designed Malibu to get a leg up on its Honda, Nissan, and Ford midsize competitors. But when all the different Malibu versions were not ready for production at launch, the brand's momentum stalled.[28]

The pioneering advantage is not inevitable.[29] Bowmar (hand calculators), Apple's Newton (personal digital assistant), Netscape (Web browser), Reynolds (ballpoint pens), and Osborne (portable computers) were market pioneers overtaken by later entrants. First movers also have to watch out for the shortcomings of being a pioneer.

Marketers have identified several weaknesses among the failing pioneers. These include new products that were too crude, were improperly positioned, or appeared before there was strong demand; product-development costs that exhausted the innovator's resources; a lack of resources to compete against larger firms entering the market; and managerial incompetence or unhealthy complacency. Successful imitators thrived by offering lower prices, continuously improving the product, or using brute market power to overtake the pioneer.

Researchers raise further doubts about the pioneer advantage.[30] They distinguish among an *inventor,* first to develop patents in a new-product category; a *product pioneer,* first to develop a working model; and a *market pioneer,* first to sell in the new-product category. Including non-surviving pioneers in their sample, they conclude that although pioneers may still have an advantage, more market pioneers fail than has been reported, and more early market leaders (who were not pioneers) succeed. Later entrants overtaking market pioneers through the years have included Matsushita over Sony in VCRs, GE over EMI in CAT scan equipment, and Google over Yahoo! in search.

A longitudinal study of 625 brand leaders in 125 categories found that leading brands are more likely to persist during economic slowdowns and when inflation is high; they are less likely to persist during economic expansion and when inflation is low.[31] Furthermore, half the leading brands in the sample lost their leading position after being a leader over periods ranging from 12 to 39 years. The data further show that the rate of brand leadership persistence has been substantially lower in recent eras than in earlier ones (e.g., more than 30 years ago) and that once brand leadership has been lost, it is rarely regained. Interestingly, the study found above-average rates of brand leadership persistence in the categories of food and household supplies, and below-average rates in durables and clothing.

Source: difenbahia/Shutterstock

>> Niche product Sriracha hot chili sauce has made LA-based Huy Fong Foods one of the fastest-growing U.S. food companies and has even enlivened the taste buds of NASA astronauts in orbit.

Identifying Niche Markets. An alternative to being a follower in a large market is to be a leader in a small market, or niche market. Smaller firms normally avoid competing with larger firms by targeting small markets of little or no interest to the larger firms. Over time, those markets can sometimes end up being sizable in their own right, as Huy Fong Foods has found.

Firms with low shares of the total market can become highly profitable through smart niche marketing. They know their target customers so well that they can meet their needs better than other firms by offering high value, but they can also charge a premium price, achieve lower manufacturing costs, and shape a strong corporate culture and vision. The **niche marketer** achieves high margin, whereas the mass marketer achieves high volume.

The guiding principle in successful nichemanship is specialization. Here are two common types of specialization:

- **Customer specialist.** The firm specializes in one type of end-use customer. For example, a *value-added reseller* customizes computer hardware and software for specific customer segments

Sriracha Hot Chili Sauce David Tran started Huy Fong Foods in Los Angeles's Chinatown in 1980, naming the company after the Taiwanese freighter that brought him to the United States as a refugee from Vietnam. Based in part on a condiment made in Si Racha, Thailand, Tan's Sriracha hot chili sauce is known as the "rooster sauce" for the distinctive rooster (Tan's astrological sign) on its green-capped squeeze bottle. A unique combination of locally sourced jalapeño peppers, vinegar, sugar, salt, and garlic created a taste that his packaging suppliers thought would be too spicy. Tran refused to change the recipe, saying, "Hot sauce must be hot. If you don't like it hot, use less. We don't make mayonnaise here." Fortunately, many consumers agreed. Huy Fong's Sriracha sauce can be bought at Walmart and enjoyed in dishes at Applebee's restaurants and in street foods in major cities. NASA has supplied it to its astronauts in space to help stave off dulled taste buds. Because of Sriracha's popularity, Huy Fong has become one of the fastest-growing U.S. food companies. Success has attracted imitators, but the firm's revenues have continued to grow, making it one of the leaders in the Asian hot sauce market.[32]

and earns a price premium in the process. The firm sells only to customers in a certain locality, region, or area of the world.

- **Product or service specialist.** The firm carries or produces only one product line or product. A copper producer may concentrate on producing raw copper, copper components, or finished copper products. A manufacturer may produce only lenses for microscopes. A retailer may carry only ties. The firm offers one or more services not available from other firms. A bank might take loan requests over the phone and hand-deliver the money to the customer.

Paul Reed Smith founded PRS Guitars to compete with big rivals Fender and Gibson and supply "the Stradivarius of guitars." PRS instruments are carefully constructed of selected mahogany and figured maple, kiln-dried and sanded five times, followed by eight very thin coats of finish. They cost from $3,000 to $60,000, but endorsements from top musicians like Carlos Santana, and distribution through well-respected retailers like Rudy's Music Shop in Manhattan, have helped the brand establish a foothold.[33]

Much like companies serving larger customer segments, nichers have three tasks: creating new markets, expanding current markets, and protecting their market position. The risk is that the niche might dry up or be attacked. The company is then stuck with highly specialized resources that may not have high-value alternative uses. Zippo has successfully addressed the problem of a fast-shrinking niche market.

Zippo With smoking on a steady decline, Pennsylvania-based Zippo Manufacturing found the market for its iconic brass and chrome "windproof" cigarette lighters shrinking from 18 million units sold in 1998 to 12 million in 2011. With the handwriting on the wall, the company decided to broaden its focus to selling "flame," warmth, and much more, reducing its reliance on tobacco-related products to 50 percent of revenue by 2010. Although an earlier attempt to diversify into tape measures, key holders, and belt buckles in the 1960s and 1970s had lost momentum in the 1990s and finally was discontinued in 2007, Zippo came close to meeting its new goal. It introduced a long, slender multipurpose lighter for candles, grills, and fireplaces; launched an Outdoors Line including hand warmers and fire starters sold through DICK'S Sporting Goods, REI, and True

>> When Zippo found the market for its cigarette lighters shrinking, the company introduced a multipurpose lighter for candles, grills, and fireplaces, launched an Outdoors Line that included hand warmers and fire starters, and acquired a knife-making company.

Source: urbanbuzz/Alamy Stock Photo

Value; and acquired W.R. Case & Sons Cutlery, a knife maker. Zippo even launched a clothing line and men's and women's fragrances as a way to become more of a lifestyle brand. The company still sells its fair share of lighters by promoting new designs as well as perennial favorites like lighters with Elvis Presley's image.[34]

Because niches can weaken, the firm must continually create new ones. The firm should "stick to its niching," but not necessarily to its niche. That is why multiple niching can be preferable to single niching. With strength in two or more niches, the company increases its chances for survival.

EXPANDING EXISTING MARKETS

When the total market expands, the dominant firm usually gains the most. If Heinz can convince more people to use ketchup, or to use ketchup with more meals, or to use more ketchup on each occasion, the firm will benefit considerably because it already sells almost two-thirds of the country's ketchup. In general, the market leader should look for new customers or more usage from existing customers.

A company can search for new users among two groups: those who have never used a product or service (*new-market segment strategy*), or those who live elsewhere (*geographical-expansion strategy*). *SBI Mutual Fund has successfully expanded the market for investments in mutual funds by reaching out to small investors in Tier 2 and Tier 3 cities.*

SBI Mutual Fund Investment in the equity markets or mutual funds was never on the wish list of low-income households in small towns and cities. Such investment products were traditionally designed for the middle class and the rich. In 2009, SBI Mutual Fund (SBIMF) launched an equity-based micro-systematic investment plan (MicroSIP) to expand the market by reaching out to low-income savers. A low investment amount of ₹100 was introduced to reduce the entry barriers for the poor. The company enrolled 100 daily wage earners as a part of its launch program. Intermediaries including NGOs, self-help groups, microfinance institutions were tapped to reach the target customers. These intermediaries helped SBIMF create awareness, acceptability and accessibility.[35] However, scaling up proved to be a challenge due to high acquisition as well as servicing costs. The learnings and experiences proved to be extremely useful when the company focused on bringing the benefits of capital markets to customers in Tier 2 and Tier 3 cities. New products, awareness campaigns and higher distribution coverage by leveraging SBI's branch network and offices enabled the company to attract new customer segments to grow the market. Products suitable for investors with lower-level risk appetites facilitated higher inclusiveness. Adoption of local languages for mass media communications including outdoor, newspaper, radio, television and extensive deployment of below-the-line (BTL) marketing programs improved reach. Increased physical presence in all cities and use of digital channels improved customer access, enabled virtual sales and enriched channel partner engagements. Simple and easy to understand videos on mutual fund products and investment solutions were used to educate customers as well as distribution partners.

SBI MUTUAL FUND
A PARTNER FOR LIFE

>> SBI Mutual Fund expanded its market by reaching out to the low-income savers.

Source: ©State Bank of India, used with permission

Training employees of the SBI's extensive branch network and engaging with the traditional distribution channel partners while activating new partners boosted market creation. Now customers in 99% of postal pin codes across the country can easily access SBIMF. The fund house is actively trying to be the change agent for inclusive growth through financial services. All these initiatives drove SBIMF's assets under management (AUM) to achieve a breakneck compound annual growth rate (CAGR) of 37% during 2017–21.[36]

In targeting new customers, the firm should not lose sight of existing ones. Daimler, maker of Mercedes-Benz, has developed a balanced approach to capitalize on both the established demand from mature markets in the European Union, the United States, and Japan and the enormous potential offered by fast-growing emerging markets. As the company's chairman Dieter Zetsche proclaimed, "You cannot do either/or. You have to maintain your strength in traditional markets and even expand it."[37]

Defending Market Position

While trying to expand total market size, the dominant firm must actively defend its current business: Boeing against Airbus, Walmart against Amazon, and Apple against Samsung. How can the leader achieve this? The most constructive response is *continuous innovation*. The front-runner should lead the industry in developing new products and customer services, distribution effectiveness, and cost cutting. Comprehensive solutions increase competitive strength and value to customers so that they feel appreciative or even privileged to be a customer, as opposed to feeling trapped or taken advantage of.

In satisfying customer needs, we can distinguish among responsive marketing, anticipative marketing, and creative marketing. A *responsive* marketer finds a stated need and fills it. An *anticipative* marketer looks ahead to needs customers may have in the near future. A *creative* marketer discovers solutions that customers did not ask for but to which they enthusiastically respond. Creative marketers are proactive market-driving firms, not just market-driven ones.[38] Many companies assume their job is simply to adapt to customer needs. They are reactive, largely because they are overly faithful to the customer-orientation paradigm and fall victim to the "tyranny of the served market." The most successful companies instead proactively shape the market to their own offerings. Instead of simply trying to be the best player, they change the rules of the game.[39]

Proactive companies create new offers to serve unmet—and maybe even unknown—consumer needs. In the late 1970s Akio Morita, the Sony founder, was working on a pet project that would revolutionize the way people listened to music: a portable cassette player he called the Walkman. Engineers at the company insisted there was little demand for such a product, but Morita refused to part with his vision. By the 20th anniversary of the Walkman, Sony had sold more than 250 million in nearly 100 different models.[40]

Even when it does not launch offensives, a company must not leave its market position exposed. The aim of a defensive marketing strategy is to reduce the probability of attack, divert attacks to less-threatened areas, and lessen the intensity of attacks. A leader strives to do anything it legally and ethically can to reduce competitors' ability to launch a new product, secure distribution, and gain consumer awareness, trial, and repeat.[41] In any strategy, speed of response can make an important difference to profit.

A dominant firm can use six main defense strategies.[42] Decisions about which strategy to adopt will depend in part on the company's resources and goals and on its expectations about how competitors will react.

- **Position defense.** Position defense means occupying the most desirable position in consumers' minds, making the brand almost impregnable. Procter & Gamble "owns" the key functional benefit in many product categories—e.g., Tide detergent for cleaning, Crest toothpaste for cavity prevention, and Pampers diapers for dryness.
- **Flank defense.** The market leader should erect outposts to protect a weak front or support a possible counterattack. Procter & Gamble brands such as Gain and Cheer laundry detergent and

CHAPTER 18

Developing New Market Offerings

Market leader Tata Motors has achieved remarkable success in the competitive market for commercial vehicles by combining customer insights, innovation and rigorous research. Its Tata Ace created a new category of low capacity mini-trucks.
Source: Tata Motors

The development of new offerings shapes the company's future. Without investing in developing new offerings, a company is destined to rely on acquiring new products developed by other companies to ensure sustained growth. The development of new offerings is the engine that drives a company's success, enabling it to challenge industry norms and apply imaginative solutions that engage and delight customers. One company that definitely understands how to shape not only its own future, but also that of its customers, is Tata Motors.

>>> Tata Motors, established in 1945, stands out as the market leader with a broad portfolio of commercial vehicles that cater to the changing needs of customers with quality products. Tata Ace is one such innovative product that revolutionized the goods transportation industry in India. Launched in 2005, Tata Ace is a mini-truck with a one-tonne capacity that comes at an affordable price. In 2001, after experiencing a significant loss, the leadership sought opportunities to drive stable growth and insulate the company from downturns in the cyclical commercial vehicles sector. Introducing a mini truck was conceived after rigorous market and customer research.[1] The research identified the opportunities for an economic mini-truck to replace the 3-wheeler cargo carriers with a

capacity of less than a tonne, and fill the gap in the mini-trucks offerings that started with a capacity of over two tonnes. The company adopted a systematic new product introduction process that involved suppliers, customers, dealers, and the marketing team to create an economic, safe and affordable last-mile distribution vehicle. Tata Ace's innovative 2-cylinder engine and truck like solid body proved very attractive to the transporters. The brand had a blockbuster debut and become a bestseller in a short span of time.[2] Sales crossed the million mark by 2012 and Tata Ace continued to be a frontrunner in the segment with a market share of 78% by 2014. The company has continuously expanded the Tata Ace range with variants that provide high fuel efficiency, power and pickup, and low maintenance to generate higher profits for transporters. With cumulative sales of over 2.3 million in sixteen years,[3] the company is now planning to stretch the brand by introducing 'Super Ace', India's first electrical commercial distribution vehicle.[4]

This chapter provides an overview of the process of developing new market offerings. Because the term *new products* is commonly used in reference to new market offerings, we use these terms are used interchangeably. Thus, the following discussion is relevant not only to new products and services but also to the development of the business models of an enterprise.

The Process of Developing New Market Offerings

Innovation is the key to developing viable new offerings. Innovation is not limited to the development of new products or services. It can involve a new technology, a new approach to brand building, a new pricing mechanism, a new way of managing incentives, new channels of communication, or a novel distribution method. Innovation is particularly important in industries that are characterized by high technological uncertainty, high market uncertainty, fierce competition, high investment costs, and short product life cycles. Innovative offerings disrupt existing business models and make companies that fail to adapt to changing market conditions superfluous by devising new ways to create market value.

THE INNOVATION IMPERATIVE

In an economy characterized by rapid change, continuous innovation is a necessity. Companies that fail to develop new products leave themselves vulnerable to changing customer needs and tastes, shortened product life cycles, increased domestic and foreign competition, and lack of awareness of the potential market opportunities opened up by new technologies.

Learning Objectives After studying this chapter you should be able to:

18.1 Explain how companies develop new offerings.

18.2 Explain how companies generate new ideas.

18.3 Describe how companies create and validate a prototype.

18.4 Summarize the key aspects of designing a business model for a new offering.

18.5 Explain how companies implement new offering strategies.

18.6 Discuss the key steps in commercially deploying a new offering.

Highly innovative firms are able to repeatedly identify and quickly seize new market opportunities. They create a positive attitude toward innovation and risk taking, "routinize" the innovation process, practice teamwork, and allow their people to experiment and even fail. One such firm is W. L. Gore.

W. L. Gore Best known for its GORE-TEX high-performance fabrics, W. L. Gore has introduced breakthrough versions of guitar strings, dental floss, medical devices, and fuel cells—while constantly reinventing the uses of the polymer polytetrafluoroethylene (PTFE). Several principles guide the company's new-product development. First, it works with potential customers. Its thoracic graft, designed to combat heart disease, was developed in close collaboration with physicians. Second, Gore has a distinctly egalitarian culture; it lets employees choose projects and appoints few product leaders and teams. The company likes to nurture "passionate champions" who convince others that a project is worth their time and commitment, and leaders have positions of authority because they have followers. Third, all research associates spend 10 percent of their work hours on "dabble time," developing their own ideas. Promising ideas are judged according to a "Real, Win, Worth" exercise: Is the opportunity real? Can we win? Can we make money? Fourth, Gore knows when to let go, although dead ends in one area can spark innovation in another: Elixir acoustic guitar strings were the result of a failed venture into bike cables. Even successful ventures may need to move on. Glide shred-resistant dental floss was sold to Procter & Gamble because Gore knew retailers want to deal with a company selling a family of health care products. W. L. Gore employs nearly 10,000 people in dozens of countries around the globe and has revenue of more than $3.5 billion.[5]

Source: W. L. Gore & Associates

>> Product development at W. L. Gore entails working closely with customers, letting employees choose their projects, giving leadership positions to passionately committed employees, allowing researchers space to develop their own ideas, and knowing when to call a halt to a venture.

Innovation ranges from minor improvements or revisions of existing products to new-to-the-world items that create an entirely new market. Fewer than 10 percent of all new products can be considered truly innovative and new to the world. Most new-product activity is concentrated on improving existing products. This form of continuous innovation can broaden a brand's meaning and force competitors to play catch-up. Many of the supermarket product launches in the past decade have been brand extensions, such as Tide Pods, Gillette Fusion ProShield, Downy Unstopables, Colgate Total Clean-In-Between, and Oreo Thins. At Sony, modifications of established products have accounted for over 80 percent of new-product activity. In fact, most established companies focus on **incremental innovation**, entering new markets by tweaking products for new customers, using variations on a core product to stay one step ahead of the market, and creating interim solutions for industry-wide problems.

The focus on minor variations of existing products is due in part to the fact that it is increasingly difficult to identify blockbuster products that will transform a market. Nonetheless, many companies continue to pursue new-to-the-world innovations. These innovations are typically associated with great risk and cost, but if they succeed, they can improve the corporate image, create a greater sustainable competitive advantage for the company, and produce significant financial rewards.[6]

Keurig pioneered the one-cup-at-a-time pod-style brewing system that has swept homes and offices alike. For the speed, convenience, and variety offered, users are willing to pay 10 times the cost of a traditionally brewed cup of coffee. This has helped Keurig sales to exceed $11 billion and its revenue-based market share of the single-cup coffee market to reach 30 percent.[7]

Successful new-product launches are exceptions rather than the rule. New products fail at rates estimated to be as high as 95 percent. The most common reasons include ignored or misinterpreted market research, overestimates of market size, high development costs, poor product performance, inadequate pricing, ineffective communication, insufficient distribution support, proactive competitive response, lack of organizational support for the new offering, and inadequate return on the company's investment. The different reasons for failure can be summed up in one sentence: The new offering fails to create superior value for its target customers in a way that sufficiently benefits the company and its collaborators.

MANAGING INNOVATION

Innovation does not happen in a vacuum. Innovative products are created by individuals, many of whom work for both small and large enterprises. Therefore, creating an environment that fosters innovation and encourages the development of new products is paramount.[8] Companies handle the organizational aspect of innovation in different ways. Some of the popular approaches to managing innovation are outlined as follows:

- **Departments in charge of current offerings.** A common approach to foster and manage innovation is to assign responsibility for developing new products and services to managers in charge of a given product category, brand, or market. The advantage of this approach is that these managers have a solid understanding of customer needs, the competitive environment, and the processes involved in designing, communicating, and delivering the company's products to its current customers. On the downside, managers in charge of offerings that already exist are often focused on these offerings and may lack the skills, knowledge, and motivation to develop successful new products.
- **New-product departments.** Large companies often establish a new-product department headed by a manager with substantial authority and access to top management, along with responsibility for generating and screening new ideas, working with the research and development department, and carrying out field testing and commercialization. Eli Lilly put *every* department engaged in the process of turning molecules into medicine—from the research and development staff to the team that seeks FDA approval—under one roof to improve efficiency and cut development time.
- **Innovation centers.** Some firms open innovation centers in new geographic locations to better design new products for those regions. For example, Microsoft has over 100 innovation centers worldwide forging partnerships with local government, universities, and industry collaborators. In the same vein, the networking giant Cisco has built a network of innovation centers located around the world, each serving as a hub to build solutions with partners and start-ups, to engage in rapid prototyping, as well as to invest in and partner with start-ups, accelerators, and universities.
- **Venture teams.** Another approach to driving innovation involves assigning new-product development to venture teams—cross-functional groups charged with developing a specific product or business. These **intrapreneurs** are relieved of other duties and given a separate budget and a longer time frame than is typical. They are also often organized in a "skunkworks" setting—informal workplaces, sometimes garages, where entrepreneurial-minded teams work to develop new products. For example, as it transformed itself from a PC company into a solutions company in the cyber-security and data center design and management business, Dell established separate headquarters for its new units, with marching orders to think entrepreneurially.[9]
- **Communities of practice.** Another organizational arrangement for new-product development involves creating forums in which employees from different departments are encouraged to share their knowledge and skills. For example, Japanese pharmaceutical maker Esai Co. has formed more than 400 innovation communities. One of these innovation centers helped develop an easy-to-swallow, jelly-like medication for Alzheimer's patients. Grocery retailer Supervalu commissioned 29 innovation community-of-practice projects, 22 of which ended up being implemented by the company.[10]
- **Cross-functional teams.** Creating project-specific teams combining different skillsets is another popular approach to fostering innovation. A particular benefit of this approach is that it brings

different types of expertise to the new-product development process, which, in turn, expedites innovation and increases the chances of creating groundbreaking new offerings. Cross-functional teams composed of both engineers and marketers help ensure that a company's research and development efforts are not driven to create a "better mousetrap" when potential customers do not need or want one.

THE STAGE-GATE APPROACH TO DEVELOPING NEW OFFERINGS

New-product development is commonly represented as a sequence of actions (stages) separated by hurdles (gates) that the new offering must overcome.[11] The stage-gate approach divides the innovation process into stages, with a gate or checkpoint at the end of each stage. The ultimate goal of using a stage-gate approach to new-product development is to ensure market success in a way that minimizes risk and optimizes allocation of the company's resources.

Stage-gate systems have evolved over the years as users have made them more flexible, adaptive, and scalable, with improved built-in governance, integrated portfolio management, incorporated accountability and continuous improvement, and ongoing input from a wide range of sources both inside and outside the company. By using a stepwise approach of formulating, testing, realigning, and pivoting, a company aims to separate the wheat from the chaff, weeding out bad ideas and investing in the ones that are most likely to produce the desired outcome. For example, at Tata Steel, about 50 to 100 ideas are generated for every one that makes it to implementation, and at any point in time, 50 to 70 product-development projects are in the pipeline before some clear the final-phase gate.[12]

There is no single stage-gate format; companies vary in the ways they define different stages of product development and the hurdles that the new offering must overcome. At the same time, there are several similarities between these approaches that can be distilled into an overarching **stage-gate framework** for managing the process of developing new offerings. This framework presents a streamlined version of the stage-gate approach, which comprises five key stages—*idea generation, concept development, business-model design, offering development,* and *commercial deployment* —separated by hurdles that aim to validate the actions taken in the previous step. This stage-gate framework for developing new offerings is depicted in Figure 18.1.

The five stages of the stage-gate approach to developing new offerings can be summarized as follows:

- **Idea generation.** The starting point for developing a new offering is uncovering an unmet customer need and coming up with an idea about how to fulfill this need better than the available alternatives. The initial idea outlines in broad strokes the ways in which the company can address the focal customer need, without going into much detail about the specifics of the market offering. Idea generation is followed by an assessment of the soundness of the idea and validation of its key assumptions.
- **Concept development.** Following validation of the idea, the next step is the development of an initial version (prototype) of the offering that has the core functionality of the proposed offering. The developed concepts are then validated by assessing their technological feasibility and potential to fulfill the uncovered customer need.
- **Business-model design.** The validated concept then becomes the core of a business model that defines the offering's target market, the value created by the offering in this market, and the key attributes of the offering. The business model is validated on the basis of the degree to which it is able to fulfill the identified customer need in a way that sufficiently benefits the company and its collaborators.
- **Offering implementation.** The validated business model is still only a plan; the company has not developed a market-ready version of the offering. To fulfill the needs of its target customers

FIGURE **18.1**
The Stage-Gate Framework for Developing New Offerings

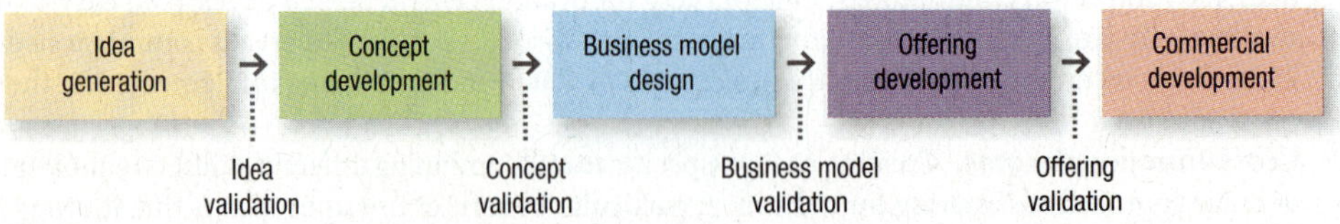

and create value for its stakeholders and collaborators, the company must develop the resources needed to create the offering and then develop a market-ready version of it.

- **Commercial deployment.** The market-ready version of the offering is then commercially deployed, meaning that it is communicated and made available to target customers. Commercial deployment often begins with launching the offering in selected markets before making the offering available to the entire target market. The commercial deployment is concomitant with continuous market testing and optimizing of the product to better meet the needs of the target customers, respond to changes in the market environment, and take advantage of any changes in the underlying technology, know-how, and business processes.

The stage-gate approach encompasses three aims. Its goal is to develop: (1) a *desirable* offering that target customers will find attractive, (2) a technologically *feasible* offering that the company will find doable, and (3) a *viable* offering that will create value for the company and its collaborators. Desirability, feasibility, and viability are integral to the process of developing an offering, although these factors play different roles. The offering's desirability is typically paramount in the idea-generation phase of product development. Both desirability and feasibility share the focus during concept development. And business-model design aims to ensure that all three of these criteria are met before implementing the final version of the offering and bringing it to market.

The high uncertainty and risk associated with new-product development implies that for every successful innovation there are many innovative ventures that did not pan out. The high rate of failure of new-product development projects suggests that in order to end up with a viable market offering, a company must start with a number of new ideas that, through a series of screening, pivoting, and realignments will produce a successful outcome. In this context, having hurdles (gates) is important for managing resource allocation, investing in projects that have a high probability of succeeding, and screening out projects that cannot be validated at the different stages of the new-product development process.

Thus, at the beginning of the process, the company might consider a large number of ideas at a relatively low cost. Many of these ideas are screened out; only a few proceed to the concept-development stage, which requires a relatively larger investment in prototyping and testing. As the projects go through the different stages of the development process, the number of viable alternatives is reduced to a few options (or often a single option) to be commercialized. At the same time, the investment per project increases, with the last two stages—commercialization and commercial deployment—typically requiring the most of the company's resources.

The stage-gate approach outlined previously represents a streamlined version of the process of developing a new offering. On many occasions, the development of a new offering might not follow a predefined series of orderly, well-delineated steps but might instead entail actions that do not follow the linear format of the stage-gate framework. I is not uncommon for a new-offering development project to pass the idea-generation stage only to fail to overcome some of the subsequent hurdles. In such cases, the company must go back to the drawing board and perhaps even reevaluate the idea and/or the concept underlying the entire project. Note, however, that even though the new-product development process might involve multiple iterations rather than a linear process in which each stage naturally transitions into the next, the stage-gate framework outlined previously offers a set of actionable guidelines that can streamline the process of developing new offerings.

THE STAGE-GATE APPROACH TO DEVELOPING NEW OFFERINGS: AN ILLUSTRATION

The stage-gate approach to business-model development can be illustrated with the following example. Consider a food-processing company seeking to introduce a new product that will increase its market presence and fuel its revenue growth. The five stages of developing a new offering can be delineated as shown here.

Idea Generation and Validation. After exploring a number of alternative ideas, the company decides to focus on creating a powder to add to milk to increase its nutritional value and taste. Next, the company must answer several questions: Who will use this product—infants, children, teenagers, young or middle-aged adults, or older adults? What primary benefit should this product provide—taste, nutrition, refreshment, or energy? On what occasion will people consume this drink—at breakfast, mid-morning, for lunch, mid-afternoon, with dinner, late evening?

After answering these questions, the company formulates several ideas: (1) an instant drink for adults who want a quick nutritious breakfast without preparation, (2) a tasty snack for children to drink as a midday refreshment, and (3) a health supplement for older adults to drink in the late evening before bed. Note that these ideas affect not only the way the product would be formulated but also the market in which it would compete. An instant-breakfast drink would compete against bacon and eggs, breakfast cereals, coffee and pastry, and other breakfast alternatives. A snack drink would compete against soft drinks, fruit juices, sports drinks, and other thirst quenchers.

After evaluating the pros and cons of different options, the company decides to go ahead with the first idea and develop an instant-breakfast drink. Next, the product idea must be fleshed out and turned into a specific product concept.

Concept Development and Validation. To turn the idea into a product concept, the company has to articulate the specific attributes of its market offering: What will be the particular *product* formulation? What ingredients will it involve and how will they be mixed? What *brand* name and associations will identify this product? What are the *price* points at which this offering will be sold? What *incentives* will be associated with this product? How will the company *communicate* this offering to its target customers? How will this product be *delivered* to its target customers?

To address these questions, the company may conduct market research to examine how its product will stand in relationship to other breakfast options. Within this category, its nearest competitors are cold cereal and breakfast bars; its most distant competitors are bacon and eggs. The company might also examine the extant market offerings—its own breakfast products as well as products offered by its competitors. Finally, the company might consider the likely size of the market for its product: Are there many customers whose needs the company's offering can address better than the competition?

Based on its evaluation of the customer market, the competitive offerings, and its own goals and resources, the company might decide to develop a mid-price product emphasizing nutrition and convenience. At this stage, the product concept is defined as "a powdered mixture added to milk to make a tasty instant breakfast that provides all daily nutrition needs in three flavors (chocolate, vanilla, and strawberry) and individual packets, six to a box, at $2.99 a box." The product concept can be thought of as the value proposition the company will offer to its target customers.

Business-Model Design and Validation. Following the development and validation of the product concept, the company must make the case for why customers will buy the company's offering and how the company and its collaborators will benefit from launching the offering. To this end, the company must articulate (1) the specifics of the target market (size of the market, core competitors, and key collaborators), (2) the value the offering creates for target customers, the company, and its collaborators, and (3) the key attributes of the offering (product, brand, price, incentives, communication, and distribution).

The *target market* for the product consists of adults who are short on time and seek a convenient, nutritious, and moderately priced breakfast meal. The customer demand estimates show that this is a sufficiently large market to enable the company to reach its revenue and profit goals. The competitive analysis further shows that even though there are several large competitors in this space, most of them compete at either the high end or the low end of the market, so there is an opportunity for a mid-range-priced breakfast offering.

The *value* that the company's offering creates in this market can be defined along three key dimensions—customer value, collaborator value, and company value.

- For *target customers*—strapped-for-time middle-class families with children—the offering will create value by providing a convenient, nutritious, and moderately priced breakfast meal.
- For *collaborators*—suppliers and distributors—the offering will create value by generating additional sales at competitive rates.
- For the *company stakeholders*, the offering will create value by providing a new stream of revenue and profit. It will also allow the company to gain market position and build a strong brand that can be used as a platform for additional offerings. Specifically, the company plans initially to sell 500,000 cases for a 2.5 percent share of the market, with a loss in the first year not exceeding $1.3 million. Over the course of five years, the company intends to gain a 12 percent market share and realize an after-tax return on investment of 12 percent.

Following definition of the target market and the offering's value proposition, the company must build on the initial concept of the *market offering* and define the attributes of the new offering in greater detail. In this context, the key attributes of the company offering might be defined as follows:

> The product will be offered in chocolate, vanilla, and strawberry flavors, in individual packets of six to a box, at a retail price of $2.99 a box. There will be 48 boxes per case, and the case price to distributors will be $78. To ensure trade support, retailers will be offered one case free for every four cases bought during the first two months, plus allowances for cooperative advertising. Free samples will be distributed in stores. Coupons for 50 cents off will appear in newspapers and online. The total sales promotional budget will be $15 million. One-third of an advertising budget of $6 million will go into television and two-thirds into online, equally split between outbound and inbound communication. Advertising copy will emphasize the benefit concepts of nutrition and convenience. During the first year, $100,000 will be spent on marketing research to buy store audits and consumer-panel information to monitor market reaction.

Offering Implementation and Market Testing. Following the design of a viable business model, the company embarks on developing the offering—that is, creating the actual product that will be made available in the market. To this end, the company must first ensure that it has the *resources* needed to make the product concept a reality. For example, the company might have to procure the manufacturing facilities and ensure the availability of the ingredients needed to produce the breakfast meal created by the food engineers in the company's research and development department.

Once the necessary resources have been secured, the company can proceed with *implementing the offering*—turning its new-product concept of a breakfast meal into a market-ready product. To this end, the company must produce the actual breakfast meal, design its packaging, create its brand identity, set retail and wholesale prices, define sales promotions for retailers and consumers, secure the communication channels that will inform target customers about the company's product, and assemble the distribution channels that will deliver this product to target customers.

Following the development of the offering, the company conducts a **market test** to validate its offering. Specifically, the company chooses Columbus, Ohio—a popular location for testing new fast-food products because it is reasonably representative demographically of the rest of the nation and is a contained market with reasonable media rates. Based on the results of the market test, the company modifies its offering by tweaking the product formula, streamlining product packaging, and updating its brand identity.

Commercial Deployment. Following the development of the offering, the company is ready for commercial deployment. To minimize risk and the initial outlay of resources involved in launching the product, and to ensure its ability to further modify the product based on market response, the company chooses to deploy its product in *selected markets*. To ensure early success of the offering and generate a stream of revenue, the company chooses to focus on a subset of its target customers who are most likely to adopt its offering and whom the company can reach to communicate and deliver its product in an effective and cost-efficient manner. In addition, rather than launching all three flavors of its breakfast meal, the company decides to launch its most popular flavor—chocolate—first and introduce the other flavors at a later point.

Once the product has been successfully launched in the primary market, has been well received by consumers, and has created a stream of revenue to partially offset the costs of developing the new offering, the company *expands* the initial market to include all customers who might benefit from the new breakfast meal. The company then scales up production, begins promoting its product beyond the primary market, and ensures that the offering is available across the entire target market. As its target market broadens, the company also broadens the available product assortment and launches the other breakfast meal flavors. In addition, it considers launching volume packs to deliver greater value to customers who have adopted its offering and consume it on a regular basis.

The key aspects of the five components of the stage-gate model—*idea generation, concept development, business-model design, offering implementation,* and *commercial deployment*—are discussed in more detail in the following sections.

Idea Generation

The search for viable ideas is the starting point of new-product development. Some of the greatest opportunities and highest leverage for new products can be found by uncovering unmet customer needs that the company can fulfill better than the completion.

GENERATING VIABLE IDEAS

Successful innovations result from identifying a novel approach to address an unmet market need. Innovation marries a customer need with a creative idea that addresses this need. Depending on the impetus of the innovation, there are two approaches to idea generation: market-driven, or top-down, and invention-driven, or bottom-up.

Top-down idea generation begins with identifying a market opportunity followed by developing an offering specifically designed to address this opportunity. The market opportunity must address an important problem faced by potential customers that it can solve better than the available alternatives can. Thus, top-down idea generation starts with a market analysis that aims to identify an important unmet need that the company can fulfill in a way that is superior to its competitors.

A number of successful products have resulted from top-down idea generation. Motiv realized that many consumers found fitness tracker bracelets and other wearable devices too bulky and uncomfortable, to say nothing of lacking in style. So it bundled a step counter, heart-rate monitor, and sleep tracker in a discreet and stylish ring that not only looks good but is water resistant and withstands the elements. Varidesk products allow users to both sit and stand while doing computer and other office tasks. The products were a direct result of widely publicized concerns about the effects of constant sitting on long-term health. Learning thermostats from Nest filled the need for temperature control that didn't require constant programming, yet saved energy and money and kept the home atmosphere comfortable. The Nest smart home-security devices that followed targeted consumers who didn't want the hassle and ongoing expense of having an outside home-monitoring system installed, yet wanted to implement security measures.

Bottom-up idea generation is the opposite of top-down generation: It starts with an invention and then seeks to identify an unmet market need. With bottom-up idea generation, the invention is driven by technological innovation rather than by an identified market need. Because it is rooted in technology, the bottom-up approach is more likely to be employed by research scientists than by marketing managers. And the market applications of technology innovation often come about accidentally.

Among the technologically innovative products that have resulted from bottom-up idea generation are *Evista,* which failed as a contraceptive but was turned into a multibillion-dollar drug to treat osteoporosis. *Strattera* started out as an unsuccessful antidepressant before it became a top-selling attention deficit/hyperactivity disorder (ADHD) drug. The iconic toy *Slinky* was the accidental outcome of a naval engineer's attempt to design a meter to monitor power on battleships, after tension springs fell to the floor and kept bouncing. An electrical engineer's research on the use of radio frequency to offset hypothermia occasioned the discovery that a cooled heart could be restarted by stimulation—and led eventually to invention of the pacemaker.

To develop a product that will ultimately become a market success, bottom-up idea generation must address a viable market opportunity. Innovative technology is not in itself a good reason for developing a new offering. New technologies can, of course, contribute to market success, but the key driver of success is the company's ability to parlay this technology into a product that effectively addresses an unmet market need. For example, the iPod was not the first Mp3 player that featured a hard drive that could store a great number of songs. Such devices were available on the market prior to the iPod, many at a lower price. Yet only when Apple launched the iPod did the entire category of hard-drive-based portable music players explode.

To turn a technological invention into a viable business idea, the company must identify an unmet customer need that this invention can address better than the competition. Thus, even though successful products can spring from technological invention, *top-down innovation is the preferable method of idea generation.* The ultimate success of an offering hinges on its ability to deliver value; therefore, a company can enhance its chances of generating a product destined for success by identifying value-creation opportunities in the marketplace at the outset.

IDEA VALIDATION

Idea validation examines the key assumptions of an idea to determine its soundness. This process involves assessing the offering's *desirability* and *viability* based on whether the offering is likely to successfully address an important unmet customer need (idea desirability) in a way that will simultaneously benefit the company (idea viability).

Companies are prone to two types of errors when they evaluate proposed ideas for new offerings. The first error involves the failure to reject an idea that has little or no merit, which will probably result in an unsuccessful market offering. The second error is based on an opposite miscalculation—the rejection of a good idea. The high rate of new-product failures might lead to the conclusion that failure to reject bad ideas is more prevalent than rejecting promising ideas. This is not necessarily the case. Many new-product failures can undoubtedly be attributed to poor ideas, but the steep rate of such failures can also be caused by a high incidence of rejecting good ideas (Figure 18.2), along with the many technological and market risks inherent in new-product development. A good idea that is poorly executed also runs the risk of failure.

The growth projections of many companies have been held hostage to the erroneous belief that it would be an easy task to educate customers to appreciate the benefits of offerings that did not address a problem (pain point) they faced. TiVo is a prime example. The company introduced the first digital video recorder at the turn of this century, fully anticipating that it would revolutionize the television industry and that customers would be quick to adopt it. The TV revolution did materialize, but at a distinctly slower rate than the company predicted. After the competition moved in, TiVo was left with a sliver of the digital video recording market. TiVo's miscalculation: failing to understand that consumers were fairly satisfied with the way they watched TV and did not see the value of TiVo's offering or feel a strong urge to acquire it. For consumers, it was a nice-to-have product, but they did not feel the need to have it.

FIGURE **18.2**

Why Good Ideas Fail: Forces Fighting New Ideas

Source: With permission of Jerold Panas, Young & Partners Inc.

MARKET RESEARCH TOOLS FOR IDEA GENERATION AND VALIDATION

Exploratory research is a mainstay of idea generation and validation.[13] This form of research helps to identify unmet customer needs, formulate research questions (hypotheses), and generate ideas. Typically used in the initial stages of new-product development, exploratory research strives to attain a general understanding of available market opportunities, rather than quantifying the obtained insights or establishing causal relationships. Common market research tools for idea generation and validation involve *observing and interviewing customers, interviewing employees and experts, analyzing the competition, and crowdsourcing*.

- **Observing customers.** Examining people's behavior in their natural environment can be an effective way to gain insights into customer needs and determine how best to address these needs. This can include observing both physical and online behavior—such as the way customers evaluate, buy, and consume the products and services they use, the websites they visit, the content on which they focus the most, and the information they share online.
- **Interviewing customers.** Questioning customers to uncover their unmet needs and gather insights about novel ways in which these needs can be fulfilled is a logical place to start the search for new ideas. After all, customer acceptance is a key factor in the success of a new offering. Yet, even though customers are an important source for generating new ideas, they are not always able to articulate their needs clearly and suggest viable new products. As Henry Ford famously said, "If I'd asked people what they wanted, they would have said a faster horse." Being overly focused on consumers who may not really know what they want, or what is possible, can result in shortsighted product development and miss potential breakthroughs. This is one of the reasons why some companies, including Apple and IKEA, tend to take consumer input with a grain of

salt in the belief that focusing on customers' current needs can lead to incremental rather than breakthrough innovation.[14]

- **Interviewing employees.** Employees can be a source of ideas for developing new products and services. For example, Toyota reports that its employees submit 2 million ideas annually (about 35 suggestions per employee), over 85 percent of which are implemented. LinkedIn launched an in-house incubator that allows any employee to organize a team and pitch a project to a group of executives. The company has also created "hackdays"—one Friday a month when employees work on creative projects.
- **Interviewing experts.** Encouraged by the open innovation movement, many firms are going outside their boundaries to tap external sources of new ideas, including scientists, engineers, patent attorneys, university and commercial laboratories, industrial consultants and publications, channel members, marketing and advertising agencies, and even competitors.
- **Analyzing the competition.** Companies can find good ideas by researching the products and services of other companies, discovering what customers like and dislike about these products. In addition, they can acquire competitors' products, reverse-engineer them, and design better ones. Knowing competitors' strengths and weaknesses can help the company establish the optimal brand positioning for a new product and the right points of parity and points of differences.[15]
- **Crowdsourcing.** The traditional company-driven approach to product innovation is giving way to a world in which companies are turning to crowdsourcing to generate new ideas and to co-create products with consumers. **Crowdsourcing** lets companies engage outsiders in the new-product development process in rich and meaningful ways and receive either unique expertise or a different perspective on the problem that might otherwise be overlooked.[16] For example, when Baskin-Robbins ran an online contest to pick its next flavor, 40,000 consumers entered. The winning entry combined chocolate, nuts, and caramel and was launched as Toffee Pecan Crunch.[17]

Because different methods have their own advantages and shortcomings, companies often use combined approaches to generate new ideas. For example, when Procter & Gamble was looking to create a dishwashing detergent "smart enough" to reveal when the right amount of soap has been added to a sink full of dirty plates, it reached out to a global network of volunteer tinkerers, including professionals, retired scientists, and students. As it happened, an Italian chemist working from her home laboratory had pioneered a new kind of dye that turns dishwater blue when a certain amount of soap is added. For $30,000 in prize money, the company had a solution.[18]

Concept Development

Concept development embodies a potentially viable idea by creating an initial version, or prototype, of the company's offering. The **prototype** is a working model of the offering that aims to flesh out the original idea and weed out potential problems before the actual offering is created. Concept development improves the chances of market success by evaluating consumer response to the offering's core benefits in order to create a product with maximum market potential.

PROTOTYPING

Concept development typically evolves from a description of the product's core features into the scaled-down prototype that introduces the offering's core concepts to target consumers. Prototypes don't have to be functional; rather, they might be rough models that offer a preliminary glimpse of how the proposed offering will fulfill an identified market need, put together solely so that the company can gauge the reaction of potential customers. As such, the prototype addresses only the most important aspect(s) of the potentially viable product or service.

The complexity of prototypes can vary widely. Prototypes can be simple representations of an offering's underlying concept—for example, a diagram that illustrates how the offering will function, a drawing that outlines the overall look and feel of the offering, or a model that incorporates only some of the core functions proposed for the market-ready model. Other prototypes might be much more advanced and may at times even approach the final version of the offering.

The level of prototype complexity is usually geared to various stages of the new-product development process. During the idea-generation and concept-development stages of the offering, simpler, more basic prototypes usually suffice. On the other hand, the more advanced stages of product development typically call for more refined prototypes. This is particularly true when the validated product concept is almost ready to be translated into a marketable offering.[19]

Firms rigorously test prototypes to see how they perform in different applications and to ensure that the final product will be well received in the market. There are two types of prototype tests: **alpha testing**, which involves an evaluation of the product within the firm, and **beta testing**, which tests the product with customers.

For example, Vibram, which makes soles for different types of shoes designed for sports that include skateboarding, cycling, and rock climbing, employs a team of experts to alpha test its products. The company evaluates its products under the most extreme conditions by executing tests directly in the field and employing a series of procedures. One Vibram executive described the way it tests products:

> If our chemist creates a new compound targeted towards road running applications, first we perform a battery of lab tests to understand the compound's physical properties. Next, we bring natural environments and surfaces into the laboratory and calculate information. Then lastly shoes are distributed to our tester team who will document things like weather/temp, distance, location, and running surfaces, etc. They'll comment on the differences in the grip of the soles. We then compile the results and make a decision on validation.[20]

Beta testing can bring consumers into a laboratory or give them samples to use at home. Procter & Gamble has on-site labs such as a diaper-testing center where dozens of parents bring their babies to take part in the studies. To develop its Cover Girl Outlast all-day lip color, Procter & Gamble invited 500 women to come to its labs each morning to apply the lipstick, record their activities, and return eight hours later in order that the remaining lip color could be measured. This resulted in a product that included a glossy moisturizer women could apply on top of the color without looking in a mirror. Microsoft has an "Insider Program" that rolls out versions of its new products months in advance to customers and developers who might be interested in what the next iteration of the Windows operating system will look like.

Business products can also benefit from market testing. Expensive industrial goods and new technologies normally undergo alpha and beta testing. During beta testing, the company's technical people observe how customers use the product, a practice that often exposes unanticipated problems of safety and servicing and alerts the company to customer training and servicing requirements. The company can also observe how much value the equipment adds to a customer's operation as an input to subsequent pricing.

CONCEPT VALIDATION

Concept validation typically assesses the soundness of the core concept underlying the proposed offering by addressing the technological *feasibility* of the offering and the way target customers view its *desirability*. Thus, to validate the concept, a manager should answer two key questions: *Can a functional prototype and, later, a fully functional version of the offering be built?* and *Does it fulfill the identified customer need better than the alternative options?*

Concept development and validation are typically guided by experimental studies designed to test the prototypes produced by the company. To this end, a study might involve varying one or more aspects of the prototype and observing the effect of these changes on customers' reactions to the offering—a process also referred to as A/B testing. Based on the outcome of the experiment, the company either proceeds to develop a business model for the offering or goes back to the drawing board to formulate new ideas and concepts that incorporate the knowledge gained from the test. Another commonly used approach is **conjoint analysis**, which involves asking respondents to evaluate a series of different combinations of attributes of an offering in order to determine the value that consumers place on specific attributes of this offering.

Business-Model Design

Up to this point, the product has existed only in the form of a description, a drawing, or a prototype. The next step represents a jump in investment that dwarfs the costs incurred so far, requiring the company to determine whether the product idea can be translated into a commercially feasible offering. **Business-model design** also takes the offering's *viability*—its value-creating capacity—into consideration, in addition to concept development's focus on the technological *feasibility* and the *desirability* of the offering. If the business model is validated, the concept can move to the development stage. If the business-model analysis suggests that the offering is unlikely to create market value for the company and its customers, the offering concept (and sometimes the underlying idea) must be revised and reevaluated.

DESIGNING THE BUSINESS MODEL

Designing the business model involves three key components (discussed in detail in Chapter 2): identifying the target market, articulating the offering's value proposition in that market, and delineating the key attributes of the market offering (Figure 18.3):

- The **target market** is the market in which the company has chosen to create value with its offering. Included in the target market are the target customers that the company has identified as potential purchasers of the offering, competitors that are also vying for the target customers, collaborators that will help the company distribute the offering and serve the target customers, the company itself, and the context of the market in which the company operates.
- The **value proposition** details the type of value that the company plans to create for its target customers and collaborators in the market, as well as the way in which the company plans to capture some of this value for itself.
- The **market offering** describes how the company will create, communicate, and deliver value to its target customers, collaborators, and the company stakeholders. This involves specifying the product, service, brand, price, incentives, communication, and distribution aspects of the company's offering.

The creation of market value is the ultimate goal of the business model. Accordingly, the success of an offering is determined by the degree to which it can create value for its target customers, collaborators, and the company. Thus, the design of a business model for a new offering is guided by three key questions: *Does the offering create value for target customers? Does the offering create value for the company collaborators?* and *Does the offering create value for the company?*

FIGURE **18.3**

The Key Components of a Business Model of a New Offering

Source: Alexander Chernev, *Strategic Marketing Management: Theory and Practice* (Chicago, IL: Cerebellum Press, 2019)

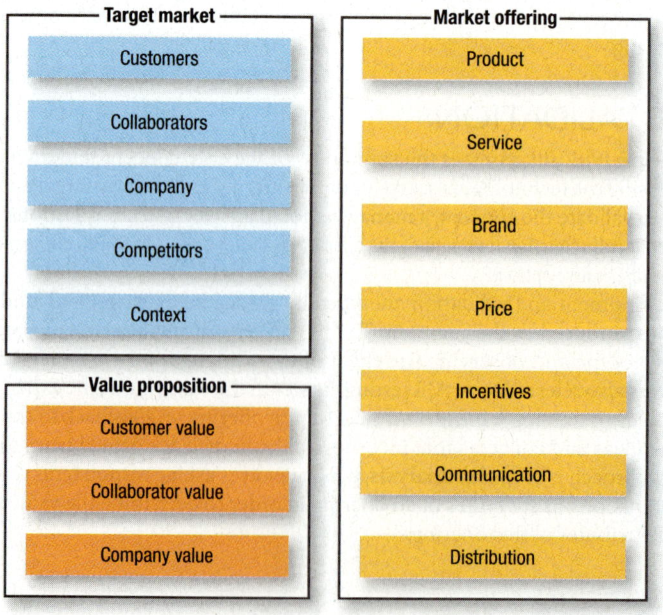

The key principles involved in developing the value proposition and the process of creating customer, company, and collaborator value were discussed in detail in Chapter 2.

BUSINESS-MODEL VALIDATION

Business-model validation aims to assess the offering's ability to create market value on three key dimensions: desirability, feasibility, and viability.

- *Desirability* indicates the extent to which target customers perceive the offering to be attractive. The desirability of an offering hinges on its ability to deliver the benefits sought by customers at a reasonable expenditure of money, time, and effort. The inability to achieve an optimal balance of benefits and costs can hinder an offering's desirability. An example is Crystal Pepsi, a clear, caffeine-free alternative to regular colas: The offering failed to gain traction in the market, despite a massive promotional campaign, because consumers did not find the concept of clear cola appealing.
- *Feasibility* indicates the extent to which the company can create an offering that delivers the functionality desired by customers. Feasibility hinges on both current technologies and a company's expertise in using these technologies. For example, a perpetual motion machine that can operate indefinitely without an energy source is not a feasible concept.
- *Viability* indicates the extent to which an offering can create value for the company. For most companies, a viable offering is one that is able to generate profits. Thus, viability is typically a function of expected revenues and the cost structure of an offering; an inability to balance revenues and costs often is an indication of impending market failure. Pets.com lost money on most sales and ultimately was unable to stay in business despite high name recognition and a high-profile promotional campaign.

Because a company's success is based on the desirability, feasibility, and viability of its offerings, to create a sustainable business model a manager must answer the following three questions: *Do target customers find the offering desirable, and does it create value for these customers? Is it feasible for the offering to be built as planned?* and *Is the offering viable—that is, able to create value for the company and its collaborators?*

An offering's desirability, feasibility, and viability are interrelated. An offering that customers do not find desirable would probably not be viable because it would not create sufficient customer demand to create value for the company. An offering that is not technologically feasible would be likely to prove undesirable because it would not be able to meet customer needs.

An important aspect of validating a company's business model in general, and an offering's viability in particular, is ensuring that the offering addresses a need that is perceived to be important to a customer segment is large enough to create value for the company. In this context, demand forecasting—a process that involves identifying the size of the potential market for the company's offering—is an integral aspect of developing new offerings.[21]

Demand forecasts are built on one of three information bases: what people say, what people do, or what people have done. Using what people say requires surveying buyers' intentions, composites of sales force opinions, and expert opinions. Building a forecast on the basis of what people do means putting the product into a test market to measure buyer response. To use the final basis—what people have done—firms analyze records of past buying behavior or use time-series analysis or statistical demand analysis. Different approaches to demand forecasting are discussed in detail later in this chapter.

Offering Implementation

Implementing the offering turns the concept into a reality. It involves two key aspects: *developing the necessary resources* to put the business model into action and *developing the market offering*.

DEVELOPING THE CORE RESOURCES

To succeed, a company must have the necessary resources to implement its business model. Often, at the time a company develops the offering's concept and designs its business model, it does not have all of the resources necessary to create and launch the market offering. Thus, after the business model has been designed, the logical next step is to develop the necessary resources by building, outsourcing, or acquiring them.

Resources required to launch a new offering involve factors such as *business facilities* that include procuring and preparing manufacturing equipment, creating call centers to service customers, and developing an information technology infrastructure; *supply channels* to obtain the materials needed to create the offering; *distribution channels* through which the offering will be delivered to target customers; *skilled employees* who can contribute the required technological, operational, and business expertise; and *access to capital* to secure the financial resources needed to implement the business model.

To gain the resources needed to successfully launch the new offering, a company might adopt one of two different strategies. First, the company might create its own resources either by internally developing its assets and capabilities or by acquiring the necessary resources from a third party. Alternatively, rather than building its own resources, a company might choose to collaborate with other entities that have the resources required to help develop, manufacture, distribute, and promote the offering, and leverage these resources without assuming ownership of them.

DEVELOPING THE MARKET OFFERING

Developing the market offering involves turning the prototype into a market-ready commodity. This involves not only creating the final product and service but also building the brand, setting both retail and wholesale prices, determining the type of sales promotions to be used, and developing a plan to effectively communicate the benefits of the offering and make it available to target customers.

The development of an offering often involves advanced prototyping and market testing to ensure that the offering will succeed in creating market value. The amount of prototyping and testing needed is influenced by a variety of factors, such as product novelty, product complexity, and the investment required to modify the offering after it has been launched. New-to-the-world products warrant more market testing than products that involve slight modifications from what is already available in the market. More complex products are more likely than simpler products to benefit from market testing. Products that will require high levels of investment in modification after launch (e.g., retooling the manufacturing plant to modify the design of a car) are in greater need of advance prototyping and market testing than products that can be modified relatively easily post launch.

An important decision involved in test marketing is determining in which markets and with which customers the offering should be tested. A number of considerations come into play for this decision. Many major global consumer-goods makers such as L'Oréal, Philips, and Nikon like to test in South Korea because its consumers are known to be demanding but fair-minded, and its well-developed marketing infrastructure helps ensure that products are in good enough shape to enter other global markets. Gucci tests many of its luxury products in China because consumer preferences there are indicative of where the luxury market is heading.

Many companies skip test marketing despite its benefits and rely on faster and more economical testing methods. Starbucks regularly launches products before they have been deemed "perfect," based on the philosophy espoused by chief digital officer Adam Brotman: "We don't think it is okay if things aren't perfect, but we're willing to innovate and have speed to market trump a 100% guarantee that it'll be perfect." The company's mobile payments app had a number of flaws that needed correcting during its first six months after launch, but it now generates three million mobile transactions a week.[22] General Mills prefers to launch new products in 25 percent of the country, an area too large for rivals to disrupt. Managers review retail scanner data, which tells them within days how the product is doing and what corrective fine-tuning is needed.

When developing a new offering, a company can create a fully functional, full-scale version of the product prior to launching it in the market. Alternatively, a company might develop a streamlined version that incorporates only features that are essential to fulfilling the customer need. The development of a streamlined version of the offering—referred to as a *minimum viable offering*—enables the company to test the offering's market performance before proceeding to develop the full-scale offering.

Commercial Deployment

Commercialization informs target customers about the company's offering and makes the offering available to these customers. Because large-scale rollouts are characterized by greater uncertainty and higher costs, companies often choose to launch the offering in a few select markets before making it available to all target customers. The key aspects of commercialization—*selective market deployment* and the subsequent *market expansion*—are outlined here.

SELECTIVE MARKET DEPLOYMENT

A key commercialization decision is whether a company should launch its new offering to all target customers delineated in its business model or initially deploy its offering only in selected markets, gradually expanding availability until the offering reaches its full market potential.[23] Many companies have adopted the **selective market deployment** approach, which allows them to conduct testing in a natural environment and observe how target customers, competitors, and company collaborators react to the offering.[24]

The smaller scale of selective market deployment provides the company with greater agility to adjust various features of the offering to maximize its impact in the marketplace. In addition to enhancing agility, selective market deployment requires fewer company resources to launch the offering and has the potential to bring in revenues to help defray the cost of the subsequent market expansion.

The subset of target customers to which the offering will initially be made available is referred to as the **primary target**. The primary target typically involves customers who are most likely to buy the company's offering and who will help the company to refine the offering and generate an initial stream of revenue.

Some products catch on immediately (roller blades), whereas others take a long time to gain acceptance (diesel engine autos). One new-product concept that quickly took hold was StubHub, an online ticket-reselling service.

StubHub The founders of StubHub, Jeff Fluhr and Eric Baker, came up with the idea for their site when they were Stanford MBA students. Realizing there were far too many unused tickets for sporting events, theater events, and concerts, they decided to set up an "eBay for tickets" where sellers could set a price higher or lower than face value, depending on demand. StubHub would take a 10 percent cut from the buyer and a 15 percent cut from the seller on every purchase. The service had to negotiate state laws restricting ticket reselling, but by 2006 it was making $100 million in revenue, split between sports (75 percent), concerts (20 percent), and theater (5 percent) in a market estimated to be worth $4 billion in the United States. StubHub was sold to eBay for $310 million in 2007 (in 2020 eBay sold StubHub to Swiss online ticket marketplace Viagogo). Original-ticket seller Ticketmaster and its Live Nation parent have fought the company from the start, threatening legal action, introducing paperless tickets that limit reselling, and launching the TicketExchange service to compete. StubHub has set its sights on being more than a ticket marketplace and becoming a multiplatform e-commerce site. With close to 40 percent of primary tickets going unsold, StubHub is also emphasizing helping consumers discover events and attend more of them.[25]

MARKET EXPANSION

Expanding the market to include all customers for whom the company's offering aims to create value is the next logical step after the company's offering has been successfully launched in its primary target market.

<< StubHub, a leader in online secondary ticket marketplaces, is considering other e-commerce options while adding a more emotional component to its core business.

Source: These materials have been reproduced with the permission of StubHub, Inc.

Market expansion typically involves three key activities: ramping up the facilities involved in the offering's production, promoting the offering to all target customers, and ensuring that the offering is available to the entire target market. During market expansion, a company typically moves upstream on the path of least resistance and the path of least resources to attract customers who are more difficult to reach and who are less likely to recognize the value of the company's offering. As a result, the company will probably expend more time, effort, and resources during market expansion than during initial market deployment.

Broader markets usually involve a wider range of customers, which frequently necessitates introducing variants of the offering to accommodate the different needs and preferences of all target customers. Thus, a company might enter the market with a single offering that appeals to its most likely adopters, and then introduce variations that appeal to the wider range of customer needs within the expanded target market. The increased assortment of company offerings associated with market expansion, in turn, calls for additional resources to ensure the market success of these offerings.

marketing INSIGHT

Understanding the Adoption of Innovations

Designing effective products that are likely to succeed in the marketplace requires a thorough understanding of the process by which customers evaluate products, knowledge of the factors on which they base their decisions, and awareness of how quickly they adopt products. The term *diffusion of innovation* refers to the way knowledge of a product, service, or idea spreads to the marketplace and the speed with which it is purchased or used. Two popular frameworks that examine customers' reaction to new offerings are outlined below.

Rogers' Model of Adoption of Innovations

Rogers' model, named after the American sociologist Everett Rogers, classifies customers according to the speed with which they adopt new offerings. This model defines level of innovativeness in terms of whether an individual adopts new ideas relatively earlier or later than other consumers. Rogers' model is based on the notion that some customers are more open than others to embracing innovative products. Depending on the timing of new-product adoption, the Rogers model divides customers into five categories (Figure 18.4):

- *Innovators* are technology enthusiasts; they are venturesome and enjoy tinkering with new products and mastering their intricacies. In return for lower prices, they are happy to conduct alpha and beta testing and to report on weaknesses in the early offering. Innovators are defined as the first 2.5 percent of adopters.
- *Early adopters* are opinion leaders who carefully search for new technologies that might give them a dramatic competitive advantage. They are less price

FIGURE **18.4**

Adopter Categorization on the Basis of Relative Time of Adoption of Innovations

Source: E. Rogers, *Diffusion of Innovations* (London: Free Press, 1962).

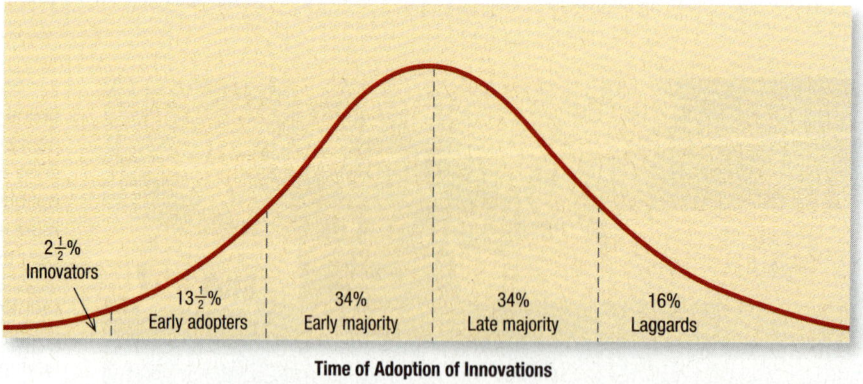

(continued)

marketing insight *(continued)*

sensitive and are willing to adopt the product if given personalized solutions and good service support. Early adopters are defined as the 13.5 percent of adopters following the innovators.

- The *early majority* includes deliberate pragmatists who adopt the new technology after its benefits have been proved and much adoption has already taken place. The early majority makes up the mainstream market and includes the next 34 percent of adopters.
- The *late majority* encompasses skeptical conservatives who are risk averse, technology shy, and price sensitive. The late majority consists of the next 34 percent of adopters following the early majority.
- *Laggards* are tradition bound and resist an innovation until the status quo is no longer defensible. The laggards make up the remaining 16 percent of the adopter population.

Each group requires a different type of marketing if the firm wants to move its innovation through the full product life cycle. In addition to or instead of targeting opinions leaders, some experts advocate targeting **revenue leaders** with a new product—those customers with higher customer lifetime value—to accelerate the path to profitability.

Rogers' model is a classification model; even though it divides individuals into five distinct categories based on the speed with which they adopt new offerings, it does not provide a decision rule that can be used to determine the category to which a particular individual is likely to belong. Furthermore, because individuals are assigned to one of the five categories based on relatively stable personality traits, this model does not account for the fact that a customer who is an innovator in one domain might be a laggard in another. Because of these limitations, the Rogers' model has limited applicability and is confined to describing five types of innovation adopters.

Moore's Model of Adoption of New Technologies

Named after organizational theorist Geoffrey Moore, **Moore's model** adapts the Rogers model specifically to technology products. It places technology adapters into five categories that more or less reflect the five categories specified by the Rogers model based on how open they are to adopting technological innovations. Here are the five classes of adopters of innovation in the Moore model:

- *Technology enthusiasts* are the innovators who are committed to technological innovations and are typically the first group to want to experience new technologies.
- *Visionaries* (early adopters) are also among the first to adopt new technologies in order to solve their problems, fulfill their needs, and take advantage of emerging market opportunities.
- *Pragmatists* (early majority) rely on innovation as a productivity tool. They are unlike enthusiasts in that they do not adopt technological innovations for their own sake. And they differ from visionaries in that they apply technology to enhance existing business models rather than to change them.
- *Conservatives* (late majority) are pessimistic about deriving significant benefits from emerging technological innovations and thus are slow to adopt them.
- *Skeptics* (laggards) tend to be very critical of technological innovations and are unlikely to adopt them despite their benefits.

Rogers' model assumes that the adoption of innovations is a continuous process and that after the innovation reaches market saturation in one segment, it will roll over into the next segment. Moore's model, on the other hand, argues that the adoption of innovations is a discontinuous process involving certain "gaps" and that the adoption of an innovation by one segment does not necessarily mean that the innovation will be adopted by another segment. This is because different consumer groups exhibit different patterns of adoption, each of which requires a different marketing strategy. For example, the fact that technology enthusiasts have embraced an innovation does not imply that it will be widely adopted by visionaries, who may view the technological innovation in a completely different light.

Moore defines the largest gap in the innovation-adoption process as the one that exists between the early adopters, the segment made up of technology enthusiasts and visionaries, and the mainstream market of technology pragmatists, conservatives, and skeptics. He defines this as the "chasm" and views it as the most significant challenge in developing technology innovations and the key hurdle that technology pioneers must overcome if they are to succeed in having their offerings widely accepted.[26]

summary

1. Innovation is the key to developing viable new offerings. Innovation can involve a new technology, a new approach to brand building, a new pricing mechanism, a new way of managing incentives, new channels of communication, or a novel distribution method. Innovative offerings disrupt existing business models and make companies that fail to adapt to changing market conditions superfluous by devising new ways to create market value.
2. Successful new-product development requires the company to establish an effective organization for managing the development process, which can include product managers (of either the new product or existing products), committees, departments, or venture teams. Increasingly, companies are adopting cross-functional teams, connecting to individuals and organizations outside the company through crowdsourcing and other means, and developing multiple product concepts.
3. New-product development is an *iterative process* of discovering a novel idea and translating this idea into a viable, successful market offering. New-product development is represented as a sequence of actions (stages) separated by hurdles (gates) that the new offering must overcome. The stage-gate approach divides the innovation process into five key stages—*idea generation, concept development, business-model design, offering development,* and *commercial deployment*—separated by gates that serve to validate the actions taken in the previous step.
4. Innovation begins with *generating an idea* that pinpoints an unmet market need and suggests a novel way to address this need. There are two basic methods of idea generation: top-down idea generation, which begins with identifying a market opportunity, and bottom-up idea generation, which starts with an invention and then seeks to identify an unmet market need that it will satisfy. Top-down idea generation is the preferred approach for developing new offerings.
5. *Concept development* embodies a potentially viable idea by creating an initial version, or prototype, of the company's offering. Concept development aims to reduce market and implementation risk by designing the offering in an expeditious and resource-efficient way. Concept development typically evolves from a description of the product's core features to a scaled-down prototype that features the offering's core functionality.
6. Designing the *business model* involves three key components: identifying the target market, articulating the offering's value proposition in that market, and delineating the key attributes of the market offering. The target market delineates the market in which a company's offering aims to create value. The value proposition describes the value that the company plans to create for target customers, collaborators, and its stakeholders. The market offering defines the ways— product, service, brand, price, incentives, communication, and distribution—in which the company will create, communicate, and deliver market value.
7. *Offering implementation* turns the conceptualized offering into an actual offering that is ready for market launch. Implementation involves gathering the necessary resources to put the business model into action and develop the market offering.
8. *Commercialization* informs target customers about the company's offering and makes the offering available to these customers. To minimize risk and resources, companies initially deploy the offering in selected (primary) markets and, upon its success, expand the availability of the offering to the entire target market. Market expansion ramps up the facilities involved in the offering's production, promotes the offering to all target customers, and ensures that the offering is available to the entire target market.
9. Two popular frameworks examine customers' reaction to new offerings. *Rogers' model* depicts the number of new adoptions, rather than total adoptions, at a given point in time and divides customers into five categories—innovators, early adopters, early majority, late majority, and laggards—based on the timing of new-product adoption. Building on Rogers' model, *Moore's model* argues that in the case of technology products, the adoption of innovations is a discontinuous process marked by distinct adoption gaps, the largest of which is the gap between the early adopters (enthusiasts and visionaries) and the mainstream market.

marketing
SPOTLIGHT

Paper Boat

Paper Boat, established in 2013 by Hector Beverage, is India's fastest growing food and beverage company known for its ethnic drinks. The company serves an exclusive range of authentic traditional Indian beverages like Aam Panna, Kokum, Jaljeera, Neembu Pani and many more. It also offers seasonal and occasion-based drinks such as Sharbat-e-Khas (available during Eid) and Panakam (available during Ram Navami). Some of its popular milk-based drinks include *thandai, badam* milk and butter milk. The company, with its authentic homemade-like fresh taste of its beverages, reflects the nostalgia of consumers connecting the tastes to their childhood memories and experiences.

In a market dominated by soft drinks majors Coca Cola and PepsiCo, customers did not have the option of a a drink that offered the traditional Indian taste and flavors. Paper Boat identified this gap and niche segment seeking the age-old traditional beverages with an authentic taste that seemed lost in the hustle-bustle of the urban lifestyle. Products by Paper Boat used both functional as well as emotional appeal to reconnect with tradition through its classic and authentic Indian beverages prepared with love and care. The company aims to preserve the traditional beverage recipes of India using innovation to make its ethnic drinks free of artificial coloring or preservatives.[27]

Paper Boat's product portfolio and promotion strategy revolve around creating the feelings of 'nostalgia, childhood and innocence' associated with the age-old recipes and memories. The company offers homemade drinks that consumers can relate with to their growing-up years, and therefore, enjoy a strong positive association. Its winning formula of ethnic flavors, unique packaging and intense digital marketing has helped Paper Boat penetrate deeper into the consumer's heart and retailer's shelves.

Paper Boat drinks set them apart from the crowd with their ethnic and authentic flavors. To ensure the traditional taste, Paper Boat takes complete care of the manufacturing process as well as the procurement of the raw materials and key ingredients. For instance, Paper Boat imported the seeds of purple carrot and started cultivating it for one of its products—Kanji, to preserve its authentic recipe which was replaced long back with red and orange carrots.[28]

Another key success factor behind the growing popularity of Paper Boat is its differentiated and eye catching packaging that sets the products apart on the retail shelves. Paper Boat follows clean and snazzy packaging design, unique for each product category, positioning the exclusivity of the brand with the help of an exceptional set of images and textures. The packs are given different color themes as per the product line with its distinctive cap designed for the convenience of unsealing the drink.[29]

Source: Paper Boat©Hector Beverages, used with permission

(continued)

Paper Boat has successfully deployed intense digital marketing techniques based on creative storytelling focused on childhood nostalgia to connect with the target audience at a personal level. The brand uses unique narratives along with out-of-the-box advertising campaigns that include a series of simple, animated ads reflecting childhood nostalgia and memories. A series of short films by Paper Boat helped the brand create an image of being an authentic homemade brand striving to preserve fond memories from childhood and traditions.

With its unique blend of success elements such as ethnic Indian flavored beverages—the true hero of the Paper Boat's success story, its unique, eye-catching and convenient packaging with snazzy look, and aggressive digital marketing communication based on stories capturing the deep emotions and childhood nostalgia, Paper Boat became one of the most popular Indian beverage brands. In a short span of time, Paper Boat expanded its business overseas by capturing the attention of NRIs in the USA, France, Britain, Canada, Australia, Netherlands, the UAE and Malaysia, thereby achieving a 20% growth in revenues as of 2020.[30]

The key factor in Paper Boat's success is its clear identification of an untapped segment in the beverage market. By staying ahead of health awareness trends, Paper Boat has firmly established itself as a valuable brand while still operating under the company's original mission —to create delicious, healthy, organic beverages with honesty, integrity, and an eye toward sustainability.

Questions

1. What role did customer insights play in developing Paper Boat?
2. What are the key factors that contributed to the success of Paper Boat?
3. How should Hector Beverages grow the Paper Boat brand?

marketing SPOTLIGHT

WeChat

Source: Piotr Swat/Alamy Stock Photo

WeChat is a Chinese social media, messaging, and mobile payment app developed by Tencent, a Chinese conglomerate that specializes in technology, gaming, and social media. WeChat is primarily used for messaging and communication, similar to Facebook and WhatsApp, and combines the functionality of apps like Twitter, PayPal, Reddit, and Uber. Users can also play video games, send money, voice chat, read news, share posts, order a taxi, and much more. WeChat's user base consists of over one billion daily active users, including companies, celebrities, and even hospitals that use the application as a promotional platform. Many Chinese cannot imagine life without this ubiquitous application.

WeChat began in 2010 as a social media and instant messaging application for smart phones. CEO Ma Huateng recognized that the future dominant platform for social media and messaging would be mobile phones rather than personal computers. He tasked an engineering team of fewer than 10 members to develop the first version of WeChat. The prototype version was capable only of sending text messages and pictures. Because instant messengers and SMS texting applications already existed with these features, consumers initially didn't see the app's value. WeChat's reception changed in May 2011 when the team upgraded the app to support voice messaging, which appealed to adults who were not used to typing on smart phones. Chinese businesspeople also found the increased functionality useful.

WeChat's user base skyrocketed in 2012 to over 100 million. There were two main reasons for this. First, overall Chinese smart-phone unit sales grew exponentially. In 2010, there were over 35 million smart-phone unit sales; by 2012, smart-phone unit sales had increased over fivefold to more than 210 million, which meant that a greater number of users were able to download and utilize the app. Second, WeChat growth was fueled by several innovations and features that provided a better user experience compared to competitor applications. WeChat introduced unique features

(*continued*)

like Shake, which randomly connected users who were shaking their phones at the same time, and Message in a Bottle, which allowed users to send messages to random recipients. WeChat's expanded platform also allowed users to read and share blog posts on Official Accounts and play games on the gaming platform. Competitor services like Feixin did not offer their application to users who did not have China Mobile, and MiTalk failed to provide a stable user experience, so WeChat overtook the messaging and social media market.

WeChat added payments to the platform in 2013. Initially, WeChat Pay was limited to microtransactions for games, virtual items for avatars, and mobile subscriptions. Tencent later expanded the payment platform and created WeChat Wallet, which lets users pay for goods and services at certified merchants and transfer money to other users. Four years after its introduction, WeChat Pay had over 600 million users.

WeChat Pay has improved the way Chinese users give each other hongbao, red envelopes filled with money, a popular tradition for the Lunar New Year. Users of the WeChat Red Packet can send their friends and loved ones hongbao in fun and addictive ways. For example, a user can put $5 from her or his WeChat Wallet into a virtual red envelope and have it distributed equally among five friends. Users can also have the first two recipients who tap the screen split the money in equal proportions or in a random cut. Red Packet became a massive success during the 2014 Lunar New Year, with more than 40 million hongbao sent to 8 million recipients. WeChat's Red Packet has grown to become a messaging medium in itself, with Chinese users frequently sending each other yuan amounts that have special meanings. For example, the number "520" is Chinese slang for "I love you."

One of WeChat's biggest selling points was the implementation of *mini programs* within the application. Mini programs, introduced in 2017, are best described as apps within the WeChat app. Mini programs are typically less than 10 megabytes that run instantly on WeChat without having to be downloaded from an app store. Programs load very quickly and are smoothly integrated within the WeChat platform. Many companies have developed mini programs for WeChat. JD.com, the second largest B2C e-commerce company in China, developed a shopping platform mini program. Tesla features a mini program where users can locate charging stations, schedule test drives, and share their experiences about driving a Tesla. Other mini programs include popular games, shared bike locators, and a payment tool for gas stations.

The wide variety of features that WeChat offers has helped the application become one of the largest mobile applications in the world. Although WeChat has been a widespread phenomenon mainly in China, Tencent has begun international expansion of WeChat, advertising the application's benefits to potential users in the United States, Malaysia, Singapore, and South Africa.[31]

Questions

1. What factors contributed to the phenomenal success of WeChat in China?
2. How important was WeChat's early-mover advantage in gaining and sustaining its dominant market position?
3. Can WeChat replicate its market success outside of China? Why or why not?

CHAPTER 19

Building Customer Loyalty

Building a community and creating an emotional attachment with customers have fueled cult.fit's expansion.

Source: ©cult.fit, used with permission

Generating a sale is not the ultimate goal of the marketing process. It is the beginning of building and managing customer relationships for the purpose of creating a loyal customer base. Cultivating loyal customers is a priority for market-driven companies that seek to gain and defend their market position. Indeed, without building customer loyalty, a company will have to constantly invest in acquiring new customers to replace disloyal customers who have switched to competitive offerings in search of a better deal.

Customer loyalty is the result of a company's efforts to consistently deliver a positive product, service, and brand experience. Although their enhanced capabilities can help companies earn strong customer loyalty, increased consumer capabilities pose challenges. Regardless, marketers must connect with customers—informing, engaging, and maybe even energizing them in the process. Customer-centered companies are adept at building customer relationships in addition to products; they are skilled in market engineering as well as product engineering. Creating user communities plays an increasing role for many companies and industries that seek new ways to satisfy customer needs and build loyalty. cult.fit is a vivid example of a company that has achieved market success by building a loyal customer base.

>>> cult.fit—India's leading health and fitness platform, was founded in 2016 by Mukesh Bansal and Ankit Nagori. It offers a one-stop solution to a variety of health and fitness-related needs, including physical as well as mental fitness. Headquartered in Bangalore, cult.fit caters to living a healthy life through its critical dimensions—physical fitness & wellness. The platform provides fitness-related services through a mix of online and offline channels, that include offline

group workouts at cult.fit Gx centres and other gym or equipment-based workouts at its own gyms and partner gyms across the country.

The unicorn startup offers a wide array of offline as well as online fitness services ranging from exercise, sports gear, food, mental wellness, preventive care and much more. The brand's online sessions by celebrity trainers, offered at a relatively lower price range than the offline sessions, boosted its growth during the COVID-19 pandemic lockdown period. Ensuring the wellbeing of its clients in the safety and convenience of home proved to be a gamechanger.[1] In 2021, with its new name cult.fit (previous name—Cult) after a rebranding exercise, the company has included many interesting and innovative customer-focused features such as online personal training, engaging and interactive group sessions, library of DIY (do-it-yourself) content, energy tracker, yoga, meditation and many more. cult.fit's 'Cult Pass' community allows members to access the complete range of service offerings that include fitness and yoga, healthy meals, mental wellbeing, medical and lifestyle care. With its omnichannel approach and success mantra of #BeBetterEveryDay, cult.fit has emerged as one of the most popular wellness brands. Community-based fitness workouts, that facilitates group workouts for its members along with trainers who instruct and coach them, drive a high level of engagement and retention among members. The company enjoys retention of over 60% with active participation among its members.

After reporting nearly 5*x* growth, the company's business expansion plans include pan-India and overseas as well.[2] It currently operates 350+ owned and partnered fitness centres/gyms in more than 25 cities across India.

Successful marketers are those who carefully cultivate customer satisfaction and loyalty. In this chapter, we spell out the some of the ways they can go about winning customers and beating competitors.

Managing Customer Acquisition and Retention

The ability to effectively acquire new customers and retain existing ones has a direct impact on the company's bottom line. To achieve success in acquiring and retaining customers, a company must have a clear understanding of the customer acquisition funnel and effectively balance its customer acquisition and retention efforts.

THE CUSTOMER ACQUISITION FUNNEL

The main steps in attracting customers can be imagined in terms of a funnel that depicts the phases in the customer acquisition process, from merely being aware of an offering to becoming loyal advocates. The **customer acquisition funnel** can be represented in terms of five relatively distinct phases: awareness, appeal, ask, act, and advocate.[3] This five-phase (or 5-A), narrowing approach to evaluating the customer acquisition process is depicted in Figure 19.1.

Learning Objectives After studying this chapter you should be able to:

19.1 Explain how a company should balance its acquisition and retention efforts.

19.2 Discuss how a company can manage customer satisfaction and loyalty.

19.3 Describe how companies manage customer relationships.

19.4 Discuss how a company should manage customer lifetime value.

FIGURE **19.1**
The 5-A Customer Acquisition Funnel

The *awareness* phase is the gateway to customers' interaction with the company's offering. It is in this phase that target customers encounter the company's offering. This encounter can be driven by the company's marketing communication, can occur at the point of sale, or may stem from advocacy by other customers and collaborators.

Awareness usually is not limited to a single offering. Often customers become aware of multiple offerings that could potentially meet their active need. This can happen when customers seek information on the different means to fulfill their need at the point of purchase or when they are exposed to the company's or competitors' marketing communication campaigns. It can also happen without any external influence when, based on prior experience, customers recall a set of available offerings.

The *appeal* phase reflects the fact that although customers might become aware of multiple offerings, they do not actively consider all of them. Instead, they tend to shortlist the most appealing offerings in order to form a consideration set composed of offerings that are most likely to fulfill their need. Thus, the appeal phase of the decision process can be viewed as a process of selective elimination, paring down the initial set of offerings that came to customers' minds.

During the *ask* phase, customers seek additional information about the offerings in their consideration set. This additional information can come from external sources such as friends and family, the media, and/or the company and its collaborators. For example, customers might call friends for advice, contact the company for more information, browse online reviews, use an app to compare prices, and even try out products at stores.

The *act* phase marks a transition from information gathering and evaluation to an action typically directed at a particular offering. Customer actions are not limited to purchase: They reflect the total ownership and usage experience, which also includes actual consumption of the product or service as well as the post-consumption experience.

The *advocate* phase reflects customers' reactions following their consumption experience. Ideally, customers' reactions will involve a certain level of loyalty to the company and its offering. These reactions can range from simply repurchasing the offering to ultimately advocating the offering to others. Active advocates recommend products, services, and brands they love without even being asked. They share positive experiences with others and often become evangelists.

The different steps of the decision funnel do not always occur in the linear process depicted in Figure 19.1; they can involve multiple iterations, reconsidering and reevaluating the available data, and gathering new information. And customers do not necessarily go through all of the Five A's; they might skip one or more of the five phases. For example, a customer might make an impulsive purchase without forming a consideration set and gathering additional information about the alternative options. Likewise, loyal advocates might not be actual purchasers of the company's offering. Apple products, such as the iPhone, iPad, and Apple Watch, for example, are often advocated by non-buyers.

BALANCING CUSTOMER ACQUISITION AND CUSTOMER RETENTION

Effective management of customer acquisition and retention involves clear understanding and accurate estimation of customer conversion and retention rates. By calculating **conversion rates**—the percentages of customers at the different stages who move to the next stage—managers can identify any bottleneck stage or barrier to building a loyal customer base. If the percentage of recent users is significantly lower than that of triers, for instance, something might be wrong with the product or service that prevents repeat buying.

The customer acquisition funnel also emphasizes how important it is not just to attract new customers but also to retain and cultivate existing ones. Research on customer retention suggests that acquiring new customers can cost several as much as satisfying and retaining current ones. Data further indicate that a 5 percent reduction in the customer defection rate can increase profits by 25 percent to 85 percent, depending on the industry. It has further been suggested that profit rate tends to increase over the life of the retained customer because of increased purchases, referrals, price premiums, and the reduced ratio of operating costs to service.[4]

Satisfied customers are the company's customer relationship capital. If the company were sold, the acquiring company would pay not only for the plant, equipment, and brand name but also for the delivered **customer base**, the number and value of customers who will do business with the new firm.

Some service providers are plagued by "spinners," customers who switch carriers at least three times a year looking for the best deal. Many mobile carriers and cable TV operators lose 25 percent of their subscribers each year at the cost of billions of dollars. Defecting customers cite unmet needs and expectations, poor product/service quality and high complexity, and billing errors. Different acquisition methods yield customers with varying levels of loyalty. One study showed that customers acquired through the offer of a 35 percent discount had about one-half the long-term value of customers acquired without any discount.[5] Many of these customers were more interested in the offer than in the product itself.

To reduce the defection rate, the company must define and measure its **retention rate**. For a magazine, a good measure of retention is its subscription renewal rate. Next, the company must identify the actionable causes of customer defection. For example, poor service, shoddy products, and high prices can all be addressed by the company, whereas issues such as customers moving out of the geographic area served by the company cannot be addressed. Finally, a company must compare the lost customer's lifetime value to the costs of reducing the defection rate. As long as the cost to discourage defection is lower than the lost profit potential, a company should spend the money to try to retain the customer.

Service outcome and customer loyalty are influenced by a host of variables. One study identified more than 800 critical factors that cause customers to switch services.[6] Among the key factors are pricing issues (high price, price increases, unfair pricing, deceptive pricing); convenience issues (location/hours, wait time for appointment and service); core service failure (service mistakes, billing errors, service catastrophes); service encounter failures (uncaring, impolite, unresponsive, unknowledgeable); response to service failure (negative response, no response, reluctant response); competition (found better service); ethical problems (cheat, hard sell, unsafe, conflict of interest); involuntary switching (customer moved, provider closed).

Regardless of how hard companies may try, some customers inevitably become inactive or drop out. The challenge is to reactivate them through win-back strategies.[7] It's often easier to reattract ex-customers (because the company knows their names and histories) than to find new ones. Exit interviews and lost-customer surveys can uncover sources of dissatisfaction and help win back only those with strong profit potential.[8]

Managing Customer Satisfaction and Loyalty

Loyalty has been defined as "a deeply held commitment to rebuy or repatronize a preferred product or service in the future despite situational influences and marketing efforts having the potential to cause switching behavior."[9] Customer loyalty can be thought of as a continuum, with different levels of loyalty varying in strength. Loyalty can range from satisfaction with the company's offering to advocacy and evangelism from customers who think of the offering as a part of their own identify and feel responsible for its success.

Godrej Interio Godrej Interio has emerged as one of the most desirable Indian furniture brands with a repute for developing and maintaining long term customer relationships. In 1923, Godrej started its furniture manufacturing business with Godrej Storewel steel cupboards (colloquially *almirah*). In 2006, Godrej Interio, established as a business unit of Godrej & Boyce, aptly connected with the customers based on the age-old trust in quality products and modern designs for offices and homes. Its premium and elegant designs that combine comfort with aesthetics have been a distinctive feature and a key differentiator. The company regularly upgrades and updates its product portfolio, designs, customer service options, operational processes and technology to meet the changing tastes and preferences of its customers. Strengthening its presence in the digital space during the COVID-19 pandemic helped the firm boost sales. Its investments in technology like AI and virtual reality (VR) enhanced the overall experience as customers shifted online. The company's mobile app is designed to provide a virtual walkthrough of the entire product range available at its physical stores and enables product experience through augmented reality. Focus on both experiences of in-store as well as online shopping, respectively, has helped Godrej Interio successfully reinforce its omnichannel presence while enabling customers to transform their dream spaces into reality with digitally driven, customized services. The customer-centric, eco-friendly and value-driven business model has driven Godrej Interio's growth. As one of the largest retailers of interiors, its extensive network covers over 400 cities through 50+ company-owned exclusive showrooms and 800 dealers. The firm's ceaseless efforts have been recognized by several accolades including the title of "India's most desirable brand" in 2021.[10]

Customer satisfaction is the key to building customer loyalty. Without fulfilling customer needs, a company would find it challenging to create a loyal customer base. The essence of customer satisfaction, the role of product and service quality as a driver of customer satisfaction, and the different approaches to measuring customer satisfaction are discussed in the following sections.

UNDERSTANDING CUSTOMER SATISFACTION

Satisfaction is a person's feelings of pleasure or disappointment that result from comparing the perceived performance (or outcome) of a product or service with expectations.[11] If the performance or experience falls short of expectations, the customer is dissatisfied. If it matches expectations, the customer is satisfied. If it exceeds expectations, the customer is highly satisfied or delighted.

Customer assessments of product or service performance depend on many factors, including the type of loyalty relationship the customer has with the brand.[12] Consumers often form more favorable perceptions of a product with a brand they already feel positive about. Research has also shown an asymmetric effect of product performance and expectations on satisfaction: The negative effect on customer satisfaction produced by failure to meet expectations is disproportionately stronger than the positive effect of exceeding expectations.[13]

Although the customer-centered firm seeks to create high customer satisfaction, that is often not its ultimate goal. Increasing customer satisfaction by lowering price or increasing services may result in lower profits. Alternatively, a company might be able to increase its profitability by means other than increased satisfaction (for example, by improving the efficiency of the manufacturing processes). Furthermore, because a company typically has many stakeholders—including employees, dealers, suppliers, and stockholders—spending more to increase customer satisfaction might divert funds from increasing the satisfaction of these stakeholders. Ultimately, the company must try to deliver a high level of customer satisfaction, while also delivering acceptable levels of satisfaction to its stakeholders, given its total resources.

How do customers form expectations? Expectations result from past buying experience, the advice of friends and associates, public information and discourse, and information and promises from marketers and competitors. If a company raises expectations too high, the buyer is likely to be disappointed. If it sets expectations too low, it won't attract enough buyers (although it will satisfy those who do buy).

Some of today's most successful companies are raising expectations and delivering performances to match. Korean automaker Kia found success in the United States by launching low-cost, high-quality cars reliable enough for Kia to offer 10-year, 100,000-mile warranties. Amazon's consistency in order fulfillment and on-time delivery has raised customer expectations of its future performance.

For customer-centric companies, customer satisfaction is both a goal and a marketing tool. Companies need to be especially concerned with their customer satisfaction level today, because the internet allows consumers to quickly spread both good and bad word of mouth to the rest of the world. Some customers set up their own websites to air grievances and galvanize protests, targeting high-profile brands such as United Airlines, Walmart, Home Depot, and Mercedes-Benz.[14]

PRODUCT AND SERVICE QUALITY AS A DRIVER OF CUSTOMER SATISFACTION

Satisfaction will also depend on product and service quality. **Quality** is often described as "fitness for use," "conformance to requirements," and "freedom from variation." A popular definition describes quality as the totality of features and characteristics of a product or service that bear on its ability to satisfy stated or implied needs.[15] This is clearly a customer-centered definition. We can say the seller has delivered quality whenever its product or service meets or exceeds customers' expectations.

A company that satisfies most of its customers' needs most of the time is called a high-quality company, but we need to distinguish between *performance* and *consistency*. Performance reflects the overall functionality of a company's products and services. Consistency, on the other hand, reflects the degree to which a company's performance remains at the same level over time. A Lexus automobile provides higher performance than a Hyundai: The Lexus rides more smoothly, accelerates faster, and runs problem-free longer. Yet both Lexus and Hyundai deliver consistency if all the units deliver their promised quality.

Product and service quality, customer satisfaction, and company profitability are intimately connected. Higher levels of quality result in higher levels of customer satisfaction, which, in turn, support higher prices. Studies have shown a high correlation between relative product quality and company profitability.[16] The drive to produce goods that are superior in world markets has led some countries to recognize or award prizes to companies that exemplify the best quality practices, such as the Deming Prize in Japan, the Malcolm Baldrige National Quality Award in the United States, and the European Quality Award.

Some companies are tempted to increase short-run profits by lowering costs and cutting corners. This may boost profits in the short run, but if quality declines as a result of these measures, customer experience and longer-term profits will suffer. Home Depot ran into trouble when it became overly focused on cost cutting.

Home Depot When Home Depot decided to expand into the contractor supply business, while also cutting costs and streamlining operations in its 1,800+ U.S. stores, it replaced many full-time workers with part-timers who soon made up about 40 percent of store staff. The chain's customer satisfaction rating dropped to the bottom among major U.S. retailers (11 points behind customer-friendly competitor Lowe's), and its share price slid 24 percent during the biggest home improvement boom in U.S. history. To turn the company around, new management set three main goals that all employees should strive to achieve—cleaner warehouses, stocked shelves, and top customer service. During new "power hours," on weekdays from 10 AM to 2 PM and all day Saturday and Sunday, employees were to do nothing but serve customers. To make sure the new strategy stuck, performance reviews were changed so that store employees were evaluated almost entirely on customer service. These and other customer-service initiatives increased store labor hours dedicated to customer interaction from 40 percent to 53 percent. Improved customer service, along with new product-assortment practices and centralized distribution centers, helped Home Depot reestablish its market leadership and distance itself from Lowe's.[17]

Source: REUTERS/Alamy Stock Photo

<< Home Depot reclaimed its market leadership position by focusing on policies geared to improving sagging customer service ratings throughout its network of stores.

Total quality is everyone's job, just as marketing is everyone's job. Nevertheless, marketing plays an especially important role in helping companies identify and deliver high-quality goods and services to target customers. How do marketers help? They correctly identify customer needs and requirements. They communicate customer expectations properly to product designers. They make sure customer orders are filled correctly and on time. They check that customers have received proper instructions, training, and technical assistance in the use of the product. They stay in touch with customers after the sale to ensure that they are, and remain, satisfied. They gather customer ideas for product and service improvements and convey them to the appropriate departments. When marketers do all this, they make substantial contributions to total quality management and customer satisfaction, as well as to customer and company profitability.

MEASURING CUSTOMER SATISFACTION

Many companies systematically measure how well they treat customers, identify the factors shaping satisfaction, and change operations and marketing as a result.[18]

Strategically minded firms measure customer satisfaction regularly because it is a key to customer retention. A highly satisfied customer generally stays loyal longer, buys more as the company introduces new and upgraded products, talks favorably to others about the company and its products, pays less attention to competing brands, is less sensitive to price, offers product or service ideas to the company, and costs less to serve than new customers because transactions can become routine.

The company needs to recognize, however, that customers define good performance differently. Good delivery could mean early delivery, on-time delivery, or order completeness, and two customers can report being "highly satisfied" for different reasons. One may be easily satisfied most of the time, and the other might be hard to please but was pleased on this occasion. It is also important to know how satisfied customers are with competitors in order to assess "share of wallet" or how much of the customer's spending the company's brand enjoys: The more highly the consumer ranks the company's brand in terms of satisfaction and loyalty, the more the customer is likely to spend on the brand.[19]

Periodic surveys can track customers' overall satisfaction directly and ask additional questions to measure repurchase intention, likelihood or willingness to recommend the company and brand to others, and specific attribute or benefit perceptions likely to be related to customer satisfaction.

Companies that do achieve high customer satisfaction ratings make sure their target market knows it. Once they achieved number-one status in their category on J. D. Power's customer satisfaction ratings, General Motors, Hyundai, American Express, and Alaska Airways (among others) communicated that fact.

Companies need to monitor their competitors' performance too. They can monitor their *customer loss rate* and contact those who have stopped buying or who have switched to another supplier to find out why. Companies can also hire *mystery shoppers* to pose as potential buyers and report on strong and weak points experienced in buying the company's and competitors' products.

Managers themselves can enter company and competitor sales situations where they are unknown and experience firsthand the treatment they receive, or they can phone their own company with questions and complaints to see how employees handle the calls. For example, IKEA's founder Ingvar Kamprad made frequent incognito visits to his own stores to ensure consistency of operations and superior service delivery.

The University of Michigan has developed the American Customer Satisfaction Index (ACSI) to measure consumers' perceived satisfaction with different firms, industries, economic sectors, and national economies.[20] Research has shown a strong and consistent association between customer satisfaction, as measured by ACSI, and a firm's financial performance in terms of ROI, sales, long-term firm value, and other metrics.[21] "Marketing Insight: Net Promoter Score and Customer Satisfaction" explains why some companies believe just one well-designed question is all that is necessary to assess customer satisfaction.[22]

BUILDING CUSTOMER LOYALTY

It is not enough to attract new customers; the company must also keep them and increase their business. Too many companies suffer from high customer defection. Yet many still focus the majority of their promotional efforts on acquiring new customers rather than on trying to retain existing ones, despite the high costs associated with the need to constantly counteract customer churn. Prioritizing customer retention by building customer loyalty is by far the more effective approach to long-term profitability than trying to acquire customers who are likely to leave the company as soon as they catch sight of a better deal.

Three of the most effective strategies for building customer loyalty include interacting closely with customers, developing loyalty programs, and building brand communities. These strategies are discussed next.

Interact Closely with Customers. Connecting customers, clients, patients, and others directly with company employees can be highly motivating and informative for the company employees. End users can offer tangible proof of the positive impact of the company's products and services, express appreciation for employee contributions, and elicit empathy. A brief visit from a student who had received a scholarship motivated university fundraisers to increase their weekly productivity by 400 percent; a patient's photograph inspired radiologists to improve the accuracy of their diagnostic findings by 46 percent.[23]

In addition to informing and motivating company employees, maintaining close relationships and interacting with customers often benefit these customers. Interacting with the company helps keep customers engaged with the company's products, services, and brands, which, in turn, helps create customers who are loyal to the company. Customers who believe that the company is listening to their concerns and is trying to fulfill their needs are more likely to stay loyal and are less likely to switch to a competitor offering a better deal.

Listening to customers is crucial to customer relationship management. Some companies have created an ongoing mechanism that keeps their marketers permanently plugged in to frontline customer feedback.

Deere & Company, which makes John Deere tractors and has a superb record of customer loyalty—nearly 98 percent annual retention in some product areas—has used retired employees to interview defectors and customers.[24]

Chicken of the Sea has 80,000 members in its Mermaid Club, a core-customer group that receives special offers, health tips and articles, new-product updates, and an informative e-newsletter. In return, club members provide valuable feedback on what the company is doing and thinking of doing. Their input has helped design the brand's website, develop messages for TV advertising, and craft the packaging.

Build-A-Bear Workshop uses a "Cub Advisory Board" for feedback and input to decisions. The board is made up of twenty 5- to 16-year-olds who review new-product ideas and give a "paws up or down" verdict. Many products in the stores are customer ideas.[25]

But listening is only part of the story. It is also important to be a customer advocate and, as much as possible, to take the customers' side, understand their point of view, and, when appropriate, modify the company's offering to create greater customer value.

Develop Loyalty Programs. Loyalty programs are a type of promotional incentive designed by companies to encourage customers to continue to patronize their business and, in some case, to increase the frequency and quantity of the products and services they purchase from the company. Loyalty programs are designed to reward customers who buy frequently and in substantial amounts. They can help build long-term loyalty with high-value customers, creating cross-selling opportunities in the process. Pioneered by airlines, hotels, and credit card companies, loyalty programs now exist in many other industries. Most supermarket and drug store chains offer price club cards that grant discounts on certain items.

Typically, the first company to introduce a loyalty program in an industry gains the most benefit, especially if competitors are slow to respond. After competitors react, loyalty programs can become a financial burden to all the offering companies, but some companies are more efficient and creative in managing them. Some loyalty programs generate rewards in a way that locks customers in and creates significant switching costs. Loyalty programs can also produce a psychological boost and a feeling of being special and elite that customers value.[26] Designer Shoe Warehouse is one firm that recognized the need to keep customers engaged in its loyalty reward program.

Designer Shoe Warehouse (DSW) Although the long-time loyalty program at DSW was running seamlessly, the shoe retailer realized the inherent danger of complacency. The online program gives customers points for each purchase and opens up levels of rewards to customers

>> To keep its long-time loyalty program fresh in the minds of customers, DSW initiated a personalized email campaign to inform customers of current deals and motivate them to earn future rewards.

Source: JHVEPhoto/Shutterstock

as they spend more. The problem with automatic rewards is that customers can easily forget about the program, which then instills no incentive to spend more and earn more points. As a way to keep its customers engaged and motivated, DSW inaugurated an active e-mail campaign to send regular reminders to customers about its loyalty reward program. Highly personalized e-mails inform customers about current deals, the number of points needed to earn a certificate for $10 off on a future purchase, the length of time they've been enrolled in the loyalty program, the number of points earned, and the amount they've saved during the past two years. Leveraging its trove of customer data enables DSW to create deeply personal e-mails that enhance the relevancy of its ongoing communication efforts and keep DSW and its loyalty program fresh in customers' minds.[27]

Club memberships, a popular form of loyalty program, aim to attract and keep those customers responsible for the largest portion of a company's business. Clubs can be open to everyone who purchases a product or service or can be limited to an affinity group or those willing to pay a small fee. Although open clubs are good for building a database or snagging customers from competitors, limited membership is often a more powerful long-term loyalty builder. Fees and membership conditions discourage those with only a fleeting interest in a company's products from joining. For example, to build loyalty, American Express offers its global Platinum Card members complimentary access to the network of The Centurion Lounges in major airports around the world.

Build Brand Communities. A **brand community** is a specialized community of consumers and employees whose identification and activities center revolve around the brand.[28] Three characteristics identify brand communities. First, they share a sense of connection to the brand, company, product, or other community members. Second, they share rituals, stories, and traditions that help convey the meaning of the community. Finally, they share a moral responsibility or duty both to the community as a whole and to individual community members.

Brand communities come in many different forms. Some arise organically from brand users, such as the Lugnet (LEGO) and Porsche Rennlist online discussion groups. Others are company sponsored and facilitated, such as SAP Community Network, My Starbucks Idea, Sephora Beauty Talk, Microsoft Xbox Ambassadors, and the Harley Owners Group (H.O.G.).

Harley-Davidson Founded in 1903 in Milwaukee, Wisconsin, Harley-Davidson has twice narrowly escaped bankruptcy to become one of the most widely recognized motor vehicle brands in the world. Harley keeps in touch with its customers by developing a strong brand community in the form of an inclusive owners' club, called the Harley Owners Group (H.O.G.). The group sponsors bike rallies, charity rides, and other motorcycle events and now numbers more than a million members in some 1,400 chapters. H.O.G. benefits include a magazine called *Hog Tales*, a touring handbook, emergency road service, a specially designed insurance program, theft reward service, discount hotel rates, and a Fly & Ride program enabling members to rent Harleys on vacation. The company also maintains an extensive website devoted to H.O.G., with information about club chapters and events and a special members-only section. Harley is also active with social media and boasts over 7.8 million Facebook fans. One fan inspired a digital video and Twitter campaign dubbed E Pluribus Unum—"Out of Many, One"—where Harley riders from all walks of life show their diversity and their pride in their bikes.[29]

Companies large and small can build brand communities. When New York's Signature Theatre Company built a new 70,000-square-foot facility for its shows, it made sure there was a central hub where casts, crews, playwrights, and audiences for all productions could mingle and interact.[30] Online, marketers can tap into social media networks such as Facebook, Twitter, Instagram, YouTube, and WeChat or create their own online community. Members can recommend products, share reviews, create lists of recommendations and favorites, or socialize together online.

A brand community can be a constant source of inspiration and feedback for product improvements or innovations. The activities and advocacy of brand community members can also substitute to some degree for activities the firm would otherwise have to engage in, creating greater marketing effectiveness and efficiency as a result.[31]

Building a positive, productive brand community requires careful thought and implementation. One set of researchers offers the following recommendations for making online brand communities more effective.[32]

- *Enhance the timeliness of information exchanged.* Set appointed times for topic discussion; give rewards for timely, helpful responses; increase access points to the community.
- *Enhance the relevance of information posted.* Keep the focus on topic; divide the forum into categories; encourage users to preselect interests.
- *Extend the conversation.* Make it easier for users to express themselves; don't set limits on the length of responses; allow user evaluation of the relevance of posts.
- *Increase the frequency of information exchanged.* Launch contests; use familiar social networking tools; create special opportunities for visitors; acknowledge helpful members.

Managing Customer Relationships

Companies are using information about customers to build long-term relationships.[33] **Customer relationship management (CRM)** is the process of carefully managing detailed information about individual customers and all customer touch points to maximize loyalty. Managing customer relationships is important because a major driver of company profitability is the aggregate value of the company's customer base. A related concept, customer value management, describes the company's optimization of the value of its customer base. **Customer value management** focuses on the analysis of individual data on prospects and customers to develop marketing strategies to acquire and retain customers and drive customer behavior.[34] Consider the experience of Dunnhumby.

Dunnhumby British customer data science company Dunnhumby (formed by husband and wife team Edwina Dunn and Clive Humby) has increased the profitability of retailers and other firms by gleaning insights from their loyalty program data and credit card transactions. The firm has helped British supermarket giant Tesco manage different aspects of its business: creating new shop formats, arranging store layouts, developing private-label products, and tailoring coupons and special discounts to its loyalty card shoppers. Tesco decided against dropping a poor-selling type of bread after Dunnhumby's analysis revealed it was a "destination product" for a loyal cohort that would shop elsewhere if it disappeared. Based on data from over 350 million people across the globe, Dunnhumby's insights have contributed to decisions about product range, availability, space planning, and new-product innovations. For a major European catalog company, Dunnhumby found that shoppers with different body types not only prefer different clothing styles, but also shop at different times of the year: Slimmer consumers tended to buy early in a new season, whereas larger folks tended to take fewer risks and wait until later in the season to see which styles proved popular.[35]

Customer relationship management enables companies to provide excellent real-time customer service through the effective use of individual account information. Based on what they know about each valued customer, they can customize market offerings, services, programs, messages, and media.

Popular strategies for enhancing customer relationship management include customization, customer empowerment, managing customer word of mouth, and dealing with customer complaints. We discuss these strategies in the following sections.

CUSTOMIZATION

Customization can encompass adapting the actual physical product and modifying the service experience. Customization involves making the company's offering as personally relevant as possible to as many customers as possible—a challenge, given that no two customers are identical. Customization calls on marketers to abandon the mass market practices that built brand powerhouses in the 20th century for new approaches that are a throwback to marketing practices from a century ago, when merchants literally knew their customers by name and designed unique products for each of them.

To customize the consumer experience, companies are using call centers, along with online, digital, and mobile tools complemented by artificial intelligence and data analytics to foster continuous contact between company and customer. Although technology can help with customer relationship management, firms have to be careful not to roll out too many automated-response phone systems or social-networking tools as ways to satisfy customer service requests. Many customers still prefer to talk to a live representative to receive more personal service—an ongoing priority in building lasting customer relationships.

Companies are recognizing the role of the personal component in customer relationship management and its influence once customers make actual contact with the company. Employees can create strong bonds with customers by individualizing and personalizing relationships. Consider the lengths to which British Airways is going to satisfy its valued customers.

British Airways British Airways took personalization to a higher level with its "Know Me" program. One goal was to centralize information about frequent fliers from all of the company's service channels—website, call center, e-mail, on board planes, and inside airports—into a single database. For any given passenger booked on a flight, British Airways knows his or her current seating location, previous flights and meal choices, and even prior complaint history. It also distributed iPads to crew members and ground staff, allowing them to access the database as well as to receive personal recognition messages about passengers on any flight. To facilitate VIP passenger identification, British Airways uses stored photos of fliers downloaded from Google Image searches. One company representative described the program as aiming to "recreate the feeling of recognition you get in a favorite restaurant when you're welcomed there, but in our case, it will be delivered by thousands of staff to millions of customers." Although some observers raised privacy concerns—even calling it "creepy"—British Airways noted that the passenger information was already available or was viewed as helpful by its most valuable fliers.[36]

While British Airways is personalizing its service experiences, BMW is figuring out ways to personalize its products. The company offers 500 side-mirror combinations, 1,300 front-bumper combinations, and 9,000 center-console combinations and provides new buyers with a video link to watch their car being "born" while waiting for delivery. Its detailed manufacturing and procurement system

Source: Kristoffer Tripplaar/Alamy Stock Photo

<< Centralizing information about frequent fliers from all sources into a single database and giving iPads to crew members and ground staff enabled British Airways to take personalized service to new heights.

takes the slack out of the production process, reduces inventory carrying costs, and avoids rebates on slow-moving sellers. Loyal customers tend to load up with options—generating more profitability for BMW and its dealers. Even Coca-Cola is getting in on the customization action. The Coca-Cola Freestyle dispensing machine can dispense 125 sparkling and still brands that consumers can mix via a touchscreen, creating a beverage to suit their particular taste.

To develop an effective customer relationship management program, marketers must know their customers.[37] The foundation of a customer relationship management program is the customer database, an organized collection of comprehensive information about individual customers or prospects that is current, accessible, and actionable for lead generation, lead qualification, sale of a product or service, or maintenance of customer relationships. In this context, customer relationship management can be viewed as a process of building, maintaining, and using customer-related data to contact customers, transact with them, and build long-term customer relationships.

Online retailers often add their own recommendations to consumer selections or purchases: "If you like that black handbag, you'll love this red top." One source estimated that recommendation systems contribute 10 percent to 30 percent of an online retailer's sales. Specialized software tools help facilitate customer "discovery" or unplanned purchases. At the same time, online companies need to make sure their attempts to create relationships with customers don't backfire, as happens when customers are bombarded by computer-generated recommendations that consistently miss the mark. Buy a few baby gifts on Amazon.com, and your personalized recommendations suddenly don't look so personal! Online retailers need to recognize the limitations of online personalization while searching for technology and processes that really work.

To adapt to customers' increased desire for personalization, while considering that not all customers want a relationship with the company and that many have privacy concerns, marketers have embraced concepts such as permission marketing. **Permission marketing**, the practice of marketing to consumers only after gaining their expressed permission, is based on the premise that marketers can no longer use "interruption marketing" via mass media campaigns. Perhaps one of the most common formats of permission marketing are newsletters sent to readers who have chosen to subscribe and thus have granted the publisher permission to send them relevant information.

Permission marketing implies that marketers can develop stronger consumer relationships by respecting consumers' wishes and sending messages only when the consumers have expressed a willingness to become more engaged with the brand. This approach can help make a company's interactions with its customers more meaningful.[38]

Permission marketing, like other personalization approaches, presumes that consumers know what they want, even though they often have undefined, ambiguous, or conflicting preferences.

"Engagement marketing" might be a more appropriate concept than permission marketing because marketers and consumers should work together to find out how the firm can best satisfy consumers.

CUSTOMER EMPOWERMENT

In recent years customers have had an increasing opportunity to control how they interact with a company. In the past, customers were often passive consumers of marketing messages, but today they are able to choose whether and how they want to engage with company marketing. This phenomenon, called **customer empowerment**, means that companies must strengthen their relationship with customers and engage with them in new ways. Because company empowerment has been matched by customer empowerment, companies have to adjust to changes in the nature of their customer relationships. To strengthen customer relationships, marketers are helping customers become evangelists for brands by providing them with resources and opportunities to demonstrate their passion. Doritos held a contest to let consumers name its next flavor. Converse asked amateur filmmakers to submit 30-second films that demonstrated how the iconic sneaker brand inspired them. The best submissions were showcased in the Converse Gallery website, and the best of the best became TV commercials.[39]

Although new technologies help customers assist or become involved in a brand's marketing, they can also help them avoid marketing. For example, many web browsers feature ad-blocking and popup-blocking software, e-mail servers offer spam filters, and mobile phones offer call-blocking options.

Although much has been made of the newly empowered consumer—in charge, setting the direction of the brand, and playing a much bigger role in how it is marketed—it's still true that only *some consumers* want to get involved with *some of the brands* they use, and even then, only *some of the time*. Consumers have lives, jobs, families, hobbies, goals, and commitments, and many things matter more to them than the brands they purchase and consume. Understanding how to best market a brand given such diversity in customer interests is crucially important.[40]

When will consumers choose to engage with a brand? Many factors can come into play, but one study revealed the following about customer pragmatism: "... most do not engage with companies via social media simply to feel connected.... To successfully exploit the potential of social media, companies need to design experiences that deliver tangible value in return for customers' time, attention, endorsement and data."[41] That "tangible value" includes discounts, coupons, and information to facilitate purchase. Many businesses overlook social media's capabilities for delivering customer value while capturing customer insights, monitoring the brand, conducting research, and soliciting new-product ideas.

MANAGING CUSTOMER WORD OF MOUTH

Although the strongest influence on consumer choice remains recommendations from friends and relatives, recommendations from other consumers are becoming an increasingly important decision factor. In an atmosphere of heightening mistrust of some companies and their advertising, online customer ratings and reviews are playing a growing role in the customer buying process.[42]

A Forrester research study, for example, found that about half of consumers won't book a hotel that does not have online reviews. Thus it's not surprising that more hotels are launching their own program to post reviews (Starwood places independent, authenticated reviews on individual hotel sites) or are using travel review sites (Wyndham streams its five most recent reviews from TripAdvisor on its site, leading to a 30 percent increase in bookings).[43] TripAdvisor has quickly become a valuable online resource for travelers.

TripAdvisor After being frustrated by the lack of detailed, reliable, and up-to-date information available to help him decide where to go on a Mexican holiday, Stephen Kaufer founded TripAdvisor in 2001. The pioneer in online consumer travel reviews, the company grew quickly and is now the world's largest travel website. It allows users to collect and share information and make bookings for a wide variety of hotels, vacation rentals, airlines, restaurants, and other travel-related locations or businesses through its hotel and air booking partners. Users can post reviews, photos, and opinions and participate in discussions on a variety of different topics. To improve the quality and accuracy of its content, TripAdvisor reviews content both manually and with advanced computer algorithms, including a verification and fraud detection system that considers the IP and e-mail address of reviewers (as well as other review attributes) and monitors suspicious patterns of postings as well as inappropriate language. TripAdvisor has more than 490 million unique visitors monthly and features over 700 million reviews. Hundreds of millions of people each month view its content on hundreds of other sites, including Hotels.com, Expedia, and Thomas Cook. TripAdvisor has innovated to improve the personalization and social nature of its services; in fact, it was one of Facebook's initial launch partners for its "Instant Personalization" project, which enables users to personalize their TripAdvisor experience by letting them see TripAdvisor content posted by their Facebook friends, subject to the friends' privacy elections. Local Picks is a Facebook app that allows users to localize TripAdvisor restaurant reviews and auto-share user reviews on Facebook.[44]

Brick-and-mortar retailers such as Best Buy, Staples, and Bass Pro Shops recognize the power of consumer reviews and have begun to display them in their stores. Despite consumer acceptance of such reviews, however, their quality and integrity can be in question.[45] In one famous example, over a period of seven years, the cofounder and CEO of Whole Foods Market posted more than 1,100 entries on Yahoo! Finance's online bulletin board under a pseudonym, praising his company and criticizing competitors. Some companies offer computer-recognition technology to monitor for fraud. Bazaarvoice helps companies such as Walmart and Best Buy manage and monitor online reviews using a process called device fingerprinting. The company caught one firm posting hundreds of positive reviews of one of its products and negative reviews of its competitor's products.[46]

Online reviews and blogging sites have struggled to police comments. To avoid attracting anonymous or biased reviews, Angie's List allowed only paid and registered subscribers to access its website. Users rate providers on price, quality, responsiveness, punctuality, and professionalism, using a report card–style scale of A to F. Other sites offer summaries of professional third-party reviews. Metacritic aggregates music, game, TV, and movie reviews from leading critics from multiple publications and combines them into a single 1-to-100 score. In the gaming industry, some game companies tie bonuses for their developers to game scores on the more popular sites. If a major new release doesn't make the 85-plus cutoff based on user reviews, the publisher's stock price may even drop.[47]

Marketers may benefit from tracking social media traffic to identify popular blogs. Bloggers who review products or services are influential because they may have thousands of followers; blogs are often among the top links returned in online searches for certain brands or categories. Firms also court the favor of key bloggers via free samples and advance information. Many bloggers disclose this special treatment from the companies they write about.

For smaller brands with limited media budgets, online word of mouth is critical. To generate prelaunch buzz for one of its new hot cereals, organic food maker Amy's Kitchen shipped out samples before its release to several of the 50 or so vegan, gluten-free, or vegetarian food bloggers that the company tracks. When favorable reviews appeared on these blogs, the company was besieged by e-mails asking where to buy the cereal.[48]

As it turns out, even negative reviews can sometimes be surprisingly impactful. For one thing, although they can hurt a well-known brand, they can create awareness about an unknown or overlooked one. They can also provide valued information. A Forrester study of 10,000 consumers of Amazon.com's electronics and home and garden products found that 50 percent found negative reviews helpful. When consumers can better learn the advantages and disadvantages of products through negative reviews, fewer product returns may result, saving retailers and producers money.[49]

DEALING WITH CUSTOMER COMPLAINTS

Some companies think they're getting a sense of customer satisfaction by tallying complaints, but studies show that even though customers are dissatisfied with their purchases about 25 percent of the time, only about 5 percent of dissatisfied customers complain. The other 95 percent either feel complaining is not worth the effort or don't know how or to whom to complain. They just stop buying.[50]

Of the customers who register a complaint, 50 percent to 70 percent might do business with the organization again if their complaint is resolved. The figure goes up to a staggering 95 percent if the customer feels the complaint was resolved *quickly*. Customers whose complaints are satisfactorily resolved tell an average of five people about the good treatment they received. The average dissatisfied customer, however, gripes to 11 people! Each person who is told about a negative experience will tell other people, so the number exposed to bad word of mouth may grow exponentially.

No matter how perfectly designed and implemented a marketing program is, mistakes will happen. The best thing a company can do—other than minimizing the chance of mistakes occurring in the first place—is make it easy for customers to complain. Suggestion forms, toll-free numbers, websites, apps, and e-mail addresses allow for quick, two-way communication. Enabling customers to provide feedback can not only help address their complaints; it can also help the company improve its products and services. The 3M Company claims that more than two-thirds of its product-improvement ideas come from listening to customer complaints.

Given that many customers may choose not to complain, companies should proactively monitor social media and other places where customer complaints and feedback may be aired. Along with its other responsibilities, Jet Blue's customer service team is charged with monitoring the airline's social media presence, including its Twitter account and Facebook page. When a customer's complaint about a fee for bringing a folded bike on board began to circulate online, Jet Blue quickly responded and decided this was not a service it should charge for.[51]

Given the potential downside of having an unhappy customer, it's critical that marketers deal with negative experiences properly and promptly. Although challenging, the following practices can help to recover customer goodwill.[52]

- Set up a seven-day, 24-hour toll-free hotline (by e-mail, online chat, phone, or fax) to make it easier for the customer to register complaints and for the company to act on them.
- Contact the complaining customer as quickly as possible. The slower the company is to respond, the more dissatisfaction may grow and lead to negative word of mouth.
- Identify the true source of customer dissatisfaction before seeking a solution. Some complaining customers are not looking for compensation so much as for a sign that the company cares.
- Accept responsibility for the customer's disappointment; do not shift the blame onto the customer.
- Resolve the complaint swiftly and to the customer's satisfaction, while taking into account the costs of resolving the complaint and the lifetime value of the customer.

Not all complaints, however, reflect actual deficiencies or problems with a company's product or service.[53] Big companies especially are targets for opportunistic customers who attempt to capitalize on even minor transgressions or generous compensation policies. Some firms fight back and even take an aggressive stance if they feel a criticism or complaint is unjustified. Others seek ways to find a silver lining in customer complaints and use them to improve the company's image and performance.

When Taco Bell began to attract negative buzz online, after rumors and a consumer lawsuit alleged that its taco mixture consisted of more filler than meat, it leaped into action with full-page newspaper ads headlined, "Thank you for suing us." In these ads, as well as in Facebook postings and a YouTube video, the company pointed out that its taco mixture was 88 percent beef, with ingredients such as water, oats, spices, and cocoa powder added only for flavor, texture, and moisture. To help spread the word, Taco Bell marketers bought the key words "taco," "bell," and "lawsuit" so that the company's official responses appeared as the first link on Google and the other search engines.[54]

Of course, a company can rarely achieve a zero level of complaints; there are always likely to be customers whose expectations surpass the benefits of a company's offerings. Instead, a company's

>> Taco Bell aggressively defends the quality of its products via social media.

Source: KENNELL KRISTA/SIPA/Newscom

goal is likely to be balancing customer satisfaction with the company's strategic and monetary goals, so that the company can create value for both its customers and its stakeholders.

Many senior executives worry about their firms using social media and the potential negative effects of cranky customers communicating online. Marketers, however, contend that the positives stemming from using social media outweigh the negatives and that steps can be taken to minimize the likelihood of such damage. One strategy for companies active in corporate social responsibility is to actively shape their public image during quiet times and then leverage that goodwill in paid or other media during difficult times. Nike was once a target of internet-savvy critics who skillfully used search engine optimization to populate unflattering portraits of the company. Now, searches for Nike yield links to sites that describe its many environmental and community initiatives (such as shoe recycling).

Managing Customer Lifetime Value

Marketing is often viewed as the art of attracting and keeping profitable customers. Yet every company loses money on some of its customers. The well-known 80/20 rule suggests that 80 percent or more of the company's profits come from the top 20 percent of its customers. Some cases may be more extreme: The most profitable 20 percent of customers (on a per capita basis) may account for over 100 percent of the company's profits. The least profitable 10 to 20 percent, on the other hand, can actually reduce profits, and the company breaks even with the middle 60 to 70 percent.[55] The implication is that a company could improve its profits by "firing" its worst customers.

Companies need to concern themselves with how efficiently they create value from the customers and prospects available. It's not always the company's largest customers who demand considerable service and deep discounts or who yield the most profit. The smallest customers pay full price and receive minimal service, but the costs of transacting with them can reduce their profitability. Midsize customers who receive good service and pay nearly full price are often the most profitable.

THE CONCEPT OF CUSTOMER LIFETIME VALUE

A key driver of shareholder value is the aggregate value of the customer base. The aim of customer relationship management is to produce high customer lifetime value.[56] **Customer lifetime value (CLV)** reflects the monetary equivalent of the value that customers will create for the company during their tenure with the company. CLV can refer to the value created by an individual customer, or it can refer to the cumulative value created by all of the company's customers—"the sum of lifetime values of all customers."[57] Customer lifetime value is also referred to as **customer equity**.

Customer lifetime value is affected by the revenue and the costs of customer acquisition, retention, and cross-selling. A profitable customer is a person, household, or company that, over time, yields a revenue stream exceeding by an acceptable amount the company's cost stream for attracting, selling, and serving that customer. Note that the emphasis is on the *lifetime* stream of revenue and cost. Indeed, from a company's perspective, what matters is the value that it receives over the course of all of its customer interactions, not on a particular transaction. Marketers can assess lifetime customer value individually, by market segment, or by channel.

To effectively manage its customer relationships, a company must be able to measure the value that each of its customers is likely to bring to the company over the course of that customer's tenure with the company. Yet, although many companies measure customer satisfaction, few measure individual customer profitability. Banks claim this is a difficult task because each customer uses different banking services, and the transactions are logged in different departments. However, the number of unprofitable customers in their customer database has appalled banks that have succeeded in linking customer transactions. Some report losing money on more than 45 percent of their retail customers.

Customer profitability analysis is often conducted with the tools of an accounting technique called activity-based costing. **Activity-based costing** aims to identify the real costs associated with serving each customer—the costs of products and services based on the resources they consume. The company estimates all revenue coming from the customer, less all costs. With activity-based costing, the costs in a business-to-business setting should include the cost not only of making and distributing the products and services but also of taking phone calls from the customer, traveling to visit the customer, paying for entertainment and gifts—all the company resources that go into serving that customer. Activity-based costing also allocates indirect costs such as clerical costs, office expenses, and supplies to the activities that use them, rather than as a proportion of direct costs. Both variable and overhead costs are tagged back to each customer.

Companies that fail to measure their costs correctly are also fail to measuring their profit correctly and, therefore, are likely to misallocate their marketing effort. The key to effectively employing activity-based costing is to define and judge "activities" properly. One time-based solution calculates the cost of one minute of overhead and then decides how much of this cost each activity uses.[58]

CUSTOMER LIFETIME VALUE AND BRAND EQUITY

The customer lifetime value (customer equity) perspective and the brand equity perspective certainly share many common themes. Both emphasize the importance of customer loyalty and the notion that we create value by having as many customers as possible pay as high a price as possible.

In practice, however, the two perspectives emphasize different things. The customer equity perspective focuses on bottom-line financial value. The main benefit of customer equity is that it yields quantifiable measures of financial performance. At the same time, it does not fully account for some of the important advantages of creating a strong brand, such as the ability to attract higher-quality employees, elicit stronger support from channel and supply chain partners, and create growth opportunities through line and category extensions and licensing. The customer equity approach can benefit from more explicitly considering the "option value" of brands and their potential to affect future revenues and costs.

The brand equity perspective, on the other hand, tends to emphasize strategic issues in managing brands and creating and leveraging brand awareness and image with customers. It provides much practical guidance for specific marketing activities. However, managers who focus on brands do not always develop detailed customer analyses in terms of the brand equity they achieve or the resulting long-term profitability they create. Brand equity approaches could benefit from the sharper segmentation schemes afforded by customer-level analyses and from more consideration of how to develop personalized, customized marketing programs—whether for individuals or for organizations such as retailers. There are generally fewer financial considerations put into play with brand equity than with customer equity.

Researchers have argued that a focus on either brand equity or customer equity depends on the way a company creates market value. In general, product-centric companies (such as like Procter & Gamble, Coca-Cola, and PepsiCo) tend to focus on brand equity as a major source of value and a key asset for future growth. In contrast, service-centric companies (such as banks, airlines, credit card companies, and cable and internet providers) tend to focus on customer equity as a key asset and performance measure. Specifically, the distinction between focusing on brand or customer equity has been attributed to the following factors:

- Firms that utilize subscription models—such as health clubs, mobile operators, and movie streaming companies—are more likely to find value in customer equity; firms that do not utilize contractual services tend to focus on brand equity.
- Companies that can uniquely identify their customers and assess their profitability tend to focus on customer equity; companies that cannot establish a direct link between a customer's behavior and performance outcomes tend to focus more on brand equity.
- Companies that produce self-expressive products such as cars, apparel, and fashion accessories tend to focus on brand equity.
- Companies that cannot readily obtain customer-level data and/or do not have direct contact with their customers are more inclined to focus on brand equity.
- Service-oriented companies are more likely to focus on customer equity than are product-oriented firms.

Despite the tendency of some companies to focus on either customer equity or brand equity, both types of equity matter. There are no brands without customers and no customers without brands. Brands serve as the "bait" that retailers and other channel intermediaries use to attract customers from whom they extract value. Customers are the tangible profit engine for brands to monetize their brand value.[59]

BUILDING CUSTOMER LIFETIME VALUE

Customer profitability analysis and the customer acquisition funnel help marketers decide how to manage groups of customers who vary in loyalty, profitability, risk, and other factors.[60] Winning companies improve that value by excelling at strategies like the following:

- ***Improving customer service.*** Selecting and training employees to be knowledgeable and friendly increases the likelihood that customers' shopping questions will be answered satisfactorily. Whole Foods woos customers with a commitment to provide fresh, high-quality food and deliver a superior service experience.
- ***Engaging customers.*** The more engaged with the company, the more likely a customer is to stick around. A large percentage of new Honda purchases replace an older Honda. Drivers cited Honda's reputation for creating safe vehicles with high resale value. Seeking consumer advice can be an effective way to engage consumers with a brand and company.
- ***Enhancing the growth potential of each customer.*** Sales from existing customers can be increased with new offerings and opportunities. Harley-Davidson sells more than motorcycles and accessories like gloves, leather jackets, helmets, and sunglasses. Its dealerships sell more than 3,000 items of clothing, and some even have fitting rooms. Licensed goods sold by others range from the predictable (shot glasses, cue balls, and Zippo cigarette lighters) to the more surprising (cologne, dolls, and cell phones). Cross-selling isn't profitable if the targeted customer requires a lot of services for each product, generates a lot of product returns, cherry-picks promotions, or limits total spending across all products.[61]
- ***Managing unprofitable customers.*** Marketers can encourage unprofitable customers to buy more or in larger quantities, forgo certain features or services, or pay higher amounts or fees. Banks, phone companies, and travel agencies all now charge for once-free services to ensure minimum revenue levels from these customers. Firms can also discourage those with questionable profitability prospects. Progressive Insurance screens customers and diverts the potentially unprofitable ones to competitors. However, "free" customers who pay little or nothing and are subsidized by paying customers—as in print and online media, employment and dating services, and shopping malls—may still create useful direct and indirect network effects, an important function.[62]
- ***Rewarding the most profitable customers.*** The most profitable customers can be treated in a special way. Thoughtful gestures such as birthday greetings, small gifts, or invitations to special sports or arts events can send them a strong positive signal. Hotels, airlines, credit card companies, and rental car agencies typically offer superior service to their best customers to ensure their loyalty, while at the same time maximizing their profitability.

A company should aim to build customer value across all of its customer touch points. A **customer touch point** is any occasion when a customer encounters the brand and product—from actual experience to personal or mass communications to casual observation. For a hotel, the touch points include reservations, check-in and checkout, frequent-stay programs, room service, business services, exercise facilities, laundry service, restaurants, and bars. The Four Seasons relies on personal touches, such as a staff that always addresses guests by name, high-powered employees who understand the needs of sophisticated business travelers, and at least one best-in-region facility, such as a premier restaurant or spa.

CREATING CUSTOMER LOYALTY BY BUILDING TRUST

What does it mean to trust a company or a brand? Research over the past 30 years has shown that trust is established and maintained via three important building blocks. One building block is competence. Companies and brands build *competence trust* when its managers have the skills required to do the job effectively, and when they meet or exceed expectations for those skills. Another building block is honesty. Firms build *honesty trust* by consistently telling the truth and keeping promises. A third building block is benevolence. Companies and brands build *benevolence trust* when they demonstrate genuine concern about the interests and goals of customers and employees.[63]

When customers are asked about how a particular company or brand performs with regard to the three building blocks, most companies learn that they are stronger with regard to some building blocks than with others. Facebook, for example, may be perceived as more competent than it is benevolent or honest. In contrast, a local bank may be perceived as more honest and benevolent than it is competent. It is therefore often overly simplistic to say that a company or brand is "trusted" or "distrusted," because companies are often trusted more with some things than with others. Companies and brands need to diagnose more specifically where their trust building blocks are strong or weak so they can more specifically develop strategies and tactics that will fortify trust where a building block may be weak.

Research by Kellogg School of Management expert on trust Kent Grayson suggests that a wide range of company activities can influence the extent to which customers trust a company or brand in terms of three building blocks: competency, honesty, and benevolence.[64]

- Consumers tend to judge **competence** by thinking about how what they experience with the company or brand is similar to or different from what they have experienced with relevant comparison cases. For example, customers who order room service at a three-star hotel are likely to assess their meal in relation to meals served at other three-star hotels and restaurants. If the customer asks for Dijon mustard and room service delivers regular mustard instead, the customer's trust in the hotel's competence will be more negatively affected if it is a five-star hotel than if it is a three-star hotel.
- Consumers tend to assess a brand's or company's **honesty** by comparing company statements with company actions. An airline that claims to have "no hidden fees" will become mistrusted by customers who find surprising fees on their airline ticket.
- Customers assess a brand's or company's **benevolence** based on whether they think they got a fair deal, and on whether those who work for the company have a clear understanding of customer needs and expectations. For example, many customers believe that charging customers different prices for the same product is not fair, so they mistrust companies that charge customers different prices depending on their ZIP code.

The activities that most strongly influence perceptions of the three building blocks of trust will differ, depending on factors such as the culture in which the company operates, the segment that the company is targeting, and customer perceptions of the company's brand. Companies that wish to effectively manage trust must therefore engage in customer research before deciding which activities require investment.

Research has shown that each of the three building blocks is differentially affected by positive and negative information. Competence is more strongly affected by positive information than by negative information. If a brand or company fails to deliver, and if the reason for the failure is related to competence, customers are often willing to forgive the behavior, especially if the brand has been competent in the past. In contrast, both honesty and benevolence are more strongly affected by negative information than by positive information. If a brand behaves in a way that demonstrates lack of honesty or benevolence, customers are less likely to forgive, even if the manager or brand has been honest and benevolent in the past.

Trust is more salient early in the development of a relationship and becomes less salient once a relationship has been established and is operating successfully. Once trust is established, companies and brands can benefit from the trust that employees and customers have. As long as a company or brand does not behave in a way that makes established customers question their trust, trust considerations move into the background of their consideration. This can sometimes encourage companies to exercise less care in their long-term relationships, or even to start cutting corners in ways that customers or employees will not notice. Although this can be an effective strategy in small measures, brands and companies cannot be too cavalier about trust with long-time employees and customers. The life-time value of long-term customers is often relatively high, and perceptions of trust violations in long-term relationships can sometimes have more significant negative effects than violations in shorter-term relationships.[65]

MEASURING CUSTOMER LIFETIME VALUE

Customer lifetime value is typically calculated as the net present value of the stream of future profits expected over the customer's lifetime purchases.[66] The company must subtract from its expected revenues the expected costs of attracting, selling, and servicing the account of that customer, applying the appropriate discount rate (say, between 10 and 20 percent, depending on cost of capital and risk attitudes). Lifetime value calculations for a product or service can add up to tens of thousands of dollars or even run to six figures.

Customer lifetime value calculations provide a formal quantitative framework for planning customer investment, and they help marketers adopt a long-term perspective. Researchers and practitioners have used many different approaches for modeling and estimating customer lifetime value.[67] Common factors in such models include the revenues generated from a given customer, the cost of acquiring and servicing this customer, the probability of customer repeat buying in the future, the customer's likely tenure with the company, and the discount rate (cost of capital for the firm). Marketers who use customer lifetime value concepts must also take into account the short-term, brand-building marketing activities that help increase customer loyalty.

When measuring customer lifetime value, it is important to consider not only the monetary value each customer is likely to directly generate for the company but also the strategic value this customer will create by endorsing the company and its offering to others. Indeed, a customer's value to a company depends in part on the ability and likelihood that he or she will make referrals and engage in positive word of mouth. As useful as earning positive word of mouth from a consumer can be, though, getting consumers to directly engage with the company and provide it with feedback and suggestions can lead to even greater loyalty and sales.

marketing INSIGHT

Net Promoter Score and Customer Satisfaction

Many companies make measuring customer satisfaction a top priority, but how should they go about doing it? Bain's Frederick Reichheld suggests that only one customer question really matters: "How likely is it that you would recommend this product or service to a friend or colleague?"

Reichheld was inspired in part by the experiences of Enterprise Rent-A-Car. When the company cut its customer satisfaction survey in 1998 from 18 questions to two—one about the quality of the rental experience and the other about the likelihood that the customer would rent from the company again—it found that those who gave the highest ratings to their rental experience were three times as likely to rent again as those who gave the second-highest rating. The firm also found that the diagnostic information managers collected from dissatisfied customers helped it fine-tune its operations. This insight eventually led to the development of the Net Promoter Score.

In a typical Net Promoter survey that follows Reichheld's thinking, customers are given a 1-to-10 scale on which to rate the likelihood of their recommending the company. Marketers then subtract *Detractors* (those who gave a score of 0 to 6) from *Promoters* (those who gave a 9 or 10) to arrive at the Net Promoter Score (NPS). Customers who rate the brand with a 7 or 8 are deemed *Passively Satisfied* and are not included. A typical set of NPS scores falls in range of 10 percent to 30 percent, but world-class companies can score over 50 percent.

Reichheld has picked up many believers through the years. American Express, Dell, and Microsoft have adopted the NPS metric, and some companies have even tied their managers' bonuses to NPS scores. Philips has focused on engaging Promoters as well as addressing the concerns of Detractors, developing a Reference Promoter program to get customers who are willing to recommend the brand to actually do so through taped testimonials.

Reichheld says he developed NPS in response to overly complicated—and thus ineffective—customer surveys. It is thus not surprising that client firms praise the NPS's simplicity and strong relationship to financial performance. When Intuit applied Net Promoter to its TurboTax product, feedback revealed dissatisfaction with the software's rebate procedure. After Intuit dropped the proof-of-purchase requirement, sales jumped 6 percent.

Despite the popularity of the Net Promoter Score, remember that it is only one of many dimensions on which customer satisfaction can be measured. Because of its simplicity, NPS cannot capture the different nuances of customer satisfaction and, hence, can produce inaccurate results. A common criticism is that many different patterns of responses may lead to exactly the same NPS. For example, NPS equals 20 percent when Promoters equal 20 percent, Passives equal 80 percent, and Detractors equal 0 percent, as well as when Promoters equal 60 percent, Passives equal 0 percent, and Detractors equal 40 percent, but the managerial implications of the two patterns of responses are very different. Another common criticism is that NPS is not a useful predictor of future sales or growth, because it ignores important cost and revenue considerations.

Others question the Net Promoter Score's actual research support. One comprehensive academic study of 21 firms and more than 15,000 consumers in Norway failed to find NPS superior to any other metrics, such as the ACSI (American Customer Satisfaction Index). Some have criticized both NPS and ACSI measures for not fully accounting for ex-customers or those who were never customers. Peoples' opinions about any of the single items or indices measuring customer satisfaction depend in part on how they value the trade-off between simplicity and complexity.[68]

summary

1. Customer loyalty reflects a deeply held commitment to patronize a particular product, service, or brand for future purchase and consumption occasions. Loyalty is a continuum, with different levels of loyalty varying in terms of their strength and ranging from satisfaction with the company's offering to advocacy and evangelism.
2. Customer satisfaction is the key to building customer loyalty. Satisfaction is a person's feelings of pleasure or disappointment that result from comparing the actual performance of a product or service to expectations. Recognizing that high satisfaction leads to high customer loyalty, companies must ensure that they meet or exceed customer expectations.
3. Customer satisfaction, product and service quality, and company profitability are intimately connected. Higher levels of quality result in higher levels of customer satisfaction, which support higher prices and (often) lower costs.
4. To ensure sustainable growth, a company must not only attract new customers; it must also keep them and increase their business. Losing profitable customers can dramatically affect a firm's profits. Three of the most effective strategies for building customer loyalty are interacting closely with customers, developing loyalty programs, and building brand communities.
5. Customer relationship management (CRM) is the process of carefully managing detailed information about individual customers and all customer touch points to maximize loyalty. The ultimate goal of CRM is to develop programs to attract and retain the right customers and to meet the individual needs of valued customers. Popular strategies for enhancing customer relationship management include customization, customer empowerment, customer word of mouth, and customer complaints.
6. Customer lifetime value (CLV) reflects the monetary equivalent of the value that customers will create for the company during their tenure with the company. CLV can refer to the value created by an individual customer, or it can refer to the cumulative value created by all of the company's customers—the sum of lifetime values of all customers. The aim of customer relationship management is to produce high customer lifetime value.
7. A company should aim to build customer value across all occasions on which a customer encounters its products, services, or brands—from actual experience to personal or mass communication to casual observation. Companies that fail to consistently deliver superior customer value are likely to see their customer base eroding over time.
8. Marketing managers must calculate the customer lifetime value of their customer base to understand the profit implications. Customer profitability analysis helps marketers identify their most valued customers and develop strategies to create value for these customers in a way that fosters long-term customer loyalty. When measuring customer lifetime value, it is important to take into account not only the monetary value each customer is likely to directly generate for the company but also the strategic value this customer will create by endorsing the company and its offerings to others.

marketing SPOTLIGHT

Infosys

In 1981, Narayana Murthy and his team of six engineers established Infosys with a capital of $250 in Pune, Maharashtra. Today, Infosys is a leading global information technology firm, valued at over $90 billion with revenues of $14.91 billion in 2021. With a nearly 280,000 multi-cultural workforce, Infosys offers consultancy services and software solutions to clients across the world. From the beginning, the founders adopted a customer-oriented, transparent and value-driven business model. In its initial days, the firm concentrated on customers in the US, considering that it was then the largest market for customized software services, and also, the global headquarters of leading multinationals across industries. In its 40 years of rich legacy, Infosys has emerged as one of the most reputed companies credited with India's emergence as the global destination for software services talent. Its pioneering 'Global Delivery Model' enabled faster completion of software projects through distributed project management by engagement teams located in multiple global locations.[69] The principle of taking work where it can be done best, makes the most economic sense with the least amount of acceptable risk, significantly improved engagement success and value realization for clients as compared to conventional delivery models for software services.

Running a business remotely with limited resources was one of the major challenges for the founding team of Infosys. The initial years were very challenging as the team operated from a small office with limited access to computing resources or even a telephone. It took a year for the start-up to get a telephone connection and 3 years and fifty trips to Delhi to get the license to import a computer.[70] But Narayana Murthy and his team believed in the virtues of patience, values and customer relationship. Customers were the most important stakeholder for the founders. Its strong relationship with its first client, Data Basics Corporation, a New York-based product company, helped Infosys establish its purpose and relevance. Infosys worked with this customer for more than 6 years. Referrals and positive word-of-mouth about quality services and ethical business practices helped Infosys win the trust of potential clients.[71]

As the company continued to develop expertise and expand its portfolio of offerings, it continued to reinforce itself as a customer-oriented company. The leaders recognized the importance of every single customer in the competitive business markets where a small set of customers generate a significant share of revenues. Infosys emphasizes working closely with each client to develop the core delivery capability and start handling multiple projects for these clients to broaden and deepen the relationship.

Along with long-term and in-depth relationships, its clients also developed a high level of dependency on the firm. In most instances, Infosys has developed its business by enlarging its share of customers' IT spending. Clients appreciate the simple and transparent system of Infosys in addition to its high quality and core delivery capabilities. The company's exemplary client relationship management practices have won itself several industry awards and accolades, including 'Best in Show' and 'Best Partnership' by the Outsourcing Institute and Vantage Partners.[72]

Many of Infosys clients, especially the Fortune-50 companies would have existing partnerships with leading technology companies like IBM, Accenture and Cap Gemini. After winning a project for a software-related assignment, Infosys would start working closely with these competitors who were already engaged by the client. The leadership has razor-sharp focus on the well-being of the client's business interests. Its healthy collaborative relationships with its competitors helped Infosys gain clients' respect across industries.

In 1993, Infosys started offering services in the domestic market, following its success in the US market as one of the most reliable IT companies. Infosys was among the very few IT companies that had identified the growing demand for customized software solutions across the world and started developing its offerings to cater to the rising tailored software needs. By the first decade of the 21st century, Infosys evolved as a strategic partner for many of its global clients in the banking, financial services and insurance vertical. Infosys would become an important part of strategic decisions by several clients. The company adopted a strategic account management approach, involving business leaders from

Source: The logo / brand name in the image is proprietary to Infosys

(continued)

Infosys and the client, to enhance the relationship value with its most important clients. More than 97% of its business is generated from the same set of clients while 3% of its annual revenues originate from new clients. Transparency and integrity are the key ingredients behind Infosys strong relationship with its clients. These are reinforced through the tagline *'Powered by Intellect, Driven by Values'*.

While strengthening its own core competencies to improve its position in the global market, the leaders collaborated with leading India software service providers like TCS and Wipro to create NASSCOM[73] —an industry association for the information technology business process management (IT BPM) sector. NASSCOM has played a stellar role in transforming the global image of Indian IT industry through its collaborative approach while working with governments to represent its 3000+ members generating an annual revenue of over $194 billion.

The company has been a trailblazer. Records include it being the first India-registered company to be listed on NASDAQ. Its employee stock options program created some of India's first salaried millionaires. Great Place to Work® and Fortune have honoured Infosys[74] as one of the best employers. Employees regularly rate the company as one of the best places to work. The company's people practices deliver excellent employee experiences. The leadership's commitment towards creating a credible and fair workplace is evident in its practices for hiring, inspiring, appreciating, developing, caring, and sharing. Employee satisfaction and productivity are directly linked to the success of its client projects. With its focus on stakeholder relationships, Infosys experienced rapid growth. The company generated revenues of $100 million in 1999, $1 billion in 2004 and $10 billion in 2017.

To ensure project performance, the management uses health indicators that revolve around touchpoints affecting the overall performance of the project. Continuous monitoring of ongoing projects on parameters such as time, budget and quality enable the teams to deliver projects and meet clients' requirements profitably. They serve as an early warning system for the leadership to take corrective actions including deployment of additional resources and expertise to support projects experiencing challenges. Customer satisfaction surveys keep track of the impact of the client relationship on the customer's business.[75]

With its focus on building and maintaining long-term customer relationships, Infosys has been a torchbearer of India's knowledge power on the global stage. As a leading technology company, Infosys enables over 1,700 clients in more than 50 countries to navigate their digital transformation.[76 & 77]

Questions

1. What explains the success of Infosys?
2. How do clients benefit from working with Infosys?
3. How does Infosys strengthen relationships with its best clients?

marketing
SPOTLIGHT

Tanishq

Tanishq is India's first retail jewellery brand from the house of Titan, a joint venture between Tata group and the Tamil Nadu Industrial Development Corporation. Known for its contemporary designs and customer-centric approach, Tanishq has emerged as India's fastest-growing jewelry brand. The brand has transformed the precious metal jewellery industry that was dominated by traditional retailers. It has redefined the Indian jewellery industry standards and set new benchmarks. However, the making of Tanishq as a retail giant has not been easy.

It all began in the late 1980s when Titan company decided to enter the jewellery market seeking to capitalize on the large demand for gold jewellery. The firm launched Tanishq for the international market with the aim to supply ethnic Indian jewellery, with a western twist, crafted for the international markets. However, the products failed to match up to the expectations of overseas customers.

After suffering losses in the international markets, Titan decided to launch Tanishq in the domestic market. In 1994, the company introduced 18-karat gold watches, followed by the opening of its first exclusive jewellery retail outlet in 1996 in Chennai, Tamil Nadu. Tanishq then went on to introduce 18-carat gold and diamond jewellery instead of the traditional 22-carat jewellery sold by local players. The intention was to attract customers with a less-expensive option of 18-karat gold ornaments through distinctive and modern designs embedded with precious stones.

Once again, Tanishq failed to understand the consumer sentiments attached to the purity of the gold jewellery. As a result, the brand lagged in gaining market acceptance and the company incurred a loss of more than ₹150 crores. In 2002, the company conducted a thorough market study to assess strategic options. The extensive research led to the introduction of 22-karat gold jewellery. The turning point came after the launch of Karatmeter, a device to check the

(*continued*)

purity of gold. Karatmeter grabbed the attention of customers by exposing the unscrupulous retailers who were selling lower karat gold while charging the customers for 22 karats. Trust on many local retailers dipped after published reports indicated that more than 60% of the jewellery sold in the retail market were of lower grade. Tanishq grabbed this opportunity to better understand the customers' point of view regarding purity of gold, and thereby, win over their trust.[78]

Soon Tanishq turned around its laggard state to a rapidly growing and trusted jewellery brand. The company crafted a system to capture information related to all touchpoints that affect the overall customer experience. The customer relationship team created customer profiles, which includes details related to the taste and preference of the customers along with important life events. These details are captured through Encircle, Titan's loyalty program that allows members to earn reward points and exclusive privileges on every purchase. Tanishq makes a conscious effort to provide a personalized touch while giving its customers a sense of belongingness by celebrating every customers' life events as well as common festivals. Tanishq greets customers on special occasions, including birthdays and anniversaries, with special promotional offers and gifts.

Inspired by the way Taj luxury hotels treat its guests, Tanishq introduced one of the most innovative concepts called 'Tanishq Way of Life' in 2012. Under this program, in-store employees were trained to improve the overall customer experience in the stores. Tanishq Way of Life was designed to delight the customer by taking care of every touchpoint of her journey, right from the moment the customer walks into the store, even if she did not buy anything during a visit.

Tanishq expanded its offerings by introducing a sub-brand, Mia, for the young professional women and Rivaah as exclusive wedding jewelry. Tanishq ran a campaign 'My Expression' to engage with prospects and customers through a design contest for ideas for Mia. Over 3,200 entries marked 'My Expression' as one of the most successful campaigns by Tanishq and served as a launchpad for Mia. Tanishq was gaining ground and winning customers' trust even before launching new brands.[79]

During the COVID-19 lockdown period, as a safety measure for its stakeholders, Tanishq boosted its digital presence to reach out to its customers at the comfort of home. Its new digital program called 'Endless Aisle' allows the customers to virtually access the complete range of product offerings. The company reported sales of more than ₹100 crores in the months of July and August 2020. Digital is rapidly emerging as the first touchpoint for many of its young customers. Titan's customers enrolled in its loyalty program, Encircle, earn and redeem reward points at the group's e-commerce portals. In its journey of more than four decades, Tanishq has continued to grow by keeping customer-centricity at the core of its business model.[80]

Source: tanishq©titan Company Ltd, used with permission

Questions

1. What is the role of customer relationship management in the luxury goods industry? What is the relationship among customer satisfaction, customer loyalty, and company profitability?
2. What are the key aspects of Tanishq's customer loyalty program? What are the key drivers of its success?
3. How should Tanishq use the recent developments in data analytics, machine learning, and artificial intelligence to enhance customer loyalty and create shareholder value?

CHAPTER 20

Tapping into Global Markets

Refocusing from volume and market share to quality, backed by a groundbreaking warranty, transformed the image of Bajaj Auto.

Source: ©Bajaj Auto, used with permission

Countries are increasingly multicultural, and products and services developed in one country are finding wide acceptance in others. Consider the globalization of the auto industry. According to a J. D. Power study, vehicles in the 2018 study were manufactured in 25 countries, 11 of which weren't present in the study five years ago. Those 11 new homes to auto manufacturing were Brazil, China, Finland, India, Italy, the Netherlands, Poland, Serbia, Spain, Thailand, and Turkey.[1] Consider, for example, the rapid ascent of Bajaj Auto.

>>> Bajaj Auto, established in 1945, has emerged as India's leading motorcycle manufacturer and exporter with operations in more than 70 countries. The company started its business as an importer of scooters, prior to its obtaining the manufacturing licence in 1959. Today it enjoys the status of *"The world's favourite Indian"* with more than 50% of its business coming from international markets. Bajaj Auto entered international markets in 2000 by launching its motorcycle brand Pulsar. The firm, after discontinuing scooter manufacturing, focused on creating world-class motorcycles for the mid-range segment seeking value-for-money bikes. The firm invested heavily in research and development to create product differentiation, specialization, partnership and diversification to capture the international markets.[2] Countries were grouped into categories depending on the size of the two-wheeler market. Partnering with the leading local distributors in countries with high market potential such as Indonesia, Nigeria and Iran helped the company establish its presence quickly. In mid-sized markets such as Mexico and Sri Lanka, Bajaj Auto sent a dedicated team to work closely with the local distributors to sharpen its marketing strategy.[3] This collaborative approach, along

with its partnerships with Kawasaki and KTM, helped the firm to emerge as the leading Indian brand in international markets such as Africa, Asia and South America. The company, with cumulative exports of over 18 million vehicles in the last ten years, stands as one of the most visible Indian brands worldwide. Its global sales have earned over $ 14 billion during the last decade.[4&5] Even during the pandemic-hit financial year 2020-21, the company exported over 2 million vehicles to 79 countries, and generated $1.65 billion in revenues.[6]

Although opportunities to compete in international markets are significant, the risks can be high. Companies selling in global industries have no choice, however, but to internationalize their operations. In this chapter, we review the major decisions involved in expanding into global markets.

Deciding Whether to Go Abroad

U.S. retailers such as The Limited and Gap have become globally prominent. Dutch retailer Ahold and Belgian retailer Delhaize earn almost two-thirds and three-quarters of their sales, respectively, in nondomestic markets. Foreign-based global retailers in the United States include Italy's Benetton, Sweden's IKEA home furnishings stores, and Japan's UNIQLO casual apparel retailer.

Several factors draw companies into the international arena. First, certain international markets might present better profit opportunities than the domestic market. Second, a company might need a larger customer base to achieve economies of scale. A company might also decide to go abroad to reduce its dependence on any one market. Another reason for going abroad could be a company's desire to counterattack global competitors in their home markets. A company's decision to go abroad might also stem from a its desire to be able to serve its global customers who require international service.

As cultures blend across countries, another benefit of global expansion is the ability to transfer ideas and products or services from one market into another. Cinnabon discovered that products it developed for Central and South America were finding success in the United States, too, given its large Hispanic population.[7]

Despite the potential appeal of going global, many companies would prefer to remain domestic if their domestic market were large enough. Managers would not need to learn other languages and laws, deal with volatile currencies, face political and legal uncertainties, or redesign their products to suit different customer needs and expectations. This reluctance is often grounded in the real challenges posed by wading into international markets.

International markets pose distinct challenges, including variations in customers' shopping habits, the need to gain social acceptance, and the absence of a communication and distribution infrastructure.[8] Going abroad involves two major types of risks.

- **General risks associated with entering a new market** (domestic or foreign). These risks involve a company's inability to understand customer needs and develop an offering to address these needs, to correctly identify competitive threat, to build effective supply and distribution networks, or to promote the offering in an effective and cost-efficient manner.

Learning Objectives After studying this chapter you should be able to:

20.1 Explain how companies decide whether to go abroad.

20.2 Discuss the factors that companies consider in deciding which global markets to enter.

20.3 Summarize the strategies companies use to enter global markets.

20.4 Explain how companies can adapt their marketing strategies for global markets.

- **Specific risks associated with doing business in a different country**. These risks involve not understanding the nuances of the foreign country's business culture and the intricacies of foreign regulations; lacking skilled managers with international experience; and having business disrupted by commercial and political changes such as tariffs, currency fluctuations, and even a government change leading to expropriation of foreign property.

Tesco Tesco introduced its Fresh & Easy gourmet mini-supermarkets to California after much research, which included spending time with U.S. families and videotaping the contents of their refrigerators. Fresh & Easy's 200 or so stores were roughly 10,000 square feet (about one-fifth the size of a standard U.S. supermarket but much bigger than a convenience store), with a focus on fresh-food offerings. Despite its significant investment, after five unprofitable years and more than $1.6 billion in losses, Tesco decided to exit the market in 2013. A host of problems plagued the retailer. Its U.S. customers were not accustomed to British-style ready meals, self-service cash registers, and unorthodox store layouts. Other complaints were that the product range was too narrow, there was no bakery, the flower department was underwhelming, and the stores were physically too cold. The United States was not the only trouble spot for Tesco. The company had exited Japan the preceding year and was encountering difficulty in Central and Eastern Europe. While it focused on geographic expansion, its core supermarket business in the United Kingdom was neglected. Stores weren't properly staffed, fresh food was not properly maintained, and new private-label products were not introduced. The attempt to add non-grocery items such as clothing and electronics proved futile in a recession, and entry into new areas like banking and telephony was a distraction. After enduring six consecutive quarters of same-store sales declines in its home market, Tesco announced a $1.7 billion program to refresh its UK stores and a pull-back of its global ambitions.[9]

The world's top three retailers—U.S.-based Walmart, UK-based Tesco, and France-based Carrefour—all have struggled to enter certain overseas markets. Consider the plight of Tesco.

The problems that plagued Tesco in the United Kingdom are a common downside of overly aggressive global expansion. In many cases, such expansion occurs at the expense of maintaining sufficient support for the home market. Selling everything from food to televisions, Carrefour, the world's second-biggest retailer, has also encountered stiff competition at home from smaller supermarkets for groceries, and from specialist retailers such as IKEA for other goods. Although strong in some parts of Europe and Asia, Carrefour (which means "crossroads" in French) has been forced to cease operations in Japan, South Korea, Mexico, the Czech Republic, Slovakia, Bulgaria, Switzerland, and Portugal.

Deciding whether to go abroad is the first of several decisions a company must make when developing its global strategy. If the company has concluded that going abroad is indeed the best course of

>> After less-than-successful attempts to expand into U.S. and other markets around the world threatened its UK stores, Tesco scaled back its global ambitions and concentrated on refurbishing its UK outlets.

Source: Ian Dagnall/Alamy Stock Photo

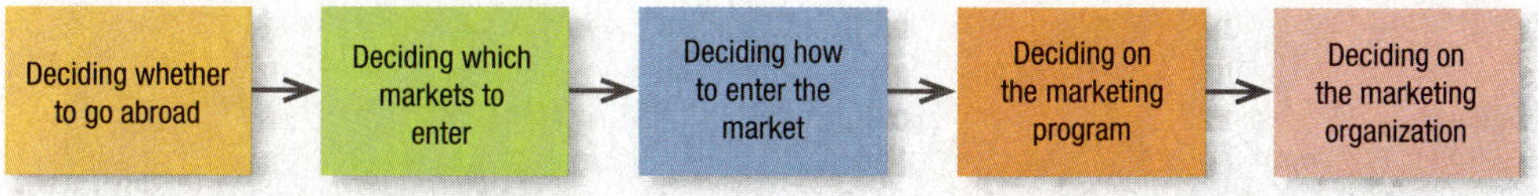

FIGURE **20.1**
Major Decisions in International Marketing

action, it must then make a set of more specific decisions, including which markets to enter, how to enter these markets, which specific marketing program to use for each market, and how to structure the marketing organization in each country. These decisions are illustrated in Figure 20.1 and discussed in the following sections.

Deciding Which Markets to Enter

In deciding to go abroad, the company needs to define its marketing objectives and policies. What ratio of international sales to total sales will it seek? Most companies start small when they venture abroad. Some plan to stay small; others have bigger plans.

DETERMINING HOW MANY MARKETS TO ENTER

The company must decide how many countries to enter and how fast to expand. Typical entry strategies are the *waterfall* approach, gradually entering countries in sequence, and the *sprinkler* approach, entering many countries simultaneously. Increasingly, firms—especially technology-intensive firms and online ventures—are born global and market to the entire world from the outset.

Matsushita, BMW, General Electric, Benetton, and The Body Shop followed the waterfall approach, which allows firms to carefully plan expansion and is less likely to strain human and financial resources. But when first-mover advantage is crucial and a high degree of competitive intensity prevails, the sprinkler approach is better. Apple, Gillette, and Unilever used the sprinkler approach for some of their products. The main risks in the sprinkler approach are the substantial resources needed and the difficulty of planning entry strategies for many diverse markets.

The company must also choose what countries to enter based on the product and on factors such as geography, income, population, and political climate. Competitive considerations come into play too. It may make sense to go into markets where competitors have already entered to force them to defend their market share, as well as to learn how they are marketing in that environment.

A critical consideration, without question, is market growth. Getting a toehold in a fast-growing market can be a very attractive option, even if that market is likely to be crowded with more competitors soon. KFC has entered scores of countries as a pioneer by franchising its retail concept and making its marketing culturally relevant.

KFC KFC is one of the most recognizable quick-service restaurant brands in the world, with more than 21,000 restaurants around the world. The company is world famous for its Original Recipe fried chicken—made with the same secret blend of 11 herbs and spices that Colonel Harland Sanders perfected more than half a century ago. KFC is the largest, oldest, most popular, and fastest-growing quick-service restaurant chain in China, with many of the more than 5,000 locations enjoying healthy margins of 20 percent per store. The company has tailored its menu in China to local tastes with items such as the Dragon Twister, a wrap stuffed with chicken strips, Peking duck sauce, cucumbers, and scallions. KFC even has a Chinese mascot—a kid-friendly character named Chicky, which the company boasts has become "the Ronald McDonald of China." Like any emerging market, China does pose challenges for KFC. Sales there took a stumble early in 2013, when state-owned Chinese media accused the company of using local suppliers that gave their chickens excessive antibiotics to stimulate faster growth. A social media firestorm followed, eventually causing KFC to apologize for not having tighter controls. Supply chain problems have posed a different challenge in Africa, KFC's next growth target. Without a domestic supply of chickens, the company had to import them, which is illegal in Nigeria and Kenya. To overcome the supply problem in Nigeria, it added fish to the menu. As it moved into more African markets, the company made sure to localize its menu—selling Ugali, a type of porridge, in Kenya and jollof rice in Nigeria—as well as to showcase local culture on store walls and in its advertising.[10]

Source: Lou-Foto/Alamy Stock Photo

>> KFC has managed to surmount global expansion challenges by tailoring its menu and advertising to the logistical and cultural requirements of specific locations.

EVALUATING POTENTIAL MARKETS

How does a company choose among potential markets to enter? One key factor is their *physical proximity*. Many companies prefer to sell to neighboring countries because they understand these countries better and can control their entry costs more effectively. It's not surprising that the two largest U.S. export markets are Canada and Mexico or that Swedish companies first sold to their Scandinavian neighbors.

At other times, *cultural proximity* determines choices. Given more familiar language, laws, and culture, many U.S. firms prefer to sell in Canada, England, and Australia rather than in larger markets such as Germany and France. Companies should be careful, however, when choosing markets according to cultural proximity. Besides overlooking potentially better markets, they may only superficially analyze real differences that put them at a disadvantage.

It often makes sense to operate in fewer countries, with a deeper commitment and penetration in each. In general, companies show preference for countries that have high market attractiveness and low market risk and in which they possess a competitive advantage.

In assessing potential markets, it may often be necessary to consider the benefits of engaging underserved populations.

Consider how the following companies successfully entered developing markets by pioneering ways to serve "invisible" consumers.[11] Grameenphone marketed cell phones to 35,000 villages in Bangladesh by hiring village women as agents who leased phone time to other villagers, one call at a time. Colgate-Palmolive rolled into Indian villages with video vans that showed the benefits of toothbrushing. And Corporación GEO builds low-income housing in Mexico, featuring two-bedroom homes that are modular and expandable.

Companies may also want to take into account the positive impact that successful relationships with collaborators can have when assessing markets. When Unilever introduced TRESemmé in Brazil, it secured the support of 40 big retailers, courted fashion bloggers, distributed 10 million free samples, and launched the company's biggest-ever single-day online ad blitz, which eventually lured 1 million fans to the brand's Brazilian Facebook page. In less than a year, sales of TRESemmé surpassed those of P&G shampoo stalwart Pantene in hypermarkets and drugstores, giving Unilever confidence to set its sights on India and Indonesia next.[12]

Marketers are learning the nuances of marketing to a broader population in emerging markets, especially when cost reductions are difficult to realize because of the firm's established supply chain, production methods, and distribution strategy, and when price premiums are hard to command because of consumer price sensitivity. Yet, getting the marketing equation right in developing markets can pay big dividends:

Source: Jorge_Adriano/Shutterstock

<< The 8R line of John Deere tractors adapts to the needs of farmers in both developed and developing markets around the world.

Smaller packaging and lower prices are often critical when income and space are limited. Unilever's four-cent sachets of detergent and shampoo were a big hit in rural India, where 70 percent of the population still lives.[13]

The vast majority of consumers in emerging markets buy their products from tiny bodegas, stalls, kiosks, and mom-and-pop stores not much bigger than a closet, which Procter & Gamble calls "high-frequency stores." In India, food is largely purchased from the 12 million neighborhood mom-and-pop outfits called kirana stores. These thrive by offering convenience, credit, and even home delivery, although modern retailing is beginning to make inroads.[14]

Successfully entering developing markets requires a special set of skills and plans, along with the ability to do a number of things differently and well.[15] Selling in developing areas can't be "business as usual." Economic and cultural differences abound, a marketing infrastructure may barely exist, and local competition can be surprisingly stiff.[16]

Many firms from developed markets are using lessons gleaned from developing markets to better compete in their home or existing markets. Product innovation has become a two-way street between developing and developed markets. The challenge is to think creatively about how marketing can fulfill the dreams of most of the world's population for a better standard of living. Many companies are betting they can do that. To feed a projected world population of 9 billion by 2050, analysts estimate that food production globally must increase by 60 percent, a challenge John Deere is addressing.

Deere & Company Deere & Company (also referred to as John Deere), a manufacturer of agricultural, construction, and forestry machinery, dates back to 1937 when John Deere established the namesake company in Illinois. Initially focused on serving the U.S. market, the company is now the largest agriculture machinery company in the world, employing over 60,000 people worldwide. Its most popular products include various types of tractors, corn pickers, sugarcane and cotton harvesters, mowers, and golf course equipment, along with accessories and associated services. John Deere's 8R line was the first tractor line designed to accommodate the needs of different farmers in 130 countries worldwide. The 8R is powerful but agile and fuel-efficient, best suited for larger farms. At the same time, it is highly customizable to suit the needs of growers in developing markets like Brazil and Russia, as well as the developed markets of the United States or Germany. To serve its diverse global customer base, Deere has a number of factories outside the United States in both developed and developing markets, including Germany, India, China, Mexico, and Brazil.[17]

Deciding How to Enter the Market

Once a company decides to target a particular country, it must choose the best mode of entry for its brands. Its broad choices are *indirect exporting, direct exporting, licensing, joint ventures,* and *direct investment,* as shown in Figure 20.2. Each succeeding strategy entails more commitment, risk, control, and profit potential.

When going global, firms often start by working with an independent agent and entering a nearby or similar country. Later, the firm establishes an export department to manage its agent relationships. Still later, it replaces agents with its own sales subsidiaries in its larger export markets. This increases investment and risk but also enlarges earning potential. Next, to manage subsidiaries, the company replaces the export department with an international department or division. If markets are large and stable, or if the host country requires local production, the company will locate production facilities there. By this time, the firm is operating as a multinational and optimizing its sourcing, financing, manufacturing, and marketing as a global organization.

We discuss the different options for entering foreign markets in the following sections.

INDIRECT AND DIRECT EXPORT

Companies typically start with exporting, specifically **indirect exporting**—that is, they work through independent intermediaries. There are three types of organizations that act as intermediaries between a company and an international market: domestic-based export agents, cooperative organizations, and export-management companies. *Domestic-based export merchants* buy the manufacturer's products and then sell them abroad. *Domestic-based export agents,* including trading companies, seek and negotiate foreign purchases for a commission. *Cooperative organizations* conduct exporting activities for several producers—often of primary products such as fruits or nuts—and are partly under their administrative control. *Export-management companies* agree to manage a company's export activities for a fee.

Indirect export has two advantages. First, there is less investment: The firm doesn't have to develop an export department, an overseas sales force, or a set of international contacts. Second, there's less risk: Because international marketing intermediaries bring know-how and services to the relationship, the seller will make fewer mistakes.

Companies may eventually decide to handle their own exports. The investment and risk are somewhat greater, but so is the potential return. **Direct exporting** happens in several ways. It may involve a domestic-based export department or division—purely a service function that may evolve into a self-contained export department operating as its own profit center. Alternatively, exporting might involve an overseas sales branch or subsidiary that handles sales and distribution and sometimes warehousing, promotion, and customer service as well. Finally, exporting might involve home-country-based traveling export sales representatives.

Many companies use direct or indirect exporting to "test the waters" before building a plant and manufacturing their product overseas. A company does not necessarily have to attend international trade shows if it can effectively use the internet to attract new customers overseas, support existing customers who live abroad, source from international suppliers, and build global brand awareness.

Successful companies adapt their websites to provide country-specific content and services, ideally in the local language, to international markets with the highest potential. Finding free information about trade and exporting has never been easier. Export-promotion offices in many states also have online resources and allow businesses to link to their sites.

FIGURE **20.2**
Five Modes of Entry into Foreign Markets

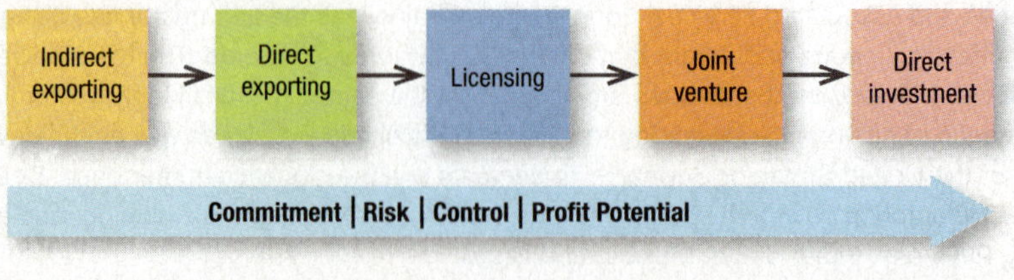

LICENSING

Licensing is a simple way to engage in international marketing. The licensor issues a license to a foreign company to use a manufacturing process, trademark, patent, trade secret, or other item of value for a fee or royalty. The licensor gains market entry at little risk; the licensee gains production expertise and/or a well-known product or brand name.

The licensor, however, has less control over the licensee than over its own production and sales facilities. If the licensee is very successful, the licensing firm has given up profits, and if and when the contract ends, it might find it has created a competitor. To prevent this, the licensor usually supplies some proprietary product ingredients or components (as Coca-Cola does with its syrup). Perhaps the best strategy is to lead in innovation so the licensee will continue to depend on the licensor.

Licensing arrangements vary. Companies such as Hyatt and Marriott sell *management contracts* to owners of foreign hotels to manage these businesses for a fee. The management firm may have the option to purchase some share in the managed company within a stated period.

In **contract manufacturing**, the firm hires local manufacturers to produce the product. Volkswagen has a contract agreement with Russian automotive conglomerate GAZ Group, whereby GAZ will build the Volkswagen Jetta, Škoda Octavia, and Škoda Yeti models in Nizhny Novgorod for the Russian market. Toshiba, Hitachi, and other Japanese television manufacturers use contract manufacturing to service the Eastern European market. Contract manufacturing reduces the company's control over the process and risks loss of potential profits. However, it offers a chance to start faster, with the opportunity to partner with or buy out the local manufacturer later.

Finally, a company can enter a foreign market through **franchising**, a more comprehensive form of licensing. The franchisor offers a complete brand concept and operating system. In return, the franchisee pays certain fees to the franchisor. Quick-service operators such as McDonald's, Subway, and Burger King have franchised all over the world, as have service and retail companies like 7-Eleven, Hertz, and Best Western Hotels.

JOINT VENTURES

Just doing business in another country may require the firm to license its product, form a **joint venture** with a local firm, or buy from local suppliers to meet "domestic content" requirements. Many firms have developed global strategic networks, with victory going to those who build the better one. The Star Alliance brings together 28 airlines—including Lufthansa, United Airlines, Singapore Airlines, SAS, and Avianca—in a huge global partnership that enables travelers around the globe to make nearly seamless connections to hundreds of destinations.

Historically, foreign investors have often joined local investors in a joint venture company in which they share ownership and control. A joint venture may be necessary or desirable for economic or political reasons. The foreign firm might lack the financial, physical, or managerial resources to undertake the venture alone, or the foreign government might require joint ownership as a condition for entry.

The value of a partnership can extend far beyond increased sales or access to distribution. Good partners share "brand values" that help maintain brand consistency across markets. For example, the fierce commitment of McDonald's to product and service standardization is one reason why its retail outlets are so similar around the world. McDonald's handpicks its global partners one by one to find "compulsive achievers" who will put forth the desired effort.

After years of growth through acquisition and buying interests in two dozen companies, the world's biggest wireless telecom operator, Vodafone, has looked outside for partners to help it leverage its existing assets.

Vodafone To spur more innovation and growth, London-based Vodafone has embraced open-source software and open platforms that allow it to tap into the creativity and skills of others. With its web portal called Betavine, both amateur and professional software developers can create and test their latest mobile applications on any network, not just Vodafone's. These developers retain intellectual property rights, but Vodafone gains early exposure to the latest trends and ensures that innovations are compatible with its network. The new apps include real-time train arrivals and departures, movie show times, and an Amazon.com widget with personalized details. With 404 million customers in 30 countries, the £46 billion company hasn't had trouble finding help from interested corporate partners. Dell has collaborated with Vodafone to design laptops and low-priced netbooks with built-in wireless broadband access over Vodafone's networks.[18]

Brand Adaptation. When they launch products and services globally, marketers may need to change certain brand elements. Even a brand name may require a choice between phonetic and semantic translations. When Clairol introduced the "Mist Stick," a curling iron, in Germany, it found that *mist* is slang for *manure*. In China, Coca-Cola and Nike have both found sets of Chinese characters that sound broadly like their names but offer some relevant meaning at the same time ("Can Be Tasty, Can Be Happy" and "Endurance Conquer," respectively).[34]

Numbers and colors can take on special meaning in certain countries. The number four is considered unlucky throughout much of Asia, because the Japanese and Chinese word for the number sounds like the word for "death." Some East Asian buildings skip not only the fourth floor but often every floor that has a four in it (14, 24, 40–49). Nokia doesn't release phone models containing the number four in Asia. Purple is associated with death in Burma and in some Latin American nations, white is a mourning color in India, and in Malaysia green connotes disease. Red generally signifies luck and prosperity in China.[35]

Brand slogans or ad taglines sometimes need to be changed too: When Coors put its brand slogan "Turn it loose" into Spanish, some read it as "suffer from diarrhea." A laundry soap ad claiming to wash "really dirty parts" was translated in French-speaking Québec to read "a soap for washing private parts." Perdue's slogan—"It takes a tough man to make a tender chicken"—was rendered into Spanish as "It takes a sexually excited man to make a chicken affectionate."[36]

Country-of-Origin Effects. Country-of-origin perceptions are the mental associations and beliefs triggered by a country. Government officials want to strengthen their country's image to help domestic marketers export and to attract foreign firms and investors. Marketers want to use positive country-of-origin perceptions to sell their products and services.

Global marketers know that buyers hold distinct attitudes and beliefs about brands or products from different countries. These perceptions can stem from a variety of factors, including the attributes of the product, the meaning of the brand, and the country of origin ("If it's French, it must be stylish"). Coca-Cola's success against local cola brand Jianlibao in China was partly due to its association with U.S. modernity and affluence. Consider the experience of Digicel:

Digicel Launched in 2001, Jamaica-based Digicel has conquered politically unstable developing countries such as Papua New Guinea, Haiti, and Tonga with mobile telecommunication products and services appealing to poor and typically overlooked consumers. The company strives for 100 percent population coverage with its networks, bringing affordable mobile service to local and rural residents who have never before had the opportunity for coverage. It operates in 31 markets in the Caribbean, Central America, and Asia Pacific. To be locally relevant, Digicel sponsors local cricket, rugby, and other high-profile sports teams in each of these areas. Well-known champion Olympic sprinter Usain Bolt is the chief Digicel Brand Ambassador for various advertising and promotions across the region. The company also runs a host of community-based initiatives in each market through the educational, cultural, and social development programs of its Digicel Foundation. The company's marketing efforts in Fiji are instructive. Pitched in a fierce battle with incumbent Vodafone only two years after entry, Digicel Fiji even added a shade of light blue from the bottom of the Fiji national flag to its own red logo to reflect the company's pride in its contributions to Fijian life and sport, as reflected in its campaign "Fiji Matters to Us."[37]

The mere fact that a brand is perceived as successful on a global stage—whether it sends a quality signal, taps into cultural myths, or reinforces a sense of social responsibility—may lend credibility and respect.[38] Research studies have found that certain countries enjoy a reputation for certain goods: Japan for automobiles and consumer electronics; the United States for high-tech innovations, soft drinks, toys, cigarettes, and jeans; France for wine, perfume, and luxury goods.

When consumers do not know where the products and brands come from, they often make inferences about their origin. In surveys, they routinely guess that Heineken is German, Nokia is Japanese, and Au Bon Pain is French (they are Dutch, Finnish, and American, respectively). Most consumers are unaware that Popov vodka, Ginsu Knives, Estée Lauder, and Häagen-Dazs originated in the United States.

Marketers must look at country-of-origin perceptions from both a domestic and a foreign perspective. In the domestic market, these perceptions may stir consumers' patriotic notions or remind them of

Source: Rafael Ben-Ari/Alamy Stock Photo

<< Efforts to stay locally relevant have enabled Digicel to bring its mobile telecom products and services to underserved customers in politically unstable countries.

Häagen-Dazs After peddling the Mattus family's homemade ice cream for more than 30 years to small candy stores and neighborhood restaurants in the Bronx, Reuben Mattus decided that ice cream lovers in New York would be willing to pay a premium for something they perceived as different, even evocative, and maybe better. To create this image, he came up with Häagen-Dazs—a fabricated name that sounded cold, crisp, luxurious, and Danish. Yet the name is not Danish (in fact, the umlaut does not exist in that language), and the name is as meaningless in Danish as it is in English. But the arresting name, reinforced by the map of Scandinavia that appeared on the cartons in which the product was sold, set the ice cream apart from its competitors and evoked an immediate association with shimmeringly clear, cold Scandinavian climes. The added cachet of the quirky name contributed to building a reputation for Häagen-Dazs as a richly textured luxury product that consumers perceived as being the best to be had.[39]

their past. As international trade grows, consumers may view certain brands as symbolically important to their own cultural identity or as playing an important role in keeping jobs in their country. More than three-quarters of U.S. consumers said that, given a choice between a product made at home and an identical one made abroad, they would choose the U.S. product.[40]

Many brands have gone to great lengths to weave themselves into the cultural fabric of their foreign markets. One Coca-Cola executive tells of a young child visiting the United States from Japan who commented to her parents on seeing a Coca-Cola vending machine—"Look, they have Coca-Cola too!" As far as she was concerned, Coca-Cola was a Japanese brand. Haier is another global brand working hard to establish local roots in other countries.

Haier As China's leading maker of refrigerators, washing machines, and air conditioners, Haier was well known and respected in its home market for its well-designed products. For rural customers, Haier sold extra-durable washing machines that could wash vegetables as well as clothes; for urban customers, it made smaller washing machines to fit in tiny apartments. At the turn of the 21st century, the company set its sights on a much bigger goal: building a truly global brand. Unlike most other Asian companies, which chose to enter Asian markets before considering Western markets, Haier decided to target the United States and Western Europe first. The company felt success there would make greater success possible elsewhere in the world. In the United States, Haier established a beachhead by tapping a neglected market—mini-fridges for homes, offices, dorms, and hotels—and securing distribution at Walmart, Target, Home Depot, and other top retailers. After some initial success, the company began to sell higher-end refrigerators and other appliances, such as air conditioners, washing machines, and dishwashers. Its goal is to be seen as a "localized U.S. brand," not an "imported Chinese brand." Thus, Haier invested in a manufacturing plant in South Carolina and became a marketing partner with the National Basketball Association. By 2018, the company's revenue from overseas markets reached 40 percent of Haier's total revenue, and Haier is now the world's top-selling home appliance brand.[41]

GLOBAL PRICING STRATEGIES

The same Gucci handbag may sell for $200 in Italy, $300 in the United States, and $400 in China. Why? Gucci must add the cost of transportation, tariffs, importer margin, wholesaler margin, and retailer margin to its factory price. Price escalation from these added costs and currency-fluctuation risk might require the price to be two to five times as high for the manufacturer to earn the same profit. In addition, prices reflect customers' willingness to pay for the benefits provided by the company's offering.

Companies have two basic choices for setting prices in different countries:

- *Set a uniform price everywhere.* PepsiCo might want to charge $1 for Pepsi everywhere in the world, but then it would earn quite different profit rates in different countries. Also, this strategy would make the price too high in poor countries and not high enough in rich countries.
- *Set a market-based price in each country.* PepsiCo could charge what each country could afford, but this strategy ignores differences in the actual cost from country to country. It might also motivate intermediaries in low-price countries to reship their Pepsi to high-price countries.

Market-based pricing can lead to scenarios in which one unit charges another unit in the same company a transfer price for goods it ships to its foreign subsidiaries. If the company charges a subsidiary too *high* a price, it may end up paying higher tariff duties, although it may pay lower income taxes in the foreign country. If the company charges its subsidiary too *low* a price, it can be accused of dumping—charging either less than its costs or less than it charges at home in order to enter or win a market. Various governments are watching for abuses and often force companies to set a price similar to prices charged by other competitors for the same product or a similar one.

Countries with overcapacity, cheap currencies, and the need to export aggressively have pushed their prices down and devalued their currencies. Sluggish demand and reluctance to pay higher prices make selling in these markets difficult. For example, when the Swedish home furnishings giant IKEA opened its first store in Beijing in 2002, local stores were selling copies of its designs at a fraction of IKEA's prices. The only way to compete in China's challenging pricing market was to drastically slash prices. By stocking its Chinese stores with Chinese-made products, IKEA has been able to slash prices as low as 70 percent below their level outside China. Although it still contends with persistent knockoffs, IKEA maintains sizable stores in 24 locations in China and continues opening new ones.[42]

GLOBAL COMMUNICATION STRATEGIES

Companies vary in the extent to which they adapt their marketing communication for each local market. A company can use one message everywhere, varying only the language and name. General Mills positions its Häagen-Dazs brand globally in terms of "indulgence," "affordable luxury," and "intense sensuality." Alternatively, a company can use the same message and creative theme globally but adapt the execution to a specific market. GE's global "Ecomagination" ad campaign substitutes creative content in Asia and the Middle East to reflect cultural interests there. Even in the high-tech space, local adaptations may be necessary.[43] A company can also develop a global pool of ads from which each country selects the most appropriate—an approach adopted by Coca-Cola and Goodyear. Finally, some companies allow their country managers themselves to create country-specific ads—within guidelines, of course.

Companies that adapt their communications wrestle with a number of challenges. They first must ensure that their communications are legally and culturally acceptable. U.S. toy makers were surprised to learn that in many countries (Norway and Sweden, for example), no TV ads may be directed at children under 12. To foster a culture of gender neutrality, Sweden also prohibits sexist advertising—a commercial that spoke of "cars for boys, princesses for girls" was criticized by government advertising regulators.[44]

A number of countries are taking steps to eliminate super skinny and airbrushed models in ads. Israel has banned underweight models from print and TV ads and runway shows. Models must have a body-mass index (BMI)—a calculation based on height and weight—of greater than 18.5. According to that BMI standard, a female model who is 5 feet, 8 inches tall can weigh no less than 119 pounds.[45]

Firms next must check their creative strategies and communication approaches for appropriateness. Comparative ads, though acceptable and even common in the United States and Canada, are less frequent in the United Kingdom, unacceptable in Japan, and illegal in India and Brazil. The EU seems to have very low tolerance for comparative advertising and prohibits bashing rivals in ads.

Companies also must be prepared to vary the appeal of their messages. In advertising its hair care products, Helene Curtis observed that middle-class British women wash their hair frequently, Spanish women less so. Japanese women avoid over-washing for fear of removing protective oils. Effective messaging in these countries must be cognizant of these differences. Language can vary, too—the local language, another language such as English, or some combination. Personal selling tactics also may need to change. The direct, no-nonsense approach favored in the United States ("Let's get down to business" and "What's in it for me?") may not work as well in Europe or Asia as an indirect, subtle approach.[46]

GLOBAL DISTRIBUTION STRATEGIES

When multinationals first enter a country, they prefer to work with local distributors who have good local knowledge, but friction often arises later.[47] The multinational complains that the local distributor doesn't invest in business growth, doesn't follow company policy, and doesn't share enough information. The local distributor complains of insufficient corporate support, impossible goals, and confusing policies. The multinational must choose the right distributors, invest in them, and set performance goals to which both parties can agree.

Distribution channels across countries vary considerably. To sell consumer products in Japan, companies must work through one of the most complicated distribution systems in the world. They sell to a general wholesaler, who sells to a product wholesaler, who sells to a product-specialty wholesaler, who sells to a regional wholesaler, who sells to a local wholesaler, who finally sells to retailers. All these distribution levels can double the consumer's price or triple the importer's price. Taking these same consumer products to tropical Africa, the company might sell to an import wholesaler, who sells to several local wholesalers, who sell to petty traders working in local markets.

Another difference is the size and character of retail units abroad. Large-scale retail chains dominate the U.S. scene, but much foreign retailing is in the hands of small, independent retailers. Millions of Indian retailers operate tiny shops or sell in open markets. Markups are high, but the real price comes down through haggling. Incomes are low, most homes lack storage and refrigeration, and people shop daily for whatever they can carry home on foot or by bicycle. In India, people often buy one cigarette at a time. Breaking bulk remains an important function of intermediaries and helps perpetuate long channels of distribution, a major obstacle to the expansion of large-scale retailing in developing countries.

Nevertheless, retailers are increasingly moving into new global markets, offering firms the opportunity to sell across more countries and creating a challenge to local distributors and retailers.[48] France's Carrefour, Germany's Aldi and Metro, and the UK's Tesco have all established global positions. But even some of the world's most successful retailers have had mixed success abroad. Despite concerted efforts and earlier success in Latin America and China, Walmart had to withdraw from both the German and the South Korean markets after heavy losses.[49]

Many multinationals are plagued by the **gray market,** which diverts branded products from authorized distribution channels either in-country or across international borders. Often a company finds some enterprising distributors buying more than they can sell in their own country and reshipping the goods to another country to take advantage of price differences.

Gray markets create a free-rider problem, making legitimate distributors' investments in supporting a manufacturer's product less productive and selective distribution systems more intensive to reduce the number of gray market possibilities. They harm distributor relationships, tarnish the manufacturer's brand equity, and undermine the integrity of the distribution channel. They can even pose risks to consumers if the product is damaged, relabeled, obsolete, without warranty or support, or just counterfeit. Because of their high prices, prescription drugs are often a gray market target, although U.S. government regulators have been looking at the industry more closely since fake vials of Riche Holding AG's cancer drug Avastin were shipped to U.S. doctors.[50]

Multinationals try to prevent gray markets by policing distributors, raising their prices to lower-cost distributors, and altering product characteristics or service warranties for different countries. One research study found that gray market activity was most effectively deterred when penalties were severe, when manufacturers were able to detect violations or mete out punishments in a timely fashion, or when both of these preventive measures were in place.[51]

marketing INSIGHT Global Similarities and Differences

The vast penetration of global connectivity, online programming, mobile communications, and social media has led to a convergence of lifestyles. Shared needs and wants have created global markets for more standardized products, particularly among the young middle class.

At the same time, global consumers can still vary in significant ways. Thus, consumer behavior may reflect cultural differences that can be pronounced across countries.[52] Academic research identifies six cultural dimensions that differentiate countries. These dimensions represent independent preferences for one state of affairs over another that distinguish countries (rather than individuals) from each other.[53]

- **Power Distance Index.** This dimension reflects the degree to which the less powerful members of a society accept and expect that power will be distributed unequally. In other words, the power distance index reflects how a society handles inequalities among people. Countries characterized by high power distance accept a hierarchical social stratification, whereas countries with low power distance strive to equalize the distribution of power and demand justification for inequalities of power.
- **Individualism vs. Collectivism.** In collectivist societies (e.g., Japan), the self-worth of an individual is rooted more in the social system than in individual achievement. In contrast, in individualistic societies (e.g., the United States), people are expected to take care of only themselves and their immediate families. A society's position on this dimension is reflected in whether people's self-image is defined in terms of "I" or "we."
- **Masculinity vs. Femininity.** This dimension measures how greatly the culture reflects assertive characteristics more often attributed to males versus nurturing characteristics more often attributed to females. The masculinity aspect represents a preference in society for achievement, heroism, assertiveness, and material rewards for success. Its opposite, femininity, reflects a preference for cooperation, modesty, caring for the weak, and quality of life.
- **Uncertainty Avoidance Index.** Uncertainty avoidance reflects the degree to which the members of a society feel uncomfortable with uncertainty and ambiguity. Countries with high uncertainty avoidance maintain rigid codes of belief and behavior and are intolerant of unorthodox behavior and ideas. In contrast, countries with low uncertainty avoidance maintain a more relaxed attitude in which practice counts more than principles.
- **Normative vs. Pragmatic Orientation.** This dimension reflects the extent to which a society links with its own past while dealing with the challenges of the present and the future. Societies with normative orientation prefer to maintain time-honored traditions and norms and are skeptical about societal change. In contrast, societies with a pragmatic orientation tend to take a more practical approach: They encourage thrift and efforts in modern education as a way to prepare for the future.
- **Indulgence vs. Restraint.** This cultural dimension represents the extent to which a society relies on strict norms to guide individual behavior. Here, indulgence stands for a society that allows relatively free gratification of basic hedonic human drives related to enjoying life. Restraint characterizes a society that subdues gratification of hedonic needs and regulates it by means of strict social norms.

The best global brands are consistent in theme but reflect significant differences in consumer behavior, brand development, competitive forces, and the legal or political environment.[54] Often heard—and sometime modified—advice to marketers of global brands is to "Think Global, Act Local." In that spirit, HSBC was explicitly positioned for years as "The World's Local Bank."

summary

1. Going abroad involves two major types of risks: general risks associated with entering a new market and specific risks associated with doing business in a different country. When deciding to go abroad, a company must carefully assess the risk–reward ratio for each global market it considers entering.
2. Deciding whether to go abroad is the first of several decisions a company must make when developing its global strategy. If the company has concluded that going abroad is indeed the best course of action, it must then make a set of more specific decisions, including which markets to enter, how best to enter these markets, the specific marketing program for each market, and the most effective way to structure the marketing organization in each country.
3. Once a company decides to target a particular country, it must choose the best mode of entry with its brands. Its broad choices are indirect exporting, direct exporting, licensing, joint ventures, and direct investment, ordered in terms of ascending commitment, risk, control, and profit potential.
4. An important decision for a company entering a new global market is to what extent it will adapt its marketing strategy to local conditions. A standardized marketing program worldwide promises the greatest consistency across individual countries. In contrast, an adapted marketing program tailors a company's offering to the specifics of each country.
5. Developing global product strategies requires knowing what types of products or services are easily standardized and what adaptation strategies are appropriate. In deciding how extensively to adapt their marketing programs at the product level, firms can pursue a strategy of straight extension, product adaptation, or product invention.
6. When entering global markets, a company must also decide how to position its brand and whether or how much to adapt the brand to the specifics of each particular market. It also must consider the country-of-origin effects that are likely to influence the way the brand is perceived in the particular market.
7. A company can benefit from adapting its price and communication strategies to the local market. The level of adaptation can vary from minor variations in the marketing program to entirely different pricing and communication policies for each target country.
8. At the distribution level, firms need to take a whole-channel view of distributing products to the final users. Firms must always consider the cultural, social, political, technological, environmental, and legal limitations they face in other countries.

marketing SPOTLIGHT

IKEA

Source: Alexander Blinov/Alamy Stock Photo

IKEA—a Swedish retailing company known for furniture, home furnishings, and appliances—has been the world's largest furniture retailer since 2008. IKEA has made a name for itself worldwide because of its affordable prices and innovative design. In 75 years of business, IKEA has expanded to over 300 stores in 25 countries across the globe, adjusting its stores and products on the basis of different consumer preferences in each location.

IKEA was founded by entrepreneur Ingvar Kamprad in 1943. The name IKEA is an acronym for Ingvar Kamprad's name; Elmtaryd, the farm where he grew up; and Agunnaryd, his hometown in Sweden. Kamprad started the business by selling pens, wallets, and watches door to door. Eventually, he added furniture to his portfolio, which was mostly sold through mail orders. IKEA found initial success in selling furniture because of its low prices. In 1953, IKEA opened its first mobile showroom in Almhult, Sweden. The showroom demonstrated the quality and functionality of its low-cost furniture. The popularity of IKEA's first showroom inspired the company to open its first retail location 5 years later in the same city. The profitability of IKEA's Almhult showroom spurred the spread of IKEA across Europe, starting with Norway in 1963. Enjoying success in European countries, the company expanded across the world, reaching the United States, Asia, and Australia by the early 21st century.

IKEA's business model is based on mass production of the same types of products, which allows it to benefit from

(continued)

large economies of scale. By securing low costs from suppliers, IKEA is able to charge low prices to consumers. Products are designed to be sleek, functional, and minimalistic so that they will appeal to the greatest number of budget-minded shoppers. In addition, IKEA keeps its prices low by assigning customers the responsibility of furniture assembly. IKEA furniture is packed neatly and tightly into cardboard boxes. IKEA attempts to remove as much air as possible from this "flat packing" to allow furniture to fit inside shipping containers without wasting any space, thus reducing the costs of shipping.

Despite its success in Europe, IKEA has faced problems replicating the business model globally. To solve these issues, IKEA identified strategic challenges in each market and has adjusted accordingly to overcome them. For example, one of IKEA's main value propositions in Europe and North America is its low-cost furniture. In China, however, IKEA's furniture is priced slightly higher than the average. IKEA realized that the same value proposition did not hold, so it began targeting young middle-class customers, who were on average wealthier, better educated, and more aware of Western style. IKEA also began locally sourcing materials and manufacturing. This enabled it to stay competitive in price. IKEA also emphasized its position as a good-quality, Western-style brand.

IKEA employs extensive market research to improve its sales in different markets by tailoring aspects such as product design and offering services. For example, IKEA's research has shown that the world's population is moving into apartments and homes with smaller living spaces. Accordingly, IKEA has designed products such as lamps and tables that have built-in wireless charging to save space from wire clutter. When research showed that the DIY packaging of IKEA products met with negative reception in China, IKEA began offering delivery and assembly fees. IKEA also opened stores in popular areas near transportation lines (as opposed to suburbs) in Asian cities, because many lack access to cars. IKEA showrooms provide model bedrooms, dining rooms, and family rooms and suggest how to furnish them, an important consideration given that home ownership in China has gone from practically zero 25 years ago to over 70 percent today. Young couples are especially drawn to IKEA's stylish, functional modern styles.

By understanding each country's different consumers and cultural nuances, IKEA is also able to create one-size-fits-all solutions instead of tweaking its products for different markets. Many customers spend time in IKEA's full-size sample rooms. Because the aesthetic of each room greatly influences whether a customer will make a purchase, IKEA shows how the same products can appeal to different regional customers. For instance, displays in Japan and Amsterdam may feature exactly the exact same beds, cabinets, and bookshelves. However, Japanese displays might pair the beds and cabinets with tatami mats. The Dutch display will have slanted ceilings, reflecting local architecture. U.S. rooms, on the other hand, fill beds with pillows and sheets.

IKEA's success can largely be attributed to the adaptation of its business model to different markets. IKEA's market research in different regions has helped the company to accelerate its expansion across the world and become a relevant competitor in each market. What will determine IKEA's future success is continuing to understand each market segment and fine-tuning its stores appropriately.[55]

Questions

1. What are some of the things IKEA is doing well to reach consumers in different markets? What else could it be doing?
2. IKEA has essentially changed the way people shop for furniture. Discuss the pros and cons of IKEA's strategy, especially as the company continues its global expansion.
3. How much should IKEA customize its products and retail environment to fit local tastes? Could excessive customization hurt its brand identity?

marketing
SPOTLIGHT

Taj Hotels

Taj Hotels, a chain of premium and luxury hotels, was founded by Jamsetji Tata with the Taj Mahal Hotel opening its doors in Bombay's Port area in 1903. It is the first Indian luxury hospitality chain, renowned for its classic Indian architecture and world-class services. Developed and refined over a century of rich legacy, the Taj hotels have become synonymous with luxury, class and comfort across the globe. The firm successfully carries the crown of being the world's strongest brand in the hospitality industry with more than 100 hotels across countries around the world, while generating over 40% of its revenue from the international markets.

Driven by Jamsetji's love for his hometown, Bombay (presently Mumbai) and his belief in the need of a good hotel for the city's advancement and enhancing tourism, he acquired two and quarter acres of land in 1898 and spent a princely sum of over ₹26 lakhs in equipping the hotel with the finest

Source: SFM GM WORLD / Alamy Stock Photo

infrastructure and accessories.[56] The Taj Mahal Hotel, located on a picturesque location facing the Arabian Sea, is an imposing building. Its palace-like architecture and world-class facilities boasted of several firsts including the first commercial building in erstwhile Bombay to be lit with electric lights and equipped with German elevator machinery, a carbon dioxide ice-making plant for cooling guest rooms, American fans, Parisian spun steel pillars for the ballroom, Turkish bath, among others. For more than half a century Taj Mahal Hotel was a stand-alone property till the group-initiated expansion in the 1970s by opening Fort Aguada Beach Resort in Goa and Taj Coromandel in Chennai in 1974, Taj President in Mumbai in 1977 and Taj Mahal Hotel in Delhi in 1978.[57]

In the late 1980s, Taj decided to spread its wings outside India by opening the Taj Sheba hotel in Yemen. Acquisition of St. James' Court Hotel marked its footprint in London. It is now known as Taj 51 Buckingham Gate Suites and Residences and St. James' Court. In the process of expanding its presence in the global market, the group banked on research for market insights and emerging trends. In the early 1990s, following extensive research, Taj decided to classify its brands under three entities—business, leisure and luxury. With its focus on world-class service delivery, Taj continued to upgrade its system and processes as per the changing needs of the customers.

One of the key success factors behind the Taj Hotel's global expansion is the positioning of the brand as synonymous with class and comfort. However, the group has changed its branding strategy twice—going from single name brand to multi-brand approach and again reverting to single brand approach. Until 2010, Taj Hotels used a single brand approach to promote and position Vivanta and Gateway which were designed for business and budget travellers respectively. In 2010, Taj removed its name from these brands to protect its flagship of being the luxury brand. Again in 2018, Taj reverted to its single brand positioning, endorsing its sub-brands under four categories: hotels, palaces, resorts and safaris.[58]

In a major move, Taj entered into a marketing alliance with Hong Kong-based hotel chain Shangri-La Hotels and Resorts in 2016. This deal helped Taj strengthen its position in the Asian market while reducing its operating expenses. In the first phase of the alliance, Taj and Shangri-La hotels integrated their loyalty membership. It offered the benefits of combined membership to their customer base of more than 6 million members worldwide. In the second phase of the alliance, the sales and distribution activities of Taj were integrated with Shangri-La, as they started promoting and cross selling each other's brands just like sister brands. As a result, the revenue contribution by Taj's loyalty programs increased by 50% as compared to the previous year 2015.[59]

In 2020, the group revisited its overseas expansion strategy during the COVID-19 pandemic by adopting 'R.E.S.E.T 2020', a 5-year overseas expansion plan. The plan envisaged hiving off non-core assets to restructure Taj into an asset-light company. Reduced operating expenses while investing for long term profitable growth was a key strategy

(continued)

to overcome the emerging challenges impacting the global travel, tourism and hospitality industries. The strategy has worked well for Taj. Despite the pandemic, Taj has been rated as one of the strongest global brands by the UK based consultancy 'Brand Finance' in 2021. In its report 'Hotels 50 2021', Brand Finance has declared Taj Hotels as the world's strongest hospitality brand on marketing investments, customer familiarity, workplace satisfaction and corporate reputation[60]. Taj has been crowned as the world's best luxury hotel chain for its world-class customer services and infrastructure.

With its vision to become a global brand, representing a blend of Asian culture through its distinct architecture blended with the world class amenities and maintaining international standards, systems and processes in place, Taj carries a rich cultural heritage embedded with luxury and world-class service for over 118 years. Taj group of hotels proudly keeps India's flag flying high in the competitive global hospitality market.

Questions

1. What factors explain the enduring global success of Taj group of hotels'?
2. What are the pros and cons of Taj Hotels' positioning as a global luxury brand? Can it have universal appeal for travelers from around the world?
3. How should Taj Hotels build its global digital media strategy in a way that increases its popularity without hurting its brand image?

World Wildlife Fund The world's leading conservation organization, the World Wildlife Fund (WWF) works in 100 countries and is supported by more than 1 million members in the United States and close to 5 million globally. Its annual budget does not allow for lavish marketing, so it relies primarily on direct marketing to solicit contributions. The organization sends about 36 million pieces of eco-friendly mail in the United States each year, garnering 65 percent of its membership revenue by that means. It is active on Facebook, Instagram, and Twitter and earns revenue through partnerships with a host of firms, including Avon, Disney, Gap, and Royal Caribbean Cruises. Partnerships sometimes include joint marketing programs; Coca-Cola donated $2 million for a campaign to help create safe areas for polar bears in Canada and other Arctic regions. WWF also tackles important wildlife issues head on, as with its multimedia anti-poaching campaign that used billboards, print ads, public service announcements, and online posters with the tagline "Stop Wildlife Crime—It's Dead Serious." WWF also offers cause marketing opportunities to for-profit companies, such as the cobranded World Wildlife Fund Visa credit card offered jointly with Bank of America.[44]

Source: Oqbas/Shutterstock

>> Coca-Cola introduced a collectible limited-edition 250ml aluminum bottle named Polar Bear to convey a message on environmental awareness.

Given the complexity of developing and implementing a successful social marketing campaign, organizations should approach these campaigns in a systematic and disciplined fashion. They should have a clearly defined goal, a well-articulated strategy, meaningful tactics that translate this strategy into a reality, a viable implementation plan, and a process for evaluating program success. Even though social marketing programs are often implemented by nonprofit organizations, they can benefit from the same strategic marketing approach that for-profit companies use. Both for-profit and nonprofit companies ultimately aim to create market value, but for-profit companies define value in monetary terms, whereas nonprofits define it in terms of benefiting society.

The concept of social marketing is related to that of *brand activism*.[45] **Brand activism** entails a company taking a stand on an important—typically controversial—social, economic, environmental, or political issue. As a form of social marketing, brand activism is associated with a focus on societal issues that customers and employees care about, rather than on issues that concern the company's bottom line. What makes brand activism stand out from other forms of social marketing is that it involves a company taking a prominent and early position on a divisive issue that has important societal implications.

An example of brand activism is Nike's decision to prominently feature former San Francisco 49ers quarterback Colin Kaepernick— the front man of an NFL player movement to kneel, during performance of the U.S. national anthem, in protest of police killings of Black Americans—in its ad campaign celebrating the 30th anniversary of its motto "Just Do It." The tagline of Nike's campaign, "Believe in something. Even if it means sacrificing everything," took a clear stance in support of the values espoused by Kaepernick's actions. This decision ultimately resulted in some customers' embracing the brand's actions and others boycotting Nike products.

Sustainability-Focused Corporate Social Responsibility

Sustainability—the ability to meet humanity's needs without harming future generations—now tops many corporate agendas. Major corporations outline in great detail how they are trying to improve the long-term impact of their actions on communities and the environment. Coca-Cola, AT&T, and DuPont have even installed chief sustainability officers (CSOs).

Consumers have put their very real sustainability concerns into words and actions, focusing on green products and endorsing a wide range of environmental issues. Consumer interest in green products has expanded to the auto, energy, and technology sectors, in addition to personal care, food, and household products. A growing number of consumers indicate their preference for buying products from environmentally responsible companies.

Many aspects of "green" culture—from organic purchase to recyclability—have gone mainstream as consumers have increasingly turned to digital devices to learn about the environment and share their green experiences.[46] Interestingly, although some marketers assume younger people are more concerned than others about the environment, some research suggests that older consumers actually take their eco-responsibilities more seriously.

Environmental issues are also playing an increasingly important role in product design and manufacturing. Many firms are considering ways to reduce the negative environmental consequences of conducting business, and some are changing the way they manufacture their products or the ingredients that go into them. In a fascinating twist, Levi Strauss found a highly creative way to address the problem of proliferating plastic bottles.

Levi's If someone said your jeans were "made of garbage," you might be insulted, but not if they were made by Levi Strauss. Twenty percent of the denim material in Levi's new "Waste<Less" jeans and jackets comes from plastic bottles and black food trays recycled from municipal sites, including about eight 12- to 20-ounce bottles per pair. Much research and development went into creating the Waste<Less line, for which the plastic is cleaned, sorted, shredded into flakes, and made into a polyester fiber that's then blended with cotton. The resulting fabric looks and feels like traditional denim except for the color of the underside, which varies according to the hue of the plastic. The jeans' retail cost ranges from $69 to $128. Levi's is not a newcomer to the market for environmentally friendly products; sustainability is a company-wide priority. Its commitment to "Water<Less" jeans helped farmers grow cotton with less water, enabled Levi's to create the popular worn-in look with less water, and educated consumers about cleaning and disposing of the garments with less water. Both lines have made a tangible difference: The Water<Less line saved more than 360 million liters of water in its first full year, and in *its* first full year, the Waste<Less line recycled 3.5 million bottles and trays.[47]

Increasingly, consumers want information about a company's record on social and environmental responsibility to help them decide which companies to buy from, invest in, and work for. Communicating corporate social responsibility can be a challenge. Once a firm touts an environmental initiative, it can become a target for criticism. Often, the more committed a company is to sustainability and environmental protection, the more dilemmas can arise, as Green Mountain Coffee Roasters has found.

Green Mountain Coffee Roasters Vermont-based Green Mountain Coffee Roasters prides itself on sustainability efforts that have helped it become one of the fastest-selling coffee brands around. The company supports local and global communities by offsetting 100 percent of its greenhouse gas emissions, investing in sustainably grown coffee, and allocating at least 5 percent of its pre-tax profits to social and environmental projects. Through its Community Action for Employees (CAFE) program, each full-time employee gets up to 52 paid volunteer hours each year to support community programs. All these activities help Green Mountain fulfill its purpose statement to "create the ultimate coffee experience in every life we touch, from tree to cup—transforming the way the world views business." The firm's 2006 purchase of Keurig and its popular single-cup brewing system posed a quandary, though: The K-Cups used with the Keurig brewing system were made of totally nonrecyclable plastic and foil. Although disposal makes up only about 5 percent of its total environmental impact—more significant effects are related to brewer use, coffee cultivation, and product packaging—Green Mountain has engaged in extensive R&D and explored numerous partnerships to find a more environmentally sound solution to make K-Cup packs recyclable, while also addressing the firm's other environmental effects in different ways.[48]

Corporate actions toward achieving sustainability take all forms. For example, Whole Foods, Wegmans, Target, and Walmart no longer sell fish caught in areas subject to overfishing or in a manner likely to harm other marine life or habitats. Other companies, in addition to conserving resources, aim to directly contribute to preserving the environment. Consider the case of FAGUO.

Source: AP Photo/Toby Talbot

>> A firm that prides itself on its sustainability efforts, Green Mountain Coffee Roasters is committed to reducing any adverse environmental impact of its popular K-Cups.

FAGUO The FAGUO fashion brand is the brainchild of French entrepreneurs Frédéric & Nicolas, who met as students in Paris and decided to launch their own brand of shoes while on a study-abroad program in China. The two men began creating collections of shoes, clothing, and accessories for customers, and what started as a student project morphed into a French start-up and ultimately into a dynamic fashion label with more than 300 shops in France and 220 shops abroad. The name of the Paris-based company, launched in 2009, is the Chinese word for "France." In addition to their commitment to fashion, the two designers felt committed to reducing the company's carbon footprint. Thus, for each FAGUO product sold, a tree is planted in France, a move that has turned unused and abandoned lands into wooded areas that can be enjoyed by all. FAGUO's partner in this sustainability project is Naudet, a nursery that specializes in maintaining and reforesting wooded areas in France. Since Faguo's 2009 inception, more than 600,000 trees have been planted in 110 new forests. A coconut button appears on all FAGUO products to symbolize the company's abiding commitment to conservation of the environment.[49]

Heightened interest in sustainability has also, regrettably, resulted in **greenwashing**—that is, providing misleading information or giving a false impression that products or practices are environmentally friendly without living up to that promise. One study revealed that half the labels on allegedly green products focus on an eco-friendly benefit (such as recycled content), while omitting information about significant environmental drawbacks (such as manufacturing intensity or transportation costs).[50] Stonyfield Farm's cofounder Gary Hirshberg is leading the charge with the "Just Label It!" campaign to provide more useful information on labels about the use of GMO (genetically modified organism) ingredients.

In response to insincere firms that have jumped on the green bandwagon, consumers bring a healthy skepticism to environmental claims. Also, many consumers are unwilling to sacrifice product performance and quality and are not necessarily willing to pay a price premium for genuinely green products.[51] Unfortunately, green products can be more expensive because ingredients are costly and transportation costs are higher for lower shipping volumes.

Even so, companies like Tom's of Maine, Burt's Bees, Stonyfield Farm, and Seventh Generation have managed to create green offerings that match customers' needs and preferences. In the same vein, part of the initial success of Clorox Green Works household cleaning products was that the company found the sweet spot for a target market that wanted to take small steps toward a greener lifestyle with a product carrying a very modest price premium and sold through a grassroots marketing program. Another company that has put sustainability at the center of its activities is Patagonia.

Patagonia Patagonia, maker of high-end outdoor clothing and equipment, has always put environmental issues at the core of what it does. Company founder Yvon Chouinard, author of *The Responsible Company*, actively promotes a post-consumerist economy in which goods are "high quality, recyclable and repairable." Under Chouinard's leadership, Patagonia even ran a full-page ad in the *New York Times* headlined "Don't Buy This Jacket." Below a photo of the retailer's R2 jacket was text explaining that despite its many positive features—"60% recyclable polyester, knit and sewn to high standards, and exceptionally durable"—the jacket still imposed many environmental costs (135 liters of water and 20 pounds of carbon dioxide were consumed in manufacturing each one). The ad concluded by promoting the Common Threads Initiative asking consumers to engage in five behaviors: reduce (what you buy); repair (what you can); reuse (what you have); recycle (everything else); and reimagine (a sustainable world). With $800 million in annual sales, privately held Patagonia is always trying to find better environmental solutions for everything it does and makes. For example, it offered the first wetsuits made from plant-based material as an alternative to neoprene. Patagonia also commits 1 percent of its total sales or 10 percent of its profit, whichever is greater, to environmental causes.[52]

Source: LWH/Alamy Stock Photo

<< Patagonia actively seeks more sustainable ways to make its outdoor clothing and equipment and dedicates a portion of its proceeds to environmental causes.

Socially responsible marketing recognizes the need to integrate environmental issues into the firm's strategic plans. Trends for marketers to be aware of include the shortage of raw materials, especially water; the increased cost of energy; increased pollution levels; and the changing role of governments.[53] Steel companies and public utilities have invested billions of dollars in pollution-control equipment and environmentally friendly fuels, making hybrid cars, low-flow toilets and showers, organic foods, and green office buildings everyday realities. More recently, Amazon.com launched a $2 billion internal venture-capital fund focused on technology investments in companies across a number of industries, including transportation, energy generation, battery storage, manufacturing, and food and agriculture to reduce the impact of climate change. The aim is to help Amazon and other companies to reduce the impact of their operations on climate, both through reduced use of fossil fuels and through investments in projects such as reforestation, and ultimately to reach a goal of "net zero" carbon emissions by 2040.[54]

Opportunities await those who can reconcile prosperity with environmental protection. Companies that innovate solutions and values in a socially responsible way are most likely to succeed.[55] Dublin-based Airtricity operates wind farms in the United States and the United Kingdom that offer cheaper and greener electricity. Vancouver-based Westport Innovations developed a conversion technology—high-pressure direct injection—that allows diesel engines to run on cleaner-burning liquid natural gas, reducing greenhouse emissions by a fourth. Illinois-based Sun Ovens International makes family-sized and institutional solar ovens that use mirrors to redirect the sun's rays into an insulated box. Used in 130 countries, the oven both saves money and reduces greenhouse gas emissions. Another company that is successfully employing eco-friendly technologies is Timberland.

Timberland Timberland, maker of rugged boots, shoes, clothing, and gear—targets individuals who live, work, and play outdoors, so it only makes sense for the firm to do whatever it takes to protect the environment. The company's actions have blazed trails for green companies around the world. Its revolutionary initiatives include putting a "nutrition label" on its shoeboxes, measuring the brand's environmental footprint—from renewable energy used in its facilities to recycled, organic, and renewable materials in its products to trees planted around the globe. Timberland also introduced a new line of shoes called Earthkeepers, which incorporates organic cotton, recycled PET, and recycled rubber (for the soles)—materials that were later expanded to multiple Timberland product categories. Outside of its products, the brand has made a major commitment to reforestation, with nearly 5 million trees planted worldwide. With sales in excess of a billion dollars, its business accomplishments prove that socially and environmentally responsible companies can be successful.[56]

Source: ronny bolliger/Alamy Stock Photo

<< Timberland strives to keep the environmental footprint of its products for outdoor enthusiasts as small as possible and carries out a major reforestation agenda.

Balancing Social Responsibility and Corporate Profitability

Business practices routinely pose ethical dilemmas. Of course, certain business practices are clearly unethical or illegal. These include bribery, theft of trade secrets, false and deceptive advertising, exclusive dealing and tying agreements, quality or safety defects, false warranties, inaccurate labeling, price-fixing or undue discrimination, and barriers to entry and predatory competition. Yet, in some cases it is not easy to draw a clear line between normal marketing practice and unethical behavior.

DEVELOPING ETHICAL MARKETING COMMUNICATIONS

Marketing communication is an area that is riddled with ethical dilemmas. To break through the clutter of messaging faced by consumers, some advertisers believe they have to push the boundaries of what could be considered ethical and sometimes even legal.

A substantial body of U.S. laws and regulations governs advertising. Advertisers must not make false claims, use false demonstrations, or create ads with the capacity to deceive, even if no one is actually deceived.[57] A floor wax advertiser can't say the product gives six months' protection unless it does so under typical conditions, and a baker of diet bread can't say its product has fewer calories simply because its slices are thinner. The challenge is telling the difference between deception and "puffery"—simple exaggerations that are not meant to be believed and that *are* permitted by law. Unfortunately, even prominent brands such Unilever's Fair and Lovely (Ajita Shashidhar (2020), 'Rebranding Fair & Lovely unlikely to impact demand for fairness creams' Business Today, June 27 , from https://www.businesstoday.in , Accessed on 23rd December 2021 News (2021)), Patanjali's Coronil ('Coronil controversy: IMA asks Patanjali to furnish documents' The Hindustan Times Mint, Feb 25, from https://www.livemint.com Accessed on 23rd December 2021), Cadbury's Dairy Milk (Dr. Shashank Shah (2020), 'When Crisis Led To Consumer Safety: The Story Of Cadbury', August 03, from http://www.businessworld.in Accessed on 23rd December 2021) and Nestle's Maggi (Webdesk (2021), 'Nestle 'unhealthy' food controversy: Looking back at the Maggi Noodles crisis in India' India Today, June 2, from https://www.indiatoday.in Accessed on 23rd December 2021) have been subject to controversies related to unethical advertisements, promoting false claims about usage, product ingredients and benefits.

POM Wonderful The Federal Trade Commission (FTC) issued a "cease-and-desist" order against POM Wonderful, saying the company had spread deceptive claims in print publications, on billboards, and online that its POM pomegranate juice could treat or prevent erectile dysfunction, prostate cancer, and heart disease. The ruling came after two years of legal wrangling. Oddly, however, POM appeared to declare victory, running a full-page ad in the *New York Times* celebrating the fact that the ruling did not force it to seek reapproval from the Food and Drug Administration (as drug companies must do). A later appeal was rejected as the FTC continued to rule against POM ads using headlines such as "Cheat Death" without stronger evidence. POM is not the only company that has run into trouble over pomegranates. Welch's settled two class-action suits for $30 million because labels on its 100% Juice White Grape Pomegranate Flavored 3 Juice Blend claimed more pomegranate than it really had—only 1 ounce in a 64-ounce bottle.[58]

Source: Denis Michailov/Alamy Stock Photo

>> POM Wonderful was told by the Federal Trade Commission to halt deceptive claims that its pomegranate juice could prevent or treat specific conditions and diseases.

Unfortunately, even prominent brands such Unilever's Fair and Lovely, Patanjali's Coronil, Cadbury's Dairy Milk and Nestle's Maggi have been subject to controversies related to unethical advertisements, promoting false claims about usage, product ingredients and benefits.

Sellers in the United States are legally obligated to avoid bait-and-switch advertising that attracts buyers under false pretenses. Suppose a seller advertises a mobile phone at $149. When consumers try to buy the advertised phone, the seller cannot then refuse to sell it, downplay its features, show a faulty one, or promise unreasonable delivery dates in order to switch the buyer to a more expensive phone.

Similar regulations apply to communication in business markets. For example, it's illegal for salespeople to misinform consumers or mislead them about the advantages of buying a product. They may not offer bribes to purchasing agents or others influencing a B2B sale. Their statements must match advertising claims, and they may not obtain or use competitors' technical or trade secrets through bribery or industrial espionage. They must not disparage competitors or their products by suggesting things that are not true.

Marketing communication can generate public controversy when marketers take unfair advantage of vulnerable groups (such as children) or disadvantaged groups (such as low-income, ethnic minority residents) or promote potentially harmful products. The cereal industry has been criticized through the years for marketing efforts directed toward children. Critics worry that high-powered appeals presented by lovable animated characters will overwhelm children's defenses and lead them to want sugared cereals or poorly balanced breakfasts. Toy marketers have been similarly criticized. A key area of concern for many consumer-protection advocates is the millions of kids who are online.

With the explosion of cell phones, tablets, software apps, and social networking sites, an important concern is protecting unknowing or unsuspecting children in an increasingly complex technological world. The 8-to-12 tween market today is highly mobile and happy to share locations via an app and communicate with others by phone, leading one trendspotting expert to characterize them as "SoLoMo" (Social Local Mobile). Only one in five parents, however, uses basic content-control features on smart phones, tablets, and game consoles. Thus, establishing ethical and legal boundaries in marketing to children online—and offline—continues to be a hot topic.[59]

Television can be especially powerful in reaching children, and marketers are using it to target them at younger ages than ever before with product tie-ins for just about everything—*Disney Princess* character pajamas, retro G.I. Joe toys and action figures, *Dora the Explorer* backpacks, and *Toy Story* playsets.

Teachers and parents are divided about the ethics of the increasingly heavy marketing push involving children. Some side with groups such as Campaign for a Commercial-Free Childhood, whose members believe that children are incredibly susceptible to advertising and that schools' endorsements of products make children believe the product is good for them—no matter what it is. Yet many schools and day care centers operating on tight budgets welcome the free resources and promotional materials that marketers offer, such as Care Bear worksheets, Pizza Hut reading programs, and Nickelodeon magazines.

Not all attempts to target children, minorities, or other special segments draw criticism. Colgate-Palmolive's Colgate Junior toothpaste has special features designed to get children to brush longer and more often. Thus, the issue is not who is targeted, but how and for what purpose. Socially responsible marketing calls for targeting that serves not only the company's interests but also the interests of those targeted.

MANAGING CUSTOMER PRIVACY

Almost every time consumers order products by mail or telephone, apply for a credit card, or take out a magazine subscription, their names, addresses, locations, and purchasing behaviors are captured and subsequently used by companies to market their offerings to these consumers. This naturally raises the concern that marketers may know too much about consumers' lives, and that they may use this knowledge to unfair advantage.[60]

Many consumers are generally aware of cookies, profiles, and other online tools that let e-commerce businesses know who they are and when and how they shop, but they are nevertheless concerned by the extent to which companies gather information about them. One area of concern is that a company's ability to pinpoint a person's whereabouts with geolocation technology enables marketers to track consumers' daily routines, frequently visited establishments, and even their movements within a retail store. When Nordstrom informed customers it was testing new technology to monitor their movements by tracking signals from their smart phones, some consumers objected, leading Nordstrom to drop the experiment.

The exploding amount of digital data created by individuals online can nearly all be collected, bought, and sold by advertisers, marketers, ad networks, data brokers, website publishers, social networks, and online tracking and targeting companies. Companies know or can find consumers' age, race, gender, height, weight, marital status, education level, political affiliation, buying habits, hobbies, health, financial concerns, vacation dreams, and much more.

The thought of such widespread transparency worries consumers. Research shows that more people, especially older consumers, are refusing to reveal private information online. At the same time, consumers are accepting more privacy intrusions every day, perhaps because they don't realize what information they are giving out, don't feel they have a choice, or don't think it will really matter. Many don't realize, for example, that buried in the fine print of their agreement to buy a new smart phone may be authorization to allow third-party services to track their every move. One such firm, Carrier IQ, receives permission from any purchaser of an EVO 3D HTC smart phone to see every call made, when and where text messages were sent, and which websites were visited. Unfortunately, once data have been collected online, they can end up in unexpected places, resulting in spam or worse.

Consumers increasingly want to know where, when, how, and why they are being watched online. Another data-tracking firm is Acxiom, which maintains a database on about 190 million U.S. individuals and 126 million households. Its 23,000 servers process 50 trillion data transactions a year as it attempts to assemble "360-degree views" of consumers from offline, online, and mobile sources. Its customers include many of the top insurance providers, retailers, telecom and media companies, retail banks, automotive manufacturers, credit card issuers, hotel companies, airlines, technology companies, and brokerage firms.

Can online data profiling go too far? New parents are highly lucrative customers, but with birth records public, a slew of companies all discover them at the same time. To beat others to the punch, Target studied the buying histories of women who signed up for new-baby registries at the store and found that many bought large amounts of vitamin supplements during their first trimester and unscented lotion around the start of their second trimester. Target then used these purchase markers to identify women of child-bearing age who were likely to be pregnant and sent them offers and coupons for baby products timed to the stages of pregnancy and later baby needs. When the practice became known, however, some criticized the company's tactics, which had occasionally been the means by which family members learned that someone in the household was expecting. Target responded by including the offers with other offers unrelated to pregnancy, and sales in the promoted pregnancy-related categories soared.

Such incidents vividly illustrate the power of database management in an internet era, as well as the worries it can create among consumers. Politicians and government officials are discussing a "Do Not Track" option for consumers online (like the "Do Not Call" option for unsolicited phone calls). Consumer-privacy advocates long ago voiced their concern that data brokers must disclose to the public what data they collect, how they collect them, with whom they share them, and how they are used. Although it is not clear how quickly legislation can be enacted, an online privacy bill that strengthens consumer rights seems inevitable. To give consumers control over their personal data, the European Union introduced the General Data Protection Regulation that requires data processors to clearly disclose any data collection, reveal the purpose of data collection, state how long data are being retained, and disclose whether the data are being shared with any third parties or outside of the European Union.

marketing INSIGHT

Environmental Concerns in the Water Industry

The huge popularity of bottled water has been a boon to many companies, but at a high cost to the environment. One estimate puts the amount of plastic used in disposable bottles at 2.7 million tons a year, which requires about 47 million gallons of oil to manufacture. Unfortunately, fewer than 20 percent of these bottles are believed to be recycled in the United States. These high environmental costs have a number of implications for marketers.

Colleges all over the country—from Western Washington University to Brown University, the University of Vermont, and the University of California at Berkeley—have banned the sale of plain bottled water, typically as part of a student-led movement toward greater sustainability on campus. The College of Saint Benedict in Minnesota equipped 31 fountains with an extra spigot to make them "hydration stations," a practice adopted by many other schools that banned bottled water. Nor are schools alone. Many public institutions, from zoos to national parks, are similarly installing water-filling stations and banning the sale of bottled water.

As more consumers seek to reduce their personal environmental footprint, sales of reusable water bottles have exploded. Sigg Switzerland sells cleverly designed lightweight aluminum water bottles for $25 to $30, choosing 100 new products from among 3,000 different designs each year. Features popular in other brands include caps with built-in micro-filtration systems.

Glass bottles are promoted for their environmental advantages over plastic and to reassure consumers who fear chemicals can leak into foods and beverages from plastic. They now account for an increasingly large percentage of water bottle sales. Glass is also being developed for greater safety if broken; for instance, PURE glass bottles use clear protective Safe-Shell coating.

>> Emphasizing product design and variety, Swiss-made Sigg caught on as sales of reusable water bottles exploded.

Source: SIGG Switzerland AG. Creators of "The Original Bottle" made in Switzerland.

(continued)

marketing insight *(continued)*

Soft drink makers face similar pressures from environmentally aware consumers. Soda Stream sells equipment that allows people to carbonate and flavor plain tap water using reusable glass bottles. The company promotes three key benefits: Using tap water is cheaper, it can be slightly more healthful, and there is no waste. Coca-Cola reports reclaiming more than one-third of its bottles and cans in North America, diverting 250 million pounds of waste from landfills each year. When PepsiCo launched Eco-Fina packaging, which uses 50 percent less plastic, for its Aquafina water brand, it estimated it would save more than 75 million pounds of plastic annually.

Perhaps the most important lesson here is that environmental concerns matter to consumers, and they expect companies to make changes to address their concerns. Furthermore, competition will emerge in all forms as companies try to find ways to better meet consumers' unmet needs, even for a sip of water.[61]

summary

1. The most admired companies in the world abide by high standards of business and marketing guidelines that dictate serving people's interests, not only their own. Raising the level of socially responsible marketing calls for pursuing a *triple bottom line* that focuses on the community and the environment, in addition to corporate profits.
2. Achieving socially responsible growth calls for marketers to invest resources to create value for the community in which a company operates. There are several domains in which community-based corporate social responsibility typically occurs: improving the workplace, engaging in corporate philanthropy, supporting low-income communities, fostering cause marketing, and engaging in social marketing.
3. A growing number of companies focus on the largest but poorest group of the world's population—commonly referred to as the bottom of the pyramid—in the belief that they can profitably serve these customers, while at the same time promoting social change.
4. Many aspects of "green" culture, from organic products or ingredients to recyclability, have gone mainstream, as consumers increasingly turn to digital devices to learn about the environment and share their green experiences. Sustainability—the ability to meet humanity's needs without harming future generations—now tops many corporate agendas. Major corporations outline in great detail how they improve the long-term impact of their actions on communities and the environment.
5. Pursuing a triple bottom line routinely poses challenges for profit-driven companies, because some of their stakeholders may not endorse corporate social responsibility that comes at the expense of corporate profits. To ensure a meaningful commitment to corporate social responsibility, a company must find the right balance between profitability and societal benefits and ensure that the chosen efforts to promote social responsibility are reflected in the company's culture and value system and have the buy-in of the company stakeholders.

marketing SPOTLIGHT

Starbucks

Source: monticello/Shutterstock

Starbucks opened its first store in 1971, at a time when coffee consumption in the United States had been declining for a decade and rival brands used cheaper coffee beans to compete on price. The Starbucks founders decided to experiment with a new concept: a store that would sell only the world's finest imported coffee beans and coffee-brewing equipment. Its original store in Seattle's historic Pike Place Market didn't sell coffee by the cup, only beans. The name, inspired by that of a character in Melville's *Moby-Dick*, evoked the romance of the high seas and the seafaring tradition of the early coffee traders.

Howard Schultz came to Starbucks in 1982. While in Milan on business, he had walked into an Italian coffee bar and had an epiphany: "There was nothing like this in America. It was an extension of people's front porch. It was

(continued)

an emotional experience." He had a vision of bringing the Italian coffeehouse tradition back to the United States and convinced the founders of Starbucks to test the coffeehouse concept in downtown Seattle, where the first Starbucks caffè latte was served in 1984. Following the success of the coffeehouse experiment, Schultz left Starbucks for a short time to start his own Il Giornale coffeehouses, which offered brewed coffee and espresso beverages made from Starbucks coffee beans. In 1987, Shultz purchased Starbucks with the help of local investors, with the aim of creating a company that would reflect Italian elegance blended with U.S. informality. He envisioned Starbucks as a "personal treat" for its customers, a comfortable, sociable gathering spot bridging the workplace and home.

The expansion of Starbucks throughout the United States was carefully planned. All stores were company owned and operated, ensuring complete control over the product and an unparalleled image of quality. Starbucks used a "hub" strategy: Coffeehouses entered a new market in a clustered group. Although this deliberate saturation often cannibalized 30 percent of one store's sales, the decrease in revenue was offset by efficiencies in marketing and distribution costs and the enhanced image of convenience. A typical customer stopped by Starbucks 18 times a month. No U.S. retailer had a higher frequency rate of customer visits. Today, Starbucks connects with millions of customers every day in its more than 24,000 retail stores in 70 countries.

Starbucks's success is often attributed to its high-quality products and services, and its relentless commitment to providing consumers with the richest possible sensory experience. Starbucks offers a range of products that customers can enjoy in its stores, at home, and on the go. These include more than 30 blends and single-origin premium coffees; handcrafted beverages such as fresh-brewed coffee, hot and iced espresso drinks, refreshers, smoothies, and teas; and fresh food—baked pastries, sandwiches, salad and grain bowls, oatmeal, yogurt parfaits, and fruit cups.

Starbucks constantly innovates the concept of the coffeehouse store. Its flagship Reserve Roastery stores, introduced in 2014, are found in major cities around the globe. According to Starbucks, Roasteries combine a coffee shop and theme-park-like experience in which "customers can immerse themselves in the world of coffee on display." Starbucks designed its Reserve stores, introduced in 2018, as scaled-down versions of Roasteries but more upscale than the regular Starbucks coffee shops. Built for nightlife, Reserve stores reintroduced Starbucks's "Evenings" program (originally launched in 2010 and discontinued in 2017) that puts premium beer, wine, and spirits on its menu.

A critical component of the success of Starbucks is its commitment to social responsibility. From the very beginning, Starbucks set out to be a different kind of company—one that not only celebrated coffee and its rich tradition but also conveyed a feeling of connection and a sense of community. Starbucks makes decisions that positively impact not only its shareholders but also its community and the environment. The company prides itself on being a responsible and ethical company and makes sure that customers are aware of its high level of involvement. From printing facts on its coffee cups to a dedicated annual report on its socially responsible endeavors, Starbucks has made corporate responsibility a company priority.

Starbucks gives back to its community in many ways, starting with its employees, whom it refers to as partners. Schultz believed that in order to exceed customers' expectations, it was first necessary to exceed employees' expectations. Starbucks was one of the first companies to offer full health benefits to eligible full- and part-time employees, including coverage for domestic partnerships. Health insurance now costs the company more each year than coffee. It was also the first privately owned U.S. company to offer a stock option program (called Bean Stock) that includes part-time employees, enabling them to participate in the company's financial success. Starbucks has also committed to hiring 10,000 veterans and military spouses over the next five years. More recently, Starbucks began offering full tuition coverage for a first-time bachelor's degree through online programs such as the one offered by Arizona State University. The Starbucks Foundation, established in 1977, aims to "create hope, discovery, and opportunity in communities" by supporting literacy programs for children and families in the United States as well as various charities and communities worldwide.

Starbucks collaborates with Conservation International, a nongovernmental organization, and follows Coffee and Farmer Equity practices, a comprehensive coffee-buying program, to ensure it purchases high-quality coffee from farmers who meet certain social, economic, and environmental standards. In 2001 Starbucks introduced ethical coffee-sourcing guidelines developed in partnership with Conservation International. The company also works continuously with farmers to improve responsible methods of farming, such as planting trees along rivers and using shade-growing techniques to help preserve forests. Over the years, Starbucks has invested more than $100 million in collaborative farmer programs and activities.

Starbucks is considered one of the leading organizations when it comes to green initiatives. From building new LEED-certified green buildings to reducing waste and improving water conservation, small changes can make a big difference in the environment. It took Starbucks 10 years to develop the world's first recycled beverage cup made of 10 percent postconsumer fiber. The company followed that with a new hot-cup paper sleeve that required fewer materials to make. These innovations conserve approximately 100,000 trees a year. Starbucks's goal is to ensure that all of its cups are recycled or reused. The company's commitment to corporate social responsibility reflects its view that Starbucks must retain a passion for coffee and a sense of

(*continued*)

humanity and continue to prove that the company "stands for something more than just profitability."[62]

Questions

1. What are the key aspects of Starbucks's strategy and tactics?
2. Where does a company like Starbucks draw the line in supporting socially responsible programs? How much of its annual budget should go toward these programs? How much time should employees focus on these programs? Which programs should Starbucks support?
3. Starbucks has worked hard to make business decisions that are both ethical and responsible. How are the results of Starbucks's socially responsible programs measured?

marketing SPOTLIGHT

Ben & Jerry's

Source: Gareth Davies/Getty Images

Ben & Jerry's was created in 1978 when founders Ben Cohen and Jerry Greenfield opened their first ice cream parlor in Burlington, Vermont. The duo "wanted to do something more fun" with their careers: Cohen was a pottery teacher and Greenfield worked as a lab technician. After taking a five-dollar course in ice cream making from Pennsylvania State University, the two managed to raise $12,000 and repurposed a gas station in downtown Burlington.

Ben & Jerry's quickly gained a loyal following of local college students because of its unique flavors and use of high-quality ingredients. Deciding that local grocery and convenience stores would be profitable outlets for their products, the pair rented factory space and began packaging their ice cream in pint-sized cartons. Although Ben & Jerry's kept its operations in the Burlington area, the ice cream received national attention in 1981, when *Time* magazine featured it as "the best ice cream in the world." Soon after the story was published, the popularity and sales of Ben & Jerry's grew dramatically. The company began opening locations outside the state of Vermont and distributing its goods across the nation.

The continued expansion of the company and high sales figures far exceeded the founders' expectations. Ben & Jerry's initially financed its growth by selling stock exclusively to residents in Vermont in order to establish local accountability and spread the wealth in the community. As the company expanded, the pair was presented with a challenging dilemma. Ben Cohen and Jerry Greenfield were unsure about keeping the business, because they were "afraid that business exploits its workers and the community." The two decided to keep the company and devised a mission statement to show how businesses could be the drivers of positive change in a community. Ben & Jerry's social mission is to "make the world a better place."

After the mission statement was established, Ben & Jerry's took many steps to fulfill its sense of corporate social responsibility. It established the Ben & Jerry's Foundation, which is dedicated to funding grassroots activism in social and environmental work through a yearly donation of 7.5 percent of the company's pretax profits. Ben & Jerry's also released products that supported various causes. Profits from the Peace Pop, an ice cream bar on a stick, were used to support various organizations that advocated for world peace. Ben & Jerry's purchased rainforest nuts for its Rainforest Crunch ice cream, which provided a demand for a rainforest good that could be grown and harvested without deforestation. Additionally, profits from this flavor were funneled back into rainforest preservation efforts.

Ben & Jerry's achieved its mission by designing its products to be environmentally friendly. The company sold its ice cream in what they called "Eco-Pints," an environmentally friendly packaging that did not use paper bleached by chlorine compounds. Ben & Jerry's sourced its milk only from regional dairy farms and used only milk that was certified hormone free. For the other ingredients, priority was placed on sources that were fair trade and organic. Ben & Jerry's also found many ways to reduce its garbage output, including feeding community farm animals with its own ice cream waste.

Even the company's advertising and product promotions displayed the value Ben and Jerry's placed on social justice and bringing together the community. Instead of purchasing

(*continued*)

large amounts of radio, television, and print advertisements, Ben & Jerry's promoted its products mainly by sponsoring events that had community value. In the past, Ben & Jerry's has sponsored peace, music, and art festivals across the country. The company has also created its own One World and One Heart festivals, each dedicated to raising awareness of many social causes.

When Unilever offered to purchase the company in 2000, Ben and Jerry were both hesitant to sell. They feared the conglomerate would undo their years of social and environmental progress and run Ben & Jerry's as a purely profit-driven enterprise. However, Ben and Jerry were presented with an offer they couldn't refuse: The company was purchased for over $300 million, with the stipulation that an executive board be created to resume carrying out its social and environmental missions. Unfortunately, the deal quickly resulted in some regression. In order to optimize its supply chain management, Unilever shut down a production plant and a distribution plant, laying off all respective workers. Some sales representatives at Ben & Jerry's headquarters were also laid off.

Despite early setbacks, the executive board eventually negotiated for autonomy. Ben & Jerry's has since doubled down on its social mission, committing further profits to supporting local farmers, reducing its environmental impact, and advocating for social and political justice. Ben & Jerry's began using only cage-free eggs in its products. In recent years, Ben & Jerry's minimum wage has been significantly higher than the national average, landing around $18/hour in 2020. Ben & Jerry's has also received B Corporation certification from a nonprofit group for holding high economic and social standards. Ben & Jerry's continues to advance its social mission, one flavor at a time.[63]

Questions

1. What role does corporate social responsibility play in the Ben & Jerry's business model?
2. Should Ben and Jerry have continued to operate Ben and Jerry's as an independent company, rather than selling it to Unilever? What were the pros and cons of going forward with the sale?
3. How can Ben & Jerry's justify the concept of a triple bottom line—profits, people, and planet—to company shareholders?

---

marketing
SPOTLIGHT

Tiffany & Co

Source: Karstu Photography/ Alamy Stock Photo

Tiffany & Co.'s roots date back to 1837, when founder Charles Lewis Tiffany opened a "stationery and fancy goods" store in New York City. Tiffany's first store quickly became the go-to destination for fashionable ladies looking for high-quality jewels and timepieces. By 1848, Tiffany had established the store's focus on fine jewelry. He hired dozens of artisans to create jewelry in a workshop located above the storefront at a time when most jewelers were simply retailers. Tiffany sought to express his own style of American jewelry that demonstrated natural beauty and simplicity. By the late 19th century, Tiffany & Co. had acquired its own facilities to cut and polish diamonds, which gave the gems a consistent, quality finish.

Diamonds and precious metals exploded in popularity in the 20th century. As a result of the increased demand for fine jewelry, Tiffany & Co. enjoyed massive growth and began expanding internationally. The company became further vertically integrated—controlling aspects such as sourcing, design, and manufacturing at locations all over the world. This allowed the company to maintain its design philosophy and to source only diamonds that met its standards. As Tiffany & Co. grew, customers became increasingly aware of the environmental concerns regarding precious metal extraction and the social injustices of the diamond industry, brought to light by various NGOs and trade organizations. Toxic chemicals such as cyanide and mercury were used to extract gold from the ground. In addition, many diamonds originated in countries with political conflicts and where the human rights of miners were severely abused. Awareness of what were known as "conflict diamonds" further increased after the 2006 release of director Edward Zwick's movie *Blood Diamond*, starring Leonardo DiCaprio.

Tiffany & Co.'s earlier steps toward vertical integration paved the way for building a sustainable and socially responsible company. Vertical integration of its supply chain allowed

(continued)

Tiffany & Co. to trace its diamonds and metals directly to the source and ensure that mining locations practiced responsible operations. The company employs a zero-tolerance policy toward purchasing conflict diamonds, and in 2006 it helped to establish the Initiative for Responsible Mining Assurance (IRMA), which became the world's first certification system for responsible mining sites. The company has also been vocal in its opposition to mines that threaten local ecosystems. Tiffany lobbied against development of the Pebble Mine in Alaska's Bristol Bay, which many believe would damage local fisheries.

The company has contributed to IRMA's mission by investing in the environmental and economic development of its mining sites. For example, Tiffany & Co. trained its workers in Botswana—where 98 percent of Tiffany's polishers are now based—to cut and polish diamonds, providing locals with job opportunities and enriching Botswana's economy by $50 million. The company has also made extensive efforts to provide its workers with an ethical standard of living. Tiffany & Co. hired an economist to calculate a fair living wage for its Cambodian workers, factoring in variables such as family size, housing, and transportation. Moreover, Tiffany & Co. provides workers with benefits such as maternity leave, free lunches, and elimination of late night/weekend shifts.

Tiffany & Co. has incorporated its sustainability mission into the company's governance, and it appointed its first chief sustainability officer in 2015, one of the first in a luxury-goods company. The CSO oversees Tiffany's social and environmental initiatives. The company has since pledged zero gas emissions by 2050, tacking on climate change as another aspect of its sustainability agenda. Tiffany & Co. has embedded its mission of sustainability into both its retail locations and its product packaging, using energy-efficient LED lighting in stores and recycled materials in its signature blue packaging. Other initiatives include conservation of coral reefs and development of urban parks.

Tiffany & Co.'s social and environmental missions have become a valuable aspect of its brand image, and its strict usage of diamonds and precious metals that are ethically sourced is an integral part of the brand's promise. In recent years, management has trained salespeople to educate customers on how Tiffany & Co.'s sourcing methods differ from those of competitor jewelry stores. The company has released collections that support various environmental initiatives, such as the Save the Wild jewelry line, with 100 percent of profits donated to Africa's Elephant Crisis Fund.

Tiffany & Co. is notable in the luxury jewelry industry for ethically sourcing precious gems and metals and supporting various social and environmental initiatives. Tiffany & Co's ability to ensure corporate social responsibility stems from the company's vertical integration, which allows it to control sourcing of diamonds and precious metals. This aspect of Tiffany & Co.'s supply chain has given it a competitive edge and has become a crucial part of its brand image.[64]

Questions

1. Should a luxury company actively engage in corporate social responsibility? What are the pros and cons of this decision?
2. Should Tiffany advertise the fact that it is supporting various social and environmental initiatives? Why or why not?
3. How important is it for Tiffany to have a chief sustainability officer (CSO)? What are the advantages and disadvantages of having a single person ultimately responsible for designing and implementing corporate social responsibility programs?

Endnotes

Chapter 1

1. G. Shainesh - Interview with KB Nagaraju - "Big Basket Introduction [Video]", (June 2020), Accessed on July 16, 2021, from https://www.edx.org
2. Knowledge @ Wharton, " Why India's online grocery battle is heating up", (April 2018), Accessed on July19, 2021, from, https://knowledge.wharton.upenn.edu
3. Katharina Neureiter and Julia Tobias (2019) "How does an online supermarket in India impact farmers", Insight, CDC Investment Works, Accessed on August 28, 2021, from https://assets.cdcgroup.com
4. Forbes India, "The secret sauce to Bigbasket's 10 million plus online deliveries",(2019), Accessed on 19 July 2021, from, https://www.forbesindia.com
5. Samreen Ahmed (2020), "BigBasket sees 84% increase in new customers as compared to pre-Covid level" Business Standard, September 1, https://www.business-standard.com/article/companies/bigbasket-sees-84-increase-in-new-customers-as-compared-to-pre-covid-level-120090101364_1.html (accessed on September 28, 2021
6. Big Basket, "Big Basket- About us", (2021), Accessed on July 16, 2021, from https://www.bigbasket.com
7. Dominique M. Hanssens and Koen H. Pauwels, "Demonstrating the Value of Marketing," *Journal of Marketing* 80, no. 6 (2016), pp. 173–90.
8. *American Marketing Association,* "Definition of Marketing," https://www.ama.org/AboutAMA/Pages/Definition-of-Marketing.aspx, accessed 11/23/2020.
9. Robert F. Lusch and Frederick E. Webster Jr., "A Stakeholder-Unifying, Cocreation Philosophy for Marketing," *Journal of Macromarketing* 31, no. 2 (2011), 129–34. See also Robert F. Lusch and Frederick E. Webster Jr., "Elevating Marketing: Marketing Is Dead! Long Live Marketing!" *Journal of Academy of Marketing Science* 41 (January 2013), pp. 389–99.
10. Peter Drucker, *Management: Tasks, Responsibilities, Practices* (New York: Harper and Row, 1973), pp. 64–65.
11. Irving J. Rein, Philip Kotler, Michael Hamlin, and Martin Stoller, *High Visibility*, 3rd ed. (New York: McGraw-Hill, 2006).
12. Philip Kotler, Christer Asplund, Irving Rein, and Donald H. Haider, *Marketing Places in Europe: Attracting Investments, Industries, Residents, and Visitors to European Cities, Communities, Regions, and Nations* (London: Financial Times Prentice Hall, 1999); Philip Kotler, Irving J. Rein, and Donald Haider, *Marketing Places: Attracting Investment, Industry, and Tourism to Cities, States, and Nations* (New York: Free Press, 1993).
13. Philip Kotler, "Marketing: The Underappreciated Workhorse," *Market Leader*, Quarter 2 (2009), pp. 8–10.
14. V. Kumar, "Transformative Marketing: The Next 20 Years," *Journal of Marketing* 82, no. 4 (2018), pp. 1–12.
15. Thomas Friedman, *The World Is Flat: A Brief History of the Twenty-First Century* (New York: Farrar, Straus & Giroux, 2005).
16. Homi Kharas, *The Unprecedented Expansion of the Global Middle Class,* (Washington, DC: The Brookings Institution, 2017).
17. Vijay Govindarajan and Chris Trimble, *Reverse Innovation: Create Far from Home, Win Everywhere* (Boston: *Harvard Business School Publishing*, 2012).
18. Rajendra Sisodia, David Wolfe, and Jagdish Sheth, *Firms of Endearment: How World-Class Companies Profit from Passion* (Upper Saddle River, NJ: *Wharton School Publishing*, 2007).
19. Jeffrey Hollender and Stephen Fenichell, *What Matters Most* (New York: Basic Books, 2004), p. 168; Alexander Chernev and Sean Blair, "Doing Well by Doing Good: The Benevolent Halo of Corporate Social Responsibility," *Journal of Consumer Research* 41, no. 6 (2015), pp. 1412–25. But corporate social responsibility efforts may not work well for some types of brands, such as luxury brands; see Carlos J. Torelli, Alokparna Basu Monga, and Andrew M. Kaikati, "Doing Poorly by Doing Good: Corporate Social Responsibility and Brand Concepts," *Journal of Consumer Research* 38 (February 2012), pp. 948–63.
20. Karey Wutkowski, "Car Makers Try to Copy Green Halo of Prius," *Reuters*, April 8, 2008; https://www.prnewswire.com/news-releases/the-car-that-changed-an-industry-toyota-marks-20th-anniversary-of-prius-with-special-anniversary-edition-301055995.html, accessed 1/30/2021.
21. For some thoughtful academic perspectives on marketing strategy and tactics, see Alice M. Tybout and Bobby J. Calder, eds., *Kellogg on Marketing,* 2nd ed. (New York: Wiley, 2010) and

Alice M. Tybout and Tim Calkins, eds., *Kellogg on Branding* (New York: Wiley, 2005).

22. Tomio Geron, "The Share Economy," *Forbes*, February 11, 2013; Georgios Zervas, Davide Proserpio, and John W. Byers, "The Rise of the Sharing Economy: Estimating the Impact of Airbnb on the Hotel Industry," *Journal of Marketing Research* 54, no. 5 (2017), pp. 687–705.
23. "New Directions: Consumer Goods Companies Hone a Cross-Channel Approach to Consumer Marketing," *The Economist Intelligence Unit Special Report*, February 2012.
24. Mark Schaefer, "The 10 Best Corporate Blogs in the World," www.businessesgrow.com, January 5, 2011; Roger Yu, "More Companies Quit Blogging, Go with Facebook Instead," *USA Today*, April 20, 2012.
25. BW Online Bureau (2017), 'Wipro Launches New Brand Identity, New Logo' Business World, May 3, Accessed on July 16, 2021, from http://www.businessworld.in
26. **Wipro, " Wipro- Partner Ecosystem", Accessed on August 5, 2021, from, https://www.wipro.com**
27. Leaders Magazine, " The Pillars of Ecology, Education and Innovation- An interview with Azim H. Premji, Chairman, Wipro Limited", Leaders Magazine Inc.,Volume 33, Issue 1,pp 49 (Jan, 2010). Accessed on August 8, 2021, from, http://www.leadersmag.com
28. ET Bureau (2017), 'Nalinikanth is President & CEO of GE Healthcare, Wipro GE Healthcare', ***Economic Times***, August 02, 2017. Accessed on July 12, 2021, from https://economictimes.indiatimes.com
29. "Case Study: Promote Iceland," www.warc.com, 2012; "How to Use a Volcanic Eruption to Your Advantage in Marketing," ICCA Best Marketing Award Entry 2010; Marc Springate and George Bryant, "Promote Iceland: Inspired by Iceland," www.warc.com, 2012; https://www.islandsstofa.is/en, accessed 11/23/2020.
30. Diane Cardwell, "At Patagonia, the Bottom Line Includes the Earth," *New York Times*, July 30, 2014.
31. For a discussion of the conditions when consumers are most likely to prefer fair-trade products, see Katherine White, Rhiannon MacDonnell, and John H. Ellard, "Belief in a Just World: Consumer Intentions and Behaviors toward Ethical Products," *Journal of Marketing* 76 (January 2012), pp. 103–18.
32. https://www.warc.com/NewsAndOpinion/News/30084, accessed 11/23/2020.
33. Alexander Edeling and Marc Fischer, "Marketing's Impact on Firm Value: Generalizations from a Meta-Analysis," *Journal of Marketing Research* 53, no. 4 (2016), pp. 515–34.
34. Constantine S. Katsikeas, Neil A. Morgan, Leonidas C. Leonidou, and G. Tomas M. Hult, "Assessing Performance Outcomes in Marketing." *Journal of Marketing* 80, no. 2 (2016), pp. 1–20.
35. V. Kumar, "Integrating Theory and Practice in Marketing." *Journal of Marketing* 81, no. 2 (2017), pp. 1–7.
36. Theodore Levitt, "Marketing Myopia," *Harvard Business Review,* July–August 1960, p. 50.
37. For a broad historical treatment of marketing thought, see D. G. Brian Jones and Eric H. Shaw, "A History of Marketing Thought," in Barton A. Weitz and Robin Wensley, eds., *Handbook of Marketing* (London: Sage, 2002), pp. 39–65. For more specific issues related to the interface between marketing and sales, see Christian Homburg, Ove Jensen, and Harley Krohmer, "Configurations of Marketing and Sales: A Taxonomy," *Journal of Marketing* 72 (March 2008), pp. 133–54.
38. For some further historical reading on the origins of brand and category management, see George S. Low and Ronald A. Fullerton, "Brands, Brand Management, and the Brand Manager System: A Critical Historical Evaluation," *Journal of Marketing Research* 31 (May 1994), pp. 173–90.
39. D. Gail Fleenor, "The Next Space Optimizer," *Progressive Grocer*, March 2009.
40. Larry Selden and Geoffrey Colvin, *Angel Customers & Demon Customers* (New York: Portfolio [Penguin], 2003).
41. For an in-depth discussion of issues around implementing a customer-based organization on which much of this paragraph is based, see George S. Day, "Aligning the Organization with the Market," *MIT Sloan Management Review* 48 (Fall 2006), pp. 41–49.
42. Frederick E. Webster Jr., "The Role of Marketing and the Firm," in Barton A. Weitz and Robin Wensley, eds., *Handbook of Marketing* (London: Sage, 2002), pp. 39–65; Colleen M. Harmeling, Robert W. Palmatier, Eric Fang, and Dianwen Wang, "Group Marketing: Theory, Mechanisms, and Dynamics," *Journal of Marketing* 81, no. 4 (2017), pp. 1–24.
43. Ibid.; Jon R. Katzenbach and Douglas K. Smith, *The Wisdom of Teams: Creating the High-Performance Organization* (Boston: Harvard Business School Press, 1993); Matias G. Enz and Douglas M. Lambert, "Using Cross-Functional, Cross-Firm Teams to Co-Create Value: The Role of Financial Measures," *Industrial Marketing Management*, 41 (April 2012), pp. 495–507.
44. Agneta Larsson, Mats Johansson, Fredrik Bååth, and Sanna Neselius, "Reducing Throughput Time

in a Service Organization by Introducing Cross-Functional Teams," *Production Planning & Control* 23 (July 2012), pp. 571–80.

45. Peter C. Verhoef and Peter S. H. Leeflang, "Understanding the Marketing Department's Influence within the Firm," *Journal of Marketing* 73 (March 2009), pp. 14–37; Pravin Nath and Vijay Mahajan, "Marketing in the C-Suite: A Study of Chief Marketing Officer Power in Firm's Top Management Teams," *Journal of Marketing*, 75 (January 2012), pp. 60–77; Christian Schulze, Bernd Skiera, and Thorsten Weisel, "Linking Customer and Financial Metrics to Shareholder Value: The Leverage Effect in Customer-Based Valuation," *Journal of Marketing*, 76 (March 2012), pp. 17–32.

46. Nirmalya Kumar, *Marketing as Strategy: Understanding the CEO's Agenda for Driving Growth and Innovation* (Boston: Harvard Business School Press, 2004).

47. George S. Day and Robert Malcolm, "The CMO and the Future of Marketing," *Marketing Management*, Spring 2012, pp. 34–43.

48. Natalie Zmuda, "Global Experience Rises as Prerequisite to Getting Ahead," *Advertising Age*, June 10, 2012.

49. For research on the prevalence of CMOs, see Pravin Nath and Vijay Mahajan, "Chief Marketing Officers: A Study of Their Presence in Firms' Top Management Teams," *Journal of Marketing* 72 (January 2008), pp. 65–81. For more discussion on the importance of CMOs, see David A. Aaker, *Spanning Silos: The New CMO Imperative* (Boston: Harvard Business School Press, 2008).

50. Rui Wang, Aditya Gupta, and Rajdeep Grewal, "Mobility of Top Marketing and Sales Executives in Business-to-Business Markets: A Social Network Perspective," *Journal of Marketing Research* 54, no. 4 (2017), pp. 650–70.

51. V. Kumarand Werner Reinartz. "Creating Enduring Customer Value." *Journal of Marketing* 80, no. 6 (2016), pp. 36–68.

52. Johanna Frösén, Jukka Luoma, Matti Jaakkola, Henrikki Tikkanen, and Jaakko Aspara. "What Counts versus What Can Be Counted: The Complex Interplay of Market Orientation and Marketing Performance Measurement," *Journal of Marketing* 80, no. 3 (2016), pp. 60–78.

53. For discussion of some of the issues involved, see Glen Urban, *Don't Just Relate—Advocate* (Upper Saddle River, NJ: Pearson Education, Wharton School Publishing, 2005).

54. For a broad historical treatment of marketing thought, see D. G. Brian Jones and Eric H. Shaw, "A History of Marketing Thought," Barton A. Weitz and Robin Wensley, eds., *Handbook of Marketing* (London: Sage, 2002), pp. 39–65. For more specific issues related to the interface between marketing and sales, see Christian Homburg, Ove Jensen, and Harley Krohmer, "Configurations of Marketing and Sales: A Taxonomy," *Journal of Marketing* 72 (March 2008), pp. 133–54.

55. Frederick E. Webster Jr., "Expanding Your Network," *Marketing Management* (Fall 2010), pp. 16–23; Frederick E. Webster Jr., Alan J. Malter, and Shankar Ganesan, "Can Marketing Regain Its Seat at the Table?" *Marketing Science Institute Report No. 03-113* (Cambridge, MA: Marketing Science Institute, 2003); Frederick E. Webster Jr., "The Role of Marketing and the Firm," in Barton A. Weitz and Robin Wensley, eds., *Handbook of Marketing* (London: Sage, 2002), pp. 39–65.

56. Jeff S. Johnson and Joseph M. Matthes. "Sales-to-Marketing Job Transitions," *Journal of Marketing* 82, no. 4 (2018), pp. 32–48.

57. For more on creativity, see Pat Fallon and Fred Senn, *Juicing the Orange: How to Turn Creativity into a Powerful Business Advantage* (Boston: Harvard Business School Press, 2006); Bob Schmetterer, *Leap: A Revolution in Creative Business Strategy* (Hoboken, NJ: Wiley, 2003); Jean-Marie Dru, *Beyond Disruption: Changing the Rules in the Marketplace* (Hoboken, NJ: Wiley, 2002); and all the books by Edward DeBono.

58. Gary Hamel, *Leading the Revolution* (Boston: Harvard Business School Press, 2000).

59. Jagdish N. Sheth, *The Self-Destructive Habits of Good Companies . . . and How to Break Them* (Upper Saddle River, NJ: Wharton School Publishing, 2007).

60. This section is largely derived from Philip Kotler, *Ten Deadly Marketing Sins: Signs and Solutions* (Hoboken, NJ: Wiley, 2004). © Philip Kotler.

61. Marketing Spotlight sources: Barbara Lippert, "Game Changers: Inside the Three Greatest Ad Campaigns of the Past Three Decades," *Adweek*, November 17, 2008; Chris Zook and James Allen, "Growth outside the Core," *Harvard Business Review,* December 2003, pp. 66–75; Adam Lashinsky, "Nike's Master Craftsman," *Fortune*, November 12, 2015; Laura Stevens and Sara Germano, "Retail Shift Pushed Nike to Amazon—Sneaker Giant Resisted for Years but Got Outflanked by e-Commerce," *Wall Street Journal*, June 29, 2017; https://about.nike.com, accessed 11/22/2020.

62. Marketing Spotlight sources: Richard Siklosc, "The Iger Difference," *Fortune,* April 11, 2008; Dorothy Pomerantz, "Five Lessons in Success from Disney's $40 Million CEO," *Forbes,* January 23, 2013; Carmine Gallo, "Customer Service the Disney Way," *Forbes,* April 14, 2011; Hugo

Martin, "Disney's 2011 Marketing Campaign Centers on Family Memories," *LA Times*, September 23, 2010; Erich Schwartzel, "Disney Lays Out Its Plan to Fight Back against Streaming Giants," *Wall Street Journal*, August 8, 2018; Brooks Barnes, "Mickey Turns 90, and the Disney Marketing Machine Celebrates," *New York Times*, November 2, 2018; https://www.thewaltdisneycompany.com/about; accessed 11/22/2020.

Chapter 2

1. Bibhu Ranjan Mishra (2020) 'InMobi Group: This Make-in-India innovator is raring to go places' (December 25), Accessed on August 10, 2021 from https://www.business-standard.com
2. InMobi. "We drive real connections", (2021), Accessed on 19 July 2021, from, https://www.inmobi.com
3. Deepak Ajwani (2014) 'InMobi has positioned itself as the go-to company in mobile advertising' (October 11), Accessed on August 10, 2021 from https://www.forbesindia.com
4. MIT Technology Review (2013) '50 Disruptive Companies 2013', Accessed on August 10, 2021 from http://www2.technologyreview.com
5. Business Wire (2021), "InMobi launches In-game advertising to global brands and agencies" (April 27), Accessed on 19 July 2021 from https://www.businesswire.com
6. Alnoor Peermohamed (2020), 'InMobi's mobile-first content platform Glance raises $145 million in funding led by Google' The Economic Times (December 23), Accessed on August 10, 2021 from https://economictimes.indiatimes.com
7. Rohin Dharmakumar (2019) 'With Glance, InMobi wants to rule Android's screens' The-Ken (March 28), Accessed on August 10, 2021 from https://the-ken.com
8. Shilpa Phadnis and Sujit John (2021), 'InMobi to list on Nasdaq by December at $15 billion valuation' The Times of India, April 1, Accessed on August 11, 2021 from https://timesofindia.indiatimes.com
9. Alexander Chernev, *Strategic Marketing Management: Theory and Practice* (Chicago, IL: Cerebellum Press, 2019).
10. Peter Drucker, *Management: Tasks, Responsibilities and Practices* (New York: Harper and Row, 1973), chapter 7.
11. https://www.google.com/about, accessed 11/23/2020.
12. https://www.ikea.com/ms/en_SG/about_ikea/our_business_idea/index.html, accessed 11/23/2020.
13. https://investor.fb.com/resources/default.aspx, accessed 11/23/2020.
14. https://www.tesla.com/about, accessed 11/23/2020.
15. https://www.starbucks.com/about-us/company-information/mission-statement, accessed 11/23/2020.
16. https://www.microsoft.com/en-us/about, accessed 11/23/2020.
17. Alok Kshirsagar (2020) 'Keep it simple': Aditya Puri on HDFC Bank's path to market leadership, McKinsey Insights (December 14), Accessed on August 20, 2021 from https://www.mckinsey.com
18. The Economist (2020), 'Star performers: Who is the world's best banker?' (October 29), Accessed on August 20, 2021 from https://www.economist.com
19. HDFC Bank (2021), Accessed on 19 July 2021 from https://www.hdfcbank.com
20. Great Place to Work, Accessed on 19 July 2021 from https://www.greatplacetowork.in
21. "HDFC is now a great place to work", (2021), Accessed on 19 July 2021 from https://www.hdfcbank.com Accessed on 19 July 2021
22. "HDFC is now a great place to work", (2021), Accessed on 19 July 2021 from https://www.hdfcbank.com Accessed on 19 July 2021
23. Beth Snyder Bulik, "Customer Service Playing Bigger Role as Marketing Tool," *Advertising Age*, November 7, 2011.
24. Robert M. Grant, *Contemporary Strategy Analysis*, 8th ed. (New York: *John Wiley & Sons*, 2013), chapter 5.
25. Biocon, Businesses (2021), Accessed on 30 August 2021 from https://www.biocon.com
26. Knowledge@Wharton, "Biocon's Kiran Mazumdar Shaw: Crafting a business model to marry risk and reward", (2012), Accessed on 27 July 2021 from https://knowledge.wharton.upenn.edu
27. Samreen Ahmad (2020), 'Biocon diversifies business model, enters digital therapeutic segment' Business Standard, (July 21), Accessed on 27 July 2021 from https://www.business-standard.com
28. This section is largely based on Alexander Chernev, *Strategic Marketing Management: Theory and Practice* (Chicago, IL: Cerebellum Press, 2019).
29. Allan D. Shocker, "Determining the Structure of Product-Markets: Practices, Issues, and Suggestions," in Barton A. Weitz and Robin Wensley, eds., *Handbook of Marketing* (London: Sage, 2002), pp. 106–25. See also Bruce H. Clark and David B. Montgomery, "Managerial Identification of Competitors," *Journal of Marketing* 63 (July 1999), pp. 67–83.
30. "What Business Are You In? Classic Advice from Theodore Levitt," *Harvard Business Review*

(October 2006), pp. 127–37. See also Theodore Levitt's seminal article "Marketing Myopia," *Harvard Business Review,*(July–August 1960, pp. 45–56.

31. For discussion of some of the long-term implications of marketing activities, see Koen Pauwels, "How Dynamic Consumer Response, Competitor Response, Company Support, and Company Inertia Shape Long-Term Marketing Effectiveness," *Marketing Science* 23 (Fall 2004), pp. 596–610; Marnik Dekimpe and Dominique Hanssens, "Sustained Spending and Persistent Response: A New Look at Long-term Marketing Profitability," *Journal of Marketing Research* 36 (November 1999), pp. 397–412.

32. Michael Porter, "How Competitive Forces Shape Strategy," *Harvard Business Review* 57 (March–April 1979), pp. 137–45; Michael E. Porter, *Competitive Strategy: Techniques for Analyzing Industries and Competitors* (New York: Free Press, 1980).

33. Alexander Chernev, *Strategic Marketing Management: Theory and Practice* (Chicago, IL: Cerebellum Press, 2019).

34. The view of customer value creation as a process of managing attractiveness, awareness, and availability is a streamlined version of the 4-A framework that delineates acceptability, affordability, accessibility, and awareness as the key sources of customer value. See Jagdish Sheth and Rajendra Sisodia, *The 4 A's of Marketing: Creating Value for Customer, Company and Society* (New York: Routledge, 1012).

35. This section is largely based on Alexander Chernev, *Strategic Marketing Management: Theory and Practice* (Chicago, IL: Cerebellum Press, 2019).

36. John Elkington, "Partnerships from Cannibals with Forks: The Triple Bottom Line of 21st-Century Business," *Environmental Quality Management* 8, no. 1 (1998): pp. 37–51; John Elkington, "25 Years Ago I Coined the Phrase 'Triple Bottom Line.' Here's Why It's Time to Rethink It," *Harvard Business Review*, June 25, 2018.

37. https://www.unilever.com/sustainable-living/our-approach-to-reporting/our-metrics, accessed 11/23/2020.

38. For other examples, see Neil Bendle, Paul Farris, Phillip Pfeifer, David Reibstein, *Marketing Metrics* 4th edition (Upper Saddle River, NJ: Pearson FT Press, 2020).

39. This section is largely based on Alexander Chernev, *Strategic Marketing Management: Theory and Practice* (Chicago, IL: Cerebellum Press, 2019).

40. This section is largely based on Alexander Chernev, *Strategic Marketing Management: Theory and Practice* (Chicago, IL: Cerebellum Press, 2019).

41. This section is largely based on Alexander Chernev, *The Marketing Plan Handbook,* 6th ed. (Chicago, IL: Cerebellum Press, 2020).

42. This marketing spotlight is largely derived from the following sources: John Gapper, "Google's Android Tactics Are Microsoft Light," *FT.com*, April 20, 2016; Jack Nicas and Jay Greene, "Google, a Cloud-Computing Upstart, Seeks Credibility" *Wall Street Journal*, March 8, 2017; Miguel Helft, "Google Introduces Impressive Array of New Hardware: Phones, Speakers, Earbuds, Cameras, and More," *Forbes,* October 4, 2017; Jack Nicas, "Google's New Products Reflect Push into Machine Learning," *Wall Street Journal*, May 19, 2016; Jack Nicas, "Google Sees Ad Growth But Earns Less for Each Click," *Wall Street Journal,* July 25, 2017; https://www.google.com/about, accessed 11/23/2020.

43. This marketing spotlight is largely derived from the following sources: Tony Hsieh, *Delivering Happiness: A Path to Profits, Passion, and Purpose* (New York: Grand Central Publishing, 2010); Sujan Patel, "10 Examples of Companies with Fantastic Cultures," *Entrepreneur*, August 06, 2015; Susan Heathfield, "Find Out the Ways That Zappos Reinforces Its Company Culture," *The Balance*, May 7, 2018; Tony Hsieh, "How I Did It: Zappos's CEO on Going to Extremes for Customers," *Harvard Business Review*, August 01, 2014; https://www.zappos.com/about, accessed 11/23/2020.

Chapter 3

1. ET (2018), 'From 2BHK to 8.3 lakh sq feet: The Flipkart story so far' The Economic Times, May 9 https://economictimes.indiatimes.com (Accessed on August 6, 2021)

2. Tanya Duber (2017), 'These Disruptions made by Flipkart over Ten Years Helped it Lead the E-commerce Sector' Busines Insider India, June 2, https://www.businessinsider.in

3. Team Flipkart Stories. "Flipkart- About us". (August 2021), Accessed on 6th August 2021, from, http://stories.flipkart.com

4. Team Flipkart Stories. "HOW A HUMAN APPROACH TO TECHNOLOGY IS ENDEARING FLIPKART TO MILLIONS", (December 2017), Accessed on 6th August 2021, from, http://stories.flipkart.com

5. Gabriela Barkho (2021) 'How the pandemic strengthened Walmart-owned Flipkart's marketshare', Global Retail, May, https://www.modernretail.co Accessed on 29th August 2021

6. ET BrandEquity (2020), "Brand Pulse: Flipkart introduces insights tool for brands", Economic Times Brand Equity, August 27, https://brandequity.economictimes.indiatimes.com (Accessed on 6th August 2021)
7. Michael R. Solomon, *Consumer Behavior: Buying, Having, and Being,* 10th ed. (Upper Saddle River, NJ: Prentice Hall, 2013).
8. Katherine N. Lemon and Peter C. Verhoef, "Understanding Customer Experience throughout the Customer Journey," *Journal of Marketing* 80, no. 6 (2016), pp. 69–96.
9. G. Hofstede, *Cultures and Organizations: Software of the Mind* (New York: McGraw-Hill, 1997).
10. Leon G. Schiffman and Leslie Lazar Kanuk, *Consumer Behavior,* 10th ed. (Upper Saddle River, NJ: Prentice Hall, 2010).
11. V. Kumar and Anita Pansari, "National Culture, Economy, and Customer Lifetime Value: Assessing the Relative Impact of the Drivers of Customer Lifetime Value for a Global Retailer," *Journal of International Marketing* 24, no. 1 (March 2016) pp. 1–21; Daniel G. Goldstein, Hal E. Hershfield, and Shlomo Benartzi, "The Illusion of Wealth and Its Reversal," *Journal of Marketing Research* 53, no. 5 (2016), pp. 804–813.
12. Delphine Dion and Stéphane Borraz, "Managing Status: How Luxury Brands Shape Class Subjectivities in the Service Encounter," *Journal of Marketing* 81, no. 5 (2017), pp. 67–85.
13. Andrea Novais, "Social Classes in Brazil," *The Brazil Business*, October 7, 2011; Edison Bertoncelo, "Social Classes in Brazil: Time, Trajectory and Immaterial Inheritance," *The Sociological Review*, May 1, 2015.
14. Leon G. Schiffman and Leslie Lazar Kanuk, *Consumer Behavior,* 10th ed. (Upper Saddle River, NJ: Prentice Hall, 2010).
15. Michael Trusov, Anand Bodapati, and Randolph E. Bucklin, "Determining Influential Users in Internet Social Networks," *Journal of Marketing Research* 47 (August 2010), pp. 643–58.
16. Elizabeth S. Moore, William L. Wilkie, and Richard J. Lutz, "Passing the Torch: Intergenerational Influences as a Source of Brand Equity," *Journal of Marketing* 66 (April 2002), pp. 17–37.
17. Kay M. Palan and Robert E. Wilkes, "Adolescent-Parent Interaction in Family Decision Making," *Journal of Consumer Research* 24 (March 1997), pp. 159–69; Sharon E. Beatty and Salil Talpade, "Adolescent Influence in Family Decision Making: A Replication with Extension," *Journal of Consumer Research* 21 (September 1994), pp. 332–41.
18. Scott I. Rick, Deborah A. Small, and Eli J. Finkel, "Fatal (Fiscal) Attraction: Spendthrifts and Tightwads in Marriage," *Journal of Marketing Research* 48 (April 2011), pp. 228–37.
19. Valentyna Melnyk, Stijn M. J. van Osselaer, and Tammo H. A. Bijmolt, "Are Women More Loyal Customers Than Men? Gender Differences in Loyalty to Firms and Individual Service Providers," *Journal of Marketing* 73 (July 2009), pp. 82–96.
20. ypulse.com/post/view/5-stats-on-millennials-teens-social-media1, accessed 1/27/2021.
21. Rex Y. Du and Wagner A. Kamakura, "Household Life Cycles and Lifestyles in the United States," *Journal of Marketing Research* 48 (February 2006), pp. 121–32.
22. Brooks Barnes, "Disney Looking into Cradle for Customers," *New York Times*, February 6, 2011; Lisa Yorgey Lester, "Expectant Parents: Tap into the Baby Boom," *Target Marketing* (September 2008); Melanie Linder and Lisa LaMotta, "How to Market to the Modern Mom," *Forbes*, January 8, 2009.
23. Zack Burgess, "An Overall Success: After 125 years, Carhartt Rolls Up Its Sleeves for the Future," *Crain's Detroit*, June 22, 2014.
24. Harold H. Kassarjian and Mary Jane Sheffet, "Personality and Consumer Behavior: An Update," Harold H. Kassarjian and Thomas S. Robertson, eds., *Perspectives in Consumer Behavior* (Glenview, IL: Scott Foresman, 1981), pp. 160–80.
25. Lucia Malär, Harley Krohmer, Wayne D. Hoyer, and Bettina Nyffenegger, "Emotional Brand Attachment and Brand Personality: The Relative Importance of the Actual and the Ideal Self," *Journal of Marketing* 75 (July 2011), pp. 35–52; Eugina Leung, Gabriele Paolacci, and Stefano Puntoni, "Man versus Machine: Resisting Automation in Identity-Based Consumer Behavior," *Journal of Marketing Research* 55, no. 6 (2018), pp. 818–831.
26. Timothy R. Graeff, "Image Congruence Effects on Product Evaluations: The Role of Self-Monitoring and Public/Private Consumption," *Psychology & Marketing* 13 (August 1996), pp. 481–99.
27. Jennifer L. Aaker, "The Malleable Self: The Role of Self-Expression in Persuasion," *Journal of Marketing Research* 36 (February 1999), pp. 45–57; Monika Lisjak, Andrea Bonezzi, Soo Kim, and Derek D. Rucker, "Perils of Compensatory Consumption: Within-Domain Compensation Undermines Subsequent Self-Regulation," *Journal of Consumer Research* 41, no. 5 (2015), pp. 1186–1203.
28. www.smartertravel.com/best-boutique-hotel-chains-2017/; www.jdvhotels.com/awards-and-accolades, accessed 1/27/2021.
29. Alexander Chernev, Ryan Hamilton, and David Gal, "Competing for Consumer Identity: Limits to Self-

Expression and the Perils of Lifestyle Branding," *Journal of Marketing* 75, no. 3 (2011): pp. 66–82.

30. Kavita Daswani, "Multitasking BB Skin Creams Becoming Popular in U.S.," *Los Angeles Times*, July 15, 2012.

31. G. Shainesh (2020), 'Interview with Amit Pande - Brand Head, The Collective & International Brands, Aditya Birla Fashion and Retail Ltd.', https://www.edx.org (Accessed on 6th August, 2021)

32. https://www.vogue.in/topics/allen-solly/ & Harish B.,"Allen Solly: My World, My Way", (July 2010), Marketing Practice, Accessed on 6th August, 2021, from, https://marketingpractice.blogspot.com

33. ET BrandEquity (2019), 'Allen Solly defines the 'Future of Bottomwear' with its latest campaign' Economic Times, March 28, https://brandequity.economictimes.indiatimes.com Accessed on 6th August, 2021,

34. Abraham Maslow, *Motivation and Personality* (New York: Harper & Row, 1954), pp. 80–106. For an interesting business application, see Chip Conley, *Peak: How Great Companies Get Their Mojo from Maslow* (San Francisco: Jossey Bass 2007).

35. Nikolaus Franke, Peter Keinz, and Christoph J. Steger, "Testing the Value of Customization: When Do Customers Really Prefer Products Tailored to Their Preferences?" *Journal of Marketing* 73 (September 2009), pp. 103–21; Aner Sela, Jonah Berger, and Joshua Kim, "How Self-Control Shapes the Meaning of Choice," *Journal of Consumer Research* 44, no. 4 (2017), pp. 724–37.

36. Margaret C. Campbell and Caleb Warren, "The Progress Bias in Goal Pursuit: When One Step Forward Seems Larger than One Step Back," *Journal of Consumer Research* 41, no. 5 (2015), pp. 1316–31.

37. Neil Stevenson, "Need Feedback? Here's 5 Ways to Reinvent the Focus Group," *Ideo*, June 6, 2016.

38. Clotaire Rapaille, "Marketing to the Reptilian Brain," *Forbes,* July 3, 2006; Clotaire Rapaille, *The Culture Code* (New York: Broadway Books, 2007); Douglas Gantebein, "How Boeing Put the Dream in Dreamliner," *Air and Space* (September 2007); Tom Otley, "The Boeing Dreamliner: A Sneak Preview," *Business Traveller*, June 3, 2009.

39. www.nbcnews.com/id/38164372/ns/business-autos/t/chryslers-pt-cruiser-hits-end-road/#.W-x7Q-JMEt, accessed 12/17/2020; www.quirks.com/articles/chrysler-dug-deep-with-archetype-research-to-shape-its-pt-cruiser.

40. Bernard Berelson and Gary A. Steiner, *Human Behavior: An Inventory of Scientific Findings* (New York: Harcourt Brace Jovanovich, 1964), p. 88.

41. University of Florida's Chris Janiszewski has conducted fascinating research looking at preconscious processing effects. See Chris Janiszewski, "Preattentive Mere Exposure Effects," *Journal of Consumer Research* 20 (December 1993), pp. 376–92, as well as some of his earlier and subsequent research. For more foundational perspectives, see also John A. Bargh and Tanya L. Chartrand, "The Unbearable Automaticity of Being," *American Psychologist* 54 (1999), pp. 462–79; and Gráinne M. Fitzsimons, Tanya L. Chartrand, and Gavan J. Fitzsimons, "Automatic Effects of Brand Exposure on Motivated Behavior: How Apple Makes You 'Think Different,'" *Journal of Consumer Research* 35 (June 2008), pp. 21–35, as well as the research programs of both authors.

42. See Timothy E. Moore, "Subliminal Advertising: What You See Is What You Get," *Journal of Marketing* 46 (Spring 1982), pp. 38–47 for an early classic discussion; and Andrew B. Aylesworth, Ronald C. Goodstein, and Ajay Kalra, "Effect of Archetypal Embeds on Feelings: An Indirect Route to Affecting Attitudes?" *Journal of Advertising* 28 (Fall 1999), pp. 73–81 for additional discussion.

43. Ross Pomeroy, "The Legendary Study That Embarrassed Wine Experts across the Globe," *RealClear*, August 18, 2014.

44. Jack Neff, "Creativity Marks This Spot: K-C Thrives in Tiny Neenah," *Advertising Age*, June 6, 2011; "U by Kotex Creates a Social Movement," *Adweek*, November 22, 2011.

45. Jonah Berger and Katherine L. Milkman, "What Makes Online Content Viral?" *Journal of Marketing Research* 49 (April 2012), pp. 192–205.

46. Scott Berinato, "The Demographics of Cool," *Harvard Business Review* (December 2011), pp. 136–37; Steve Stoute, *The Tanning of America: How Hip-Hop Created a Culture That Rewrote the Rules of the New Economy* (New York: Gotham, 2012).

47. Katherine Halek, "Retro Marketing Tactics That Work Better Than Ever," *Relevance* (May 2014).

48. Vladas Griskevicius, Noah Goldstein, Chad Mortensen, Jill Sundie, Robert Cialdini, and Douglas Kenrick, "Fear and Loving in Las Vegas: Evolution, Emotion, and Persuasion," *Journal of Marketing Research* 46, no. 3 (2009), pp. 384–95.

49. Deborah Small and Nicole M. Verrochi, "The Face of Need: Facial Emotion Expression on Charity Advertisements," *Journal of Marketing Research* 46, no. 6 (2009), pp. 777–87.

50. For additional discussion, see John G. Lynch Jr. and Thomas K. Srull, "Memory and Attentional Factors in Consumer Choice: Concepts and Research Methods," *Journal of Consumer Research* 9 (June 1982), pp. 18–36; and Joseph W. Alba, J. Wesley Hutchinson, and John G. Lynch Jr., "Memory and Decision Making," in Harold

H. Kassarjian and Thomas S. Robertson, eds., *Handbook of Consumer Theory and Research* (Englewood Cliffs, NJ: Prentice Hall, 1992), pp. 1–49.

51. Jonah Berger and Eric M. Schwartz, "What Drives Immediate and Ongoing Word of Mouth?" *Journal of Marketing Research* 48 (October 2011), pp. 869–80.

52. Based in part on Figure 1.7 from George Belch and Michael Belch, *Advertising and Promotion: An Integrated Marketing Communications Perspective*, 8th ed. (Homewood, IL: Irwin, 2009).

53. Marketing scholars have developed several models of the consumer buying process through the years. See Mary Frances Luce, James R. Bettman, and John W. Payne, *Emotional Decisions: Tradeoff Difficulty and Coping in Consumer Choice* (Chicago: University of Chicago Press, 2001); James F. Engel, Roger D. Blackwell, and Paul W. Miniard, *Consumer Behavior,* 8th ed. (Fort Worth, TX: Dryden, 1994); and John A. Howard and Jagdish N. Sheth, *The Theory of Buyer Behavior* (New York: John Wiley & Sons, 1969).

54. David Court, Dave Elzinga, Susan Mulder, and Ole Jorgen Vetvik, "The Consumer Decision Journey," *McKinsey Quarterly* 3, no. 3 (2009), pp. 96–107.

55. Geoffrey Precourt, "How Unilever Uses Online Data to Map the Path to Purchase," www.warc .com (April 2012).

49. Janet Schwartz, Mary Frances Luce, and Dan Ariely, "Are Consumers Too Trusting? The Effects of Relationships with Expert Advisers," *Journal of Marketing Research* 48 (Special Issue 2011), pp. S163–S174.

56. Min Ding, John R. Hauser, Songting Dong, Daria Dzyabura, Zhilin Yang, Chenting Su, and Steven Gaskin, "Unstructured Direct Elicitation of Decision Rules," *Journal of Marketing Research* 48 (February 2011), pp. 116–27; Michaela Draganska and Daniel Klapper, "Choice Set Heterogeneity and the Role of Advertising: An Analysis with Micro and Macro Data," *Journal of Marketing Research* 48 (August 2011), pp. 653–69; John R. Hauser, Olivier Toubia, Theodoros Evgeniou, Rene Befurt, and Daria Dzyabura, "Disjunctions of Conjunctions, Cognitive Simplicity and Consideration Sets," *Journal of Marketing Research* 47 (June 2010), pp. 485–96; Erjen Van Nierop, Bart Bronnenberg, Richard Paap, Michel Wedel, and Philip Hans Franses, "Retrieving Unobserved Consideration Sets from Household Panel Data," *Journal of Marketing Research* 47 (February 2010), pp. 63–74. For some behavioral perspectives, see Jeffrey R. Parker and Rom Y. Schrift, "Rejectable Choice Sets: How Seemingly Irrelevant No-Choice Options Affect Consumer Decision Processes," *Journal of Marketing Research* 48 (October 2011), pp. 840–54.

57. Benedict G. C. Dellaert and Gerald Häubl, "Searching in Choice Mode: Consumer Decision Processes in Product Search with Recommendations," *Journal of Marketing Research* 49 (April 2012), pp. 277–88. See also Jun B. Kim, Paulo Albuquerque, and Bart J. Bronnenberg, "Mapping Online Consumer Search," *Journal of Marketing Research* 48 (February 2011), pp. 13–27.

58. Robert E. Smith and William R. Swinyard, "Attitude-Behavior Consistency: The Impact of Product Trial versus Advertising," *Journal of Marketing Research* (1983), pp. 257–67.

59. Paul E. Green and Yoram Wind, *Multiattribute Decisions in Marketing: A Measurement Approach* (Hinsdale, IL: Dryden, 1973), chapter 2; Richard J. Lutz, "The Role of Attitude Theory in Marketing," in H. Kassarjian and T. Robertson, eds., *Perspectives in Consumer Behavior* (Lebanon, IN: Scott Foresman, 1981), pp. 317–39.

60. This expectancy-value model was originally developed by Martin Fishbein, "Attitudes and Prediction of Behavior," in Martin Fishbein, ed., *Readings in Attitude Theory and Measurement* (New York: John Wiley & Sons, 1967), pp. 477–92; for a critical review, see Paul W. Miniard and Joel B. Cohen, "An Examination of the Fishbein-Ajzen Behavioral-Intentions Model's Concepts and Measures," *Journal of Experimental Social Psychology* (May 1981), pp. 309–39.

61. Michael R. Solomon, *Consumer Behavior: Buying, Having, and Being,* 10th ed. (Upper Saddle River, NJ: *Prentice Hall*, 2013).

62. Daniel Kahneman, *Thinking, Fast and Slow* (New York: Farrar, Straus and Giroux, 2011); Meng Zhu, Yang Yang, and Christopher K Hsee, "The Mere Urgency Effect," *Journal of Consumer Research* 45, no. 3 (2018), pp. 673–90; Bart De Langhe and Stefano Puntoni, "Productivity Metrics and Consumers' Misunderstanding of Time Savings," *Journal of Marketing Research* 53, no. 3 (2016), pp. 396–406; Aaron M. Garvey, Margaret G. Meloy, and Baba Shiv, "The Jilting Effect: Antecedents, Mechanisms, and Consequences for Preference," *Journal of Marketing Research* 54, no. 5 (2017), pp. 785–98.

63. Richard H. Thaler and Cass R. Sunstein, *Nudge: Improving Decisions about Health, Wealth, and Happiness* (New York: Penguin, 2009); Michael Krauss, "A Nudge in the Right Direction," *Marketing News*, March 30, 2009, p. 20.

64. Richard E. Petty, *Communication and Persuasion: Central and Peripheral Routes to Attitude Change*

(New York: Springer-Verlag, 1986); Richard E. Petty and John T. Cacioppo, *Attitudes and Persuasion: Classic and Contemporary Approaches* (New York: McGraw-Hill, 1981).

65. Martin Fishbein, "Attitudes and Prediction of Behavior," in M. Fishbein, ed., *Readings in Attitude Theory and Measurement* (New York: John Wiley & Sons, 1967), pp. 477–92.

66. For an examination of the use of *Consumer Reports*, see Uri Simonsohn, "Lessons from an 'Oops' at *Consumer Reports*: Consumers Follow Experts and Ignore Invalid Information," *Journal of Marketing Research* 48 (February 2011), pp. 1–12.

67. Margaret C. Campbell and Ronald C. Goodstein, "The Moderating Effect of Perceived Risk on Consumers' Evaluations of Product Incongruity: Preference for the Norm," *Journal of Consumer Research* 28 (December 2001), pp. 439–49; James R. Bettman, "Perceived Risk and Its Components: A Model and Empirical Test," *Journal of Marketing Research* 10 (May 1973); Bowen Ruan, Christopher K. Hsee, and Zoe Y. Lu, "The Teasing Effect: An Underappreciated Benefit of Creating and Resolving an Uncertainty," *Journal of Marketing Research* 55, no. 4 (2018), pp. 556–70.

68. Yangjie Gu, Simona Botti, and David Faro, "Seeking and Avoiding Choice Closure to Enhance Outcome Satisfaction," *Journal of Consumer Research* 45, no. 4 (2018), pp. 792–809.

69. Richard L. Oliver, "Customer Satisfaction Research," in Rajiv Grover and Marco Vriens, eds., *Handbook of Marketing Research* (Thousand Oaks, CA: Sage Publications, 2006), pp. 569–87.

70. Albert O. Hirschman, *Exit, Voice, and Loyalty* (Cambridge, MA: Harvard University Press, 1970).

71. John D. Cripps, "Heuristics and Biases in Timing the Replacement of Durable Products," *Journal of Consumer Research* 21 (September 1994), pp. 304–18.

72. Marketing Insight sources: Daniel Kahneman, *Thinking, Fast and Slow* (Farrar, Straus and Giroux, 2011); James Bettman, Mary Frances Luce, and John Payne, "Constructive Consumer Choice Processes," *Journal of Consumer Research* 25 (December 1998), pp. 187–217; Itamar Simonson, "Getting Closer to Your Customers by Understanding How They Make Choices," *California Management Review* 35 (Summer 1993), pp. 68–84; Richard Thaler, "Mental Accounting and Consumer Choice," *Marketing Science* 4 (Summer 1985), pp. 199–214; Richard Thaler and Cass Sunstein, *Nudge: Improving Decisions about Health, Wealth, and Happiness* (Yale University Press, 2008); Dan Ariely, *Predictably Irrational* (New York, NY: HarperCollins Publishers, 2008).

73. Court, D., Elzinga, D., et al (2009). The Consumer Decision Journey. McKinsey Quarterly, June 1, 2009. McKinsey & Company. Retrieved from https://www.mckinsey.com (Accessed on October 8, 2021)

74. David Court, Dave Elzinga, Susan Mulder, and Ole Jørgen Vetvik (2009), 'The consumer decision journey', McKinsey, https://www.mckinsey.com (Accessed on 30th August 2021)

75. McKinsey blog (2017), "Ten years on the consumer decision journey: Where are we today?", McKinsey, https://www.mckinsey.com(Accessed on 30th August 2021)

76. Aravind Eyecare System, "Vision and Mission", (August 2021), Accessed on 6th August, 2021, from, https://aravind.org/vision-mission/ and https://aravind.org https://www.aurolab.com/genesis.asp (Accessed on September 17, 2021)

77. Aravind Eyecare System, "How to Support an Eye Camp?", (August 2021), Accessed on 6th August, 2021, from, https://aravind.org

78. Aravind Eyecare System, "Our Story", (August 2021), Accessed on 6th August, 2021, from, https://aravind.org

79. Aravind Eyecare System, "Activity Report, 2019–2020", pp 22–23 &25, Accessed on 11th August 2021, from, https://aravind.org

80. Sadna Samaranayake. "Three Decades in the Making, How the Aravind Model Came into Focus – NextBillion", (18 November 2011), Next Billion, Accessed on 6th August 2021 from https://nextbillion.net

81. Mehta, P. and Shenoy, S., (2011). Infinite Vision: How Aravind became the world's greatest business case for compassion'. Berrett-Koehler Publishers.

82. Rangan, V.K. and Thulasiraj, R.D., 2007. Making sight affordable (innovations case narrative: the Aravind eyecare system). Innovations: Technology, Governance, Globalization, 2(4), pp.35–49

83. Shirish C. Srivastava & G. Shainesh, (2015) "Bridging The Service Divide Through Digitally Enabled Service Innovations: Evidence From Indian Healthcare Service Providers", ***MIS Quarterly***,Vol. 39 No. 1 (March), pp. 245–267.

84. Shah, J. and Murty, L.S., 2004. Compassionate, high quality health care at low cost: The Aravind mode; In conversation with Dr G Venkataswamy and RD Thulasiraj, *IIMB Management Review, September, pp. 31–43.*

85. Insights (2019) 'Paytm: Solving problems to create opportunity', KPMG, September https://home.kpmg (Accessed on 11th August 2021)

86. Research Briefs (2017), 'Paytm Has 200 Million Users—And Plenty Of Room To Grow, In India

Marketing Context," *Marketing Science* 30 (September–October 2011), pp. 924–40; Anita Luo and V. Kumar, "Recovering Hidden Buyer–Seller Relationship States to Measure the Return on Marketing Investment in Business-to-Business Markets," *Journal of Marketing Research* 50 (February 2013), pp. 143–60.

47. Das Narayandas and V. Kasturi Rangan, "Building and Sustaining Buyer–Seller Relationships in Mature Industrial Markets," *Journal of Marketing* 68 (July 2004), pp. 63–77; D. Eric Boyd and P. K. Kannan. "(When) Does Third-Party Recognition for Design Excellence Affect Financial Performance in Business-to-Business Markets?" *Journal of Marketing* 82, no. 3 (2018), pp. 108–23.

48. Joseph P. Cannon and William D. Perreault Jr., "Buyer–Seller Relationships in Business Markets," *Journal of Marketing Research* 36 (November 1999), pp. 439–60; Doug J. Chung and Das Narayandas, "Incentives versus Reciprocity: Insights from a Field Experiment," *Journal of Marketing Research* 54, no. 4 (2017), pp. 511–524.

49. Jan B. Heide and Kenneth H. Wahne, "Friends, Businesspeople, and Relationship Roles: A Conceptual Framework and Research Agenda," *Journal of Marketing* 70 (July 2006), pp. 90–103.

50. Joseph P. Cannon and William D. Perreault Jr., "Buyer–Seller Relationships in Business Markets," *Journal of Marketing Research* 36 (November 1999), pp. 439–60.

51. Thomas G. Noordewier, George John, and John R. Nevin, "Performance Outcomes of Purchasing Arrangements in Industrial Buyer–Vendor Arrangements," *Journal of Marketing* 54 (October 1990), pp. 80–93; Arnt Buvik and George John, "When Does Vertical Coordination Improve Industrial Purchasing Relationships?" *Journal of Marketing* 64, no. 4 (October 2000), pp. 52–64.

52. Robert W. Palmatier, Rajiv P. Dant, Dhruv Grewal, and Kenneth R. Evans, "Factors Influencing the Effectiveness of Relationship Marketing: A Meta-Analysis," *Journal of Marketing* 70 (October 2006), pp. 136–53; Jean L. Johnson, Ravipreet S. Sohli, and Rajdeep Grewal, "The Role of Relational Knowledge Stores in Interfirm Partnering," *Journal of Marketing* 68 (July 2004), pp. 21–36; Fred Selnes and James Sallis, "Promoting Relationship Learning," *Journal of Marketing* 67 (July 2003), pp. 80–95.

53. Kevin Lane Keller and David A. Aaker, "Corporate-Level Marketing: The Impact of Credibility on a Company's Brand Extensions," *Corporate Reputation Review* 1 (August 1998), pp. 356–78; Robert M. Morgan and Shelby D. Hunt, "The Commitment–Trust Theory of Relationship Marketing," *Journal of Marketing* 58, no. 3 (July 1994), pp. 20–38; Christine Moorman, Rohit Deshpande, and Gerald Zaltman, "Factors Affecting Trust in Market Research Relationships," *Journal of Marketing* 57 (January 1993), pp. 81–101; Glen Urban, "Where Are You Positioned on the Trust Dimensions?" in *Don't Just Relate—Advocate: A Blueprint for Profit in the Era of Customer Power* (Upper Saddle River, NJ: Pearson Education/Wharton School Publishers, 2005).

54. Corine S. Noordhoff, Kyriakos Kyriakopoulos, Christine Moorman, Pieter Pauwels, and Benedict G. C. Dellaert, "The Bright Side and Dark Side of Embedded Ties in Business-to-Business Innovation," *Journal of Marketing* 75 (September 2011), pp. 34–52.

55. Akesel I. Rokkan, Jan B. Heide, and Kenneth H. Wathne, "Specific Investment in Marketing Relationships: Expropriation and Bonding Effects," *Journal of Marketing Research* 40 (May 2003), pp. 210–24.

56. Kenneth H. Wathne and Jan B. Heide, "Relationship Governance in a Supply Chain Network," *Journal of Marketing* 68 (January 2004), pp. 73–89; Douglas Bowman and Das Narayandas, "Linking Customer Management Effort to Customer Profitability in Business Markets," *Journal of Marketing Research* 61 (November 2004), pp. 433–47; Mrinal Ghosh and George John, "Governance Value Analysis and Marketing Strategy," *Journal of Marketing* 63 (Special Issue, 1999), pp. 131–45.

57. Kenneth H. Wathne and Jan B. Heide, "Opportunism in Interfirm Relationships: Forms, Outcomes, and Solutions," *Journal of Marketing* 64 (October 2000), pp. 36–51.

58. Mark Vandenbosch and Stephen Sapp, "Opportunism Knocks," *MIT Sloan Management Review*, 52 (Fall, 2010), pp. 17–19.

59. Mark B. Houston and Shane A. Johnson, "Buyer–Supplier Contracts versus Joint Ventures: Determinants and Consequences of Transaction Structure," *Journal of Marketing Research* 37 (February 2000), pp. 1–15.

60. Aksel I. Rokkan, Jan B. Heide, and Kenneth H. Wathne, "Specific Investment in Marketing Relationships: Expropriation and Bonding Effects," *Journal of Marketing Research* 40 (May 2003), pp. 210–24.

61. Paul King, "Purchasing: Keener Competition Requires Thinking outside the Box," *Nation's Restaurant News*, August 18, 2003, p. 87; www.aramark.com/about-us, accessed 1/25/2021.

62. Shradha Sharma (2019), 'The making of India's fastest unicorn Udaan: how this B2B online marketplace is fueling a billion dreams', YourStory,

August 21, https://yourstory.com (Accessed on September 5, 2021)

63. Peerzada Abrar (2021), 'B2B e-commerce startup Udaan to tap $100-bn opportunity in small-town India', Business Standard, July 21 https://www.business-standard.com (Accessed on August 30, 2021)
64. ET Bureau (2021), 'Udaan helps over 400 sellers in electronics category notch sales worth Rs 1 cr each', Economic Times, March 15, https://retail.economictimes.indiatimes.com (Accessed on September 5, 2021)
65. Maleeva Rebello (2020), 'The road less taken: Udaan co-founder on working for Flipkart, starting his own company & success in B2B space', Economic Times, January 29, https://economictimes.indiatimes.com (Accessed on August 30, 2021)
66. DigBijay Mishra (2021), 'Udaan back to pre-second wave levels with GMV of $4-5 billion', Economic Times, ETTech July 06, https://economictimes.indiatimes.com (Accessed on September 10, 2021)
67. Vanishka Bagaria, "The Success Story of B2B Startup Udaan", (October, 2020), Accessed on 11th August 2021, from, https://blog.finology.in
68. DigBijay Mishra (2021), 'Udaan back to pre-second wave levels with GMV of $4-5 billion', Economic Times, ETTech July 06, https://economictimes.indiatimes.com/tech/startups/udaan-back-to-pre-second-wave-levels-with-gmv-of-4-5-billion/articleshow/84151772.cms?from=mdr Accessed on September 10, 2021
69. Peerzada Abrar, (2021) 'Udaan names co-founder Vaibhav Gupta as CEO, eyes IPO in 18–24 months', Business Standard, September 11, https://www.business-standard.com (Accessed on September 16, 2021)
70. Marketing Spotlight sources: Mi Ji, Jee Eun Lee, W. Chan Kim, and Renee Mauborgne, "Salesforce.com: Creating a Blue Ocean in the B2B Space," *Blue Ocean Strategy Institute* No. 313-019-1, Fontainebleau, France: *ECCH*, 2013; Gallagher, Dan, "Salesforce Grows the Old-Fashioned Way," *Wall Street Journal*, May 29, 2018; David Gelles, "Marc Benioff of Salesforce: 'Are We Not All Connected?'" *New York Times*, June 15, 2018; www.salesforce.com/company/about-us, accessed 11/23/2020.

Chapter 5

1. George Foster and Sandy Plunkett, "Executive Cases: Interviews with Senior Executives of Early-Stage Companies," *World Economic Forum*; Ron Miller, "Analysts Weighing in on $8B SAP-Qualtrics Deal Don't See a Game Changer," *Tech Crunch* (November 2018); Stephanie Nicola and Joyce Koh, "Germany's SAP to Buy Qualtrics for $8 Billion in Cash," *Bloomberg Businessweek*, November 11, 2018; Jay Greene and Rolf Winkler, "SAP to Buy Market-Analytics Startup Qualtrics for $8 Billion," *Wall Street Journal*, November 11, 2018; Matt Weinberger, "Qualtrics Is Going Public Less than 2 Years after SAP Bought the Utah-Based Cloud Software Company for $8 Billion," *Business Insider*, July 26, 2020; https://www.qualtrics.com/about, accessed 11/24/2020.
2. Jessica Shambora, "Wanted: Fearless Marketing Execs," *Fortune*, August 15, 2011, p. 27.
3. Ellen Byron, "Wash Away Bad Hair Days," *Wall Street Journal*, June 30, 2010.
4. Natalie Zmuda, "Tropicana Line's Sales Plunge 20% Post-Rebranding," *Advertising Age*, April 2, 2009.
5. Adapted from Arthur Shapiro, "Let's Redefine Market Research," *Brandweek*, June 21, 2004, p. 20; Kevin Ohannessian, "Star Wars: Thirty Years of Success," *Fast Company*, May 29, 2007.
6. www.pgcareers.com/career-areas, accessed 1/27/2021.
7. Stephanie L. Gruner, "Spies Like Us," *Inc.*, August 1, 1998; Darren Dahl, "10 Tips on How to Research Your Competition," *Inc.*, May 11, 2011.
8. Brad Smith, "Figure Out the Customer," *Bloomberg BusinessWeek*, April 12, 2012.
9. Ned Levi, "What's the Future for U.S. Airline Inflight Entertainment?" www.consumertraveler.com, April 9, 2012.
10. Fiona Blades, "Real-Time Experience Tracking Gets Closer to the Truth," *International Journal of Market Research* 54, no. 2 (2012), pp. 283–85; Emma K. Macdonald, Hugh N. Wilson, and Umut Konus, "Better Consumer Insight—in Real Time," *Harvard Business Review* (September 2012), pp. 102–08.
11. Ashley Lutz and Matt Townsend, "Big Brother Has Arrived at a Store Near You, *Bloomberg Businessweek*, December 19, 2011.
12. For a detailed review of some relevant academic work, see Eric J. Arnould and Amber Epp, "Deep Engagement with Consumer Experience," in Rajiv Grover and Marco Vriens, eds., *Handbook of Marketing Research* (Thousand Oaks, CA: Sage Publications, 2006). For a range of academic discussion, see the following special issue: "Can Ethnography Uncover Richer Consumer Insights?" *Journal of Advertising Research* 46 (September 2006). For some practical tips, see Richard Durante and Michael Feehan, "Leverage Ethnography to Improve

8. Christopher Steiner, "The Perfect Ski," *Forbes*, February 28, 2011.
9. James H. Gilmore and B. Joseph Pine II, *Markets of One: Creating Customer-Unique Value through Mass Customization* (Boston: Harvard Business School Press, 2000); B. Joseph Pine II, "Beyond Mass Customization," *Harvard Business Review*, May 2, 2011; Don Peppers and Martha Rogers, *The One-to-One Manager: Real-World Lessons in Customer Relationship Management* (New York: Doubleday, 1999).
10. This section is largely based on Alexander Chernev, *Strategic Marketing Management: Theory and Practice* (Chicago, IL: Cerebellum Press, 2019).
11. George S. Day, "Closing the Marketing Capabilities Gap," *Journal of Marketing* 75 (July 2011), pp. 183–95.
12. C.K. Prahalad and Gary Hamel. "The Core Competence of the Corporation." *Harvard Business Review* (May–June, 1990); Gary Hamel and C.K. Prahalad. "Competing for the Future," *Harvard Business Press*, 1996.
13. George S. Day and Paul J. H. Schoemaker, *Peripheral Vision: Detecting the Weak Signals That Will Make or Break Your Company* (Cambridge, MA: Harvard Business School Press, 2006); Paul J. H. Schoemaker and George S. Day, "How to Make Sense of Weak Signals," *MIT Sloan Management Review* (Spring 2009), pp. 81–89.
14. Eva Ascarza, "Retention Futility: Targeting High-Risk Customers Might Be Ineffective," *Journal of Marketing Research* 55, no. 1 (2018), pp. 80–98; Sebastian Tillmanns, Frenkel Ter Hofstede, Manfred Krafft, and Oliver Goetz, "How to Separate the Wheat from the Chaff: Improved Variable Selection for New Customer Acquisition," *Journal of Marketing* 81, no. 2 (2017), pp. 99–113.
15. Todd Wasserman, "Unilever, Whirlpool Get Personal with Personas," *Brandweek*, September 18, 2006, p. 13; Daniel B. Honigman, "Persona-fication," *Marketing News*, April 1, 2008, p. 8; Lisa Sanders, "Major Marketers Get Wise to the Power of Assigning Personas," *Advertising Age*, April 9, 2007.
16. Jack Nicas, "Allegiant Air: The Tardy, Gas-Guzzling, Most Profitable Airline in America," *Wall Street Journal*, June 4, 2013; "Heard of Allegiant Air? Why It's the Nation's Most Profitable Airline," *Fast Company* (September 2009); https://www.allegiantair.com/about-allegiant, accessed 1/26/2021.
17. Barry Silverstein, "Hallmark—Calling Card," www.brandchannel.com, June 15, 2009; Brad van Auken, "Leveraging the Brand: Hallmark Case Study," www.brandstrategyinsider.com, January 11, 2008; https://corporate.hallmark.com/news-article/hallmark-launches-four-new-multicultural-card-lines/ accessed 11/25/2020.
18. https://www.wedinsights.com/report/the-knot-real-weddings, accessed 11/25/2020.
19. Eric Klinenberg, "The Solo Economy," *Fortune*, February 6, 2012.
20. Zhong, Raymond, "Alibaba's Singles Day Sales Top $30 Billion. The Party May Not Last," *New York Times*, November 11, 2018; https://www.cnbc.com/2020/11/12/singles-day-2020-alibaba-and-jd-rack-up-record-115-billion-of-sales.html, accessed 11/25/2020.
21. For some consumer behavior findings on gender, see Kristina M. Durante, Vladas Griskevicius, Sarah E. Hill, Carin Perilloux, and Norman P. Li, "Ovulation, Female Competition, and Product Choice: Hormonal Influences on Consumer Behavior," *Journal of Consumer Research* 37 (April 2011), pp. 921–34; Valentyna Melnyk, Stijn M. J. van Osselaer, and Tammo H. A. Bijmolt, "Are Women More Loyal Customers Than Men? Gender Differences in Loyalty to Firms and Individual Service Providers," *Journal of Marketing* 73 (July 2009), pp. 82–96; Robert J. Fisher and Laurette Dube, "Gender Differences in Responses to Emotional Advertising: A Social Desirability Perspective," *Journal of Consumer Research* 31 (March 2005), pp. 850–58.
22. Molly Soat, "Tide Equips Mr. Mom," *Marketing News Exclusives*, January 17, 2013; Jack Neff, "Ogilvyism for New Era? Consumer Is Not a Moron. He Is Your Husband," *Advertising Age*, October 17, 2011; Heather Chaet, "The Manscape," *Adweek*, September 24, 2012.
23. Ellen Byron, "Does Your Razor Need a Gender?" *Wall Street Journal,* February 1, 2020.
24. "Gillette, Olay Co-Brand Razor," *Chain Drug Review*, February 27, 2012; Jenn Abelson, "Gillette Sharpens Its Focus on Women," *Boston Globe*, January 4, 2009, accessed 11/21/2020.
25. Ashutosh Sinha, Kushdesh Prasad and Praveen Tripathi (2018), 'Indian Socio Economic Classification 2018' MRSI https://www.mrsi.co.in (Accessed on August 31, 2021)
26. Max Chafkin, "Star Power," *Fast Company*, December 2012/January 2013, pp. 91–96, 126; Rolfe Winkler, "Is It Time Local Site Called for Yelp?" *Wall Street Journal*, January 17, 2013; "How Yelp's Business Works," *Business Insider*, March 2012.
27. Scarlett Lindeman, "Jell-O Love: A Guide to Mormon Cuisine," *The Atlantic*, March 24, 2010; Julie Zeveloff, "These Cities Love Ice Cream the Most," *Business Insider*, July 20, 2012; Jim Farber, "New York Is the King of Country," *Daily News*, August 9, 2012.

28. https://claritas360.claritas.com/mybestsegments, accessed 11/21/2020.
29. Jenni Romaniuk, "Are You Blinded by the Heavy (Buyer) . . . Or Are You Seeing the Light?" *Journal of Advertising Research*, 51 (December 2011), pp. 561–63.
30. Gina Chon, "Car Makers Talk 'Bout G-G-Generations," *Wall Street Journal*, May 9, 2006.
31. www.strategicbusinessinsights.com/vals/presurvey.shtml, accessed 1/25/2021.
32. Daniel Yankelovich and David Meer, "Rediscovering Market Segmentation," *Harvard Business Review* (February 2006), pp. 1–11; Sharon E. Beatty, Pamela M. Homer, and Lynn R. Kahle, "Problems with VALS in International Marketing Research: An Example from an Application of the Empirical Mirror Technique," Michael J. Houston, ed., *Advances in Consumer Research*, volume 15 (Provo, UT: Association for Consumer Research, 1988), pp. 375–80.
33. Justin Nelson and Chance Mitchell, "The LGBT Economy Is America's Future," *Advocate*, January 2, 2018; Jeff Green, "LGBT Purchasing Power Near $1 Trillion Rivals Other Minorities," *Bloomberg*, July 20, 2016, accessed 11/21/2020.
34. Adapted from Thomas V. Bonoma and Benson P. Shapiro, *Segmenting the Industrial Market* (Lexington, MA: Lexington Books, 1983).
35. Piet Levy, "Reeling in the Hungry Fish," *Marketing News*, May 30, 2009, p. 6; Stephen Baker, "Timken Plots a Rust Belt Resurgence," *Bloomberg BusinessWeek*, October 15, 2009; Matt McClellan, "Rolling Along," *Smart Business Akron/Canton* (October 2008); "Strong Energy Market to Propel Timken," *Metal Bulletin Daily*, January 27, 2012, p. 64; https://www.timken.com/about, accessed 1/27/2021.
36. Marketing Insight sources: Chris Anderson, *The Long Tail* (New York: Hyperion, 2006); Erik Brynjolfsson, Yu "Jeffrey" Hu, and Michael D. Smith, "From Niches to Riches: Anatomy of a Long Tail," *MIT Sloan Management Review* (Summer 2006), p. 67; Anita Elberse, "Should You Invest in the Long Tail?" *Harvard Business Review* (July–August 2008), pp. 88–96; "Rethinking the Long Tail Theory: How to Define 'Hits' and 'Niches,'" *Knowledge@Wharton*, September 16, 2009.
37. Marketing Spotlight sources: Andrew Roberts, "L'Oréal Quarterly Sales Rise Most since 2007 on Luxury Perfume," *Bloomberg BusinessWeek*, April 22, 2010; "Primping for the Cameras in the Name of Research," *New York Times*, February 7, 2006; Richard C. Morais, "The Color of Beauty," *Forbes*, November 27, 2000; Jack Neff, "How L'Oréal Zen Master Menesguen Shares Best Practices around the Globe," *Advertising Age*, June 11, 2012; Victoria Gomelsky, "L'Oréal's Technology Incubator: Creating the Future of Beauty," *New York Times*, March 30, 2017; https://www.loreal.com, accessed 11/25/2020.
38. Ayanangsha Maitra (2015), 'Mjunction runs world's largest e-marketplace for Steel and Coal' The CEO Magazine, https://www.theceo.in (Accessed on September 17, 2021)
39. Thimmaya Poojary (2019), "How B2B ecommerce marketplace mjunction has balanced surging business volumes and nonstop growth", Yourstory, September 5, Accessed on September 14, 2021, from, https://yourstory.com
40. Rakhi Mazumdar (2018), ' B2B ecommerce co mjunction puts its e-procurement app on cloud' The Economic Times, June 13, https://economictimes.indiatimes.com (Accessed on August 31, 2021)
41. Sandeep Sinha (2021), 'mjunction targets 25% top line growth in FY22; conducts 27,000 e-auctions in FY21' MoneyControl, April 10, https://www.moneycontrol.com (Accessed on August 31, 2021)
42. V Rishi Kumar, (2021) "mjunction transforms from e auction solutions provider to integrated e marketplace", The Hindu Businessline, July 27, Accessed on September 14, 2021 from https://www.thehindubusinessline.com
43. Tata Steel, Corporate, Our Organusation, Tata Group of Companies, Accessed on September 14, 2021 from, https://www.tatasteel.com
44. Jayajit Dash, "Shift to digitisation and e-commerce will fuel growth: Mjunction CEO", Business Standard, (26th April 2019), Accessed on September 14, 2021 from, https://www.business-standard.com
45. ET Bureau (2020), mjunction conducts first e-auction on new tea e-marketplace at Jorhat, *The Economic Times (June 1, 2020)*, accessed on January 15, 2021, from https://economictimes.indiatimes.com
46. Asit Ranjan Mishra (2021), 'GeM to standardize bidding process for projects of govt', HT Mint, August 16 https://www.livemint.com (Accessed on September 28, 2021)

Chapter 7

1. Jio, "Jio- Press Release", (2021), Accessed on 12th August 2021, from, https://www.jio.com/en-in/press-release
2. Peerzada Abrar (2021), 'Reliance Jio among the most competitive telcos, says Sunil Bharti Mittal', Business Standard, 16th April, Accessed on 16th Sept 2021, from, https://www.business-standard.com
3. Mohanbir Sawhney, " Reinventing The Customer Experience: Lessons from Jio", (August 2020),

Forbes, Accessed on 12th August 2021, from, https://www.forbes.com

4. The following discussion of the three types of customer value is reprinted from Alexander Chernev, *Strategic Marketing Management: Theory and Practice* (Chicago, IL: Cerebellum Press, 2019).
5. For an interesting approach to assess customer product perceptions and market structure online, see Thomas Y. Lee and Eric T. Bradlow, "Automated Marketing Research Using Online Customer Reviews," *Journal of Marketing Research* 48 (October 2011), pp. 881–94.
6. Al Ries and Jack Trout, *Positioning: The Battle for Your Mind, 20th Anniversary Edition* (New York: McGraw-Hill, 2000).
7. Brian Sheehan, *Loveworks: How the World's Top Marketers Make Emotional Connections to Win in the Marketplace* (Brooklyn, NY: *PowerHouse*, 2013).
8. Piet Levy, "Express Yourself," *Marketing News*, June 15, 2009, p. 6.
9. Harish Bhat (2021), 'A Titan of Our Times', #TataStories, Penguin Random House India, Gurgaon, pp. 25–28.
10. Vinay Kamath (2018),' The music of Mozart' The Hindu, December 27, https://www.thehindu.com
11. G. Shainesh, (2018) 'Customer relationship management: Concepts and Applications',, Accessed on 8th Sept 2021, from, https://www.edx.org
12. D Shivakumar (2019) 'Titan: Inside India's Most Successful Consumer Brand- Vinay Kamath", Business World, 3rd Jan, Accessed on 16th Sept 2021, from, http://www.businessworld.in
13. Titan, "About us- Heritage", Titan, (2021), Accessed on 16th Sept 2021, from, https://www.titancompany.in
14. Karuna Sharma, "How design has helped Titan to differentiate itself in the market and become the country's biggest and the world's 5th largest watchmaker", (Feb 2021), Advertising and Media insider, Accessed on 16th August 2021 from, https://www.businessinsider.in
15. Bureau (2008) 'Titan re-branding itself with new logo and tagline", India Retailing, July, Accessed on 16th August 2021, from, https://www.indiaretailing.com
16. David A. Aaker, *Brand Portfolio Strategy: Creating Relevance, Differentiation, Energy, Leverage, and Clarity* (New York: Free Press, 2004); Rebecca Wright, "The Next Frontier for Nutrition Bars," *Nutraceuticals World* (January/February 2011).
17. Robert Klara, "The Tough Sell," *Adweek*, July 9, 2012, p. 40.
18. Kevin Lane Keller, Brian Sternthal, and Alice Tybout, "Three Questions You Need to Ask about Your Brand," *Harvard Business Review* (September 2002), pp. 80–89.
19. Patrick Barwise, *Simply Better: Winning and Keeping Customers by Delivering What Matters Most* (Cambridge, MA: Harvard Business School Press, 2004); Gregory S. Carpenter, Rashi Glazer, and Kent Nakamoto, "Meaningful Brands from Meaningless Differentiation: The Dependence on Irrelevant Attributes," *Journal of Marketing Research* 31 (August 1994), pp. 339–50; Elizabeth M. S. Friedman, Jennifer Savary, and Ravi Dhar, "Apples, Oranges, and Erasers: The Effect of Considering Similar versus Dissimilar Alternatives on Purchase Decisions," *Journal of Consumer Research* 45, no. 4 (2018), pp. 725–42.
20. Hamish Pringle and Peter Field, "Why Emotional Messages Beat Rational Ones," *Advertising Age*, March 2, 2009, p. 13; Hamish Pringle and Peter Field, *Brand Immortality: How Brands Can Live Long and Prosper* (Philadelphia: Kogan Page, 2009).
21. James H. Gilmore and B. Joseph Pine II, *Authenticity: What Consumers Really Want* (Cambridge, MA: Harvard Business School Press, 2007); Felicitas Morhart, Lucia Malär, Amélie Guèvremont, Florent Girardin, and Bianca Grohmann, "Brand Authenticity: An Integrative Framework and Measurement Scale," *Journal of Consumer Psychology* (2014).
22. Jack Neff, "Welch's Local-Sourcing Story Core to Outreach," *Advertising Age*, January 24, 2011.
23. Business Standard, " ARIES AGRO LTD. (ARIES) - COMPANY HISTORY", Business Standard, (2021), Accessed on 16th Sept 2021, from, https://www.business-standard.com/company/aries-agro-12476/information/company-history
24. G. Shainesh, (2018) 'Customer relationship management: Concepts and Applications',, Accessed on 8th Sept 2021, from, https://www.edx.org/course/customer-relationship-management
25. Aries Agro, "Company overview", (2021), Accessed on 8th Sept 2021, from, https://ariesagro.com/company-overview/
26. G. Shainesh, (2020), 'Services Marketing: Concepts & Applications", IIMB edX, Accessed on 8th Sept 2021, from, https://www.edx.org
27. Jennifer Cirillo, "Energy's MVP," *Beverage World* (August 2012), pp. 35–42; www.redbull.com/us-en, accessed 1/27/2021.
28. Thomas A. Brunner and Michaela Wänke, "The Reduced and Enhanced Impact of Shared Features on Individual Brand Evaluations," *Journal of Consumer Psychology* 16 (April 2006),

pp. 101–11; Ioannis Evangelidis and Stijn M. J. Van Osselaer, "Points of (Dis)parity: Expectation Disconfirmation from Common Attributes in Consumer Choice," *Journal of Marketing Research* 55, no. 1 (2018), pp. 1–13; Jannine D. Lasaleta and Joseph P. Redden, "When Promoting Similarity Slows Satiation: The Relationship of Variety, Categorization, Similarity, and Satiation," *Journal of Marketing Research* 55, no. 3 (2018), pp. 446–57.

29. E. J. Schultz, "New Miller Time Spots Unveiled: MillerCoors Explains the Return," *Advertising Age*, March 22, 2012.

30. "Credit Cards: Loyalty and Retention—US—November 2007," *Mintel Reports* (November 2007).

31. L. Joshua Sosland, "Dunkin' Donuts' Strategy," *Food Business News*, May 18, 2011; Chris Barth, "Can Dunkin's New Deal Brew Enough Growth to Catch Starbucks?" *Forbes*, January 4, 2012.

32. Amna Kirmani, Rebecca W. Hamilton, Debora V. Thompson, and Shannon Lantzy. "Doing Well versus Doing Good: The Differential Effect of Underdog Positioning on Moral and Competent Service Providers," *Journal of Marketing* 81, no. 1 (2017), pp. 103–17.

33. Jim Henry, "BMW Still the Ultimate Driving Machine, Not That It Ever Wasn't," *Forbes*, May 31, 2012; "No Joy Here from BMW Ad Switch," *Automotive News*, April 12, 2010.

34. For a classic analysis of perceptual maps, see John R. Hauser and Frank S. Koppelman, "Alternative Perceptual Mapping Techniques: Relative Accuracy and Usefulness," *Journal of Marketing Research* 16 (November 1979), pp. 495–506. For some contemporary perspectives on measurement techniques for positioning, see Sanjay K. Rao, "Data-Based Differentiation," *Marketing Insights* (Spring 2013), pp. 26–32.

35. Michael E. Porter, *Competitive Strategy: Techniques for Analyzing Industries and Competitors* (New York: Free Press, 1980).

36. Makiko Kitamura and David Wainer, "Similar but Not the Same," *Bloomberg Businessweek*, March 25, 2013, pp. 19–20.

37. E. J. Schultz, "Muscling Past Mayhem: Geico Rides Giant Ad Budget Past Allstate," *Advertising Age*, July 8, 2013; Tim Nudd, "You Know the 'Fifteen Minutes' Line by Heart, But Did You Also Know . . . ," *Adweek*, July 1, 2013; www.geico.com, accessed, 1/27/2021.

38. The following discussion of the strategies for creating a sustainable competitive advantage is derived from Alexander Chernev, *Strategic Marketing Management: Theory and Practice* (Chicago, IL: Cerebellum Press, 2019).

39. 27 CFR 5.22—"The Standards of Identity," Alcohol and Tobacco Tax and Trade Bureau; U.S. Department of Treasury.

40. ET Brand Equity (2017), 'Bandhan Bank's ad campaign aims to make an impact and resonate with people', (2nd Nov 2017), ET Brand Equity, Accessed on 16th Sept 2021, from, https://brandequity.economictimes.indiatimes.com

41. Best Mediainfo (2018), "Bandhan Bank shows how to earn and save at the same time", (25th Sept 2018), Best Mediainfo, Accessed on 16th Nov 2021, from, https://bestmediainfo.com

42. David Dubois, Derek D. Rucker, and Adam D. Galinsky, "Dynamics of Communicator and Audience Power: The Persuasiveness of Competence versus Warmth," *Journal of Consumer Research* 43, no. 1 (2016), pp. 68–85; Daniella Kupor and Zakary Tormala, "When Moderation Fosters Persuasion: The Persuasive Power of Deviatory Reviews," *Journal of Consumer Research* 45, no. 3 (2018), pp. 490–510.

43. Melissa Korn, "Wanted: Gurus with Actual Experience," *Wall Street Journal*, July 2, 2013.

44. Randall Ringer and Michael Thibodeau, "A Breakthrough Approach to Brand Creation," *Verse, The Narrative Branding Company*, www.versegroup.com, accessed 3/7/2014.

45. Patrick Hanlon, *Primal Branding: Create Zealots for Your Brand, Your Company, and Your Future* (New York: Free Press, 2006).

46. Ashlee Vance, "It's a Doc in a Box," *Bloomberg Businessweek*, May 7, 2012, pp. 45–47.

47. Daniel Roberts, "The Secrets of See's Candies," *Fortune*, September 3, 2012, pp. 67–72.

48. Jason Ankeny, "Building a Brand on a Budget," *Entrepreneur* (May 2010), pp. 48–51.

49. Rob Walker, "The Cult of Evernote," *Bloomberg Businessweek*, February 28, 2013; https://evernote.com, accessed 1/26/2021.

50. Marketing Insight sources: Andrew Ross Sorkin and Andrew Martin, "Coca-Cola Agrees to Buy Vitaminwater," *New York Times*, May 26, 2007; www.vitaminwater.com, accessed 1/27/2021.

51. Marketing Spotlight sources: Robert Berner, "How Unilever Scored with Young Guys," *Bloomberg BusinessWeek*, May 23, 2005; Randall Rothenberg, "Dove Effort Gives Packaged-Goods Marketers Lessons for the Future," *Advertising Age*, March 5, 2007; Jack Neff, "In Dove Ads, Normal Is the New Beautiful," *Advertising Age*, September 27, 2004; Kim Bhasin, "How Axe Became the Top-Selling Deodorant by Targeting Nerdy Losers," *Business Insider*, October 10, 2011; Jonathan Salem Baskin, "The Opportunity for Dove to Get Real with Its Branding," *Forbes*,

March 7, 2013; Jack Neff, "Campaign Has Won Lots of Awards, Sold Heap of Product. But Has It Changed Perceptions?" *Ad Age*, January 22, 2014; Tim Nudd, "Axe Tackles 'Toxic Masculinity' by Revealing How Deeply Young Men Struggle with It," *AdWeek*, May 17, 2017; *Unilever 2017 Annual Report*; www.dove.com/us/en/stories/campaigns .html, accessed 2/5/2021; www.unilever.com/ brands/personal-care/axe.html; accessed 2/5/2021.

52. ET Bureau (2012), A website for students: How Peyush Bansal become a successful entrepreneur' Economic Times, January 30, https:// economictimes.indiatimes.com (Accessed on Oct 6, 2021)
53. Bloomberg TV India, "Lenskart: Largest online eyewear in India", Bloomberg TV India, (1st Oct 2015), accessed on 17th Sept 2021, from, https:// www.youtube.com
54. Saritha Rai, "SoftBank-backed Lenskart raises $220 million as India's tech industry booms", Business Standard, (19th July 2021), Accessed on 17th Sept 2021, from, https://www.business-standard.com
55. CNBC TV18, "Young Turks -In Conversation with Lenskart CEO Peyush Bansal", CNBC TV18, (7th July 2018), Accessed on 17th Sept 2021, from, https://www.youtube.com
56. Techcircle, " Softbank-backed Lenskart turns profitable in FY20, revenue up 89.81%", (Feb 2021), accessed on 12th August, 2021, from, https://www.techcircle.in

Chapter 8

1. Jordan Golson, "Tesla Model 3 Announced: Release Set for 2017, Price Starts at $35,000," *The Verge*, March 31, 2016; Charles Duhigg, "Dr. Elon & Mr. Musk: Life inside Tesla's Production Hell," *Wired*, December 13, 2018; Niall McCarthy, "The Tesla Model 3 Was the Best-Selling Luxury Car in America Last Year [Infographic]," *Forbes*, February 8, 2019; Peter Valdes-Dapena, "Against the Odds, Tesla's Model 3 Became the Best-selling Luxury Car in America," *CNN*, February 7, 2019; Tim Higgins and Heather Somerville, "Tesla 'Battery Day' Spotlights Elon Musk Plan for $25,000 Electric Car," *The Wall Street Journal*, September 23, 2020.
2. Some of these bases are discussed in David A. Garvin, "Competing on the Eight Dimensions of Quality," *Harvard Business Review* (November–December 1987), pp. 101–9.
3. Joshua Brustein, "Even Finns Don't Want Nokia Phones Anymore," *Business Week,* May 29, 2013; Juhana Rossi, "Nokia CEO Sticks to Company's Strategy," *Wall Street Journal,* May 7, 2013; Anton Troianovski and Sven Grundberg, "Nokia's Bad Call on Smartphones," *Wall Street Journal,* July 18, 2012; www.nokia.com/about-us/who-we-are/our-history, accessed 1/28//2021.
4. Marco Bertini, Elie Ofek, and Dan Ariely, "The Impact of Add-On Features on Product Evaluations," *Journal of Consumer Research* 36 (June 2009), pp. 17–28; Tripat Gill, "Convergent Products: What Functionalities Add More Value to the Base?" *Journal of Marketing* 72 (March 2008), pp. 46–62; Robert J. Meyer, Sheghui Zhao, and Jin K. Han, "Biases in Valuation vs. Usage of Innovative Product Features," *Marketing Science* 27 (November–December 2008), pp. 1083–96.
5. Debora Viana Thompson, Rebecca W. Hamilton, and Roland Rust, "Feature Fatigue: When Product Capabilities Become Too Much of a Good Thing," *Journal of Marketing Research* 42 (November 2005), pp. 431–42.
6. David Kesmodel, "No Glass Ceiling for the Best Job in the Universe," *Wall Street Journal*, June 29, 2010.
7. Cheryl Jensen, "Honda Repeats, Ford Surges and Mercedes Tumbles in 2011 Consumer Reports Study," www.wheels.blogs.nytimes.com; Gail Edmondson, "Mercedes Gets Back Up to Speed," *Bloomberg BusinessWeek,* November 13, 2006, pp. 46–47; www.mercedes-benz.com/ en/mercedes-benz/classic/history, accessed 1/28/2021.
8. Bernd Schmitt and Alex Simonson, *Marketing Aesthetics: The Strategic Management of Brand, Identity, and Image* (New York: Free Press, 1997).
9. Subramanian Balachander, Esther Gal-Or, Tansev Geylani, and Alex Jiyoung Kim. "Provision of Optional versus Standard Product Features in Competition," *Journal of Marketing* 81, no. 3 (2017), pp. 80–95; Ulrike Kaiser, Martin Schreier, and Chris Janiszewski, "The Self-Expressive Customization of a Product Can Improve Performance," *Journal of Marketing Research* 54, no. 5 (2017), pp. 816–31.
10. Rupal Parekh, "Personalized Products Please but Can They Create Profit?" *Advertising Age*, May 20, 2012; www.us.burberry.com/store/ bespoke; Paul Sonne, "Mink or Fox? The Trench Gets Complicated," *Wall Street Journal*, November 3, 2011.
11. Ravindra Chitturi, Rajagopal Raghunathan, and Vijay Mahajan, "Delight by Design: The Role of Hedonic versus Utilitarian Benefits," *Journal of Marketing* 72 (May 2008), pp. 48–63.
12. Virginia Postrel, *The Substance of Style: How the Rise of Aesthetic Value Is Remaking Commerce,*

Culture, and Consciousness (New York: HarperCollins, 2003).

13. Ulrich R. Orth and Keven Malkewitz, "Holistic Package Design and Consumer Brand Impressions," *Journal of Marketing* 72 (May 2008), pp. 64–81; Freeman Wu, Adriana Samper, Andrea C. Morales, and Gavan J. Fitzsimons, "It's Too Pretty to Use! When and How Enhanced Product Aesthetics Discourage Usage and Lower Consumption Enjoyment," *Journal of Consumer Research* 44, no. 3 (2017), pp. 651–72.
14. Rachel Lamb, "How Will Bang & Olufsen's Lower-End Product Line Affect the Brand?" *Luxury Daily*, January 12, 2012; Jay Green, "Where Designers Rule," *Bloomberg BusinessWeek*, November 5, 2007, pp. 46–51; www.bang-olufsen.com/en, accessed 1/28/2021.
15. Drake Baer, "How a Top Houseware Brand Reinvents Perfectly Designed Kitchen Gadgets," *Business Insider,* March 4, 2016.
16. Haydn Shaughnessy, "How Samsung Competes with Apple in Design," *Forbes*, April 19, 2013; Melissa J. Perneson, "An Inside Look at Samsung's Approach to Product Design," *Tech Hive*, January 9, 2013; http://design.samsung.com/global/index.html, accessed 1/28/2021.
17. In reality, Tide's product line is actually deeper and more complex. For current product offerings, see https://tide.com.
18. A. Yesim Orhun, "Optimal Product Line Design When Consumers Exhibit Choice-Set-Dependent Preferences," *Marketing Science* 28 (September–October 2009), pp. 868–86; Robert Bordley, "Determining the Appropriate Depth and Breadth of a Firm's Product Portfolio," *Journal of Marketing Research* 40 (February 2003), pp. 39–53; Peter Boatwright and Joseph C. Nunes, "Reducing Assortment: An Attribute-Based Approach," *Journal of Marketing* 65 (July 2001), pp. 50–63. For branding advantages of a product system, see Ryan Rahinel and Joseph P. Redden, "Brands as Product Coordinators: Matching Brands Make Joint Consumption Experiences More Enjoyable," *Journal of Consumer Research* 39 (April 2013), pp. 1290–99.
19. Ryan Hamilton and Alexander Chernev, "The Impact of Product Line Extensions and Consumer Goals on the Formation of Price Image," *Journal of Marketing Research* 47 (February 2010), pp. 51–62.
20. This illustration is found in Benson P. Shapiro, *Industrial Product Policy: Managing the Existing Product Line* (Cambridge, MA: Marketing Science Institute, 1977), pp. 3–5, 98–101.
21. Joann Muller, "How Volkswagen Will Rule the World," *Forbes*, April 17, 2013; Travis Okulski, "Is Skoda Secretly Volkswagen's Best Brand?" *Jalopnik*, January 15, 2014.
22. Chris Trimble & Liang Liao," Infosys in a Distinct Business: Finacle", Tuck School of Business at Dartmouth, (2008), Accessed on 20th Sept 2021, from, https://mba.tuck.dartmouth.edu
23. Infosys Finacle, "The story of Infosys Finacle : Our journey over the years" (2017), Accessed on 30th August 2021, from, https://www.youtube.com
24. Swathi Moorthy, "Infosys' Finacle is finally having a moment two decades after launch", Money Control, (Sept 2020), Accessed on 31st August 2021, from, https://www.moneycontrol.com
25. Brett R. Gordon, "A Dynamic Model of Consumer Replacement Cycles in the PC Processor Industry," *Marketing Science* 28 (September–October 2009), pp. 846–67; Raghunath Singh Rao, Om Narasimhan, and George John, "Understanding the Role of Trade-Ins in Durable Goods Markets: Theory and Evidence," *Marketing Science* 28 (September–October 2009), pp. 950–67.
26. Tim Higgins, "Mercedes Adds Coupe to U.S. C-Class Line in Bid to Top BMW: Cars," *Bloomberg Businessweek*, September 26, 2011; Aner Sela and Robyn A. LeBoeuf, "Comparison Neglect in Upgrade Decisions," *Journal of Marketing Research* 54, no. 4 (2017), pp. 556–71.
27. John Gourville and Dilip Soman, "Overchoice and Assortment Type: When and Why Variety Backfires," *Marketing Science* 24 (Summer 2005), pp. 382–95; Alexander Chernev, "When More Is Less and Less Is More: The Psychology of Managing Product Assortments," *GfK Marketing Intelligence Review* 3, no. 1 (2011); Sungtak Hong, Kanishka Misra, and Naufel J. Vilcassim. "The Perils of Category Management: The Effect of Product Assortment on Multicategory Purchase Incidence," *Journal of Marketing* 80, no. 5 (2016), pp. 34–52.
28. Nirmalya Kumar, "Kill a Brand, Keep a Customer," *Harvard Business Review* (December 2003), pp. 86–95.
29. David Englander, "Crocs Strides toward a Comeback," *Barron's*, January 19, 2013; Jennifer Overstreet, "How Crocs Is Building a Brand Bigger than the Clog," *National Retail Federation,* August 29, 2012; Edward Teach, "How Crocs Regained Its Footing," *CFO Magazine*, May 15, 2012; https://careers.crocs.com/about-us/default.aspx, accessed 1/28/2020.
30. Ellen Byron, "Tide Turns 'Basic' for P&G in Slump," *Wall Street Journal*, August 6, 2009; Dan Sewell, "P&G Ends 'Tide Basic' Test, No Word on Plans," *Bloomberg Businessweek*, June 23, 2010.
31. Timothy B. Heath, Devon DelVecchio, and Michael S. McCarthy, "The Asymmetric Effects of Extending Brands to Lower and Higher Quality," *Journal of Marketing* 75 (July 2011), pp. 3–20.

32. Kennedy (2016), ' Comparison: Maruti Nexa Showroom vs Maruti Dealership' Drivespark, March 16, Accessed on 30th August 2021, https://www.drivespark.com

33. TOI (2021), 'Maruti Suzuki True Value clocks 4 million sales in 20 years' Times of India, February 4, Accessed on 30th August 2021, https://timesofindia.indiatimes.com

34. Julio Sevilla, Jiao Zhang, and Barbara E. Kahn, "Anticipation of Future Variety Reduces Satiation from Current Experiences," *Journal of Marketing Research* 53, no. 6 (2016), pp. 954–98; Jordan Etkin and Aner Sela, "How Experience Variety Shapes Postpurchase Product Evaluation," *Journal of Marketing Research* 53, no. 1 (2016), pp. 77–90.

35. www.bmw.com, accessed 10/28/2020.

36. Katherine White, Lily Lin, Darren W. Dahl, and Robin J. B. Ritchie, "When Do Consumers Avoid Imperfections? Superficial Packaging Damage as a Contamination Cue," *Journal of Marketing Research* 53, no. 1 (2016), pp. 110–23; Veronika Ilyuk and Lauren Block, "The Effects of Single-Serve Packaging on Consumption Closure and Judgments of Product Efficacy," *Journal of Consumer Research* 42, no. 6 (2016), pp. 858–78.

37. Eva C. Buechel and Claudia Townsend, "Buying Beauty for the Long Run: (Mis)predicting Liking of Product Aesthetics," *Journal of Consumer Research* 45, no. 2, (2018), pp. 275–97.

38. Howard Fox, "The Secret Language of Colour," *Brands & Branding*, October 2010, pp. 48–50. See also Lauren Labrecque and George Milne, "Exciting Red and Competent Blue: The Importance of Color in Marketing," *Journal of the Academy of Marketing Science* 40 (September 2012), pp. 711–27; and Niki Hynes, "Colour and Meaning in Corporate Logos: An Empirical Study," *Journal of Brand Management* 16 (July–August 2009), pp. 545–55.

39. Melissa Stanger, "How Brands Use the Psychology of Color to Manipulate You," *Business Insider*, December 29, 2012; Lauren Labrecque and George R. Milne, "Exciting Red and Competent Blue: The Importance of Color in Marketing," *Journal of Academy of Marketing Science* 40 (September 2012), pp. 711–27.

40. Stuart Elliott, "Tropicana Discovers Some Buyers Are Passionate about Packaging," *New York Times*, February 23, 2009; Linda Tischler, "Never Mind! Pepsi Pulls Much-Loathed Tropicana Packaging," *Fast Company*, February 23, 2009; Natalie Zmuda, "Tropicana Line's Sales Plunge 20% Post-Rebranding," *Advertising Age*, April 2, 2009.

41. Daniel Milroy-Maher, "Japan Has a Dangerous Fetish for Packaging," *Vice*, September 25, 2014.

42. John Pflueger, "How Dell Turned Bamboo and Mushrooms into Environmental-Friendly Packaging," *MIT Sloan Management Review*, July 17, 2012; Caroline Lennon, "5 Companies Producing Products with Eco-Friendly Packaging," *One Green Planet*, April 2, 2013.

43. Sarah Skidmore, "SunChips Biodegradable Bag Made Quieter for Critics," *Huffington Post*, February 24, 2011; Suzanne Vranica, "Snack Attack: Chip Eaters Make Noise about a Crunchy Bag," *Wall Street Journal*, August 18, 2010.

44. Sean Poulter, "How Food Labels Can Mislead Shoppers about Fat Content," *Daily Mail*, September 1, 2010.

45. Alexander Chernev, *Strategic Marketing Management: Theory and Practice* (Chicago, IL: Cerebellum Press, 2019).

46. Ibid.

47. Tao Chen, Ajay Kalra, and Baohung Sun, "Why Do Consumers Buy Extended Service Contracts?" *Journal of Consumer Research* 36 (December 2009), pp. 611–23.

48. For an empirical study, see Junhong Chu and Pradeep K. Chintagunta, "Quantifying the Economic Value of Warranties in the U.S. Server Market," *Marketing Science* 28 (January–February 2009), pp. 99–121.

49. Alexander Chernev, *Strategic Marketing Management: Theory and Practice* (Chicago, IL: Cerebellum Press, 2019).

50. Marketing Insight sources: Alexander Chernev, "When More Is Less and Less Is More: The Role of Ideal Point Availability and Assortment in Consumer Choice," *Journal of Consumer Research* 30 (September 2003), pp. 170–83; Alexander Chernev, Alexander, "Decision Focus and Consumer Choice among Assortments," *Journal of Consumer Research*, 33 (June 2006), pp. 50–59; Alexander Chernev, Ulf Böckenholt, and Joseph Goodman, "Choice Overload: A Conceptual Review and Meta-Analysis," *Journal of Consumer Psychology* 25, no. 2 (2015), pp. 333–58; Alexander Chernev and Ryan Hamilton, "Assortment Size and Option Attractiveness in Consumer Choice among Retailers," *Journal of Marketing Research* 46 (June 2009), pp. 410–20; Kristin Diehl and Cait Poynor, "Great Expectations?! Assortment Size, Expectations, and Satisfaction," *Journal of Marketing Research* 46 (April 2009), pp. 312–22; Sheena Iyengar and Mark Lepper, "When Choice Is Demotivating: Can One Desire Too Much of a Good Thing?" *Journal of Personality and Social Psychology* 79, no. 6 (2000), pp. 995–1006; Joseph P. Redden and Stephen J. Hoch, "The Presence of Variety Reduces Perceived Quantity,"

Journal of Consumer Research 36 (October 2009), pp. 406–17.

51. Marketing Spotlight sources: Peter Burrows, "Rock On, iPod," *Bloomberg BusinessWeek,* June 7, 2004, pp. 130–31; Ellen Terrell, "Apple Computer, Inc.," *Business Reference Services* (April 2008); Catherine Clifford, "Former Apple CEO John Sculley: What I Learned from Steve Jobs," *CNBC*, May 29, 2018; Mikey Campbell, "Apple R&D Spending Continues to Grow in Lockstep with iPhone, AR Projects," *Appleinsider*, May 2, 2018; *Apple Annual Report* 2018; www.apple.com; accessed 11/26/2020.
52. Marketing Spotlight sources: Tanya Dua, "How $300 Million Mattress Startup Casper Is Shaking Up Advertising," *Business Insider*, July 11, 2017; Robert J. Dolan, "Casper Sleep Inc.: Marketing the 'One Perfect Mattress for Everyone,'" *HBS* No. 9-517-042 (Boston: Harvard Business School Publishing, 2017); Khadeeja Safdar, "Casper, a Web Pioneer, to Open 200 Stores," *Wall Street Journal*, August 8, 2018; Nathaniel Meyersohn, "How Casper Drove Mattress Firm into Bankruptcy," *CNN*, October 6, 2018; Sandra Upson, "How Casper Wants to Sell You Sleep," *Wired*, June 21, 2016; https://casper.com/about, accessed 11/26/2020.
53. Marketing Spotlight sources: Charles Fishman, "No Satisfaction at Toyota," *Fast Company,* December 2006–January 2007, pp. 82–90; Brian Bemner and Chester Dawson, "Can Anything Stop Toyota?" *Bloomberg BusinessWeek*, November 17, 2003, pp. 114–22; Mike Ramsey, "Toyota Calls Hybrids 'Sturdy Bridge' to Automotive Future," *Wall Street Journal,* September 30, 2013; www.toyota-global.com/company/history_of_toyota, accessed 11/26/2020.

Chapter 9

1. Leonard L. Berry, *On Great Service: A Framework for Action* (New York: Free Press, 2006), as well as others of his texts.
2. Chandra R Srikanth (2021), 'In 1990, there was an offer to buy us out for Rs 2 crore. Infosys has Rs 6.5 lakh crore m-cap now: NR Narayana Murthy on 1991 reforms' *MoneyControl*, July 21, Accessed on 23rd Sept 2021, from, https://www.moneycontrol.com
3. Harvard Business Review, " "Why Don't We Try to Be India's Most Respected Company?", (2011), Accessed on 18th August 2021, from, https://hbr.org
4. G. Shainesh (2018), 'Interview with Kris Gopalakrishnan - Customer relationship management: Concepts and Applications', Accessed on 8th Sept 2021, from, https://www.edx.org
5. PTI (2021), 'Infosys becomes 4th Indian company to touch $100 bn market capitalisation' *Business Standard*, August 25, https://www.business-standard.com
6. Case Study (2017) 'Expanding Access to Low-Cost, High-Quality Tertiary Care' The Commonwealth Fund, November 9 https://www.commonwealthfund.org
7. N Madhavan, " Biggest Innovations: Narayana Health has successfully married affordability, quality health care", Business Today (25th May 2014), Accessed on 12th Oct 2021, from, https://www.businesstoday.in
8. Interview with Devi Shetty, interviewed by Tarun Khanna, Boston, MA, October 10, 2017, Creating Emerging Markets Oral History Collection, Baker Library Special Collections, Harvard Business School, Accessed on 12th Oct 2021, from, https://www.hbs.edu
9. Phillip Nelson, "Information and Consumer Behavior," *Journal of Political Economy* 78 (March–April, 1970), pp. 311–329.
10. Allan Adamson and Chekitan Dev, "Can Carnival Recover from the Damage to Its Brand?" *Marketing Daily*, April 12, 2013; Lateef Mungin and Steve Almasy, "Crippled Cruise Ship Returns; Passengers Happy to Be Back," *CNN*, February 15, 2013; www.carnival.com/about-carnival/about-us.aspx, accessed 1/28/2021; Hannah Sampson, "A Carnival Corp. ship had the biggest coronavirus outbreak in the industry. Now Congress is probing the company." *Washington Post*, May 1, 2020.
11. For discussion of how the blurring of the line distinguishing products and services changes the meaning of this taxonomy, see Christopher Lovelock and Evert Gummesson, "Whither Services Marketing? In Search of a New Paradigm and Fresh Perspectives," *Journal of Service Research* 7 (August 2004), pp. 20–41; and Stephen L. Vargo and Robert F. Lusch, "Evolving to a New Dominant Logic for Marketing," *Journal of Marketing* 68 (January 2004), pp. 1–17.
12. Theodore Levitt, "Marketing Intangible Products and Product Intangibles," *Harvard Business Review* (May–June 1981), pp. 94–102; Leonard L. Berry, "Services Marketing Is Different," *Business* (May–June 1980), pp. 24–29.
13. Bernd H. Schmitt, *Customer Experience Management* (New York: John Wiley & Sons, 2003); Bernd H. Schmitt, David L. Rogers, and Karen Vrotsos (2003), *There's No Business That's Not Show Business: Marketing in an Experience Culture* (Upper Saddle River, NJ: Prentice Hall Financial Times, 2004).

14. www.sportsbusinessdaily.com/Journal/Issues/2018/04/30/Marketing-and-Sponsorship/Naming-rights-deals.aspx; accessed 12/28/2020.

15. For some emerging research results on the effects of creating time and place service separation, see Hean Tat Keh and Jun Pang, "Customer Reaction to Service Separation," *Journal of Marketing* 74 (March 2010), pp. 55–70.

16. "The Client: Larry Traxler and Dave Horton, Hilton," *Hospitality Style*, November 15, 2012; "Hilton Brand Unveils New Lobby Look," *National Real Estate Investor*, April 19, 2011.

17. Rebecca J. Slotegraaf and J. Jeffrey Inman, "Longitudinal Shifts in the Drivers of Satisfaction with Product Quality: The Role of Attribute Resolvability," *Journal of Marketing Research* 41 (August 2004), pp. 269–80; Rebecca W. Hamilton, Roland T. Rust, Michel Wedel, and Chekitan S. Dev, "Return on Service Amenities," *Journal of Marketing Research* 54, no. 1 (2017), pp. 96–110.

18. The material in this paragraph is based in part on Valarie Zeithaml, Mary Jo Bitner, and Dwayne D. Gremler, "Service Innovation and Design," *Services Marketing: Integrating Customer Focus across the Firm*, 7th ed. (New York: McGraw-Hill, 2017), chapter 8.

19. John DeVine, Shyam Lal, and Michael Zea, "The Human Factor in Service Design," *McKinsey Quarterly*, January 2012; G. Lynn Shostack, "Service Positioning through Structural Change," *Journal of Marketing* 51 (January 1987), pp. 34–43.

20. Vikas Mittal, Wagner A. Kamakura, and Rahul Govind, "Geographical Patterns in Customer Service and Satisfaction: An Empirical Investigation," *Journal of Marketing* 68 (July 2004), pp. 48–62.

21. Jeffrey F. Rayport, Bernard J. Jaworski, and Ellie J. Kyung, "Best Face Forward: Improving Companies' Service Interface with Customers," *Journal of Interactive Marketing* 19 (Autumn 2005), pp. 67–80; Asim Ansari and Carl F. Mela, "E-Customization," *Journal of Marketing Research* 40 (May 2003), pp. 131–45.

22. W. Earl Sasser, "Match Supply and Demand in Service Industries," *Harvard Business Review*, November–December 1976, pp. 133–40.

23. Steven M. Shugan and Jinhong Xie, "Advance Selling for Services," *California Management Review* 46 (Spring 2004), pp. 37–54; Eyal Biyalogorsky and Eitan Gerstner, "Contingent Pricing to Reduce Price Risks," *Marketing Science* 23 (Winter 2004), pp. 146–55.

24. Sriram Sivaraman, "Explaining Ola and Uber's surge pricing", The Hindu Express, (2016), Accessed on 30th August 2021, from, https://www.thehindu.com

25. Nicas, Jack, "Now Prices Can Change from Minute to Minute," *Wall Street Journal*, December 14, 2015.

26. Karl Taro Greenfeld, "Fast and Furious," *Bloomberg Businessweek*, May 9, 2011.

26. Roland T. Rust and Ming-Hui Huang, "Optimizing Service Productivity," *Journal of Marketing* 76 (March 2012), pp. 47–66.

27. "Two Top Stock Picks for 2019: Innovative Industrial Properties and Twilio," *Forbes*, January 24, 2019; www.twilio.com/company, accessed 2/4/2021.

28. Matthew Dixon, Karen Freeman, and Nicholas Toman, "Stop Trying to Delight Your Customers," *Harvard Business Review* (July–August 2010), pp. 116–22.

29. Chi Kin (Bennett) Yim, Kimmy Wa Chan, and Simon S. K. Lam, "Do Customers and Employees Enjoy Service Participation? Synergistic Effects of Self- and Other-Efficacy," *Journal of Marketing* 76 (November 2012), pp. 121–40; Zhenfeng Ma and Laurette Dubé, "Process and Outcome Interdependency in Frontline Service Encounters," *Journal of Marketing* 75 (May 2011), pp. 83–98; Detelina Marinova, Sunil K. Singh, and Jagdip Singh, "Frontline Problem-Solving Effectiveness: A Dynamic Analysis of Verbal and Nonverbal Cues," *Journal of Marketing Research* 55, no. 2 (2018), pp. 178–92.

30. Kimmy Wa Chan, Chi Kin (Bennett) Yim, and Simon S. K. Lam, "Is Customer Participation in Value Creation a Double-Edged Sword? Evidence from Professional Financial Services across Cultures," *Journal of Marketing* 74 (May 2010), pp. 48–64.

31. Valarie Zeithaml, Mary Jo Bitner, and Dwayne D. Gremler, *Services Marketing: Integrating Customer Focus across the Firm*, 7th ed. (New York: McGraw-Hill, 2017).

32. Rachel R. Chen, Eitan Gerstner, and Yinghui (Catherine) Yang, "Customer Bill of Rights under No-Fault Service Failure: Confinement and Compensation," *Marketing Science* 31 (January/February 2012), pp. 157–71; Michael Sanserino and Cari Tuna, "Companies Strive Harder to Please Customers," *Wall Street Journal*, July 27, 2009, p. B4.

33. James L. Heskett, W, Earl Sasser Jr., and Joe Wheeler, *Ownership Quotient: Putting the Service Profit Chain to Work for Unbeatable Competitive Advantage* (Boston, MA: Harvard Business School Press, 2008).

34. D. Todd Donovan, Tom J. Brown, and John C. Mowen, "Internal Benefits of Service Worker Customer Orientation: Job Satisfaction,

Commitment, and Organizational Citizenship Behaviors," *Journal of Marketing* 68 (January 2004), pp. 128–46.

35. Jeffrey Hollender, "Lessons We Can All Learn from Zappos CEO Tony Hsieh," *The Guardian*, March 14, 2013; Tricia Morris, "Using Metrics to Create a Zappos-Like Customer Service Culture," *Parature*, November 13, 2012; Mig Pascual, "Zappos: 5 Out-of-the-Box Ideas for Keeping Employees Engaged," *U.S. News*, October 30, 2012; Helen Coster, "A Step Ahead," *Forbes*, June 2, 2008, pp. 78–80; Paula Andruss, "Delivering Wow through Service," *Marketing News*, October 15, 2008, p. 10; Jeffrey M. O'Brien, "Zappos Knows How to Kick It," *Fortune*, February 2, 2009, pp. 55–60; Brian Morrissey, "Amazon to Buy Zappos," *Adweek*, July 22, 2009; Christopher Palmeri, "Now for Sale, the Zappos Culture," *Bloomberg BusinessWeek*, January 11, 2010, p. 57.

36. Frances X. Frei, "The Four Things a Service Business Must Get Right," *Harvard Business Review* (April 2008), pp. 70–80.

37. Christian Gronroos, "A Service-Quality Model and Its Marketing Implications," *European Journal of Marketing* 18 (1984), pp. 36–44.

38. Detelina Marinova, Jun Ye, and Jagdip Singh, "Do Frontline Mechanisms Matter? Impact of Quality and Productivity Orientations on Unit Revenue, Efficiency, and Customer Satisfaction," *Journal of Marketing* 72 (March 2008), pp. 28–45.

39. Ad de Jong, Ko de Ruyter, and Jos Lemmink, "Antecedents and Consequences of the Service Climate in Boundary-Spanning Self-Managing Service Teams," *Journal of Marketing* 68 (April 2004), pp. 18–35; Michael D. Hartline and O. C. Ferrell, "The Management of Customer-Contact Service Employees: An Empirical Investigation," *Journal of Marketing* 60 (October 1996), pp. 52–70; Christian Homburg, Jan Wieseke, and Torsten Bornemann, "Implementing the Marketing Concept at the Employee-Customer Interface: The Role of Customer Need Knowledge," *Journal of Marketing* 73 (July 2009), pp. 64–81; Chi Kin (Bennett) Yim, David K. Tse, and Kimmy Wa Chan, "Strengthening Customer Loyalty through Intimacy and Passion: Roles of Customer–Firm Affection and Customer–Staff Relationships," *Journal of Marketing Research* 45 (December 2008), pp. 741–56.

40. Gregory Jones, "Jim Weddle Is Positioning Edward Jones to Be the Top of Mind Choice," *Smart Business*, May 31, 2013; https://www.edwardjones.com/financial-advisor-value/index.html, accessed 1/28/2021.

41. Loizos Heracleous and Jochen Wirtz, "Singapore Airlines' Balancing Act," *Harvard Business Review* (July–August, 2010); James Wallace, "Singapore Airlines Raises the Bar for Luxury Flying," *Seattle Post Intelligencer*, January 18, 2007; Elaine Glusac, "Can 18 Hours in the Air Be Bearable? Airlines Bet on Ultra-Long-Haul Flights," *New York Times*, October 15, 2018.

42. Paul Hagen, "The Rise of the Chief Customer Officer," *Forbes*, February 16, 2011.

43. "Butterball, LLC," *Hoover's Company Records*, October 15, 2012; Stephanie Warren, "Turkey 911! Butterball's Hotline Saves Your Thanksgiving," *Popular Mechanics*, November 23, 2011; www.butterball.com/about-us/turkey-talk-line; accessed 12/7/2020.

44. Jena McGregor, "When Service Means Survival," *Bloomberg BusinessWeek*, March 2, 2009, pp. 26–30.

45. Asia Private Banking Awards (2020), 'Best Domestic Private Bank in India 2020', AsiaMoney (July 23), Accessed on September 23, 2021 from https://www.asiamoney.com

46. Features (2021), 'Evolving trends in Wealth Management in India' MoneyControl (June 29), Accessed on September 23, 2021 from https://www.moneycontrol.com

47. Kotak Mahindra Bank, "Kotak Wealth Management", (2021), Accessed on September 23, 2021 from https://www.kotak.com

48. Neil Borate (2020), "Banks move towards advisory for HNIs, distribution for retail", The Mint (September 8, 2020), Accessed on 23rd Sept 2021, from, https://www.livemint.com

49. Mark Bowden, "The Man Who Broke Atlantic City," *The Atlantic* (April 2012).

50. Dave Dougherty and Ajay Murthy, "What Service Customers Really Want," *Harvard Business Review*, September 2009, p. 22; for a contrarian point of view, see Edward Kasabov, "The Compliant Customer," *MIT Sloan Management Review* (Spring 2010), pp. 18–19.

51. Jeffrey G. Blodgett and Ronald D. Anderson, "A Bayesian Network Model of the Customer Complaint Process," *Journal of Service Research* 2 (May 2000), pp. 321–38.

52. Jeroen Schepers, Tomas Falk, Ko de Ruyter, Ad de Jong, and Maik Hammerschmidt, "Principles and Principals: Do Customer Stewardship and Agency Control Compete or Complement When Shaping Frontline Employee Behavior?" *Journal of Marketing* 76 (November 2012), pp. 1–20; James G. Maxham III and Richard G. Netemeyer, "Firms Reap What They Sow: The Effects of Shared Values and Perceived Organizational Justice on Customers' Evaluations of Complaint Handling," *Journal of Marketing* 67 (January 2003), pp. 46–62; Nita Umashankar, Morgan K. Ward, and Darren W. Dahl. "The Benefit of Becoming

Jean-Noel Kapferer, *The New Strategic Brand Management*, 5th ed. (London, UK: Kogan Page, 2012); Leslie de Chernatony, *From Brand Vision to Brand Evaluation: The Strategic Process of Growing and Strengthening Brands*, 3rd ed. (Oxford, UK: Butterworth-Heinemann, 2010); and David A. Aaker and Erich Joachimsthaler, *Brand Leadership* (New York: Free Press, 2000).

6. Steven Shepherd, Tanya L. Chartrand, and Gavan J. Fitzsimons, "When Brands Reflect Our Ideal World: The Values and Brand Preferences of Consumers Who Support versus Reject Society's Dominant Ideology," *Journal of Consumer Research* 42, no. 1 (2015), pp. 76–92; Mathew S. Isaac and Kent Grayson, "Beyond Skepticism: Can Accessing Persuasion Knowledge Bolster Credibility?" *Journal of Consumer Research* 43, no. 6 (2017), pp. 895–912.
7. Lara O'Reilly, "Real Madrid Beat Man U to World's Richest Football Team Spot," *Marketing Week*, April 18, 2013; Steven G. Mandis, *The Real Madrid Way: How Values Created the Most Successful Sports Team on the Planet* (Dallas, TX: BenBella Books, 2016); www.realmadrid.com/en, accessed 1/30/2021.
8. Rajneesh Suri and Kent B. Monroe, "The Effects of Time Pressure on Consumers' Judgments of Prices and Products," *Journal of Consumer Research* 30 (June 2003), pp. 92–104; Aaron M. Garvey, Frank Germann, and Lisa E. Bolton, "Performance Brand Placebos: How Brands Improve Performance and Consumers Take the Credit," *Journal of Consumer Research* 42, no. 6 (2016), pp. 931–51.
9. Rosellina Ferraro, Amna Kirmani, and Ted Matherly, "Look at Me! Look at Me! Conspicuous Brand Usage, Self-Brand Connection, and Dilution," *Journal of Marketing Research* 50 (August 2013), pp. 477–88; Alexander Chernev, Ryan Hamilton, and David Gal, "Competing for Consumer Identity: Limits to Self-Expression and the Perils of Lifestyle Branding," *Journal of Marketing* 75 (May 2011).
10. Pankaj Aggarwal and Ann L. McGill, "When Brands Seem Human, Do Humans Act Like Brands? Automatic Behavioral Priming Effects of Brand Anthropomorphism," *Journal of Consumer Research* 39 (August 2012), pp. 307–23. For some related research, see Nicolas Kervyn, Susan T. Fiske, and Chris Malone, "Brands as Intentional Agents Framework: How Perceived Intentions and Ability Can Map Brand Perception," *Journal of Consumer Psychology* 22 (2012), pp. 166–76, as well as commentaries on the article published in that issue.
11. Matthew Thomson, Jodie Whelan, and Allison R. Johnson, "Why Brands Should Fear Fearful Consumers: How Attachment Style Predicts Retaliation," *Journal of Consumer Psychology* 22 (2012), pp. 289–98; Shirley Y. Y. Cheng, Tiffany Barnett White, and Lan Nguyen Chaplin, "The Effects of Self-Brand Connections on Responses to Brand Failure: A New Look at the Consumer-Brand Relationship," *Journal of Consumer Psychology* 22 (2012), pp. 280–88.
12. Shally Seth Mohile (2018) 'Trip, Trend, Tryst: Treebo launches three sub-brands for hotel portfolio' *Business Standard*, November 22, https://www.business-standard.com
13. G. Shainesh (2018) 'Interview with Sidharth Gupta, CEO – Treebo' https://www.edx.org
14. Sarika Anand, "Treebo Hotels - Putting Dignity Back into Budget Travel", (March 2021), Accessed on 18th August 2021, from, https://startuptalky.com
15. Tilde Heding, Charlotte F. Knudtzen, and Mogens Bjerre, *Brand Management: Research, Theory & Practice* (New York: Routledge, 2009); Rita Clifton and John Simmons, eds., *The Economist on Branding* (New York: *Bloomberg Press*, 2004); Rik Riezebos, *Brand Management: A Theoretical and Practical Approach* (Essex, UK: Pearson Education, 2003).
16. Joffre Swait and Tulin Erdem, "Brand Effects on Choice and Choice Set Formation under Uncertainty," *Marketing Science* 26 (September–October 2007), pp. 679–97; Tulin Erdem, Joffre Swait, and Ana Valenzuela, "Brands as Signals: A Cross-Country Validation Study," *Journal of Marketing* 70 (January 2006), pp. 34–49; Leslie K. John, Oliver Emrich, Sunil Gupta, and Michael I. Norton, "Does 'Liking' Lead to Loving? The Impact of Joining a Brand's Social Network on Marketing Outcomes," *Journal of Marketing Research* 54, no. 1 (2017), pp. 144–55; Danielle J. Brick, Gràinne M. Fitzsimons, Tanya L. Chartrand, and Gavan J. Fitzsimons, "Coke vs. Pepsi: Brand Compatibility, Relationship Power, and Life Satisfaction," *Journal of Consumer Research* 44, no. 5 (2018), pp. 991–1014.
17. Scott Davis, *Brand Asset Management: Driving Profitable Growth through Your Brands* (San Francisco: Jossey-Bass, 2000); Mary W. Sullivan, "How Brand Names Affect the Demand for Twin Automobiles," *Journal of Marketing Research* 35 (May 1998), pp. 154–65.
18. Brian Braiker, "New Coke Pops . . . 34 Years Later," *Advertising Age*, May 25, 2019.
19. Xueming Luo, Sascha Raithel, and Michael A. Wiles, "The Impact of Brand Rating Dispersion on Firm Value," *Journal of Marketing Research* 50 (June 2013), pp. 399–415.

29. Michael A. Wiles, Neil A. Morgan, and Lopo L. Rego, "The Effect of Brand Acquisition and Disposal on Stock Returns," *Journal of Marketing* 76 (January 2012), pp. 38–58.

21. Natalie Mizik and Robert Jacobson, "Talk about Brand Strategy," *Harvard Business Review* (October 2005), p. 1; Baruch Lev, *Intangibles: Management, Measurement, and Reporting* (Washington, DC: Brookings Institution, 2001). For a detailed examination, see Nigel Hollis, *The Meaningful Brand: How Strong Brands Make More Money* (New York: Palgrave Macmillan, 2013).

22. Other approaches are based on economic principles of signaling (e.g., Tulin Erdem, "Brand Equity as a Signaling Phenomenon," *Journal of Consumer Psychology* 7 [1998]), pp. 131–57) or on more of a sociological, anthropological, or biological perspective (e.g., Grant McCracken, *Culture and Consumption II: Markets, Meaning, and Brand Management* [Bloomington: Indiana University Press, 2005]). For a broad view of consumer psychology perspectives on branding, see Bernd Schmitt, "The Consumer Psychology of Brands," *Journal of Consumer Psychology* 22 (2012), pp. 7–17.

23. For an overview of academic research on branding, see Kevin Lane Keller, "Branding and Brand Equity," in Bart Weitz and Robin Wensley, eds., *Handbook of Marketing* (London: Sage Publications, 2002), pp. 151–78; Kevin Lane Keller and Don Lehmann, "Brands and Branding: Research Findings and Future Priorities," *Marketing Science* 25 (November–December 2006), pp. 740–59.

24. Kevin Lane Keller, *Strategic Brand Management*, 5th ed. (Upper Saddle River, NJ: Pearson, 2019).

25. Kusum Ailawadi, Donald R. Lehmann, and Scott Neslin, "Revenue Premium as an Outcome Measure of Brand Equity," *Journal of Marketing* 67 (October 2003), pp. 1–17.

26. Deborah Roedder John, Barbara Loken, Kyeong-Heui Kim, and Alokparna Basu Monga, "Brand Concept Maps: A Methodology for Identifying Brand Association Networks," *Journal of Marketing Research* 43 (November 2006), pp. 549–63.

27. PTI (2011), 'Mahindra & Mahindra to use 'Rise' as new brand positioning' Economic Times, January 17, Accessed on August 19, 2021 from https://economictimes.indiatimes.com

28. BS Reporter, (2013) 'Rise' is Mahindra's new mantra' Business Standard, January 20, Accessed on August 19, 2021 from https://www.business-standard.com

29. Delshad Irani, " Mahindra & Mahindra's new logo to reflect global brand identity", The Economic Times (Jan 2013), Accessed on 18th August 2021, from, Mahindra & Mahindra's new logo to reflect global brand identity - The Economic Times https://economictimes.indiatimes.com

30. M. Berk Ataman, Carl F. Mela, and Harald J. van Heerde, "Building Brands," *Marketing Science* 27 (November–December 2008), pp. 1036–54.

31. Marina Puzakova and Pankaj Aggarwal, "Brands as Rivals: Consumer Pursuit of Distinctiveness and the Role of Brand Anthropomorphism," *Journal of Consumer Research* 45, no. 4 (2018), pp. 869–88.

32. "No Matter How You 'Like' It, 42BELOW Vodka Encourages Everyone to Celebrate National Coming Out Day," *PR Newswire*, October 7, 2011.

33. Alina Wheeler, *Designing Brand Identity*, 5th ed. (Hoboken, NJ: John Wiley, 2017).

34. Eric A. Yorkston and Geeta Menon, "A Sound Idea: Phonetic Effects of Brand Names on Consumer Judgments," *Journal of Consumer Research* 31 (June 2004), pp. 43–51; Tina M. Lowery and L. J. Shrum, "Phonetic Symbolism and Brand Name Preference," *Journal of Consumer Research* 34 (October 2007), pp. 406–14.

35. John R. Doyle and Paul A. Bottomly, "Dressed for the Occasion: Font–Product Congruity in the Perception of Logotype," *Journal of Consumer Psychology* 16 (2006), pp. 112–23; Kevin Lane Keller, Susan Heckler, and Michael J. Houston, "The Effects of Brand Name Suggestiveness on Advertising Recall," *Journal of Marketing* 62 (January 1998), pp. 48–57; for an in-depth examination of how brand names are developed, see Alex Frankel, *Wordcraft: The Art of Turning Little Words into Big Business* (New York: Crown Publishers, 2004).

36. For some interesting theoretical perspectives, see Claudiu V. Dimofte and Richard F. Yalch, "Consumer Response to Polysemous Brand Slogans," *Journal of Consumer Research* 33 (March 2007), pp. 515–22.

37. For a marketing academic point of view of some important legal issues, see Judith Zaichkowsky, *The Psychology behind Trademark Infringement and Counterfeiting* (Mahwah, NJ: LEA Publishing, 2006) and Maureen Morrin, Jonathan Lee, and Greg M. Allenby, "Determinants of Trademark Dilution," *Journal of Consumer Research* 33 (September 2006), pp. 248–57; Larisa Ertekin, Alina Sorescu, and Mark B. Houston, "Hands Off My Brand! The Financial Consequences of Protecting Brands through Trademark Infringement Lawsuits," *Journal of Marketing* 82, no. 5 (2018), pp. 45–65.

38. Rupal Parekh, "Meet the Woman behind the Michelin Man," *Advertising Age*, June 11, 2012.

39. Judith Anne Garretson Folse, Richard G. Netemeyer, and Scot Burton, "Spokescharacters: How the Personality Traits of Sincerity, Excitement, and Competence Help to Build Equity," *Journal of Advertising* 41 (Spring 2012), pp. 17–32.
40. Eddie Pells, "Despite Numbers, Burton Still Bullish on Boarding," *Bloomberg Businessweek*, February 12, 2013.
41. Jennifer Aaker, "Dimensions of Brand Personality," *Journal of Marketing Research* 34 (August 1997), pp. 347–56. See also Aparna Sundar and Theodore J. Noseworthy, "Too Exciting to Fail, Too Sincere to Succeed: The Effects of Brand Personality on Sensory Disconfirmation," *Journal of Consumer Research* 43, no. 1 (2016), pp. 44–67.
42. Jennifer L. Aaker, Veronica Benet-Martinez, and Jordi Garolera, "Consumption Symbols as Carriers of Culture: A Study of Japanese and Spanish Brand Personality Constructs," *Journal of Personality and Social Psychology* 81 (March 2001), pp. 492–508.
43. Yongjun Sung and Spencer F. Tinkham, "Brand Personality Structures in the United States and Korea: Common and Culture-Specific Factors," *Journal of Consumer Psychology* 15 (December 2005), pp. 334–50.
44. David A. Aaker, *Brand Portfolio Strategy: Creating Relevance, Differentiation, Energy, Leverage, and Clarity* (New York: Free Press, 2004).
45. Michael Krauss, "The Glamour of B-to-B," *Marketing News*, February 2013, pp. 22–23.
46. Stuart Elliott, "Lipton Goes Back to Basics with a Tea Bag," *New York Times*, January 9, 2013; Heather Landi, "High Tea," *Beverage World*, July 2011, pp. 18–22; https://www.bloomberg.com/news/articles/2020-01-30/unilever-reviews-tea-business-after-slowest-growth-in-a-decade, accessed 11/26/2020.
47. Nirmalya Kumar, "Kill a Brand, Keep a Customer," *Harvard Business Review*, December 2003, pp. 87–95.
48. Jing Lei, Niraj Dawar, and Jos Lemmink, "Negative Spillover in Brand Portfolios: Exploring the Antecedents of Asymmetric Effects," *Journal of Marketing* 72 (May 2008), pp. 111–23.
49. For comprehensive corporate branding guidelines, see James R. Gregory, *The Best of Branding: Best Practices in Corporate Branding* (New York: McGraw-Hill, 2004). For some B-to-B applications, see Atlee Valentine Pope and Ralph Oliva, "Building Blocks: Ten Key Roles of B-to-B Corporate Marketing," *Marketing Management*, Winter 2012, pp. 23–28.
50. Guido Berens, Cees B. M. van Riel, and Gerrit H. van Bruggen, "Corporate Associations and Consumer Product Responses: The Moderating Role of Corporate Brand Dominance," *Journal of Marketing* 69 (July 2005), pp. 35–48; Zeynep Gürhan-Canli and Rajeev Batra, "When Corporate Image Affects Product Evaluations: The Moderating Role of Perceived Risk," *Journal of Marketing Research* 41 (May 2004), pp. 197–205.
51. Vithala R. Rao, Manoj K. Agarwal, and Denise Dalhoff, "How Is Manifest Branding Strategy Related to the Intangible Value of a Corporation?" *Journal of Marketing* 68 (October 2004), pp. 126–41. For an examination of the financial impact of brand portfolio decisions, see Neil A. Morgan and Lopo L. Rego, "Brand Portfolio Strategy and Firm Performance," *Journal of Marketing* 73 (January 2009), pp. 59–74; and S. Cem Bahadir, Sundar G. Bharadwaj, and Rajendra K. Srivastava, "Financial Value of Brands in Mergers and Acquisitions: Is Value in the Eye of the Beholder?" *Journal of Marketing* 72 (November 2008), pp. 49–64.
52. Chuck Carnevale, "United Technologies Has Transitioned Itself for Accelerated Growth," *Forbes*, March 22, 2013; William J. Holstein, "The Incalculable Value of Building Brands," *Chief Executive*, April–May 2006, pp. 52–56; www.utc.com/Who-We-Are/Pages/Key-Facts.aspx, accessed 1/30/2021.
53. Deborah Roedder John, Barbara Loken, and Christopher Joiner, "The Negative Impact of Extensions: Can Flagship Products Be Diluted?" *Journal of Marketing* 62 (January 1998), pp. 19–32.
54. Vanessa Fuhrmans, "Mercedes Pins Hopes on Sleek S-Class," *Wall Street Journal*, May 16, 2013.
55. Yuxin Chen and Tony Haitao Cui, "The Benefit of Uniform Price for Branded Variant," *Marketing Science* 32 (January–February 2013), pp. 36–50.
56. Marcus Cunha Jr., Mark R. Forehand, and Justin W. Angle, "Riding Coattails: When Co-Branding Helps versus Hurts Less-Known Brands," *Journal of Consumer Research* 41, no. 5 (2015), pp. 1284–1300; Ann-Kristin Kupfer, Nora Pähler vor der Holte, Raoul V. Kübler, and Thorsten Hennig-Thurau. "The Role of the Partner Brand's Social Media Power in Brand Alliances," *Journal of Marketing* 82, no. 3 (2018), pp. 25–44.
57. Tansev Geylani, J. Jeffrey Inman, and Frenkel Ter Hofstede, "Image Reinforcement or Impairment: The Effects of Co-Branding on Attribute Uncertainty," *Marketing Science* 27 (July–August 2008), pp. 730–44; Ed Lebar, Phil Buehler, Kevin Lane Keller, Monika Sawicka, Zeynep Aksehirli, and Keith Richey, "Brand Equity Implications of Joint Branding Programs," *Journal of Advertising Research* 45 (December 2005); Abhishek Borah and Gerard J. Tellis, "Halo (Spillover) Effects in Social Media: Do

Product Recalls of One Brand Hurt or Help Rival Brands?" *Journal of Marketing Research* 53, no. 2 (2016), pp. 143–160.

58. Hannes Datta, Kusum L. Ailawadi, and Harald J. van Heerde. "How Well Does Consumer-Based Brand Equity Align with Sales-Based Brand Equity and Marketing-Mix Response?" *Journal of Marketing* 81, no. 3 (2017), pp. 1–20.

59. Philip Kotler and Waldermar Pfoertsch, *Ingredient Branding: Making the Invisible Visible* (Heidelberg, Germany: Springer-Verlag, 2011).

60. Kalpesh Kaushik Desai and Kevin Lane Keller, "The Effects of Brand Expansions and Ingredient Branding Strategies on Host Brand Extendibility," *Journal of Marketing* 66 (January 2002), pp. 73–93.

61. Martin Bishop, "Finding Your Nemo: How to Survive the Dangerous Waters of Ingredient Branding," *Chief Executive*, March 15, 2010.

62. Kevin Lane Keller, *Strategic Brand Management*, 4th ed. (Upper Saddle River, NJ: Prentice Hall, 2013). See also Philip Kotler and Waldemar Pfoertsch, *B2B Brand Management* (New York: Springer, 2006).

63. Tatiana M. Fajardo, Jiao Zhang, and Michael Tsiros, "The Contingent Nature of the Symbolic Associations of Visual Design Elements: The Case of Brand Logo Frames," *Journal of Consumer Research* 43, no. 4 (2016), pp. 549–66; Yuwei Jiang, Gerald J. Gorn, Maria Galli, and Amitava Chattopadhyay, "Does Your Company Have the Right Logo? How and Why Circular- and Angular-Logo Shapes Influence Brand Attribute Judgments," *Journal of Consumer Research* 42, no. 5 (2016), pp. 709–26; Ryan Rahinel and Noelle M. Nelson, "When Brand Logos Describe the Environment: Design Instability and the Utility of Safety-Oriented Products," *Journal of Consumer Research* 43, no. 3 (2016), pp. 478–96.

64. Kevin Lane Keller and Don Lehmann, "How Do Brands Create Value?" *Marketing Management*, May–June 2003, pp. 27–31. See also Rajendra K. Srivastava, Tasadduq A. Shervani, and Liam Fahey, "Market-Based Assets and Shareholder Value," *Journal of Marketing* 62 (January 1998), pp. 2–18; Shuba Srinivasan, Marc Vanheule, and Koen Pauwels, "Mindset Metrics in Market Response Models: An Integrative Approach," *Journal of Marketing Research* 47 (August 2010), pp. 672–84.

65. Larry Light and Joan Kiddon, *Six Rules for Brand Revitalization: Learn How Companies Like McDonald's Can Re-Energize Their Brands* (Upper Saddle River, NJ: Wharton School Publishing, 2009).

66. Jonathan R. Copulsky, *Brand Resilience: Managing Risk and Recovery in a High-Speed World* (New York: Palgrave Macmillan, 2011).

67. Rebecca J. Slotegraaf and Koen Pauwels, "The Impact of Brand Equity and Innovation on the Long-Term Effectiveness of Promotions," *Journal of Marketing Research* 45 (June 2008), pp. 293–306.

68. John Kotter, "Burberry's Secrets to Successful Brand Reinvention," *Forbes*, February 26, 2013; Angela Ahrendts, "Burberry's CEO on Turning an Aging British Icon into a Global Luxury Brand," *Harvard Business Review*, February 2013; www.statista.com/topics/3458/burberry, accessed 11/26/2020.

69. See also Eric A. Yorkston, Joseph C. Nunes, and Shashi Matta, "The Malleable Brand: The Role of Implicit Theories in Evaluating Brand Extensions," *Journal of Marketing* 74 (January 2010), pp. 80–93; Tom Meyvis, Kelly Goldsmith, and Ravi Dhar, "The Importance of the Context in Brand Extension: How Pictures and Comparisons Shift Consumers' Focus from Fit to Quality," *Journal of Marketing Research* 49 (April 2012), pp. 206–17; Susan Spiggle, Hang T. Nguyen, and Mary Caravella, "More than Fit: Brand Extension Authenticity," *Journal of Marketing Research* 49 (December 2012), pp. 967–83; Keisha M. Cutright, James R. Bettman, and Gavan J. Fitzsimons, "Putting Brands in Their Place: How a Lack of Control Keeps Brand Contained," *Journal of Marketing Research* 50 (June 2013), pp. 365–77.

70. Kevin Lane Keller, *Strategic Brand Management*, 4th ed. (Upper Saddle River, NJ: Pearson, 2013). See also Alokparna Basu Monga and Deborah Roedder John, "Cultural Differences in Brand Extension Evaluation: The Influence of Analytical versus Holistic Thinking," *Journal of Marketing Research* 33 (March 2007), pp. 529–36; Rohini Ahluwalia, "How Far Can a Brand Stretch? Understanding the Role of Self-Construal," *Journal of Marketing Research* 45 (June 2008), pp. 337–50.

71. Pierre Berthon, Morris B. Holbrook, James M. Hulbert, and Leyland F. Pitt, "Viewing Brands in Multiple Dimensions," *MIT Sloan Management Review*, Winter 2007, pp. 37–43.

72. Andrea Rothman, "France's Bic Bets U.S. Consumers Will Go for Perfume on the Cheap," *Wall Street Journal*, January 12, 1989.

73. Valarie A. Taylor and William O. Bearden, "Ad Spending on Brand Extensions: Does Similarity Matter?" *Journal of Brand Management* 11 (September 2003), pp. 63–74; Sheri Bridges, Kevin Lane Keller, and Sanjay Sood, "Communication Strategies for Brand Extensions: Enhancing Perceived Fit by Establishing Explanatory Links," *Journal of Advertising* 29 (Winter 2000), pp. 1–11.

74. Ralf van der Lans, Rik Pieters, and Michel Wedel, "Competitive Brand Salience," *Marketing Science* 27 (September–October 2008), pp. 922–31.

75. Beth Newhart, "Monster Fights with Coca-Cola over Competing Energy Drinks," *BeverageDaily*, November 12, 2018.
76. Al Ries and Jack Trout, *Positioning: The Battle for Your Mind*, 20th Anniversary Edition (New York: McGraw-Hill, 2000).
77. David A. Aaker, *Brand Portfolio Strategy: Creating Relevance, Differentiation, Energy, Leverage, and Clarity* (New York: Free Press, 2004).
78. https://www.nytimes.com/interactive/2018/10/23/us/metoo-replacements.html, accessed 11/25/2020.
79. Alice M. Tybout and Michelle Roehm, "Let the Response Fit the Scandal," *Harvard Business Review*, December 2009, pp. 82–88; Kathleen Cleeren, Harald J. van Heerde, and Marnik G. Dekimpe, "Rising from the Ashes: How Brands and Categories Can Overcome Product-Harm Crises," *Journal of Marketing* 77 (March 2013), pp. 58–77.
80. Norman Klein and Stephen A. Greyser, "The Perrier Recall: A Source of Trouble," Harvard Business School Case #9-590-104 and "The Perrier Relaunch," Harvard Business School Case #9-590-130.
81. Christine Moorman, "Covid Drives Digital as Marketers Pivot into Stronger and Leaner Roles," *The CMO Survey*, June 18, 2020.
82. Rob Walker, "Nike's Secret for Surviving the Retail Apocalypse, *Medium*, April 6, 2020.
83. Melissa Pasanen, "How the Pandemic Propelled King Arthur Flour into the National Spotlight," *Seven Days*, June 23, 2020.
84. www.bain.com/about/media-center/press-releases/2017/press-release-2017-global-fall-luxury-market-study/
85. Stellene Volande, "The Secret to Hermès's Success," *Departures*, November–December 2009, pp. 110–12.
86. www.subzero-wolf.com/sub-zero, accessed 1/30/2021.
87. Martinne Geller and Uday Sampath Kumar, "Bacardi to Buy Out Patrón Tequila in $5.1 Billion Deal," *Reuters*, January 22, 2018; www.patrontequila.com/our-story.html, accessed 1/30/2021.
88. Ariel Adams, "Montblanc on How to Be a Luxury Brand for Many," *Forbes*, March 14, 2013; www.montblanc.com/en-us/discover/about-montblanc/about-us.html, accessed 1/30/2021.
89. Delphine Dion and Stéphane Borraz, "Managing Status: How Luxury Brands Shape Class Subjectivities in the Service Encounter," *Journal of Marketing* 81, no. 5 (2017), pp. 67–85.
90. Kevin Lane Keller, "Managing the Growth Tradeoff: Challenges and Opportunities in Luxury Branding," *Journal of Brand Management* 16 (March–May 2009), pp. 290–301.
91. Marketing Spotlight sources: Brenden Gallagher, "The Greatest Travel Brand on Earth: A History of Louis Vuitton, Luggage and the LV Monogram—Louis Vuitton Monogram History," *Grailed*, February 21, 2018; Derek Thompson. "Branding Louis Vuitton: Behind the World's Most Famous Luxury Label," *The Atlantic*, May 13, 2011; Robert Johnston, "King Louis," *GQ*, September 11, 2017; https://us.louisvuitton.com, accessed 1/30/2021.
92. Marketing Spotlight sources: Diana Budds, "How Muji, Japan's Most Famous Anti-Brand, Plans to Win America," *Fast Company*, July 9, 2018; Carren Jao, "How Muji Created a Cult Following of Design Enthusiasts," *Entrepreneur*, July 23, 2015; Masaaki Kanai, "The Chairman of Ryohin Keikaku on Charting Muji's Global Expansion," *Harvard Business Review*, January 4, 2018; Molly Young, "At Muji, Design Intelligence Meets Dried Squid," *New York Times*, January 19, 2018; https://www.statista.com/statistics/870917/muji-overseas-store-numbers, accessed 11/26/2020.

Chapter 11

1. Edmund Lee, "Netflix Is Raising Prices. Here's Why," *New York Times*, January 15, 2019; Julia Alexander, "Netflix Raises Prices on All Streaming Plans in US," *The Verge*, January 15, 2019; Mike Snider, "Netflix Price Increases Could Cause Some Subscribers to Downgrade, Cancel Streaming Service," *USA Today*, January 17, 2019.
2. Yasmin Ahmed, "Netflix is increasing prices but you don't have to worry about it in India", India Today, (30th Oct 2020), accessed on 5th October 2021, from, https://www.indiatoday.in
3. Lata Jha, "Netflix subscriber additions drop in Q2", Live Mint, (July 2021), Accessed on 19th August, 2021, from, https://www.livemint.com
4. Cassie Lancellotti-Young, "Groupon Case," Glassmeyer/McNamee Center for Digital Strategies, Dartmouth College, 2011; https://press.groupon.com, accessed 1/30/2021. For relevant academic research, see Xueming Luo, Michelle Andrews, Yiping Song, and Jaakko Aspara, "Group-Buying Deal Popularity," *Journal of Marketing* 78 (March 2014), pp. 20–33.
5. Christian Homburg, Ove Jensen, and Alexander Hahn, "How to Organize Pricing? Vertical Delegation and Horizontal Dispersion of Pricing Authority," *Journal of Marketing* 76 (September 2012), pp. 49–69.
6. For a thorough review of pricing research, see Chezy Ofir and Russell S. Winer, "Pricing: Economic and Behavioral Models," in Bart Weitz and Robin Wensley, eds., *Handbook of Marketing*

(London: Sage Publications, 2002). See also Ray Weaver and Shane Frederick, "A Reference Price Theory of the Endowment Effect," *Journal of Marketing Research* 49 (October 2012), pp. 696–707; Kwanho Suk, Jiheon Lee, and Donald R. Lichtenstein, "The Influence of Price Presentation Order on Consumer Choice," *Journal of Marketing Research* 49 (October 2012), pp. 708–17; Stephen A. Atlas and Daniel M. Bartels, "Periodic Pricing and Perceived Contract Benefits," *Journal of Consumer Research* 45, no. 2 (2018), pp. 350–64.

7. Eric Wilson, "Why Does This Pair of Pants Cost $550?" *New York Times*, April 26, 2010; Denise Crosby, "Abercrombie & Fitch Is Cool Again. But Does the Formerly Oversexed and Overpriced Brand Deserve a Second Chance?" *The Beacon-News*, September 3, 2018.

8. For a comprehensive review, see Tridib Mazumdar, S. P. Raj, and Indrajit Sinha, "Reference Price Research: Review and Propositions," *Journal of Marketing* 69 (October 2005), pp. 84–102. For a different point of view, see Chris Janiszewski and Donald R. Lichtenstein, "A Range Theory Account of Price Perception," *Journal of Consumer Research* 25 (March 1999), pp. 353–68. For business-to-business applications, see Hernan A. Bruno, Hai Che, and Shantanu Dutta, "Role of Reference Price on Price and Quantity: Insights from Business-to-Business Markets," *Journal of Marketing Research* 49 (October 2012), pp. 640–54.

9. Adapted from Russell S. Winer, *Pricing*, MSI Relevant Knowledge Series (Cambridge, MA: Marketing Science Institute, 2006); Ellie J. Kyung and Manoj Thomas, "When Remembering Disrupts Knowing: Blocking Implicit Price Memory," *Journal of Marketing Research* 53, no. 6 (2016), pp. 937–53; Meghan R. Busse, Ayelet Israeli, and Florian Zettelmeyer, "Repairing the Damage: The Effect of Price Knowledge and Gender on Auto Repair Price Quotes," *Journal of Marketing Research* 54, no. 1 (2017), pp. 75–95.

10. For a discussion of how "incidental" prices outside the category can serve as contextual reference prices, see Joseph C. Nunes and Peter Boatwright, "Incidental Prices and Their Effect on Willingness to Pay," *Journal of Marketing Research* 41 (November 2004), pp. 457–66; Thomas Allard and Dale Griffin. "Comparative Price and the Design of Effective Product Communications," *Journal of Marketing* 81, no. 5 (2017), pp. 16–29.

11. Glenn E. Mayhew and Russell S. Winer, "An Empirical Analysis of Internal and External Reference-Price Effects Using Scanner Data," *Journal of Consumer Research* 19 (June 1992), pp. 62–70.

12. Robert Ziethammer, "Forward-Looking Buying in Online Auctions," *Journal of Marketing Research* 43 (August 2006), pp. 462–76. See also Caroline Ducarroz, Sha Yang, and Eric A. Greenleaf, "Understanding the Impact of In-Process Promotional Messages: An Application to Online Auctions." *Journal of Marketing* 80, no. 2 (2016), pp. 80–100.

13. John T. Gourville, "Pennies-a-Day: The Effect of Temporal Reframing on Transaction Evaluation," *Journal of Consumer Research* 24 (March 1998), pp. 395–408. See also Anja Lambrecht and Catherine Tucker, "Paying with Money or Effort: Pricing When Customers Anticipate Hassle," *Journal of Marketing Research* 49 (February 2012), pp. 66–82; Ajay T. Abraham and Rebecca W. Hamilton, "When Does Partitioned Pricing Lead to More Favorable Consumer Preferences? Meta-Analytic Evidence," *Journal of Marketing Research* 55, no. 5 (2018), pp. 686–703.

14. Wilfred Amaldoss and Sanjay Jain, "Pricing of Conspicuous Goods: A Competitive Analysis of Social Effects," *Journal of Marketing Research* 42 (February 2005).

15. "Ferrari Focuses on Exclusivity," www.warc.com, May 10, 2013; Roger Bennett, "Gained in Translation," *Bloomberg Businessweek*, April 2, 2012.

16. Eric T. Anderson and Duncan Simester, "Effects of $9 Price Endings on Retail Sales: Evidence from Field Experiments," *Quantitative Marketing and Economics* 1 (March 2003), pp. 93–110.

17. Anderson and Simester, "Mind Your Pricing Cues," *Harvard Business Review*, September 2003, pp. 96–103; Monica Wadhwa and Kuangjie Zhang, "This Number Just Feels Right: The Impact of Roundedness of Price Numbers on Product Evaluations," *Journal of Consumer Research* 41, no. 5 (2015), pp. 1172–185.

18. Anderson and Simester, "Mind Your Pricing Cues," *Harvard Business Review*, September 2003, pp. 96–103.

19. Daniel J. Howard and Roger A. Kerin, "Broadening the Scope of Reference-Price Advertising Research: A Field Study of Consumer Shopping Involvement," *Journal of Marketing* 70 (October 2006), pp. 185–204.

20. Thomas T. Nagle, John E. Hogan, and Joseph Zale, *The Strategy and Tactics of Pricing*, 5th ed. (Upper Saddle River, NJ: Pearson, 2011).

21. Katherine N. Lemon and Stephen M. Nowlis, "Developing Synergies between Promotions and Brands in Different Price–Quality Tiers," *Journal of Marketing Research* 39 (May 2002), pp. 171–85.

22. Alexander Chernev, *Strategic Marketing Management: Theory and Practice* (Chicago, IL: Cerebellum Press; 2019).

23. Based on information from Thomas T. Nagle, John E. Hogan, and Joseph Zale, *The Strategy and Tactics of Pricing*, 5th ed. (Upper Saddle River, NJ: Pearson, 2011).

24. Brett R. Gordon, Avi Goldfarb, and Yang Li, "Does Price Elasticity Vary with Economic Growth? A Cross-Category Analysis," *Journal of Marketing Research* 50 (February 2013), pp. 4–23; Harald J. Van Heerde, Maarten J. Gijsenberg, Marnik G. Dekimpe, and Jan-Benedict E. M. Steenkamp, "Price and Advertising Effectiveness over the Business Cycle," *Journal of Marketing Research* 50 (April 2013), pp. 177–93; Huachao Gao, Yinlong Zhang, and Vikas Mittal. "How Does Local–Global Identity Affect Price Sensitivity?" *Journal of Marketing* 81, no. 3 (2017), pp. 62–79.

25. Marco Bertini, Luc Wathieu, and Sheena S. Iyengar, "The Discriminating Consumer: Product Proliferation and Willingness to Pay for Quality," *Journal of Marketing Research* 49 (February 2012), pp. 39–49.

26. Nirmalya Kumar, "Strategies to Fight Low-Cost Rivals," *Harvard Business Review*, December 2006, pp. 104–12; Jan-Benedict E. M. Steenkamp and Nirmalya Kumar, "Don't Be Undersold," *Harvard Business Review*, December 2009, pp. 90–95.

27. Nirmalya Kumar, "Strategies to Fight Low-Cost Rivals," *Harvard Business Review*, December 2006, pp. 104–12.

28. Miller Magazine, " Solix from Buhler for guaranteed revenue increase", (2021), Accessed on 19th August 2021, from, https://millermagazine.com

29. Anupam Mukerj, "Monsoon Marketing," *Fast Company*, April 2007, p. 22.

30. Marco Bertini and Luc Wathieu, "How to Stop Customers from Fixating on Price," *Harvard Business Review* (May 2010), pp. 85–91.

31. For a discussion of some theoretical issues with auctions, see Amar Cheema, Dipankar Chakravarti, and Atanu R. Sinha, "Bidding Behavior in Descending and Ascending Auctions," *Marketing Science* 31 (September–October 2012), pp. 779–800; and Jason Shachat and Lijia Wei, "Procuring Commodities: First-Price Sealed-Bid or English Auctions?" *Marketing Science* 31 (March–April 2012), pp. 317–33.

32. Nick Brown, "Kodak Patent Sale Plan Gets Bankruptcy Court Approval," *Reuters*, January 11, 2013.

33. Eric Savitz, "SAP to Buy Ariba for $4.3B," *Forbes*, May 22, 2012; Ashlee Vance, "For an Online Marketplace, It's Better Late than Never," *New York Times*, November 20, 2010.

34. Using expected profit for setting price makes sense for the seller that makes many bids. The seller that bids only occasionally or needs a particular contract badly will not find it advantageous to use expected profit. This criterion does not distinguish between a $1,000 profit with a 0.10 probability and a $125 profit with an 0.80 probability. Yet the firm that wants to keep production going would prefer the second contract to the first.

35. Sandy D. Jap, "The Impact of Online Reverse Auction Design on Buyer–Supplier Relationships," *Journal of Marketing* 71 (January 2007), pp. 146–59; Sandy D. Jap, "An Exploratory Study of the Introduction of Online Reverse Auctions," *Journal of Marketing* 67 (July 2003), pp. 96–107.

36. For an illustrative academic application, see Adib Bagh and Hemant K. Bhargava, "How to Price Discriminate When Tariff Size Matters," *Marketing Science* 32 (January–February 2013), pp. 111–26.

37. Dana Mattioli, "On Orbitz, Mac Users Steered to Pricier Hotels," *Wall Street Journal*, August 23, 2012; Christopher Elliott, "Do Travel Companies Raise Prices Based on Who You Are?" *Huffington Post*, September 1, 2013.

38. Ricard Gil and Wesley R. Hartmann, "Empirical Analysis of Metering Price Discrimination: Evidence from Concession Sales at Movie Theaters," *Marketing Science* 28 (November–December 2009), pp. 1046–62.

39. R. Venkatesh and Vijay Mahajan, "The Design and Pricing of Bundles: A Review of Normative Guidelines and Practical Approaches," in Vithala R. Rao, ed., *Handbook of Pricing Research in Marketing* (Northampton, MA: Edward Elgar Publishing Company, 2009), pp. 232–57.

40. Dilip Soman and John T. Gourville, "Transaction Decoupling: How Price Bundling Affects the Decision to Consume," *Journal of Marketing Research* 38 (February 2001), pp. 30–44; Ramanathan Subramaniam and R. Venkatesh, "Optimal Bundling Strategies in Multiobject Auctions of Complements or Substitutes," *Marketing Science* 28 (March–April 2009), pp. 264–73.

41. Anita Elberse, "Bye-Bye Bundles: The Unbundling of Music in Digital Channels," *Journal of Marketing* 74 (May 2010), pp. 107–23.

42. Bob Donath, "Dispel Major Myths about Pricing," *Marketing News*, February 3, 2003, p. 10. For an interesting historical account, see Meghan R. Busse, Duncan I. Simester, and Florian Zettelmeyer, "'The Best Price You'll Ever Get': The 2005 Employee Discount Pricing Promotions in the U.S. Automobile Industry," *Marketing Science* 29 (March–April 2010), pp. 268–90.

43. For a classic review, see Kent B. Monroe, "Buyers' Subjective Perceptions of Price," *Journal of*

Marketing Research 10 (February 1973), pp. 70–80. See also Z. John Zhang, Fred Feinberg, and Aradhna Krishna, "Do We Care What Others Get? A Behaviorist Approach to Targeted Promotions," *Journal of Marketing Research* 39 (August 2002), pp. 277–91.

44. Margaret C. Campbell, "Perceptions of Pricing Unfairness: Antecedents and Consequences," *Journal of Marketing Research* 36 (May 1999), pp. 187–99; Lan Xia, Kent B. Monroe, and Jennifer L. Cox, "The Price Is Unfair! A Conceptual Framework of Price Fairness Perceptions," *Journal of Marketing* 68 (October 2004), pp. 1–15; Eric T. Anderson and Duncan Simester, "Does Demand Fall When Customers Perceive That Prices Are Unfair? The Case of Premium Pricing for Larger Sizes," *Marketing Science* 27 (May–June 2008), pp. 492–500; Xiaomeng Guo and Baojun Jiang, "Signaling through Price and Quality to Consumers with Fairness Concerns," *Journal of Marketing Research* 53, no. 6 (2016), pp. 988–1000.

45. Kusum L. Ailawadi, Donald R. Lehmann, and Scott A. Neslin, "Market Response to a Major Policy Change in the Marketing Mix: Learning from Procter & Gamble's Value Pricing Strategy," *Journal of Marketing* 65 (January 2001), pp. 44–61.

46. Laura Heller, "Publix the Walmart Slayer Wins Another Round with Low Prices," *Forbes*, July 30, 2013.

47. Nirmalya Kumar, "Strategies to Fight Low-Cost Rivals," *Harvard Business Review* (December 2006), pp. 104–12. See also Adrian Ryans, *Beating Low Cost Competition: How Premium Brands Can Respond to Cut-Price Rivals* (West Sussex, England: John Wiley & Sons, 2008); Jack Neff, "How the Discounters Hurt Themselves," *Advertising Age*, December 10, 2007, p. 12.

48. Scott Neslin, "Sales Promotion," in Bart Weitz and Robin Wensley, eds., *Handbook of Marketing* (London: Sage, 2002), pp. 310–38.

49. Rajkumar Venkatesan and Paul W. Farris, "Measuring and Managing Returns from Retailer-Customized Coupon Campaigns," *Journal of Marketing* 76 (January 2012), pp. 76–94.

50. For a summary of the research on whether promotion erodes the consumer franchise of leading brands, see Robert C. Blattberg and Scott A. Neslin, "Sales Promotion: The Long and Short of It," *Marketing Letters* 1 (December 2004). For a related topic, see Michael J. Barone and Tirthankar Roy, "Does Exclusivity Pay Off? Exclusive Price Promotions and Consumer Response," *Journal of Marketing* 74 (March 2010), pp. 121–32.

51. Harald J. Van Heerde, Sachin Gupta, and Dick Wittink, "Is 75% of the Sales Promotion Bump Due to Brand Switching? No, Only 33% Is," *Journal of Marketing Research* 40 (November 2003), pp. 481–91.

52. Kusum L. Ailawadi, Karen Gedenk, Christian Lutzky, and Scott A. Neslin, "Decomposition of the Sales Impact of Promotion-Induced Stockpiling," *Journal of Marketing Research* 44 (August 2007); Eric T. Anderson and Duncan Simester, "The Long-Run Effects of Promotion Depth on New versus Established Customers: Three Field Studies," *Marketing Science* 23 (Winter 2004), pp. 4–20; Luc Wathieu, A. V. Muthukrishnan, and Bart J. Bronnenberg, "The Asymmetric Effect of Discount Retraction on Subsequent Choice," *Journal of Consumer Research* 31 (December 2004), pp. 652–65.

53. Rebecca J. Slotegraaf and Koen Pauwels, "The Impact of Brand Equity Innovation on the Long-Term Effectiveness of Promotions," *Journal of Marketing Research* 45 (June 2008), pp. 293–306.

54. Kusum L. Ailawadi, Bari A. Harlam, Jacques Cesar, and David Trounce, "Promotion Profitability for a Retailer: The Role of Promotion, Brand, Category, and Store Characteristics," *Journal of Marketing Research* 43 (November 2006), pp. 518–36.

55. Abhijit Guha, Abhijit Biswas, Dhruv Grewal, Swati Verma, Somak Banerjee, and Jens Nordfält, "Reframing the Discount as a Comparison against the Sale Price: Does It Make the Discount More Attractive?" *Journal of Marketing Research* 55, no. 3 (2018), pp. 339–51; Andong Cheng and Cynthia Cryder, "Double Mental Discounting: When a Single Price Promotion Feels Twice as Nice," *Journal of Marketing Research* 55, no. 2 (2018), pp. 226–38; Fengyan Cai, Rajesh Bagchi, and Dinesh K. Gauri, "Boomerang Effects of Low Price Discounts: How Low Price Discounts Affect Purchase Propensity," *Journal of Consumer Research* 42, no. 5 (2016), pp. 804–16.

56. He Jia, Sha Yang, Xianghua Lu, and C. Whan Park, "Do Consumers Always Spend More When Coupon Face Value Is Larger? The Inverted U-Shaped Effect of Coupon Face Value on Consumer Spending Level," *Journal of Marketing* 82, no. 4 (2018), pp. 70–85.

57. Prasad Vana, Anja Lambrecht, and Marco Bertini, "Cashback Is Cash Forward: Delaying a Discount to Entice Future Spending," *Journal of Marketing Research* 55, no. 6 (2018), pp. 852–68.

58. Franklin Shadd and Ayelet Fishbach, "Seller Beware: How Bundling Affects Valuation," *Journal of Marketing Research* 54, no. 5 (2017), pp. 737–51.

59. Steven K. Dallas and Vicki G. Morwitz, "'There Ain't No Such Thing as a Free Lunch': Consumers' Reactions to Pseudo-Free Offers," *Journal of Marketing Research* 55, no. 6 (2018), pp. 900–15.

60. Miguel Gomez, Vithala Rao, and Edward McLaughlin, "Empirical Analysis of Budget and Allocation of Trade Promotions in the U.S. Supermarket Industry," *Journal of Marketing Research* 44 (August 2007). Norris Bruce, Preyas S. Desai, and Richard Staelin, "The Better They Are, the More They Give: Trade Promotions of Consumer Durables," *Journal of Marketing Research* 42 (February 2005), pp. 54–66.

61. Kusum L. Ailawadi, "The Retail Power-Performance Conundrum: What Have We Learned?" *Journal of Retailing* 77 (Fall 2001), pp. 299–318; Koen Pauwels, "How Retailer and Competitor Decisions Drive the Long-Term Effectiveness of Manufacturer Promotions," *Journal of Retailing* 83 (2007), pp. 364–90.

62. Alexander Chernev, *Strategic Marketing Management: Theory and Practice* (Chicago, IL: Cerebellum Press, 2019).

63. Robert Klitzman, "Huge Price Hikes by Drug Companies Are Immoral," CNN, September 18, 2018.; Wayne Drash, "Report: Pharma Exec Says He Had 'Moral Requirement' to Raise Drug Price 400%," CNN, September 12, 2018; Daniel Kozarich, "Mylan's EpiPen Pricing Crossed Ethical Boundaries," *Fortune*, September 27, 2016; Cynthia Koons and Robert Langreth, "How Marketing Turned the EpiPen Into a Billion-Dollar Business," *Bloomberg Businessweek*, September 23, 2015; Sara Berg, "How Are Prescription Drug Prices Determined?" *AMA*, September 14, 2018.

64. Marketing Spotlight sources: Keith Loria, "The Real Deal: Inside Priceline.com's Digital Strategy," *CMO*, August 21, 2017; Stella Yifan Xie, "After a Comeback and a Name Change, Priceline Bets Big on China," *Wall Street Journal*, December 28, 2018; Leonard A. Schlesinger and Anish Pathipati, *The Priceline Group: Booking a Place for the Future* (Harvard Business School Publishing, 2016, case 9-316-177); Robert J. Dolan, *Priceline.com: Name Your Own Price* (Harvard Business School Publishing, 2000, case 9-500-070); Darren Huston, *Priceline's CEO on Creating an In-House Multilingual Customer Service Operation* (Harvard Business Review, 2016, case R1604A).

65. Marketing Spotlight sources: Avery Hartmans and Nathan McAlone, "The Story of How Travis Kalanick Built Uber into the Most Feared and Valuable Startup in the World," *Business Insider*, August 1, 2016; Youngme Moon, *Uber: Changing the Way the World Moves* (Harvard Business School Publishing, 2017, case 9-316-101); Thales Teixeira and Morgan Brown, *Airbnb, Etsy, Uber: Acquiring the First Thousand Customers* (Harvard Business School Publishing, 2018, case 9-516-094); Thales Teixeira and Morgan Brown, *Airbnb, Etsy, Uber: Growing from One Thousand to One Million Customers* (Harvard Business School Publishing, 2018, case 9-516-108; Virginia Weiler, Gerry Yemen, and Kusum Ailawadi, *Uber Pricing Strategies and Marketing Communications* (Darden Business Publishing, 2016, case UV6878; Feng Zhu and Angela Acocella, *Fasten: Challenging Uber and Lyft with a New Business Model* (Harvard Business School Publishing, 2018, case 9-616-962).

Chapter 12

1. G. Shainesh (2018), 'Interview with Vivek Sharma, Chief Marketing Officer – Pidilite', EDX Courses, Customer Relationship Management, Accessed on 19th August 2021, from, https://www.edx.org

2. ETBrandEquity (2020). 'Unlock 1: Fevicol urges change in strategy to fight Covid' Brand Equity, The Economic Times, July 5, Accessed on 19th August 2021, from, https://brandequity.economictimes.indiatimes.com

3. Opinion (2021) 'Advertisers should join the battle against covid' LiveMint, April 1, Accessed on 19th August 2021, from, https://www.livemint.com

4. Campaign India Team, " Fevicol's Social Experiment delivers a pointed message on social distancing", (March 2021), Accessed on 19th August 2021, from, https://www.campaignindia.in

5. Bureau (2019) 'Fevicol 'Sofa' campaign depicts 60 years of the brands existence' Adgully, August 24, Accessed on 19th August 2021, from, https://www.adgully.com

6. Norris I. Bruce, Kay Peters, and Prasad A. Naik, "Discovering How Advertising Grows Sales and Builds Brands," *Journal of Marketing Research* 49 (December 2012), pp. 793–806.

7. E. K. Strong, *The Psychology of Selling* (New York: McGraw-Hill, 1925), p. 9; Robert J. Lavidge and Gary A. Steiner, "A Model for Predictive Measurements of Advertising Effectiveness," *Journal of Marketing* (October 1961), p. 61; Everett M. Rogers, *Diffusion of Innovation* (New York: Free Press, 1962), pp. 79–86.

8. John R. Rossiter and Larry Percy, *Advertising and Promotion Management*, 2nd ed. (New York: McGraw-Hill, 1997). See also Russell H. Colley, *Defining Advertising Goals for Measured Advertising Results* (New York: Association of National Advertisers, 1961).

9. Stephen Williams, "Rivals Gang Up on Ford Trucks as Dodge Ram Joins Battering," *Advertising Age*, February 20, 2012.

10. Debora Viana Thompson and Rebecca W. Hamilton, "The Effects of Information Processing Mode on Consumers' Responses to Comparative

Advertising," *Journal of Consumer Research* 32 (March 2006), pp. 530–40.

11. Leigh McAlister, Raji Srinivasan, Niket Jindal, and Albert A. Cannella, "Advertising Effectiveness: The Moderating Effect of Firm Strategy," *Journal of Marketing Research* 53, no. 2 (2016), pp. 207–24.

12. Rajesh Chandy, Gerard J. Tellis, Debbie MacInnis, and Pattana Thaivanich, "What to Say When: Advertising Appeals in Evolving Markets," *Journal of Marketing Research* 38 (November 2001); Gerard J. Tellis, Rajesh Chandy, and Pattana Thaivanich, "Decomposing the Effects of Direct Advertising: Which Brand Works, When, Where, and How Long?" *Journal of Marketing Research* 37 (February 2000), pp. 32–46; Peter J. Danaher, André Bonfrer, and Sanjay Dhar, "The Effect of Competitive Advertising," *Journal of Marketing Research* 45 (April 2008), pp. 211–25.

13. Dan Horsky, Sharon Horsky, and Robert Zeithammer, "The Modern Advertising Agency Selection Contest: A Case for Stipends to New Participants," *Journal of Marketing Research* 53, no. 5 (2016), pp. 773–89.

14. Anat Keinan, Francis Farrelly, and Michael Beverland, "Introducing iSnack 2.0: The New Vegemite," Harvard Business School Case, April 2012; Ruth Lamperd, "Vegemite Product Renamed Vegemite Cheesybite after iSnack 2.0 Was Dumped," *Herald Sun*, October 7, 2009.

15. Diana T. Kurylko, "Goofy Ads, Variants Help Mini Rule Its Own Little World," *Automotive News*, May 20, 2013; Micheline Maynard, "BMW's Bold Plan to Build Lots More Minis," *Forbes*, July 9, 2012; Douglas B. Holt and John A. Quelch, "Launching the New Mini," HBS Case# 9-505-020, 2004; www.mini.com/en_MS/home.html, accessed 1/30/2021.

16. Some of these definitions are adapted from the American Marketing Association.

17. Amna Kirmani and Akshay R. Rao, "No Pain, No Gain: A Critical Review of the Literature on Signaling Unobservable Product Quality," *Journal of Marketing* 64 (April 2000), pp. 66–79.

18. Sean Corcoran, "Defining Earned, Owned and Paid Media," *Forrester Blogs*, December 16, 2009. For an empirical examination, see Andrew T. Stephen and Jeff Galak, "The Effects of Traditional and Social Earned Media on Sales: A Study of a Microlending Marketplace," *Journal of Marketing Research* 49 (October 2012), pp. 624–39.

19. Andrew T. Stephen and Jeff Galak, "The Effects of Traditional and Social Earned Media on Sales: A Study of a Microlending Marketplace," *Journal of Marketing Research* 49 (October 2012), pp. 624–39; Ezgi Akpinar and Jonah Berger, "Valuable Virality," *Journal of Marketing Research* 54, no. 2 (2017), pp. 318–30; Peter J. Danaher and Harald J. van Heerde, "Delusion in Attribution: Caveats in Using Attribution for Multimedia Budget Allocation," *Journal of Marketing Research* 55, no. 5 (2018), pp. 667–85; Anatoli Colicev, Ashwin Malshe, Koen Pauwels, and Peter O'Connor, "Improving Consumer Mindset Metrics and Shareholder Value through Social Media: The Different Roles of Owned and Earned Media," *Journal of Marketing* 82, no. 1 (2018), pp. 37–56.

20. Steve McClellan, "Costs for TV Spots Rocket 7%," *Media Daily News*, January 29, 2013; "4As Television Production Cost Survey," 4As, January 21, 2013.

21. Chen Lin, Sriram Venkataraman, and Sandy Jap, "Media Multiplexing Behavior: Implications," *Marketing Science*, 32 (March–April 2013), pp. 310–24; Courtney Paulson, Lan Luo, and Gareth M. James, "Efficient Large-Scale Internet Media Selection Optimization for Online Display Advertising," *Journal of Marketing Research* 55, no. 4 (2018), pp. 489–506.

22. Alexander Konrad, "Bigger Than Craisins," *Forbes*, December 2, 2013; "Ocean Spray's Pop-Up Restaurant Emerges from 2,000 lbs. of Cranberries inside a Cranberry Bog in Rockefeller Center," *Business Wire*, September 29, 2011; www.oceanspray.com/Our-Story, accessed 2/23/2021.

23. www.statista.com/statistics/217134/total-advertisement-revenue-of-super-bowls/, accessed 10/24/2020.

24. Jeffrey Dorfman, "Super Bowl Ads Are a Bargain at $5 Million," *Forbes*, February 4, 2017.

25. Prashant Malaviya, "The Moderating Influence of Advertising Context on Ad Repetition Effects: The Role of Amount and Type of Elaboration," *Journal of Consumer Research* 34 (June 2007), pp. 32–40; Christine Köhler, Murali K. Mantrala, Sönke Albers, and Vamsi K. Kanuri, "A Meta-Analysis of Marketing Communication Carryover Effects," *Journal of Marketing Research* 54, no. 6 (2017), pp. 990–1008.

26. Marshall Freimer and Dan Horsky, "Periodic Advertising Pulsing in a Competitive Market," *Marketing Science* 31 (July–August 2012), pp. 637–48.

27. Werner Reinartz and Peter Saffert, "Creativity in Advertising: When It Works and When It Doesn't," *Harvard Business Review*, June 2013, pp. 107–12; Norris I. Bruce, B.P.S. Murthi, and Ram C. Rao, "A Dynamic Model for Digital Advertising: The Effects of Creative Format, Message Content, and Targeting on Engagement," *Journal of Marketing Research* 54, no. 2 (2017), pp. 202–18.

28. John R. Rossiter and Larry Percy, *Advertising and Promotion Management*, 2nd ed. (New York: McGraw-Hill, 1997).

29. Ayn E. Crowley and Wayne D. Hoyer, "An Integrative Framework for Understanding Two-Sided Persuasion," *Journal of Consumer Research* 20 (March 1994), pp. 561–74. Roger D. Blackwell, Paul W. Miniard, and James F. Engel, *Consumer Behavior*, 10th ed. (Mason, OH: South-Western Publishing, 2006).

30. C. I. Hovland, A. A. Lumsdaine, and F. D. Sheffield, *Experiments on Mass Communication*, vol. 3 (Princeton, NJ: Princeton University Press, 1949).

31. H. Rao Unnava, Robert E. Burnkrant, and Sunil Erevelles, "Effects of Presentation Order and Communication Modality on Recall and Attitude," *Journal of Consumer Research* 21 (December 1994), pp. 481–90.

32. Gillian Naylor, Susan Bardi Kleiser, Julie Baker, and Eric Yorkston, "Using Transformational Appeals to Enhance the Retail Experience," *Journal of Retailing* 84 (April 2008), pp. 49–57.

33. Michael R. Solomon, *Consumer Behavior*, 12th ed. (Upper Saddle River, NJ: Pearson Prentice Hall, 2016).

34. Rik Pieters and Michel Wedel, "Attention Capture and Transfer in Advertising: Brand, Pictorial, and Text-Size Effects," *Journal of Marketing* 68 (April 2004), pp. 36–50.

35. Herbert C. Kelman and Carl I. Hovland, "Reinstatement of the Communication in Delayed Measurement of Opinion Change," *Journal of Abnormal and Social Psychology* 48 (July 1953), pp. 327–35.

36. Timothy P. Derdenger, Hui Li, and Kannan Srinivasan, "Firms' Strategic Leverage of Unplanned Exposure and Planned Advertising: An Analysis in the Context of Celebrity Endorsements," *Journal of Marketing Research* 55, no. 1 (2018), pp. 14–34.

37. Lucia Moses, "What Do These Real People Think of Ads Starring Real People?" *Adweek*, May 1, 2012.

38. C. E. Osgood and P. H. Tannenbaum, "The Principles of Congruity in the Prediction of Attitude Change," *Psychological Review* 62 (January 1955), pp. 42–55.

39. Derek D. Rucker, *Advertising Strategy*, 5th ed. (Acton, MA: Copley Custom Textbooks, 2018).

40. The material in this section has been developed by Derek D. Rucker, Kellogg School of Management, Northwestern University.

41. Shrihari Sridhar, Frank Germann, Charles Kang, and Rajdeep Grewal. "Relating Online, Regional, and National Advertising to Firm Value," *Journal of Marketing* 80, no. 4 (2016), pp. 39–55; Peter Pal Zubcsek, Zsolt Katona, and Miklos Sarvary, "Predicting Mobile Advertising Response Using Consumer Colocation Networks," *Journal of Marketing* 81, no. 4 (2017), pp. 109–26.

42. Millie Elsen, Rik Pieters, and Michel Wedel, "Thin Slice Impressions: How Advertising Evaluation Depends on Exposure Duration," *Journal of Marketing Research* 53, no. 4 (2016), pp. 563–79.

43. Oliver J. Rutz, Garrett P. Sonnier, and Michael Trusov, "A New Method to Aid Copy Testing of Paid Search Text Advertisements," *Journal of Marketing Research* 54, no. 6 (2017), pp. 885–900.

44. Peter J. Danaher and Tracey S. Dagger, "Comparing the Relative Effectiveness of Advertising Channels: A Case Study of a Multimedia Blitz Campaign," *Journal of Marketing Research* 50 (August 2013), pp. 517–34; Garrett A. Johnson, Randall A. Lewis, and Elmar I. Nubbemeyer, "Ghost Ads: Improving the Economics of Measuring Online Ad Effectiveness," *Journal of Marketing Research* 54, no. 6 (2017), pp. 867–84.

45. Marketing Insight sources: Natalie Zmuda and Rupal Parekh, "More Than a Pitchman: Why Stars Are Getting Marketing Titles," *Advertising Age*, February 10, 2013; Tim Nudd, "Dos Equis Invites You to Call the Most Interesting Voicemail in the World," *Adweek*, November 9, 2012; Lucia Moses, "Get Real," *Adweek*, April 30, 2012; Irving Rein, Philip Kotler, and Martin Scoller, *The Making and Marketing of Professionals into Celebrities* (Chicago: NTC Business Books, 1997); https://variety.com/2018/biz/news/older-celebrities-make-better-brand-endorsements-survey-finds-1202960720, accessed 11/26/2020.

46. Marketing Spotlight sources: "Red Bull and Auto Racing: Sponsor or Own a Formula One Team?" Case Study, *Stanford Graduate School of Business*, June 04, 2007; Daniel Engber, "Who Made That Energy Drink?" *New York Times*, December 6, 2013; Robert Katai, "10 Lessons Red Bull Can Teach You about Marketing," May 23, 2018; Nitin Pangarkar and Mohit Agarwal, "The Wind Behind Red Bull's Wings," *Forbes*, June 24, 2013; Brad Spurgeon, "Meet the Red Bull Tribe," *New York Times*, May 24, 2013; James Ayles, "From Cliff Diving To Formula One and Football: How Red Bull Built A World-Class Sporting Empire," *Forbes*, January 14, 2020; www.redbull.com, accessed 11/26/2020.

47. Marketing Spotlight sources: Dawn Emery, "The Truth about the 'Best Job in the World,' According to the Man Who First Won It," *The Independent*, April 01, 2017; Anthony Hayes, "'The Best Job in the World' & Beyond in a Brave New Marketing World," *Campaign*, September 7, 2011; Dylan Kissane, "Case Study: The Best Job in the World," *DOZ*, January 12, 2015; Mark Sweney, "'Best Job in the World' Campaign Storms Cannes Lions

Advertising Awards," *The Guardian*, June 23, 2009; www.tourism.australia.com, accessed 2/6/2021.

Chapter 13

1. Lydia Dishman, "How Dr. Dre's Burgeoning Headphones Company Stays True to Its Bass-Thumping Roots," *Fast Company*, September 13, 2012; Andrew J. Martin, "Headphones with Swagger (and Lots of Bass)," *New York Times*, November 19, 2011; Burt Helm, "How Dr. Dre's Headphones Company Became a Billion-Dollar Business," *Inc*. (May 2014); Colin Finkle, "Beats by Dre: A Lifestyle Brand Case Study," brandmarketingbolog.com, October 12, 2018; www.drdre.com, accessed 11/26/2020.
2. Rajeev Batraand and Kevin Lane Keller, "Integrating Marketing Communications: New Findings, New Lessons, and New Ideas," *Journal of Marketing* 80, no. 6 (2016), pp. 122–45.
3. Adapted from Kevin Lane Keller, *Strategic Brand Management,* 4th ed. (Upper Saddle River, NJ: Pearson, 2013).
4. Don E. Schultz and Heidi Schultz, *IMC, The Next Generation: Five Steps for Delivering Value and Measuring Financial Returns* (New York: McGraw-Hill, 2003).
5. "Ouch! Advertising Icon Can't Duck Injury of His Own," *PR Newswire*, January 8, 2012; Daniel P. Amos, "How I Did It: Aflac's CEO Explains How He Fell for the Duck," *Harvard Business Review* (January–February 2010); Stuart Elliott, "Not Daffy or Donald, but Still Aflac's Rising Star," *New York Times*, April 22, 2009; www.aflac.com/about-aflac/default.aspx, accessed 11/26/2020.
6. Song Yao, Wenbo Wang, and Yuxin Chen, "TV Channel Search and Commercial Breaks," *Journal of Marketing Research* 54, no. 5 (2017), pp. 671–86.
7. Jeffrey Dorfman, "Super Bowl Ads Are a Bargain at $5 Million," *Forbes*, February 4, 2017.
8. www.pewresearch.org/topics/state-of-the-news-media, accessed 1/11/2021.
9. Glen Urban, Guilherme (Gui) Liberali, Erin Macdonald, Robert Bordley, and John Hauser, "Morphing Banner Advertising," *Marketing Science* 33 (January–February 2014), pp. 27–46; Michael Braun and Wendy Moe, "Online Display Advertising: Modeling the Effects of Multiple Creatives and Individual Impression Histories," *Marketing Science* 32 (September/October 2013), pp. 753–67; Lara Lobschat, Ernst C. Osinga, and Werner J. Reinartz, "What Happens Online Stays Online? Segment-Specific Online and Offline Effects of Banner Advertisements," *Journal of Marketing Research* 54, no. 6 (2017), pp. 901–13.
10. Anja Lambrecht and Catherine Tucker, "When Does Retargeting Work? Information Specificity in Online Advertising," *Journal of Marketing Research* 50 (October 2013), pp. 561–76.
11. Peter J. Danaher, Janghyuk Lee, and Laoucine Kerbache, "Optimal Internet Media Selection," *Marketing Science* 29 (March–April 2010), pp. 336–47; Puneet Manchanda, Jean-Pierre Dubé, Khim Yong Goh, and Pradeep K. Chintagunta, "The Effects of Banner Advertising on Internet Purchasing," *Journal of Marketing Research* 43 (February 2006), pp. 98–108.
12. Max Chafkin, "Ads and Atmospherics," *Inc.* (February 2007).
13. Abbey Klaassen and Andrew Hampp, "Inside Outdoor's Digital Makeover," *Advertising Age: Creativity*, June 14, 2010, p. 5.
14. Michael A. Wiles and Anna Danielova, "The Worth of Product Placement in Successful Films: An Event Study Analysis," *Journal of Marketing* 73 (July 2009), pp. 44–63.
15. "Grow the Heineken Brand," *Heineken Annual Report 2012*; Guy Lodge, "The Skyfall's the Limit on James Bond Marketing," *The Guardian*, October 23, 2012; Marc Graser, "'Skyfall' a Windfall for Product Placement," *Variety*, November 9, 2012.
16. Ram Bezawada, S. Balachander, P. K. Kannan, and Venkatesh Shankar, "Cross-Category Effects of Aisle and Display Placements: A Spatial Modeling Approach and Insights," *Journal of Marketing* 73 (May 2009), pp. 99–117; Pierre Chandon, J. Wesley Hutchinson, Eric T. Bradlow, and Scott H. Young, "Does In-Store Marketing Work? Effects of the Number and Position of Shelf Facings on Brand Attention and Evaluation at the Point of Purchase," *Journal of Marketing* 73 (November 2009), pp. 1–17.
17. John R. Hauser, Glen L. Urban, Guilherme Liberali, and Michael Braun, "Website Morphing," *Marketing Science* 28 (March–April 2009), pp. 202–23; Peter J. Danaher, Guy W. Mullarkey, and Skander Essegaier, "Factors Affecting Web Site Visit Duration: A Cross-Domain Analysis," *Journal of Marketing Research* 43 (May 2006), pp. 182–94; Philip Kotler, *According to Kotler* (New York: American Management Association, 2005).
18. "Automotive Brand Websites Drive Trials," www.warc.com, January 31, 2013.
19. Avi Goldfarb and Catherine Tucker, "Why Managing Consumer Privacy Can Be an Opportunity," *MIT Sloan Management Review* (Spring 2013), pp. 10–12.
20. Ron Berman and Zsolt Katona, "The Role of Search Engine Optimization in Search Marketing," *Marketing Science* 32 (July–August 2013),

pp. 644–51; Oliver J. Rutz, Randolph E. Bucklin, and Garrett P. Sonnier, "A Latent Instrumental Variables Approach to Modeling Keyword Conversion in Paid Search Advertising," *Journal of Marketing Research* 49 (June 2012), pp. 306–19; Oliver J. Rutz and Randolph E. Bucklin, "From Generic to Branded: A Model of Spill-over in Paid Search Advertising," *Journal of Marketing Research* 48 (February 2011), pp. 87–102.

21. Christian Schulze, Lisa Schöler, and Bernd Skiera, "Not All Fun and Games: Viral Marketing for Utilitarian Products," *Journal of Marketing* 78 (January 2014), pp. 1–19.

22. Ashish Kumar, Ram Bezawada, Rishika Rishika, Ramkumar Janakiraman, and P. K. Kannan. "From Social to Sale: The Effects of Firm-Generated Content in Social Media on Customer Behavior," *Journal of Marketing* 80, no. 1 (2016), pp. 7–25; Yuchi Zhang, Michael Trusov, Andrew T. Stephen, and Zainab Jamal, "Online Shopping and Social Media: Friends or Foes?" *Journal of Marketing* 81, no. 6 (2017), pp. 24–41.

23. "Lay's 'Do Us a Flavor' Contest Is Back: Fans Invited to Submit Next Great Potato Chip Flavor Idea for the Chance to Win $1 Million," *PR Newswire*, January 14, 2014.

24. Andrew Yoo, "Logo Ideas: Crowdsourcing the Next Big Hit," *Digital Initiative*, March 20, 2017.

25. For an academic discussion of chat rooms, recommendation sites, and customer review sections online, see Dina Mayzlin, "Promotional Chat on the Internet," *Marketing Science* 25 (March–April 2006), pp. 155–63; and Judith Chevalier and Dina Mayzlin, "The Effect of Word of Mouth on Sales: Online Book Reviews," *Journal of Marketing Research* 43 (August 2006), pp. 345–54.

26. Rebecca Walker Naylor, Cait Poynor Lamberton, and Patricia M. West, "Beyond the 'Like' Button: The Impact of Mere Virtual Presence on Brand Evaluations and Purchase Intentions in Social Media Settings," *Journal of Marketing* 76 (November 2012), pp. 105–20.

27. Jae Young Lee and David R. Bell, "Neighborhood Social Capital and Social Learning for Experience Attributes of Products," *Marketing Science* 32 (November–December 2013), pp. 960–76.

28. Olivier Toubia and Andrew T. Stephen, "Intrinsic vs. Image-Related Utility in Social Media: Why Do People Contribute Content to Twitter?" *Marketing Science* 32 (May–June 2013), pp. 368–92.

29. Thales Teixeira, "The New Science of Viral Ads," *Harvard Business Review*, March 2012, pp. 25–27; Thales Teixeira, Michel Wedel, and Rik Pieters, "Emotion-Induced Engagement in Internet Video Advertisements," *Journal of Marketing Research* 49 (April 2012), pp. 144–59. See also Jonah Berger and Katherine L. Milkman, "What Makes Online Content Viral?" *Journal of Marketing Research* 49 (April 2012), pp. 192–205.

30. Matthew Creamer and Rupal Parekh, "Ideas of the Decade," *Advertising Age*, December 14, 2009.

31. Simon Owens, "Is It Time to Regulate Social Media Influencers?" *Intelligencer*, January 17, 2019.

32. Nicholas Confessore, Gabriel Dance, Richard Harris, and Mark Hansen, "The Follower Factory," *New York Times*, January 27, 2018.

33. Yi Zhao, Sha Yang, Vishal Narayan, and Ying Zhao, "Modeling Consumer Learning from Online Product Reviews," *Marketing Science* 32 (January–February 2013), pp. 153–69; Rebecca Walker Naylor, Cait Poynor Lamberton, and David A. Norton, "Seeing Ourselves in Others: Reviewer Ambiguity, Egocentric Anchoring, and Persuasion," *Journal of Marketing Research* 48 (June 2011), pp. 617–31; Yang Wang and Alexander Chaudhry, "When and How Managers' Responses to Online Reviews Affect Subsequent Reviews," *Journal of Marketing Research* 55, no. 2 (2018), pp. 163–77. See also Itamar Simonson and Emanuel Rosen, *Added Value* (New York: HarperCollins, 2014).

34. "Nielsen: Global Consumers' Trust in 'Earned' Advertising Grows in Importance," April 10, 2012.

35. Sinan Aral, "The Problem with Online Ratings," *MIT Sloan Management Review* (Winter 2014), pp. 47–52. See also Shrihari Sridhar and Raji Srinivasan, "Social Influence Effects in Online Product Ratings," *Journal of Marketing* 76 (September 2012), pp. 70–88; Wendy W. Moe and Michael Trusov, "The Value of Social Dynamics in Online Product Ratings Forums," *Journal of Marketing Research* 48 (June 2011), pp. 444–56.

36. Zoey Chen and Nicholas Lurie, "Temporal Contiguity and Negativity Bias in the Impact of Online Word of Mouth," *Journal of Marketing Research* 50 (August 2013), pp. 463–76; Yubo Chen, Qi Wang, and Jinhong Xie, "Online Social Interactions: A Natural Experiment on Word of Mouth versus Observational Learning," *Journal of Marketing Research* 48 (April 2011), pp. 238–54.

37. Jacob Goldenberg, Gal Oestreicher-Singer, and Shachar Reichman, "The Quest for Content: How User-Generated Links Can Facilitate Online Exploration," *Journal of Marketing Research* 49 (August 2012), pp. 452–68.

38. Zsolt Katona, "Competing for Influencers in a Social Network," working paper, Haas School of Business, University of California at Berkeley (2014); Michael Trusov, Anand V. Bodapati, and Randolph E. Bucklin, "Determining Influential Users in Internet Social Networks," *Journal of Marketing Research* 47 (August 2010), pp. 643–58; Bart de Langhe, Philip M. Fernbach, and Donald R. Lichtenstein, "Navigating by the Stars: Investigating the Actual and Perceived Validity of Online User Ratings," *Journal of Consumer Research* 42, no. 6 (2016), pp. 817–33.

39. "Mobile Continues to Steal Share of US Adults' Daily Time Spent with Media," *eMarketer*, April 22, 2014.

40. Preethi Chamikuttyl, "Wharton Professor David Bell, on Brand Building in the Offline and Online World," *Your Story*, September 3, 2013.

41. Sunil Gupta, "For Mobile Devices, Think Apps, Not Ads," *Harvard Business Review* (March 2013), pp. 71–75.

42. Diana Ransom, "When the Customer Is in the Neighborhood," *Wall Street Journal*, May 17, 2010.

43. Farhan Thawar, "2013: The Breakout Year for Mobile Commerce," *Wired,* March 15, 2013.

44. Bettina Cornwell, Michael S. Humphreys, Angela M. Maguire, Clinton S. Weeks, and Cassandra Tellegen, "Sponsorship-Linked Marketing: The Role of Articulation in Memory," *Journal of Consumer Research* 33 (December 2006), pp. 312–21.

45. T. Bettina Cornwell, Clinton S. Weeks, and Donald P. Roy, "Sponsorship-Linked Marketing: Opening the Black Box," *Journal of Advertising* 34 (Summer 2005).

46. www.factorytour.com, accessed 1/9/2021.

47. Noah Joseph, "Buy a Car, Get a Trip: How European Delivery Works," *Car and Driver*, December 8, 2017.

48. Barak Libai, Eitan Muller, and Renana Peres, "Decomposing the Value of Word-of-Mouth Seeding Programs: Acceleration versus Expansion," *Journal of Marketing Research* 50 (April 2013), pp. 161–76, Oliver Hinz, Bernd Skiera, Christian Barrot, and Jan U. Becker, "Seeding Strategies for Viral Marketing: An Empirical Comparison," *Journal of Marketing* 75 (November 2011), pp. 55–71; Angela Xia Liu, Jan-Benedict Steenkamp, and Jurui Zhang, "Agglomeration as a Driver of the Volume of Electronic Word of Mouth in the Restaurant Industry," *Journal of Marketing Research* 55, no. 4 (2018), pp. 507–23; David Dubois, Andrea Bonezzi, and Matteo De Angelis, "Sharing with Friends versus Strangers: How Interpersonal Closeness Influences Word-of-Mouth Valence," *Journal of Marketing Research* 53, no. 5 (2016), pp. 712–27.

49. Thales Teixeira, "How to Profit from 'Lean' Advertising," *Harvard Business Review* (June 2013), pp. 23–25; Jing Peng, Ashish Agarwal, Kartik Hosanagar, and Raghuram Iyengar, "Network Overlap and Content Sharing on Social Media Platforms," *Journal of Marketing Research* 55, no. 4 (2018), pp. 571–85; Daniel Mochon, Karen Johnson, Janet Schwartz, and Dan Ariely, "What Are Likes Worth? A Facebook Page Field Experiment," *Journal of Marketing Research* 54, no. 2 (2017), pp. 306–17; Andrew M. Baker, Naveen Donthu, and V. Kumar, "Investigating How Word-of-Mouth Conversations about Brands Influence Purchase and Retransmission Intentions," *Journal of Marketing Research* 53, no. 2 (2016), pp. 225–39.

50. Rob Walker, "Mixing It Up," *New York Times*, August 24, 2008; www.blendtec.com/pages/about, accessed 11/26/2020.

51. Scroll.in, "Behind that viral video of a vada maker is a common sense idea and a determined Indian", (2018), Accessed on 19th August, 2021, from, https://scroll.in

52. Jessica Naziri, "Dollar Shave Club Co-founder Michael Dubin Had a Smooth Transition," *Los Angeles Times*, August 16, 2013; Emily Glazer, "A David and Gillette Story," *Wall Street Journal*, April 12, 2012; https://www.cnbc.com/2019/03/23/dollar-shaves-dubin-admits-a-business-built-on-simplicity-can-get-complicated .html, accessed 11/26/2020.

53. David Godes and Dina Mayzlin, "Firm-Created Word-of-Mouth Communication: Evidence from a Field Test," *Marketing Science* 28 (July–August 2009), pp. 721–39; Sarah Gelper, Renana Peres, and Jehoshua Eliashberg, "Talk Bursts: The Role of Spikes in Prerelease Word-of-Mouth Dynamics," *Journal of Marketing Research* 55, no. 6 (2018), pp. 801–17; Zoey Chen and Jonah Berger, "How Content Acquisition Method Affects Word of Mouth," *Journal of Consumer Research* 43, no. 1 (2016), pp. 86–102; Grant Packard and Jonah Berger, "How Language Shapes Word of Mouth's Impact," *Journal of Marketing Research* 54, no. 4 (2017), pp. 572–88.

54. Jonah Berger and Raghuram Iyengar, "Communication Channels and Word of Mouth: How the Medium Shapes the Message," *Journal of Consumer Research* 40 (October 2013), pp. 567–79. See also Mitch Lovett, Renana Peres, and Roni Shachar, "On Brands and Word of Mouth," *Journal of Marketing Research* 50 (August 2013), pp. 427–44; Jonah Berger and Eric M. Schwartz, "What Drives Immediate and Ongoing Word of Mouth?" *Journal of Marketing Research* 48 (October 2011), pp. 869–80.

55. Matteo De Angelis, Andrea Bonezzi, Alessandro M. Peluso, Derek D. Rucker, and Michele Costabile, "On Braggarts and Gossips: A Self-Enhancement Account of Word-of-Mouth Generation and Transmission," *Journal of Marketing Research* 49 (August 2012), pp. 551–63. See also Yinlong Zhang, Lawrence Feick, and Vikas Mittal, "How Males and Females Differ in Their Likelihood of Transmitting Negative Word of Mouth,"

Journal of Consumer Research 40 (April 2014), pp. 1097–1108; Ana Babić Rosario, Francesca Sotgiu, Kristine De Valck, and Tammo H. A. Bijmolt, "The Effect of Electronic Word of Mouth on Sales: A Meta-Analytic Review of Platform, Product, and Metric Factors," *Journal of Marketing Research* 53, no. 3 (2016), pp. 297–318.

56. "A Purr-fect Fit: CeeLo Green and Purrfect Remix the Meow Mix Cat Food Jingle," PRWeek Awards 2014; Rebecca Cullers, "CeeLo Green Creates a Purrfect Meow Mix Remix with His Cat," *Adweek*, May 10, 2012.

57. This section is largely based on Alexander Chernev, *Strategic Marketing Management: Theory and Practice* (Chicago IL, Cerebellum Press, 2019).

58. Marketing Insight sources: Marketing Insight sources: Rose Leadem, "The ROI of Social Media," *Entrepreneur*, July 7, 2018; Josh Bernoff, "A Balanced Perspective on Social ROI," *Marketing News*, February 28, 2011; Frahad Manjoo, "Does Social Media Have a Return on Investment?," *Fast Company*, July/August 2011; David A. Schweidel, Wendy W. Moe, and Chris Boudreaux, "Social Media Intelligence: Measuring Brand Sentiment from Online Conversation," *MSI Report 12-100* (Cambridge, MA: Marketing Science Institute, 2012).

59. Marketing Spotlight sources: Julie Jargon, "Burger King Returns to Its Roots," *Wall Street Journal*, March 9, 2016; Julie Jargon and Tess Stynes, "Burger King Profit Rises on Lower Costs," *Wall Street Journal*, February 13, 2014; Chris Kelly, "Disruptor of the Year: Burger King," *Marketing Dive*, December 3, 2018; Mallory Russell, "How Burger King Went from McDonald's Greatest Rival to Total Train Wreck," *Business Insider*, April 15, 2012; www .statista.com/statistics/266462/burger-king-revenue, accessed 3/6/2021; Chantal Tode, "Burger King's 5-Step Plan for Hacking Pop Culture," *Marketing Dive*, June 18, 2018; Laura Healy, *Can 3G Capital Make Burger King Cool Again?* (INSEAD, 2018, case 6402).

60. Marketing Spotlight sources: Terence Baker, "6 Ways AccorHotels Is Transforming Its Digital Strategy," *Hotel News Now*, September 5, 2018; Brad Howarth, "How AccorHotels Is Building Emotional Connections with Customers," *CMO Australia*, March 8, 2017; David Dubois, Inyoung Chae, Joerg Niessing, and Jean Wee, *AccorHotels and the Digital Transformation: Enriching Experiences through Content Strategies along the Customer Journey* (INSEAD, 2016, case 08-2016-6241); Jill Avery, Chekitan S. Dev, and Peter O'Connor, *Accor: Strengthening the Brand with Digital Marketing* (Harvard Business School Publishing, 2017, case 9-315-138).

Chapter 14

1. Credit Access Grameen, " Grameen Kota Reaches a milestone with 1 million micro finance customers", (2015), Accessed on (23th August 2021), from, https://www.creditaccessgrameen.in

2. Great Place to work, "Why Credit Access Grameen Limited is a great place to work", (2020), Accesses on 23rd August, 2021, from, https://www.greatplacetowork.in

3. Software group, " Success Stories- Credit Access Grameen Finance Limited", (2019), accessed on 23rd August, 2021, from, https://www.softwaregroup.com

4. AB Ravi, "Here's The Success Story Of The Udaya Kumar Hebbar ", Making It Big Episode 12, CNBC TV, (Feb 2019), Accessed on 11th Oct 2021, from, https://www.youtube.com

5. Nathaniel N. Hartmann, Heiko Wieland, and Stephen L. Vargo. "Converging on a New Theoretical Foundation for Selling." *Journal of Marketing* 82, no. 2 (2018), pp. 1–18.

6. Some of the following discussion is based on a classic analysis in W. J. E. Crissy, William H. Cunningham, and Isabella C. M. Cunningham, *Selling: The Personal Force in Marketing* (New York: Wiley, 1977), pp. 119–29.

7. Simon J. Blanchard, Mahima Hada, and Kurt A. Carlson, "Specialist Competitor Referrals: How Salespeople Can Use Competitor Referrals for Nonfocal Products to Increase Focal Product Sales," *Journal of Marketing* 82, no. 4 (2018), pp. 127–45.

8. Christian Homburg, Michael Müller, and Martin Klarmann, "When Should the Customer Really Be King? On the Optimum Level of Salesperson Customer Orientation in Sales Encounters," *Journal of Marketing* 75 (March 2011), pp. 55–74.

9. Raghu Bommaraju and Sebastian Hohenberg, "Self-Selected Sales Incentives: Evidence of Their Effectiveness, Persistence, Durability, and Underlying Mechanisms," *Journal of Marketing* 82, no. 5 (2018), pp. 106–24.

10. Pranav Jindal and Peter Newberry, "To Bargain or Not to Bargain: The Role of Fixed Costs in Price Negotiations," *Journal of Marketing Research* 55, no. 6 (2018), pp. 832–51.

11. Joel E. Urbany, "Justifying Profitable Pricing," *Journal of Product & Brand Management* 10 (2001), pp. 141–59.

12. Rajesh Bagchi, Nevena T. Koukova, Haresh Gurnani, Mahesh Nagarajan, and Shweta S. Oza, "Walking in My Shoes: How Expectations of Role Reversal in Future Negotiations Affect Present Behaviors," *Journal of Marketing Research* 53, no. 3 (2016), pp. 381–95.

13. Brent Adamson, Matthew Dixon, and Nicholas Toman, "Dismantling the Sales Machine," *Harvard Business Review* (November 2013), pp. 103–9.

14. V. Kumar, Rajkumar Venkatesan, and Werner Reinartz, "Performance Implications of Adopting a Customer-Focused Sales Campaign," *Journal of Marketing* 72 (September 2008), pp. 50–68; George R. Franke and Jeong-Eun Park, "Salesperson Adaptive Selling Behavior and Customer Orientation: A Meta-Analysis," *Journal of Marketing Research* 43 (November 2006), pp. 693–702.

15. www.tupperwarebrands.com/company/heritage, accessed 11/26/2020.

16. "The View from the Field," *Harvard Business Review* (July–August 2012), pp. 101–9.

17. Shrihari Sridhar, Murali K. Mantrala, and Sönke Albers, "Personal Selling Elasticities: A Meta-Analysis," *Journal of Marketing Research* 47 (October 2010); Raghu Bommaraju, Michael Ahearne, Zachary R. Hall, Seshadri Tirunillai, and Son K. Lam, "The Impact of Mergers and Acquisitions on the Sales Force," *Journal of Marketing Research* 55, no. 2 (2018), pp. 254–64.

18. Brent Adamson, Matthew Dixon, and Nicholas Toman, "The End of Solution Sales," *Harvard Business Review* (July–August 2012), pp. 60–68.

19. Ashwin W. Joshi, "Salesperson Influence on Product Development: Insights from a Study of Small Manufacturing Organizations," *Journal of Marketing* 74 (January 2010), pp. 94–107; Philip Kotler, Neil Rackham, and Suj Krishnaswamy, "Ending the War between Sales & Marketing," *Harvard Business Review* (July–August 2006), pp. 68–78.

20. "The View from the Field," *Harvard Business Review* (July–August 2012), pp. 101–9.

21. Shailesh Menon, "Why it still pays for Eureka Forbes to knock on doors despite extending sales online", Economic Times, (12th July, 2016), Accessed on 20th October 2021, from, https://economictimes.indiatimes.com

22. Nikolaos G. Panagopoulos, Adam A. Rapp, and Jessica L. Ogilvie, "Salesperson Solution Involvement and Sales Performance: The Contingent Role of Supplier Firm and Customer–Supplier Relationship Characteristics," *Journal of Marketing* 81, no. 4 (2017), pp. 144–64.

23. Michael Ahearne, Scott B. MacKenzie, Philip M. Podsakoff, John E. Mathieu, and Son K. Lam, "The Role of Consensus in Sales Team Performance," *Journal of Marketing Research* 47 (June 2010), pp. 458–69; Huanhuan Shi, Shrihari Sridhar, Rajdeep Grewal, and Gary Lilien, "Sales Representative Departures and Customer Reassignment Strategies in Business-to-Business Markets," *Journal of Marketing* 81, no. 2 (2017), pp. 25–44.

24. Øystein Daljord, Sanjog Misra, and Harikesh S. Nair, "Homogeneous Contracts for Heterogeneous Agents: Aligning Sales Force Composition and Compensation," *Journal of Marketing Research* 53, no. 2 (2016), pp. 161–182.

25. For distinctions between bonuses and commissions, see Sunil Kishore, Raghunath Singh Rao, Om Narasimhan, and George John, "Bonuses versus Commissions: A Field Study," *Journal of Marketing Research* 50 (June 2013), pp. 317–33.

26. Madhu Viswanathan, Xiaolin Li, George John, and Om Narasimhan, "Is Cash King for Sales Compensation Plans? Evidence from a Large-Scale Field Intervention," *Journal of Marketing Research* 55, no. 3 (2018), pp. 368–81.

27. Daniel H. Pink, "A Radical Prescription for Sales," *Harvard Business Review* (July–August 2012), pp. 76–77.

28. Tony Ritigliano and Benson Smith, *Discover Your Sales Strengths* (New York: Random House Business Books, 2004).

29. Sonke Albers, "Sales-Force Management—Compensation, Motivation, Selection, and Training," in Bart Weitz and Robin Wensley, eds., *Handbook of Marketing* (London: Sage, 2002), pp. 248–66.

30. Yashar Atefi, Michael Ahearne, James G. Maxham III, D. Todd Donavan, and Brad D. Carlson, "Does Selective Sales Force Training Work?" *Journal of Marketing Research* 55, no. 5 (2018), pp. 722–37.

31. Gaurav Sabnis, Sharmila C. Chatterjee, Rajdeep Grewal, and Gary L. Lilien, "The Sales Lead Black Hole: On Sales Reps' Follow-up of Marketing Leads," *Journal of Marketing* 77 (January 2013), pp. 52–67.

32. Michael Ahearne, Son K. Lam, John E. Mathieu, and Willy Bolander, "Why Are Some Salespeople Better at Adapting to Organizational Change?" *Journal of Marketing* 74 (May 2010), pp. 65–79; Constantine S. Katsikeas, Seigyoung Auh, Stavroula Spyropoulou, and Bulent Menguc, "Unpacking the Relationship between Sales Control and Salesperson Performance: A Regulatory Fit Perspective," *Journal of Marketing* 82, no. 3 (2018), pp. 45–69.

33. Jeff Green, "The New Willy Loman Survives by Staying Home," *Bloomberg Businessweek*, January 14, 2013, pp. 16–17.

34. Barbara Giamanco and Kent Gregoire, "Tweet Me, Friend Me, Make Me Buy," *Harvard Business Review* (July–August 2012), pp. 88–93.

35. Willem Verbeke and Richard P. Bagozzi, "Sales-Call Anxiety: Exploring What It Means When Fear

Rules a Sales Encounter," *Journal of Marketing* 64 (July 2000), pp. 88–101. See also Douglas E. Hughes and Michael Ahearne, "Energizing the Reseller's Sales Force: The Power of Brand Identification," *Journal of Marketing* 74 (July 2010), pp. 81–96; Jeffrey P. Boichuk, Willy Bolander, Zachary R. Hall, Michael Ahearne, William J. Zahn, and Melissa Nieves, "Learned Helplessness among Newly Hired Salespeople and the Influence of Leadership," *Journal of Marketing* 78 (January 2014), pp. 95–111.

36. Sebastian Hohenberg and Christian Homburg. "Motivating Sales Reps for Innovation Selling in Different Cultures." *Journal of Marketing* 80, no. 2 (2016), pp. 101–20.

37. Mark W. Johnston and Greg W. Marshall, *Sales-Force Management,* 12th ed. (New York: Routledge, 2016). See also Eric G. Harris, John C. Mowen, and Tom J. Brown, "Reexamining Salesperson Goal Orientations: Personality Influencers, Customer Orientation, and Work Satisfaction," *Journal of the Academy of Marketing Science* 33 (Winter 2005), pp. 19–35.

38. Ashutosh Patil and Niladri Syam, "How Do Specialized Personal Incentives Enhance Sales Performance? The Benefits of Steady Sales Growth," *Journal of Marketing* 82, no. 1 (2018), pp. 57–73.

39. Thomas Steenburgh and Michael Ahearne, "Motivating Salespeople: What Really Works," *Harvard Business Review* (July–August 2012), pp. 70–75.

40. Ibid.

41. Sarang Sunder, V. Kumar, Ashley Goreczny, and Todd Maurer, "Why Do Salespeople Quit? An Empirical Examination of Own and Peer Effects on Salesperson Turnover Behavior," *Journal of Marketing Research* 54, no. 3 (2017), pp. 381–97.

42. Ran Kivetz and Itamar Simonson, "The Idiosyncratic Fit Heuristic: Effort Advantage as a Determinant of Consumer Response to Loyalty Programs," *Journal of Marketing Research* 40 (November 2003), pp. 454–67.

43. Sneha Jha, "Here's how going completely digital helped Digit Insurance acquire 1.5 lakh customers in less than 4 months", Economic Times, 30th August 2018, Accessed on 16th October 2021, from, https://cio.economictimes.indiatimes.com

44. Debangana Ghosh, "Digit Insurance is India's newest unicorn, valued at $1.9 bn", TMT, (Jan 2021), Accessed on 24th August 2021, from, https://www.vccircle.com

45. Bob Stone and Ron Jacobs, *Successful Direct Marketing Methods,* 8th ed. (New York: McGraw-Hill, 2007). See also David A. Schweidel and George Knox, "Incorporating Direct Marketing Activity into Latent Attrition Models," *Marketing Science* 32 (May–June 2013), pp. 471–87.

46. Xi (Alan) Zhang, V. Kumar, and Koray Cosguner, "Dynamically Managing a Profitable Email Marketing Program," *Journal of Marketing Research* 54, no. 6 (2017), pp. 851–66.

47. Matt Schifrin, "Master Class," *Forbes*, January 17, 2011, pp. 54–55.

48. Nora Aufreiter, Julien Boudet, and Vivien Weng, "Why Marketers Keep Sending You E-mails," *McKinsey Quarterly* (January 2014).

49. www.grainger.com/content/cat_print, accessed 2/15/2021.

50. "Internet & Mail-Order Retail Industry Profile," www.firstresearch.com, January 10, 2018.

51. Barbara Feder Ostrov, "Annoying Robo-Calls Are At 'Epidemic Levels' This Health Open-Enrollment Season," *Washington Post,* November 11, 2018; Jake Swearingin, "The Beginning of the End of Robocalls," *Intelligencer*, February 14, 2019.

52. Marketing Insight sources: Noel Capon, Dave Potter, and Fred Schindler, *Managing Global Accounts: Nine Critical Factors for a World-Class Program*, 2nd ed. (Bronxville, NY: Wessex Press, 2008); Peter Cheverton, *Global Account Management: A Complete Action Kit of Tools and Techniques for Managing Key Global Customers* (London, UK: Kogan Page, 2008); Malcolm McDonald and Diana Woodburn, *Key Account Management: The Definitive Guide*, 2nd ed. (Oxford, UK: Butterworth-Heinemann, 2007).

53. Marketing Spotlight sources: Rebecca Stuart, "Avon's Global Marketing Boss on How It's Rebranding for the Instagram Generation," *The Drum*, November 27, 2018; Hakki Ozmorali, "Will Avon's Turnaround Be Real This Time?" October 8, 2018; Phil Wahba, "Here Are 5 Reasons Avon Fell Apart in the U.S.," *Fortune,* December 17, 2015; Phil Wahba, "How Avon's CEO Failed to Fix the Company," *Fortune*, August 3, 2017; Polly Mosendz, "The Avon Lady's Makeover, *Bloomberg Businessweek*, March 7, 2017; https://www.prnewswire.com/news-releases/natura-co-to-close-acquisition-of-avon-creating-the-worlds-fourth-largest-pure-play-beauty-group-300980823.html, accessed 11/26/2020.

54. Marketing Spotlight sources: Avi Dan, "How Progressive's CMO Jeff Charney Made 'Flo' More Loveable than Ducks and Geckos," *Forbes*, May 3, 2012; Giselle Abramovich, "How Progressive Got Its Social Flow," CMO.com, December 11, 2013; E. J. Schultz, "Progressive Goes Flo-less in Corporate Image Campaign," *Ad Age*, September 23, 2013; E. J. Schultz, "Flo Gets More Company as Progressive Rolls out

'The Box,'" *Ad Age,* December 5, 2012; Andrew Bary, "How Progressive Is Driving Growth in Auto Insurance," *Barron's*, December 1, 2018; https://www.statista.com/statistics/737860/progressive-revenue, accessed 11/26/2020; www.progressive.com/about, accessed 11/26/2020.

Chapter 15

1. Finshot, "The Asian Paint's story", (Jan 2021), Accessed on 24th August 2021, from, https://finshots.in
2. Robert Palmatier, Louis W. Stern, and Adel I. El-Ansary, *Marketing Channel Strategy,* 8th ed. (New York, NY: Routledge, 2017).
3. Andreas Fürst, Martin Leimbach, and Jana-Kristin Prigge, "Organizational Multichannel Differentiation: An Analysis of Its Impact on Channel Relationships and Company Sales Success," *Journal of Marketing* 81, no. 1 (2017), pp. 59–82.
4. Sarah E. Needleman, "Dial-a-Mattress Retailer Blames Troubles on Stores, Executive Team," *Wall Street Journal,* July 14, 2009, p. B1.
5. For an academic treatment of related issues, see Elie Ofek, Zsolt Katona, and Miklos Sarvary, "'Bricks and Clicks': The Impact of Product Returns on the Strategies of Multichannel Retailers," *Marketing Science* 30 (January–February 2011), pp. 42–60.
6. V. Kumar and Rajkumar Venkatesan, "Who Are Multichannel Shoppers and How Do They Perform? Correlates of Multichannel Shopping Behavior," *Journal of Interactive Marketing* 19 (Spring 2005), pp. 44–61.
7. Tarun Kushwaha and Venkatesh Shankar, "Are Multichannel Customers Really More Valuable? The Moderating Role of Product Category Characteristics," *Journal of Marketing* 77 (July 2013), pp. 67–85.
8. Rajkumar Venkatesan, V. Kumar, and Nalini Ravishanker, "Multichannel Shopping: Causes and Consequences," *Journal of Marketing* 71 (April 2007), pp. 114–32.
9. For a detailed conceptual model, see Jill Avery, Thomas J. Steenburgh, John Deighton, and Mary Caravella, "Adding Bricks to Clicks: Predicting the Patterns of Cross-Channel Elasticities over Time," *Journal of Marketing* 76 (May 2012), pp. 96–111.
10. Peter C. Verhoef, Scott A. Neslin, and Björn Vroomen, "Multichannel Customer Management: Understanding the Research-Shopper Phenomenon," *International Journal of Research in Marketing* 24, no. 2 (2007), pp. 129–48.
11. Xubing Zhang, "Retailer's Multichannel and Price Advertising Strategies," *Marketing Science* 28 (November–December 2009), pp. 1080–94; Kitty Wang and Avi Goldfarb, "Can Offline Stores Drive Online Sales?" *Journal of Marketing Research* 54, no. 5 (2017), pp. 706–719; Dmitri Kuksov and Chenxi Liao, "When Showrooming Increases Retailer Profit," *Journal of Marketing Research* 55, no. 4 (2018), pp. 459–473; Dhruv Grewal, Carl-Philip Ahlbom, Lauren Beitelspacher, Stephanie M. Noble, and Jens Nordfält. "In-Store Mobile Phone Use and Customer Shopping Behavior: Evidence from the Field," *Journal of Marketing* 82, no. 4 (2018), pp. 102–26.
12. ET Auto, "Mercedes-Benz presents 'Retail of the Future' model in India for direct sales", Economic Times, (22nd October 2021), Accessed on 26th Oct 2021 from, https://auto.economictimes.indiatimes.com
13. Hugo Martin, "Outdoor Retailer Patagonia Puts Environment Ahead of Sales Growth," *Los Angeles Times,* May 24, 2012.
14. Mary Wagner, "IRCE 2011 Report: Learn It on the Web, Use It Cross-Channel," www.internetretailer.com, June 20, 2011; Monte Burke, "A Conversation with REI Chief Executive, Sally Jewell," *Forbes*, May 19, 2011; https://www.rei.com/about-rei, accessed 11/26/2020.
15. Asim Ansari, Carl F. Mela, and Scott A. Neslin, "Customer Channel Migration," *Journal of Marketing Research* 45 (February 2008), pp. 60–76; Edward J. Fox, Alan L. Montgomery, and Leonard M. Lodish, "Consumer Shopping and Spending across Retail Formats," *Journal of Business* 77 (April 2004), pp. S25–S60.
16. Sara Valentini, Elisa Montaguti, and Scott A. Neslin, "Decision Process Evolution in Customer Channel Choice," *Journal of Marketing* 75 (November 2011), pp. 72–86.
17. Katrijn Gielens and Marnik G. Dekimpe, "The Entry Strategy of Retail Firms into Transition Economies," *Journal of Marketing* 71 (April 2007), pp. 196–212.
18. www.thebalancesmb.com/apple-retail-stores-global-locations-2892925, accessed 3/3/2021.
19. David Segal, "Apple's Retail Army, Long on Loyalty but Short on Pay," *New York Times*, June 23, 2012; Gardiner Morse and Ron Johnson, "Retail Isn't Broken. Stores Are," *Harvard Business Review* (December 2011), pp. 78–82; www.macrumors.com/roundup/apple-retail-stores; accessed 12/18/18.
20. Joydeep Srivastava and Dipankar Chakravarti, "Channel Negotiations with Information Asymmetries: Contingent Influences of Communication and Trustworthiness Reputations," *Journal of Marketing Research* 46 (August 2009), pp. 557–72.
21. "Why STIHL Chooses Independent Dealers," www.stihlusa.com, accessed November 2, 2013; Ken

Waldron, "How Stihl Fulfilled Brand Promise of Superior Product, Customer Service," *Advertising Age*, December 10, 2009; Timothy Appel, "Too Good for Lowe's and Home Depot?" *Wall Street Journal*, July 24, 2006.

22. Vivian Giang, "McDonald's Hamburger University: Step inside the Most Exclusive School in the World," *Business Insider*, April 12, 2012.

23. www.greatharvest.com/company/franchise-business-philosophy, accessed 2/9/2021.

24. Raji Srinivasan, "Dual Distribution and Intangible Firm Value: Franchising in Restaurant Chains," *Journal of Marketing* 70 (July 2006), pp. 120–35.

25. Anne Coughlan and Louis Stern, "Marketing Channel Design and Management," in Dawn Iacobucci, ed., *Kellogg on Marketing* (New York: John Wiley & Sons, 2001), pp. 247–69; Michaela Draganska, Daniel Klapper, and Sofia B. Villa-Boas, "A Larger Slice or a Larger Pie? An Empirical Investigation of Bargaining Power in the Distribution Channel," *Marketing Science* 29 (January–February 2010), pp. 57–74.

26. These bases of power were identified in John R. P. French and Bertram Raven, "The Bases of Social Power," in Dorwin Cartwright, ed., *Studies in Social Power* (Ann Arbor: University of Michigan Press, 1959), pp. 150–67.

27. V. Kasturi Rangan, *Transforming Your Go-to-Market Strategy: The Three Disciplines of Channel Management* (Boston: Harvard Business School Press, 2006).

28. Stefan Wuyts, Stefan Stremersch, Christophe Van Den Bulte, and Philip Hans Franses, "Vertical Marketing Systems for Complex Products: A Triadic Perspective," *Journal of Marketing Research* 41 (November 2004), pp. 479–87.

29. Arnt Bovik and George John, "When Does Vertical Coordination Improve Industrial Purchasing Relationships?" *Journal of Marketing* 64 (October 2000), pp. 52–64; Elizabeth Aguirre, Dominik Mahr, Ko de Ruyter, Dhruv Grewal, Jan Pelser, and Martin Wetzels, "The Effect of Review Writing on Learning Engagement in Channel Partner Relationship Management," *Journal of Marketing* 82, no. 2 (2018), pp. 64–84.

30. www.citizensbank.com, accessed 2/9/2021.

31. Cotton Timberlake, "In the iPhone Era, Leica Tries Its Own Stores," *Bloomberg Businessweek*, June 18, 2012.

32. For a detailed case study example, see Jennifer Shang, Tuba Pinar Yildrim, Pandu Tadikamalla, Vikas Mittal, and Lawrence Brown, "Distribution Network Redesign for Marketing Competitiveness," *Journal of Marketing* 73 (March 2009), pp. 146–63.

33. Xinlei Chen, George John, and Om Narasimhan, "Assessing the Consequences of a Channel Switch," *Marketing Science* 27 (May–June 2008), pp. 398–416.

34. Edward Moltzen, "Apple Grows, But So Does Channel Conflict," *CRN*, July 27, 2007; Steven Burke, "Apple Partners Speak Out on Channel Conflict," *CRN*, October 12, 2015.

35. Moeen Naseer Butt, Kersi D. Antia, Brian R. Murtha, and Vishal Kashyap, "Clustering, Knowledge Sharing, and Intrabrand Competition: A Multiyear Analysis of an Evolving Franchise System," *Journal of Marketing* 82, no. 1 (2018), pp. 74–92.

36. For a more thorough academic examination that shows the benefits to suppliers from Walmart expanding its market, see Qingyi Huang, Vincent R. Nijs, Karsten Hansen, and Eric T. Anderson, "Wal-Mart's Impact on Supplier Profits," *Journal of Marketing Research* 49 (April 2012), pp. 131–43.

37. Tony Haitao Cui and Paola Mallucci, "Fairness Ideals in Distribution Channels," *Journal of Marketing Research* 53, no. 6 (2016), pp. 969–87.

38. For some examples of when conflict can be viewed as helpful, see Anil Arya and Brian Mittendorf, "Benefits of Channel Discord in the Sale of Durable Goods," *Marketing Science* 25 (January–February 2006), pp. 91–96.

39. Danny T. Wang, Flora F. Gu, and Maggie Chuoyan Dong, "Observer Effects of Punishment in a Distribution Network," *Journal of Marketing Research* 50 (October 2013), pp. 627–43; Sara Van der Maelen, Els Breugelmans, and Kathleen Cleeren, "The Clash of the Titans: On Retailer and Manufacturer Vulnerability in Conflict Delistings," *Journal of Marketing* 81, no. 1 (2017), pp. 118–35.

40. This section draws on Robert Palmatier, Louis W. Stern, and Adel I. El-Ansary, *Marketing Channel Strategy,* 8th ed. (New York, NY: Routledge, 2017). See also Jonathan D. Hibbard, Nirmalya Kumar, and Louis W. Stern, "Examining the Impact of Destructive Acts in Marketing Channel Relationships," *Journal of Marketing Research* 38 (February 2001), pp. 45–61; Alberto Sa Vinhas and Erin Anderson, "How Potential Conflict Drives Channel Structure: Concurrent (Direct and Indirect) Channels," *Journal of Marketing Research* 42 (November 2005), pp. 507–15.

41. Niraj Dawar and Jason Stornelli, "Rebuilding the Relationship between Manufacturers and Retailers," *MIT Sloan Management Review* (Winter 2013), pp. 83–90.

42. Nirmalya Kumar, "Living with Channel Conflict," *CMO Magazine* (October 2004).

43. Kersi D. Antia, Xu (Vivian) Zheng, and Gary L. Frazier, "Conflict Management and Outcomes in Franchise Relationships: The Role of Regulation," *Journal of Marketing Research* 50 (October 2013), pp. 577–89. Kersi D. Antia, Sudha Mani, and Kenneth H. Wathne, "Franchisor–Franchisee Bankruptcy and the Efficacy of Franchisee Governance," *Journal of Marketing Research* 54, no. 6 (2017), pp. 952–67.

44. Andrew Kaplan, "All Together Now?" *Beverage World* (March 2007), pp. 14–16.

45. Debra Hoffman, "Gartner Supply Chain Top 25," www.gartner.com, May 30, 2013.

46. "The Total Package," *Bloomberg Businessweek*, Special Advertising Section, November 28, 2011; Geoff Colvin, "The Trade Tracker," *Fortune*, November 7, 2011; Helen Coster, "Calculus for Truckers," *Forbes*, September 12, 2011; "All the Right Moves," *Fortune*, Special Advertising Section, May 2, 2011.

47. Marketing Insight sources: "Showrooming Threat Hits Major Chains," www.warc.com, March 1, 2013; "'Showrooming' Grows in U.S.," www.warc.com, February 4, 2013; Miriam Gottfried, "How to Fight Amazon.com, Best Buy–Style," *Wall Street Journal*, November 20, 2016; Ruth Bolton, "Can E-Commerce Save Retail?," *Entrepreneur*, October 19, 2020.

48. Marketing Spotlight sources: Kasra Ferdows, Michael A. Lewis, and Jose Machuca, "Rapid-fire Fulfillment," *Harvard Business Review* 82, no. 11 (2004), pp. 104–17; Thompson, Derek, "Zara's Big Idea: What the World's Top Fashion Retailer Tells Us about Innovation," *The Atlantic*, November 13, 2012; Martin Roll, "The Secret of Zara's Success: A Culture of Customer Co-creation," MartinRoll.com, August 11, 2018; Stephen Wilmot, "Zara's Blues: What's Keeping World's Most Valuable Fashion Retailer Down," *Wall Street Journal* (March 12, 2018); Rodrigo Orihuela, "Zara Owner's Lean Business Model Helps It Cope With Pandemic," *Bloomberg*, September 16, 2020; www.zara.com, accessed 11/26/2020.

49. G. Shainesh (2018) 'Interview with Titan and Tanishq Managers', EDX Courses,), Accessed on 25th Oct 2021, from https://www.edx.org

50. Dreaming Reality, "Channel Management the case of Titan watches", Academia (2021), Accessed on 25th Oct 2021, from https://www.academia.edu

51. Ajita Shashidhar, "The New Titan", Business Today (16th May 2021), Accessed on 22nd October 2021, from, https://www.businesstoday.in

52. Samar Srivastava, "Titan Looking Beyond Tanishq To Fast-Track Growth", Forbes (23rd June 2014), Accessed on 22nd Oct 2021, from, https://www.forbesindia.co

Chapter 16

1. Chad Bray and Vanessa Friedman, "Yoox to Merge with Net-a-Porter in All-Share Deal" *New York Times*, March 31, 2015; Lucy Yeomans, "The Net Set: Meet the Team Who Persuade You to Spend £500 Every Time You Log on to Net-A-Porter," *Evening Standard*, February 13, 2013; Lucy England, "The Spectacular Life of Net-a-Porter Founder Natalie Massenet," *Business Insider*, September 3, 2015; www.net-a-porter.com/en-us/content/about-us, accessed 11/26/2020.

2. https://www.wholefoodsmarket.com/company-info, accessed 11/26/2020.

3. Ann Zimmerman and Kris Hudson, "Chasing Upscale Customers Tarnishes Mass-Market Jeweler," *Wall Street Journal*, June 26, 2006.

4. Robert P. Rooderkerk, Harald J. van Heerde, and Tammo H. A. Bijmolt, "Optimizing Retail Assortment," *Marketing Science* 32 (September–October 2013), pp. 699–715; Xiaoyan Deng, Barbara E. Kahn, H. Rao Unnava, and Hyojin Lee, "A 'Wide' Variety: Effects of Horizontal versus Vertical Display on Assortment Processing, Perceived Variety, and Choice," *Journal of Marketing Research* 53, no. 5 (2016), pp. 682–98.

5. Richard A. Briesch, William R. Dillon, and Edward J. Fox, "Category Positioning and Store Choice: The Role of Destination Categories," *Marketing Science* 32 (May–June 2013), pp. 488–509.

6. George Anderson, "Why Are Trader Joe's Customers the Most Satisfied In America?" *Forbes,* July 30, 2013; Beth Kowitt, "Inside the Secret World of Trader Joe's," *Fortune*, August 23, 2010; Christopher Palmeri, "Trader Joe's Recipe for Success," *Bloomberg BusinessWeek*, February 21, 2008; www.traderjoes.com/our-story, accessed 11/26/2020.

7. Robert Klara, "Something in the Air," *Adweek*, March 5, 2012, pp. 25–27.

8. Jean Wee, Amitava Chattopadhyay, "Fabindia: Branding India's Artisanal Craft for Mass Retail", Insead case study, (2015), Accessed on 1st Sept 2021, from, https://amitavac.com

9. Amrita Bose, "A fab experience", The Hindu, (22nd Sepr 2018), Accessed on 27th Oct 2021, from, https://www.thehindu.com

10. Varun Jain, " Fabindia bets big on Experience stores; witnesses better sales from the format", ET Retail, (2019), Accessed on 1st Sept 2021, from, https://retail.economictimes.indiatimes.comq

11. Velitchka D. Kaltcheva and Barton Weitz, "When Should a Retailer Create an Exciting Store Environment?" *Journal of Marketing* 70 (January 2006), pp. 107–18; Jennifer J. Argo and Darren W. Dahl, "Standards of Beauty: The Impact

of Mannequins in the Retail Context," *Journal of Consumer Research* 44, no. 5 (2018), pp. 974–90.

12. Dave Hodges, "Fans Welcome Bass Pro Shops to Town," Tallahassee.com, September 5, 2013; Seth Lubove, "Bass Pro Billionaire Building Megastore with Boats, Guns," *Bloomberg Businessweek,* June 3, 2013; Brian Hauswirth, "Missouri-Based Bass Pro and Cabela's Officially Join Forces," Missourinet, September 25, 2017; https://about.basspro.com, accessed 11/26/2020.

13. Venkatesh Shankar and Ruth N. Bolton, "An Empirical Analysis of Determinants of Retailer Pricing Strategy," *Marketing Science* 23 (Winter 2004), pp. 28–49.

14. Karsten Hansen and Vishal Singh, "Market Structure across Retail Formats," *Marketing Science* 28 (July–August 2009), pp. 656–73.

15. Samuel Hine, "High Times at the House of Bijan," *GQ*, August 27, 2018.

16. www.lumberliquidators.com, accessed 11/26/2020.

17. Paul W. Miniard, Shazad Mustapha Mohammed, Michael J. Barone, and Cecilia M. O. Alvarez, "Retailers' Use of Partially Comparative Pricing: From Across-Category to Within-Category Effects," *Journal of Marketing* 77 (July 2013), pp. 33–48; Jiwoong Shin, "The Role of Selling Costs in Signaling Price Image," *Journal of Marketing Research* 42 (August 2005), pp. 305–12.

18. For a comprehensive framework of the key image drivers of price image formation for retailers, see Ryan Hamilton and Alexander Chernev, "Low Prices Are Just the Beginning: Price Image in Retail Management," *Journal of Marketing* 77 (November 2013), pp. 1–20.

19. Michael Tsiros and David M. Hardesty, "Ending a Price Promotion: Retracting It in One Step or Phasing It Out Gradually," *Journal of Marketing* 74 (January 2010), pp. 49–64; Kusum L. Ailawadi, Yu Ma, and Dhruv Grewal, "The Club Store Effect: Impact of Shopping in Warehouse Club Stores on Consumers' Packaged Food Purchases," *Journal of Marketing Research* 55, no. 2 (2018), pp. 193–207.

20. David R. Bell and James M. Lattin, "Shopping Behavior and Consumer Preference for Retail Price Format: Why 'Large Basket' Shoppers Prefer EDLP," *Marketing Science* 17 (Spring 1998), pp. 66–68.

21. Paul B. Ellickson, Sanjog Misra, and Harikesh S. Nair, "Repositioning Dynamics and Pricing Strategy," *Journal of Marketing Research* 49 (December 2012), pp. 750–72.

22. Stephanie Clifford and Catherine Rampell, "Sometimes, We Want Price to Fool Us, *New York Times,* April 13, 2013; "Why Walmart Can Pull Off 'Everyday Low Prices' but Everyone Else Keeps Failing," *Business Insider,* September 3, 2012; Alexander Chernev, "Why Everyday Low Pricing Might Not Fit J.C. Penney," www.bloomberg.com*,* May 17, 2012.

23. "How Mobile Coupons Are Driving an Explosion in Mobile Commerce," *Business Insider,* August 12, 2013.

24. Sam K. Hui, J. Jeffrey Inman, Yanliu Huang, and Jacob Suher, "The Effect of In-Store Travel Distance on Unplanned Spending: Applications to Mobile Promotion Strategies," *Journal of Marketing* 77 (March 2013), pp. 1–16.

25. Lauren Brousel, "5 Things You Need to Know about Geofencing," *CIO*, August 28, 2013; Dana Mattioli and Miguel Bustillo, "Can Texting Save Stores?" *Wall Street Journal*, May 8, 2012.

26. https://cvshealth.com/about/facts-and-company-information, accessed 3/11/2021.

27. K. C. Ifeanyi, "Burberry Makes It Rain in Taipei," *Fast Company*, April 27, 2012; Barry Silverstein, "The Future of Retail: Reinventing and Preserving the In-Store Experience," www.brandchannel.com, March 22, 2013.

28. Anthony Dukes and Yunchuan Liu, "In-Store Media and Distribution Channel Coordination," *Marketing Science* 29 (January–February 2010), pp. 94–107; Pierre Chandon, J. Wesley Hutchinson, Eric Bradlow, and Scott Young, "Does In-Store Marketing Work? Effects of the Number and Position of Shelf Facings on Brand Attention and Evaluation at the Point of Purchase," *Journal of Marketing Research* 73 (November 2009), pp. 1–17.

29. Ashley Lutz, "Why the Lingerie Industry Can't Compete with Victoria's Secret," *Business Insider,* September 2, 2013; Sapna Maheshwari, "Victoria's Secret Channels Mad Men into Hottest Limited," *Bloomberg Businessweek,* November 12, 2012; Kristina Monllos, "Why Victoria's Secret Won't Be Mailing Out Any More Catalogs," *Adweek*, May 24, 2016; https://www.lb.com/our-brands/victorias-secret, accessed 11/26/2020.

30. Sarah Frier, "Gilt Groupe CEO Seeks to Prove Flash Sales Are No Fad," *Bloomberg Businessweek,* August 1, 2013; Shelley Dubois, "What's Gilt Groupe's Secret Weapon?" *Fortune,* March 5, 2012; Claire Cain Miller, "Flash-Sale Site Shifts Its Model," *New York Times*, August 14, 2011.

31. Alexis K. J. Barlow, Noreen Q. Siddiqui, and Mike Mannion, "Development in Information and Communication Technologies for Retail Marketing Channels," *International Journal of Retail and Distribution Management* 32 (March 2004), pp. 157–63.

32. Ankita Rai, "Lifestyle stores adopt an omnichannel and tech-led strategy for growth",

Financial Express 22nd April 2019, Accessed on 5th November 2021, from, https://www.financialexpress.com

33. Mini Tejaswi, "Landmark Group eyes 40% sales via omni channels", The Hindu 20th Feb, 2020, Accessed on 5th November 2021, from, https://www.thehindu.com

34. E. J. Schultz, "Grocery Shoppers Continue to Spend Less, Embrace Private Label," *Advertising Age*, June 10, 2011.

35. Matthew Boyle, "Even Better than the Real Thing," *Bloomberg Businessweek*, November 28, 2011.

36. Lien Lamey, Barbara Deleersnyder, Jan-Benedict E. M. Steenkamp, and Marnik G. Dekimpe, "The Effect of Business-Cycle Fluctuations on Private-Label Share: What Has Marketing Conduct Got to Do with It?" *Journal of Marketing* 76 (January 2012), pp. 1–19.

37. Kusum Ailawadi and Bari Harlam, "An Empirical Analysis of the Determinants of Retail Margins: The Role of Store-Brand Share," *Journal of Marketing* 68 (January 2004), pp. 147–65.

38. Anne ter Braak, Marnik G. Dekimpe, and Inge Geyskens, "Retailer Private-Label Margins: The Role of Supplier and Quality-Tier Differentiation," *Journal of Marketing* 77 (July 2013), pp. 86–103.

39. For a detailed analysis of contemporary research on private labels, see Michael R. Hyman, Dennis A. Kopf, and Dongdae Lee, "Private Label Brands: Benefits, Success Factors, and Future Research, *Journal of Brand Management* 17 (March 2010), pp. 368–89. See also Kusum Ailawadi, Koen Pauwels, and Jan-Benedict E. M. Steenkamp, "Private Label Use and Store Loyalty," *Journal of Marketing* 72 (November 2008), pp. 19–30; Kristopher O. Keller, Marnik G. Dekimpe, and Inge Geyskens, "Let Your Banner Wave? Antecedents and Performance Implications of Retailers' Private-Label Branding Strategies," *Journal of Marketing* 80, no. 4 (2016), pp. 1–19.

40. Matthew Boyle, "Even Better Than the Real Thing," *Bloomberg Businessweek*, November 28, 2011.

41. Grant Surridge, "Brands of the Year: Rediscovering the Loblaw Story," *Strategy*, September 28, 2012; Jim Chrizan, "Loblaws Reverses Private Label Trend," *Packaging World*, January 22, 2010; "Loblaw Launches a New Line of Discount Store Brands," *Store Brand Decisions*, February 16, 2010; www.loblaw.ca/en/about-us.html, accessed 11/26/2020.

42. Jan-Benedict E. M. Steenkamp and Nirmalya Kumar, "Don't Be Undersold," *Harvard Business Review* (December 2009), p. 91; Nirmalya Kumar and Jan-Benedict E. M. Steenkamp, *Private Label Strategy: How to Meet the Store-Brand Challenge* (Boston: Harvard Business School Press, 2007).

43. www.amerisourcebergen.com/abcnew/about-our-history, accessed 11/26/2020.

44. www.arrow.com/en/about-arrow/overview and http://fortune.com/fortune500/arrow-electronics/ accessed 11/26/2020.

45. Marketing Insight sources: Alexander Chernev, *Strategic Marketing Management: Theory and Practice* (Chicago, IL: Cerebellum Press, 2019); Alexander Chernev and Ryan Hamilton, "Price Image in Retail Management," Katrijn Gielens and Els Gijsbrechts, eds., *Handbook of Research on Retailing* (Northampton: Edward-Elgar Publishing, 2018), pp.132–52; Ryan Hamilton and Alexander Chernev, "Low Prices Are Just the Beginning: Price Image in Retail Management," *Journal of Marketing* 77, no. 6 (2013), pp. 1–20.

46. Marketing Spotlight sources: David Aaker, "6 Reasons Why Uniqlo Is Winning," *Prophet* (June 19, 2018); Jeff Chu, "Cheap, Chic, and Made for All: How Uniqlo Plans to Take Over Casual Fashion," *Fast Company*, June 18, 2012; Stuart Emmrich, "What's Smoother Than a Federer Backhand? His $300 Million Uniqlo Deal," *New York Times,* September 8, 2018; Martin Roll, "Uniqlo—The Strategy behind the Japanese Fast Fashion Retail Brand," MartinRoll.com, August 9, 2018; Jack Houston, "Sneaky Ways Stores Like H&M, Zara, and Uniqlo Get You to Spend More Money on Clothes," *Business Insider*, January 15, 2019; www.uniqlo.com, accessed 11/26/2020.

47. Croma, "Croma-About-us", (2021), Accessed on 2nd September 2021, from, https://www.croma.com

48. Nandana James, "Croma sees big growth for its private brands in three years", The Hindustan Business line, (Oct 2018), Accessed on 2nd September 2021, from, https://www.thehindubusinessline.com

49. Sangeeta Tanwar, "Retail chain Croma getting back on track on refreshed omnichannel strategy", Business standard, (May 2018), Accessed on 2nd Sept 2021, from, https://www.business-standard.com

Chapter 17

1. FT Bureau (2003) 'Maruti Ropes In SBI Arms For Car Finance' Financial Express, June 29,https://www.financialexpress.com Accessed on 2nd Nov 2021.

2. G Balachandar (2018), 'Maruti tops J D Power customer service study for 17th consecutive year' The Hindu BusinessLine, January 16, Accessed on 2nd Nov 2021, from https://www.thehindubusinessline.com

3. Rajeev Dubey, "Behind the Maruti success story", Business Today 20th Dec 2017, Accessed on 2nd Nov 2021, from, https://www.businesstoday.in
4. Mayank Dhingra, "Suzuki reveals its 5-year plan", Auto car India 27th Feb 2021, Accessed on 2nd Nov 2021, from, https://www.autocarindia.com
5. Igor Ansoff, *Strategic Management* (New York, NY: *John Wiley & Sons*, 1979).
6. Diane Mermigas, "ESPN Could Be Digital Sports Nirvana," www.mediapost.com, January 14, 2011; www.worldofespn.com, accessed 11/26/2020.
7. "Merck: Acquisitions & Divestments," www.merckgroup.com, October 23, 2010; www.crunchbase.com/organization/merck-co-inc/acquisitions/acquisitions_list#section-acquisitions, 11/26/2020.
8. Peter Svensson, "Sprint's Nextel to Be Shut Off as Early as June 2013," *Huffington Post*, May 29, 2012.
9. Alok R. Saboo, Amalesh Sharma, Anindita Chakravarty, and V. Kumar, "Influencing Acquisition Performance in High-Technology Industries: The Role of Innovation and Relational Overlap," *Journal of Marketing Research* 54, no. 2 (2017), pp. 219–238.
10. Theodore Levitt, "Innovative Imitation," *Harvard Business Review* (September–October 1966), p. 63. Also see Steven P. Schnaars, *Managing Imitation Strategies: How Later Entrants Seize Markets from Pioneers* (New York: Free Press, 1994).
11. Amir Efrati, "Clone Wars Roil App World," *Wall Street Journal,* March 4, 2013; Ben Rooney, "Rise of a Cloner Draws VC Fans and Critics," *Wall Street Journal,* May 17, 2012; Brian Caulfield, "The Predator," *Forbes*, March 12, 2012.
12. www.ralstonfoodservice.com/ralstonbrands.html, accessed 3/11/2021.
13. Claire Ruckin, "RLPC-Distressed Debt Investors Eye Spain's Telepizza–Bankers," *Reuters,* March 8, 2013; https://www.globalconveniencestorefocus.co.uk/features/happiness-delivered-by-spains-telepizza, accessed 11/26/2020.
14. Felix Gillette, "Inside Big Pharma's Fight against the $75 Billion Counterfeit Drug Business," *Bloomberg Businessweek*, January 17, 2013.
15. "Pretty Profitable Parrots," *The Economist*, May 12, 2012.
16. Rajendra S. Sisodia, David B. Wolfe, and Jagdish N. Sheth, *Firms of Endearment: How World-Class Companies Profit from Passion & Purpose* (Upper Saddle River, NJ: Wharton School Publishing, 2007); Ashlee Humphreys and Gregory S. Carpenter. "Status Games: Market Driving through Social Influence in the U.S. Wine Industry," *Journal of Marketing* 82, no. 5 (2018), pp. 141–59; Alexander Edeling and Alexander Himme, "When Does Market Share Matter? New Empirical Generalizations from a Meta-Analysis of the Market Share–Performance Relationship," *Journal of Marketing* 82, no. 3 (2018), pp. 1–24.
17. William M. Bulkeley, "Xerox Tries to Go beyond Copiers," *Wall Street Journal*, February 24, 2009, p. B5; Ellen McGirt, "Fresh Copy," *Fast Company* (December 2011–January 2012), pp. 130–38; Christa Carone "Xerox's Brand Repositioning Challenge," *Advertising Age,* March 12, 2013; www.xerox.com/en-us/about, accessed 11/26/2020.
18. Priya Raghubir and Eric A. Greenleaf, "Ratios in Proportion: What Should the Shape of the Package Be?" *Journal of Marketing* 70 (April 2006), pp. 95–107; Valerie Folkes and Shashi Matta, "The Effect of Package Shape on Consumers' Judgments of Product Volume: Attention as a Mental Contaminant," *Journal of Consumer Research* 31 (September 2004), pp. 390–401.
19. Sarah Nassaur, "The Psychology of Small Packages," *Wall Street Journal*, April 15, 2013.
20. Samarpita Banerjee (2020), 'Why Cadbury Dairy Milk's ongoing campaigns on the theme of generosity became even more important in 2020', BusinessInsider, December 24, Accessed on November 15, 2021, from https://www.businessinsider.inadvertising
21. John D. Cripps, "Heuristics and Biases in Timing the Replacement of Durable Products," *Journal of Consumer Research* 21 (September 1994), pp. 304–18.
22. "Creative New Monroe Marketing Campaign Reminds Consumers to Replace Worn Shocks and Struts," www.monroe.com, March 18, 2013.
23. Gregory S. Carpenter and Kent Nakamoto, "Consumer Preference Formation and Pioneering Advantage," *Journal of Marketing Research* 26 (August 1989), pp. 285–98.
24. William T. Robinson and Sungwook Min, "Is the First to Market the First to Fail? Empirical Evidence for Industrial Goods Businesses," *Journal of Marketing Research* 39 (February 2002), pp. 120–28.
25. Kurt A. Carlson, Margaret G. Meloy, and J. Edward Russo, "Leader-Driven Primacy: Using Attribute Order to Affect Consumer Choice," *Journal of Consumer Research* 32 (March 2006), pp. 513–18.
26. Gerald Tellis and Peter Golder, *Will and Vision: How Latecomers Can Grow to Dominate Markets*

(New York: McGraw-Hill, 2001); Rajesh K. Chandy and Gerald J. Tellis, "The Incumbent's Curse? Incumbency, Size, and Radical Product Innovation," *Journal of Marketing Research* 64 (July 2000), pp. 1–17. See also Dave Ulrich and Norm Smallwood, "Building a Leadership Brand," *Harvard Business Review* (July–August 2007), pp. 93–100; V. Kumar and Anita Pansari, "Competitive Advantage through Engagement," *Journal of Marketing Research* 53, no. 4 (2016), pp. 497–514.

27. Sungwook Min, Manohar U. Kalwani, and William T. Robinson, "Market Pioneer and Early Follower Survival Risks: A Contingency Analysis of Really New versus Incrementally New Product-Markets," *Journal of Marketing* 70 (January 2006), pp. 15–35. See also Raji Srinivasan, Gary L. Lilien, and Arvind Rangaswamy, "First In, First Out? The Effects of Network Externalities on Pioneer Survival," *Journal of Marketing* 68 (January 2004), pp. 41–58.

28. Tim Higgins, "GM's First Mover Disadvantage," *Bloomberg Businessweek*, October 1, 2012.

29. Venkatesh Shankar, Gregory S. Carpenter, and Lakshman Krishnamurthi, "Late Mover Advantage: How Innovative Late Entrants Outsell Pioneers," *Journal of Marketing Research* 35 (February 1998), pp. 54–70; Elena Reutskaja and Barbara Fasolo, "It's Not Necessarily Best to Be First," *Harvard Business Review* (January–February 2013), pp. 28–29.

30. Peter N. Golder, "Historical Method in Marketing Research with New Evidence on Long-term Market Share Stability," *Journal of Marketing Research* 37 (May 2000), pp. 156–72; Peter N. Golder and Gerald J. Tellis, "Pioneer Advantage: Marketing Logic or Marketing Legend?" *Journal of Marketing Research* 30 (May 1993), pp. 34–46.

31. Peter N. Golder, Julie R. Irwin, and Debanjan Mitra, "Long-term Market Leadership Persistence: Baselines, Economic Conditions, and Category Types," MSI Report 13-110, Marketing Science Institute (2013).

32. Frank Shyong, "Sriracha Hot Sauce Purveyor Turns Up the Heat," *Los Angeles Times*, April 12, 2103; Caleb Hannan, "Burning Sensation," *Bloomberg Businessweek*, February 21, 2013, pp. 66–69.

33. Karsten Strauss, "Sound Judgment," *Forbes*, April 15, 2013, pp. 68–69.

34. Robert Klara, "Burning for You," *Adweek*, May 21, 2012; James R. Hagerty, "Zippo Preps for a Post-Smoker World," *Wall Street Journal*, March 8, 2011; Michael Learmonth, "Zippo Reignites Brand with Social Media, New Products," *Advertising Age*, August 10, 2009, p. 12; Thomas A. Fogarty, "Keeping Zippo's Flame Eternal," *USA Today,* June 24, 2003; www.zippo.com/pages/about-us, accessed 11/26/2020.

35. ET Bureau, " SBIMF launches Micro SIP", *Economic Times (15th April 2009)*, Accessed on 8th November 2021 from, https://economictimes.indiatimes.com

36. The Mint (2021), 'SBI MF becomes first mutual fund house to cross ₹5 lakh crore AUM mark' *HT Mint, April 8*, https://www.livemint.com (Accessed on December 25, 2021)

37. "Daimler Takes Balanced Approach," www.warc.com, November 28, 2012.

38. Nirmalya Kumar, Lisa Sheer, and Philip Kotler, "From Market Driven to Market Driving," *European Management Journal* 18 (April 2000), pp. 129–42; Sudhir Voleti, Manish Gangwar, and Praveen K. Kopalle. "Why the Dynamics of Competition Matter for Category Profitability," *Journal of Marketing* 81, no. 1 (2017), pp. 1–16.

39. Much of the remaining section on proactive marketing is based on an insightful book by Leonardo Araujo and Rogerio Gava, *The Proactive Enterprise: How to Anticipate Market Changes* (Hampshire, UK: Palgrave Macmillan, 2012). See also Eelco Kappe, Sriram Venkataraman, and Stefan Stremersch, "Predicting the Consequences of Marketing Policy Changes: A New Data Enrichment Method with Competitive Reactions," *Journal of Marketing Research* 54, no. 5 (2017), pp. 720–36.

40. Jonathan Glancey, "The Private World of the Walkman," *Guardian,* October 11, 1999.

41. For some contemporary perspectives on defense strategies, see Timothy Calkins, *Defending Your Brand: How Smart Companies Use Defense Strategy to Deal with Competitive Attacks* (New York: Palgrave Macmillan, 2012).

42. These six defense strategies, as well as the five attack strategies, are taken from some classic work by Philip Kotler and Ravi Singh, "Marketing Warfare in the 1980s," *Journal of Business Strategy* (Winter 1981), pp. 30–41.

43. Jaideep Prabhu and David W. Stewart, "Signaling Strategies in Competitive Interaction: Building Reputations and Hiding the Truth," *Journal of Marketing Research* 38 (February 2001), pp. 62–72.

44. Yuhong Wu, Sridhar Balasubramanian, and Vijay Mahajan, "When Is a Preannounced New Product Likely to Be Delayed?" *Journal of Marketing* 68 (April 2004), pp. 101–13; Barry L. Bayus, Sanjay Jain, and Ambar G. Rao, "Truth or Consequences: An Analysis of Vaporware and New-Product Announcements," *Journal of Marketing Research* 38 (February 2001), pp. 3–13.

45. Marshall Eckblad, "Sara Lee No More: A Hillshire Is Born," *Wall Street Journal*, June 6, 2012; Emily Bryson York, "Sara Lee to

Split into Two Businesses," *Los Angeles Times*, January 28, 2011.

46. E.J. Schultz, "Kraft's New Grocery Company Plans Marketing Boost in Search of 'Renaissance,'" *Advertising Age,* September 7, 2012; Paul Ziobro, "Kraft Defends Split," *Wall Street Journal*, September 8, 2011; www.kraftheinzcompany.com/company.html, accessed 11/26/2020.
47. Theodore Levitt, "Exploit the Product Life Cycle," *Harvard Business Review* 43 (November–December 1965).
48. Rajesh J. Chandy, Gerard J. Tellis, Deborah J. MacInnis, and Pattana Thaivanich, "What to Say When: Advertising Appeals in Evolving Markets," *Journal of Marketing Research* 38 (November 2001), pp. 399–414.
49. Dennis K. Berman, "Zipcar: Entrepreneurial Genius, Public-Company Failure," *Wall Street Journal,* January 2, 2013; Mark Clothier, "Can Hertz Outrun Zipcar in Hourly Car Rentals?" *Bloomberg Businessweek,* March 29, 2012; Paul Keegan, "The Best New Idea in Business," *Fortune*, September 14, 2009, pp. 42–52; www.zipcar.com/about, accessed 11/26/2020.
50. Rita Gunther McGrath, "Transient Advantage," *Harvard Business Review* (June 2013), pp. 62–70.
51. Simon Zekaria, "Electrolux Moves to Add Sizzle to Its Brand," *Wall Street Journal*, September 30, 2012; Ola Kinnander and Kim McLaughlin, "Electrolux Wants to Rule the Appliance World," *Bloomberg Businessweek*, March 28, 2011; Trond Riiber Knudsen, "Escaping the Middle-Market Trap: An Interview with CEO of Electrolux," *McKinsey Quarterly* (December 2006), pp. 72–79; www.electroluxappliances.com/About-Electrolux/About-US/, accessed 11/26/2020.
52. Jorge Cauz, "Encyclopædia Britannica's President on Killing Off a 244-Year-Old Product," *Harvard Business Review* (March 2013), pp. 39–42.
53. Laurence P. Feldman and Albert L. Page, "Harvesting: The Misunderstood Market Exit Strategy," *Journal of Business Strategy* (Spring 1985), pp. 79–85; Philip Kotler, "Harvesting Strategies for Weak Products," *Business Horizons* (August 1978), pp. 15–22.
54. Stuart Elliott, "Those Shelved Brands Start to Look Tempting," *New York Times*, August 21, 2008.
55. Rajan Varadarajan, Mark P. DeFanti, and Paul S. Busch, "Brand Portfolio, Corporate Image, and Reputation: Managing Brand Deletions," *Journal of the Academy of Marketing Science* 34 (Spring 2006), pp. 195–205; Nirmalya Kumar, "Kill a Brand, Keep a Customer," *Harvard Business Review* (December 2003), pp. 86–95.
56. Youngme Moon, "Break Free from the Product Life Cycle," *Harvard Business Review* (May 2005), pp. 87–94.
57. John E. Swan and David R. Rink, "Fitting Market Strategy to Varying Product Life Cycles," *Business Horizons* (January–February 1982), pp. 72–76; Gerald J. Tellis and C. Merle Crawford, "An Evolutionary Approach to Product Growth Theory," *Journal of Marketing* 45 (Fall 1981), pp. 125–34.
58. Theodore Levitt, "Exploit the Product Life Cycle," *Harvard Business Review* (November–December 1965), pp. 81–94.
59. Katy McLaunghlin, "Macaroni Grill's Order: Cut Calories, Keep Customers," *Wall Street Journal*, September 16, 2009, p. B6.
60. Hubert Gatignon and David Soberman, "Competitive Response and Market Evolution," in Barton A. Weitz and Robin Wensley, eds., *Handbook of Marketing* (London, UK: Sage Publications, 2002), pp. 126–47; Robert D. Buzzell, "Market Functions and Market Evolution," *Journal of Marketing* 63 (Special Issue 1999), pp. 61–63.
61. Marketing Insight sources: Venkatesh Shankar, Gregory Carpenter, and Lakshman Krishnamurthi, "Late-Mover Advantage: How Innovative Late Entrants Outsell Pioneers," *Journal of Marketing Research* 35 (February 1998), pp. 54–70; Gregory S. Carpenter and Kent Nakamoto, "The Impact of Consumer Preference Formation on Marketing Objectives and Competitive Second-Mover Strategies," *Journal of Consumer Psychology* 5 (1996), pp. 325–58.
62. G. Shainesh, (2018), " CRM Interview With Siddarth Gupta, CEO - Treebo', MOOCs on CRM, edX, Accessed on 2nd Nov 2021, from https://www.edx.org
63. ETtech (2021),'Treebo raises $16 million Series D funding from Accor and others' Economic Times, June 30, Accessed on 2nd Nov 2021, from https://economictimes.indiatimes.com
64. Anumeha Chaturvedi (2019) 'Treebo launches unbundled offering 'Hotel Superhero', 100 properties sign up in pre-launch phase' Economic Times, August 15, Accessed on 2nd Nov 2021, from https:// f.indiatimes.com
65. Sindhu Kashyap, "How Treebo Hotels is gunning for profitability by 2021 with steps to reduce cash burn", Yourstory (18th November 2019), Accessed on 11th November 2021, from, https://yourstory.com
66. Marketing Spotlight sources: American Express, "Membership Rewards Program from American Express Adds Practical Rewards for Tough Economic Times," February 19, 2009; "American Express Company," *Encyclopaedia Britannica*; Charles Duhigg, "Amex, Challenged by Chase,

Is Losing the Snob War," *New York Times*, April 14, 2017; https://about.americanexpress.com, accessed 11/26/2020.

Chapter 18

1. Krishna G. Palepu & Vishnu Srinivasan, "Tata Motors: The Tata Ace", The Harvard Business School Publication, (2007), Accessed on 6th Sept 2021, from, https://hbsp.harvard.edu
2. N. Madhavan, "Biggest Innovation: How Tata Ace has transformed both Tata Motors and commercial vehicle industry", Business Today (2014), Accessed on 6th Sept 2021, from, https://www.businesstoday.in
3. Tata Motors, "Tata Ace crosses 16 Years and 23+ lakh sales in 2021", May 21, 2021, Accessed on December 12, 2021, from https://ace.tatamotors.com
4. Malyaban Ghosh, "Tata builds small ECV, gears up for year-end launch", Live Mint (March 2021), Accessed on 6th Sept 2021, from, https://www.livemint.com
5. Robert Safian, "Terry Kelly, the 'Un-CEO' of W. L. Gore, on How to Deal with Chaos: Grow Up," *Fast Company*, October 2012; "Gary Hamel, "W. L. Gore: Lessons from a Management Revolutionary," *Wall Street Journal*, March 18, 2010; www.gore.com/about, accessed 11/26/2020.
6. Saim Kashmiri and Vijay Mahajan, "Values That Shape Marketing Decisions: Influence of Chief Executive Officers' Political Ideologies on Innovation Propensity, Shareholder Value, and Risk," *Journal of Marketing Research* 54, no. 2 (2017), pp. 260–78.
7. Eddie Yoon and Linda Deeken, "Why It Pays to Be a Category Creator," *Harvard Business Review* (March 2013), pp. 21–23.
8. Eric (Er) Fang, Jongkuk Lee, Robert Palmatier, and Shunping Han, "If It Takes a Village to Foster Innovation, Success Depends on the Neighbors: The Effects of Global and Ego Networks on New Product Launches," *Journal of Marketing Research* 53, no. 3 (2016), pp. 319–37; Tereza Dean, David A. Griffith, and Roger J. Calantone, "New Product Creativity: Understanding Contract Specificity in New Product Introductions," *Journal of Marketing* 80, no. 2 (2016), pp. 39–58.
9. Anne VanderMey, "Dell Gets in Touch with Its Inner Entrepreneur," *Fortune*, December 12, 2011.
10. John Bessant, Kathrin Moslein, and Bettina Von Stamm, "In Search of Innovation," *Wall Street Journal*, March 22, 2009; JC Spender and Bruce Strong, "Who Has Innovative Ideas? Employees," *Wall Street Journal*, June 14, 2012.
11. The section on the stage-gate approach to developing new offerings is adapted from Alexander Chernev, *Strategic Marketing Management: Theory and Practice* (Chicago, IL: Cerebellum Press, 2019).
12. Richard Barrett, "Tata Steel's Cutting Edge," *Metal Bulletin Weekly*, August 13, 2012.
13. Andrew T. Stephen, Peter Pal Zubcsek, and Jacob Goldenberg, "Lower Connectivity Is Better: The Effects of Network Structure on Redundancy of Ideas and Customer Innovativeness in Interdependent Ideation Tasks," *Journal of Marketing Research* 53, no. 2 (2016), pp. 263–29.
14. Jens Martin Skibsted and Rasmus Bech Hansen, "User-Led Innovation Can't Create Breakthroughs; Just Ask Apple and Ikea," *Fast Company*, February 15, 2011.
15. Baojun Jiang and Hongyan Shi, "Intercompetitor Licensing and Product Innovation," *Journal of Marketing Research* 55, no. 5 (2018), pp. 738–51.
16. Hidehiko Nishikawa, Martin Schreier, Christoph Fuchs, and Susumu Ogawa, "The Value of Marketing Crowdsourced New Products as Such: Evidence from Two Randomized Field Experiments," *Journal of Marketing Research* 54, no. 4 (2017), pp. 525–39; Woojung Chang and Steven A. Taylor. "The Effectiveness of Customer Participation in New Product Development: A Meta-Analysis," *Journal of Marketing* 80, no. 1 (2016), pp. 47–64; B. J. Allen, Deepa Chandrasekaran, and Suman Basuroy, "Design Crowdsourcing: The Impact on New Product Performance of Sourcing Design Solutions from the 'Crowd,'" *Journal of Marketing* 82, no. 2 (2018), pp. 106–23.
17. Bruce Horovitz, "Savvy Marketers Let Consumers Call the Shots," *USA Today*, March 24, 2011; www.baskinrobbins.com/content/baskinrobbins/en/aboutus.html, accessed 11/26/2020.
18. Barrett Sheridan, "It's Getting Crowded in Here," *Newsweek*, September 11, 2008.
19. Rupinder P. Jindal, Kumar R. Sarangee, Raj Echambadi, and Sangwon Lee. "Designed to Succeed: Dimensions of Product Design and Their Impact on Market Share," *Journal of Marketing* 80, no. 4 (2016), pp. 72–89.
20. Cindy Atoji Keene, "Shoe Tester Puts His Sole into the Job," *Boston Globe*, November 4, 2012.
21. Ashish Sood and V. Kumar, "Analyzing Client Profitability across Diffusion Segments for a Continuous Innovation," *Journal of Marketing Research* 54, no. 6 (2017), pp. 932–51.
22. Austin Carr, "Starbucks's Leap of Faith," *Fast Company*, June 2013, pp. 46–48; www.starbucks.com/about-us/company-information, accessed 11/26/2020.

23. Amalesh Sharma, Alok R. Saboo, and V. Kumar, "Investigating the Influence of Characteristics of the New Product Introduction Process on Firm Value: The Case of the Pharmaceutical Industry," *Journal of Marketing* 82, no. 5 (2018), pp. 66–85.

24. Jessica Müller-Stewens, Tobias Schlager, Gerald Häubl, and Andreas Herrmann, "Gamified Information Presentation and Consumer Adoption of Product Innovations," *Journal of Marketing* 81, no. 2 (2017), pp. 8–24; Nooshin L. Warren and Alina Sorescu, "Interpreting the Stock Returns to New Product Announcements: How the Past Shapes Investors' Expectations of the Future," *Journal of Marketing Research* 54, no. 5 (2017), pp. 799–815; Nooshin L. Warren and Alina Sorescu. "When 1 + 1 > 2: How Investors React to New Product Releases Announced Concurrently with Other Corporate News," *Journal of Marketing* 81, no. 2 (2017), pp. 64–82; Taewan Kim and Tridib Mazumdar, "Product Concept Demonstrations in Trade Shows and Firm Value," *Journal of Marketing* 80, no. 4 (2016), pp. 90–108.

25. Ted Marzilli, "Fresh Ticket Oak Campaign a Boost for StubHub Perception," *Forbes,* May 23, 2013; Mallory Russell, "Five Questions with StubHub's CMO," *Ad Age,* October 23, 2012; Dinah Eng, "StubHub: Anatomy of a Game-Changing Idea," *Fortune,* July 23, 2012; https://chainstoreage.com/ebay-completes-multi-billion-dollar-sale-stubhub, accessed 11/26/2020; www.stubhub.com/about-us, accessed 11/26/2020.

26. Marketing Insight sources: Everett M. Rogers, *Diffusion of Innovations* (New York: Free Press, 1962); Geoffrey Moore, *Crossing the Chasm: Marketing and Selling High-Tech Products to Mainstream Customers* (New York: HarperBusiness, 1991); Alexander Chernev, *Strategic Marketing Management: Theory and Practice* (Chicago, IL: Cerebellum Press, 2019).

27. Rajesh Srivastava," Paper Boat: Riding on a wave of nostalgia", Founding Fuel, (2016), Accessed on 6th Sept 2021, from, https://www.foundingfuel.com

28. Rashmi Pratap, "How Paper Boat rowed against the tide to find success ", The Hindu Business line, (Jan 2018), Accessed on 6th Sept 2021, from, https://www.thehindubusinessline.com

29. ET Brand Equity," Paper Boat: "It identified a clear need gap in Indian flavoured drinks", (2018), Accessed on 6th Sept 2021, from, https://brandequity.economictimes.indiatimes.com

30. Startuptalky, " Paper Boat Company Profile | Success Story of The Juice Company", (June 2021), Accessed on 6th Sept 2021, from, https://startuptalky.com

31. Marketing Spotlight sources: Alex Pasternack, "How WeChat Became China's App for Everything," *Fast Company*, June 29, 2017; Shannon Liao, "How WeChat Came to Rule China," *The Verge*, February 1, 2018; Thomas Graziani. "What Are WeChat Mini-Programs? A Simple Introduction," *WalktheChat*, November 14, 2017; Arjun Kharpal, "Everything You Need to Know about WeChat-China's Billion-User Messaging App," CNBC, February 3, 2019.

Chapter 19

1. Mansvini Kaushik, "How we survived: cure.fit, reimagining fitness", Forbes, (March 2021), Accessed on 7th Sept 2021, from, https://www.forbesindia.com

2. Exchange4Media, "cure.fit renamed as cult.fit", (may 2021), Accessed on 7th Sept 2021, from, https://www.exchange4media.com

3. Philip Kotler, Hermawan Kartajaya, and Iwan Setiawan, *Marketing 4.0: Moving from Traditional to Digital* (John Wiley & Sons, 2016). See also David Court, Dave Elzinga, Susan Mulder, and Ole Jørgen Vetvik, "The Consumer Decision Journey," *McKinsey Quarterly* (June 1, 2009).

4. Frederick F. Reichheld, *Loyalty Rules* (Boston: Harvard Business School Press, 2001); Frederick F. Reichheld, *The Loyalty Effect* (Boston: Harvard Business School Press, 1996). See also Sungwook Min, Xubing Zhang, Namwoon Kim, and Rajendra K. Srivastava, "Customer Acquisition and Retention Spending: An Analytical Model and Empirical Investigation in Wireless Telecommunications Markets," *Journal of Marketing Research* 53, no. 5 (2016), pp. 728–44; V. Kumar, Agata Leszkiewicz, and Angeliki Herbst, "Are You Back for Good or Still Shopping Around? Investigating Customers' Repeat Churn Behavior," *Journal of Marketing Research* 55, no. 2 (2018), pp. 208–25; Christophe Van Den Bulte, Emanuel Bayer, Bernd Skiera, and Philipp Schmitt, "How Customer Referral Programs Turn Social Capital into Economic Capital," *Journal of Marketing Research* 55, no. 1 (2018), pp. 132–46.

5. Michael Lewis, "Customer Acquisition Promotions and Customer Asset Value," *Journal of Marketing Research* 63 (May 2006), pp. 195–203; see also Romana Khan, Michael Lewis, and Vishal Singh, "Dynamic Customer Management and the Value of One-to-One Marketing," *Marketing Science* 28 (November–December 2009), pp. 1063–79.

6. Susan M. Keaveney, "Customer Switching Behavior in Service Industries: An Exploratory Study," *Journal of Marketing* 59 (April 1995), pp. 71–82.

7. Jacquelyn S. Thomas, Robert C. Blattberg, and Edward J. Fox, "Recapturing Lost Customers," *Journal of Marketing Research* 61 (February 2004), pp. 31–45.

8. Werner Reinartz and V. Kumar, "The Impact of Customer Relationship Characteristics on Profitable Lifetime Duration," *Journal of Marketing* 67 (January 2003), pp. 77–99; Werner Reinartz and V. Kumar, "The Mismanagement of Customer Loyalty," *Harvard Business Review* (July 2002), pp. 86–97.

9. Gary Hamel, "Strategy as Revolution," *Harvard Business Review*, July–August 1996, pp. 69–82; Leonard L. Berry and A. Parasuraman, *Marketing Services: Computing through Quality* (New York: Free Press, 1991), pp. 136–42.

10. Godrej Press Release "Godrej Interio boosts its digital drive to drive richer consumer experience", Godrej Press Release (24th August 2021), Accessed on 18th November 2021, from, https://www.godrej.com

11. Michael Tsiros, Vikas Mittal, and William T. Ross Jr., "The Role of Attributions in Customer Satisfaction: A Reexamination," *Journal of Consumer Research* 31 (September 2004), pp. 476–83. For a succinct review, see Richard L. Oliver, "Customer Satisfaction Research," in Rajiv Grover and Marco Vriens, eds., *Handbook of Marketing Research* (Thousand Oaks, CA: Sage Publications, 2006), pp. 569–87; for an in-depth discussion, see Richard L. Oliver, *Satisfaction: A Behavioral Perspective on the Consumer* (Armonk, NY: M. E. Sharpe, 2010).

12. Jennifer Aaker, Susan Fournier, and S. Adam Brasel, "When Good Brands Do Bad," *Journal of Consumer Research* 31 (June 2004), pp. 1–16; Pankaj Aggrawal, "The Effects of Brand Relationship Norms on Consumer Attitudes and Behavior," *Journal of Consumer Research* 31 (June 2004), pp. 87–101; Florian Stahl, Mark Heitmann, Donald R. Lehmann, and Scott A. Neslin, "The Impact of Brand Equity on Customer Acquisition, Retention, and Profit Margin," *Journal of Marketing* 76 (July 2012), pp. 44–63.

13. Vikas Mittal, William T. Ross, and Patrick M. Baldasare, "The Asymmetric Impact of Negative and Positive Attribute-Level Performance on Overall Satisfaction and Repurchase Intentions," *Journal of Marketing* 62 (January 1998), pp. 333–47.

14. James C. Ward and Amy L. Ostrom, "Complaining to the Masses: The Role of Protest Framing in Customer-Created Complaint Sites," *Journal of Consumer Research* 33 (September 2006), pp. 220–30.

15. For a thorough conceptual discussion, see Peter N. Golder, Debanjan Mitra, and Christine Moorman, "What Is Quality? An Integrative Framework of Processes and States," *Journal of Marketing* 76 (July 2012), pp. 1–23.

16. For influential, classic research, see Robert D. Buzzell and Bradley T. Gale, "Quality Is King," *The PIMS Principles: Linking Strategy to Performance* (New York: Free Press, 1987), pp. 103–34. (PIMS stands for Profit Impact of Market Strategy.)

17. Jena McGregor, "Putting Home Depot's House in Order," *Bloomberg BusinessWeek*, May 14, 2009; Katie Benner, "The Other Side of Home Improvement," *Fortune*, October 29, 2012; https://corporate.homedepot.com/about/history, accessed 11/26/2020.

18. Neil A. Morgan, Eugene W. Anderson, and Vikas Mittal, "Understanding Firms' Customer Satisfaction Information Usage," *Journal of Marketing* 69 (July 2005), pp. 131–51.

19. Timothy L. Keiningham, Lerzan Aksoy, Alexander Buoye, and Bruce Cooil, "Customer Loyalty Isn't Enough. Grow Your Share of Wallet," *Harvard Business Review*, October 2011, pp. 29–31.

20. Eugene W. Anderson and Claes Fornell, "Foundations of the American Customer Satisfaction Index," *Total Quality Management* 11 (September 2000), pp. S869–82; Eugene W. Anderson, Claes Fornell, and Sanal K. Mazvancheryl, "Customer Satisfaction and Shareholder Value," *Journal of Marketing* 68 (October 2004), pp. 172–85.

21. For a thorough and insightful review, see Vikas Mittal and Carly Frenna, "Customer Satisfaction: A Strategic Review and Guidelines for Managers," *Fast Forward Series*, (Cambridge, MA: Marketing Science Institute, 2010). See also Claes Fornell, Sunil Mithas, Forrest V. Morgeson III, and M. S. Krishnan, "Customer Satisfaction and Stock Prices: High Returns, Low Risk," *Journal of Marketing* 70 (January 2006), pp. 3–14.

22. For an empirical comparison of different methods to measure customer satisfaction, see Neil A. Morgan and Lopo Leotto Rego, "The Value of Different Customer Satisfaction and Loyalty Metrics in Predicting Business Performance," *Marketing Science* 25 (September–October 2006), pp. 426–39.

23. Adam M. Grant, "How Customers Can Rally Troops," *Harvard Business Review*, June 2011, pp. 96–103.

24. Frederick F. Reichheld, "Learning from Customer Defections," *Harvard Business Review*, March 3, 2009, pp. 56–69.

25. Dinah Eng "How Maxine Clark Built Build-A-Bear," *Fortune*, March 19, 2012.

26. Joseph C. Nunes and Xavier Drèze, "Feeling Superior: The Impact of Loyalty Program Structure on Consumers' Perception of Status," *Journal of Consumer Research* 35 (April 2009), pp. 890–905; Joseph C. Nunes and Xavier Drèze, "Your Loyalty Program Is Betraying You," *Harvard Business Review* (April 2006), pp. 124–31.

27. Lindsey Peacock, "10 Examples of Innovative Customer Loyalty Programs," *Shopify*, September 4, 2018; https://www.designerbrands.com/our-brands/designer-shoe-warehouse, accessed 11/26/2020.

28. James H. McAlexander, John W. Schouten, and Harold F. Koenig, "Building Brand Community," *Journal of Marketing* 66 (January 2002), pp. 38–54; Albert M. Muniz Jr. and Thomas C. O'Guinn, "Brand Community," *Journal of Consumer Research* 27 (March 2001), pp. 412–32; Susan Fournier and Lara Lee, "Getting Brand Communities Right," *Harvard Business Review* (April 2009), pp. 105–11.

29. Joseph Weber, "Harley Just Keeps on Cruisin'," *Bloomberg BusinessWeek*, November 6, 2006, pp. 71–72; Robert Klara, "A Whole Different Hog," *Adweek*, July 23, 2012, p. 40; www.harley-davidson.com, accessed 11/26/2020.

30. Christina Chaey, "How to Create Community," *Fast Company* (February 2012), p. 16.

31. Scott A. Thompson and Rajiv K. Sinha, "Brand Communities and New Product Adoption: The Influence and Limits of Oppositional Loyalty," *Journal of Marketing* 72 (November 2008), pp. 65–80.

32. Mavis T. Adjei, Charles H. Noble, and Stephanie M. Noble, "Enhancing Relationships with Customers through Online Brand Communities," *MIT Sloan Management Review* (Summer 2012), pp. 22–24.

33. For a comprehensive set of articles from a variety of perspectives on brand relationships, see Deborah J. MacInnis, C. Whan Park, and Joseph R. Preister, eds., *Handbook of Brand Relationships* (Armonk, NY: M. E. Sharpe, 2009).

34. Peter C. Verhoef and Katherine N. Lemon, "Customer Value Management: Optimizing the Value of the Customer's Base," *Fast Forward Series* (Cambridge, MA: Marketing Science Institute, 2011); Eva Ascarza, Peter Ebbes, Oded Netzer, and Matthew Danielson, "Beyond the Target Customer: Social Effects of Customer Relationship Management Campaigns," *Journal of Marketing Research* 54, no. 3 (2017), pp. 347–63.

35. www.dunnhumby.com/about-us, accessed 11/26/2020.

36. Tim Hume, "BA Googles Passengers: Friendlier Flights or Invasion of Privacy?" CNN, August 22, 2012; https://www.britishairways.com/en-us/information/about-ba, accessed 11/26/2020.

37. V. Kumar, Rajkumar Venkatesan, and Werner Reinartz, "Knowing What to Sell, When, and to Whom," *Harvard Business Review* (March 2006), pp. 131–37.

38. Mike Isaac, "The New Social Network That Isn't New at All," *New York Times*, March 19, 2019.

39. Rob Walker, "Amateur Hour, Web Style," *Fast Company* (October 2007), p. 87.

40. Martin Mende, Ruth N. Bolton, and Mary Jo Bitner, "Decoding Customer–Firm Relationships: How Attachment Styles Help Explain Customers' Preferences for Closeness, Repurchase Intentions, and Changes in Relationship Breadth," *Journal of Marketing Research* 50 (February 2013), pp. 125–42.

41. Carolyn Heller Baird and Gautam Parasnis, *From Social Media to Social CRM* (Somers, NY: IBM Corporation, 2011).

42. For some behavioral perspectives on recommendations and reviews, see Rebecca Walker Naylor, Cait Poynor Lamberton, and David A. Norton, "Seeing Ourselves in Others: Reviewer Ambiguity, Egocentric Anchoring, and Persuasion," *Journal of Marketing Research* 48 (May 2011), pp. 617–31.

43. Amy Farley, "Hotel Handbook," *Travel + Leisure* (June 2012), p. 168.

44. Josh Constine, "TripAdvisor Aims to Beat Yelp with Social, Revives Restaurant 'Local Picks' Facebook App," www.techcrunch.com, June 20, 2012; https://tripadvisor.mediaroom.com, accessed 11/26/2020.

45. Shrihari Sridhar and Raj Srinivasan, "Social Influence Effect in Online Product Ratings," *Journal of Marketing* 76 (September 2012), pp. 70–88; Joanna Stern, "Is It Really Five Stars? How to Spot Fake Amazon Reviews," *Wall Street Journal*, December 20, 2018.

46. Shelley Banjo, "Firms Take Online Reviews to Heart," *Wall Street Journal*, July 29, 2012.

47. Nick Wingfield, "High Scores Matter to Game Makers, Too," *Wall Street Journal*, September 20, 2007, p. B1; see also Yubo Chen, Yong Liu, and Jurui Zhang, "When Do Third-Party Product Reviews Affect Firm Value and What Can Firms Do? The Case of Media Critics and Professional Movie Reviews," *Journal of Marketing* 75 (September 2011), pp. 116–34.

48. Candice Choi, "Bloggers Serve Up Opinions," *Associated Press*, March 23, 2008; Maura Smith, "What Agencies Need to Know about the FTC's Influencer Guidelines," *Forbes*, December 13, 2018.

49. Jonah Berger, Alan T. Sorensen, and Scott J. Rasmussen, "Positive Effects of Negative Publicity: When Negative Reviews Increase Sales," *Marketing Science* 29, no. 5 (2010), pp. 815–27; Elizabeth Holms, "When Shopping Online, Can You Trust the Reviews?" *Wall Street Journal*, November 29, 2016.

50. Piyush Sharma, Roger Marshall, Peter Alan Reday, and WoonBong Na, "Complainers vs. Non-Complainers: A Multi-National Investigation of Individual and Situational Influences on Customer Complaint Behaviour," *Journal of Marketing Management* 26 (February 2010), pp. 163–80.

51. Andrew McMains, "Airline Lost Your Luggage? Tell It to Twitter," *Adweek*, February 20, 2012, p. 12.

52. Philip Kotler, *Kotler on Marketing* (New York: Free Press, 1999), pp. 21–22; Jochen Wirtz, "How to Deal with Customer Shakedowns," *Harvard Business Review* (April 2011), p. 24.

53. Lea Dunn and Darren W. Dahl, "Self-threat and Product Failure: How Internal Attributions of Blame Impact Consumer Complaining Behavior," *Journal of Marketing Research* 49 (October 2012), pp. 670–81.

54. Julie Jargon, Emily Steel, and Joann S. Lublin, "Taco Bell Makes Spicy Retort to Suit," *Wall Street Journal*, January 31, 2011.

55. Timothy L. Keiningham, Terry G. Vavra, Lerzan Aksoy, and Henri Wallard, *Loyalty Myths* (Hoboken, NJ: John Wiley & Sons, 2005).

56. Roland T. Rust, Valerie A. Zeithaml, and Katherine A. Lemon, "Measuring Customer Equity and Calculating Marketing ROI," in Rajiv Grover and Marco Vriens, eds., *Handbook of Marketing Research* (Thousand Oaks, CA: Sage Publications, 2006), pp. 588–601.

57. Robert C. Blattberg and John Deighton, "Manage Marketing by the Customer Equity Test," *Harvard Business Review* (July–August 1996), pp. 136–44.

58. "Easier Than ABC," *The Economist*, October 25, 2003, p. 56; Robert S. Kaplan and Steven R. Anderson, *Time-Driven Activity-Based Costing* (Boston MA: Harvard Business School Press, 2007); "Activity-Based Accounting," *The Economist*, June 29, 2009. See also Morten Holm, V. Kumar, and Carsten Rohde, "Measuring Customer Profitability in Complex Environments: An Interdisciplinary Contingency Framework," *Journal of the Academy of Marketing Science* 40 (May 2012) pp. 387–401.

59. Robert Leone, Vithala Rao, Kevin Lane Keller, Man Luo, Leigh McAlister, and Rajendra Srivatstava, "Linking Brand Equity to Customer Equity," *Journal of Service Research* 9 (November 2006), pp. 125–38; Niraj Dawar, "What Are Brands Good For?" *MIT Sloan Management Review* 46 (Fall 2004), pp. 31–37. For an insightful analysis of the relationship between brand equity and CLV, see Florian Stahl, Mark Heitmann, Donald R. Lehmann, and Scott A. Neslin, "The Impact of Brand Equity on Customer Acquisition, Retention, and Profit Margin," *Journal of Marketing* 76 (July 2012), pp. 44–63. For an in-depth analysis of customer equity, see Peter Fader, *Customer Centricity: Focus on the Right Customers for Strategic Advantage*, 2nd ed. (Wharton Executive Essentials).

60. Michael D. Johnson and Fred Selnes, "Diversifying Your Customer Portfolio," *MIT Sloan Management Review* 46 (Spring 2005), pp. 11–14; Crina O. Tarasi, Ruth N. Bolton, Michael D. Hutt, and Beth A. Walker, "Balancing Risk and Return in a Customer Portfolio," *Journal of Marketing* 75 (May 2011), pp. 1–17.

61. Denish Shah and V. Kumar, "The Dark Side of Cross-Selling," *Harvard Business Review* (December 2012), pp. 21–23; Denish Shah, V. Kumar, Yingge Qu, and Sylia Chen, "Unprofitable Cross-buying: Evidence from Consumer and Business Markets," *Journal of Marketing* 76 (May 2012), pp. 78–95.

62. Sunil Gupta and Carl F. Mela, "What Is a Free Customer Worth?" *Harvard Business Review* (November 2008), pp. 102–9.

63. Shankar Ganesan (1994), "Determinants of Long-Term Orientation in Buyer-Seller Relationships," *Journal of Marketing* 58 (April), pp. 1–19; Peter Kim, Donald Ferrin, Cecily Cooper, and Kurt Dirks (2004), "Removing the Shadow of Suspicion: The Effects of Apology versus Denial for Repairing Competence- versus Integrity-Based Trust Violations," *Journal of Applied Psychology* 89, no. 1, pp. 104–18; Roger Mayer, James Davis, and F. David Schoorman, "An Integrative Model of Organizational Trust," *Academy of Management Review* 20, no. 3 (1995), pp. 709–34.

64. Kent Grayson and Tim Ambler, "The Dark Side of Long-Term Relationships in Marketing Services," *Journal of Marketing Research* 36, no. 1 (1999), pp. 132–41; Susan Fiske, Amy Cuddy, and Peter Glick, "Universal Dimensions of Social Cognition: Warmth and Competence," *Trends in Cognitive Science* 11, no. 2 (2007), pp. 77–83.

65. The material in this section was developed by Professor Kent Grayson at the Kellogg School of Management, Northwestern University.

66. V. Kumar, "Customer Lifetime Value," in Rajiv Grover and Marco Vriens, eds., *Handbook of Marketing Research* (Thousand Oaks, CA: Sage Publications, 2006), pp. 602–27; Sunil Gupta, Donald R. Lehmann, and Jennifer Ames Stuart, "Valuing Customers," *Journal of Marketing Research*

or Vanishing Differences?" *Marketing Science* 27 (September–October 2008), pp. 844–60.

29. For some organizational issues in adaptation, see Julien Cayla and Lisa Peñaloza, "Mapping the Play of Organizational Identity in Foreign Market Adaptation," *Journal of Marketing* 76 (November 2012), pp. 38–54.

30. Paulo Prada and Bruce Orwall, "A Certain 'Je Ne Sais Quoi' at Disney's New Park," *Wall Street Journal,* March 12, 2003.

31. Mallory Schlossberg, "26 Crazy McDonald's Items You Can't Get in America," *Business Insider*, July 1, 2015.

32. Global Brand Counterfeiting Report, 2018.

33. David Meyer, "Yes, Chinese Piracy Has Lost Microsoft a Lot of Windows Revenue. But the Story Isn't So Simple," *Fortune*, November 2, 2018.

34. Marc Fetscherin, Ilan Alon, Romie Littrell, and Allan Chan, "In China? Pick Your Brand Name Carefully," *Harvard Business Review* (September 2012), p. 706. See also Valentyna Melnyk, Kristina Klein, and Franziska Völckner, "The Double-Edged Sword of Foreign Brand Names for Companies from Emerging Countries," *Journal of Marketing* 76 (November 2012), pp. 21–37; Rajeev Batra, Y. Charles Zhang, Nilüfer Z. Aydinoğlu, and Fred M. Feinberg, "Positioning Multicountry Brands: The Impact of Variation in Cultural Values and Competitive Set," *Journal of Marketing Research* 54, no. 6 (2017), pp. 914–31.

35. Zeynep Gürhan-Canli and Durairaj Maheswaran, "Cultural Variations in Country-of-Origin Effects," *Journal of Marketing Research* 37 (August 2000), pp. 309–17.

36. Mark Lasswell, "Lost in Translation," *Business 2.0,* (August 2004), pp. 68–70; Richard P. Carpenter and the *Globe* Staff, "What They Meant to Say Was...," *Boston Globe,* August 2, 1998.

37. Bernard Condon, "Babble Rouser," *Forbes*, August 11, 2008, pp. 72–77; Elenoa Baselala, "Digicel's New Look," *Fiji Times*, November 4, 2010; www.digicelgroup.com/en/about/history.html, accessed 11/27/2020.

38. Douglas B. Holt, John A. Quelch, and Earl L. Taylor, "How Global Brands Compete," *Harvard Business Review* 82 (September 2004), pp. 68–75; Jan-Benedict E. M. Steenkamp, Rajeev Batra, and Dana L. Alden, "How Perceived Brand Globalness Creates Brand Value," *Journal of International Business Studies* 34 (January 2003), pp. 53–65.

39. Richard D. Lyons, "Reuben Mattus, 81, the Founder of Häagen-Dazs." *New York Times*, January 29, 1994.

40. Consumer Reports, "How to Decipher 'Made in the USA' Claims," *Boston Globe*, April 7, 2013.

41. Joel Backaler, "Haier: A Chinese Company That Innovates," *China Tracker*, www.forbes.com, June 17, 2010; Patti Waldmeir, "Haier Seeks to Boost European Sales," *Financial Times*, June 18, 2012; Fan Feifei, "Haier Benefiting from Localization," *China Daily*, August 31, 2018.

42. Mei Fong, "IKEA Hits Home in China: The Swedish Design Giant, Unlike Other Retailers, Slashes Prices for the Chinese," *Wall Street Journal,* March 3, 2006, p. B1; Helen H. Wang, "Why Home Depot Struggles and IKEA Thrives in China," *Forbes*, February 10, 2011.

43. Geoffrey Fowler, Brian Steinberg, and Aaron O. Patrick, "Globalizing Apple's Ads," *Wall Street Journal*, March 1, 2007.

44. Matthew Day, "Swedish Toy Catalogue Goes Gender Neutral," *The Telegraph*, November 26, 2012.

45. Ray A. Smith and Christina Binkley, ""Israel's New Year's Resolution: No Overly Thin Models," *Wall Street Journal*, January 1, 2013.

46. John L. Graham, Alma T. Mintu, and Waymond Rogers, "Explorations of Negotiation Behaviors in Ten Foreign Cultures Using a Model Developed in the United States," *Management Science* 40 (January 1994), pp. 72–95.

47. Rajdeep Grewal, Alok Kumar, Girish Mallapragada, and Amit Saini, "Marketing Channels in Foreign Markets: Control Mechanisms and the Moderating Role of Multinational Corporation Headquarters–Subsidiary Relationship," *Journal of Marketing Research* 50 (June 2013), pp. 378–98; Rajdeep Grewal, Amit Saini, Alok Kumar, F. Robert Dwyer, and Robert Dahlstrom, "Marketing Channel Management by Multinational Corporations in Foreign Markets," *Journal of Marketing* 82, no. 4 (2018), pp. 49–69.

48. Katrijn Gielens, Linda M. Van De Gucht, Jan-Benedict E. M. Steenkamp, and Marnik G. Dekimpe, "Dancing with a Giant: The Effect of Wal-Mart's Entry into the United Kingdom on the Performance of European Retailers," *Journal of Marketing Research* 45 (October 2008), pp. 519–34.

49. Miguel Bustillo, "After Early Errors, Wal-Mart Thinks Locally to Act Globally," *Wall Street Journal*, August 14, 2009; Holman W. Jenkins Jr., "Wal-Mart Innocents Abroad," *Wall Street Journal*, April 25, 2012.

50. Christopher Weaver, Jeanne Whalen, and Benoît Faucon, "Drug Distributor Is Tied to Imports of Fake Avastin," *Wall Street Journal*, March 7, 2012.

51. Kersi D. Antia, Mark E. Bergen, Shantanu Dutta, and Robert J. Fisher, "How Does Enforcement Deter Gray Market Incidence?" *Journal of Marketing* 70 (January 2006), pp. 92–106.

52. For examples, see Ana Valenzuela, Barbara Mellers, and Judi Stebel, "Pleasurable Surprises: A Cross-Cultural Study of Consumer Responses to Unexpected Incentives," *Journal of Consumer Research* 36 (February 2010), pp. 792–805; Praveen K. Kopalle, Donald R. Lehmann, and John U. Farley, "Consumer Expectations and Culture: The Effect of Belief in Karma in India," *Journal of Consumer Research* 37 (August 2010), pp. 251–63; Carlos J. Torelli, Aysegül Özsomer, Sergio W. Carvalho, Hean Tat Keh, and Natalia Maehle, "Brand Concepts as Representations of Human Values: Do Cultural Congruity and Compatibility between Values Matter?" *Journal of Marketing* 76 (July 2012), pp. 92–108.

53. Geert Hofstede, *Culture's Consequences* (Beverley Hills, CA: Sage, 1980); www.hofstede-insights.com/models/national-culture, accessed 11/27/2020.

54. For some in-depth treatments of branding in Asia in particular, see S. Ramesh Kumar, *Marketing & Branding: The Indian Scenario* (Delhi: Pearson Education, 2007) and Martin Roll, *Asian Brand Strategy: How Asia Builds Strong Brands* (New York: Palgrave Macmillan, 2006).

55. Marketing Spotlight sources: Jemma Goudreau, "How IKEA Leveraged the Art of Listening to Global Dominance," *Forbes,* March 8, 2013; "How IKEA Adapted Its Strategies to Expand and Become Profitable in China," *Business Today*, December 6, 2013; Beth Kowitt, "It's IKEA's World, We Just Live in It," *Fortune*. March 10, 2015; www.ikea.com/ms/en_US/this-is-ikea/the-ikea-concept/index.html, accessed 11/27/2020.

56. Harish Bhat (2021) 'Why Did Jamsetji Tata Build the Taj' in #Tatastories: 40 Timeless Tales to Inspire You', Penguin Business, Gurgaon: pp. 158–162.

57. Nita," The story of one of India's biggest brands – the Taj", Word Press Blog (24th November 2006), Accessed on 6th December 2021, from, https://nitawriter.wordpress.com Accessed on December 1, 2021

58. BusinessLine Bureau, " Indian Hotels makes Taj its master brand", The Hindu BusinessLine (12th January 2018), Accessed on 6th December 2021, from, https://www.thehindubusinessline.com Accessed on December 1, 2021

59. Bidya Sapam, "Taj ties up with Shangri-La in bid to expand global footprint", Live Mint (30th November 2016), Accessed on 6th December 2021, from, https://www.livemint.com

60. Team Indian Express, " 'Taj' rated as strongest hotel brand in world", The Indian Express (25th June 2021), Accessed on 6th December 2021, from, https://indianexpress.com

Chapter 21

1. Casey, P., 2021. The Story of TATA: 1868 to 2021. Penguin Random House India Private Limited.

2. Rachna Tyagi, "Tata Trusts: A role model for philanthropy", The Week (14th October 2018), Accessed on 21st December 2021, from, https://www.theweek.in

3. Tata Group, "About-Tata Trusts", Tata Group (2021), Accessed on 22nd December 2021, from, https://www.tatatrusts.org

4. Shally Seth Mohile (2018), 'One Tata': Group firms collaborate with Tata Trusts' Business Standard, January 9, https://www.business-standard.com Accessed on December 29, 2021

5. Prince Mathews Thomas (2018) 'Tata Trusts to cross Rs 1,000 crore in disbursals, doubles outlay in eight years' MoneyControl, April 18, https://www.moneycontrol.com Accessed on December 29, 2021

6. Harish Bhat (2017), 'Jamsetji – The Tata who never went away' The Economic Times, March 3, https://economictimes.indiatimes.com Accessed December 22, 2021

7. 19th Annual Global CEO Survey (January 2016), www.pwc.com/ceosurvey, accessed 11/27/2020.

8. David Hessekiel, "Cause Marketing Leaders of the Pack," *Forbes*, January 31, 2012.

9. "Growth on Principle: The Unconventional Leadership of Stonyfield Farm," *Center for Customer Insights*, February 12, 2014; Gary Hirshberg, *Stirring It Up: How to Make Money and Save the World* (New York: Hyperion, 2008); Melanie D. G. Kaplan, "Stonyfield Farm CEO: How an Organic Yogurt Business Can Scale," *SmartPlanet*, May 17, 2010; www.stonyfield.com/our-story/history, accessed 11/27/2020.

10. https://consciouscompanymedia.com/workplace-culture/hr-innovations/6-ways-corporate-social-responsibility-benefits-employees, accessed 11/27/2020.

11. ICICI Direct Research (October 30, 2021). Gokaldas Exports (GOEXP). Retrieved from https://www.icicidirect.com Accessed on December 22, 2021

12. Gokaldas Exports CSR Team," Gokaldas Exports Limited- Corporate Social Responsibility Policy", Gokaldas Exports Limited (2019), Accessed on 23rd December 2021, from, https://www.gokaldasexports.com

13. www.fairtradecertified.org/why-fair-trade, accessed 11/27/2020.

14. Daniel Korschun, C. B. Bhattacharya, and Scott D. Swain, "Corporate Social Responsibility, Customer Orientation, and the Job Performance of Frontline Employees," *Journal of Marketing* 78 (May 2014),

pp. 20–37; Saurabh Mishra and Sachin B. Modi. "Corporate Social Responsibility and Shareholder Wealth: The Role of Marketing Capability," *Journal of Marketing* 80, no. 1 (2016), pp. 26–46; Charles Kang, Frank Germann, and Rajdeep Grewal, "Washing Away Your Sins? Corporate Social Responsibility, Corporate Social Irresponsibility, and Firm Performance," *Journal of Marketing* 80, no. 2 (2016), pp. 59–79; Alexis M. Allen, Meike Eilert, and John Peloza, "How Deviations from Performance Norms Impact Charitable Donations," *Journal of Marketing Research* 55, no. 2 (2018), pp. 277–90.

15. Paul Newman and A. E. Hotchner, *Shameless Exploitation in Pursuit of the Common Good: The Madcap Business Adventure by the Truly Oddest Couple* (Waterville, ME: Thorndike Press, 2003); www.newmansownfoundation.org, accessed 11/27/2020.

16. Ronald McDonald House Charities, www.rmhc .org, accessed 11/27/2020.

17. Jennifer Aaker, Kathleen D. Vohs, and Cassie Mogilner (2010), "Nonprofits Are Seen as Warm and For-Profits as Competent: Firm Stereotypes Matter," *Journal of Consumer Research* 37 (August), 224–37; Steve Hoeffler and Kevin Lane Keller (2002), "Building Brand Equity through Corporate Societal Marketing," *Journal of Public Policy & Marketing* 21 (Spring), pp. 78–89; Kevin Lane Keller and David A. Aaker, "The Impact of Corporate Marketing on a Company's Brand Extensions," *Corporate Reputation Review* 1 (July 1998), 356–78; Sankar Sen, C. B. Bhattacharya, and Daniel Korschun (2006), "The Role of Corporate Social Responsibility in Strengthening Multiple Stakeholder Relationships: A Field Experiment"" *Journal of the Academy of Marketing Science* 34 (Spring), 158–66.

18. Isabelle Maignan, O. C. Ferrell, and G. Tomas M. Hult (1999), "Corporate Citizenship: Cultural Antecedents and Business Benefits," *Journal of the Academy of Marketing Science*, 27 (October), pp. 455–69; Xueming Luo and C. B. Bhattacharya (2006), "Corporate Social Responsibility, Customer Satisfaction, and Market Value," *Journal of Marketing* 70 (October), pp. 1–18; John Peloza and Jingzhi Shang (2011), "How Can Corporate Social Responsibility Activities Create Value for Stakeholders? A Systematic Review," *Journal of the Academy of Marketing Science* 39 (1), pp. 117–35.

19. Lois A. Mohr, Deborah J. Webb, and Katherine E. Harris (2001), "Do Consumers Expect Companies to Be Socially Responsible? The Impact of Corporate Social Responsibility on Buying Behavior," *Journal of Consumer Affairs*, 35 (Summer), pp. 45–72; Daniel Kahneman and Jack L. Knetsch (1992), "Valuing Public Goods: The Purchase of Moral Satisfaction," *Journal of Environmental Economics and Management* 22 (January), pp. 5–70; Diogo Hildebrand, Yoshiko DeMotta, Sankar Sen, and Ana Valenzuela, "Consumer Responses to Corporate Social Responsibility (CSR) Contribution Type," *Journal of Consumer Research* 44, no. 4 (2017), pp. 738–58.

20. Alexander Chernev and Sean Blair, "Doing Well by Doing Good: The Benevolent Halo of Social Goodwill," *Journal of Consumer Research*, 41 (April 2015), 1412–25; Tom J. Brown and Peter A Dacin, "The Company and the Product: Corporate Associations and Consumer Product Responses," *Journal of Marketing*, 61, (January 1997), pp. 68–84.

21. C. K. Prahalad, *The Fortune at the Bottom of the Pyramid* (Upper Saddle River, NJ: Wharton School Publishing, 2010); Vijay Govindarajan and Chris Trimble, *Reverse Innovation: Create Far from Home, Win Everywhere* (Boston, MA: Harvard Business School Publishing, 2012).

22. Erik Simanis, "Reality Check at the Bottom of the Pyramid," *Harvard Business Review* (June 2012), pp. 120–25.

23. ITC Limited. '20 years of ITC e-choupal'. Retrieved from https://www.itcportal.com Accessed December 30, 2021.

24. www.danone.com/about-danone/at-a-glance .html, accessed 11/27/2020.

25. G. Shainesh (2018), 'Interview with Manoj Kumar, CEO- Naandi Foundation' https://www.edx.org Accessed on December 20, 201

26. Clayton M. Christensen, Stephen Wunker, and Hari Nair, "Innovation vs. Poverty," *Forbes*, October 13, 2008; Nomaswazi Nkosi, "Nokia Still Top SA Choice," *Sowetan Live*, August 15, 2012.

27. "How Dawn Saves Wildlife," www.dawnsaveswildlife .com, accessed 11/27/2020; www.marketwatch .com/press-release/dawn-commemorates-40-years-of-helping-save-wildlife-2018-07-20; accessed 11/27/2020.

28. Christian Homburg, Marcel Stierl, and Torsten Bornemann, "Corporate Social Responsibility in Business-to-Business Markets: How Organizational Customers Account for Supplier Corporate Social Responsibility Engagement," *Journal of Marketing* 77 (November 2013), pp. 54–72; Alexander Chernev and Sean Blair, "Doing Well by Doing Good: The Benevolent Halo of Social Goodwill," *Journal of Consumer Research* 41 (April 2015), pp. 1412–25; C. B. Bhattacharya and Sankar Sen, "Consumer-Company Identification: A Framework for Understanding Consumers' Relationships with Companies,"

Journal of Marketing 67 (April 2003), pp. 76–88; Sankar Sen and C. B. Bhattacharya, "Does Doing Good Always Lead to Doing Better? Consumer Reactions to Corporate Social Responsibility," *Journal of Marketing Research* 38 (May 2001), pp. 225–44.

29. "2013 Cone Communications Social Impact Study: The Next Cause Evolution," www.conecomm.com.

30. (Goldman Sachs. 'Goldman Sachs 10,000 Women in India'. Retrieved from https://www.goldmansachs.com Accessed on December 22, 2021).

31. (NSRCEL Team, IIMB, "IIM Bangalore re-Launches Goldman Sachs 10,000 Women" , Indian Institute of Management, Bangalore (22nd October 2018), Accessed on 22nd December 2021, from, https://www.iimb.ac.in).

32. Paul N. Bloom, Steve Hoeffler, Kevin Lane Keller, and Carlos E. Basurto, "How Social-Cause Marketing Affects Consumer Perceptions," *MIT Sloan Management Review* (Winter 2006), pp. 49–55; Stephen Hoeffler and Kevin Lane Keller, "Building Brand Equity through Corporate Societal Marketing," *Journal of Public Policy and Marketing* 21 (Spring 2002), pp. 78–89; Jenny G. Olson, Brent McFerran, Andrea C. Morales, and Darren W. Dahl, "Wealth and Welfare: Divergent Moral Reactions to Ethical Consumer Choices," *Journal of Consumer Research* 42, no. 6 (2016), pp. 879–96.

33. For some related research, see Ann Kronrod, Amir Grinstein, and Luc Wathieu, "Go Green! Should Environmental Messages Be So Assertive?" *Journal of Marketing* 76 (January 2012), pp. 95–102; Katherine White, Rhiannon MacDonnell, and John H. Ellard, "Belief in a Just World: Consumer Intentions and Behaviors toward Ethical Products," *Journal of Marketing* 76 (January 2012), pp. 103–18; Michael Giebelhausen, HaeEun Helen Chun, J. Joseph Cronin Jr., and G. Tomas M. Hult, "Adjusting the Warm-Glow Thermostat: How Incentivizing Participation in Voluntary Green Programs Moderates Their Impact on Service Satisfaction," *Journal of Marketing* 80, no. 4 (2016), pp. 56–71.

34. Kevin Lane Keller and Lowey Bundy Sichol, "Product(Red): Building a Social Marketing Brand," *Best Practice Cases in Brand Management* (Upper Saddle River, NJ: Pearson Prentice Hall, 2015); www.red.org, accessed 11/27/2020.

35. Stefanie Rosen Robinson, Caglar Irmak, and Satish Jayachandran, "Choice of Cause in Cause-Related Marketing," *Journal of Marketing* 76 (July 2012), pp. 126–39.

36. One Sight, www.onesight.org, accessed 11/27/2020.

37. www.worldwildlife.org/partnerships, accessed 11/27/2020.

38. TeamVCC (2021), 'Former Nike, Apple execs launch Plaeto footwear brand for children' VCCircle, October 21, https://www.vccircle.com Accessed on December 22, 2021

39. BW Online Bureau (2021), 'Plaeto To Power Untapped Indian Market For Kids' Footwear', Business World, December 3, http://www.businessworld.in Accessed on December 22, 2021

40. Arijit Barman, "New playbook: Is Plaeto out to disrupt kids' sneaker market dominated by Bata, Nike and Campus?", Economic Times (12th November 2021), Accessed on 23rd December 2021 from, https://economictimes.indiatimes.com

41. Philip Kotler and Gerald Zaltman "Social Marketing: An Approach to Planned Social Change, *Journal of Marketing*, 35 (July 1971), pp. 3–12.

42. Philip Kotler, David Hessekiel, and Nancy Lee, *Good Works: Marketing and Corporate Initiatives That Build a Better World . . . and the Bottom Line* (Hoboken, NJ: John Wiley & Sons, 2012); Alan Andreasen, *Social Marketing in the 21st Century* (Thousand Oaks, CA: Sage, 2006).

43. Nancy R. Lee and Philip Kotler, *Social Marketing: Behavior Change for Social Good,* 6th ed. (Thousand Oaks, CA., 2020).

44. Andrew Adam Newman, "Avoiding Violent Images for an Anti-Poaching Campaign," *New York Times*, February 19, 2013; www.wwf.org, accessed 11/27/2020.

45. Christian Sarkar and Philip Kotler, *Brand Activism: From Purpose to Action* (Houston, TX, Idea Bite Press, 2018).

46. Monic Sun and Remi Trudel, "The Effect of Recycling versus Trashing on Consumption: Theory and Experimental Evidence," *Journal of Marketing Research* 54, no. 2 (2017), pp. 293–305.

47. "Levi's Introduces New Waste<Less Jean Using Recycled Materials," *Daily News*, August 21, 2013; Susan Berfield, "Levi's Has a New Color for Blue Jeans: Green," *Bloomberg Businessweek*, October 18, 2012; https://www.levistrauss.com/how-we-do-business/use-and-reuse, accessed 11/27/2020.

48. Scott Kirsner, "An Environmental Quandary Percolates at Green Mountain Coffee Roasters," *Boston Globe*, January 3, 2010; Natalie Zmuda, "Green Mountain Takes on Coffee Giants Cup by Cup," *Advertising Age*, June 1, 2009, p. 38; www.gmcr.com/coffee, accessed 11/27/2020.

49. www.faguo-store.com/en/faguo-universe/introduction, accessed 11/27/2020.

50. David Roberts, "Another Inconvenient Truth," *Fast Company*, March 2008, p. 70; Melanie Warner, "P&G's Chemistry Test," *Fast Company* (July/August 2008), pp. 71–74.

51. For related consumer research, see Alexander Chernev and Sean Blair. "When Sustainability is Not a Liability: The Halo Effect of Marketplace Morality." *Journal of Consumer Psychology* (September 2020); Julie R. Irwin and Rebecca Walker Naylor, "Ethical Decisions and Response Mode Compatibility: Weighting of Ethical Attributes in Consideration Sets Formed by Excluding versus Including Product Alternatives," *Journal of Marketing Research* 46 (April 2009), pp. 234–46; Johannes Habel, Laura Marie Schons, Sascha Alavi, and Jan Wieseke, "Warm Glow or Extra Charge? The Ambivalent Effect of Corporate Social Responsibility Activities on Customers' Perceived Price Fairness," *Journal of Marketing* 80, no. 1 (2016), pp. 84–105.

52. Mat McDermott, "Patagonia's New Wetsuits Will Be Made from Plants," TreeHugger.com, November 19, 2012; Tim Nudd, "Ad of the Day: Patagonia," *Adweek*, November 28, 2011; www.patagonia.com/company-info.html, accessed 11/27/2020.

53. Philip Kotler, "Reinventing Marketing to Manage the Environmental Imperative," *Journal of Marketing* 75 (July 2011), pp. 132–35; Subhabrata Bobby Banerjee, Easwar S. Iyer, and Rajiv K Kashyap, "Corporate Enviromentalism: Antecedents and Influence of Industry Type," *Journal of Marketing* 67 (April 2003), pp. 106–22; Wenbo Wang, Aradhna Krishna, and Brent McFerran, "Turning Off the Lights: Consumers' Environmental Efforts Depend on Visible Efforts of Firms," *Journal of Marketing Research* 54, no. 3 (2017), pp. 478–94.

54. Dana Mattioli, "Amazon to Launch $2 Billion Venture Capital Fund to Invest in Clean Energy," *Wall Street Journal*, June 23, 2020.

55. John A. Quelch and Nathalie Laidler-Kylander, *The New Global Brands: Managing Non-Government Organizations in the 21st Century* (Mason, OH: South-Western, 2006); Philip Kotler and Nancy Lee, *Corporate Social Responsibility: Doing the Most Good for Your Company and Your Cause* (New York: Wiley, 2005).

56. Mark Borden and Anya Kamentz, "The Prophet CEO," *Fast Company* (September 2008), pp. 126–29; Tara Weiss, "Special Report: Going Green," Forbes.com, July 3, 2007; Matthew Grimm, "Progressive Business," *Brandweek*, November 28, 2005, pp. 16–26; www.timberland.com/en/about-timberland, accessed 11/27/2020.

57. Anita Rao and Emily Wang, "Demand for "Healthy" Products: False Claims and FTC Regulation," *Journal of Marketing Research* 54, no. 6 (2017), pp. 968–89.

58. "In Lawsuit Brought by POM Wonderful, a Federal Jury Finds Juice Maker Welch's Intentionally Misled Consumers," *Reuters*, September 15, 2010; Alicia Mundy, "FTC Bars Pom Juice's Health Claims," *Wall Street Journal*, January 16, 2013. For a discussion of the possible role of corrective advertising, see Peter Darke, Laurence Ashworth, and Robin J. B. Ritchie, "Damage from Corrective Advertising: Causes and Cures," *Journal of Marketing* 72 (November 2008), pp. 81–97.

59. Bruce Levinson, "Does Technology Change the Ethics of Marketing to Children?" *Fast Company*, April 11, 2013; Heather Chaet, "The Tween Machine," *Adweek*, June 25, 2012.

60. Avi Goldfarb and Catherine Tucker, "Shifts in Privacy Concerns," *American Economic Review: Papers & Proceedings* 102, no. 3 (2012), pp. 349–53; Avi Goldfarb and Catherine Tucker, "Online Display Advertising: Targeting and Obtrusiveness," *Marketing Science* 30 (May–June 2011), pp. 389–404; Alessandro Acquisti, Leslie John, and George Loewenstein, "The Impact of Relative Judgments on Concern about Privacy," *Journal of Marketing Research* 49 (April 2012), pp. 160–74; Charles Duhigg, "How Companies Learn Your Secrets," *New York Times*, February 16, 2012.

61. Marketing Insight sources: Stephanie Strom, "Wary of Plastic, and Waste, Some Consumers Turn to Glass," *New York Times*, June 20, 2012; "Bottled Water and the Damage Done: Coping With Plastic Pollution," *Bloomberg Law*, May 21, 2018; https://www.nationalgeographic.com/environment/2019/08/plastic-bottles, accessed 11/27/2020.

62. Marketing Spotlight sources: Howard Schultz and Dori Jones Yang, *Pour Your Heart into It: How Starbucks Built a Company One Cup at a Time* (New York: Hyperion, 1997); Francesca Landini, "Coffee Rivals Square Off in Italy Ahead of Starbucks Invasion," *Reuters*, September 18, 2017; Adam Campbell-Schmitt, "Starbucks Opened Its First Reserve Store (and It Serves Booze)," *Meredith Corporation Allrecipes Food Group*, February 27, 2018; Adam Campbell-Schmitt, "Roastery, Reserve Bar, Regular Starbucks: What's the Difference?" *Meredith Corporation Allrecipes Food Group*, December 20, 2018; Kevin Johnson, "Starbucks New Sustainability Commitment," *Starbucks Stories and News,* January 21, 2020; www.starbucks.com/about-us/company-information, accessed 11/27/2020.

63. Marketing Spotlight sources: Paula Kepos, ""Ben & Jerry's Homemade, Inc.," *International Directory* *of Company Histories*, Vol. 10 (Detroit, MI: St. James Press, 1995); David Gelles, "How the Social Mission of Ben & Jerry's Survived Being Gobbled Up," *New York Times*, August 21, 2015; O. C. Ferrell, John Fraedrich, and Terry Gable "Managing Social Responsibility and Growth at Ben & Jerry's," Daniels Fund Ethics Initiative, University of New Mexico (2011); Genevieve Roberts, "Ben & Jerry's Builds on Its Social-Values Approach," *New York Times,* November 16, 2010; www.benjerry.com/about-us, accessed 11/27/2020; https://www.benjerry.com/values/issues-we-care-about/climate-justice, accessed 11/27/2020.

64. Marketing Spotlight sources: A. J. Agrawal, "How Tiffany & Co. Built a Marketing Empire," *Forbes*, August 09, 2016; Frederic Cumenal, "Tiffany's CEO on Creating a Sustainable Supply Chain," *Harvard Business Review*, February 21, 2017: *Tiffany Sets Ambitious Commitments for the Future Across the Pillars of Product, People, and Planet*, http://press.tiffany.com/News/NewsItem.aspx?id=389; www.tiffany.com/worldoftiffany, accessed 11/27/2020.

Glossary

A

activity-based costing accounting procedures that can quantify the true profitability of different activities by identifying their actual costs.

administered vertical marketing system a marketing structure in which one of the members coordinates successive stages of production and distribution.

advertising the presentation and promotion of ideas, goods, services, and brands using paid media.

agents the brokers, manufacturers' representatives, and sales agents that search for customers and may negotiate on the producer's behalf but do not buy or resell the goods.

alpha testing the evaluation of a product or service within the company.

anticipatory pricing the raising of prices by more than the cost increase, in anticipation of further inflation or government price controls.

areas of dominant influence the geographic or market areas on which the communication budget is focused.

attitudes a person's enduring evaluations, emotional feelings, and behavioral tendencies toward an object or idea.

auction pricing the setting of prices through competitive bidding.

average cost the cost per unit at a specific level of production.

B

behavioral research a means of obtaining data to gain a better understanding of customers' purchasing, consumption, and decision-making processes.

behavioral segmentation the division of target customers into groups based on their actions.

belief a conviction that something is true or real, regardless of whether it is or is not.

beta testing the evaluation of a product or service by customers.

bottom of the pyramid (BOP) a socioeconomic concept that refers to the poorest group of the world's population.

bottom-up idea generation a process that starts with an invention and then seeks to identify an unmet market need.

brand a name and/or design element intended to identify the goods or services of a company and differentiate them from competitive offerings.

brand activism a company's stance on a controversial social, economic, environmental, or political issue.

brand associations all thoughts, feelings, perceptions, images, experiences, beliefs, and attitudes that are attributed to the brand.

brand audit an assessment of the health of the brand and its position in the market.

brand character a brand symbol with human characteristics that enhances brand likability and relatability.

brand dilution the weakening of the power of a brand.

brand equity the monetary value of a brand that reflects the premium placed on a company's valuation because of its ownership of the brand.

brand extension a company's use of an existing brand for an offering in a different product category or price tier.

brand hierarchy a reflection of the way in which a company's brands are related to its products and services, as well as to one another.

brand mantra a succinct articulation of the essence of the brand.

brand personality the human traits attributed to a particular brand.

brand personification a means to determine consumers' brand associations by asking them to equate the brand to a person, animal, or object.

brand portfolio the set of all brands owned by a company.

brand power the ancillary value that the brand contributes to a product or service.

brand tracking the use of quantitative data to provide consistent information about how brands and marketing programs are performing.

brand value chain an assessment of the way marketing activities create brand value.

branded variants specific brand lines supplied to specific retailers or distribution channels.

branding the process of endowing products and services with the power of a brand.

business markets all the organizations that acquire goods and services used in the production of other products or services that are sold, rented, or supplied to others.

business-model design the process of determining the ways in which a product or service will create market value.

C

cause marketing the linking of a firm's contributions to a designated cause with its customers' revenue-producing transactions.

channel captain an entity responsible for managing the partnerships within a distribution channel.

channel conflict actions by one channel member that prevent another channel member from achieving its goal.

channel power the ability to alter channel members' behavior so they take actions they would not have taken otherwise.

cobranding two or more brands marketed together.

commercialization the process of informing target customers about the company's offering and making the offering available to them.

communication objective the specific task to be accomplished with a specific audience within a specific period of time.

company demand the company's estimated share of market demand in a given time period.

company sales forecast the expected level of company sales for a given time period based on market trends and company marketing efforts.

company sales potential the upper limit of sales that a company can achieve in a specific market in a given time period.

competitive advantage a company's ability to create market value in a way that competitors are unable to match.

competitive-parity budgeting an approach to communication budgeting based on what the competition is spending.

competitive pricing the setting of prices based on competitors' prices.

concept validation an assessment of the feasibility and attractiveness of the core concept underlying the proposed offering.

conformance quality the degree to which all produced units are identical and meet promised specifications.

conjoint analysis measurement of the value that consumers place on specific attributes of an offering.

consumer incentives the rewards offered to customers to encourage purchase.

containerization the placement of goods in containers for easy transfer between transportation modes.

contextual placement the purchase of ads on sites related to the product being advertised.

contract manufacturing the use of local manufacturers to produce the company's product in a specific market.

contractual vertical marketing system a group of independent firms at different levels of production and distribution that contractually integrate their programs to obtain greater economies or sales impact.

conventional marketing channels systems of independent producers, wholesalers, and retailers.

conversion rate the percentage of customers who move to the next stage of the customer acquisition process.

core competency expertise in an area that gives a company a competitive advantage.

corporate culture the shared experiences, stories, beliefs, and norms that characterize an organization.

corporate vertical marketing system a strategy that combines successive stages of production and distribution under a single entity.

cost inflation a circumstance in which rising costs unmatched by productivity gains squeeze profit margins and lead companies to regular rounds of price increases.

creative brief a succinct document that outlines the specific communication approach to be used in a creative assignment.

crowdsourcing the gathering of data and opinions from the public to enrich the marketing process.

customer acquisition funnel a depiction of the phases of the process of attracting new customers.

customer base customers who are loyal to the company and its offerings.

customer-centricity a focus on the customer that underlies all company offerings and activities.

customer empowerment the ability of customers to choose how they want to engage with the company.

customer equity the total sum of the lifetime values of all company customers.

customer lifetime value the total amount a customer is expected to spend during his or her tenure with the company.

customer profile the observable demographic, geographic, behavioral, and psychographic customer descriptors.

customer profitability analysis a means of assessing and ranking customer profitability.

customer relationship management the process of managing detailed information about individual customers and all customer touch points to maximize loyalty.

customer touch points the occasions on which a customer encounters the brand, product, or service.

customer value analysis assessment of how consumers view the company's strengths and weaknesses relative to the competition.

customer value management analysis of customer perceptions of an offering's value to develop marketing strategies to acquire and retain customers and drive purchase behavior.

customer value proposition the value the company aims to create for its target customers.

D

demand forecast an estimation of the size of the potential market for the company's offering.

design the totality of features that affect the way a product looks, feels, and functions.

design thinking a process of developing design concepts.

direct exporting the sale of a company's offering in other countries by the company itself.

direct investment the process by which a foreign company can buy a partial or full interest in a local company or build its own manufacturing or service facilities.

direct marketing channel a manufacturer selling directly to the final customer.

distribution channel a set of interdependent organizations participating in the process of making a product or service available to the target market.

diversification strategy a move to enter a new market with an offering that is new to the company.

diversified portfolio a fairly broad assortment of multiple product lines.

divesting the process of selling an asset of a company or the company itself.

dual-level channel a distribution channel that contains two intermediaries, typically a wholesaler and a retailer.

E

economic-value-to-customer pricing the setting of the price a consumer is willing to pay based on the perception of the product's value.

elaboration likelihood model a description of the process by which consumers make evaluations in both low- and high-involvement circumstances.

ethnographic research a particular observational research approach that uses concepts and tools from anthropology and other social science disciplines to provide deep cultural understanding of how people live and work.

everyday low pricing (EDLP) a consistently low retail price with little or no price promotion or special sales.

exclusive distribution the use of a highly limited number of intermediaries.

expectancy-value model the process by which people evaluate products and services by combining their assessments according to the weighted importance of those assessments.

experience-curve pricing the setting of a lower price based on the future ability to lower production costs through experience.

external marketing the process of designing, communicating, and delivering a product or service to customers.

F

facilitators the transportation companies, independent warehouses, banks, and advertising agencies that assist in the distribution process but do not take title to goods or negotiate sales.

fad a short-lived mode of behavior that has no social, economic, or political significance.

fixed costs costs that do not vary with changes in production level.

flagship product an offering that best represents or embodies the brand.

flanking an attack on a competitor's weak spot to steal market share.

focus group a small group of people who are selected based on certain demographic, psychographic, or other considerations and brought together to discuss various topics of interest.

forward buying the purchase of a greater quantity of favorably priced goods than a retailer can immediately sell.

frame of reference a benchmark against which customers can evaluate the benefits of a company's offering.

franchising granting permission to use a company's know-how, procedures, intellectual property, business model, and brand to sell its branded products and service.

frontal attack a move to match a competitor's marketing strategy and tactics.

G

geofencing a mobile promotion strategy that targets customers when they are within a defined geographic space, typically near or in a store.

geographic segmentation the division of the market into geographic units such as nations, states, regions, counties, cities, or neighborhoods.

goodwill an accounting term that includes brand equity and signifies the monetary value of all intangible assets of a company.

gray market the diversion of branded products from authorized distribution channels.

greenwashing providing misleading information or giving the impression that products or practices are more environmentally friendly than they really are.

guarantee the assurance that if a product fails to function as promised or as customers expect, the company will provide some type of compensation to the purchaser.

guerrilla attack a series of small, intermittent attacks on the competition.

H

harvesting the reduction of investment in an offering to reap the greatest possible profit.

heuristics rules of thumb that facilitate the decision process.

high–low pricing higher retailer prices on an everyday basis, with frequent promotions featuring prices temporarily lower than EDLP-level prices.

horizontal channel conflict a dispute between channel members at the same level of the distribution network.

horizontal marketing systems two or more unrelated companies pooling resources or programs to exploit an emerging marketing opportunity.

I

image pricing the act of setting prices higher to make an offering more desirable in the eyes of consumers.

incentives the typically short-term sales promotion tools designed to stimulate the purchase of a product or service.

incremental innovation a minor improvement of an existing offering or process.

indirect exporting the use of independent intermediaries to sell a company's offering in other countries.

influencer marketing the use of a popular figure to promote a product, service, or brand within his or her social media sphere.

informational appeal an elaboration of product or service attributes or benefits to influence the consumer purchasing decision.

institutional market schools, hospitals, nursing homes, prisons, and other entities that provide goods and services to people in their care.

integrated marketing the coordination of all marketing activities and programs aimed at designing, communicating, and delivering consistent value to consumers.

integrated marketing communication an approach to managing a communication campaign through the coordinated use of different communication tools.

intensive distribution the placement of goods or services in as many outlets as possible.

interactive marketing the company's encouragement of, and response to, consumer perspectives and behaviors regarding an offering or brand.

internal marketing the hiring, training, and motivating of employees to serve customers in a way that reflects the company's goals.

intrapreneur a company employee whose duties are focused on fostering product, service, and process innovation within the company.

J

joint venture a business enterprise engaged in by two or more otherwise separate entities.

just-in-time inventory management the ordering of production components as needed, to save on warehousing costs and improve cash flow.

L

laddering a series of increasingly specific questions that can reveal consumers' motivations and deeper goals.

licensing granting permission to manufacture and sell a company's offering in a specific market.

line extension the addition of new products to a company's current product line.

line filling a lengthening of a company's product line by adding more items to the existing range.

line stretching an expansion of the product line beyond its current range.

localized marketing program an approach that tailors its marketing activities to individual target markets.

long-term memory the capacity to remember and store information indefinitely, or even permanently.

loss-leader pricing the setting of a low price for a product to attract greater consumer traffic.

M

macromodel of marketing communication description of the interaction between the sender (company) and the recipient (consumer) of the communication message.

macroscheduling decision the allocation of communication expenditures related to seasons and the business cycle.

market demand the total volume of a product that would be bought by a defined customer group in a defined geographic area in a defined time period in a defined marketing environment under a defined marketing program.

market-development strategy a focus on expanding sales of a product or service to new target markets.

market expansion a move that makes an offering available to the entire target market.

market forecast the market demand projected for a future time period.

market leader the company with the largest share of the market in which it competes.

market logistics infrastructure design and control of the flow of materials and goods from manufacturer to customer.

market offering the actual good that the company deploys in order to fulfill a particular customer need.

market-penetration strategy a focus on increasing sales of the company's current offerings to its existing customers.

market position a company's share of the market in which it competes.

market potential the maximum sales that can be achieved in a specific market in a given time period.

market segmentation the division of a consumer group into subsets that share a similar set of needs and/or profile characteristics.

market skimming the setting of a relatively high price to make the offering affordable only to customers with the greatest willingness to pay.

market test a means of validating the offering in a portion of the market or in the entire market.

marketing the identification and meeting of individual and social needs in a way that harmonizes with the goals of the organization.

marketing communication the means by which firms inform, persuade, and remind consumers about the products and brands they sell.

marketing dashboards a structured way to disseminate the insights gleaned from marketing metrics and marketing-mix modeling.

marketing management the art and science of choosing target markets and getting, retaining, and growing customers by delivering superior value.

marketing mix the attributes (product, service, brand, price, incentives, communication, and distribution) that define the company's offering.

marketing network the company and its supporting stakeholders, with whom it has built mutually profitable business relationships.

marketing-mix models a way to analyze data from multiple sources to understand the effects of specific marketing activities.

markup pricing a pricing method that adds a standard markup to the product's cost.

mass customization the use of mass production techniques to produce offerings that can be customized to meet the needs of individual customers.

mass marketing addressing the entire market with a single offering.

merchant wholesalers the intermediaries that buy directly from the manufacturer, store the product, and then sell it to the customer.

merchants the wholesalers and retailers that buy and resell the offering to consumers.

micromodel of marketing communication description of consumers' specific responses to communications.

microscheduling decision the allocation of communication expenditures within a short time period to obtain maximum impact.

mission a clear, concise, and enduring statement of the reasons for an organization's existence.

Moore's model an adaptation of the Rogers' model for technology products.

multichannel conflict a dispute between two or more channels that sell to the same market.

N

native advertising a form of advertising that resembles the medium's editorial content but is intended to promote the advertiser's product.

net price analysis the "real price" of the offering after discounts and advertising and promotion costs are deducted.

niche marketer a company that caters to a subset of customers with an offering exclusively tailored to their needs.

O

objective-and-task budgeting an approach for determining the communication budget based on the specific task to be achieved.

observational research a means of obtaining data by unobtrusive observation of customers' shopping or consumption habits.

opinion leader a person who offers informal advice or information on how best a specific product or product category can be used; also known as an influencer.

optimal value proposition the value an offering creates for customers, collaborators, and the company.

order-to-payment cycle the time between an order's receipt, delivery of the product or service, and payment.

organic growth an increase in the company's revenues, profits, and/or market position through the use of its own resources.

P

penetration pricing the setting of a low price to maximize market share.

perception the process of selecting, organizing, and interpreting information to create a meaningful picture of the world.

perceptual map a visual representation of consumer perceptions and preferences.

performance marketing the financial and nonfinancial returns to business and society from marketing activities and programs.

permission marketing the practice of marketing to consumers only after gaining their expressed permission.

personality a set of distinguishing human psychological traits that lead to relatively consistent responses to environmental stimuli, including buying behavior.

personal selling the face-to-face interaction between the salesperson and the buyer.

personas the detailed profiles of one or more target consumers that depict the typical consumer in the target market.

points of difference (PODs) attributes or benefits that differentiate the company's offering from the competition.

points of parity (POPs) attributes or benefits that are not unique and are shared with other brands.

positioning statement a summary of a product or brand's strategy that aims to guide the company's actions.

positioning designing a company's offering and image to occupy a distinctive place in the minds of the target market.

price discrimination sale of the same offering at different prices to different customers.

price elasticity of demand the degree to which a change in price leads to a change in quantity sold.

price image the general perception that consumers have about the level of prices at a given retailer.

price indifference band a range within which changes in price have little or no effect on consumer purchases.

pricing cues a means of prompting customers to rely on price to infer the value of a product.

primary data information gathered for a specific purpose or project.

primary target the subset of target customers for which an offering will initially be made available.

principle of congruity psychological mechanism by which consumers like to view seemingly related objects as being as similar as possible in favorability.

private label a proprietary brand developed and sold by retailers and wholesalers.

product-development strategy the creation of new products or modifications to existing products in the target market.

product life cycle the length of time between the introduction of an offering in the market and its removal from the market.

product line a group of related products sold by the same company.

product–market growth framework a grid that outlines the different growth strategies; also known as the Ansoff matrix.

product-mix pricing the setting of prices in a manner that maximizes profits on the total mix of company offerings.

product portfolio the total number of products offered by a company, including various product categories and product lines.

product-value analysis the assessment of a product's value by examining ways components or processes can be modified to reduce costs without adversely affecting product performance.

projective technique a process of presenting consumers with an incomplete or ambiguous stimulus, such as word association or choice ordering, in order to get a better understanding of their thought processes.

prototype a model of an offering that aims to weed out potential problems before the actual offering is created.

psychographic segmentation the division of target customers into groups based on psychological traits, lifestyles, or values.

psychological resistance a reluctance to change established preferences or opinions that are barriers to purchase.

public relations a variety of programs designed to promote a company's image among the relevant stakeholders.

publicity the securing of editorial content to promote an offering, idea, organization, or image.

pull strategy the use of advertising, promotion, and communication to persuade consumers to demand the product from intermediaries.

push strategy the selling of a product to end users through collaborators.

Q

quality the degree to which a product or service fulfills customer expectations of value.

questionnaire a set of questions presented to respondents to collect primary data.

R

reference groups all groups that have a direct or indirect effect on an individual's beliefs, decisions, and behavior.

reference prices pricing information a consumer retains in memory that is used to interpret and evaluate a new price.

relationship marketing the development of mutually satisfying long-term relationships with key constituents to earn and retain their business.

retailing the activities involved in selling goods or services directly to final consumers for nonbusiness use.

retention rate the number of customers that continue to do business with a company over a defined period of time.

revenue leaders the group of customers that represent the highest customer lifetime value to the company.

reverse-flow channel a distribution channel in which goods flow backward from the user to the producer, typically for recycling, resale, or disposal.

reverse innovation the use of a successful product as a base for creating an inexpensive alternative for developing markets.

Rogers' model a classification of consumers according to the speed with which they adopt new offerings.

S

sales force incentives the means used to motivate the sales force, such as bonuses and trips.

sample size the number of people who should be surveyed to provide credible results that can be extrapolated to the entire target population.

sampling procedure a means of choosing survey respondents that makes the sample more representative of the total target population.

sampling unit the respondents who should be surveyed to glean information about a specific market, product, or behavior.

search engine marketing (SEM) the practice of paying search engine companies for one's product, service, brand, or organization to be featured in the results of particular keyword searches.

search engine optimization (SEO) the activities designed to increase the likelihood that a link for a company or brand ranks as high as possible in the order of all nonpaid links that appear during online searches.

secondary data existing information collected for another purpose.

selective attention the process of focusing on specific environmental stimuli while ignoring others.

selective distortion the tendency to interpret information to fit our preconceptions.

selective distribution the use of a number of carefully selected intermediaries willing to carry a particular product.

selective market deployment an approach that deploys the company's offering only to specific areas of the target market to test market reaction.

service an intangible act that one entity performs for another that does not result in a change in ownership.

service blueprint a mapping of the service provided by the company from the customer's point of view.

short-term memory the capacity to keep a limited amount of information in mind for a short time.

showrooming examination of a product in a store before purchasing it from a different retailer, typically to secure a lower price.

single-level channel a distribution channel that contains one selling intermediary, such as a retailer.

social marketing marketing done by a nonprofit or government organization to further a cause, such as "say no to drugs."

specialized portfolio a fairly narrow assortment of one or a few product lines.

stage-gate framework a multiphase model for managing the process of developing new offerings.

standardized marketing program a strategy that uses the same strategic and tactical approach across different markets and countries.

strategic brand management the design and implementation of marketing activities and programs to build, manage, and measure brands.

strategic business unit (SBU) a single business or collection of related businesses that can be planned separately from the rest of the company, with its own set of competitors and a manager who is responsible for strategic planning and profit performance.

strategic targeting a focus on customers whose needs the company can fulfill better than the competition.

strategy a company's game plan for achieving its goals.

subliminal perception messages that consumers are not consciously aware of but that affect their behavior.

supply chain management the procurement of inputs and their conversion into finished products that are dispatched to the final destinations.

sustainability avoidance of the depletion of natural resources by reducing the impact of human activity on the environment.

systems buying the purchase of a total solution to a business problem or need from one company.

systems selling a marketing approach to attract buyers that prefer to buy entire systems from one company.

T

tactical targeting identifying the means to reach strategically viable customers to communicate and deliver the company's offering.

tactics the marketing mix that makes the company's strategy come alive and defines the key aspects of the offering developed to create value in a given market.

target attractiveness the ability of a market segment to create value for the company.

target compatibility a reflection of the company's ability to fulfill the needs of target customers.

target market the market in which a company aims to create and capture value.

target-rate-of-return pricing the setting of a price that will yield the desired rate of return.

targeting the process of identifying those customers for whom the company will optimize its offering.

time-and-duty analysis an hour-by-hour breakdown of activities to help employees understand how they might increase their productivity.

top-down idea generation a product-development process that begins with identifying a market opportunity.

total costs the sum of the fixed and variable costs for a given level of production.

total customer benefit the perceived functional, psychological, and monetary value that customers derive from a market offering.

total customer cost the perceived functional, psychological, and monetary costs that customers incur to evaluate, obtain, use, and dispose of an offering.

trade incentives the rewards offered to members of the distribution channel.

trend a change in behavior or sequence of events that has momentum and durability.

triple bottom line the concept that a company has a responsibility to stakeholders, which include employees, customers, and society as a whole.

V

value proposition the type of value that the company plans to create for target customers.

variable costs costs that vary directly with the level of production.

vertical channel conflict a dispute between members at different levels of the distribution network.

vertical marketing system a marketing system in which producers, wholesalers, and retailers work together as a unit.

visualization a way for marketers to gain insight into people's perceptions by asking them to create a collage or drawing.

W

warranties formal statements of expected product performance by the manufacturer.

wholesaling all activities involved in selling goods or services to those who buy for resale or make large purchases for business use.

word association a research method that involves asking respondents what words come to mind when they hear the brand name.

Y

yield pricing a pricing strategy based on anticipating and influencing customers' behavior.

Z

zero-level channel a distribution channel that involves a manufacturer selling directly to the final customer; also called a direct marketing channel.

zone of tolerance the range in which customers will deem company service satisfactory.

Name Index

Company, Brand, and Organization

C

D

L

M

N

T

Subject Index

D

Q